THE BUILDINGS OF ENGLAND

FOUNDING EDITOR: NIKOLAUS PEVSNER

WARWICKSHIRE

CHRIS PICKFORD
AND
NIKOLAUS PEVSNER

Warwickshire

- - - Boundary of this Volume
Coventry
For Coventry suburbs see
map pp. 278–9

'A' roads
Motorway
+—+ Railway

STAFFORDSHIRE

LEICESTERSHIRE

BIRMINGHAM
AND
BLACK
COUNTRY

No Mans Heath
Newton Regis
Austrey
Seckington
Shuttington
Alvecote
Warton
Polesworth
Tamworth
Grendon
Dordon
Baddesley Ensor
Freasley
Baxterley
Merevale
Wood End
Hurley
Kingsbury
Botts Green
Middleton
Wishaw
Lea Marston
Curdworth
Water Orton
Nether Whitacre
Over Whitacre
Shustoke
Coleshill
Maxstoke
Birmingham
Little Packington
Great Packington
Hampton-in-Arden
Eastcote
Knowle
Dorridge
Packwood
Bentley Heath
Nuthurst
Lapworth
Baddesley Clinton
Wroxall
Beausale
Umberslade Park
Tamworth-in-Arden

Atherstone
Mancetter
Bentley
Hartshill
Oldbury
Ansley
Arley
New Arley
Galley Common
Astley
Fillongley
Corley
Meriden
Berkswell
Eastern Green
Balsall Common
Barston
Temple Balsall

Caldecote
Nuneaton
Bramcote
Weston-in-Arden
Bulkington
Shilton
Ansty
Hawkesbury
Exhall by Coventry
Bedworth
Arbury

Burton Hastings
Wolvey
Copston Magna
Wibtoft
Withybrook
Willey
Monks Kirby
Newbold Revel
Easenhall
Harborough Magna
Churchover
Pailton
Stretton-under-Fosse
Combe Fields
Combe Abbey
King's Newnham
Little Lawford
Church Lawford
Long Lawford
Rugby
Clifton-upon-Dunsmore
Bilton Grange
Dunchurch
Wolston
Brandon
Baginton
Bubbenhall
Princethorpe
Ryton-on-Dunsmore
Stretton-on-Dunsmore
Bourton-on-Dunsmore
Thurlaston
Frankton

COVENTRY

Stoneleigh
Ashow
Honiley
Kenilworth

Leicester
M1
A5
M69
M6
M42
M45
M40
M6
A14
A45
A46
A452
A34
Avon
Coventry Canal
Anker
Tame
Sowe

20 km
10 miles

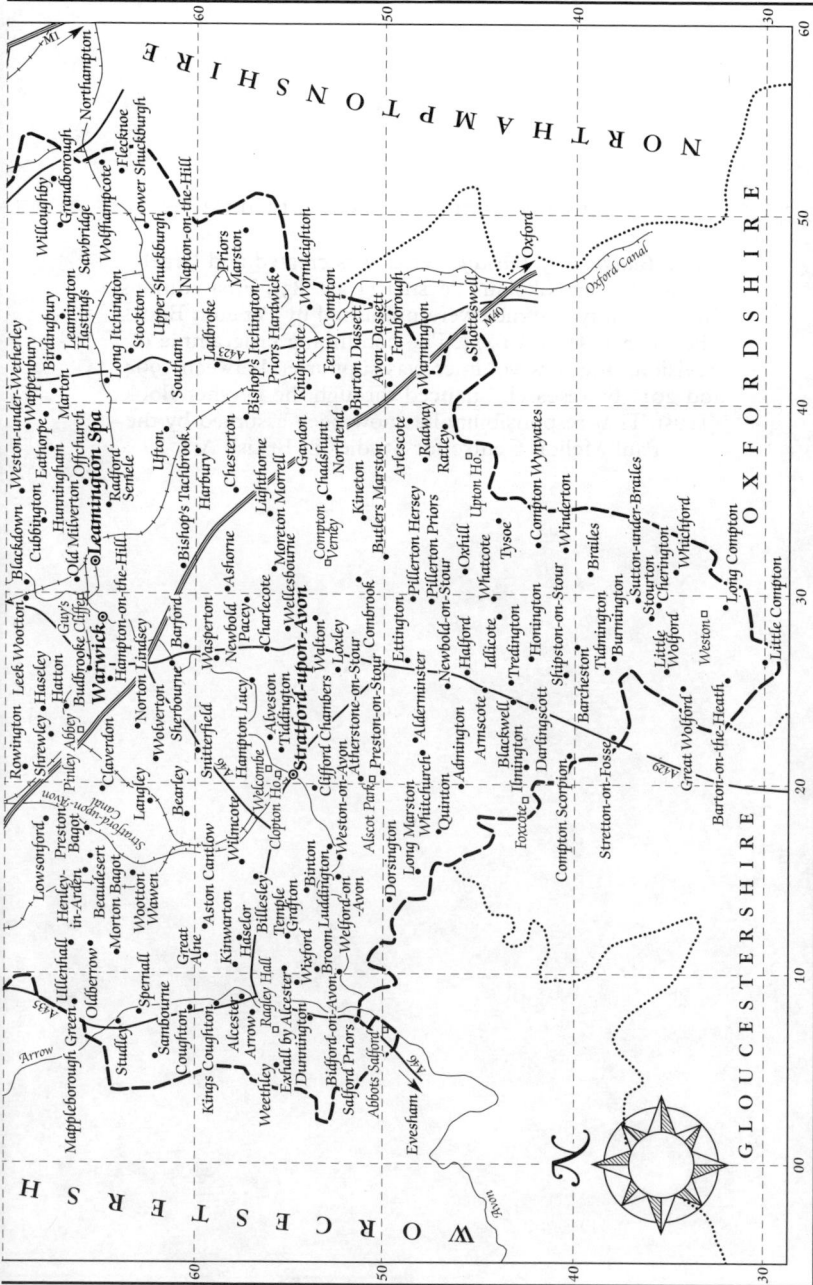

NORTHAMPTONSHIRE
OXFORDSHIRE
GLOUCESTERSHIRE
WORCESTERSHIRE

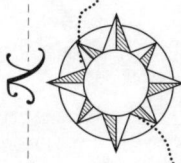

M1
Northampton
Willoughby
Grandborough
Flecknoe
Wolfhampcote
Lower Shuckburgh
Upper Shuckburgh
Napton-on-the-Hill
Sawbridge
Priors Marston
Ladbroke
Wappenbury
Birdingbury
Hunningham
Leamington Hastings
Marton
Stockton
Southam
Long Itchington
Bishop's Itchington
Priors Hardwick
Wormleighton
Weston-under-Wetherley
Blackdown
Cubbington Eathorpe
Old Milverton
Offchurch
Leamington Spa
Radford Semele
Ufton
Harbury
Chesterton
Gaydon
Lighthorne
Moreton Morrell
Knightcote
Fenny Compton
Burton Dassett
Avon Dassett
Warmington
Shotteswell
Farnborough
Oxford
Oxford Canal
M40
Compton Verney
Chadshunt
Northend
Kineton
Butlers Marston
Radway
Ratley
Upton Ho.
Arlescote
Pillerton Hersey
Pillerton Priors
Oxhill
Whatcote
Tysoe
Compton Wynyates
Winderton
Rowington
Leek Wootton
Haseley
Hatton
Guy's Cliffe
Budbrooke
Warwick
Hampton-on-the-Hill
Norton Lindsey
Barford
Sherbourne
Wasperton
Newbold Pacey
Charlecote
Wellesbourne
Waspertorn
Ashorne
Bishop's Tachbrook
Shrewley
Claverdon
Wolverton
Snitterfield
Hampton Lucy
Alveston
Tiddington
Stratford-upon-Avon
Loxley
Combrook
Ettington
Newbold-on-Stour
Halford
Idlicote
Tredington
Honington
Shipston-on-Stour
Barcheston
Tidmington
Burmington
Long Compton
Little Compton
Weston
Cherington
Stourton
Sutton-under-Brailes
Brailes
Whichford
Little Wolford
Great Wolford
Burton-on-the-Heath
Stretton-on-Fosse
Darlingscott
Armscote
Blackwell
Ilmington
Foxcote
Admington
Quinton
Long Marston
Whitchurch
Preston-on-Stour
Atherstone-on-Stour
Clifford Chambers
Wixford
Dorsington
Compton Scorpion
Aston Cantlow
Wilmcote
Welcombe
Clopton Ho.
Alscot Park
Weston-on-Avon
Binton
Temple Grafton
Ardens Grafton
Broom
Luddington
Welford-on-Avon
Bidford-on-Avon
Salford Priors
Abbots Salford
Evesham
Avon
Lowsonford
Preston Bagot
Henley-in-Arden
Beaudesert
Morton Bagot
Wootton Wawen
Langley
Bearley
Hasely
Kinwarton
Haselor
Billesley
Great Alne
Alcester
Arrow
Exhall
Dunnington
Ragley Hall
Weethley
Kings Coughton
Coughton
Sambourne
Studley
Oldberrow
Ullenhall
Mappleborough Green
Spernall
Arrow
Stratford-upon-Avon Canal
N

Warwickshire

BY

CHRIS PICKFORD

AND

NIKOLAUS PEVSNER

THE BUILDINGS OF ENGLAND

YALE UNIVERSITY PRESS
NEW HAVEN AND LONDON

YALE UNIVERSITY PRESS
NEW HAVEN AND LONDON

302 Temple Street, New Haven CT 06511
47 Bedford Square, London WC1B 3DP
www.pevsner.co.uk
www.lookingatbuildings.org.uk
www.yalebooks.co.uk
www.yalebooks.com

Published by Yale University Press 2016
2 4 6 8 10 9 7 5 3 1

ISBN 978 0 300 21560 1

Printed in China
through World Print
Set in Monotype Plantin

The dedication of the 1st edition of Warwickshire was

to

MESSRS WILLIAM CLOWES AND SONS
with the admiration due to them
for having printed The Buildings of England
ever since the first volume
and still not being sick of them

The revised edition is

for

HEATHER

CONTENTS

LIST OF TEXT FIGURES AND MAPS

Every effort has been made to trace or contact all copyright holders. The publishers will be glad to make good any errors or omissions brought to our attention in future editions.

MAPS

PHOTOGRAPHIC ACKNOWLEDGEMENTS

The photographs were almost all taken by John Roan Photography. We are also grateful for permission to reproduce the remaining photographs from the sources as shown below.

Reproduced courtesy of Arbury Hall: 53, 62

© Bildarchiv Monheim Gmbh/Alamy Stock Photo: 65

Reproduced courtesy of Chris Firth: 38

Chris Pickford: 16, 77

© Christopher Simon Sykes/Hulton Archive/Getty Images: 37

Reproduced courtesy of David Nicholls: 94

© Historic England: 31, 122; (Christopher Dalton Collection): 9

Reproduced courtesy of the Landmark Trust: 68

Reproduced courtesy of Michael Fetherston-Dilke: 33

© National Trust Images/Rupert Morris: 36

© National Trust Images/Matthew Antrobus: 43

© Peter Cook: 124

Reproduced courtesy of Princethorpe College: 92

Reproduced courtesy of the Rugby School: 95

© Roger Rosewell: 25

MAP AND ILLUSTRATION REFERENCES

The numbers printed in italic type in the margin against the place names in the gazetteer of the book indicate the position of the place in question on the INDEX MAP (*pp. ii–iii*), which is divided into sections by the 10-kilometre reference lines of the National Grid. The reference given here omits the two initial letters which in a full grid reference refer to the 100-kilometre squares into which the county is divided. The first two numbers indicate the *western* boundary, and the last two the *southern* boundary, of the 10-kilometre square in which the place in question is situated. For example, Abbots Salford (reference 0040) will be found in the 10-kilometre square bounded by grid lines 00 (on the *west*) and 10, and 40 (on the *south*) and 50; Wroxall (reference 2070) in the square bounded by the grid lines 20 (on the *west*) and 30, and 70 (on the *south*) and 80.

The map contains all those places, whether towns, villages or isolated buildings, which are the subject of separate entries in the text.

ILLUSTRATION REFERENCES are given as marginal numbers for photographs, and as marginal *italic* cross-references for images on other pages of the text.

FOREWORD AND ACKNOWLEDGEMENTS

The first edition of this volume was published in 1966 as *Warwickshire* under the joint authorship of Nikolaus Pevsner and Alexandra Wedgwood. As was explained in the Foreword to that edition, Wedgwood did the preparatory research for the whole volume and wrote the whole description for Birmingham. Pevsner did the rest, accompanied on his visits by Michael Taylor, whose entertaining account of their travels together in 1965 offers a perceptive insight into the manner in which the original version was compiled and written. It was, of course, all done in a single university vacation, at a breathtaking speed and with unbelievable intensity. Such was the man and thus was his approach to the task. His achievement was all the more remarkable for it, as has been constantly impressed on me throughout my work on this revision.

This revised edition is different. It omits Birmingham altogether and its coverage differs in other respects from that in the original. But Warwickshire as defined for the purposes of this volume is still an artificial construction, since it spans administrative areas that are technically no longer in the administrative or ceremonial county. Official boundaries and definitions are thus not especially helpful. Suffice it to say that for present purposes Warwickshire includes all the historic county – including Coventry and the rural part of Solihull Metropolitan Borough in the so-called Meriden gap – outside the greater Birmingham area. For practical simplicity the route of the M42 motorway south and south-east of Birmingham and Solihull has been used as the dividing line, with all the area within to be covered in a separate volume (in preparation, 2016) to be titled *Birmingham and the Black Country*. The division may not be ideal but it should have at least one advantage over following the real boundaries, namely complete clarity.

Even allowing for the reduced coverage, Warwickshire is still a big county whose urban centres include a major city, Coventry, as well as five large towns. It is also rich in major castles, important country houses and fine churches. This new edition has been prepared with a much more generous timescale for visiting, although the total span of almost six years is certainly longer than the publishers had intended. For their forbearance and constant support I am especially grateful. In general terms the chief task has been to check, correct and where necessary supplement Pevsner's original gazetteer entries. The established principles of the series have been followed. I have either seen things myself or been able to check on them from reliable and recent accounts (e.g. photographs and detailed surveys). Where such checks have not been possible then the entries appear in brackets. Wherever possible Pevsner's writing has been left unaltered or merely tweaked to avoid replacement. Quite often, however, changes to buildings or subsequent re-interpretation through deeper research have made his observations obsolete. In such cases new entries have been required, but even these retain much of the original descriptive text – along with those distinctively Pevsnerian comments that characterize the series. As to its extent, the revised gazetteer runs to over two and a half times the original. Many of the descriptions are expanded and more buildings of all periods and types have been included. This means that information ought to be as complete as the format of the series permits for churches and other places of worship before 1945 and only a little more selective for the period thereafter. The range of secular buildings is not limited by date and many built within the last decade or in progress are mentioned if they are thought likely to be of future architectural interest. Nevertheless, what appears here is still but a selection of the buildings in the county and inevitably a somewhat personal and subjective one guided by the reviser's own likes and interests. There is certainly some emphasis on Victorian and later buildings, on church restorations, on stained glass and on buildings which, perhaps unremarkable in the bigger picture, represent the best works of the better local architects. Pevsner's opinions have been retained unless no longer relevant or true. I have ventured few of my own, except by way of selection for inclusion.

It has been a particular pleasure to re-explore my native county after an absence of twenty years or so when employment took me to other parts of the country. To explain, between the late 1960s and the mid 1980s I visited every church, most country houses and a great many other buildings in the county to examine and record bells and belfries – a particular lifelong interest, stemming from being both a bellringer and a historian of bells and ringing. The buildings were always of equal interest and my project involved a fair amount of architectural and local history research too. So returning after a gap has allowed me to renew my acquaintance with the county and made me especially aware of the changes that have taken place in the intervening years. It has also given me an ideal outlet for my earlier research and enabled me to complete unfinished business. It has been pleasantly reassuring to find how much still seems familiar yet also a delight to discover places and buildings I had not fully appreciated before. To add to that, it has been particularly touching to meet a handful of people who remembered Pevsner's original visits. Not only have I retraced my own footsteps, but I have also followed in his.

Research has been referred to. It is not easy to convey an idea of just how much fresh material has become available since the original edition appeared in 1966. The quantity is vast, and still only a portion of what exists in print, online or in archival sources has been fully exploited. But the length of time it has taken to complete the revision is due in no small measure to the efforts made to find answers where important questions of date and attribution would otherwise be left uncertain.

My first acknowledgement must be to the staff, past and present, of the Warwickshire County Record Office, especially to the late Michael Farr (formerly County Archivist), Monica Ory, Mark Booth, Richard Chamberlaine-Brothers and Rob Eyre. The ecclesiastical archives for the area are divided between four different archives, and the help of staff at the Worcestershire Archive and Archaeology Service, the Lichfield Record Office of the Staffordshire and Stoke-on-Trent Archive Service, the Birmingham Archives, Heritage and Photography Service, and the Gloucestershire Archives must also be gratefully acknowledged. Thanks are also due to the Coventry Diocesan Registrar and to Jill Russell at the Registry for allowing access to material still held there. Also to Lambeth Palace Library, whose holdings include the extensive archive of the Incorporated Church Building Society, richer in detail than the selection in Church Plans Online (*www.churchplansonline.org*) suggests. Other record offices and libraries to whose staff I owe thanks include the Shakespeare Centre Library and Archives at Stratford (Bob Bearman, Mairi Macdonald and Delia Garratt), Solihull Library (Tracey Williams), Coventry History Centre, the Oxfordshire History Centre, the library of the Society of Antiquaries (especially Adrian James), the Royal Institute of British Architects' library and drawings collection, and the Historic England Archive at Swindon (formerly the English Heritage National Monuments Record Centre) where Pevsner's original notes are held. Other archives have been helpful in answering enquiries, including those of the major banks (HSBC, Lloyds and RBS), the Church of England Record Centre, the Birmingham Archdiocesan Archives (Rev. Dr John Sharp), Oxford College archives (Magdalen and Christ Church), the Institution of Civil Engineers and several local repositories.

Next, it is my pleasure to acknowledge the contributions of a great many people who sent snippets of information and corrections to the Buildings of England office between 1966 and the commencement of the revision. The names are too numerous to list but thanks are due to all who have assisted in this way. However, special mention should be made of Malcolm Airs, Peter Bolton, George McHardy, Richard Hewlings, Peter Reid, D.M. Palliser, the late Sir Howard Colvin and the late Professor Andor Gomme who all made frequent contributions. Specialists who offered such help included R. Neville Hadcock (religious houses), Adam White (church monuments), Paul Thompson (William Butterfield), Bob Hakewill (Henry Hakewill) and Jon Bayliss (Elizabethan and Stuart monuments; indicated as (JB) in the gazetteer).

Since I embarked on this revision, many people have come to my aid, and for all their help and contributions I am most grateful. Indeed, the resulting volume would have been considerably the poorer without their input. Willingness to answer queries or forward pieces of useful information is such a great help in a task like this. Alan Brooks has been a constant pillar of support in this respect. Not only did he accompany me on my initial visits to get me started, but he willingly gave me access to his research files on Victorian stained glass and school buildings. Moreover any queries are always swiftly answered – and he usually has the answers. They are acknowledged by his initials (AB) against the entry. It has been helpful to work alongside Andy Foster in Birmingham, sharing information and discoveries across our agreed boundary line. For churches, Aidan McRae Thomson has been more than helpful. For Roman Catholic churches collaboration with Andrew Derrick and his team at the Architectural History Practice working on the 'Taking Stock' project was fruitful, and Johanna Roethe helped specially with the Coventry entries. Of those who shared their knowledge while accompanying me on my visits or showing me round particular towns, villages or buildings, special mention should be made of Bob Bearman (Stratford-upon-Avon and Butlers Marston), Professor Louise Campbell (Warwick University), James Mackay and Christine Hodgetts (Warwick), Bruce Bailey (country houses), Vince Taylor (Bedworth and Exhall), Richard Russell (Cherington and Sutton-under-Brailes), Steven Parissien and Cranmer Webb (Compton Verney), Dr Christopher Powell-Brett (Forest Hall, Meriden), Amanda Slater (Allesley and other Coventry suburbs), Adrian King (Guy's Cliffe), the Rev. Tony Upton (Foleshill and Knowle), David Eaves and Sheila Woolf (Stoneleigh Abbey), David McGrory (St Mary's Hall, Coventry), Peter and Gillian Ashley-Smith (Kineton), Eddie Tolcher (Princethorpe), Rusty MacLean (Rugby School), Gervald Frykman (Warwick School), Rob Phillips (King Henry VIII School, Coventry), David Adams (Chesterton), Paul Maddocks (Coventry Charterhouse), Gary Hall (Coventry Old Grammar School), Chris Kirby (Coventry Whitefriars), Colin Jones (Warwick Shirehall) and Andy Main (Newbold Revel). To this list must be added the many owners of private houses and custodians of churches and other buildings – not forgetting the National Trust, Landmark Trust and people at properties now used at hotels or in shared ownership – who permitted access and provided helpful guidance to me when I visited. While limits of space dictate that they must remain anonymous, they must not go unthanked.

Special thanks are reserved, though, for the owners of larger private houses where access is a special privilege. That owners are willing to allow visits, give of their time and share their often considerable knowledge for the benefit of the *Buildings of England* series is a matter for public gratitude as well as personal thanks. Among them are Lord Hertford (Ragley), Lord Aylesford (Packington), Viscount Daventry (Arbury), Sir Matthew Dugdale (Merevale), Lady Dugdale (Blythe Hall), Michael Fetherston-Dilke (Maxstoke), Marian Carter (Clifford Chambers), Martin Taylor (Ilmington), David Richards (Radway), Hamish Cathie (Barton-on-the-Heath), Emma Holman-West (Alscot), Camilla Holman-West (Atherstone-on-Stour), Benjamin Wiggin (Honington), Ludo de Walden (Arlescote), Sir James Shuckburgh (Shuckburgh), Guy Ward (Little Wolford), Roger Hancox (Grimshaw Hall),

Charles Mallinder (Pooley Hall), Fiona Meyrick (Fenny Compton), Michael Macdonald (Burmington) and Henry Warriner (Weston Park). Only a handful of refusals were received and these, while regrettable, are not difficult to understand. This is a reminder that a firm statement is necessary here to emphasise that the inclusion of any building in the gazetteer does not mean that it is open to the public.

Next, there are those who have shared their expertise and made available information from unpublished researches during the course of the work – in some cases through frequent and extended correspondence. They include Nat Alcock (vernacular architecture), James Bettley (Ernest Geldart), Dr John Bland (north Warwickshire parishes), Tim Booth (mills), Geoff Brandwood, Tim Clayton (churches in Birmingham diocese), Max Craven, George Demidowicz (Coventry; denoted (GD) in the gazetteer), Fr Brian Doolan (Roman Catholic churches), Robert Eberhard (stained glass), Geoffrey Fisher (C17 and C17 church monuments and sculptors; his attributions denoted (GF) in the gazetteer), Keith Geary (Nonconformist chapels), Professor Jane Geddes (ironwork), Rob Gill (Coventry), John Goodall (castles), Jeremy and Caroline Gould (C20 Coventry), Nigel Harrison (Clough Williams-Ellis), Elain Harwood (C20 architecture), Jeffrey Haworth (National Trust), Will Hawkes (Sanderson Miller; denoted (WH) in the gazetteer), Peter Howell, Gill Hunter (William White), Stanley R. Jones (timber-framed buildings), Michael Kerney (stained glass), Nicholas Kingsley, Hugh Martin (C20 houses), Chris Mawson (T. H. Mawson), John Minnis (railway architecture), the late Richard K. Morris (Kenilworth), Julian Osley (Post Offices), Maurice Rogers (geology), Roger Rosewell (wall paintings and stained glass), Fr Edward Stuart (Roman Catholic churches), Paul Tindall (organs and organ cases), Dr Charles Tracy (medieval woodwork), Geoffrey Tyack (country houses), Susannah Wade Martins (model farms), Philip Ward-Jackson (memorials), plus many others – architects, clergy, local historians – who have responded to specific queries. Special thanks here must go to Stuart Palmer who willingly agreed to summarize the county's early past in the separate chapter on prehistoric, Roman and Anglo-Saxon Warwickshire.

Finally, for the gazetteer, there are the local informants who have helped with their towns or villages and, in many cases, read and commented on the drafts – a task also performed by some of the other people already mentioned above. They include Richard Churchley and Cyril Johnson (Alcester), Brian Johnson (Alveston), Margaret Antill (Ansley), Judy Vero and John Austin (Atherstone), Sarah Richardson and Jill Burgess (Avon Dassett), Peter Britton (Barcheston), Ann McDermott (Barford), Deborah Kirkham (Barston), Chris Brett (Baxterley), John and Lynne Burton (Bedworth), Sandra Parker (Bidford-on-Avon), Canon Nicholas Morgan (Brailes), Peter Sheen (Bubbenhall), Verna Scott and Tim Clamp (Caldecote), Dorothy Bancroft (Clifton-upon-Dunsmore), Michael Bryant (Hampton-in-Arden), Rosemary Tyler and Jean Lapworth (Hartshill), Margaret Hunt (Haseley),

John Parr (Haselor), Robin Leach, Norman Stevens and Graham Gould (Kenilworth), Jeremy Ashbee (Kenilworth Castle), Carole Haines (Kingsbury), Janet Erzen and Kathy Jephcott of the Knowle Society (Knowle), Peter Hill (Lapworth), Paul Eldridge (Leek Wootton), Colin Such (Lighthorne), Paul Harvey (Morton Bagot), Fr Philip Wells (Polesworth), Liz Pride of MJP and Lizzie Morrison (University of Warwick), Lady Elizabeth Hamilton (Walton), Pamela Bromley (Warwick Castle), Steven Wallsgrove and Jolyon Hall (Warwick), Alan F. Cook (Weddington), Peter Bolton (Wellesbourne), Brian and Christine Sanderson (Wolfhampcote), Geoff Lewis (Wolvey), Keith Chambers (Wolston) and Jeremy Wheeler (Wormleighton). To these I would add the conservation and planning officers who have taken interest in the revision for their areas, especially Katherine Moreton (Nuneaton and Bedworth), Paul Varnish (Rugby), Martin Saunders (Solihull) and Chris Patrick who gave considerable help with the draft for Coventry.

Turning to the commissioning and production team at Yale, my first debt of gratitude is to Charles O'Brien for his patient support throughout this project. Invariably wise and helpful, he made a great many insightful and sensitive suggestions to improve my drafts and encouraged me through moments of difficulty. Simon Bradley and Sally Salvesen have been similarly supportive, as have colleagues working on other revisions. When work began, the research and fieldwork was funded by the Pevsner Books Trust. At that stage Gavin Watson's guidance was invaluable. Funding is now provided by the Paul Mellon Centre whose ongoing support is gratefully acknowledged. In the office, Elizabeth O'Rafferty has been responsible for co-ordinating the illustrations and Linda McQueen for assembling them for the inset and also for steering the manuscript through to publication. John Roan and his team took the commissioned photographs and the maps and plans were prepared or redrawn by Martin Brown. Thanks are also due to the copy-editor, Katy Carter, the proof-reader, Charley Chapman, the indexer, Judith Wardman, and to the volunteer researchers – Karen Evans and Michael Breen – for seeking out information from libraries and archives in the capital.

There is one more, and an important one. The dedication is to my wife, Heather, who has encouraged me throughout, helping in many ways and often accompanying me on my visits. Without her love and patient support this revision would never have been completed and for that, and much besides, I owe her more than mere gratitude.

To anyone overlooked or whose contribution has been under-acknowledged I can only apologize. I must apologize too for such errors as will inevitably remain. Users of this book are invited to make these, and any serious omissions, known to me through the publishers.

Chris Pickford
2016

INTRODUCTION

Warwickshire is Mid-Land indeed, geographically situated both in the middle of the country and at the heart of the Midlands region. At Meriden is a cross in the place said to be the centre of England. As far as this volume is concerned, it should be explained at the outset that Warwickshire means the area outside the conurbation around Birmingham but including Coventry and the rural belt – the so-called Meriden gap – between Coventry and Solihull. Thus defined, Warwickshire is about midway in size among English counties, having an approximate area of 840 square miles (2,180 square kilometres) and a population of around 940,000.*

Within this area, Coventry alone accounts for over one-third of the total population. Other big urban centres include Nuneaton and Bedworth, Rugby, Leamington, Stratford-upon-Avon and Warwick. Outside these places, however, Warwickshire is a predominantly rural county. Its smaller towns include Atherstone, Knowle, Kenilworth, Southam, Alcester and Shipston-on-Stour, and there are large villages such as Bidford-on-Avon, Henley-in-Arden, Kineton and Wellesbourne.

As to TOPOGRAPHY, Warwickshire has the high ground of the Birmingham plateau to the NW and a high ridge above Atherstone and Nuneaton on the N. But the SW is Cotswolds. Warwickshire LANDSCAPE is also mid-land landscape. The highest heights are no more than about 850 ft (259 metres) along the SE boundary to Oxfordshire and Northamptonshire, with Ebrington Hill, Edge Hill, and Brailes Hill. Cliffs, not high, but impressive, are along the Avon at Warwick and Guy's Cliffe. The N is flat, but really flat flat-land is rarely met apart from the plain below the Edge Hill escarpment and the pasturelands in the thinly populated belt E of Southam and S of Rugby. Most of Warwickshire is rolling country, well wooded – even without any large areas of forest – and friendly. And as varied as its landscape and its building materials are its monuments of architecture and art. Not many, though some, are among England's outstanding treasures (e.g. Warwick and Kenilworth castles, Ragley Hall, Coventry Cathedral), but there is an immense amount of more than local interest and more than average value.

* These are the very approximate combined totals for the current administrative areas covering the 'county', i.e. Warwickshire, Coventry and part of Solihull Metropolitan Borough Council.

GEOLOGY AND BUILDING STONES*

Several places in Warwickshire claim to be the 'centre' of England and, as if arranged to support these claims impartially, the rivers of the county run down to almost all the possible seas – the Cole–Blythe–Anker system to the North Sea by way of the Trent and Humber, the Arrow–Alne–Avon to the Bristol Channel and the Atlantic, and in the extreme SE of Warwickshire a tiny group of headwater streams drains the Cotswold ridge to the Thames. So also do the rocks reflect a kind of geological centrality, for they straddle across the transition from the 'hard' rocks of West and Northern England to the 'soft' rocks of the South and East. Thus both physiographically and stratigraphically Warwickshire is essentially midland. It is therefore consistent with this pattern, albeit not strictly logical, to start a GEOLOGICAL DESCRIPTION with the middle unit of the complete rock succession, since this underlies the Forest of Arden, the heart of Warwickshire.

The formation on which the Forest of Arden lies is MERCIA MUDSTONE of hard, red marls formed from the dusts blown into this zone in the dry, desert conditions of the TRIASSIC about 230 million years ago. The countryside floored by this assemblage of soft red or chocolate-coloured mudstones and shales, sometimes with green or white streaks, is, as might be expected, flattish, or only very gently featured. Where it is broken by low rounded hills or ridges – as in the Alcester–Henley-in-Arden–Knowle country – these interruptions are produced by slightly harder sandstone units within the main mass of the marls. A thicker and more persistent SANDSTONE (part of the NEW RED SANDSTONE group or SHERWOOD SANDSTONE group, the rock strata prevalent in the Midlands and so called because it underlies Sherwood Forest in Nottinghamshire) lies immediately below the marls, and forms the E flank of the two Warwickshire 'table-lands' – the Birmingham region in the NW, and the Kenilworth–Tamworth upland in the centre and N. This BROMSGROVE SANDSTONE (in the past known as Keuper Sandstone) is a handsome compact medium-grained rock which may vary in colour from light red or brown to a green-grey and even a pale near-white. This is one of the most commonly used local stones from the medieval period onwards and in different areas it obtained the appellation of the places in which it was quarried. Stone extracted at Attleborough, S of Nuneaton, was already known as Attilburgh Sandstone in the C14 and was a true freestone, i.e. bedrock which could be split into slabs or large blocks, in use from the C11 to the late C19. It is the buff grey stone used not only for the abbey church of St Mary at Nuneaton and the market crosses in the same town but also for much later buildings nearby such as Arbury Hall.

---

*This chapter is a revision and expansion of the text by Terence Miller in the first edition of this volume. I am grateful to Alan F. Cook, Maurice Rogers and Hugh Jones for providing much essential information on the use and distribution of the county's building stones.

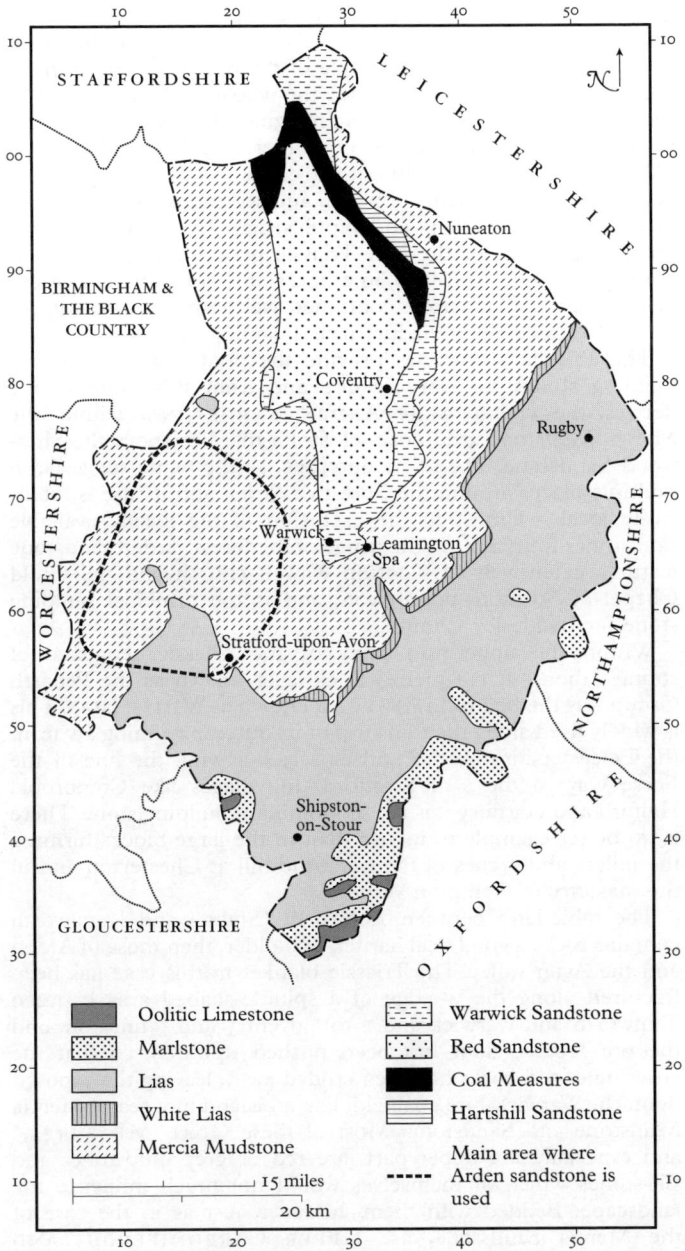

Geological map of Warwickshire

There is evidence that that it was transported to sites several miles away, possibly along the Anker. St Michael's church at Coventry is the principal example of the red-toned Bromsgrove Sandstone, but it is also used for the whole of the church of St Mary, Newton Regis, and in its grey guise it is widely employed in the buildings of Warwick (and therefore known locally as 'Warwick Sandstone') including the castle and St Mary's church. Near Warwick, fragments of plants and scorpions, and footprints of primitive amphibians and reptiles, have been found in this rock, suggesting, for the Late Triassic period, a region of temporary lakes and sand-flats, in a hot, semi-arid climate. The use of Bromsgrove Sandstone continued well into the C19, e.g. for the Milverton railway viaduct near Leamington Spa.

The Triassic sandstones provide the predominant group of building stones for Warwickshire and from this same source derives the creamy-white ARDEN SANDSTONE, within the Mercia Mudstone group of rock strata that lies above the Sherwood Sandstone. The stone outcrops, as the name suggests, in multiple places around the Forest of Arden and its use is intensively local – almost to the exclusion of the locally available sandstones from around the fringe of the forest. Arden sandstone features extensively in Wootton Wawen church and the Guild Chapel at Stratford-upon-Avon, and is the principal building stone for Baddesley Clinton.

Within the uppermost layer of the Triassic sequence of strata – the 45-ft (14-metre) thick layer known as the Penarth Group – is the bed of LIMESTONE known as WHITE LIAS. This is widely used along the thin strip of its outcrop running SW from the Leicestershire border and closely following the line of the Fosse Way to the S of Stratford. In villages like Combrook, Halford and Harbury it is the predominant building stone. There is no better example of its use than in the large blocks forming the pillars and arches of the C17 windmill at Chesterton and in the masonry of Compton Verney.

The table-land between Tamworth (Staffs.) and Kenilworth contains rocks a good deal harder, and older, than those of Arden and the Avon valley. The Triassic blanket in this case has been fractured along the W edge of a spindle-shaped area between Tamworth and Warwick and E to Coventry and Nuneaton, and the pre-Triassic floor has been pushed upwards, so that the covering of soft rocks has been eroded away, leaving the exposed floor, the Warwickshire coalfield, like an island in a sea of Mercia Mudstone and Sandstone. Most of these COAL MEASURES,* and especially the upper part, are red or grey mudstones and silt-stones which of themselves would not much influence the landscape. Bedded with them, however, just as in the case of the Mercia Mudstone, are UPPER CARBONIFEROUS AND

---

* The Middle Coal Measures, which contained the workable seams, crop out along the E side of the spindle and around its N end, but as they dip under the Upper Measures, pits were opened in, and driven down through, the 'barren' Upper Measures, to the coal-bearing layers below.

PERMIAN SANDSTONES, collectively known as the Warwickshire Group and formed from river sediments laid down some 250 million years ago, which produce a more rolling country, with occasional low scarp ridges, as for example about Meriden, near Coventry. Within this central area darker red, as well as buff, sandstones from the Coal Measures can be seen. The formations have a multiplicity of names specific to their locality, such as the Ashow formation, whose red sandstones are the predominant building stone for that village, or Kenilworth, whose stones are much used locally. Apart from Kenilworth Castle the good examples are the w door of St Nicholas, Kenilworth, and the e range of Stoneleigh Abbey, but the varied types of sandstone from this district may also be seen in the churches and other buildings at Allesley (All Saints), Temple Balsall, Nether Whitacre, Over Whitacre and Shustoke. The latter is a good demonstration of how medieval masons needed to build close to the site of the stone's extraction, for the church was built 3 miles away from the village on the hill where its sandstone outcrops. To have transported it to the settlement would have been prohibitively expensive.

Still older rocks, which were formerly part of the floor on which, in their turn, the Carboniferous peat swamps grew, appear at the surface in the narrow, NW–SE-trending Hartshill ridge which overlooks Nuneaton. These are red and purple CAMBRIAN shales and quartzites (sandstones hardened into a tough, compact rock by a silica cement), 500–600 million years old, with slightly younger bodies of igneous rock (diorite) injected into them. Both the quartzites and the diorites have been extensively quarried for road-metal (aggregates) but the unyielding nature of the diorites makes them unsuitable for building other than walling, although the walls of the nave at St Mary, Atherstone, appear to be of this. Nevertheless the very hard, purplish HARTSHILL SANDSTONE (grey colour streaked with purple and green) is to be found employed in the building of Hartshill Castle and in the 1840s at Holy Trinity, Hartshill, as well as the ruins of the medieval priory of St Mary Nuneaton. A narrow strip of PRE-CAMBRIAN volcanic rocks stretches for 2 miles NW from Nuneaton, but is of little importance topographically. These rocks were quarried for setts and paviours for roads.

The southernmost 'lobe' of Warwickshire, and practically all the ground e of the Fosse Way, is based on rocks younger than the Mercia Mudstone. The first of these, the JURASSIC LOWER LIAS, has a low, interrupted, w-facing scarp looking across the main Avon valley, and forming almost a mirror-image of the Arden country beyond. This region, known to geographers as the 'Felden', is one of heavy, ill-drained soils, waterlogged in winter, deeply fissured in dry summers. Like the lower-lying, less sandy parts of the Forest of Arden, the Felden carries fewer villages than is usual for the county. This area was never heavily wooded and accordingly little of the timber-framed tradition that provides the main alternative to stone building up to the C17 can be seen here. The Vale of the Red Horse, below Edge Hill, and the battlefield of Kineton are typical of this part. Within the Lias Group the oldest beds are the BLUE LIAS, which lies on top of the Triassic White Lias, formed of layers of limestone and clay. This fossil-rich Blue Lias was widely used in the southern half of the county and quarries at Wilmcote gave their name to the best of this limestone, which is frequently employed for the plinths on which are raised the timber-framed houses so numerous in the neighbourhood, e.g. Palmer's Farm, Wilmcote, or as slabs for flooring etc. A notable fashion over a long period in various places is to see White or Blue Lias laid together in alternating courses or alternating with bands of sandstone and ironstone, e.g. at Ladbroke Hall (c. 1670) and Stockton St Michael (1847). The industrialized burning of Blue Lias for lime for CEMENT was carried on at Wilmcote, Southam and Stockton from the C19 and there were also quarries at Bishop's Itchington which served the local cement works until 1970. The formation known as Rugby Limestone continues to be quarried as the aggregate for the production of Rugby Cement.

Edge Hill, and the general SW–NE scarp of which it is the most prominent sector, is built of the next youngest Jurassic formation, the MARLSTONE ROCK. This is a quite thin (150-ft (46-metre)) band of rich brown sandstones and ironstones, with some clays, well seen in the cutting at Warmington, S of Farnborough. It is best observed immediately below the church of St Michael (itself built of the same stone) through which the main Warwick–Banbury road climbs the scarp to the high plateau of north Oxfordshire. Familiarly also known as 'Hornton stone', this ferruginous ironstone has a warm, if not hot, dark brown toffee colour and fossily grain. It was formerly quarried at Burton Dassett, and was used fairly generally along the Edge Hill ridge, for example in the church at Avon Dassett, the houses and cottages of Tysoe and *Sanderson Miller*'s Edgehill Tower. Medieval masons' concerns about marlstone's structural limitations may be the explanation for the decision to build the C13 broach spire of Crick church (Northants.) from sandstone brought from Coventry, 25 miles away, rather than use the marlstone available immediately around them and of which the rest of the church is built. Dressed as ashlar it is the defining material of All Saints, Chadshunt. Marlstone is also the sole material for major buildings like the gatehouse at Wormleighton and much in evidence in that village. Indeed it is employed as a building stone for many houses of C16, C17 and C18 date. In church work it seems more commonly to be intermingled with other stone or favoured for dressings: one sees it used for quoins, buttresses and windows in many places, notably Holy Trinity, Stratford-upon-Avon.

Next in sequence, although much less apparent, are the Middle Jurassic inferior OOLITIC (or OOIDAL) LIMESTONES. There is a small area of this bedrock within Warwickshire's boundary e.g. at the southern tip around Long Compton. Stretton-on-Fosse is a village almost entirely composed of such stone but the majority of these limestones in Warwickshire buildings unquestionably derive from the Cotswolds to the SW, for example the beds of Birdlip Limestone just across the border into Worcestershire.

As one goes N from Edge Hill towards Rugby, the main escarpment loses height and bears gently to the E away from the county boundary; SW of Rugby the rather drab Lower Lias Clay country is varied by the wide expanse of Dunsmore Heath, a thick 'pad' of superficial glacial deposits. The topographical effects of these 'superficial deposits' are of great importance in Warwickshire, as in all the English Midland counties. They consist of more or less unconsolidated materials either dumped directly by the great ice-sheets which lay, a thousand feet or more in thickness, across England and Wales during the PLEISTOCENE era more than 10,000 years ago, or reworked from such dumps by the meltwater rivers which flowed out from the ice during the warm spells between glacial advances. A large fraction of the surface of Warwickshire is covered (although no further S than Edge Hill), and the bedrock obscured, by these glacial (or inter-glacial) sands and gravels peppered with assorted stones ('erratics') of all sizes up to boulders several tons in weight. The thickness of this veneer varies from a few inches of sandy soil, or a scatter of foreign pebbles, to 200 ft (60 metres) or more, where a pre-glacial valley or hollow has been filled up. One of the more obvious results of this patchy distribution is the preferred location of villages and ancient settlements on patches of glacial sand in the clay-based areas, where reliable water supplies, otherwise unobtainable, could be got from shallow wells. In the buildings of these villages it is accordingly typical to find cobbles and boulders providing the principal walling materials for churches and other buildings, for example at St Mary, Clifton-upon-Dunsmore, where the great variety of rubble used confirms the lack of good building stone in the vicinity.

Indeed, few medieval buildings are of exclusively one stone or another; a great many of the churches in the sandstone areas are composed of more than one variety, expressing their evolution, so that for example the tower may be of Bromsgrove Sandstone, the nave of Arden, the chancel of something else again. Transporting stone was hugely expensive so medieval masons needed to acquire their stone near the working site – a figure of no more than 400 yds has been given as the limit of the distance. However, because such a large proportion of Warwickshire is underlain by comparatively soft rocks, and because none of the more important building stones of England occur within its borders, it seems to have been from the earliest times an importer of FREESTONE, not least for the finer work required in the carving of tracery and the piers of church arcades. As has been noted, Cotswold Stone and Cotswold 'slates' for roofing were in easy reach to the SW and the Lincolnshire Limestones to the NE. Bath Stone from Wiltshire to the S was brought in for the construction of Moreton Hall, Moreton Morrell, in 1905–8. There are also isolated instances of the orangey ironstones more common in Northamptonshire, notably in the tower of Grandborough church, which lies just a few miles from the county boundary. But the widespread importing of stone for building is primarily the effect of the C19 revolution in transportation along the canals and railways that enabled the import of more durable stones e.g. for church restorations, notably the quartz-rich Hollington Sandstone from Staffordshire which in its natural state is, as Alec Clifton-Taylor wrote in his *Pattern of English Building*, 'extraordinarily soft; large blocks, weighing up to six tons each, can be cut out like cheese. Fortunately it becomes much harder on exposure to air and as it possesses a very even texture it lends itself to carved detail better than most sandstones'. It is the stone used for the construction of *Spence*'s Coventry Cathedral and the refacing of Warwick's Shire Hall in 1948.

There are of course more building materials than stone in Warwickshire; for its timber framing *see* pp. 28–31, and brick *see* p. 32.

PREHISTORIC AND ROMAN WARWICKSHIRE
BY STUART PALMER

The Warwickshire landscape in the PALAEOLITHIC era (*c.* 950,000–8000 B.C.) was very different from today. Some 760,000 years ago (Lower Palaeolithic), when Britain was a peninsula of Eurasia, a huge artery known now as the River Bytham drained much of what was to become the Midlands region. Evidence for Warwickshire's earliest human presence was found in Bytham sediments in the base of a gravel quarry at Waverley Wood Farm, Bubbenhall. This nationally important site has yielded a group of hand-axes associated with evidence for the local environment some half a million years ago. Over 260 Lower and Middle Palaeolithic stone implements have been collected from fields and quarries in the county. Most were deposited north of Warwickshire and arrived here through glacial activity. Particular concentrations from Wolvey, Burton Hastings, Little Alne near Alcester and along the Avon valley are attributable to specialist collectors but these important discoveries provide a direct link to the early hominins which are otherwise absent in the fossil record.

Evidence for Upper Palaeolithic and Final Upper Palaeolithic activity, the period when anatomically modern humans (*Homo sapiens*) began colonizing the peninsula (*c.* 40,000–8000 B.C.), is rare, though a small flint tool assemblage was found at the Gloucestershire border on Ebrington Hill, near Ilmington.

The end of the last Ice Age (*c.* 8500 B.C.) was marked by a period of global warming as the open tundra landscape was gradually colonized by forest and rising sea levels cut our peninsula from mainland Europe. Technologically this MESOLITHIC period (*c.* 8000–4000 B.C.) is defined by the making and use of a wide range of small retouched flint blades (microliths) and the introduction of the flaked axe or adze. The earlier Mesolithic toolkit was based on broad blades and obliquely blunted points which have been found sporadically in fields across the county. An important assemblage of over 4,000 was recovered from Blacklow Hill, Leek Wootton.

In the later Mesolithic (*c.* 6000–4000 B.C.) assemblages become dominated by narrower blades and are in a wider variety of forms associated with the growth and spread of mixed deciduous woodland that necessitated the development of new hunting techniques. These tool types are widespread across the county but in a few places occur in sufficient numbers to suggest temporary camp sites, for example at Over Whitacre and two sites in Corley. At Polesworth, a fishing camp has been identified on a low-lying sand bar within a former channel of the River Anker.

The emergence of NEOLITHIC ideas concerning ancestry, relations with nature, values and ideals at *c.* 4000 B.C. is manifest in the introduction of pottery and polished stone tools, the construction of communal monuments and the importation of cereals and domesticated animals. This new world view was gradually adopted and adapted by the indigenous population but the absence of some classic early monuments in Warwickshire could indicate that the transition occurred later here than in other regions. Nevertheless, scatters of Mesolithic and Early Neolithic flint tools beneath Neolithic monuments at Rollright and King's Newnham indicate that some Mesolithic locations remained important throughout this transition.

Evidence for a Neolithic 'farming revolution' has failed to emerge across most of lowland Britain where a largely mobile herding population may have used rudimentary horticultural plots, but were still heavily dependent on wild resources. Their polished stone axes, leaf-shaped flint arrowheads and blade-derived flint flaked tools are found scattered throughout the county. Polished stone axes demonstrate long-distance exchange networks, revealing links as far away as Cumbria and Cornwall, while a possible axe factory has been posited near Nuneaton. In locations that seem to have been regarded as significant, items that were invested with meaning were selected for burial within pits. Round-bottomed pots, flintwork, and less durable material including food items which have sometimes survived as carbonized fossils, were mixed with the ashes from hearths after episodes of feasting and have been found at Wasperton, Barford, Warwick, Church Lawford and King's Newnham.

By far the majority of Warwickshire's early communal MONU-MENTS are found in complexes along the River Avon which was then a major artery for travel and communication. The earliest elements within the Avon complexes were constructed *c.* 3000 B.C. (Middle Neolithic) and include two large, segmented enclosures, closely related to the earlier causewayed enclosures of southern Britain. An example at Wasperton was devoid of internal features but at Church Lawford the enclosure was associated with a range of ritual pits revealing that the locale was frequented for over a thousand years.

The complexes at Longbridge (Warwick), a site to its E at Barford Sheds, NE of Barford itself, and Charlecote were founded on Middle Neolithic cursus monuments. These long, 'processional' monuments are probably related to oblong enclosures, long barrows and mortuary enclosure, although the date and function of those excavated at Charlecote, Wasperton, King's Newnham and Barford remains uncertain.

Two possible Early Neolithic megalithic tombs at Little Compton and Rollright, both on the Oxfordshire border, are probably outliers of the distinctive Cotswold–Severn group. Warwickshire's only standing stone (the King's Stone at Long Compton) forms part of the Rollright complex, of which the King's Men stone circle and the Whispering Knights portal dolmen both lie across the Oxfordshire border.

During the third millennium B.C. a transformation occurred in religious and social practices as the cult of the ancestor gave way to theism. The new forms of monuments, such as the complex of four earthwork henges recently excavated at Bidford-on-Avon and the hengiform ring-ditches added to the complexes at Barford and Wasperton, attest to the rise of ritual authority structures. Other certainly LATE NEOLITHIC (c. 3000–2200 B.C.) monuments are scarce, though some of the region's many ring-ditch cropmarks could be Neolithic in origin, as are those excavated at Charlecote, King's Newnham and Barford. Grooved Ware, the classic tub and barrel shaped pottery style of this period intimately associated with pig bones and feasting, is present in the special pit deposits at Wasperton, Church Lawford and Salford Priors.

In the EARLY BRONZE AGE (c. 2600/2200–1800 B.C.) there is a proliferation of élite burials in the single grave tradition. Over 130 barrows and/or ring-ditches have now been recorded, predominantly as cropmarks, often in groups or cemeteries and incorporated into earlier monument complexes along the Avon valley. A concentration of barrows at Wolvey, at the head of the Anker valley, may indicate a new area of occupation.

ROUND BARROWS are mostly associated with the European-derived 'prestige goods economy' evinced by the fancy goods 'Beaker package'. These finely made pottery vessels accompanied changes in flint technology such as thumbnail scrapers, barbed-and-tanged arrowheads, flaked knives and daggers, ground-stone maceheads and battle axes and metalwork. The arrival of Beakers marks the advent of the Bronze Age, although there are no precise dates yet for the introduction of metal into Warwickshire.

There is as yet no evidence for Early Bronze Age settlement, but significant cultural items were deposited in pits at Oversley and Church Lawford. During the second millennium B.C. the mortuary tradition includes both inhumation and cremation burial, often accompanied by new forms of pottery such as food vessels, while collared and biconical urns can also be found in isolated contexts.

Across Britain the MIDDLE BRONZE AGE (c. 1500–1000 B.C.) is a time of conspicuous social change engendered by new conceptions of identity and territory. The landscape was increasingly divided and as clearance and new settlement increased so did new manifestations of prestige, authority and regional diversity.

In Warwickshire a growing number of burnt mounds have been found adjacent to streams. These isolated piles of heat-cracked pebbles have variously been interpreted as the remains of sweat lodges or cooking sites. There is an increase in the quantity of metal artefacts in circulation from this period onward. Axes, palstaves, other weapons and gold objects have been recovered either by chance or more often now by metal detectorists.

After the construction of burial and ritual monuments ceased towards the end of the second millennium B.C., flat cremation CEMETERIES become common. At Ryton-on-Dunsmore and Coton near Rugby, ashes were buried in large urns of the Deverel–Rimbury tradition.

The climatic downturn in the LATER BRONZE AGE AND EARLY IRON AGE (c. 1000–400 B.C.) may well have provoked social and economic pressures in the growing population. Along parts of the Avon and Arrow valleys smaller tributaries were used to define land units, while at Wasperton the earliest constructed boundary is dated c. 1300–850 B.C. At Church Lawford, in the centre of the newly deforested Dunsmore plateau, alignments of closely spaced posts were erected between surviving stands of trees c. 920–410 B.C. Structural evidence for settlement consistently occurs later than the boundary features, although early settlements like those at Barford (Park Farm) and Coton were quite ephemeral and are difficult to recognize.

Social rituals of feasting and conspicuous consumption were carried out on an enormous midden site at Whitchurch, where vast quantities of metalwork have been recovered. This important site remains the only place at which a higher status can be inferred in this period.

By the Early Iron Age some settlements were enclosed within a ditch, which although not always defensive may well have been invested with symbolic attributes. Further settlement locations of this date are indicated by ceramic assemblages recovered from fields at Alderminster, Ettington, Idlicote and Halford, and from pits at Burton Dassett and High Cross.

Some of the county's fourteen possible HILLFORTS may date from this period, although the defences at Nadbury at least (see Ratley) were not erected until much later. Hillforts have been associated with communal stores, meeting places and community retreats in times of trouble, but locally none have been sufficiently excavated to determine their function, and the absence of such sites in large parts of the county raises many questions as to their role as central places or élite residences.

The burial record in this period is almost unknown save for a highly unusual high-status cremation performed within a mini-ring-ditch at Salford Priors, in which three rare bronze cauldrons were included on the pyre.

The population expansion during the Middle and Later Iron Age (c. 400 B.C.–A.D. 43) prompted new episodes of clearance, initially for pasture and later for cultivation. Earlier notions of belonging and exclusion were fortified with the construction of EARTHWORK BOUNDARIES like the massive Hobditch at

Lapworth. On Dunsmore a network of boundaries formed by alignments of closely spaced pits radiate from a single nodal point in the centre of the plateau, forming the blueprint for medieval township boundaries on Dunsmore. Similar pit alignments occur along the major river valleys and often precede the explosion of settlement sites throughout the county.

Individual SETTLEMENTS generally comprise one or two roundhouses used by an extended family unit, set within a rectilinear ditched enclosure, but other settlements take the form of buildings clustered alongside earlier boundary features. The majority of buildings demonstrate a local tradition of conical thatched roofs supported on turf walls rather than on vertical posts like those in other regions. Doorways generally lack the porch structures common elsewhere, although a group on Dunsmore have hugely elongated versions with only Continental parallels.

Enclosed farmsteads have been excavated at Salford Priors, Wasperton, Barford, Rollright, Brandon and Bretford, and Church Lawford. Unenclosed settlements have been excavated alongside boundaries at Walton near Wellesbourne and Coton. Other settlements have been examined at Coleshill, Tiddington and Warwick University but at no site have contemporary field systems been identified. The occupants were largely self-sufficient farmers, engaged in a mixed agricultural regime of cereals, legumes, cattle and sheep; pigs, horses and dogs were also kept.

The dead were generally laid out and exposed to the elements, though a few individuals were buried in pits: examples have been found at Wasperton and Walton adjacent to a pyre site and covered by a stone cairn. At Church Lawford a group of exposure platforms could probably be seen from a mortuary enclosure within an adjacent land unit. The tradition of depositing significant artefacts in pits finds new currency in the Iron Age. At Walton several pits contained complete animals and special pits are known from Nadbury, Church Lawford, High Cross, Rollright and Wellesbourne. Many settlement sites reveal similarly special deposits in threshold features such as the terminal ends of enclosures and eaves drip gullies, and at Meon Hill hillfort (see Quinton) and Park Farm (Barford) iron ingots known as currency bars were buried.

Comparisons made between excavated ceramic assemblages seem to imply that communities to the north of the Avon valley had cultural links to the east and that those within and to the south of the valley traded to the south-west. This division is broadly supported by the sporadic finds of Iron Age COINS, which appear to demonstrate a north–south divide.

Unlike in SE England, where there is evidence for Continental trade and influence before the arrival of the legions in A.D. 43, ROMANS only become apparent in Warwickshire during the late 40s with the construction of MILITARY SITES. A fort on a ridge overlooking the River Arrow at Alcester was soon replaced by another in the valley around which the town then developed.

The fort at Baginton included a remarkable horse-training *gyrus*, which is unique in Britain. A vexillation fortress at Mancetter was initially occupied by a legionary detachment with auxiliary troops, but was later reoccupied on a smaller scale, perhaps to police the region after the Boudican rebellion. It was finally abandoned in the mid to late 70s. Major Roman ROADS such as the Fosse Way, Watling Street, Icknield Street and the Salt Way are likely to have had military origins as they link forts.

The immediate effects of the new order on the majority of the population are difficult to recognize in the archaeological record, because the pre-conquest settlement patterns and building techniques continue well into the C2. While this may merely reflect the relative pace of the spread of these innovations, it may also imply a reluctance to engage with the Roman economy. Indigenous society based on kin groups holding land or estates as agricultural and economic units and subject to partible inheritance is likely to have continued, although some diversification is evident with the development of a pottery industry and more rarely metal working.

The principal SETTLEMENT in Roman Warwickshire was Alcester (Alauna), where substantial public buildings indicate that it had local government status. Still one of the most extensively excavated small towns in Britain, it was partly fortified with ditch and rampart in the C2 and a wall in the C4. The second most significant town developed along the Fosse Way at Chesterton. This classic local 'central place' midway between adjacent tribal centres has no known military phase, but geophysical survey has demonstrated a spread of settlement extending far outside the extant earthwork defences. Further along the Fosse Way at Princethorpe a small town may have developed from a defended enclosure, which is visible as a cropmark but is mostly known from a pottery scatter recovered from ploughed fields. Small-scale excavations have demonstrated some C2 activity along the roadside. The focus of the extensive settlement at Coleshill, situated on the tribal boundary between the Cornovii and the Corieltauvii, was a major stone-built temple complex. At Churchover (Tripontium), a stone-built *mansio* with bath house has been recorded, although the full extent of the settlement remains uncertain. Extensive excavations around the village at Tiddington have revealed an important pre-Roman market place which thrived throughout the Roman period and where pottery was manufactured and agricultural produce was processed. Timber rectilinear buildings were in use during the mid C2 and it may have been defended in the C4.

The distribution of VILLA sites in the county broadly correlates with proximity to the major road network and significant river valleys. The most extensively excavated villa at Salford Priors has a dispersed layout quite unlike the villas of the Cotswolds or SE England. It appears to have developed from multiple Iron Age farmsteads located within a single land unit along the Arrow valley, with the first villa type buildings erected in the C3. Walls and mosaic floors have been uncovered at Ewefields Farm, Chesterton, but the range and extent of the villa complex is still unknown. A mosaic floor within a probable substantial villa was uncovered at Pillerton Priors which seems likely to have developed from an Iron Age precursor. A villa site at Radford Semele was proven by limited excavation, although very little data was recovered there, and a villa has been recognized from field survey and limited excavation at Long Itchington. Three possible villa sites indicated by surface scatters of artefacts at Lighthorne, Gaydon and Kineton are testimony to the possibility of discovering more through concerted local prospection. Excavations on two adjacent enigmatic building sequences at Crewe Farm and Glasshouse Wood, both near Kenilworth, revealed evidence for later Roman buildings, but these sites remain imperfectly understood. A stone-walled structure associated with combed flue tile was found at Burton Dassett and an aisled building was recorded at Fenny Compton.

A complex of substantial stone buildings excavated on the edge of a Roman road at Billesley Manor Farm, midway between the urban centres of Alcester and Tiddington, included two corn-driers, prompting speculation that the site could have been a specialized crop-processing centre. A small farmstead at Ling Hall Quarry, Church Lawford, developed from an Iron Age precursor but was abandoned during the C2. An unusual figure-of-eight feature found in the same land unit is thought to have been a small shrine.

Less 'Romanized' farmsteads at Abbots Salford and Bidford Grange had curvilinear enclosures and few demonstrable signs of Romanization other than each having corn-drying ovens, while at Wasperton a substantial enclosure and field complex represented a shift in settlement foci from the preceding Iron Age period, but again, other than corn-drying ovens, little evidence for Romanization.

POTTERY KILNS which produced a distinctive greyware have been excavated at Bubbenhall, Wappenbury and Ryton-on-Dunsmore, while sufficient pottery kilns have been found at Mancetter and Hartshill to suggest the base of a major industry with significance both to the local economy and nationally in terms of the range and distribution of its products. At Lapworth pottery kilns date from the C2. Tile kilns have been discovered at Ullenhall, Arbury, Griff Quarry, Nuneaton, and Chase Woods near Kenilworth: tiles stamped T C M were found along with wasters near Cherry Orchard (Kenilworth).

There is an almost total absence of briquetage, the crude ceramic vessels used to transport salt, in the county, which is of particular interest given the proximity of the important salt production centre at Droitwich, Worcestershire, and the Salt Way which passed through Alcester and Stratford-upon-Avon.

BURIALS have been recorded at a number of sites, although datable examples have all been later Roman; several at Tiddington had been decapitated, which may have been a cult practice. The absence of early Roman burials may well reflect a continued adherence to Late Iron Age funerary practices.

ANGLO-SAXON WARWICKSHIRE
BY STUART PALMER

The withdrawal from Britain by Imperial Rome in A.D. 410 is an event not demonstrable in the archaeological record of Warwickshire. The chronology of the end of a trading infrastructure, the demise of the pottery and manufacturing industries, the absence of coinage and the cessation of the construction of stone buildings is not refined further than the late C4.

However, there is mounting evidence that agrarian society continued in the ANGLO-SAXON period much as it did in the Iron Age, albeit with a modified archaeological footprint. There is currently no sign of continued town life but there is compelling evidence for continuity of settlement at Tiddington and Stretton-on-Fosse, dislocated new settlement foci at Salford Priors and Barford and, significantly, the continued use of cemeteries at Wasperton and Alveston.

In the C5 and C6 the richly furnished Avon valley burial grounds at Wasperton, Alveston, Bidford, Longbridge (Warwick) and others, demonstrate the transformation of the proto-English culture. They show that Warwickshire's native majority rapidly opted to identify with the cultural traits of an incoming minority warrior élite, although some isolationist Roman Christian (Primitive Welsh) enclaves are inferred by the place name Exhall both S of Alcester and N of Coventry, and it remains possible that the Anglo-Saxon tongue was not fully adopted until the C9. Nevertheless most settlements are named in the favoured new language, and burial goods indicate an eastern trading link with Anglia; but in the early C6 the S and W are demonstrably part of the Hwiccan kingdom which covered a similar area to the Iron Age Dobunni tribe.

It is in this period that we see new architectural forms such as sunken floored buildings, which survive as rectangular pits with post-holes generally along the axis but occasionally in the corners and along the sides. Establishing the superstructure of these buildings is far from straightforward, but the copious amounts of detritus which survive in the sunken part show that a range of crafts were undertaken; distinctive ceramic loom weights are particularly common. Small groups of these features have been found at Broom and more sporadically at Hampton Lucy, Barford, Wolston and Welford. The other type of structure commonly found of this date is the rectangular wooden hall, only evidenced as an arrangement of post-holes at Broom.

The whereabouts of Warwickshire's MIDDLE SAXON population (C7–C9) has been spectacularly difficult to establish. Evidently they did not use pottery at all and the buildings they
constructed must have had a very light footprint, as none have
been found. It is only recently with the assistance of precision
radiocarbon-dating that any evidence for them has been
recovered despite place name evidence clearly indicating sprouting new settlement. In Ratley and Upton skeletal material from
at least four graves on the ridge atop Edge Hill dates to
650–820 and a skeleton from a previously assumed Roman
cemetery at Tiddington returned a date of 640–770. On the
Staffordshire border at Middleton a fish weir has been dated to
650–890. An enigmatic possible temple with burials was
recorded at the tantalizingly named Blacklow Hill; one of the
burials was accompanied by a distinctive type of sword or seax
of C8 date.

Given what is known of post-Roman settlement in the county,
it is surprising that for ANGLO-SAXON ARCHITECTURE
Warwickshire is singularly barren. There are just two main exam-
3   ples, both important. At Wootton Wawen, where a Saxon monastery was founded in the C8, the central tower of the late C10
or early C11 church has N and S entries to a *porticus* on each side.
5   At Tredington, reputedly of 961, there is the shadow of a nave
with a wooden W gallery high up. Rather later, there is also the
shadow of a former *porticus* at Wolston. There is also the possibil-
8   ity of a former late Anglo-Saxon octagon at Berkswell, but the
present fabric is no earlier than the late C12. At Ashow, probably
later too, the N aspect is distinctly Saxo-Norman in scale and
9   form. There is a fragment of C10 carving at Billesley and another
with interlaced carving at Whitchurch, and there is C11 carving
at Barton-on-the Heath too.

MEDIEVAL CHURCHES

NORMAN ARCHITECTURE is richer than Anglo-Saxon, though
not as rich as in some counties. Many doorways survive, but
4   few ambitious ones (Kenilworth, Salford Priors), many arcades,
many fonts, few more or less complete churches. Norman arcades
usually have short round piers. The development through the
C12 goes from square abaci to round abaci, from unmoulded
arches via arches with bold roll mouldings to slightly chamfered
and properly chamfered arches, from round to pointed arches,
and from big single- or double-scalloped or elementary volute and
leaf capitals to many-scalloped flat capitals and trumpet-scallops,
waterleaf, and finally crocket and stiff-leaf capitals. There is no
fixed order, and early motifs of one kind meet later motifs of
another. At Butlers Marston e.g. are unmoulded pointed arches
and its flatness compares with similar arcades of round openings
at Warmington and Shotteswell. On the whole Warwickshire is

conservative. Herringbone masonry, usual as a sign of the CII, occurs in contexts of the full CI2 (e.g. Billesley, Loxley, Studley and Whitchurch), and waterleaf capitals occur (e.g. Berkswell, Curdworth and Tysoe) in contexts of general primitivity. An especially fine long arcade with clerestory of as early as c. 1130 is preserved at Polesworth, a nunnery church. At Nuneaton, another nunnery church, the mighty crossing piers are still largely there. If one is looking for relative completeness, Stoneleigh and Berkswell are perhaps the most rewarding larger churches, Curd-10 worth, Wyken (Coventry) and Corley (early and late CI2) and perhaps Ryton-on-Dunsmore (of before 1100) the most rewarding small churches. Stoneleigh and Berkswell both have remarkably wide naves. Berkswell in addition, of c. 1170–80, has a crypt 8 of extreme interest, far too little known. It is rib-vaulted and consists of two parts, the western one being an octagon with eight ribs. The possibility that this reflects a then still existing Saxon octagon above has already been mentioned. Another heavily rib-vaulted Norman crypt is below part of St Mary at Warwick. Stoneleigh has a rich chancel arch, a tympanum with some raw fauna in the Anglo-Danish tradition, blank arcading in the chancel, and provision for a chancel rib-vault. Provision for a rib-vault is also to be seen at Beaudesert.

Decorated TYMPANA are rare.* Alveston has one, Halford   p. 102
another, and at Billesley a part of another has been found. The Halford example has a beautiful seated angel holding a scroll. It   7
has affinities in style with Worcester Cathedral. At Halford also, two niches have been found l. and r. of the chancel arch, and in one of them was a badly damaged figure, probably of the Virgin in relief, no doubt to go with the former rood. The Billesley   9
fragment is associated with the Herefordshire School and dated to c. 1140–50. Patterned tympana occur too, e.g. at Corley, Farnborough and Whichford. A minor item of figure sculpture is three almost identical square panels at Studley, Tysoe and Whitchurch, with a lamb and stylized foliage in the corners of a kind already more CI3 than CI2. Norman pillar piscinae are to be found in Clifford Chambers, Loxley, Tidmington and Whitchurch.

Norman FONTS of course abound, as in nearly all counties, and among them some are notable: Curdworth for being so baf-flingly barbaric, Oxhill for the thin upright trails or shrubs and the thin figures of Adam and Eve standing up in narrow blank arcading, Stoneleigh for the twelve Apostles standing similarly but clothed in draperies with the excited criss-cross of Anglo-Saxon derivation, and Coleshill for figures of the same kind, but   6
also a Crucifixion framed in a ring with the Virgin and St John standing, as it were, behind the ring and cut by it.

To the EARLY ENGLISH STYLE Warwickshire contributes little, the best at Merevale, Pillerton Hersey and Temple Balsall. At Merevale the refectory of the abbey and the parish church are

---

* The whole of Warwickshire has been fully surveyed for the Corpus of Romanesque Sculpture (CRSBI) and detailed reports are available online.

E.E., the refectory with impressively closely spaced big shafts
with fillets inside and nearly as closely spaced chamfered buttresses outside, the church surprisingly short and wide and aisled.
Pillerton Hersey has a fine chancel. At Temple Balsall, the whole
church looks as if it were the chancel of a non-existing church.
It has extremely original late C13, i.e. Late Geometrical, windows.
The shape of Temple Balsall is explained by the fact that it was
the chapel of a preceptory of the Templars, the shapes at Merevale by the fact that it was the *capella ante portas* of the abbey.
Stray examples of E.E. worth noting include the tower and spire
at Austrey, the plain but relatively intact chancel at Wappenbury
and the chancel at Sutton-under-Brailes, which has both lancets
and bar tracery.

So perhaps this is the place to interpolate a brief account of
MONASTIC ARCHITECTURE in Warwickshire. Remains are
extant of thirteen houses or, including the Templars, fourteen.
The Benedictine nunneries of Polesworth (where there is also
a Norman doorway into the cloister and early C14 gatehouse)
and Nuneaton (fragment of the church, traces of the cloister E
range, brewhouse) have already been referred to. Wroxall was
another Benedictine nunnery. Here we have part of the church
(late C13) and small bits by the cloister. The most famous Benedictine house for monks was Coventry Priory. What remains
belonged to the church, which had a Norman crossing tower
and long aisled nave, partly Romanesque but E.E. in its W parts.
One sees a small part of a C13 radiating E chapel, the outline of
the nave, part of the NW tower, and the base of the E.E. W front.
Monks Kirby was also Benedictine. Something of the church
remains in the present parish church, but it is far from telling.
Of Augustinian priories Kenilworth has quite a lot, though little
fully standing, apart from the gatehouse and probably the guesthouse, both of the C14. Much was excavated but only some
parts remain exposed. It dates from the Norman of shortly after
the foundation in 1119 to the C15. The most interesting Norman
feature was the straight chancel E wall. The Norman nave was
aisleless. The C13 enlargement of the chancel also had a straight
E wall running in front of chancel, narrow chancel aisles, and
wide outer aisles divided crosswise into chapels. Of Studley the
only fragment is one window. Maxstoke, founded as late as
1336–7, has the surviving base of its crossing tower, octagonal
as if it were a friars' tower – which is a reflection of what orders
were leading in the C14 – and its gatehouse. Then the Cister-
cians, busy colonizing. Their houses, Stoneleigh and Combe,
have in common the fact that the remains of both have become
part of later mansions. In both cases the churches have
disappeared,* courtyards represent the cloisters, and the
Norman chapter house entrance and adjoining parts survive – at
Combe part of the C15 cloister, at Stoneleigh part of the dormitory undercroft and a complete gatehouse of 1346 with attached

11

14

p. 199

p. 580

---

* Though at Stoneleigh blocked arches represent the S aisle arcade, and one capital
of a crossing pier and the arch from S aisle into S transept are still visible.

guesthouse. Merevale, also Cistercian, has been mentioned a little earlier. Pinley was a Cistercian nunnery. Little survives of the church, but a timber-framed house of *c.* 1500 may have been the abbess's dwelling or the refectory. Warwickshire had one Charterhouse, at Cheylesmore outside Coventry. It was established in 1381, and one range stands, conveying confused evidence. Coventry, being at that time among the four or five greatest towns of England, also had two friars' houses. Of the Greyfriars we have the crossing tower with its noble spire; of the Whitefriars again only one range but a much more telling one, and the area of the church has been excavated. Friars had houses also at Warwick (Dominicans) and Atherstone (Austin friars).* Nothing remains at Warwick, but what remains at Atherstone, the present parish church, incorporates the octagonal crossing tower and the chancel of the friars' church of the last quarter of the C14. It is typical of the orders of friars in England that they had these octagonal towers, placed on a transverse space separated from nave and chancel by walls opened in arches or not. The steeple of the Greyfriars at Coventry also stood in just such a position, and the Whitefriars excavations confirmed the same.

Coventry also had major parish churches, and they are in their present form of the same time as the friars' churches. But both St Michael (later the cathedral and gutted in the Blitz) and Holy Trinity were already substantial churches in the THIRTEENTH CENTURY, to which we can now return. Both have no more preserved than a porch, but that of Holy Trinity especially is quite a sumptuous job. It dates from the mid C13, but Warwickshire (like e.g. adjoining Leicestershire) only came into its own in the LATE THIRTEENTH AND EARLY FOURTEENTH CENTURIES. During these decades there was rebuilding and enlarging going on everywhere. Chancels, especially, received attention as buildings were embellished for the celebration of the Mass, for example at Priors Hardwick, Long Itchington and Alderminster. Caldecote, though greatly restored, is a complete church of the late C13. Temple Balsall (*see* above) is a particularly sumptuous and inventive building. As a rule inventiveness was valued little. Tracery is of the Y- or the intersecting type, sometimes uncusped but mostly cusped, or else of three stepped lancet lights under one arch, cusped and sometimes pointed with top or spandrel trefoils. Piers are only too often just octagonal in section, and arches just double-chamfered. These two, called standard elements in the gazetteer, were to be continued with relentless stolidity throughout the C14 and C15. Quatrefoil piers (Grendon, Harborough Magna) or quatrefoil piers with thin shafts in the diagonals (Austrey and – in a more original version – Snitterfield) also appear and are more gratifying, Burton Dassett in the late C13 adds fun to its octagonal piers by letting beasties run along the abaci, and after 1300 or 1310 tracery accepts the ogee arch and gets ready for the games of flowing tracery and the

118

13

* The existence of a house of Austin friars at Shuttington seems to have been brief.

DECORATED style, even if this was played for low stakes in Warwickshire. The moment of the coming ogee is illustrated by Wroxall Abbey with its conservative date, 1315, the same windows with slight ogees in the outer lights also appearing at Lapworth. An example of enterprising flowing tracery is at Salford Priors, another at Aston Cantlow, a third with a pentagram at Warmington. Dunchurch had an E window with unusual geometrical tracery, replaced in 1908 and now on permanent display at the Victoria and Albert Museum. A big straight-headed Dec window with ballflower ornament at Exhall near Alcester reminds us that straight-headed windows are by no means a late Perp innovation. In addition a few churches are entirely or mostly Dec: the parish church of Astley, which was the chancel of a very large collegiate church begun in 1343, the parish church of Maxstoke also of c. 1340, and looking like a large chancel, the chapel of the Hospital of St John at Coventry (the Old Grammar School), and the smaller churches of Ratley (where the piers and arches have continuous mouldings) and Tanworth-in-Arden. Leamington Hastings church has a good N aisle of this period, with a fine porch. As a postscript the very curious bell-turret of Baginton must be appended. It is polygonal with a spirelet and stands over the junction between nave and chancel, as if it were part of a

Dunchurch, St Peter,   Salford Priors, St Matthew,
former east window.   nave north window.

Engravings, c. 1840

miniature friars' church. It necessitated tripartite arches to its w
and its E, i.e. a nave E set and a chancel W set. There is no way
of dating this odd piece. It may just as well be late as early C14,
i.e. Perp just as well as Dec.

The PERPENDICULAR STYLE started relatively early in Warwickshire, and there are no datable late examples of the Dec.
The earliest firm Perp date is the beginning of the Perp work at
St Michael Coventry, i.e. the cathedral, which took place in 1371.
Other dates are the start on the chancel of Atherstone shortly
after 1375, of Holy Trinity, Coventry, in 1391, and the completion
of St Mary Warwick in 1392. St Michael was one of the largest
parish churches in England; Holy Trinity is of a spectacular size   23
too, and both have, around the nave, aisles and chancel, divers
chapels built by guilds, but the chancel of St Mary Warwick is
more interesting than either, on account of its vaulting pattern
including flying ribs. In 1443 the Beauchamp Chapel was begun   25
s of St Mary – at first quite detached. It is among the most ornate
ecclesiastical interiors of its date in England, and the sculpture
around the E window is about the most up to date of the moment   22
in the country. Soon the chapel was linked to the chancel by a
narrow lobby and a tiny chapel, and as the chancel has in addition on the N side a polygonally projecting chapter house as well,
the whole of the E end of St Mary is one of the most manifold
groups of Perp structures in England. Another impressive group
is Lapworth, high, not long, and compact. Wholly or essentially   17
Perp are also Knowle, begun before 1400, St John Coventry, built   18
as a collegiate chapel, Coughton with much of its original furnishing, Weston-on-Avon, and the Guild Chapel at Stratford-
upon-Avon, close in style to the splendid chancel of the Stratford
parish church with its four-light windows. The latter was started
c. 1480. As in many other cases at about the same time the nave
received a clerestory and the tower a spire. The Stratford clerestory is of twelve closely spaced windows and the same is true of
Brailes, a type of design more familiar in East Anglia than in the   16
Midlands. As for spires, Warwickshire is not a spire county like
Northamptonshire, but of the medieval ones nearly all are
recessed and not of the broach or splay-foot types. Most of them
of course are W towers, and a number are crossing towers, but
Warwickshire was readier than many counties to experiment with
towers in odd positions too. Thus Lapworth is detached, three
are in a NW, one in a SW, one in a N, and one in a S position.

To these capital examples of the Perp style in Warwickshire – and the chancel of Merevale is yet another, equally complete, if not equally large – the following comments on individual
features must be added. Piers in the last fifty years or so before
the Reformation tend to show more inventive forms than the
mere octagon, or indeed the nationally popular section of four
shafts and four diagonal hollows. We now find finely moulded
sections basically of a lozenge shape with the longer side towards
the arch opening, the shorter to nave and aisle. Details are not
all standardized. Examples are Brinklow, Coughton, Coventry
Holy Trinity and St John, Monks Kirby, Newbold-on-Avon, and   23

Willoughby. Steeple details do not need any remarks, except perhaps the impressive arrangement of bell-openings in twins of two lights each with a transom and the same blank on the l. and

27   r. Thus it is at Coleshill, a tower which belongs in a group with Kings Norton, Bromsgrove and Kidderminster in Worcestershire. Other towers have very pronounced and almost triangular hoodmoulds or gables for doorway, w window, and even the tiny staircase windows (e.g. Wellesbourne). This beetle-browed appearance extends to windows in other places as well (e.g.

17   Lapworth s aisle); often the hoodmould stops are rather sinister bat-like or giant-insect-like monsters (e.g. Lapworth and Wootton Wawen clerestories), and one of these occurs as the w corbel of the n aisle at Henley-in-Arden. Of timber roofs little will be found in the gazetteer. Warwickshire roofs are nothing special. The majority are of low pitch with tie-beams and decorated bosses, but some also resemble barn roofs, and these are usually the more impressive. Timber porches are also an exception (Berkswell).

There is only one more note required on the Perp style. How long did it go on? We shall see that a break between survival and revival can hardly be made. Later datable examples include the

28   near identical towers at Baddesley Clinton and Packwood, paid for by Nicholas Brome, who died in 1517. Coughton's later Perp e end is of about the same date, its windows glazed with money left in 1518 by Sir Robert Throckmorton. The Marler Chapel at Holy Trinity, Coventry, is of c. 1526–7. Walsgrave-on-Sowe (*see* p. 303) and Foleshill (pp. 288–9) both have three-light square-headed windows of simple form, datable to c. 1540.

Now we must turn to CHURCH FURNISHINGS, not touched upon so far. The oldest piece of church equipment in wood is the crozier head of c. 1200 at Baxterley. Then there is a gap, and even c14 church furnishings are rare. With the late Middle Ages evidence of course increases in quantity, though in Warwickshire it does not increase in quality. Nor is there any great novelty in style.

Norman FONTS have been considered already. Of the plain tub sort, hard to place chronologically or stylistically, there are many. At Brailes, the font is octagonal with Dec traceried patterns on each side. Some fonts with heads sticking out from the underside of the bowl (e.g. Aston Cantlow, Lapworth, Snitterfield and Wootton Wawen) are assigned to the early c14. Tysoe, also c14, has figures of saints under crocketed gables. Barcheston is profusely ornamented with ballflower. Perp fonts deserve little comment, except Tredington, which has traceried panels in the manner of the earlier one at Brailes.

Developments in the liturgy of the Mass brought with them grander chancels with more elaborate facilities. Fairly typical are the E.E. PISCINA and SEDILIA in the chancel and s transept at Wolston, and in Kingsbury chancel. Those at Aston Cantlow, Long Itchington and Priors Hardwick are of the later c13, and more elaborate. Dec at Brailes, plain but with projecting seats and arm-rests. At Ladbroke there are crocketed pinnacles, and at Warmington crocketed ogee arches. Some of the Perp examples have canopies with carving, e.g. at Knowle, Coleshill and Holy Trinity, Stratford-upon-Avon. A piscina at Newton Regis has a Kentish barb. There is an especially fine Perp one in the s chapel at Wootton Wawen. Ladbroke also has a Dec EASTER SEPULCHRE, and one of these at Withybrook has traces of painting.

Knowle and Astley have STALLS with MISERICORDS. The Astley stalls of *c.* 1365–90 are particularly interesting in that their backs are painted with large single figures of Prophets and Apostles. The misericords there are by a carver also working at Worcester Cathedral in 1379. At Coventry, a set of C15 misericords originally in the Whitefriars church has been shared out between Holy Trinity, the Old Grammar School and King Henry VIII School. The late C15 misericords at Holy Trinity, Stratford-upon-Avon, are especially entertaining. The first RENAISSANCE forms appear in the stalls at Snitterfield, and they look 1530s.

SCREENS, on the whole, are uneventful. Screens at Long Itchington, Shotteswell and Wolfhampcote may belong to the second third of the C14. They are characterized by shafts with shaft-rings instead of the later moulded mullions. Of Perp screens, the best are those at Wormleighton and Knowle. The former was originally at Southam. At Alcester is an especially ornate early C16 screen in the N aisle. The one at Merevale is especially interesting, because it is of the veranda type, although of wood, and because it has its original loft with a square balcony in the middle. In some places the lower parts survive (e.g. Tredington) and others preserve sections of carved woodwork or panelling (e.g. Caldecote).

Among PULPITS, one stands out. This is the stone pulpit attached to the SE crossing pier at Holy Trinity, Coventry, *c.* 1400. The same church also one of the familiar big eagle LECTERNS of brass, early C15. Of medieval seating there is little, and nothing of real note. Carved bench ends occur at Tredington, Tidmington and Shotteswell. There are examples of simple seating forms at Oxhill, Tysoe, Aston Cantlow and Packwood.

Moving from furnishings to the decorative arts, we come to WALL PAINTINGS. Here there is more. First should be noted the early decoration in the reveal of a late C11 upper nave window at Tysoe, the painting probably concealed when the opening was filled in for the addition of the C12 S aisle. Norman windows at Curdworth have extensive remains of painted decoration too. Burton Dassett has remains of a C13 Doom above the chancel arch, over-painted in the C14. Further C13 painting in the N transept too. Middleton has C13 fragments. At Packwood there are the figures of the Three Quick of a painting formerly of the Three Quick and the Three Dead, early C14. Of outstanding quality and remarkably complete is the Doom of *c.* 1430–40 at Holy Trinity, Coventry, finely conserved in 2002–4. Of similar date, a Crucifixion on the refectory wall at the Charterhouse in the same city. Wyken (Coventry; *see* p. 307) has a large fragment of St Christopher of *c.* 1500. Of other paintings it is enough to

p. 24

Coventry, Holy Trinity, pulpit.
Engraving, *c.* 1840

mention the Doom over the chancel arch of the Guild Chapel at
Stratford, also *c.* 1500.

Then medieval STAINED GLASS, for which Warwickshire is
well represented by online photographs in the Corpus Vitrearum
Medii Aevi (CVMA). Much of what survives is fragmentary but
often charming – a bishop at Avon Dassett, music and instruments at Wixford, a censing angel at Nether Whitacre, and the
usual figures and faces and heraldry (e.g. the C14 Mohun family
at Whichford). In the surviving usually very beautiful stained
glass of the early C14 the most complete is the Tree of Jesse at
Merevale, while at Wroxall the N windows are of one scheme
(early C14) well restored in 1869. At Kinwarton there is a single

panel datable by its inscription to *c.* 1316. Of later C14 fragments
the best are at Coventry Cathedral, where there are pieces in the   19
windows of the Chapel of Unity and St Michael's Hall, and more
in the restored s porch of the ruins of St Michael's. Fragments,
too, over the road in St Mary's Guildhall. Complete windows of
patterned and emblematic glass have survived at Whitchurch and
Weston-on-Avon, late C15. Coughton has a number of complete
figures from the scheme installed under the will of Sir Robert
Throckmorton, who died in 1518. But the finest glass of all is in
the Beauchamp Chapel at St Mary's, Warwick, executed after   22
1447 by *John Prudde* of Westminster, the king's glazier, using
foreign glass 'with no glass of England', richly coloured and
jewelled. Much of the E window survives along with the tracery
lights in the side windows. These have choirs of angels with
scrolls of plainsong music, the Gaudeamus on the N and Ave
Regina on the s. Of foreign glass, the best is the Netherlandish
and German pieces of the early C16 in Rugby School chapel.

Then MONUMENTS including brasses up to the early C16. For
FUNERARY MONUMENTS we go back to the mid C12. Supposedly of this date is an effigy of an abbess at Polesworth. The
flatness of the draperies, the ironed-out folds, and the whole
tightness of the carving might easily tempt one to support such
an early date. Then at Avon Dassett is an early C13 slab of Forest
marble with a tonsured deacon in vestments, flatly carved and
severely stylized. Then there is a gap until after 1250. Of the late
C13 is the exceptionally beautiful, though alas headless, effigy of
a knight at Merevale, the bust under a trefoiled arch marking a
heart burial at Hampton-in-Arden, and the delightful coffin-lid
with a foliated cross at Studley.* Early C14 knights, cross-legged
and slender, and early C14 ladies have been preserved in several
places – the lady at Hillmorton (*see* p. 551) being of particularly
high quality.

Among monuments of that time, curious and very attractive
are those slabs where of the deceased only the bust and the feet
appear, usually sunk in a quatrefoil and a half-quatrefoil; the rest
is the slab itself carved with a decorative cross. This type, also
existent in other counties, is represented by a monument at
Willey and one at Tysoe, and one at Newton Regis with, in addition, two kneeling acolytes and, at the top, the soul of the
deceased in a napkin,. The best later C14 monument in the
county by far is that to Thomas Beauchamp at Warwick. He died
in 1369, and the effigies are as accomplished as the small mourners against the tomb-chest.

English brass at its best is of course found in funerary brasses,
and there Warwickshire has quite a number of the first class, none
very early – all except for one (Sir Richard Bingham †1476, at
Middleton) are of between 1400 and 1430. They are at Warwick
(Thomas Beauchamp II †1401, Baginton †1407, Wixford †1411   p. 715
and †1418, Merevale †1412, and Quinton †1430, and the figures
are between 3 ft (90 cm.) and 6 ft 3 in. (1.9 metres) in size. At

*A lead casket with a heart of unknown date was found at Clifton-upon-Dunsmore.

Warwick also is the crowning achievement of English C15 metal-craft, the monument to Richard Beauchamp, Earl of Warwick, in the middle of the Beauchamp Chapel. This dates from 1449–53. The effigy with the hands raised in prayer but detached from one another is as good as any in the Netherlands, and so are the mourners. The figures are of latten, cast by *William Austen*, probably from the models of *John Massingham*.

No stone or indeed alabaster monument in Warwickshire is as good as this. The earliest alabaster piece is at Kingsbury, the second is the best, that of Thomas Beauchamp I at Warwick, †1369. There are six more down to 1450. Astley has three of †1457, c. 1483, and c. 1530, incongruously united on one tomb-chest. Coleshill has a good alabaster effigy (†1520) and Coughton the big richly cusped tomb-chest without an effigy to Sir Robert Throckmorton, who died in 1518.

In funerary monuments the date of the first Renaissance forms is later. A Ferrers monument at Baddesley Clinton, †1535, has no Renaissance detail, and Sir William Feilding at Monks Kirby who died in 1547, Reginolde Digby at Coleshill who died in 1549, William Willington at Barcheston who died in 1555, John and Anne Digby at Coleshill who died in 1558, and Sir Fulke Greville at Alcester who died in 1559, have only rudimentary Renaissance bits (crude balusters or colonnettes on the tomb-chests) applied without much conviction.

MEDIEVAL SECULAR BUILDINGS

In the field of secular architecture of the Middle Ages, Warwickshire has much to contribute without which the national patrimony would be the poorer. If we begin with CASTLES, the series starts with the mighty Kenilworth keep of c. 1124–30. It continues with the early C13 curtain walls of Warwick and Kenilworth, the two major castles of Warwickshire, both proving up to date in substituting for defence by keep defence by a curtain wall with towers, with the excavations at Brandon Castle revealing an oblong early C13 keep. The principal mid-C14 castle is Maxstoke, oblong, with angle towers and in the middle of one long side a gatehouse. This is of the type established in Britain by the 1190s, later seen at Harlech of 1283–9, yet also in transition towards the form of Bolton Castle in Yorkshire of 1378 and Bodiam in Sussex of 1385 which look externally more or less the same but are really fortified houses with four ranges round a courtyard. At Maxstoke the gatehouse side never had permanent buildings against it. Concurrently Caludon Castle near Coventry received what must have been a fine great hall with large windows, of which one wall still stands. Concurrently also the provision of bigger towers began at Warwick, culminating in Guy's Tower of 1394. The state rooms at Warwick were in the place where they are now, as is proved by the extensive vaulted C14 undercrofts. In all of these, there is much use of polygonal forms – very much a Midlands feature in castle design.

Somewhere between castle and manor house must be placed the FORTIFIED HOUSES of Baginton (late C14; foundation only), Kingsbury Hall, and Astley Castle, solid oblong blocks, together with the C13 remains at Hartshill. But the climax of military as well as domestic architecture in Warwickshire is John of Gaunt's Great Hall at Kenilworth Castle, dating from about 1377 and being, next to Westminster Hall, undoubtedly the most splendid English hall of before 1400. It is 90 by 45 ft (27.4 by 13.7 metres), with large windows to the courtyard as well as the outer bailey, a spacious bay window to the courtyard, and another to the outer bailey, matched in appearance by the Strong Tower projecting from the lower end of the hall and containing buttery, pantry, and other service rooms. This tower is vaulted throughout. Below the Great Hall was another vaulted undercroft, and the hall itself was accessible by a sumptuous portal reached by way of a spacious outer staircase. Towards the outer bailey – this must be repeated – the hall range presented a symmetrical façade, although hall bay (Saintlowe Tower) and service tower (Strong Tower) were functionally completely different. It is among the earliest examples in English domestic (as against military) architecture of such an imposed symmetry. Large chambers continued the living accommodation in the S range of the castle. They were also on the upper floor. Moreover, beyond the large lake W of the castle Henry V built a Pleasance in the Marsh. Only the earthworks survive, as the building itself was timber-framed.

Before leaving castles, brief mention should be made of the numerous smaller MOTTE-AND-BAILEY examples, mainly Norman, for which only earthworks remain. These included Beaudesert, Brailes, Brinklow, Fillongley (two), Kineton, Ratley and Seckington. The best preserved are at Brinklow and Ratley, the former – like Beaudesert on its Mount – sited quite dramatically. The other lost castle of note was at Coventry whose site and minor remains are now subsumed within the group of buildings around St Mary's Hall and the Council House.

Some of the county's MEDIEVAL BRIDGES are worth noting. A bridge over the Avon with a long raised causeway to the S existed at Bidford-on-Avon by 1240. Part of the structure is still medieval, with irregular arches. The ruined bridge below the castle at Warwick dates from 1374–83, and there are well-preserved bridges with causeways at Halford, Marton and Stare Bridge at Stoneleigh. These three all by-passed now. The Clopton Bridge at Stratford-upon-Avon with fourteen arches is especially notable, built in *c.* 1480–90. Bishop Vesey built the bridge at Water Orton *c.* 1520. Narrow packhorse bridges survive at Bradnocks Marsh in Hampton-in-Arden and remotely on the Knee Brook towards Ditchford at Tidmington.

Of DOMESTIC ARCHITECTURE there are examples from the C12. The complex story of Middleton Hall, a minor manor house, begins with a blocked Norman window on the ground floor. Burmington Manor has an *in situ* blocked late C12 twin

35

opening within a round arch, and inside there are stone stiff-leaf trumpet capitals to the timber arcades of a two-bay aisled hall dendro-dated to 1194–5. The Old Rectory at Avon Dassett has a C13 twin window in one wing. Of the royal manor at Cheyles-more in Coventry, only the heavily restored gatehouse survives, but a part of the house with a C14 crown-post roof survived until 1956.

By far the most prevalent form of construction among the SMALLER MEDIEVAL HOUSES is TIMBER FRAMING, which plays a large part in medieval building in Warwickshire, especially in the Forest of Arden where (just as with sandstone) timber was abundant. Other areas like the Feldon were served badly for stone and for timber, which explains their empty landscape. Manor houses often and farmhouses nearly always are timber-framed and so too are many smaller houses, such that the timber-framed tradition encompasses the social range – from high-status owners living on rents, through the very large class of people earning a living from the land or trades, to the lowest agricultural labourer. The earliest evidence is frequently concealed within later structures of stone or brick and more of these houses might be known to us but were cleared away as unsanitary in the C20.

For the ordinary houses in towns and villages, it is worth noting that ongoing research and dendrochronological (tree-ring) analysis and radiocarbon-dating to establish the felling dates of timbers and, therefore, likely dates of construction are providing us with a more complete picture of when and how these were built. Warwickshire is well known for its cottages and streets of timber-framed houses which have tended to be blanket dated to the C16 or C17. As dated examples in the gazetteer will show, earlier dates of the C14 and C15 are by no means rare, e.g. at Alcester, Coleshill, Henley-in-Arden and Stratford-upon-Avon. At Coventry the original and imported buildings in Spon Street exhibit typical features of different periods, mainly C15. Best of all, Nat Alcock's analysis of the villages of Stoneleigh and Ashow provides a uniquely detailed insight of the evolution of their buildings across a range of types – in timber, stone and brick – from the C15 onwards.

The essential feature at the centre of the medieval house is the OPEN HALL with a central hearth for living. The earliest surviving timber-framed houses in Warwickshire are AISLED HALLS which, as that suggests, were constructed rather in the manner of medi-eval barns with aisles flanking the central space of the hall and increasing the width of the hall floor and the height of the main space by raising the tie-beam of the roof on posts. The roof of the aisled hall in Burmington's Manor House, already men-tioned, had passing braces for structural lateral stability and such braces are a characteristic of other aisled hall roofs. Another aisled hall revealed in the county is the Old Hall, Temple Balsall, which was built by the Knights Templar in the late C12.

Otherwise, the smaller medieval house in Warwickshire seems to be notable, as Nat Alcock has written, for its lack of extrava-gance. In Warwickshire, as in a large area of the Midlands, the dominant technique in smaller medieval house is the CRUCK TRUSS, i.e. timbers curved by nature and used so as to join and form an arch. No structural distinction arises between main wall timbers and main roof timbers. To date, some seventy-five cruck houses have been identified in Warwickshire among hundreds in the Midland counties, although the nature of their construction is typically concealed externally unless the truss itself is exposed in the end walls e.g. No. 34 High Street, Polesworth, and Phoenix Cottage (No. 1 Birmingham Road), Stoneleigh, built c. 1480. The earliest examples known are Cruck Cottage, Haselor, dated to 1384–5, and The Chestnuts, Water Orton, dated to 1398–9, both with arch-braced open trusses over the hall; these were built at a time of recovering prosperity after the Black Death, but the vast majority of examples recorded belong to the C15, e.g. Anne Hathaway's Cottage, Shottery, a three-bay house with timbers dated to 1462–3. After about 1500, the cruck tradition was superseded by box framing (see below).

The drawback of the aisled form of house is the imposition of arcade posts between the hall and aisles, encumbering the internal living space. The cruck house was similarly limited by its construction to halls of restricted width. By the C14 solutions were being found to overcome this problem, leading to the development of other forms of construction that could span the width of the space without need for intermediate support. One option was for the truss spanning the hall of Mancetter Manor House to take the form of a BASE CRUCK, which in spite of the name follows a slightly different tradition from true or full crucks in that the curved blades extend only to the height of a collar- or tie-beam which supports the roof. This enables the blades to be more widely spaced so the area of the open hall is increased. This has been identified as the structure of the earliest timber building in the whole of the county (after the aisled halls), at No. 21 High Street, Alcester, whose timbers are dated to 1257–64. Few houses have, as yet, yielded such an early date and the other recorded base cruck houses in Warwickshire date from the early C14: Mancetter Manor House; Manor Farm, Wasperton and Old Manor House, Cubbington, all of which also have spere (partition) trusses of aisled form. Later examples are Hopkins, Long Marston, of 1339–40, and Priory Farm, Shustoke (C15).

The typical plan of the smaller medieval Warwickshire house has all the rooms in line in a single range, and at the centre the open hall of one or two bays (i.e. with an open truss over the centre of the hall) with a single bay adjoining it to contain the service rooms at one end and a sleeping chamber at the other. Anne Hathaway's Cottage, Shottery, was of this kind. Others might have a bay only for the chamber or services rather than both. Over time plans evolved to four or even five bays. The entrance would probably have been towards the low end of the hall just as in the larger medieval houses. The first notable variation to this type of plan comes with the addition of a gabled CROSS-WING which is no longer in line but projects forward at the front or back or both. This would be two-storey and would either have a chamber over the service rooms or a chamber over a parlour at the 'high' end of the hall. Mancetter Manor House already had a cross-wing *c.* 1330; among smaller houses The Chestnuts, Water Orton, has a cross-wing added to the earlier hall in the first quarter of the C15; and Oakdene, Bretford (Brandon) is another example of a cross-wing added in the late C15 to an earlier C15 open hall. The more impressive H-plan with cross-wings at both ends is much less common among smaller village houses and only found at the higher end of the scale, for example the Old Rectory, Clifford Chambers, dated to *c.* 1433–4. It is more commonly a plan of the greater C16 houses.

ROOFS, in particular, often disclose early timbers, as at Old Manor House, Cubbington, dendro-dated to *c.* 1314–41. By the C14 carpenters were worried that frames would collapse lengthways – what is known as 'racking' – and to counter this the rafters of the roof were stiffened by the introduction of PURLINS supported by a CROWN-POST on the tie-beam. This is the common form of roof in many English smaller houses but actually rare in Warwickshire; the hall in Manor Farm, Wasperton, bears the remains of an elaborate crown-post roof, and another occurs in the cross-wing of 1345 to No. 150 High Street, Henley-in-Arden.

BOX FRAMING, which appears in some parts of the Midlands in the late C13 and C14, superseded cruck framing as the dominant form of construction in the C15. The frames of post-and-truss construction are sometimes raised on a low stone plinth to protect the timbers from damp. The typical pattern in medieval Warwickshire, as elsewhere, is for the frame to have SQUARE PANELS of quite large dimensions but with the beginning of the C15 these square panels diminish in size and at the same time the fashion grows for CLOSE STUDDING in which the vertical posts (or studs) of the frame are placed very close together. This is already the style of the Old Rectory, Clifford Chambers, in the 1430s. There seems to be little structural justification for this and many examples of close studding seem primarily for display. The combination, with ground-floor close studding and square panels above, is not uncommon in the Midlands. It can be seen at Netherstead Hall, Morton Bagot, built *c.* 1649. The frames of C15 and C16 houses also employ CURVED BRACES for strength. The earlier houses have as a rule downward-curving braces, while the later ones are curved upwards. The infill of the frame is wattle or laths infilled with daub.

Tredington's old rectory incorporates substantial C15 remains and this is one of the more important medieval stone houses in Warwickshire, although much altered by *D. R. Hill* in 1840–1. Turning to the use of stone leads us to Coventry, where the TOWN HOUSES of the wealthier inhabitants in the C14 were built above vaulted undercrofts of a type also found in other medieval towns such as Chester and Southampton. Of these a number remain, even though everything old above ground has been replaced. Among these are examples under Nos. 19–22 High

Street, and beneath the former City Architect's Department in the Earl Street side of the Civic Centre. Medieval houses take some forms that are similar to the rural types but also new forms specifically suited to their location, where constraints of plots for building encouraged the placing of houses at right angles to the street – especially where shops were placed at the front of the ground floor and the owner's hall moved to the back, with services beyond. No. 111 High Street, Coleshill, has behind its C18 façade an early C14 frame, partly preserving the open hall with its crown-post roof. In the same street is another medieval survival, No. 95, in which the house has one part parallel to the street and a longer rear wing. The principal living space was the chamber at first-floor level. In Henley-in-Arden the Heritage Centre (No. 150 High Street; dated in one part to 1345 but with a secondary phase for the hall) is an example of a house with internal jetties. The hall is partly floored i.e. open to the roof for one part but with the area of the chamber over projecting into it.

The best run of urban houses is of course Spon Street, Coventry; however, one must remember that some have been moved from more than one location in the city and have been heavily restored. The Spon Street houses include WEALDEN HOUSES, in which the cross-wings project just a little and the eaves of the roof continue across the space between them and are sometimes supported by curved braces. These are an important reminder not only that the type occurs well beyond the limits of Kent and Sussex but also that beyond the south-east of England it is an essentially urban form; it is found also in Warwick and Stratford-upon-Avon in the C15 and C16. Within medieval houses in Coventry there is some variety of planning with a mixture of open halls parallel to the street and others with the halls set to the rear, an indication that in towns the varying purposes to which houses were put resulted in more than one type of house plan.

JETTIES are a feature of Warwickshire houses from the late C14 at least, for example No. 169 etc. in Spon Street, Coventry, and the front of the Guildhall, Stratford, built c. 1417, which has a long jetty of the kind frequently found in towns in the C15, C16 and C17. Along Malt Mill Lane, Alcester, these are a defining feature, and they are found in the C16 houses in Warwick's High Street that were spared by the fire in the town in the late C17. In the towns, buildings may be jettied on more than one floor and with jettied gables, e.g. Lychgate Cottages, Coventry, dated to 1414–15.

In the cities and towns, the secular and religious worlds met in the GUILDS. Rooted in the trades yet also tied closely to the church, the guilds played a significant role in public administration in medieval times, making it convenient for their buildings to pass into municipal hands at the Reformation. C15 guildhalls survive in smaller communities like Knowle, Aston Cantlow and Henley-in-Arden, but the more important ones are at Coventry, Warwick and Stratford-upon-Avon. St Mary's Guildhall at Coventry, a grand hall added by the Trinity Guild to the premises of

41
39
40
29

1340–2 of the Merchant Guild, stands on a vaulted stone undercroft of the kind found in the merchant houses of the town. The
hall itself is of *c*. 1394–1414 and is stone, probably replacing an
earlier timber-framed one, and Perp with lavish detailing. At
Warwick, the medieval guildhall is now within the Lord Leycester
Hospital and the chapel above the West Gate also belonged to the
guild. At Stratford the present Guild Chapel was remodelled for
the guilds amalgamated in 1403, whose guildhall of *c*. 1417 stands
alongside. In all these, stone was sparingly used if at all, and only
for the higher status areas (e.g. chapels). The same is true, too, of
later foundations in Coventry such as Bablake School of *c*. 1500,
Ford's Hospital of 1529 (founded 1509) and Bond's Hospital
(established 1506), noted in 1581 as 'newly built'.

Some of Coventry's town walls are also preserved, with two
minor gates, and Warwick has two much more impressive gates,
with again some of the town wall close to one of them.

For the visual arts, two major pieces at St Mary's Hall in
Coventry merit attention: first, the splendid Great Chair of the
mid to late c14, an elaborate Gothic piece acquired in 1579; and
second, the Flemish tapestry of *c*. 1495–1500. It represents the
Assumption with the twelve Apostles, Henry VI and his queen
kneeling, and at the top Justice (a c17 replacement) and angels
and saints. Outstanding by any standard.

TUDOR, ELIZABETHAN AND JACOBEAN

So we come to the c16 and the first significant appearance of
BRICK among the most important Tudor mansions in Warwickshire. Pooley Hall, Polesworth, of 1509, is all brick (and quite
irregular), as is Wormleighton Manor House begun 1516 – the
fragment of which, with its large, square-headed windows, makes
one regret the loss of most of it. Compton Wynyates, begun
c. 1500, and Coughton Court, built *c*. 1510, are both mixed. At
Coughton Court, Sir Robert Throckmorton's house, the gatehouse of *c*. 1520 is of stone, but the two back wings, once the
side ranges of a courtyard house, have timber-framed upper
floors, and at Compton Wynyates it is the mixture of brick with
some half-timber, of windows with cusped and uncusped lights,
and the total absence of any symmetries which make the house
so supremely picturesque. It is the very opposite of Maxstoke,
or, within its own dates, of Thornbury in Gloucestershire of
c. 1521. Yet at Baddesley Clinton the new gatehouse and chamber
ranges of 1526 and 1536 are all of grey Arden stone. The preference for stone here is easily explained by its having been quarried
at a short distance from the house.

Among SMALLER HOUSES, however, the tradition of timber
framing flourished through the c16 with some attendant changes
in appearance and plan. In this period new houses are routinely
floored throughout, the open hall having been in decline through

30
39
p. 727
36
37
38

the C16, and in older houses it became increasingly common to insert a floor into the former space of the hall resulting in two-storey interiors throughout with the principal chamber over the hall. This internal subdivision takes place over a long period in the C16 and C17, and it both prompted the need for, and coincided with, the introduction of smoke bays and chimneystacks to convey smoke from the fire out of the building. This also created a change in the internal planning of houses and the formation of the typical lobby entry plan, with the entrance to the house in line with the chimneystack that divides the rooms of the ground floor. Netherstead Hall, built c. 1649, is a good example, with the entrance covered by a very fine two-storey porch. The central positioning of the stack gave such houses two hearths on each floor.

The houses remain of great interest quite apart from being highly picturesque with their bargeboards, their oriel windows, and their close-spaced vertical studs. Indeed what might be regarded as the glory of Warwickshire's timber-framed buildings is the DECORATION of the frame in the late C16. Much of what one sees now in places such as Stratford's High Street or the High Street of Henley-in-Arden was covered over from the C18 and only revealed in the enthusiasm for the (often misguided and over-enthusiastic) restoration of such houses in the early C20 to conform to an ideal of black-and-white houses as the true image of 'Shakespeare Country'. In common with other Midland counties (e.g. Worcestershire) there is a fashion for herringbone pattern bracing between the studs (e.g. in the cross-wing of Palmer's Farm, Wilmcote, built c. 1569 and Oken's House in Warwick) or the creation of lozenge and quatrefoil patterns within the square panels. All three patterns can be seen at Grimshaw Hall, Knowle, built c. 1560, and among urban houses a very good example is Southam Manor House (where in addition to the curved patterns of the bracing there are fleurs-de-lys and heart-shaped cusping). Perhaps less common (or at least with less visible evidence now) is the tradition of carving the studs and rails of the frame, although this does occur at the (admittedly heavily restored) Harvard House, Stratford, dated 1596, where there are in addition Renaissance decorative motifs including console brackets carved with acanthus leaves. The same house also retains some rare domestic WALL PAINTING in the form of fictive panelling. But otherwise this is a most uncommon survival in Warwickshire houses. At Netherstead Hall, Morton Bagot, some very early examples of mid-C17 sgraffito painting can be seen.

Prevalent and decoratively creative as the use of timber was in the county, no major ELIZABETHAN AND JACOBEAN MANSIONS in Warwickshire are timber-framed. At the same time they still were in Shropshire, Cheshire, and Lancashire, and even in High Holborn's Staple Hall in London as late as 1586. These houses start in the county in the very year of the queen's accession to the throne with Charlecote, completed in 1558. Its builder, Thomas Lucy, inherited in 1551 and his work at Charlecote symbolizes the rise of the new gentry under the Tudors and the way in which their social aspirations were emphasized through their houses. Charlecote has been interfered with, however, and even the seemingly original features of porch and gatehouse are now dated to *c.* 1572 and *c.* 1605 respectively. The porch, with its ribbed ceiling inside as if to imitate Gothic vaulting, has coupled columns above coupled columns, i.e. Renaissance elements, and a composition much like that of the porches of Northamptonshire type at Dingley Hall, Deene Park and Kirby Hall, all of *c.* 1560–72, and Gorhambury (Herts.) of 1568. Another Elizabethan porch is that built by Robert Dudley, Earl of Leicester, at Kenilworth *c.* 1570, alongside his powerful new gatehouse. He also built a completely new range in continuation of John of Gaunt's. This, with its large mullioned-and-transomed windows, is fully Elizabethan in style, big, very chary of external ornament, and with strong emphasis on unmitigated verticals and horizontals. It is of brick, while Leicester of course built in the local red sandstone. Sir Thomas Leigh's remodelling of Stoneleigh Abbey *c.* 1570–1600 is intensely conservative when compared to what Leicester was up to, even though Kenilworth is so close. Of another house of these years, Arbury (*c.* 1580), only some internal features and one re-set bay window remain. Fine internal features in other houses are the sumptuous chimneypieces at Little Wolford Manor and Baddesley Clinton.

Neither the year 1600 nor the year of Queen Elizabeth's death, 1603, marked any break in style. In houses nothing changed. In fact the first quarter of the C17 can be called the climax of the Elizabethan style nationally, but in Warwickshire there are no major Jacobean houses as exemplified by Aston Hall and Castle Bromwich near Birmingham. Plain gables, mullioned and mullioned-and-transomed windows, and maybe some exuberance around the main entrance were the norm, as at Billesley Manor, *c.* 1610–20, early C17 Birdingbury, and Barton House, *c.* 1636. But shaped gables were altogether fashionable among the owners of the middling houses in the county, more so perhaps than elsewhere. Examples are Salford Hall at Abbots Salford of 1602 and the part with ogee gables at Combe Abbey of *c.* 1590–1605. The fashion continued through to Marble House, *c.* 1640, and St John's, *c.* 1667–70, both in Warwick. There were others now lost, e.g. Wroxall Abbey, *c.* 1613, and the priory at Warwick, *c.* 1620. Other dated Jacobean buildings are Stone House, Allesley, of 1608, and the mighty gatehouse of Wormleighton of 1613. Finally, Stone Building at Claverdon keeps itself entirely to itself. It is like a late-comer among North Country tower houses, with large windows only on the upper floor. It has no date but seems to be late C16.

Late C16 and early C17 churches and furnishings

As with major domestic architecture, there is little to say. For the late C16, not a single church or major part of a church falls into this category, except perhaps the chancel at Claverdon which could be Elizabethan. That is all, and hardly any piece of church furnishing or church equipment merits notice either.

It is different with FUNERARY MONUMENTS. They abound in the last quarter of the C16, starting with a curiously alien piece at Weston-under-Wetherley (1573) with reliefs of the Resurrection and the Ascension and small kneeling figures, German rather than English. But the standard type of monument with the recumbent effigy or effigies on a free-standing tomb-chest also continues (Monks Kirby †1580, Coleshill †1586, St Mary's in Warwick †1590, Holy Trinity at Stratford †1592) and, alongside it, the same type, but against a wall and with a superstructure of anything between a flat arch on columns (Robert Dudley, Earl of Leicester, †1588, at Warwick, with a splendid display of radiating flags against the back wall) and a four-poster or six-poster (Coughton †1580).* In addition there is the popular Elizabethan type of kneeling effigies at a prayer-desk (Churchover †c. 1595, and also, a little less standardized, Newbold-on-Avon, c. 1583). Most of these monuments are of alabaster, and it is easy to recognize the same workshop for many of them, e.g. Monks Kirby †1547, Coleshill †1558 and Alcester †1559, and Monks Kirby †1580, Newbold c. 1583, and Chesterton †1585. As Jon Bayliss has shown, these are from Burton upon Trent, where the principal carvers were *Richard Parker* (fl. 1534–69), *Richard and Gabriel Royley* (1540s–70s), *Garrat Hollemans* (1584–96) and *Jasper Hollemans* (1598–1625) as attributed in the gazetteer. They were not the only suppliers. Monuments at Coughton †1570 and St Mary's, Warwick, †1584 and †1590, for instance, are attributed to the *Cure* workshops at Southwark.

Moving into the early C17 there is a little more when it comes to church fabric. Minor C17 works are noted at Exhall near Coventry (1609), Baxterley (before 1615), Farnborough (1611), Haselor (1622), Wolvey (1624 and 1630) and Hillmorton, Rugby (1640). These are repairs or minor embellishments, of course, and in the traditional mode as might be expected. The style is still Perp, handled with perfect ease and obviously without any self-consciousness. The more major work at Astley, where the w tower and chancel are of 1607–8, is just the same. Although documents suggest that Withybrook tower was partly built in 1632 there is nothing C17 about its appearance. Willoughby tower, Dec in details, might date from 1636. If that is the date, as conjectured, then it is a fine piece of Gothic survival. Later still, Budbrooke tower, 1668, has Y-tracery and Gothic pinnacles but C17 mouldings to the string courses. The s chapel at Stoneleigh of 1665 has Perp tracery and a convincingly medieval vault, and at exactly the same time the chapel of Compton Wynyates, a two-naved edifice, is Perp too. At Compton Wynyates the position of the pulpit is interesting and determines the building

---

*A recumbent effigy also is that of Nicholas Lane †1595 at Alveston, but it is – most exceptionally – carved in such a way that it must always have been intended to be put up vertically, not horizontally.

at once as C17. It is set in the middle of one side wall, a proof of the paramount importance of the sermon in the C17.

As to CHURCH FURNISHINGS, many of the pulpits mentioned in the gazetteer are described as Jacobean. Few in Warwickshire are dated (Bourton-on-Dunsmore 1607, Earlsdon, Coventry, 1661), and there is – from national evidence – every reason to believe that most of them, even if Jacobean-looking, are in fact of the years of Archbishop Laud, i.e. the 1630s. Again of the 1630s are the screen at Baddesley Clinton (1634) and Butlers Marston pulpit (1632). The screen to the Bromley vault at Baginton is dated 1677 and yet is still fully Jacobean in style. The organ cases at Bilton and Brownsover are two parts of the former organ case from St John's College, Cambridge, the earlier part at Bilton once thought to be of 1635, now dated to 1661; the part at Brownsover early C18.

JACOBEAN FUNERARY MONUMENTS are plentiful, but not of much typological interest. Business among the aforementioned alabasterers and the tomb-makers in stone flourished and went on as usual to 1625 and well beyond. An uncommonly fine alabaster tomb-chest with recumbent effigies is that at Charlecote with the date of death 1600. Another at Charlecote of five years later has the figure of the widow kneeling on the ground in front of the tomb-chest. The type of tomb-chest with a coffered arch over is represented by the Earl of Totnes at Stratford who died in 1629. It is an early work by *Edward Marshall*. At Ettington Park is a four-poster (†1633), at Warwick a six-poster (1st Lord Brooke, †1628, by *Thomas Ashby*, without any effigy). Kneeling figures facing each other across a prayer-desk are at Seckington (†1603; by *Jasper Hollemans*), at Caldecote (†1616), Clifford Chambers (†1622), and even still at Moreton Morrell (†1635) and Churchover (1641). At Newbold-on-Avon there are two couples, one above the other (†1635). Single kneeling figures are at Caldecote (1629) and Middleton (†1638). A variation on this theme is at Preston-on-Stour, where two wives kneel in the usual way, but the husband (†1624) kneels frontally. A type not so far found in the county is the frontal demi-figure. This is a type favoured in all England for divines and scholars, and it is therefore eminently interesting to see that it was chosen for Shakespeare's monument at Stratford (†1616; by *Gerard Johnson*). Finally, there are tablets without any effigies. One at Brailes with the date of death 1639 has an attractive still-life of books, their spines all to the rear. But by the 1630s a general loosening of iconographical conventions is to be noticed everywhere in the country, and this belongs in a different context. It is first emphatically heralded by the monument to Margaret Clarke at Salford Priors. She died in 1640, and hers is a standing figure in a niche with a shell top.

We ought not leave this period without a passing reference to PUBLIC BUILDINGS. Alcester has a town hall of 1618 with semi-circular stone arches (blocked) and columns to the street and a timber-framed chamber above. Of almshouses there are two notable groups, first the long range facing the green at Stoneleigh, originally timber-framed, 1574, but cased in red sandstone in 1594. At Leamington Hastings there is only the preserved façade of the original buildings, 1633. Of schools established in these years there are none with surviving buildings, apart from those that set themselves up in former monastic properties (e.g. Atherstone, Coventry and Stratford).

EARLIER SEVENTEENTH CENTURY TO EARLY EIGHTEENTH CENTURY

What we must do now is to trace the development of the CLASSICAL STYLE in Warwickshire, wherever it occurs, between the 1630s and the 1680s. Nationally speaking, it had of course begun with Inigo Jones in 1616 and 1619. But architectural followers were few before the middle of the century, and it is not until 1684 at Honington church that the Wren style appears, with arcades on Tuscan columns and a shallow segmental plaster vault. It is rather on the small scale of the FUNERARY MONUMENTS that the desire for a classical as against the Jacobean style found expression. The key works in Warwickshire are a tablet at Baginton attributed to *Maximilian Colt* with the date of death 1632 and no effigy, though with Mannerist statuettes of Faith, Hope, and Charity; a convex tablet at Coleshill (†1642; probably by *Edward Marshall*) with a long inscription, treated as if it were part of a column by adding an Ionic capital on top; and a large tablet at Warwick with no figures at all. This was made by *Nicholas Stone* in 1639. Stone was the leading English sculptor of these years. Even where he goes on with the recumbent effigies on a tomb-chest, his style is at once recognizable as post-Jacobean. He uses white and black marble, an Italo-Dutch choice, and he carves his effigy with a freedom, a naturalism of detail, and an expressiveness unprecedented in England. A monument at Compton Verney (†1630) is not one of his best. Stone did two more monuments in the county: at Charlecote (†1640, with *John Schorman*), where she is recumbent and he semi-reclining, and where there is just such a still-life of books as at Brailes at exactly the same time (*see* above); and at Chesterton, 1637–9, where there are two busts in an architectural surround. *John Stone*, his son, repeated the same composition at Chesterton a few years later (†1643) and architecturally with greater purity. The bust was the favourite representation of the deceased in those years. It occurs in a circular recess (Bidford †1655, Upper Shuckburgh †1656 by *Peter Bennier*), or in an oval recess (Newbold Pacey †1668, by *Thomas Stanton*, a demi-figure rather than a bust; Mancetter †1689), or in the round without a recess. This is a later type and part of a general development towards the liberation of the figure from the architectural framework. The Warwickshire examples are Stratford †1649 (demi-figures, holding hands – by *Thomas Stanton*), Leamington Hastings †1656, where the bust (possibly

by *Bushnell*) is not even strictly frontal, Compton Verney †1668
(*C. G. Cibber*), Leamington Hastings †1676 (two busts, again not
frontal, also attributed to Bushnell), Upper Shuckburgh †1683
(Catherine Shuckburgh, with one bare breast; attributed to *James
Hardy*), Holy Trinity, Coventry (†1691, three busts by *Edward
Hurst*), and Nuneaton (†1703, two busts and a haunting skeleton
in a winding sheet as the predella). Other than busts, monuments
of these years hardly need inclusion here. The monument to
Duchess Dudley at Stoneleigh (†1668) was executed by *William
Wright c.* 1648 and inscribed by *Thomas Stanton* in 1669. It is in
white and black marble, and the effigy is recumbent in a
shroud – much as Stone might have done. The monument to the
2nd Lord Digby †1661 at Coleshill (1672, possibly by *Cibber*) is
a square pedestal and a large urn in the round on it. Finally the
monuments to the Willoughby family †1665–88 (*c.* 1690, by
Hardy) at Middleton and Thomas Archer †1685 at Tanworth-in-
Arden are large affairs without effigies but with cherubs' heads
and Baroque cartouches – on the way into the C18.

52

Of DOMESTIC ARCHITECTURE nothing later than work in the
Jacobean style has yet been introduced. The wind of change is
first felt in the windmill at Chesterton. No wonder it is popularly
attributed to Inigo Jones. It has a date 1632 and yet none of the
Jacobean frills. The court style seems already fully absorbed.

46

The archway from Chesterton churchyard towards the former
mansion is quite different and represents, even if in a very
subdued form, what Sir John Summerson called the Artisan
Mannerism of the mid C17. It is of brick, pedimented, and with
all the parts and mouldings of brick too. The mansion, on the
other hand, which was built *c.* 1657–62 and exists no longer, was,
to judge from illustrations, a building in the Inigo Jones–John
Webb style and probably the first in the county. Its designer was
probably *John Stone*. Warwickshire has no Artisan Mannerism
proper. But much of the minor brick building is in a similar
transitional state between the ornamental early C17 and the anti-
ornamental late C17 (in terms of exterior architecture only), with
its brick pilasters, brick quoins, moulded brick string courses,
and occasional stepped or shaped gables. At Eastcote, Wharley
Hall and Eastcote House, both of 1669, are early examples of
purely brick houses, and Wharley Hall not only makes use of
moulded brickwork but has windows framed by pilasters and
pediments. Built for a prospering family, the Fishers, it is the
beginning of the end of the vernacular house and the start of the
regular square plan house with hipped roof so characteristic of
the C18. Other examples of this stylistic trend are the stables
of Packwood House of the 1660s by *Roger Hurlbutt*,* the stables
of Arbury of *c.* 1670, the service wings of Honiley of a little later,
and Packington Old Hall, Great Packington, of 1679–80, and so
to Ansty Hall of 1678, which is really classical but betrays its

---

*Apropos Packwood and the Mannerism of the mid C17, a word must be said about
the Yew Garden of Packwood, this curious conceit of a garden said to represent in
terms of trimmed yew trees the Sermon on the Mount.

Ettington Park, loggia (from Coleshill).
Engraving by W. Niven, 1876

prior allegiance by a certain trickiness of detail. A specially instructive instance of the transitional character of this provincial architecture is a doorway at Lower Tysoe, dated 1671. This has a classical segmental pediment (like e.g. Packington Old Hall) but, to make doubly sure, also a hoodmould on big lozenge-stops.

Internally two things are typical of the second third of the century. The first is panelling no longer of the small, oblong, eternally repeating Jacobean kind and not yet of the large scale of William and Mary and Queen Anne, but in square units with the corners bastion-like projecting as little squares. This is to be found e.g. in the NE block at Stoneleigh Abbey and no doubt corresponds to the rainwater-head date of 1655. The other typical feature of the 1630s to 1660s or 1670 is staircase railings not with balusters (though balusters of course go on and go their own way from Jacobean to stronger and shapelier forms, to the dumb-bell shape and finally the twisted shape*) but with pierced panels, first of abstract shapes and in the end of lush acanthus scrolls. The abstract form occurs at Whateley Hall Farm and at Wolvey Hall, still in 1677, though the foliage form – admittedly still rudimentary – was used at Stoneleigh Abbey already in 1655.

From this Mannerism one road turned away to the restrained classical style already mentioned. But another continued into the BAROQUE. This road was chosen much more rarely by the English. We can see how it proceeded by a glance at the loggia from Coleshill Park removed to Ettington Park, and also minor

*The latter already at Packington Old Hall in 1680.

fragments over the orangery portal of Ansley Hall. As regards
dates these pieces are probably later C17. But the full exuberance
of this ornamental style belongs to interiors, and here it is often
the same houses that display it which externally kept so silent
and forbidding an appearance. Thus it is most grandly at Combe
Abbey, where *William Winde* in 1682–4 made additions including
a saloon noble and classical to the outside but with a glorious
stucco ceiling inside by *Edward Gouge*, one of the greatest of the
English plasterers. Of *c.* 1669–81 is the splendid stucco (by *Pettifer
& Pelton*) and woodwork (by *Roger & William Hurlbutt*) in
Warwick Castle, and 1678 is the date of the chapel ceiling at
Arbury (by *Edward Martin*).

For Arbury, *Wren* in 1674 did a design for the doorway of the
stables. It was not carried out, or was carried out with great
modifications, but is yet the earliest fully classical portal in Warwickshire. It is a little more ornate than this earliest classical style
is otherwise in the county. Thomas Archer, father of Thomas
Archer the architect, lived at Umberslade. Umberslade was
rebuilt *c.* 1695–1700 and became a large, very plain stone
mansion, entirely classical in the details and certainly not by
Archer. The builder was one of the *Smiths* of Warwick, and they
are C18 rather than C17 men, and we are not ready for them yet.
That classical façades tend to be restrained to the verge of the
purely utilitarian is also the case at Honington in 1682 (where,
however, the busts of Roman emperors in niches add a certain
richness), at Farnborough Hall after 1684, at Wootton Wawen in
1687, and at Upton House in 1695 – apart from Combe Abbey
referred to previously. Other houses of this period to note include
Alveston House (1689), Clopton (*c.* 1665–70) and Arlescote
(*c.* 1685).

p. 199
53
p. 637
54

EARLY EIGHTEENTH CENTURY TO
EARLY NINETEENTH CENTURY

So we have arrived at 1700, and now, for a while, Warwickshire
architecture moves from its relatively phlegmatic existence into
the forefront of events. They concern two different trends: the
Baroque and the Gothic Revival. In neither did the original initiative lie in the county. The ENGLISH BAROQUE had originated
with John Webb's King Charles Block at Greenwich in 1665,
Hugh May's chapel in Windsor Castle of 1675 etc., and Wren's
later style, from the 1680s onward, and that of the Office of
Works about 1700, i.e. a Wren–Hawksmoor mixture. The Gothic
Revival also, although there are a multitude of single antecedents,
established itself in the work of Wren on some of the City
churches. The English Baroque culminated in Vanbrugh and
Hawksmoor and also Thomas Archer whose work is exemplified
nearby by his Birmingham Cathedral (1709–15 and 1725 tower).

What constitutes the WARWICKSHIRE BAROQUE is the work of the brothers *William Smith* and *Francis Smith*, the latter of Warwick. Their works are fully enumerated and analysed in Andor Gomme's study of *Smith* of Warwick. William was born in 1660, Francis in 1672. They were builders, but also designers of buildings. We know that they worked to the designs of Sir William Wilson, of Archer, and at least twice of Gibbs. Their work at Umberslade has already been mentioned but they were busiest with major building in the years from about 1715 to about 1730. The climax of their work is Francis's Stoneleigh Abbey, i.e. the W range of the mansion, which was built in 1720–6. Here, at its most grandiose, are all the elements of the Smith style, a style derived originally from a mixture of the grand Baroque way of John Webb at Greenwich in the 1660s which had gone on to Talman at Chatsworth (1687 etc.) and of the blunter, more domestic way of the late Wren office (see e.g. the chapter house of St Paul's and Marlborough House), but also practised by others already before 1700 (Ven House, Somerset, 1698) and shortly after 1700 (Winde at Buckingham House in 1703–5, John Prince at Cound, Shropshire, in 1704, Wotton House, Buckinghamshire, *c.* 1704, etc.). On the grand side, with ashlar facing and giant columns and pilasters and a top balustrade, the key buildings before the Smiths are Hawksmoor's Easton Neston, Northants, of 1702, and then Cannons, Middlesex, of 1713–20, and Gibbs's works. The Smiths' characteristics are those of their predecessors, including on the more modest, domestic side, an attic above the cornice carried by giant pilasters, or angles with rustication of even length of blocks. Examples of their work or style are the Court House, Warwick, of 1725–6, No. 10 Market Place, Warwick, of 1714, Stone House at Stoneleigh of 1716, Newbold Revel of 1716, Meriden Hall of 1721–4 and possibly houses in Priory Row and Little Park Street, Coventry. There are more, and they will be found in the gazetteer.

56

p. 473

They were not the only exponents of the Baroque. Nor were they quite the earliest, tempting though it is to associate the Smiths with the three Baroque corner houses at the crossroads in the middle of Warwick, *c.* 1696. There were, for instance, later C17 houses at Knowle and Snitterfield with similar detailing, now lost. Nor was it all grand or attributable. Elements of the Baroque are to be seen in smaller houses of the early Georgian period too, e.g. at Hurley, Atherstone-on-Stour and Kites Hardwick (Leamington Hastings). Among the major houses Compton Verney, once attributed to the Smiths, has been convincingly reassigned to *John & William Townesend* of Oxford. The date is 1711–14. Radbrook Manor (Quinton) of the 1720s is probably by the *Woodwards* of Chipping Campden, who are among the candidates for the design of Foxcote in the hills above Ilmington. Neither the date nor authorship of this fine Baroque house has been established with certainty. But another exponent of the Baroque was *Sir William Wilson*, exemplified by Moat House of *c.* 1700 at Sutton Coldfield (formerly in Warwickshire). He brings us back to Warwick and to the Smiths, but also takes us in an altogether different direction.

55

Wilson had been a mason like the Smiths, but owing to an advantageous marriage rose to be a squire and a knight. The Smiths worked to Wilson's designs early on, and this was at St Mary, Warwick. This, as rebuilt in its w parts after the fire of the town in 1694, is the most important church of the EARLY GOTHIC REVIVAL outside the City of London. It was begun in 1698 and completed in 1704. Wren and Hawksmoor had made drawings too, also Gothic, but they were not accepted. Wilson's tower is Gothic in its motifs, but lacks the Gothic sense of growth of which Wren at St Dunstan and St Mary Aldermary proved himself fully aware. It consists of motif after motif and tier after tier. The interior of nave and aisles on the other hand – although of the hall-church type, uncommon in English Gothic churches – is surprisingly correct in the mouldings, even if the capitals are graced with small acanthus foliage. The ornamental portal from the s transept to the Beauchamp Chapel dates from 1704 and is emphatically Gothic too, though quite different. It is by *Samuel Dunckley*, and so playful and crowded with Gothic motifs taken from the equally crowded Beauchamp Chapel itself that, for a short time, it might well deceive.

And Warwickshire has more early Gothic Revival church work than that. Around 1711–12 the tower of Wishaw was built in a kind of basic medievalism, and in 1773–4 *Thomas Squirrell*'s tower of Lighthorne has the familiar large quatrefoils and Y-tracery of the C18 Gothic. Alcester is much more interesting. It dates from 1729–30 and is by the *Woodwards* of Chipping Campden 'under the advise, direction and Government' of *Francis Smith*. The Woodwards had already in 1725 at Blockley (Glos.) done a perfectly convincing neo-Perp tower, modelled on the Campden parish church. Their Gothic windows at Alcester (widened and altered in Preedy's 1870 restoration) were equally convincing, though the inside of the church is unhesitatingly classical. So here is final proof that we are dealing with revival, not survival, if after the evidence of St Mary, Warwick, further proof were needed.

There are, indeed, plenty of examples of Gothic church building. At Warwick, the chapel of St Peter above the East Gate has a pretty tower of *c.* 1730 and the rest is later C18, although the traditional attribution to Francis Hiorne, 1788, now seems doubtful. At the castle, the 1st Earl Brooke's chapel was Gothicized in the 1740s. The tower and spire of St Nicholas were rebuilt in 1748, and *Thomas Johnson* rebuilt the rest of the church in Gothic in 1779–80. Outside the county town there is Preston-on-Stour, for which *Edward Woodward* in 1752 made an elaborate Gothic design. It was much simplified in execution, but the window tracery is quite correct. Mention should be made of the lost Gothick work at Kineton of 1755–6, but that was by *Miller* whose earlier essays in the style have yet to be mentioned. Astley has internal Gothick features of the 1750s or 60s. The Gothic tower and courtyard front of Guy's Cliffe chapel, 1764, might be by *Timothy Lightoler*. Arrow church has a w tower of 1767 and Maxstoke's little bell-turret is faintly Gothic, 1773–4.

Preston-on-Stour church, proposed elevation.
Drawing by Edward Woodward, 1752

Middleton's NW vestry or schoolroom has intersecting tracery, 1784. Then there is Lighthorne of 1773–4, already mentioned, and *Joseph Eglington*'s plain but correct church at Leek Wootton, 1790–2, and *Thomas Johnson*'s surviving tower of Ettington new church, 1795–8.

So much for churches. What of secular works? Alscot Park of *c.* 1750–64 is Gothic, but this time decidedly Gothick, i.e. with Gothic decoration applied to a Georgian body. It was built in two phases, the first part in the early 1750s and the rest in 1762–4. The *Woodwards* were the builders, working to designs by two London carpenter-surveyors, *John Phillips* and *George Shakespear*. The date, nationally speaking, is very early. Hawksmoor at All Souls of course had been earlier still, and Kent at Esher Place and Hampton Court. But Horace Walpole started at Strawberry Hill only in 1748 or 1749, and the most Gothic of the rooms are of between 1753 and 1762. Warwickshire is earlier, thanks in the first place to *Sanderson Miller*, squire-architect of Radway Grange and consulted from Wiltshire to Cambridgeshire and Essex. He built the thatched cottage on Edge Hill in 1744, the tower, also on the hill, before 1749, and in those years added to Radway Grange Gothic adornments such as two bay windows. Arbury Hall, perhaps the finest of all early Gothic Revival houses in England, is largely the creation of owner-architect *Sir Roger Newdigate*, influenced in the early stages by Miller. He came in

63

67,
p. 520
62

1749 to teach Sir Roger how to draw Gothic arches but they later disagreed over political matters. Work on the Gothicizing of the Elizabethan mansion began in 1750–2, and the similarity of the two bay windows to those of Radway Grange is striking. Also involved at Arbury were the mason-architect brothers *William & David Hiorne*, principally as builders, but William was also paid in 1748 for a plan. The Hiornes were among those mason-architects who acted both as builder and designer – like the Smiths, the Woodwards, and Wilson – and their works included the fine Gothick church at Tetbury (Glos.), 1776–81. The library at Arbury was 'fitted up Gothic' by 1755 (and still has a classical ceiling* – a sign of a certain half-heartedness), and after that the Gothicizing proceeded with great gusto right up to 1792. The climax is the rooms designed by *Henry Keene*, Surveyor to Westminster Abbey, from 1762 onwards and inspired by Henry VII's Chapel. They are every bit as enchanting as the rooms of the same years at Strawberry Hill, and on a larger scale. Their stucco fan-vaults are their great feature.

At Warwick, Francis Greville (Earl Brooke, and later 1st Earl of Warwick of the new creation) began Gothic improvements at the castle *c.* 1748. *Timothy Lightoler*'s grand new entrance and dining room are of 1763–4. The earl also built a Gothic hunting lodge in the park, Spiers Lodge. This, as Tim Mowl has observed, bears a striking resemblance to a lodge illustrated in *Lightoler*'s 1762 pattern book.

Pretty C18 Gothic is often considered as frivolous, playful and indulgent – definitely not serious. Michael Hall has shown, however, that there was nothing light-hearted about the Gothick at Arbury by which Newdigate harked back to ancient authority as validation of his secret Jacobite political beliefs. Likewise at Warwick the earl was using historical architectural forms to demonstrate the antiquity of his lineage, best exemplified by the historicist recreation of the towers of 1768 and 1775 on the castle mound. In both instances the motives for using Gothic lay much deeper than in architectural form alone.

So these are more than just stirrings of the Gothic, even though this remained the age of the classical to which we will return presently. On a smaller scale, ogees, quatrefoils, pinnacles and other Gothic features can be seen for example in the wings flanking the gatehouse at Coughton Court, the stable block at Astley Castle, a porch at Cherington, an octagonal dovecote at Idlicote, *p. 605* outbuildings at Combe Abbey and a major town house near the Guild Chapel in Stratford-upon-Avon. With these examples, the field of the secular C18 Gothic is covered.

But perhaps too much prominence has been given to Gothic. It was, after all, the exception, even in Warwickshire. Side by side with it, normal GEORGIAN BUILDINGS went up, and other buildings received normal Georgian decoration – some of it of grandeur, of beauty, and of considerable interest. Georgian CHURCHES have little to contribute. Honiley of 1723 has a rather Baroque w

---

* Etruscan in taste, incidentally, which is remarkably early.

tower and spire. Its architect is unknown, although there are
several notable names among the possible candidates. Over Whitacre, although as late as 1765-6, is even more Baroque, including   71
its spire which replaced the original humpish dome in 1850. It is   p. 498
probably an early work by *Francis Hiorne*, strikingly similar to his
later church at Tardebigge (Worcs.). *Capability Brown*'s chapel at
Compton Verney (1772) is very plain but has a pretty, Adamish
interior. Binley, Coventry (1771-3), has been attributed to *Adam*   72
himself, but Terry Friedman gives it jointly to *Brown* and *Henry
Couchman*. Ansley chancel, 1760, and the sister towers at Priors
Marston (1721) and Napton-on-the-Hill (1731), all mingle Gothic   69
details with their mainly classical forms. The rest is minor (Barston
1721, Weddington (Nuneaton) 1733, Walton 1750, Dorsington
1758, Birdingbury 1774-5 and Stockingford, Nuneaton, by *John
Russell*, 1822-3 – all partially Gothicized by the Victorians), with
the one exception of Great Packington, and that is best considered in the context of Packington Hall (below).

Of CHURCH FURNISHINGS little need be said. One outstanding piece, however, is *Lightoler*'s Gothic reredos and the relief of
the Annunciation by *William Collins* in the Beauchamp Chapel
at Warwick, *c.* 1765. Bulkington has a font of 1789 by local squire-
sculptor *Richard Hayward*, whose work there also includes a
carved stone (probably from an altar) and a family memorial,
1781. Preston-on-Stour has stained glass of 1754 by *William Price*.
For the rest there are C18 seating arrangements with box pews
at Ansley, Hillmorton and Honiley, an ensemble of 1723 fittings
at Baginton and a 1731 s gallery at Berkswell. There are pulpits
with pretty marquetry (e.g. Offchurch, Birdingbury, Maxstoke
and Hillmorton). There are baluster fonts (e.g. Birdingbury), a
tapering pillar at Harbury and a font at Honiley of *c.* 1723 which
is tellingly Georgian in being no more than a small bowl half let
into the wall; no enthusiasm under any circumstances. And there
are a number of fine communion rails, some of wrought iron
(Astley, Chadshunt, Preston-on-Stour and Ullenhall, 1735).
Some of the best early C18 wrought-iron work in Warwickshire
is by *Nicholas Paris* of Warwick.

In FUNERARY MONUMENTS there are sometimes hints of the
Rococo. A typical example is a large tablet at Honington with a
big putto and completely asymmetrical paraphernalia. The date
of death is 1763* and the design is associated with *Sir Robert
Taylor* (c.f. Rochester and Ludlow). The other aspects of the C18
funerary monument are represented thinly in the county. The
Baroque trend shows itself in standing effigies: a couple at Honington †1712 and 1713 attributed to *William Palmer* and another
at Newbold-on-Avon †1716 signed by *John Hunt* of Northampton. Both have two standing figures. Two standing figures and
one semi-reclining is the motif of the much later major work of   74
the minor sculptor *J. F. Moore* (Ettington, 1775); one standing
figure is on a monument by *John Hickey* at Tanworth-in-Arden,

---

*But already in 1706 a tablet at Austrey has in its predella a death's head with
wings exactly as daringly asymmetrical.

†1778. The classical trend appears at its best in the monument to Baron Dormer †1712 at Budbrooke, attributed to *Francis Bird*: no effigy, no figure – the greatest reticence all round. One monument exists in Warwickshire by *Rysbrack* (Stratford, 1756), and it is on the whole dull, and one by *Peter Scheemakers* (Studley †1759), and that is nothing special either. More rewarding are the monuments of *Richard Hayward* whose work at Bulkington church has been mentioned already. There are good monuments there (†1781 and †1788), but where he tried his hand at something bigger and more dramatic and looked to Roubiliac for inspiration (Nether Whitacre, 1775), he failed. He also carved a chimneypiece at Arbury Hall. In Ilmington churchyard there is an elaborate Georgian Gothic monument, †1750, most likely by *Edward Woodward* of Chipping Campden. Here a brief mention should be made of the lesser churchyard memorials of later C18 and early C19 date, some of worthwhile quality, of stone in the S and often of slate in the N, doubtless imported from Charnwood Forest in nearby Leicestershire.

It may be just as well to continue with funerary monuments into the 1820s. There is little to report. The principal names occur, but few principal works: five by the *Flaxmans* (father and son) †1798 to †1813, none of the first order; several by the prolific *Bacons*, among them an excellent one by the father at Berkswell, 1795, and a good one by the son, †1818, at Newbold-on-Avon; numerous *Westmacotts*, three of them (Preston-on-Stour †1797, Ilmington †1806, Honington †1821) virtually the same, another (Berkswell †1818, with two embracing angels) wholly Victorian already in its sentiment; and good *Chantreys* (Rugby School Chapel 1824, Alcester 1828).

At this point, CHAPELS need to be introduced, although there is not much to say and less to see. Despite the strength of Nonconformity in the county it never produced any really notable buildings. Sadly, a great many chapels have either gone altogether or been converted beyond worth, and that is as true of the C19 as it is for the earlier period under review here. There are early Quaker meeting houses at Ettington (1684–9), Armscote (1705) and Warwick (1695), and one at Shipston-on-Stour (*c.* 1689) converted to a library. Long Compton has a group of early chapels or former chapels of most denominations. At Stretton-under-Fosse a former Presbyterian chapel (later Congregational) registered as 'new erected' in 1781 survives, at least externally. Alcester's Baptist church of *c.* 1737 stands alongside a later one and part of Wolvey Baptist church is of 1803. Bedworth's Old Meeting is of 1726. All these are humble and utilitarian, Georgian with occasional use of Gothic. Chapels of this sort continue into the early and even mid C19, but they are all merely typical rather than outstanding in any way. Warwick Unitarian chapel is of 1781 but much altered and Gothicized in 1862–3. For the Roman Catholics, Brailes is unusual and interesting, because the chapel on the upper floor of a barn was fitted out in 1726, some years before the Acts of 1778 and 1791 allowing the Mass and permitting Catholic chapels. Also ahead of the building spree that began after 1830 were the Catholic chapels at Wappenbury, 1795, the private chapel built by *John Tasker* in 1813 in the grounds of Wootton Wawen Hall, and *John Russell*'s original classical chapel (now the Seventh Day Adventist mission) in Leamington, 1828.

To return to the Georgian mainstream, we come to major houses of the period. Of the leading architects of GEORGIAN COUNTRY HOUSES two are represented in Warwickshire: *Gibbs* and *Robert Adam*. To these great names might be added those of *James* and *Samuel Wyatt*. Gibbs did the stables of Compton Verney, 1736–8, and the remodelling *c.* 1750 of late C17 Ragley Hall, including the splendid entrance hall with its pairs of giant pilasters and rich plasterwork. A slightly earlier gorgeous entrance hall is at Honington Hall, *c.* 1741, where in 1751–2 *John Freeman* and *William Jones* created the remarkable octagonal saloon. There is yet another grand entrance hall and more mid-C18 rooms at Farnborough Hall. There the Rococo aspect is reflected, as it is in the interior decoration of other mid-C18 houses (e.g. Honington and Ragley again, and Sherbourne Park). Robert Adam at Compton Verney, early in his career (*c.* 1761–6), refaced one side and added long wings. The centre received a portico, but much of Adam's future elegance is still lacking, and little of his original interior has survived. Adam's design influence is to be seen elsewhere, of course, with touches of Adamish decoration occurring widely through this period, e.g. especially at Packington Hall (below) but also at Ragley, Newbold Revel, Wellesbourne Hall, etc. *James Wyatt* added the grand portico and external steps at Ragley, and probably the stables and lodges too, 1778–83. *Samuel Wyatt* was the designer of Coton House (Churchover), a fine Neoclassical house of 1784 badly damaged by fire in 2010 and currently awaiting refurbishment. Two Late Georgian oddities might be referred to here: *Francis Hiorne*'s Kites Nest at Beausale, 1788, with three-storied octagonal centrepiece and lower wings each side, and The Folly at Halford with two octagons placed side by side as canted bays, *c.* 1790. Not everything conforms to standard styles and plans. Later Georgian manifestations include the semi-derelict classical villa by *Edward Gyfford* at Ryton-on-Dunsmore, 1806–7, and Fillongley Hall with Greek Revival interiors by *George Woolcot & Bryan Browning*, 1824–5.

But to see a range of Georgian work from the relatively ordinary to the definitely *avant garde* one must visit Packington. Here there are Palladian stables by *William & David Hiorne*, 1756–8, arranged around a quadrangle and with low corner towers (c.f. Hagley and Croome, both in Worcs.). The Hall was enlarged and completely remodelled for the 3rd Earl of Aylesford in 1766–72 by *Matthew Brettingham* the elder, assisted by *Henry Couchman* who took over following the former's death in 1769. The earlier interiors are Adamish in style, but under Heneage Finch, the 4th Earl who inherited in 1777, stylistic adventures began. The showpiece is the Pompeian Room, and that, with its painting by *J. F. Rigaud*, was designed by *Joseph Bonomi*. This was a gallery designed to display the earl's collection of Greek vases. It has

Pompeian-style painting on a black background derived from a book on the decoration of the Baths of Titus in Rome, published in 1786. The earl, a talented artist, had certainly sketched the ancient ruins he had visited in Italy on the Grand Tour in 1771–3. Italian-born Bonomi came to England to work for the Adams in 1767, setting up on his own account in 1781, and he was first engaged to work at Packington in 1782. He tutored the earl in architecture and perspective drawing, and together they designed the interiors, completed one by one from 1784 including the Pompeian Room in 1787. This was the most complete Pompeian scheme in England, but it is not the most startling or original creation by the duo of the earl and his architect. That is Great

73 Packington church, designed in 1787–8, built in 1789–92 and probably the most interesting church of its date anywhere in England.

The style of this amazing building derives from classical models from the ancient world, known to Bonomi and the earl either from their visits or illustrated in books available in England by the 1780s. These buildings were admired by both men for what Geoffrey Tyack has described as their 'qualities of almost brutal strength'. While some elements had been tried in England previously, e.g. the inscribed cross plan used by Wren more than once and the arrangement of corner towers taken over from Archer's St John Smith Square, the manner of usage here and the adoption of the Greek Doric style were adventurous and new. This was radical for the times, ahead of the most daring French architects of the moment, men like Boullée and Ledoux, or the angry young men of the Académie de France à Rome, or of Soane in England. Anyway, there it is, a rude brick block, with stone used only for the top of the four corner towers – the towers being a motif. The windows are all lunettes, large and small, and the vaulted interior designed on the Byzantino-Venetian plan has Greek Doric columns which in 1789 were also a motif still accepted by only very few. There is nothing in Wren and little at the time in Europe to compare with the beautiful, completely sheer ashlar groin-vaults of the church. As to authorship, it now seems that the earl himself called the shots in terms of style and primary features of the design, while Bonomi skilfully knitted it all together into the remarkable building we see today. It no longer has the massive marble font originally placed right in the centre of the building, but the decidedly un-English altarpiece remains. Set in a marble aedicule, this is a fresco painting by *Rigaud* completed in 1791 and slightly altered in 1793.

We cannot leave Aylesford and Bonomi without referring to the latter's Forest Hall at Meriden, built for the Woodmen of Arden, 1787–8. In it, a fine bust of the earl by *Thomas Banks*, 1795. In Warwickshire, Bonomi also designed Springfield Hall, Temple Balsall, 1790–1, and the original Barrells Park at Ullenhall, 1792–4 (recently reconstructed from its ruins along the original lines). But neither here nor anywhere else among Bonomi's executed works is there anything quite like Packington for originality and power.

The church lies in the grounds of Packington Hall, and this brings us to C18 LANDSCAPES. No more than a brief summary is necessary, as the subject is now well covered elsewhere (*see* Further Reading) and its relevance here is chiefly limited to the setting for buildings erected to enhance the landscape. But here Warwickshire again comes centre stage owing to the influence of *Sanderson Miller* of Radway. His diary, edited by Will Hawkes, shows just how widely he advised on landscape and architecture and how active he was. He was busy at Edge Hill on his own estate as early as 1739, building Egge Cottage (1744) and his castle on the hill (1745–50). He advised, among others, at Arbury, Upton House, Alscot, Honington, Farnborough and Packington, although not all his schemes were implemented. He certainly worked at Honington, where the Rococo landscape with its Chinese summerhouse and cascade was delightfully recorded in views by artist Thomas Robins in 1759. At Farnborough, Miller's landscape includes a terrace laid out by 1742; there is a game larder nearby, and along the terrace walk are the Ionic temple, Oval Pavilion and obelisk all attributed to *Miller* and *William Hiorne*. At Walton, Miller did the delightful bath house of 1749 on the hillside above the house. At Upton he did a temple by the lake, *c.* 1757. The grounds at Packington were landscaped not by Miller but by *Capability Brown*, who was also busy in Warwickshire. His plans for Packington are dated 1751. He worked at Ragley Hall in the 1750s, at Compton Verney in 1768–74 and also at Newnham Paddox (Monks Kirby; from 1746), Warwick Castle (from 1749), Charlecote (1757–61) and Combe Abbey (1771–6). Combe's park buildings include two lodges and a menagerie, possibly designed by *Henry Holland Jun.*, who was Brown's son-in-law. Landscape survival is patchy, but some tell-tale signs of Brownian water and planting remain at all these. After Brown came *Repton*, whose chief work in the county was at Stoneleigh Abbey where work began *c.* 1810. Among the buildings there are the castellated stables and riding school by *C. S. Smith*, the one designed in 1814, the other in 1820. Of the same years, the real tennis courts at Combe, 1817.

It was during the C18 in connexion with the growth of towns that PUBLIC BUILDINGS assumed importance. Even so, one must be mentioned of before the C18: *William Hurlbutt*'s Market Hall of Warwick of 1669–70. It survived the Great Fire of 1694, unlike Hurlbutt's near contemporary Shire Hall and county gaol in Northgate Street which were destroyed. Their successors, the major public buildings of the county town, are the main interest here. The Shire Hall of 1753–8 was designed by *Sanderson Miller*. It is surprising to see the amateur Gothicist capable of so disciplined and so dignified a performance in a mature Palladian style. Next to the Shire Hall in 1779–83 *Thomas Johnson* built the county gaol, and this, with its row of giant Doric columns (intended originally by him to be Greek Doric), is in its own way as amazing as Aylesford and Bonomi's Great Packington Church. Who was Johnson to be in his columniation among the pioneers in the whole of Europe? The gaol was continued round the

67

66
68

p. 50

76

Warwick, Shire Hall, elevation and plan.
Engraving by Francis Hiorne, 1768

corner by *Henry Couchman* (County Surveyor) in 1792–3 in as
77 menacing a way. Coventry had its own County Hall and gaol, of
which the hall by *Joseph Eglington*, 1784, and adjacent Governor's
House remain. Of town halls the best is *Francis Smith*'s Court
House of 1725–6 in Warwick representing the Warwickshire
Baroque, while *Robert Newman*'s at Stratford-upon-Avon, 1767–8,
is a civilized, urban, Palladian job. Both have contemporary
statuary: at Warwick, a figure of Justice by *Thomas Stayner*, 1731,
and at Stratford, a lead statue of Shakespeare by *John Cheere* in
an alcove specially designed by *Timothy Lightoler*, c. 1769. The
next significant public building is *John Russell*'s Old Town Hall
of Leamington Spa, 1831 and modestly classical.

Founded in 1677, the hospital (almshouses) at Temple Balsall,
although rebuilt in the early C18, retains the original plan around
three sides of a spacious courtyard. This follows the C16 tradition
of Bond's and Ford's Hospitals at Coventry and Leycester's
Hospital at Warwick. Other almshouses are in the form of single
buildings (e.g. Dunchurch, 1693 (rebuilt 1818), and Oken's and
Eyffler's at Warwick, 1696) or rows of cottages (e.g. Shustoke,
85 1699, Mancetter of 1728 and a second group with pretty iron
veranda of 1822). For pre-Victorian healthcare, the former infirmary and dispensary at Southam, built in a simple Gothic style
from 1818, is the best example. Here one might also mention the
Pump Rooms at Leamington Spa of 1813–14 by *C. S. Smith*, of
which only the front colonnade survives. Of schools built like

large houses, there are the old Boughton Free School at Dunchurch by *Francis Smith*, 1707–9, and the Old School House in
Kenilworth, 1724. More formal and of grander appearance is the
first group of buildings for Rugby School, by *Henry Hakewill*,
1809 etc., castellated but dull. Nethersole School at Polesworth,
rebuilt in 1818 by *Joseph Potter*, is in the Tudor Gothic style.

It should be observed that the conservatism already seen in
churches of the C17 is noticeable in other ways as well. SMALL
HOUSES with mullioned windows occur as late as 1711 (Ilmington) and 1714 (Shipston-on-Stour) and even with mullioned-
and-transomed windows (Newbold-on-Stour, 1714). Much more
typical of general trends in window design from the late C17 is
the cross-window with casements. This is the form found at
Grove Farm, Warmington, built *c.* 1700, and this is the county's
earliest example of a symmetrical double-pile house on a square
plan with hipped roof and inside four rooms per floor and a
staircase within the central hall. Sash windows begin to appear
in houses at about this time. There is also a long overlap between
the old and new traditions of building, and Hines House, Clifford
Chambers, built *c.* 1720, demonstrates the use of brick for the
façade for reasons of fashion and show but the continuation of
timber framing for everything behind.

For housing it otherwise need only to be said that the C18 and
early C19 saw widespread rebuilding as part of TOWN IMPROVE-
MENTS, the best examples of which can be picked up from the
perambulations (e.g. Atherstone, Alcester, Stratford-upon-Avon
and Shipston-on-Stour). Special importance attaches to the town
planning and design of Warwick as rebuilt after the Great Fire
of 1694. Here there was controlled variation within a uniform
design framework set by the Commissioners, best seen in the
High Street, Old Square and Northgate Street where brick and
stone houses are standard products of the rebuilding during the
C18. There was growth too, of course, reflected in the newer
buildings around what were then the outer areas of the expanding
towns and villages. At Coventry where land for expansion was
not available, it is interesting to see how close to the centre the
early C19 terraces were. Here remain some of the typical
WEAVERS' HOUSES with so-called top-shops having closely set
large second-floor windows behind which stood the loom. In the
towns too, especially in Coventry, Atherstone, Bedworth and
Nuneaton, were the overcrowded, insanitary courts inhabited by
the poorer classes. In the countryside, the effects of PARLIAMEN-
TARY ENCLOSURE can be seen in the construction of isolated
farmhouses associated with newly allocated landholdings outside
the village centres. Such farms are typical of the Warwickshire
landscape.

Of specific house types, PARSONAGES deserve special note
because they are particularly well documented as to designers
and dates. Dated examples include Wellesbourne (1698–9),
Hampton Lucy (1721–4, by *Francis Smith*), Kinwarton (1788)
and Alcester (1796). Other C18 rectories and vicarages without
definite dates but of some architectural refinement include those
at Atherstone-on-Stour, Long Compton, Warmington, Offchurch

and Whichford. Architect-designed Georgian parsonages of the early C19 include Leamington Hastings (*William Slater* of Derby, 1822), Corley (*C. S. Smith*, 1824–5), Coughton (*Charles Edge*, 1829–30) and Whitchurch (*William Kendall*, 1839).

Then there are the VILLAS of the 1830s, often lining the roads leading out of the towns, for instance along Binley Road in Coventry, at Radford, Coundon and Keresley on the other side of the same city, Emscote Road in Warwick, Bilton and Clifton roads in Rugby and Warwick Road in Stratford-upon-Avon. But for villas the paradise is Leamington, where fashionable development began in the late C18, accelerating with the creation of the New Town N of the River Leam from 1808. The high point for secular building was between 1820 and 1840. The villas are late classical, Gothic, Tudor, Jacobean, Italianate, they are all there in a leafy setting, and they were all there when Victoria ascended the throne. Of the 1820s there are a few examples of *P. F. Robinson*'s *cottage orné* style. There are terraces, squares and crescents too, notably Victoria Terrace (*William Thomas*, 1836–8) near the parish church, Clarendon Square (*c.* 1828–32) and Lansdowne Crescent (1838, again by *Thomas*). Smaller developments like Clarendon Crescent (*Samuel Nicklin*, 1830–9) and Lansdowne Circus (*c.* 1834–8, by *Thomas*) are also noteworthy.

To conclude the pre-Victorian era we must turn to transport and industry. For TRANSPORT in the C18 this means the roads and canals. The turnpiking of the main ROADS saw the erection of tollhouses, recognizable by their look-out windows angled towards the road. A few examples remain, notably Gothick Tollgate Cottage at Over Whitacre, 1769, and one by *William Eborall* on the Banbury Road south of Warwick, 1787. There are others at Arrow (*c.* 1825), Weethley (*c.* 1826), Kinwarton (*c.* 1814) and Wootton Wawen (*c.* 1814), all near Alcester. The C18 also saw improvements to river crossings in the form of new bridges, especially those for which the county was responsible. For those, work was generally supervised by the County Surveyor or Bridgemaster. Among the more important surviving bridges of these times are Polesworth (*Thomas Sheasby Sen.*, 1776–9), Maxstoke (also *Sheasby*, 1780), Offchurch (1785), Ryton (*Henry Couchman*, 1786–7), Barford (also *Couchman*, 1792–5), Wixford (*Couchman*, 1800–1) and the causeway to Halford Bridge (*John Nichol*, 1832). Other bridges were built privately or at parish expense, including Warwick Castle Bridge (1789–93) and Leafield Bridge in the park (*Robert Mylne*, 1772–6), Stoneleigh Park Bridge by *John Rennie*, 1813–14, and a bridge at Grendon (*Joseph Potter*, 1825). Attached to Clopton Bridge at Stratford-upon-Avon is a Gothick tollhouse built when the bridge was widened in 1814.

As to CANALS, the years from the 1770s to the 1820s were altogether the great canal years; in the county there are parts of the Grand Union Canal, which connected Birmingham and the North with London by way of the Grand Junction Canal,*

---

*Birmingham–Warwick–Napton 1793–4, Grand Junction completed 1805, Grand Union begun 1810.

the Coventry Canal (1768–90), the Oxford Canal (1768–90), and the Stratford Canal (1816). Altogether canal architecture can be very attractive. Among the notable features are a tunnel at Curdworth engineered by *Smeaton* and completed in 1789, the stone aqueduct over the Avon at Emscote between Warwick and Leamington, the flight of twenty-one locks at Hatton, and a horse tunnel at Shrewley, all of *c.* 1799, and the canal pumping station of 1821 at Hawkesbury. Edstone or Bearley Aqueduct by *William Whitmore*, 1813, is the longest in England, 250 yds (229 metres) long, and there is a shorter one of the same date at nearby Wootton Wawen. There are cast-iron bridges, one from Walsgrave (relocated to Spon End in Coventry) by the *Horseley Iron Works*, Tipton, to a design by *C. B. Vignoles*, 1832–4, and another at Hawkesbury cast at the *Britannia Foundry*, Derby, 1837. There are canal yards at Hillmorton (Rugby), Hatton and Hartshill, the latter rebuilt by *John Sinclair*, the resident engineer, *c.* 1840. The Stratford Canal has distinctive barrel-roofed lengthman's cottages (e.g. Lowsonford and Preston Bagot) of *c.* 1810–13.

79

80

The improved transport networks were especially important to trade and industry. INDUSTRIAL BUILDINGS remain near the canal and river wharves, e.g. the old timber yard at Stratford-upon-Avon, the Leicester Row warehouses at Coventry and groups of canalside commercial buildings at Atherstone and Polesworth. In Warwick, the group of industrial buildings round the Saltisford canal basin (mostly removed since the first edition of this guide) includes the former gas works, with two octagonal gas holders of 1822. Early industrial premises are generally scarce now, though Atherstone still has some surviving early C19 hat factory buildings. In Chapelfields and Earlsdon, Coventry, there are watchmakers' workshops of the 1840s, and in New Buildings in central Coventry a ribbon factory of 1849. But these stretch the date range for this section, intended to cover the pre-Victorian years.

The coming of the railways is best considered with the Victorian age, but at Stratford-upon-Avon the second bridge over the Avon belongs to the horse tramway opened from Stratford wharf to Moreton-in-Marsh (1826) and its branch line to Shipston-on-Stour (1836). *John Urpeth Raistrick* was the engineer and William James was the chief promoter. Long sections of the track bed, some bridges and other features remain along the route.

VICTORIAN AND EDWARDIAN

'The Victorian Age offers a fine harvest to those ready to gather it, and there are – it is pleasant to record – more and more of them.' So began this section in the first edition of this guide. Re-reading it now reminds us that back in 1965–6 Victorian architecture was still largely despised and disliked. Since then not only have interest and appreciation been rekindled but also our

Stretton-on-Dunsmore church, perspective.
Lithograph, 1839

knowledge of the period has been considerably expanded. Many of the leading Victorian architects have modern biographies and there are detailed studies of building types, period decoration and so on. It follows that this revision has involved a fair amount of updating in this respect. Moreover, the number of examples to select from for this overview is much increased.

We start with CHURCHES. Many were rebuilt or newly built in the second quarter of the century. A list of them is appended as a note.* The majority of them are of the type of the Commissioners' churches, i.e. aisleless, with tall, slender windows, lancet or two-light Perp, narrowly placed thin buttresses, a w tower or no tower, and a short chancel. The most interesting of them are two by *Thomas Rickman* and his partners of the time. Rickman of course was a scholar – he gave us our terminology of E.E., Dec and Perp – and his depth of knowledge of medieval churches is demonstrated at Hampton Lucy (*Rickman & Hutchinson*, 1822–6) and Stretton-on-Dunsmore (*Rickman*, 1835–7). The former is on a grand scale and the tower especially successful, but for the aisle windows cast-iron tracery was used. At Stretton the tracery is more accurate. Both, however, are high and narrow,

*The surviving churches are Hampton Lucy 1822–6; Great Wolford and Newbold-on-Stour 1833; Bidford-on-Avon 1835; Stretton-on-Dunsmore 1835–7; Alveston, St Mary Leamington, and Long Lawford, all 1839; St Peter, Hillfields, Coventry[†] 1840–1; St Matthew, Rugby, 1841; Wilmcote 1841; Attleborough[†] (Nuneaton), and Stretton-on-Fosse 1841–2; St Paul, Warwick, 1844; and Keresley,[†] Coventry, 1844–5. The daggers indicate Commissioners' churches built with the aid of the second Parliamentary grant. Churches demolished or replaced are omitted from this list.

their ashlar walls are smooth and they had (Stretton still has) short chancels. They are thus of their time, despite the apparent correctness of the architectural detail. The other building of interest here is Bidford (*John Lattimer* of Stratford, 1834–5), although it doesn't fit the narrative at all. It is C17 semi-classical, semi-Gothic, and most unusual. 90

So at this date not even Rickman could design churches which were archaeologically convincing. He used medieval elements with great accuracy but never aimed at a total facsimile. That, though, was the avowed aim of Pugin, who succeeded where he had enough money. But he certainly succeeded as a church decorator and furnisher and, moreover, he established, by his fervent writings more than his buildings, a duty to build churches truly as Gothic churches, i.e. as churches such as they would have been built in the Gothic centuries and preferably the decades of the Second Pointed, i.e. the late C13 and earliest C14. *G. G. Scott* was Pugin's most successful follower, and his two very early churches of Westwood Heath, Coventry (*Scott & Moffatt*, 1842–4) and Wasperton (*Scott*, 1843–52) are patently post-Commissioners, i.e. designed to be what Gothic village churches were. That they remain recognizable at once as Victorian is another matter. It is due – if we make a statement applying generally to Victorian churches – to the regularity of the window tracery, i.e. that lack of the haphazard fenestration of genuine buildings, buildings grown and not made; to the preference for NW or SW or N or S towers over W towers; and to the naturalism of leaf and flower carving inside. Baddesley Ensor (*Clutton*, 1845–6) is another church that fits this model, and Scott's restoration of the Late Geometrical church at Temple Balsall, 1848–9, still demonstrates the same crispness and neatness of finish.

Post-Commissioners also is the Leamington parish church, the grandiose enterprise of a crazy incumbent, *Dr John Craig*, who was largely his own architect. He started in 1843 and went on undaunted into the seventies, despite bitter disputes with professional advisers and acrimony within the parish. The result is bold, monumental, and ignorant. The style is Continental Gothic, not at all correct in the details.

Briefly a fashion of the forties was the NEO-NORMAN, the parallel to the much more successful *Rundbogenstil* in Germany. Christ Church, Leamington, by *P. F. Robinson*, unfortunately destroyed, was of 1825 and thus a pioneer of the mode. Among the local examples are the mortuary chapel of Princethorpe Priory by *Hansom*, completed in 1843, *Harvey Eginton*'s Spernall of 1844 (much like his church at Trimpley, Worcs.), and *T. L. Walker*'s Hartshill of the same years with its unbelievable portal of six orders with voussoirs of vitrified dark blue bricks. Another, in brick, is the workhouse chapel of 1842 at Alcester, and a further one is the Church of England chapel in Coventry Cemetery, *c.* 1846. A still later example, clearly influenced by Kilpeck (Herefs.) where the donor's family had connections, is Pailton by *William Chick*, the Herefordshire County Surveyor, 1883–4. 93

Tempting though it is to look at parallel developments in secular buildings, we will continue with churches of the Gothic Revival although they are not entirely separable from their associated buildings, i.e. parsonages and schools. Moving into the 1850s we reach the High Victorian era and the great names in Warwickshire are Scott and Butterfield. *Scott's* maturity was marked by Holy Trinity, Rugby, of 1852–4 (demolished 1983) and the sumptuous estate church of Sherbourne, which cost £20,000 to build in 1862–4. His work of the intervening years is significant too: the soaring apsed chancel at Hampton Lucy, 1856–8, the tower and spire at Ansty, 1856, chancels at Whitnash (1855) and Tysoe and Farnborough (1858), and the superb interior restoration of 1854–6 at Holy Trinity, Coventry, where he also designed the sadly demolished timber belfry. Rugby was to be Butterfield's later on but in the 1850s Scott, who did the School Field building in 1852, still held sway.

Butterfield like Scott appeared early in Warwickshire with small buildings e.g. Wilmcote school (1845–6) and vicarage (1846–8) and Aston Cantlow school (1847–8), only marginally Gothic and much rather sensibly domestic in the way Pugin could be, who was indeed the great formative influence on Butterfield, as he was on Scott. This can be seen in his combined church, school and teacher's house of 1849 at Thurlaston. But soon, before 1850 in fact, Butterfield became Butterfield, hard-hitting, not afraid of the ugly, provided it had character, strident in his insistence on polychromy and always forceful. None of this is now evident in his early work at Aston Cantlow church, 1850, as his High Church furnishings have been whittled away to nothing. But the move towards sharply distinctive tracery is seen in the s aisle, and in the restorations at Kinwarton (1847) and Barton-on-the-Heath (1851). Cubbington chancel furnishings, 1852, certainly have the Butterfield hallmark. His muscular style came to Warwickshire 103 later, but was in full force at Rugby School from 1867 and at St Andrew's, Rugby, from 1877. His New School of 1867, extended s in 1885, has a bold polychromatic façade to the street ingen-94, 95 iously unexpected in composition and details. The school chapel is a little later – 1872 is the year – and much calmer. With its three bays wide shallow transepts and soaring piers, it is both functionally ingenious and most noble. St Andrew's, the principal parish church, is yet later – 1877–85, with tower and spire later still, 1895–6. Although restrained in colour externally, it has all the might associated with its architect and there is plenty of polished stone and brass within.

By the third great name of the period, *G. E. Street*, there is little – a minor school at Barton-on-the-Heath of 1854–5, restorations at Henley-in-Arden (1856) and Lapworth (1860), and a remarkably plain church at Shipston-on-Stour (1854–5). His later work is no more distinguished, e.g. Dordon and New Bilton (both 1867–8) and restorations at Polesworth, Seckington and Tanworth-in-Arden. But of the 1850s there is *John Gibson's* awkwardly fussy estate church for the Lucys at Charlecote, 1851–3. He also did Combrook for the Verneys, 1866–7. Both are highly

Dec. *Henry Woodyer*'s 1862–3 restoration at Long Compton also fits in the context of this phase of the Gothic Revival.

But if Street was dull, the same cannot be said of Warwickshire's own High Victorian architect, *James Murray* of Coventry. In a short but intensely busy career – he died in 1863 at the age of thirty-two – he was responsible for two major churches, St James at Stratford-upon-Avon (from 1853) and All Saints, Emscote, at Warwick (1854–61). Both are now demolished, but Murray's virile Gothic can still be seen in his other work of period (e.g. the Bluecoat School in Coventry, 1856–7).

The savage 'rogue architects' of the High Victorian period, those who prized originality higher than beauty, are thinly represented in Warwickshire. There is nothing by E.B. Lamb, and *S. S. Teulon*'s sole commission – at Eastern Green, where he designed the church, parsonage and school – came right at the end of his life. But the county had a 'rogue' of its own in *G. T. Robinson* (the archidiaconal architect) whose hand is plainly to be seen in his restoration at Brinklow (1862) and in the chunky capitals of St Mark's in Coventry (*Paull & Robinson*, 1868–9). His most striking works are both outside the county – at Earlswood (or Salter Street) where he did the polychromatic w tower of 1860, and at St Luke's, Blakenhall, Wolverhampton, a complete build of 1860–1. Warwickshire's best example is not by Robinson but by *John Croft*, whose Lower Shuckburgh church of 1863–4 is every bit as perverse as an extreme Teulon or even a Lamb church. 97

The use of Gothic was to continue through the rest of the Victorian age and into the early C20 and it is only necessary to pick out a few interesting or typical examples. From national architects we have *J. P. Seddon*'s Ullenhall church of 1875, still striving for originality but more restrained than in the previous decade, more knowledgeable, but also decidedly odd in external and internal motifs. Winderton by *William Smith* (1876–8) is in p. 711 similar vein, still with originality though less adventurous. The one church by *J. L. Pearson* at Newbold Pacey (1880–1) is but a minor work. The first work in the county by *Ewan Christian* was a restoration at Austrey in 1844–5. His work is generally serious and even pedestrian, as at Bishop's Itchington (1872–3) and Claverdon (1876–7) but his St John's at Kenilworth (1851–2) is more impressive than one might expect. We have a clutch of vigorous churches by *John Cotton*, at Luddington (1871–2), Longford, Coventry (1873–4), Atherstone-on-Stour (1875–6) and Hockley Heath, Nuthurst (1879–80), and *J. A. Chatwin*'s Mappleborough Green (1888) is more rewarding inside than its rock-faced exterior would suggest. Two especially pleasing churches are those at Radway (1865–6) and Avon Dassett (1868–9) by *C. E. Buckeridge* of Oxford, the latter being done in a range of medieval styles. The deliberate contrast is most effective. Hatton (*William Young*, 1878–80) is dull. Worcestershire has several good churches by *W. J. Hopkins* of Worcester, but his only one in this county (Wixford, 1880–1) is nothing special. The work of *Frederick Preedy* is generally rewarding, e.g. his complete churches at Binton (1875–6) and

99 Temple Grafton (1875). So too are the major Leamington churches of *John Cundall*, St Paul's in Leicester Street (1873–5) and St John the Baptist (1877–88) in Tachbrook Street. The later routine forms of Gothic are also exemplified in Leamington in the completions of the parish church (*Sir Arthur Blomfield*, 1898–1902) and Holy Trinity (*W. Hawley Lloyd*, 1913–14).

By 1890 this sort of style was already out of fashion in favour of a lighter and gentler form of Gothic, aesthetic not mighty, Perp with touches of the Renaissance and Queen Anne, not stubbornly English C13–C14. One of the authors of this change was *Thomas Garner*. He was born in Warwickshire, and worked with Scott at Sherbourne in 1862–4. In 1865–6 he delightfully restored the chapel of the Lord Leycester Hospital at Warwick, restoring Beaudesert in 1864, Wroxall in 1867–8 and building a small church at Balsall Common in 1871. He became a partner with *G. F. Bodley* in 1868. The Warwickshire churches of *Bodley & Garner* at Oldberrow (1875–6) and New Bilton (completed 1881) are not especially distinguished, nor is their more major work at Bedworth (1888–90). But the lightness of their distinctive style, coupled with the aesthetic quality of the furnishings, can be seen in their restoration work, especially at Bilton (1871–2), Rowington (1872), Clifton-upon-Dunsmore (1872 and 1893) and Holy Trinity, Stratford-upon-Avon (1885–98). For later Gothic developments we must also take note of St

100 Mark's, New Milverton, Leamington (1876–9). It is the most important surviving work of *George Gilbert Scott Jun.* who also designed the Queen Anne revival vicarage nearby (now Leamington House, 1873–6). For now, that brings our summary of Victorian and Edwardian churches nearly to a close, apart from a brief mention of the Arts and Crafts Gothic of Holy Trinity new church at Ettington (1902–3) and at St Peter's Rugby (1909) by *C. Ford Whitcombe*.

The character of CHURCH RESTORATIONS differed little from the mainstream work of new building. Some have already been noted and so only a few more instances need be given. Among the early, serious and 'correct' jobs were Austrey (*Ewan Christian*, 1844–5), Temple Balsall (*Scott*, 1848–9) and Coleshill (*William Slater*, 1858–9). The remodelling of St Nicholas, Kenilworth (*William Smith*, 1864), might be regarded as drastic, while in the restoration at Monks Kirby (*G. E. Street*, 1868–9) several of the windows were 'corrected' and the same architect's concurrent work at Polesworth was harshly done too. In contrast *Scott*'s restoration at Ladbroke (1876) left a good example of what the Victorians thought a church should be, conservatively repaired (albeit with improvements) and decently furnished within. Hatred for the Georgian was shown in the heavy-handed conversions of round-headed windows to Gothic ones at Weddington, Nuneaton (*A. W. Blomfield*, 1880–1), and Barston (*E. H. Lingen Barker*, 1899–1900). Some restorations were just messy and undistinguished (e.g. Napton-on-the-Hill and Lillington), some (e.g. Bubbenhall, 1865–6) undertaken by builders feeling no need for professional advice, or by clergy unaided (e.g. Studley). Of later restorations, *Thomas Garner*'s work at Wolverton (1869–70) is especially rewarding, and generally the best are those by *Bodley & Garner* and the Arts and Crafts practitioners like *C. Ford Whitcombe*.

CHURCH FURNISHINGS are often integral to new builds and restoration, though not always. In Warwickshire, we must note examples of metalwork by *Francis Skidmore* of Coventry's Victoria Art Metal Works, particularly the superb brass candelabra at Holy Trinity, Coventry (*c.* 1855), the altar rails at Cubbington (1852), several pieces at Hampton Lucy (*c.* 1858) and much at Sherbourne (1862–4). For woodwork, Warwick produced some quality pieces, for instance at Combrook (*T. H. Kendall*, 1867), Warwick St Paul (*Kendall, c.* 1870) and probably the 1850s ensemble at Upper Shuckburgh. Warwick woodcarvers' secular pieces are more famous (e.g. the Kenilworth buffet at Warwick Castle by *Cookes & Sons*, 1851). As to stone carvers, there is work from the usual firms: *Earp, Harry Hems, Farmer & Brindley* (woodwork also) and *Boulton* of Cheltenham. There are the usual sanctuary floors richly paved with encaustic tiles, e.g. Caldecote (*Minton*, 1857) and Pailton (*Godwin*, 1884) and complete ensembles of choir and clergy stalls in chancels, e.g. Coventry St John (*J. O. Scott*, 1886). Individually distinctive pieces include a High Victorian stone pulpit at Bishop's Tachbrook by *G. T. Robinson* with relief carving signed by *S. P. Wood*, 1861. Wellesbourne has an alabaster reredos by *T. H. Wyatt*, 1873, inlaid with mosaics by *Salviati*. Fonts include an extraordinary alabaster angel at Mappleborough Green (1888), and Pailton (1884) with Normanesque detailing from Kilpeck (Herefs.). Alveston has an especially fine screen and pulpit by *Temple Moore*, 1904, the carving by *James Elwell* of Beverley. Many churchyards have Victorian lychgates, that at Ladbroke by *J. T. Irvine*, 1884, being a nice example. Clifton-upon-Dunsmore has a memorial cross by *Bodley*, 1898.

As to STAINED GLASS, there is much variety and all the big names appear, *Willement, Wailes, Clayton & Bell, Gibbs, Preedy, Morris & Co., Heaton, Butler & Bayne, Lavers, Barraud & Westlake* (later *Lavers & Westlake*), *Burlison & Grylls, Kempe* etc. These need little discussion, since by the time of Willement's accurately medieval E window at Hampton Lucy (1837) the stylistic direction was already set. With the proximity to Birmingham, there are numerous *Hardman* windows too, some of the earlier ones to *Pugin* designs. There are also some from the Smethwick studios. Warwick was a centre of stained glass from the 1830s, and the work of *William Holland*, Frenchman *Tony Dury* (working mainly for Roman Catholic churches), *Holland & Holt* and *F. Holt & Co.* run successively until after the Great War.

With MONUMENTS, plain tablets persisted but Wootton Wawen has one with a Gothic surround and rib-vault, yet with an urn and mourning woman (*John Ternouth*, †1836). From the 1830s appear overblown Gothic forms with crocketed pinnacles, ogees etc. Examples are at Stratford (*Wm Moysen*, Birmingham, †1841), Alveston (by *Peter Hollins*, Birmingham, †1848 and one

101

of two there), the Shuckburgh tablets at Bourton-on-Dunsmore, Newbold-on-Avon (†1868) and Ansley (*Hollins* still, †1873). There is the revival of MEMORIAL BRASSES from the 1840s, mostly by *Hardman*, as at Sherbourne (†1845). They were especially popular in Roman Catholic churches, as at Coughton (†1843 and †1851), Kenilworth (†1845), Rugby (†1848) and elsewhere. One at Holy Trinity, Coventry, is by *Francis Skidmore*, 1878. Turning to the memorials of the upper classes, Arrow (†1870) and Alcester (†1880) both have Seymour memorials by *Count Gleichen*, the former with a recumbent effigy, the latter with a seated effigy. Among the rich collection of all periods at Upper Shuckburgh are two by *H. H. Armstead* (†1876 and †1884). Stoneleigh has a fine set too, including a recumbent effigy in a vaulted polygonal recess with late C13 Gothic carving, possibly by *Scott*, †1851. Another by Scott has an alabaster relief by *J. Birnie Philip*, 1861, and there are others by *J. Forsyth* of Worcester, 1867, by *Butterfield*, 1863, and one in the Quattrocento taste, signed by *E. Orlandini* of Florence, 1886. Wroxall has an ornately carved Dugdale memorial and reredos, typical *Bodley & Garner*, 1896–7.

In parallel chronologically came the provision of new PARSON-AGES, sometimes done by the same architects and often quite close in date to the restoration or improvement of churches. While Gothic was often the style it was not slavishly used and many new rectories and vicarages were in a modest domestic style, albeit sometimes with fashionable dashes of the time. For instance Monks Kirby (*Scott & Moffatt*, 1842–3) has diapered brickwork and fish-scale tiling. Even works by the outlandish *G. T. Robinson* (Long Itchington, 1862) and *John Croft* (Lower Shuckburgh, 1862–3) are relatively tame in comparison with their churches, as is *Yeoville Thomason*'s Sherbourne, 1863. Some are big and rambling, e.g. Quinton (*Medland & Powell*, 1880–1). Others are rather gaunt, like Oldberrow by *R. Bradshaw* of Leamington (1878) and *Ewan Christian*'s Gaydon (1880–1). It will suffice to illustrate the range of styles, materials and designers. Tanworth-in-Arden (*J. B. Harper*, 1835) is Tudor. There are Jacobean gables at Grandborough (1844), Rowington (*Horace Francis*, 1850) and on *T. L. Walker*'s remodelling of St Nicolas, Nuneaton (1845–6). Walton (*William Kendall*, 1843) and Burton Dassett (partly *John Plowman*, 1846–7) have bargeboarded gables. Withybrook has quoins and keystones (*Joseph Nevill*, 1854). Wilmcote (*Butterfield*, 1846–8) is early Gothic while Newbold-on-Stour (*John Prichard*, 1867–8) is muscular, like the architect's nearby Ettington Park. Polesworth (*John Douglas*, 1876) is in a delightful Arts and Crafts Tudor with half-timbering. As to materials, Bilton (*R. C. Hussey*, 1853) is gault brick, Haselor (*Joseph Lattimer*, 1868) is rendered, Ashow (*Charles E. Davis*, 1866) and Nether Whitacre (*Robert Jennings*, 1873) are in plum brick and Hartshill (*Jennings*, 1853) and Astley (*F. C. Penrose*, 1884) are rock-faced. Hockley Heath (*W. H. Bidlake*, 1896) typifies the ordinary house that became standard. Exceptionally, the building of grand parsonages continued into the C20, notably at

p. 507

Alveston (*Temple Moore*, 1903–4), Honiley (*Osborn, Pemberton & White*, 1923) and Lighthorne (*Coleridge, Jennings & Soimenow* of Westminster, 1929–30). Many, of course, are composites of several dates, for instance Butlers Marston (in four phases, 1838–80), Bidford-on-Avon (part *H. J. Ingram*, 1859, part *W. J. Hopkins*, 1888), and Fenny Compton (by Oxford architects *H. J. Underwood*, 1842, and *Harry Drinkwater*, 1887). Before leaving parsonages, it is worth noting that the Rev. John Sandford's vicarage at Dunchurch had grounds landscaped by *J. C. Loudon*, 1837.

The classic C19 grouping is of church, parsonage and school, as at Eastern Green already mentioned. Other such groups now regrettably lost included Emscote in Warwick, and Keresley near Coventry where *Benjamin Ferrey* did the school (1852) and vicarage (1868) as well as the church (1844). The school was particularly good. Victorian S C H O O L S have not fared well in Warwickshire owing to the strictly utilitarian and cost-conscious policies of the local education authorities. The accretions obscuring the schools at Wilmcote and Temple Grafton exemplify this. Closed schools have done better, either as houses (e.g. Alderminster) or as village halls (e.g. Wroxall). There have been widespread demolitions too. Those that remain range from the simple box-like form of Kenilworth's St Nicholas National School, 1836, resembling a Nonconformist chapel, through various phases of Gothic to the plain council schools of the early C20 (e.g. Galley Common, 1897, and Arley, 1913) by the County Architect (or County Surveyor).

The interest is chiefly in the village schools, usually consisting of one or more classrooms with a house for the teacher alongside. These were built as National Schools from the early C19, but in greater numbers after the passing of the Elementary Education Act of 1870. Great Alne (*J. B. Harper* of Henley, 1840) is Italianate, a style also used for the same architect's Claverdon, 1848. Gothic, of course, became the norm. Radway (*D. G. Squirhill*, 1851), Long Itchington (*William Hey Dykes* of York, 1855–6), Tysoe (*Scott*, 1857–9), Wroxall (1863), Quinton (*Preedy*, 1864), Butlers Marston (*William White*, 1871) and Fillongley (*John Cotton*, 1877) are among the more rewarding of the mid C19. Not all are architect-designed, and Southam (1859) and Tiddington (1867) offer rather amusing examples of diapering and polychromy as conceived by builders. Of the later Board Schools, apart from Warwick (above) the best are perhaps at Exhall by Coventry (1876–7) and Polesworth (1881) by *George Taylor*, Long Lawford (1878), Henley-in-Arden (*W. Hawley Lloyd*, 1883–4), Westgate School, Warwick (*G. H. Cox*, 1883–4, Queen Anne *p. 62* style), Atherstone (*W. Millican* of Leicester, 1882) and several in Leamington (e.g. Clapham Terrace by *Frederick Foster*, 1889–90). To grammar schools and public schools we will return later.

We must turn now to the places of worship of the other denominations, beginning with R O M A N   C A T H O L I C   C H U R C H E S. The repeal of restrictive legislation in 1829 led to a rush of building activity, spurred on by the old Catholic families like the

Warwick, Westgate School, perspective.
Engraving, 1883

Throckmortons at Coughton and the Ferrers at Baddesley
Clinton, incomers including Captain Washington Hibbert at
Bilton Grange and converts like Lord Denbigh at Newnham
Paddox. The range of buildings included priories and convents
with schools, Catholic parish churches with presbyteries, schools,
and dedicated cemeteries. Nearly all have complex building
histories.

Of the religious communities, the buildings at Princethorpe
Priory and Baddesley Clinton (Poor Clares) remain. There were
others at Atherstone (St Scholastica's), Monks Kirby and Southam
as well as shorter-lived ones elsewhere (e.g. Coventry and Rugby).
At Princethorpe building began in 1833, initially under *John
Russell* of Leamington, whose extensive but sparing brick buildings went up at great speed. The original church was built in
1835–7. After 1837 *J. A. Hansom* became involved, and he did the
Neo-Norman mortuary chapel and nuns' cemetery (now the
Roundhouse) in 1843. Later Hansoms worked here until 1892
although the grand but rather vacuous church of 1898–1901 is
by *P. P. Pugin*. Baddesley Clinton is essentially of one build,
including the church, by *Benjamin Bucknall*, 1870. The Southam
convent began in 1876 and had a rather gaunt main building 'by
a German architect', 1897.

These convent and priory buildings accommodated a wide
range of Catholic welfare activities. In that context, mention
should be made of Coleshill and the large complex of buildings
belonging to the children's 'garden city' begun in 1902 by Fr
George Hudson. The earliest were by *Henry Sandy*, and after the
Great War *Harrison & Cox* took over. The octagonal central
office building is particularly memorable.

Of Catholic parish churches, the earliest is at Hampton-on-
the-Hill (1819; enlarged by *John Russell*, 1830). The older part is
in a fanciful Gothic (also noted at Wappenbury). The rest is Perp,

as is the adjoining presbytery. Many of the early churches started on a small scale, as at Nuneaton (*J. A. Hansom*, 1838, enlarged in 1910–11 and 1936). From the Pugins we have St Augustine, Kenilworth (*A. W. N. Pugin*, 1841–2, enlarged by *G. R. Blount*, 1849–52), Rugby (*Pugin's* 1845–7 church is now the N aisle, grandly enlarged by *E. W. Pugin* 1864–7 with a splendid tower and spire by *Bernard Whelan*, 1872), Warwick (*E. W. Pugin*, 1859–60) and Stratford-upon-Avon (*E. W. Pugin*, 1865–6). P.P. Pugin's contribution at Princethorpe has been noted already.

From other architects we have three by *Charles Hansom*: St Osburg's in Coventry (1843–5 with a steeple finished in 1852), then Coughton (1851–3) and Studley (1853), both with presbyteries. At Coughton there was also a Catholic school of 1858 by *C. A. Buckler* who did the church at Atherstone (1859) and a school at Ilmington (1864), later converted into a church. For the rest, there are Avon Dassett church and presbytery (*Thomas Meyer*, 1854–5), *Clutton's* ambitious C13 French church at Leamington (1861–4 with slender tower 1877–8), Weston-in-Arden (1869) by *Gualbert Saunders*, Alcester (1888–9) by *A. J. C. Scoles* and Foleshill (1914–16) by *Harrison & Cox*. Coventry architect *T. R. Donnelly* did three, Bedworth (1882–3, tower 1899), St Mary & St Benedict, Coventry (1893), and Wootton Wawen (1904, but with fittings from the old chapel including painted glass by *Samuel Lowe*, 1814). Besides those already mentioned there are Catholic schools at Atherstone (*Robert Jennings*, 1859–60), Stratford-upon-Avon (*G. H. Cox*, 1883) and Kenilworth (1893); presbyteries at Kenilworth (*G. R. Blount*, c. 1849), Leamington (*Clutton*, 1861–6), Southam (1886) and Stratford (*G. H. Cox*, 1889); and separate cemetery chapels at Coughton (1867), Wootton Wawen (1872) and the Denbigh Mausoleum Chapel at Monks Kirby by *F. A. Walters*, 1897–8. Lastly, mention should be made of the former private chapels at Wolvey Hall (*R., J & J. Goodacre* of Leicester, 1889) and Bourton Hall (*H. A. Peto*, 1908).

The general paucity of NONCONFORMIST CHAPELS has been mentioned already so it will not be surprising to learn that there are few C19 examples of note. Many are small and nondescript, but an increase in wealth and numbers through the century gave congregations new architectural confidence. Moving on from chapels of the ordinary Georgian sort we find chapels with more refined classical details, for instance Brook Street Congregation in Warwick (refronted and enlarged by *T. S. Whitwell*, 1825–6), Stratford-upon-Avon Baptist (1835), Spencer Street Congregational in Leamington (*John Russell*, 1836) and Hartshill Congregational (1840). Alcester Baptist (*Joseph Lattimer*, 1859) is still classical. Later still are two classical chapels in Stratford-upon-Avon, the Primitive Methodist (*T. T. Allen*, 1865–6) and the added front of Birmingham Road Methodist (*Frederick Foster*, 1883). Baddesley Ensor Congregational (1863) is Italianate. Elements of the same style appear elsewhere, as in *E. Axten's* Studley Methodist, 1872, and Rugby Primitive Methodist (now Evangelical Free Church) by *James Kerridge & Sons* of Wisbech, 1877.

Simple Gothic forms appear in the 1830s, for instance with lancets at Coleshill Congregational (*D. R. Hill*, 1834) and Hampton-in-Arden Providence Chapel (now Coptic Orthodox) (1836), and the Gothic windows and big crenellated front of Atherstone Methodist (1836). Southam Congregational (1836) has a pretty Gothick front. Plain forms continue at Ratley Wesleyan (1865) and Shipston Baptist (1866) with Y-tracery and banded headers. Holly Walk Congregational in Leamington (*Squirhill*, 1849) is more enlightened with its diapering and Perp tracery. By the 1860s a particular form of chapel Gothic had arrived, examples including Kenilworth United Reformed (*G. & I. Steane*, 1872–3), Radford Semele Baptist (1874) and Radford Road Methodist in Leamington (1876–7) both by *John Cundall*, Stratford-upon-Avon Congregational (*H. J. Paull*, 1878–80) and Cubbington Methodist (*Frederick Foster*, 1888). Warwick Northgate Methodist (*J. L. Ball* 1893) is in a specially churchy Gothic, as is Earlsdon Methodist, built in 1923 to an earlier design by *Crouch & Butler*, 1909.

There were specialist chapel architects. *George Ingall* of Birmingham designed the Gothic Baptist churches at Henley-in-Arden (1867), Dunnington (1878) and the ambitious one at 98 Umberslade (1877). The prolific *John Wills* of Derby did Shipston-on-Stour Methodist (1880), Manor Court Road Baptist in Nuneaton (1899) and the Gothic street front of Rugby Wesleyan (now Christian Fellowship) (1898). Local Methodist *T. T. Allen* of Stratford did Kineton (1893) and Henley-in-Arden (1894). Bilton (1893) and Fillongley (1892–3) chapels are by Birmingham Methodist architect *Ewen Harper*, but the Fillongley homes for Wesleyan preachers (1898–9) are by *F. J. Yates*, who carried out numerous Methodist commissions in Nuneaton.

Queens Road Baptist in Coventry (1883–4) by *G. & I. Steane* is Gothic, but the same firm's Warwick Road Congregational (1889–91) nearby is in free Renaissance style with domed towers. The move away from formal styles characterized chapel building 111 around the turn of the C20. Nuneaton United Reformed church (*Ingall & Son* of Birmingham, 1903–4) is a large chapel in a free Gothic style, while Heath End Free Methodist church at Chilvers Coton (*F. J. Yates*, 1903) and Bedworth Baptist church (*T. R. J. Meakin*, 1912) are free Perp. Kenilworth Methodist (*Crouch & Butler*, 1902–3) is Gothic, but with a freestyle stone porch. Of the free Perp style of *George & R. Palmer Baines* there are four chapels, the best at Rugby (1905–6) and others at Nuneaton (1905), Foleshill (1923–4) and Stoke (1928–9). Chapels at Ryton near Bulkington (1911) and Whitacre Heath, Nether Whitacre (*A. McKewan*, 1914) have large Diocletian windows. *F. W. B. Yorke*'s Wellesbourne Methodist (1915) is fully Arts and Crafts.

Of the religious denominations not yet mentioned, we should note the Coventry Synagogue and Rabbi's House in Barras Lane by *Thomas Naden* of Birmingham, 1870, and the Rugby Quaker meeting by *H. Bedford Tylor* of Bournville, 1909.

Finally, to conclude this review of C19 and early C20 religious buildings we should turn to CEMETERIES and their chapels.

These originated in steps taken to tackle the health problems associated with interments in town centre churchyards and burial grounds. The provision of greenfield sites was the answer, with existing churchyards being closed for burials. The new cemeteries were provided with boundary walls, lodges and chapels, usually one for the Church of England and another for the dissenters, burials taking place respectively in consecrated and unconsecrated areas. The earliest and best is in Coventry, where the London Road Cemetery has finely landscaped grounds on 81

Coventry, London Road Cemetery,
memorial to Sir Joseph Paxton †1865.
Engraving, 1867

the site of an old quarry. The layout was by *Paxton & Stokes*, 1846–7, and the buildings include a Neo-Norman chapel for the Anglicans, a Grecian one for the dissenters, an Italianate lodge and a prospect tower. Just inside the gates is a monument to *p. 65* Paxton (†1865), and among the others are the memorials of two Coventry architects, J. L. Akroyd (†1856) and James Murray (†1863). The first superintendent was *Richard Ashwell*, who later advised on the landscaping of cemeteries at Birmingham (1862) and Nuneaton (1874). Leamington has an original lodge (*Squirhill*, 1852) but the remaining chapels (*Cundall*, 1868) belong to a later extension. There are good chapels at Warwick (1857–61), Rugby (*G. Bidlake*, 1863) and Shipston-on-Stour (*W. H. Knight*, 1864), the latter being especially well designed with a tower and spire over the arch between the two chapels. Stratford-upon-Avon has a lodge, boundary walls and the damaged remains of the chapels (*T. T. Allen*, 1881). Later urban cemeteries exist at Holbrooks and Foleshill in Coventry, Stockingford and Attleborough in Nuneaton, and at Kenilworth (*Sholto Douglas*, 1912–13). There are village cemeteries with minor buildings at Harbury, Bishop's Itchington and Wolston.

We must step back now to the beginning of Queen Victoria's reign or, to be more precise, to the eve of it. The architecture of these decades has already been described as bold, monumental and ignorant. The same is true if we turn to COUNTRY HOUSES, 86, 87 where the period begins with Studley Castle (1834–7) by *Samuel Beazley*, who was best known for theatrical work. It is still symmetrical – a sign of Georgian allegiance – and combines a towering Norman keep with Gothic fenestration. It harks back in form and concept, though not in style, to *Robert Lugar*'s Weddington Hall of *c.* 1805–10, demolished in 1928. Also demolished is Neo-Tudor Grove Park (*C. S. Smith*, 1833–8), another example of the genre, like the same architect's stables and riding school at Stoneleigh Abbey already mentioned. Grendon Hall (*Joseph Potter*, 1825) was another. Goldicote at Alderminster (1830) is a survivor.

Bold and monumental and not at all ignorant is *Edward Blore*'s 88 Merevale Hall, a castle with embattled tower rising on a wooded hill. Its style is certainly more refined than the same architect's earlier Weston House (1827–30), now demolished, although lodges around the park reflect its nature. Merevale was built 1838–44, and *Henry Clutton* assisted Blore from 1842 and then apparently, very young, took over. It is completely asymmetrical and much enlivened with gables, turrets, parapets and pinnacles. *p. 156* *Pugin* did one mansion in Warwickshire, Bilton Grange, 1841–7, and that also is asymmetrical. Bilton Grange of course is Gothic, but Merevale Hall is as much Jacobean as it is Gothic. In fact the Elizabethan – or, as it was then called, Tudor – arrived early in Warwickshire: Blythe House, Barston, is of 1829, and Stretton House at Stretton-on-Fosse is a highly creditable imitation of a Cotswold manor house and seems to date from 1836. In the same years much was done at Charlecote, which is indeed more Early Victorian than Elizabethan. The hall was remodelled from

1828–37 with *C. S. Smith* doing the architectural work while *Willement* did the interiors. More, especially the N front and forecourt wings, was done by *John Gibson* after 1849. Gibson's Woodcote at Leek Wootton (1861–2) is also Neo-Elizabethan, as was Myton Grange in Warwick (1857), of which only a later lodge (1883) survives. Tudor also is the Manor House at Hampton-in-Arden by *William Giles* of Derby, 1855.

Here we come to *Scott*, at work in the county as early as 1842, who did two mansions. The first was spiky Brownsover Hall, Rugby (1857), and Walton Hall (1858–62), which also cost about £30,000 to build. Both are in his favourite Middle Pointed style, with hints of French Gothic at Walton. Not far away from Walton is another ambitious house of the same years, this time emphatically High Victorian. Ettington Park is by *John Prichard* of Llandaff, begun in 1858 and completed in 1862. Greatly admired by Eastlake, it is strong stuff, resourceful in composition and grouped excellently.

102

Ettington leaves the other High Victorian mansions of Warwickshire far behind: Eathorpe Park by *Robert Clarke* of 1860, Wroxall Abbey of 1866 by *Walter Scott* of Liverpool (who had been G. G. Scott's clerk of works at Walton), Jacobean Welcombe of 1867 (cost over £35,000) jointly by *Clutton* and *Thomas Newby*, Ettington Chase by *Martin & Chamberlain* of 1867, Coleshill Park by *Middleton & Goodman* of 1872–3, *William Young*'s Haseley Manor House of 1873–5, Chadwick Manor (Temple Balsall) of 1875 and *R. J. & J. Goodacre*'s Caldecote Hall of 1879–80. Above all these, though, one would put *Eden Nesfield*'s mighty wing of Combe Abbey, built in 1863–5, demolished but now partially recreated, and his clock tower (1872) at Hampton-in-Arden Manor House.

p. 696

p. 356

105

In other styles, we have Italianate Bitham Hall at Avon Dassett and Knowle Hall, both of c. 1849–50, and *H. E. Kendall*'s slightly

Walton Hall, perspective showing additions by G. G. Scott.
Engraving, 1860

later refronting of Shuckburgh Hall. An unexpected addition
here is Town Thorns at Easenhall, by *Alfred Waterhouse*, 1873–5.
Newnham Paddox (demolished) was in the French Renaissance
style by *T. H. Wyatt*, 1875. In Leamington, *E. W. Pugin*'s demolished Harrington House (1869) was in what Pevsner described
in the first edition as 'a dissolute Gothic-cum-Italian-cum-
French' style.

With Nesfield and his one-time partner Norman Shaw we
come to the intimate, pretty LATE VICTORIAN. It starts early,
too early really for any pigeon-holing. *Nesfield*'s row of cottages
at Hampton-in-Arden and the lodge of the manor house have
tile-hanging, white pargetting, and a general air of daintiness and
yet date – the cottages at least – from 1868. Yet earlier uses were
on Nesfield's stables at Combe Abbey, *c.* 1863. While these
characteristics of the Old English and the Queen Anne style that
followed are common enough in the county (e.g. schools) they
do not occur among the mansions, except in some details of *F. C.
Penrose*'s Ardencote near Claverdon, 1876 and *William Tasker*'s
Park Hall at Salford Priors, 1879. The story up to the Great War
really ends with a few more houses: Tudor Dunsmore House at
Clifton-upon-Dunsmore by *W. H. Ward* of 1881; Avon Carrow
at Avon Dassett by *W. E. Mills*, 1889, also Tudor; two Arts and
Crafts houses by *P. Morley Horder* at Bishops Tachbrook (Greys
Mallory of 1903–4 and Mallory Court of 1914–15); *H. B. Creswell*'s
Stone Edge at Leek Wootton (1909) and an enlargement of
Cawston House at Dunchurch (1907); and the grand Queen
Anne revival Dunchurch Lodge of 1907 by *Gilbert Fraser* of Liv-
erpool in grounds landscaped by *T. H. Mawson*. Altogether more
lavish are the houses built for wealthy American families, *Edward
Goldie*'s Neo-Elizabethan Ashorne Hill House (1895–7) and two
at nearby Moreton Morrell, Neo-Palladian Moreton Hall
(1905–8) and now demolished Moreton Paddox (1909), both by
W. H. Romaine-Walker. Just before the war, *Clough Williams-Ellis*
appears in the county, and his delightful small extension to
Wolverton Court (1912) marks a fitting end-point for this review.

VILLAS, smaller houses and ordinary dwellings are too numerous to cover in any detail. Suffice it to say that Stratford-upon-
Avon and Warwick both have 1830s 'new town' areas, north
Leamington is especially rich in Early Victorian examples across
a range of styles, in Rugby there are several 1850s houses with
diapered brickwork, The Quadrant in Coventry preserves a row
of 1860s Italianate villas, and for the 1840s to 1880s Emscote
Road in Warwick has some variety. Later, Rugby has substantial
houses of the 1880s and 1890s as well as its distinctive streets
of terraced housing running down towards the railway. For
ARTISAN HOUSING, there is Chapelfields in Coventry, mainly
1840s–50s, while Odibourne Terrace and Lower Ladyes Hills
in Kenilworth represent the 1860s–80s. For later Victorian
upmarket, architect-designed housing, the best concentrations
are perhaps off Welcombe Road in Stratford-upon-Avon, the
Moultrie Road area in Rugby, New Milverton in Leamington,
Spencer Park at Coventry, the Manor Court Road district in

104

p. 316

112

Nuneaton and the countryside in the suburban hinterland around Knowle, Dorridge, Packwood and Lapworth.

For rural housing, there are ESTATE COTTAGES. Wormleighton has Althorp estate housing by *Blore*, 1848. The Alscot estate built at Alderminster, Wimpstone (Whitchurch) and Preston-on-Stour, 1858–63. At Combrook, Chesterton and Kineton there are Compton Verney estate cottages, 1860s (*William Lait*). Of social and INDUSTRIAL HOUSING, schemes to be noted include the cottages erected for the Labourers' Dwelling Company in Stratford, 1876–7, and the Nelson Village at Emscote, Warwick, with houses of concrete erected for workers at the gelatine works, 1889. At Bermuda in Chilvers Coton the Griff Colliery Company built a village of ninety houses in 1893.

Of major PUBLIC BUILDINGS, most lack distinction. In some places the use of older buildings continued. Nuneaton and Rugby have nothing of this period and nearly all the Victorian corn exchanges and smaller town halls have gone. In Coventry there are *James Murray*'s dark red sandstone adjuncts of 1863 to St Mary's Guildhall, continuing along Bayley Lane and into St Mary's Street where they were seamlessly rebuilt by *Harry Quick*, 1896. They now form a consolidated group behind the Council House by *Garratt & Simister* (1913–17 etc.), a rather tired and late imitation of the great town halls of the north. Much more ambitious is Leamington Town Hall by *J. Cundall* (1883–4), in 107 mixed style with giant entrance and a tall clock tower.

Of the public buildings erected under the auspices of the County Surveyors are the magistrates' courts, police stations and lockups, as at Kenilworth, Kineton, Polesworth and Henley-in-Arden, all by *William Kendall*, 1857–9. Shipston's courthouse of 1874 was designed by architects in private practice, *Medland & Son*. Warwick's Italianate County Offices in the Butts, later the police headquarters, is by *William Lait*, County Surveyor, 1882–3. Nuneaton's former police station and courthouse (now the Yorkshire Bank) by *John Willmot*, 1896–7, is more substantial and noteworthy. Related institutions include the county gaol in Warwick (*D. R. Hill*, 1853–60) of which only the blue-brick Governor's House and an outbuilding remain, and some fragmentary bits of the same architect's Reformatory (1856) at Weston-under-Wetherley. Hill, it should be noted, was also the architect of Winson Green Prison (1845–9) in Birmingham.

Among the Poor Law Union WORKHOUSES, the best survivor is at Alcester (*Bateman & Drury*, 1836–7) where Sir Charles Throckmorton of Coughton gave stone for the front and Sir F. L. H. Goodricke of Studley Castle gave the adjacent chapel, 1842. The main block of Shipston (*John Plowman*, 1837–9) also survives. The rest were adapted as hospitals or demolished. Of purpose-built HOSPITALS, the best of the C19 examples have gone: the Warneford at Leamington (*Joseph Bateman*, 1832–4), Coventry (*Nevill & Son*, 1864–5) and Stratford-upon-Avon (*E. W. Mountford*, 1883–4). Stratford's has been replaced by a hotel of similar appearance, retaining the original clock turret. Mountford's other hospital, at Shipston (1896), still remains. p. 563

Kineton, Pittern Hill House, perspective of garden front.
Photo lithograph, 1901

(1934–9). These represent an evolved style still rooted in the Arts and Crafts.

Warwickshire's image of a county of pretty timber-framed buildings in fact created a HISTORICAL REVIVAL against the tide of architectural fashion. In Stratford-upon-Avon, especially, from the opening decade of the C20 people were busily removing Georgian accretions to get back to the older timber framing. The impressive gabled front of the Shakespeare Hotel is an example of a recreation, largely by *Albert Callaway*, 1919–20. It had looked very different only a few years earlier. So had the Tudor House nearby, an earlier uncovering of 1903 by *Holtom & Yorke*, largely at the expense of the writer Marie Corelli who keenly advocated such schemes. In addition, there were new houses built from old timbers – Bradley Lodge in Tiddington Road was built in 1924 by Major *Kenneth Hutchinson Smith* using substantial elements from Bradley Hall, Kingswinford, Staffs., including a splendid three-storey porch of 1596. Longfield at Bubbenhall is another (*H. T. Jackson*, 1932–4). New houses, altogether more generously proportioned and comfortable than their historic counterparts, were erected too, e.g. in Shottery Road at Stratford (*Osborn, Pemberton & White*, 1921–2),

To find the first serious engagement with the functional style emanating from the United States and on the Continent one must turn to Stratford and *Elizabeth Scott*'s rebuilding of the theatre, 1928–32. Though unexceptional by the Continental standards of the time, it was for England quite sensational in its novelty, especially in such a traditional location as Stratford. Its brickwork, and especially the brick sculpture, is influenced by North Germany.

Art Deco and modern were the styles favoured for CINEMAS, and there are surviving examples at Leamington (the Bath Cinema, *Horace G. Bradley*, 1925), Coventry in Coventry

University's Ellen Terry building (built as the Gaumont, by *W.H. Watkins* of Bristol, 1931), and the Ritz in Nuneaton (*Verity & Beverley*, 1937). ART DECO is also to be seen in a house at Stivichall, Coventry, *Frederick Gibberd*'s first work, 1931, and rather splendidly in the platform facilities at Leamington Station (*P.E. Culverhouse*, 1939). The county's greatest exponent of the style was *H. N. Jepson* of Nuneaton, where several buildings for the Co-operative have Art Deco features. He also did St Thomas More R.C. School, Nuneaton (1937), with an emphatic tower over the central entrance.

Next we might consider the evolution of the high street and the emergence of corporate branding made visible through architectural identity. While the Co-op sometimes favoured the Art Deco, as just mentioned, Boots the Chemist went for ornamental Baroque and the use of terracotta, as seen at Nuneaton (1907) and more exuberantly at Rugby (1912), both by *Albert N. Bromley*. The later extension to the Rugby Boots (*Percy Bartlett*, 1935) is Art Deco with pharmaceutical sculpture. Woolworths, Marks & Spencer and Timothy Whites adopted their own styles too, moving in the 1920s towards the modern. The stores of Montague Burton's the tailors, always with snooker halls above, are especially distinctive, generally fronted in dark polished marble, as at Nuneaton (1929), Leamington (1931), Stratford-upon-Avon (1937) and Rugby (1938) by in-house architects *Harry Wilson* and his successor *Nathaniel Martin*. At Stratford commercial identity came second to local character, as delightfully illustrated by the quasi-Tudor W.H. Smith's (*Osborn, Pemberton & White*, 1920–1), Costa (*F.C.R. Palmer* for National Provincial Bank, 1924) and No. 6–7 High Street (in-house designers for Timothy Whites, 1937). The most impressive of the inter-war commercial buildings is *Palmer & Holden*'s Neoclassical NatWest Bank in Coventry, 1929–30, with its rich American Beaux-Arts interior.

Brewers also sought to assert their identity through the design of PUBS, built in large numbers between the wars to serve the new housing estates around the towns and as roadhouses for the motor age. Of so-called Brewer's Tudor, Coventry has several instances, e.g. the Biggin Hall at Stoke (1923), the Maudslay at Chapelfields (1928), and the City Arms at Earlsdon (1930). The Pilot at Radford, however, is distinctively *moderne*, especially inside (*W.S. Clements* for Atkinson's Brewery, 1938–9). Pubs of these years in a range of other styles will be found in the gazetteer but they do not need singling out here.

Of PUBLIC BUILDINGS, the only one to merit attention is the town hall at Nuneaton, a Neo-Georgian job with a grand colonnaded front. It is by *Peacock & Bewlay*, 1934. Coleshill has a simple town hall on a domestic scale with half-timbered gables, by *S.H. Wigham*, 1925–6.

A major focus of public building programmes in these years was HOUSING. Coventry developed vast estates at Stivichall from 1921, Radford and Coundon begun in 1924, and Canley commenced 1938, all with shopping centres and other amenities.

Council housing developments are noted at Warwick (*Crouch, Butler & Savage*, 1920) and Kenilworth (*Sholto Douglas*, UDC Architect, 1920–5), Nuneaton (the Middlemarch Road Estate, 1931) and in the villages. Of private schemes, there is Ernest Parke's housing at Butlers Marston, begun in 1905–13 but developed by *S. Alex Wilmott*, the Bournville Village Trust architect, in 1926–36. Another is the little group of estate cottages at Clifford Chambers by *Deane & Braddell*, 1923–7. A model village was built at Long Itchington for cement workers (*Charles M. C. Armstrong*, 1912–13) and a small garden suburb at Radford, Coventry (*Raymond Unwin*, 1912–14).

So what of CHURCHES? There are interesting beginnings of change in *P. Morley Horder*'s roughcast and timber-framed church at Galley Common, 1909. The direction for both the Anglicans and the Roman Catholics was to be towards the Early Christian or Byzantino-Romanesque style favoured by the leading Birmingham ecclesiastical architects from the years immediately before the Great War. Early examples there are St Basil, Deritend (*A. S. Dixon*, 1911–12), and St Germain, Edgbaston, by *E. F. Reynolds*, 1915–17. In Warwickshire the type is best represented for the Anglicans by Rugby St Philip (*H. B. Creswell*, 1914) with tripartite lunettes and Celtic stone decoration and in Coventry by blue pantile-roofed St Mary Magdalene, Chapelfields (*Harold T. Jackson*, 1932–4). For the Catholics, there are the Precious Blood & All Souls, also at Chapelfields, Coventry (*George Cave*, 1923–4, continued by *E. Bower Norris*, 1938–9), Southam (*Sandy & Norris*, 1925) and Coleshill (*Harrison & Cox*, 1938–42). Of course, Gothic continued too, e.g. at the Rugby School Memorial Chapel (*Sir Charles Nicholson*, 1922) whose pale and almost feeble exterior belies a powerfully moving interior. It is evident also in two late Coventry works of *Paley & Austin* (Earlsdon St Barbara, 1930–1, and Great Heath St Barnabas, 1931). But St Luke's at Holbrooks and St George's in Barker's Butts Lane, Coundon, Coventry, both by *N. F. Cachemaille-Day*, 1938–9, signal a new direction. St Luke's, indeed, anticipates in some respects the later design of Coventry's future cathedral.

Of church furnishings, it is worth noting the stained glass of *Richard Stubbington* (e.g. Balsall Common, Lapworth and Packwood), of *Geoffrey Webb* (e.g. Curdworth and Quinton), *Arild Rosenkrantz* (e.g. Churchover) and the superb W window at Ansley by *Karl Parsons*, 1931. Lapworth church has a small monument by *Eric Gill* (1928).

As to chapels, this was not a busy time for building, but the Methodist Central Hall at Coventry (*Claude Redgrave*, 1931–2) with its Gothic tower and lumpish exterior is an extraordinary building for a period when the movement nationally (influenced by J. Arthur Rank) was seeking to escape from churchiness. Modern, though, are its cinema-style seats. More interesting is *John W. Wilson*'s Germano-Scandinavian Congregational chapel at Knowle, 1932.

POST-WAR TO CONTEMPORARY

It was undoubtedly the calamity of wartime devastation that finally brought about the adoption of broader C20 architectural conceptions in Warwickshire. Replanning and reconstruction at Coventry began before the Second World War, but it was only the extent of damage caused by bombing that allowed the scheme to be transformed into a total redevelopment of the city centre on an integrated plan with buildings of modern design. Coventry's rapid growth necessitated development in the suburbs too. The scheme was masterminded by *Sir Donald Gibson* as City Architect and planner, and continued from 1956 by his successor, *Arthur Ling.* They were assisted by many of the rising stars of the day who went on to make their own names as municipal architects and planners elsewhere. The *œuvre* of the City Architect's Department was prodigious but private firms were also involved (e.g. for the towers at the ends of three wings of the Precinct). The detailed study (2009) and subsequent book (2016) by Jeremy and Caroline Gould both tell the full story and place Coventry in the context of other post-war developments in the UK and abroad. Readers are referred to these (*see* Further Reading) for a full analysis, but a summary together with a description of the scheme as it survives today will be found in the gazetteer. In hindsight, Coventry is considered more remarkable for its planning than for its architecture, and many buildings of the period have been significantly altered or replaced. Particularly important buildings are Broadgate House (1948–53), the Belgrade Theatre (1955–8) and Alpha House (1961–3), where the Jackblock construction technique was pioneered. Specially successful and significant is the railway station (*Architect's Department, British Railways, London Midland Region* 1960–2). p. 264

Something of the same sort was attempted in Nuneaton, also bombed, where *Frederick Gibberd* and Borough Surveyor *R. C. Moon* prepared a development plan in 1947, resulting in a new road scheme, a civic district (represented by the library of 1961–2) and several housing projects (1950–73). At Kenilworth the redevelopment of bomb-damaged Abbey End began along similar lines but never extended beyond the immediate locality. Warwick's Market Street also belongs to a central redevelopment area, 1965–75. Bedworth town centre was redeveloped in the early 1970s.

For HOUSING, as well at the Coventry estates of the 1950s (e.g. Tile Hill, Bell Green and its satellite neighbourhoods, Willenhall) other urban schemes worth noting include Lillington and Leamington (e.g. Kennedy Square and Sydenham Farm) by *Gibberd* and the Borough Housing Architect, *Henry Fedeski.* With these might be bracketed private housing developments, of which some successful examples include Fields Court in Warwick (*Ling & Johnston,* 1966–7), two in Barford (Verdon Place by *Denys Hinton & Associates,* 1967, and prairie-style Ryland Road by *Roy A. Geden,* 1973–4) and the Langlands in Hampton Lucy (*Architects*

Design Group, 1975). Walsgrave has a Scandinavian-style development of 1962–5 by *John Thorne Barton & Associates* who also did an intriguing group of four hexagonal houses at Lillington, 1964.

Coventry also experimented with SCHOOL design, especially in its successful partnership with *Stirrat Johnson-Marshall*'s team at the Ministry of Education. Some of the best schools of the period have been demolished or replaced (e.g. Whitley Abbey and Lyng Hall) but original buildings at Limbrick Wood (1951–2) remain. Nuneaton, also an independent education authority, only produced schools of fairly conventional design. Through the 1950s, however, the county council under County Architects *G. R. Barnsley* (†1959) and his successor *Eric Davies* produced schools of modest quality, often with artworks such as sculptures by *Walter Ritchie*. Among the survivors are Coleshill (1956) and Henley-in-Arden (*Barnsley* with *Gibberd*, 1957).

The origins of Coventry's two UNIVERSITIES also lie in postwar reconstruction and planning, at least as far as sites and buildings are concerned. Coventry University came into existence in 1992, but its core buildings are those of the former City Council College of Technology, originally by *Gibson* and *Ling* and on Miesian lines. Warwick University, on the SW edge of the city, was conceived in 1958 and its campus plan by *Ling* and *Alan Goodman* was published in 1964. However, the main campus buildings of the first main phase are by *Yorke, Rosenberg and Mardall* (*YRM*) in long blocks originally with the firm's trademark white tile cladding – also to be seen at their IBM office in Warwick, 1979–82. Now much expanded, the universities possess some of the most important and distinctive architecture of the later C20 and early C21 in the county – the Maths Houses at Warwick by *Howell Killick Partridge & Amis*, 1968–70, and at Coventry the Frederick Lanchester Building (*Alan Short Partnership*, 1998–2001) with its silver-topped ventilating towers and the silver sloping Engineering & Computing Building (*Arup Associates*, 2009–12).

But for international distinction and undiminished public acclaim, Coventry Cathedral stands alone. *Sir Basil Spence*'s design won the competition in 1951 and the completed building was consecrated in 1962. The cathedral abandons all period forms without abandoning what might be called a Gothic spirit. Moreover, Spence programmatically made it a receptacle of the decorative arts, from so easily acceptable a piece as *Epstein*'s St Michael to so difficult an object as the cross on the flèche by *Geoffrey Clarke*, from the woodwork of the stalls, Sir Basil's own ingenious design, and *Ralph Beyer*'s movingly simple inscriptions and symbols to the confusing richness and violence of the stained glass. *Graham Sutherland*'s tapestry all the same succeeds in dominating the interior.

Spence also designed three small suburban churches in similar vein (Tile Hill, Willenhall and Wood End, all completed 1957), built simply and cheaply but nonetheless convincing. They follow a common form varied in design detail and in the configuration of church, parsonage and hall. The churches, though, all have the traditional plan of chancel and nave rather than with the central altar Bishop Gorton had hoped to incorporate in the cathedral design. Such a church was built soon afterwards at Allesley Park (Coventry) at *Cachemaille-Day*'s St Christopher's (the Bishop Gorton Memorial Church) of 1959–60. Another church influenced by the Liturgical Movement is St George at Rugby by *Denys Hinton & Associates* (1962–3) where the baptistery is especially striking.

Of other post-war Anglican churches, mention should be made of Chilvers Coton (Nuneaton), rebuilt by German prisoners of war under *H. N. Jepson*, 1944–7, after wartime destruction. St Paul's, Foleshill (Coventry), is another post-war replacement, by *Nicholson & Rushton*, 1951–3, respectably neutral in style. More innovative are Cheylesmore (Coventry; *A. H. Gardner & Partners*, 1954–7) with good interior fittings, Stivichall (Coventry), where the architects (*W. S. Hattrell & Partners*, 1955–65) adopted a modern Gothic style to complement the existing fabric of 1810–17, and Radford (Coventry; *Lavender, Twentyman & Percy*, 1953–5) where the church is hangar-like with inward-sloping walls.

For the Roman Catholics, this was a time of much activity. The best church of the era following the Second Vatican Council in 1962 is Lillington (*Rayner & Fedeski*, 1962–3), along the lines of Gerard Goalen's slightly earlier Harlow church; in the Coventry suburbs are: Holy Family, Whitmore Park (*Peppard & Duffy*, 1966–7); tent-like St Patrick's at Bell Green (*Desmond Williams & Associates*, 1968–9); and Sacred Heart at Stoke (*Williams & Winkley*, 1978–9) with its Brutalist interior. More recently there is St Francis of Assisi at Kenilworth (*Rathbone & Taylor*, 1992–3).

116

Of other places of worship few merit attention here. The Methodists, busy building in the 1950s and 60s, escaped from traditional forms but went for functional simplicity. Two practitioners (or their firms) were responsible for most of the work in the county, *Claude Redgrave* of Coventry and *W. H. Cripps* of Oxford. Rugby (*Peter Thimbleby*, 1983–4) is a notable exception. For the other denominations, only two chapels by *Keith Corrigan* are of more than passing interest, Bedworth Zion Baptist (1978) and the Elim Pentecostal in Coventry (1979–80). Hillfields in Coventry has a high concentration of mosques and temples, and near the boundary between Leamington and Warwick there is an especially dominant Sikh temple (2008–9; *see* p. 661).

Turning to PUBLIC BUILDINGS, Rugby Town Hall (*J. C. Prestwich & Sons*, 1959–61) is unadventurous architecturally. The *County Architect*'s Modernist Shire Hall extensions of 1955–66 in Warwick are surprisingly successful for their setting at the head of the historic market square, although the Brutalist block of 1972–3 dominating the approach to the town from Saltisford fits less comfortably. Coventry's Civic Centre was built in phases by the *City Architect's Department*, 1951–76. It includes two ranges around a courtyard used to exhibit building materials, a tower block and the unashamedly modern brick corner block with its bridge to the Council House. Of other major public buildings it is worth noting the Justice Centres at Nuneaton (*Frank Shaw Associates*, 2005) and Leamington (*HLM Architects*, 2009–10), already replacing the County Architect-designed police and court buildings of a generation earlier.

We might end this review by giving a short miscellany of other later c20 and early c20 buildings of interest. Of its type, the Oakley Wood Crematorium, Bishop's Tachbrook (*Sir Guy Dawber, Fox & Robinson*, 1969–71) is considered notable. For theatres and cinemas, there are *Gibberd*'s Royal Spa Centre (1970–2) in Leamington and *Michael Reardon*'s Swan Theatre (1984–6) in the shell of the Victorian theatre at Stratford. Among commercial projects, mention might be made of the NFU Mutual office complex at Tiddington (*Robert Matthew, Johnson-Marshall & Partners*, 1982–4), the Network Rail Development Centre at Westwood Heath (*MacCormac Jamieson Prichard* for Cable & Wireless, 1994) and the British Film Institute's master film store at Gaydon (*Edward Cullinan*, 2010–11). Of private houses one might pick just a few apart from the norms of their times, e.g. *Erno Goldfinger*'s Whitley Piece (1947–8) at Henley-in-Arden, the replacement Denbigh house at Newnham Paddox (*Garnett Cloughley Blakemore*, 1980), the *Kulodotschko* house at Dorsington (2005), and a little cluster of architect-designed houses at Alveston of the 1960s to 1980s. Of particular local importance, though, are the varied, quirky and resourceful houses of *Robert Harvey* (*Yorke, Harper & Harvey*), 1954–80 (e.g. at Ilmington).

As to comparisons between Warwickshire in 1965–6 and the period of this revision in 2010–15, there have been few major losses. Of these, we might note among houses the demolition of Grove Park, significant reductions to the remains of Ansley Hall, and the loss of *E. W. Pugin*'s Harrington House in Leamington. The *Lutyens* extensions at Clifford Chambers Manor, although mentioned in the first edition, had already gone. Among religious buildings, several Victorian churches have been destroyed, among them Coventry (St Thomas), Leamington (St Alban), Warwick (All Saints, Emscote) and Rugby (Holy Trinity). The demolition of *Scott*'s Rugby was especially shameful. The Roman Catholic priory at Atherstone and the Southam convent have also gone, along with numerous Nonconformist chapels. Hams Hall power station and its cooling towers (illustrated in the first edition) have also disappeared from the landscape. But there have been resurrections too, notably in the saving of Stoneleigh Abbey and Compton Verney, where major houses whose futures seemed uncertain have found new uses and undergone careful restoration. Similarly, the Landmark Trust adaptations of the Walton bath house and Astley Castle have brought these buildings back from the brink of destruction, while at Barrells Hall, Ullenhall, a private owner has created a new mansion within the ruined shell of the old house. An interest in the wellbeing of vernacular buildings is exemplified by the restoration of Netherstead at Morton Bagot, and in the rediscovery of the weavers' houses with internal jetties at Spon End in Coventry. In Coventry, too, it is hoped that an ambitious scheme to develop a heritage park s of the city will see the restoration of the Charterhouse under the Historic Coventry Trust. The Old Grammar School, long disused and derelict, has recently been restored. In Warwick, mention should be made of the revival of the Hill Close Gardens and the restoration of the houses along Northgate Street. Among the smaller towns, Alcester and Shipston-on-Stour remain delightful. Henley-in-Arden demonstrates how the historic character of the main street has been retained despite intensive infilling and peripheral development. Atherstone still hovers between neglect and renewal but has good buildings that could still be successfully reused and saved. Rugby is much the same. Post-industrial Nuneaton has become a much more pleasant place where the quality of its Victorian and C20 buildings can now be enjoyed. Stratford-upon-Avon, though, has not come through the past half-century unscathed from the harmful effects of tourism. Leamington has regained something of its graceful Regency character. Perhaps Warwickshire's historic image and its pivotal place in the tourism economy will continue to help safeguard the undoubted richness and variety of the county's built heritage.

FURTHER READING

GENERAL COUNTY WORKS begin with the *Victoria County History* (VCH) published in eight volumes between 1904 and 1969, the final volume covering Coventry and Warwick. For a shorter general history of the county there is Terry Slater's *A History of Warwickshire* (1981). Of the older architectural guidebooks P. B. Chatwin's third edition of the Warwickshire *Little Guide* (1930) still has some value. Douglas Hickman's *Shell Guide* (1979) is certainly useful, and it is beautifully illustrated.

Articles on Warwickshire local history, sometimes on architectural subjects, will be found in *Warwickshire History*, published twice yearly since 1969. An index to the journal and a Warwickshire bibliography will be found on the Warwickshire Local History Society's website at *www.warwickshirehistory.org.uk*. The Dugdale Society has been publishing volumes of original archive source material for the county since 1921 and has also produced a series of occasional papers. Details are also online at *www. dugdale-society.org.uk*.

As to BUILDINGS, the Royal Commission on Historical Monuments has never published an inventory for Warwickshire. Thus the architectural descriptions in the volumes of the VCH (mainly 1945–55) were the main source of background information for the first edition of this volume – for which, incidentally, one should see Michael Taylor's brilliant 'With Pevsner in Warwickshire' in *The Buildings of England: A Celebration Compiled to Mark*

Fifty Years of the Pevsner Architectural Guides, edited by Simon Bradley and Bridget Cherry (2001). Now the detailed descriptions of individual listed buildings in the National Heritage List for England (NHLE) are available online. The official Historic England website at *www.historicengland.org.uk/listing/the-list* is the primary listing but Images of England at *www.imagesofengland.org.uk* helpfully includes photographs, although the contents and descriptions are no longer up to date. There is another version on British Listed Buildings at *www.britishlistedbuildings.co.uk*.

The EARLY HISTORY is Sir William Dugdale's *Antiquities of Warwickshire*, first published in 1656 and revised and illustrated in a second edition by W. Thomas, 1730. These are still remarkably valuable, not least for church monuments. W. Smith's *History of Warwickshire* (1830) and the parish descriptions in C19 and C20 Directories (e.g. Kelly's) can still be surprisingly useful too. One must not forget that Matthew Holbeche Bloxam, the author of *The Principles of Gothic Architecture* (various editions from 1829) lived at Rugby, and this book contains numerous Warwickshire examples, also used for J.H. Parker's *Glossary of Architecture* (1st edn 1838 and subsequently). Bloxam was one of the likely authors (with William Stanton) of the anonymous two-volume *Churches of Warwickshire* (1847 and 1858) which, sadly, only ever covered the Deanery of Warwick. For its superb illustrations and level of detailed description it remains a work to treasure and enjoy.

On the subject of ILLUSTRATIONS, mention should be made of three important collections of drawings of Warwickshire churches and houses. One is in the Aylesford Collection at the Birmingham Archives. These date from *c.* 1792–1810. A second collection is that of Captain James Saunders (1773–1830) of Stratford-upon-Avon and it is at the Shakespeare Centre Library and Archives. There is a third major collection at the Herbert Museum and Art Gallery in Coventry. For the present administrative county there is a remarkably useful collection of old photographs and illustrations on the Windows on Warwickshire website, at *www.windowsonwarwickshire.org.uk*. This draws together material from several museums, libraries and archives, making it all accessible in one place. For Coventry there is a similar collection on the Historic Coventry Forum website (*http://forum.historiccoventry.co.uk*). These, of course, are in addition to the now numerous published books of old photographs available for many towns and villages (e.g. under the Amberley, Sutton, Francis Frith and Tempus imprints). A local venture deserving particular mention is the series of booklets for North Warwickshire villages (e.g. *Arley Remembered*) by John Bland, Rita Callwood and Colin Hayfield published in the 1980s.

For ARCHAEOLOGY the starting point for exploration is the County Historic Environment Record, available through the Warwickshire Museum website at *http://timetrail.warwickshire.gov.uk*. As well as giving summaries of information on each site, this also provides references to published and unpublished research information. The *Transactions of the Birmingham and Warwickshire Archaeological Society* (*BAST*), published since the late C19, is the principal journal. It still publishes articles on architectural topics. The *Archaeological Journal* 128 (1972) includes the proceedings of the Royal Archaeological Institute's tour of the county with short studies of numerous sites and buildings. A similar volume, highly useful for the buildings it describes, is the volume of papers from the 2007 British Archaeological Association conference in 2007, published as Linda Monckton and Richard K. Morris (eds), *Coventry: Medieval Art, Architecture and Archaeology in the City and Its Vicinity*, BAA Conference Transactions 33 (2011) (cited hereafter as BAA 33 (2011)).

For RELIGIOUS HOUSES there is surprisingly little at a general level, although there are details for each abbey, priory and convent in the VCH vol. 2 (1908). As to particular houses, on Combe Abbey there is Warwick Rodwell's 2007 paper in BAA 33 (2011). The papers from a 1993 symposium on *Coventry's First Cathedral: the Cathedral and Priory of St Mary* were edited by George Demidowicz (1994), but updated accounts following the Phoenix Project millennium excavations are *The Archaeology of the Medieval Cathedral and Priory of St Mary, Coventry* by Margaret Rylatt and Paul Mason (2003) and the papers by Richard Plant, George Demidowicz and Richard K. Morris in BAA 33 (2011). The same volume also includes two papers on the Coventry Charterhouse. The Coventry Whitefriars has *The Church of Our Lady of Mount Carmel and some conventual buildings at the Whitefriars, Coventry*, by Charmian Woodfield (2005). For Kenilworth, BAA 33 (2011) has a paper on the Kenilworth Abbey Barn and there is also *Kenilworth: the Story of the Abbey* (1995) by Harry Sunley and Norman Stevens. For Stoneleigh Abbey there is *Stoneleigh Abbey: the House, Its Owners, Its Land*, edited by Robert Bearman (2004), in which the papers by Morris, Ramey and Demidowicz are especially helpful for the early period.

On CHURCHES there is no single modern work, apart from Mike Salter's *The Old Parish Churches of Warwickshire* (1992), useful more than anything for its phased plans. Like other works, though, it draws heavily on the VCH and on the first edition of this guide. For overall coverage, W. Hobart Bird's *Old Warwickshire Churches* (undated) is still helpful. Especially useful, though not entirely comprehensive, is the selection of photographs on Aidan McRae Thomson's Warwickshire Churches website at *http://warwickshirechurches.weebly.com*.

Regarding specific aspects of churches, Warwickshire falls within the *Corpus of Anglo-Saxon Stone Sculpture: Vol. X: Western Midlands* by Richard Bryant (2012). Romanesque sculpture has been recorded and photographed – chiefly by the late Harry Sunley – and the individual church records are in the Corpus of Romanesque Sculpture in Britain and Ireland (CRSBI) at *www.crsbi.ac.uk*. Medieval stained glass is likewise represented by online photographs in the Corpus Vitrearum Medii Aevi (CVMA) at *www.cvma.ac.uk*. However, neither the CRSBI nor

CVMA gives any indication of the likely dates of the pieces illustrated and described. Much new information on Warwickshire churches of the period is to be found in Terry Friedman's *The Eighteenth-Century Church in Britain* (2011). Extensive use has been made of the contemporary reports of C19 and early C20 church restorations in the reports and papers of the Associated Archaeological Societies (the Worcestershire society being one of the associates) and in the *Worcester Diocesan Church Calendar*. A great many church guides, articles and websites have been consulted, but a handful of works on particular churches should be mentioned. The ruined cathedral has a new study in George Demidowicz and Heather Gilderdale Scott, *St Michael's Coventry: the Rise and Fall of the Old Cathedral* (2015). Of the many books and articles on Coventry's new cathedral the most useful is Louise Campbell's *Coventry Cathedral: Art and Architecture in Post-war Britain* (1996), but there are also her exhibition catalogue *To Build a Cathedral: Coventry Cathedral 1945–62* (1987); 'Towards a New Cathedral: the Competition for Coventry Cathedral' in *Architectural History* 35 (1992); and a chapter on the cathedral in *Basil Spence: Buildings and Projects* (2012). There is *The Collegiate Church of Saints John the Baptist, Laurence and Anne of Knowle* (1966) by Anthony A. Upton who also, as vicar, produced a particularly informative guide to the church at Foleshill in outer Coventry. From John D. Austin there is *Merevale Church and Abbey* (1998). Holy Trinity at Stratford-upon-Avon has *Shakespeare's Church: a Parish for the World* by Val Horsler et al. (2010). On St Mary's, Warwick, there is 'Fit for a King? The Architecture of the Beauchamp Chapel' by Linda Monckton in *Architectural History* 47 (2004).

Warwickshire CHAPELS have their own section in Christopher Stell's Royal Commission *Inventory of Nonconformist Chapels and Meeting-houses in Central England* (1986). For places of worship generally, but especially for chapels, Keith Geary's edition of *The 1851 Census of Religious Worship: Church, Chapel and Meeting Place in Mid-nineteenth Century Warwickshire*, Dugdale Society 47 (2014), is helpful for dates.

For ROMAN CATHOLIC CHURCHES collaboration with the Architectural History Practice meant that I had early access to the completed *Taking Stock* report (2015) on the churches of the Birmingham archdiocese, and we shared the use of unpublished research material. In print, however, are J.J. Scarisbrick's *History of the Diocese of Birmingham, 1850–2000* (2008) with a short illustrated account of each church, and Roderick O'Donnell's *The Pugins and the Catholic Midlands* (2002).

COUNTRY HOUSES are particularly well covered in Geoffrey Tyack's *Warwickshire Country Houses* (1994) which updates or supplements the same author's earlier occasional papers for the Warwickshire History Society: *The Making of the Warwickshire Country House 1500–1650* (no. 4, 1982), *Warwickshire Country Houses in the Age of Classicism* (no. 2, 1980) and *The Country Houses of Warwickshire 1800–1939* (no. 7, 1989). Together these provide a comprehensive account, their usefulness enhanced by careful referencing. Houses and their parks and gardens are often best studied together and so the appearance of *Historic Gardens of Warwickshire* (2011) by Timothy Mowl and Diane James was especially timely for this volume. Warwickshire is also included in Peter Reid's *Burke's & Savills Guide to Country Houses* vol. II (1980). Many individual houses, especially those close to Stratford-upon-Avon, are described in articles by Dr Robert Bearman in *Focus* magazine. Others are described and illustrated in *Country Life*. Michael Holmes's *The County House Described: an Index to the Country Houses of Great Britain and Ireland* (1986) picks up references hidden in a range of C19 and C20 titles as well as indexing the major articles in *Country Life*.

Books of particular interest on specific houses include: Robert Bearman's *Compton Verney: a History of the House and its Owners* (2000), supplemented by Andor Gomme's 'Compton Scarsdale or Sutton Verney' in *English Heritage Historical Review* 2 (2007). For Stoneleigh Abbey there is Bearman's *Stoneleigh Abbey* (as above) and the chapters by Gomme, Tyack and Fryer. On Baddesley Clinton there is 'Baddesley Clinton: Architectural Responses to Social Circumstances' by Nathaniel W. Alcock and Robert A. Meeson in the *Antiquaries Journal* 87 (2007).

For CASTLES and greater medieval houses there are two main works. Warwickshire's major castles are all thoroughly covered in John Goodall's *The English Castle 1066–1640* (2011). There is some overlap with Anthony Emery's *Greater Medieval Houses of England and Wales 1300–1500* vol. 2 (2000) which, however, also looks in detail at manors, granges and unfortified houses. 'Castles in Warwickshire' by Philip B. Chatwin in *BAST* 67 (1947–8) is dated but still useful, as is Mike Salter's little volume on *The Castles and Moated Mansions of Warwickshire* (1992). Caludon has its own *A History of Caludon Castle* by George Demidowicz and Stephen Johnson (2014). Kenilworth is covered not only in Richard K. Morris's guidebook (3rd edn, 2015) but also in his two articles, 'Sidelights on the 14th-century Architecture at Kenilworth Castle' in BAA 33 (2011) and '"I was never more in love with an olde howse nor never newe worke coulde be better bestowed": the Earl of Leicester's remodelling of Kenilworth Castle for Queen Elizabeth I' in the *Antiquaries Journal* 89 (2009). For Maxstoke, there is 'Maxstoke Castle, Warwickshire' by N.W. Alcock et al. in the *Archaeological Journal* 135 (1978). At Warwick I was given access to the *Warwick Castle Conservation Plan* prepared by Rodney Melville & Partners (2012) which contains an up-to-date overview of research discoveries, including documentary findings by the late Michael Farr and the detailed investigations by Richard Morris (1986), Nicholas Palmer and Mark Booth (1992 and 2010). David Buttery's *Canaletto and Warwick Castle* (1992) is too enchanting to be omitted.

Our knowledge of VERNACULAR ARCHITECTURE has developed hugely in the past fifty years. Warwickshire is well covered in Nat Alcock and Dan Miles's *The Medieval Peasant House in*

Midland England (2012), and Alcock's *People at Home: Living in a Warwickshire Village 1500–1800* (1993) is of much wider value than for its detailed information on the buildings of Ashow and Stoneleigh. The same author's 'After the Stamp Collecting: the Context of Vernacular Architecture' in *Transactions of the Ancient Monuments Society* 46 (2002) also illustrates several Warwickshire examples as case studies. The journal *Vernacular Architecture* includes numerous articles on Warwickshire buildings, and the Vernacular Architecture Group's dendrochronology database – listing tree-ring dates, with relevant journal references – is online at *http://archaeologydataservice.ac.uk/archives/view/vag_dendro*. The background to the collection in Spon Street, Coventry, is entertainingly chronicled in 'From the Black Prince to the Silver Prince: Relocating Mediaeval Coventry' by Robert Gill in *Twentieth Century Architecture* 7 (2004) and there is a helpful booklet on the buildings, *Spon Street Townscape Scheme: a Guide to the History of the Street and the Buildings in the Scheme* (1993).

On BUILDING MATERIALS besides timber there is Hugh Jones, *A Ramblers' Guide to Building Stones in Warwickshire* (2006), and the *English Heritage Strategic Stone Study: a Building Stone Atlas of Warwickshire* (2011). We might follow this with a short round-up of miscellaneous titles on specific BUILDING TYPES : *Warwickshire Breweries* by Joseph McKenna (2006); *The Obelisks of Warwickshire* by the Warwickshire Gardens Trust (2013); *Coventry Car Factories: a Centenary Guide* (1995); and two on mills, *Windmills in Warwickshire: a Contemporary Survey* by Wilfred A. Seaby and Arthur C. Smith (1977), and *Warwickshire Watermills* by D.T.N. Booth (1978). Here mention should also be made of *Wind and Water Mills* 16 (1997) which contains a thorough account of the Chesterton watermill. Although there are many books on railways, the Warwickshire Railways website (*www.warwickshirerailways.com*) is an excellent portal for all enquiries. Similarly there are websites on Post Office buildings (*http://britishpostofficearchitects.weebly.com*) and cinemas (*http://cinematreasures.org*) which, among others, have been much used.

For CITIES and TOWNS, *Alcester* by David Green (1993) in the Towns and Villages of England series provides a useful start. *Atherstone: a Pleasantly Placed Town* by Nat Alcock and Margaret Hughes (2008) contains a particularly thorough and well-researched account of the town's buildings. Bob Meeson's *Coleshill Buildings c. 1350–1850* (2006) does likewise for that town. Coventry has *A Guide to the Buildings of Coventry: An Illustrated Architectural History* by George Demidowicz (2003). There is a near contemporary account of the city's post-war reconstruction in G. Lewison and R. Billingham, *Coventry New Architecture* (1969), but Jeremy and Caroline Gould's *Coventry: the Making of a Modern City 1939–1973 (Informed Conservation)* (2016) provides an updated assessment, based on their more detailed study *Coventry Planned: the Architecture of the Plan for Coventry 1940–1978* (2009), which includes summaries for individual buildings. For Leamington there is Lyndon Cave's *Royal Leamington Spa: a History* (2009), and the booklets by Paul Edwards on *The Regency*

Style of Leamington (2005) and Janet Storrie on *William Louis de Normanville: Engineer, Architect & Inventor (1843–1928) and His Role in Creating Royal Leamington Spa* (undated) are helpful. Rugby has E.W. Timmins, *Rugby: a Pictorial History* (1990). Robert Bearman's *Stratford-upon-Avon: a History of its Streets and Buildings* (2007) is supplemented by *The Frieze: Shakespeare's Town, Stratford-upon-Avon* (2013), which uses an unfolding panorama to document the buildings along the town's historic spine. Warwick was covered by Alec Clifton-Taylor in *Six More English Towns* (1981) and has *The Buildings of Warwick* by Ken Hoverd and Richard K. Morriss (1994) and Michael Farr's edition of the papers of the Warwick Fire Commissioners in *The Great Fire of Warwick* 1694 (Dugdale Society 36, 1992). But for these towns and for the villages there are also vast numbers of histories, guides, articles and websites to be explored.

For ARCHITECTS, the standard biographical dictionaries must be consulted: Sir Howard Colvin's *Biographical Dictionary of British Architects 1660–1840* (4th edn 2008), the two-volume RIBA *Directory of British Architects, 1834–1914* (2001), and *Edwardian Architecture: a Biographical Dictionary* by A. Stuart Gray (1986). The companion volumes of the *Biographical Dictionary of Civil Engineers*, for 1500–1830 by Sir Alec Skempton (2002) and 1830–1890 by Peter Cross-Rudkin and Mike Chrimes (2008) and 1890–1920 by Robert McWilliam and Mike Chrimes, may be useful too. A number of monographs and articles on individual architects and firms are especially relevant to Warwickshire. Among them (in rough chronological order by working period) are Andor Gomme's *Smith of Warwick: Francis Smith, Architect and Master Builder* (2000); two on Sanderson Miller, an edition of *The Diaries of Sanderson Miller of Radway* by William Hawkes, Dugdale Society 41 (2005) and Jennifer Meir's *Sanderson Miller and His Landscapes* (2006); Andor Gomme's chapter on 'William and David Hiorn' in Roderick Brown (ed.), *The Architectural Outsiders* (1985); M.H. Port on 'Thomas Rickman (1776–1841): "A name to whom we owe, perhaps, more than any other"' in Christopher Webster (ed.), *Episodes in the Gothic Revival: Six Church Architects* (2011); and *The Architectural Achievement of Joseph Aloysius Hansom (1803–1882)* by Penelope Harris (2010), which covers his Warwickshire years. For the Victorians there are Paul Thompson, *William Butterfield* (1971), Gordon Barnes, *Frederick Preedy* (1984), Jennie McGregor Smith, *John Cotton: the Life of a Midlands Architect 1844–1934* (2002), Geoff Brandwood and Martin Cherry, *Men of Property: the Goddards and Six Generations of Architecture* (1990), Gavin Stamp, *An Architect of Promise: George Gilbert Scott Junior (1839–1897) and the Late Gothic Revival* (2002), and Michael Hall, *George Frederick Bodley and the Later Gothic Revival in Britain and America* (2014). For the whole period, *Birmingham's Victorian and Edwardian Architects* (2009) edited by Phillada Ballard covers some twenty-six architects practising in the city. Then (since their Warwickshire work is mainly later) *The Architecture of Sharpe, Paley and Austin* by Geoff Brandwood (2012); and coming towards the end of the C20 are

Alan Clawley, *John Madin* (2011), Alan Powers, *In the Line of Development: F. R. S. Yorke, E. Rosenberg and C. S. Mardall to YRM, 1930–1992* (1992), and an article 'Against the grain: the domestic architecture of Robert Harvey' by Louise Campbell in *Twentieth Century Architecture* 4 (2000).

As to other craftsmen, there are the standard works on SCULPTORS. The early period is covered by Adam White's 'A Biographical Dictionary of London Tomb Sculptors *c.* 1560– *c.* 1660' in *Walpole Society* 61 (1999) and its supplement in 71 (2009). The original listing for the next period by Rupert Gunnis has been superseded by *A Biographical Dictionary of Sculptors in Britain 1660–1851* by Ingrid Roscoe et al. (2009), and its supporting database is accessible online (*www.henry-moore.org/hmi/library/ biographical-dictionary-of-sculptors-in-britain*). Works on display in the county are covered in the Warwickshire, Coventry and Solihull volume (no. 6) of the *Public Sculpture of Britain* series (2003) by George T. Noszlopy. Of particular local importance is *The Woodcarvers of Warwick* by Ann Stevens (1980). For STAINED GLASS, books dealing with artists and makers based locally include Stanley A. Shepherd, *The Stained Glass of A. W. N. Pugin* (2009), Michael Fisher, *Hardman of Birmingham: Goldsmith and Glasspainter* (2008), Michael Kerney, *The Stained Glass of Frederick Preedy (1820–1898): a Catalogue of Designs* (2001), and the books by Roy Allbutt including *The Stained Glass Windows of A. J. Davies (1877–1953) of the Bromsgrove Guild, Worcestershire* (2002) and *An Introduction to the Stained Glass Window Designers and Makers of the Birmingham School of Art* (2013). Of related interest is Quintin Watt (ed.), *The Bromsgrove Guild: an Illustrated History* (1999).

Finally PRIMARY SOURCES. These are surprisingly complicated owing to historical, administrative and ecclesiastical arrangements and boundary reorganizations. The chief archive repository is the Warwickshire County Record Office (WCRO) in Warwick, but there are very important holdings too at Coventry History Centre, Birmingham Archives, the Shakespeare Centre Library and Archives (SCLA) at Stratford, and at Solihull Library. Some catalogues – those for SCLA and WCRO – are now available online, at least in part. WCRO is the Diocesan Record Office for Coventry and covers parts of Birmingham and Gloucester too, but older church records are also to be found in their historic locations, i.e. the Worcestershire Archive and Archaeology Service, the Lichfield Record Office of the Staffordshire and Stoke-on-Trent Archive Service, and the Gloucestershire Archives. Centrally held faculty records at these repositories are especially important when looking at churches, as are the plans and related papers for parsonage building. The central records for Coventry diocese after 1918 are held at the registry, but unfortunately the all-important faculty papers have not been preserved. Of major archives consulted elsewhere only three need be singled out: first, the Incorporated Church Building Society material at Lambeth Palace Library dealing with the restoration of churches from 1818 until 1982. Although the plans are available online (*www.churchplansonline.org*), the supporting papers in the archive provide a great deal more information. Second, the unpublished church notes of Sir Stephen Glynne (1807–74) at the Flintshire Record Office contain descriptions of buildings either before or shortly after restoration. Third is the RIBA Drawings Collection which holds, among many others, a small collection of drawings by the Coventry architect John Murray (†1863).

As to newspapers and periodicals, use has been made of the standard journals *The Builder* and *Building News*. For local newspapers there are good holdings at WCRO and in local libraries, but access is becoming easier and easier with the increasing number of titles (especially for Leamington and Coventry) searchable online through the British Newspaper Archive (*www.britishnewspaperarchive.co.uk*). Much use has been made of this, with considerable success in identifying names of architects and clarifying dates for key works. Lastly, the availability of almost comprehensive coverage of large-scale Ordnance Survey maps from the 1880s to the late C20 via the Old Maps website (*www.old-maps.co.uk*) really does make possible a degree of checking that would have been totally impossible until now for multiple sites and buildings.

GAZETTEER

ABBOTS SALFORD

1 m. sw of Salford Priors

SALFORD HALL HOTEL. A large stone house. It began as a 45
retreat for the monks of Evesham Abbey, partially rebuilt and
much enlarged after 1600 in the Elizabethan stylefor Sir John
Alderford (†1606) and his son-in-law Charles Stanford. The
entrance is through a gatehouse with timber-framed gables
(herringbone struts) over the archway. The N front has the
porch dated 1602 (incorrectly re-carved as 1662) dividing the
newer work from the old. The service wing to the r. has a
timber-framed gable, and its w side is of c. 1480 with two big
stone chimney-breasts and a tower-like projection. The upper
parts here are timber-framed, with irregular gables. Back on
the N side, the early C17 work is in Lias with golden ashlar
quoins, mullions and transoms. Attractively varied in height
and in the configuration of windows, with shaped gables to
each bay. The E front is more monumental than the entrance
side. E-plan, with three three-storeyed bay windows with
shaped gables, and the two-storeyed parts lying back between
them. The windows are of five and four lights and transomed.
The main staircase (with a solid timber-framed core) is in the
inner angle between the hall and this wing. The E wing had
the principal rooms, large chambers on the first floor and a
long gallery above – all now subdivided. A community of
Benedictine nuns (afterwards at Stanbrook Abbey, Worcs.)
resided here from 1807 to 1838 and there was a Roman Catholic chapel in the hall until it was sold by the Eyston family in
1948. The hall later became a hotel, suffering decay and
damage in the early 1980s but carefully restored in 1987–9.
Some C17 panelling inside, and a fine C18 moulded doorcase
in the main entrance hall.

On Evesham Road, the RED HOUSE, c. 1770, with covered
entrance and Gothick fanlight, gauged brickwork, etc.

ADMINGTON

ADMINGTON HALL. C16, of brown stone, with mullioned windows and gables at the rear. The S front is 1801, not regular, but formal. In the middle a (later) Tuscan porch and, above it, a tripartite window on the first and second floors. The ground-floor windows of the front have pediments. Added service wing, 1813. By the drive, stucco-faced STABLES with Soanish details and gabled C17 DOVECOTE.

In the village, N of the hall, C18 LOWER FARM is brick with quoins. TOP FARM, S on Armscote Road, is a C17 stone farm-house with mullioned-and-transomed windows, hipped roof and dormers.

ALCESTER

The town (pronounced 'All-ster') lies at the confluence of the rivers Alne and Arrow. Its origins as a town lie in the Roman period but there is evidence of earlier occupation back to Neolithic times. Two Roman roads cross here, Icknield Street running N–S and the E–W Salt Way from Droitwich. The Romans arrived around A.D. 47 and their settlement grew into a substantial town, Alauna. There are no standing remains, but the site – mainly S of the present town, between the Stratford and Evesham roads and the River Arrow (e.g. around Bleachfield Street) – has been extensively excavated. Many of the finds are on display in the Roman Alcester Heritage Centre in Globe House. A finely carved Saxon Tau cross (now in the British Museum) found in the rectory gardens in the C19 gives an indication of the later prosperity of the settlement. A Saxon silver bracelet has also been found. Ralph de Boteler founded a Benedictine abbey N of the town in 1140. Again nothing remains, but the foundations were discovered during excavations in 1939. The Botelers and their successors as lords of the manor, the Beauchamps, created a new town N of the Roman site. Instead of Icknield Street, they chose the road towards Wootton Wawen (now Henley Street) as the main street. In 1274 Alcester obtained the rights to hold weekly markets and, in 1292, a fair. The plan of the medieval town shows classic signs of the provision for commerce, with a market place N of the church and the Bull Ring at the S end of the High Street where the road widens like a funnel towards the T-junction with Swan Street. Alcester remained a manorial borough, and still maintains a ceremonial court leet and manorial traditions today. As well as holding a market well into the late C19, Alcester had a thriving trade in the clothing industry, especially in linen, knitting and glove-making, with the addition of needle-making from the C17 to the C20. The town was also on a major coaching route and thus supported several good inns. In terms of size, Alcester's population was fairly static at around 2,400 through the C19 and

right up to the Second World War. Until then, the town was
mainly within the loop on the w bank of the Arrow. Since 1951,
when the population was 2,924, there has been substantial
expansion (the 2011 figure being 6,939), with new housing,
schools, amenities and industrial areas on the NE side towards
Kinwarton and N towards Kings Coughton. There has also been
some infilling towards the line of the 1866 railway to the w. The
town was by-passed to the w and s in 1990.

CHURCHES

ST NICHOLAS. w tower of Arden sandstone, late C13 below with
lancets and an arch to the nave with three continuous chamfers. Dec w window and a golden stone Perp-style parapet,
doubtless C18. Indeed, the nave and aisles are of 1730–3, by
Edward & Thomas Woodward of Chipping Campden, 'under the
advise, direction and Government' of *Francis Smith* of Warwick.
There were two contracts, one for the N aisle and a slightly
later one for the s aisle and chancel, showing that the scheme
evolved as work progressed. The exterior is Gothic with battlements and pinnacles, originally with regular two-light
windows. Ogee mouldings to w doorways of aisles. Bishop
Pococke in 1756 refers to its 'light plain Gothic architecture'.
But the interior is entirely classical, i.e. five bays with Doric
columns on pedestals, flat aisle ceilings, coved nave ceiling.
Terry Friedman suggested that this separation of contrasting
styles had French precedents, with this being an early British
manifestation. The E end is of 1870–1 by *Preedy* who added
the chancel and transepts in place of the typical C18 meagre
'altar recess' and s vestry described in 1858. Preedy's work on
the rest of the church was limited to the widening and

Alcester, St Nicholas.
Etching by Allan E. Everitt, *c.* 1858

replacement of the aisle windows with three lights and re-seating, but the scale and style of the chancel hints that a rebuilding might have been contemplated. – FONT and STONE PULPIT, 1871. Caen stone, carved by *Mr Boulton* of Cheltenham. – SCREEN. Part of an early C16 screen, as ornate as a Devon screen, at the E end of the N aisle. – BENEFACTIONS BOARD dated 1683. An odd composite forming a triptych to frame donations recorded on parchment. Side panels with crude paintings of Acts of Charity and scriptural texts in C16 style. The top frieze Early Georgian. – CHANDELIER. Brass, given by the Bishop of Worcester, 1733. Not large but very graceful. – STAINED GLASS. E window and one in S chapel, *Clayton & Bell*, 1879 and 1885. – By *Mayer & Co.* the W window 1893, and chancel sides, 1903. – In S aisle, one by *Alan Younger*, 1997. – MONUMENTS. Sir Fulke Greville †1559 and his wife Elizabeth (Willoughby) †1565, by *Richard & Gabriel Royley* of Burton upon Trent, 1558 (JB). Alabaster. Two recumbent effigies, not as skilful as some but as forceful as any. Just look at the sharp cut of his beard, the Romanesque power of the lion, and the unmitigated shape of her skirts (and also try to look up them). Against the tomb-chest thin twisted colonnettes and stiffly standing children. Against one short end shield held by two grotesque cherubs. The inscription is still in black letter. – John Brandis †1724. By *Edward Woodward*. With columns, an open segmental pediment, and putto heads. – William Halford †1731. Small tablet with three steep pyramids at the top, and also three putto heads. Quaint, not beautiful. – Francis Ingram Seymour Conway, 2nd Marquess of Hertford, †1822 (cf. Ragley Hall). By *Francis Chantrey*, 1828. White marble. The figure sitting up on a Grecian couch, but the background Gothic. – Sir Hamilton Seymour, †1880. By *Count Gleichen*, 1882. White seated effigy, a rug or drape over his knees; lifelike. – WAR MEMORIAL. Triptych by *Stephen Dykes Bower*, 1951.

Churchyard wall with simple GATEPIERS and lamp facing High Street.

OUR LADY OF THE ISLE & ST JOSEPH (R.C.). By *Rev. A. J. C. Scoles* of Bridgwater, 1888–9. Also used as a school initially, with teacher's house (now the PRESBYTERY) alongside. Stone. E.E., but side windows changed to Dec in 1903. Nave and chancel with central spirelet. Interior with W gallery and large statues in canopied surrounds. – STAINED GLASS. E window, 1888, and others 1903–4 by *Hardman*. – Two W windows by *Arthur Wybo* of Brussels, 1910.

BAPTIST CHURCH, Church Street. *Joseph Lattimer*, 1859. Latish classical. Inside a gallery and a pretty ceiling rose. Alongside, in MEETING LANE, the former CHURCH registered as 'lately built' in 1737. Brick with arched windows and hipped tile roof. Sunday School wing added 1817. – MONUMENTS. Pleasant late C18 and early C19 tablets. A Baptist church here was in existence by 1655.

CEMETERY, Birmingham Road. Laid out by *Edward Holmes*, 1861, but his chapel has been demolished. Lychgate 1908.

PUBLIC BUILDINGS

TOWN HALL, Church Street. 1618; given by Sir Fulke Greville. The stonework by *Simon White* of Chipping Campden. Only the ground floor is of stone. To the long side there are six round arches on Doric columns. Until 1873 the arched openings were open. The upper room is timber-framed with close studding, rendered externally. Rough hammerbeam roof, dated 1641. Pitched roof to the outside.

Former RURAL DISTRICT COUNCIL OFFICES (now Rotary International), Kinwarton Road. By *F. B. Andrews & Son*, 1959–62. Opposite, the GREIG HALL, 1958, with flat-roofed circular foyer and colonnade in the angle between the wings.

CIVIC BUILDINGS, Priory Road. By the County Architect (*Eric Davies*), 1969. Low group of separate blocks for Magistrate's Court, Police, Library and Health, with FIRE STATION in Seggs Lane behind. SCULPTURE by *Walter Ritchie*. The court building nearest the roundabout rebuilt as GLOBE HOUSE for Stratford District Council in 2001, and now (2014) occupied by the town council and the Museum of Roman Alcester. Clock tower on one corner. Mural of Roman Alcester by *Andy Hazel* on road frontage.

ALCESTER GRAMMAR SCHOOL, Birmingham Road. Established 1582. New school by *F. P. Trepess*, 1912. Arts and Crafts Georgian. Extension by *Jackson & Edmonds*, 1955. New sixth form centre etc. by *Marson Rathbone Taylor*, *c.* 2012.

PERAMBULATION

All on a nice modest scale. Nothing imposes itself, nothing hurts. In 1814 Brayley noted perceptively that 'the chief houses have now received modern fronts, but the interior of many is yet unaltered, and here may be seen the massy timbers and abundant carvings of past days'. Behind the frontages there is still much timber framing. Moreover, for some we have dates, all earlier than the C16 or C17 so readily assumed for such work.

It is best to begin W of the church and head first into BUTTER STREET. Facing, the former RECTORY, 1796, brick, three bays, two and a half storeys, with typical diagonally placed, painted lintel stones. Rear extension by *Preedy*, 1871. A sculptured human torso built into a wall adjoining the rectory is probably Roman work and depicts a bearded male figure wearing a tunic. The narrow street curves round the W of the church, with battlemented CASTLE HOUSE (No. 6) of *c.* 1820 facing S and nestling against the churchyard wall. Heading N, a pretty early C19 double shopfront (Nos. 7–9). Then a pair of cottages (Nos. 3–5), originally a hall house with timbers dendro-dated to 1444–5. As the street widens, it becomes HENLEY STREET with the town hall (*see* Public Buildings) in the middle of the space N of the church. On the l., CHURCHILL HOUSE, dated 1688 with initials TEL on the rainwater heads showing it was refronted – not built – for Thomas and Elinor Lucas. Small, but once quite opulent. Brick, three bays. Unfortunately the ground floor is altered. The middle window above has an open scrolly segmental pediment on brackets, and the window frames and modillion frieze are carved too. (There is said to be a fine plaster ceiling on the first floor.) Past the town hall the road narrows. GREYHOUND HOUSE (Nos. 29–31), formerly an inn, has box framing and a jettied first floor with moulded bressumer supported on carved scroll brackets. No. 25 with a covered way leading to the yard behind was also an inn, the RED HORSE, still with late C19 pub windows. Another dendro-date, *c.* 1400, at CRUCK HOUSE (No. 19). On the w side, the timber framing continues at intervals to School Lane near GUNNINGS BRIDGE (mentioned in 1270) over the Arrow, rebuilt *c.* 1814. Returning on the E, HENLEY STREET has ARDEN HOUSE (No. 28) with two uneven gables, one jettied. Nos. 40–44 towards the corner of Meeting Lane, again box-framed, with good carved struts to bressumer and an exposed bit of lath and plaster.

To the E and s of the church is CHURCH STREET, beginning with the Baptist church (*see* Churches) facing the town hall and a row of varied and grander C18–C19 fronts overlooking the churchyard. An attractive and impressive group. Most are stuccoed and painted in pastel colours, with only No. 6 displaying naked brickwork. Nos. 4–5, once the ANGEL INN, has an archway again, and a carving of Tobias and the Angel high up. THE LIMES (No. 7) is a Late Georgian house with two canted bay windows. Then No. 8, a bigger one of *c.* 1820–30 with giant fluted pilasters and Soanian incised ornament. Lastly on the E, No. 10 with a handsome cast-iron balcony.

MALT HOUSE (Nos. 11–12) is on the s and at the corner of MALT MILL LANE, early C16, timber-framed and with jetty and two gables. It continues in the lane with a long leaning front, all closely spaced studs. So nearly cleared away in the 1970s, Malt Mill Lane is Alcester's showpiece – as it always was. It survived thanks to the foresight of Alcester District Council, who were persuaded by the Fine Arts Commission and the Historic Buildings Council to compulsorily purchase the whole street, create a conservation area and work with partners to restore the buildings for new uses. After Malt House there are further buildings of similar type on both sides lower down, and then attractive groups of C19 brick cottages (e.g. Nos. 32–34), again on a curve. Restoration and development began in 1972–3 with the refurbishment of the E side with new sheltered housing behind in COLEBROOK CLOSE, and continued in phases until the completion of CHESTNUT COURT on the adjacent reclaimed industrial site in 1992. The whole represents a visually and socially successful blending of the old and the new, all carried out by *Associated Architects* (initially under *Walter Thomson*), 1972–1992.

Now into the HIGH STREET, where frequent renewal and alteration means there is generally less of interest. Nevertheless, the whole street remains varied and pleasant, predominantly brick.

First on the E side a box-framed house with a reported date of 1625, having concave-sided lozenges to the panels in the gables. Then VICTORIA HOUSE (No. 6) with canted bays at first floor with early C19 Gothick glazing bars. On a narrow plot on the opposite side, No. 21 is a base cruck house (now brick-fronted) whose timbers have been dendro-dated to 1264. Further down, the only real intrusion is the unfortunate block of shops by *James A. Roberts*, 1969, on the site of the former Italianate Corn Exchange (*Edward Holmes*, 1857; demolished 1967). Facing up the street at the far S end, LLOYDS BANK in Stratford Road, C18, brick, three bays, with Venetian and lunette windows.

Nice minor houses in other streets as well, e.g. a mixed group in BLEACHFIELD STREET and a little to the w in EVESHAM STREET early C19 Neoclassical ACORN HOUSE and its attractive coach house with partially blind round-headed openings, louvred turret and weathervane. In PRIORY STREET leading N towards the Birmingham road, just beyond the Catholic church, is THE PRIORY (No. 81), a crazy Early Victorian Gothic folly house with mock battlements and quatrefoil panels.

Former MINERVA MILL, Station Road. Built as a needle-making 109 factory for William Allwood & Son, *c.* 1878. Monumental. Brick. Three storeys and twenty bays. Now restored and refurbished as offices.

OVERSLEY BRIDGE, ½ m. SE of the church on Stratford Road at Oversley Green. Once dated 1600. Six segmental stone arches over the Arrow, below the confluence with the Alne.

OVERSLEY HOUSE, Kinwarton Road, ¼ m. NE. A rare survival of a former WORKHOUSE, little altered externally although adapted as retirement housing in 1984–7. By *Bateman & Drury*, 1836–7, with an inscription on the parapet stating that Sir Charles Throckmorton gave the stone for the front. The rest is in brick. Front of eleven bays and two and a half storeys. Heavy porch. Single-storey pavilions either side of the main block, also stone-fronted. Behind, the usual brick wings, cruciformly arranged with an octagonal centre carrying a cupola with clock and weathervane. Alongside, the former CHAPEL, given by Sir F.L.H. Goodricke, 1842. Brick, simple Neo-Norman, like the donor's home at Studley Castle.

BEAUCHAMP COURT. *See* King's Coughton.

ALDERMAN'S GREEN see p. 277

ALDERMINSTER 2040

ST MARY AND HOLY CROSS. Cruciform and externally almost entirely early C13, i.e. with lancet windows, dignified and

reticent. The texture is harsh and uniform, the result of *Preedy*'s
attentions in 1873–4 (chancel, transepts and tower) and 1884–5
(nave), largely faithful in detail though with much necessary
rebuilding. Each face of the crossing tower has two widely
spaced lancets, with a quatrefoil below and another in the
parapet. There are pinnacles and gargoyles. The chancel is
entirely early C13, except one original C14 S window in the
sanctuary. Inside, the story becomes more complicated. It
starts in the C12. The nave is in fact essentially Norman, with
small (restored) windows N and S and doorways each side of
the nave. The S doorway was redone in 1884 but the N doorway
is genuine. It has one order of columns and a very curiously
decorated arch with a double row of back-to-back cusping and
short cylindrical projections within the arch. This seems late
Norman and links stylistically with the crossing, rebuilt after
the church passed to Pershore Abbey in 1193. Here there are
four arches with one slight continuous chamfer and one order
of shafts with the capitals similar to the doorway arch. But the
arches are now pointed. The transepts and chancel followed
in the C13, though the N transept W window is Norman. The
S transept W window is a good lancet. In the chancel there are
two AUMBRIES, one of them behind the organ casing. The
church was re-consecrated in 1286. – FITTINGS largely by
Preedy, 1874–85, including the very E.E. FONT with figurines
of the Evangelists and four relief scenes. – Another FONT, in
the porch, probably of *c.* 1661–2. – STAINED GLASS. E window,
T.F. Curtis, Ward & Hughes, 1898. – Chancel side windows all
Lavers, Barraud & Westlake, 1885. – W window 1884, *Heaton,
Butler & Bayne*, and another, 1882. – Others by *Preedy*, 1885,
Clayton & Bell c. 1885 and *G. Maile*, 1976.

At Alderminster the trackbed of the former Stratford and
Moreton TRAMWAY, 1826, is especially well preserved, both
on the approaches and through the village where the road now
follows its course. ALDERMINSTER LODGE, NW of the
churchyard, 1830s Gothic with ogee-headed porch. Across the
main road, late C17 stone-fronted OLD RECTORY with canted
bay to brick garden front. Further N, HIGH MEADOW, *c.* 1790,
has gauged brickwork to the windows. Nearby in Sutcliffe
Avenue, COUNCIL HOUSING by *Yorke & Barker*, 1952, nicely
grouped in linked pairs and triplets. S of the church is the
former SCHOOL, 1871, brick with plate tracery and bell-turret,
sympathetically enlarged from 1991 and incorporating a near-
matching window* in the added gabled end. Beyond, a low
row of two-storey houses, *c.* 1830.

At the edges of the village on Shipston Road two groups of Alscot
estate houses (cf. Preston-on-Stour and Whitchurch): seven
pairs of cottages (Nos. 1–14) on widely spaced plots N towards
Stratford, 1858–9, and five pairs (Nos. 30–40) to the S towards
Shipston, 1862–3. The architect may have been *J. Ross* whose
design won a prize from the Royal Agricultural Society in 1861.

*From the demolished school at Radford Semele.

Tudor, gabled but with subtle variations in all details. The groups symmetrical but most of the pairs asymmetrical.

GOLDICOTE HOUSE, 2 m. NE. Built for Gustavus Thomas Smith, 1830; in parkland and on the site of older houses. Regency Gothic, brick with stone dressings and an oriel over the porch. N wing demolished. Now apartments, but used as a residential training centre 1953–1999 when additional buildings were constructed in the grounds.

ALLESLEY see p. 277

ALLESLEY PARK see p. 280

ALSCOT PARK
½ m. NE of Preston-on-Stour

2050

Alscot Park is one of the two most rewarding early Gothic Revival houses of Warwickshire. Arbury is the other. The Gothic is emphatically pre-archaeological in the manner of Batty Langley and William Kent. Howard Colvin referred to Alscot's 'delightfully frivolous Gothic that lacked even Strawberry Hill's pretensions to mediaeval scholarship', which is much what Richard Jago meant when he wrote in *Edgehill* (1767) of its 'fretted spires, Of fairest model, Gothic or Chinese'.

The history of the house is like this. James West, Joint Secretary to the Treasury and a noted collector and antiquary, bought the estate in 1747. He found a C17 house close to the River Stour described by Mrs West in contemporary letters as 'the comicalest little old house that you ever saw' yet also 'a very bad one'. It stood at right angles to the river. Of this, which is within the N wing of the present T-plan house, he kept a certain amount. The evidence is not clear but the middle section (towards the join of the T) clearly incorporates older work. The plan, with pairs of dainty canted bays E and W, suggests an earlier form, and the bays on the E have mullioned basement windows. There are straight joints to the adjoining parts both S and N. Inside the ceilings are low. Parts of the N end must be old too, perhaps belonging to improvements for Richard Mariett in the 1720s, but this section was made square and refaced in ashlar in West's first phase of improvements in the 1750s. It has a canted bay facing the river, larger than those on the sides (i.e. as above) which were refaced and given new windows at the same time. Smooth golden ashlar. Battlements. The windows mainly ogee-headed. Bills show that *Edward Woodward*, the Chipping Campden mason (*see* Alcester and Preston-on-Stour) and his father *Thomas Woodward* worked here with two London carpenter-surveyors, *John Phillips* and

George Shakespear in the early 1750s. In 1762 West retired from the Treasury, and he then added to the house a higher and larger S wing with a broad façade. This was completed externally and internally by 1764–5. The S front is symmetrical, seven bays wide, of two storeys, with two higher, merely decorative, polygonal turrets with blank panelling flanking the three-bay centre. The ends to W and E have each a broad canted bay window. The details follow the earlier styles, i.e. ashlar, battlements and ogee heads. The matching S porch is an addition *ante* 1820, by *Thomas Hopper*.

The finest thing about Alscot Park is the internal composition or procession of rooms. Notable too the exuberance of the Rococo-Gothick in the main rooms, light and playful, with none of the archaeological earnestness to be seen at Arbury. The ENTRANCE HALL has, in white stucco, giant panels of thin shafts and ogee arches and, in the centre of the ceiling, a fan-like Gothic motif. The plasterwork is by *Robert Moore*. The fireplaces with their odd curved trefoiled tops are in their way intended to be Gothic too. Above them, in the overmantels, busts of William Shakespeare (by *Rysbrack*, 1759) and Matthew Prior, and another of Isaac Newton over the door facing the entrance.* To the l. of the entrance hall is the DRAWING ROOM with a very rich fan-vault pattern of papier mâché in the ceiling by *Thomas Bromwich*, 1765. Gothick cornice. This room has an exquisite chimneypiece by *John Hinchliffe*, 1769, with Ionic columns and inlaid with Blue John. To the r. of the hall is the SITTING ROOM with a heavy Early Victorian ceiling of 1844–5, Jacobethan with pendants, and carved oak doors and window surrounds. The decoration probably by *William Holland*, the woodcarving perhaps by *George Clark*.† From the entrance hall the middle door leads to the principal STAIR-CASE. This is Victorian with steps only bonded into the walls, a cast-iron balustrade, and an oblong skylight. Gothic wall panels. From here one enters on the same axis the N wing. A passage with ogee-headed doors gives access to the W and E to library and kitchen. The LIBRARY ceiling is again an Early Victorian replacement. Still continuing the same axis there follows the secondary STAIRWAY in the N wing under an oval skylight. It runs through three storeys with interesting differences of level. Delightful Gothic and Rococo stucco decoration, doubtless of the 1750s. The wrought-iron handrail with scrolly balusters may be earlier, possibly belonging to Mariett's improvements in the 1720s. Finally the sequence ends with the middle room towards the river. It is hexagonal. On an upper floor another passage with more ogee-headed doors and again

---

*The Shakespeare bust is a plaster replica of the original which is now at Birmingham Museum and Art Gallery. The Newton bust is attributed to *Peter Scheemakers*, *c.*1760 (GF).
†In the basement a gorgeous SIDEBOARD made for this room (then the dining room) by *Cookes & Sons* of Warwick, dated 1851. It is thickly carved with hunting implements, game birds, a dying stag, etc. modelled by *Hugues Protat*, and has excellent ironwork to the doors.

top-lit. The skylight has early C19 painted glass in delicate colours and the walls have painted *trompe l'œil* decoration by *Linda LeGrice*, 1974, with Gothic arches, plants etc.

In the grounds, the walls of the former parterres and the approach with monumental walling between the two lakes, all by *George Clark*, 1850s. To the S, a fine though plain STABLE BLOCK of 1753 with clock turret and cupola. By the weir N of the house, a delightful ogee-capped GAUGING STATION by *The Heritage Practice*, Bristol, for the Environment Agency, 1999. It pays homage to the architecture of the house, as do the 1760s-looking Gothick LODGES on the Stratford Road to the E, actually by *Richard Hulls*, 1813.

ALVECOTE   *2000*

In the Anker valley and across the river from Shuttington. By the railway, two long terraces of miners' cottages of *c.* 1900. By the canal, a marina created in 1995–7 on the site of a brick-works. Buildings by *Hilton Architectural* of Atherstone.

ALVECOTE PRIORY, founded in 1159. In ruins, but standing remains include the lower walls of a rectangular building and an arched doorway. Also the lower walls of a dovecote.

ALVESTON   *2050*

ST JAMES. 1837–9 by *William Walker*, but completed under *William Kendall* after Walker fell into financial difficulties. Typical of the date, with lancets and many thin buttresses. Grey stone with brick and stucco dressings, W tower, no aisles. Broad hammerbeam roof to nave. Original short chancel replaced in 1875–6 by *Preedy*'s present E end with side chapels. The chancel ceiling, and other decoration of 1903–6, by *Temple Moore*. W end reordered by *Brown Langstone Matthews*, 1989. – REREDOS carved by *Martin & Evans* of Cheltenham with painted panels by *Preedy*, 1876. – Marvellous SCREEN and PULPIT by *Temple Moore*, 1904, the carving by *James Elwell* of Beverley. – STAINED GLASS. E window by *Preedy*, 1876. – S chapel and tower window also *Preedy*, 1877. – Two in nave S by *Holland*, 1860. – Nave N, two by *Clayton & Bell*, †1887 and 1892. – MONUMENTS. Two big Gothic memorials to Higgins family, by *Peter Hollins*, Birmingham, 1870s.

OLD CHURCH, ¼ m. N in Mill Lane. The nave and central turret were demolished after 1839, leaving only the chancel which had been rebuilt after 1802 in brick with raised quoins. Restored 1945 and 2006. Of the two Norman tympana from the old nave, one lies face down in the churchyard, its carving

Alveston, Old Church, tympanum.
Drawing by Captain James Saunders, early C19

gone. The other is inside. It has a lower strip, hardly recognizable now but mid-C19 sketches and photographs of 1905 show
some of the lost detail. It has snaky Viking-type interlace with
beads and patterning of interlaced quatrefoils. In the centre
an angel, although all that remains is the lower part of its
attire resembling a bird's tail. The upper part has more quatrefoil patterning between two animals. The capitals are of
the two-scallop and the volute type. – PULPIT, C18; plain.
– WOODWORK. Fragments of tracery from the former screen.
– MONUMENT. Nicholas Lane †1595. Re-set in the wall in
pieces with strapwork panels alongside and inscription above.
The orientation is puzzling. The effigy itself would suit a table
tomb, lying flat, his hands clasped in prayer. But attached (i.e.
part of the same stone) are kneeling figures either side of his
feet. They would have looked absurd horizontally.

OLD VICARAGE, early C16 timber-framed house by the side of
the old church. Close studding. Jettied first floor on N side.

In parkland opposite, ALVESTON HOUSE. A fine William and
Mary house, built in 1689 for Thomas Peers. Seven-bay E
front, chequer brick, recessed three-bay centre and hipped roof
with dormers, the type of Honington (q.v.), but smaller. The
middle window below the pediment has a rusticated brick surround. The quoins are of stone and raised too. The porch on
the S side must be of c. 1750. Roman Doric columns and fine
carving of the triglyph frieze. There was once a grotto by the
river bank. An avenue of trees led to the old church.

N of the new church, three notable architect-designed houses of
the later C20. Among them are *Patric Guest*'s WHITE HOUSE
in the Rookery, 1968; *Peter Womersley*'s CEDAR LAWN, 1964;
and *Michael Tastard*'s COURT LEYS, 1983. They stand in the
grounds of ALVESTON LEYS (now a residential care home),
one of many villas built in the late C18 and early C19 when
Alveston became a fashionable location for prosperous families. Another nearby, KISSING TREE HOUSE, is a late C18

farmhouse aggrandized in the early C19 and more so recently, stuccoed with classical details. HEMINGFORD HOUSE in Church Lane (youth hostel), again stuccoed, has a Doric porch, blind niches on the ground floor with blind windows above in the wings, and panelled parapets. Over Wellesbourne Road, BARASET was originally built for William Harding, 1800–1. The house was demolished in 1928, but its surviving service wing was repaired by *Neville Hawkes* in 1955 and extended and remodelled as a Regency-style house by *Trevor Edwards*, 2007.

On a smaller scale, but of the same period, further houses by the green. THE WOODLANDS has a Georgian stuccoed front. THE LODGE, *c.* 1840, is stuccoed, Tudor-style with dummy loopholes in the gables. There were more along the main road towards Stratford, all since replaced by modern housing.

By the WAR MEMORIAL, ¼ m. SW of the church, a succession of vicarages. Between Main Street and the Avon is the RED HOUSE, originally by *John Gibson*, 1859, but much altered. It was built for the vicar who purchased it when he retired in 1900. Another (now the OLD RECTORY) was built across the Wellesbourne Road by *Temple Moore*, 1903–4. L-plan, rough-cast with gables. Alongside, the present VICARAGE, by *Robert Harvey*, 1979.

See also Tiddington (p. 630) and Bridgetown, Stratford-upon-Avon (p. 613).

ANSLEY

A village partly rural and partly post-industrial. Church End is the old centre of the parish which extends further W to Monwode Lea (Over Whitacre). Ansley village (1 m. SE) and Ansley Common (2 m. NE) expanded after the opening of the Ansley Hall colliery in 1874. Based in Coleshill Road, close to Ansley Hall, the pit closed in 1959. Many miners' houses remain.

ST LAURENCE. A big church with an impressive Perp W tower, its pinnacles of 1790. Two-light bell-openings with transoms. W door and three-light W window with lions' heads as hood-mould stops, the surrounds almost triangular. But the church itself is Norman – see the pilaster buttresses of nave and chancel, the re-set N doorway (the aisle was added in 1913), the plain S doorway, a blocked chancel S window, and the interesting chancel arch. Restored and perhaps altered by *A. Bickerdike* in 1875, this has capitals with volutes above a band of upright leaves or lancet-like flutes. On the N side, level with the capital, a carved stone with a tree with curling roots on one face, and on the side a man being eaten up by two monsters. They are just swallowing his arms. Is this re-set and older than the C12 arch? The clerestory of course is Perp, as is

the roof (one dated corbel refers to repairs in 1786). The surprise is the chancel, extended by John Ludford in 1760. Its E
pediment is classical, but it has Gothic details – the ogee-
headed priest's doorway and a N window with intersecting
tracery. Inside it is wholly classical with coved ceiling, cornice
and frieze and a central roundel with a dove. It is cleverly done,
with the reredos and inner arch perfectly framed by the chancel
arch when viewed from the nave. The overall effect is almost
theatrical. – Its FURNISHINGS are largely of 1760. The
REREDOS rather tight, with two black and gilded Tuscan
columns and a semicircular top, the IHS lit from behind by
the small quatrefoil in the E wall. The ALTARPIECE is a painting, Dutch and probably early C17. COMMUNION RAIL, semi-
oval in plan with turned balusters. – BOX PEWS of c. 1749 in
the inner chancel, lowered in 1975 and now used as stalls.
– STAINED GLASS. In the chancel N window ancient fragments,
heraldic l. and C15 Coventry glass r. – In the inner chancel, N
by *Jones & Willis*, †1872, and s by *Clayton & Bell*, †1897. – Two
by *William Morris & Co. Ltd* (Westminster), 1921 and 1928.
– The best, the superb W window by *Karl Parsons*, 1931. Christ
in Majesty with angels, saints and rainbow with Nativity scene
below. Strong sparkling colouring, deep blue prevailing.
– MONUMENTS. In the E chancel arch two big square pedestal
monuments with urns. They are of †1700 and †1727, the latter
erected 1761. – On the E wall, two Ludford memorials by
Hollins of Birmingham, one Gothic, †1827, the other still classical, 1829. – S of these, a spiky Gothic one by *Peter Hollins*,
†1873.

In the churchyard, the PARISH ROOM by *Kenneth Holmes
Associates*, 2003. In the style of an early C19 schoolroom, brick
with tripartite end windows.

CONGREGATIONAL CHURCH (Providence Chapel), Birmingham Road. Lean Gothic, 1822. Now a house, incorporating
the adjoining CONGREGATIONAL SUNDAY SCHOOL by
William Fidler, 1924.

NURSERY HILL SCHOOL, Coleshill Road, Ansley Common. A
large council school, 1906, with bold gabled street front. Four
gables, each with three windows. Higher transverse range
behind with ventilator turret on roof.

Of ANSLEY HALL, rather less remains than when described by
Pevsner in 1966. Abandoned after the closure of the colliery
in 1959 it fell to ruin and parts were demolished in 1978–9.
But in 1998–9 the surviving elements were incorporated in a
housing development on the site. It was a large and rather
confusing mansion, much enlarged in the C18 and in 1810–11.
'Irregular but very respectable', said *The Beauties of England
and Wales* in 1814. The garden front retains the appearance of
the C16 house. Four gables, each with pointed windows with
intersecting tracery in the glazing in imitation of the final state
of the original. A stone canted bay in the middle. The range
on the r. extending ten bays to the N has gone, or rather is only

represented now by fragments of brickwork. On the l., the c18 ORANGERY with alternating stone quoins and arched openings. Above the middle window a jumble of c17 stone fragments, probably from elsewhere, including two Ionic capitals on the piers above the blind oculus. Of the Early Georgian castellated entrance range and stables fronting the road only the lower walls remain. It was built in 1733. There were in the grounds a Chinese temple based on designs by *Sir William Chambers*, 1767, and a curious hermitage that was there by 1758. Over the road, remains of the walled garden with a corner tower.

At Church End, the former VICARAGE, its w side an extension of 1868 by *Thomas Pearson*.

Across the main road, the old SCHOOL (now ARC SCHOOL). *Dunlop, Bryant & Naylor* of Westminster, 1872–3. Wild Gothic, the window heads in alternating yellow and blue brick and once with frilly bargeboards to the gables. Ill-fitting extensions of 1896 by *R. Scrivener & Sons*, and the usual later accretions.

Towards Ansley Common, 1920s COLLIERY buildings remain. Single-storey office block with rounded corner and flat roof. Tall tower with long windows.

ANSTY

ST JAMES. Transformed into a Victorian estate church by *Scott's* two-stage restoration, 1856 and 1876. The church had already been re-roofed in 1841 and the gables rebuilt in stone. They had been timber-framed, like the existing division between nave and chancel. The date 1615 on a chancel roof beam doubtless relates to this phase. Simple c13 chancel. The N arcade perhaps c14 (standard elements). Meagre w porch tower with spire, by *Scott*, 1856. The tower square at the base, turning octagonal low down where the buttresses carry pinnacles with seated figures of Prudence and Fortitude. Above the door an image niche with crocketed canopy and statue of a knight in armour. Rich interior, largely *Scott's*, mainly 1876 and mostly paid for by the Adams family. Stencilled walls and painted panels in the chancel. *Godwin* tiles. – Gothic SCREEN by *Scott* (carved by *John Thompson*), 1876. – FONT, also 1876. – PAINTING of the baptism of Prince Peada, by *George Ostrehan*, 1896. – STAINED GLASS. Three Adams memorial windows in chancel, †1846 to †1851. – Nave s, *Kempe & Co.*, 1907. – N chancel, *Burlison & Grylls*, 1887. – s chancel, with astronauts, Concorde, etc., *Caldermac Studios*, 1974. – N aisle E, 1868 by *Hardman*, who also did two in the nave, 1872 and 1885. – MONUMENT. Simon Adams †1801 and wife Sarah †1833, by *Cooke* of London, with weeping woman at tomb.

ANSTY HALL. Built for Edward Taylor in place of an older house. Dated 1678 on the doorway which has a broken pediment on brackets with details connecting back to the so-called Artisan Mannerism of *c.* 1650–60. Brick, seven bays, with long-and-short quoins and a pedimented three-bay centre. The back of the house in the same style but a different rhythm, three–one–three. The doorway here without pediment and tied together with the window above. Originally two-storey. The heightening of *c.* 1800 is especially obvious at the rear. Also widened with recessed bays each side, later given curved single-storey quadrants at the front, probably 1894–5. Inside, an open-well C17 staircase with carved balustrade. Reused early C17 panelling in the entrance hall and a wooden screen with archway. Late C18 internal remodelling to dining room. Pillared screen with Ionic columns and antae. C19 grey marble fireplaces in two rooms. The Adams family lived at Ansty from 1744 until 1986 when it became a hotel. Two-storey extension on the r. *c.* 1986. Behind, the orangery with dark glass and rounded brick columns, 2000.

ARBURY

ARBURY HALL. Arbury Hall is one of the finest examples of the early Gothic Revival in England – some may say *the* finest, and every bit as good as Strawberry Hill. The hall stands on the site of an Augustinian priory, of which nothing except the quadrangular plan remains, and which was replaced by a mansion about 1580, of which something remains, but not many features. In the s range on the courtyard side is a mullioned-and-transomed window. The chimney-breasts projecting outside are also probably Elizabethan. The estate was sold to John Newdegate in 1586, and the rest of the story is all Newdegate (or from the mid-C17 Newdigate). Inside the great survival is the LONG GALLERY on the first floor, filling the N front. The panelling here was installed in 1606 and the big stone fireplace with crazy side pilasters and a wooden overmantel with pilasters, columns and obelisks look of the same period, or perhaps a little earlier, *c.* 1590. The flat balusters of the main staircase also belong to this period (though may have come from Astley Castle) and the semicircular stair itself is not unlike that shown on Henry Beighton's bird's-eye view of 1708. The long gallery ceiling, though, is of the 1750s and the windows are Gothick.

The STABLES are a large brick block with a central projecting archway and angle pavilions. The windows are all of the cross type, the gables boldly shaped. The date is 1675–7 but the building accounts fail to identify a designer completely. It is known from correspondence that in 1674 Sir Richard

Newdigate consulted *Sir Christopher Wren* on the portal and received two drawings. They were not used, and *William Wilson*, the Leicestershire carver and architect, whose name appears in the accounts for the porch, was also involved. Did Wilson perhaps design the stables themselves as well? They are rather conservative for him, and the portal is certainly too crude for Wren. But it is entirely classical, with two pairs of unfluted Ionic columns. The garlands by the coat of arms are decidedly poor.

The other principal job undertaken by Sir Richard was the making or decoration of the CHAPEL in the NE corner of the house. It is a long, low room, but it is made glorious by the superb stucco work of the ceiling, done by *Edward Martin* 53 in 1678. He was to be paid £48 'besides comeing and going and goate's haire'. It is of a familiar type but done with a *bravura* matched only by the best. Leaf-wreaths, flowers, almost totally detached, fruit, cherubs and so on. One knows the apparatus yet is every time again amazed at the skill. The white-painted woodwork is contemporary and may be by *Grinling Gibbons* who was paid for the chapel wainscot and later designed family monuments at Harefield. – FURNISHINGS. C16 Flemish triptych, acquired by a later family member *c.* 1900. – Painted PANELS with the Ten Commandments, 1631. – Exquisite door LOCK and hinges by *John Wilkes* of Birmingham, *c.* 1680, and a reinstated ORGAN purchased from London organ builder *Henry Holland*, 1787.

All the rest that one sees and admires at Arbury Hall is due to *Sir Roger Newdigate*, who started Gothicizing the house almost to the year that Horace Walpole started at Strawberry Hill, kept at it longer, and in any case could work on a larger scale. He had, when he began, in the county as the natural adviser *Sanderson Miller* of Radway Grange, whose Gothic bows there date from 1746 and whose Gothic front and hall at Lacock in Wiltshire – very comparable to Arbury – date from 1754–5. Miller was indeed here in 1749, teaching Sir Roger how to draw Gothic arches. Work started with the library bay window built in 1750–2 but designed in 1749. Next came Lady Newdigate's dressing room (above the library) which was 'fitted up Gothic' by 1755. This was done by the mason-architect brothers *William & David Hiorne*, to Miller's scheme, although Miller's own mason *William Hitchcox* was employed in 1752 for the bow at the W of the S front. Newdigate and Miller had disagreed over political matters in 1754 and after 1756 Miller was less involved, but his influence can still be seen in the matching bow on the E, done in 1760–1. From 1762 onwards *Henry Keene*, Surveyor to Westminster Abbey and busy at Oxford too, was in charge. He received £15 15s. in 1762 for drawings. In 1762–3 the drawing room was fitted up, i.e. the SE room with the other bow. The S front centrepiece with 62 the dining room within dates from 1769–73. The plasterer was *G. Higham*. Keene died in 1776, and his successor was the local mason-entrepreneur *Henry Couchman*, who remained until his dismissal for being 'very unreasonable' over pay in 1789. The saloon in the centre of the E front is his, but was probably still done from Keene's designs. The dates referring to it are 1786 for plastering (*William Hanwell*) and 1793 for the windows, i.e. the great bow. Couchman also did, for convenience's sake, the N and E cloisters (finished in 1785). The porte cochère (1792–6) and work on the W front (1801–3) followed, *John Alcott* being the carver.

Only then, after over fifty years, could Sir Roger sit back and enjoy his completed house. As for the designing, it is so much of a piece throughout the principal rooms that he must have had a say himself. An accomplished perspective artist, he produced both sketches and architectural designs from as early as the 1750s and through to the 1790s, as Michael McCarthy has shown.★ Whatever the role of others, Sir Roger's was the steering hand: he controlled the masterplan and he must himself have taken chief responsibility for much of the design.

With the exception of the work of the last ten or twelve years, which is simpler and perhaps a little tired – the porte cochère, the entrance hall, and the cloisters – the unifying features at Arbury are great elaboration and consistent finesse of execution inside as well as outside, and a sustained preference for the late Perp of such regal buildings as Henry VII's Chapel and the Divinity School at Oxford.

There are not many further comments required on the exterior and the rooms. The exterior in grey ashlar from Attleborough is castellated and articulated by the porte cochère, the bows – one wide one to the E, two smaller but two-storeyed ones, very much like those of Miller's Radway – and the chimney-breasts. Only the W range is later. The windows otherwise all have four-centred heads. The E bow is notable for its charming Rococo-Gothic glazing bars and the decorative frieze and cresting alternating between pinnacles and fleurs-de-lys. The S front is obviously of two builds, part 1750 and part after 1769. The earlier bows l. and r. in the slightly projecting wings (which are the typical wings of an Elizabethan E-front) are much more playful than the later centrepiece, three big proper Perp windows of four lights with panel tracery and an ornate high cresting.

The INTERIOR is taken in the order in which it is shown, except for the LIBRARY in the SW corner, which is not open to the public, but must here come first, as the earliest room. This room was apparently being got ready in 1754–6, the plasterer being *Robert Moore*. It already has ogee-gabled bookcases, Gothick panelling, and the most charming pierced fretwork in the arch and tympanum of bow window and back recess. But the gently segmental ceiling still has classical painting (by *William Wise*, 1761), medallions, etc., an extremely early case of the use of so-called Etruscan motifs. Negatively speaking,

★ Michael McCarthy, *The Origins of the Gothic Revival* (1987).

however, this classical idiom is a sign that the ideal – i.e. most
Rococo – Gothic treatment of ceilings has not yet been hit
upon. This was of course the use of fan-vaulting, the liveliest,
busiest, most playful of English Gothic vaults. It is exactly the
vaulting Horace Walpole used in his long gallery at Strawberry
Hill in 1762–3. This appears in the SCHOOL ROOM (once the
Chaplain's Room) of as late as 1788, where the window reveals
and the shutters are moreover closely panelled in the Perp way.
The charming coloured marble chimneypiece with ogee arch
is by *Joseph Alcott*, 1796–1800. The room lies S of the chapel,
facing E, and shares an arch above its doorway with the
entrance to the LITTLE SITTING ROOM (Small Dining
Room) to the S. The same elements are found here, but this
room has, however, a classical white marble chimneypiece of
c. 1740. The centre of the E front is the SALOON, again late
(1786–94). The room is tripartite, with fan-vaults and especially the peculiar use of feigned fans starting, it seems, from
pendants, which is the hallmark of Henry VII's Chapel. Keene
was probably responsible for the idea of using this motif. In
the bow are eight little pendants arranged apsidally; it is the
gayest place in the house. Delicate Rococo-Gothic window
bars echoing the panelling in the first and last bays of the apse.
The light columns below the vaults are of coloured marble
with cute little capitals. In the N wall is a diapered recess with
two slender columns. The DRAWING ROOM occupies the SE
corner. Here the ceiling is a four-centred tunnel-vault panelled
transversely. This is again a Henry VII motif, but this time that
of the vestibule to the chapel. Keene, it has been mentioned,
was designing this room in 1762. Panelled walls, each panel
with a crocketed ogee gable. Large panels for painting in the
side and back walls. In the bow window lacy fan-vaulting. The
chimneypiece is inspired by the canopy of the monument to
Aymer de Valence in Westminster Abbey – Dec, not Perp. The
two buttress strips are broader than in the original. The cusps
are of grey marble, the top of the gable and the fireplace surround of brown marble. These C18 materials make some difference to the C14 design. The chimneypiece was carved in
1763–4 by *Richard Hayward* of Weston Hall (*see* Bulkington)
who was a neighbouring squire as well as a noted sculptor. The
DINING ROOM in the middle of the S front was formerly the
entrance hall and must more or less correspond to the Elizabethan Great Hall. Remodelling took place in 1769–73, the key
elements being the fan-vaulting and the three Gothic arches
to the one-storeyed extension on the S. The room has a very
large chimneypiece in the back wall, the overmantel decorated
with a row of little niches projecting triangularly. In the walls
are tall canopied Gothic niches (as at Lacock), and in them
casts of ancient Roman statues. Similarly there is a relief of
Endymion framed by the elaborate Gothic surround in the E
wall. Below it, an ancient Roman relief of Bacchus and below
that a later Roman sarcophagus front. Both were brought from

Rome by Sir Roger in 1775. That he could still mix the classical
piece with his Gothic decoration shows that he belonged to
the first generation of the Gothicists. Pevsner thought Newdigate's Gothic, like Horace Walpole's, to be gay, amusing,
pretty – not at all venerable, as Gothic architecture had been
ever since the Romantics. However, Michael Hall has shown
that for Newdigate, Gothic represented a validation of his
secret Jacobite political beliefs by ancient authority, much
more than mere architectural form.* Of this, indeed, there is
evidence here in the Dining Room, where the Stuart rose and
star in stained glass adorn an upper window. The glass is by
James Brooks & Son, 1784.

In the GARDENS immediately W of the S range a later wall
with an openwork Jacobean top balustrade and then, re-erected,
against the wall of the kitchen garden a major Elizabethan
bay window from the house: five lights, one transom. It is followed by a four-centred door head and another such bay
window. Before reaching the stables from the N drive one
passes through a simple GATEHOUSE, said to be 1754, and to
the E of the stables is a charming wrought-iron GATE, dating
from *c.* 1710–25.

As to landscaping, Arbury once had formal gardens with
gazebos, walled enclosures etc. These were probably laid out
for Sir Richard Newdigate in the decades either side of 1700.
N of the house, a semicircle of classical 'terms' represent this
earlier period. The rebuilding of the house from the late 1740s
was carried out alongside a transformation of the grounds.
David Hiorne received payments for several garden structures
– including the now derelict TEA HOUSE in the park NE of the
hall – in 1748. The garden buildings and landscape shown in
Beighton's view of 1708 were swept away in favour of lawns,
lakes and flower gardens to the S, and woodland to the E of
the house. Sanderson Miller certainly influenced the earlier
stages, advising on the cascade in 1752. The present landscape,
hardly changed since the early C19, is of rolling lawns, artificial
lakes and trees.

The N lodge 1 m. away on Arbury Road is known as the
ROUND TOWERS. It is indeed a gatehouse of rough red sandstone with round towers and four-centred archway. The lodges
are cottagey. Similarly TOWER FARM, ½ m. W, is a combination of a round tower with domestic accommodation. Might
these by *Miller* and *c.* 1750 as Tim Mowl suggests? Or, as Will
Hawkes observed, are they too lumpy to be his? Another lodge
at Astley (p. 118), a square tower, may also be by *Miller*. The
third lodges, a pair at Griff, are two plain cubes with Y-tracery,
Gothick glazing and openwork parapet, perhaps by *Couchman*,
c. 1780.

(TEMPLE HOUSE, ½ m. WNW. A sandstone house with a square
turret and gables, said to incorporate the remains of a C15 hall,
but very largely second quarter C19 and later. The windows

* Michael Hall (ed.), *Gothic Architecture and its Meaning 1550–1830* (2002), pp. 18–19.

are straight-headed with pointed lights and hoodmoulds. C17 woodwork and fireplaces inside. NHLE.)

ARLESCOTE

1½ m. NW of Warmington

Arlescote nestles under the Edgehill scarp. The hamlet is clustered round a small green set in a landscape of ridge-and-furrow field systems.

ARLESCOTE HOUSE is one of the most delightful of its type in the county. The composition of the S front seems late C17 but, as examination shows, it is not all of one build. Its origins are in the late C16 and early C17 – see the plain and irregular N and E sides with cross-mullioned windows. The not quite symmetrical chimneystacks are a giveaway too. It was probably William Goodwin jun. who remodelled the house and laid out the grounds *c.* 1685. The resulting S front gives the house its distinction. Of Hornton stone, two-storeyed with projecting two-bay wings and a hipped roof. The wings with sash windows are 'archetypal post-Restoration' (Tim Mowl) but the recessed three-bay centre belongs to the earlier house. It has mullioned-and-transomed windows, symmetrically arranged: three–two–three lights. The doorway has an open scrolly pediment. On the W, a brewhouse range of *c.* 1710. Further extension beyond with well-matched stables and garage by *Alp Arikoglu*, 2005. Three late C17 garden PAVILIONS, one-storeyed with tiled ogee roofs. Two symmetrically in front of the house, linked by a raised walk; a third on the N. In the gardens, two separate sections of stone-lined canal from once well-landscaped grounds.

ARLEY

A rural village until the opening of the pit in 1901. Much of the development was at New Arley (p. 470) but the old village expanded too.

ST WILFRID. The nave N wall is partly Norman – see the flat buttress and the round-headed window at the W end. E of this a window with stepped ogee lights (i.e. a form a little earlier than Dec) imitated in the Victorian S window. The rest mostly Dec, the W tower and the chancel with its ogee-headed priest's doorway and side windows with Kentish tracery. Chancel N windows of graduated height, with a stepped sill course. Cusped intersecting tracery to E window. Restoration by *Bodley & Garner*, 1872–3, including the chancel arch, painted and stencilled chancel ceiling, boarded nave roof and s porch. w window restored during alterations by *Mansell & Mansell*, 1909. – CHANCEL PANELLING by *Jones & Willis*, 1897, and REREDOS by *J.A. Swan*, 1928. – Red sandstone FONT, octagonal with Dec tracery panels, 1912. – Carved oak ROOD SCREEN with cross above, by *Bodley & Garner*, 1873. – Good Gothic ORGAN CASE in tower arch, 1938. – STAINED GLASS. In a chancel N window early C14 pieces including heads in roundels, a priest, St John and (possibly) a seated Virgin. – Three by *Burlison & Grylls*, the E window and two chancel side windows, all 1893. – w window in tower, *James Powell & Sons*, 1930. – Bright Good Shepherd nave window, 1951. – MONUMENT. Recumbent priest, two angels at his pillow; *c.* 1350. The recess is over-restored.

METHODIST CHURCH. 1920. Brick with white stone-headed Gothic windows, coping and finials.

S of the church a C17 brick building with plain latticed windows and steps to the upper room, used as a SCHOOLROOM in the early C19. Nearby in Oak Avenue, the former ELEMENTARY SCHOOL and rendered teacher's house, 1875, enlarged in 1908. The end facing the road is High Victorian with black bands in the brickwork, stone window mullions and transom and a tympanum with polychromatic nogging.

HERBERT FOWLER JUNIOR SCHOOL, Church Lane. Probably by *Willmot, Fowler & Willmot*, 1913. Brick. L-shaped.

WAGGON LOAD OF LIME, Ansley Lane. A purpose-built pub of *c.* 1914 with big chimneys and sweeping roofs with dormers.

ARMSCOTE

2040

The two principal C17 houses are similar and both well hidden. In walled grounds on the N side of the hamlet, the MANOR HOUSE. Cotswold type, mid-C17. Front with two gabled wings. Mullioned windows. Restored and enlarged by *E. Guy Dawber* for Capt. Yorke, 1914. Said to have a priest hole in one of the gables. At the s end, ARMSCOTE HOUSE alongside a pond, shielded on the E by partly C17 thatched outbuildings and on the s by a wall with gatepiers. The house again Cotswold type, H-plan, with mullioned windows and stone slate roof. ARMSCOTE FARM, further w, is similar. In Middle Street, a pair of pretty late Arts and Crafts cottages, 1930s.

FRIENDS' MEETING HOUSE, privately owned since 2002. George Fox, founder of the Quaker movement, was arrested on a visit to Armscote in 1673. A meeting had been established and a barn acquired a little earlier. Christopher Stell suggests that the present building is probably a new structure erected on the site of the barn in 1705. Plain, gabled, of mixed stone. Original bench seating. Altered *c.* 1900, the roof continues down over a sheltered area on the s.

ARROW

The Ragley (q.v.) estate village.

HOLY TRINITY. Across a field by the river. Norman S doorway, much re-cut. Also two C13-style S windows with intersecting tracery, the W one a Victorian replacement. The chancel is Dec and good. Roughcast Gothick W tower with quoins, embattled parapet and panelled pinnacles, 1767. The Earl of Hertford was the patron. The quatrefoil windows are convincingly C18, and the cusped Y-tracery in the bell-openings seems contemporary too. The lower stage with buttresses and Tudor doorway must be earlier. The chancel restoration and E window by *Solomon Hunt*, 1854. *Preedy* added the N aisle, N chapel and vestry in 1865, re-setting two low Dec tomb recesses in the N aisle wall. Lias masonry and banded stonework. Rich opening to the chapel from the chancel. – PULPIT. Mid-C17, the panels with the familiar exclamation-mark decoration. – REREDOS. Alabaster, by *Earp, Son & Hobbs*, 1884. – C18 Gothick ALTAR RAILS. – STAINED GLASS. Medieval fragments in two chancel windows. – Good E window, †1851. – Three by *Preedy*, 1865–6. – Others by *Burlison & Grylls*, 1879, by *Heaton, Butler & Bayne*, 1884 and 1909, and *Clayton & Bell*, 1901. – MONUMENT. Sir George Francis Seymour of Ragley, †1870. By *Count Gleichen*, his son-in-law. Recumbent effigy; white marble. LYCHGATE, 1903.

Early C19 OLD RECTORY with pretty Gothic details and big chimneys. In 1866 *Preedy* added a large E wing, since demolished, but the canted bay on the S side must be his.

Attractive cottages on the main road, mostly timber-framed. The OLD SCHOOL (now offices) is by *Preedy*, 1865–6, extended 1884. Polychromatic brick, with chimney-cum-bell-turret and lancets. Dormers added 1986. Former TOLLHOUSE to the Evesham and Worcester roads, *c.* 1825 with Gothick glazing. Towards Alcester, the big iron WATERWHEEL of the former pumping station, 1879.

MILL, ¼ m. S of the church. (Now a restaurant). C18. Waterwheel, gearing and stones from Bubbenhall Mill.

OVERSLEY CASTLE. *See* Ragley Hall.

ASHORNE

Newbold Pacey

ASHORNE HILL HOUSE, 1¼ m. NE. 1895–7 by *Edward Goldie* for an American couple, Arthur and Ethel Tree, who separated in 1899. Charles Tuller Garland (cf. Moreton Hall, p. 466) subsequently lived here. Good, large: 'already quite cubic and indeed clearly on the way to the Lutyens style' was Pevsner's impression, but more apt would be comparisons with contemporary American mansions on Long Island and in the Hudson Valley.* The entrance side is of stone but with blue brick below the gables, Neo-Elizabethan, and nearly but not quite symmetrical, e.g. the bay windows in the fronts of the two projecting wings differ. The garden side on the other hand is quite asymmetrical: hall bay window, and to the l. staircase tower and another big bow, to the r. a projecting subsidiary wing. Rich interiors were illustrated in *The Builder* in 1895 and 1898. The galleried hall has Neo-Jacobean details, there are panelled rooms with carved fireplaces and plastered ceilings, classical opulence in the drawing room and Rococo decoration in the octagonal boudoir. The house has been in corporate use since 1939 and is now the Ashorne Hill Management College. Big STABLE BLOCK, 1897, converted for government wartime use by *Armstrong & Gardner*, 1940. Large 1970s block s of the house refaced with new garden front by *Callingham Associates*, 2011.

In the village, the former SCHOOL by *B. Bradshaw*, 1875. Red brick with yellow bands and louvred clock turret above the porch. Further w down a lane, TOAD HALL (once the Congregational chapel) of 1843 has pineapples on the corner piers.

ASHOW

A secluded Stoneleigh estate village in a loop of the River Avon. The church is at the very end of the village, reached by a footpath.

ASSUMPTION OF OUR LADY. Picturesquely situated on a bank above the river. C12, although the N side is distinctly Saxo-Norman in proportion. Nave and chancel with putlog holes and small Norman windows set high in the walls. N doorway with chamfered imposts and plain arch mouldings. Immediately E of this a second doorway (also blocked): E.E. with stiff-leaf capitals. It must be re-set, but why? In the SE nave buttress a re-set Norman lintel with small saltire crosses. Chancel E end Perp. W tower Perp too. All in red sandstone so far. Then the s wall of nave, of grey ashlar, *c.* 1794.† Simple Gothic with Y-tracery. Tall nave. Open timber roof with carved bosses on the tie-beams, supposedly C16 but reconstructed after 1793. Chancel arch removed in 1958 but what remains is Norman. In the chancel, blank arcading N and S arcading: probably C19 Neo-Norman.‡ – ALTARPIECE. Two parts of a Flemish Crucifixion triptych, *c.* 1550. – PULPIT. Late C18.

---

* I am grateful to Michael Whitaker and Michael Hall for this comparison.
† The old wall fell in 1793. The bill and plans detailing the repairs are undated.
‡ The whole church was stuccoed internally in 1841–2.

– BOX PEWS, *c.* 1794. – DECALOGUE etc., painted by *James Cherry* of Coventry, 1818. ROYAL ARMS. George III. – STAINED GLASS. E window by *Hardman*, 1932.

Former RECTORY N of the church by *Charles E. Davis* of Bath for the Hon. and Rev. Cecil Fiennes, 1866. Plum brick with stone detailing.

Mixed housing in the village. Some timber framing, including cruck- and box-framed TRINITY COTTAGE dendro-dated to 1464–75. C18 brick farmhouses. In the middle, two pairs of 'picturesque' cottages with steep gables, playful half-timbering and Tudorish chimneys. By *James Murray* for Lord Leigh, *c.* 1860.

ASTLEY

3080

ST MARY THE VIRGIN. A remarkable building and an interesting story. What we see now, which is on a monumental scale, belongs to the collegiate church built in 1343 by Sir Thomas Astley of Astley Castle. Dugdale records that Astley's cruciform church had a chancel with side chapels, nave, transepts and a central tower with a tall wooden spire. The spire was such a notable landmark in the Arden Forest woodland that it was called the 'Lanthorn of Arden'. The college was dissolved in 1545 and its grand building was afterwards neglected and robbed of materials until the tower fell *c.* 1600. In 1607 Richard Chamberlaine decided to re-establish it as a parish church, and it was he who converted the original chancel of three bays into the nave and built the present W tower and chancel, doubtless reusing old materials.

Of the original chancel, the PISCINA and SEDILIA survive behind the stalls on the nave S side. Red and pink sandstone walls with grey ashlar dressings. Large three-light windows on each side with flowing tracery of two patterns, curvilinear and almost flamboyant. What is 1–2–1 on the S is 2–1–2 on the N. Above the windows the ogee-headed hoodmoulds are carried up to figured corbel tables along N and S eaves with foliage, shields, carved heads and ballflower decoration. Between the windows are slender buttresses, originally supporting pinnacles. The walling of the original C14 E end is again grey stone, with crocket mouldings to the ogee-headed window opening and on the coping. In the gable a rose window, rather archaic for 1343. Below the remains of an enormous later, i.e. Perp, E window of seven lights, its blocked panel tracery visible inside and out.

Then the additions. First, the W tower. Substantially of 1607 (eroded date on SW buttress) but possibly incorporating portions of the central tower of the collegiate church. The arch between the tower and nave is C14 and not C17. Massive and in red sandstone, it is a remarkably successful facsimile of a

Perp tower, except that the distribution of the windows strikes one as unusual. Small square-headed openings in the lower stages and bigger Perp ones above. Embattled parapet with eight pinnacles. Shields and other carved stonework re-set in the masonry. Awkward multi-layered buttressing.

Next the chancel. Grey stone, small-scale, dated 1608 yet still in the Gothic tradition. The E window and the two three-light side windows are convincingly Perp. Only the openwork parapet looks post-medieval. The two blocked windows with cusped Y-tracery are Gothick and may belong to an C18 remodelling of the interior. The chancel again embellished with shields.

Inside, the tall nave contrasts with the low chancel beyond. The chancel arch, 1608, is below the wide opening of the blocked C15 E window. Either side are canopied image niches. In the sides of the nave are doorways, on the N (now blocked) with ogee head and crocketed hoodmould and on the S to the porch. The chancel has a plaster ceiling with traceried panels and Gothick details, doubtless associated with a remodelling for Sir Roger Newdigate (cf. Arbury). Possibly by *Sanderson Miller*, c. 1750–5, or *Henry Keene*, mid 1760s, or even – as Will Hawkes has suggested – by *Newdigate* himself. Plasterwork probably by *Robert Moore*. Restored by *F.C. Penrose*, 1876. His the flat panelled ceiling in the nave with painted shields and the inner arch to the tower enclosing the first-floor vestry with ringing room above. Load-bearing walls underpinned for the National Coal Board under *H. Goldstraw*, 1951–2: the system specially developed by consulting engineers *Pynford Ltd*. Interior repairs by *Chatwin & Son*, 1954–5. Further restoration under way in 2009–10. – PULPIT and LECTERN. Late C17 and finely carved. Probably for Sir Richard Newdigate of Arbury who acquired the advowson in 1674 and regarded Astley almost as a private family church. – STALLS. In the nave. An important set of c. 1365–90, nine (8 + 1) each side. The stalls themselves of the double-screen type, with thin shafts and shaft rings, cusped heads, painted foliate frieze and crenellation above. But the backs have PAINTINGS of Apostles (N side) and Prophets (S), a unique set in this context for Britain and probably Europe. The Latin texts on scrolls overpainted in English, 1624. The seats have MISERICORDS with foliage, the head of a lady, a dog, a boar, a wyvern séjant etc., possibly by the same carver as those in Worcester Cathedral of 1379. – Chancel stalls Gothick, presumably contemporary with Newdigate's C18 alterations. – PAINTING. Late C16 Flemish triptych, acquired in 1904. – LAMPS. A pair of State Gondola lanterns from Venice with pennants depicting the lion of St Mark, given by Sir Francis Newdigate in 1903. – WALL PAINTINGS. Framed strapwork panels with scriptural texts on the nave walls, six on the S and three on the N. A single scheme, c. 1610. Conserved by *Tobit Curteis*, 2010. – On E wall, the Ten Commandments in Gothic lettering under, perhaps late C17 scrollwork. – COMMUNION RAIL. Wrought-iron, c. 1700. – STAINED GLASS. C14 fragments in two chancel windows, and also in tops of windows in nave and tower. – One nave N window with near-complete beasts and angels. – S chancel, †1902, probably *Burlison & Grylls*. – MONUMENTS. Brass fragment of a woman of *c.* 1400. The size of the fragment is 29½ in. (75 cm.). – Three alabaster effigies incongruously united on one tomb-chest as if they belonged together. They are (N) Sir Edward Grey, Lord Ferrers, †1457; (S) Cecily Bonneville, wife of Edward Grey, Lord Lisle, †*c.* 1483; and the shorter one (centre) probably Elizabeth Talbot, wife of Thomas Grey, 1st Marquess of Dorset, †*c.* 1530. The Talbots' head and crest in oak on an iron bracket nearby must relate to this memorial.

ASTLEY CASTLE. Rescued from near ruin by *Witherford Watson Mann* for the Landmark Trust in 2010–13, Astley was a substantial fortified manor house on a moated site. A licence to crenellate was obtained in 1266. The Astley family (*see* above) were here from the C14 until 1420 when the estate passed to the Greys, Lady Jane Grey's family. Her father's participation in the Wyatt rebellion against Mary Tudor in 1554 brought their ownership to an end. Later owners remodelled the castle. The date 1627 inside the E front relates to alterations for Richard Chamberlaine. The Newdigates of Arbury bought Astley in 1674 and in the later C18 Sir Roger made some further improvements. It was a hotel from 1952 until a devastating fire in 1978, after which it was abandoned.

It stands on its own NE of the church, protected by a well-preserved moat. The curtain wall and gatehouse may belong to an early phase of development. The castle itself is mostly Elizabethan or later, but some C15 elements have been uncovered. It was a long rectangle with an embattled parapet all round. The windows mostly square-headed with mullions and transoms. Of this the E front is intact but windowless. The W side is similar, but on the N and S large areas of new walling have been inserted. Inside, the areas within the E front are partly open to the sky with all features exposed. These include fireplaces either side of the big central chimney. The new accommodation is at the back and on two floors. The upper room is like a great hall with a wide widow at the S looking towards the church. The restoration preserves every jagged corner of the old fabric as it was at the point when work began. Thin Danish bricks have been used for the new masonry. All surfaces are unplastered and so the joins are entirely visible. The effect is certainly unusual, but the starkness of the contrast between old and new is softened by the subtle use of colours, textures and materials.

The Gothick STABLE BLOCK to the S is of Roger Newdigate's time, *c.* 1765.

Tightly clustered village S of the church and castle. Two short rows of houses and a farm, and a SCULPTURE on the green, *Johnny White*'s red sandstone 'Lantern of Arden', 2009. The former SCHOOL, dated 1871, was enlarged by *T.R. Kydd* in 1885. By the crossroads to the SE is rock-faced GLEBE HOUSE, built as the vicarage by *F. C. Penrose*, 1884. Further N on the road to Nuneaton, ASTLEY LODGE at the S approach to Arbury. Square with embattled parapet. Later C18 Gothick with C19 additions.

ASTON CANTLOW

Approached through a traditional LYCHGATE by *J. A. Chatwin & Son*, 1956, the church, former school and Old Vicarage form a group.

ST JOHN THE BAPTIST. *William Butterfield* worked here for the Tractarian vicar, the Rev. Henry Hill. Although their High Church furnishings have been whittled away, the fabric still bears *Butterfield*'s imprint. In 1850 he rebuilt the S side of the nave, did the chancel arch with its low screen wall and gates and re-roofed the nave. The W tower E.E. to the lancet stage, and above that Perp. Late C13 the fine chancel. The S windows with their three variations on cusped and enriched Y-tracery are delightful. The SEDILIA and PISCINA go well with them. One N chancel window with bar tracery no doubt corresponds too. Of about the same time as the chancel or a little later the rough N arcade of four bays with octagonal piers. A surprise is the large Dec (though ogeeless) E window in the N aisle with the five-lobed motif in the head. It does not go with anything else in the church and may, as the VCH suggested, come from elsewhere. Equally surprising the W turret of the N aisle, possibly (cf. Salford Priors) for a beacon to help travellers cross the River Alne. It has a small round window with a mouchette wheel, i.e. Dec, as are also the aisle windows. Over the N door, a niche with a Nativity, the Virgin Mary recumbent; uncertain date, perhaps early. – FONT. Octagonal, Perp, with quatrefoils and bearded heads looking out from the underside. – PULPIT. Early C17 (cf. Wootton Wawen), yet with foiled and ogee panels separated by crocketed ribs. – Carved PANELLING, some formerly incorporated in a REREDOS, probably of domestic origin, C17. – BENCH ENDS. Two with poppyheads, and more made up into chancel chairs in 1939. – ALTAR RAILS, by *Butterfield*; wood, with big tracery. – STAINED GLASS. Old fragments in two N aisle windows. – Two by *O'Connor*, †1852 and c. 1860. – By *Kempe*, the E window, 1898, and N aisle E window, 1902.

Former SCHOOL and TEACHER'S HOUSE, S of the church. By *Butterfield*, 1847–8. A delightful composition, clearly following *The Ecclesiologist*'s recommendation of 1847 that a school should be by the church and be the 'prettiest building in the village'. The house especially picturesque, designed not only for the master but also for the accommodation of boys to be educated as choristers. The school of stone with small lancets and big chimneys. Only the main part and the w wing are original; the E part in brick, 1883.

OLD VICARAGE, W of the church tower, a good C18 double-pile two-storey house, with C19 additions.

GUILD HOUSE, in the main street facing the small green. Originally the hall of the Guild of St Mary founded in the mid C15. Impressive frontage with overhang and closely set studs. Restored in 1961 by *Andrews & Hazzard*, with a new VILLAGE HALL behind.

On the opposite side of the village green, the KING'S HEAD pub with C16 timber framing. Nearby, two neat rows of brick cottages, some with Lias foundations. The CLUB and a pair of High Victorian ESTATE COTTAGES S of the Guild House built for Thomas Wood, 1875–6. In Bearley Road and in the lane N of the church, white-painted and timber-framed cottages.

A large parish, extending towards Newnham and Bearley Aqueduct (p. 143) in the E and Little Alne and Shelfield in the N and NW.

NEWNHAM, 2 m. E, is an isolated settlement. REDLANDS FARM has a C16 cross-wing with close studding below and square framing above.

At LITTLE ALNE, 1 m. N, HOLYOAKE FARMHOUSE: timber-framed, the end facing the road with late C16 or early C17 panels in the gable forming concave-sided lozenges. The ground floor closely studded.

SHELFIELD, 3 m. NW, has several good farms. THE POPLARS with remarkable decorated brick chimneystack dated 1688. SHELFIELD HOUSE, brick with stone quoins, *c.* 1700, three bays, two storeys, hipped roof and dormers; doorway with Doric pilasters and triglyph frieze. Behind, a square gabled DOVECOTE, Elizabethan or Jacobean, restored by *F.W.B. Yorke*, 1945–6.

ATHERSTONE

3090

Atherstone is on Roman Watling Street, but its history as a town really begins in the C13 when the abbot of Bec encouraged its development. The first market charter was obtained in 1246. There had been a Domesday settlement here and a chapel existed by 1125 but Atherstone remained a chapelry of Mancetter until 1825 and only became a separate civil parish in 1866.

By laying out burgage plots at right angles to Watling Street and creating a market place to the N, the monks established the street plan that exists to this day. The main street, rightly called Long Street, follows the Roman road. With a major highway through the town, transport links have always underpinned Atherstone's prosperity – the number of inns giving an indication of its importance in the coaching era. The canal from Coventry came in 1771 and opened to Fazeley in 1790. The Trent Valley

Railway (West Coast main line) was opened in 1847. The town's by-pass was completed in 1964.

From the C17 until the last factory closed in 1999, felt-making and hatting were the predominant industries. There was hosiery too and ribbon-making, and coal from the nearby collieries was transported via the town.

As to local builders and architects, *Benjamin Harris* (*fl.* 1775–1800) was one of the contractors (with *John Cheshire*) for the present church tower in 1782. He was a developer who is known to have built extensively in the town. In the C19, the *Fox* family of Atherstone builders restored numerous churches and built widely in the north Midlands.

Atherstone's local architect for much of the C19 was *Robert Jennings* (*fl.* 1845–70) who worked initially with Clutton at Merevale Hall before setting up his own practice. His *œuvre* included the former Italianate Corn Exchange (1854, dem.) and the grammar school (1864) in the town. He also worked quite widely in the locality.

Despite some significant losses and insensitive redevelopment, Atherstone remains a place of character and visual interest. The clearance of the 'yards' of lowly courtyard dwellings was, in the main, nothing but an improvement. They had, nevertheless, been a feature of the town. The opening up of the main square with the demolition of the large and undistinguished town hall certainly affords better views of some of the finer buildings near the church.*

CHURCHES

St Mary. Once tucked away behind buildings, the church now stands open to the market place on the S. It consists of a large nave and aisles entirely of 1849–50 (by *Wyatt & Brandon*), an octagonal crossing tower, and a chancel of three bays. The history explains the oddity. The chancel was once an independent chapel served from Mancetter and in existence by 1125. This was taken over when, *c.* 1375, an Austin friary was founded here. The friars were building in 1383, as a legacy shows, and this probably meant a new church in the friars' tradition in England (cf. Greyfriars and Whitefriars in Coventry) – i.e. a nave, then a cross-space – in the middle of which stands a tower, often octagonal – and then a chancel. The interior is indeed of this type. The division between nave and aisles and the cross-space is an arch from each of the aisles plus a tripartite arching from the nave. The middle arch corresponds to the base of the tower. A recess in the wall between cross-space and chancel is certainly original (perhaps an Easter sepulchre), and so is the whole of the chancel. The arch between tower and

---

*Major losses include Atherstone Hall (dem. 1963) and St Scholastica's Convent (by *J.A. Hansom*, 1837–58, and *Edward J. Hansom*, 1873; dem. 1967), along with individual buildings listed by Pevsner – particularly Ratcliffe House in North Street and Tannery House in Long Street – whose demolition is to be regretted.

chancel is tall and entirely unmoulded. *Wyatt & Brandon* left all this unaltered in 1849. They built an aisled nave to which the area under the tower served as a temporary chancel. The building E of the crossing was not then part of church (it was used by the grammar school until 1864 and not returned to use as the chancel until 1888). The chancel windows are of a type which may well be early Perp: three lights, the two l. and r. lancets, but the middle one taken up with straight mullions into the main arch. The windows of the old nave as shown in an engraving of 1791 appear to have been the same. The large five-light E window is certainly Perp, but the quatrefoils in the tracery lights are still Dec touches.

Outside, what one sees now is the late C14 chancel, the rather harsh rock-faced nave and aisles of 1849–50 and the delightful octagon tower. The top of the tower rebuilt by *Henry Couchman* in 1782 with two-light bell-openings each with a rose window over, and an open parapet with pinnacles, rather dwarfed by the nave roof. On the N side of the chancel, a re-set C12 doorway from the old church at Baddesley Ensor (dismantled in 1848), incorporated in a private entrance from now demolished Atherstone Hall. S transept remodelled as the Lucy Chapel with a heavy marble ALTAR brought from St Scholastica's Convent in 1967. The W end of the church was converted into a lounge, 1985. – REREDOS and panelling, by the *Warham Guild* to designs by *F.E. Howard*, 1926. – FONT. Octagonal, Perp, with trefoil panels and alternate Symbols of the Evangelists and Instruments of the Passion. On Victorian columns and with a good carved wooden cover, 1853. – STAINED GLASS. E window by *Kempe*, 1896, the lower panels rearranged by *Kempe & Co.*, 1927. – Chancel side windows N and S also *Kempe*, 1899 and 1911. – Big war memorial W window, *T.F. Curtis, Ward & Hughes*, 1920. – S chapel Annunciation, *Roger Fifield*, 1972. – S aisle windows, three by *Cakebread Robey & Co.*, 1899–1909.

ST BENEDICT (R.C.), Owen Street. In a cluster of buildings with the adjacent presbytery and – further away and now separated – the former Catholic school of 1859–60 by *Robert Jennings* at the junction of Coleshill Road and South Street. The church by *C.A. Buckler*, 1859. Brick with apse and bellcote. Open timber roof. – REREDOS. Another part of the altar brought from St Scholastica's Convent in 1967. – Stone ALTAR, AMBO and FONT, 1989. – STAINED GLASS in apse by *Hardman c.* 1859, and two nave windows by *Norgrove Studios*, 1986 and *c.* 1993.

Former INDEPENDENT CHAPEL (now THE CLOISTERS), North Street. 1826–7. Brick with arched windows and a doorway with a ribbed band round the arch resting on two Ionic columns *in antis*. Former SUNDAY SCHOOL, 1837, to the rear.

TRINITY METHODIST/UNITED REFORMED CHURCH, Coleshill Road. Originally Wesleyan. Bold front with Gothick windows and crenellated eaves. 1836, with later porch.

PUBLIC BUILDINGS

NORTH WARWICKSHIRE BOROUGH COUNCIL OFFICES,
South Street. *Conder Winchester* design and build, 1979–81. An
L-shaped range, sprawling, brick with mansard roof.

CIVIC PRECINCT, Long Street. Bland LIBRARY, 1966, 1962
MEMORIAL HALL, and 1975 SWIMMING POOL by the
County Architect's Department (J.C.E. Tainsh) now within the
LEISURE CENTRE (refronted with a pointy steel tower with
glazed sides *c.* 2003).

GRAMMAR SCHOOL (now part of Queen Elizabeth School and
Sports College). Austere three-storey buildings on the Long
Street frontage. The school moved to this site in 1864 and the
original buildings were by local architect *Robert Jennings.*
Assembly hall with large six-light Perp-style window to the
rear, but otherwise undistinguished. The main campus of the
COLLEGE is now further E on Witherley Road, developed
around low blocks of classrooms by the *County Architect's
Department*, 1929.

ROWAN CENTRE, at the corner of North Street and Ratcliffe
Road. The Board School by *W. Millican* of Leicester, 1882.
Red brick, sandstone dressings, ogee window heads (some
topped by fleurs-de-lys), and a high tower in lighter brick with
a French pavilion roof – a landmark in Atherstone.

ARTS CENTRE, Owen Street. The 1893 GIRLS' SCHOOL. Wide
and plain, but with terracotta date plaques at each end with
foliage.

Present schools mostly standard *County Architect's Department*
work of the 1950s and 1960s, but ARDEN HILL SCHOOL in
Shortlands has a contemporary sculpture, *Tumbler*, by *Walter
Ritchie*, 1952.

Former RAILWAY STATION, Station Street. By *J.W. Livock*,
1847. Tudor, brick, with gables and chimneys.

PERAMBULATION

Begin at the church where the open space to the S was created
by the removal of the old town hall in 1963. The streets which
connect this enlarged market place with Watling Street are
Market Street on the E and Church Street on the W. At the
top end of MARKET STREET are CHAPEL HOUSE, erected as
a dower house for Atherstone Hall (dem. 1963) in 1728, and
ST MARY'S HOUSE, built for the schoolmaster, then the SWAN
ARCHWAY through which a new roadway into North Street
was created in 1798. From here can be seen the jettied timber
framing at the back of Nos. 11–13 Market Street. Back in the
square, BEECH HOUSE (No. 19) built by William Eyre in 1708
is a fine Queen Anne house, with a good doorcase and well-
preserved interiors. Nos. 15–17 and 11–13 have contrasting
fronts, the former still gabled and C17 with massive brick
chimneys, the latter refronted in the C19. Further S is the ex-
Servicemen's Club (No. 9), *c.* 1830 with giant pilasters with

incised ornament. Almost at the junction with Long Street, an engraved ceramic mural 'We are here' by *Justin Sanders*, 1998.

On the s side of Market Place, a striking single-bay brick façade of two and a half storeys with Venetian window under round arch and a Diocletian window above. The w side is Church Street, and the top end towards The Angel, facing the church, has Georgian exteriors of varied height and style. THE ANGEL itself, refronted in the 1920s in Tudor style, has internal woodwork of *c.* 1500–20. Lower down, No. 8 Church Street has C15 timbers in the attic. On the l. corner (No. 82 Long Street), a big Regency building in which the COFFEE TAVERN opened in 1878.

In LONG STREET, w of Church Street, No. 74 (N side), Late Georgian, two and a half storeys with windows on the first floor in circular surrounds, and a lunette in the attic story which has curved ends to the gable; and No. 63 (s side), dated 1875 and Gothic, with one short fat column between doorway and shop doorway carrying an oriel. The E end of the street is grander than the w, with fine three-storey buildings (especially Nos. 88–108), some Regency and others showing Italianate and later Victorian influences, some stone-fronted and some with well-preserved shopfronts. The inns and commercial buildings are here. On the N side No. 102, four bays, brick, with a doorway with broken pediment on Tuscan columns. At the corner of Ratcliffe Street, the Midland Bank (now HSBC), reticently classical and by *Joseph Hansom*, 1838, refronted in 1913. Opposite on the s, OLD BANK HOUSE (No. 129) with a not contemporary date 1711 and the principal features rather 1775: tripartite ground-floor windows with thin columns and a doorway with a pediment on Adamish columns. Then at No. 112 the ALBERT HALL (originally a mission hall and now a nightclub), 1876, with Italian Gothic detail. Further E, DENHAM HOUSE (No. 122) in Flemish bond with Ionic capitals to doorway. On the s side at the junction of Woolpack Way, the CONSERVATIVE CLUB (originally Atherstone House), late C17, H-plan with two projecting wings, quoins, and a hipped roof. The centre party infilled. Facing, a rather oppressive block of Waterloo Housing Association flats, 1980s, at Nos. 132–134 replaces Tannery House, described by Pevsner as Atherstone's stateliest house 'with two canted bay windows and in the centre a Venetian window with nicely carved details above the doorway'.

Back to the other side of Long Street, 75 yds E is the OLD SWAN, the best timber-framed house in the town, with close studding and also some diagonal braces, an overhang, and on the ground floor two canted bay windows and an oriel. It is mostly C16 work, but the w elevation is a mock-up added when Welcome Street was cut through in 1855. 175 yds further E by the old grammar school (*see* Public Buildings) more nice groups of Georgian houses on both sides. On the s side HILTON HOUSE (No. 215) has tripartite windows with thin columns. On the N, No. 212 with classical porch and fanlight.

Just beyond at the start of WITHERLEY ROAD, a pair of big Victorian houses with steep, trussed gables, 1870s.

WELCOME STREET, s of Long Street, leads to an area of artisan housing developed from 1855 into the early C20, with good examples in Stafford Street and the Grove.

On the edge of town down SOUTH STREET, several large houses for prosperous businessmen, including bargeboarded THE GABLES and rock-faced ARDEN HILL by *Robert Jennings* for Hanson Sale, 1860. The County Council acquired Arden Hill as a home for old people in 1953, the conversion and extensions by *G. R. Barnsley*, County Architect.

GRENDON LODGE, Long Street, ¼ m. w of Church Street. Built in 1828 for Mary Satterthwaite. An important house – a Regency gem – set in quiet grounds with contemporary outbuildings behind. In the garden a Gothic folly with carved heads, possibly from Merevale Abbey. The house was originally a perfect cube, of two storeys and with a symmetrical front of three bays and a Greek Doric porch. The symmetry was spoiled by the addition of short wings to the e and w *c.* 1864. Inside a central staircase with iron balustrading, lit from a skylight above.

PEEL HOUSE, No. 79 Witherley Road. 1868, in stone and gault brick with pretty bargeboards, iron finals and carved initials and date in the gables.

HATTON'S HAT FACTORY, behind No. 50 Long Street. One of the more notable remaining buildings associated with the industry, remodelled after a fire in 1841.

Former BRITANNIA WORKS (Wilson & Stafford), Coleshill Road, SE of the canal. The last of Atherstone's felt factories. C19, three-storey, with a varied frontage in three distinct sections. Nearby on the canal, the COAL WHARF with its pretty little canalside office.

ATHERSTONE-ON-STOUR

ST MARY. Closed in 1977 and in private ownership since redundancy in 1993. By *John Cotton*, 1875–6. Rock-faced, with chancel, nave and sw porch tower with crocketed pyramid spire. w rose window. Otherwise Dec. Most FITTINGS removed before the church was sold, including the STAINED GLASS e window. It was by *C. E. Tute*, a pupil of Kempe, 1893 and good.

e of the church, ATHERSTONE HOUSE, a big double-plan farmhouse, *c.* 1720, with hipped roof and added dormers. Modillion cornice. Five symmetrical bays to garden front. Restored in 1999.

To the w, the former RECTORY (now flats). An awkwardly proportioned Early Georgian five-bay brick house of three storeys with segment-headed windows. Giant angle pilasters. The third floor may be a later addition. It has its own pilasters. Dull side elevation. Two-storey rear extensions, *c.* 1875. Renovated 1984.

ATHERSTONE HILL FARMHOUSE, ½ m. SW. On a hilltop site with all-round views, especially towards Meon Hill and the Cotswolds. Built *c.* 1710 for Dr William Thomas, the editor of Dugdale's *Antiquities*, and bought by James West of Alscot in 1751. Red brick in Flemish bond with vitrified headers. Plain five-bay front of two storeys with raised brick quoins.

AUSTREY 2000

ST NICHOLAS. The tower and spire are of the C13. The rest of 14 the church is of one build in the early C14 and remarkable for its unity and completeness. Faithful restoration by *Ewan Christian* – who later described this job as 'the first foundation stone of success' – in 1844–5 at the instigation of the Rev. Roger Bass (†1844) whose widow provided the funds enabling his successor to complete the work. The material is a light grey stone and the roofs are of slate. Angle buttresses to the E.E. tower which carries a broach spire with two tiers of lucarnes. It has typical late C13 windows, with pointed-trefoiled lights and foiled circles over. S window below the bell-openings oddly has a transom and shafts instead of a mullion. Splendidly spacious interior with steeply pitched roofs to the chancel and clerestoried nave and very tall four-bay arcades. Tower arch towards the nave very steep and triple-chamfered. Roof-line on the E face above indicates the outline of the preceding church. Piers of the arcades and chancel arch quatrefoil with very thin shafts in the diagonals. Arches with two chamfers and sunk-quadrant mouldings. Aisles and clerestory windows have cusped lights, the cusping resulting in a distinctive droplet shape. Aisle E windows cusped intersected but with ogee-headed lights. Chancel windows redone with Geometrical tracery by *Christian* in 1844–5 but in a C14 style, the roofs of chancel and nave of the same date. – FURNISHINGS. In a pre-Ecclesiological manner and largely of 1844–5, including the altar rails, the Commandment boards on gabled panels in the sanctuary, the choir stalls, nave seating and the encaustic tiles in the chancel.* – STAINED GLASS. Some early fragments in the head of the SE window in the S aisle. – E window of S aisle, †1844 ascribed to *George Rogers* of Worcester. – MONUMENT (N aisle). Three sons of Thomas Monck, erected in 1706, with the death's head in the predella, composed with its wings

---

*The front of the contemporary carved cube LECTERN noted by Pevsner remains disused (and damaged) at the back of the church.

completely asymmetrically and hence rather frighteningly alive.

In the CHURCHYARD, numerous slate headstones.

BAPTIST CHURCH, Main Road. Built 1819 for a church formed in 1808. Brick with a gabled W front. Round-arched windows with keystones and imposts. Some original fittings remain including a W gallery with iron columns. Several good slate headstones (some signed) in the burial ground, now laid flat.

The old SCHOOL (now the VILLAGE HALL), 200 yds SE of church. 1850, with an extension of 1888. Diapered brickwork and patterned tiled roof. Casement windows.

Opposite the church, the former VICARAGE with C18 façade of brick, five bays with rusticated quoining and a later (Regency?) porch. Outside the pub E of the church, the village CROSS of 1897 on the ancient octagonal base and steps.

Main Road leads N to the centre of the village where Bishops Cleeve, Warton Lane and No Mans Heath Lane form a square. Here there are several large farmhouses and houses once separated by open space but now linked by later infilling and development. On the E side of Warton Lane is FLAVEL HOUSE, late C18 and typical of the larger village houses in the area. Further round on the N side is the MANOR HOUSE, C17 with later alterations, two and a half storeys and a range of five windows. Opposite, splendid C16 timber-framed BISHOP'S FARM has close studding with plastered infill and a later open porch. Originally T-plan, but the rear section largely rebuilt in brick. Inside, a ground-floor room with C17 panelling has a fine overmantel dated 1621 with carved terminal figures.

AVON DASSETT

4040

ST JOHN THE BAPTIST. By *Charles Buckeridge*, 1868–9. In the care of the Churches Conservation Trust since 1989. On the site of an earlier church on a steep bank, the spire silhouetted against a backdrop of trees. All of Hornton stone. W tower with broach spire and a re-set W window of intersecting tracery. It was a complete rebuild and externally the new church is quite unlike the old, but inside Buckeridge recreated a Norman N arcade. Otherwise the details are C13, with plate as well as bar tracery. The deliberate contrast is most effective. Raised chancel and sanctuary with *Godwin*'s tiles. – Heavy Butterfieldian Purbeck marble REREDOS. – FONT also Purbeck marble. – STAINED GLASS. In the W window, a small figure of a bishop among old glass quarries. C15. – E window by *Clayton & Bell*, 1870. – In N aisle, a *Powell* window of 1884, brought from a house in Wimbledon and installed here by the Boyles (cf. Avon Carrow, below) in 1904. – MONUMENT in a tomb recess with cusped ogee arch and ballflower decoration, *c.* 1330. The effigy is of a tonsured deacon in vestments and older, now thought to be early C13. Slab of Forest marble. The figure is flatly carved and severely stylized. One hand is raised, the other lowered and holding a scroll. The arms keep immediately close to the sunk figure. The head under an arch on thin shafts; architectural features on the arch. At his feet are stiff-leaf foliage and a bird biting at a leaf. The slab is on a low chest, with just three short colonnettes.

OLD RECTORY, s of the church. C17 stone front with mullioned-and-transomed windows, with an older wing adjoining the churchyard. On this wing facing E a C13 twin window, the arch and sub-arches with rolls. The shaft has a leaf capital which looks c. 1200. The wing is buttressed.

ST JOSEPH (R.C.), 330 yds SSW, 1854–5 by *Thomas Meyer* of London for Joseph Knight of Bitham Hall. E.E. with chamfered lancet windows and a poor NW porch tower with clock dial and slate pyramid spire. – Carved stone REREDOS, FONT and PULPIT, all 1855. – Hanging CRUCIFIX by *Francis-Xavier Pendl*, 1859. – STAINED GLASS. All by *Hardman*, mostly 1855–7 but some 1874 and 1877. The church links through the sacristy to the PRESBYTERY on the s, also by *Meyer* and 1854–5. To the r. ST JOSEPH'S COTTAGE, dated 1679. Used as a convent and orphanage, 1874–1910. Doorway with typical oversized, lozenge-shaped hoodmould stops. Mullioned windows.

BITHAM HALL, 50 yds NW. Built for the horticulturalist Joseph Knight (†1855) and afterwards the home of his former business partner Thomas Aloysius Perry, who had married Knight's niece in 1840. Italianate, c. 1850. Simple five-bay centre and higher projecting wings. Now flats. In the grounds, a splendid iron-framed GLASSHOUSE, c. 1860. Original mid-C19 GATE-PIERS at s entrance, and late C19 TOP LODGE high above the village. Further NE, LIME COTTAGE, 1852, was its lodge.

AVON CARROW, 300 yds S. By *W.E. Mills* of Banbury for Captain Cecil Boyle, 1889. Tudor-style, on the courtyard plan with tall castellated tower at the centre of the s front and low service wings with corner pavilions at the rear. Now subdivided.

BADDESLEY CLINTON

ST MICHAEL. Perp, except for the C13 masonry of part of the nave. One N window with Y-tracery. Clerestory and W tower paid for by Nicholas Brome, who died in 1517. The tower is strikingly similar to nearby Packwood, also funded by Brome. Both perhaps c. 1495 to 1505, and Baddesley has a contemporary bell. A somewhat later inscription – in Roman lettering – records that Brome 'did new build the steeple in the reigne of King Henry the Seaventh'. The square-headed chancel side windows are of 1634, when, according to another inscription, the chancel was rebuilt. Barrel-vaulted roof.

Modest restoration and seating by *Payne & Talbot*, 1874.
– Handsome and unusual SCREEN, dated 1634. The cross-
members in the doors, side panels and in the arch above are
reminiscent of the decorative braces of contemporary timber-
framed houses. – STAINED GLASS. The E window with sacred
and armorial glass, originally given by Sir Edward Ferrers
(†1535). It is C16 in style and origin, but restoration by *Hardman*
in 1965 confirmed that little early glass remains. Mostly C18 or
later with much by *Camm Bros*, 1874. – CHAMBER ORGAN.
Sarah Green of Isleworth, 1797, in plain wooden case. –
MONUMENT. Sir Edward Ferrers †1535 and other members of
the family, latest †1564. Tudor-style tomb-chest with richly
cusped quatrefoils containing shields, and Latin inscription
round the edge. No effigies. Recess with cresting. Plain English
inscription on tablet.

ST FRANCIS (R.C.), Rising Lane. In a group with presbytery,
school (closed in 1990) and Poor Clares Convent (closed in
2011). All 1870, by *Benjamin Bucknall*, then of Swansea, but
replacing earlier buildings on the site begun with the building
of a Franciscan academy in 1793. The Poor Clares arrived in
1850. Catholicism at Baddesley, though, extends back to the
C16 with the Ferrers family at the Hall. Plain CHURCH in
French Gothic style with lancets. Chunky columns on the
entrance front, also below the clerestory inside. High interior
with panelled roof. – STAINED GLASS. Two S windows, probably by *Tony Dury*, c. 1870. – The rest by *Hardman*, one 1913
(N) and another 1960s (baptistery). The CONVENT CHAPEL
adjoins the church. It has cinquefoiled side windows and an
open bellcote on the end gable. Simple Gothic details to the
CONVENT and PRESBYTERY.

38   BADDESLEY CLINTON HALL. As you approach Baddesley
Clinton Hall, it stands before you as the perfect late medieval
moated manor house, admired by Romantics since at least the
C18. The entrance side of Arden stone quarried on the estate,
the small Queen Anne brick bridge across the moat, the
gateway with a porch, higher than the roof and embattled – it
could not be better. But it is not entirely what it seems.

First, the history. Belonging to the Clintons, Baddesley
originated as a fortified manor on a moated site in the C12 or
C13. It passed to John Brome of Warwick, a lawyer, in 1438.
From this date the building history becomes clearer, as will be
seen. On the death of Nicholas Brome in 1517 it went to his
daughter's husband, Sir Edward Ferrers. After the Reformation the family remained Catholic. Henry Ferrers (1549–1633),
the antiquary, who provided Dugdale with much material, was
among the later owners. Baddesley remained in direct family
descent until 1884. A Ferrers widow, Rebecca Dering (*née*
Orpen), lived in the house until 1923. Acquired in 1940 by
Thomas Walker, a distant relation, it later passed to his son
Thomas Ferrers-Walker through whose efforts it passed to the
National Trust in 1980, opening to the public in 1982. The
Derings and the Walkers undertook various repairs and

BADDESLEY CLINTON HALL

ground floor plan

brew-house

moat room

the building

0   10   20   30   40ft

J.W.B 1939

scullery

modern

larder

wing

N

gateway

bridge

dining room

kitchen

little hall

great hall

drawing room

moat surrounding

servants' hall

pantry

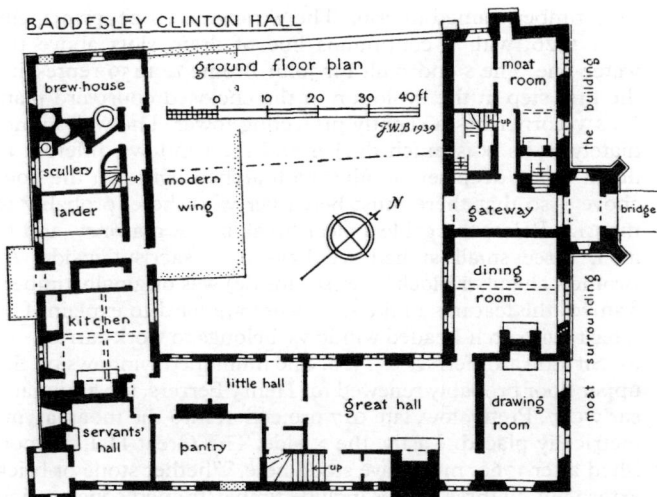

Baddesley Clinton Hall.
Plan

alterations, and a thorough restoration for the Trust was carried
out by *S.T. Walker & Partners*, 1980–2.

The house is surrounded on all four sides by a moat and
approached by a bridge on the E side.* Seemingly C15, the
entrance front proves to be later and more complex than previously thought, as disclosed by the recent researches by Alcock
and Meeson. This range is substantially of *c.* 1536 for Sir
Edward Ferrers: cf. the gateway and porch with its diagonal
buttresses, arrowslits, and arched lights in the side openings,
and the two windows to the r. of the gateway and their arched
lights. The entrance to the porch has a four-centred arch set
in a larger blank basket arch. But the great transomed six-light
window above is an alteration contemporary with the creation
of the Great Parlour for Edward Ferrers in 1633, and the battlements, which replaced a gable, are early C19. The windows
to the l. of the gateway are replacements too. The two S end
bays were refronted in stone matching the earlier work,
c. 1790. Handsome tall brick chimneys, star-shaped in plan.

Next, the exterior going clockwise. To the moat the S range
presents an even, though irregularly windowed brick front – a
surprise and a happy one.† The quality of the brickwork is very
high. The uniformity is broken by a big stone chimney-breast
to the hall, and stone elements r. (the *c.* 1790 refronting) and
l. (the SW corner). The brickwork, of course, is C18 masking

*The front of the house is actually NE but here it is given as E, following the orienta-
tion used in the National Trust's guide.
†The staircase window was enlarged in 1940.

for a timber-framed interior. The w range is stone, principally
of *c.* 1526, with a continuous line of drain slots above the
water-line. The s end built for John Brome *c.* 1459 represents
the first step in the evolution of the enclosed courtyard plan.
Its sw corner has a slightly projecting tower. The wall immediately to its w is much thicker and the windows different in
detail – one deep-set, another with arched lights on the floor
above – so that there must be earlier work here, probably of
the c14. Below the gable a clear break in the masonry, and to
its l. three small arched windows to a sacristy inside. As
Brome's chamber block here (see inside) was originally timber-
framed, the features in the stonework are hard to explain. The
n part, with arch-headed windows, belongs to work carried out
for Sir Edward Ferrers *c.* 1526. The mullioned windows on the
upper floor probably renewed for Henry Ferrers, the antiquary,
early c17. Pretty, low, late c17 projection into the moat, asymmetrically placed. Lastly, the n side. The Great Hall, demolished after 1760, must have stood here. Whether stone or brick
externally, all three ranges include timber-framed construction
within.

Through the archway over the bridge one enters through an
oak-panelled and studded Tudor door, then past the guard-
room. One reaches an inner courtyard, not too big, quite
intimate and informal. Looking N, one sees the moat past the
space where the Great Hall stood. In front, a Victorian service
block, stone below and timber-framed above with a N gable to
the moat, designed by *Edward Dering*, 1890. This shields the
w range of *c.* 1526. In the sw corner, the two lower timber-
framed gables are later, *c.* 1574, but mask out Brome's chamber
block of *c.* 1459. The three higher gables of the s wing represent the hall range as altered *c.* 1579–85 for Henry Ferrers. The
1530s E side, much altered, has a big six-light mullioned-and-
transomed window and timber-framed gable belonging to the
Great Parlour, 1633. The variety of height and decoration in
the gables is especially pleasing.

The s range now contains the HALL. It has moulded c16
beams, uncovered in 1940, and a large, ornate Elizabethan
stone chimneypiece, moved from the room above the gateway
in 1752. The pillars l. and r. of the fireside opening are of the
most fanciful type, reminiscent of c16 architectural writer
Wendel Dietterlin; above them are termini Atlantes. There is
heraldic STAINED GLASS in the windows here and in other
rooms. The earliest date is 1582, but there is much earlier glass
as well.

Upstairs, several wooden early c17 chimneypieces, one in
the LIBRARY dated 1634. Others noted in Henry Ferrers's
diary as carved by *Radcliffe*, 1629, must include those in the
two bedrooms. On the upper floor, also in the w range, is the
domestic chapel, made in 1875 and recreated after 1940. There
are PRIEST HOLES in this part of the house. The wall between
the chapel and SACRISTY seems to have been originally a

screen with plain muntins, i.e. late C15 or early C16. At the entrance to the sacristy is a fragment of timber with two immediately adjoining small doorways, perhaps originally leading from the screens passage to kitchen and pantry. Over the gateway is the GREAT PARLOUR, its end windows and barrel-vaulted ceiling 1633. The original LONG GALLERY here had already been subdivided by 1574.

The STABLES are of brick, 1714, with a pretty timber-framed clock turret renewed in 1981. Nearby BARN (the restaurant), 1721–2. Next to them C18 garden WALLS.

At the entrance from Rising Lane, a Tudor LODGE, 1890, probably by *Edward Dering*.

BADDESLEY ENSOR

2090

ST NICHOLAS. Replacing a C12 church W of the village whose distributed remains include voussoirs reassembled as an arch outside the new one. Other fragments in Church Row (below) and a doorway at Atherstone (p. 121). By *Henry Clutton* – his first independent church commission – for W. S. Dugdale of Merevale Hall, 1845–6. Chancel and nave with stocky SE tower and short spire. Hartshill stone with slate roofs. Externally all in one style, C13 with thin cusped lancet windows and a band of stylized beakheads under the parapets. Broad aisleless nave, still the proportions of the Commissioners' churches. Inside, the chancel is almost High Victorian, with larky details to the paired N windows and the (later?) arch and stone screen to the S vestry (access to the pulpit is via the tower steps – a novel feature). Stylistic differences accentuated by the memorial REREDOS (1882) continue round the sanctuary walls as cinquefoiled stone panelling by *W. Davis*, 1886. Tiling and other chancel improvements of the same date. – PULPIT, from the old church but used in the Methodist church until 1996. C17, hexagonal with tester. – STAINED GLASS. Composite E window largely by *Willement*, 1846, restored in 1947 after wartime bomb damage. W window probably also by *Willement*. N chancel by *A. L. Moore*, 1886. One in N nave, *Jones & Willis*, 1925. The rest by *Claude Price*, 1970–2.

Two former CHAPELS in KEYS HILL (both disused in 2010). At the top, the old Quaker Meeting of *c.* 1768 behind the plain brick Wesleyan chapel of 1895. Lower down, the former Congregational chapel: 1863, in simple Italianate style with raised gable. Ornamental stonework and blue banding. Sympathetic porch addition, 2000, after the building became Trinity Methodist Church.

In CHURCH ROW, the former Church House Inn, with built-in fragments from the old church. Pointed windows and a small ogee-arched light.

Until the closure of the pit in 1989 Baddesley was a coal-mining village. On the common in Maypole Lane, the MINING MEMORIAL, 1991. Iron pit-head wheel on a stone pedestal.

BAGINTON

3070

An ancient settlement on elevated ground s of Coventry. In a curve of the River Sowe on the w and bounded by the Avon on the e towards Bubbenhall. In the village was BAGINTON HALL (by *Francis Smith*, 1714–23 with extensions of 1733–5, also by *Smith*) built for William Bromley, Speaker of the House of Commons. The Hall was destroyed by fire in 1889 but the ruins remained standing until the 1920s and the gatepiers of the entrance drive remain.

ST JOHN THE BAPTIST. Small, with a distinctive central bell-turret. Largely C13 in two main phases, one early and the other later, but it is a complicated building made more so by subsequent alterations. Triple lancet e window of *c.* 1840. Two s nave windows with trefoil lights by *J. L. Akroyd*, 1840, replacing Georgian round-headed windows but based on the fragment of tracery of *c.* 1300 now in the blocked N door and said to be from the nave w window. Present w window a quatrefoil of *c.* 1798 in the infill of a once larger opening. Original E.E. details in the chancel include the priest's doorway and lancets in the N and s walls. The low vestry under a continuous sloping roof to the N of the chancel seems to be contemporary. The nave has a C13 blocked s door and a C14 w door inserted in older masonry. On the w the church appears to have an asymmetrical nave (explained inside) and an added N aisle with its own gable. Here, too, the materials differ. The s side in red sandstone and the outer N aisle in light-coloured sandstone ashlar. The N aisle has three small lancet windows and a two-light e window with pointed tracery, but the w window of one light is Dec with an ogee head.

The whole church heavily buttressed, especially on the s. The biggest is below the stone bell-turret over the junction between nave and chancel. The turret is most unusual. It is corbelled out below, then square and then pulled in to make an octagonal top stage with short spire. It is perhaps modelled on the friars' churches (e.g. Atherstone and Coventry) which would imply a C14 date. The result of this can be seen inside in the thickness of the wall between nave and chancel, where there are deep triple arches with tall openings facing the nave and lower ones on the chancel side. The lower parts of the side arches probably contained altars. They were opened up in the C18 when box pews (since removed) were constructed for the parson and squire. But another surprise remains – a double arcade of three bays between the nave and N aisle. The inner arcade with round piers and round abaci opens to a narrow aisle under a continuous sloping roof with the nave – explaining the asymmetry visible outside. This seems to have been a chapel aisle containing an altar and the tomb of Thomas de Ednesour †1285. The outer arcade has piers of four chamfered shafts and opens to a wide and lofty N aisle. The outer aisle is most likely the chantry chapel endowed in 1292, originally separated from the body of the church by pier-to-pier parclose screens in the arcades as shown by cut-outs in the bases and capitals. The N lancet aisle windows have square-headed cinquefoiled arches internally. In the N wall a plain tomb recess. On the S a C13 piscina.

Largely C18 interior, the chancel 'beautifyed' by Speaker Bromley in 1723 and the nave done slightly later. Some internal reordering by *A.B. Chatwin* in 1966–8 when the Bromley vault in the N aisle was removed and the N side of the church re-seated with open benches. – Wainscot PANELLING and COMMUNION RAIL in chancel, all 1723. – PULPIT, DESK and BOX PEWS on S side of nave, mid-C18. – WEST GALLERY, on cast-iron columns, by *Edward Bradford*, 1797. – SCREEN. Dated 1677. From the 'Repositorium Bromleighorum', i.e. originally with the Bromley vault but now enclosing a vestry at the W end of the N aisle. Still essentially Jacobean. – SCULPTURE. St John the Baptist by *Peter Eugene Ball*, 1992. – WALL PAINTING. In the chancel arches, C14 or C15, with rosettes, flowers, etc. On N wall, the outline of a saint. – STAINED GLASS. Heraldic glass in W window of N aisle, Bagot arms of *c.* 1400 and C17 Bromley arms. – E window by *Hardman*, 1876. – Quatrefoil W window by *Shrigley & Hunt*, 1932. – MONUMENTS. Sir William Bagot †1407 and wife Margaret. Large and very accomplished brasses, the figures 4 ft 9½ in. (1.46 metres) long, restored by the *Wallers c.* 1840 when the colouring was renewed. – Mrs Ellen Campion †1632, attributed to *Maximilian Colt* (GF). Remarkably classical for its date; no trace of the Jacobean style. Two black columns, open scrolly pediment, statuettes of Faith, Hope, and Charity at the top, and the bust of a cherub sitting by an hourglass in a roundel at the foot. – Mrs Elizabeth Bromley †1742. Big tablet with bust in a circular recess at the top. – Bromley family, 1813. By *Flaxman*. Large, white, seated, amply draped female in profile; dull.

BAGINTON CASTLE. Medieval earthworks NW of the church. Also the foundations of a rectangular building, probably of the late C14 when Sir William Bagot owned the castle. Oblong, with the responds of rib-vaults to five apartments and a projecting spiral staircase. It was probably a tower house of the North Country type.

The old village is approached from the W over an C18 ashlar sandstone BRIDGE with semicircular arches and past the MILL (now a pub and restaurant). Also past 1920s and 1930s bungalows and houses up Mill Hill and Coventry Road, some using an early form of concrete block.

Opposite the church, the old RECTORY. Stone, built after 1675. L-plan with stone-coped gable-ends with kneelers and ball finials. In Church Road, the former Lucy Price SCHOOL of 1873 in the Tudor style in brick with stone dressings (the front now rendered) and the adjoining flat-roofed SCHOOLROOM by *Harry Quick*, 1933. Several timber-framed and brick cottages in the central village area, and polychromatic HOME FARM of *c.* 1865 facing into Church Road. Across the green to the SE, THE ROW, late C18 brick cottages.

THE LUNT, Coventry Road. The excavated foundations of an extensive Roman fort, with reconstructions of the eastern defences and other buildings erected by the Royal Engineers 1971–7.

COVENTRY AIRPORT, E of the village. Developed from Baginton Airfield, which was planned in 1935–6 as a municipal airport but sited alongside the Armstrong Whitworth aircraft factory. Large numbers of aircraft used in the Second World War were produced at the Baginton factory. As yet the airport lacks any buildings of merit.

BALSALL COMMON
Temple Balsall

Balsall Common developed from a cluster of small settlements at the edges of Temple Balsall and Berkswell parishes. These became linked by inter-war ribbon development to create a new village around the crossroads on the Kenilworth Road. With further expansion since the 1970s it has become almost a small town, encompassing parts of Berkswell S and E of the railway.

ST PETER, Holly Lane. *Thomas Garner*, 1871. Originally a chapel of ease known as the Balsall Street Chapel, and therefore simple and plain. Dec. Brick, nave and chancel in one. Weatherboarded bell-turret and spirelet. Plain interior with heavy roof timbers. Extensions wrapped round the W end by the *Hellberg Harris Partnership*, 1989, and contemporary S vestry. – STAINED GLASS. Fine Arts and Crafts E window by *Richard Stubbington*, 1915. – W window by *Claude Price*, 1954, two roundels from its lower section re-set in narthex cupboard doors in 1989.

S of the church, the VICARAGE, 1935; brick, five bays, with hipped roof and pretty fan pediment with statue above the porch.

BLESSED ROBERT GRISSOLD (R.C.), Meeting House Lane. *John D. Holmes*, 1994–5, on the site of a church of 1948. Church and meeting room conjoined, the church with turret and cross. Brick, with shallow-pitched roofs and gables with minimalist wooden tracery.

METHODIST CHURCH, Station Road. Replacing an 1825 Wesleyan chapel in Kenilworth Road. Plain concrete-framed hall, previously used by Plymouth Brethren. Enlarged for the Methodists in 1964 by *Claude Redgrave* with flat-roofed foyer, octagonal-sided porch and thin copper-covered spire.

PRIMARY SCHOOL, Balsall Street East, 1913, by *Willmot, Fowler & Willmot*. L-plan, single-storey with two-storey block in the angle. Keystoned windows. Sympathetic extensions, 1931 and later.

The beginnings of the modern village are represented by developments around the Station Road roundabout. On one corner, REGENT HOUSE is a 1920s corner block with half-timbered upper storey. Almost diagonally opposite, the temple-like NATWEST BANK (originally National Provincial) is by *A.S. Parker* of Plymouth, 1928–9. A good recent addition further N is the LIBRARY, oblong with central ridge and sidelights. By the *Building Design Group* of Solihull MBC, 2002.

HOLLY GRANGE, 1¼ m. s of the crossroads in Holly Lane. A sizeable Late Victorian house, with steep gables and canted window bays. By *Hartland & Urry* for George Lewis, 1894.

BERKSWELL WINDMILL (or BALSALL WINDMILL), 1 m. SE. 1826, and the best preserved tower mill in the Midlands, with much of its machinery intact. Tapering brick tower, awaiting reinstatement of its boat-shaped cap and four sails. Restored in 2013.

In Hob Lane, 1 m. further SE, MOAT FARMHOUSE, *c.* 1530: timber-framed with curved braces and close studding on the first floor, original roof timbers within.

At Mere End, 2 m. s, ST RICHARD'S HOUSE, built as a mission church in 1929. By *F.B. Osborn* in the form of a Tudor barn with timber framing and brick nogging, chimneys with decorated brickwork, tiled roof and dormer belfry over main door. Closed in the 1970s and neatly converted into a house.

BARCHESTON 2030

ST MARTIN. Notable for its leaning NW tower with priest's chambers on two upper floors. Both chambers have fireplaces. On the first floor a blocked doorway to the nave. Stone window seats on the floor above. The lean to the W is evident in the coursing of the masonry inside and outside. Up to the second stage the E and S walls seem to be of C13 date, represented outside by original masonry abutting the later SW and NE buttresses. The N and W walls and the entire top stage are C15 with Perp details but incorporating C13 shafts and capitals in the openings. Diagonal buttresses with nice cresting towards the top. On the W an added buttress cutting into a window opening. So the structural problems must have been addressed first by partial rebuilding with thicker walls in the C15, and later by additional buttressing. How the settlement affected the N aisle is not entirely clear. The N wall has C17 windows with mullion-and-transom crosses. Although an inscription dated 1631 on one pier has been taken as evidence of rebuilding there is nothing C17 about the N arcade. It seems late C12 with round piers, with one trumpet-scallop capital and another moulded. The W respond has a corbel held up by a hand. The arcade has double-chamfered pointed arches. So here there is little evidence of any disturbance after the construction of the C13 tower. Of the rest, the two S doors represent the oldest parts. They appear late C12 and early C13, but probably belonging to different builds. The priest's doorway in the chancel is barely pointed and Romanesque. The arch of the main S doorway is amply moulded and later. The chancel arch has one trumpet capital and one with a little nailhead. The chancel also has a N lancet but otherwise is largely Dec, as is the tall W window of the nave. In the C16 the S chapel was built E of the early doorway and cutting into it.* Its arcade has piers and arches of two continuous chamfers. Clerestory above S chapel only. Elizabethan plain parapets and finials to nave and S chapel. Cotswold slate roofs. The roofs and seating all belong to the restoration of 1869–70 by *Ewan Christian.* – C19 stone ALTAR, perhaps from the 1840 restoration by *J.M. Derrick* of Oxford. – FONT. Octagonal, Dec with cusped panels, alternate carved heads and ballflower ornament and a tracery-panelled stem with more ballflowers round the base. – STAINED GLASS. Fragments of C18 painted glass in head of S chancel window. – E window by *Hardman*, 1891, and S aisle E window also theirs, 1893. – S chancel window by *Clayton & Bell*, †1880. – N chancel, *A.O. Hemming*, 1905. – W window, late Arts and Crafts, by *Donald Brooke* of Long Compton, 1944. – MONUMENTS. Brass to Hugh Humphray M.A., †1530 (13 in. (33 cm.)). – Incised slab to a layman, *c.* 1500 or later, defaced for reuse as a memorial to a rector †1746. – William Willington †1555 and wife Anne, attributed to *Richard & Gabriel Royley* of Burton upon Trent (JB). Alabaster. Free-standing, high tomb-chest. Thin, spiral-fluted angle colonnettes. Shields and stiffly standing figures against the chest. The effigies recumbent and praying. His hands rest on a tiny prayer-book. – Rustic wood and marble wall tablet to William Brent †1675. Strapwork and broken pediment, lions' heads and supporters with pointed ears and breasts. – Arts and Crafts memorial to the C17 Barcheston weavers, 1939, with flowers painted on stone. LYCHGATE by *E. Adams Jun.*, 1911.

Near the church, just the former RECTORY and the MANOR HOUSE. By tradition, William Sheldon started his tapestry weaving at the MANOR in 1560 and Richard Hyckes, the queen's Arras Maker, lived here until his death in 1620. The E front of the present house, only three bays wide, with a

---

*One small capital then removed became a corbel for the S aisle roof.

symmetrical front with transomed windows, is of this period.★
The OLD RECTORY, with N wing added by *Matthew Hastings*
of Eynsham, 1840.
The village was depopulated in the C16 and the main settlement
is ¾ m. S at WILLINGTON, with attractive C17 stone houses.
The best is THE COTTAGE in two builds, part ashlar and part
rough stone. BRIDGE FARMHOUSE, now rendered, has stone
quoins and a datestone, 1728.

BARFORD   *2060*

ST PETER. Perp W tower, broad, low and sturdy. The rest 1843–4
by *R.C. Hussey*. Perp, quite big, but not in any way showy.
Wide aisles with five-bay arcades. Hammerbeam roof to nave.
Minor work by *Thomas Garner*, 1861, when the S entrance
through the tower was formed. NE organ chamber by
John Oldrid Scott, 1883–4, paid for by Miss Ryland (*see*
Sherbourne). – BOX PEWS, 1844, modified 1891. – STAINED
GLASS. E window by *Holland* of Warwick, 1844. It belongs to
a complete glazing scheme of sixteen windows, the rest largely
stamped quarries, borders and scrolls. Some lights replaced
with clear glass but chancel and N side intact. All restored
1996–2000. – MONUMENTS. Totally defaced C14 female
effigy. – Thomas Dugard †1683. Uncommonly excellent tablet,
the details of the open scrolly pediment very progressive
indeed. At the foot a putto head. – John Mills, rector, †1791.
Tablet with a small urn in front of an obelisk. – Then the urns
go independent: Mrs Cattell, daughter of Mills, †1795 by *King
& Son* of London; Mrs John Mills †1807, also by *King*; William
Mills †1820 by *Henry Westmacott*; Charles Mills †1826; Mrs
Charles Mills, 1844 by *J. Browne* – all these with a big urn,
draped or undraped, on a pedestal. Some of these monuments
were re-set in Gothic niches in 1844.
Stone BRIDGE by *Henry Couchman*, County Bridgemaster,
1792–5, replacing one of 1484 described by Leland as 'a greate
stone Bridge over Avon with 8 fayre Arches'. Couchman's
bridge has brick-lined arches and circular flood-water openings
(cf. Wixford). The 2007 bridge for the Barford by-pass is
alongside.
PERAMBULATION. Start at the bridge to explore this rewarding
village, which has decent small-scale brick houses of the C18
and C19 as well as older timber framing and some thatch. On
the W side is BRIDGE HOUSE, with stone quoins, flared red
brick lintels with stone keyblocks, *c.* 1800 although looking a
century older. At the corner of Church Street, CEDAR HOUSE,

★ The C16 linenfold panelling from Barcheston Manor was removed to the Birmingham Museum and Art Gallery in the 1930s.

late C17 or *c.* 1700, five by four bays, brick, with a hipped roof and a later porch. Along Wellesbourne Road is BARFORD HOUSE, quite an impressive Regency house in the manner of Soane, built for George Kitchin, 1809–10. White stucco, of nine bays, with, in the centre, four attached giant unfluted Ionic columns, then giant angle pilasters, and then end bays, slightly lower and slightly more decorated. In the grounds, an early C19 GAZEBO with columns and leaded dome.

From Cedar House into Church Street, noting SUN COTTAGE (No. 18), with pretty C19 doorcase carved by *Thomas Keyte*, and late C18 IVY HOUSE (No. 24) with Venetian windows. Beyond, the former SCHOOL, 1850, with bell gable over the entrance and fish-scale tiled roof. At the corner of Church Lane, the one-time RECTORY, 1897, large with tile-hanging and half-timbered gables. The WAR MEMORIAL in the churchyard wall, opposite, by *Charles M.C. Armstrong*, 1921. Beyond the church, the later C18 GLEBE HOTEL was built as a rectory by the Rev. John Mills but became a hotel in 1948. Three storeys and three bays with projecting centre and pilasters round the entrance. A fine cedar tree in front. Nearly opposite, a varied group beginning with JOSEPH ARCH'S COTTAGE, a thatched cottage adjacent, chequer brick STATION HOUSE with chunky Italianate stone windows, and its neighbour with an iron canopied porch.

Here the road becomes HIGH STREET. What catches the eye is the remarkable wooden porch of WATCHBURY with its musical figures, twisted columns and spandrel decoration. The house (now subdivided into three) has a low, rambling timber-framed front, but behind the roof rises to a considerable height. It belonged to the Whitehead and Greaves families through the C19, for whom two rear bays with good plaster ceilings were added *c.* 1810. Grand staircase in the raised section. Further work in 1871, with dated stained glass. Fireplace by *Thomas H. Kendall* of Warwick, 1888, and imported woodwork. Kendall may have done the porch too. Behind, accessible via Church Lane, is the former tollhouse from Longbridge on the Stratford–Warwick road, re-erected as a LODGE for Watchbury in 1872. *Cottage orné* style, by *D.G. Squirhill*, 1843.

Two later C20 housing developments of note. On the site of the Red House opposite the church, VERDON PLACE by *Denys Hinton & Associates*, 1967. Further N, RYLAND ROAD by *Roy A. Geden*, 1973–4, influenced by Frank Lloyd Wright's 'Prairie' style. Higher on the wooded bank of the Avon, demolished in 1954, was BARFORD HILL HOUSE (*Henry Hakewill* for Charles Mills *c.* 1810), later the home of the Rylands. Its stable block survives across the road as CLOCK COTTAGE. N again, close to the river, DEBDEN HOLLOW, by *Robert Harvey* (*Yorke, Harper & Harvey*) for R.J. Povey, 1969. Concrete and glass with a strongly horizontal emphasis, lying low against the bank. Sympathetically extended by *Project Direct* (*James Pain*), 2011.

BARSTON

ST SWITHIN. A chapelry of Berkswell until 1893. The present church is largely of 1721–6, replacing the old chapel which had fallen into disrepair. 'The roof thereof being fallen' Thomas Fisher (cf. Eastcote Hall, Eastcote) embarked on a rebuilding as recorded on the now eroded panel over the w door. Small, brick, with stone quoins. w tower with parapet. Georgian round-headed windows in tower and E end, but the poor Victorian Gothic side windows belong to *E.H. Lingen Barker*'s insensitive restoration, 1899–1900. Barker re-roofed the church and added the s vestry and organ chamber. Inside, the chancel arch is pure High Victorian, with fruit and flowers, now brightly painted. All this thirty years out of date by 1899. Earlier re-pewing and reordering by *Dudley Male*, 1853–4. – COMMUNION RAIL. Probably *c.* 1721. Still with twisted balusters. – Oak PULPIT and Gothic stone FONT by *Male*, 1854. – STAINED GLASS. E window, *William Holland*, 1869, restored 2008. – Nave N, farming scenes, *A.N. Yoxall & E. Whitford*, 1970. – Nave s, *Art of Glass*, 2000.

In the churchyard, a few late C17 memorials and CHURCH-YARD CROSS with medieval base and later top.

ST SWITHIN'S HOUSE, the former vicarage. C18, brick, with hipped roof. Restored in 1989–90.

MEMORIAL INSTITUTE AND HALL, w of the church, is a former malthouse, extended with rendered addition and simple wooden Gothic window, surprisingly of 1897. Adapted as a village hall *c.* 1920.

BARSTON HALL, ¼ m. E. An C18 farmhouse, with pyramid-roofed DOVECOTE in yard and long embattled garden wall on Barston Lane.

BLYTHE HOUSE FARM, ¾ m. E, was built for Edward Barber of Barston Hall. Formerly dated 1829 on its E gable. Playful. Straight-headed windows with Tudorish hoodmoulds and close and pretty cast-iron Gothic glazing bars. Square symmetrical plan. Two high storeys and attic, originally with steep triangular gables on each elevation. Whitewashed brick. Gables replaced by a hipped roof, 1969.

w of the village, the Tudor-style GATEHOUSE of the 1870s, built for William Shenstone. Opposite, C17 BLYTHE COTTAGE with timber framing and brick nogging. Beyond, towards Eastcote (p. 318), THE FIRS, a three-story square-plan Georgian farmhouse with hipped roof, pretty gatepiers with ball finials, and an C18 brick L-plan barn behind.

BARTON-ON-THE-HEATH

ST LAWRENCE. There was probably an Anglo-Danish church here, for one chancel N window has a remodelled head of the early CII with loose interlace and a serpent. Then followed a late Norman church, and of this substantial parts remain: the nave W window in its deep reveal, the chancel arch with semi-circular responds carrying trumpet-scalloped capitals, and the (re-set?) centrifugal chevrons lateral to the internal face of the window with the Anglo-Danish head outside. On the E side of the chancel arch one area of carving with a scroll and a quad-ruped with long pointed ears and a pointed tail (a pig or a hare?), apparently later than the arch itself. The simple S doorway with its edge roll and its plainer blocked N counter-part are probably a little later. Also later but still CI2 the lower parts of the small, unbuttressed W tower. Its top stage is early CI4 and has a saddleback roof. Early CI4 also the S chapel and the chancel E wall which has ballflower decoration on the window and under the gable. One big straight-headed Perp N window in the nave. Then came *Butterfield*'s restoration in 1851, sympathetic in its treatment of the old fabric yet making significant changes: the porch, the gable crosses and the tidy narrow arch between the chapel and nave. The roof and many of the FITTINGS are *Butterfield*'s too. – FONT. CI5, with flowers in pointed quatrefoils. – STAINED GLASS. CI4 fragments in two N chancel windows, one with a date of 1350. – E window, 1902 by *Swaine Bourne & Son*. – S chancel window, mainly of stamped quarries, by *James Powell & Sons*, 1850. – In the S aisle, E by *Clayton & Bell*, 1858 and S by *Ward & Hughes*, 1876. – Cathie memorial window in nave by *Christian Shaw*, 1995, when the six CI5 falcons in yellow stain from the previous window were relocated to the SW end of the nave. – MONU-MENT. Brass to Edmund Bury †1558, 22½ in. (57 cm.) figure (chancel floor) set in a stone laid by his widow, Elizabeth Tawyer, for a family memorial in 1608. – Tablets to the Bird family in S chapel by *Bacon*, †1817 and †1838.

BARTON HOUSE, N of the church. Golden limestone. Begun as an H-plan Tudor house of Cotswold type. Reworked for Walter Overbury in 1636. Its character, however, is that of the remod-elling by *E. Guy Dawber & Whitwell* for Col. Stanley Arnold in 1898. Dawber added a new wing linking the house to the old dairy and brewhouse and adorned the house with varied gables and finials. The big round connecting arch over the hall window pre-dates Dawber's work. It is probably by *T.H. Wyatt* who undertook alterations for Major Bird *c.* 1870. This earlier refronting retained the CI7 porch towers but the pediments of the two doorways were cut down to fit in the space they now occupy. Inside, a CI7 staircase with square balusters. The downstairs sitting room or Oak Room has CI7 panelling and an armorial plaster ceiling by *Hayles & Howe*, 1996. Upstairs the library has a fireplace and stucco ceiling of *c.* 1741 for the Bird family. Late C20 additions for the Cathie family are in the style of Inigo Jones; inspired by the tradition that Jones was the architect for the house in 1636. The billiard room has a stone fireplace (1992) by *Cecil Haslam* based on Jones drawings. In the grounds a 1990s tennis pavilion by *Helen*

Cathie modelled on the Jones portico of St Paul's, Covent Garden.

Opposite the entrance to the drive of Barton House, with its C17 gatepiers and nearby LODGE, a small triangular green. On it the WELL-HOUSE with a hemispherical dome supported on three stone columns rising from a polygonal plinth. Inside, an urn with grapes, foliage and drapery. On the base a lion's-head spring. Erected as a memorial 1875, but stylistically of the C17 or C18. Perhaps by *Wyatt*. E of the green, the old SCHOOL (now the Parish Hall) by *G.E. Street*, 1854–5. Small, simple Gothic with sharply pitched Cotswold slate roof and big chimney. Several substantial Cotswold stone farmhouses and cottages round the green and in the village centre, mostly C17 or C18 and one, ROSE COTTAGE, dated 1724. To the W, the former RECTORY, a mid-C18 two-storey brick house of five bays with fanlight over door in the middle and stone ranges l. and r.

BAXTERLEY

CHURCH. C12 origin with C14 S aisle and Victorian additions for the Rev. Hugh Bacon (rector 1854–1907): the N aisle, timber-framed porch and general restoration by *Paull & Bickerdike*, 1874–5, the vestry by *Alfred Bickerdike*, 1891. The chancel was redone in 1871 by *G.T. Robinson*. His, the triple lancet E window. The surprise is the late C16 or early C17 W front – said to have been remodelled for Hugh Glover (†1615) – with nave and original S aisle under one roof and a stone bell-turret in the middle: round-headed windows, buttresses with ogee gablets, the turret with straight-headed bell-openings and plain battlements and pinnacles. Inside, the chancel is of *c.* 1200 – see the narrow slit side windows, the priest's doorway to the N with nailhead decoration on the outside (now in the vestry) and the chancel arch with incised leaf-forms on the responds. In the S wall of the chancel an unglazed lowside window with bars and shutter. Within the nave stand the supporting walls of the bell-turret, the E side having a simple round-headed arch. Wide nave incorporating the original S aisle in one without arcade. Victorian N arcade of three bays. – FONT. C15, octagonal. – CROZIER HEAD, found in 1958 during reconstruction of chancel arch because of mining subsidence. Of wood, *c.* 1200, with leaves and a dragon head, a rare survival. – STAINED GLASS. E window by *R.B. Edmundson & Son*, 1871. – S aisle E window by *Samuel Evans*, 1875. – N aisle W window by *Hardman*, 1883. – Others in nave and aisle by *Clayton & Bell* †1879 and †1890, and *Burlison & Grylls* †1878, †1882 and †1887. The 1882 window commemorates the thirty-two men who died in the Baddesley pit disaster. – MONUMENTS. Wall tablet to the Boultbee family, †1806 etc., by *R. Blore*. – Another,

with cameo portrait, to the Rev. Hugh Bacon †1907. – Bronze
war memorial tablet by the *Bromsgrove Guild*, 1926.

At the entrance to the churchyard, a LYCHGATE by *Bickerdike*,
1897. Alongside, the tiny parish SCHOOLROOM, 1839: a
humble structure, stuccoed with slate roof and gable cross.

Before the opening of the coal mines in the mid C19, Baxterley
was a village of scattered farms with a cluster of houses at the
crossroads towards Wigston Hill 1m. ESE of the church. Here
stood BAXTERLEY OLD HALL, now an C18 farmhouse but
still with moat and stone perimeter walls. The modern settlement is now in Main Road to the N near the former
BADDESLEY COLLIERY site where the offices of *c.* 1876 and
long row of single-storey buildings remain. On the green opposite, the former RECTORY and, adjacent, the early C19 OLD
STONEHOUSE (formerly two cottages) with a pretty quatrefoil
window. At the entrance to the Colliery Bowling Club, a stone
LODGE once marking the approach to Baddesley Hall: solid,
L-plan with polygonal turret and Tudor details, but probably
C18. (In the former hall grounds, two FOLLIES cut into the
rock with brick vaulting and sandstone elevations. One – the
HOUSE UNDERGROUND – may have been a smoke-house for
meat. Both, as Hickman observed, feel inspired by Piranesi.)

BEARLEY

ST MARY. C12 in origin although few early elements remain
except the plain N door. Largely rebuilt by *Neville Hawkes* in
1961–2, retaining the key features from *Edwin Dolby*'s 1875
restoration. The meagre brick tower 1820s, its transverse
gabled roof a reworking of Dolby's Victorian top after gale
damage in 1946. Dolby's, too, the roof-lights to the W gallery.
Nave and chancel in one. – FONT. C15, octagonal with quatrefoil panels. – FURNISHINGS mostly by *Hawkes*. Simple but
good. – STAINED GLASS. Tiny E window high up in the wall
by *Hardman*, 1886. – S window by the *Art of Glass* (Earlswood),
2001. – Two porch windows by *H. Vernon Spreadbury*, 1962.

Entrance to the CHURCHYARD through a simple Late Victorian LYCHGATE.

The former RECTORY, W of the church, also by *Dolby*, 1875,
for the Rev. R.T. Kempthorne. Brick with semicircular projection to stair and timber-framed gables on the main front. Now
much extended.

Round the old village centre several C16 and C17 cottages. The
STONE HOUSE of *c.* 1660 in Church Lane has an added
timber-framed wing, close-studded with arched braces. This
came from a house in Stratford-upon-Avon demolished
c. 1928. On the N side of Snitterfield Road, behind C17 TUDOR
COTTAGE, is C16 and C17 BEARLEY MANOR. Long and irregular, with a taller middle section with pyramid roof and Doric

porch to main entrance. Facing the manor, the COACH HOUSE of *c.* 1820 is Gothic with crude pointed windows and a clock dial with pediment and ball finials. In School Lane, the former BOARD SCHOOL, 1877–8 by a *Mr Swift*, originally just a classroom with entrance porch. Tucked up a bank off Ash Lane is the 1863 WESLEYAN METHODIST CHAPEL (now CHAPEL COTTAGE) with plain pedimented front.

STATION HOUSE, ¾ m. w. *c.* 1860 (when the railway first opened from Stratford to Hatton) and probably by *William Clarke*. Patterned polychromatic brick with slate roof. Now a private house, but thoroughly in keeping with its original use.

BEARLEY (or EDSTONE) AQUEDUCT on the Stratford Canal, 1¼ m. w. Thirteen big tapering brick piers carrying the waterway in a straight cast-iron trough. Built by canal engineer *William Whitmore*, 1813. 250 yds (229 metres) long; the longest canal aqueduct in England. ₇₉

79

BEAUDESERT

1060

Now part of Henley-in-Arden, but Beaudesert is the older settlement and began as a small village at the foot of The Mount to the E on which the de Montforts built their castle soon after the Norman Conquest. The River Alne separates the two villages and Beaudesert extends into the rural area well N of Henley.

ST NICHOLAS. A puzzling church, although some of the architectural problems are doubtless explained by its altered plan. It is a Norman church, once on a considerable scale but later reduced, the nave being lower and narrower than the chancel. Whether this resulted from a collapse or some other cause is unclear but there must have been problems with the ground to the N. The rebuilt nave N wall stands within the original building line (*see* below) and is well buttressed. The C15 tower built into the W wall stands at the far S of the axis, in line with the nave S wall. It is buttressed on the N too. Inside, the nave roof is C16 or C17, perhaps the best indicator of when the N wall was rebuilt. Before *Thomas Garner*'s restoration in 1864, when the present nave windows were inserted, there were three large round-headed windows on the N. These were probably of C17 date rather than Norman. The chancel is completely Norman, with two large N windows and an E window shafted outside and inside, and moreover with an arch outside, the chevron of which stands at right angles to the wall – usually a sign of late Norman date. Yet the interior is so sturdy in its proportions that one would like to be allowed an earlier date. The chancel is fully and impressively rib-vaulted. These two bays of vaults are of 1864 but the wall piers and corbels call for them, even if the elementary shapes of the ribs may have no authority. The chancel arch is very sturdy too and very

richly arched. Although much restored, it is sufficiently reliable. Here also the chevron is partly at right angles. Until 1864
the l. side of the chancel arch was partially concealed in the N
wall of the narrowed nave. When it was restored, Garner
ingeniously provided a Dec half-arch to fully expose it. In the
N wall, a re-set plain C12 doorway. The S wall of the Norman
nave is *in situ* but originally went a little further W and was
higher than now, as is proved by one blocked opening high up
in the wall, W of the doorway. The S doorway, which stands
forward, has an elaborately carved arch, reconstructed from
surviving fragments, again with lateral chevron mouldings.
The Perp W tower is of soft grey Arden stone. Small in scale
but finely detailed. – BENCH ENDS. Simple, Perp, with arms.
– LECTERN. Neo-Norman, by the *Bromsgrove Guild*, †1930.
– STAINED GLASS. E window by *Holland*, 1853. – Five nave
windows N and S by *Morris & Co.*, 1864–5. Individual figures
by *Philip Webb*, *Burne-Jones*, *Ford Madox Brown* and *Morris*
himself. – Two by *Wailes*, one in chancel, 1871, and W window,
1875. – Two in N chancel, possibly by *Holt*, 1890 (AB).

Open timber-framed LYCHGATE at the churchyard entrance,
1898. Immediately W, the former ealy C19 SCHOOLROOM, now
attached to the CHURCH HALL of 1954. Behind the church,
the OLD RECTORY, red brick in 'early Geometrical style' by
J.W. Hugall, 1878.

MOTTE-AND-BAILEY CASTLE, on the Mount, ENE of the
church. The castle belonged to the de Montforts. At the E end
of the enclosed area bumps seem to indicate masonry towers,
perhaps belonging to a C13 modernization of the late C11
earthworks. Exploration in 2001 concluded that the castle may
not have had a great stone keep as once thought, but remains
of a large hall and solar were found. Certainly the main enclosure was walled in stone.

Immediately N of Henley, in parkland W of the main road, three-
storeyed BEAUDESERT PARK (now flats), early C19, stuccoed
with hipped slate roof. On Birmingham Road further N, a
curving row of detached houses, L-plan with flat-roofed
porches, by *Major G.H. Jones*, 1935.

BEAUSALE

Beausale is rich in farmhouses and farm buildings. The most
substantial is BEAUSALE HOUSE, late C17 square red brick
house of five bays with stone dressings, quoins, cross-windows
and hipped roof. The best is sandstone KITES NEST, 1788, by
Francis Hiorne (†1789), whose will refers to his 'new erected
messuage or tenement called Kyte's Nest at Bewsall'. Three-
storey octagonal centrepiece with shaped parapets to the lower
flanking wings, which have windows set in blind arches. Late
C18 farm buildings too, again with blind arches.

In Wedgnock Lane, towards Leek Wootton and Warwick, late
C17 grey ashlar BULLOAK FARM. SE in Wedgnock Park,
PROSPECT FARM, dated 1743.
IRON AGE HILLFORT, ½ m. SE, near Camphill Farm. The site
consists of a single bank and ditch, best preserved on the S,
enclosing a roughly oval area of 5½ acres (2.2 ha). The rampart
has been considerably reduced by ploughing.

BEDWORTH

3080

In the first edition of this guide, Pevsner thought Bedworth
'a depressing small town', the church 'architecturally too good
and too solid for it'. In the *Shell Guide*, Douglas Hickman was
similarly dismissive, describing it as 'a dreary mining town,
with Edwardian and interwar houses, and . . . around the High
Street, . . . some run-down Georgian houses'. When consulted in
the 1960s by the Bedworth Urban District Council about
improvements, Ian Nairn famously advised them to do nothing
and to retain the charm and eccentricity of the old town. That
advice was ignored and the centre of old Bedworth soon afterwards disappeared in wholesale redevelopment. Had it survived,
it might well have been viewed more favourably now, especially
since what replaced it is so architecturally undistinguished.

There was mining here from the late C17 until the closure of
the last colliery in 1982. Bedworth was also a centre for the
weaving of silk ribbons, an industry founded by French Protestant refugees. There were once many weavers' houses or top-
shops, with large top-floor windows, but the best of these in Mill
Street disappeared in the 1970s redevelopments. The strength of
nonconformity in the town is reflected in the number of chapels
of various denominations, many with roots in the C18 and C19.

CHURCHES

ALL SAINTS, High Street. By *Bodley & Garner*, 1888–90 for the
Rev. F.R. Evans, and a dignified replacement for a rather
mangled ancient church* of which only the plain Perp W tower
in grey Attleborough stone remains. In contrast, *Bodley &
Garner*'s work is of substantial Runcorn red sandstone ashlar.
Perp style: nave and aisles, chancel with pinnacled bellcote, S
chancel chapel, and N vestries with stair-turret. No clerestory.
Dark interior with sober furnishings, the W end reordered as a
narthex with rooms above by *David Slade*, 2000. The old
chancel SCREEN, 1929, now fronts the partition to the nave,
flanked by awkward oriels to the aisles. – REREDOS and panelling by *Bodley & Hare*, 1918. – Iron SCREEN in tower arch, by

---

*Its N aisle rebuilt 1766, the chancel 1686, the nave and S aisle by *William Thomas*
1827 and further enlargements by *J.L. Akroyd*, 1851.

Barkentin & Krall, 1901. – STAINED GLASS. Good E window: Tree of Jesse with Crucifixion and largish individual figures from the Old and New Testaments, on brown branches. *Burlison & Grylls*, 1890. – others by *Burlison & Grylls* in S chapel and aisle, 1898 and 1902–6. – In S aisle, the former E window of stamped quarries, †1845, re-set. – N transept window, brilliant, by *Harry Clarke* of Dublin, 1929. – S aisle W by *Florence, Robert & Walter Camm*, 1948. – Tower window by *Roger Fifield*, 1965.

ST ANDREW, Smorrall Lane, Bedworth Heath. *H.N. Jepson & Partners*, 1963–4. Functional dual-purpose church and hall.

ST FRANCIS OF ASSISI (R.C.), Rye Piece Ringway. By *T.R. Donnelly* of Coventry, 1882–3, for a mission established in 1877. The original chancel, separated from the nave by a light iron screen, is now the narthex. Orientation reversed and the present chancel added in 1923. Tall brick tower with slate pyramid roof, 1899, and other later additions. – TABERNACLE, ALTAR, PULPIT, FONT and SCULPTURES all by Maltese sculptor *Carmel Cauchi*, 1973 and later. – STAINED GLASS. Roundel of St Francis and four lancets in side windows, by *Hardman*, 1883, originally in the other end of the church. – In aisles, ornamental glass by *S. Evans* of Smethwick, 1883.

In a group with the PRESBYTERY and former SCHOOLS, 1894.

OLD MEETING (United Reformed), off Leicester Street. Founded by Julius Saunders in 1686. Built 1726 and remodelled 1808. Flemish bond brickwork and slate hipped roof. Lightly Gothic upper windows doubtless 1808. Inside, pitchpine galleries on cast-iron columns, *c.* 1890. – STAINED GLASS. A complete Arts and Crafts scheme, †1936–54.

ZION BAPTIST CHURCH, Newdigate Road. *Keith Corrigan*, 1978, replacing the previous chapel of 1798 in the High Street. Modernist brick church with sweeping monopitch slate roofs, the S side top-lit by high oblong windows separated by brick columns. Behind, tombstones from the old graveyard relaid between sections of brick wall.

METHODIST CHURCH, Mill Street. *C.F. Redgrave*, 1953, on the site of a chapel of 1845 destroyed by fire in 1941. Plain brick with a white cross on its short tower and round-headed glazing bars in the rectangular windows. Inside, abstract STAINED GLASS by *Abbott & Co.* of Lancaster, *c.* 1953.

COLLYCROFT METHODIST CHAPEL, Orchard Street. The Ebenezer (Primitive Methodist) church of 1851, rebuilt 1878. Group with schoolroom, rendered. Round-headed windows.

BAPTIST CHURCH, Coventry Road. *T.R.J. Meakin*, 1912. Free Gothic: red rendering, with white bands and window surrounds.

PUBLIC BUILDINGS

The High Street S of the church has become Bedworth's civic centre, with a range of public buildings. Most striking is the

Bedworth, Chamberlaine Almshouses.
Engraving, 1839

CIVIC HALL, originally by *Gelsthorpe & Savidge* for Bedworth
UDC, 1973; refurbished and refronted 2005. Opposite is the
HEALTH CENTRE fronting two sides of a small square facing
the church. By *French Thorpe Consultancy*, 1996, with aluminium and glass canopy to the entrance. Further s, the 1980s
LIBRARY and the POLICE STATION, 1991, with banded brickwork breaking into angled patterns round the gables and
doorways.

CHAMBERLAINE ALMSHOUSES, N of the church. The finest
buildings in Bedworth. By *Thomas Larkins Walker*, 1839–40.
They replaced the earlier almshouses which shared a site with
the schools, also founded by Nicholas Chamberlaine in 1715,
alongside the church. The move to a new site allowed for
rebuilding on an altogether more ambitious scale and the result
is impressive. Red brick, Tudor with cloister walks, castellated
chimneys and lattice windows. The Governors' Hall in the
middle of the recessed front, with an ogival-roofed clock turret
above. Inside, the Hall has a Perp stone fireplace, wooden
panelling with coats of arms and a gallery. In the middle of the
courtyard, the PUMP HOUSE with pumps dated 1840. The
GATEHOUSE (r.) has gone, but the PARSONAGE opposite
remains, alongside the NURSES HOUSE, set at an angle to the
courtyard and retaining timber framing in the basement. All
now screened from the street by an attractive water feature set
among shrubs.

Behind, in Chapel Street, is CHAMBERLAINE COURT, an
associated development for the Trust by *Corporate Architects
Ltd*, of Leicester, 2009. On a corner site, two-storey
Neo-Georgian.

NICHOLAS CHAMBERLAINE TECHNOLOGY COLLEGE, Bulkington Road. Built as a secondary modern school, 1953. The
main building is a T-shaped, flat-roofed three-storey block,
typical of its times. Also in Bulkington Road, *G. Taylor*'s 1882

infants' school (ALL SAINTS) has been rebuilt, but the teacher's house remains.

RACE LEYS SCHOOL, N of the town. Former Leicester Road Council School, 1912. Two-storey administration block at the centre with single-storey wings. Doubtless by *Willmot, Fowler & Willmot.*

WATER TOWER, outside the centre, to the SW. Bedworth's most notable feature, standing at the heart of a 1990s housing development. 1898, brick with tiled pyramid roof, 148 ft (45.1 metres) high. *H. Bertram Nichols* of Birmingham was the engineer.

PERAMBULATION

A 1970s any-town centre, where All Saints Square replaced the old market place. Uniform shops of uniform height, the monotony broken only by the distant presence of taller buildings. Opposite the church, the mildly Art Deco CO-OP, 1929, probably by *H.N. Jepson.* Immediately E of the centre in King Street is KINGS HOUSE, a seven-storey concrete tower block by *W.S. Hattrell & Partners*, 1976–8. Shops on N side of King Street and round into All Saints Square belong to the same scheme, also by *Hattrell*, 1975–8.

CEMETERY, Coventry Road. 1874, neatly laid out with the WAR MEMORIAL by *Major H.C. Corlette*, 1920.

MINERS' WELFARE PARK, SE across the Ringway. 1923. In it, the pit-head wheel from Newdigate Colliery at Bedworth Heath, re-erected in 1986, and *Stella Carr*'s horti-sculpture of a miner, 2000.

BELL GREEN *see* p. 281

2090

BENTLEY

CHAPEL. 1 m. S of Bentley Common. The medieval chapel of Bentley in Shustoke, some 5 m. from the parish church. It was 'decayed' in 1589. Now just one pathetic E wall in a field. It has a straight-headed Perp two-light window with fragmentary remains of panel tracery.*

At BENTLEY COMMON, the former SCHOOL of 1844. Built for W.S. Dugdale of Merevale Hall. More like a chapel or industrial building than a school. Brick with slate roof, with a bellcote at each end. Round-headed windows. Of five bays divided by brick pilaster buttresses. Nearby, the SCHOOL HOUSE of 1859. By the road on the Common, a stone POUND with a date 1846.

---

*ST JOHN, the church erected nearer to Bentley Common in 1837, was demolished in 1972.

BENTLEY HEATH

Dorridge

Originally an area of open farmland in the s of the parish of Solihull, from which it was transferred to Dorridge in 1940.

Former SCHOOL (now a house), Widney Road. 1869–70, by a *Mr Watson* – possibly *W.A. Watson* of Birmingham. Built as a dual-purpose church and school with an endowment from George Homer of Solihull on a site given by the Rev. J.H. Short of Temple Balsall, whose forebears had owned Widney Manor. Crude Gothic in polychromatic brickwork, with serrated gables. Extension of 1902.

ST JAMES and PRIMARY SCHOOL, Widney Close. 1978. Replacing the above, and again dual-purpose. The worship area was extended and improved in 1999–2000. The chancel end has full-height side windows and an E end of brick with an inlaid cross in Cotswold stone.

BENTLEY HEATH COTTAGES, Tilehouse Green Lane. Three groups of cottages, each around three sides of a courtyard. The two N blocks of 1934 (Nos. 1–10) and 1935 (Nos. 11–20), both single-storey in brick, by *Watson & Johnson*. They have canted bays with plain stone mullions and alternating black-and-white and brick nogging in the gables over the windows. To the s, the third group by *Horace W. Stokes*, 1966–7. The side ranges single-storey, and the centre block two-storey with a wavy roof over the sheltered walkway facing the courtyard.

THE GRANGE, No. 46 Four Ashes Road. The best of a group of substantial Edwardian houses. By *J.P. Osborne* for Joseph Petit, 1902. Arts and Crafts style with an impressive central hall leading right through to the garden.

BERKSWELL

ST JOHN THE BAPTIST. Berkswell is easily the most interesting Norman village church in Warwickshire. Its chancel is complete, it has two crypts and there is more Norman work in the nave. The W crypt is one of the riddles of the county's architecture. It is octagonal, and Pevsner conjectured that it may have been built below a Late Anglo-Saxon E octagon as at St Augustine, Canterbury. As will be seen, it is now understood that the present fabric here is no earlier than the late C12. However, there is evidence of a pre-Conquest shrine at Berkswell and the nearby well (*see* below) may have had religious significance, so there remains a possibility that an earlier plan was retained in a Norman rebuilding.

The ensemble of chancel and crypts requires an overview before a detailed description. The octagonal chamber is below the E end of the nave and W of the chancel arch. The portion

of the nave above the octagon is raised and there are three
further steps to the chancel, which was designed to occupy an
elevated position. The crypt beneath the chancel is lit by
windows above ground level. It was originally reached and left
by small stairs N and S of the chancel arch. So the crypt and
chancel were clearly planned together, with a linking arch to
the inner chamber.

Externally the chancel is in red sandstone in evenly coursed
ashlar blocks, with semicircular buttresses, meeting very close
to the angles, and with corbel table and shafted windows. The
crypt windows are set within chimney-like buttresses carried
up to the string course. There was some renewal *c.* 1855 when
Perp insertions on the S were replaced by Norman windows
matching the others. The E end has three evenly spaced
windows of equal size, two smaller ones above and a round
one near the top of the gable. The capitals of the window shafts
include waterleaf, so *c.* 1170–80. Inside, the E windows are also
shafted. The capitals have ribbed stylized leaves. Heads as
hoodmould stops. The chancel arch has strong responds with
many-scalloped capitals and a single-step arch.

Now the crypt. As already noted, it is in two parts. The E
part under the chancel is rectangular, with the stairs either side.
It has two big rib-vaulted bays, the vaults on short wall-shafts.
The capitals are scalloped again, waterleaf also occurs again,
and the ribs have a slight chamfer, another late C12 sign. The
crypt windows are deeply splayed. Then the octagon – a complete surprise, and indeed unique – wider than the rest of the
crypt. The rib-profiles and capitals are in no way different but,
as the straight joints prove, it was built separately. It must be
marginally later than the E section. Interestingly, the octagon
has been formed within a space under the nave represented by
earlier masonry, which is visible through the aperture on the
SE. There are low stone seats round the walls of the crypts and,
at the E end, traces of later medieval painting above the
window.

The nave has a Norman N arcade with round pier, square,
scalloped capital, and single-step arches, i.e. just later than the
chancel arch, but the arcade stops short of the area of the
octagon, and here there is a later wide arch. The S arcade is
of three normal bays with unusual capitals having demi-
octagonal lobes set on plain octagonal piers. It is probably of
c. 1300. There is indeed a window of that date (intersecting
tracery) in the S aisle, with others of the C14. The N aisle
windows are Perp, the simple oblong clerestory windows probably post-medieval, and the squat, grey stone, unbuttressed W
tower of two stages is late C15. The S entrance is a re-set
Norman doorway, again with one order of columns, waterleaf
capitals and a depressed arch. Then the magnificent timber-
framed porch of *c.* 1500: two-storeyed with an external stair
on the W, the upper room also accessible from the gallery. The
upper storey is jettied and has closely set studding and a gable
just like a cottage. The base is partly open-sided.

Restorations by *Jethro Cossins c.* 1881, the chancel by *W.D. Caröe* 1909, the N aisle and Lady Chapel by *Sir Charles Nicholson* 1928, the crypt by *Charles M.C. Armstrong* 1925, and minor works by *A.H. Gardner* 1949–61. CHURCH ROOMS, joined on the N side of the church, by *Brown Matthews*, 2004: sandstone, two-storey, mullioned side windows and end windows in simplified Gothic with stone crosses in panels at the top. – Lavish chancel FURNISHINGS by *Caröe*, 1909. – SCREENS in S aisle. Pretty, Perp, of one-light divisions. – Several pieces by *Robert Thompson* of Kilburn, including the PULPIT, 1926, the Lady Chapel SCREEN and ALTAR RAILS, 1928, and the wooden FONT, 1946. – SOUTH GALLERY of 1731, altered in 1795 and lit by dormer windows designed by *Gardner* in 1961, but still preserved, a rare survival. – BOX PEWS. Some at the back, 1746. – ROYAL ARMS, 1791. – Brass CANDELABRUM, by *J. Haywood*, Birmingham, 1780. – Wooden SUNDIAL on tower, 1774. – STAINED GLASS. Two by *Powell & Sons*, the E window, 1909, and one in chancel, 1930. – Two S chancel windows (one in storage), patterned with medallions, but providing evidence of fabric alterations, 1853–5. – War memorial window, *c.* 1920, probably *Percy Bacon* (AB). – MONUMENTS. Lady Eardley, by *John Bacon*, 1795. Excellently carved large putto holding an inscription plaque. An urn above. – John Eardley Eardley-Wilmot †1815, by *(Sir) Richard Westmacott*, with sarcophagus. – (Mrs) Elizabeth Emma Eardley-Wilmot †1818, aged 29, by the same. Two embracing angels, their wings symmetrically spread, an engaging composition, though rather sentimental for Westmacott in 1818. To l. and r. of the inscription identical vignettes of a sickle and a rose. – Lt. Col. William Eardley †1805, by *Chantrey*, 1820.

89

In the churchyard, a CROSS, 1850, but on a high medieval base of six steps. Further E, the Gothic WAR MEMORIAL, by *Sir Charles Nicholson*, 1921; shrine-like, with open tracery in the sides and embattled parapet above.

BERKS WELL nearby, described by Dugdale as 'a large spring which boileth up on the south side of the churchyard'. In a stone-walled basin 16 ft (4.9 metres) square, restored in 1851. Was it used for immersion baptisms?

WELL HOUSE (the old rectory), S of the church. Dated 1718 on a downpipe, but looking late C17, still with big shaped gables. Brick and stone dressings. Quoins. Moulded window surrounds.

Between the church and green, the Tudorish PRIMARY SCHOOL, 1839, enlarged 1906. Brick with cream-painted dressings. Central teacher's house with schoolrooms either side. Sash windows. The classroom windows have hoodmoulds continued upwards into the gables. The central portion has an oriel.

On the tidy little green the village STOCKS, and the gabled brick ALMSHOUSES of 1853 with an older timber-framed building (the MUSEUM) behind. GARDEN HOUSE is an C18 square brick house with pretty trellis porch. Several former estate COTTAGES at the crossroads, in Lavender Hall Lane and along

Meriden Road, some with bargeboards, others with fish-scale tiling and a few with machicolation-like supports to the projecting upper-floor windows. N on Meriden Road the READING ROOM by *H. W. Chattaway*, 1900, with painted beasts' heads on the brackets supporting the gable above the wide Queen Anne-style window.

BERKSWELL HALL, in landscaped grounds NW of the church. Now flats. At its core, the house built for Samuel Marow between 1663 and 1674. Remodelled externally for John Eardley Eardley-Wilmot in 1814, but plain apart from the Neoclassical E front with projecting pedimented centre. Doric columns to first floor under pediment. The Italianate gatepiers and cast-iron railings in front of the house go with the improvements undertaken for Thomas Walker, who bought the estate in 1860. Walker built the substantial brick STABLES of 1869, also Italianate, which once had an imposing clock tower, removed in 1971.

THE MOAT, off Coventry Road, is a C17 farmhouse enlarged after 1874 for John Feeney, the proprietor of the *Birmingham Post and Mail* and a major benefactor and trustee of the Birmingham Museum and Art Gallery. The house itself falls short of what one might expect of a great patron of the arts, but it has a rock-faced S LODGE in Spencers Lane, 1892, and later buildings on the estate are by *Charles M.C. Armstrong* of Warwick, including a pair of traditional brick and timber-framed COTTAGES off Benton Green Lane, 1910.

Further out towards Coventry, HILL HOUSE with an 1857 lodge at the drive. The house part early C19 Neoclassical, stuccoed with crested Victorian hipped roof, and part 1850s and brick. Alongside model farm buildings, *c.* 1870, probably for Thomas Walker who added Hill House to the Berkswell estate in 1866.

RAM HALL, ½ m. SSE in Baulk Lane. House of *c.* 1680, part brick and part stone, with coped gables, mullioned two-light windows and panelled brick chimney with quoins. Inside, enriched chimneypieces and an original staircase.

NAILCOTE HALL, 1¾ m. SE, now a hotel and much extended, but partly C16 with many-gabled timber-framed front and brick chimneys.

At BRADNOCKS MARSH at the far W of the parish towards Hampton, a PACKHORSE BRIDGE (p. 349). For BERKSWELL WINDMILL and MOAT FARMHOUSE, *see* Balsall Common.

BIDFORD-ON-AVON

ST LAURENCE. The churchyard stretches down to the river. The church is a surprise and remains one. Rugged and tight, the embattled W tower is clearly medieval and could belong in the borderlands of South Wales. The chancel is E.E. with trefoiled lancets, but quite evidently Victorianized. It was indeed treated by *H.J. Ingram*, 1865, and later by *W.J. Hopkins*, 1886,

including the chancel arch with its chunky capitals. The nave 90
and aisles have three-bay arcades of round piers and arches.
The aisles have four windows each, and they are of three lights,
straight-headed, and arranged exactly symmetrically with the
centres of the three-bay arcades – like one hand doing common
time and the other doing triplets. What does all this add up
to? C17 semi-classical, semi-Gothic? The answer is 1834–5 and
the architect was *John Lattimer* of Stratford. The narrower part
by the tower, flanked by N porch and S vestry, was originally
galleried. – Heavy stone REREDOS and carved PISCINA canopy
by *Ingram*. – STAINED GLASS. E window by *Hardman*,
1895. – In the chancel N, two by *J.B. Capronnier*, 1885; rigidly
pictorial. – Others in chancel by *Cox & Son*, 1864 to †1872. – In
the end of the S aisle, E by *Hardman*, 1886, and S by *F. Holt
& Co.*, 1911. – W tower by *William Pearce Ltd*, 1901. – High
over vestry door, abstract sacraments of baptism by *Norgrove
Studios* (*Clare Johnson*), 2005. – MONUMENTS. Lady Skipwith
†1655. Frontal bust in a roundel, with painted arms
above. – Some by local masons, including one to John Slatter
†1785, by *Thomas Laughton* of Cleeve Prior, and several by
Davis of Bidford, 1820s.

BIDFORD BRIDGE. C13 in origin, but much rebuilt; irregular
arches, some medieval and one raised for the passage of river
traffic. Cutwaters upstream. The raised causeway to the S was
in place by 1240.

PERAMBULATION. The main street is that of a little town, widening out into a small square which once had a market cross. The
houses line the street with few breaks, those N of the square
pleasantly varied in height, style and colour. Facing into the
square at the W is BANK HOUSE, Lias with Cotswold stone
mullions. On the S, KING GEORGE HOUSE (No. 11) of *c.* 1800
stands by the entrance to the former VICARAGE: C17 timber-
framed with roughcast exterior, extended by *Ingram*, 1859, and
further enlarged in 1888 by *Hopkins* whose stone S wing incorporates Ingram's Gothic bay window resited below a half-
timbered gable.

At the corner of Church Street and High Street the former
FALCON INN, a stately though irregular stone house, of
coursed oölite and Lias. Mullioned and mullioned-and-transomed windows. On the N side and to the rear are parts with
timber-framed gables. Opposite the lychgate, 1898, Church
Street has the former SCHOOLROOM of 1846, stone, and adjacent brick cottage for the teacher.

Back in High Street towards the E, FOSBROKE HOUSE is a
plain C18 house with a triangular-headed window in a side
extension. Further E, TOWER CLOSE (No. 2) is Late Georgian, *c.* 1835, with trellis porch.

W down High Street, two former pubs by the bridge, the
WHITE LION (No. 53) with rounded corner and rusticated
stucco frontage, *c.* 1830, and opposite, the NEW SAXON (No.
72) with C18 imitation ashlar front. Further W, Nos. 90–92,
C16 with Lias ground floor and square-framed timbering
above.

In Victoria Road to the w, the OLD SCHOOL HOUSE is a token replacement for *F. R. Kempson*'s National School of 1871–2, the rest of the site occupied by a Poundbury-style development, 2003.

At BARTON, ⅝ m. SE, over the river, a good cluster of houses. The MANOR HOUSE built for John Payton, 1663, is Lias with mullioned windows, as is the smaller MALT HOUSE opposite. WISSON HILL nearby is partly stone but with varied timber framing above.

BILLESLEY

ALL SAINTS (Churches Conservation Trust). Pre-Conquest in origin but rebuilt in a rustic classical style for Bernard Whalley, 1692. Small, with enclosed bellcote and added w porch. The chunky quoins and late C17 windows are at once recognizable. To the s a chapel-like family pew with an oculus window and a chimney. Inside, box pews and w gallery. The unexpected apse suggests a Romanesque predecessor. Traces of that early church remain, including herringbone masonry on the s and work in the N wall, which also has a blocked medieval doorway. Under the gallery stairs, the w respond of the former Norman N arcade. – Two important SCULPTURES mounted in the vestry. – One is from a free-standing cross or from the jamb of an arch. With a Romanesque Christ figure on one side, probably from a Harrowing of Hell, it was found in 1980 to have Anglo-Saxon carvings too. One is a foliage pattern (cf. a C10 slab excavated at St Oswald's Priory, Gloucester), the other a lozenge pattern of similar date. – The lively tympanum, rediscovered in 1980, shows a man pursued by evil forces. It and the Christ figure are identifiable as the work of a leading carver of the Herefordshire school of sculptors (cf. Kilpeck and Eardisley), *c.* 1140–50, and the use of north Cotswold oolitic limestone suggests they were carved locally and not imported as worked Herefordshire stone. – MONUMENTS. To the Mills, Knottesford and Getley families, mainly by *William* and *Peter Hollins* of Birmingham, †1820–1859.

BILLESLEY MANOR. Of Lias, built *c.* 1610–20 for Sir Robert Lee, son of a London merchant. The principal Jacobean front of seven windows faces s. Of the four dormer gables only two, at the ends, are original. The others belong to later adjustments, including the one above the projecting porch. The off-centre porch itself has Renaissance columns under a Tudor arch. Six-light mullioned-and-transomed windows, some renewed. Restored by *Detmar Blow* for Charles Hanbury Tracy after 1906. Blow also added the present entrance range at right angles on the E end, also with six-light windows. On the upper floor are two panelled rooms which also have Jacobean chimneypieces. Close to one of them was a priest hole. C18 library at the W end of the hall range. The galleried hall was created by *M. Eyre Walker & A.W. Harwood* for H. Burton Tate in 1921 but the heavily carved chimneypiece is old. Now a hotel and much extended, with a gabled ivy-clad block W of the original house, 1982. Various C17 and C18 outbuildings and barns. C18 rusticated gatepiers with urns to E and NE drives.

In the grounds S of the hall a MOUND, once thought to be an ancient tumulus but shown by excavation in 1927 to be the burial place of a favourite horse, probably C18.

SE of the church, earthworks and the moat of the old manor near the DOVECOTE mark the site of Billesley Trussell, a substantial pre-Conquest village deserted in the late C14.

BILTON GRANGE

½ m. NE of Dunchurch

4070

Alongside an earlier C19 house still standing at the NW, the Grange was built by *Pugin* for Capt. J. H. Washington Hibbert, a relative by marriage of the Earls of Shrewsbury. Hibbert, who also commissioned St Marie's in Rugby (p. 533), was Pugin's most difficult client. The first designs were prepared in 1841 but Hibbert wanted something grander. The plans were revised in 1844 and the main works were completed 1846–7. *George Myers*, the builder, worked here from 1841 to 1851. Their creation was described in 1861 as 'one of the best modern examples of Tudor Architecture in the kingdom'. The whole is emblazoned with family initials, crests and insignia, most notably in the open-work black-letter inscription in the balustrade on the garden terrace wall.

The Grange has been a school since 1887, with additions including the chapel and wing lining both sides of the approach to the main entrance. But Pugin's house is readily identifiable as the middle part with the grand entrance tower with its stepped pyramid roof, the Great Hall immediately to the r., and the wing projecting on the garden side. The wing has four even gables and four even canted bay windows below them. The portion adjoining this at right angles is also Pugin's in the part nearest to the centre. All red brick with black brick initials and patterns. Gothic windows, dormers and embattled tops to the bays. Inside, a gallery, 103 ft (32 metres) long, running right through. Off it, the library and drawing room fronting the terrace. In the N range, a fine staircase with carved beasts and painted ceiling. This rises from the passage leading to the dining hall which resembles the hall of a university college. Grand fireplace, screen and gallery and a splendid roof with curved principals and Y-shaped rafters. – Rich internal decoration by Pugin (executed by *J. G. Crace*), mainly 1846–8. All

Bilton Grange, aerial perspective.
Engraving, 1861

now more readily appreciated thanks to late C20 restoration and the reintroduction of brightly coloured wallpapers. Several excellent chimneypieces and a fine patterned floor of *Minton* tiles in the entrance hall (presently carpeted over). Heraldic STAINED GLASS by *Hardman*.

The added S WING has the initials of Walter Earle, the headmaster, and the date 1891 in the brickwork. The style neatly complements Pugin's.

The CHAPEL was built in 1889–92; by *Garlick & Sykes* of Preston, with apse and octagonal belfry. Collegiate-style interior. – STAINED GLASS probably by *Burlison & Grylls*, c. 1890, but one N window is older. – War memorial PANELLING by *S. Gambier Parry*, 1919.

Service wing and courtyard with stabling and coach house to NW, all pre-1861. On Rugby Road, a LODGE of 1853 and, opposite, 'model cottages for labourers' (Nos. 97–99 Rugby Road) with polychromatic brickwork, by *John Birch*, 1873. Another lodge on Ashlawn Road at the end of the N carriage drive created for John Lancaster after 1861.

BINLEY *see* p. 281

BINLEY WOODS *see* p. 282

1050   BINTON

ST PETER. Entirely rebuilt 1875–6 by *Preedy*. It cost £3,500, towards which the Marquess of Hertford gave £2,000. Lias

and golden stone. SW porch tower, nave, chancel and transepts. E.E. style with lancets and geometrical, intersecting and
plate tracery. Pierced tracery parapet to tower. Simple interior
with bare plaster walls and mostly contemporary fittings. Tomb
recesses over coffin-lids in N, S and E walls. – FONT. C15,
octagonal. FONT COVER. Said to be 1640, of ogee ribs,
diamond-studded (cf. Idlicote). At the top an urn. – Light oak
SCREEN, 1924. – CHEST. Dug-out type, 8 ft 2 in. (2.5 metres)
long, medieval. – STAINED GLASS. E window by *Lavers,
Barraud & Westlake*, 1876. – Three by *Kempe & Co.*, 1910–15.
N window, 1913, incorporating the C15 Greville arms from the
old church. The W window, 1915, commemorates Captain
Robert Falcon Scott and his ill-fated polar expedition in 1912.
Scott was married to the rector's daughter.

At the CHURCHYARD entrance, steps by the gate. SE of the
porch, the stump of the CROSS adapted as a sundial.

The GRANGE (former rectory), S of church with good aspect to
the Avon valley. H-plan in stuccoed brick with hipped tile roof,
C18. N front by *Robert Payne*, 1821.

Facing Church Bank, the curved stone wall to Stonebank has a
DRINKING TROUGH AND FOUNTAIN with lion's head and
pipe in an arched recess dated 1868. An added stone with
inscription above, 1870. Round the corner, another recess and
water hole, 1872. All with the initials of William Jackson, who
provided this delightful amenity.

Binton has one long street, MAIN ROAD, rising up the bank
from the church. Some timber-framed cottages, some brick but
mostly local Blue Lias and many thatched. The VILLAGE
HALL (former school) and adjacent house, 1873, possibly by
Preedy. Further up, the EBENEZER CHAPEL, 1866, and manse,
now one house, form a good group. The chapel with round-
headed windows, the house with segmental window arches,
unified with fish-scale tiling.

Outside the village centre, an 1830s brick farmhouse with hipped
slate roof at LOWER BINTON, ½ m. E. In the Avon valley, W
of the bridge, the remains of BINTON STATION, including
goods shed and station building, both Lias, probably 1879.

At REDHILL, 2 m. N, a Georgian stone farmhouse on an awkward
site by the Alcester–Stratford road. Alongside, THE STAG,
with Victorian Gothic windows re-set in the range facing the
road.

BIRDINGBURY

4060

ST LEONARD. Built in 1774–5 to replace a medieval church with
funds left by Charles Biddulph in 1752. A Georgian front with
four Doric pilasters, pediment and octagonal cupola. In the
front just a doorway. Then, in 1875, the Victorians made it

'more church like'[*] and, being so sure of the rightness of their convictions, raised the roof, dwarfed the façade, altered the windows, and added a full-blown Gothic polygonal apse, thickly shafted, and vaulted. *John Cundall* of Leamington was the architect. Inside, the apse has a richly painted ceiling and encaustic floor tiles. C18 WEST GALLERY now contained within three tall Victorian arches. – FONT. Of stone, with a baluster stem. – PULPIT, C18. With pretty marquetry. – BOX PEWS. – STAINED GLASS. One N window by *Hardman*, 1876, the rest 1875 and 1879, probably by *Clayton & Bell*.

BIRDINGBURY HALL, N of the church. Large, symmetrical, Jacobean mansion, built for the Shuckburgh family in the early C17 and owned by the Biddulphs from 1687 to 1914. U-plan with mullioned-and-transomed windows. N wing rebuilt after a fire, 1859. In the centre, a late C19 porch with Tuscan columns and keyed archway. Galleried entrance hall with ornate C19 fireplace. In the S wing a staircase of *c.* 1630 with a thick openwork balustrade and carved finials. The Georgian domestic staircase is said to come from Kenilworth Castle. To the NE, the former STABLES (converted to residential use *c.* 1979) with cupola, built for Sir Theophilus Biddulph, 1742–5, probably by *Richard Trubshaw*. LODGE by *H.B. Creswell*, who also did alterations to the hall itself in 1910–11.

Former RECTORY, S of the church, *c.* 1830. Stuccoed with Doric porch and elliptical fanlight.

BISHOP'S ITCHINGTON

ST MICHAEL. 1872–3 by *Ewan Christian*, retaining parts of the E and S of the old church. Large, with N aisle and vestry, S porch and W tower with pyramid roof. Dec detail. Blue Lias with Bath stone dressings and Sherwood Sandstone columns. Additional rooms N of the church, 1981. Nave and aisles re-seated with chairs. Striking open stair to upper room under the tower. Tower restored by *Mark Evans*, 2011. – Marble, mosaic and *Minton* tile REREDOS, by *Christian*, 1878. – SCREEN and low wooden PULPIT, late Gothic, 1940. – STAINED GLASS. E window, 1873. – N aisle *Holland & Holt*, 1881. – Chancel *Hardman*, 1882.

CEMETERY, ½ m. N, with small apsed chapel by *Francis P. Trepess*, 1903–4.

Former CONGREGATIONAL CHAPEL, Chapel Street. 1836. Three-bay front with two tiers of pointed windows under a large pedimental gable. Lancet side windows. A house since 1981.

---

[*]As George Miller observed in 1889.

OLD SCHOOL with teacher's house in Fisher Road, 1871 with later additions. Brick, minimal Gothic. Nearby in Poplar Road, the separate infants' school by *Trepess*, 1902.

A large village with extensive housing for the workers at the Blue Lias quarries and cement works which closed in 1970. Among the earliest are terraces of brick cottages in Old Road, Fisher Road and Hambridge Road, boldly dated 1892 and 1902. In 1914 *Clough Williams-Ellis* prepared plans for a small development to be called Lakin's Hamlet, but only one cottage (No. 21 Station Road) seems to have been built. In Fisher Road the MEMORIAL HALL has a reinforced concrete frame with local aggregate blocks. Designed and built by *Wilson Lovatt & Sons* of Wolverhampton, 1921.

Immediately w of the church, the OLD VICARAGE, partly of 1821 but modernized and refaced in 1873. E of the church, although fronting Fisher Road, was THE MANOR (or The Mansions), a C17 house demolished in 1964–5.

THE COTTAGE, ½ m. NNE. By *Voysey* for M.H. Lakin, a proprietor of the cement quarries, 1888. Enlarged in 1900 when two N wings were added. W porch 1982. The original main entrance was on the s. The older part is Voysey's first country house, but his hallmark style is already fully developed. Roughcast, with varied fronts, decorative buttresses with much batter, a big, comfortable roof, and horizontal windows in the Jacobean tradition. The principal rooms are the central entrance hall, entered by an off-centre s porch; the main window is in the middle instead. In the rear courtyard, a kind of gallery with a square bay and plenty of window. Voysey's original scheme also included the layout of the gardens.

BISHOP'S TACHBROOK   3060

ST CHAD. Nave and chancel Norman in outline but only discernible in the angles of the nave and in blocked windows (partially obscured) to the vestry on the N side of the chancel. The resited N doorway is also Norman and has one order of columns and pellets in the hoodmould. Good N and s arcades of similar form, the piers and arches with continuous mouldings. The s arcade has shallow bases with chamfers, late Dec. On the N the bases are deep with mouldings and the whole arcade is finer and later, probably early Perp. The windows of both aisles and also the clerestory windows are straight-headed, with ogee-headed lights. Perp w tower with high arch to the nave. Chancel restored by *James Murray*, 1854–5, with refaced side walls, new window tracery on the s, rebuilt chancel arch and new E end. Piecemeal later C19 restoration including work by *John Cundall*, 1885, and the vestry by *F.G. Cundall*, 1898. – Two FONTS, one Victorian, the other with a plain bowl, probably C12, recovered in 1928. – PULPIT with attached

LECTERN and low SCREEN wall. High Victorian, with coloured bands, inlaid cross and marble shaft. Brass and iron
fittings for lectern and lamp. By *G. T. Robinson*, with relief
carving signed by *S. P. Wood*, 1861. – STAINED GLASS. E
window by *Heaton, Butler & Bayne*, 1893 (replacing one by
Holland, 1858). – Others by the same in S aisle, E and S, 1893
and 1909. – N aisle E by *Morris & Co.*, 1863, commissioned by
Thomas Garner whose first recorded independent work this
was. In memory of John Garner, the architect's uncle. The
Presentation scenes (by *William Morris* himself) are described
by Charles Sewter as Morris's most elaborate and ambitious
figure compositions. Background and emblems by *Philip Webb*.
– Three in N aisle †1871–4, probably by *Wailes* (AB). – The rest
by *Hardman*, †1888 to 1935 and (W window) 1982. – MONU-
MENTS. John Rous †1680, wife †1686/7, and Lady Crewe
†1696. Uninspired and old-fashioned. Attributed to *Thomas
Cartwright I*, *c.* 1696 (GF). – Sir Combe Wagstaffe †Jan 1667/8,
but probably made by *Andrew Carpenter c.* 1712–15 (GF). Big.
Of reredos type, grey and white marble. Corinthian columns;
arms and garlands at the top. No figures. – Sir John and Alice
Wagstaffe (*née* Stanton), both †1681. Nowy-headed tablet with
columns, shield and flaming urns. By *Edward Stanton*, made *c.*
1710 (GF). – Sir Thomas Wagstaffe †1708 and Frances †1706.
Again by *Stanton*, and also of grey and white marble. Also of
reredos type, but smaller. Segmental top, urn with weeping
putti.

Around the church are a number of timber-framed cottages,
mainly box-framed, some thatched. Otherwise a village of C20
housing. Former SCHOOL at the foot of the hill E of the church,
by *G. T. Robinson*, 1863. Nearby THE LEOPARD has a cruck
dendro-dated to 1413–14. In Savages Close opposite, the C16
MANOR is H-plan with three gabled bays and C19 extensions.
Further N, TACHBROOK MALLORY HOUSE has dates 1570
and 1609. Both said to have good C16 and C17 interiors. In
between them is CHAPEL HILL FARM, where the shell of a
stone chapel survives in the rear wing of a later farmhouse.
The chapel is first mentioned in 1336 but fell into disuse after
1505. Until the 1970s there was fragmentary evidence of the E
window and the division between nave and chancel was represented by internal buttresses.

Outside the village, two good early C20 Arts and Crafts houses
by *P. Morley Horder*. On Banbury Road, GREYS MALLORY
(originally called Greystoke) of 1903–4 for A.E. Batchelor,
with lodge and archway to the road. Stables and clock turret.
Jacobethan-style house restored following a fire in 2010.
MALLORY COURT (now a hotel) on Harbury Lane was built
for J. T. Holt, 1914–15. C17 vernacular with steep gables and
tall brick chimneys. Wood-panelled interior with simple stone
fireplaces. The pool garden behind the house belongs to
Horder's contemporary landscape design.

GUIDE DOGS NATIONAL BREEDING CENTRE, Banbury
Road. By *Broadway Malyan*, 2010–11. Separate gull-winged,

glulam-roofed pavilions round a central courtyard with facilities for breeding 1,550 puppies a year.

OAKLEY WOOD CREMATORIUM, 1¼ m. SSW off Wellesbourne Road. *Sir Guy Dawber, Fox & Robinson (Christopher Robinson)*, 1969–71, for the Mid-Warwickshire Crematorium Committee. In mature woodland, with the buildings almost hidden among the trees. Two chapels, the larger to the S with curved walls but based on a hexagon plan indicated internally by six concrete pilasters. Vertical windows and copper-clad spike. The N chapel smaller and in brick. The chapels are separate but linked by covered walkways and pedestrian courtyards.

OAKLEY WOOD CAMP, SE of the crematorium. Roughly triangular in plan. The principal enclosure covers about 9 acres (3.6 ha) with further earthworks beyond. The best preserved portion is on the N, where the bank still stands 12 ft (3.64 metres) high and 27 ft (8.23 metres) wide. Gaps in the embankments on the E and W are probably the original entrances. Now regarded as a medieval woodland management feature rather than an Iron Age fort as was once believed. Acle or Ocle (i.e. Oakley) wood is mentioned in documents from the late C12.

BLACKDOWN
3060

A rural area between the N side of Leamington and the River Avon, including outlying parts of Cubbington, Lillington and Old Milverton. In the later C19 it became fashionable for residences of successful business and professional families.

BLACKDOWN HALL (originally Blackdown Hill) is Jacobean with mullioned windows and gables built in 1859 for Leamington solicitor Algernon Sydney Field, along with a lodge with cross-loopholes at the Sandy Lane entrance. Now flats (badly damaged by fire, 2014). For Field's son Henry, *Horace Field* designed THE QUARRY (now a clinic) in Sandy Lane towards Old Milverton, 1891–2; red brick Jacobethan, with large shaped gables. BERICOTE HALL on the ridge above Blackdown is a gloomy plain house of the late 1860s, built for John Whitehead Greaves, proprietor of the Llechwedd slate quarries in North Wales and chairman of the Blaenau Ffestiniog Railway. Across the Stoneleigh Road towards Cubbington is WESTHILL, an Italianate house of *c.* 1875 by *Payne & Talbot* for Henry Ellis, with lodges. On the Kenilworth Road, WOODLAND GRANGE (now a hotel with substantial additions). Neo-Tudor of *c.* 1889 with half-timbered gables, built for Major Warner Brooks. CASTELL FROMA (*see* Lillington, p. 429) also belongs with these houses for the well-to-do.

BLACKDOWN MILL, on the Avon in Hill Wootton Road. The mill is said to have medieval evidence, but the main three-storey structure is C18 on the river side and C19 on the w. The mill-wheel survives, visible through a central archway. Timber-clad lucam also central. Tall brick chimney behind. Converted to residential use, with plenty of quaint late C20 embellishments. MILL HOUSE opposite, probably C18.

BLACKWELL
1 m. W of Tredington

A small hamlet. Cotswold stone and brick, but pleasantly varied. C17 BLACKWELL GRANGE is stone, L-plan, with a thatched BARN nearby. GABLES FARM, also C17, has gabled dormers and mullioned windows and a brick extension, 1897. Early C19 HOME FARM has chequered brickwork. Further E, LOWER FARM, dated 1627. The former humble CHAPEL, C19, is stone-fronted but with brick end wall.

BOTTS GREEN

BOTTS GREEN HOUSE. The date 1593 on the gable above the porch is not ancient, but a later C16 date fits the house. It is large and timber-framed with the timbers exposed (and in parts just painted on). Much herringbone strutting, also concave-sided lozenges and cusped concave-sided lozenges. There are also two panels with the timbers formed into fleurs-de-lys. The l. and r. ranges have C16 windows projecting forwards on bracketed sills. The porch is of sandstone, with a fluted frieze above the doorway and in the sides cusped concave-sided lozenges of stone which could be medieval. Inside, the entrance is through a stone vaulted passage separating two fireplaces. The main room has a massive fireplace with a Tudor arch. On it a frieze of shallow pilasters carved with fleurs-de-lys and fluting, the initials RB and IB at the ends, and above the centre a treble rose carved in stone. In the grounds, a two-storey outbuilding with sandstone base and pretty timber framing above. Gatepiers and garden walls.

To the S, THE BOTHIE. Part timber-framed and part stone, incorporating a C15 cruck-built open hall with C17 additions.

BOURTON-ON-DUNSMORE

ST PETER. Low, with a SW steeple. C14, but much restored. The chancel masonry is medieval with intersecting Y-tracery in the

E window. Inside there are medieval parts left including the S arcade. Restored in 1842 and 1850 under *J. L. Akroyd*.* The chronology is uncertain, but work began with the chancel, vestry and partial re-seating of the nave in 1842. The external remodelling of the nave, S aisle and steeple came later. The top stage of the tower turns octagonal and carries a stone spire with lucarnes. N aisle added 1858. Big N transept or Shuckburgh family chapel. – FONT. Octagonal, with bald pointed trefoils under gables. Early C14? – PULPIT. Dated 1607. A two-decker. Some decorated panels. – COMMUNION RAIL. Jacobean. – BOX PEWS, 1842. – STAINED GLASS. Chancel windows, 1842, and further patterned glass in N chapel, *c.* 1850, all with the Shuckburgh motto. – In the S aisle one by *Kempe*, 1902, another by *Heaton, Butler & Bayne*, 1925. – MONUMENT. Effigy of a lady; *c.* 1300. She wears a wimple. By her pillow two defaced angels. – In the N transept, a good assembly of C18 floor slabs, hatchments and C19 Gothic wall monuments to the Shuckburghs.

Former BAPTIST CHURCH (now a house) at Draycote, ½ m. E. Rebuilt 1869 for a church established in 1811. Lancets.

BOURTON HALL. The seat of the Shuckburghs from the late C16 to 1906. The present stately ashlar house was begun by John Shuckburgh in 1791. The S side with symmetrical canted bay windows is typically Later Georgian and the three-bay pediment on the entrance front must be original too. Extensions *c.* 1880, including an extensive N service wing. Remodelled with pedimented window surrounds and balustraded parapets by *Charles M. C. Armstrong* for James Shaw in 1906–7. *Armstrong* also did the Italianate SW loggia, in brick with Venetian window and delicate stone columns. Then in 1908 *Harold A. Peto* added the private ROMAN CATHOLIC CHAPEL and its linking two-storeyed wooden quadrant gallery. The chapel has a Quattrocento façade and a marble portal with a copy in relief of Raphael's *Sposalizio* in the tympanum. Inside, marble walls and a gilded panelled wood ceiling. *Peto* laid out the gardens, and *Armstrong* designed the STABLE BLOCK and entrance LODGE. After years of decay Bourton was restored for Ingersoll from 1981 and is now in multiple commercial occupancy.

In the village, the former SCHOOL, founded 1836 and rebuilt 1847. Schoolroom and teacher's residence with Gothick details. Nearby typical Victorian ESTATE COTTAGES, one dated 1856.

VILLAGE HALL at the corner of Frankton Road, by *Lathams*, 2006. Attached to it is a delightful curiosity, a C19 gault brick building which began as an ornamental cottage for a poor widow built for Lady Shuckburgh, i.e. after her husband's death in 1837. Bowed veranda with slender iron columns,

---

* *Joseph Potter* of Lichfield, who remodelled the former rectory in 1840, is generally credited with the restoration, but this may be an error. Only *Akroyd*'s name occurs in the documents.

radiating arms, curved eaves brackets, central chimney and fish-scale slate roof.

BRAILES

A long village straddling the Shipston–Banbury road. There are two main settlements. The church is at Lower Brailes, while Upper Brailes is on the w towards Shipston. Winderton (q.v.) is another. Brailes was a place of some importance at the time of Domesday and achieved the right to hold a market and fair in 1248. Its prosperity in medieval times is reflected in the grandeur of the church. Later, Brailes remained a large village instead of developing into a small town.

16 ST GEORGE. A large church with a commanding w tower – 'the Cathedral of the Feldon'. C13–15, but mostly 1325–72. Restored by *William Smith* (who became William Bassett Smith *c.* 1882), 1877–9, included the rebuilding of the chancel arch and the whole N aisle and clerestory. Smith also created the charming Sanctus-bell turret on the E gable. N organ chamber and vestry enlarged 1892–3. There must have been an earlier church but the oldest part of the present building is the s aisle, with typical late C13 windows (three stepped lancet lights, three-light cusped intersecting). The s doorway has three continuous mouldings, two of them of an unusual profile. Pretty, close corbel table with heads, monsters, etc. On this side only the broad s porch and the openwork parapet are Perp. The tower Perp too, tall and thin, yet still mighty. Big five-light w window. Twin two-light transomed bell-openings. The chancel is Dec with red sandstone window details. The large five-light E window is later and not of red stone. Its tracery is reticulated. On the s, a big four-light Perp window inserted. Dec also the N aisle and the clerestory, their windows of two lights and straight-headed. On both sides, tall crocketed central pinnacles on the nave parapets. The clerestory has twelve windows on either side corresponding to six bays inside, unusual in this region but very impressive inside. The six-bay arcades have octagonal piers and double-chamfered arches, but they differ in many ways. The s arcade comes first. Its bases and capitals are far from uniform. Part of the arcade is probably late C13, part early C14. The N arcade is Dec, but rebuilt. Tower arch tall, with three continuous hollow chamfers.

In the chancel Dec SEDILIA, the seats proper seats with stone arms, these rather crudely heightened. Ogee arches. – REREDOS with pink marble cross and shafts, 1879. Elaborately carved, with an imitation of the s aisle parapet on top. – FONT. Dec, of the pattern-book type, with eight different tracery patterns. Good wooden cover by *Bassett Smith*, 1886.

– CHEST, C15 also with traceried carving. – SCULPTURE. Part of a reeded shaft. On it foliage and a sow with piglets. – Two carved spandrels from the W doorway, one dated 1649 when the church was repaired after Civil War damage. – ROYAL ARMS, 1722. – STAINED GLASS. In five S aisle windows, six C16 or C17 Flemish pieces, restored and re-set 2000. – W and E windows *Ward & Hughes*, 1878 and 1880. Associated memorial tiles alongside the E window. – Two in clerestory, *A. L. Moore*, 1879. – N aisle (E to W) by *Ward & Hughes* 1884, *Joseph Bell & Co.* (*Geoffrey Robinson*) 1995, *Clayton & Bell* 1914, *William Glasby* 1925 and (W) *T. F. Curtis, Ward & Hughes* 1910. – S aisle E, *A. L. & C. E. Moore*, 1928. – S aisle W, *Ward & Hughes*, 1879. – MONUMENT. Tomb-chest with plain panels and a defaced effigy; C15. – Richard Davies †1639. On top of the tablet a carefully arranged still-life of books, their spines to the rear.

In the CHURCHYARD a fine open Gothic LYCHGATE, 1910. On the E wall of the chancel, a memorial to John Austin, Roman Catholic priest, †1809. To the N, a granite memorial with bronze sphinxes to Henry John, 'last of the Sheldons', †1896.

ST PETER AND ST PAUL (R.C.). On the upper floor of a barn attached to the RECTORY FARM, E of the church. Adapted and fitted out for Fr George Bishop in 1726, some years before the Acts of 1778 and 1791 allowing the Mass and permitting Catholic chapels. Contemporary panelling, COMMUNION RAIL and ALTARPIECE of the Crucifixion. Wooden cross-windows, evenly spaced. PRESBYTERY alongside, also in converted premises. All restored 1992–3.

At Lower Brailes, the OLD PARSONAGE. Of many dates, with a stone wall on the side adjoining the churchyard. Enlarged by *Matthew Hastings*, 1817, and altered by *William Smith*, 1864. On the road below, the INSTITUTE, 1886, like a schoolroom. W of the green, 1840s LOWER BRAILES HOUSE, double-fronted and bargeboarded, has an intricate porch with columns and openwork pediment. Good corner group beyond The George, where an archway has the datestone 'H.A. 1844'. This led to the yard of Attwoods, the Brailes builders who built and restored several schools and churches in the area from the 1840s to 1880s. The OLD SCHOOL, nearby, by *Smith*, 1858–9, was built by *Attwood*.

Opposite, the driveway to BRAILES HOUSE, in parkland N of the road. Built in 1822 for the Sheldons after they vacated Weston Park. A plain house. Brick-walled KITCHEN GARDENS to rear.

Towards Shipston, NOOK FARM at the corner of Sutton Road also by Attwood, 1858.

The pretty rock-faced hexagonal LODGE at the corner of Castle Hill Lane belonged to SPRINGFIELD HOUSE behind. The house early C19, stuccoed with Greek Doric porch. The lodge, *c.* 1860. The earthworks on CASTLE HILL belong to the C12 motte-and-bailey castle of Roger Newburgh, Earl of Warwick. A crescent-shaped platform instead of a bailey proper.

70

In Upper Brailes, the former PRIMITIVE METHODIST CHAPEL at the back of the green, 1863, with round-arched keystoned windows. Along the road a good mix of brick and stone, slate and thatch. Early C19 HILLSIDE HOUSE is three storeys, brick with quoins, slate roof and Greek Ionic porch. Further N, ironstone GABLE END has the top of a two-light Dec window re-set in the gable.

BRAMCOTE

1½ m. NE of Bulkington

3080

BRAMCOTE HOSPITAL. 1913; small. Built as a Sanatorium for Consumptives and later adapted as an isolation hospital. W extension to admin block by *R. C. Moon*, the Nuneaton Borough Surveyor, 1937. Additional buildings to the rear.

GAMECOCK BARRACKS. Began as an airfield in the Second World War, transferred to the Royal Navy as HMS Gamecock in 1946 and used by the army since 1959. The M69 motorway was built over the runway. Wartime buildings include the concrete, flat-roofed control tower, and five large hangars. Traditional post-war admin building by the main gate. (Chapel with E window by *Camm*, 1950s.)

BRANDON

4070

BRANDON CASTLE, across the Avon from Wolston church (q.v.). All that is visible is earthworks and a few small fragments of rubble. Excavations have shown the castle to be of C12 origin, with a late C13 oblong keep.

The AVON VIADUCT on *Robert Stephenson*'s London to Birmingham Railway was completed in 1835–8; *Samuel Henning*, contractor. Elliptical arches, rusticated voussoirs and strong detailing.

The viaduct separates the castle from the village, which has some timber framing and thatch, but also larger houses of brick. In the main street are the BRANDON CLUB, 1885, and former SCHOOL, 1888, both built for the Beech family of Brandon Hall.

NW of the village, BRANDON HALL HOTEL is built around the early C19 lodge built by *Robert Lugar* for Lord Grey de Ruthin. Of the rustic villa illustrated in Lugar's *Plans and Views* (1811), sections of the S and E façades remain recognizable.

At BRETFORD, 1¼ m. ENE, an C18 BRIDGE of five arches carrying the Fosse Way over the Avon. To the N, timber-framed OAKDENE has large framing with curved braces and a jettied gable-end to the cross-wing. Recent study has identified three main periods of construction, starting with the hall of *c.* 1420 and ending with the cross-wing in *c.* 1471.

BRINKLOW

4070

On the Roman Fosse Way, which is crossed N of the village by the Oxford Canal (1774) and the Trent Valley Railway (1847). From the canal there are arms leading to wharves in Stretton and Brinklow.

ST JOHN THE BAPTIST. E.E. chancel. The rest late Perp. On a sloping site, with a steep rise in floor levels from E to W. Chancel with lancets N and S. E window of intersecting tracery. Perp aisle windows and timber N porch. The N doorway has a straight-sided arch and is panelled in reveals and soffit. The W tower has panelling l. and r. of the doorway, and the diagonal W buttresses (four sides of a hexagon) end in canopied niches. Inside, the arcades are of five narrow bays with typical late Perp section and no capitals. The bases are stepped as the ground rises. Rood stair exposed in angle between chancel and S aisle. The chancel seems entirely Victorian within. The restoration was by *G. T. Robinson*, 1862. He was respectful of the old fabric but his rogueish hand is also visible in the roof, chancel arch and pastry-cutting round the windows, and the FURNISHINGS. – By Robinson the stone AMBO, PULPIT and panelled ends to N chapel ALTAR. – CHOIR STALLS and nave SEATING Robinson's too. – FONT. Octagonal, Perp, with fleurons. – TILING in the chancel, 1864. Victorian; *azulejos*, the Spaniard would say. – STAINED GLASS. Original bits in N and S aisle windows. Among them charming C15 roundels of fairly naturalistic birds, including a dead-frontal peacock. – E window by *Francis Barnett* of Leith, 1863. A N chancel window also 1863. – One S chancel window by *Edwin Horwood* of Frome, 1872. – W window by *Hardman*, 1870. – In S aisle W, figure of St George, from Coventry All Saints, by *Powell*, 1921. Installed here 1972.

UNITED REFORMED CHURCH (Congregational), Broad Street. 1827 with extension towards the street by *Walter Hattrell*, 1913–4. Classical front.

MOTTE-AND-BAILEY CASTLE, E and SE of the church. Norman, although on a hilltop site previously fortified by the Romans. There are no standing remains but the earthworks are impressive. The motte is at the E end, 40 ft (12.2 metres) high and 60 ft (18.3 metres) wide at the top; two baileys to its W. The castle helped to guard the Fosse Way.

SCHOOL, NE of the church. Begun 1827 and enlarged 1895, but mainly by *James Murray*, 1855. The house on the street with faintly Butterfieldian details, the schoolrooms behind, long and low.

Much variety along the village street, with some handsome houses among the timber-framed and thatched cottages. At the N end beyond the school, Tudor-style blue brick fronted CARLTON HOUSE, built *c.* 1840 for John Ferguson, resident engineer of the Oxford Canal. Then 1820s LOVEITTS FARM in yellow gault brick. Nearly opposite the church Nos. 31–35 The Crescent were originally one house, probably C15, timber-framed with jettied cross-wings at the ends. By the church the street widens into a small green. On the W lower down the COMMUNITY HALL, whose half-timbered front belongs to the original building by *Charles J. Hair* of Southampton, 1902. Nearer the S end, mid-C18 DUNSMORE HOUSE with rusticated stucco lintels to the windows and unusual arched windows and *œil de bœuf* in the upper storey.

In Coventry Road W, the OLD RECTORY, 1813–14 (*David Jones*, mason, and *Benjamin Tomlinson*, carpenter), again yellow brick. Further W, THE LODGE, also early C19. Three-storey, red brick with keyblock lintels. Doric porch with fanlight.

BROOM

1050

Former MISSION CHURCH (St Matthew), Mill Lane. *W. J. Hopkins*, 1878. Simple Gothic with lancets and bellcote. Residential conversion, 1994.

BROOM HALL pub, Bidford Road. Perhaps C16. Timber-framed on a stone plinth with closely set studding and four-gabled front.

BROOM COURT, ½ m. s. Incorporating parts of a substantial house built on a moated site for Sir Simon Clarke, *c.* 1618. C18 ashlar front with re-set Jacobean porch with Tuscan columns. Inside, C17 stairs and armorial windows. In the grounds, a stone wall with embattled parapet bears a shield with the Clarke arms, as re-set on the house.

BUBBENHALL

3070

ST GILES. A C13 church – see the red sandstone parts of the chancel with its lancets, the W tower with two late C13 Green Men as head corbels of the arch towards the nave (naturalistic foliage), and the nave with a finely moulded S doorway, but also Dec features (N doorway). The chancel arch is E.E. too, but has been moved a little to the E (inside it intersects the window opening), done in 1865–6 when the church was restored by *James Marriott* of Coventry. A builder's restoration, with *George Punshon* as Clerk of Works. The chancel E end was rebuilt, the N vestry added, the church re-roofed and, following local fashion, a stone AMBO and PULPIT* (cf. Stretton-on-Dunsmore and Marton) were placed in front of the resited chancel arch. The arch has two side arches and although this arrangement seems to be Victorian it too follows local precedent (cf. Baginton). Tower top C14, and W wall crudely buttressed with C19 brickwork. S porch rebuilt 1897, but retaining roof timbers dated 1616. NW extension by *Kenneth Holmes Associates*, 1999. – REREDOS of the Last Supper, by *W.J. Hopkins*, 1878 (carved by *Boulton*). – STAINED GLASS. E window by *Clayton & Bell*, 1866. – By *Kempe*, five chancel windows, 1888–9, and a nave window, 1902.

On Leamington Road, the three-storeyed OLD RECTORY with bold porch, 1840s, and bargeboarded Tudor SCHOOL by *W. Trepess*, dated 1864 in the brickwork. In Spring Hill, LONGFIELD, a half-timbered house created in 1932–4 by *H. T. Jackson* for Leonard Lee with much reused timber and fittings from C16 houses. Towards Baginton, ¾ m. WNW, a stone BRIDGE over the Avon, 1884.

BUDBROOKE

2060

ST MICHAEL. The blocked N doorway Norman with one order of shafts and a billet hoodmould. The chancel E.E. with lancet windows, one of them of the lowside type. The E window is Perp. There was formerly an E.E. S aisle too, its W part already demolished before the E bay was converted into a S transept by *D. G. Squirhill* in 1838. The outline of the arcade and a pier can be seen outside, datable by the now eroded dogtooth on the abacus. N transept added 1838. The gables and windows of both transepts are of *John Cotton*'s restoration, 1874–5. W tower, dated 1668, has a clumsy variety of Y-tracery and crocketed pinnacles but C17 mouldings on the string courses. Inside, both transepts have fully moulded arches with responds to the nave, one completely different from the other. Probably redone in a further restoration in 1882, a nice illustration of Victorian historicism. Internal reordering, 1995. – STAINED GLASS. E window by *William Holland*, 1846. – Tracery lights with early C19 glass in two S windows. – Chancel S window, probably by *Holland & Holt*, †1872. – MONUMENT. Rouland, 4th Baron Dormer of Wing, †1712, attributed to *Francis Bird* (GF). Outstandingly good, decidedly metropolitan tablet. Large inscription between pilasters, open segmental pediment with an urn and two trumpets, beautiful harpy-like angels outside the pilasters, drapery at the foot.

Immediately E, the CHURCH CENTRE by *Donald James*, 1992. Former VICARAGE, altered by *Cotton*, 1876, to the N. Otherwise the church stands alone.

---

*Removed in the 1950s.

On the site of Budbrooke Barracks, built in 1876–7 and demolished 1964, is HAMPTON MAGNA. A complete new village
with school, pub and shops, begun in 1965–6 by *Thorne &
Barton* for a private developer and since extended w. Mostly
unadventurous architecturally, apart from a group of late 1960s
houses with steeply monopitched roofs in Tithe Barn Close
and Old Budbrooke Road.

GROVE PARK. *See* Hampton-on-the-Hill.

BULKINGTON

A large parish including the hamlets of Bramcote (p. 166) and
Weston-in-Arden (p. 701). Bulkington was a centre of the ribbon-
weaving industry. The C18 brought access to the Coventry Canal
and later the Ashby-de-la-Zouch Canal near the parish boundaries. The Trent Valley Railway arrived in 1847. From 1894 until
1932 Bulkington had its own Urban District Council.

ST JAMES. High grey sandstone w tower, nicely decorated with
crocketed gables and a niche under the s belfry window. Of
the North Warwickshire type (cf. Curdworth), with almost
triangular openings and heavy carving, e.g. the winged beasts
as stops to the hoodmoulds. The tower arch and w window
surround both have mouldings more Dec than Perp, but nevertheless the tower must be mid-C15. The rest of the church
was re-roofed, re-seated and over-restored by *G. T. Robinson*
in 1865. Despite his intervention the chronology is clear. C12
fragments re-set in the porch. Then comes the s arcade of five
bays, early C13 with octagonal piers, double-chamfered arches
and elementary crocket capitals. The N arcade is later, but
probably not after 1300. The elements are the same. The N
wall of the same date has a tomb recess, finely moulded. In
the s aisle is what appears to be an untouched s window of no
later than 1300. Inside, it has Y-tracery cusped, with rolls. But
it may be Victorian, as an early C19 drawing (Aylesford Collection) shows this window with just a mullion and transom.
C14 s aisle and chancel but with renewed tracery. Perp clerestory with windows on the s side only. Straight-headed Perp
windows in the N wall too and another, with a tomb recess
below, in the s aisle. The Victorian chancel arch and the arch
to the N vestry are by *Robinson*, 1865, and try to beat the C13
at its own game. Enjoyably chunky. s porch rebuilt 1907. New
meeting rooms and facilities at the back of the nave, 2008–10.
– FONT. On an antique Roman column drum of coloured
marble brought back from the Grand Tour by *Richard Hayward*
of Weston Hall and given to the church in 1789. Hayward was
a gentleman sculptor of no mean achievement, as the pieces
here show. The first is his small white font bowl with figurines
like those on chimneypiece lintels. The Baptism of Christ is
represented, and also gifts being brought to the Virgin. The

four feet have panels with dolphin carvings. – Also by *Hayward* the oblong stone in the chancel, possibly from an ALTAR, with a small oval relief of the Last Supper. – Again by him, Carrara marble MONUMENT to his parents and family, made in 1781. Two angels l. and r. of the inscription, and above a graceful relief of a woman among Gothic fragments and in front of a ruinous Gothic building. – Mary and Richard Hayward †1788 and †1800. Circular relief with the mourning sister by a sarcophagus. Probably begun by *Hayward* and finished after his death. Erected by his sister. – ORGAN CASE, semi-classical and designed to complement the font below, by *Keith Robinson*, vicar, 1992. – NAVE SEATING, from a church in Rugby, 1992–3, replacing *John Russell*'s box pews of 1821 with light Gothic detailing. – Carved CRUCIFIX in the chancel arch, also by *Keith Robinson*. – STATUE of Our Lady in N aisle, by *John Letts*, 2000. – STAINED GLASS. E window probably by *Burlison & Grylls*, 1893. – N chancel by *William Holland & Son*, 1868.

ROMAN CATHOLIC CHURCH. *See* Weston-in-Arden.

CONGREGATIONAL CHAPEL, School Road. In a group with the manse, schoolroom and courtyard cottages. The chapel 1811, restored 1883. Plain pedimented front with round-arched windows. Galleries inside. The chapel and MANSE, 1821, have chequered brickwork.

RYTON METHODIST CHURCH, Rugby Road. 1911. Brick with white bands, fussy Arts and Crafts detail over main entrance and big Diocletian window.

A large and largely modern village. A pair of timber-framed cottages survives in Church Street (No. 4), and some pre-C20 cottages in Chequer Street, School Road and New Street. Otherwise redeveloped. No longer is the village street 'lined by late-18th-century houses and cottages' (VCH), nor do the three-storey ribbon-weavers' houses with broad windows on the top floor survive.

To the W, the former STATION on the Trent Valley Line by *J. W. Livock*, 1847. Tudorish, with ball finials on the gables.

BURMINGTON 2030

ST BARNABAS AND ST NICHOLAS. Traces of earlier fabric in the N chancel wall and in the foundations, but essentially a Victorian rebuilding. In 1849 *Thomas Johnson* re-cased or rebuilt the existing church,* adding a N vestry and extending the nave W. The NW tower with pyramid roof is also 1849, the spiral stair leading to the W gallery inside. Smooth ashlar walls. Lancets. The chancel arch has two big reused late C12 corbels, one with a trumpet-scallop capital. – Furnishings mostly 1849, including a square stone PULPIT with entrance from the vestry

---

* Sketch plans in the vestry illustrate its development. A partial collapse in 1688 necessitated major work in 1693, but of this nothing can be seen.

behind. – STAINED GLASS. A complete scheme of 1883, probably by *Ward & Hughes* (AB).

Stone MANOR HOUSE, immediately SW of the church, with timber framing on the side facing the church and a wall incorporating a late C12 blocked twin opening within a round arch, all in golden Cotswold stone, and an early C16 three-light window. These are not re-set as might be supposed. The twin opening is *in situ* and belongs to the solar range, altered in the C16 when new floors were inserted. But that is not all. W of the solar there are substantial remains of a two-bay aisled hall with timber arcades. Dendrochronology indicates a date of 1194/5. The main features are now exposed. The ends of the arcades are supported on stone stiff-leaf trumpet capitals. The centre has wooden pillars with capitals, one with well-preserved carving. The C16 roof incorporates smoke-blackened timbers from the original roof, enabling the form of the C13 roof structure to be determined.

A long village with the main buildings on a single street. N of the church and manor, the pretty little symmetrical, bargeboarded SCHOOL (now the VILLAGE HALL), founded in 1845 and enlarged seamlessly in 1871. The style is wholly 1840s. BURMINGTON FARM, 175 yds E, is C17 but has a street frontage in brick with stone quoins, dated 1730 on a stone panel set in a diamond of blue bricks. Alongside, a timber-framed granary with brick infill and slate pyramidal roof, on staddle-stones. Further E, the former RECTORY (now Hazlewood House) standing back from the road, 1848. At the crossroads BURMINGTON HALL, a large mid-Victorian three-storey house with classical porch and blue brick quoins.

BURMINGTON MILL (the House of Bread retreat), ¼ m. WNW by the Stour. A substantial four-storey building. With the nearby MILL HOUSE dated 1732 and adjacent cottages it forms an attractive group.

BURTON DASSETT

Burton Dassett is at the N end of the Dassett Hills, the site of the ancient village and former market town being on the western slopes of Church Hill (692 ft (211 metres)). The Black Death in 1348–9 and enclosure under Sir Edward Belknap around 1500 resulted in depopulation, so Northend and Little Dassett (p. 476) and Knightcote (p. 401) became the main settlements. The hilltop area, now in the country park, was extensively quarried for ironstone.

ALL SAINTS. On a sloping site, the E end dug into the hillside. An unforgettable church, not only for its position, but also because it seems so delightfully unrestored. Restored it was, but unobtrusively by *Jethro Cossins* with advice from SPAB in

1888–9 and again by *P. B. Chatwin*, 1935–7. It is of ironstone with two re-set Norman doorways and the NE quoin of the Norman nave, a good C13 N aisle and N transept (pairs of lancets and groups of stepped lancets, in the transept N window a circle above the group of four), a chancel of *c.* 1300 (Y- and intersecting tracery at the E end) with Dec windows in its W part (including a tall, transomed lowside window), a Dec ogee-headed N porch entrance, and Perp S aisle and S transept windows. The porch and W tower said to be *c.* 1335. C15 clerestory. Inside, seventeen steps from the tower to the altar. The interior is as varied as the exterior. It starts with the chancel arch, which has shafts with shaft-rings, a crocket capital on the N, but still with late Norman trumpet scallops on the S. Then follows the S arcade (octagonal piers, round capitals without carving, double-chamfered arches) and the arch into the S transept, and after that (or before it?) the N arcade with the same elements but a lot of most entertaining carving along the capitals and abaci, a foliage trail and plenty of beasties walking on the abacus. They include hounds and a rabbit, dragons, and also a man holding branches. Dogtooth on one capital. The date cannot be later than the late C13. A pity it is all so artless. The W arch into the N transept is later than its S counterpart. In the N transept N wall is a C13 tomb recess. Nice C15 traceried spandrels in N aisle roof. The long chancel is pleasantly white and bare inside and the whole interior remains plastered. – Overbearing wooden PULPIT, heavily carved with nailhead, ballflowers and fussy floral panels, 1920. – TILES. Many, C14 and others. – BENCHES. Two in the nave, with simple rounded ends. – WALL PAINTINGS discovered in 1966 and restored by *Eve Baker* in 1968. Above the chancel arch, painted over a C13 Doom of which traces are visible lower down, two censing angels with the Virgin Mary and St John. C14. The Virgin's face delightful, and the angels vigorous. – In the N transept, extensive C13 decoration on the N wall and in the window reveals, a figure holding his own severed head on one side and opposite a king raising up a covered gift. – In the nave and aisles more, C16 and C17. – MONUMENTS. Tomb-chest (N transept), plain, late C16. – John Temple †1603. Wall tablet with columns and painted coats of arms. Restored by *Sanderson Miller* for Earl Temple of Stowe, 1751–2. – Tomb-chest with scrolls etc. to John Swain †1658 and his wife Anne †1677 (S transept).

HOLY WELL, on the green N of the church. The well-house is of 1840, with a vaulted chamber and Grecian details to the entrance surround. Eroded inscription and carved roundels.

Former VICARAGE, N of the church. Dated 1696, but largely rebuilt by *John Plowman* of Oxford, 1846–7 with prominent bargeboarded gables.

BEACON, on the hill, ½ m. N. C15. Probably built as a tower mill, later converted into a look-out. Round, like a Martello tower, with top corbels resembling machicolations and a conical roof.

BURTON HASTINGS

St Botolph. Chancel C14. Perp w tower, oblong, ashlared and probably early C16. Nave with Perp tracery in N and S windows. Inside, a late Tudor arch within original opening to tower. Restoration by *H. Percy Smith* of Worcester, 1915–17, including chancel roof and S porch. – FONT. Of *c.* 1300. Pointed-trefoiled arches and in the tympanum rosettes and fleurs-de-lys. – Wrought-iron LECTERN, painted and decorated; a rather jolly piece, perhaps by *Skidmore & Co.*, 1860s. – STAINED GLASS. N window by *Roger Fifield*, 2001.

Among the slate headstones in the CHURCHYARD, two stone tomb-chests, 1850s and Graeco-Egyptian in style. Another on a mitred square column with an urn on top.

Facing the church, a decent C18 three-storey brick house, and another, GROVE FARM, to the W. Down Mill Lane, a stone BRIDGE over the Ashby Canal, *c.* 1800, and the MILL. The building unexceptional, but containing important C19 machinery and waterwheel.

In Hinckley Road NE of the church, pretty bargeboarded HOLLY HOUSE, an Overstone estate cottage, 1856. Then, 1½ m. NE, over the motorway, the OLD VICARAGE, in Queen Anne style by *Isaac Barradale* of Leicester, 1888.

At Stretton Baskerville, on Watling Street, STRETTON HOUSE with stables and outbuildings by *Goddard & Co.* of Leicester for Col. E. C. Atkins, 1912.

BUTLERS MARSTON

St Peter and St Paul. Externally an ironstone Perp w tower, a C14 S aisle remodelled in the C17, but otherwise mostly Victorian. *Thomas Naden* of Birmingham rebuilt the N wall, redid the chancel and added the vestry and S porch, 1867–8. Inside, a three-bay late Norman S arcade of round piers with flat leaf capitals, square abaci, and unmoulded but pointed arches. Flat mouldings round the arches (cf. Shotteswell and Warmington). No bases to the intermediate piers. The tower, restored in 1891, has carvings on the string course under the embattled parapet. – FONT. Octagonal, Perp, with quatrefoils. Carved wooden cover, 1934. – PULPIT. Octagonal with columns and carved panels, 1632. – Traditional chancel SCREEN, 1934. – Gothick S DOOR surviving from repairs under *William Kendall*, 1838. – BENEFACTION BOARD. Rustic, 1711. – STAINED GLASS. E window by *Holland*, 1863. – The rest by *Clayton & Bell*, 1869 (two) and 1875. – MONUMENT above S arcade. William Woodward †1684. Inscription on feigned drapery. Attributed to *William Stanton* (GF).

MONKSBRIDGE, S of the church, was exchanged for use as a vicarage and largely rebuilt by *H. J. Underwood* of Oxford, 1838–9. Extended and improved in 1846, 1868 and 1880.

N of the churchyard, THE MANOR, a substantial stone house with hipped roof. Five-bay S front, long rear section of nine bays and shorter N range. Largely *c.* 1660 for William Abraham, but in two builds and perhaps extended for the Newshams after 1682. Rainwater heads of 1848 relate to refurbishment for Letitia Woodward.

Former SCHOOL. By *William White*, 1871. Gothic with bell-turret, sympathetically extended since conversion as a house.

A compact village of grey and brown stone houses, including some built for Ernest Parke, an associate of George Cadbury, who embraced Cadbury's ideals by providing decent housing for agricultural workers. First, Nos. 9–10 in Bank Close, 1905, and then HALL COTTAGES to the S, curving round the corner of Fish Lane, 1913. Arts and Crafts style, with irregular quoins. Hall Cottages also have circular stones on the front and patterns in big stone blocks in the gable-ends. In 1926 Parke gave these cottages to the Bournville Village Trust whose architect *S. Alex Wilmott* added further cottages in Bank Close in 1926–7 (Nos. 38–41) and 1936 (Nos. 29–32). Beyond, the OLD CHAPEL (formerly Wesleyan), 1923; stone, pointed windows. Then, past C17 gatepiers with eccentric C20 gates and ironwork, is WESTMEADS. Probably built for William Woodward in the 1670s. Low with recessed front and hipped roof. Lumpish SE extension by *Seymour, Orman & Adie*, 1937.

CALDECOTE

3090

ST THEOBALD (formerly St David) AND ST CHAD. There are only three dedications to St Theobald in England. Rock-faced in Hartshill Quartzite with Attleborough sandstone dressings. Nave and chancel and small stone bell-turret with spirelet replacing a square brick tower of 1768. Late C13 bar tracery, mostly renewed by *Ewan Christian* in 1857. Christian's the imposing hammerbeam roof with angels, the seating and the added N vestry. Untouched only the actual arch of the chancel arch and the N door. *Minton* tiles throughout, those in the sanctuary richly coloured. This thorough restoration cost £2,200, borne by Kirby Fenton of Caldecote Hall. N organ chamber, 1885. – SCREEN. Fragment with intricate tracery, C14. – Superb carved and gilded REREDOS by the Rev. *Ernest Geldart*, 1896. – IRONWORK. S door with very long, thin hinges having loose profiled scrolls ending in stamped terminals, *c.* 1300. Style copied on C19 N door. – STAINED GLASS. Some medieval fragments in the W windows and the N vestry, set in quarry glass by *Powell*'s in 1857. – *Powell* quarries in nave windows, 1857. – Chancel S windows by *Kempe*, 1897, the rest – including the angels in the E window above the reredos – by *Kempe & Co.*, 1910. – MONUMENTS. Of the Purefoy family. Against the W wall two tablets with columns and entablature to Michael †1570 and Joyce †1585. – In the chancel, to their son William †1616 and his son Francis †1613. Large alabaster tablet with columns, obelisks, achievement, 1617. Kneeling figures, too large for the arched space allowed them. – Opposite, Michael (†1627), 1629. Kneeling figure, also between columns. – Adjacent, George Abbott (†1648). Alabaster, purely architectural, 1649.

CALDECOTE HALL. Victorian, but replacing a house dating back to the C15, home to the Purefoy, Abbot and Wright families and to Thomas Fisher, who refronted the old mansion in 1781. The present house is by *R. J. & J. Goodacre* of Leicester for Captain Henry Townshend, 1879–80. It cost almost £22,000. Two linked blocks, the main house (or w wing) and the E wing to the s. Red brick, free Jacobean with big stone porch to entrance front on NE side. It is not an inspired or an inventive design, the monotony of near symmetry in the elevations relieved only by minor variations (e.g. chimney configurations). After 1925 it was in institutional use, and after a fire in 1955 the E wing was converted into flats and part of the main block rehabilitated. The rest remained unrestored until residential conversion in 2008. To the s, a large STABLE range with clock tower, by the *Goodacres*, dated 1880. On Watling Street to the NE, a lodge.

An estate village with some C18 and early C19 buildings including a three-storey pedimented block with flanking cottages on the main street E of the hall's gates. Otherwise mostly by the *Goodacres*.

On Weddington Road to the N, the former SCHOOL (now the VILLAGE HALL), 1898. Alongside, a pair of ESTATE COTTAGES, both with black-and-white half-timbering.

The architect J.A. Hansom lived here, *c.* 1834–41, and built a house for himself (no longer extant) at the Mill Farm.★

CALUDON *see* p. 282

CANLEY *see* p. 283

3050   CHADSHUNT

ALL SAINTS (Churches Conservation Trust). A humble church, quite long, among trees on a bank above the road. w tower, nave, Early Georgian chancel and N chapel. Hornton stone. The nave is Norman, see the plain N and s doorways with their heavy mouldings and simple capitals, probably first half of the C12. The church was extended w in the C13 and heightened by the addition of the clerestory in the C15. The nave roof sturdy, with tie-beams and kingposts. The w tower is an addition of

★He was agent to Dempster Hemming of Caldecote and is said to have designed the Hansom cab while living here.

c. 1660 (bells 1669) although the lower part may be older. The chancel has a Venetian E window and a large round-arched window on the S. White panelling inside. Andor Gomme cites bank account evidence that the chancel may have been done by *Francis* and *William Smith* for the Newshams, *c.* 1734–5. The N chapel with its raised FAMILY PEW is of similar date but with significant Victorian alterations. It has its own elliptical-headed N doorway with direct access to the adjacent Hall (i.e. Chadshunt House). Discreet restorations in 1866, in 1905 by *C. Ford Whitcombe*, in 1933 by *P.B. Chatwin* and since 1988 for the Trust by *Rodney Melville & Partners.* – FONT. In the Norman style with arcaded decoration, but dogtooth ornament round the rim, so early C13. On a multiple moulded plinth. – Early Georgian COMMUNION RAILS, of wrought iron, part *in situ* and part removed to the chancel arch. – STAINED GLASS. In the N transept C16 glass brought from Italy by Robert Knight (†1772), Earl of Catherlough. It carries the date 1558. It was installed by one of the Knights in 1855. Their arms are depicted and one window has a monogram F.E.K. (possibly for Frances Knight). – MONUMENTS. Walter and Fridayswed Newsham, 1621. Pilasters with funerary emblems. – Michael Askel †1697 and others †1697–1712, erected by Susannah Askel, 1713. Large marble wall tablet by *Robert Taylor.* Mostly architectural, but with two small seated putti, one clasping a skull.

In the CHURCHYARD, the base of a medieval CROSS. Many fine ironstone headstones and chest tombs, C17 and C18.

CHADSHUNT HOUSE, N of the church, is a large but plain house altered in 1841–6 for Robert Knight, who acquired the estate in 1837, and for Edward Bolton King, who became tenant *c.* 1845. It replaced a gabled stone house built in 1631 for the Newshams who lived here from 1552 until 1764. Features of the Newsham parkland remain, including the brick boundary wall with gatepiers and C18 iron gates, the lake and avenues of trees to the N and W. The present house is rendered. Front of seven bays and return side of five bays, both with central pediments. At the back a later stone-mullioned window to the staircase. Victorian estate buildings mostly after 1837 (Knight spent £9,253 on improvements 1838–46) and later for King, who inherited by marriage in 1855. Knight built CHADSHUNT FARM in 1843. Work for King included the brick and stone stable block with courtyard, small groups of estate cottages and a pretty 1860s lodge on the Southam Road.

CHAPELFIELDS *see* p. 284

CHARLECOTE

Charlecote is an estate village. The Lucys have held the manor from the early C13, if not the C12. It was passed on in direct male descent till 1786, when John Hammond, grandson of Alice Lucy, assumed the name of Lucy. In 1892 another female Lucy, Ada Christina, married Sir Henry Ramsay-Fairfax, and the name was changed to Fairfax-Lucy. The house and park were handed over to the National Trust in 1946 but the Fairfax-Lucys still live here.

ST LEONARD. By *John Gibson*, 1851–3, replacing a medieval church on the same site. Built by Mary Elizabeth Lucy as a memorial to her husband, George, who died in 1845. Expensively done, lavishly detailed and heavily adorned with Lucy emblems and commemorative and religious inscriptions. Grey Warwick sandstone and highly Dec, the walls of a rather fussy hammered surface. Gabled buttresses and gargoyles. s tower with spiky spire. Chancel E end with a big Dec window. Family chapel N of the chancel with an E roundel and three N windows of spherical triangle form. Also a small NW turret and spire to the chapel. Nave of four bays simpler, w front again with a roundel. While the exterior was designed to look dignified from the house, the vaulted interior is serious and refined. Real stone tierceron vaults throughout, in the chancel liernes too. The chancel E window has a giant panelled arch inside with canopied niches at the ground level. The panelling continues round the arches of the family chapel and organ chamber on the N. – Contemporary wooden FURNISHINGS including CHOIR STALLS, the SCREEN to the family chapel, PULPIT and DESK, all carved by *Davis* of Taunton. – Ornate stone FONT, carved by *J. Tolmie*. Also Dec. Figurines against the stem. A lot of crocketing on the bowl. – STAINED GLASS. E window and Lucy Chapel E window by *Willement*, 1852. – Chancel and nave s windows by *O'Connor*, 1852–64, also w window, 1852. – Two N windows by *William Holland*, 1852. – One by *Kempe*, 1891, nave. – One, 1912, nave. – MONUMENTS. Three Lucys only: in the family chapel. Sir Thomas †1600 and wife. Alabaster. Tomb-chest with two recumbent effigies, very good in quality. – Sir Thomas †1605, or probably him. No inscription. Attributed to *Bartholomew Atye* and *Isaac James*. Also alabaster. Also recumbent effigy. Two black columns, two obelisks outside. His widow kneeling on the ground in front, the children in relief against the tomb-chest. – Sir Thomas †1640 and wife. White and black marble. Four closely set black columns in front carrying arches. Small top pediment. She is recumbent, he behind and a little above her, semi-reclining. Both are white. Behind on the r. a still-life composition of books. A book has Lucy's initials, T.L. The titles read Homer, Horace, Virgil, Cato, Pliny, Xenophon, Winter's Ayres. On the l. instead a landscape with Sir Thomas on horseback. Sir Thomas's effigy was carved by *John Schorman*,[*] but the overall design of the monument seems to have been by *Nicholas Stone*. The canopy

[*] It is documented in a transcript of a list of Schorman's works dated 1643.

has similarities with Stone's 1638 Spencer monument at Great Brington, Northants, where Schorman was one of his assistants.

CHARLECOTE PARK. As one approaches it through its broad gatehouse, the house strikes one as Elizabethan. What becomes clear on drawing closer is that it is largely a C19 interpretation of the Elizabethan style, skilfully worked into a genuine Elizabethan frame.

In outline, the building phases are these. Beginning soon after he inherited in 1551 Thomas Lucy, who became Sir Thomas in 1565, did away with the older house on the site, completing the present one by about 1558. The gatehouse came later, c. 1605. The C17 saw the establishment of formal gardens in the fashionable Dutch style with canals, pavilions and parterres for Captain Thomas Lucy in the 1670s. These were over-written by later changes, as was C18 work on the house by local architects – *Francis Smith, William & David Hiorne* and *Timothy Lightoler*. After their marriage in 1823, George and Mary Elizabeth Lucy set about a major remodelling of the house to make it more comfortable while preserving its Elizabethan character. When American writer Nathaniel Hawthorne described Charlecote in 1855 as a 'time-honoured hall' displaying 'a perfection of comfort and domestic taste and an amplitude of convenience' he confirmed that the Lucys had accomplished what they had hoped to achieve.

The remodelling left the footprint and outer walls of the 1551–8 house unaltered. The main changes were within the courtyard, clearly visible in the varied styles of brickwork but limited to subtle changes to the windows, gables and parapets. Inside, though, the changes were much more radical. There were two main phases, the first in 1828–37 and the second, for Mary Elizabeth alone, from 1849 until 1867. For the first phase the Lucys initially obtained plans from *Benjamin Dean Wyatt* in 1825 but concern about the expense forced them to rethink. In the event, the architectural work was handled by *Charles Samuel Smith* of Warwick, while the interior design was brilliantly done by *Thomas Willement*. For most of the work after 1849 *John Gibson* was the architect. His the canted bays to the forecourt of the house, 1852, alterations to the S wing, 1866, and other buildings in the park.

One begins at the GATEHOUSE, which dominates the approach. Long thought to be Elizabethan, and part of Thomas Lucy's original scheme of 1551–8, it is now dated to c. 1605, as the heraldry on the first-floor bay window is that of the 3rd Sir Thomas Lucy who succeeded in that year (Jeffrey Haworth). Like the house, it is of brick with grey stone dressings. It has polygonal angle turrets to the outside with ogee caps and vanes. The arch is round, and above it, also only to the outside, is an oriel window. The windows are mullioned-and-transomed, the lights no longer arched. Some of the windows are of two lights, i.e. of the cross-type. Along the flat top of the building runs a pierced balustrade with elongated rosette motifs. The passageway has a rib-vault with pendants, and to the l. and r. niches with shell apses, the details stylistically of the first decade of the C17.* The iron GATES with the initials of William Lucy are by *Nicholas Paris* of Warwick, 1722.

Next the house, the outside first. It is of 1551–8 and later, as already noted. Elizabethan in form is the PORCH, which is an example of the Northamptonshire type of Dingley, Deene and Kirby, all of *c.* 1560–72, and also Gorhambury (Herts.) of 1568. But is it of 1558 or, as Geoffrey Tyack suggests, of *c.* 1572, i.e. a showpiece erected for the visit of Queen Elizabeth in that year? Unfortunately much of the detail is C19 pastiche including the initials TL and IL for the first Thomas Lucy and his wife above the door; the royal arms and initials ER also seem to belong to this tinkering. It has two storeys, the lower with a round arch framed by pairs of fluted Ionic pilasters, the upper with pairs of Corinthian columns awkwardly projected on corbels with a fish-scale pattern. The top balustrade, possibly C17, has a Catherine wheel and heraldic beasts holding vanes. Inside the porch is a ceiling, ribbed and provided with a pendant as if it were a vault. The porch belongs to the recessed centre of the house, which has projecting wings. This façade faces E, and the porch is asymmetrically placed in the medieval way, l. of the Great Hall with its oriel window. The brickwork helps with dates here: diapering to the Tudor work, blackish-blue brick for the alterations of 1829–33 and plain brick generally later. The strapwork balustrading is a C19 feature. The three equal gables over the whole centre are not original. The two WINGS are far-projecting and have two gables and cross-windows to the forecourt. Each wing ends with one broad gable, a two-storey canted bay window (1852) beneath it, and an outer stair-turret. This arrangement of long wings and stair-turrets at their ends is typical of the mid C16 and compares e.g. with Long Melford and Rushbrooke, both in Suffolk.

The N front is an interesting example of composition, made very deliberately asymmetrical by the placing of the chimneys. At the two ends are, once more, turrets with ogee caps. Between them are three gables, two cut by the chimneys in two different places, one not cut at all. This is probably as originally built. The bird's-eye view of the house of 1696 shows that the gables and chimneys on the W front were of identical form. The W front is close to the River Avon. It has a single-storey extension by *C. S. Smith* dated 1833. The brick used here is blackish-blue again. Big symmetrical bay windows with angle pilasters and pinnacles. To the S, a large added wing in different red brick with Tudor-style dressings. The main block with the skimpy turrets is of 1829, but the S end with ogee-capped turrets dated 1866 is *Gibson*'s.

---

*I am grateful to Jeffrey Haworth for these suggestions regarding the date and style of the gatehouse.

Inside, the GREAT HALL was remodelled in the earlier phase under *Willement c.* 1830, the original oriel window to the fore-court being rebuilt and enlarged. The ribbed wood-looking ceiling of four-centred section is of plaster and an Elizabethan-looking chimneypiece boldly dated TL 1558 is part of the deceit too. The walls are hung with portraits and there are several busts.* The red and white floor of Venetian marble was laid in 1844. In the windows, original heraldic glass of *c.* 1558 by *Nicholas Eyffeler* of Warwick, brought up to date (1558–1823) by *Willement.*

The two rooms behind the hall, facing W, are the DINING ROOM and the LIBRARY. They are both of 1833, within the extension by *C. S. Smith* who did the stucco ceilings with pendants. The richly patterned flock wallpapers are by *Willement,* who also did the heraldic glass in the dining room (1016–1313) and library (1313–1600). In the DINING ROOM the gorgeous carved wooden SIDEBOARD is by *James Morris Willcox* of Warwick. It was made in 1858. On the top is Ceres with a huntsman and a fisherman. Below them, representations of the fruits of land and sea and much else. In the LIBRARY, the chimneypiece and bookcases are of one scheme, executed by *Theophilus Taylor* to *Willement's* designs, 1833.

To the N of the hall is the principal STAIRCASE. It belongs to the alterations done by *Francis Smith,* 1717–23, as the dainty twisted balusters show. The wood carver was *Joel Lobb.* In the N wing are two rooms redone by *Gibson* in association with Mary Elizabeth Lucy, doubtless in 1852 when the end bay window of the drawing room was altered. In the DRAWING ROOM a mid-C18 marble chimneypiece in the style of Robert Adam. This and the adjoining BILLIARD ROOM have Jacobean-style ceilings by *George Trollope & Sons,* 1856.

The private quarters are in the S wing of the forecourt, in the C16 part of the house, but the exterior was largely redone by *Gibson.* Inside, a secondary STAIRCASE of about 1700 with a flat ceiling painted entirely in the Verrio-Laguerre style. On the wall a large PAINTING of the Battle of La Hogue (which took place in 1692). The service wing immediately to the S, containing the kitchen range, was added in 1829, and later extended further S (as already indicated above) in 1866.

The GATES from the wings to the N and S are again by *Nicholas Paris* and were made in 1722. On the S they lead to the STABLES and the BREWHOUSE, two Elizabethan build-ings. The bricks may come from a pre-Elizabethan house. Mullioned windows, gables. Extensive C19 alterations and improvements, including the range with the cupola over the archway leading to the outer stables.

---

*The splendid *pietra-dura* table comes from the Borghese Palace in Rome. George Lucy acquired this and many other pieces at the sale of contents of William Beck-ford's Fonthill Abbey in 1822.

NE of the house, two buildings of interest. First, the charming little rustic SUMMERHOUSE. Built of logs and thatched, it
is in the Swiss chalet style. Inside, there are shields of twigs in
the ceiling and pretty fireplaces. The stained glass dated 1826
and 1828 with the initials of Mary Elizabeth Lucy is by *Willement*, 1839, whose catalogue describes the building as 'the
cabinet of natural history'. Slightly to its E, the ORANGERY
(now the tea room) has tall cross-windows and is by *Gibson*,
1857. At the entry from the forecourt to the orangery are a
pretty shepherd and shepherdess in lead, by *Edward Hurst*,
1718.

The gardens were laid out by *Capability Brown*, 1757–61. The
terrace garden W of the house was redone in 1858 by *Gibson*,
who also renewed other garden walls in the Jacobean style.
Gibson's, too, the boundary railings and iron gates E
of the house, 1861, and the Jacobean-looking GATEWAY
ARCH and LODGE at the Stratford entrance on the W edge of
the park, 1865. Lastly, the stone BRIDGE within the park W
of the house was built in 1867, and at the same time
Brown's CASCADE where the River Dene joins the Avon was
redesigned.

In the VILLAGE, a single street with a mixture of timber-framed
and 1830s ESTATE COTTAGES. Simple SCHOOL (now the
VILLAGE HALL), 1838. Opposite the church, a large brick
farmhouse dated 1831 with kneelered gables and tall chimneys.
To its N, the OLD VICARAGE, 1836 with elaborate Tudor
detail to the stone bay at the front. Further S, CHARLECOTE
GARDENS, dated 1839, has diapered brickwork and belonged
originally to the kitchen gardens. Boldly remodelled and
extended, perhaps 1970s, with a steel and glass section sandwiched between parts with patterned brickwork. Cast-iron
columns in the projecting porch and in the added E wing. It
stands by the River Dene, E of the BRIDGE built by *David
Hiorne* for George Lucy in 1755–7 after the road had been
diverted away from the park. Rusticated segmental arch. End
piers with ball finials.

On the River Avon towards Hampton Lucy are CHARLECOTE
MILL and the adjoining late C18 MILL HOUSE. The three-
storey brick mill with weatherboarded lucam was rebuilt in
1806. Inside, working C19 machinery restored since 1978.

CHERINGTON

ST JOHN THE BAPTIST. Largely C13, repaired and beautified in
1768 and restored without an architect in 1865 and 1876–7.
Roof repaired by *C. Ford Whitcombe*, 1909, and organ chamber
added by *J. A. Chatwin & Son (Philip B. Chatwin)*, 1926. C13
the simple S doorway, and then, probably later, the chancel E

window, one nave s window, and the N aisle E window. They are all varieties of the type of three stepped lancets or lancet lights. The three N aisle N windows with Y-tracery must be of 1768. Inside they are in original surrounds but have little finials above the tracery. The parapet and the funny obelisks with blank quatrefoils probably 1768 too. The w tower, begun before 1300 (arch to the nave of three continuous chamfers), has a c15 bell-stage and c18 parapet, again with obelisk pinnacles. In the nave on the s side one large straight-headed four-light Perp window, redone in 1865 when the window above was added. Perp also the clerestory. Inside, again late c13, the two-bay N arcade which is continued to the E by an ill-fitting tomb with gloriously Dec carving to the arched canopy. c16 chancel arch and s side of chancel redone, 1877. – Jacobean ALTAR with Corinthian columns, painted cherubs and gilded sunburst. Acquired as a reredos from the R.C. chapel at Weston in 1780, dismantled 1877 and reassembled in 1909. – FONT. *Jones & Willis*, 1877. – STAINED GLASS. Three in chancel by *Lavers, Barraud & Westlake*, 1877. The E window still High Victorian, the others in later Gothic style. – In N aisle, one by *Donald Brooke*, 1970. – The rest all in fragments, some from Weston and elsewhere but mostly from Kiddington Manor, Oxon, and dating from the early c14 (one piece N aisle E) to the c18. Nearly all was collected by the Rev. John Warner, rector 1741–80. Some pieces are very good, e.g. the early c16 fragments in the big nave s window. Mostly heraldic, but some pictorial, sacred and secular. – Lavish Dec MONUMENT squeezed uncomfortably between N arcade and chancel arch under a rich depressed ogee arch with big cusping and much decoration. It consists of a high tomb-chest with, to the aisle, a built-in PISCINA. The effigy, *c.* 1320, represents a franklin, his head supported by angels and his feet resting on a dog. Hidden in the carving, a small hare. – WAR MEMORIAL triptych by *Miss F. Brooke* of Barford, 1920. Arts and Crafts with good carving of St George and the Dragon.

Immediately s, the OLD RECTORY, *c.* 1835. Big square house, double-depth plan, five bays and two storeys, with hipped roof. One Gothick ground-floor window.

CHERINGTON HOUSE, ¼ m. sw. Partly c17 but dated 1711 on a tablet on the w front. The very pretty, delicate Gothick porch must be of *c.* 1750–60, possibly by *Sanderson Miller* (Will Hawkes). Early c19 rear range with polygonal end.

Main Street w of the church has several good stone houses dated 1716 to 1724 including five-bay HOME FARM HOUSE. Quoins and coped gables are a common feature. Probably all built after the old cottages were destroyed by fire in 1716. Further datestones of 1746 to 1761. Towards the w, surviving c17 stone houses at DICKINS DAIRY (or THURLYANS).

At Featherbed Lane, Cherington conjoins Stourton (p. 587). c18 OLD SCHOOL HOUSE at the corner of Burmington Lane is in

Cherington. Further w, CHERINGTON MILL has a former granary to the rear in Flemish bond with local bricks in red and yellow, 1850.

3050

CHESTERTON

Chesterton is an eerie place which lost its heart when it lost the Peyto mansion, pulled down in about 1802. It is a scattered village with only a few buildings, yet there was once much more here. There are archaeological remains from all periods, especially from Roman times and – though more recently discovered – from the Middle Ages and Tudor period too. The Peyto family lived here from the C14, and the C17 work for which they are best known came at the end of a long sequence of building projects. Evidence is emerging of a large late medieval house* with extensive pleasure grounds and gardens N of the church, represented now by the terrace between the archway from the churchyard and the stream. This in turn was replaced by the grand and curious mansion built further N in about 1657–62. Its designer was probably *John Stone*, the greater Nicholas's son (*see* below). It had a façade eleven bays long which was a rustic version of Inigo Jones's Banqueting House in Whitehall (whose mason Nicholas Stone had been), not as gauche, as Howard Colvin observed, as Brympton d'Evercy in Somerset, nor as classical as Coleshill in Berkshire. Of the Peytos' interest in building there can be no doubt, for Sir Edward Peyto (†1643) had a large collection of architectural works in his library. He and his son, also Edward, were together responsible for the remarkable assembly of distinguished buildings at Chesterton, of which the main survivors are the windmill, the watermill and the archway (*see* below).

ST GILES. A long, narrow, low church, its appearance perhaps influenced by its position in the vista from successive Peyto mansions. Only slight differentiation between the nave and chancel. Heavily buttressed and much altered. The fabric presents a confusing picture of its development and it is hard to be certain what is *in situ* and what is not. One needs to begin by looking at later alterations. The E end, certainly, is largely Victorian, partly of *John Gibson*'s first restoration in 1862 and the s chancel windows of 1868. The continuous embattled parapet bringing unity to the whole building is a Victorian addition, entirely of 1884. But the length was already there before these changes, suggesting that the Peytos had previously extended the church for visual effect – and also to house the

---

*Some of the heraldic glass from its hall, as described by Dugdale, has recently been found on the site.

monuments which, until 1862, were in the chancel. The squat
w tower is an addition of the C17, in two stages of unequal
dimensions but structurally of one build. What of the rest?
There are fragments of C12 masonry (scalloped capitals)
embedded in the N and S walls of the nave. Next the simple N
doorway (blocked), probably early C13. The most enjoyable
piece the Dec S doorway (possibly resited), which has all along
one moulding of jambs and arch big ballflowers connected by
a long trail. Dec, or rather early C14, one specially nice N
window. The adjacent window is Perp. Late Perp the square-
headed S windows, and Perp also the nave roof of low pitch
with cambered, moulded tie-beams. The S porch with basket-
handle arch and stone seats probably C16. – SCULPTURE.
Outside, above the porch, a carved fragment with headless
figures. Probably an Adoration of the Magi and probably
from a reredos, maybe 1400 or a little later. The Virgin is
missing. – In the sanctuary a Dec canopy with nodding ogee
head, ribs and carved boss, discovered in 1890 and resited in
the S wall as a PISCINA. – DECALOGUE etc., a three-piece set,
painted on canvas by *J. Woodley*, 1836, and near contemporary
ROYAL ARMS of William IV. – STAINED GLASS. Original bits
in one N window. – The E window by *A. O'Connor*, 1862. – Two
S chancel windows, one by *William Holland* (also the donor),
1868, the other by *Hardman*, 1885. – Nave S by *Geoffrey Robinson*, 1999. – MONUMENTS. Humphrey Peyto †1585 and wife
Anna †1604, attributed to *Garrat Hollemans* of Burton upon
Trent (JB). Alabaster tomb-chest with two recumbent effigies.
Note her puppy. Against the chest the most rudimentary balusters. Shields between them. The inscription still in black
letter. Back panels with ten doll-like children, their names
noted. – William Peyto †1609 and his wife Eleanor †1636/7.
By *Nicholas Stone*, 1637–9. Reredos type with pilasters and a
pediment containing a smaller segmental pediment. The
centre of the composition is a recess with sloping arch and two
busts, rather dull for Stone. – Sir Edward Peyto †1643 and wife
Elizabeth. According to the engraving in Dugdale by *John
Stone*, Nicholas's son, and a great improvement on the previous
one, at least as regards purity of architecture and animation of
features. Black-and-white, with detached columns and a simple
pediment. Two frontal busts again. – Floor slab to Sir Edward
Peyto the younger †1658, also by *John Stone*, 1660. – WAR
MEMORIAL, *c.* 1919. Oblong alabaster tablet with gilded
inscription and ornate foliate cross and crests carved in relief
against a blue-green background.

Of the surviving Peyto remains, the first is the ARCHWAY from
the churchyard to the gardens of the old manor N of the
church. Of brick, pedimented and with moulded, cut and
rubbed bricks to create a lively rustication. Influenced by, if
not actually by, *Inigo Jones* and resembling one of his churchyard gateways flanking St Paul's, Covent Garden, of 1631,
illustrated in *Vitruvius Britannicus*. Most likely for Sir Edward
Peyto, *c.* 1630, but a later date in the 1650s has been

suggested too. Restored by *Eric Davies*, the former County Architect, in 1990.

46 Next the White Lias WINDMILL, on a hilltop, exposed and alone ¾ m. NW. Its purpose has been much debated – was it a mill, an observatory, a summerhouse, a folly or even a working folly? Building accounts for 1633 show that it was, indeed, built as a windmill. It is circular, and consists of a high open ground floor with six pillars and raking round arches, an upper storey with small one-light and larger cross-windows, a low domed cap, and four sails. Originally there was a central timber structure containing the staircase and hoist. The mill gear remains. On the cap is 'EP 1632', identifying Sir Edward Peyto as its instigator. He may well have been the designer too, although an unshakeable popular attribution to Inigo Jones persists. Again, a case of Jones's influence in the court style of the day rather than direct authorship? The windmill was restored, including the machinery, by Warwickshire County Council (*Eric Davies*, County Architect) in 1966–74.

Lastly, stranger still, the MILL HOUSE, a handsome three-bay limestone house, *c.* 1660, restored since 2000. Symmetrical, with cross-windows, a pedimented doorway on Tuscan columns, and an arched niche over. Again, theories abound, especially that this was an earlier Peyto house (which it wasn't), converted to a watermill after the mansion was built. Its primary use as a watermill is beyond doubt, since it stands alongside the mill pool created by a dam across the Tach Brook, ½ m. NW of the two main Peyto residences. It seems, as Peter Bolton observes, that the Peytos dressed their windmills and watermills in elegant architectural clothing.

In the village, the former SCHOOL and teacher's house. By *William Lait*, the Compton Verney estate architect, 1862. Stone with red and blue brick dressings. Nicely converted to a house.

HARWOOD'S HOUSE on Banbury Road at the Fosse Way crossroads. On the site of an older house. Possibly by *John Standbridge* of Warwick who was paid £88 'for building of Harrod's House' in 1765. Four-window range with stone pedimented entrance in second bay. Two storeys and attic with dormers. All as shown in a perspective view on an undated estate map of the 1770s.

ROMAN TOWN site, on the Fosse Way ½ m. S of the Harbury Lane crossroads. The settlement straddles the road, mainly on the E but also extending up the hillside to the W. Fortified part represented by a roughly rectangular earthwork with a maximum length of 660 ft (201 metres) enclosing about 8 acres (3.24 ha). Partial excavation and associated finds indicate Roman occupation from the C2 to C4. A stone wall was erected in the C4. Outlying villa found in 1992 when a tessellated pavement was revealed at Ewefields Farm, 1½ m. SW of the main settlement. A satellite settlement was found W of the town in 1999.

CHEYLESMORE *see* p. 285

CHURCH LAWFORD

4070

St Peter. By *Slater & Carpenter*, 1871–3, incorporating elements from the previous church including the simple s doorway
of *c.* 1210 and a C13 s window of two lancets. w tower, aisled
nave and chancel. Rock-faced. Dec. Nicely proportioned with
fine detailing (e.g. the w door surround and other carving by
Harry Hems). Inside, three bays of the N arcade are C14, striped
red and cream, with standard elements and an ogee piscina
below the E corbel. Open roof with carved decoration on the
main beams, some reused. Walls of unpainted plaster. *Minton*
tiles and handsome CORONA in the chancel. – FONT. Like a
coarse octagonal capital, C14, and oak cover, †1931. – PULPIT.
Jacobean with carved panels of snarling beasts. – COMMUN-
ION RAIL. C18. – PANELLING. Re-set in the chancel and aisles,
including a section dated 1618 behind the sedilia. – ARCHI-
TECTURAL FRAGMENTS in the tower, corbels and coffin-lids.
– STAINED GLASS. Two in chancel by *Kempe*, one s, 1884, and
E window, 1887. – N aisle E window by *Lavers, Barraud &
Westlake*, 1884. – Several in chancel and N aisle by *Heaton,
Butler & Bayne*, 1899 to 1920. – One in chancel N by *A. L.
Wilkinson*, 1947.

MANOR, w of the church. C16 and later. H-plan. Late C19 N front
in Tudor style with brick nogging, pargetting and a gabled
two-storey porch with carved capitals to the columns.

VILLAGE HALL, School Street. *Bilton Design & Build*, 2007–8.
Brick with blue dressings, gabled frontage and clock turret. On
the site of the 1912 reading room, with the 1923 WAR MEMOR-
IAL in front.

CHURCHOVER

5080

HOLY TRINITY. Perp w tower, the plain parapet probably post-
Reformation. The top of the C15 spire rebuilt in 1885. The rest
externally all Victorian (1896–7 by *W. Bassett Smith*), except
for the s doorway, which is E.E. Inside, the s arcade of three
bays with standard elements may be of *c.* 1300. The N arcade
belongs to the rebuilding. – FONT. Norman. Of flowerpot
shape, with a rope moulding. Carved wooden hexagonal FONT
COVER, 1673. – ROOD SCREEN with bold columns and light
classical ornamentation, by *H. S. Goodhart-Rendel*, 1951.
– SCULPTURE. In the s aisle w wall, re-set, a Norman capital
with symmetrical stylized foliage. – STAINED GLASS. Bright
Arts and Crafts E window by *Arild Rosenkrantz*, 1918. – Chancel
s window by *Kempe*, 1897. – MONUMENTS. Robert Price, his

wife and her parents, erected *c.* 1595 but without memorial inscriptions. Large standing monument. Two couples kneeling and facing each other across prayer-desks. They kneel on the same level. Children below. The couples are flanked and separated by three columns. Strapwork decoration. – Charles Dixwell †1591 and wife Abigail †1635, erected 1641. Larger couple, kneeling the same way. The children below are demi-figures with rather comical faces, looking as if they were standing in water.

In the village, C17 timber-framed WHITE HOUSE opposite the church has initials T B K B on the gable. N, behind the early C19 yellow brick MANOR, is an C18 thatched cattle shelter. N of these, a group of three cottages with tile-hung gables, built for Arthur James of Coton House, 1893. In School Street, opposite the VILLAGE HALL given by James in 1895, late C18 brick cottages (Nos. 1–4) with keystoned lintels and a moulded stone eaves cornice. To the E, the plain Late Georgian SCHOOLROOM, 1841.

COTON HOUSE, 1 m. SE. A fine Neoclassical house, designed by *Samuel Wyatt* for Abraham Grimes in 1784. Ashlar-faced. Two-storeyed. The three-bay main front has an ample bow with shallow dome to which a circular room corresponds inside. Either side of the bow are tripartite windows with slim unfluted Ionic columns and blank segmental arches. The sides of five bays are studiedly plain but with blank recessed panels between the ground- and first-floor windows. Coton was privately owned until 1948 when it became an apprentice hostel for British Thomson-Houston. It then became a Postal Management College in 1970 and the Post Office restored the interiors, including the fine top-lit staircase, starting in one flight and returning in two. It has a sparse iron balustrade. Several good alabaster chimneypieces. Upper floors badly damaged by fire in 2010. The college closed in 2012. Extensive post-1948 development on the site, but the big two-storey STABLE BLOCK remains; long ranges either side of a central archway with clock and cupola above, probably 1856–7.

ROUND BARROW, 300 yds SW of Coton House and just E of the A426 by the motorway junction. 70 ft (21.3 metres) in diameter and 10 ft (3 metres) high, with traces of what appears to be a ditch on the S and E. Once considered to have been a Bronze Age burial site, the mound is now thought more likely to have belonged to a windmill, i.e. the base for a post mill.

TRIPONTIUM. This Roman settlement lay in the extreme E part of the parish, both sides of Watling Street and just N of Holywell House. Nothing in the way of structures can be seen on the ground, but the fields in the area are strewn with pottery and building debris. Excavations since 1962 have located traces of a *mansio* with a bath house. The settlement was at its most prosperous in the C2. Defences were erected in the later C3 and Tripontium fell into decline in the C4.

CLAVERDON

ST MICHAEL. Mainly of 1876–7 by *Ewan Christian*, whose aisled and clerestoried nave quickly replaced the nave and S aisle rebuilt in Tudor style in 1828–30 by *J. B. Harper* of Henley-in-Arden. Of earlier work, the upper portion of the chancel arch is ascribed to the C14 and the side walls have late C16 mullioned-and-transomed windows with oblong panels. The Perp W tower of grey stone may be of *c.* 1454 when the Bishop of Worcester granted indulgences for contributions to work on the church. Christian's work, which included many of the FURNISHINGS, is predictably indifferent. – Good Arts and Crafts ALTAR RAILS, 1910. – STAINED GLASS. E window by *Kempe, c.* 1890. – War memorial windows in S aisle by *James Powell & Sons*, 1921. – One in N aisle by *A. J. Davies* of Bromsgrove, 1948. – Millennium window in S aisle, *Roger Sargent*, 2000. – MONUMENT. Thomas Spencer, son of Sir John Spencer of Althorp. Two black columns, shallow coffered arch. The surfaces covered with rustically treated foliage trails. Tomb-chest with half-columns along the front. No effigy, but Dugdale's engraving shows a now lost sarcophagus, which held the surviving inscription. Curiously, this tells us when the father died, in 1586, but not the son. The Spencers acquired the manor in 1568 and Thomas died in 1630. The monument looks Elizabethan rather than Jacobean, but the inscription suggests a date after the marriage of Thomas Spencer's daughter Anne to Sir Thomas Lucy in 1610.

OLD VICARAGE, E of the church. By *Henry Rowe* of Worcester, 1816, enlarged to the rear by *J. B. Harper*, 1829, and on the E in 1862. A plain Georgian red brick house. A little E, PARK COTTAGE with curious Gothic windows. N, at the junction of Church Road and Station Road, the charming SMITHY, timber-framed and brick, with a wooden horseshoe surround to the main door.

At the junction of Station Road and Langley Road, ¼ m. w, the former NATIONAL SCHOOL and adjacent teacher's house. The school by *Harper*, 1848, is Italianate with overhanging eaves and round-headed blue brick windows. The house, in red brick with blue dressings, is by *George Clark*, 1857.

THE OLD HALL, Lye Green Road, is part C16, although extended and much restored. H-plan, mostly timber-framed with brick nogging, but with stone portion to ground floor on l. side and big stone chimney to r. Good C18 gatepiers with ball finials.

In Manor Lane, ¾ m. NE, two notable buildings. First, the MALTHOUSE, C16 and later. A long range, of different depths. Stone, with close-studded timber framing above. Then the STONE BUILDING, late C16, apparently built for Thomas Spencer whose monument is in the church. It was doubtless associated with Spencer's 'very fair house', since demolished, and may have been a hunting lodge or banqueting house. It is of a type very rare in the Midlands: a tower house in the north English sense, not fortified but defensible within bounds.

Ground-floor doorway and two three-light ground-floor windows. The larger, mullioned-and-transomed windows all on the first and second floors, and even then mostly on one side. In the NW corner the staircase rising higher than the rest. Inside, an arched doorway dated 1593. The main first-floor room is brick-lined, with a number of recesses, probably for books and rolls. The tower was restored and a single-storey accommodation block added by *George G. Pace*, 1967.

ARDENCOTE HOUSE, ¾ m. NNE, off The Cumsey. By *F.C. Penrose* for Catherine Phillips, 1876. Red brick, in the so-called Queen Anne style. Rather dull, and now much encumbered by late C20 hotel and country club additions. Of the gardens, originally laid out by *Arthur Markham Nesfield*, an oval box maze remains.

IRON AGE HILLFORT, in Barnmoor Wood, 600 yds NW of C16 Kington Grange. On high ground, with good all-round views, especially over the valley to the W. The fort is of univallate construction, enclosing an oval area of 3½ acres (1.4 ha), with entrances W and NE. Not excavated.

See also LANGLEY and PINLEY ABBEY.

CLIFFORD CHAMBERS

ST HELEN. Both nave doorways are Norman, that on the S side with scallop capitals. There is also a Norman PILLAR PISCINA. The chancel is too restored to be valid evidence, but Glynne (1868) described the chancel arch as Norman too. The E.E. lowside lancet re-set in the Victorian organ chamber came from the chancel N wall. One early Dec S chancel window remains. On the N side of the church a re-set window, shafted inside, oddly set in a blocked larger arch belonging to a lost transept, but again from the chancel and not *in situ*. The W tower has Perp features and good gargoyles, but may be older in its masonry. Square-headed Perp windows to nave. Restored in 1886–7 by *John Cotton* who added the organ chamber and vestry, rebuilt the S porch and enlarged the chancel, the latter with stone carving by *William Naylor* of Birmingham. Chancel re-seated in 1931 by *Stratton Davis & Yates*, who also enlarged the N vestry in 1937. – PULPIT. Jacobean, with blank arches. – COMMUNION RAIL. Mid- or later C17. – STAINED GLASS. Fragments in organ chamber window, including small canopies. – E window *T.F. Curtis, Ward & Hughes*, 1899. – Nave N, pretty Arts and Crafts, †1905, probably *Paul Woodroffe* (AB). – Two Elizabethan BRASSES. Hercules Rainsford †1583 and wife Elizabeth. – Elizabeth Marrowe †1601. – MONUMENT. Sir Henry Rainsford †1622 and wife Anne. Big tablet with the two figures kneeling and facing one another across a bulgy prayer-desk. Two columns; the architrave raised semicircularly in the middle. Three stiff children in the predella.

WAR MEMORIAL on the street NW of the church, by *Comper*, 1920.

The OLD RECTORY, s of the churchyard. Timber-framed, with closely set studs. Stone chimney-breast. The house is of the hall type with two gabled and jettied cross-wings. Dendro-dating indicates that it was built *c.* 1433–4 when John Bokeland was rector. Two C15 stone chimneypieces in the parlour wing, both with blank shields.

The MANOR HOUSE, in enclosed grounds behind iron gates, a little s of the church. A pre-Conquest manor later owned by the monks of Gloucester, for whom an impressive timber-framed grange was built in the C15 or C16. Later additions included a N range built for the Dighton family *c.* 1700, and a s wing added by *Tudor Owen* for John Gratrix after 1903. In 1909 the house was purchased by Kathleen Wills, shortly before her marriage to Dr Edward Douty (†1911). The whole was gutted by fire in 1918 but afterwards rebuilt by *Lutyens*, 1919–22. This included a replacement guest house in the style of the C15 grange, but this was demolished in the 1950s along with other Lutyens extensions to the house. What remains is the broad brick façade of the Dightons' house with a Lutyens interior, largely in empathy with the pre-fire house. Galleried entrance hall. Several C16 to C18 chimneypieces brought in. SUMMERHOUSE by *Edward Douty, c.* 1910.

One long street leads from the manor to the main road with many timber-framed cottages, some refronted in brick. A pleasant group in the SQUARE by the church, with chequer brick CHURCHSIDE (No. 28) at the end. Across the street, set back, the former SCHOOL, 1882. Behind its plain white front CLIFFORD COTTAGE (No. 19) is predominantly C17 but has fragmentary remains of C14 timber framing. C18 CLIFFORD LODGE alongside has rusticated gatepiers with ball finials. Further N on the E side, a group of estate cottages by *Deane & Braddell* (*Darcy Braddell*), 1923 (Nos. 5–8) and 1927 (Nos. 9–11), dignified and well planned. Just before these the angular brick-fronted JUBILEE HALL, by *L. L. Dussault*, 1935. On Campden Road, gaunt Victorian RED HILL HOUSE and lodge, built for the Rev. W. A. Pippet, 1896.

Former MILL, ⅜ m. N on the Stour. Totally rebuilt 1853. Now converted, but the river frontage with its chimney still recognizable. Behind, the CLIFFORD FORGE was an C18 mill house, enlarged with a plain stucco front *c.* 1820.

HINES HOUSE FARM, off Banbury Road, 1½ m. E. Built *c.* 1720, yet timber-framed with integral brick front for show.

CLIFTON-UPON-DUNSMORE

5070

ST MARY. Restored late C12 window and s door in chancel. Otherwise the chancel C13 with lancets, paired lancets, and in the E wall three stepped lancets. C13 also the much patched s arcade. The characteristic feature is the round abacus on an

Clifton-upon-Dunsmore, Townsend Memorial Hall, perspective.
Photo lithograph, 1885

octagonal pier. Of *c.* 1300 the N and S aisle details, including
Y-tracery. Also the lower part of the W tower with intersecting
tracery in the W window. Above it a quadruped in a traceried
opening. The tower top seems C16 and once carried a spire,
removed in 1639. Perp N arcade and clerestory. W ORGAN
GALLERY, possibly from alterations by *W. Nixon*, 1806.
Chancel arch Victorian. Chancel restored 1872 and again with
the rest of the church by *Bodley & Garner*, 1893. N vestry
(designed as an organ chamber), 1893. S porch, 1897. N porch
extension, *GSS Architecture*, 2010. – FITTINGS mainly 1893,
including a chunky stone FONT with carved wooden cover,
PULPIT and chancel STALLS. – Painted and stencilled vestry
SCREEN, very *Bodley & Garner*. – STAINED GLASS. W window
by *Hardman*, 1873, another 1882. – Patterned glass in chancel
by *Powell*, 1884. – Two aisle windows probably by *Burlison &
Grylls*, †1881 and 1893. – N aisle by *Kempe*, 1896. – S aisle E,
1920. – MONUMENTS. A drum-shaped lead casket was found
in 1893 beneath the chancel. It contained a heart. – Sir Orlando
Bridgeman †1721. Big tablet. White and grey marble. A black
sarcophagus at the top, a cartouche at the foot.
In the CHURCHYARD, a good Townsend memorial, by *Bodley*,
1898. LYCHGATE, 1906.
Opposite the church, the TOWNSEND MEMORIAL HALL. By
G. G. Woodward, 1885. Village club, with cottages in adjoining
courtyard. Attractively designed, but disappointing in
execution.
PRIMARY SCHOOL, at the corner of Station Road. By *Frederick
Wood*, and boldly dated 1850 in diapered brickwork. Nicely
extended.
CLIFTON MANOR in walled grounds E of the church has an C18
front, and a Queen Anne revival extension, 1895, with portico
and Venetian window.
Further E along Lilbourne Road, DUNSMORE HOUSE by *W.H.
Ward* for P.A. Muntz, a Birmingham industrialist (brother of
G.F. Muntz Jun.; cf. Umberslade Park), 1881. A large Tudor-
style house in ironstone with limestone dressings. Gabled
dormers, mullioned-and-transomed windows and big chimneys. Rescued from near dereliction, 2009–10, and now a hotel.

GOOD SHEPHERD, Newton, 1 m. N. Brick mission church by *T. W. Willard*, 1901, with wide pointed windows and polygonal apse. Nearby, the former Congregational chapel in Silver Street, built 1871 and refronted by *J. T. Franklin*, 1905.

CLOPTON HOUSE
1¾ m. N of Stratford-upon-Avon

2050

Approached from the S through housing encroaching on the parkland, leaving a pair of C17 gatepiers isolated on the verges in Clopton Road.

At first glance across the park, the house seems late C17. A handsome SW front of brick with stone dressings. Symmetrical, of seven bays with three-bay projection with steep pediment. Hipped roof and dormers. Stone doorway with segmental pediment. The SE front has seven tighter bays. This is all of 1665–70 when, following an advantageous marriage, John Clopton rebuilt and enlarged the old, moated C16 house which lies behind. This is grouped round a small courtyard, to which the C17 parts form two sides. On the NE front is the porch, originally a free-standing gatehouse inside the moat (cf. Brockhampton, Herefs.), built for George Carew, *c.* 1605. Stone ground floor; two small caryatids l. and r. of the entrance arch. Upper floor timber-framed. Also on the NE, a little r. of the porch, a C16 canted bay window with pilasters and crosswindows. The house was extensively restored for C.T. Warde in 1839–46, restored again for Arthur Hodgson in 1904, and converted to flats in 1986. Inside, the hall had panelling and an overmantel of *c.* 1600. The staircase is C17, and before conversion so were the principal upper rooms, with thin, rather coarse stucco work. There was a chapel under the roof, with a communion rail with massive balusters, also late C17. These features are said to survive.

The COACH HOUSE and clock turret of 1843 on the NW belong to Warde's improvements.

CLOPTON TOWER, 500 yds SE of the house. Lias with Cotswold stone dressings. Polygonal, with higher stair-turret and battlements. Built *c.* 1850, again for Warde. Extended in matching style, 1991.

COLESHILL

2080

A sizeable town distinguished for its hilltop church and prominent spire. The coaching era brought prosperity, with many of the older houses being refronted or rebuilt in the later C17 through to the C19. The diversion of the main road to Northeast England through Birmingham in 1835 – and the lack of direct access either to a canal or a mainline railway – led to a decline. Coleshill nevertheless remained moderately prosperous and retained its older buildings until the post-war period without major rebuilding. Having gained its tree-lined by-pass in the 1930s Coleshill escaped the damage inflicted on many towns in the interests of road improvement. It suffered greatly, though, in the 1960s when redevelopment removed much of its charm while failing to provide many replacement buildings of any merit. The loss of the buildings lining the High Street up the hill on the approach from the N is especially to be regretted, the more so since had they lasted even another decade they would have been appreciated for their variety and interest.

CHURCHES

St Peter and St Paul. A large C14–C15 church with a tall steeple with slender spire, all heavily restored by *William Slater* in 1858–9. The restoration was faithful, ecclesiologically correct but rather dull. The geometrical tracery of the aisles, especially, looks mechanically regular. There is ample compensation, though, in the fine detailing of the tower and spire and in the bold, pinnacled Perp chancel. The tower bell-openings are two twins with transom, and there are blank twins each side. It is Perp of the North Warwickshire type (cf. Curdworth and Middleton) with the same sharp-headed openings and chunky carving. The spire (partially rebuilt by *Bodley & Garner* in 1888) is crocketed up the edges and has three tiers of lucarnes. The chancel has large five-light windows, a seven-light E window, and battlements and pinnacles. Grotesque carvings and winged angels on the parapets. Pretty battlemented C19 vestry on N side of chancel with windows of trefoil-headed lights surmounted by quatrefoils.

Inside the first four bays of the nave come first, early C14 with a clear join in the pier linking them to the three bays to the W, completed when the tower was begun. Big diagonal tower buttresses within W end of aisles. The tower arch to the nave is tall and in its mouldings still close to the Dec. So a beginning date of *c.* 1385, as implied by Dugdale, is quite acceptable. The W bays of the arcades are fully Perp. The chancel evidently mid-C15, with big openings making walls of glass. On the S, remains of vaulted SEDILIA, now too low down. The N doorway surround, quite swagger. – FONT. An outstandingly good Norman piece of the mid C12, drum-shaped, with arcading. In the arcading single figures in very excited late Norman draperies, with expressive folds, alternating with vertical foliage scrolls. One only of these scrolls is symmetrical in itself. Also the arcading is interrupted on the E side for a Crucifixus with the Virgin and St John. The Crucifixus is of a type hardly possible before 1200, and a circular band surrounds him which cuts in front of the Virgin and St John, as though they stood behind it. – Elaborate wooden PULPIT with carved tracery panels, C19. – TOWER SCREEN. *J. J. Hackett* of Birmingham, 1913. The rooms within the tower later, 1989. – SCREEN to S chapel, 1957, designed by *H. W. Hobbiss* and carved by *Pancheri*. – STAINED GLASS. In the chancel all by *Clayton & Bell*, the excellent E window and two side windows, 1859, and two more, a facing pair, 1882. Theirs, too, the W window (now largely obscured by ceilings in the space under the tower), 1888. – In the nave and aisles, three by *Hardman*, 1871–92. – W window of S aisle by *T. W. Camm*, 1894.

– MONUMENTS. An uncommonly rich collection. First two cross-legged knights in chain-mail, one holding his shield up high. They are of the early C14 (N aisle, S aisle) and believed to be two successive John Clintons. – Then in the chancel three brasses: William Abell, vicar, †1500 (12½ in. (32 cm.)), Alice Clifton †1506 (25½ in. (65 cm.)), and Sir John Fenton †1566 (18½ in (47 cm.)). – The other monuments in the chancel all Digbys. Simon †1519 and wife Alice (N side). Alabaster. Two recumbent effigies on a tomb-chest with cusped lozenges. – Reginolde †1549 and wife Anne (S side), by *Richard and Gabriel Royley*. Incised alabaster slab on a tomb-chest with primitively spiral-fluted colonnettes. – John and Anne, both †1558 (N side), also by the *Royleys*. Alabaster. Two recumbent effigies. On the tomb-chest shields and also spiral-fluted colonnettes. – Sir George †1586 and wife Abigail (S), by *Jasper Hollemans*, 1599 (JB). Recumbent effigies. Against the tomb-chest kneeling children. – 1st Lord Digby †1642 and others, attributed to *Edward Marshall* (GF). A very interesting tall, narrow tablet to fit in the space between two N chancel windows. The inscription on a convex surface, representing part of a big column; for it is crowned by an Ionic capital. – 2nd Lord Digby †1661 in Dublin. Erected by his widow, Mary, in 1672, and possibly by *C. G. Cibber* (GF). Square pedestal and full-round big urn of ample shape with shield and supporters on front. – WAR MEMORIAL. In the churchyard. *Bodley & Hare*, 1920. Hollington stone cross on a pedestal. Life-sized statues of a soldier and a sailor at the cross base.

SACRED HEART AND ST TERESA (R.C.), Coventry Road. 1938–42 by *Harrison & Cox* (*G. B. Cox*) of Birmingham, replacing a previous church of 1882 nearby. Large, of brick, with a crossing tower and Byzantino-Romanesque details. Plain plastered interior without an E window. Low arcades with carved capitals and narrow passage aisles. West gallery. Well-proportioned and dignified, enhanced by good contemporary fittings including marble altars and mosaic Stations of the Cross. – STAINED GLASS. One S chancel window by *Hardman*, 1882, brought from the old church in 1987. – Big N transept window (the three mysteries of the Rosary), and nave clerestory windows (the Ten Commandments) probably by *G. E. Sheedy*, *c.* 1950; excellent. The church stands alongside the former buildings of the Father Hudson Homes etc. (*see* Perambulation).

UNITED CHURCH (originally Wesleyan), Coventry Road. Plain, but with quirky and minimal decoration on the street front, 1900. Possibly by *Ewen Harper*.

Former CONGREGATIONAL CHAPEL, Birmingham Road. 1834 by *D. R. Hill*. Brick with lancets.

PUBLIC BUILDINGS

TOWN HALL, High Street. By *S. H. Wigham*, 1925–6. Domestic scale, brick with half-timbering. Large hall to rear.

THE COLESHILL SCHOOL, Coventry Road. By the *County Architect* (*G.R. Barnsley*), 1956. It replaced the grammar school. Main block of four storeys. Oblong reinforced concrete frame with curtain walling.

BRIDGE, ⅜ m. N, over the River Cole. Six round sandstone arches with cutwaters, C16 or earlier. The E face well-preserved despite later widening and repairs.

PERAMBULATION*

The place to begin is in CHURCH HILL. This was the market square. At the top, two good brick houses. Late Georgian OLD BANK HOUSE, of three storeys, with two full-height canted bays whose windows are of Gothic shape, and Early Georgian DEVEREUX HOUSE, five bays with giant Ionic angle pilasters and a hipped roof with dormers. Immediately W, mediocre CHURCH HILL FLATS by *John Tetlow & Partners* for Meriden RDC, 1969. Low down on the N, converted cottages with the Institute upstairs and once open archways on the ground floor. PILLORY or whipping post outside. On the corner, HSBC, 1910 by *T. B. Whinney* for the London, City & Midland Bank, and matching extension on High Street by *Whinney, Son & Austen Hall*, 1953–4.

The HIGH STREET is reached at the point where the SWAN HOTEL stands, rendered, of seven bays, early C18 with sashed windows, consoles and dormers. In the coaching era the carriage entrance to the courtyard (now a doorway) was in the middle. From here the High Street turns N down to the river. On the E, a long and dreary run of shops but including No. 95, whose internal features are dendro-dated to 1456. The W side has fared better. Nos. 84–86 is a decent example of post-war improvement by *Ewen Harper & Co.* for George Mason stores, 1949–50. Brick with brick-mullioned windows and dormers. It sits well in a run of mixed Georgian buildings, some brick, some stuccoed, between the Swan and the Green

*Coleshill is particularly well served by the excellent publications of its Civic Society, and especially the book on *Coleshill Buildings c. 1350–1850* by Bob Meeson (2006). Information from these sources is gratefully acknowledged.

Man. Much further down, early C18 LABURNUM HOUSE (No. 38), with symmetrical three-bay façade to the High Street and an irregular frontage to Penn's Lane. Brick with heavy stone detailing, white-painted. Nearly opposite, No. 37 has exposed timber framing with curved braced on the upper floor, probably C15. At the bottom of the hill, ST PAUL'S HOUSE (No. 1) is the best of the C18 houses. Elegant front of five bays and three storeys. Symmetrical, with rusticated corners, lintels and decorated keystone. Central door with Doric pilasters and open scrolled pediment against rustication. From 1884 it was St Paul's Home for Boys (*see* Coventry Road, below). Beyond this just the bridge (*see* above).

Now for the rest of the High Street, heading s. From the Swan, the w side continues with varied C18 and C19 fronts, mainly brick, but Nos. 107–109 (E side, once the Three Tuns) has fine timber-framed gables, exposed and restored in 1972. The framing has small panels of squares in squares. Stone plinth at the front and under the integral archway to the courtyard. Inside No. 111, remnants of a medieval house including a crown-post roof, probably early C14. Again on the E, the LYCHGATE at the town entrance to the churchyard, 1929. Here the character is still predominantly Georgian, but diminishing in scale after LLOYDS BANK (No. 121), which has an added single-storey wing with elaborate porch and Gibbsian window surrounds. Then the POST OFFICE, an uncompromising *Ministry of Works* job (*W. T. Vale*, architect), 1967. Next door, QUEEN ANNE HOUSE (No. 131). Late C17, with delightful portico consisting of a segmental tympanum richly decorated with fat swags, flowers and foliage, supported on thin Roman Doric pillars. The 1840s façade of Nos. 138–140 conceals evidence of a medieval house with open hall and cross-wing.

W in SUMNER ROAD, the COLEHAVEN ALMSHOUSES, by *H. W. Weedon* for Sir John Sumner. Two blocks set in neat gardens, the main group on the N, 1931–2, and another opposite, 1934. Tudor-style, with diapered brickwork, carved stone dressings and big chimneys.

Back in the High Street, opposite the town hall, the grounds of CHANTRY HOUSE. It belonged to the Digbys and was formerly the vicarage, later used as Meriden District Council offices. At the centre is a mid-Georgian block of five bays with keystoned windows and portico. The main extension is by *Jackson & Edmonds*, 1958–60, but their council chamber (1962) was demolished in 1989. Again on the E side COLESHILL HOUSE (No. 141) with a Roman Doric porch. This was the house of the Digbys.

Beyond the United Church the High Street becomes COVENTRY ROAD. Off to the r., in PARKFIELD ROAD, the former PAROCHIAL SCHOOL (converted to housing). By *Middleton & Goodman* of Cheltenham, 1871–2, with an extension by *G. H. Cox*, 1887. Brick with blue bands, ashlar dressings, steep gables and plate tracery.

Further s on the e side of Coventry Road, a large complex of Roman Catholic institutional buildings, developed as a children's 'garden city' by Fr George Hudson, appointed secretary of the Birmingham Diocesan Rescue Society in 1902. It was to succeed the St Paul's Home (*see* High Street). Particularly memorable is the Neo-Georgian Central Office (Father Hudson's Society), 1923 by *Harrison & Cox*; an irregular octagon with canted entrance bay and projecting wings. The other buildings (some replaced as part of the redevelopment of the site, 2014–15) included St Edward's Boys' Home, 1905–6, St Gerard's Orthopaedic Hospital of 1912–13, both by *Henry Sandy*, and others by *Harrison & Cox* from 1923; the Cottage Homes of 1925, St Joan's Home for Girls (s of the church) in 1931, schools and other facilities to 1961.

Nearly opposite, No. 64 Coventry Road is a modest house by *Buckland & Farmer*, 1902. On the same side, further s, the GEORGE & DRAGON (No. 154), in Tudor style by *Satchwell & Roberts*, 1923–4.

ST ANDREW'S HOUSE, No. 37 Blythe Road, ¼ m. e. Stuccoed, Regency. Five-bay s front with recessed centre containing the Greek Doric porch.

COLESHILL PARK, 1 m. w, in an elongated triangle of farmland between motorways. The Digby family built a low gabled house to the w of the town in the c16. It was pulled down in 1810 but the former outbuildings were incorporated in the home farm. In 1872–3 John Wingfield-Digby commissioned *Middleton & Goodman* of Cheltenham (*John Middleton*) to design a new house some ½ m. w of the old one. Red and blue brick, Gothic, with a porte cochère tower, matching outbuildings and a similar N lodge at Gilson. Carved beasts in stone on the main front. It is rather gaunt and can never have been cheerful or welcoming. The family left before the First World War. Coleshill Park became a retreat for Birmingham diocese and then a hospital before falling derelict in the 1990s. It has been restored as COLESHILL MANOR since 2002 by *Abacus* for IM Properties for commercial use, with new buildings alongside in the park.

COMBE ABBEY

Combe Abbey was Cistercian, founded in 1150. In the late c13 it was by far the richest monastic house in the county. It was dissolved in 1539. At the end of the c16 it was in the hands of Lord Harington. In 1622 the estate was sold to Lady Craven, widow of Sir William, a Lord Mayor of London. Her son (of Hamstead Marshall in Berkshire) was the first Lord Craven. It remained Craven property until 1923 when it was sold to John

The upright of the new building at Comb Abey

The West Front
B B B Sr. Isaac Gibson's Building

Combe Abbey, elevation.
Drawing by William Winde, c. 1682

Gray, a Coventry builder. Gray retained the w wing but sold its original fittings and demolished substantial parts of the building. The house and 280 acres (113 ha) of the park were bought by the City of Coventry in 1964. The grounds opened to the public as a country park in 1966 and since 1994–5 the abbey has been extended and developed as a country house hotel.

Despite its partial demolition Combe remains an *abrégé* of English architecture from Norman times to the 1860s. Of the pre-Reformation abbey substantial parts remain, including late Norman work of *c.* 1180–90 and parts of the C15 cloisters. The late C16 is represented by parts of the w wing, adapted for domestic use for the Haringtons. The E wing was similarly altered and a splendidly ornate fan-vaulted garden porch was added *c.* 1605, but these parts were lost in the Victorian alterations.

Combe is exceptionally well illustrated from the mid C17 and the improvements carried out by *William Winde* for Lord Craven (or rather for his cousin and prospective heir, Sir William Craven, who lived here) after 1681 are documented with correspondence as well as architectural drawings. These sources also show that Lord Craven's godson, agent and tenant, Sir Isaac Gibson, had built a three-bay gabled block at the sw corner in 1667–9. Winde's work on the w and N sides of the house remains, but his NW kitchen block was a casualty of the early C20 demolitions. The C18 saw the erection of several distinctive buildings within the park as part of *Capability Brown*'s landscaping for the 6th Lord Craven from 1771, but only minor changes to the house. Then from 1861 Combe underwent a transformation under that rare and highly talented architect *W. Eden Nesfield*, who created a very original E range on top of the Norman parts in 1863–5. This was 350 ft (107 metres) long and cost about £60,000. It was one of Nesfield's major works and its early C20 demolition was a great loss, partially rectified in 1994–5 by the creation of a new E wing (extended in 1999) in a rather diluted Nesfield style by *Alan Johnson Associates*.

One approaches the house today from the S along a long avenue of trees, among which are several small mounds of uncertain origin.[*] It leads across the C19 moat by a Victorian medieval bridge into a courtyard with buildings to E, N and W. This courtyard represents the abbey cloister, which had the church on the S rather than on the N as would have been more usual. On the E side is still the entrance into the chapter house with the standard twin windows l. and r. All this is red sandstone, and the architectural details belong to the late C12: chevron applied also at right angles to the wall, waterleaf in a capital, etc. The shafts of the twin windows are three in depth and the middle one of them is paired. The surrounding arches are of an unusual horseshoe shape. Warwick Rodwell's reinterpretation has shown that the sub-dorter stood N of the chapter house. Its doorway is pointed. Then, round the N corner, just one small doorway of *c.* 1200 survives but it is *ex situ*. To the S of the chapter house is the doorway into a room which adjoined the N transept of the church. The Neo-Norman vaulted passage in front was created by *Nesfield* but represents two bays of the original cloister. Here and behind the chapter house entrance some details are original, but unlikely to be *in situ*. These include angle shafts for the cloister vaulting and medieval masonry in the plinths of the Victorian arches in the hotel foyer. The E range ends towards the S by a kind of semi-circular bastion projecting into the moat and displaying an adjoining portcullis. Although said to be based on excavated foundations this is essentially Nesfield's. The rebuilt upper floors of 1994–5 with big mullioned-and-transomed windows, oriels and demi-conical roofs replicate Nesfield's lost wing. The E front and added E wing of 1999 are similar, with gables, semicircular bay, tourelle and round corner tower. Although in the same spirit, it is all less varied and vibrant than what it replaced.

The cloister walks themselves were rebuilt in the C15 and their four-light windows remain on the N and W sides.[†] On the N side part of the back wall has four bays of blind trefoil-headed arcading and Romanesque leaf and chevron details. Otherwise the W range was rebuilt *c.* 1540–80. The upper parts are timber-framed with oriels on the first floor facing the courtyard. They all project on little brackets, as was usual in timber-framed building. Harington's work included two bays of the S front with their Dutch gables and mullioned-and-transomed windows (altered). One first-floor window is of seven lights and has three transoms. Inside there was a fireplace (sold in 1925) with Harington's arms, dated 1590. The

---

[*] Once thought to be round barrows but now regarded as of uncertain function and date.

[†] Dugdale mentions a gift of £30 in 1509 to build the S side of the cloister. This section no longer exists.

third bay, also Dutch gabled, belongs to Sir Isaac Gibson's addition of 1667–9 and continues on the W front with three bays, the middle one projecting, and three plain gables. On the W the windows were mullioned and mullioned-and-transomed but were later sashed.

Then come *William Winde*'s additions and alterations of 1682–4. He provided a new W front immediately N of Gibson's short one (which in 1682 Craven contemplated replacing to create a long front of fifteen bays with a recessed centre), a NW kitchen range (demolished) and a grand saloon on the N side, behind Lord Harington's building and facing N. The surviving W range is of seven bays and two storeys, all done with great breadth. Quoins, three-bay quoined and pedimented centre. In the pediment ornamental carving by *Edward Pearce*. The windows have moulded surrounds, the doorway and the first- and last ground-floor windows pediments on brackets. The rainwater heads say 1684. Here we have an early documented use of sash windows, although none of the originals survive.

The NORTH SALOON is of five bays, with four windows and a central chimney projection. This and the angles are quoined. Inside, this room (called Cloisters) has a mighty and not ornate chimneypiece, doorcases with big segmental pediments on corbels, a date-plate 1684, and a splendid plaster ceiling by *Edward Gouge*. By him no doubt also the even bolder frieze of flowers in the Lady Craven room on the first floor of the W front. In the ground-floor Walnut Restaurant room, panelling, a back screen of four fluted Ionic columns, and a late C18 chimneypiece. Otherwise little of note. The 1990s décor and fixtures of the hotel's public areas are eclectic and quirky, representing a range of periods and styles from classical to C18 Gothick. Enjoyable enough if not taken too seriously.

Immediately N of the house is the former REAL TENNIS COURT, 1817, top-lit with slate-lined interior walls. Converted into function rooms on two floors and now called The Courthouse. NE of this, the C18 STABLE BLOCK (The Abbeygate), enlarged and altered by Nesfield in 1863 with a pretty central clock turret and a tile-hung porte cochère on the N. NE again, the walled KITCHEN GARDENS (derelict in 2015), 1863–5, with chunky stone columns and brick arches facing the house. Nesfield's tile-hanging is replicated on the red brick bedroom block, PRIORY PARK: *Hitchman Stone Partnership*, 2007–8.

The FORMAL GARDEN W of the house was thought to have been designed by *William Andrews Nesfield* when his son was working at Combe *c.* 1863–5. At that time a channel was dug to link the moat to the lake, and this forms the boundary of the garden. The two tulip-shaped parterres are later (after 1873), and by the head gardener, *William Miller*, whose 1897 plan of the gardens shows them in this form. Re-set carved stones from the abbey ruins in the garden walls. In the garden wing of the lake, a sculpture of fisherman and nymph by *Percy George Bentham*, 1968.

The GROUNDS were landscaped by *Capability Brown* in 1771–6. Lord Torrington, who visited in 1789, was not impressed. Brown's landscape has largely disappeared but its form is recorded on an estate map of 1778 showing a classic serpentine lake, shelterbelts and planting. The map also shows the Menagerie in the loop of the lake at the W end of the park, a boat house, dog kennels (demolished) along the S avenue, and drives to the W and E Lodges on the Coventry–Brinklow road. While the landscaping was Brown's, it has been argued by Mowl and James that the buildings may be by his son-in-law *Henry Holland Jun*. Whatever, they are a remarkable group of buildings, all of *c.* 1771–8.

The MENAGERIE, 1 m. W of the house, was a private zoo, on the model of Versailles. Associated buildings to the N originally housed animals and provided accommodation for the keeper and staff. The main building has two two-storey corner towers with pyramid roofs. They are red sandstone and may belong to an earlier structure, perhaps a hunting lodge. The rest is in grey ashlar, with a Palladian domed octagon at one corner. Restored 2005–9.

The WEST LODGE stands at the Coventry entrance towards Binley, ⅝ m. from the abbey. Triumphal arch with Corinthian pilasters, urns and raised section over the archway with swags and pyramid roof. Rusticated stonework on side facing the park. Its sophistication could well indicate the hand of a designer such as Holland. It is certainly quite unlike the former dog kennels, which were castellated Gothick with a spired turret.

The EAST LODGE, 1 m. ESE towards Brinklow, is Gothick. Hexagonal centre with quatrefoils, ogee windows and dummy arrowslits. Decorative parapet, originally pinnacled.

The S avenue has a pair of rusticated GATEPIERS with decorated panelled tops, relocated from the Griffin Gate in the 1960s. On the l. of the drive, the VISITOR CENTRE, by *Purcell Miller Tritton and Partners*, 1993: red brick with a portico at each end, like a market hall in plan and design. Nearby, several sculptures in wood by *John Wakefield*, 1996–9.

COMBE FIELDS

Combe Fields is the parish for Combe Abbey. Chiefly rural apart from some industrial development on the W edge towards Coventry.

PETER HALL. An C18 red brick farmhouse incorporating substantial stone elements of a C14 and C15 chapel. It was the church of the Domesday parish of Smite, whose settlement was deserted in the later Middle Ages. Walls of nave, chancel and S aisle partially extant with buttresses and blocked windows. A C14 N doorway. Also a C15 chancel roof, with secondary roof above.

COMBROOK

3050

An estate village in the valley below Compton Verney.

ST MARY AND ST MARGARET. By *John Gibson* (*see* Compton Verney), 1866–7, but keeping the chancel of 1831 by *John Nichol* of Wellesbourne, restored in 1863. Grey and brown stone, very free Gothic, with a plethora of angels leaning forwards. They appear e.g. on the big animated bell-turret and the W doorway with its openwork-cusped gable. Between the two a rose window. Spherical triangles too. The style of Gibson's work is *c.* 1300, rather over-cusped. Inside especially typical the naturalistic leaves and flowers of the roof corbels. Devonshire marble shafts, including the chancel arch which Gibson replaced at his own cost. – FITTINGS mostly 1866–7, the wooden PULPIT and DESK carved by *Kendall* of Warwick. – STAINED GLASS. E window by *Willement, c.* 1863. – W window given by Gibson, 1867. – E end of aisles, probably *Burlison & Grylls*, †1887 and 1896. – In S aisle, two by *Powell*, 1912 and 1928.

VILLAGE HALL (former school). 1855, enlarged 1907. Probably by *Gibson*. Nothing special.

Several good C17 and C18 stone houses, predominantly White Lias, some with mullioned windows, some thatched. Varied ESTATE HOUSES, of grey and brown stone, perhaps 1840s through to 1880s in differing styles, some of the earlier ones possibly by *Gibson* but after 1860 more likely by the estate office (i.e. *William Lait*, the Compton Verney Clerk of Works). Nos. 8–9 with diamond-pane windows. Nos. 3–4 have canted bays with mullioned-and-transomed windows. Nos. 18–20 with grouped lancets. Nos. 40–41 later with blue brick bands and mild polychromy. Two WELL-HEADS, both 1860s. One with ogee arch, the other (alongside No. 4) with shaped gable.

COMPTON SCORPION

2040

Originally Compton Scorfen, a sizeable medieval village now represented only by earthworks SW of the Manor House.

Cotswold stone MANOR HOUSE. The N entrance front late C17, symmetrical, with mullioned windows. The other façade C18 with sashed windows, dormers and coped gables with ball finials.

A little N, COMPTON SCORPION FARMHOUSE, built 1824–5 for the Weston Park estate. Limestone ashlar with mullioned windows and stone porch. Good range of contemporary farm buildings, also 1824. Nearby, a pair of chequer brick ESTATE COTTAGES with fish-scale tile roofs, by *Johnson & Son* of Lichfield, 1853.

COMPTON VERNEY

3050

The greatest beauty of Compton Verney is its superb position by a large lake, crossed by a handsome Georgian bridge. There are ample cedar trees about as well. The C18 setting is by *Lancelot 'Capability' Brown* and the first part of the house to come into view is *Robert Adam*'s E front of 1761–6. But the site is altogether more historic.

On the E bank of the pool by the bridge was the medieval village, depopulated in the C15. Compton Verney – or Compton Murdak as it was known until about 1500 – belonged to the Murdak family, whose ancient manor stood on the site of the house. The Verneys came in 1435, rebuilding the manor which was subsequently enlarged. Hollar's view of *c.* 1655 shows a long gabled and chimneyed s range with polygonal turrets at each end.

The present house incorporates older fabric, but represents two principal phases of C18 rebuilding linked to significant events in the history of the Verneys. In 1696 Richard Verney became the 11th Lord Willoughby de Broke, having established his claim to the barony. When his son George inherited in 1711 he decided to remodel the house and landscape the grounds. All but the E side of the house is of this phase, which George Vertue tells us was completed in 1714. The Baroque design has been speculatively attributed to the Smiths of Warwick, Hawksmoor and Vanbrugh. Altogether more convincing is the recent suggestion by Richard Hewlings* that *John & William Townesend* of Oxford were responsible. Compton Verney exhibits several features (e.g. hanging keystones and rusticated lesenes) found in other examples of their work, while any traces of Hawksmoor's influence might derive from the Townesends' contemporary involvement with him in Oxford.

Francis Smith is known to have prepared an unexecuted scheme, perhaps *c.* 1735, for completing the remodelling. At that date, the house was still on the courtyard plan, entered from the E through an archway with a cupola. Also, the s side was asymmetrical, the r. side lower and tighter than the surviving l. section. The stables were built in this period, but nothing major was done to the house.

---

* Richard Hewlings is credited with this suggestion by Andor Gomme in 'Compton Scarsdale or Sutton Verney' in *English Heritage Historical Review* vol. 2 (2007) pp. 60–69.

The second major building phase came in the 1760s with alterations for John Peyto Verney, 14th Lord Willoughby de Broke, who came of age in 1759. He had inherited the Chesterton estates of the Peytos, adding considerably to his wealth. After a long minority and evidently eager to remodel the house, Verney commissioned *Robert Adam*, the first of whose nine surviving drawings for Compton Verney is dated 2 September 1760. The remodelling of the E front was undertaken in 1761–6. Verney's account with Hoare's Bank records a total spend of over £10,000 of which some £8,000 was paid to *William Hiorne*, the Warwick builder who supervised the work. Plans of the house were published in *Vitruvius Britannicus* in 1771. Adam's work on the house was followed by a landscaping of the grounds by *Capability Brown* in 1768–74 along with several new buildings to his designs. The main landscaping works cost some £4,000.

The later Verneys made some changes, notably in 1824 when *Henry Hakewill* remodelled the dining room and from the mid C19 (most likely after 1863 for the 18th Baron) when *John Gibson* made various alterations. The 19th Lord Willoughby de Broke was forced to sell in 1921 and the house suffered depredations and sales of contents under subsequent owners and wartime occupation. Then came decades of empty neglect. Acquisition by Christopher Buxton in 1984 offered hope of a rescue but the failure of his plans to use the house as a hotel alongside an opera house by the lake left the house still semi-derelict. In 1993, it was bought by the Peter Moores Foundation as an independent art gallery run by Compton Verney House Trust. It was repaired and conserved by *Rodney Melville & Partners*, working alongside *Stanton Williams* who were responsible for the internal adaptations and for the new block (on the site of the old service wing) adjoining the N side. The principal exhibition gallery and visitor services are in the new block. The initial work was completed in 1996–8, with further work in 2003–4 on the attic conversion to house the Folk Art Collection and the creation of a new learning centre and offices between the old brewhouse and stables.

Of the house itself the architecturally most successful part is the WEST RANGE attributed to the *Townesends*, built after 1711 for George Verney, 12th Lord Willoughby de Broke, and Dean of Windsor. The style is broadly speaking Vanbrugh's, decidedly North Country. Stone, two storeys, in a 3–5–3 rhythm of fenestration. The centre of ashlar and raised, with a balustrade, the side-pieces of smaller stones with ashlar dressings. All windows are large and arched with hanging keystones. The quoins have strips of blocks, alternatingly rusticated. The centre has giant Tuscan pilasters. Doorway with attached columns and triglyph frieze. 55

The s front belongs partly to the post-1711 house, extended E and made uniform by *Adam*, whose drawing of 1760 is titled 'Design for an addition . . . corresponding to the old part of the house as much as possible'. The old part had pediments over the end bays of the four-window range. With Adam's additions the front now has eight bays and three pediments, the division not quite symmetrical and with blocking for pilasters. His lengthening was repeated on the N side. And thus to the E he had to cope with a centre and two overlong wings, creating a deep forecourt. The windows of the forecourt wings are widely spaced, and their E ends have on the ground-floor Venetian windows of the Adam type with arches over the whole triplet and solid tympana. Lunettes in the pediments. To accentuate the centre sufficiently, Adam gave it a portico of four giant unfluted Corinthian columns. Inside the portico is a coffered ceiling and a rich garland frieze. The latter, however, belongs to C19 alterations made by *Gibson*. Adam abstained from a pediment. At the sides of the portico are older staircase bays, brought forward by Adam. Their corners create rather painful joints both to the portico and to the slightly higher wings. He was no doubt forced to make them higher by changed standards of interior grandeur. The details on the other hand are very fine. Adam's work, especially round the portico, is unmistakably in his early style, the style of Shardeloes, Buckinghamshire (1759–61), and the Bowood Mausoleum, Wiltshire (1761–3). Adam had returned from Italy only in 1758, when he was thirty. Later his work is more elegant and less masculine.

Adam did little inside and only two rooms display his style. The ADAM HALL has a screen of four columns on the l. and a grand coffered ceiling on a deep cove. Marble floor. The plaster picture frames on the walls are probably by *Joseph Rose*, although *Robert Moore* also worked here. These originally contained paintings by *Antonio Zucchi*, Adam's collaborator, sold in 1931. The coving and the hunting scene on the frieze over the screen are by *Gibson*, c. 1863, and doubtless contemporary with his alterations to the portico immediately outside. In the WEST GALLERY (previously the dining room or saloon) in the centre of the W front are pairs of columns l. and r. screening apses. The MORNING ROOM in the S wing is *Adam*'s too, but it was delightfully refurnished as a ladies' boudoir in the 1860s with bookcases, corner cabinets and fireplace. In the restoration since 1993 the interior has been adapted for the display of works of art. The new work by *Stanton Williams* has finishes in white with oak and stainless steel.

On the N, the new block by *Stanton Williams*, 1997–8. Simple and understated externally, with plain stone, glass sheets and grey metal finishes. This links to Stanton Williams's LEARNING CENTRE and OFFICES in the old brewhouse, completed 2003–4.

Then the LANDSCAPE, essentially *Brown*'s as we see it today. In 1768–74 he removed nearly all traces of the formal gardens, avenues and the canal W of the house shown in detail on James Fish's map of 1736. He also cleared away the old chapel in 1772 and rearranged the old mill pools to create a single sheet of water. In place of the garden design associated with the house of 1711–14 he created a naturalistic landscape with grassland and trees, opening up views of the house from the three main sides. Associated with this work are the UPPER BRIDGE on the approach road through the park, of three arches with balustraded parapet and sphinxes, *c.* 1770, and the road bridge on the W side of the grounds, 1772. Beyond is the lower lake, enlarged by *William Whitmore* 1814–15, with an 1860s boathouse believed to be by *Gibson.* Also by *Brown,* the thatched ICE HOUSE near the Upper Bridge, 1771. Restored by *John Goom,* 2011. NW of the house was *Brown's* ORANGERY (or Green House), built in 1769–70 but demolished in the 1950s. A new house with a replica façade has been erected by *Brock Charles Architects,* 2010–13.

STABLES, NE of the house. By *James Gibbs,* but built by *Francis Smith,* 1736–8. Nine-bay front of one and a half storeys. Three-bay pediment in centre with a bust in a roundel. Doorways and windows with the typical Gibbs surrounds. Cupola added 1823. Courtyard floor raised and the building converted to apartments, *c.* 1989.

CHAPEL, immediately NW of the house. Built in 1776–9 by *Brown* to replace the medieval chapel by the lake, whose site is marked by an obelisk, 1848, at the entrance to the vault. It cost £981. The chapel became a parish church in 1852. Externally a plain rectangle with arched windows, a Venetian E window, and a front with niches and pediment, all rather 1740- than 1770-looking. The bellcote 1852. Inside, fine, sparing decoration of walls, close to Adam in style, by *William Hiatt,* 1777. Fluted pilasters l. and r. of the former altar and to the window above. The heavy ceiling panels and the decorated surrounds to the side windows probably 1860s. WEST GALLERY on paired Tuscan columns. Restoration of the chapel as a venue for music and other events will commence in 2016. – The SEATING is arranged college-chapel-wise with a three-decker PULPIT at the far end on the S side. – STAINED GLASS. Only window heads remain with C18 glass.* – MONUMENTS. Brasses to Anne Verney †1523 (23 in. (58 cm.) figure), to Richard Verney(?) †1526 and family (24 in. (61 cm.); she is taller than he), and to George Verney †1574 (23 in. (58 cm.)). – Sir Richard Verney †1630 and wife Margaret. By *Nicholas Stone,* 1630/1. The monument cost £90. Free-standing tomb-chest and recumbent effigies. White and black marble. – Sir Greville †1642 and other Verneys †1648–9. Three similar incised floor slabs with heraldic carving and inlaid brass, attributed to *Edward Marshall.* – Sir Greville Verney, Lord Willoughby de Broke, †1668. Attributed to *C. G. Cibber* (GF). Bust of the young man in the round, with a full wig. Black architectural background. – John Verney †1741 and his wife Abigail †1760. A noble piece. Strigillated sarcophagus in front of an obelisk. On the sarcophagus a medallion with the two heads in

*The C15 to C17 heraldic glass, transferred from the old chapel in 1776–9, was removed in the 1920s and sold in 1931. Some of it is at Warwick Museum, some in the Burrell Collection in Glasgow and more in the USA.

profile. – Lady Lewisham †1798. By *Richard Westmacott I.* White, figureless, with a garland. – Lord Willoughby de Broke †1852. By *Peter Hollins* of Birmingham. White, with a draped portrait medallion. – Also a fine set of mid-C17 ledger stones of black marble and brass.

LODGE up the hill towards the Fosse. Altered, but originally one-storeyed. Heavy rusticated quoins and window surrounds. No doubt by *Gibson*, 1860s.

3040

COMPTON WYNYATES

37 Compton Wynyates was in the olden days known as Compton-in-the-Hole, a graceless way of saying that the house lies in a hollow, with hills – low hills – rising on all sides. The house is essentially still that built by Sir William Compton in two main phases between 1493 and 1528, although it replaced an earlier house of the Comptons who had owned property here since the C13. Sir William held court appointments under Henry VIII. His grandson Henry became Lord Compton in 1572 and Henry's son was made Earl of Northampton in 1618. In 1812 the 9th Earl, Charles, was given the rank of Marquess. But from the 1570s the family lived mainly at Castle Ashby in Northamptonshire until the 7th Marquess made Compton Wynyates his main home in 1978. Of its history, mention should be made of the tradition preserved by Leland that materials from the C15 Fulbroke Castle, near Warwick, were incorporated in Sir William's new house. The 1st Earl undertook some internal remodelling in the early C17 but both the house and the adjacent church suffered damage in the Civil War. Rainwater heads indicate repairs in 1723 and the E range was altered in 1732. In 1774, however, the contents were sold and the house remained unfurnished and unoccupied until *Matthew Digby Wyatt*'s restoration for the 3rd Marquess in 1859–67. Internal improvements and garden landscaping followed in the later C19. An extensive refurbishment was undertaken by *Forsyth Lawson & Morris* for the 7th Marquess in 1978–82.

It is the perfect picture-book house of the early Tudor decades, the most perfect in England in the specific picturesque, completely irregular mode, the very opposite to the roughly contemporary Herstmonceux (East Sussex), Oxburgh (Norfolk), or Thornbury (Glos.). It does not pretend to be fortified. It is a courtyard house which began with a basic quadrangle, later enlarged with irregular additions. Anthony Emery suggests a beginning after 1503, and a second phase of 1515–20. It originally had a moat, partially filled after the Civil War. It is of brick, partly with diapering and with just two timber-framed gables on the W or entrance side.

Take that side in detail. The porch first of all is not in the centre. It is two-storeyed, the entrance with a four-centred arch and decorated spandrel, the top with battlements. The arch is enriched with little carvings up its jambs. There is a projection on the l. of the porch, a higher projection further out on the r. The two half-timbered gables, needless to say, do not match either. They have replacement bargeboards in the original style. The projections and the porch, and other projections on the N and S sides, have straight joints, i.e. were added to a house with plainer frontages. The house in that form may have been of *c.* 1500. The principal projection on the S side is a big, quite irregular embattled tower, its r. part recessed and higher than the rest. To the r. of the tower follows the wall of the chapel with a five-light window with arched lights at the top and also below a transom. The windows immediately l. and r. of the chapel window are symmetrically arranged. The E side of the house was doubled in depth in the early C18 (rainwater heads 1732), but the present front with its shallow Gothic bay and battlements is *Wyatt*'s, *c.* 1860. Behind it lies the principal staircase.

The windows of Compton Wynyates are a riddle which may never be solved. They are of all kinds, although all are square-headed, but the lights are cusped or uncusped, and the arches of the lights two-centred or four-centred. Their dates vary between *c.* 1500, *c.* 1520, and the C19. They are particularly puzzling in the courtyard. The back (E) range is the hall range. The big bay window of the 1520 type with uncusped lights, a transom, a decorated frieze, and battlements is said to come from Fulbroke Castle.* Also varied are the chimneys, all in brick, in a range of configurations and patterns.

The HALL still has its screens passage with linenfold panelling. The buttery (with its original doorway) is surrounded by wooden partitions as well. The hall roof has been shortened by one bay and may have come from Fulbroke, although today this suggestion has little support. Side windows in two tiers; they may be original. Big grey chimneypiece. Its style goes with rainwater heads on the courtyard side which are also dated 1732. The STAIRCASE in the E wing is by Wyatt, *c.* 1860. The DINING ROOM ceiling has strapwork panels. It is supposed to be genuine, i.e. Elizabethan. The ceiling in the DRAWING ROOM above this room is also said to be genuine. The chimneypiece certainly is. It is of wood, richly, if not very sophisticatedly carved, and was transferred from Canonbury House, London, *c.* 1867. The CHAPEL DRAWING ROOM is half above the chapel and was presumably originally the family pew. The plasterwork again is called Jacobean, but all these ceilings look a little suspicious. The ceiling of HENRY VIII's BEDROOM on the other hand is obviously C17, with its Stuart badges, broad bands and unusual shapes. In the second-floor

*Anthony Emery agrees that the external head originally belonged in another context, but stops short of associating it with Fulbroke.

room in the tower is the COUNCIL ROOM with another Jacobean-looking ceiling. There are six doors to this room. On the floor above there is a PRIEST'S ROOM. The CHAPEL in the house needs little comment, but has pale STAINED GLASS by *Comper*, 1930, and a C17 chamber organ from Northampton with a finely carved case.

ST MARY (private chapel), detached, N of the house. C13 origins. Damaged in the Civil War and afterwards rebuilt by the 3rd Earl of Northampton. The rainwater heads have 'I N / 1665'. The top of the W tower with the curious M-like frieze must be C17 although the main structure may be pre-Reformation. The church was reported as 'newly erected' in 1674, but then 'there was as yet neither pulpit, seates, not any bookes, vestments or utensils provided for it'. It is two-naved and has two E windows and to the N and S two windows each, symmetrically placed. The window details are correctly Perp, but the pilaster-strips between them are most oddly C17, and so are the hoodmould stops. The S doorway has a surround of alternating rustication. Inside, the two naves are separated by an arcade with quatre-foil piers. The W respond is but a corbel, and this is placed immediately above the low tower arch. The PULPIT stands elevated between the two S windows. It has an ogee cap. – BOX PEWS. – FONT. Probably *c.* 1680. Of stone, oval in shape. Baluster stem. – COMMUNION RAIL. Three-sided; C18. – PAINTED PLASTER fragments depicting the sun and moon with lively faces, from the 1665 ceiling taken down in 1911. – HATCHMENTS. A splendid set of seventeen: late C17 to early C18. – HELM, GAUNTLETS, etc. Suggested to come from an early C16 monument. – MONUMENTS. A number of terribly damaged alabaster effigies, probably the victims of Civil War vandalism: lady late C15, Sir Thomas Compton †1528(?), knight late C16, two ladies late C16. – Sir William Compton †1663. Attributed to *Jasper Latham* (GF). Big tablet, purely architectural, and entirely classical. At the top a vase in a broken segmental pediment. Garland at the foot.

³/₈ m. SW of the house is COMPTON PIKE, a beacon, assigned to the late C16. Stone pyramid with ball finial.

For the WINDMILL, *see* Tysoe.

COPSTON MAGNA

A Denbigh (Newnham Paddox) estate village, with a small group of farms and cottages on a green near the church.

ST JOHN. By *Wyatt & Brandon* for the Earl of Denbigh, 1848–9, as a chapel of ease to Monks Kirby. It replaced an earlier chapel, mainly C15. Nave, chancel and bellcote, with contem-porary chimneyed S vestry. The style is Dec of *c.* 1300. E window tracery renewed in 1887 by *E. Swinfen Harris*, County

Surveyor for Buckinghamshire, whose wife Emily (*née* Toone)
came from Copston. – Traceried stone PULPIT, original, 1849.
– STAINED GLASS. Toone memorial E window, *Lavers & West-
lake*, 1887. – Sexfoil rose W window with patterned glass, *James
Powell & Sons*, 1849.
HOLLIES FARM, C19, has good outbuildings.

CORLEY

2080

CHURCH. Red sandstone. Norman, of early and late C12. Short
nave with added N aisle. The nave windows small with wide
reveals and continuous roll mouldings inside on the S, and
another in the original outside wall on the N, cut away when
the aisle was built. Arcade of two bays. Thick round piers with
round capitals decorated by scallops with various minor
enrichments. The large head etc. of the E respond is proud of
the circumference and possibly contemporary. Chancel arch
of the earlier building, just single-stepped. Round-headed S
doorway has one order of shafts with capitals with two spiral
volutes. Monolithic tympanum with rows of chip-carved
saltire crosses. Is this all early or late C12? The chancel is
ashlar-faced and of *c.* 1300 (Y- and intersecting tracery),
restored with new roof in 1865. Low central turret over E end
of nave, ancient in form but rebuilt by *John Ladds*, 1884–5. Also
by Ladds, the W end of the nave with Neo-Norman detailing.
Boarded nave ceiling, 1905. Plain N vestry added by *Gardner
& Baldwin*, 1967. – Normanesque PULPIT and READING
DESK, 1894–5, carved in Corley oak by the rector, the *Rev. R.
Potter*. – FONT. Circular, without features of interest, but
inscribed 1661. – PAINTING. Hardly recognizable fragments of
a St Christopher (N wall). – STAINED GLASS. In the chancel,
three by *Heaton, Butler & Bayne*, the E window, 1882, and side
windows, 1885.
At the NE entrance to the churchyard, a timber-framed Great
War memorial lychgate, by *C. J. Johnson* of Leicester, *c.* 1920.
S of the church, CORLEY MANOR, by *C. S. Smith*. Built as the
vicarage, 1824–5. Rendered, double-pile plan with Doric
portico. Plain brick rear extension, now a separate dwelling,
dated 1833. On the main road to the N, the former SCHOOL
HOUSE by *J. L. Akroyd*, 1848, enlarged 1879–80. In Church
Lane W of the church, the VILLAGE HALL, 1964, with low
vestibule and long rock-faced frontage. Further along, the
CORLEY CENTRE, built as a residential school for Coventry
City Council by *Arthur Ling*, 1959, with contemporary sculptures. On the lawn, Children Playing Fivestones by *Bob
Dawson*. On the driveway wall, Children, Cat and Elephant in
carved brick by *James C. Brown*. CHURCH FARMHOUSE is
partly C17 but with an E end of 1784 with quoins and gable
with oculus window.

CORLEY HALL, ½ m. NE. Timber-framed, H-plan with cross-gables. Early C16 but much altered and now rendered. On the E side a four-centred timber door head. (In an upper room a series of Early Renaissance panels with heads, some in medallions, c. 1530. Also an elaborate overmantel with pilasters and arches, late C16. VCH.)

At CORLEY MOOR, 1½ m. W, a former iron church in Watery Lane, 1886. Disused but hanging on. Further W, the old WINDMILL. A tower mill, converted to a house in 1973.

On the M6 ¾ m. N of the village, the MOTORWAY SERVICE STATION, originally by *Garnett, Cloughley, Blakemore & Associates*, 1970–2. Much altered, but the distinctive overbridge remains, rather like a railway carriage crossing the motorway.

IRON AGE HILLFORT, SE of the village by Corley Rocks and Burrow Hill. The fort is roughly square in plan and the univallate defences enclose an area of 7 acres (2.8 ha). The earthwork is still a conspicuous monument, despite ploughing, and stands to a height of 6 ft (1.83 metres) in places. A single entrance occurs in the middle of the W side. Excavation has shown the rampart to be of earth and rubble construction revetted with a well-built dry-stone wall on its outer face and strengthened internally by means of wooden tie-beams.

COUGHTON

ST PETER. All Perp, and all late C15 to early C16. The lower parts of the W tower are suggested to come first, but there is little difference in the details such as mouldings. Only the top stage is obviously different, but might just be C16. Nave and aisles, clerestory of three-light windows, chancel and two-bay chapels. The E end was the end chronologically. Sir Robert Throckmorton, who died in 1518, left money for the glazing of the three main E windows. The aisle windows are clearly earlier also than the chapel windows, which are the only ones with uncusped lights (cf. Coughton Court below). On the N, a brick and stone turret for the rood stair. The N aisle doorway has decorated spandrels, the S doorway a Gothick porch with ogee arch and quatrefoils of c. 1780 (cf. also Coughton Court). The arcades of three bays have piers with a typical late Perp section, basically lozenge-shaped (i.e. thinner to the nave than to the arch openings), and in detail with four hollow-chamfered projections, continued by concave-sided capitals and hollow-chamfered four-centred arches. The chapel arcades are less sophisticated. The pier has the customary section of four shafts and four hollows, the arches have wave mouldings. The chancel arch goes well with the chapel arcades. Attractively re-roofed and re-seated by *Charles Edge*, 1829–30. The seating since altered (the central aisle originally narrowed in the first bay of the nave) but the neat Gothic bench ends remain.

Proper and respectful for the date. Only minor restorations and alterations since.

The FURNISHINGS are exceptional in quantity and variety. – FONT. A composite, the bowl square but cut to octagonal. It stands on a short C13 stem with central column and four supports. – PULPIT, 1891. With traceried panels and linenfold panels from the medieval rood screen, reused. Further panels were used in the reredos, 1897, removed in 1973. – STALLS with traceried fronts and linenfold backs, C19 but incorporating C16 woodwork. Some of the same, very simple, poppy-heads (two with little figures) repeat in BENCH ENDS. – SCREENS to both chancel and chapels. Of one-light divisions. – Much of this evidently belongs to the original furnishings. – BREAD DOLE BOARD. 1717. With a whole fence of little balusters (s aisle). – STAINED GLASS. In the s and N chapel window heads many parts of the original glass, including a number of complete small figures. Sir Robert Throckmorton in his will stipulated that the E window should have the Doom, the N chapel E window the Seven Sacraments, and the s chapel E window the Seven Works of Mercy. In the E window the three sibyls (heads C19) were originally dated 1530 and placed in a different window. Their style is Flemish. Above heraldic glass and fragments. In the other windows the Apostles, the Evangelists, and many small bits. – Good w window, 1890, by *Powell* (designer *Henry Holiday*), now hidden by the ringing gallery of 1991. – One N window by *Hardman*, 1901. – MONU-MENTS. In the nave central aisle a big tomb-chest prepared for Sir Robert Throckmorton, who died in the Holy Land in 1518. Richly cusped quatrefoils with shields. The monument had of necessity remained empty and was appropriated by a later Sir Robert †1791. – Sir George †1553 and Dame Katherine (chancel N), the dates of death left blank. Tomb-chest with 3-ft (0.91-metre) brasses in the dress of 1530–40. He in armour, his head resting on the helmet. Small children below their feet. The large tomb-chest is of Purbeck(?) marble and has just two quatrefoils on its long side. – Sir Robert †1570 (chancel s), probably by *William Cure* the elder (GF). Alabaster tomb-chest with grey conglomerate slab and pilasters. Finely carved shields on the sides. – Sir John †1580 and wife Marjorie (chancel s). Alabaster six-poster of fluted Corinthian columns with high attic, containing heraldic shields between figures. Two recumbent effigies holding hands. They lie on straw mats – the Netherlandish tradition. The features are rather dull. Against the tomb-chest kneeling children, facing outwards. – Sir Robert †1862 and wife Elizabeth †1850 (chancel N). Tomb-chest with black marble lid and brass and enamel cross. Early revival brasses by *Hardman*, one designed by *Pugin*, 1843. On the end a plate commemorating Dame Elizabeth Throckmorton, the last abbess of Denny Abbey, Cambs., who returned to Coughton after the Dissolution in 1539 and continued to live by the rule of her order, accompanied by two other nuns, until her death in 1547. The remains of three nuns were discovered during the construction of the tomb. – Wall tablet in S aisle to Thomas Barr OSB, †1823, 'Pastor to the Roman Congregation of this Place during 38 Years'. Rare in a parish church, even one in the shadow of a Catholic stronghold.

In the churchyard a CROSS BASE and on it a C17 column with sundial and ball finial.

ST PETER, ST PAUL AND ST ELIZABETH (R.C.). Built for the Throckmortons by *Charles Hansom*, 1851–3. Very stately, and within a stone's throw of the old parish church. Large and as one composition with the well-composed, asymmetrical priest's house also by *Hansom*, c. 1853. The church is aisleless but with NE chapel-cum-private pew with its own entrance. Nave, chancel and spindly polygonal SW turret reminiscent of the early Christian towers in Ireland or Scotland. The style is c. 1300. W gallery inside. Panelled chancel ceiling with painted and stencilled decoration. – Carved stone PULPIT and FONT, c. 1855. – STAINED GLASS mostly by *Hardman*, 1855–62, and another †1916. – One S window by *F. Holt & Co.*, 1902. – Plain memorial window with inscriptions, 2004.

COUGHTON COURT. The Throckmorton family has lived at Coughton Court from the early C15 to the present day. They were a God-fearing family. They rebuilt the church in the late C15 and early C16, as we have seen, and Sir Robert went to the Holy Land in 1518. They remained Catholics after the Reformation, they were involved in the plot against Queen Elizabeth in 1583, suffered penalties and disabilities and never flinched. The house has its genuine priest holes, and a large part of the S wing was used in the C18 and C19 as a chapel, until in 1851–3, again as we have seen, they could build a separate Catholic church. Coughton was given to the National Trust in 1946 and the baronetcy died out in 1994, but Throckmorton descendants continue to live there and have initiated recent improvements to the property, notably in the stables, the gardens and in the grounds.

The fabric may conceal portions of an earlier building but the oldest visible part of the house is the lower part of the GATEHOUSE. The grey stone differs from the golden upper part, and the turrets above are polygonal, whereas their substructure is square. The upper part is assigned to after 1518, as the end of a building campaign which started under Sir Robert c. 1510 and continued under Sir George (†1553).

As originally built, the house was of the courtyard type with the gatehouse at the W and had a moat around. The brick and timber-framed N and S ranges remain. But in 1688 the hall range, i.e. the E range, was damaged by anti-Catholic rioters. Largely abandoned, it was eventually demolished about 1780 and in 1783 the moat was filled in. So what remains is the W range and two long N and S wings extending to the E. What is now clear, although unknown until quite recently, is that late C18 improvements transformed Coughton Court into what it is now. These were begun under Sir Robert Throckmorton,

4th Baronet, in about 1780 and continued after his death in 1791 by his grandson and heir, Sir John. Sadly, the name of their architect has not yet been discovered. *William Smith*, who supervised, does not seem to have been the designer. There are plans, unfortunately neither signed nor dated.

We must now look at the w front in more detail. The gatehouse itself is little altered externally and a remarkable piece of early Tudor domestic architecture. It bears both the royal arms and the Throckmorton arms. The opening has a four-centred arch and decorated spandrels with shields and foliage. Above is a two-storeyed canted oriel both to the w and the E. The windows have depressed-arched lights, uncusped. On the first floor they have two transoms, on the second only one. The angle turrets are also broken up in windows, an effect typical of the years when building went on (cf. e.g. Thornbury Castle, Glos., of *c.* 1521). Astonishingly the bays on each side, although their stone colour and mouldings match the gatehouse, are not Tudor but of the 1780s, as their internal arrangement confirms. These bays are two storeys in height with square-headed mullioned-and-transomed windows and hoodmoulds. The continuation of the w front is symmetrical N and S. First come three unmistakably Gothick ogee-headed windows in slightly recessed bays each side, and then two end bays of two storeys with square-headed windows. Illustrations show that the two outer bays once had C17 shaped gables. The final alterations came in 1835 when the plain low parapet and gables to the five end bays on each side were replaced by the unifying embattled parapets. These have blind quatrefoils, echoing the originals on the 1780s bays, on the otherwise featureless deep parapet. These later parts are cement-rendered. So, the late C18 work paid homage to the Tudor, and the 1835 alterations respected the Gothick.

Into the courtyard next. The S and N ranges were built in the early C16 but do not align equally with the gatehouse. They are timber-framed on a brick ground floor and much restored. The big Perp doorway in the S range, leading to the former chapel, is reused *ex situ*, possibly from the demolished E range. The E end of the S range shows the outline of three Gothic pointed windows of the former chapel. The gables on the N and S sides differ in number and rhythm. The pretty carved bargeboards and finials of the two S gables are particularly fine, with smaller ones on the dormers on the roof above. The top floor and the gables of the N wing are of about 1600. At about the same time the S range was widened. Sir Francis Throckmorton extended the house in 1663–5, adding a two-storeyed SW block with a new parlour and dining room. The additions are in brick with stone dressings and a big shaped gable, similar to those once on the W front (the one in the SW corner having been of 1663–5 too). The N range, presumably *c.* 1690, also received addition on the N where there are three projecting bays with hipped roofs. The extension is rendered and has quoins but still mullioned-and-transomed windows.

As regards the INTERIOR, one enters through the gatehouse with its delicate C18 plaster fan-vaulting – the grand new entrance created in the 1780s and originally lit with armorial windows, replaced by oak double doors in 1835. The open-well stair on the S – in one of the C18 Tudor bays flanking the gatehouse – was under construction in 1784–5. On the first floor, the BLUE DRAWING ROOM with a Gothic frieze in plaster. To the N, the YELLOW DRAWING ROOM has an C18 fireplace. A spiral stair leads up to the TOWER ROOM above, with an original chimneypiece with foliage in the spandrels. In the NE turret of the gatehouse are two priest holes, one below the other. From the gatehouse roof, good views of the complex roofscape. Also the parkland to the W and the gardens and open country to E and SE

Back down on the first floor, the panelled dining room in the S wing has a carved oak frieze with foliage and medallions characteristic of *c.* 1530. The panelling below and the chimneypiece with coupled black marble columns in two tiers looks *c.* 1620. The Tribune adjoining the dining room, also panelled, leads to a stair down to the SALOON at the E end, where the chapel was. The panelled double-flight staircase was brought in from Harvington Hall in Worcestershire, another Throckmorton property. It was, of course, altered in the re-setting. The Saloon has internal arcading on the N side, by *James Hart* of Bristol, 1910. N of the gatehouse is the study, with very fine later C17 panelling. The giant pilasters and the peculiar shape of the panels are equally typical of their date. At the N end is a C17 staircase with vertically symmetrical balusters. On the first floor is a wooden chimneypiece also from Harvington. Good early C16 beamed ceilings in the N wing.

An OUTBUILDING of stone to the N (marked as the brewhouse on a 1746 plan), also C16 and once connected to the N range by a bridge. The windows have arched lights, and the doorway a four-centred arch.

Later C18 STABLES N of the house and abutting the above. Symmetrical W front with central archway and bell-turret above. Pavilions at each end, the S pavilion being the hipped-roofed end of the outbuilding. Through the archway, a courtyard and linked mid-C19 coach house.

Coughton stretches along the ancient Icknield (or Ryknield) Street (now Birmingham Road) which runs N–S through the parish, becoming Haydon Way to the N and continuing S into Kings Coughton (p. 399). Just the Court and its parkland on the E through the village, the old houses in the park having been cleared away in the 1780s leaving only the caged stump of the village CROSS at the crossroads and earthworks near the C20 entrance LODGE. S of Coughton Fields Lane at the crossroads, three-storey early C19 COUGHTON CROSS FARM. On the W side opposite a low range of cottages, once ALMSHOUSES founded in the C16 but rebuilt. Up Coughton Lane,

several black-and-white and C19 estate cottages. Here, too, was
the Catholic school, by *C. A. Buckler*, 1858, but now gone. On
the corner, the former POST OFFICE, timber-framed and brick
behind as seen from the lane but Georgian with bow windows
on the street front. Heading N on the W side, the old FORGE
adjoining a brick and timber cottage the corner of Sambourne
Lane. In the lane, the old NATIONAL SCHOOL, 1860. Brick
with polychromatic patterning, with a matching extension.
Then the burial ground and CHAPEL, 1867. Gothic, soft cream
and red brick with stone dressings. Back on Birmingham Road,
the OLD VICARAGE set back from the street. An old building
acquired by the vicar in 1786 in exchange for a house pulled
down by Sir Robert to improve the park. Refronted and
enlarged, 1829–30, by *Charles Edge* who was then working on
the church. Next COUGHTON HOUSE, a substantial C16 or
C17 timber-framed house with an added wing of painted brick,
1840s. Then the low timber framing of COUGHTON LODGE,
once the estate office, now a hotel. Over the bridge the ground
rises, with further estate cottages (dates 1896–7) and the much
altered THROCKMORTON ARMS before cottages. A little N,
PARKFIELD LODGE, a square brick house, *c.* 1830. The
windows have stone lintels on consoles.

COUNDON *see* p. 286

COVENTRY

INTRODUCTION

Through the ages Coventry has seen great prosperity but the vicissitudes of economic development have also brought times of hardship. Development began in the early C11 with the Benedictine priory (*see* p. 234) founded by Leofric, Earl of Mercia, and Countess Godiva, and the town that grew up on a triangular site to the w. The priory was consecrated in 1043 and became a cathedral during the short period of Coventry as a bishop's see (1102–88). In about 1139 the Earl of Chester built a castle E of Broadgate. From these origins emerged a city with distinct areas associated with the two principal churches, the prior's estate being served by Holy Trinity and the earl's domain by St Michael's. The story continues with the rise of commerce in the C13, incorporation in 1345, the erection of city walls with twelve gates between 1356 and 1423, and the acceptance as a county in 1451. The C14 saw the climax of medieval prosperity. Coventry was the fourth city in England then (after London, York and Bristol) in wealth, though not in size. The C14 population is estimated at *c.* 5,000. The Merchant Guild of St Mary was granted in 1340, and three more guilds established themselves in the 1340s. The Holy Trinity Guild followed in 1364. In 1392 four of these were united and soon afterwards rebuilt St Mary's Guildhall (p. 247). Of merchants' houses a few undercrofts remain. Also, always a sign of prosperity, Coventry had, apart from its ancient Benedictine priory, houses of the Greyfriars and Whitefriars, a hospital and, outside, a charterhouse. Of all these remains are preserved.

The source of Coventry's wealth was wool first, cloth soon after. Then, after an undeniable decline, the city rallied in the C18 with the specialities of ribbon-making and watch-making. Ribbon-making (Cash's) became an industry in the period 1820–50, and out of watch-making grew sewing-machine-making and then, in the 1870s, bicycle-making. The foundation of Daimler's motor-car factory dates from 1896 and Siddeley-Deasy (later Armstrong Siddeley) commenced aircraft production in 1915. By

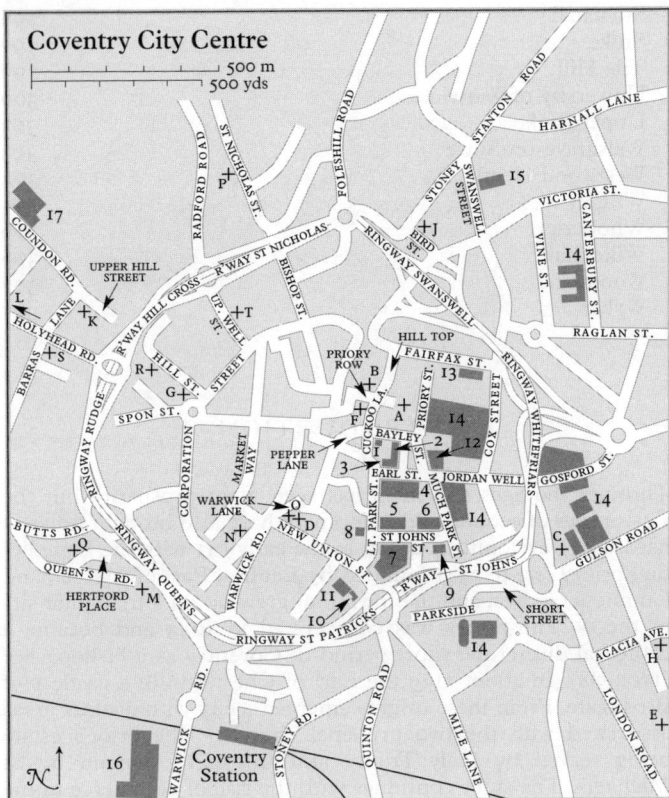

Coventry City Centre

A Coventry Cathedral and ruins
   of St Michael's Cathedral
B St Mary's Cathedral and Priory
C The Whitefriars
D Greyfriars
E Charterhouse of St Anne
F Holy Trinity
G St John the Baptist
H St Anne and All Saints
J St Mark (former)
K St Osburg (R.C.)
L Great Meeting House
M Queens Road Baptist Church
N United Reformed church
O Methodist Central Hall
P St Columba's United
   Reformed Church
Q Elim Pentecostal
R Friends' Meeting
S Synagogue and Rabbi's
   House (former)
T Salvation Army Centre

1 St Mary's Guildhall
2 Public Offices
3 Council House
4 Civic Centre
5 Magistrates' Court
6 Crown & County Court
7 Police Headquarters
8 Telephone Exchange
9 Severn Trent Water
   Operations Centre
10 Government Offices
11 Job Centre
12 Herbert Art Gallery and
   Museum
13 Sports and Leisure Centre
14 Coventry University
15 Coventry City College
16 King Henry VIII School
17 Bablake School

the mid 1960s the motor-car and accessories industries employed 45,000. However, the boom years came to an abrupt end with the loss of 46 per cent of manufacturing jobs between 1974 and 1982. A shift towards business and the creative industries brought a recovery, coupled with the emergence of the two universities as major employers. Coventry University (1987) in the city centre developed from earlier institutions while the University of Warwick, on the southern outskirts, was founded anew in 1965.

Industrial prosperity brought expansion. From a population of *c.* 12,000 in 1750 Coventry grew to 16,000 in 1801, 37,000 in 1851 and 70,000 in 1901, after which boundary extensions, most significantly in 1927 and 1932, added to the totals. Migration of workers to Coventry between the wars fuelled an increase from 114,197 in 1921 to 260,685 in 1951, making it the fastest growing UK city in the inter-war period. Today the population stands at 337,400 (2014). With this growth came physical expansion, with larger factories outside the city centre and new housing estates at Stivichall from 1921, Radford and Coundon begun in 1924 and Canley commenced in 1938.

Coventry benefited from its central location for ease of communications, especially after *Telford*'s new Holyhead Road put the city on the main road from London to Birmingham in 1824–9. The canal basin N of the city opened in 1769, initially for the transport of coal from Bedworth, but eventually connecting by 1777 to the canals towards Oxford and Tamworth from Hawkesbury junction. Coventry station on the London to Birmingham railway opened in 1838, followed by branches to Milverton (later to Leamington) in 1844 and to Nuneaton in 1850. Of other road improvements, mention should be made of the southern and western by-pass completed in 1937–9 and the city centre's inner ring road in 1974.

Architecturally Coventry reached its zenith between the mid C14 and mid C15, as can be seen at St Mary's Guildhall, Holy Trinity, and St John the Baptist, and in the remains of St Michael's and Whitefriars. As well as developing a particularly distinctive Perp style, Coventry was also a significant centre for stained glass, most notably represented by *John Thornton*, who contracted for the great E window of York Minster in 1405. The medieval city, hemmed in at the edges by large landed estates E and S and by the freemen's commons W and SW, was densely populated and compact. Right into the C20 it was characterized by narrow streets of timber-framed buildings, many with high-quality decorative detail from the C15 onwards.

Of local architects, only *Joseph Eglington* (1780s–90s) and *Thomas Stedman Whitwell* (1820s–30s) stand out until the mid C19. *Charles Hansom* practised in Coventry from 1838 until 1847, serving as City Surveyor 1840–3. Then came *J. L. Akroyd* (†1856), *Joseph Nevill* (fl. 1840s–60s), and local 'rogue architect' *G. T. Robinson* (fl. 1860s). The most notable was *James Murray* (†1863), who made a huge impact on Coventry in his short but active career. He is commemorated by a fine monument in the London Road Cemetery (*see* p. 285). Later Victorian and Edwardian architects included the *Steanes* (George †1914 and Isaac †1908), notable for Nonconformist churches, factory architects *Harry Quick* and *E.J. Purnell (Jun.)*, busy general practitioner *T.F. Tickner*, and *T.R. Donnelly* (†1908), who was responsible for several Roman Catholic churches. In the inter-war years *T.R.J. Meakin* and *Harold T. Jackson* were among the more adventurous local designers.

For Coventry in the C20, we must turn to public architecture. City Engineer *J.E. Swindlehurst* (retired in 1924) designed the old fire station in 1902 and the Carnegie Libraries in 1911–12, and oversaw the city's early council-house building programme. His successor, *E.H. Ford*, coped with a widening brief including responsibility for planning. He was greatly involved in the development of the suburbs, meeting the constant demand for new housing. His projects included the laying out of Corporation Street (1931), the clearance of the historic but by then shabby and constricting Butcher Row to create Trinity Street (1937) and the construction of the outer by-pass (1937–9). His war work as surveyor and engineer in a city devastated by bombing in 1940–1 earned him the OBE. Despite these achievements his reputation has suffered from his ill-remembered involvement in the post-war reconstruction of the city.

Given the influx of workers for the factories it is hardly surprising that the Labour Party won control of the city council in November 1937, remaining in power until 1968. An early act of the new socialist administration was to create a new City Architect's Department headed by *(Sir) Donald Gibson* who took up his post in January 1939. His staff transferred from the Engineer's Department included *Gwyn H. Morris*, joined by *Percy Johnson-Marshall*. Gibson's team produced proposals for 'Coventry of Tomorrow' in 1939, one of the first schemes for city-centre replanning.* The devastation of the city in the air raids of 1940 and 1941 rendered it obsolete. In the civic and commercial core only 31 out of 975 buildings were unscathed. Acting swiftly, the council instructed Gibson and Ford, still in control of planning, to draw up reconstruction plans. As they could not agree, separate schemes were prepared, Ford producing a pragmatic and essentially conservative plan offering little change. Gibson's more visionary scheme for comprehensive redevelopment was adopted in February 1941, undergoing several revisions before implementation got under way.† Nevertheless, the scale of the Gibson plan is still among the most impressive in Britain and its key elements, especially the pedestrianized precincts and the ring road, mark it out from others. That it could be drawn up, developed and largely put into operation was due to the lucky combination of prospering industrial private enterprise with a Labour council under George Hodgkinson as chairman of the Planning and Redevelopment Committee.

---

*Jeremy Gould indicates that Southampton also had a pre-war redevelopment plan.
†According to Gould, Plymouth became the first UK city to implement its post-war plan.

Rebuilding began in 1948 and Gibson became City Architect and Planner after Ford retired in 1949. His principals then were *Douglas Beaton* (city centre), *William Glare* (schools), *Gwyn Morris* (housing) and (Sir) *Wilfred Burns* (planning). Gibson was always keen to give credit to key team members.* Other assistants under Gibson included *Edmund C. Tory*, *F. Lloyd Roche*, *Fred Pooley*, *Kenneth G. King*, *Raymond Ash*, *John C. Barker*, *David Percival* and *Brian Bunch*, while *James C. Brown* was often responsible for the artworks. Gibson's successor was *Arthur Ling* (1955–64), whose assistants included *Audrey Lees*, *J. Michael McLellan*, *Terry Long*, *Bill Berrett* and *Alan Robinson*. Then came *Terence Gregory* (1964–73) and *Harry Noble* (1973–94) who succeeded when Gregory became Chief Executive. Later assistants included *Roger Arlidge* and *Rex Chell*. The names are worth listing because so many of them went on afterwards to hold senior posts elsewhere as County or City Architects, or in planning, in teaching (e.g. Gibson and Ling), and (e.g. Pooley, Burns and Roche) to high office in professional bodies. This, of course, reflects the wider influence and impact of 'new Coventry'.

Under Gibson and Ling the output was prodigious – not only the city centre, but also council buildings, colleges, schools, housing estates, etc. Of necessity some projects were carried out in partnership with private practices (e.g. Hillman House with *Arthur Swift & Partners*). Local practices closely associated with the 1950s and 1960s redevelopment included *W. S. Hattrell & Partners*, *Rolf Hellberg* (later *Hellberg & Harris*), *C. F. Redgrave* (later *Redgrave & Clarke*) and *W. H. Saunders & Son*.

Although widely acclaimed at the time, Coventry's post-war buildings have not fared very well. Many have been demolished and replaced and a high percentage of those which remain are now much altered. Redevelopment is actively ongoing (2015). In the first edition of this guide Pevsner could justifiably state that the centre of Coventry in 1964 could only be treated in C20 terms. Now the work of that time must be seen as just one major change in the city's evolution and viewed in the context of national post-war rebuilding. The recent study by Jeremy and Caroline Gould, drawing comparisons with other war-ravaged cities like Plymouth, Exeter, Southampton and Bristol, should help to foster appreciation of what remains and to dispel Coventry's undeserved reputation as a city without buildings of architectural merit.

CITY CENTRE

The area is roughly defined by the Ringway, built in stages and completed in 1974. This takes in nearly all the area of the

---

*For brevity, works by the City Architect's Department are identified in the gazetteer under the names of Gibson and his successors Ling, Gregory and Noble. Project architects are sparingly named without stating their precise roles.

medieval walled city. However, some other buildings in the inner suburbs that might be regarded as central are included (e.g. places of worship, the railway station and parts of Coventry University straddling the boundary).

CATHEDRAL OF ST MICHAEL

118   Coventry was raised to cathedral rank in 1918. St Michael, the prime parish church, became the cathedral. On 14 November 1940 it was largely destroyed but the immediately declared ambition to rebuild meant that the ruins remained a potent symbol of the city's fortitude, and open-air ceremonies continued within its shell. The first scheme for rebuilding was developed by *Sir Giles Gilbert Scott*, appointed in 1942, and envisaged incorporating the apse and tower of the church into the new building, with the former nave as a cloister. This plan was given up in 1946 in the face of resistance from Bishop Gorton who wanted a fresh start, a building for modern worship and right for Gibson's new city. Scott initially tried to accommodate the demands of the bishop but eventually resigned. A restricted site was one of the difficulties, resolved when additional land was acquired in 1948. When a competition for a new building was held in 1950–1 there were no prescriptions as to style, orientation, materials or plan. Gorton secured provision for special features, including a Chapel of Unity, but was unable to insist on the central altar he so greatly favoured. Of the 219 entries, many followed the conventional design of nave and aisles with altar at the E end. Some were traditional Gothic. The winner was *Basil Spence* (of *Basil Spence & Partners*) who was knighted in 1960 for his work at Coventry. The principal features of his design had come to him when he first visited the site: the placing N–S and the use of the ruin of the old church as a forecourt. The design, when made known, was blamed by the moderns as not modern enough, by the traditionalists as too modern, by the man in the street as jazzy. Those initial controversies are over now that the building has been complete for fifty years and its importance as the principal monument of England's reconstruction and artistic flowering after the war is recognized,* but many still maintained after its consecration in 1962 that Sir Basil's brief was wrong and that a church in the mid C20 ought to have been planned not like one of the past, but in accordance with what called itself the Liturgical Movement, that is, like the 'theatre in the round' with the altar in the centre and the faithful all turned towards it. This is arguable – objections have e.g. been raised on the grounds that what is good for a parish church is not necessarily good for a cathedral – but has nothing to do with the architectural appreciation to which we must now proceed.

---

*It was listed Grade 1 in 1988 and in 1999 was voted Britain's favourite C20 building in a poll carried out by Channel 4 with English Heritage.

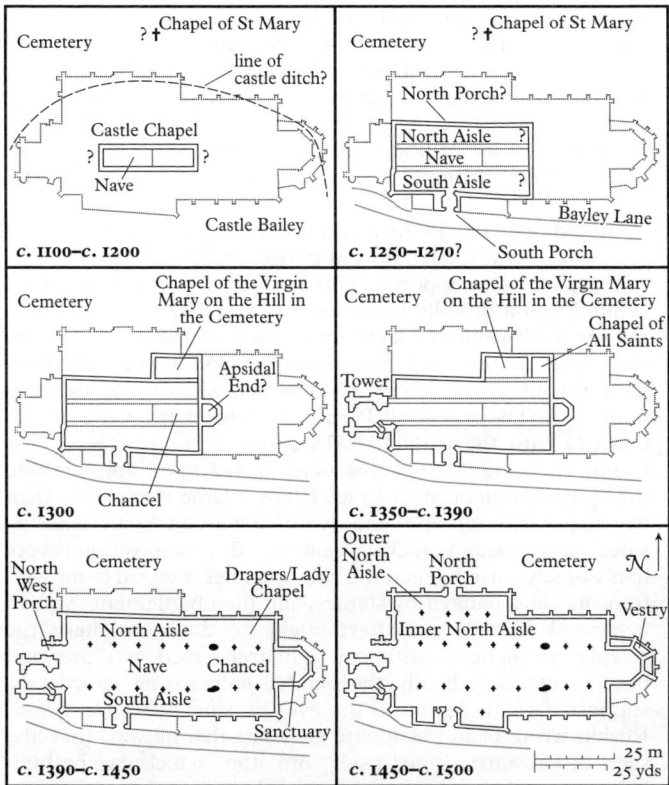

Coventry, Cathedral of St Michael.
Phased plan showing development from *c.* 1100 to *c.* 1500

Pevsner's description and assessment of the old and new cathedrals needs little amendment and is repeated here largely unaltered.*

The cathedral is small – only 270 ft (82.3 metres) long – but Sir Basil managed to make it appear large. It is built of red sandstone – the traditional local material – and is entered from the E (ritually s) or the s (ritually w). To the s remain the outer walls of the church of ST MICHAEL and to their w the steeple, 295 ft (90 metres) high. St Michael, with a floor area of 24,000 sq. ft (2,230 sq. metres), was one of the largest English parish churches. It began in the C12 as the chapel for the castle, sitting

*Minor corrections of errors of fact or dating have been made and some further details added at the suggestion of Louise Campbell (LC) and George Demidowicz (GD) for whose contributions I am very grateful.

within the castle bailey. By the later C13 a small aisled church
stood within the footprint of the later nave and S aisle. This
was extended in the C14, especially on the N side where chapels
were added with crypts below as necessitated by the sloping
ground. Then came the great rebuild, *c.* 1390 to *c.* 1450, followed by further additions on the N (the outer N aisle) and S
(the chapels flanking the earlier S porch) in the later
C15 (GD).

One should first tarry in the forecourt and examine what survives
after 1940 of this splendid old parish church. The oldest surviving part is the S porch. This is *c.* 1250–70, with moulded
capitals and a broadly trefoil-cusped arch. Below the outer N
aisle is a rib-vaulted CRYPT of *c.* 1300 consisting of two by
three bays. To the E is a later extension. Both crypts were built
with chapels above, afterwards replaced when the N aisle was
built (GD). The rest is all Perp but stretches from the mid to
late C14 into the early C16. In about 1371 the steeple was
begun. Its octagon was constructed in the 1430s and work on
the spire commenced in 1444. It has a large W window, then
two stages with tall one- and two-light windows with concave-
sided or ogee-sided crocketed gables – the composition is very
handsomely varied – then the bell-openings, two tall twins with
transoms and flanked by statues, and then battlements and an
octagonal storey – an afterthought no doubt to make the
steeple yet higher – with two-light transomed windows and
battlements, and finally the banded spire rising effortlessly,
supported (so it seems to the eye) by slim flying buttresses.
Ruskin wrote of it, passionate geologist that he was, that 'the
sand of Coventry' binds itself 'into stone which can be built
half-way to the sky' (1874). Inside, the tower was open right
up to a lierne-vault just below the octagonal stage, but this was
altered when the bells were repositioned low down in the tower
in 1986–7. There is a viewing platform above the bells from
which the vault (reinstated to a new design by *John Oldrid Scott*
as part of his thorough restoration of the steeple, 1888–90) can
be seen.

As one stands inside one will notice at once the great and undeniably painful anomaly of the church. The nave was considerably
wider than the steeple. To its N there is enough space for a
whole porch and portal with a lierne-vault inside. The reason
is that the steeple was built to stand W of the C13 (or C12) nave,
possibly explaining the curious lengths of bare wall between
steeple and nave (GD). The widening of the nave is part of a
somewhat later and even more ambitious building programme.
When the wealthy of Coventry embarked on it we do not
know, but the work is datable to *c.* 1390 to *c.* 1450. Work
started with the chancel and proceeded quickly. The chancel
has a polygonal apse, a rarity in England (cf. Lichfield) and
especially at so late a date. With its decorated battlements and
pinnacles it now stands higher than the rest of the walls. The
windows are of four lights with ample panel tracery. There are
subsidiary vestry rooms at the foot of the apse. Of the

five bays three date from the late C15. The two on the SE completing the range are by *John Oldrid Scott*, 1886–7. As one turns N or S, one first sees the seven-light chancel aisle E windows (N four plus four intersecting, S three plus one plus three) and then the large N and S windows, the latter now entirely without mullions and tracery. But from about midway to the W one does not see outer walls of the aisles any longer; for late in the C15 chapels were added E as well as W of the porches. The E window of the SE chapel has the pretty quatre-foils in the tracery of which we are to find much more at St John the Baptist(*see* p. 243).

As for the interior, it must be hard for anyone to remember it to visualize its scale and character. The piers are marked in the ground. Only one pier stands fully: in the SE chapel. But in this state, like the arena of a martyrdom, this bare space open to the sky is deeply moving, and as, already under its canopy, one descends twenty steps into the porch of the new cathedral, one is ready for whatever spiritual impact may come. The survival of the steeple was an untold boon to competitors for the new building; for the C20 style had not been able to create anything anywhere both as elegant and as powerful as a late medieval steeple. But the relation between the walls of the church and the new building was all Sir Basil Spence's. The motif of his design which hit his many imitators most forcibly was the sawtooth walls N and S.* The sharp rhythm of com-pletely bare rose sandstone walls pointing half-w and each section rising along the skyline towards the W, and equally completely grid walls of stone and glass pointing half-E and thus throwing their coloured light towards the altar, establishes at once a poignancy which will be found in many other places and ways. The E wall is entirely bare, except for a large cross in relief and the batter of the angle buttresses. The Lady Chapel N and S walls have a rather smaller rhythm of long oblong and small square windows. To the S near the E end projects the concrete CHAPEL OF CHRIST THE SERVANT with its slate fins. To the N near the W end is the dodecagonal CHAPEL OF UNITY, also concrete, with its much more complex slate but-tresses and irregularly detailed slit windows. Opposite it the S wall curves outward gently and has a bold stone grid of a dif-ferent pattern from that of the windows. Behind this is the font. Finally the PORCH. It is open to N and S (again ritually speak-ing). The main entrance, unless one passes through the Perp forecourt, is from the S, where a flight of steps leads up to it. Here to the r. is *Epstein*'s St Michael and Lucifer, one of his last works. It is large, of bronze, and the two figures are kept entirely separate. St Michael hovers over Lucifer, but Lucifer, although reclining, reclines nowhere. It is a sentimental piece, its expressionism more in feature and gesture than in emo-tional intensity of forms. In Sir Basil Spence's taste it marks

---

*The directions in the following pages are all taken ritually, i.e. the altar end is called E though it faces N, etc.

the one extreme. The other we shall find later, and the two never in the cathedral reach a full reconciliation. Similarly the porch itself differs in style from the rest of the church. Its design was in fact revised at the end, and as it was finally built it is closer to the University of Sussex than to the sawtooth walls of Coventry. Earlier Spence was sharp, later Spence (under Le Corbusier's influence: Maisons Jaoul) is more massive. The piers of the porch are circular and extremely high. They are sheer, except that very convincingly just under the top they stop and disclose the much thinner gauge of concrete doing the real carrying job. Canopies jut out or grasp out to N, S, and W.

Having the steeple of St Michael, the new cathedral needed no beacon of its own. But some vertical accent on the flattish roof seemed to be called for, and so Sir Basil decided on a flèche. This also went through a number of phases. It ended up as a tall, transparent space-frame, looking – in spite of *Geoffrey Clarke*'s thorny, abstract cross, so amazingly lowered into position by an RAF helicopter – like a piece of television apparatus. One could imagine that one day Sir Basil himself might have wished to change this flèche.

One enters through doors which are part of a W wall completely of glass. At Coventry the distinction between architectural description and description of the furnishings loses its sense. The two are too much part of one conception. What was made for, and went into, the cathedral between the laying of the foundation stone in 1956 and the consecration in 1962 was what Sir Basil wanted and went where he wanted it. The WEST WINDOW is engraved with saints and angels by *John Hutton*, long, gaunt figures more stylized than Epstein's St Michael, but, in the Expressionist way, telling their story by intensified gesture and tense drapery. Henry Moore's wartime drawings are evidently the source of style.

The first impression in looking through the glass wall or passing through the doors is undeniably Gothic. This is due to four causes: the proportions, the existence of nave and aisles, the slenderness of the piers, and the semblance of a ribbed vault. As for proportion, it is not only a matter of width to height of nave, although that matters greatly, but also of length to both of them, i.e. the uninterrupted vista along many piers to a distant altar wall. There is in fact no altar wall, as there is no vault, but the mind interprets the visual data that way. The piers are cruciform, set diagonally, and taper outward as they rise. They could be slenderer yet at the bottom, and once again Sir Basil decided to demonstrate this structural fact by giving them a girth of much smaller section. The engineers building train sheds for railway stations had done that for nearly a hundred years. From the piers issue concrete ribs creating a vaulting grid of folded square panels filled in with wooden slats in two directions, an exciting pattern of exactly the same fighting energy as the sawtooth walls. In fact all this has nothing to do with vaulting the building in the Gothic sense. Piers and

120

ribs form a canopy from W end to altar space and keep detached from the real concrete roof.* This is not easily noticed, and those who ask for structural truth will not be satisfied with the very narrow gap between walls and canopy. It is only when one looks back from the Lady Chapel that one realizes that a man can stand upright between the two.

Next to the piers and vaults the side walls speak most powerfully. Owing to the sawtooth plan one sees only them and no windows, and they are entirely sheer, except for *Ralph Beyer*'s monumental inscriptions. The walls are harled, to use the Scottish term for a Scottish architect's choice, i.e. roughcast a whitish grey, i.e. not made to look precious. The large inscription tablets are done in a script of Roman capitals very much with the carver's irregularities; there is no machine transmission here. The sculptor who designed them cut them himself. They are of biblical passages, and each is illustrated by a very simple, primeval symbol: a dove, a chalice, the sun. *Ralph Beyer* also designed the dedication inscription for the floor at the W end, and this is carried out in brass letters, 3 ft (0.9 metres) high. The floor is of white and black marble and might compete unfavourably with the greys above, if it were not for the permanently set rows of stacking chairs (designed by *Russell, Hodgson & Leigh*).

But before the inscriptions can be read and the visitor proceeds towards the chancel, there is a double halt, almost immediately after the entry. On the S is the baptistery, on the N the access to the Chapel of Unity. The BAPTISTERY curves out very gently to hold the FONT, which is an enormous raw boulder brought from Bethlehem, another of those poignant ideas in which Sir Basil's mind was so fertile. The concave wall is a three-dimensional stone grid filled entirely by STAINED GLASS 119 designed by *John Piper* and made by *Patrick Reyntiens*. It is among the best English glass of the C20, entirely abstract, but its colours expressing a perfectly convincingly presented message. The message is *per aspera ad astra*, to a sun-like yellow with actually a white centre, from dark blue at the top, dark red along the sides, a dark green lower down, and a busier mixture of colours down below, where we are. The detail is largely organized in forms parallel to those of the grid, which results in a sense of order and direction and so finally in repose.

Opposite is the one long stretch of bare wall simply at right angles to the entry wall. The access to the CHAPEL OF UNITY is low and flanked by two areas of absolutely plain clear glass, release from the intensity of the interior mood of the cathedral. The passage leading to the chapel is funnel-shaped, functionally appropriate and at the same time in accordance with the *leit-motif* of diagonals which runs throughout the building (except for the porch). The walls here are once more clear glass. But the chapel is mysterious, more concentratedly perhaps than any other part of the building. What Sir Basil has done is to

---

* *Ove Arup* was the structural engineer for this.

alternate round the room between angular stretches of high walling, each taking in an angle of the dodecagon, and deep funnel-shaped recesses like the jambs of windows in a keep, ending (on the outer surface of what seem buttresses externally) with irregularly shaped small panels of coloured glass all the way up. The *dalle-de-verre* glass, again entirely abstract, is by *Margaret Traherne*. But in order not to keep the chapel too much in darkness unfiltered light was needed, and this Sir Basil provided by the thinnest slits all the way up between walls and recesses. The floor mosaic is by *Einar Forseth*.

As one returns to the cathedral proper and proceeds eastward one becomes aware first of the STAINED GLASS of the aisle windows, each 80 ft (24.4 metres) high. The windows, as has already been said, all face diagonally towards the altar, and they are seen only as one looks back in bay after bay. There are ten of them, and they were designed and made by *Lawrence Lee*, *Geoffrey Clarke* and *Keith New*. They are all one in style, even if individually distinguishable. They are essentially abstract, and whereas John Piper's is mostly rectilinear and, whatever its colour coherence, self-contained in each of the panels, these can only be read as a whole each, and they are, some aggressively diagonal and criss-cross in pattern, some rounder and weightier. The symbols in them are based on Rudolph Koch's *Book of Signs* (LC). Also in some of them objects can be discovered, while others keep away entirely from representation. The first l. (*K. New*) and r. (*K. New*) with much yellow are restless and full of conflict, the second l. (*L. Lee*) introduces more red, and in the second r. (*L. Lee*) flowers are distinguishable. The third l. (*G. Clarke*) is quite different, with larger areas of rounded form, whereas the third r. (*K. New*), with much red, is still restless. Then number four l. (*G. Clarke*) introduces deep blue, and number four r. (*G. Clarke*) is the darkest of them all. Finally, five l. (by all three of the artists) returns to the yellow of the beginning but now in a more controlled composition, and five r. (*L. Lee*) is also pale and one of the most harmonious. That the progress is meant to be towards the divine will be patent from this inadequate description. If the description remained inadequate, that is due to a certain extent to the essentials of the so-called Abstract Expressionism. Its message can be strong but not explicit. One can enthuse about it, but not formulate precisely.

The chancel begins with PULPIT and LECTERN, designed by Sir Basil, and the lectern given as a book rest an eagle (the traditional motif) modelled brilliantly by *Elisabeth Frink* and carried out in bronze. Against the E walls of the aisles stand the ORGAN pipes, in Sir Basil's own ingenious arrangement, a complete success as the subsidiary *point de vue* for the aisles. Meanwhile in the centre the CHOIR STALLS insist on attention. Sir Basil accepted the Gothic principle of canopies and the most prominent canopy for the bishop's throne, but interpreted them in terms of slender-membered three-pointed stars, their tips or some of their tips carrying the centre of the next star. Each star is somewhat like the Mercedes trademark interpreted three-dimensionally. The whole is an intricate, ever-changing pattern, reminding everybody, especially from a distance, of birds in flight. In themselves they are exhilarating, but as part of the total vista towards the E wall they may be too insistent.

The ALTAR, a long, heavy piece with short legs and massive top, stands free at this point for the clergyman to minister towards the congregation. On the altar the silver-gilt CROSS, by *Geoffrey Clarke*, an abstract interpretation of both the cross and the agonized pain of the Crucified. The candleholders attached to the altar are also by *Clarke*. The large ceramic CANDLESTICKS l. and r. are by *Hans Coper*. To approach the Lady Chapel one goes through a low passage on the l. with, by one's side, some STAINED GLASS saints by *Einar Forseth*.

The LADY CHAPEL, and of course the whole cathedral, is dominated by *Graham Sutherland*'s TAPESTRY, made in France by *Pinton Frères* at Felletin. It is 75½ ft (23 metres) high ('the largest tapestry in the world') and cost £17,500, a very reasonable sum. It is undoubtedly the climax of the building, and was meant from the beginning to fulfil that function. Not only its scale and the size of the figure of Christ, but also the colouring, have no peer. Everything visible as one progresses was muted in colour, to enhance the effect of the intensity of the green background of the tapestry. It is a nature-green, very full and rich, and very pure, neither yellowy nor blueish. Against it Christ seated in a white garment with yellow lights against a dun-coloured *mandorla*. He is seated frontally and his hands are raised – a figure obviously inspired by Early Christian mosaics, yet not imitating them. The *mandorla* has a frame of golden yellow, as if it were brass, and this metallic frame extends, as for the wings of a polyptych, to frame the symbols of the four Evangelists. They are, against the directness of representation in the Christ, disturbed, thorny beings and have reds and purples and browns. The frame also extends above as if intended to secure the whole of the figurework to the walls and roof. At the top are rays, and between Christ's feet stands a tiny man. Below this are the chalice and the serpent of eternity, and right below, ash-grey, like a predella, is Christ crucified, again thorny and fierce. The tapestry receives full light, as high and narrow clear glass windows, again not at once visible, are to its l. and r. The tapestry has come in for much criticism. One of the two most important arguments is that the design was not made with a view to the tapestry-making technique, but that is hardly convincing; for where the size is as great as it is here, the individual square which is the maker's unit need no longer tell in the whole. The other crucial criticism of the tapestry is that it is corny and too obvious, i.e. too directly representational.

Now this criticism is one which runs parallel to one raised against Sir Basil Spence as well, and to answer it we ought now to see the two last parts not yet looked at. One is the CHAPEL OF

CHRIST THE SERVANT or Guilds Chapel, the Cinderella of the cathedral, with its even light and its lack of atmosphere – in spite of the Crown of Thorns by *Geoffrey Clarke* hanging in the middle as a baldacchino with the cross and nails. This has integral light fittings to illuminate the robust form of the altar table set on massive legs upon a plinth lettered by *Beyer*, complemented by the massive ceramic candleholders by *Coper*. These components are carefully coordinated (LC).

The other is the CHAPEL OF GETHSEMANE, the smallest in the cathedral. There are only a few benches in it, for intimate devotion, and the feeling is one of being in a cave. On the back wall in ceramics are the large, consciously Byzantine angel of Gethsemane and a panel of the sleeping disciples by *Steven Sykes*. The entrance side is a screen with a large wrought-iron Crown of Thorns designed by Sir Basil himself. So here we are back at the criticism of the furnishings and the building as corny.

What is meant by that? That it appeals to all? For it does: two years after the consecration thousands still came on the pilgrimage and queued outside to be let in. Did they come to pray in the house of God which was bombed and rebuilt? No – they came to admire a work of architecture and works of art. And they were the same who wrote only a short time earlier: 'this unusually ugly factory ... resembling a cockroach ... the gasholder on one side and the glorified dustbin on the other ... an utter monstrosity ... a concrete disgrace.' These were the people who wanted their cathedrals still imitation-Gothic or imitation-Early Christian. Could Sir Basil Spence have convinced them so spectacularly in such a short time, if he had not thought from the beginning in terms of a building conducive to worship? Had he been entirely uncompromising, he would not only have had no chance of winning the competition and building the building, he would also have had no chance of winning those for whom he built. And to think of them in the first place surely is true, spiritual, functionalism.

At the same time there is of course a danger to aesthetic values nowadays in thinking exclusively of pleasing the consumer. We all know what happens in show business, where that is the sole consideration. The letter from which I have just quoted shows that this was not Sir Basil's attitude. He visualized something fully to satisfy himself and yet capable of convincing worshippers at large. And satisfying himself implied of course satisfying other modern architects, critics of architecture, and those laymen susceptible to architecture in the C20. In this also, at least in my opinion, he has succeeded. Even internationally speaking, the cathedral acts with a high emotive power. And it has moreover plenty of subtleties which can be appreciated coolly – such as the walls of the Chapel of Unity, the position and shape of the baptistery, the interlocking of old and new building.

Not that a building on this scale can hope to silence all criticism. Criticism from those in whom religious emotions do not exist can perhaps be neglected. But those also who insist on a church being a church and who are moreover sympathetic to Sir Basil's modes of expression are left in doubt on certain major points. I can only sum up my own. They are these. If the rib-vault is not a rib-vault but a canopy, it ought to have been separated more demonstratively from the walls. If the stained glass of the aisles was intended to throw all light on to the altar, it ought not to have been given the clear glass wall at the w end as a competitor: w in the cathedral is s, and so on a fine day light streams in from the entrance, and silences the stained glass of the aisles. The form of the flèche is perhaps not a major point. But it does not seem to participate in the mood of the rest of the building.

A last major point, however, is the furnishings. The canopies of the choir stalls tend to interfere with the fullness of the impact of the tapestry. And, more subtly, the process of appreciating Geoffrey Clarke and the process of appreciating Epstein are so different that one may not find it easy to apply both of them in the same building. One can fully understand Sir Basil's intention. Here, he felt from the start, is the c20 cathedral. It must not be an architect's drawing-board job, it must be alive like its medieval predecessors. And they, at the time when they were the centre of spiritual life, were cram-full of ornaments and fitments, nor was there one man to impose his style or taste on them. So let this new building also be representative of the good things going on now, the easier ones and the hard ones, provided once again they would – in Sir Basil's conviction – have a chance of conveying their message.

This is as far as one can go, or at least as I can go. The same arguments might have been used and the result might have been an aesthetic nonentity or an aesthetic disaster. If that is not so, if the cathedral as a whole and with what it contains has become a contribution to English c20 art, this is due to the genuine humility, the resourcefulness and the imagination of its begetter.

Pevsner's account ends there, but some additions are necessary. The cathedral and its main furnishings are largely unchanged, but in 2000 an area off the N stairway was adapted by *Acanthus Clews* as the MILLENNIUM CHAPEL OF THE STALINGRAD MADONNA. Curved glass screen, simple wooden floor, bench and altar and a copy of a drawing, *The Stalingrad Madonna*, by *Kurt Reuber*, a German soldier, in 1942. Then in the cathedral there are additional works of art. – SCULPTURE. *John Bridgeman*'s Mater Dolorosa in the Lady Chapel, 1970. – The Plumbline and the City, a metal collage in the s aisle by *Clarke Fitzgerald*, 1971. – The Czech Cross, a figure of Christ carved in a simple wooden cross, carved during the war by *Jindrich Severa* who gave it to Coventry in 1968. – STAINED GLASS from old St Michael's is now in various locations at the cathedral.* Six medieval panels of angels restored by the *York*

---

*Including those in the Cappers' Room (*see* below). Much else is in store, having been rediscovered in *Dennis King*'s Norwich workshops in 2003 and returned to a specially designed store at the cathedral in 2009.

Glaziers Trust in 1981 are fixed across the windows of St
Michael's Hall in the basement. Further panels restored in
1992 are on display in cases placed around the Chapel of
Christ the Servant in 2002.*

The area within the ruins of St Michael's serves as a public space
for prayer and reflection with particular emphasis on peace and
reconciliation. Placed here are first the poignant symbols of
hope in the face of desolation: the RUBBLE ALTAR and the
CROSS of charred beams erected in the apse by *Jock Forbes* for
Provost Howard in 1941.† The open space is used to display a
range of artworks. – SCULPTURE. Ecce Homo in Italian
marble, by *Epstein*, 1934–5, placed by the S wall of the ruined
S aisle, 1969. – Also in the S aisle, on the N side near the apse,
a figure of Christ, cast in concrete, by *Alain John* (†1943), one
of Bishop Gorton's pupils at Blundell's School. – In the outer
N aisle, Reconciliation by *Josefina de Vasconcellos*. A cast made
in 1995 from an original at Bradford University, 1977, but
originally designed after the war. – MONUMENT. Bishop
Yeatman-Biggs †1922. Table tomb with a recumbent effigy in
bronze by *Sir William Hamo Thornycroft*, 1924–5. The bishop
holds a model of the old cathedral.‡ Contemporary with the
new cathedral are two rooms in the S porch. In the upper
chamber is the CAPPERS' ROOM, restored with new window
tracery and furnished by *Basil Spence & Partners* in 1953–7. It
has some of the elements of the cathedral interior: panelled
timber ceiling, a tapestry by *Edinburgh Weavers* and furniture
made by *Heals* (LC). Underneath is the BISHOP HAIGH
MEMORIAL CHAPEL, with plain stone altar, simple chairs and
some of the best fragments of medieval STAINED GLASS,
installed in the S and N windows by *King & Son* of Norwich
in 1965.

REMAINS OF RELIGIOUS HOUSES

ST MARY'S CATHEDRAL AND PRIORY. The Benedictine priory
of Coventry was founded by Earl Leofric and Countess Godiva
c. 1020–30 and consecrated in 1043. The priory became the
richest house in the whole region, not excluding Evesham,
Tewkesbury and Pershore. From 1102 its church was the cathedral of a joint see, still called Coventry and Lichfield after the
bishops removed to Lichfield. St Mary's was the only cathedral
church in England to be completely demolished at the Reformation. Parts of the three towers survived into the C17, the
lower parts of the NW tower being subsequently incorporated

---

* Excluded from revised editions of *The Buildings of England* but deserving of note
here are PLATE, much of the C20, e.g. two chalices, four silver-gilt patens, a flagon,
and a salver by *Gerald Benney*, and VESTMENTS. Copes, chasubles and dalmatics
designed by *John Piper*. He also designed two BANNERS but the whereabouts of
these are now unknown.
† The cross is a replica, put up in place of the original which was moved inside the
cathedral in 1978.
‡ This was a sole survivor of the bombing.

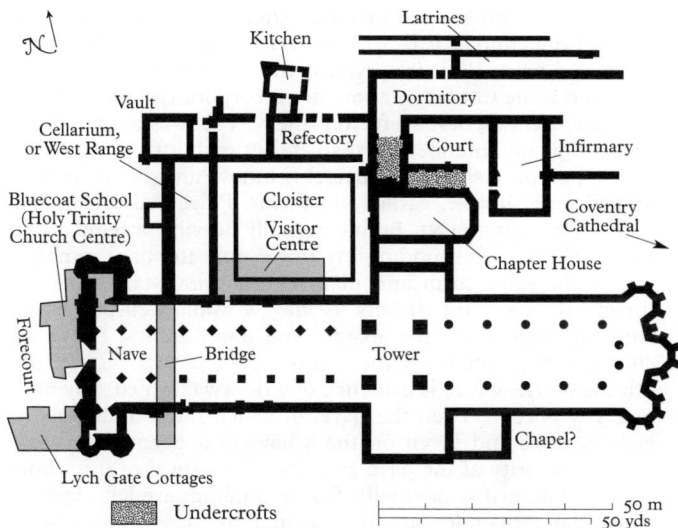

Coventry, St Mary's Cathedral and Priory.
Plan

in *James Murray*'s 1856–7 Bluecoat School (p. 255). Work on the
school in 1856 also revealed the foundations of the W front,
afterwards left exposed. Much more was uncovered as a result
of the Phoenix Initiative (p. 269) excavations in 1999–2001.
The site is now open with a VISITOR CENTRE by *MacCormac
Jamieson Prichard* (*MJP*), 2001–2, and a viewing bridge over
the ruins leading to the Bluecoat School which was refurbished
as Holy Trinity Church Centre.

As a result of the archaeological discoveries and associated
documentary research much more is known about the cathedral and priory than hitherto. As completed the old cathedral
was about 425 ft (130 metres) long, apparently built in stages
between *c.* 1100 and *c.* 1250. It was cruciform with an aisled
nave of nine bays. The W end was still incomplete by 1189
when the monks were expelled. The W front was begun *c.* 1220.
Completion is suggested by a royal grant of oaks in 1247–51.
A new S porch was added before 1299 and royal mason *Master
Hugh de Titemersshe* may have been responsible for work
c. 1312. The C14 saw piecemeal refenestration and in the mid
C14 there were problems with the crossing tower, which may
have been rebuilt on its existing Romanesque piers. A vaulted
transept was added *c.* 1400, and in the late C14 or early C15 a
polygonal chevet with chapels was added at the E end.

The conventual buildings were largely rebuilt after *c.* 1200
and included cloisters N of the church reconstructed in the
mid C13, a chapter house of *c.* 1310–30 (with later paintings
c. 1360–70), and a refectory of *c.* 1340 above a mid-C13 undercroft. The cloisters were substantially renovated in the C15.

What one can see are first the extensive remains of the W front of the church, E.E. with towers outside (i.e. wider than) the aisled nave. Best preserved is the NW tower of which the base and some C13 fabric above are incorporated in the former Bluecoat School, best seen from the N. This was altered more than originally intended in 1856–7, but early C19 drawings of the upper part showed a lancet window and blank trefoil-arched arcading, i.e. earlier C13 forms. Polygonal turrets NW with spiral stair and NE, both externally heavily battered at the base. Of the corresponding SW tower only the base remains, but of the same form and plan with a spiral stair in its SW turret. Between the towers is the W wall, well-preserved, with the responds of the arcades and tower arches. These are clustered with fillets on the shafts, again *c.* 1220–30. In the middle of the W wall is evidence of a doorway which may have had a W porch.* Then the nave, of which the foundations of eight N piers and seven on the S have now been discovered, i.e. the majority of the nave and about one-third of the whole church. The two W bays with E.E. mouldings are left exposed while the remainder are represented by York stone blocks under glass. The piers on the S were Romanesque and of *c.* 1110–30 (cf. Ely, Peterborough and Dunstable). Those on the N were lozenge-shaped and E.E. The side walls of the N and S aisles are also represented although mostly by later walling. Three of the four crossing piers have been located but remain buried. All Norman. Beyond Priory Row and right by the new cathedral are the remains of two polygonal radiating chapels of the chevet at the E end of the church, late C14 or early C15.

The priory buildings stood to the N, the W part of the cloister being represented by the visitor centre garden. The cellarium stood to the W and the refectory to the N. On the E were the slype and chapter house, with dormitories and infirmary to the NE. There are no standing remains, but during the Phoenix Project the remains of C13 undercrofts were found N of the chapter house. These are on permanent display in the specially designed basement of Youell House (*see* Perambulation 1) and visible through glass from Priory Place. There are two chambers, W and S, both originally vaulted. The W chamber is two-naved and has three bays. It was entered from a spiral stair in the S wall. In the S chamber are remains of an E.E. triplet window originally opening to a yard on the N. When the undercrofts were restored in 2003–4 by *Brownhill Hayward Brown* a storage room was created alongside under the pedestrian link from Hill Top to Priory Place. This houses stonework from the whole priory site.

The visitor centre displays some of the worked stones and architectural fragments, including carved heads, bosses, canopies and statues, together with C14 heraldic tiles. Espe-

---

*Suggested in earlier accounts of the remains. There is no proof either way but Richard Morris and George Demidowicz consider this unlikely.

cially appealing is a piece with a tiny but exquisite painted fragment of three crowned heads from the Apocalypse in the chapter house, *c.* 1360–70. Also displayed is a section of the underside vaulting to the C14 refectory pulpit with original polychromy.

THE WHITEFRIARS, uncomfortably close to the Ringway and flyover at the head of London Road. This was a Carmelite settlement founded in 1342. Building commenced immediately and went on into the second quarter of the C15. There are references to an enlargement of the living quarters in 1414 and to the completion of the cloister of 1506. What survives is the E range of the cloister. The church stood to the N and the exposed foundations belong chiefly to its choir and the remains of a walkway leading S through a vestibule to the cloister. The C14–C15 friary church was cruciform and exceptionally large, being 303 ft (92.4 metres) long from W to E. It had a nave of nine bays, with lozenge piers, separated from the six-bay chancel by the typical mendicant cross-piece carrying (as at the Greyfriars, and at Atherstone) the tower. The excavated foundations show that the cross-piece was early altered to a square crossing with shallow transepts, perhaps after 1384 when Lord Basset of Drayton left money to enlarge the church. The first tower collapsed in 1446 and its successor fell in 1572. By then the friary had been dissolved (in 1538) and much of the church demolished. John Hales acquired the remains, adapting the cloister as part of his residence, called Hales Place. The medieval stalls and misericords were later put to use by Coventry's Free Grammar School in the medieval hospital of St John.* From 1801 the buildings were used as a workhouse and in 1965 Whitefriars became a museum (now closed). All the later additions have been stripped away.

The surviving two-storey cloister range of red sandstone is of *c.* 1343–50. Stumps of the N and S ranges also remain. The W side facing the cloister garth is buttressed. The ground-floor openings are three per bay, cusped and ogee-headed. Square-headed upper windows, some of three lights mullioned, and some of five lights mullioned and transomed. In the centre a pretty oriel window, probably added by Hales. The cloister is vaulted with star-like lierne-vaults, i.e. two tiercerons rising from each corner of a bay to a central lozenge. The ribs have one elongated chamfer. In the middle of the range was the chapter house on the E, entered through a big, cusped archway. In the thick wall of the short entrance passage l. and r. are two small doorways. The surviving part of the chapter house vault has a big grid pattern of ribs. Either side of the chapter house N and S are rooms with plain rib-vaults. Upstairs above these vaults were the dormitory and the *studium generale* with a fine open roof dendro-dated to 1475 and 1493–4 (felling dates). Big

---

*The surviving elements are described under the Old Grammar School (p. 268), Holy Trinity (p. 240), and King Henry VIII School (p. 254). There is another seat (not mentioned below) at the Herbert Art Gallery & Museum.

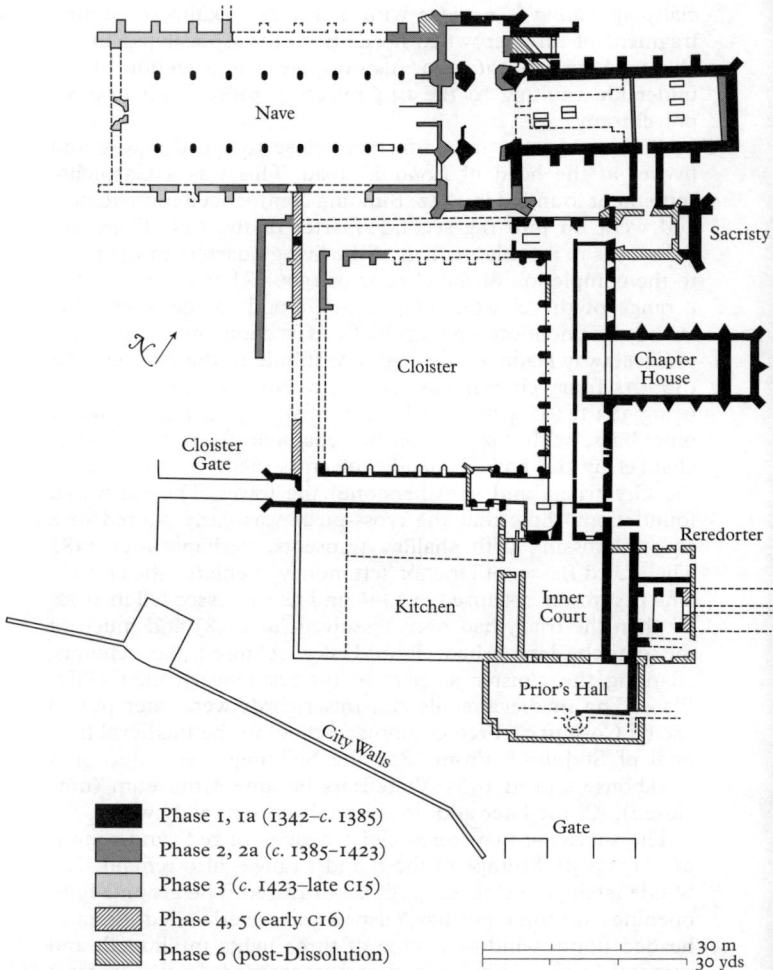

Phase 1, 1a (1342–c. 1385)
Phase 2, 2a (c. 1385–1423)
Phase 3 (c. 1423–late C15)
Phase 4, 5 (early C16)
Phase 6 (post-Dissolution)

30 m
30 yds

Coventry, The Whitefriars.
Plan

traceried windows in each end of the dormitory. In the middle a large open fireplace. At the N end of the range is a former doorway, at the S end another.

GREYFRIARS, Warwick Lane. The house was established in 1234. All that remains is the splendid steeple built *c.* 1350 – the third of Coventry's three famous spires. It is 230 ft (70 metres) high and stood, as was customary with the friars, over the centre of a cross-passage between aisled nave and aisleless chancel. In 1830–2 a church, called CHRIST CHURCH, was added by *Rickman & Hutchinson* to the remaining steeple, making the space under it the chancel. The church was bombed in 1941 and never restored, a new church at Cheylesmore (*see* Outer Suburbs) with the same dedication being erected to replace it in 1954–7. The Greyfriars steeple and some of the 1830s ashlar-faced additions either side of it survive, including a spherical triangle window. When the remains were restored by *Redgrave & Clarke* in 1970 the fancy C19 Gothic work in the E and W openings was removed to reveal the original arches of *c.* 1358. The steeple is octagonal, as friars' steeples often are. It has two-light windows but in the diagonals on the W side are blank three-light panels with reticulated tracery. The belfry stage and parapet much restored in 1970, with the loss of the previously openwork parapet shown in late C18 illustrations. The space under the tower is partly visible from the outside.

CHARTERHOUSE OF ST ANNE, ¼ m. E of the London Road Cemetery. The sixth in foundation date of England's nine Carthusian priories. Initiated in 1381 when the first monks settled in Coventry. Construction began in 1385 when Richard II and Queen Anne laid the foundation stone for the church. The inscription on the Crucifixion painting indicates that the building was finished when William Soland was prior, i.e. 1409–37.* It accommodated the prior and twelve monks, the latter living around a rectangular cloister where foundations of two-storeyed eremitic cells have been excavated. After the Dissolution in 1539 Charterhouse became a private house owned latterly by Col. William Wyley, who left it to the city in 1940. Several decades of mixed use left the building unscathed but in poor condition. In 2012 it passed to a local trust (incorporated in the newly formed Historic Coventry Trust in 2015), which has plans for a sensitive restoration of the house and for creating a heritage park (taking in the cemetery and a tract of land along the River Sherbourne).

What remains is much of the perimeter wall and one range of red sandstone ashlar with an Elizabethan timber-framed N end. The church stood to the N and a substantial length of its S wall still stands in the garden. The surviving range contained the refectory, with the prior's quarters to the S with a low passageway beyond. The refectory was on the ground floor and stood to the full height of the N end, lit on the E by two large pointed windows whose surrounds are visible outside at first- and second-floor levels. In the prior's quarters a spiral stair (now blocked) led from the panelled ground-floor room r. of the entrance to an upper chamber with a big chimneypiece corbelling forward towards the lintel. The upstairs rooms were reconfigured in the C16 with an additional floor and internal partitions. On the top floor, several C15 tie-beams with gracefully traceried carving. Good mouldings on transverse beams too. In the corridor the head of a carved wooden door frame

---

*Prior William's term of office, previously dated to 1411–17, is now known to have been longer than once thought. The inscription also mentions Thomas Lambard (†1440) as procurator.

from one of the eremitic cells has been reused. Also reused is the stone mensa from the altar as an overmantel to a fireplace. In the same room, traces of moulded surrounds in a W window and two carved stone corbels. More corbels to the ground-floor passageway at the S end of the house. Worked stones re-set in modern walling in the garden. Especially prominent externally are the five tall brick chimneystacks, probably Elizabethan. – WALL PAINTINGS. On the first floor of the refectory S wall are the remains of a Crucifixion with large seated figures at each side and groups of smaller figures at the base of the cross. It was originally 23 ft (7 metres) wide and 13 ft (4 metres) high. Only the lower part remains, complete with the inscription (as above) now interpreted as suggesting a date of c. 1430–5 for the painting. The arms of Edward, Lord Clinton (†1585), have been inserted in grisaille. The upper part was lost during the late C16 alterations but fragments survive on re-set stones on the second floor. – Also in grisaille, a painting on an Elizabethan partition on the first floor. It has Italianate antiquework and the arms of Sampson Baker, a late C16 owner. – On the second floor, a fictive tapestry painting, again C16 and on an inserted partition.

HOSPITAL OF ST JOHN, Hales Street. *See* Perambulation 6.

PARISH CHURCHES

In and immediately around the city centre only four parish churches remain (one disused). Of Christ Church only the medieval Greyfriars spire remains (*see* p. 238). All Saints (*Paull & Robinson*, 1868–9) and St Thomas (*Sharpe & Paley*, 1848–9), both just outside the Ringway, have been demolished.

HOLY TRINITY, Priory Row, is one of only two medieval parish churches in the city, close to the original market place and occupying the prime site on the crown of the hill. It is hemmed in tightly between the old cathedral and priory site on the N and St Michael's (*see* Coventry Cathedral) to the SE. Holy Trinity served the priory estates in the northern half of the town. Holy Trinity is first mentioned in 1113 and was badly damaged by fire in 1257, by when there must have already been a substantial church, of which the N porch remains. Later medieval rebuilding and embellishment made Holy Trinity one of the longest parish churches in England (194 ft (59 metres)). It has a quite uncommonly high crossing tower with spire, totalling 237 ft (72 metres) in height – second to St Michael's among Coventry's famous three – an aisled chancel with chapels, transepts, a nave with aisles, and in addition outer N chapels. All this dates from between c. 1360 and c. 1535–40, but the only firm date we have is the beginning of the chancel in 1391. So the church is mainly Perp but externally over-restored: the tower was re-cased in 1826 by *Rickman* and redone in Woolton stone under *T. G. Jackson* in 1915–18. *Joseph Eglington* re-cased the E end in Bath stone in 1786. The

23

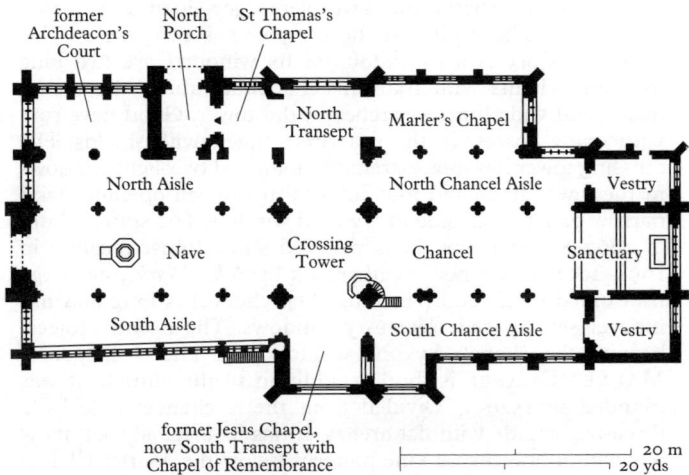

former
Archdeacon's
Court

North
Porch

St Thomas's
Chapel

North
Transept

Marler's Chapel

North Aisle

North Chancel Aisle

Vestry

Nave

Crossing
Tower

Chancel

Sanctuary

South Aisle

South Chancel Aisle

Vestry

former Jesus Chapel,
now South Transept with
Chapel of Remembrance

20 m
20 yds

Coventry, Holy Trinity.
Plan

w end was similarly treated by *R. C. Hussey* in 1843, followed
by the rest of the church, 1843–9. The church escaped major
damage in the war and its survival makes it an especially
important monument to the medieval prosperity and cultural
richness of the city, a fine building handsomely decorated and
furnished.

The story begins with the INNER N PORCH. This is E.E. and
survives from an earlier building. It is elegantly rib-vaulted,
the ribs springing from corner shafts with stiff-leaf capitals,
and the doorway into the church has two orders, formerly
also with crocket capitals, and a finely moulded arch. From
the porch to the E is a twin doorway of the later C13, the two
arches pointed-trefoiled and with a large circle above. So there
must have been a chapel in this place, and it later became
ST THOMAS'S CHAPEL.* The porch has a vaulted crypt
underneath and a later priest's room above. Otherwise we
know little of the church before the present one, except that
the outer NW chapel has high in its E wall (the porch W wall)
a re-set window with elongated reticulated tracery.

Stylistically the oldest part after those of the C13 is the N
transept. The arches from the N aisle and N chancel chapel
into it have round abaci, whereas everywhere else the abaci are
polygonal. This is so for the nave arcades and the crossing
arches, which are similar in character. The crossing piers have

23

* George Demidowicz suggests this might be where Holy Trinity absorbed the
earlier chapel of the Virgin Mary on the Hill. The blocked windows and rough
walling suggest it belonged to a separate building at one time.

round respond shafts, the nave piers ogee-sided and filleted projections. The capital of the SW pier has two shields. The nave clerestory is a C15 addition. Its windows are two long mullioned lights with transoms. Panelling above the arches inside and wide buttress arches to the tower. Good nave roof with many bosses. In the spandrels angels with shields. The crossing tower has four extremely elongated two-light windows in the lower stage and four unusual triple bell-openings with narrow panels each side of a glazed window. The spire, rebuilt in 1667–8 and many times restored since (most recently in 1995–2001 with a new weathercock by *John Clark*), has large transomed lights and panelling. The chancel is long and has nine closely spaced clerestory windows. The E end projects beyond the chapels by one window bay. The N chapel or MARLER CHAPEL is the last addition to the church. It was founded in 1526–7. Divided from the N chancel aisle by a three-bay arcade with flat arches. It has its original roof, its W bay with a fine carved vine pattern. Below the Marler Chapel are a vaulted crypt and a charnel house in use 1528–1660 and still intact. The outer N porch belongs to the C15. It has very thin shafts and a panelled four-centred vault. In the later C15 a public passageway was created through the S transept which was adapted to contain an elevated JESUS CHAPEL. Of the Jesus Passage the blocked archway remains. The former upper chapel is recognizable by the outer staircase and the PISCINA high up inside. The transept was refurnished as a Chapel of Remembrance with light wooden screen and altar rails by *Sir J. N. Comper*, 1949–52. E of the S transept is the choir vestry, with another good original roof. This room may originally have been the Lady Chapel.* The S aisle has pairs of closely spaced two- and three-light windows.

Scott began an interior restoration in 1854 when the galleries were removed. His are e.g. the timber vault inside the tower† and the excellent seating in the nave with superb brass candelabra by *Francis Skidmore*. The CHANCEL interior is Scott's too, with contemporary fittings, more Skidmore light standards and a sanctuary pavement of encaustic tiles, 1855–6. The painted decoration on the side walls (possibly by *F. Holt & Co.*) was completed in 1909. – REREDOS of Caen stone by *Farmer & Brindley*, 1873. – CHOIR STALLS, 1855–6, but incorporating misericords from the Whitefriars stalls now at the Old Grammar School (*see* pp. 237 and 269). These include addorsed cockatrices, addorsed eagles, a hunting scene, a lion and a man, a Green Man, a head in profile, a lion, a traceried door, a lion

---

*Holy Trinity was full of separate named chapels. It had a dyers' chapel, and St Thomas's Chapel seems to have been founded in 1296. In addition the tanners had the W end of the S aisle as their chapel, the butchers had another chapel, and there were also chapels of St Andrew and All Saints, besides chantries of Holy Cross and the Lodynton and Percye families.
†After Scott removed the lower floors in the tower to open up the lantern to view, the bells were removed to a pretty weatherboarded wooden BELL TOWER N of the church. This was Scott's, 1856. It was removed in 1967.

and a man with a club, a griffin, and an angel. More of the same set are at King Henry VIII School (p. 254). – LECTERN. Brass, with an eagle top, an often imitated type, but here original, i.e. East Anglian, early C15. Thirty-three examples from the same moulds are known, one of them at Urbino Cathedral in Italy. – PULPIT. An excellent Perp stone piece, *c.* 1400, attached to the SE crossing pier. Leaf corbel, panelled underside, openwork balustrade, ribbed underside of the lectern. – FONT. Octagonal, big, Perp, with panelled stem and quatrefoils on the bowl. Painted. – ALMS BOX. Column with carved scrollwork and bowl, C17. – In the W wall of the NW chapel a long, narrow CUPBOARD for banner-staves. – WALL PAINTING. Last Judgment, above the W crossing arch, *c.* 1430–40, restored in 2002–4 by *Granville & Burbidge*.* Remarkably complete and vividly detailed. Central figure of Christ with the Apostles seated either side. An angel blows the last trumpet. On the l., shrouded figures rising from their graves. On the r., harrowing scenes with demons and the mouth of hell right at the bottom. – STAINED GLASS. Many fragments assembled in one NW chapel window, probably C15. – The Victorian E and W windows were both destroyed in the war. The replacements are by *Comper* (E) and *Hugh Easton* (W), both completed 1955. – One S chapel window by *Geoffrey Webb*, 1933. – Alongside, one with re-set heraldic roundels from the former E window by *David Evans* of Shrewsbury, 1833. – N chapel E window, *Heaton & Butler*, 1860. – Three on N side by *Heaton, Butler & Bayne*, 1870, 1885 and 1894. – Marler Chapel E window by *Hardman*, 1873. – One in the St Thomas's Chapel by *Kempe & Co.*, 1921. – MONUMENTS (all in the NW chapel). Mawtun (or Morton) monument of the Purbeck type but of local stone. Small tomb-chest, two piers originally carrying carved figures. Back wall formerly with brasses. Depressed pointed arch, canopy with heavy cresting. – John Whitehead †1600 (or 1597?). Brass plate in simple stone surround. He stands behind a table, the two wives kneel l. and r. Children below. – John Bohun †1691 with wife and daughter, both Mary. By *Edward Hurst*. Architectural background and three busts, his a little higher than the others. – John Howells †1857, by *G. T. Robinson*, depicted in the *Illustrated London News* in 1859. Angel holding the inscription, below a florid canopy and on a triple grey marble shaft. – Memorial brass to J.J. Hook †1836, one of two by *Francis Skidmore & Son*, 1878. The other (apparently lost) commemorated the Rev. W.F. Hook †1875. – WAR MEMORIAL reredos in the St Thomas's Chapel (moved from the S aisle *c.* 2014), by *Temple Moore & Moore*, *c.* 1920.

ST JOHN THE BAPTIST, Spon Street. St John was a collegiate church, built by Queen Isabella as a chantry to her 'late dear

p. 24

21

---

* *The Last Judgement: The Coventry Doom Painting and Holy Trinity Church* (undated, *c.* 2004) and 'The Doom in Holy Trinity Church and Wall-Painting in Medieval Coventry' by Miriam Gill in *BAA* 33 (2011).

lord', King Edward II. It was also the church of the Guild of St John the Baptist. The guild was founded in 1344. Building went on from then to the end of the C14. However, most of what we see now appears C15 work. The college was dissolved in 1548. In the early C17 the building was restored for occasional sermons and lectures. It became a parish church in 1734. Tower and transepts restored in 1858 by *G. G. Scott*, who restored the rest in 1875-7. Extensive stonework renewal by *Bucknall*, 1908, and further repairs after wartime damage. Vestries N of the church, 1877, extended as a church hall by *Milner & Craze*, 1974, and refurbished by *Mark Evans*, 2004.

The church is cruciform but on a most irregular plan. Few walls are quite parallel. Red sandstone, the crossing tower with odd tourelles or bartizans. These are shown in the earliest views of the building and evidently original, though the embattled tops are Victorian additions. The tower windows long and thin, of two lights and straight-headed, as in the crossing tower of Holy Trinity. The church is entirely Perp, but not at all uniform, and more study ought to be devoted to the problem of surviving parts of the C14. Changes of plan are visible in several places. The S aisle windows are not in axis with the S arcade and continue where now the S transept is. So they belong to a plan without a transept. The E responds of the arcades of the chancel aisle presuppose an arcade different from that which was built. And the W crossing piers were begun without a vault for the tower in mind, whereas the E piers made provision for it. The vault, opened to view in 1877 but now concealed, is of lierne type. The Perp tracery of St John is almost throughout characterized by transoms represented by friezes of quatrefoils. This is already so in the S aisle. The chancel clerestory again has the extremely elongated thin form with more than one transom to which we have already referred. Inside, the vault below the windows is panelled. The extremely elongated windows are continued in the nave clerestory on the S side. But on the N side Dec – i.e. C14 – windows were reused instead. The arcade piers of nave and chancel are of different patterns too, but both with the fine shafts and the hollows of the Perp style, and both basically of lozenge shape. Nice doorway to the tower staircase in the N transept, and yet nicer corbel to the staircase higher up in the W arch of the tower. The function is fulfilled by a big horizontal man. – REREDOS. Gothic, alabaster, with figures of Christ and the Apostles based on a Giotto painting at Padua, 1879. – CHANCEL SCREEN, GATES and CHOIR STALLS. By *John Oldrid Scott*, 1886. – LECTERN carved posthumously to a design by *Sir G. G. Scott*, 1887. – Penkridge stone PULPIT by Scott, 1877. – Perp stone FONT by *Hubert Adderley* (Lord Norton) 1929. – ROYAL ARMS. Painted on sheet metal fixed between four cast-iron columns, the city emblem and Prince of Wales feathers l. and r., 1812. – STAINED GLASS. Some pre-war survivors, including fragments from the W window of

1874 by *F. Barnett & Son*, and 1877 by *Lavers, Barraud & Westlake* in s chapel and transept. – Four by *Burlison & Grylls*, s transept 1885 (upper parts), s chapel 1922, and N aisle 1931 (two). – In the s aisle one by *Kempe*, 1897. – Of the post-war replacements the best is the fine E window by *M.E. Aldrich Rope*, 1952. – s chapel E, *Goddard & Gibbs* (*A. E. Buss*), 1951. – N chapel N, *George Cooper-Abbs*, 1960. – N transept, *Harry Clarke Studios*, Dublin, 1963.

St Anne and All Saints, Acacia Avenue. A workers' institute and canteen for the nearby motor works, built for the Ministry of Munitions as part of a wartime housing scheme, 1917. Adapted as a church with the addition of a NW porch tower and apse by *Henry E. Farmer*, 1930. – STAINED GLASS. E window by *Powell*, 1930.

Former St Mark, Bird Street. 1868–9 by *Paull & Robinson* who also designed All Saints (dem.; *see* p. 272). Renovated by *Harry Quick*, 1895. Following redundancy in 1973 it was in hospital use until 2006 and is now (2015) used by a Christian charity. Red and rock-faced. Double bellcote of two transparent lancets over the W end of the N aisle. The style is C13 and the inside more interesting than the outside. Normal round piers, but enormous abaci and chunky capitals. The chancel arch on two brackets in the form of capitals, and the roofs all decidedly odd. – PAINTING. The whole altar wall a Resurrection by *Hans Feibusch*, 1962–3.

OTHER PLACES OF WORSHIP

St Osburg (R.C.), Hill Street. 1843–5 by *Charles Hansom*, then City Surveyor. Steeple completed 1851–2. Damaged in the Second World War and afterwards repaired by *Harrison & Cox*, 1944–52. Further restoration and reordering, 2010–11, by *Brownhill Hayward Brown* (*BHB*) of Lichfield. Crazy-paving stonework. E.E. style, with a sw steeple. Broach spire. The interior humble and plain, but not small. Circular piers. Clerestory with columns supported on gilded and painted angel corbels. Two-bay side chapels to chancel, both with sexfoil windows high in the E walls which have bright mosaic decorations. – ALTAR and sanctuary FURNISHINGS, 2010–11. The altar has glazed openings shielding alabaster STATUETTES of St Mary, St Lawrence and St Denis, the male figures from Charterhouse, C15. – STAINED GLASS. Richly coloured E window by *Earley Studios*, Dublin, 1952. – Others in the style of Harry Clarke, also by Earley Studios, 1950s. – Etched glass doors under W gallery, 2011. – MEMORIAL BRASS. Fulford family, *c.* 1845, by *Hardman*.

The three-storey PRIORY building N of the church is also a post-war replacement, by *Harrison & Cox* (*G. B. Cox*), 1961. On the s side, the HALL of 1938, restored 1957, with a statue high up in a blind arch on the Upper Hill Street end.

GREAT MEETING HOUSE (Unitarian), Holyhead Road. The successor of a city meeting founded in 1662 whose chapel was built in 1700. Relocated to present site in 1936–7. By *G. A. Steane* in red brick with tower. Round-headed traceried windows. Rib-arch plaster ceiling inside. Some furnishings from previous chapel, including the FONT. – STAINED GLASS, probably by *F. S. Trickett*, 1937 (AB).

QUEENS ROAD BAPTIST CHURCH, by the Ringway. By *George & Isaac Steane* of Coventry, 1883–4. Large, red brick, late C19 Perp, with a corner tower shortened in the 1990s. Galleried interior with organ at the front. Porch added 1974, and extended in 2004–5 by *Mayway Construction* to create a glass-fronted CHURCH CENTRE with curvy roof. STAINED GLASS in side windows. Scenes from *Pilgrim's Progress*, 1920s.

UNITED REFORMED CHURCH (Congregational), Warwick Road. *G. & I. Steane* again, 1889–91. Free Renaissance style front flanked by polygonal towers with domed caps. Brick with stone dressings. Inside, oval with apse. Galleries on thin cast-iron columns. Projecting vestibule added by *Gardner & Baldwin*, 1964.

METHODIST CENTRAL HALL, Warwick Lane. 1931–2 by *Claude Redgrave*. Reactionary Gothic. Lumpish exterior resembling an office building with a churchy tower. Facilities on the ground floor and main hall above. Galleried interior with organ at front. Cinema-style seating on gallery. Union Street entrance and its redesigned interior by *Kenneth L. Holmes*, 1988–90.

ST COLUMBA'S UNITED REFORMED CHURCH (Presbyterian Church of England), Radford Road. *Spalding & Myers*, 1931. Red brick with canted front and steeply pitched roof with dormers. Interior with concrete ribs to roof. Pierced wooden panels on each side of the organ at the W end.

ELIM PENTECOSTAL, The Butts. *Keith Corrigan*, 1979–80. Single storey with flat roof. Triangular skylight above the fan-shaped meeting area.

FRIENDS' MEETING, Hill Street. A plain domestic building by *A. H. Gardner & Partners*, 1953.

SYNAGOGUE and adjoining RABBI'S HOUSE (both disused in 2015), Barras Lane. By *Thomas Naden* of Birmingham, 1870. Simplified Romanesque style. STAINED GLASS by *Hardman*, 1953–61.

SALVATION ARMY CENTRE, Upper Well Street. *HSSP Architects*, 2003–5, with hall, offices and café area with brick arches and windows overlooking part of the C15 city wall with a bastion.

PUBLIC BUILDINGS

This section deals with the public buildings in the civic quarter defined in the Gibson plan (*see* p. 222), and since further developed. These are chiefly the Council House and its associated buildings (including the medieval St Mary's Guildhall) and the public buildings in the zone defined by Little Park Street,

Earl Street and Jordan Well. Coventry University has its own section (*see* p. 251). There is a separate brief section for colleges and schools. Other public and semi-public buildings are described in the perambulations.

COUNTY HALL, Cuckoo Lane, and the adjoining GOVERNOR'S HOUSE. *See* Perambulation 1.

ST MARY'S GUILDHALL, Bayley Lane. One of the most notable surviving medieval guildhalls in Britain. Begun in 1340–2 as the hall of St Mary's Guild, newly established in 1340, it was built in stages and not completed until the mid C15. It stands at the edge of the former castle site, and immediately E of its bakehouse in what is now Castle Yard. The first phase is represented by the vaulted undercroft, originally of only four bays with a hall above (probably timber-framed), first used in 1342. Service buildings were added to the s on land acquired in 1342–8 and by 1393 these conjoined a low stone tower where so-called Caesar's Tower now stands. On the E was a yard with access from Bayley Lane, but the hall itself did not extend N to the street until later. The new Trinity Guild was formed by amalgamating four earlier guilds in 1392 and shortly afterwards the hall was rebuilt in stone. This phase included the erection of the street frontage with a separate undercroft below. It is said to have been completed in 1414. The service buildings and the kitchen were also improved and a 1420s dendro-date for the armoury on the upper floor indicates a later completion of this wing. Improvements to the entrance from Bayley Lane and the chambers above came in the final phase, again in the 1420s, with later alterations to the access to the Great Hall through a gallery entrance at the s end of the courtyard. The guilds were dissolved in 1547 and in 1552 St Mary's Hall, which had been used for Common Council meetings in earlier times, passed formally to the corporation. There was a restoration under *Thomas Stedman Whitwell* in 1824–6 and further work under *Harold Brakspear* in 1913. Caesar's Tower was badly bomb-damaged in 1940 and in 1941 the roof of the Great Hall was burned by incendiaries. Post-war restoration was completed in 1952–3 under *Granville Berry*, City Engineer, and in 1956 an internal bridge was built to link the hall to the Council House behind.

Although within the Council House complex, St Mary's Hall is distinguishable as a group of buildings around a courtyard entered from Bayley Lane. The long side, glimpsed down Castle Yard, has a pretty oriel and, at the far end, Caesar's Tower. The N façade has the late C14 added section of the hall on the r. with a shallow Perp window of nine lights (3:3:3) above a row of nine canopied niches, and the entrance and windows to the N undercroft at street level below. Alongside to the l. a plain wall to the archway from the street and a two-storey block beyond. The entrance has a carriage arch and a blocked side entrance that led to the Mercers' Room. After the plain exterior the gateway comes as a surprise. One enters

under a fine tierceron star-vault with big bosses including a
Green Man. The centre boss is a Coronation of the Virgin, a
Victorian replacement. The inner arch has a panelled four-
centred vault. The opening to the courtyard is carried on
excellent, though worn, figured corbels l. and r. On the r. of
the courtyard, the low windows lighting the vaulted undercroft,
which is entered at the far end. The main part has two naves
and four bays. The piers are short and octagonal and have no
capitals. Heavy single-chamfered ribs. The added N bay is
separated from the rest by an original wall. The Freeman's
Guild Room beyond has five small windows and a doorway to
the street. S of the courtyard is the timber-framed gallery
entrance to the hall and the jettied ante-room above, with the
kitchen and a cluster of rooms beyond. The E side of the
courtyard again timber-framed, but much restored in the C19.
The staircase to the hall is in this range and has C15 carved
wooden handrails. From here a short passage leads to the
hall.

The hall itself is of 1394–1414 and 76½ ft by 30 ft (23.3
metres by 9.1 metres) in size. To the N, i.e. the street, it has
the grand window of nine lights. Close to this end is the customary oriel window on the W. Its very high, narrow arch is
matched on the other side by an altered one giving access to
the Mayoress's Parlour. Perp side windows of two, four and
four lights. Splendid panelled roof with angels making music
and heraldic bosses, restored 1952–3 but reusing salvaged C15
carvings. Then on the S side the minstrels' gallery, narrow and
of wood. Below there are three doorways, the usual arrangement on the services side of medieval halls. The middle one
connects by a staircase with the kitchen below and the rooms
l. and r. ought originally to have been buttery and pantry. The
Prince's Chamber (r.) is panelled and has a wooden chimneypiece of the early C17 not belonging to St Mary's Hall. The
Old Council Chamber (l.) was restored in 1935 and has a
tapestry frieze by *Morris & Co.* – In the Old Council Chamber
is the GREAT CHAIR, an elaborate Gothic piece of the mid to
late C14 acquired in 1579. Among the carvings a Virgin.

Much of the STAINED GLASS in the hall's N window is
original work of *c.* 1492, depicting Henry VI and his forebears.
Coventry had a special affection for the king who made the
city an independent county and had his court here during the
Wars of the Roses. – Fragments in the oriel window, assembled
in 1893 by *Burlison & Grylls*, and in the Old Council Chamber,
some by *John Thornton* of Coventry, *c.* 1420–2. – Hall side
windows by *Clayton & Bell*, 1930, and richly coloured S window
above the minstrels' gallery also theirs (designer *Reginald Bell*),
1926. – TAPESTRY. This famous piece was evidently made for
its position below the N window. Flemish, *c.* 1495–1500. It
represents the Assumption of the Virgin with the Apostles and
the kneeling figures of Henry VI (again) and his queen, and
above, Justice, a later replacement for a Christ in Judgment.
To the l. and r. are angels with the Instruments of the Passion
and saints. – SCULPTURE. In the bay window two C16 statues,

supposed to have formed part of the 1544 market cross originally, and a plaster statue of Lady Godiva by *William Calder Marshall*, 1854.

A passage in the sw angle of the Old Council Chamber leads through to the low yet heavily rib-vaulted Treasury Room on the middle floor of Caesar's Tower. The rebuilt vault is a tierceron star, and the ribs have long chamfers and a thin soffit (cf. the surviving vaulted cellars in High Street and Earl Street). Re-set medieval tiles in the floor.

From the hall a spiral stair leads up to the timber-framed ante-room above the passage linking from the E range. Higher still, the armoury, again timber-framed and dendro-dated to the 1420s. Good bearded stone corbel and a good timber roof. Behind on the recreated top floor of Caesar's Tower is the Mary Queen of Scots Room, with restored stone fireplace and a loophole window.

Back down through the hall, the Mayoress's Parlour (now called the Drapers' Room) over the entrance was refurbished for Mayor George Eld in 1834–5. Good Gothic ceiling (reusing C15 bosses), fireplace and carved doors. Two two-light windows to the street and a five-light C19 window to the courtyard replacing a Venetian window incongruously inserted in 1785. – In the Mayoress's Parlour, a small SCULPTURE of Godiva on horseback, by *William Behnes*, c. 1844.

Lastly, the kitchen. The area below the Old Council Chamber has a low ceiling and C14 timber framing is visible on the E where the kitchen has a higher ceiling. The N wall has an octagonal pier and two arches with a figured E corbel. These openings seem to have connected to a kitchen aisle towards the courtyard. Along the E and s walls (concealed) are the four enormous fireplaces of the medieval kitchen.

Immediately E are the PUBLIC OFFICES, fronting Bayley Lane and originally entered from St Mary's Street. By *James Murray*, 1863. Red sandstone. Gothic. Facing St Michael's, a symmetrical front with oriels in the end bays. Murray also built a police station and superintendent's house extending about halfway along St Mary's Street. This whole front was remodelled or rebuilt to designs by *Harry Quick*, 1896. Quick had won the competition for new municipal buildings in 1895 but the scheme was unable to proceed. This section was built, but to an alternative design. It blends almost seamlessly with the taller and later section of the Council House to the s.

The COUNCIL HOUSE faces s onto Earl Street. Built in the manner of the great Victorian town halls of the north, but too timidly and too late. It reflects the medieval past rather than the city's emerging industrial future. After the 1895 scheme (*see* above) had to be abandoned a further competition was held in 1910, won by *Edward Garratt* and *H. W. Simister* of Birmingham.* Mainly built 1913–16 but not officially opened

---

* *Buckland & Farmer* were also associated with the winning competition entry, but only Garratt & Simister are named as architects on the 1920 plaque on the building.

until 1920. Runcorn stone, Tudor, symmetrical front of fifteen bays with gables, oriels in alternate first-floor bays, a central gabled accent with a timber turret above, and a totally asymmetrical tower at the corner of St Mary's Street. On the tower a clock dial with gilded angel projecting diagonally, statues between the louvred belfry windows and St Michael on top. The entrance bay is over-ornamented with statuary, Arts and Crafts branches with shields and gilded squares with animals and birds. The statues of Leofric, Godiva and Justice are by *Henry Wilson*, pre-1920 and 1926. Inside, nice Arts & Crafts detailing to the open wooden stair and attractive plaster decoration to the walls and ceilings, especially in the panelled corridor outside the Council Chamber. The seats in the Council Chamber are by *Wilson*, 1916, finely carved, and there is stained glass by *Goddard & Gibbs*, 1951 (post-war replacement).

To the E, on the opposite side of Earl Street, is the CIVIC CENTRE, designed by the *City Architect's Department* and built in four phases. First came CIVIC CENTRE 1, two copper-roofed blocks set at right angles, begun under *Gibson* and completed by *Ling*, 1951–7. A block of six shops with colonnade nearby (Nos. 26–31 Earl Street) with flats above, also by *Gibson*, is contemporary. Then in 1957–9 *Ling* filled the gap on the Earl Street front, adding a brick block with ground-floor colonnade on the E by the shops and completing the N side with a curtain-walled block. This is CIVIC CENTRE 2, which originally housed the Architecture and Town Planning Departments, its ground floor open on pilotis except for a big glazed part for exhibitions (the ROOTS GALLERY). Underneath the E range are the vaulted cellars of the former Old Star Inn (*see* p. 261). The group was completed by *Noble* (principals *Chell* and *Arlidge*) in 1974–6 with the corner block in the NW angle, unashamedly different. CIVIC CENTRE 3 is brick with sloping copper roof, chamfered corners and deep-set windows. It is linked to the Council House by a copper-clad bridge over Earl Street. The whole complex encloses a courtyard, paved with sample materials used as a palette for the city centre rebuilding.

Along the Little Park Street side of the Civic Centre there is open space in front of the buildings in what was once the ancient Palace Yard. From it leads Meschede Way, a pedestrian corridor between two blocks of public buildings. At its E end is the sixteen-storey tower block, CIVIC CENTRE 4 (*Terence Gregory*, 1971–3; principal *McLellan*). To the S are the MAGISTRATES' COURT (*Harry Noble*, 1984–7; principal *Arlidge*) building fronting Little Park Street, and the CROWN & COUNTY COURT (*PSA Midland Region* with *John Madin Design Group*, 1986–8) towards Much Park Street.

Belonging to Gibson's plan, although both of utilitarian design, are two more public buildings in Little Park Street, completing the intended boulevard leading S from the Council House. On the E, the POLICE HEADQUARTERS round a courtyard, by

Gibson, 1954–7 (principal *W. G. Sealey*). On the w, the TELE-PHONE EXCHANGE by the *Ministry of Works*, 1955.

With these one might also group some later government and public utility buildings in the same part of the city. In St John Street is the SEVERN TRENT WATER Operations Centre, by *Associated Architects* and *Webb Gray*, 2008–10. Seven storeys around a central atrium, with aquamarine glass louvres of differing heights on the three bays of the w front. Further w, outside the defined civic quarter, are the 1930s GOVERNMENT OFFICES in Cheylesmore and the adjacent JOB CENTRE by *PSA Services*, 1991–3.

HERBERT ART GALLERY AND MUSEUM, Jordan Well. 1954–60 by *Herbert, Son & Sawday*. Hornton stone and sparingly diapered brick. Of varied grouping. The ground floor of the w wing with its brown pillars was open and the shops opposite (Nos. 26–31 Earl Street) repeated the same brown arcading. w wing alterations by *Haworth Tompkins*, 2002, involving conversion of the ground floor to a café and addition of a rooftop pavilion with zinc-clad angled roof-lights. To the N, a glass and laminated timber grid-shell roofed extension by *Pringle Richards Sharratt*, 2006–8. On the E end of the s front, two sculpture panels of Man's Struggle by *Walter Ritchie*, 1957–9, relocated from the Upper Precinct, 1994.

SPORTS AND LEISURE CENTRE, Fairfax Street. The SWIMMING BATHS (designed 1956) by *Ling* and *Gregory* (principal *McLellan*), 1962–6. Four main stanchions outside supporting butterfly-winged cantilevered roofs. Large areas of glazing. This is linked to the LEISURE CENTRE, known locally as 'The Elephant', wholly clad in silver grey zinc sheeting and raised on concrete legs over Cox Street. By *Noble* (*McLellan*), 1974–6. Pool and sports hall are closing in 2019.

RAILWAY STATION, off Warwick Road. *See* Perambulation 4.

COVENTRY UNIVERSITY

Coventry University came into being in 1992 but its history links back to 1829 through former institutions such as the Mechanics Institute, the Technical Institute (later Technical College), the School of Art etc. The immediate predecessors were the Lanchester College of Technology and the Coventry College of Art, which combined in 1970 as Lanchester Polytechnic, known as Coventry Polytechnic from 1987 to 1992. In the plan for post-war rebuilding the two colleges were co-located E of the cathedral, in the square bounded by Priory Street, Fairfax Street, Cox Street and Jordan Well. This is still the main site but to cater for a student population of 27,000 (2013) the campus has spread within the city centre and beyond the Ringway E and s. The buildings were originally lettered (e.g. C Block) but are now named after people associated with the city or University.

The first buildings, of course, were by the *City Architect's Department*, for the then city-controlled College of Art on Cope Street

and the Lanchester College to its w and s. They were planned
as a series of interlocking buildings around open spaces, with
a few surviving gravestones of St Michael's churchyard on the
Priory Street frontage. As originally completed, with the now-
demolished Frank Whittle Building on the s, the buildings of
1957–64 by *Ling* (principals *Roche* and *Long*) comprised a neat
little Miesian group. Of these, the survivors are CHARLES
WARD (the original College of Art), 1952–5 (*Gibson*), and the
FOUNDATION BUILDING and ALAN BERRY, both *Ling*,
1962–4. All low with simple framed structures and glass. The
administration building (Alan Berry) has an added green
portico on the cathedral front. Behind, and also of the original
college, are GEORGE ELIOT, a transverse seven-storey curtain-
wall block with pale green opaque glass, by *Ling*, 1957–60
(principal, *Barker*), and the splendidly long (560-ft (171-
metre)) and uncompromising JAMES STARLEY BUILDING
along Cox Street, blue steel and white glass, 1961–3 (principal
Roche). The first student residence, PRIORY HALL, consisted
of three separate blocks, beginning with the twenty-storey
tower block in Priory Street by *Ling*, 1965–6, with panels of
concrete cladding and vertical fins. This faces the e end of the
cathedral and trumps it. Along Fairfax Street to the N, six
blocks with arches in the ground floor and five to six storeys
above. Then a six-storey link block with a lower tower in the
middle. These additions are by *Gregory*, 1969–74.

On the main site there have been few significant changes. To
George Eliot was added, in 1991–2, the single-storey HILLMAN/
HUMBER BUILDING in brick by *Grantham Parsons & Nolan*,
1991–2, with a circular restaurant and lecture theatres in the
style of Greek amphitheatres with curved and sloping angles.
More recently, the s end of the site towards the Herbert Art
Gallery (*see* p. 251) and Jordan Well has been redeveloped. The
space is now occupied by THE HUB, a six-storey L-shaped
glass box by *Hawkins Brown*, 2010–11. Dark and clear glass
and irregular vertically striped bands. It has a roof garden.

The first 'off-site' development was the GRAHAM SUTHERLAND
BUILDING, built to replace the original Art College, by
Gregory, 1966–7 (principal *John Smith*). At right angles to Cox
Street towards the Ringway, with a low workshop range
extending s towards Gosford Street. The main block has seven
storeys, the lower part with wide windows against dark panels
between thin concrete pillars, the upper with narrow windows
all along and thin concrete mullions attached. Attached on the
N side is the BUGATTI BUILDING, by the *Hellberg Harris
Partnership*, 2002–4. To the N, the MAURICE FOSS BUILDING
by *Noble*, 1986.

To the s of Jordan Well, the area bounded by Much Park Street
on the w and White Friars Street on the e has further university
buildings. RICHARD CROSSMAN by *Gregory*, 1971, was the
library (now Health and Life Sciences). Brick with narrow
windows each side of exposed concrete piers and flat panels of
brown brick above the first floor with its TV-shaped windows.

To its s, the functional two-storeyed SIR JOHN LAING BUILD-
ING by *Noble*, 1976. Back on Jordan Well, the ELLEN TERRY
BUILDING was originally the Gaumont Cinema (later Odeon),
by *W. H. Watkins* of Bristol, 1931. Adapted for the university
by the *Hellberg Harris Partnership*, 2000. Art Deco pale faience
front with coloured stylized Egyptian capitals. With it is the
white-tiled and domed WHITE FRIARS BUILDING at the
corner of White Friars Street and the range of shops down
the side, originally Coliseum Buildings with ballroom and café,
by *T. R. J. Meakin* for Frank Turner in 1920–2. After 1931 it
became a ballroom attached to the Gaumont as the Palace
Ballroom. To the s, the SPORTS CENTRE with curved roof by
HB Architects, 2003.

Two more groups E on Gosford Street beyond the flyover. On
the l., a little group on a thumb of land hemmed in by the
Ringway, the JAGUAR BUILDING, 1978 (refurbished by
Robothams). Behind is ARMSTRONG SIDDELEY (the original
Engineering and Computing building, now (2015) Mathematics and Information Sciences) by *Gregory*, 1972–3, with white
concrete external columns and projecting boxes on the top
floor. To the E and originally separate, WILLIAM LYONS by
Noble, 1982–3, its front curtain wall with a canopy supported
on ten brick piers. It is on three sides of a hexagon, giving it
a curved appearance. The five-storey link building between
them is by the *Design Büro*, 2003.

The university's most adventurous buildings are on the site
across Gosford Street through to Gulson Road. First, the
WILLIAM MORRIS BUILDING on Gosford Street. The main
block was erected by *Harry Quick* as the Hotchkiss armaments
works in 1915–16, afterwards taken over for motor manufacture in 1923 by Morris who added a second (E) block to the
frontage. The additions are by *T. D. Griffiths*, 1924. Red brick
with concrete floor bands and large windows. Acquired by the
university in 1993 and converted with two added floors and
curved roof by *Percy Thomas Partnership*, Birmingham, 1993–4.
Immediately s, the FREDERICK LANCHESTER BUILDING
(Library) by *Alan Short Partnership*, 1998–2001. Simple square
plan made visually arresting by the arrangements of the projecting wings and silver-topped convection ventilating towers.
To the E, the GOSFORD STREET CAR PARK by *RMJM*, 2008,
with vertical stainless steel panels and rounded corners. More
daring still, the ENGINEERING & COMPUTING BUILDING   125
by *Arup Associates*, 2009–12. Double L-shaped blocks with
sloping hexagonally patterned sides. Silver again. The final
building here is the STUDENT CENTRE by *HB Architects*,
2006.

On separate sites in PARKSIDE, s of the Ringway, are the university's TECHNOLOGY PARK and INNOVATION VILLAGE,
1998–2007. At the entrance from Deasy Road, the re-erected
wrought-iron GATEHEAD of the Armstrong Siddeley works
(later Rolls Royce), *c*. 1919 (re-erected 1997). Development
began with the TECHNO CENTRE in Parkside by the *Hellberg*

Harris Partnership, 1996–8. The TECHNOLOGY PARK, opened in 2007, has three main blocks, all in brick with distinctive curved blue roofs. The INNOVATION CENTRE, on Cheetham Way and Puma Way, has eight similar blocks by *PDD Architects*, 2006–7, around a central car park. The ACT-UK building by the Deasy Road roundabout is by *Robothams*, 2009.

Lastly, a few outliers. First, two former industrial buildings towards Hillfields NE of the Ringway. The ALMA BUILDING, Alma Street, is of no architectural interest but it occupies the site of Francis Skidmore's noted Victorian Art Metal works (est. 1859). A little N, in Canterbury Street, is SINGER HALL on the site of the motor works and retaining its French chateau-style office block, 1891. The student accommodation is in neat groups of two- and three-storeyed blocks scaled to resemble the nearby terraced houses. By the *Hellberg Harris Partnership*, 1993–4. Another residence is QUADRANT HALL in Manor House Drive, originally built as a YMCA hostel by *Redgrave & Clarke*, 1970.

COLLEGE AND SCHOOLS

COVENTRY CITY COLLEGE, Swanswell Street. The City College was established after the merger of the Technical College in the Butts and Tile Hill College in 2002, relocating to the new Swanswell premises from 2007. Two five-storey blocks with irregular curved frontages to a small green. Grey and silver, with some areas of red brick. Both by *Robothams*, the NORTH BUILDING completed 2007 and the SOUTH BUILDING in 2009.

KING HENRY VIII SCHOOL, Warwick Road. 1884–5 by *Edward Burgess*. Red brick and stone dressings, spacious, with an irregular front in the Tudor style. The centre has the scholastically much favoured gatehouse motif derived from Lupton's Tower at Eton. The façade survived air-raid damage in 1941 but the internal structure is post-war. Later additions include the handsome school hall and covered walkway by *W. S. Hattrell & Partners*, 1951, and typical 1950s and 60s extensions. At the city end, the junior school and dining room by *Temple Cox Nicholls*, 1996. At the rear, the sports hall by *Viner Associates*, 2002, and the swimming pool with wavy aluminium roof by *CA Design*, 2009. In the Archive Room created in 2014 are displayed three C15 MISERICORDS, originally from Whitefriars (p. 237) brought here from the Old Grammar School (p. 269).

BABLAKE SCHOOL, Coundon Road. *John Giles, Gough & Trollope*, of London, 1889. Late Tudor style in red brick with stone mullioned-and-transomed windows. Embattled tower with oriel and clock dial over the main entrance. Swimming baths by *Redgrave & Clarke*, 1962–3; music and drama building, 1999–2000, one of several projects on the site by *VB Architects*, Kenilworth, including the science laboratories and CDT department.

In the first edition of this guide, a great deal of coverage was given to the new schools built in the 1950s and early 1960s by the City Architect's Department under *Gibson* and *Ling*. The availability of central government funding from 1997 for school replacement has resulted in the loss of several significant schools of this pioneering period. Among these are BINLEY PARK SCHOOL, 1957–9, closed in 1990 (its site is now a business park); LYNG HALL, by *Ling* in association with *Stirrat Johnson-Marshall's* team at the Ministry of Education, 1953–5, replaced by new buildings on another part of the site; and CALUDON, 1951–4, which has been demolished, as has WHITLEY ABBEY, 1955–8, which stood by a lake in the landscaped grounds of the old mansion and was highly praised in its time. The survivors are mentioned under the localities below.

PERAMBULATIONS

1. Around the cathedral: the historic core

The area round the cathedral, a sort-of close, makes a good starting point. The streets are all cobbled and the old churchyards of St Michael's and Holy Trinity have trees and grass. The N side is PRIORY ROW, a narrow lane running E from Trinity Street to the cathedral. It begins with LYCHGATE COTTAGES (Nos. 3–5). Timber-framed with close studding and diagonal braces on the upper floors. Three-storeyed with two overhangs. Dendro-dated to 1414–15, perhaps surprisingly since the appearance seems late C16 even though the form of the façade seems to be original. The group belongs to a once longer range, of which only these four bays remain. The taller adjunct at the W end is part of the Priory Gate Offices (now the Flying Standard pub) facing Trinity Street (*see* p. 271). Immediately E, No. 1 is an additional cottage to the rear, overlooking the deep ruins of the priory (*see* p. 234). Half-timbered and gabled with patterned tile roof. It is approached by a pretty open staircase and gallery and its front is raised on stilts. This and the muscular Gothic sandstone BLUECOAT SCHOOL buildings behind are by *James Murray*, 1856–7, the Lychgate Cottages being restored in 1855–6 too. Before the excavations, the N side here was Holy Trinity churchyard (*see* Parish Churches).★

After that some C18 and C19 brick houses with iron railings in front. PELHAM LEE HOUSE (No. 7, Diocesan Offices), *c.* 1800, of five bays with painted quoins, keystoned windows and dentil cornice. Central door with rusticated pilasters, open pediment on console brackets and fanlight. Pedimented window above. No. 8, perhaps *c.* 1790, has a porch with Greek

★ On it was *Scott's* detached wooden BELL TOWER, 1856, regrettably demolished in 1967, which Pevsner in the first edition of this guide thought 'sufficiently unexpected and direct in expression to please us greatly today'.

Doric columns. From here a narrow cobbled alley, HILL TOP, leads N towards Pool Meadow. On the E side it has low brick buildings adapted for cathedral outreach work. Opposite is YOUELL HOUSE (cathedral offices) by *MacCormac Jamieson Prichard (MJP)*, 2002–3,* as a PHOENIX PROJECT replacement for *Spence*'s John F. Kennedy House, built as a residential youth centre for the cathedral, 1965. Back on Priory Row, Nos. 9–10 are similar in style and scale to No. 8. Then No. 11 with an extremely fine Early Georgian front, described in 1741 as 'the new mansion house'. Set back in a courtyard with a fine wrought-iron gateway. Five bays, brick, two storeys and plain attic. Giant fluted Ionic pilasters. Doorway with a Gibbs surround and a pediment. Although the front is preserved, the house is entirely by *A. H. Gardner & Partners*, 1953. Between No. 11 and the cathedral, the exposed foundations of the E chevet of the priory (*see* p. 236).

CUCKOO LANE separates the two churchyards, running S from the E end of Holy Trinity. Immediately S of the church is the COVENTRY CROSS, designed by *Rolf Hellberg* with carved statues by *George Wagstaffe, Philip Bentham, Wilfred Dudeney* and *George Ford*, 1976. The cross is a red ferro-concrete version of one erected in 1541 and taken down in 1771. In the manner of an Eleanor Cross, with blind panelling at the bottom, canopied niches with statues and tapering top with flags and crown. It stands in a small square alongside COUNTY HALL (now The Establishment bar), by *Joseph Eglington*, 1784. Five bays, of ashlar, with rusticated blank-arched ground floor. Above, three-bay attached Doric portico and pediment. Inside, some courtroom fittings remain in the galleried bar. Attached on the S side, along Pepper Lane, the GOVERNOR'S HOUSE, probably *c.* 1772. Brick, seven bays, with quoins, rusticated doorcase and a three-bay pediment. Top storey added awkwardly, before *c.* 1800.

HAY LANE leads S, short and narrow with decent C18–C19 fronts, mainly brick although some (e.g. Nos. 10 and 10A) have timber framing behind. At the corner the GOLDEN CROSS is on the r., reputedly of 1583 but heavily restored. Timber-framed and jettied. Opposite, a gabled corner block of 1991, sandstone-faced, on the site of St Michael's Baptist Church (*Murray*, 1858; destroyed 1940). BAYLEY LANE continues E, twisting between the old cathedral on the l. and St Mary's Guildhall (p. 247) on the r. On the bend, THE COTTAGE (No. 22) is a fine piece of *c.* 1500 with a boldly traceried angle post and, on the first floor, buttress-shafts and carved window surrounds. At the far end on the S, beyond the late C19 Public Offices (p. 249) and St Mary Street, the DRAPERS' HALL by *Rickman & Hutchinson*, 1832. Greek Revival, irregular, of stone, with a porch *in antis* of unfluted Ionic columns. E wing added by *Nevill & Son*, 1864. Entrance hall and two principal rooms,

---

*It stands above a basement specially designed to display the priory undercrofts (*see* p. 236).

entirely top-lit as the site was surrounded by other buildings. Good decorative plaster ceilings. Under refurbishment as a music centre with an extension to the s by *PCPT Architects*, 2015–16. Opposite, in brick on the pavement of the Herbert Art Gallery (p. 251), is an outline marking the position below of a vaulted medieval UNDERCROFT of a merchant's house (formerly Nos. 38–39 Bayley Lane), of which nothing remains above ground.

E of the cathedral is COVENTRY UNIVERSITY (p. 251). s of Bayley Lane is the Council House (p. 249).

2. Broadgate and the precinct: the post-war city

BROADGATE is the city's central square, as it was before the war. As reconstructed in 1948 it became a large traffic island with, in the middle, its corny bronze equestrian STATUE of Lady Godiva by *Sir William Reid Dick*, 1949. The statue was turned 90 degrees to face down the precinct in 1990 and in 2012 the square was pedestrianized. The E side was developed later than the rest and has the CATHEDRAL LANES SHOPPING CENTRE by *Chapman Taylor Partnership*, 1986–90: undistinguished, with central arch, rounded corner towers and a glazed central area within. It blocks the connection to the cathedral area, although the two spires of St Michael and Holy Trinity can be seen above the roof-line from the opposite site of the square. On the N side is PRIMARK (originally Owen Owen), by *Rolf Hellberg & Maurice Harris*, 1953–4, a curtain-wall job with wide glazed front, less restless now than it was originally. On the W side, the r.-hand block (originally the LEOFRIC HOTEL) is by *W. S. Hattrell & Partners*, 1953–5, designed to balance BROADGATE HOUSE on the other side, the first of *Gibson*'s new city centre buildings, erected in 1948–53 (principal *Frank Moate*). These two blocks display the characteristic features setting the tone for the redevelopment: walkways with columns clad in Hornton stone; thin concrete window surrounds in the brick-work; balconies with light iron railings; and green slate-clad pilaster strips between the bays. Broadgate House continues at right angles along the s side to link up with *Palmer & Holden*'s pre-war NatWest Bank (*see* Perambulation 3) with a projecting clock tower in the middle. This has the whimsical GODIVA CLOCK, with a small balcony, painted backdrop and two doors emblazoned with heraldry through which moves a figure of Lady Godiva on horseback; in the triangular opening above appears Peeping Tom by *Trevor Tennant*, 1953. On the W side of the clock the building formed a bridge over a road (blocked since the road was closed in 1969) and on the E an opening for pedestrians into Hertford Street. On the back are Tennant's sculpted figures of The People of Coventry, and just inside at street level is *H. R. Hosking*'s mosaic of the Coventry Martyrs, all 1953.

In the middle of the w side of Broadgate the pedestrianized PRECINCT begins. It was first planned in 1941 and begun in 1948. It was the first scheme for a large-scale pedestrian precinct in Britain although not the first to be built. Its design pre-dated Exeter's Princesshay (1945, built 1949), Plymouth (1944, built 1951) and, in the European context, the Lijnbaan in Rotterdam (1951–3). It is in two halves, the UPPER PRECINCT to the e and the LOWER PRECINCT to the w, intersected in the middle by SMITHFORD WAY and MARKET WAY at right angles to the N and S. On the E–W axis the site slopes gradually to the w and the two halves are on different levels. In each precinct there are shops with covered walkways on two levels, echoing the Rows at Chester. The Upper Precinct was completed first in 1951–6, the Lower Precinct in 1957–60. Both have later undergone substantial remodelling.

Entering the UPPER PRECINCT from Broadgate, a central walkway (1979–81) leads to the upper level of shops and there are passages at the sides into the main square. Here, under the bridge, is *Trevor Tennant*'s LEVELLING STONE, laid in 1946 to inaugurate the redevelopment. The link blocks on either side of the square are by *Hattrell & Partners*, 1954–6. These remain unaltered, but what has changed is the access from the square to the upper level. Gibson's elegant curved staircases have been crudely replaced, the walkways widened and the planting and artworks removed.* Worst of all, there is an ugly and intrusive green cage for the escalators.

The crossing in the middle of the precinct is crucial to the design, and it is only from here that one can appreciate how it was intended to work. To the E, the middle distance is closed by the narrowing of the entrance between the two Broadgate blocks, with the spire of St Michael's in between them beyond. This was Gibson's concept. The addition of towers at the end of the other three wings stemmed from Ling's amendments to the plan. To the N on Smithford Way is eighteen-storey HILLMAN HOUSE (*Ling* (and *McLellan*) with *Arthur Swift & Partners*, 1965), with protruding triangular windows and an odd pyramid roof on the tank. The w end of the Lower Precinct terminates with a tower of twenty-two storeys, MERCIA HOUSE by *Ling* and *Gregory* (principals *McLellan* and *Chell*), 1967, facing broadside to the precinct. The final tower, to the s on Market Way, is COVENTRY POINT by *John Madin Design Group*, 1972–5.

The crossing itself is marked by near-symmetrical blocks on each corner, all breaking forward from the line of the link blocks beyond to define the area of the four precincts. Marks & Spencer on the NE corner is by *Norman Jones Sons & Rigby* of Southport, 1953–5. The SE block (BHS) is by *George Coles* of London, 1951–5, and the SW block, the first part of the Lower Precinct, by Woolworth's in-house architect (*Harold*

---

* Sculpted panels of Man's Struggle by *Ritchie*, 1957–9, were removed from the Upper Precinct Bridge to the Herbert Art Gallery (p. 251) in 1994.

Winbourne), 1952–4. The fourth corner of the crossing came later, built by *Ling* (principal *Beaton*) with *Kett & Neve*, 1958–60. This was the Locarno Ballroom. Its upper floors have criss-cross windows with mosaic decoration by *Fred Millett*. The original ballroom entrance was a completely glazed staircase block standing out into Smithford Way, replaced after the building became the Central Library in 1986 by a bland red steel and glass structure closer to the building line.

The Smithford Way and Market Way shops were always two-storeyed and modest, but the N arm of the precinct now leads to the WEST ORCHARDS SHOPPING CENTRE by *John Clark Associates* of London, 1986–91. Six levels of shops with an open area in the middle under a wide glass dome.

Continuing W, one reaches the LOWER PRECINCT by *Ling*, 1957–60. The main shopping blocks have low-pitched gables. Redesigned with a covered roof (by *Aukett Associates*), widened walkways and new escalators and stairs in 2002. The circular CAFÉ (*Bill Pearson*, assistant), an original feature (although altered), still stands in the precinct like a mushroom. In the narrow passage out to Corporation Street at the far end, a delightful ceramic MURAL by *Gordon Cullen*, 1958 (relocated from the ramp between the precincts and the surviving parts restored in 2002). Illustrating the history of the city, it is especially valuable for its representation of the post-war masterplan and buildings. Also part of the original scheme are the eight neon panels by *James Brown* representing Coventry industries, 1958 and 1961. In alternate bays on the top floor, they were restored in 2002. 117

From the Lower Precinct Sherbourne Arcade leads to *Ling*'s circular MARKET HALL, 1956–7 (principals *Beaton* and *Kenneth Bradley*, with City Engineer *Granville Berry*). It has a central ring and the 276-ft (84-metre) diameter hall supported a rooftop car park, a novel idea at the time.* Inside, a mural at one end by *Jürgen Seidel*, presented by the city of Dresden, 1961.

The S end of Market Way is continued in SHELTON SQUARE (*Ling* with *Ardin & Brookes*, 1958), which links up with the CITY ARCADE (*Ling*, 1960–2; *Frank Barnett*) towards Queen Victoria Road. It is a dog-leg arcade of small shops with offset two-way canted fronts, top-lit. The wing E of Shelton Square leads into BULL YARD, completed 1965–8 (*Ling*: principals *Chell* and *Berrett*). Above the archway is a carving of Guy slaying the Dun Cow by *Alma Ramsey*, 1952, relocated from Broadgate House in 1983. In Bull Yard, the façade of the THREE TUNS pub (*W.S. Hattrell & Partners* for Bass Breweries) has an extraordinary abstract relief in cast concrete by *W.G. Mitchell*, 1966.

From here, HERTFORD STREET leads back to Broadgate. Following the closure of the road to traffic in 1969 the w side was redeveloped by *W.S. Hattrell & Partners*, 1971. This

*It also had a spindly skeletal clock tower, demolished in 2006.

included a large office block to the w, the covered section of
the street and the stepped shops at the s end with moulded
dark fibreglass panels, again by *Mitchell*. Older buildings on
the e, but of interest only the former POST OFFICE (No. 71)
by *W. T. Oldrieve*, 1902, with alterations and additions by *D. N.
Dyke*, 1923, and the Hertford Street elevation of the NatWest
Bank which begins the next perambulation.

3. The High Street and east

Starting again in Broadgate, begin in the se corner with the
NATWEST BANK. By *Palmer & Holden*, architects to the
National Provincial Bank, 1929–30. Neatly conjoined to Gibson's Broadgate House in the post-war reconstruction. Proudly
Neoclassical with a Doric portico of Portland stone and a little
altered American Beaux-Arts interior. Entrance doors made by
the *Birmingham Guild*, with beaten panels in stainless steel. In
the banking hall a semicircular glass ceiling and good plasterwork. Holden was responsible for the decorative scheme,
which uses emblems from ancient British and Greek coinage,
motifs which appear in the metopes of the portico's frieze. Its
neighbour, LLOYDS BANK, is also monumental. By *Buckland
& Haywood*, 1932, with the entrance recessed in a giant classical arch at the front and stylized fluted demi-columns down
the sides. Otherwise the HIGH STREET is conventional banks
and offices, mostly pre-war as this area escaped heavy damage
in the Blitz. A typical example is YORKSHIRE BANK (originally Barclays, Nos. 7–11) by *Peacock, Bewlay & Cooke*, 1919.
BARCLAYS opposite (No. 25) with Hornton stone facings and
glass panelled windows is by *Barclays Property Division*, 1981.
Further e the glass-fronted COVENTRY BUILDING SOCIETY
(Nos. 19–20) by *Redgrave & Clarke*, 1974–5, has vaulted medieval cellars below. The vaulting of four by two bays has heavy
ribs with a long chamfer and a thin soffit. The cellars extend
under the HALIFAX (No. 22) as well. The High Street ends
with two blocks with rounded corners facing the Council
House (p. 249). On the n, Nos. 16–17 at the corner of Hay
Lane (*see* Perambulation 1), late c19 Italianate in brick with
stone dressings. On the s, continuing round into Little Park
Street, THE EARL OF MERCIA (No. 18) by *F. B. Osborn* was
built as the London, City & Midland Bank, 1897. Ornate, with
Free Renaissance details and balustrading.
Beyond this there are just a few buildings not already covered.
The area is largely occupied by the Civic Centre (*see* Public
Buildings) and Coventry University (p. 251).
On its w side LITTLE PARK STREET has two fine c18 houses
overlooking the open area in front of the Civic Centre. The
first, No. 7, is one of the most splendid in Coventry and similar
to the one in Priory Row (No. 11). It was built for a silk mer-
chant, with a plainer warehouse at the side, set back. Early
Georgian. Brick and stone dressings. Five bays, two storeys,

and an attic. Giant Corinthian pilasters. Narrow doorway with pilasters with triglyph-like fluted capitals (cf. Stoneleigh Abbey). The window above with side volutes and garlands (cf. Stoneleigh too). In the attic the middle window is arched. The other windows are segment-headed with aprons. Set back from the street, KIRBY HOUSE (No. 16) is of the same type. Probably by *Francis Smith*, *c.* 1725 (Andor Gomme) but remodelled about 1780. Giant pilasters, but Adamish oval paterae in the frieze above the capitals. Aprons to the windows. Doorway with segmental pediment on unfluted Ionic columns, the window above again with extravagant scrolls flanking. Staircase with two twisted and one fluted baluster to the tread. Restored as an office in 1982–3 by *Crouch Butler Savage Associates*, sympathetically enfolded in their dark brick SUN ALLIANCE BUILDING with simple round-headed windows. Between these, WHITEFRIARS HOUSING (No. 9) by *Redgrave & Clarke* for the Liverpool Victoria Friendly Society, 1971–2, attempts to mimic the style of the two C18 houses in an unashamedly C20 manner and on a bigger scale. Brick and glass, but with cream ribs representing pilasters and segmental curves in the concrete courses above the first floor and at the top.

EARL STREET has been wholly redeveloped. For the Council House and its post-war extensions *see* p. 249. It shows no hints of its medieval past, except below ground. Under the former Department of Architecture & Planning in Civic Centre 2 (s side, p. 250) there are vaulted cellars of the Old Star Inn, two by two bays with ridge ribs. Heavy ribs with a long chamfer and a thin soffit. On the N side, DRAPERS bar by *Baynes & Co.*, 1998, with rough Hollington stone base and coppered curved roof supported on timber poles above a glazed area with timber-lined roof inside.

The continuation of Earl Street is JORDAN WELL (for its buildings *see* Coventry University, p. 251). Opposite the Herbert Art Gallery (p. 251) is MUCH PARK STREET, also dominated by the university buildings but once home to some of the medieval timber-framed buildings now residing in Spon Street (*see* Perambulation 5). Surviving the systematic clearance is a ruined stone building at the s end of the university's Sir John Laing Building on the E side. Possibly a wealthy merchant's house, this C14 structure is two-storeyed, rectangular with gabled ends. There is a fireplace in the s wall of the principal chamber, which had a stone vaulted cellar below. A little further s, close to the Ringway, is the WHITEFRIARS GATE, again mid-C14, of red sandstone and Lias. It is thought to have been adapted as a gateway leading to Whitefriars by John Hales in the later C16. Single stone arches on both sides. Converted to two cottages with a timber-framed floor visible within the tops of the archways.

Back on Jordan Well past the converted Gaumont Cinema of 1931 (now the Ellen Terry Building of Coventry University, p. 253) and its white-tiled corner group stretching round into

WHITE FRIARS STREET. Here the road to the E becomes
GOSFORD STREET. On the corner, THE PHOENIX pub, 1906
(probably by *T. F. Tickner* for James Eadie Ltd), with brown
glazed tiles at street level, ribbed black bands between the
floors, little circular bays at first-floor level and shaped gables.
On the same side, Nos. 114–115, with crown-post roof dendro-
dated to *c.* 1335. Originally a two-bay hall house with floors
inserted later. Now a pub (the WHITEFRIARS).

4. South to the railway station

Start from Broadgate again. Hertford Street (*see* Perambulation
2) was first created in 1812 to relieve congestion in GREYFRI-
ARS LANE, until then a main thoroughfare of the old city. It
was and is but a narrow lane, leading inauspiciously S between
the two grand High Street banks and past the back of the old
Hertford Street Post Office, from where a range of timber-
framed buildings stand out ahead. These belong to FORD'S
HOSPITAL ALMSHOUSES. The hospital was founded in 1509
by William Ford, whose original endowment was increased by
others in 1517 and 1529. The buildings must have been put up
immediately and belong chiefly to the second decade of the
C16. They were badly bombed in 1940 but carefully restored
by *W. S. Hattrell & Partners*, 1951–3. Profusely decorated with
rich carving, Ford's Hospital is perhaps the finest of Coventry's
surviving timber-framed buildings. The street front has three
oriels and three gables. The carving includes buttress-shafts on
both floors overlaying the close studding, moulded and carved
bressumers, fine traceried windows in the oriels, bargeboards
and gable pendants. The central doorway leads directly into a
narrow, long courtyard, closed at the far end as well. Here the
details are similar, again with buttress-shafts, moulded bressumers at first-floor and eaves levels, and bargeboarded gables.
The doorways in the courtyard have foliage carving in the
spandrels. Oak seats in the corners and lead rainwater heads
dated 1784. The side outer elevations have close studding with
curved braces.

Immediately S, the EVENTIDE HOMES, a complementary group
of old people's homes by *Redgrave & Clarke*, 1968. Two-storey
with tile-hanging. Square bays of stone blocks. Courtyard to
rear.

Ahead is CHRISTCHURCH HOUSE, a five-storey office block
with curved corners and U-shaped ground-floor windows, by
Gregory, 1974–5. This is at the back of SPIRE HOUSE, an
earlier part of the same development, 1971–2, and behind this
is the steeple of the Greyfriars (*see* p. 238). Spire House fronts
onto NEW UNION STREET, constructed in place of a web of
old streets and designated as the professional precinct of the
post-war city. All of this period, except the 1930s pub, THE
SQUIRREL, at the corner of Greyfriars Lane. The N side has

two blocks by *Ling*, single-storey UNION BUILDINGS at the
E, 1958, and three-storeyed Nos. 20–42, 1964–5. At the W end
on the S, a rather monotonous seven-storey block (No. 163)
by *W.H. Saunders & Son*, 1973. Along the rest of the S side, a
continuous three-storey office block (Nos. 101–161) by *Hellberg, Harris & Partners*, 1969. Especially successful, with an
arcade with tiled columns at street level, first-floor windows of
even size subtly spaced and an asymmetrical projecting bay
towards the W. This identifies an archway connecting through
to a courtyard, behind which the REGISTER OFFICE occupies
part of the restored gatehouse of CHEYLESMORE MANOR.
Originally established in the mid C13, Cheylesmore became a
royal manor in the C14, chiefly associated with Queen Isabella
and the Black Prince. A solar wing of the manor house with a
crown-post roof was demolished as recently as 1956. What
remains is the three-bay gatehouse with its archway and two
cross-wings. The SE wing is C14 with square framing with
diagonal bracing. The gatehouse and NW wing are close-
studded and C15. Restored by *F. W.B. Charles* for the corporation 1966–8, with an added staircase clad in weatherboarding.
The extension by *Gregory* (principals *McLellan* and *Chell*),
1970–1, is in dark brown brick and glass, blending with the
office range on the N side of the courtyard. The side to Manor
House Drive has narrow windows spaced to resemble the
timber framing.

Further S in Manor House Drive are the former youth hostel
(now Coventry University's Quadrant Hall, p. 254) and two
government office buildings. Tall, glass-sided FRIARS HOUSE
by the *Hellberg Harris Partnership*, 1989–90, with a SCULPTURE
('Cofa's Tree') by *Deborah Ford* in the lobby. SHERBOURNE
HOUSE in silver-grey with curved frontage, by *Alan Johnson
Associates*, 2002.

Now to Greyfriars spire (p. 238) to head S down GREYFRIARS
GREEN towards Warwick Road. The tree-lined green widens
to the S. On it, statues to Coventry benefactor Thomas White
(†1566) by *W. W. & T. W. Wills*, 1883, and to industrialist
James Starley (†1881) by *Joseph Whitehead & Sons*, 1884. On
the W side WARWICK ROW typifies the lingering small-town
character of Coventry's central area, mostly three-storey,
mainly brick, some stuccoed. Only the five-bay REFORM
CLUB (No. 5) with classical porch and the United Reformed
church (*see* Other Places of Worship) stand out. Opposite,
THE QUADRANT, a long Italianate terrace, some (maybe all)
by *Murray*, 1855. The only modern building here is BANK
HOUSE (No. 23), by *Twentyman Percy & Partners* for Martin's
Bank and the Royal Insurance Group, 1965. To the S, right by
the Ringway, two later Victorian villas in their gardens (Nos.
25 and 29) with the glass tower of Friars House (*see* above)
behind.

The railway station lies beyond the Ringway in an area undergoing redevelopment (2015), partly replacing the 'foothold of the

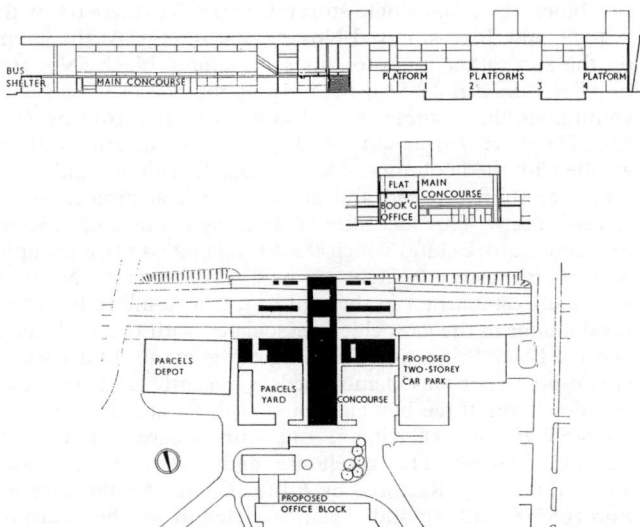

Coventry, railway station.
Sections and site plan, 1962

new Coventry' described in the first edition of this guide.* Of
the 1960s STATION SQUARE nothing will remain except the
STATION itself. This is of 1960–2 by the *Architect's Department,
British Railways, London Midland Region* (*W. R. Headley*,
regional architect; *Derrick Shorten*, job architect). One of the
best stations of the period in England, influenced by Scandinavian models and taking its high glass sides and open structure from Nervi's unrealized design of 1954 for Naples central
station. It was a passenger-centred design. As Shorten wrote,
'the concept was simple – to enable the passengers to see the
trains as soon as they came into the concourse, and to see the
bridges to the far platforms. Similarly, passengers arriving
should be able to see the way out at a glance.' A very clear
plan, cross-shaped, with the main wing under one big slab roof
and the cross-wing much lower. The latter runs parallel with
the rails. The former contains the concourse and the ample
bridge across the rails. The concourse is continued out to
Station Square (on the city side) by a big canopy projecting so
far that the bus shelter with its own long slab roof stands easily
below it, projecting far to the l. and r. Spacious, clearly articulated ticket hall with marbled floor and varnished hardwood
ceiling. Much use of glass, white tiles and timber. The signage
was by *Jock Kinneir*. The waiting room in the r. cross-wing is
divided from the refreshment room by a little planted patio.

---

*The Friargate development is intended to include a civic centre with new council
offices etc. The decking over the Ringway (completed 2015) improves pedestrian
access between the station and the city.

5. *West*

We head next to the zone outside the central shopping area between Warwick Road and Bishop Street, past St John's church and the Belgrade Theatre. Along Greyfriars Road and Queen Victoria Road there is nothing of note except the wavy-roofed and subtly toned VICROFT COURT flats in Queen Victoria Road, by *Roger P. Dudley & Associates*, 2007. Then the IKEA building at the corner of Croft Road. Distinctive blue with areas of yellow, silver and grey, by *Capita Ruddle Wilkinson Architects*, 2007. To its w, the SKYDOME ARENA and the associated SKYDOME entertainment complex, both by *S & P Leisure Architects*, 1999. The Skydome is on the site of the former Rudge cycle works and its N façade towards Spon Street is sympathetically built in factory style in brick with large windows.

SPON STREET is Coventry's historic quarter or, rather, its museum of historic buildings. Between St John's church and the Ringway it is lined with timber-framed buildings. Many occupy their original sites and belong here, but others were re-erected here after 1969. The street is one of the ancient main roads into the city and continues beyond the Ringway to Upper Spon Street and Spon End (*see* Inner Suburbs: North-west). Being extra-mural it was always wider than those within the city. It escaped major damage in the war but fell into neglect until a scheme was launched in 1967 to restore its remaining timber-framed buildings and to relocate others here from elsewhere in the city, principally from Much Park Street (*see* Perambulation 3). In doing this, the city council under *Gregory* worked with *F. W. B. Charles*, an architect with a particular enthusiasm for and expertise in timber-framed buildings. But Charles, as Robert Gill has pointed out, was a Modernist at heart and had learned to appreciate timber-framed structures from Gropius. He admired them more for their function and form than for nostalgia and charm. Now one might well question the appropriateness of removing such buildings from their original sites. Moreover the methods of repair were a far cry from those of today.* Yet the result, generally, is a happy one.

At the w end, on the N side, Nos. 159–162 are the surviving end of a C15 terrace with Wealden fronts to the recessed hall-bays and jettied bays in between. Nos. 163–164 alongside came from Much Park Street (Nos. 8–10) in 1971–4. Again C15. Three storeys with two overhangs, reconstructed first-floor windows with tracery and two doorways with carved spandrels. Then a two-storeyed group with jettied fronts *in situ*, of which the last (No. 169) with curved braces was the first to be restored, 1969–70. Its crown-post roof has been dendro-dated to c. 1395.

41

---

*In essence, only the frames were preserved. Even at the time, SPAB was critical.

Opposite, a handsome C18 group (Nos. 26–28) of brick, three-storeyed with keystoned windows and an infilled carriage arch to the l. of No. 26. The OLD WINDMILL pub (No. 22) is stuccoed but the jettied front reveals its C16 timber framing. Nos. 20–21 belong to the Green Dragon Inn (Nos. 122–123 Much Park Street), re-erected here 1982–4. Double-depth, the front block with overhang of *c.* 1500 and the rear part mid-C15. Attached on the r. is part of the carriage arch of its former neighbour (No. 124). Opposite, an electricity substation unconvincingly concealed by a stout timber fence with painted panels. This abuts the former Rising Sun pub (Nos. 180–181) of 1896 and FAIRFAX HOUSE, 1901, both with Victorian half-timbering. The N side ends with a shop, dated 1909, at the corner of Lower Holyhead Road in which, on the l., is a group of three-storey brick cottages (Nos. 12–23) with top-shop windows on the second floor, 1819.

Back in Spon Street, No. 16 on the S has square framing, *c.* 1700. This was moved from 142–143 Spon Street in 1974. Alongside, TUDOR HOUSE (Nos. 14–15) is the finest of Spon Street's own buildings. Later C15, with curved coving below the windows in the outer wings and under the roof in the centre. The wide door on the l. was an entrance to the courts behind. Nos. 11–12, *in situ*, represent the two right-hand bays of a C14 Wealden house, the curved braces at the eaves of No. 11 marking the position of the recessed centre hall-bay. Double-depth No. 9 was relocated from No. 7 Much Park Street in 1971–2. The museum ends round the corner with Nos. 1–2, originally in Spon Street W of the Ringway (Nos. 54–57) and originally four early C15 hall houses with alternate Wealden and jettied bays. No. 1 (No. 54) has only one bay but has a cross-passage behind. In front of these is a low stone wall representing the city wall leading to the Spon Gate (dem. 1771) which stood across the road just W of St John's church (*see* Churches). A small section of original city wall can be seen in the end of No. 190 facing the churchyard.

N of Spon Street is HILL STREET, with Bond's Hospital and Bablake School, a complex site comprising both the former collegiate buildings belonging with the nearby church of St John and the hospital endowed by Thomas Bond in 1506. Until it relocated to new premises in 1890 Bablake School (p. 254) was here too. The buildings are timber-framed and in three ranges. They stand to the E, N and W of a courtyard with a big lime tree, open to St John's to the S. The courtyard is entered from the E by a stone gateway of 1832. The oldest range is the E range, BABLAKE SCHOOL itself, which has a long back to the street, with a stone ground floor and mullioned windows, and all close studding above and no gables. To the courtyard there are open galleries instead, on the ground as well as the first floor. The openings have four-centred arches. Inside in the centre is the former hall with tie-beams, big arched braces and wind-braces. All this seems to date from *c.* 1500. Probably in 1681 the staircase with twisted balusters was put in (there is a date on one fireplace). There is also in one room an ornate wooden chimneypiece with the date 1629. The overmantel is divided by groups of triple colonnettes. The chimneypiece comes from a house in Little Park Street. The N range is BOND'S HOSPITAL, described in 1581 as newly built. Heavily restored with the addition of enormous stone chimneys. The W end was mostly rebuilt in 1832–4 by *Rickman & Hutchinson*. The work carried out at that time is remarkably conscientious archaeologically. In 1846–8 the street front was refaced and extended along Hill Street. The gable end to the street has carved bressumers, and an oriel with buttress-shafts and traceried lights. The side N of the courtyard with big stone chimneys has at the W end a group of two gables, and further E three more gables. On the first floor are oriels with buttress-shafts on coving. The lintels are carved. Some of the windows have original small-scale tracery, and there is an admirable diversity of bargeboards, illustrated by Ferrey and Pugin in *Ornamental Timber Gables* (1839). The street front has a specially elaborate gable. Inside is another staircase with twisted balusters. The W range is entirely of 1898. The city walls were immediately W of the W and N of the N range, and across Hill Street there was another gate (i.e. in addition to the Spon Gate to the S).

On the other side of Hill Street, BOND'S COURT ALMS-HOUSE by *Stewart Anderson & Keith Berry* for the Coventry Church Charities, 1985. Further out, a restored group of late C18 brick cottages with top-shop windows at Nos. 34–44 Hill Street and Nos. 1–3 Ryley Street.

Now back to St John's to follow CORPORATION STREET NE round to Bishop Street. This was a new street, created by *E.H. Ford* in 1931 and retained in the post-war rebuilding as the periphery of the central precinct (*see* Perambulation 2). On the S side, a 1930s Neo-Georgian pair (Nos. 2–12) and then the CO-OP store (Nos. 14–20) by *G. S. Hay*, CWS architect, 1955–6, with incised line drawings by *John Skelton* on the columns to its ground-floor walkway. Opposite, a continuous 1950s four-storeyed block (Nos. 49–63) with green slate columns, and another (Nos. 65–73) of brick with concrete columns at street level continuing under the Corporation Street frontage of the Belgrade Theatre.

The BELGRADE THEATRE was designed by *Ling* (principals *King* and *Beaton*) and built in 1955–8. It was the first municipal theatre built in England after the war. The name derives from the support shown by the people of Belgrade for the city's reconstruction; their donation of Yugoslavian beech was used for the curved sound reflectors in the ceiling. African hardwood had to be used for the walls. Original features include the spirals of brass lights as CHANDELIERS in the stairwell by *Bernard Schottlander* and the large MURAL inside by *Martin Froy*, 1958. On the outside wall, the Belgrade relief in *ciment fondu* by *James C. Brown*, 1958, based on a 1684 engraving of the city. The theatre was refurbished in 1984 and in 2002–7 when *Stanton Williams* added a boxy new black, grey and red minimalist wing.

In Belgrade Plaza, a FOUNTAIN by *Rawstorne Associates*, 1986, and *Norelle Keddie*'s 1962 memorial to theatre director Bryan Bailey, originally fibreglass but remade in bronze in 2008. To the N, on Upper Well Street, a large block containing PREMIER INN, shops and apartments, by *S. R. Davis*, 2008–10. Behind the Salvation Army Citadel opposite, a section of the C15 CITY WALL with a semicircular bastion. Back at the junction with Corporation Street, the former offices of the Coventry Evening Telegraph by *L. A. Culliford & Partners*, 1957–60. Green slate, concrete and glass, with balconied covered entrance in the angle at the corner. The angled frontage of WEST ORCHARDS HOUSE opposite belongs to the extremity of the Smithford Way wing of the precinct, with Hillman House towering above. All by *Ling* with *Arthur Swift & Partners*, 1962.

Continue E, with smaller scale ORCHARD HOUSE on the S and taller blocks with walkways on the N, either 1950s or following the scale and style. On the N, an eight-storey block, ST GEORGE'S HOUSE (Nos. 167–173), by *Fitzroy Robinson & Partners*, 1972–3. This adjoins No. 175 which is linked by a bridge over Well Street behind to a taller tower block. Both by *Alan Johnson & Associates* for Equity & Law (afterwards AXA), 1989. All these have been turned into the STUDY INN student village, 2014–15, re-clad in red, grey and dark grey panels.

The S side of Corporation Street ends with the half-timbered and gabled TUDOR ROSE pub, 1928–31, on the diagonal corner at the junction with The Burges. Built as the Wine Lodge by *Hattrell & Wortley* for Truman, Hanbury, Buxton & Co.

6. North

Continuing from the Tudor Rose, look first to the S into THE BURGES which preserves a short stretch of its pre-war streetscape, unremarkable but little altered. The COVENTRY CROSS pub is probably C16 behind its later façade, and others here have concealed timber framing. To the N there is little, although at the top end of Bishop Street can be seen the footbridge leading over the Ringway to the canal basin (*see* Inner Suburbs: North-west). E, however, at the beginning of HALES STREET is the OLD GRAMMAR SCHOOL, in fact a fragment of the HOSPITAL OF ST JOHN founded in 1155, of which the base of a C12 pier was formerly preserved in the building. What remains is a large red sandstone hall, apparently built in the earlier C14, with a separate N chapel licensed in 1343. The main hall is now thought to have been a chapel at its E end, with an aisled infirmary to the W, although these have been traditionally referred to as the chancel and nave. After 1545 it was acquired by John Hales and used as a school from 1557 until 1885 when the grammar school relocated to Warwick Road

(p. 254). The Dec E window is complete and finely moulded inside but the chapel was revamped in 1794 with a fanciful W front in Gothick style with panelled parapets, tall pinnacles and leaded cupolas – all replaced by the present façade in 1852 with its W window with curious flowing tracery. In 1794, too, a library wing to the S with timber-framed upper storey was removed. The NW tower retains the outline of a blocked Dec window but has a remodelled W doorway and carries a Victorian bell-turret. The interior is lofty, divided into a nave of two bays with a stilted pointed arcade on piers, blocked both sides, and with capitals chiselled back flush with the wall. Chancel of two bays with deeply moulded windows, blocked up in their lowest quarter. Apart from the fenestration, there is no differentiation between nave and chancel, both being covered by a continuous roof springing from a continuous chamfered stone cornice. The present ceiling of slatted boards dates from 1965 but conceals a plaster tunnel-vault, probably C18. The N aisle has a three-light window and a three-light E window with flowing tracery, again partly blocked. Below floor level a piscina was found in the N chapel during excavations in 2013. Two-storey Gothic additions to the N, 1852. – STALLS. c. 1380–84. Mostly relocated from the Whitefriars church c. 1557. Four incomplete ranges of back-stalls providing evidence for 44 from a probable total of 52 former seats. Of high quality workmanship, though much abraded and defaced during three centuries of school use. They were rearranged school-wise, with the Master's reading desk under the E window, consisting of a salvaged tracery panel with wide ogee arch and panel tracery spandrels. Three ranges of original panelled and traceried desk-fronts and poppy-head ends are preserved. The back-stalls were later raised, and the original choir-boys' benches mostly disposed of. The MISERICORDS have been removed but some still exist elsewhere.* Also, on the NW, six chunkier open-ended stall standards from a different set, also late C14. Possibly salvaged from the demolished St Mary's Cathedral and Priory (p. 234). The whole complex has been restored in 2014–15 by *Marsh Grochowski Architects* as an extension for the COVENTRY TRANSPORT MUSEUM, whose main building lies E on the NW side of Millennium Place.

MILLENNIUM PLACE is the centrepiece of *MacCormac Jamieson Prichard*'s 'Phoenix Initiative', 1999–2003, which redeveloped an area along a route from the cathedrals to the Garden of International Friendship on the N. The WHITTLE ARCHES, representing Coventry's aviation history, tower over the crossroads as a kind of gateway leading into the city via Trinity Street and as the entry to Priory Place (below). Designed by *MJP* with *Whitbybird*, engineers. Beneath the arches, a statue

---

*Complete examples, partial remains and watercolour drawings evidence the survival of 33. Today they can be found at Holy Trinity church (p. 240), King Henry VIII School (p. 254) and at the Herbert Art Gallery & Museum which also has another Whitefriars seat standard (*Ex.inf.* Dr Charles Tracy).

of Sir Frank Whittle by *Faith Winter*, 2007. The arches also
define the wedge-shaped forecourt of the museum, which has
a timeline (*Françoise Schein*), public bench (*Jochen Gerz*) and
a wall covered in plaques commemorating friendships and
reconciliation. Overall, it fails to impress. The setting is
impaired by the retention of poor-quality buildings on several
sides, especially the brick terrace at the bottom of Trinity
Street and Sainsburys (*Pick, Everard, Keay & Gimson*, 1963–4)
opposite. But if the arches (imaginatively illuminated at night)
resemble a pair of boomerangs back to back, what of the elevated walkway leading out of Millennium Place to the N? This
is by *MJP* and *Alexander Beleschenko*. It is bright blue, has a
spine-like structure with fins and rises from Millennium Place
in a spiral before lunging its way N over the gardens. It's all
entertaining enough, yet feels ephemeral and impermanent. At
the far end is the GARDEN OF INTERNATIONAL FRIENDSHIP
where a tall sandstone wall with irregular openings marks the
termination of the Phoenix site. A maze-like box garden fills
the remaining part of the area. *Rummey Design Associates* were
the landscape architects.

Altogether more comfortable is LADY HERBERT'S GARDEN
alongside, laid out in 1930–1 and 1937–8 by *Albert Herbert* for
his cousin Sir Alfred Herbert in memory of Florence, Lady
Herbert (†1930); with two blocks of six almshouses, 1935 (N)
and 1937 (S), boundary wall with attractive metalwork, bronze
gates and a garden shelter with seats in four alcoves. These lie
inside a well-preserved section of the medieval CITY WALL
with C15 gates N and S. At the N end, COOK STREET GATE.
A small tower with a four-centred archway, restored in 1918.
The SWANSWELL GATE at the S is of very similar appearance,
but its archway is blocked.

Opposite the Swanswell Gate is the OLD FIRE STATION by
City Engineer *J. E. Swindlehurst*, 1902. Free Renaissance style,
with archways on the street front, brick and stone banding
above, centre bay with oriel and shaped gable, and a louvred
tower behind. At the corner by the Whittle Arches and extending along Fairfax Street is the BUS STATION in Pool Meadow,
with a classical portico at each entrance, by the city *Property
Services Department* for Centro, 1992–4. Also in Pool Meadow,
the BINGO HALL by *Simons Design* of Lincoln, 2002. The
eight-storeyed BRITANNIA HOTEL (originally De Vere) by
G. R. Stone & Associates, 1973, stands above the road, which
continues towards Priory Hall (*see* Coventry University) and
the swimming baths (*see* Public Buildings). Between the hotel
and the arches one sees the side of PRIORY PLACE, the main
retail, commercial and residential section of *MJP*'s Phoenix
Initiative. Irregular sandstone base and columns under the
three uniform floors of apartments. A narrow entrance between
the mountings of the arches leads into the open space of Priory
Place and on to the Priory Visitor Centre beyond. Facing the
old priory tower at the N end of the Bluecoat School (p. 255)
in New Buildings is the restored RIBBON FACTORY, 1849,
with large multi-pane workshop windows on both sides.

The lane from New Buildings leads to TRINITY STREET. Opposite is a small square called Ironmonger Row and far ahead
the dome of West Orchards Shopping Centre and Hillman
House (for both, *see* Perambulation 2). On the l. the back of
Primark (p. 257). Burges House on the r. by *W. S. Hattrell &
Partners*, 1962, has been turned into student accommodation
(the STUDY INN) re-clad in red, grey and dark grey panels,
with a mural of world nations' flags on the brickwork, 2014–15.
At the top of Trinity Street are the Priory Gate offices (now
the FLYING STANDARD pub), *c.* 1938–9. Steel-framed but
dressed up in half-timbered cladding with pairs of gables, oriels
and balconies. It was a token substitute for the loss of Butcher
Row and the other historic properties destroyed when Trinity
Street was created to ease traffic flow in 1937. Its s end, though,
is nicely married to the Lychgate Cottages facing Trinity
churchyard, which is where the central perambulations began.

INNER SUBURBS

Broadly this section covers the area immediately outside the
Ringway, beginning N of the city and going round clockwise. The
sectors are divided by the main roads leading in and out of the
city. However, parish churches and other places of worship (*see*
p. 240) and major public buildings (*see* p. 246) in this zone are
included in the main sections above, as is Coventry University
(*see* p. 251), whose large site straddles the Ringway.

North-east: Foleshill Road (B4113) to Sky Blue Way (A4600)

The area NE of the city towards the SWANSWELL POOL was
developed under an Act of Parliament of 1844. NORTON
HOUSE at the corner of Norton Street and Bird Street is a
survivor of this development, a small double-fronted villa of
the 1850s. The pool is in a public park, with former St Mark's
(*see* Parish Churches) in the NW corner. Beyond stood the
original Coventry & Warwickshire Hospital (*Nevill & Son*,
1864–5). The main hospital building has been demolished but
on Stoney Stanton Road some associated buildings remain
(awaiting reuse, 2015). The most striking is the octagonal OUT-
PATIENTS' DEPARTMENT, by *A. Hessell Tiltman* and *H. W.
Chattaway*, 1909, with Dalek-like louvred flèche. Single-storey
consulting rooms round the base. To the NE, the former NURSES'
HOME by the same architects, 1906 with 1930s additions. Life-
sized crocodiles in the half-timbered gables of the original
block. NE again, parts of the site used for new city centre
healthcare buildings, most notably SWANSWELL POINT on a
tapering site by *Aedas Architects*, 2003–4, and the multi-coloured
COVENTRY HEALTH CENTRE by *Sonnemann Toon*, 2009–11.
Beyond these is the City College (*see* College and Schools).

Around the Ringway below Hillfields (p. 291), Swanswell Street leads to PRIMROSE HILL STREET and the KASBAH night-club, built as the Globe Theatre by *J. H. Gilbert*, 1913. Ornate Neoclassical frontage, partially intact. Opposite, the SIDNEY STRINGER ACADEMY, by *Sheppard Robson*, 2011–12.

Continuing clockwise, one comes to Alma and Raglan Streets, created in 1855. In the narrow tapering junction between them THE FORESTERS pub, with a rounded end.* This was an area of 1850s terraced housing and factories including the Singer Works in Canterbury Street. Coventry University (p. 251) has residences and other facilities here.

South-east: Sky Blue Way (A4600) to London Road (A4114)

The River Sherbourne passes under the road near the round-about. Here the Gosford Gate and its bridge chapel marked the edge of the walled city and the main entrance from Rugby and Leicester. Here Gosford Street (in the city) becomes FAR GOSFORD STREET (without), retaining several C14–C16 houses *in situ* from the approach to the medieval city. Unlike those in Spon Street (p. 265) these are set among later develop-ments and can be viewed in the context of social and economic change.

First, on the S is the office block of the former CALCOTT WORKS by *E. J. Purnell Jun.* (son of the City Surveyor), 1896. Brick front in Free Renaissance style with terracotta dressings and Dutch gables. The factory produced cycles, then motor-cycles from 1905, and turned over to making cars in 1913. A little E in Vecqueray Street are the former ALL SAINTS SCHOOL (now Scholars), 1877, and PARISH ROOMS (*H. W. Chattaway*, 1905).

In Far Gosford Street on the l. two C15–C16 houses (Nos. 32–33), under restoration in 2015, and a nicely restored group (Nos. 38–40) illustrate the humble yet significant surviving buildings. Higher up and opposite, a good C16 block (restored) at Nos. 122–124 with exposed square framing. Other proper-ties are known to have concealed framing and early features within. On the l. is the site of All Saints (*Paull & Robinson*, 1868–9), built at the same time as St Mark's (*see* Parish Churches). It was demolished in 1970, but the tree-lined churchyard and boundary wall remain. No. 120 on the S is the former Hand and Heart pub, inter-war, probably built for Lucas & Co. in Neo-Tudor brick with stone mullioned windows and canted bays at ground-floor level. Carved stone panel in the gable symbolic of the former name. On the N further E, a group of five three-storeyed top-shops (Nos. 67–71) with big windows (seven by five panes) on the second floor at the back as well as on the street front. The l. pair are early

*There was another pub, now gone, in the narrow angle between Alma Street and Lower Ford Street.

C19, the r. side 1840. A further example on the other side at No. 93.

Beyond the former Humber Motor Works (Lloyds Bank, Nos. 86–88) Far Gosford Street widens out to GOSFORD GREEN, dividing into Walsgrave Road (N) and Binley Road (S). The far edge of the green has an embankment which originally carried the railway loop built in 1914 to link the Rugby–Birmingham and Coventry–Nuneaton lines. The route of the line is now PHOENIX WAY, a road linking Binley Road with the north of the city, and a 1¼-mile (2-kilometre) section N of the Thackhall Street bridge is impressively lined with decorative brickwork by *Derek Fisher*, 1997. The design is based on original C18–C19 patterns for silk ribbon weaving.

Between Far Gosford Street and London Road are the Gulson Road campus of Coventry University (p. 253) and Whitefriars (p. 237), and in the valley to the S is the Charterhouse (p. 239). Mainly terraced housing otherwise, although at the E end of GULSON ROAD is an ELECTRICITY SUBSTATION, *c.* 1924. A large brick hall with gabled ends and high arched windows.

South: London Road (A4114) to Warwick Road (A429)

To the E of this sector are the London Road Cemetery (*see* Outer Suburbs: Cheylesmore) and the Coventry University Technology Park and Innovation Village (*see* Coventry University) on the site of the former Rolls Royce (Armstrong Siddeley) Parkside works.

QUINTON CYCLE WORKS, at the corner of Parkside and Quinton Lane. By *Harry Quick*, 1890. Restored and converted to the Ibis Hotel, 1998–9. One of the earliest production sites of the Coventry motor industry, light cars being produced here commercially from 1898.

MARTYRS MEMORIAL, on a grassed area in the middle of the Ringway traffic island, by *G. Maile & Son*, 1910. A plain granite cross to the Coventry martyrs burned for their religious beliefs nearby in 1510 to 1555.

STONEY ROAD ALLOTMENTS, S of the railway in the arc between the branch line from Leamington and Stoney Road, an area of 'guinea gardens', some with later C19 and early C20 summerhouses.

For the station and its forecourt buildings *see* Perambulation 4.

WARWICK ROAD S of the railway opposite and beyond King Henry VIII School (*see* College and Schools) was once lined with large later Victorian villas, mostly now replaced by apartment blocks. Survivors include the HYLANDS HOTEL (No. 153) with shaped gable and castellated canted bay facing the road, 1880s, and HAMPTON HALL (No. 157) half-timbered with tile-hung gables, 1885. In brick with stone dressings and big double window to the main stairway, DALECOTE (No. 165) of 1878 is now the Coventry Masonic Hall. At the intersection of the Warwick and Leamington roads is

Kenilworth Court, a group of flats with an eleven-storey tower, by *G. R. Stone*, 1960–1. The Spencer Park area w of Warwick Road is similar, with late C19 housing and replacement flats. In the park, s of Spencer Avenue, a square pavilion with veranda and clock turret by *J. E. Swindlehurst* (Borough Engineer), 1915.

South-west: Warwick Road (A429) to Holyhead Road (A4114)

Between the station and Albany Road, past Queens Road Baptist Church (*see* Other Places of Worship), there is not a great deal. In Queens Road, No. 48 (originally Mills & Rockley) by *J. D. & B. Y. Tetlow*, 1960, was an early intruder on the residential street. Four-storey, set transverse to the road and running through to Hertford Place behind, with plain grey ends. In the Butts, the Ramada Hotel, a seventeen-storey tower block by *W. B. Harries Baker* of Bridgend, 1974, refurbished as a hotel 2005. Flats at the corner of the Butts and Albany Road now occupy the site of St Thomas (*Sharpe & Paley*, 1848–9; dem. 1976). Thomas House alongside is the former vicarage, 1897–8.

Earlsdon Park Premier Inn (Nos. 53–55 Butts Road) occupies the refurbished buildings of the former Coventry Technical College, which closed when the college relocated to Swanswell in 2008. Originally by *A. W. Hoare*, 1933–5,[*] and converted to a hotel 2012. The building was steel-framed but faced with Clipsham stone. The exterior conservatively classical with a big portico, but entirely functional where display ceased. Main façade preserved, along with the tiled and columned foyer inside. Within the central courtyard is the Albany Theatre, refurbished and reopened in 2013. Auditorium with segmental roof and Art Deco ceiling lights.

Spon End Estate, along the ne side of Butts Road, is the better preserved of the two Comprehensive Development Areas (CDAs) of the *Ling* era. The other was Hillfields (q.v.). Designated 1957. Three ten-storey blocks (George Poole House, Givens House and Spon Gate House) of 1960 with butterfly-wing roofs and balconies, rather in the London County Council style. Alongside two of these are clusters of four-storey brick-faced reinforced concrete-framed four-storey flats (e.g. Grindlay House and Winslow House), 1964. Newer housing on the n side of the River Sherbourne, with *Gregory*'s four-storey blocks of deck-access flats at Trafalgar House, 1968–9, nestling round the base of *Ling*'s seventeen-storey Meadow House. A little w off Sherbourne Street, a group of single-storey copper-roofed old people's houses in Wellington Gardens by *Gibson*, 1953. A *Walter Ritchie*

---

[*]Hoare had won an open design competition in 1913–14 for a new college on a different site. He produced a new design for this site in 1919 but delays prevented building until 1933.

sculpture from the demolished community building was re-erected in the gardens, 2011.

The resited CANAL BRIDGE from Walsgrave links the areas N and S of the river. Re-erected here in 1969. Cast-iron, single-span, by the *Horseley Iron Works*, Tipton, to a design by *C. B. Vignoles*, 1832–4.

SPON END RAILWAY VIADUCT carries the Coventry–Nuneaton line across the Sherbourne valley. Originally of twenty-eight sandstone arches, 1848–50, it was mostly rebuilt in blue brick after it collapsed in 1857.

S of the viaduct, a cluster of older houses at SPON END, a significant outer suburb when Upper Spon Street was the old main road into the city. SPON BRIDGE was built in 1771, partly with materials from old Spon Gate near St John the Baptist's church. On the parapets the stumps of stone obelisks, once with lamps on top. By the bridge on the Coventry side the ruinous CHAPEL OF ST JAMES AND ST CHRISTOPHER, probably built by the city weavers before 1395. Two windows with four-centred heads remain, to the S and E, without mullions or tracery, and the W arch.

The WEAVER'S HOUSE and BLACK SWAN TERRACE on UPPER SPON STREET (Nos. 119–123) are survivors of the medieval street. Six cottages of three rooms, the two end cottages becoming the Black Swan in the early C19. Dendro-dated to c. 1455 and built as one structure. Restored by *John C. Goom* for the Spon End Building Preservation Trust, 2002–7. Some adapted as offices for community organizations, with the Weaver's House (No. 122) being restored close to its medieval form with hall, rear chamber and solar above. Of particular significance are the internal jetties supporting upper floors. 1930s street fronts preserved.

ROTHESAY TERRACE, Nos. 27–57 Barras Lane. Sixteen three-storey houses on rising ground, 1887–8. Red brick with terracotta dressings. Opposite, the synagogue (*see* Other Places of Worship). Off Barras Lane in Gloucester Street, to the r., STEEPLE HOUSE with thin spirelet and chequerboard gable was St John's School, by *N. W. Vickers* of Liverpool, 1884. Rather altered.

North-west: Holyhead Road (A4114) to Foleshill Road (B4113)

The final part of the circuit round the inner suburbs begins with *Telford*'s new HOLYHEAD ROAD, created in 1824–9. Mainly an area of modest later C19 housing. Beyond the Unitarian church (*see* Other Places of Worship) is a cast-iron RAILWAY BRIDGE, 1848.

From Day's Hotel, Barras Lane leads N towards St Osburg's Roman Catholic Church (*see* Other Places of Worship). Directly E of the church, Nos. 58–64 UPPER HILL STREET, a terrace of four three-storey houses built in blue brick with painted stone dressings, perhaps 1850s. COUNDON ROAD leads NW past more substantial Victorian houses towards Bablake School (see College and Schools) and the railway crossing beyond. Level crossing with a vehicular underpass on one side. By the crossing a small sandstone cottage for the stationmaster, c. 1850. Coundon Road station closed in 1956 and the platforms and buildings have gone.

Returning SW down Coundon Road and l. on Middleborough Road, past Naul's Mill Park is a seventeen-storey skyscraper, NAULS MILL HOUSE, by Gregory, 1968. Quite uncompromisingly white concrete bands and, a little retracted, glass bands. On the other side of Radford Road there are two more, also seventeen storeys. These are SAMUEL VALE HOUSE, between St Columba's Close and St Nicholas Street, and WILLIAM BATCHELOR HOUSE, off Leicester Row, both by Ling, 1966.

This area is DRAPER'S FIELDS, around the basin at the city end of the Coventry Canal. The basin opened in 1769. It is on high ground above the city, with GRAIN WAREHOUSES along LEICESTER ROW to the SE begun in the C18 and already extensive by 1807. Some C19 rebuilding and C20 renewal.* The upper floors of the warehouses are level with the canal. In the basin, an early C19 WEIGHBRIDGE OFFICE. These buildings were restored for the Coventry Canal Trust in 1984. Along the N side of the basin and over the steps in the SW corner are new buildings of an appropriate scale and character, mainly 1993–5, including THOMAS YEOMAN HOUSE and JOHN SINCLAIR HOUSE by the City Architect's Department.

From here the canal follows a winding route to Hawkesbury Junction. By the first bridge, ¾ m. N on the canal towards Foleshill, are CASH'S TOPSHOPS (now apartments). Two blocks of weavers' cottages, one fronting the canal and the other on Cash's Lane. By James Murray, 1857, for silk-ribbon manufacturers John & Joseph Cash. Three-storeyed, of brick with half-timbered gables to the projecting bays at the centre and ends of each range. Large top windows to the workshops. All windows have vaguely Gothic tops. These particular cottages were considered model dwellings at a time of sordid conditions in such weavers' cottages.

Other factories include the office block (now Harp Place) of the former DAIMLER WORKS in Sandy Lane, 1907–8. Four storeys, brick with white banding and mitred corner. On the former MOTOR MILL site by the canal, a large POWER HOUSE, also a Daimler remnant, again 1907. Contemporary, the CHALLENGE CYCLE WORKS offices, 1906–7, on Foleshill Road (Nos. 203–269). Probably by Frederick Foster of Leamington and Coventry. Long front with classical columns to the entrance. Ornamental end blocks with stone bands, blind balustrading and curved parapets.

---

*Inside there are cast-iron pillars dated 1914 on the first floor.

OUTER SUBURBS

ALDERMAN'S GREEN
3 m. NE

METHODIST CHAPEL, Alderman's Green Road. The original Wesleyan building of 1840 is still Georgian in character. Pointed windows, with charming fancy iron glazing bars. To the l. the successor chapel by *T. F. Tickner*, 1896–7, also classical, but far on the way to Italianate. To the r. of both, the Gothic JUBILEE HALL, 1908.

ALLESLEY
4 m. WNW

One of the old villages brought within the boundaries of the expanding city. Allesley was by-passed in 1966 and retains its village character, especially along Birmingham Road.

ALL SAINTS. Norman origins, but mainly E.E. and Victorian. The Georgian s side and chancel were rebuilt when *James Murray* restored the church in 1862–3. E.E. the w tower up to the bell-openings, which have bar tracery. Carved heads below the plain parapet. The w doorway has stiff-leaf capitals. Only the spire is a little later. It has three sets of lucarnes in alternating directions, the lower ones with Y-tracery. Inside, the two w bays of the s arcade are Norman. Round piers, probably heightened,* flat, square, scalloped capitals, single-stepped arches. The N arcade is E.E. with standard capitals and a little nailhead. These elements were repeated in the E bay of the s arcade in 1862–3. E.E. also the tower arch. The chancel is entirely of 1862–3. Church hall extension on the N, *Kenneth Holmes Associates*, 1992–3. – Gloomy Gothic REREDOS and ALTAR, 1919. – Carved oak PULPIT on stone columns, 1863. – FONT, 1863. Caen stone, octagonal, on marble columns with encaustic tiles round the base. – N aisle SCREEN, by *Charles M. C. Armstrong*, 1929. – PEWS in nave and aisles by *Robert Thompson's Craftsmen*, 1980, with carved mice. – STAINED GLASS. Five by *Heaton, Butler & Bayne*, 1864–7, all deeply coloured and well-drawn. The best is the s aisle E window, 1864: scenes of Ruth and Boaz. – In the N aisle, one by *Ward & Hughes*, 1897, and another by *T. F. Curtis, Ward & Hughes*, 1920. – MONUMENTS. Quite a number of tablets, starting from the late C17, in the tower and at the back of the church. – Henry Neale †1730 by *Francis Smith*, who may have also done the memorials to Thomas Tristram †1730 and Francis Blyth †1734 (Andor Gomme).

Birmingham Road enters the village from the E through a deep cutting below the churchyard belonging to *Telford*'s Holyhead

---

*If so, it was before 1862–3. A pre-restoration view of the C18 interior shows the arcade as it is now.

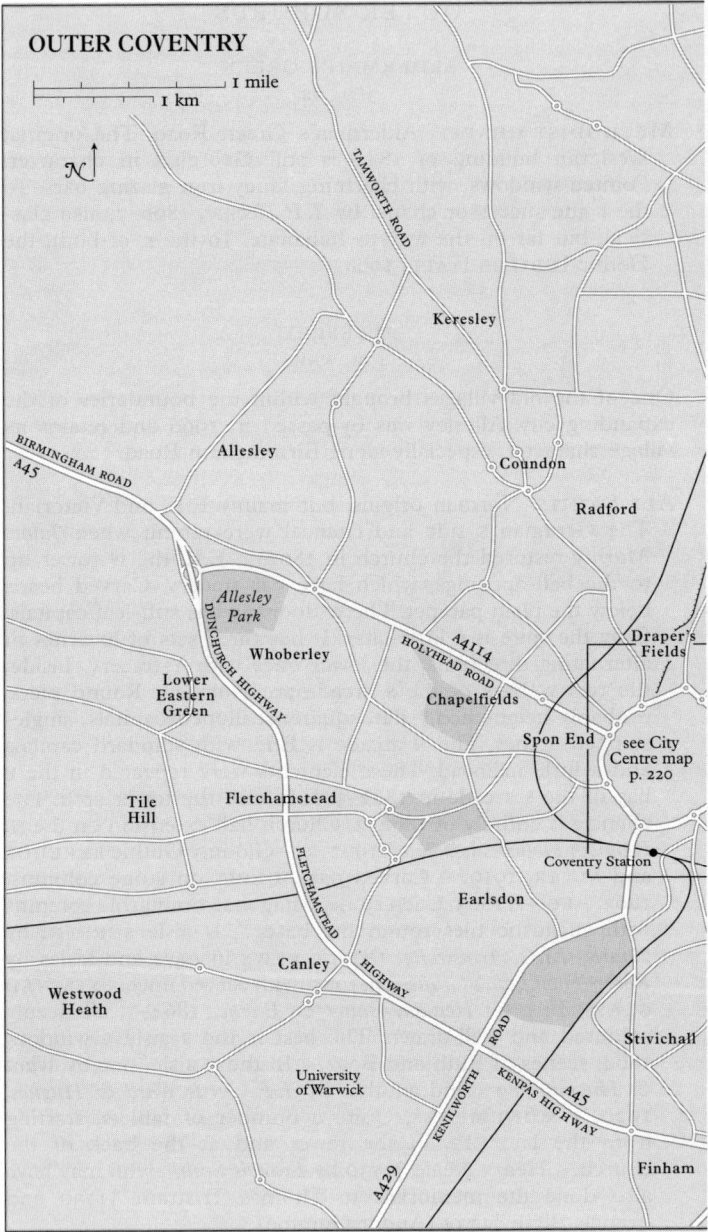

OUTER COVENTRY

1 mile
1 km

N

TAMWORTH ROAD

Keresley

BIRMINGHAM ROAD
A45

Allesley

Coundon

Radford

Allesley Park

DUNCHURCH HIGHWAY

Whoberley

HOLYHEAD ROAD
A4114

Chapelfields

Draper's Fields

Lower Eastern Green

Spon End

see City Centre map p. 220

Tile Hill

Fletchamstead

FLETCHAMSTEAD HIGHWAY

Coventry Station

Earlsdon

Canley

Westwood Heath

University of Warwick

KENILWORTH ROAD
A429

KENPAS HIGHWAY
A45

Stivichall

Finham

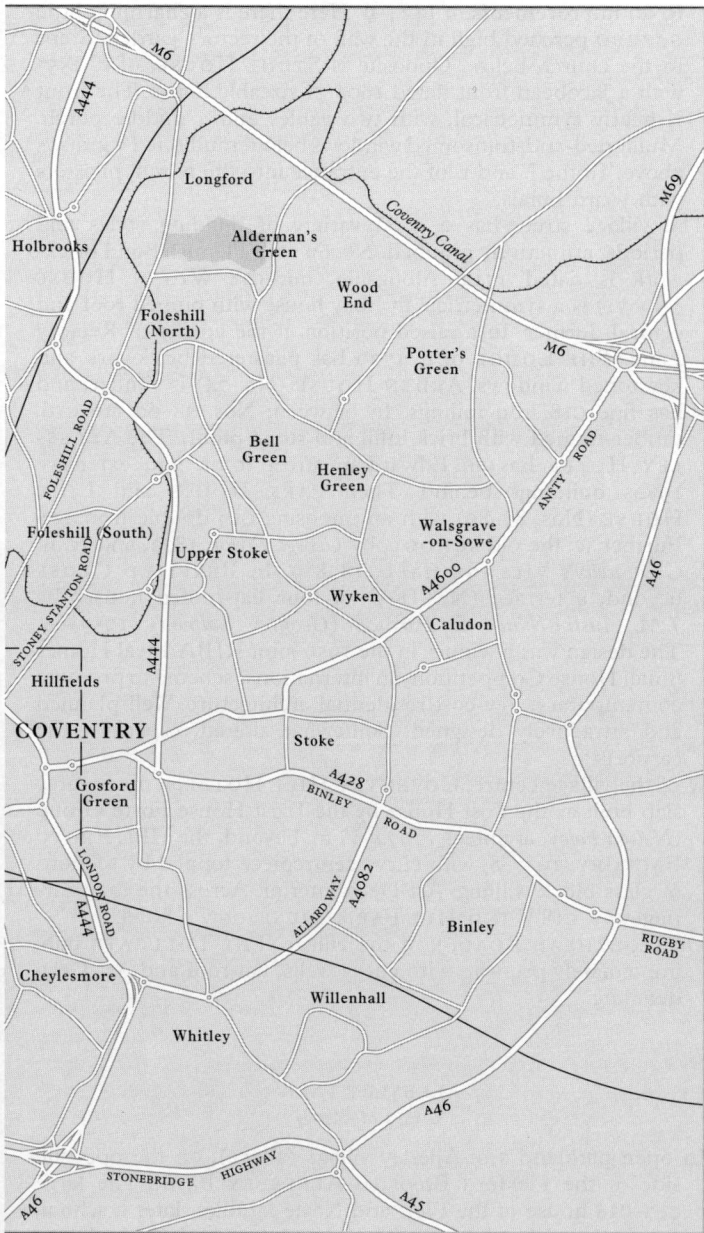

Road improvements of 1824–9. Here there is a charming little
GAZEBO perched high in the wall of the rectory garden. Steps
to the church below. Opposite is STONE HOUSE, of *c.* 1557
with a Jacobean front dated 1608. A sizeable house. The front
is nearly symmetrical, with two gables and a middle porch.
Mullioned-and-transomed windows below, mullioned windows
above. To the l. and r. of the entrance into the porch, pilasters
with weird finials.

The village street has a good variety of building styles and
periods, attractively grouped. No. 69 with Flemish bond brickwork is dated 1712. Alongside, mid-C18 WIGAN HOUSE
(No. 71) is a symmetrical five-bay house with hipped roof and
central dormer. In a raised position at the corner of Rectory
Lane, THE LODGE of *c.* 1720 has pilastered brickwork and
keystoned windows. ARDEN HOUSE (No. 74) is similar, and
has fine C18 iron railings. In between, Nos. 58–60 are C16,
timber-framed with brick infill and stone plinth. The ALLES-
LEY HOTEL has an Edwardian street front, and extensive
1970s buildings behind. Then PARK HOUSE and LION
HOUSE (Nos. 87–89) with an imposing C19 double frontage.
Further w, the old SCHOOL, by *George Taylor*, 1873, and *H. W.
Chattaway*'s VILLAGE HALL, 1898–9. In BEXFIELD CLOSE
beyond, a terrace (Nos. 1–7) of four flat-roofed houses by
J. M. Austin-Smith & Partners (Geoffrey Salmon), 1959–60.
The design was a winner in the 1959 joint RIBA/Ideal Homes
Small House Competition, an international scheme to promote
contemporary, low-cost residential architecture. Well planned
and attractively designed. Somewhat altered, especially the
carports.

w of the village centre, COVENTRY HILL HOTEL, a nine-storey
slab built as the Post House by the Trust House Forte Group
(*Nelson Foley*, architect), 1972. ¼ m. beyond, the HPL PROTO
FACTORY, 1937–8, with curvy centrepiece topped by sections
of glass block walling. Art Deco interior. Across the dual carriageway, C18 WINDMILL FARMHOUSE, now a hotel.

On HOLYHEAD ROAD, E of the village, THE TOLLGATE pub:
immediately pre-war, with curvy walls, flat roof and Art Deco
detailing.

ALLESLEY PARK
½ m. s of Allesley

In open parkland s of Allesley village (above), on the opposite
side of the Pickford Brook, is ALLESLEY PARK. The large
C17–C18 house of the Flint and Neale families, later a school,
was replaced by the present rendered Arts and Crafts house
built for William Iliffe in 1910. From the old house the pretty
C18 circular DOVECOTE with conical tile roof, STABLES and a
WALLED GARDEN remain. The house and parkland were given
to the city of Coventry by Lord Iliffe in 1937. The area s of

the house was developed in the 1950s, with Allesley Park becoming a separate suburb.

ST CHRISTOPHER (Bishop Gorton Church), Winsford Avenue. By *N. F. Cachemaille-Day*, 1959–60. In the form of a cross with a centrally placed altar in homage to the bishop (†1955) who had pressed unsuccessfully for such an arrangement at the new cathedral. Raised roof with clerestory over the centre. – CORONA and hanging CROSS above the altar. – *Dalle-de-verre* GLASS by *Goddard & Gibbs* in the clerestory windows.

The locality centres on the Winsford Avenue Housing Estate, with small-scale WESTMEDE SHOPPING CENTRE by *Willoughby Fletcher & Associates*, 1968. Nearby, the ALLESLEY PARK NEIGHBOURHOOD CENTRE, by the *Design Büro*, 2012. Alongside, ST JOHN'S SCHOOL, by *W. S. Hattrell & Partners*, 1965. On the corner of Allesley Road, ST CHRISTOPHER'S SCHOOL by *Gibson*, 1950–4, with a *Walter Ritchie* sculpture, 1952.

BARRAS HEATH *see* UPPER STOKE, p.303

BELL GREEN
2½ m. NNE

As Jeremy and Caroline Gould observe, the route from the city to Bell Green is marked with tower blocks 'like milestones' along the way. All by *Ling*, these are seventeen-storey FALKENER HOUSE off Stoney Stanton Road at the bend in Great Heath, ten-storey PARADISE HOUSE (1961) in Eden Street, and another of seventeen storeys, LONGFIELD HOUSE, at Courthouse Green. The route terminates with another seventeen-storey tower, DEWIS HOUSE (1961–5), at the heart of the BELL GREEN Designated Development Area. Here Ling and his City Architect's Department created a neighbourhood centre with a pedestrian shopping plaza, RILEY SQUARE, and four long and low blocks of flats. A successful composition and a pioneering work of its time both in concept and design.

The City Council's Bell Green Housing Estate included several distinct neighbourhoods. They are Courthouse Green (SW), Henley Green (E), Manor Farm (far E) and Wood End (N), each with a green enclosed (or partly enclosed) by housing. These (where mentioned) are treated separately (q.v.).

For the Bell Green churches, *see* Alderman's Green (p. 277), Foleshill (North) (p. 288), Henley Green (p. 290), Potters Green (p. 295) and Wood End (p. 307).

BINLEY
2¾ m. E

ST BARTHOLOMEW. A small ashlar-faced church, built in 1771–3 on the site of an earlier one for William, 6th Lord Craven, of Combe Abbey. Palladian in style and said to be by

Robert Adam, but recently attributed by Terry Friedman jointly to *Henry Couchman* and *Capability Brown*. The evidence is plausible though not conclusive. The main entrance is from the w: Tuscan columns *in antis*, arched windows l. and r., and an octagonal bell-turret with cupola. The sides have arched windows too, and the e end is a low apse. To the n a family chapel, whose original n doorway with Tuscan columns was moved outwards in the c19 when the vestibule was added, in closely matching style and materials. Visiting in 1789 Lord Torrington, never a kind critic, described the interior as in the 'Venetian ballroom taste'. It has a segmental plaster vault, as has the family chapel. The chapel is separated from the church by a small but lavish alabaster screen, probably later. The chancel arch has marble columns with Tower of the Winds capitals, reminiscent of Adam. Also Adamish is the very sparing stucco decoration on the walls and ceiling with garlands and medallions delicately highlighted against contrasting coloured backgrounds. The ceilings are (since redecoration, 2012) in Wedgwood blue, the walls in cream. – The marble ALTAR is like a side-table, on two legs and with a shaped front. – COMMUNION RAIL of wrought iron and WEST GALLERY also original. – STAINED GLASS. The e window by *William Peckitt* of York, 1772, after del Sarto's Corsini Madonna: typical of the enamelled glass of the later c18. – s window by *Powell* (designer *George Woolliscroft Rhead*), 1892. – N, mid-c19 patterned glass with figure of St Bartholomew.

CORPUS CHRISTI (R.C.), Langbank Avenue, Ernesford Grange. By *Jennings Homer & Lynch* of Brierley Hill, 1957–8. Designed as a hall for a church never built, with school, 1959, and presbytery, 1961, nearby. Simple with plain interior. – STAINED GLASS. Good w window, 1970s, probably from a Dublin studio. – Side windows, pre-1999.

BINLEY WOODS (just outside the city) is an inter-war 'shack and track' development s of Rugby Road. The land was sold off as building lots in 1923. Many of the original houses were of timber construction, now largely replaced. The generous plots have shaped subsequent redevelopment. THE ROSEYCOMBE pub, Rugby Road, is by the *Northampton Brewery Co.* in-house architects, 1934. At the SCHOOL (*Geoffrey Barnsley*, County Architect, 1956), off Coombe Drive, an ovoid SCULPTURE relief of Alice in Wonderland by *Walter Ritchie*, 1956.

CALUDON

2½ m. E

Caludon is a suburban area of Wyken, between the Ansty and Binley Roads. Stoke and Walsgrave lie to the w and e. Mainly inter-war and later housing including the St Austell Road Estate (*Gregory*, 1965–7) with the last of Coventry's high-rise flats, ten-storey VINCENT WYLES HOUSE and fifteen-storey WILLIAM MALCOLM HOUSE.

HOLY CROSS, St Austell Road. A church hall by *N. F. Cachemaille-Day*, 1939, refurbished and converted into a dual-purpose church and pastoral centre in 1992.

CALUDON CASTLE. Just one remaining fragment and parts of the moat in a public park. What remains is of the early C14, not large but decidedly impressive. It is a wall with two of at least four large transomed two-light windows on the upper floor. They evidently represent the outer wall of the great chamber, overlooking a mere to the N as at Kenilworth. C19 illustrations show that the now-lost tracery was Dec (single reticulation units). Smaller windows for the undercroft. Grey stone with red sandstone dressings. It was begun by Stephen Segrave as a fortified manor house in the early C13. Licence to crenellate was obtained by Sir John Segrave in 1305 and the surviving parts followed in *c.* 1320–50. There was a major rebuilding in 1580–1 when the castle belonged to the Berkeley family and in the later C17 it was a residence in two parts with a combined total of twenty rooms. By 1748 most of it had been demolished and replaced by a farmhouse (since demolished) on the E side of the site.

CANLEY

2 m. SW

Canley was developed from 1938 but with increasing urgency during the war years when the city desperately needed additional housing. *Gibson* experimented here. Much of the original housing has been replaced, but survivors from 1941 include a terrace of four two-storey houses (Nos. 27–35 Sherriff Avenue) and a semi-detached pair (No. 1 Mayor's Croft).

ST STEPHEN THE MARTYR, Charter Avenue. *A. H. Gardner & Partners*, 1954, enlarged 1978. Functional. – STAINED GLASS. Three reused figures by *Morris & Co.* from All Saints, Edgbaston, Birmingham, 1923.

ST JOSEPH THE WORKER (R.C.), De Montfort Way, Cannon Park. Brick church, 1981, linked to smaller hall by *John D. Holmes*, 1994. Both square with pyramid roof and spike. Plain interior with high roof.

CANLEY CREMATORIUM, Charter Avenue. Planned 1935, approved 1938 but not opened until 1943. Completed under *Gibson*, evidently to an inherited design by *E. H. Ford*, the City Engineer. The CHARTER CHAPEL and CREMATORIUM cruciform in plan and churchy Tudor in style. Red brick with Guiting stone dressings. Large extension including the CANNON HILL CHAPEL, with round-arched windows and pantile roofs. By *Coventry Property Services Department*, 1992–3. Bronze SCULPTURE, Pax, by the German émigré sculptor *Georg Erlich*, 1945. Commissioned and given by the German-born industrialist Siegfried Bettmann who was mayor of Coventry in 1913–14.

CHAPELFIELDS

1¼ m. w

Chapelfields is the area N of Earlsdon and W of Spon End, between Hearsall Lane and the Holyhead Road.

St Mary Magdalene, Sir Thomas White's Road. *Harold T. Jackson*, 1932–4, with W extension and octagonal porch of 1985–6 by *Nicol Thomas Viner Barnwell* of Coventry. Byzantine. Brick exterior with shocking blue pantiled roof. Dignified interior in brick and stone of close-matching colours. Aisled nave, chancel with semicircular apse, N organ chamber and S chapel. Good detailing to the carved stonework and ornamental features of the barrel roofs. – REREDOS, ALTAR and ALTAR RAILS of artificial marble, white, grey and blue. – CHOIR STALLS with Jackson's typical animal carvings (cf. St Barnabas, Foleshill, p. 289). – STAINED GLASS. In the S chapel by *Harvey & Ashby*, 1933–4 in the apse and post-war on the S. – Striking W window of Christ with Mary Magdalene by *Glass Mountain Studios* (*Patrick Martin*), 1986, and a small panel in N aisle by the same, †1989. – S aisle W window by *Goddard & Gibbs* (*A. E. Buss*), 1964, brought here in 1986. Originally at St Thomas, Albany Road (dem. 1976).

The Precious Blood and All Souls (R.C.), Kingsland Avenue. Built in stages beginning with the aisled nave by *George Cave*, 1923–4, followed by the apsidal sanctuary, transepts and tower by *E. Bower Norris*, 1938–9. Bomb-damaged in 1940 and restored 1952–62, with later addition of narthex by *John D. Holmes*, 1996–7. Romanesque throughout. Red brick exterior, with blind arcading and chequerwork gable on the street front. Stone and plaster inside, with round-arched arcades and vaulted ceilings. The sanctuary lined with Swedish marble. – PULPIT with mosaic depiction of Christ speaking from the boat on the Sea of Galilee, 1962. – STAINED GLASS mainly by *Hardman*, mostly 1952–71.

Hearsall Baptist Church, Queensland Avenue. *Redgrave & Clarke*, 1960–61. Brick with tall round-arched windows and a stone-faced vestibule and memorial chapel. To the N, the CHURCH ROOMS (originally the Sunday School) in crazy brickwork with open-topped corner tower by *G.A. Steane*, 1928.

Chapelfields' later C19 watch-making industry centred on a small cluster of streets off ALLESLEY OLD ROAD. At Nos. 23–29 a group of master watchmakers' houses of *c.* 1846 front the main road. The workshops were behind. In Craven Street, Duke Street and Lord Street there are blocks of top-lit workshops in two-storeyed wings attached to the main house fronting the Old Road. Williamson's, behind No. 49, may be by *Thomas Pratt*, 1857. The surrounding streets have terraced houses for the artisans and their families, and several contemporary pubs. The best of the 1840s and 50s houses are in Craven Street.

Further out on Allesley Old Road, THE MAUDSLAY pub by *T.D. Griffiths* for Bass & Co., 1928: Tudor style, with mullioned-and-transomed ground-floor windows and half-timbering above.

CHEYLESMORE
1¼ m. SSE

CHRIST CHURCH, Frankpledge Road. A suburban replacement for bombed Christ Church, Greyfriars, in the city centre. 1954–7 by *A. H. Gardner & Partners*, with adjoining hall, 1956. More expensive than the contemporary Spence churches, but also more appealing through the quality of the artworks. Big oblong tower with chequerboard top. Figure of Christ the Sower by *John Skelton* and copper-covered canopy over main door. Slim concrete columns and undulating roof to street façade, also inside. Pastel paintwork, lightly coloured wood-work and grey-green flooring. – Wooden LECTERN, marble FONT, angel CARVINGS behind the altar, Evangelists on the PULPIT and cherubs round the CLOCK also by *Skelton*. – Wickerwork hanging LAMPS with caged angels. – STAINED GLASS. By *Pierre Fourmaintraux*, 1955. Square *dalle-de-verre* panels set in windows of mainly clear glass. The CHURCH HALL has a timber lamella roof.

QUINTON PARK BAPTIST CHURCH. By *F.B. Andrews & Son* of Birmingham, 1957, replacing the bombed Hay Lane church in the city. Simple contemporary style, but with lantern and cross above at one end. – STAINED GLASS. Full-height baptis-tery window by *Hardman*, 1957.

CEMETERY, London Road. Conceived by *Joseph Paxton* and laid out 1846–7. Paxton was assisted by *Richard Ashwell* and by his son-in-law *G. H. Stokes*. Ashwell became cemetery superinten-dent in 1848, subsequently designing cemeteries elsewhere (e.g. Birmingham and Nuneaton). The landscaping and plant-ing were especially successful. There was a medieval quarry on the site and loose rubble was used to create a terrace along the roadside boundary. One of the chapels is perched on a bluff. Between the walkways are hillocks and hollows to create intimate spaces, shielded by trees. Stokes was probably respon-sible for the buildings. The LODGE is Italianate, in the villa mood, and very typical of the 1840s. With it, the entrance gates and a PROSPECT TOWER (restored 1996) by the road. Equally typical is the choice of Neo-Norman for the Church of England CHAPEL. Chancel, nave and N tower with pyramid roof. Good Romanesque detailing to the W front and over the tower door. The Dissenters' CHAPEL, further S, is Grecian. The façade has fluted Ionic columns *in antis* and a pediment. On each side are low, short, pillared pavilions (now roofless, 2014). Among the MONUMENTS, one to Paxton (†1865), who became M.P. for Coventry in 1854, near the N entrance. A highly Gothic pillar with shafts of Aberdeen granite crowned by two tabernacles of diminishing size. Designed by *Joseph Goddard* and carved by

81

p. 65

Samuel Barfield, both of Leicester, 1868. Elsewhere are memorials to Coventry architects James Lloyd Akroyd (†1856) and James Murray (†1863), the latter with panels depicting the architect drawing plans (front), a sculptor carving an angel (left), and a painter at an easel (right). James Starley's memorial (†1881) with cameo portrait is by *Joseph Whitehead & Sons*.

Of Cheylesmore as a suburb, hardly anything of note except the long parade of SHOPS facing Quinton Park in Daventry Road, 1936–9. In mixed style, with hints of Art Deco in the canted blocks at each end.

CORLEY *see p.* 211

COUNDON
1½ m. NW

ST GEORGE, Barker's Butts Lane. *N. F. Cachemaille-Day*, 1938–9. Brick, with side walls relieved by narrow curved-sided projections. Short and massive tower with heavy diagonal buttresses, octagonal top (rather like Kenilworth) and slate spire with tall lucarnes. Diagonal concrete ribs inside. Wide concrete arches to the two-bay N arcade. Baptistery under the tower. – STAINED GLASS. E window by *W. T. Carter Shapland*, 1965. – SCULPTURE. Incised St George on S side of tower, by *George Deeley*, 1939.

CHRIST THE KING AND OUR LADY OF LOURDES (R.C.), Westhill Road. *W. H. Saunders & Son*, 1971–2, replacing a wooden church of 1933. Front with arched entrances added 1982. – Carrara marble ALTAR and LECTERN, 2003. – Brightly coloured STAINED GLASS in the clerestory by *Abbey Studios*, Dublin, 1988.

St George's stands in a tree-lined road with a long view to the steeples of St Michael and Holy Trinity churches. The surrounding streets, some also tree-lined, have almost uniform housing of the late 1920s and early 1930s. Of this period, a group of buildings in MOSELEY AVENUE associated with the large housing estate on streets radiating from Radford Circle, 1924–7. The RIALTO was built as a picture palace, by *Meakin & Son*, 1928. It was bomb-damaged in 1940, but rebuilt as part of RIALTO PLAZA. Opposite, a terrace of shops and flats, 1926–7. On the corner across Barker's Butts Lane, LLOYDS BANK, Neo-Georgian with curved frontage, by *T. D. Griffiths*, 1928.

To the N, towards Tamworth Road at Keresley, are several larger houses that once enjoyed a rural setting in close proximity to the city. COUNDON LODGE, Coundon Green, is a C19 house said to have a carved wooden chimneypiece of 1666. Plum brick Gothic outbuildings. COUNDON COURT (now part of Coundon Court school), Northbrook Road, was built for George Singer, the industrialist, in 1891. Austere exterior, but good interior with an intricate galleried staircase. The OLD HALL, near Keresley church, early C19 Neoclassical, later a hotel (empty 2014), was originally Keresley Hall.

To the w in the garden of No. 14 BEAUMONT CRESCENT is the c15 stone-built ST CATHERINE'S WELL, with a lancet-shaped opening and a well 128 ft (39 metres) deep. It is supposed to have been the head of the conduit leading to the priory.

EARLSDON

1½ m. SW

Development began in 1852 when the Coventry branch of the Freehold Land Society purchased an estate and laid out eight streets with 250 building plots. Earlsdon became part of the city in 1890. Earlsdon and Chapelfields (p. 284) were noted as the centre of the watch-making industry.

ST BARBARA, Rochester Road. 1930–1 by *Austin & Paley* of Lancaster in association with *Harold T. Jackson* of Coventry. Incomplete to w and N. Dignified and restrained, though conventional in style. The chancel is Dec. The rest is Perp. All still entirely late c19 Gothic, untouched by c20 developments. Nave and chancel, aisles, polygonal apse. Brick and artificial stone dressings, the chancel lined with stone and quite lavish. Lady Chapel (s), with fine woodcarving by *Robert Bridgeman & Sons*. – Chancel PANELLING by *A. H. Gardner & Partners* with delightful narrow frieze carved by *Walter Ritchie*, 1954. – PULPIT. Dated 1661. Big, with fluted angle colonnettes and panels with gristly details. Bulbous foot. Donated in 1931 but the provenance is unknown. – Stone FONT and carved wooden LECTERN from the previous church in Palmerston Road by *T. R. J. Meakin*, 1912–13. – CHOIR STALLS by *Robert Thompson* of Kilburn. – STAINED GLASS. Mainly *Shrigley & Hunt*, c. 1931–1947. – One s window by *Derek Hunt*, 2008.

METHODIST CHURCH, Albany Road. *Crouch, Butler & Savage*; designed in 1909 but not built until 1923. Late Victorian Gothic with banded gable and side turrets. Cruciform with fine open roof. Side porch and interior conversion by *Kenneth Holmes Associates*, 2000. Church hall and Sunday School adjoining, 1959–60.

LIBRARY, Earlsdon Avenue North. One of the three Carnegie Libraries of 1911–12 (cf. Foleshill and Stoke). All by *J. E. Swindlehurst*, City Surveyor.

Earlsdon centres on the crossroads where Albany Road and Earlsdon Street meet Earlsdon Avenue. On the SE corner is the CITY ARMS, a large Tudor-style pub of 1929–30 by *Quick & Lee* for Flower & Sons. BERKELEY ROAD SOUTH has a pair of weavers' cottages (Nos. 89–91), c. 1854, with workshop windows on the top floor, and a block of three-storey houses opposite (Nos. 102–110) of similar date. The CRITERION THEATRE occupies the former Wesleyan school chapel by *William Tomlinson*, 1884. At the s end of the road, HENNESSY'S retains the blue tiled frontage of a former corner shop and off-licence. In Clarendon Street, another pair of 1850s houses (Nos. 15–17). Clarendon House (No. 15) was the childhood home of the architect Sir Frederick Gibberd.

The ALBANY CLUB in EARLSDON STREET is much altered, but recognizable as the rather grand coffee tavern of 1899. In ALBANY ROAD the red brick castellated front of NEXUS is that of the Broadway Cinema (later the Astoria), 1922. Alongside, a typical Coventry Co-operative Society shop of 1915. Near the railway, the ALBANY pub by *T.D. Griffiths* for Marston Thompson & Evershed, 1907.

See also Chapelfields (p. 284) and Kenilworth Road (p. 293).

EASTERN GREEN *see* p. 318

FINHAM

2 ¼ m. s

An estate of the 1920s and 30s on the s edge of the city, beyond the A45 and towards Stoneleigh.

ST MARTIN IN THE FIELDS, Green Lane. *E. E. Lofting*, 1938. Neo-vernacular. White walls with stone dressings. Mullioned windows, stone at the ends and timber on the sides. Dormers. Leaded bell-turret. Pleasant timber-framed interior. Entrance and reception area by *Keith Berry* of Wolston, 2006, enhancing the existing link between the church and the round-roofed *Reema* CHURCH HALL of 1963.

FLETCHAMSTEAD

2 ½ m. w

An area w of the outer ring road, part of which is called the Fletchamstead Highway, towards Tile Hill. Mainly 1930s houses and factories. Also known as Lime Tree Park.

ST JAMES, Tile Hill Lane. *Harold T. Jackson*, 1936–7. Buff brick and very plain. Lancets. Street front with five stepped windows over three pointed doorway openings. Slate roof. Heavy concrete ribs inside. E end and hall completed by *Denys Hinton & Partners*, 1969.

Nearly opposite, the NEWLANDS pub, in Tudor style with unusually ornate carving on the half-timbered gables. By the in-house building department for *Atkinsons Brewery*, 1292–30.

FOLESHILL (North)

2 ½ m. NE

The ancient parish of Foleshill covered much of north Coventry, parts of which are now in Holbrooks (p. 292) and Longford (p. 294). The area covered here is just the original settlement round the old church. The district is more generally known as Bell Green (p. 281), while the name Foleshill more commonly refers now to the s end towards the city (below).

ST LAURENCE, Old Church Road. Perp w tower, ashlar-faced. N aisle *c.* 1540. Inside the N arcade responds both Perp too. That is the medieval evidence. The rest is all a mix of dates, architecturally modest yet interesting. The chancel was rebuilt in 1782 and heightened when *T. F. Tickner* restored the church in 1888. Alongside is a NE vestry of brick dated 1812. The N aisle was raised and the S aisle added by *Line & Johnson* of Coventry in 1816. The S aisle W wall is stone, the S wall of brick with windows with Y-tracery. N vestry 1904, mid-Victorian S porch and S transept chapel by *Meakin & Son* to *Tickner*'s designs, 1927. Both the aisle arcades have long, bald cast-iron piers, 1816. Along the top, elegantly decorated cornices of 1958 on the concrete beams supporting the roof trusses of 1880 still charred from wartime damage in 1940. – FONT. Norman, round, with two big zigzag bands. – REREDOS by *Roddis & Nourse* of Birmingham, 1909, with painted panels by *Henry Mileham*, 1923. – STAINED GLASS. In aisles, two by *William Pearce Ltd*, 1901–2. – Three in E wall of S transept, by (l. to r.) *Goddard & Gibbs*, 1988, probably *Pearce & Cutler*, 1927, and *Hardman*, 1932; and a S window, 1927. Others unidentified, including Art Nouveau w window of S aisle, 1910.

The OLD VICARAGE, S of the church, 1745. Front porch and polygonal SE rear wing by *George Steane*, 1871; *C. S. Smith* and *William Lunn* also worked here in 1852 and 1884 respectively.

FOLESHILL ROAD UNITED REFORMED CHURCH, in a large graveyard at the junction with Old Church Road. The original 1795 chapel has gone and the 1848 BRITISH SCHOOL building is now used. Pilasters, dentil mouldings and fish-scale tiling.

Former METHODIST CHURCH, Old Church Road. 1848, but still undebased classical. Rendered with arched windows and a plain pediment.

FOLESHILL (South)
1½ m. NNE

The southern part of Foleshill towards the city is now divided from the rest by the A444 main road and includes the areas known as Great Heath and Edgwick.

ST PAUL, Foleshill Road. Originally by *J. L. Akroyd*, 1840–1, but largely destroyed in 1940. Part of the w tower was incorporated in the new church by *Nicholson & Rushton*, 1951–3. Plain brick with round-headed windows. Interior plain and decent, with contemporary Renaissance-style oak FITTINGS throughout. – STAINED GLASS. Two E windows of *c.* 1953, perhaps by *G. E. R. Smith* (AB), again with Renaissance details.

ST BARNABAS, Cromwell Street, Great Heath. *Paley & Austin*, 1931, under the supervision of their Coventry associate, *Harold T. Jackson*. Perp style. w end unfinished. Adapted for shared community and church use after 2004 redundancy. – LECTERN and CHOIR STALLS designed by *Jackson*, 1932–3, with good carved decoration. – STAINED GLASS. E window in *dalle-de-verre* by Brother *Gilbert Taylor*, 1981.

St Elizabeth (R.C.), Eld Road. *Harrison & Cox (G. B. Cox)*, 1914–16, restored and enlarged after war damage in 1940 by the same firm (*Bernard V. James*), 1961–2. Dec. Brick with stone and terracotta dressings. Aisled and clerestoried nave. The additions of 1962 include the short sanctuary and tall s clock tower. – STAINED GLASS. *Hardman*, 1962.

Baptist church, Broad Street. *George Baines & Son*, 1923–4. Their usual free Perp.

Bethel Apostolic Church (originally Free Methodist), Station Road West. *George & Isaac Steane*, 1880. Brick with blue bands and banded headers to doorways and windows.

Durbar Avenue Evangelical Church, at junction with Boston Place. By *Redgrave & Clarke* for the Free Methodists, 1958. Brick with reconstituted panels.

Nanaksar Gurdwara Gursikh Temple, Foleshill and Edmund roads. Built as a cinema, 1933. Art Deco. Converted as a temple and enlarged, 1979.

Former Broad Heath School (now Broad Street Young People's Centre). By *G. & I. Steane*, 1910. Two-storeyed with projecting gabled blocks at intervals. Attractively carved date-stone on the Broad Street side.

Carnegie Library, Broad Street. By *J. E. Swindlehurst*, the City Surveyor, 1911–12 (cf. Earlsdon and Stoke).

Former General Wolfe pub, at the corner of Station Road West. By *T. F. Tickner* for Phipps & Co., 1899–1900; terracotta, with ornate gables and copper-covered corner turret.

Former Courtaulds works, Foleshill Road. Probably by *Harry Quick*, 1904 onwards. Sturdy brick, segmental windows and tall clock tower of 1912–13. Refurbished as a business centre, late 1990s. Also the remains of the chimney (originally 365 ft (111 metres) high) on Kingfield Road, 1924, and 1950s satellite office buildings in Lockhurst Lane.

Ordnance Works, off Red Lane and in a loop of the Coventry Canal. Established by a consortium of shipbuilders in 1905 for the manufacture of 15-inch guns for battleships. The vast gun shop is 815 ft (248 metres) long and 205 ft (62 metres) wide. It was the longest industrial workshop in Europe when it was built in 1906.

Cooperative Emporium, Foleshill and Holmsdale roads. 1930s Art Deco, faience tiled frontage.

GREAT HEATH *see* FOLESHILL (South)

HAWKESBURY *see* p. 359

HENLEY GREEN

2¾ m. NE

One of the districts of the Bell Green Estate (p. 281).

St Patrick (R.C.), Deedmore Road. *Desmond Williams & Associates*, 1968–9 (*Jack Edmondson*, project architect) with *Ove*

Arup as structural engineers. An exciting design with a complex steel-framed structure. Tent-like exterior with aluminium-sheathed roof and tall spike. Semicircular plan. The roof unfolds like a fan. Lady Chapel between the church and presbytery with a statue by *A. Breen*, 1969. – STAINED GLASS. Large Crucifixion behind the altar and St Patrick in the entrance foyer, by *Dublin Glass*, 1969. Both back-lit (i.e. internal). – Contemporary coloured glass in the side walls by *John Hardman Studios*.

HENLEY COLLEGE COVENTRY, Henley Road, ⅜ m. SE of Bell Green, has been much expanded but retains the original central block built for the college of further education by *Ling*, 1961–4. CLASP system with concrete plank cladding.

On Henley Road, MANOR FARMHOUSE has a massive stone chimney dated 1624. The rest part C17 timber-framed and part C18 and later brick. Separated from nearby development by green space, but overshadowed by seventeen-storey CARADOC HALL (originally John Fox House), the centrepiece of the city council's MANOR FARM ESTATE begun in 1964. The tower itself was built 1966–8. The estate is predominantly two-storeyed and laid out on the Radburn system.

HILLFIELDS
½ m. NE

At one time known as Harnall, Hillfields runs from Stoney Stanton Road down to Sky Blue Way, and on the E to the A444 (Phoenix Way; see p. 273).

ST PETER'S CENTRE, Charles Street. Church and community centre with glass spirelet over the worship area. *Kenneth Holmes Associates*, 2001. – STAINED GLASS by *Elegance in Glass Ltd*, 2001. The old church (CEPHAS COURT) alongside was converted into seventeen apartments on four storeys by *Latham Architects* of Derby, 2007–8, with additions above the original roof-line and a SE staircase block. A Commissioners' church by *Robert Ebbels*, 1840–1. Red brick, lancets and many buttresses. The W tower square and surprisingly substantial. Short chancel. – STAINED GLASS. E window, 1955–6, partially replicating one by *W. Pearce Ltd*, 1913.

ST MARY & ST BENEDICT (R.C.), Raglan Street. Church and original PRESBYTERY (rebuilt after 1985) by *T. R. Donnelly*, 1893. The two-storey Lady Chapel on the N belongs to the older convent, built in 1861–2. The church E.E., brick with stone dressings. Marian cross in stone on E wall of apsidal chancel. Rose window to S chapel. Cloistered narthex at W end by *Rayner & Fedeski*, 1975–6, along with the CHURCH CENTRE behind. Inside, open timber roof. W gallery. – Stone REREDOS, marble ALTAR, PULPIT and FONT all designed by *Donnelly* and carved by *A. B. Wall* of Cheltenham, 1893.

– STAINED GLASS mostly *c.* 1950. – Bright *dalle-de-verre* glass to narthex, *c.* 1976.

ST STANISLAUS KOSTKA (R.C.), Springfield Road. The Polish church, by *Kazimierz Kuźmiński*, 1961, with quirky tower added 1974. Contemporary artworks inside by *Adam Bunsch* of Kraków including the painting of the patron saint in the sanctuary. Bunsch also designed the STAINED GLASS, made by *Hardman*, 1963.

HILLFIELDS EVANGELICAL BAPTIST CHURCH, Waterloo Street. *Peter Thornton* of Bournemouth, 1975. Octagonal, with copper-covered gabled valley roofs and central spike.

Former METHODIST CHURCH, Stoney Stanton Road, by *Harrison & Hattrell*, 1898. Brick with Hollington stone dressings. Castellated frontage. Tower with octagonal top-stage and spire with a lantern towards the top. The congregation moved to the CORNERSTONE METHODIST CENTRE, a combined church and family centre by *Kenneth L. Holmes* at the corner of Howard Street, in 1985–6.

REDEEMED CHRISTIAN CHURCH OF GOD, Albert Street. Built as the Coventry Howitzer Club by *Hellberg, Harris, Reyner & Partners*, 1971–4. Hall with semicircular brick stacks between the windows. Taken over by the church in 2009.

Also in this district, several sizeable and distinctive non-Christian places of worship: the Islamic MOSQUE in Eagle Street East, originally *c.* 1969 but since enlarged; and in Harnall Lane West the SIKH TEMPLE, 1965 with later additions, and the SHREE KRISHNA HINDU TEMPLE, 1992.

Hillfields is dominated by the remaining tower blocks erected in the designated Comprehensive Development Area (CDA) under *Ling* in 1957 (*see also* Spon End, p. 274). There were ten originally, described by Lewison and Billingham as 'the sterile megaliths of Hillfields'. What remain are three ten-storey blocks (e.g. HILLFIELDS HOUSE) with what Pevsner called 'butterfly excrescences' on top (cf. Spon End) and two of seventeen storeys, PIONEER HOUSE and THOMAS KING HOUSE. Of the early Hillfields development, a few houses of *c.* 1840 remain near St Peter's (e.g. 1–3 Charles Street).

HOLBROOKS
(including Whitmore Park)
2½ m. N

ST LUKE, Rotherham Road. By *N. F. Cachemaille-Day*, 1938–9, and modelled on a modernistic church at St Denis, Paris. Its design illustrates a root of the style of Spence's Coventry Cathedral. Of brick. Windows with concrete patterns and grids. Brick piers square, placed diagonally. Concrete roof beams across and a longitudinally folded roof. Apsidal chancel. Outer pulpit and outer altar. Repaired after war damage, 1948. Enlarged in 1968–9 with a plain N aisle and Lady Chapel.

– STAINED GLASS. Coloured glass in apse windows. – One N window by *G. Maile Studios*, 1977.

HOLY FAMILY (R.C.), Penny Park Lane, Whitmore Park. By *Peppard & Duffy* of Dublin, 1966–7. Cruciform with a prominent steel cross (originally much taller) on the roof over the centre. Side walls of diagonal blocks linked by glass. W front with triangular arch over main entrance. Complex timber roof. Reordered internally 1989–90. – STAINED GLASS. E window of the Holy Family, 1990.

HOLBROOKS EVANGELICAL CHURCH, Parkgate Road. Successor of a Congregational church established 1911. By *Peter Thornton* of Leicester, 1969–70. Clerestoried, with aluminium-framed end windows and copper spirelet. Baptistery in one end. Connected to the 1973 hall by a link area with curved roof, 2010–11.

ST PAUL'S CEMETERY, Holbrooks Lane. Laid out in 1892. Small brick chapel, 1930s. In the cemetery, a memorial by *Richard Ormerod* to speedway rider Tom Farndon, 1935, with streamlined motor cycle and rider.

KENILWORTH ROAD

The Kenilworth Road leads SW out of the city. Beyond the War Memorial Park and outer ring road (A45) the road runs straight for 1¾ m. with a broad sward each side and large houses set back behind trees. Along or close to this route there are several significant houses, mainly around Gibbet Hill.

Among them, several in the manner of Frank Lloyd Wright's prairie houses. Three are by *Yorke, Harper and Harvey (Robert Harvey)*, at No. 114 Kenilworth Road, for Harvey's brother, 1957–9; No. 9 Gibbet Hill Road, for D. Daley, 1963; and SOUTH WINDS in Cryfield Grange Road, for R.M. Wilson, 1965–6. Mainly by *Roy Geden*, a related group of individual houses in a sylvan setting at The Spinney, 1967–8; and Mistral (No. 145 Kenilworth Road), for Dr Minton, 1968.

Also of interest is No. 7 Leighton Close, by *H. N. Jepson & Partners (Michael Jepson)* for F.H. Clarkson, 1959, extended 2001.

CRYFIELD GRANGE, Cryfield Grange Road. C15 origins with vaulted cellar. C16 decorative timber-framed porch and C17 stairs inside. Later brick additions.

KERESLEY
2½ m. NNW

At the rural NW edge of the city. The area near the church was a fashionable residential district in the mid C19, but the remaining houses are mainly in Coundon (p. 286) on the other side of the Tamworth Road. To the N was the Coventry Colliery, opened in 1911.

St Thomas, Tamworth Road. 1844–7 by *Ferrey*.* Red sandstone in a Gothic style still pre-archaeological, showing few
signs of Ferrey becoming a leading architect of the correct
antiquarian school. Slender windows and buttresses, no aisles,
and a short chancel. Hammerbeam roof to nave, rather thin
and busy. The w tower is slight too but has a splay-footed
spire. Its windows have plate tracery. There are dummy loopholes and corner pinnacles. Interior reordered but still with
enclosed pews with simple poppyheads. w gallery on iron
columns, with new stair access from the nave. se vestry added
1970 and the Galilee Room on the n, 1989. – STAINED GLASS.
e window group, *Heaton, Butler & Bayne*, 1874. – MONU-
MENT. Thomas Wilmot †1846. Memorial brass by *Hardman*,
1851, in a stone setting signed by *Peter Hollins*.

KERESLEY GREEN MEDICAL CENTRE, Bennetts Road South,
by *Robothams*, 2005. Brick, render and cedar outside, with a
circular corner tower. Open timber beams inside.

ROYAL COURT HOTEL, Tamworth Road. Built (as Keresley
Hall) for motor manufacturer William Hillman, c. 1908. Later
(1928–68) used as a hospital. Hillman's half-timbered Tudor
house and its lodge remain, now surrounded by later hotel
buildings. Further out towards Corley, KERESLEY HOUSE,
c. 1775, has an arboretum said to have been laid out originally
by *Joseph Paxton*, c. 1850, for the Rev. William Thickins.

In Sandpits Lane, an attractive group of older buildings around
C16 AKON HOUSE and the brick-fronted BEECHWOOD
HOTEL, which retains C16 timberwork inside.

The COVENTRY COLLIERY site has been wholly redeveloped as
PROLOGIS PARK, with the loss of the main office buildings
and *J. H. Forshaw*'s Pithead Baths, 1935. Keresley End, to the
n, was the mining village. Its COMMUNITY CENTRE, 1999, has
a striking front with red-painted steelwork and blue and red
tile decoration.

LONGFORD

3¼ m. NNE

St Thomas, Longford Road and Hurst Road. 1873–4 by *John
Cotton*, with vestry extension 1907. A town church in a townish
street. Red brick and Attleborough stone dressings and lancets.
NW steeple over porch. Octagonal bell-stage accompanied
by big pinnacles. Short spire. The buff Nuneaton brick is
exposed inside. Internal reordering completed 2006. – Wooden
REREDOS, PULPIT, LECTERN etc., all 1915–18. – Alabaster
FONT, 1916. – STAINED GLASS. Mostly *Jones & Willis*,
†1897–1910. – St Christopher, 1952, possibly by *Walkers Glass
Co.* (AB).

SALEM BAPTIST CHAPEL, Lady Lane. Built in 1872 for a
congregation established in 1765. Red and blue brick with

---

*Ferrey also designed the school, 1852, and vicarage, 1868, both demolished.

rendered pilasters. Large, with raised entrance to pedimented front.

UNION PLACE BAPTIST CHURCH, Oban Road, 1827. Rendered brick walls and hipped slate roof. Good galleried interior. Long extension with round-headed windows, 1885.

CEMETERY, Windmill Road, 1908–9. Boundary wall, entrance gates, lodge and Gothic chapel with tower above porte cochère, all by *T. F. Tickner*.

This area of north Coventry is dominated by the RICOH ARENA which occupies the site of the old Foleshill Gasworks. The arena is a football stadium with additional sporting and leisure facilities. By *Holmes Miller* of Glasgow, 2004–5. Prominent tubular steel framework supporting the roof canopy.

LOWER EASTERN GREEN
1 m. SSW of Allesley

ST JOHN VIANNEY (R.C.), Bishopton Close, Mount Nod. *W. S. Hattrell & Partners*, 1962. Functional rectangular building with galleried nave.

POTTER'S GREEN
3¼ m. NE

At the far E of Bell Green (*see* p. 281), adjoining the N end of Walgrave and Wyken (qq.v.).

ST PHILIP DEACON, Ringwood Highway. *W. H. Saunders & Son*, 1963–4, but the roof redesigned and lowered in height by *Viner Associates*, 1991.

UNITED REFORMED CHURCH, Woodway Lane. Founded 1820, but rebuilt 1865. Brick with lancets, now rendered. Adjacent church hall, 1892. A humble group.

GRACE ACADEMY, Wigston Road. A new build by *Swanke Hayden Connell*, 2009–10, on the site of the former Woodway Park School.

RADFORD
1 m. NW

Originally within the priory manor of Coventry, Radford has a well-documented topography from medieval times, although no early buildings remain.

ST NICHOLAS, Engleton Road. *Lavender, Twentyman & Percy* of Wolverhampton, 1953–5. Brick, with a tower formed as a high slab with rounded outline. The nave of hangar shape, with inward-leaning walls. Innovative, but now (2014) unsafe and facing demolition. The HALL, by *Arcon*, 1949, is used as the church.

ST FRANCIS OF ASSISI, Links Road, North Radford. 1957–9 by *N. F. Cachemaille-Day*, in cubic shapes and light brick that would have looked progressive in the 1930s. Frugally furnished but with simple baldacchino.

St Augustine (R.C.), Heathcote Street, 1979. Plain, but with contemporary clerestory stained glass by *Abbey Studios*, Dublin, and a Belgian carved oak altar, *c.* 1830.

Radford Garden Suburb is a development of forty large houses with big gardens by *Raymond Unwin*, 1912–14, for Coventry Garden Suburbs Ltd. The first erected were in Middlemarch Road and Lydgate Road (Nos. 1–15) facing the recreation ground and with views towards the city. Others were intended in Shepperton Way, Cheveral Avenue and Bede Road.

Jubilee Crescent, North Radford. On the E is a grand 1930s parade in the Georgian style. The w side much weaker, but including *Ling*'s library, 1966–7, on the corner plot of Links Road.

At the junction of Catesby and Burnaby roads, The Pilot pub, by *W.S. Clements* for Atkinson's Brewery, 1938–9. Red brick front of nine bays between canted cross-wings. Good interior with surviving *moderne*-style features.

For Cash's houses *see* Inner Suburbs: North-west (p. 276).

STIVICHALL
1½ m. s

One of the villages absorbed into the expanding city in the c20. Styvechale is an alternative name, nowadays preferred. Stivichall Hall stood in parkland E in a loop on the Leamington Road.* It was sold in 1927 and soon afterwards demolished. A straight road was created through the park *c.* 1930 and housing sprang up on either side of it.

St James, Leamington Road. The history here is of a small Norman and Perp church rebuilt in 1810–17 and then remodelled and enlarged 1955–65 to serve the new suburb. The 1817 church was built by *James Green* at the expense of Francis Gregory. It has lost its fanciful Gothick tower, but the nave remains as the chancel of the enlarged building. The chancel has become the apse chapel, ashlar-faced and castellated. Screened off inside, the chapel has pilasters and a pretty ribbed ceiling vault in plasterwork. The rest is by *W.S. Hattrell & Partners*, the broad nave and baptistery in 1955, the s vestries in 1958–9 and the porch tower in 1965. The nave strives to complement the Gothick.† Inside, a handsome boarded timber roof with laminate beams. – font, octagonal, with plain rolls

---

* Stivichall Hall was built by the *Hiornes* for Arthur Gregory to a design by *Flitcroft*, 1755–60, and enlarged in the early c19. A Stivichall chimneypiece by *Richard Hayward* is now at Loxley Hall.

† In the first edition of this guide Pevsner described it 'reactionary beyond belief . . . as if nothing had happened in the world since 1900'.

to separate the panels, hard to date but looking more 1660s than Perp (Pevsner). – STAINED GLASS by *Hardman*, 1948, originally in the E window but moved to the baptistery in 1955. The CHURCH HALL at the NE corner of the churchyard is by *N. F. Cachemaille-Day*, 1939, rather obscured by additions.

ST THOMAS MORE (R.C.), Watercall Avenue. *W. H. Saunders & Son*, 1966–8, replacing a temporary church by the same firm, 1946. Square plan, with N side chapel. Margaret Roper Room and covered entrance added by *Viner Associates*, 1993. Brick with low-pitched aluminium roof. Narrow windows relieved with irregular white panels. Interior with W gallery and suspended ceiling of plywood pyramids. – ALTAR and REREDOS of Irish marble. – STAINED GLASS. Two E windows by *Patrick Pollen*, 1967.

WEST ORCHARD UNITED REFORMED CHURCH, The Chesils, Baginton Road. *G. A. Steane*, 1952, with hall and ancillary buildings. It replaced a city centre chapel (by *T. S. Whitwell*, 1820) destroyed in the Blitz. Mottled brick. Rectangular with rounded corners. Round-headed windows. Low tower. Projecting porch. – STAINED GLASS. *F. S. Trickett*, 1952.

STIVICHALL CROFT, the old village street, has a cluster of C17 and C18 buildings at the S end, including the SMITHY and a former ANIMAL POUND, and the C18 MANOR (No. 28 Leamington Road) at the other. In between, No. 8, with hints of Art Deco distinguishing it from its more conventional neighbours of the same decade, was *Frederick Gibberd*'s first commission, designed for his parents, 1931. Crossing the W end of the road is rock-faced COAT OF ARMS BRIDGE. This has large shields over the arch with the arms of Arthur Francis Gregory one side and his wife's on the other. Erected for the London and Birmingham Railway Company, 1844, as a condition of being allowed to build the railway over the Gregorys' land.

W of the railway is the WAR MEMORIAL PARK, laid out in 1921. At the city end, the WAR MEMORIAL. A white, towering structure, oddly reminiscent of the Russian Stalin style. By *T. F. Tickner*, completed in 1927.

STYVECHALE GRANGE, off Lonscale Drive, ½ m. SW of the church. A four-bay ashlar-faced house, probably C16 but externally of *c.* 1635. It has four small triple mullioned windows on the two upper storeys, completely symmetrical and divided by string courses. The blocked ground-floor doorway however is asymmetrical and has a four-centred head. Restored after 1975 by *Lyndon F. Cave* and converted to flats with a dark brick extension alongside.

See also Kenilworth Road (p. 293).

STOKE

1½ m. E

Once a village of several hamlets, the church on its own ½ m. N of the main centres of Stoke Green, Stoke Aldermoor and Biggin.

It also included Barras Heath and Stoke Heath in Upper Stoke (p. 303) to the N.

St Michael, Walsgrave Road. Much enlarged but retaining the Perp w tower of cream-coloured stone and the w parts of the nave and s aisle. The red sandstone aisle is of *c.* 1320–30, i.e. with two windows having intersected and one having reticulated tracery. Inside, the three w bays of the s arcade have standard elements. Enlargement began in 1822 when *William Line* added a N aisle with plain arcade and typically mean windows. In 1860–1 *James Murray* extended the nave and aisles by two bays and rebuilt the chancel in C14 style. Pretty s porch rebuilt 1921. The NW vestry and hall are by *H. W. Whiteman*, 1929–30. The chapel and organ chamber N and s of the chancel completed 1952. – FONT. Octagonal, Perp. – SCULPTURE. Under the PISCINA is a fine late C13 capital with a head. – The Victorian FURNISHINGS include the CHOIR STALLS, 1872, and PULPIT, 1899. – TOWER SCREEN. Stone. Gothic. By *T. F. Tickner*, 1907. – STAINED GLASS. In the w window fragments of Perp figures, but mostly heraldic panels. – C14 figures with fragmentary texts in s aisle window too. – E window, 1864, possibly *Wailes.* – Two s aisle windows by *F. Holt & Co.*, 1918, and another by *Walkers Glass Co.*, 1948. – In N aisle three by *Hardman*: two 1954–5 and one *c.* 1970. Also *Hardman*, s aisle w, 1960. – MONUMENT. Lively cartouche to Joseph Harwar †1722.

St Margaret of Antioch, Walsgrave Road, Ball Hill. *Harry Quick*, 1910–11. Perched above the road. Brick with stone dressings in a free Perp style. A large church, with clerestoried nave, aisles and transepts. – STAINED GLASS. E window a replacement by *Hardman*, 1955, for war-damaged glass by *Pearce & Cutler*, 1926, of which the upper sections remain. – N chapel windows also *Pearce & Cutler*, 1931–2.

Sacred Heart (R.C.), Harefield Road. *Williams & Winkley*, 1978–9. Brutalist interior with exposed concrete frame. Plain brick exterior with greenhouse roof. – STAINED GLASS. Porthole windows by *Goddard & Gibbs*, 1979. Old church alongside by *George Bernard Cox*, 1933–4, now used as a hall.

United Reformed church, Harefield Road. *George Baines & Son*, 1928–9. A typical sub-Perp job, and a late example of their style of twenty years earlier.

Stoke Library, on Walsgrave Road near St Margaret's, is one of the three Carnegie Libraries given to the city (cf. Earlsdon and Foleshill), all by *J. E. Swindlehurst*, 1911–12.

Stoke Green is lined with substantial C19 houses, also erected along the broad section of the Binley Road and in Brays Lane. Further E, the Biggin Hall pub by *Tickner*, 1923. In 'olden time' style with half-timbering and still retaining most of its original plan. Good fittings, including an inglenook in a rear room. Towards Binley is Copsewood Grange, by *John Cundall* for ribbon manufacturer James Hart, 1870–2. Elaborate portico, but otherwise plain. Derelict but awaiting conversion to apartments (2014).

TILE HILL

3 m. w

The church (St Oswald) needs to be seen in the context of the whole development, which is therefore to be considered first.

A Designated Development Area, Tile Hill was regarded as the most successful of the earlier city estates (begun 1951) planned and designed by *Gibson*'s City Architect's Department. This is largely due to the site, with several patches of wood left untouched, and vertical accent provided by the three blocks of eleven storeys at the heart of the estate. These blocks in FERRERS CLOSE, were completed in 1953. In themselves they are far from distinguished, but their role in the visual play is most important. To the s is the SHOPPING CENTRE on JARDINE CRESCENT with curtain-wall blocks of four storeys with arcades, completed after 1955 by *Ling*. w of these is the church and facing an open green beyond is a long CRESCENT of three storeys with an unbroken roof, known as the 'Banana flats'. On the s end of the green is the replacement LIBRARY by *Armstrong Burton Architects*, 2008. To the N, the copper roofed BLACK PRINCE by *W.S. Hattrell & Partners*, 1958. Around this core, expanses of Wimpey 'no-fines' housing – i.e. built using concrete with no fine sand in the mix.

ST OSWALD. By *Sir Basil Spence*, 1957. The best of the three churches (cf. Willenhall and Wood End) built for Bishop Gorton, who wanted good modern buildings for the new estates provided economically. St Oswald cost £19,790, an amazingly low sum, although more expensive than the others. It fulfilled the brief very well at the time, and it is still admired by some. It is an aisleless rectangle and its free-standing tower on the spacious green is just an open concrete frame with some vertical timber studding in two or three of the framed areas, originally with small coloured enamelled panels here and there between the studs. The parish hall,* linked to the church by a connecting porch, also forms part of the group. At Willenhall and Wood End Spence used the same elements and varied the grouping and some details. At St Oswald the w wall is bare except for two slit windows l. and r. and a horizontal slit at the top and the E wall is windowless. On the w front a plain cross. On the E end a Crucifixus without Cross by American sculptor *Carroll Harris Simms*. The side walls have only a row of small oblong windows low down and a row of smaller square windows high up. The structure of the church is reinforced concrete. The walls are of what was then called 'no-fines' (*see* above) and roughly roughcast. Inside, a fine large wall-covering in appliqué work covers the E wall. It is by *Gerald Holtom* and depicts St Aidan and St Oswald. On the w wall, a REREDOS of 1952 by *J. N. Comper* from All Saints, Emscote, Warwick, installed here *c.* 1990. Spence designed FITTINGS

---

*A later replacement, not by Spence.

for Tile Hill, Willenhall and Wood End, but here his pulpit and lectern have gone.

OUR LADY OF THE ASSUMPTION (R.C.), Tile Hill Lane. 1957 with additions, 1980, and porch, 1995. Featureless exterior. – STAINED GLASS. Two 1980s windows in chancel. – Other windows with Gothic tops, including set in nave depicting the seven sacraments, by *John Bradley*, 2001–2.

LIMBRICK WOOD BAPTIST CHURCH, Faseman Avenue. *J. Roland Sidwell*, 1957.

The Tile Hill SCHOOLS of the 1950s have fared better than those in other parts of the city where many have been replaced. Here, *Gibson*'s City Architect's Department worked in collaboration with the Ministry of Education Development Group under *Stirrat Johnson-Marshall*. LIMBRICK WOOD SCHOOL, 1951–2, is on a grid plan and uses aluminium pre-cast panelling. WOODLANDS ACADEMY in Broad Lane, 1953–5, has detached 'houses' in what became the Coventry custom, the grouping done in a sensitive way. A little S, TILE HILL WOOD SCHOOL, Nutbrooke Avenue, 1955–7, was also built in houses and the same plan has been followed for the later N group.

CROMWELL COTTAGE. *See* WESTWOOD HEATH (p. 304).

UNIVERSITY OF WARWICK
2¾ m. SW, W of Kenilworth Road

Warwick is now (2014) a large university occupying a 750-acre (304-ha) site, with some 23,500 students and 5,400 staff. *Arthur Ling* and *R. S. Johnston* produced a concept design for a University College at Coventry in 1958 but it was not until 1961 that planning began in earnest. Another scheme, by *Ling* and *Alan Goodman*, was published in 1964. However, the main campus and the first buildings on site were planned and designed by *Yorke, Rosenberg & Mardall* (*YRM*) who were involved by 1963. The university first opened to students and gained its charter in 1965. The first phase allowed for only 5,000 students although right from the start an eventual student population of 15,000 or more was planned. The first Vice-Chancellor, Jack Butterworth, envisaged an American-style university closely linked to local industry. Further Master Plans by *Shepheard & Epstein*, 1972, *Casson Conder*, 1992–5, and *MacCormac Jamieson Prichard* (*MJP*), 2007, have guided subsequent developments. All have retained the campus concept, an evolved gridiron plan, open spaces and water. Now the centre of the site has become very crowded. But there is no high-rise and although few buildings excite a high standard of design and landscaping continues to be maintained.

The earliest buildings are on the EAST SITE at GIBBET HILL where an original multi-purpose building survives. By *Grey, Goodman & Associates*, 1964–5, with lecture theatre cantilevered over a courtyard. It is now part of the MEDICAL SCHOOL, whose additions include the LIFE SCIENCES BUILDING

(Quinton Hazell wing), 1997, the CLINICAL TRIALS UNIT by *MJP*, 2009, and the MECHANOCHEMICAL CELL BIOLOGY BUILDING, by *Boswell Mitchell Johnston Architects* (*BMJ*), 2012. In 1968–70 when this zone belonged to the mathematics department, Professor Christopher Zeeman secured funds to erect the MATHS HOUSES for scholars who came to Warwick on long stays with their families. They are by *Howell Killick Partridge & Amis* and consist of six cubic blocks – five individual houses and one containing two flats – round a small green, all in yellow brick with flat roofs, rounded corners and discreet windows. In each house, a study with an all-round blackboard.

Heading through Tocil Wood and over the brook towards the campus centre, one first encounters BLUEBELL HALLS. A successful group of four butterfly or X-plan blocks by *Page/Park Architects* of Glasgow, 2012.

On the main campus the principal early buildings are all by *YRM*, i.e. mainly by *Eugene Rosenberg*, a pupil of Le Corbusier, and *David Allford*. On a regular plan, in long blocks, and originally all with YRM's trademark white Twintile cladding and grey-green panels – all very striking and modern then. Owing to problems with the tile fixing, all except the Humanities Building have been re-clad. The main academic buildings by *YRM* are HUMANITIES, the now enlarged LIBRARY, 1964–6 (phased refurbishment by *MJP* 2007–13), and ENGINEERING (refurbished by *Broadway Malyan*, 2011). Also the ROOTES RESIDENCES, the first block (ROOTES 1), 1965–6, originally tiled, but ROOTES 2, 1968–9, is brick. Especially striking internally is the ROOTES SOCIAL BUILDING, 1965–6, with its refectory and the 'Lounge' recalling YRM's work at Gatwick Airport. Close by is BENEFACTORS HALL, 1965–6, built for American exchange students, with double-height reading room in the centre and two-tier accommodation above (under refurbishment, 2015). In Red Square near these, *Bernard Schottlander*'s abstract 3B Series 1 sculpture, 1968.

A new plan by *Shepheard & Epstein* in 1972 signalled a desire to escape from the well-ordered neatness of the YRM period and its homogenized style. The TOCIL FLATS, 1972, irregularly grouped, are of this period. *Shepheard Epstein & Hunter* designed the SOCIAL STUDIES block at the corner of Gibbet Hill Road and Library Road, 1978, using red brick with irregular windows, balconies and angled corners. The buildings are arranged round separate courtyards.

From this period too, the ARTS CENTRE, by the *Renton Howard Wood Levin Partnership*. In three main phases. First came the THEATRE, 1974–5, then the BUTTERWORTH HALL, 1981 (refurbished by *ADP* in 2009–10), and lastly the cinema, bookshop and MEAD GALLERY, 1983–5. Varied masses and stepped roofs, with steel and coloured cladding for visual relief. Mostly in white-painted breezeblock, but the HELEN MARTIN STUDIO added by *ADP*, 2009, is partly faced in sandstone. On an exterior wall a cast aluminium sculpture by *Geoffrey*

Clarke, 1964, re-erected here in 1992. Outside is the WHITE KOAN by *Liliane Lijn*, 1972, with rotating ellipses of neon lit at night. Nearby, *Richard Deacon*'s Let's Not Be Stupid, 1991.

In the centre, also worthy of note is the STUDENTS' UNION by *Goodman & Short* in association with *Knowles Knowles*, 1976. Additions here are by the *Casson Conder Partnership*, 1996, including the student shops, and by *MJP*, 2010. At the junction of Library Road and Gibbet Hill Road, the RAMPHAL BUILDING (Social Studies) 1996, by *John Miller & Partners*. L-plan around a drum-shaped auditorium separated by an attractive triangular covered foyer. *Miller* also did the initial stages of the WARWICK BUSINESS SCHOOL opposite, from 1999. It has extensions by *Robothams*, 2005, and *Associated Architects*, 2015.

E of University Road and aligned with Library Road through the centre of the campus, a newly created academic square around a grassed area with a small water feature. The concept derived from the *Casson Conder* masterplan and the landscaping is by *BDP*. Three of the main buildings are by *Edward Cullinan Architects*. The first and largest at the entrance to the square is the INTERNATIONAL MANUFACTURING CENTRE, 1993–5. At the far end, the ADVANCED PROPULSION CENTRE UK (built as the International Institute for Product Service and Innovation, 2011–12). On the SW, the INTERNATIONAL DIGITAL LABORATORY, 2007–9. Common features include the use of engineering brick, towers with rounded corners and prow-like canopies. The two buildings on the NE are by *RHP Architects*: the COMPUTER SCIENCE building, 2000, and the ZEEMAN BUILDING (mathematics and statistics), 2003–4, linked by a glass bridge. Tucked behind the Digital Laboratory is the associated PHYTOBIOLOGY BUILDING, an environmentally controlled greenhouse by *BMJ*, 2013, who had previously designed the MATERIALS AND ANALYTICAL SCIENCES BUILDING completed alongside the existing Physics Block in 2011.

Several RESIDENCES N and E. WHITEFIELDS, near the Students' Union, are by *Goodman & Short*, 1975. Of the following decade are JACK MARTIN, *Danks & Love*, 1988. Then ARTHUR VICK by *David Robotham Ltd*, 1993, and CLAYCROFT by the *Casson Conder Partnership* in association with *Robothams*, 1995–6.

Further N the SCIENCE PARK, and former National Grid Offices (by *Watkins Gray International*, 1993), taken over as UNIVERSITY HOUSE in 2003. The planned NATIONAL AUTOMOTIVE INNOVATION CENTRE, due for completion in 2017, has also been designed by *Cullinan*. Then WESTWOOD CAMPUS, around the former Coventry College of Education, N of Kirby Corner. The surviving college buildings include an estate of residences by *W. S. Hattrell & Partners*, 1957–9 and 1960–2, and the Dining Rooms with hyperbolic paraboloid roof. Newer buildings include the TENNIS CENTRE with curved roof and metal cladding by *Berman Guedes Stretton Architects*, 2008.

Lastly, the university has expanded w along Scarman Road. More residences, including *Robothams'* LAKESIDE, 2000, *ADP*'s HERONBANK, 2003, and SHERBOURNE. The last of these is a group of six four-storey blocks with brightly coloured panels, by *Robothams*, 2011–12. Further s the older CRYFIELD residences by *Perry & Rathbone*, 1975, are being partially replaced by *RHP*'s new CRYFIELD RESIDENCES, 2015–17. Nearby, discreetly fronting Whitefield Coppice, a new Combined Heat and Power ENERGY CENTRE by *Cullinan Studios*, 2013–14.

UPPER STOKE

1½ m. NE

Stoke Heath and Barras Heath ½ m. NW of Stoke Church have areas of green space preserved when the area was developed.

ST ALBAN, Mercer Avenue, Stoke Heath. By *H. B. Creswell*, 1928–9. Byzantine, of red brick, with pantiles; tunnel-vaults inside, but pointed arcades and, oddly enough, the larger windows pointed with two mullions. The bellcote is set transversely. All these elements are the same in Creswell's earlier St Philip at Rugby (q.v.). Reordered internally by *Kenneth L. Holmes* with w end partitioned off, 1994–5. – Elegant carved FONT in Forest of Dean stone, 1929. – STAINED GLASS. E window, *Reginald F. Hallward*, 1929. – w windows, *John Hayward*, 1955.

On BARRAS GREEN (at Barras Heath) is ALPHA HOUSE, a pioneering venture in Jackblock construction (the floors finished on ground level and jacked into position as the tower was assembled) by *Ling*'s City Architect's Department, 1961–3, refurbished 2009–10. Sheer and impressive. Seventeen storeys, 180 ft (55 metres) high. The ground floor is retracted. The composition includes a row of one-storeyed white-brick cottages and a small hall. It makes an excellent group.

WALSGRAVE-ON-SOWE

3 m. ENE

ST MARY. A waterleaf capital in the churchyard belongs to an earlier church here, rebuilt and enlarged from *c.* 1300. The red sandstone chancel is of that period – see the Y-tracery and the mouldings of the s doorway. The s aisle was C14 too, but the outer walls were rebuilt in grey stone with straight-headed windows. There is documentary evidence to suggest a date, *c.* 1550. Wills show that the N aisle, also with square-headed Perp windows, dates from *c.* 1540. Described in 1544 as 'the new aisle before St Oswald' its features resemble the N aisle at Foleshill (p. 288). It once had timber-framed gables as at Foleshill again, and Ansty. Grey Perp w tower. N vestry added during remodelling, 1822. The nave clerestory belongs to *Street*'s restoration, 1865. Inside, the arcades have standard elements but differ, the s C14 with rood stair and the N late

Perp. Interior reordered 1982–3. Wrapped round the SW corner, the PARISH CENTRE by *Hinton Brown Langstone*, 1980–1, with the OCTAGON ROOM in the SW angle. – FONT. Norman, of flowerpot shape, with arcading, each arch having its own two thin shafts. – STAINED GLASS. C16 angels with armorial shields in tracery of S aisle E window. – E window by *Goddard & Gibbs*, 1958. – One good Victorian S chancel window, †1865, probably *Lavers & Barraud*. – N aisle W and N *Clayton & Bell*, 1913. – S aisle *Christopher Lund*, 1992. – Otherwise a rather dispiriting collection of partial remains.

BAPTIST CHURCH, Hinckley Road. The original chapel of 1840 became a schoolroom when the present one was built in 1901. Enlarged with addition of L-shaped block with corner tower alongside the façade, 1985–6.

The neighbourhood is dominated by the vast UNIVERSITY HOSPITAL by *Nightingale Associates*, 2002–6, replacing the previous Walsgrave Hospital of 1968 by *S. N. Cooke & Sons*. Relocation of the Coventry & Warwickshire Hospital from the city centre in the 1960s led to the provision of housing N and E of the old village, including a varied development of Scandinavian-style houses around OSLO GARDENS and NORDIC DRIFT by *John Thorne Barton & Associates*, 1962–5.

WESTWOOD HEATH

3⅛ m. SW

ST JOHN THE BAPTIST. Built 1842–4 as a daughter church of Stoneleigh, largely at the expense of Lord Leigh. By *Scott & Moffatt*, i.e. by the future Sir George Gilbert Scott, and one of the first archaeologically conscientious churches in England. Quite small, just nave and chancel and a (remodelled) bellcote, but how different from the Commissioners' type with lancets and thin buttresses and a nave with a barn roof. Here is an attempt at least at recreating the local village church, even if such a church would not be likely to have windows of identical form varied only in the tracery detail. The roof also is still a bit thin, but the attitude is unmistakably the Victorian as against the pre-Victorian. S vestry, 1875. L-plan CHURCH CENTRE wrapped round SW corner, by *K. C. White & Partners*, 1980–1. Interior wholly reordered, but retaining the octagonal FONT with ballflower ornament below the bowl, and the oddly pre-Tractarian DECALOGUE BOARDS on the E wall. – STAINED GLASS. E window by *Horace Wilkinson*, †1916. – One S window by *F. Holt & Co.*, 1886. – W window 1936, possibly by *Percy Bacon* (AB). – WAR MEMORIAL TABLET in nave, by *Comper*, 1919–20.

GREEK ORTHODOX, Westwood Heath Road. Built as a National School, 1870, and converted as a church in 1977–8. Since enlarged. Behind, ST GEORGE'S HALL by *Michalakis Tzirki*, 1993–4.

CROMWELL COTTAGE on Cromwell Lane, just S of Tile Hill Station. Part stone and part timber framing with early brick infilling. Previously thought to have been C17, but dendro-dating in 2007 only produced dates between 1547 and 1580. This suggests later C16 building dates for both parts of the cottage, although the construction history is complex. It incorporates a massive tie-beam from elsewhere, and reclaimed materials from a nearby grange of Stoneleigh Abbey may have been used.

The BUSINESS PARK includes the NETWORK RAIL DEVELOP-MENT CENTRE on Westwood Heath Road by *MacCormac Jamieson Prichard* for Cable & Wireless 1994, faced with faience tiles. An oval court at the centre. The EON headquarters (built for Powergen) in Westwood Way is by *Bennetts Associates*, 1993–4.

WHITLEY

2 m. SSE

ST JAMES, Abbey Road. Dual-purpose church, now the hall, by *C. F. Redgrave & Partners*, 1950. Larger church and contemporary vicarage alongside by *Redgrave & Clarke*, 1967–8. Bare brick interior, sparsely furnished.

MORMON CHURCH, Riverside Close, off London Road. By the *LDS Church Architect's Department*, 1967–8. Usual spindly tower and spike.

PUMPING STATION and LODGE, London Road. By *Thomas Hawksley* for Coventry Corporation, 1893–5. Ruskinian Gothic, like his earlier one at Darlington (1873–9). Awaiting conversion to apartments (2014).

WHITLEY ACADEMY, Abbey Road. *Henry Boot Construction* (project architect *Rob Lavers*), 1999–2000. It replaced WHITLEY ABBEY COMPREHENSIVE SCHOOL, 1955–7, a showpiece of Coventry's post-war educational developments, which stood SW of the lake that belonged to Whitley Abbey, demolished in 1953.* Taking advantage of the landscaped grounds, *Ling* and his team had a field day here. The school was on the Coventry system of 'houses' with steel frame and aluminium cladding. The present academy was built on the opposite side of the lake in preparation for the redevelopment of the school site as a business park with the Jaguar Engineering Centre. It now stands closer to the 1960s PRIMARY SCHOOL and ALICE STEVENS SCHOOL, which remain.

Two BRIDGES over the River Sherbourne. One at ABBEY ROAD on the original crossing: *c.* 1760, single-span with keystone and blocks to the arch, buttressed piers. The other further N on *Telford*'s LONDON ROAD, 1826, widened and much altered in 1938.

---

*Whitley Abbey was a late Elizabethan house altered by *Soane* in 1810–12 and partially rebuilt in 1879 after a fire.

WHOBERLEY

2 m. w

A small but distinctive estate by *Gregory*, 1967–8, s of Brookside Avenue. Single-storey brick houses in terraces (e.g. either side of Overdale Road), with walled front and rear gardens. Similar two-storey terraces to the w (between Wildcroft Road and the Dunchurch Highway). The grouping includes a school and two clusters of low-rise apartment blocks.

WILLENHALL

2½ m. ESE

Willenhall lies between the River Sowe and the A46, bounded by the railway on the N and the Stonebridge Highway on the s. The London Road to Tollbar End was one of the old main roads out of the city.

St John the Divine, Robin Hood Road. By *Sir Basil Spence*, 1955–7. One of the three designed by Sir Basil for Bishop Gorton (cf. Tile Hill and Wood End). The chief external feature is the detached bell-tower, of concrete, an open framework, at different levels in different directions filled in by concrete studs and between them a few small green panels. The tower connects to the church by an open passage. The main entrance is s of the w front, grouping with hall and vicarage, here alone both by Spence and in largely original form. The w front is all glazed and has just one large steel crucifix made of I-beams. The church is plain, oblong, without aisles or structurally exposed chancel. Harled walls, as at Spence's cathedral. Small low side windows. Solid E wall. One s window to light the altar, high and narrow with five small square openings. A wider two-light floor-to-ceiling window opposite. Ceiling of coloured fibreboard panels. The nave has been re-seated with chairs but the furnishings designed by Spence for the choir and sanctuary remain.

St Anne (R.C.), Dunsmore Avenue. *H. J. Harper*, 1979. Octagonal, with featureless brick walls and low pitched roof with raised lantern over the sanctuary lighting a tapestry on the E wall by *Mother Regina* of Stanbrook. – stained glass by *Pendle Stained Glass Ltd*, c. 2011. Free-standing Celtic cross in grounds, 1999.

Willenhall was a Designated Development Area in *Gibson*'s plan. The large expanse of housing to the s and E is the Willenhall Wood Estate, 1959–65 by *Ling*'s City Architect's Department. Two- to four-storeyed buildings in 'no-fines' concrete. All have exclusively pedestrian front access, and access for vehicles at the back – the so-called Radburn-type dual-access. First phase encircled by Middle Ride, 1958–9, and then the group within St James' Lane and Yarningale Road in two phases, 1960 and 1962–5. The later groups more varied in facing materials and detailing.

The square in Remembrance Road N of St John's, 'indifferent as architecture' in Pevsner's opinion, was redeveloped by *Kingham Knight Associates* in 1998, with a new COMMUNITY LIBRARY at the s end. Single-storey with tiled roof and dormers. Opposite, the PRIMARY CARE CENTRE by the *Design Büro*, 2002–3. Red brick with yellow banding, shallow-pitched roof and monumental corner tower.

THE CHACE, London Road. Built as a private house for C.W. Iliffe, 1897. Gabled front with half-timbering and projecting porch. Now a hotel, with 1930 matching extensions on the road side and large accommodation block behind by *Hubbard Ford & Partners*, 1970.

WOOD END
2¾ m. NE

Wood End was one of the three Bell Green estates by *Gibson*'s City Architect's Department, begun in 1950.

ST CHAD, Hillmorton Road, was the pilot of three churches designed for the new estates by *Sir Basil Spence* for Bishop Neville Gorton to an economically very tight specification. It was opened in May 1957, followed soon afterwards by the others at Tile Hill (p. 299) and Willenhall (p. 306). They all consist of a concrete-framed aisleless church, detached campanile, hall and vicarage. The grouping varies and certain details vary also. Here there is a clerestory of small square windows, while Willenhall has none. Also both w and E ends are glazed and there are crosses of plain I-section steel beams are against both ends. The others have solid E walls. The campanile here is the most basic of the three. – Wooden CRUCIFIX carved by *Eric Gill*'s pupils at Blundell's School, Tiverton, Devon, when Gorton was headmaster in the 1930s.

WYKEN
2¼ m. ENE

Towards the E of the city, but still semi-rural thanks to the preservation of a generous area of open space along the River Sowe N and E of the old church. For the area of Wyken s of Ansty Road *see* CALUDON (p. 282).

ST MARY MAGDALENE, Wyken Croft. Norman almost throughout, though the simple red sandstone Norman w doorway is not *in situ*. It has one order of columns. There are traces of the jambs of a N and a s doorway in the nave. Moreover, the nave has a N window, and the chancel one N, one s, and traces of two out of three E windows inside. The grey stone tower has a pretty Victorian timber top, a truncated pyramid, followed by the low bell-openings and a pyramid proper. It dates

from *George Steane*'s restoration in 1866. Chancel ceiling, 1686.
WEST GALLERY. – FONT. Norman, round, with blank arcading. – STAINED GLASS. E window, 1867, probably *Lavers &
Barraud*. – WALL PAINTING. On the N wall, a large fragment
of St Christopher of *c.* 1500 uncovered in 1956. The child on
his shoulder is preserved, and a bit of riverside landscape with
a wooden windmill of the post mill type.
RISEN CHRIST, alongside. *Trehearne & Norman, Preston & Partners*, 1966–7. Church and hall. A simple box. W gable with
cross and battlement-like parapet. – Coloured GLASS in N
window.
ST JOHN FISHER (R.C.), Tiverton Road. Church and presbytery
by *Desmond Williams & Associates*, 1972 (cf. the same architects' Holy Spirit (R.C.), Runcorn, Cheshire, 1971). Low and
square with a raised lantern over the sanctuary carrying a tall
cross. Plain interior lit by a clerestory band. Brick wall with
crucifix behind the altar. The adjoining parish centre by *J. D.
Holmes*, 1992, has a pyramid roof and peaked skylight.
LYNG HALL SCHOOL, Blackberry Lane. The girls' comprehensive school by *Ling* in conjunction with *Johnson-Marshall*'s
team at the Ministry of Education, 1953–4, has been demolished and replaced piecemeal by new school buildings.

3060   CUBBINGTON

ST MARY. On a bank above the street. Red sandstone exterior.
Norman W tower with clasping buttresses. Awkward bell-
openings, the two lancets on the N not convincingly C13. S
doorway C13 with continuous mouldings. Cusped intersecting
and Dec tracery to S aisle windows but this must be Victorian,
as Glynne (*c.* 1840) tells us that these had 'all lost their tracery'.
Dec chancel with reticulated tracery. Low Perp N aisle and
small clerestory. Inside, the S arcade is Norman again, and
probably earlier than the tower. Short round piers, square,
multi-scalloped capitals. Single-step arch in the middle, two
later re-cut arches l. and r. The N arcade probably Dec. Octagonal piers and – an oddity – single-chamfered arches. In the
chancel plain ogee-headed SEDILIA and EASTER SEPULCHRE.
Tie-beam roof with collar-beams and queenposts. Chancel
restoration by *Butterfield*, 1852. Nave and aisles re-seated and
restored by *G. F. Smith* (the Milverton builder) in 1885. SE
vestry added by *F. G. Cundall*, 1896. – Good CHANCEL FUR-
NISHINGS by *Butterfield*, 1852. Brass ALTAR RAILS made by
Francis Skidmore with delicate leaf decoration. Heavy wooden
REREDOS and CHOIR STALLS. – STAINED GLASS. Three
chancel windows by *Warrington*, 1852.* – By *Clayton & Bell*
the E window, 1902, and two chancel windows, 1909. – Two in

*They also did an E window in 1850, replaced in 1902.

N aisle by *Hardman*, 1900 and 1904. – In S aisle, two by *F. Holt & Co.*, 1899 and 1909, and one by *Powell*, 1956. – ESCUTCHEON with ROYAL ARMS. A splendid oddity. Not really a memorial, nor just royal arms. Oval wooden tablet richly emblazoned with foliage, cherubs and shield inscribed 'ABRA MURCOTT, Marriner, 1702'. At the foot a boat, a sailor, Neptune and fishes. Murcott (b. 1662), shipwrecked off the Scilly Isles in 1703, did not die until 1708.

METHODIST CHURCH (Wesleyan). *Frederick Foster* of Leamington, 1888. Simple Gothic with rose window and side tower alongside the entrance for gallery stairs. LEDBROOK HALL in High Street (now residential), 1844, was the previous chapel.

SCHOOLS, S of the church, by *Squirhill*, 1846–7. Brick and stone, with Perp windows and fish-scale tile roofing.

Cubbington is separate from Leamington but seems like a suburb, especially on Rugby Road and NW abutting Lillington. The High Street is the old village centre. Near the church a good group around the crossroads. On the W, raised above the road, THE MANOR. C17 and C18, half stone and half brick with stone quoins and timber-framed within. To the S, the OLD MANOR HOUSE has a timber-framed E wing along New Street. The hall in the red sandstone part facing High Street has a base cruck with crown post dendro-dated to *c.* 1314–41. The C17 W wing is grey ashlar with quoins, mullioned windows, stringband and cornice. In Church Hill, No. 2 is a good 1850s house.

Surrounded by modern housing in Pinehurst is the former VICARAGE, by *John Bradford*, 1821. Brick (now painted) with Doric portico.

On Welsh Road towards Offchurch, C18 HAM FARMHOUSE has unusual half-round gables.

CURDWORTH

1090

ST NICHOLAS AND ST PETER AD VINCULA. Nave and chancel are Norman, i.e. the body of the C12 two-cell church, the N side particularly well preserved. Original windows remain, and also the pilaster buttresses and traces of N and S doorways. Of the latter two jamb shafts survive. Partial refenestration in the early C14 – the Dec four-light E window in the chancel with intersecting tracery and windows on the S chancel and nave, the tracery largely renewed at the restoration by *Bodley & Garner* in 1895–6. The nave extended W in the C15 and the well-proportioned Perp W tower added *c.* 1460. This has thickly crocketed window and portal gables – almost triangular – as found so often in this area. Inside, the pink and grey sandstone chancel arch is Norman and helps to date the job. Waterleaf capitals and keeled rolls mean *c.* 1170–90. The arch has a single row of chevron lateral to the face. On the r. a two-light squint, C15. That on the l. is a copy. In the reveal of the first N window in the nave is a pretty C15 image niche with some original colouring, and a C20 Madonna and Child. Arch-braced roof of 1895–6 to nave, replacing one of 1800 when the church was re-roofed and re-fitted by *Samuel Bennison*. The open seats in the nave – cut down and reworked – retain the feel of the 1800 scheme. – Dominant, the carved wooden ORGAN GALLERY in front of the chancel arch. In the style of a Dec rood loft and by *Bodley & Garner* 1895–6. – Of *Comper*'s English altar, 1907, no trace remains. – FONT. Discovered buried in 1895. Norman, strong and barbaric. Round at base but square at top with rounded angles. Carved on it are, in no order, the Lamb, grotesque lion mask, an Atlas-like figure, two pairs of standing men, a winged monster, etc. At the top some inches are missing. – SCULPTURE. Big bracket with an angel, perhaps C16, found at Water Orton bridge and placed here 1926; defaced. – Fine Angel of the Annunciation, perhaps from a reredos. Medieval. – WALL PAINTING. C13 or earlier? In the reveals of all surviving Norman windows in the nave and chancel. One in the chancel has Lombardic letters and figures of saints. – TILES. Just three, a king, a flower and one with the alphabet, each line running r. to l. – A huge dug-out CHEST, early C13. – STAINED GLASS. E window by *Geoffrey Webb*, side lights 1912, centre 1919. Panel in N window also by *Webb*, 1925. – Millennium window in nave s, *Lawrence & Co.*, 2001. – MONUMENTS. Thomas Wakefield †1837. By *Hollins* of Birmingham. Sarcophagus and weeping willow. – On nave N wall, a group of minor mural tablets signed by *Hollins* †1826 and other Birmingham sculptors †1842 to †1870. – Painted wooden war memorial boards by *Geoffrey Webb*, 1925 and *c.* 1945. – Rev. Lancelot Mitchell, with elongated gilded figure of a priest by *Holland W. Hobbiss*, 1949.

Through the open timber lychgate N of the church, the hexagonal CHURCH HALL. By *J. L. Osborne*, 1966.

CANAL TUNNEL, ¼ m. N, on the Birmingham and Fazeley Canal, engineered by *John Smeaton* and completed in 1789. Short. Between here and Fazeley, a sequence of eleven LOCKS.

DUNTON HALL, I m. ENE. Plain, late C17, brick, five bays, two and a half storeys, hipped roof. Late C18 extension wing to l. with an ogee-headed window with Gothic glazing bars. Dr Samuel Johnson's maternal grandparents lived here.

DARLINGSCOTT

ST GEORGE. By *William Thompson*, 1873. Nave, chancel and N porch; bellcote. Decorative roof slates. Bleak bar tracery. Quirky carved capitals to chancel arch. Brick schoolroom and vestry on s, screened from the church.

In the village, N and E of the church, several substantial C16 to C18 stone houses. In Potters Lane, SUNDIAL COTTAGE, part dated 1681, is Lias with Cotswold stone dressings. Long low MANOR HOUSE and nearby CAMPERDOWN HOUSE have mullioned windows, the latter with a coped gable on one side. On the road to Blackwell a striking range with WELL COTTAGE, of Lias, between Cotswold stone houses. On the l. C18 DARLINGSCOTT HOUSE has a re-set sundial, 1621.

LONGDON MANOR, ⅓ m. SW. Again stone, mullioned windows, C14 and later. Also an C18 brick DOVECOTE in an attractive group of farm buildings.

DORDON

2000

A coal-mining village, part of Polesworth parish until 1948. Birch Coppice Colliery (known locally as Hall End Pit), S of Watling Street, operated from 1875 to 1987. There were brickworks here too. The site of Dordon's medieval chapel in the Anker valley at Polesworth was found during the construction of the railway in 1846. The obelisk erected to mark the site was moved to a new position in 1901 (*see* p. 509).

ST LEONARD. 1867–8 by *Street*, whose S extension of 1878 was replaced when *W. H. Bidlake* again enlarged the church in 1901. So the nave and chancel, of multi-hued local brick, are Bidlake's and the N aisle and vestry are Street's. The stone windows follow the original C14 style. Polygonal stone bell-turret and spirelet on W gable of N aisle. Inside, the nave arcade between is by Bidlake but follows Street's 1878 plan with half-arches at each end. Plain arches without capitals. – REREDOS and wooden panelling by *Jones & Willis*, 1939. – FONT. A square stone column, 1968. – STAINED GLASS. E window by *Cox, Sons & Buckley*, 1882, moved here in 1901. – W window by *Curtis, Ward & Hughes* (designer *George Parlby*), 1917.

In the churchyard E of the church, the SUNDAY SCHOOL of 1884. Gothic in red brick with blue-lined pointed windows.

CONGREGATIONAL CHURCH, Long Street. Simple Gothic of 1908 in brick with pointed stone windows. SUNDAY SCHOOL, 1937, alongside. Similar, but all brick.

DORDON HALL, ¾ m. NE. Early Georgian front of stone with older timber-framed parts behind. The front has four bays of segment-headed windows. A door surround of cyclopean rustication to the slightly projecting third bay. The end gables are stepped. By 1715 or 1720 when this was done such details were already archaic.

Elizabethan HALL END HALL, the home of the Corbins, has gone but HALL END FARM (formerly Holt Hall) survives. A rambling late C17 house with later additions, and gabled outbuildings dated 1902 in the brickwork facing Watling Street.

In Long Street and New Street, rows of terraces and small-scale housing with dates from 1879 to 1923. Some with moulded terracotta decoration from the local brickworks. On the corner of Church Road the DEREK AVENUE ESTATE. Old people's flats and community centre for Atherstone Rural District Council, 1971. Lower down Long Street at Woodlands Close, two groups of single-storey, two-room houses for old people with a rhythm of rising and falling monopitch roofs by *H. N. Jepson & Partners*, 1962.

For Freasley, *see* p. 333.

DORRIDGE

The arrival of the Oxford and Birmingham Railway in 1852 began the transformation of a hamlet of scattered farmhouses into the substantial community that exists today. The Muntz family of Umberslade, the major landowners, initiated development in the 1870s. In the decades that followed, new housing sprang up within reach of the railway. By the time of the Second World War there had been quite extensive but low-density development – sizeable properties in large grounds. After the war, and especially from the 1960s and again in the 1990s, the pace of development quickened with the number of houses increasing from around 600 in 1955 to over 2,500 by 2000. However, development has always been held in check by those wishing to maintain the character of the area, its affluence represented by the so-called 'golden triangle' of showy housing E of the railway.

On the E, Dorridge and Knowle (qq.v.) merge indistinguishably.

ST PHILIP, Manor Road, W of the station. (Total replacement planned, 2016.) The original North Packwood mission church of 1878 by *Payne & Talbot* remains, little altered, as the nave of a much grander church begun by *J. A. Chatwin* with the building of the chancel and E end in 1896–7. The nave low and brick. The chancel, chancel chapel, organ chamber and vestry all higher and stone. Chatwin's intended nave and tower were never built. The contrast is strange outside and more so within, especially the join between old and new. N of the church are The Hall by *S. T. Walker & Partners*, 1969, and The Link by *Kelly & Surman*, 1985. – FITTINGS including a sculptured alabaster REREDOS, probably *c.* 1897, and decent carved oak CHOIR STALLS and PULPIT by *John P. Osborne & Son*, 1953. – STAINED GLASS. E window by *Jones & Willis*, 1912. – War memorial window on chancel S by *Hardman*, 1921. – W window (the E window of the original church), pictorial and by *Swaine Bourne*, 1878.

Former VICARAGE (N of the church) by *W. H. Bidlake*, 1928.

ST GEORGE AND ST TERESA OF THE CHILD JESUS (R.C.), Station Road. The Dorridge mission commenced in a chapel in the garden of John Tarleton Hardman, the fourth generation head of the Hardman firm, in 1905. The first church of 1917 was destroyed by fire in 1934. The present nave is by *J. Arnold Crush*, 1934–5. Brick with round-headed windows and pantiled roof. Extended and orientation reversed in 1977 by *Cyril Horsley*, and parish centre added by *Brownhill Hayward Brown*, 2005–6. – STAINED GLASS mainly by *Hardman*, 1937 to *c.* 1960, and an internal panel to commemorate the centenary of the original mission, 2005. – One chapel window by *Roberto & Georgiou*, 1990. – SCULPTURE of Risen Christ, above the altar, by *John Petts*, 1977. Behind, the L-shaped PRESBYTERY by *Harrison & Cox*, 1922.

METHODIST CHURCH, Mill Lane. *W. H. Cripps* of Oxford, 1965. Concrete-framed with brick- and stone-clad exterior, with flat-roofed hexagonal tower and cross. Alterations by *R. D. D. Smith* in 1983. Extensions to the church and hall with stone-clad frontages, 1996.

Dorridge begins at the area round the station where *G. F. Muntz Jun.* laid out two estates for well-to-do villas in 1878. In Arden Road, SW of the railway, a row of substantial 1880s villas, some three-storey in gault brick with red brick bands (e.g. BANK-FIELD) and some with half-timbering and others two-storey with hipped roofs (e.g. FAIRFIELD). Others in Knowle Grove, E of the railway, including HILLSIDE in Temple Road, with late 1870s polychromatic brickwork (cf. Kenilworth Road cottages in Knowle).

Of this period, too, the row of SHOPS in Station Approach and Muntz's FOREST HOTEL, making an attractive group, with the station (rebuilt in the 1930s) at the top and the shops curving round on falling ground leading down to Station Road. All brick with half-timbering, steep gables with pierced boards and bands of fish-scale tiles in the roofs. Possibly by *George Ingall*, who did much other work for Muntz around 1880.

For Bentley Heath, *see* p. 149.

DORSINGTON

1040

Once a small village of timber-framed and thatched properties. Some remain, but a fire in the village centre in 1753 destroyed a farm, its outbuildings and seven cottages as well as damaging the church.

ST PETER. Built in 1758 (datestone up the tower with initials 'I M Builder'). Humble, of red and yellow chequered brick on a stone foundation. Stone quoins too. Thin W tower with feeble pinnacles. The original round-arched windows Victorianized and the chancel rebuilt by *T. T. Allen* of Stratford-upon-Avon, 1870. Restoration commemorated by pretty painted panel in nave matching the benefaction board opposite.

– FONT. Octagonal, the bowl Perp, the foot probably of the 1660s. C17 graffiti on the bowl. – PULPIT. Jacobean and late C17 panels. – STAINED GLASS. E window by *Preedy*, 1872. – S window in nave, *T. F. Curtis, Ward & Hughes*, 1897. – N window, *Harry Harvey* of York, 1975.

Red brick NEW HOUSE FARM on the small green must be *c.* 1755. Immediately E of the church, MOAT HOUSE, a mainly C17 farmhouse on the site of a moated medieval grange. Major late C20 additions and a glass-sided garden room over the moat by *Glenn Howells*, 2003.

Further E, the OLD RECTORY with a C19 garden front in Blue Lias with a hipped roof and central gablet and a projecting triangular window below.

OLD MANOR, 250 yds S. Originally five cottages, expensively restored as a single house for Felix Dennis in the 1990s. Heavy thatched gables. In the grounds, OLD MANOR LODGE COTTAGE, similarly restored. Behind is HIGHFIELD, a residential 'party' house by *Lyons, Sleeman & Hoare*, 1997. On three levels with swimming pool and areas for work, relaxation and dining within a green oak-framed aisled barn. In the grounds, bronze sculptures commissioned by Dennis for his GARDEN OF HEROES.

DORSINGTON HOUSE, Barton Road. By *Igor Kulodotschko* and *Granville Lewis*, 2005, for Kulodotschko himself. Pre-cast concrete panels with Lias limestone facing. Around two courtyards, with open-plan accommodation and recreational facilities. Gardens designed by *Les Baker*.

DUNCHURCH

4070

ST PETER. A large church with C12 remains, extensively rebuilt in the C14. Restored for the Vicar John Sandford by *R. C. Hussey*, 1841, and again by *S. Gambier Parry*, 1907–8, when the N chancel aisle was added. The unusual geometrical tracery of the original E window, tamely replaced in 1908, is now on permanent display at the Victoria and Albert Museum. Dec the flowing tracery in the big S aisle windows. Curvilinear windows in N aisle. Ambitious Perp W tower. Red sandstone, but the very top dark grey. Big W window of three lights. Bell-openings of two twins with transom and blank tracery below, the details all rather wild. Top frieze of quatrefoils etc. High SE stair-turret. Elaborate cusped doorway to main W entrance. Inside, the tower has a very high arch towards the nave. At its apex a plaster rib-vault. The sides of the arch have Gothic plaster panelling, probably 1841. The three-bay S arcade is Dec. One capital has ballflower enrichment. The abaci are castellated. The piers incidentally stand on late C12 bases with angle spurs. The N arcade, slightly lower and slightly later, is Perp. N

p. 20

chapel arcade with fleurons, by *Gambier Parry*, 1908. Ringing gallery and access stairs by *HB Architects*, 2010. – Carved wooden REREDOS with inset oil paintings, *Gambier Parry*, 1908. – FONT. †1848. – WOODWORK. Traceried panels, including a three-leg pattern, from the pulpit or bench ends, re-set in the later furnishings. – ORGAN CASE in the Organ Reform style, by *Grant, Degens & Bradbeer (Frank Bradbeer)*, 1972. – STAINED GLASS. E and W windows by *Herbert Bryans*, 1908. – The rest by *Shrigley & Hunt*, †1894 to 1923. The sons of Arthur Hunt were educated at Dunchurch and one of them succeeded his father as the firm's senior partner. – MONUMENT. Thomas Newcomb, the king's printer, †1681. Diptych with open doors. Attributed to *John Bushnell* (GF). – BRASSES (chancel). Daniel Augustus Sandford, †1849, and Elizabeth Sandford, †1853, both by *Hardman*.

METHODIST CHURCH, Cawston Lane. *Franklin, Newman & Press*, 1935. – STAINED GLASS, †1946, perhaps by *Camm & Co.* (AB).

INFANT SCHOOL (Boughton Endowed School), off Dew Close. By *Buckland & Haywood*, 1928. Single-storey, with hipped roof and cupola.

PERAMBULATION. W of the church an irregular square opening out towards the main S–N road, with the tall octagonal WAR MEMORIAL cross, 1921, on an island in the roadway. On the S side of this space, GUY FAWKES HOUSE (formerly LION INN), timber-framed with close vertical studding and a few big diagonal braces. First floor continuously jettied, one gable at the end with its own jetty. The house is supposed to have been dated 1663, but must be C16. More or less diagonally opposite the old BOUGHTON FREE SCHOOL, by *Francis Smith*, 1707–9. Brick, with quoins and originally seven bays under a low hipped roof. Stone plaque below the central window. Rather savagely converted into two houses, 1930. Alongside, ALMSHOUSES founded by the will of Thomas Newcomb (†1691) in 1693 but rebuilt 1818: brick with keystoned windows, big chimneys and gabled porches. A little to the N, STATUE of landowner and M.P. Lord John Scott, by *Joseph Durham*, 1867.

Turn r. here to Rugby Road and Vicarage Lane. On the E, the OLD VICARAGE, partially by *D. G. Squirhill*, 1836, in grounds landscaped by *J. C. Loudon* in 1837 for the Rev. John Sandford, who wished to unify the vicarage grounds and the churchyard, separated only by an openwork metal fence. Further ENE, WHITE LODGE (No. 3 Vicarage Lane) is a three-bay house with a very handsome C18 wrought-iron gate. Opposite it a garden gateway with another such wrought-iron gate.

Back to the statue, and to its W the DUN COW HOTEL with a heavy Early Victorian porch across the pavement and a carriage arch to the courtyard. In front of the hotel the MARKET CROSS, adapted in 1813 as a milestone with an obelisk inscribed with distances to London, Holyhead etc. N of it the STOCKS and a thatched SHELTER.

s along Southam Road, several groups of thatched cottages. On the l., in walled grounds is DUNCHURCH HALL, Regency with Ionic porch, its pedimented lodge and former stables fronting the road. ¼ m. further on by the motorway bridge, TOFT EDGE, a striking house designed by *David Collins* for his own occupation, 2012.

DUNCHURCH LODGE, in extensive grounds E of the church. In an elevated situation, with fine views towards Northampton-shire. On the site of a house built for Richard Tawney, the engineer of the Oxford Union Canal, 1804. Rebuilt for John Lancaster by *Gilbert Fraser* of Liverpool, 1907, in gardens land-scaped by *T. H. Mawson*. Queen Anne revival style. Stables, lodges, screen walls and gates also by *Fraser*, 1907–9. Used as an industrial training centre for many years, it became a hotel in 2003.

CAWSTON HOUSE, 1¼ m. NW. In 1585 Edward Boughton built a mansion here using stone from the Whitefriars' church in Coventry. The estate was bought in 1743 by the 2nd Duke of Montagu and later belonged to the Dukes of Buccleuch, who rebuilt Cawston in 1829. In 1907 the house was remodelled and much enlarged by *H. B. Creswell* for the 6th Duke. Large, symmetrical mansion with hipped roof and Georgian windows. Originally roughcast in the Voysey manner. After 1918 it passed through various hands and uses until restored in 2004. Now at the centre of LIME TREE VILLAGE, a development of retire-ment homes.

See also Bilton Grange and Thurlaston.

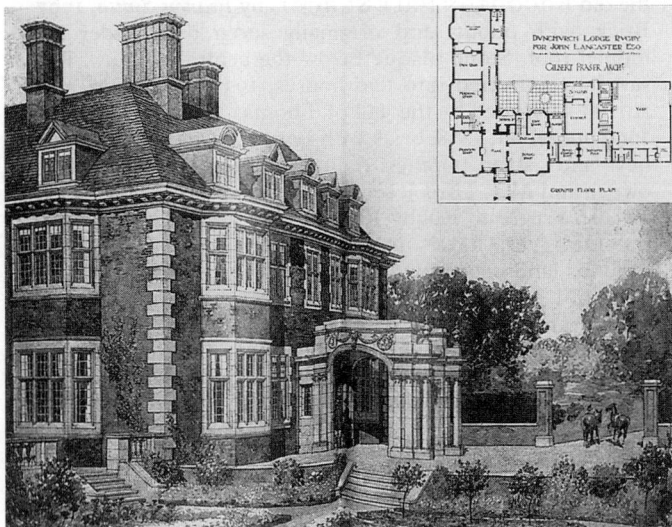

Dunchurch, Dunchurch Lodge, perspective.
Photo lithograph, 1908

DUNNINGTON

SCHOOL (C of E). 1876, originally doubling as a chapel. Lias and grey limestone with lancets and the stump of a chunky E bell-cote over the porch. Later school extensions.

BAPTIST CHURCH. By *G. Ingall*, 1878. Plain exterior with faint C13 details. Inside, rostrum pulpit and immersion baptistery. Parts of the previous chapel, 1841, retained as meeting rooms at E end. A good group with the former MANSE to the S, *c.* 1890, and HALL and COTTAGE to the N, by *F. C. B. Dabbs* of London, 1909, in Arts and Crafts style.

To the S, CONWAY COTTAGE, *c.* 1830, square with pairs of steep bargeboarded and pinnacled gables on each side and square-headed windows with Gothic glazing. Probably built for the Ragley estate.

EARLSDON *see* p. 287

EASENHALL

A southern hamlet of Monks Kirby (q.v.). Single street with a small green at each end. Older buildings include C17/C18 cottages and a farm, but the village was improved by Edward Wood of Newbold Revel in 1871. His architect was *Joseph Goddard* of Leicester.

The gatekeeper's cottage at the former SE entrance to the estate, EASENHALL LODGE, is at the W end of the village. Circular tower in the angle and large moulded stone corbels under the bargeboarded gable on the main elevation. Also *Goddard*'s, several distinctive pairs of estate cottages on either side of the street: High Victorian, with steep gables and elaborate barge-boards, and blue brick bands but varied in their details. Facing the upper green, the former CONGREGATIONAL CHAPEL, 1873.

TOWN THORNS, I m. W, beyond the railway. Large Italianate house, an unexpected style for *Alfred Waterhouse*. His client was an American, Washington Jackson, 1873–5. Brick with rusticated stone quoins, modillion cornice, ball finials and pediment on the N front with pilasters. Porte cochère on N front and bowed bay S, both with Doric columns. It became an evacuation centre for Coventry children in 1940 and from 1954 it was a special school run by the city council. Alterations included the demolition of the large service wing and erection of new school buildings, since replaced by the large CARE HOME flats, 1990. On the Brinklow road, three Italianate lodges, also by *Waterhouse*, 1873.

1080

EASTCOTE

A distinct settlement at the crossroad on the road from Hampton-in-Arden to Knowle. Several interesting houses.

WHARLEY HALL and EASTCOTE HOUSE are both dated 1669, and are, indeed, sister-houses. Important for their early use of decorative brickwork and hipped roof, innovative for the area. The characteristic feature is the use of pilaster-strips at the angles and to flank the windows. They also have brick pediments to the ground-floor windows. Eastcote House was built for the Fisher family (cf. Barston church) as indicated by initials GF TF on the re-set datestone. Wharley has the initials T.W. in a panel above the doorway. Timber-framed EASTCOTE MANOR stands between them. C16, but its showy black-and-white framing (known from illustrations) is much altered. Large early C20 extensions in similar style.

Further W, EASTCOTE HALL, though much enlarged and modernized, has in its centre a C15 hall with a spere-truss to the screens passage. Alterations here by *William de Lacy Aherne* for Samuel Jevons in 1901.

SW of Eastcote Hall, HENWOOD HALL FARM, a brick house of 1824 near the site of Henwood Priory, a Benedictine nunnery.

To the S of the crossroads off Knowle Road, two big late C19 houses on what was Reddings Farm: THE RIDDINGS, 1893, and EASTCOTE GRANGE, 1894. Both built for the Gladstone family, of Mackie & Gladstone, the Birmingham and Liverpool wine merchants. The Riddings with yellow gault brick in its half-timbered gables by *Martin & Chamberlain*, The Grange by *E. H. Mansell* bigger and more refined in its use of Tudor detailing. Now divided into apartments, The Grange was used as a hospital from 1948 until the 1970s.

2080

EASTERN GREEN

A group of church, school and vicarage built to serve the rural area W of Allesley (Coventry), largely through a bequest from Mrs Elizabeth Morgan of Cheltenham. *S. S. Teulon* was the architect, although he died in May 1873 before work commenced.

ST ANDREW. 1875. Brick with blue bands and restless stone dressings. N tower with polygonal stair-turret. Octagonal belfry stage and shingled spire. Plate tracery. Aisleless interior, the brick (now painted) not concealed. Cheap domestic S extension by *Hinton, Brown, Madden & Langstone*, 1975, and gallery over W end of nave. – Ill-matched late C20 chancel furnishings, including CHOIR STALLS and ALTAR RAIL, by the same architects, 1984. – STAINED GLASS. E window †1901, possibly *Jones & Willis*.

SCHOOL and SCHOOL HOUSE, E of the church, also 1875. Blue-banded brick again. Plate tracery to schoolroom.

VICARAGE (now Glebe House) to the W, 1876. Similar, with segment-headed windows and tall chimneys.

EATHORPE

EATHORPE HALL, S of the village centre, was built on the site of an older house for the Vyner family, 1759. Central section of five bays with hipped roof and dormers, and later recessed two-bay wings each side. To it belonged the LODGE and the polychromatic COACH HOUSE and STABLES, 1875.

On a hill E of the Fosse, EATHORPE PARK (originally Highfield House) built for Robert Singlehurst; by *Robert Clarke* of Nottingham, 1860. Enlarged N for Francis Sumner, 1892. A LODGE, 1860, cut off by the re-routed road.

In the main street, ESTATE COTTAGES dated 1860 and 1861 built for Samuel Shepheard, who owned the Eathorpe estate from 1858 to 1866. He also built the BRIDGE over the River Leam, 1862.

ETTINGTON

Ettington (formerly Eatington) has two main settlements. Upper Ettington, the present village, is on the main Stratford–Banbury road. Ettington Park is at Lower Ettington 1¼ m. SSW. The village is unusual in having had three separate churches on three different sites, and the more so since parts of all three buildings survive.

The ancient church in Ettington Park (*see* below) was abandoned in 1802 in favour of a new one in the village: ST THOMAS BECKET by *Thomas Johnson*, 1795–8. Mostly pulled down in 1913; only the tower and the W wall of the nave survive. The details were of the elementary Gothic of *c.* 1800. Officially declared redundant in 1972–5. The tower has since been restored as part of a private house.

HOLY TRINITY. 1902–3 by *C. Ford Whitcombe*, succeeding the church of St Thomas. Brown stone, Neo-Perp, with nice S attachment. NE tower completed by *W. K. Shirley*, 1908–9. Ogee-headed belfry windows enfolding inscribed panels below the pierced sections of the parapets. Rooms at the back of the church by *Brown Matthews Architects*, 2009. – PULPIT. Late C18, doubtless from the predecessor church. – FONT, 1841, with cover, 1914. – STAINED GLASS. E window by *Christopher Whall*, 1906. – BRASSES from the old church. Thomas and

Elizabeth Underhill †1603. – MONUMENT. Margaret Underhill †1784. Large marble mural tablet.

Good LYCHGATE, by *C. Ford Whitcombe*, 1905.

Near the ruins of St Thomas, the former vicarage (now ETTING-
TON GRANGE) by *John Nichol*, 1830, enlarged by *Benjamin
Bradshaw*, 1867.

Off Halford Road S of the village, the FRIENDS' MEETING
HOUSE. Built in 1684–9. A stone house, 18 ft by 24 ft (5.5
metres by 7.3 metres), with a later mullioned window in the E
gable. Enlarged in 1986 and the interior gently modernized in
1996. Some of the plain furniture is original.

In the village, on Banbury Road a little E of Holy Trinity, the
former SCHOOL, built by the Shirleys 1813 and enlarged in
1871, with spindly clock tower of 1873. Alongside, the SCHOOL
HOUSE. Random rubble, mildly picturesque. This resembles
the pair of Shirley ESTATE COTTAGES much further E (Nos.
60–62) dated 1850. The POST OFFICE (No. 29 Banbury Road)
has a good C19 shopfront. On the W side, a former TOLL-
HOUSE (No. 24), mid-C19, brick with canted front to the street.

At opposite ends of the village, two substantial houses built for
branches of the Lowe family. Near the Fosse, ETTINGTON
CHASE (originally called Foss Hill), by *Martin & Chamberlain*
for William Bevington Lowe, 1867. Gothic with traceried hall
window. It is now at the heart of a large hotel complex. In
Rookery Lane, S of the church, Jacobean-style ETTINGTON
HALL, 1871, built for Lowe's widowed sister, Sarah Gibbins,
and her son William Bevington Gibbins. Possibly by *Cundall*,
who later designed the nearby Gothic LODGE for Mrs Gibbins.

ETTINGTON PARK

102   Ettington was the ancient seat of the Shirleys, whose ownership
can be traced back to Domesday. From the C16 until 1641 the
Underhills were tenants here. A branch of the Shirley family,
whose main estates were elsewhere (Derbyshire, Leicestershire
and in Ireland), returned to Ettington after 1717. Of the old
house the only visible trace is one Gothic arch inside. The later
Shirleys made various improvements in the C18 and earlier C19
before Evelyn Philip Shirley embarked on a total remodelling in
1858–62 to create the most important and impressive High Victorian house in the county. Street was Shirley's first choice as
architect and he submitted plans, but the eventual commission
fell to *John Prichard* of Llandaff whose designs were, in the words
of Geoffrey Tyack, more extrovert and passionate. The work here
is by Prichard alone, although he was in partnership with J.P.
Seddon at the time. The style is C13 Gothic, and – as Eastlake
observed – of 'consummate skill in the details' and of 'genuine
and unstrained architectural effect'. The remarkable thing to us
is the relative symmetries always ingeniously broken. For instance
the main front has a porte cochère in the middle, pierced, arched
screen walls l. and r. to hide the recessed centre, and symmetrical
gables on that recessed centre, but then in its angles a round

turret l., a higher square turret r., and in the projecting wings a
rounded bay window l., a canted one r. And so on, on the E and
N sides. On the N side a back entry next to a projecting lower
wing which ends in the later house chapel, 1865, with a polygonal
apse. Window shapes of several types include, on the ground
floor, straight-headed ones with shafts and a dividing shaft and
vertical pieces on top of the shafts. The house is of yellow and
grey stone in bands, and in other respects also Ruskinian. This
Eastlake noticed too. In addition he stresses that the use of First
Pointed, i.e. the earlier E.E., for the purposes of a private mansion
was something quite new. A special glory of Ettington Park is all
the sculpture, many narrative reliefs, carved by *Edward Clarke* of
Llandaff to designs by *H. H. Armstead*. They all represent events
in the history of the Shirley family. The canted bay S of the W
front and the upper portion below the SE tower are also deli-
ciously ornamented with statues and carving. The interior is
disappointing as it lacks the vigour of the exterior. Indeed, many
of the rooms belong to the older house and reflect the tastes of
earlier generations, especially that of Evelyn John Shirley who
inherited in 1810.* The survival clearly shows that Prichard
undertook a remodelling and not a rebuilding. Everywhere, the
Shirley motto 'Loyal je suis' and extensive use of heraldry in tiles
and carving.

Prichard's rib-vaulted PORTE COCHÈRE and seven-bay screen
lead to the ENTRANCE HALL with *Minton* tiles and a sumptuous Elizabethan chimneypiece carved in wood by *Willcox* of
Warwick, 1857, under the overall supervision of *William
Holland*. Of 1810–11 the narrow top-lit STAIRCASE HALL in a
French Renaissance-cum-Elizabethan-cum-some-Dixhuitième
style. On the S, the Regency Gothic LIBRARY decorated in 1820,
with a pinnacled doorway and traceried ogee arch. The *Coade*
stone chimneypiece, 1817, is based on one at Windsor, but the
C13 two-light window with bar tracery comes from 'an old
chapel near Campden'. It has brightly coloured kings in stained
glass, looking 1820s but apparently by *Clayton & Bell*, 1860.
Alongside, the GREAT DRAWING ROOM was remodelled by
Prichard and has a Neo-Gothic beamed ceiling and Neo-
Gothic chimneypiece. On it the Shirley motto again. Back into
the passage, a genuine C15 or C16 doorway leads to the OAK
DINING ROOM in the C18 part of the house, which has a
Frenchy ceiling of 1843 but a genuine late C18 chimneypiece
and inlaid panelling with shields by *Charles Steinitz*, 1860.
Beyond the dining room, the CHAPEL with stained glass and
remains of murals, 1865. On the top floor, the LONG GALLERY
lined with bookcases is again Prichard's, although restored in
1979 after fire damage.

* Geoffrey Tyack (*Warwickshire Country Houses*, pp. 81–7) chronicles the early C19
alterations in detail and discusses unexecuted schemes as well as work by *Rickman
& Hutchinson*, 1824–6, largely swept away by later changes.

Ettington ceased to be the family residence in 1912 and for much of the C20 it was let to tenants or used for other purposes. It was restored as a hotel in 1984–6, with a new accommodation block to the rear, sympathetic in style with gables, banded stonework and shouldered window openings.

p. 39 Behind the house is a LOGGIA of the later C17, brought here from Coleshill Park by Evelyn John Shirley after 1810. It has two arches separated by a square, fluted pillar. The angles are rusticated and have above hanging garlands. In the spandrels of the arches big flower or leaf motifs still reminiscent of Perp portals. Along the top scrolly acanthus frieze. Pineapple finials.

STABLES, N of the house, erected by *Edward Woodward* for George Shirley, 1766, and remodelled in the classical style by *William Walker*, 1832.

LODGE to Ettington Park at Newbold-on-Stour (q.v.) in the same style as the house.

HOLY TRINITY (also called St Nicholas), the ancient parish church, stands just SE of the house. Partially demolished *c.* 1803 after the erection of the new church in the village (*see* above) and retained as a romantic landscape feature. In ruins except for the S transept, adapted as a mortuary chapel to which a small sanctuary was added, 1881. Broad Norman tower with flat buttresses and a flat broad clasping staircase projection. The bell-openings are of *c.* 1200: twins, with a shaft and pointed arches under a round arch. The tower arch is late C12 with decorated trumpet-scallop capitals and an arch with one step and two slight continuous chamfers. The former bell chamber re-fitted as a Gothic library after 1803 and the whole tower restored 1972–4 by *Gardner & Baldwin*. C14 N arcade with hexagonal piers. One has three small faces on the capital. Double-chamfered arches. Perp clerestory. Aisle W window with two-centred arch but just three mullions. That would go (as a repair) with the S windows, which are probably of 1674–6 when the S side of the church was repaired. The S doorway is typical of the early C14. Of the chancel only the S wall remains. Red sandstone windows, one of *c.* 1300, the other Perp. The chancel is continued in an avenue of trees. The S transept has one W lancet, but the rest is restoration of 1825 by *Thomas Rickman*. Distinctively his the panelled plaster ceiling and the doorway and spherical triangle windows in the archway to the old nave. The bellcote and fussy S window apparently 1875.

The added side chapel of 1881 has tiled dado and paving. – Imitation Norman FONT with chevron and rope decoration. – Cast-iron BENCH ENDS, by *Rickman*, 1825. – STAINED GLASS. Two windows by *Evie Hone*: the E window, excellent primitive Expressionism, 1948–9; the S window more conventional. The glass replaces that returned from here to the chapel of Winchester College, from which it had strayed to Ettington in 1825. – MONUMENTS. Ralph Shirley †1327 and wife. Two defaced recumbent effigies. He had crossed legs. Angels by her pillow. – Dame Frances Freckleton †1633. A documented work by *Nicholas Stone*. Plain four-poster with Corinthian capitals.

The effigy of stone and not especially good, but already less
stiff than Jacobean effigies. – Robert, Earl Ferrers, †1717, his   74
second wife, Selina, †1762 and their son George who commissioned it. Intended for Staunton Harold but erected here
instead. By *J. F. Moore*, 1775. The earl and countess stand l.
and r., George higher up, semi-reclining. Obelisk back. The
figures are white, the framework of various marbles. The atti-
tudes rather rigid, and the expressions dull. – Phyllis Byam
Shirley †1836. By the *Patent Works, Westminster*. With a vase at
the top. – Others by the *Patent Works*, †1832–6, and the *Westminster Marble Company*, †1830. – John Evelyn Shirley †2009.
Simple black tablet with Celtic decoration.

EXHALL BY ALCESTER   *1050*

St Giles. Norman origins – see the N door – but rebuilt and
much altered by *Solomon Hunt* of Harvington, 1861–2, amid
protests from the Worcester Diocesan Architectural Society.
Some windows are Victorian, especially the lancets at the w
end, but Hunt was more respectful of the old fabric than might
be imagined. The C13 chancel retains two N lancets and a Dec
E window. The nave s window *in situ* with ballflower decoration
and straight top outside. Its three lights are ogee-headed.
Opposite, a large rectangular N window with tracery of two
cusped crosses. It is illustrated *c.* 1800, but was probably then
where the s porch is now. Inside the two facing windows have
segmental arches, that on the s with ballflower. *Hunt* raised the
roof and added the s porch. The stone bellcote with copper-
covered spirelet (originally shingled) is of 1862. – Decent contemporary furnishings by *Hunt*, 1861–2, including wooden
PULPIT with carved panels replicating the tracery of the N
window. – STAINED GLASS. E window, *Charles E. Steel*, 1916.
– w windows, *Harry Harvey*, 1977. – BRASSES. John Walsing-
ham †1566 and wife; figures 23 in. (54 cm.)
A single street, with black-and-white cottages, some on Lias
foundations. Towards the s, HUNTERS HILL, built as a rectory
by *Robert Jennings* of Atherstone, 1870; not Gothic. Further s
and opposite, EXHALL COURT farmhouse, gabled with wavy
bargeboards, brick with stone windows, rebuilt and enlarged
for the Bomford family, *c.* 1860.

EXHALL BY COVENTRY   *3080*

St Giles. Chancel of *c.* 1300, the E window with intersecting
tracery. Perp w tower, grey sandstone. Good Dec s aisle and
porch of 1842–3 by *Charles Hansom*. The N aisle began as a

two-bay chapel for the Hales family, 1609, with a perfectly normal late Perp N window. Enlarged to the W by *William Tomlinson* of Coventry, 1885. The vestry also 1885. – Caen stone PULPIT with red marble pillars, *Jones & Willis*, 1892. – STAINED GLASS. E window, *Hardman*, 1867. – Chancel S, one *Hardman*, 1866, the other *Usher & Kelly*, 1872. – Two more by *Hardman*, W tower, 1890, and N aisle W, 1955–6. – In S aisle S, two by *T. W. Camm*, 1900 and 1905. – N aisle, *Florence, Robert & Walter Camm*, 1921. – S aisle W, *Shrigley & Hunt*, 1932. – S aisle E, *Norgrove Studios (Noel Sinclair)*, 1999. – MONUMENTS. John Phillips †1716. Corinthian pilasters. – Anne Brooks †1839. Grecian. By *W. Morgan* of Exhall, i.e. a local monumental mason.

In the churchyard, two late C17 sandstone CHEST TOMBS with architectural details, an old FONT bowl and a C19 column with SUNDIAL.

NW of the church a group of former SCHOOL buildings. Facing the road, the original school endowed by W. Bentley. A plain house, now rendered, by *Richard Booth*, 1813. To the rear, the SUNDAY SCHOOL by *J. L. Akroyd*, 1841: brick, with pretty timber roof trusses inside.

In Church Lane, the former VICARAGE (now BHALLA RESIDENCE) is a solid traditional parsonage by *Harry Quick*, 1909.

½ m. ENE, beyond the M6 motorway in Exhall Green, the former BOARD SCHOOL (now the Community Centre), by *George Taylor*, 1876–7: red brick with blue dressings, single-storey, segment-headed windows and terracotta finials on the gables. The house alongside, detached, now roughcast.

NEWLAND HALL FARMHOUSE, 1 m. W. Only the ashlar-faced ground floor concerns us. It has mullioned C17 windows with hoodmoulds. But on the E front are four small heads of *c.* 1300 or earlier which must have been label stops or corbels. It was a moated site, with fishponds, belonging to Coventry Priory.

FARNBOROUGH

ST BOTOLPH. The church as seen from the house impresses one as a Victorian estate church. It was, indeed, transformed by *Scott* for Archdeacon Charles William Holbech. First, in 1858, he restored the chancel, already high-roofed and on a grander scale than the rest. Then, in 1874–5, he restored the nave and raised its roof, added the N aisle[*] and heightened the tower by adding the belfry stage and spire. But otherwise the church is medieval. It has a Norman S doorway with jamb shafts clasped intermittently in a very curious way. Chevron arch with a cogwheel edge and tympanum with a neat, small-scale pattern

---

[*]Replacing a N transept added in 1839.

of tipped or slanting fish scales, *c.* 1140. In the nave also a lancet window. Dec chancel with reticulated tracery in E window. The 1858 chancel arch reuses a Norman lozenge chain probably from the original arch. Dec the tower arch to the nave with mouldings dying into the jambs. Back outside, the S porch entrance also Dec. The second stage of the tower dated 1611 has square mullioned windows. Scott's splay-footed spire is recessed, set behind a low parapet. – FURNISHINGS mainly by *Scott*, e.g. chancel STALLS, seating in nave and aisle and SCREEN in tower arch. – STAINED GLASS. E window by *Wailes*, 1858. – Others by *Wailes* in chancel, †1858, and nave and N aisle, 1875. – Two heraldic windows in chancel by *Willement*, 1839, probably from the transept. – In the nave, one by *James Cameron*, 1885, and another by *Powell*, 1918. – In the N aisle, an excellent Arts and Crafts window, †1936, probably by *B. J. Warren*. – MONUMENTS. Head of an effigy of *c.* 1200, with mail coif. Found in the churchyard in the 1940s. – Mrs Mary Wagstaffe †1666/7. Brass inscription with wide stone band of very pretty leaf and scroll motifs, still entirely Jacobean. The inscription goes like this:

> Ten children of their mother are bereft;
> And them for pledges shee a saint hath left
> With their father, till it please God to call
> For those deare pledges, and himself and all:
> A better freind [*sic*], a wife, and a mother
> Could never bee: shew mee such another:
> Now for to lose such a good wife as this;
> Judg you how great, and what a losse was his:
> Then if a saint on earth you ever see
> Think you of her: for such a one was shee.

Jeremiah Hall †1711. Cartouche with an open book, an unusual motif. The decoration also very conservative. – William Holbech †1777. Purely architectural tablet, rather 1740- than 1770-looking. – LYCHGATE, 1875, presumably *Scott*.

Close by, the former RECTORY, a stuccoed Regency house, 1814, with an added red brick service wing (now GLEBE HOUSE), 1875.

In the village, FARNBOROUGH GRANGE is a late Tudor house with additions by *Walter E. Mills*, *c.* 1903. Facing each other at the W end of the main street, the former SCHOOL, 1831, and the old PARISH ROOM, 1890. Both ironstone, Tudor-style.

FARNBOROUGH HALL. Acquired by the National Trust in 1960, Farnborough has been the home of the Holbech family since 1684 when Ambrose Holbech bought the manor. His son William (†1717) began a reconstruction of the earlier house around the time of his marriage in 1692. Work continued to about 1705. The next William (†1771) made extensive improvements to the house and landscaped the grounds in the 1740s, much influenced by what he had seen in Italy while on his Grand Tour in the previous decade. His advisers included

Sanderson Miller, here in strictly classical mode, who was engaged in the grounds from *c.* 1742 to 1755 and on the hall in 1746–7. Among the craftsmen were *William Hiorne* of Warwick and the plasterer *William Perritt* of York. Later, in 1813–16, another William Holbech commissioned *Henry Hakewill* to design a new service wing, since demolished, and to improve the stables.

The house has two principal fronts: to the W and to the N. The W façade is of *c.* 1701 and attributed by Andor Gomme to *William & Francis Smith* of Warwick; of hot brown Hornton ironstone with grey Warwick sandstone dressings. Seven bays wide and two storeys high with a balustrade and a hipped roof. The middle bay is stressed by a slight projection, by being faced with grey stone, by having a raised, pedimented dormer, and by a broad doorway with segmental pediment, only just fitting in. The N side is of *c.* 1746–7 and by *Miller*, nine bays wide with slightly projecting two-bay wings. The windows have architraves and are comfortably spaced. Doorway with attached Tuscan columns, a triglyph frieze, and a pediment. Blank arched niches to the inside of the wings. The S front is simpler, also *c.* 1746–7, with the centre five of the seven bays set forward. The doorway here has skirted architraves and a pediment on brackets (cf. Hagley, Worcs.).

The Palladian ENTRANCE HALL on the N side was formed *c.* 1750 to house the treasures collected by William Holbech in Italy. It has a panelled stucco ceiling with pretty Rococo motifs, busts of Roman emperors and classical goddesses in front of oval recesses at the top of the walls, a beautiful chimneypiece with big corbels, frontal and in profile, and a leaf frieze. The plasterwork by *Perritt*, the carved wooden overmantel probably by *Benjamin King* of Warwick. The STAIRCASE runs up round three sides of an oblong well. Of *c.* 1700, it has fluted balusters, and the walls are decorated by stucco panels. Oval skylight, and, at its foot, a gorgeous, thick garland of flowers. This is probably by *Edward Gouge*, *c.* 1695, although the rest of the decoration is by *Perritt*, 1750. The DRAWING ROOM (formerly the dining room) on the S was also created *c.* 1750. It has again delightful Rococo panels framing paintings by *Canaletto* and *Giovanni Paolo Panini* (replaced by copies in 1929), and decoration round the oval mirror between the windows. This is Rococo in the extreme, i.e. asymmetrical. There is a bill from *Perritt* for the plasterwork here, although the decoration round the paintings may be by *Francesco Vassalli* (cf. Hagley again) and that round the mirror by *Thomas Roberts* of Oxford (cf. Kirtlington Park, Oxon.). On the W side of the house, the DINING ROOM with an C18 painted ceiling partially uncovered. In the LIBRARY, bookcases and furnishings of *c.* 1812.

Immediately NW of the house, the C18 STABLES remodelled by *Hakewill* 1815–16 and the new COACH HOUSE of the same date. By *Hakewill*, too, the forecourt wall N of the house, with delicate iron gates for which there are drawings dated 1816.

The real delight of Farnborough is the winding TERRACE WALK following the ridge to the S of the house, with fine views towards Edgehill and the Dassett Hills. It extends almost half a mile, with ornamental buildings at intervals. Below, a meandering pool. *Sanderson Miller* was responsible for the landscape design, and probably for the buildings too. *William Hiorne* was the builder. There are no firm dates, although the terrace itself had been laid out by 1742 and the pentagonal summerhouse (no longer extant) beyond the far end of the terrace was of 1746. The buildings of *c.* 1750 attributed to *Miller* and *Hiorne* are these. First, the GAME LARDER, through a wall to the l. of the terrace. Hexagonal, with Tuscan columns around. In the louvre is still the wheel from which the game was suspended. Next, on the r. of the terrace walk, the IONIC TEMPLE. It has a pedimented portico of four columns with fluted frieze. Then the grey stone OVAL PAVILION or look-out among trees on the l. further along the terrace. The ground floor is a loggia with Tuscan columns. Ionic pilasters above, and a low dome. Rococo plasterwork by *Perritt* in the upper room. The pavilion much resembles the 1630s summerhouse at Ecton Hall, Northants, a place known to Miller and Hiorne. Lastly, the OBELISK marking the far end of the terrace. Built by 1746 (although dated 1751), but rebuilt in 1823.

Other landscaping included the lakes, a cascade and the planting of clumps of trees. This work continued under Miller, 1745–55. There is also an C18 ICE HOUSE SW of the house.

FENNY COMPTON

ST PETER AND ST CLARE. Dedications to St Clare are rare among medieval churches (cf. Bradfield, Suffolk). The church is of Hornton stone. Late C14 W tower with recessed spire. N doorway Dec with characteristic continuous mouldings. Tower arch similar. Dec also the chancel arch and the N arcade, varied in detail. The arcade five bays long, but on a small scale. The whole S aisle and its arcade are of 1862 by *Edward G. Bruton*, but in a complementary style. Small Perp N clerestory. Chancel with reticulated E window and three identical cinque-foiled S windows. Porch partly remodelled 1675. Restoration by *T. G. Jackson*, 1879; his are the good chancel STALLS. – PULPIT. Plain, 1670s. – COMMUNION RAIL. C17. – STAINED GLASS. Patterned E window, *Cox & Sons*, 1871. – N aisle, *Lavers, Barraud & Westlake*, 1885. – BIER with much bright brass, 1907. – MONUMENT. Elizabeth Croke †1719, with *putti* and flaming urn.

OLD RECTORY, over the churchyard wall. A plain gabled house of 1842 by *H .J. Underwood*, enlarged on the E by *Harry Drinkwater*, 1887. This is a Corpus Christi living and Oxford architects were employed.

By the entrance to the churchyard a cottage with good Victorian Gothic tracery. Opposite, in Church Street, C17 HOPE COTTAGE with delicately moulded doorway and window surrounds. Just N is RED HOUSE, the rectory until 1842. Its brick front of five bays and two storeys is dated 1707. Only the r. side quoined. Hipped roof. Stone doorway with big broken segmental pediment in the second bay, not centrally. This may well indicate an earlier interior. The front room r. of the door has caryatids on the wall and ornate plasterwork, but the latter may be C20 Arts and Crafts imitation. The overmantel of c. 1600 was probably brought in. The staircase on the other hand is of 1707 (twisted balusters).

At the N end of Church Street, three SCHOOLS. The old NATIONAL SCHOOLROOM, 1833, stands near its much altered 1864 INFANT SCHOOL replacement by *Bruton*, now subordinate to the pretty mixed SCHOOL, 1889–90, by *Drinkwater*, which is in a free Tudor style reminiscent of Jackson. Considerate additions, 1995.

In High Street, N of the school, the METHODIST CHURCH (Wesleyan), 1838, at the end of a narrow alley. Galleried interior.

In BRIDGE STREET several good houses. WOAD HOUSE is L-shaped and has under its front gable an upper two-light Dec window. The other windows are mullioned. The doorway is classical. Another part dated 1593. All extensively restored by *F. W. B. Yorke*, 1931–3. Opposite, OLD TOFT has a flat front with mullioned windows. Further N, CONTONE HOUSE, again mullioned, was 're-edified' in 1668.

THE LODGE, Avon Dassett Road. A neat ironstone house, Late Georgian with Tuscan doorcase. Gothic oriel window on rear wing facing The Slade, perhaps from alterations by *W. E. Mills*, c. 1900.

OXFORD CANAL, 1 m. E. When opened in 1776 the canal passed through a tunnel, ⅝ m. long. This was dismantled in stages between 1838 and 1870, leaving a deep cutting. In the middle of the cutting near the road bridge, a mid-C19 cast-iron ROVING BRIDGE. The RAILWAY runs parallel to the canal.

FILLONGLEY

ST MARY AND ALL SAINTS. On a bank above the village, approached through a lychgate by *Thomas Garner*, 1902. The W tower is E.E., except for the Perp top parts. The arch to the nave is triple-chamfered. The roof-line above it shows that the nave at that time was lower than it is now. The nave was rebuilt and widened about 1300 (see the Y-tracery and the windows of three stepped lancet lights with trefoil heads). It is indeed very wide – hall-like, as Douglas Hickman observed. Only the E.E. S doorway was made use of and re-set. The clerestory of course is Perp, but the chancel is again of *c.* 1300, or at least its obvious features; traces of former E windows inside show that the masonry here is Norman. Late Perp N chapel of two bays. Fine ceiling with moulded beams and bosses. Good restoration by *Bodley & Garner*, 1887–8, including panelled ceiling to nave. N extension by *Alfred Gardner*, 1981. – REREDOS given by *Garner*, 1891; carved stone, painted and gilded. – BENCH ENDS. The very boldly done and very varied tracery panels of the stall-front (in N chapel) and the prayer-desk are probably former bench ends. Linenfold panelling on nave seats and PULPIT too. – FONT. An odd, clumsy piece, round, with vertical ribs dividing convex panels from each other. Probably C15. – Old CHEST with painted inscription and donor's arms, 1729. – Gilded MAJESTAS designed to hang in the chancel arch, by *Comper & Bucknall*, 1961. – STAINED GLASS. Good C14 fragments in a N window. – In the N chapel C15 donor and family. Also small C16 Netherlandish panels. – Otherwise mostly by *Burlison & Grylls*, 1887–1933, including one in S chancel (†1872) and adjacent window designed by *Garner*, 1890. – One in S nave by *T. W. Camm* for *R. W. Winfield & Co.*, 1891, and two to W by *Heaton, Butler & Bayne*, 1896–7. – MONUMENT. Mrs Anne Daniel and daughter Elizabeth, erected by Lord Leigh, 1725. Purely architectural and quite up to date. – Wall monument, also architectural, to Holbeche family, by *Richard Squire* of Worcester, *c.* 1772.

In the CHURCHYARD, remains of two CROSSES, one C15, restored by *Bodley & Garner*, 1896. Also good C17 table tombs.

Former (Wesleyan) METHODIST CHAPEL, Church Lane, and adjoining house, by *Ewen Harper*, 1892–3; residential conversion 1984. Further NW, in BERRYFIELDS, a group of seven COTTAGES, built by prominent Methodist David Barr as homes for retired Wesleyan preachers. By *F. J. Yates*, 1898–9.

BOURNEBROOK SCHOOL, Coventry Road. By *John Cotton*, 1877. Brick with dark bands, pierced bargeboards and fish-scale tiled roofs. L-plan facing the church. Apsidal end with carved animal heads fronting the street. To the N, the SUNDAY SCHOOL erected for Joseph Johnson in 1840, with modest side extension by *J. J. Raggett*, 1910. Brick with segment-headed windows.

In the village centre, old cottages W of church. Brick and timber-framed ALPHA HOUSE of *c.* 1612, once a pub, with brick frontage and steps. To its N, a former shop with pointed Gothick first-floor window. In the dip, THE MANOR pub dominates; its street front C18, the S side a decent C20 adaptation. On the bank to the S, Regency ARDEN HOUSE.

Fillongley has two CASTLE sites, one alongside Nuneaton Road to the NE and the other at Castle Yard SE of the village. Both have earthworks, and the latter a fragment of masonry of a rectangular building which may indicate a late C13 keep.

FILLONGLEY HALL. 1824–5 by *George Woolcot & Bryan Browning* for the Rev. Bowyer Adderley. Extended and improved by *J. L. Akroyd* of Coventry, 1840–1. Restored since 1993 for the

8th Lord Norton. *Woolcot & Browning*'s two-storey house was Neoclassical, rich within yet plain outside. Akroyd's additions give it distinction. Front of five bays, two storeys, ashlar, and in the middle loggia of two unfluted Ionic columns in antis. Pedimented doorway on brackets. Long veranda on cast-iron columns on s side and projecting wing on the w. (Inside quite a grand entrance hall with, in the corners, four red giant columns. Circular glazed skylight with some stucco surrounds. Library with more scagliola columns, the ensemble described by Gervase Jackson-Stops as 'one of the great unsung interiors of the Greek Revival in England'.) On Broad Lane to the NE, a single-storey LODGE of stuccoed brick with balustraded parapet and Doric portico, perhaps by *Akroyd, c.* 1835.

Fillongley is an extensive parish, rich in farms and houses of architectural diversity and interest. One can only summarize by locality.

In the E, FILLONGLEY GRANGE, *c.* 1840, double-pile with Doric portico. Further E on Breach Oak Lane, BIG HOUSE FARM, a typical square North Warwickshire C18 farmhouse with hipped roof.

Far w beyond the hall, GROVE COTTAGE with late C18 Gothick windows, rugged early C17 stone-mullioned STONE HOUSE FARM, and COLLIERS OAK FARM, partly 1587 with huge sandstone chimneystacks and brick stables dated 1611. N of this at SHAWBURY VILLAGE, a gated estate of *c.* 1990 on the site of former Birmingham Industrial School for Outcast Boys, established 1868 and enlarged in 1890. Of the largely utilitarian SHAWBURY SCHOOL buildings hardly anything remains.

N towards Arley, off Tamworth Road, FILLONGLEY LODGE. Small country house, *c.* 1830. Stuccoed brick with balustraded parapet. Two storeys, front of five bays with Doric tetrastyle portico. Projecting canted bay on w side. LODGE COTTAGE at the entrance to drive has a rustic veranda shading Gothic windows.

Finally in the s, FILLONGLEY MOUNT, largely of *c.* 1840 with lozenge lattice windows and shark's teeth bargeboarding. Beyond the motorway at Chapel Green, OLD FILLONGLEY HALL, a C16 brick house remodelled with new stone gabled projections, *c.* 1840. Towards Meriden, HAYES HALL FARM, an C18 house with striking red brick farm buildings.

FINHAM *see* p. 288

FLECKNOE

A hilltop village and the main settlement in Wolfhampcote parish. Several ironstone farmhouses and cottages.

ST MARK. By the *Rev. R. O. Assheton*, rector of Bilton and Rural Dean, 1891. Small, brick, unremarkable. – Plain octagonal FONT, from Effingham (Surrey). – STAINED GLASS, assembled by *Assheton* in 1891 with panels by *Burlison & Grylls* and texts by *Heaton, Butler & Bayne* set among 'debris given to him from other churches' and *Powell*'s Cathedral glass.

MANOR HOUSE. Fine C18, in brick with rusticated alternating quoins and five-bay gabled front. Gault brick C19 farm buildings (now residential) to rear.

Former VICARAGE, Vicarage Lane. By *F. G. Cundall*, 1899, replacing the new parsonage built at Wolfhampcote (q.v.) less than twenty years earlier.

FLETCHAMSTEAD see p. 288

FOLESHILL see p. 288

FOXCOTE

1040

1¼ m. SW of Ilmington

A large, impressive, early C18 Baroque house, superbly situated on the S side of Windmill Hill, with long views towards Stow. Beyond the gardens, the ground drops steeply to the valley below, where there are lakes. The house occupies the site of an earlier one and the deserted medieval settlement of Foxcote must have been nearby.*

The N and S fronts have nine bays, two storeys and attic, with vases and hipped roof. The pedimented centres have giant attached angle columns of the Doric order and there are giant pilasters separating the outer bays; that might mean the angle bays are an enlargement. If so, the original had giant angle pilasters. A Doric frieze runs round the whole building. The triglyphs would not please a C5 Athenian. To the garden a fine doorway with fluted attached Corinthian columns carrying an open segmental pediment. (In the entrance hall panelling with garlands. The staircase with cast-iron handrail is late C18.)

But what is the date? And who was the architect? The arms formerly over the main entrances (noted by Neale) belonged to Francis Canning II who inherited in 1734. Later, in 1760, the house and offices were described as 'all in a few Years past built by the said Mr. Canning', i.e. the same Francis Canning (II) who was the head of the family until 1766. As to the

---

*This entry owes much to Pearl Mitchell and Margaret Fisher, the authors of a detailed study of Foxcote and its estate (privately printed), and to Nicholas Kingsley, who kindly provided information on Coscombe and shared his thoughts on the identification of Foxcote's architect.

designer, Andor Gomme suggested the *Smiths* of Warwick, and John Harris attributed the house to *Edward Woodward*, a view backed by Howard Colvin who regarded the distinctive bell *guttae* below the triglyphs as identifying marks of the Woodward brothers (cf. Honington Hall, and Radbrooke Manor, Quinton), and there are stylistic similarities in their pediments elsewhere too. A third candidate is the carpenter *John Phillips* of Broadway; annotated views discovered among the Phillipps MSS suggest that he may have been the architect here and also at Coscombe, Glos., a vanished Baroque house built for Robert Tracy *c.* 1715–20. There was a striking resemblance between the two.

After the last of the Cannings married into the Howard family of Corby Castle, Cumberland, in 1843 the house was let to tenants and finally sold in 1934. It has been restored with tasteful additions for the present owner by *Donald Insall & Associates*, since 1997–8.

To the garden a former Catholic CHAPEL projects, a plain four-bay structure with arched windows, connected to the house by a contemporary piazza or cloister. Built for Francis Michael Canning in 1814 and used for private and parish worship until 1934. An adjoining building was used as a presbytery. The STABLE range of *c.* 1814 too, stone-fronted but with plain brick on the side facing the walled kitchen gardens.

To the NNE, DUNSTALL BUILDINGS, an early C19 barn dressed up as an eyecatcher from the house. Triple lancets and gables with ball finials are its distinctive features.

FRANKTON

ST NICHOLAS. Grey stone with red sandstone dressings. Short W tower, C13 below, Perp above. The top stage has deeply recessed bell-openings with panelled soffits. Pinnacles 1976, but a C17 one with carved decoration is preserved inside. The rest restored or rebuilt by *Scott*, 1872–3, except the E end of the chancel which is C18 brick, with an inserted window of 1858. Inside, the S arcade responds seem to be of *c.* 1300 or a little later. – FITTINGS mainly by *Scott*, 1873, including the SCREEN, ALTAR RAILS and excellent CHOIR STALLS. – *Godwin* TILES. – ORGAN GALLERY, 1952. – STAINED GLASS. E window, probably *Ward & Hughes*, †1857. – IRONWORK. C14 straps re-fixed on S door.

MANOR HOUSE, NW of the church. C17 and later, but much altered by *Charles M.C. Armstrong* for Col. W.H. Biddulph in 1925–6. The stately William-and-Mary-looking doorway of Hornton stone with a hood on brackets is of 1926. Inside a Georgian staircase with two turned balusters to each tread came from The Priory at Warwick at the same date, along with some panelling and two mantelpieces.

OLD RECTORY, across the valley to the S, *c.* 1830: Flemish bond brick, hipped roof and bold Doric porch with Soanian incised decoration.

FREASLEY

A little hamlet around a green. Close to the M42 motorway and not far from the former Birch Coppice colliery at Dordon yet sheltered and pleasant. Several old cottages.

ST MARY. Mission church, 1894, with two-storey verger's cottage attached. Brick base to the church, timber-framed upper stage and tiled roofs.

FREASLEY HALL. Late C17 in style but dated 1723 on the W front. Brick, five by three bays, with a hipped roof and quoins. The chimneys each with an arched panel. The central bay on the W side has a segmental pediment over the door and rusticated stonework above.

GALLEY COMMON

A former mining village at the far W of the Stockingford district of Nuneaton but originally an area of common land at the edge of three parishes. Mining at Haunchwood Tunnel Colliery (also known as the Tunnel Pit) began in 1891. At its peak before the First World War the mine produced 480,000 tons and had 1,354 employees. After closure in 1967 virtually all signs of the mine were cleared away, the spoil heap being landscaped in 1972–3 and many of the miners' houses demolished in 1979. An industrial estate now occupies part of the colliery site and the village has been redeveloped for housing – a dramatic transformation of a once heavily industrialized landscape.

ST PETER. By *Percy Morley Horder*, 1909. Built with contributions from the miners. Roughcast, domestic and unremarkable outside. Constructed of hollow pink terracotta blocks, visible as facing within, with pretty wooden Arts and Crafts arcades to the aisles and transepts. Open timber roof. Restored within a completely new exterior shell by *Stainburn Taylor Architects*, 2005, with the original structure supported on a steel skeleton frame. Encapsulation ingeniously solved serious structural problems while preserving the rewarding interior intact. – SCREEN with integral pulpit and reading desk, 1911, in memory of Sir Alfred Hickman, the founder of the colliery.

The SCHOOL, N of the church, 1897. Low, brick with later rendering. Symmetrical front, retaining separate entrances for boys and girls.

In the village, a few miners' cottages of the 1890s. The HAUNCH-WOOD SOCIAL CLUB (formerly the Miners' Institute) in Valley Road is the only significant colliery building to survive. Loosely Arts and Crafts, *c.* 1914.

GAYDON

ST GILES. 1852–3 by *D. G. Squirhill* of Leamington, retaining the N doorway from the previous chapel. Toffee-coloured ironstone. Simple Dec style. Provincially competent if rather ignorant for its date. NW tower with octagonal top and spire. Inside, a passage behind the reading desk giving access from N aisle and chancel. – FITTINGS, mostly 1852–3. – STAINED GLASS. E window, *Lavers, Barraud & Westlake*, 1879. – S window by *F. Holt & Co.* (designed by *William Wheildon* whose parents it commemorates), 1894. – Another, *William Aikman*, 1923.

In Church Road, the rustic 1886 VILLAGE HALL (originally thatched) faced with split-log poles, ornamentally arranged. Nearby, thatched and Lias OLD BAKEHOUSE dated 1714, and a brick house opposite dated 1773 with pretty doorcase. E of the church, the OLD HOUSE dated 1665 and POPLARS FARM, late C17 in Lias with ironstone dressings and recessed centre. On Banbury Road, a group of substantial cottages built on the Bolton King (Chadshunt) estate, 1884–5. Off the Warwick Road, the rather cheerless OLD VICARAGE by *Ewan Christian*, 1880–1.

(On the wartime airfield site 1 m. NW, a concentration of buildings of the British motor industry at the JAGUAR LAND ROVER GAYDON CENTRE, late 1970s onwards. Also ASTON MARTIN, whose stone-fronted HEADQUARTERS, 2001–3, and DESIGN CENTRE, 2008, are by the *Weedon Partnership*.) At the SE of the site, the circular Art Deco-style HERITAGE MOTOR CENTRE by *Temple Cox Nicholls*, 1992–3, enhanced with new mezzanine gallery by *Metz Architects* of Leicester, 2006–7.

(Also at Gaydon, the MASTER FILM STORE by *Edward Cullinan* for the British Film Institute, 2010–11: a sustainable and high-tech storage facility for the national archive of volatile nitrate films and acetate reels. A sleek design with concrete fins, stainless steel cladding and angled sedum roof.)

GRANDBOROUGH

ST PETER. The church is of red sandstone, the W tower of grey ashlar. The church is mostly Dec – see the S doorway and windows, the chancel windows, the N windows, the N and S arcades (four bays, standard elements). Only the exceptionally fine steeple is Perp. The bell-openings are twins with transom and blank tracery below. The spire is recessed behind battlements, once with pinnacles. Chancel restored 1849. Nave and aisles re-roofed and clerestory added by *G. R. Clarke*, 1862–3. Wooden vaulting in tower, probably 1868 after the tower arch was opened out. – COMMUNION RAIL. C18. – Caen stone REREDOS, 1849. – Brass CORONA in chancel, *c.* 1863. – MONUMENTS. Gothic Watson memorials in chancel, early to mid-C19.

PRIMITIVE METHODIST CHAPEL, 1856.

In the village, the former SCHOOL, 1840. Chequered brickwork and wide-arched windows. Old VICARAGE, E of the church. 1844, for the Rev. W.J. Wise. Jacobean-style with shaped gables. Further N, the three-storey WATERMILL, converted as a house by *Willard Son & Ellingham*, 1931.

At Woolscott, ½ m. NNE, impressively timber-framed C16 HARROW HOUSE. To the W, CASTLE FARM with C16 range of banded stone, and another later C17 range with quoins.

GREAT ALNE

ST MARY MAGDALENE. A humble church of nave, N aisle, and chancel, with a polygonal W porch turret. Lias with limestone dressings. There is medieval masonry preserved – see one lancet and the priest's doorway in the chancel and one C15 window in the nave N wall. The brick vestry, N of the chancel, was added as a Sunday School in 1835 and extended in 1996. Church enlarged in 1837 by *William Walker* of Stratford. His the turret with lion heads on the string course below the octagonal belfry stage, the W end of the nave and the W gallery inside. N aisle and improvements to chancel arch and E wall by *Butterfield*, 1860. The diarist the Rev. Richard Seymour was largely responsible for the C19 improvements. – Of *Butterfield*'s chancel fittings only the carved oak ALTAR RAILS remain. – STAINED GLASS. E window by *Hardman*, 1860. – Good N aisle E window, *Yoxall & Whitford*, 1968.

A linear village. At the E end, a LODGE to the demolished hall (*G. H. Hunt* for Daniel Ratcliff, 1878). *Hunt*'s WEST LODGE, Old English style, also survives in Park Lane, and on the corner of Mill Lane there are ESTATE COTTAGES in similar style, *c.* 1880. The hall site (again under redevelopment 2014) was taken over by the Maudslay Motor Co. in 1941.

Near Mill Lane, C17 WOODBINE COTTAGE has square panel framing. To the S, the former MILL with cowled top to the raised section. In use until 1966 but converted to balconied apartments, 1989. Back to the street, ALNE HOUSE at the corner of Park Lane is of mottled brick with an Italianate feel, *c.* 1840. Down the lane are white-painted STUART COTTAGE with Gothick details and the *c.* 1900 stables and clock tower of YEW TREE FARM, converted to housing, 1980.

Towards the church, THE LODGE, *c.* 1800 has Gothick details and light trellis porch. Off the road W of the church, C17 MANOR HOUSE with later additions including, again, Gothick windows. Then the former STATION, by *William Clarke*, 1876. The line closed in 1944 but the main building still preserves its platform and awnings. Opposite, the VILLAGE HALL by *W. Norman Twist*, 1921, originally thatched. Former SCHOOL and teacher's house by *J. B. Harper* of Henley, 1840. Italianate, with a further classroom on the E, 1870.

GREAT PACKINGTON

ST JAMES.* If one were to name the most important and the most impressive English church of the ending C18, Great Packington would be the first to come to mind. It is a leading monument of the Neoclassical revival and one of European importance. It was built on the site of the medieval church by Heneage, 4th Earl of Aylesford, in 1789–92. Eclectic and international in style, it was once thought a remarkable work by *Joseph Bonomi* alone. Now, however, it is understood to be the result of a creative partnership between patron and architect in which Aylesford himself is due more than a little of the credit. Both men were fascinated by classical antiquities, both had travelled and sketched in Italy, and Aylesford had been tutored by Bonomi in architecture and perspective. It may have been the prospect of work at Packington that lured Bonomi back from Italy in 1784. He was at work in the Hall (*see* below) later that year and his drawings for the church were exhibited at the Royal Academy in 1787–9. Aylesford had the willing agreement of his tenantry and was ready to build in the spring of 1787, but an objector – anxious to safeguard the resting place of his parents under the E wall of the new church – caused delays in construction. Thus 1787 the design, 1789–92 its realization. One wonders what the contemporary reaction was to such an uncompromising building. It certainly implies a ruthless take-it-or-leave-it attitude on the part of the patron and his architect.

So why its importance? Simply that it is utterly distinctive and earlier than anything comparable, for here we see the first internal use of Doric forms in English architecture and the then wholly novel use of Greek columns with arches. As Marcus Binney has shown, the inspiration came direct from Italy – from Rome and Paestum. He also argued that Aylesford contributed the architectural elements, especially the Greek

---

*Since formal redundancy in 1994, the church has become a private chapel of the Aylesford family.

orders which particularly interested him, leaving Bonomi to turn it – with great skill – into a cogent and practical design.

Standing alone in the great park, the exterior is starkly forbidding – its solid squareness, the featureless brick walls, the very large Diocletian windows rising into big broken pediments, and the four short corner towers. This arrangement of towers is that of Archer's St John Smith Square, which Bonomi must have known. In their lower stages they each have two small lunettes, one above the other. Only the tower tops are of stone. They carry shallow lead domes with ball finials and weathervanes. The entrance – the doors with strong cast-iron plates – is on the W, but otherwise the external elevations are all similar, though the E wall has a blind arch in place of the lunettes on the other sides. In the NE corner, an added vestry (octagonal inside) projects uncomfortably and there are steps leading to the crypt.

After the rudely utilitarian, completely and totally unornamented exterior, the interior is overwhelming. It is all painted to resemble smooth ashlar stone, walls as well as vaults. It is on the cross-in-square plan, with square centre, four short arms, and four lower corner rooms. That is a Byzantine scheme, but one which, via Venice and Holland, Sir Christopher Wren picked up. So Bonomi could have known it from Wren's St Anne and St Agnes in London. But, as Peter Meadows has noted, the inspiration may have been just such a church in Naples that Bonomi had sketched in 1784. The centre vault and the corner vaults are groined, and the arms tunnel-vaulted between broad, entirely unmoulded transverse arches. But set in the corners of the centre, as if to carry the vault, are four rose-coloured sandstone columns, and they are of the Greek Doric order, excessively sturdy, with an exaggerated entasis and weighed down by a piece of triglyph frieze. The centrepiece was originally a large marble font, its footprint still visible in the paving. This was swept away when the church was refurnished in a more conventional English style in the C19. – ALTARPIECE. The painting of the IHS sign in clouds, worshipped by angels, is by *Jean François Rigaud* (*see* below, Packington Hall). It and the marble columns and pediment look straight out of an Italian church. – The COMMUNION RAIL of marble. – PULPIT, five sides of a hexagon, in coloured marble with narrow strips of mosaic in the angles between the panels. – The READING DESK similar. These marble fittings might be original. All seem to be of one period, but the church accounts refer to a 'new pulpit' in 1876. – The ORGAN, built in 1750 by *Thomas Parker* (working for *Richard Bridge*) for Charles Jennens of Gopsall (Leics.) to a specification provided by G.F. Handel in 1749. Jennens was Handel's librettist and the cousin of the 3rd Earl of Aylesford, to whom he left the instrument at his death in 1773. – MONUMENT. Recumbent plaster images of husband and wife with beasts at their feet, from a monument to two generations of the Fisher family. The elaborate canopy and one pair of effigies are lost. Identification

73

uncertain, but Elizabethan in style and probably John Fisher
(†1570) and wife Mary rather than Sir Clement (†1619) and
Katherine.

PACKINGTON OLD HALL. Built for Sir Clement Fisher in 1679–
80. It was apparently just a farmhouse, and not the main residence of the Fishers. Brick, and in the Artisan Mannerist style.
The front is of two storeys plus dormers, and the three-storeyed
porch is not quite in the middle. The dormers have gables, the
porch a segmental pediment, and whereas otherwise angles are
strengthened by raised brick quoins, the second floor of the
porch has angle pilasters (with sunk panels) and capitals. All
such irregularities are very engaging and partly attributable to
alterations of c. 1700 to the front elevation. The windows have
wooden crosses, the storeys are separated by heavily moulded
brick courses, and the garden wall has oval stone peepholes, placed horizontally. These are motifs as characteristic of
c. 1670–80 as are the heavily twisted balusters of the staircase
and the plasterwork on the first floor. The large room above
the hall has only a garland frieze (dated 1680), but the small
room above the porch has a wreath tied together with a big
ribbon.

Behind the house an oblong brick late C17 DOVECOTE
with well over 1,000 nesting places. To the NW, the two-
storey VENISON HOUSE (now a garage), late C18 with blocked
round-headed openings to each side wall and a low-pitch slate
roof.

PACKINGTON HALL. Approached from the E through open
parkland made especially private by the diversion of the road
away from the park in the C18. Built initially in 1693 by Sir
Clement Fisher, a nephew of the other Sir Clement, it was
enlarged and completely re-cased for the 3rd Earl of Aylesford
in 1766–72. *Matthew Brettingham* the elder was the architect,
assisted by *Henry Couchman* who took over following Brettingham's death in 1769. *Couchman* and afterwards *Joseph
Bonomi* and *Jean François Rigaud* did the interiors for the 4th
Earl, who succeeded to the title in 1777. *Bonomi*'s first schemes
were prepared in 1782 and executed, mainly by *Rigaud* who
died at Packington in 1810, over a period of almost twenty
years. The house suffered a serious fire in 1979, the subsequent
restoration being carried out by *Rodney Melville & Partners*
who have also overseen the reinstatement of some of the C18
interiors.

The house is of stone, nine by five bays in size and two and
a half storeys high. The E FRONT (entrance) side is staid and
well-mannered. The ground floor is rusticated. The three-bay
centre has upper giant pilasters and a pediment. That is about
all, except for the portal with two square Ionic pillars and two
Ionic columns. The W SIDE is a little more eventful. Here the
centre has attached giant unfluted Ionic columns, a pair, then
two singles, then again a pair. Originally they were free-
standing, i.e. until 1828 there was an open loggia behind them.
The main windows of the angle bays are a little stressed, and

64

above each is a blank panel with a garland. The first-floor windows are balustraded.

The ENTRANCE HALL on the E is T-shaped, with a narrower back part behind two Roman Doric columns. Here elements of *Brettingham*'s original scheme remain and the decoration is mainly by *Couchman*, 1778. The TAPESTRY ROOM to the l. has an Adamish ceiling. It is the link to the POMPEIAN ROOM, the showpiece of the house, designed by *Bonomi* after 1782 to house the 4th Earl's collection of Greek vases. To this room belonged a set of klismos chairs, designed by *Bonomi* too and earlier than anything of the kind popularized by Thomas Hope after 1800. The carved chimneypiece is by *Bonomi*. The painting on the walls and ceilings by *Rigaud* is derived from a book on the decoration of the Baths of Titus in Rome published by Nicolas Ponce in 1786. *Benedetto Pastorini* (painter of the wall compartments), *Domenico Bartoli* (scagliola), *Giovanni Borgnis* (gilder) and *Joseph Rose* (plasterer) were also at work here in 1785–8. It is the most complete Pompeian scheme in England, and much more serious in character than any Adam work in the Etruscan taste. The room fills the whole S front and is tripartite, being divided with Corinthian columns. In the two ends there were originally bookcases, the Pompeian-style painting on a black ground being convincingly extended when they were removed *c.* 1970. Behind this room is the main STAIRCASE, with a very modest cast-iron handrail and a glazed circular lantern in a squared setting. Simple in form yet pleasing, with plasterwork and doorcases all by *Bonomi* (his drawings are in the Pierpont Morgan Library). The MUSIC ROOM (or Saloon) in the W wing is to a scheme by *Bonomi* but was never painted. The ceiling is very fresh and pretty with its flower garland and medallions. The plasterwork on the walls has musical details. The organ now at the church was once in this room. Painted panels of Packington scenes on canvas now fill the roundels, by *Marcus May*, 2000. The office to the N (once the LITTLE DINING ROOM) has another Adamish ceiling. In the LIBRARY the ceiling has *Rigaud*'s last painting, *c.* 1810. The bookcases were designed by *Henry Hakewill* in 1828. *Hakewill* also did a top-lit BILLIARD ROOM on the first floor, destroyed in the 1979 fire. Lastly in the DINING ROOM, a ceiling with classical figures in panels separated by floral scrolls, again by *Bonomi* and *Rigaud*.

The former STABLES (now offices) lie some little distance N of the house, arranged around a quadrangle. They are more monumental if smaller than the house, having a heavy loggia of Tuscan pillars and columns with a pediment and at the corners the low towers with pyramid roofs so much favoured by the English Palladians. Here can be seen the influence (cf. Hagley and Croome in Worcs.) of *Sanderson Miller*, who advised the future 3rd Earl in 1749, and also of *Brown*, who landscaped the grounds in 1751–2. Attributed and dated variously in the past, the stables are now known to be by *William & David Hiorne* of Warwick, 1756–8.

GROUNDS. Immediately around the house, the S and W terraces were laid out by *Hakewill* for the 5th Earl in 1812. To the SE and N near the stables are GATEPIERS with vermiculated rustication and Adamish tops. A Victorian range by *William Burn* (1862) with conservatory and aviary between the house and the stables was demolished apart from the low side entrance on the N. Beyond the hall, the landscaping we see now is essentially as shown in *Brown*'s 1751 plan, with the winding lake S and W of the house, the distant trees and a stone bridge on the main drive. Before this, Packington had been known and admired for its fine gardens, canals, vistas and 'places of delight' – the C17 creation of the Fishers, largely swept away by *Brown* for the 3rd Earl. The GREAT POOL is a survivor of the earlier scheme, albeit altered by Brown who added a cascade. On the edge of the PARK there are LODGES at the main entrances. The best is late C18 BEECH LODGE to the SE on the old approach road from Meriden, with facing building opposite. Both are square with slate pyramid roofs and pedimented elevations.

GREAT WOLFORD

ST MICHAEL. Replacing a medieval church on the same site. By *James Trubshaw*, the builder of Weston House, 1832–5. Ashlar, broad and aisleless, with a W steeple and recessed spire. The sides with tall C13-style two-light windows and narrowly placed buttresses typical of the date. The short chancel was never lengthened. The E end has big octagonal pinnacles and a Perp-style E window of four lights. Interior with shallow-pitched and panelled roof, the trusses having braces with carved spandrels. Interior, originally with W gallery, reordered by *J. E. K. Cutts*, 1885. His the choir stalls enclosed by a low wooden screen, nave pews and pulpit. – STAINED GLASS. The E window, with large single figures of the Evangelists, by *P. G. Heinersdorf & Co.* of Berlin, 1886. Faded and discoloured. – MONUMENTS in chancel and at W end of nave to Ingrams, from the old church. C17 and C18.

On the green, the old SCHOOL, 1821, enlarged and part rebuilt 1874; stone with square-headed windows and thin tall bellcote. Also mid-C19 ESTATE COTTAGES for Lord Redesdale (Batsford estate), stone with diamond quarry windows. Former RECTORY, SW, a plain two-storey house of three bays by *James Hastings* of Enstone, 1824–5; altered.

GRENDON

ALL SAINTS. A rich and rewarding church, although more for its furnishings than for the building itself. Impressive and stately W tower of 1845–6, by *John Sinclair* of Hartshill, the resident engineer to the Coventry Canal Co. It is indeed an engineer's job, built in blue brick faced with ashlar and with a jack-arched ceiling to the ground-floor vestry. In character, it is still pre-archaeological and the flatness of the Perp tracery is ignorant. It replaces an older tower that escaped rebuilding when the church was done over by *Joseph Potter* for Sir George Chetwynd of Grendon Hall in 1824–5. *Potter*'s the tracery of some S windows and the present plaster nave roof with moulded ribs and foliage bosses. Slightly earlier the stuccoed S porch dated 1820. The church itself is long and low. The nave follows the C12 outline but all the details are later. The N aisle has a C13 doorway, and the arcade, of standard elements, but with nailhead decoration, may well be late C13 too. The S aisle is Dec, with a finely moulded doorway and much renewed windows. The buttresses have a little decoration. The S arcade is Dec and in good condition. Three bays. Quatrefoil piers with fillets, arches with two sunk quadrants. The chancel arch is the same, although the chancel is clearly C13, as the N lancets and the remains of the S lancets show. Later alterations include geometrical tracery of 1863 in the E window and the arch between chancel and the Chetwynd pew at the E end of the S aisle – a quite inventive Victorian connexion – of 1864.

– FONT. C15, octagonal. – Also in the S aisle, an C18 font with oval basin. – PULPIT with Jacobean carved panels. The mahogany base made of timber from the old chancel screen removed in 1863. – SCREENS. In the S aisle, enclosing the private pew, a screen of c. 1680 with arches on square pillars and putto heads in the spandrels. Achievement and two hovering angels at the top. – Under the organ gallery at the back of the nave, a complete box pew with back, sides, front and roof. The front and sides have pretty, scrolly openwork volutes. On the front is the inscription 'Richard Drakeford / Stephen Winkle / Churchwardens / Anno Domini 1618'. This came from St Mary, Stafford, where it is said to have been the mayor's pew. – REREDOS. Elaborate carving of Christ blessing, two cherubs' heads and decoration of c. 1740, probably from the top of a reredos. – COMMUNION RAIL. Late C17, with twisted balusters, the main posts decorated with small figures and at the top a frieze of cherubs' heads. – STAINED GLASS. In the S aisle E window of the family pew, glass with Chetwynd heraldry, by *Joseph Hale Miller*, c. 1825. Also from *Miller*'s collection the Risen Christ in later glass in the W window of same aisle. – Others by *Clayton & Bell*, the E window, 1863, and N chancel window, 1870. – N aisle E by *Francis H. Spear*, 1946, and W by *F. S. Trickett*, 1947. – MONUMENTS. Alabaster effigy of a lady, mid-C15 – see the headdress. Nearly all the others of Chetwynds. Margaret †1539, incised slab with a babe in swaddling clothes by her side. She looks just like a playing-card. – Panel of figures and black-letter inscription to John †1592 and second wife, Margery (Middlemore), †1602 with stunted balusters and shields below. It came from Ingestre, Staffs., and seems to have been part of a bigger monument with a tomb-chest. By *Garrat Hollemans* of

Burton upon Trent. – Several from the second half of the C17. John Chetwynd †1652. Tablet. Attributed to *Edward Marshall* (GF). – Two memorials of the 1670s attributed to *Joshua Marshall*: architectural tablet to Frances Chetwynd †1673, and cartouche of 1676 to Sir William Chetwynd †1612. – Lady Dixey †1686. Architectural tablet in the style of *Joshua Marshall*. – Two fine memorials of the 1690s attributed to *Edward Pearce* (GF): William Chetwynd †1691 (garlanded drapery on a tablet); Walter Chetwynd †1653 (cartouche). – Mary †1750. In a recess. Standing, life-size figure crying by an urn. By *Sir Robert Taylor*. – Nicholas Penny †1745 and wife Frances, handsome, late C18 tablet. – Sir George †1850. An interesting case of strapwork revival.

The former RECTORY, alongside the church, rebuilt by *Robert Jennings*, 1852. Victorian Tudor-style in brick with stone dressings.

Over the River Anker S of the church, GRENDON BRIDGE of 1825 by *Joseph Potter*. Nearby CROFT HOUSE of 1781 above the site of an old mill. Original front of three bays, the centre gable with pediment and lunette window. Early C19 Tuscan porch.

Near the canal at Bradley Green, 1 m. SE, the old SCHOOL built for the Chetwynds in 1871 and enlarged by *R. Scrivener & Sons* in 1904. Gothic with matching extensions, 1996.

Of GRENDON HALL, an early C17 courtyard house massively enlarged in the Jacobean style by *Joseph Potter* for Sir George Chetwynd in 1825–6, only a corner of stuccoed brickwork with octagonal pinnacles remains. It was demolished in 1933. Some of the C18 outbuildings, now converted to dwellings, survive, along with a gabled NORTH LODGE of 1878 (1 m. NW near a canal bridge). In the park between hall and lodge, the old BRIDGE over the River Anker. C15 with four chamfered arches and cutwaters.

The parish extends S, with the main settlement along Watling Street and towards Grendon Common. Few buildings of note. The METHODIST CHURCH, mid-C19 with round-headed cast-iron windows, extended in 1885 and altered in 1905. On the N side of Watling Street towards Tamworth is SWAN FARM, built for the Chetwynds in 1853.

GUY'S CLIFFE

Guy's Cliffe house in its ruinous state and the neglected, almost tropical growth of vegetation around make a picture moving, exciting, and at the same time sordid. Much as we may like that, it ought to be said all the same that the house should never have been allowed to fall into decay like this, and a fire in the ruins in 1992 has caused further damage. Nevertheless, the walls have been stabilized, some buildings are in use and the whole site is under active guardianship. Although the house still looks crowded by trees from a distance, the vegetation close to is controlled.

The earliest primary source relating to Guy's Cliffe is a royal writ of 1334 referring to a hermitage at Gybeclyve. However, the C15 historian John Rous (†1491) served as a chantry priest here and his writings tell us of a hermitage in 1153 and of Guy of Warwick, a legendary chivalric hero and saintly hermit who lived in the C10. Guy ended his days in a cave here; so the story goes. By the late C12 the legend of Guy of Warwick was extremely popular. His Christian ideals were exemplary. His deeds as a knight in the service of Christ were remarkable. It is needless to distinguish between fact and fiction in either the legend or in Rous's account of Guy's Cliffe. Their importance lies in what they tell us of medieval traditions, all rolled up with the ideals of chivalry and the aspirations of the Beauchamp family of Warwick Castle. From the C13 the Beauchamps promoted the legend and adopted its hero, Guy, as their forebear. It strengthened their family status. The 10th Earl of Warwick, born c. 1272, was named Guy, and we have the late C14 Guy's Tower at Warwick Castle. Thus Richard Beauchamp endowed a chantry here in 1422–3, and thus much of the history as told by Rous.

The caves are much of the story but there were buildings too, certainly by the C14. As we shall see, the chapel is partly C15, and under the will of the 13th Earl (†1439) an existing house here was rebuilt. Under King Henry VIII, the property passed to Sir Andrew Flammock in 1546–7 and became a house. This was illustrated by Hollar for Dugdale in the mid C17. A small house in the position of the W front was built for William Edwards, a Kenilworth surgeon, in the opening decades of the C18. Then in 1751 Samuel Greatheed bought the estate and added a new E wing in the Palladian style behind the Edwards house. The whole house was reworked in stages between 1813 and 1824 by Bertie Greatheed, who was his own architect, followed by further embellishment by *John Gibson* in 1871–2. A sturdy tower extension was built in 1898 by a young Newcastle architect *Guy Wilfred Hayler*, doubtless through an Alnwick connection, as Lord Algernon Percy had inherited Guy's Cliffe in 1891. Decline set in after Percy's death in 1933. After the Second World War a sequence of events led to the abandonment of the house and its eventual decay.

The HOUSE faced W, the main front originally visible from the Coventry Road down a long tree-lined avenue. To the river on the E it presented a massive and varied aspect, raised on its cliff after the manner of Warwick. The courtyard is on the S, with the chapel at the far end. The S face of the Palladian house is still discernible, the doorway approached up a double flight of stairs above a doorway leading into a vaulted undercroft. This side was of seven bays with pediments over the projecting first and last bays, a rusticated basement, and two storeys. Doorcase, originally pedimented, with unfluted Ionic columns.

On the corner, the polygonal block dated 1898. The W front is an early C19 addition to the Edwards house. Surprisingly, illustrations show that this front with its Tudor parapets and shaped gables really was of 1819, although Gibson may have improved the details later. In the same Tudor style was the front to the river, 1815–17, a thickening of the Palladian house. It has a bold splay-footed tower on the r., arches in the base and a large oriel above. To the l., polygonal projections, shaped gables, strapwork parapets and another oriel, mostly original but with some details clearly by Gibson again. Behind and rising above the roof-line was what looked almost like a keep, solid-looking with square corner towers, but entirely a sham, 1814. To the E of the main house, Bertie Greatheed created a new KITCHEN with three big Tudor chimneys towards the river and five stepped lancets to the courtyard. The lancets are round-headed but cusped, separated by thin rolled shafts and under a hoodmould. This is not a ruin.

Linked to the kitchen is the CHAPEL OF ST MARY MAGDALENE, also in use. Parts of the fabric are C14 (cf. two blocked windows), but much of it dates from 1454–5 when two new altars were consecrated. The external appearance is largely later C18 with Y-traceried windows, quatrefoils and Gothick parapets. Front of five irregular bays. In the centre a projecting tower partially rebuilt by Samuel Greatheed, 1764. The date and style suggest *Timothy Lightoler* as the architect. The lower stage of the tower is the porch with a later C15 fan-vault. Parts of the outer bays C15 too. Inside, the chapel is two-naved, divided by a two-bay arcade of 1454–5 with continuous mould-ings. Plaster tierceron vault, probably of 1802 when Bertie Greatheed repaired the chapel.* The end bays on each side have parallel four-centred ribs. The chapel was restored in 1875 (by *Gibson*) and again in 1933. Further restoration since the building was taken over for Masonic use in 1974. Undercroft below, and a large chamber in the roof-space above. – STAINED GLASS. Mostly by *Three Spires Glass Co.* of Coventry, 1987, but incorporating surviving bits of the windows installed by *Holland & Holt*, 1875. – Prominently placed, hewn out of the live rock, a STATUE of Guy, over 8 ft (2.4 metres) high. The style is that of the 1330s and in 1395 a carver was paid to cut the ancient arms of the Earls of Warwick on it. He wears chain-mail and knee plates and carries his shield. It must once have looked very thrilling in here. – C15 DOOR from Wellesbourne church formerly in the chapel is still in store on site.

CHAMBERS are carved in the rock all along the S and E sides of the courtyard, some medieval, others later. At the E end, the STABLES, vaulted inside. Facing the Palladian house, a row of eight barrel-vaulted chambers with round-headed openings to the courtyard. The shape and proportions of these openings suggest a mid-C18 date. More at river level, including GUY'S

*The date 1813–24 is sometimes quoted, but the work at that time seems to have been on the house rather than on the chapel.

CAVE, which once had an inscription 'in Saxon characters' found in the early C19.* This is where Guy is supposed to have died. HARRIS'S CAVE, 50 yds E of the chapel, was created in the C18. It has four small alcoves dug into the rock each side of a central aisle, with two more at the far end. The bays are separated by rock-hewn monolithic pillars. Along the under-cliff W of the house is GUY'S WELL.

One leaves the courtyard through a jolly GATEWAY, rusticated with a fanciful concave-sided top and side openings topped by urns. Probably mid-C18. On the Coventry Road, a plain stone LODGE dated 1831. Boundary wall and gatepiers by *Gibson*, 1872.

SAXON MILL, Coventry Road. A picturesque spot with the mill, a wooden footbridge over the River Avon and views down-stream towards the ruined house. The MILL is stone and has one iron waterwheel still in place. Along the side, a pretty wooden balcony under overhanging eaves, first added by Bertie Greatheed in 1812 and since extended. Towards the road, early C18 stone ashlar MILLER'S HOUSE and former warehouse, partly timber-framed. The mill buildings became a restaurant in 1952.

GAVESTON'S CROSS, ¼ m. N. On Blacklow Hill beyond the Warwick by-pass, without a path. Erected by Bertie Greatheed *c.* 1822–5 to mark the site of the execution of Piers Gaveston, favourite of King Edward II, in 1312. Heavy short cross on a high pedestal of four mighty square piers. The inscription is not complimentary to poor Piers, nor to his king: 'The minion of a hateful king, in life and death a memorable instance of misrule.'†

HALFORD

2040

ST MARY. The church possesses a Norman tympanum (in the N doorway) which is the best piece of Norman sculpture in the county. It represents an angel, seated frontally but only visible to the knees, and holding a scroll with a later painted inscrip-tion. The composition with spread wings, scroll, and fluttering drapery is absolutely symmetrical. The figure is slender, the head small but strong, the knees come out l. and r. Deborah Kahn‡ has suggested that the sculptor of the angel was prob-ably aware of Anglo-Saxon manuscripts. She also notes a

*This is no longer decipherable, but it can only have been part of the medieval fiction.
†The inscription was composed by Dr Samuel Parr, *c.* 1822. Tim Mowl has pub-lished evidence that the cross existed by 1825, so it cannot be by *J. G. Jackson*, 1832, as previously suggested on the evidence of his signed and dated drawing.
‡Deborah Kahn, 'The Romanesque Sculpture of the Church of St Mary at Halford', in *Journal of the British Archaeological Association* 133 (1980).

similar carved angel at Worcester Cathedral. On the r. capital of this doorway, an intricately carved bearded figure in a tunic. The arch mouldings resemble the N door at Whatcote. A simple Norman doorway also in the nave S wall. Inside the church is a Norman chancel arch. The abaci of the responds are continued as a frieze. One side (r.) has flat diamonds on edge over a cable, the other (l.) has flat sawtooth carving. To the r. of the arch, fairly high up, a blind niche with shafts was discovered in 1960 when the plaster was removed. In it, in relief, was a Norman figure in profile, alas much defaced. There was another niche to the l. The figures were probably the Virgin and St John the Evangelist, and they would have corresponded to a rood. The tower stands to the SW and is of the C13, with lancets. The arch to the E is of two continuous chamfers and not centrally placed. Above it but central a former E window. To its E a S aisle almost entirely Victorian. In fact the whole church was fiercely restored by *Poulton & Woodman* in 1862. The chancel received its big leaf corbels carved by *James Ansell* of Leamington in 1879. Of original details remained the curious late C13 three-light N window in the nave, of red sandstone and of three lancet lights. Of about the same date the S aisle E window. But the arcade of the aisle is all rebuilt. – FONT. Octagonal, with flat tracery panels. The pretty FONT COVER is probably early C16 work. Its top knob is five bishops' heads. – STAINED GLASS. E window by *F. Holt & Co.*, 1906. – CURIOSUM. Two fire-hooks to pull down burning thatch.

OLD MANOR HOUSE, N of the church, C17, irregular. One part has a timber-framed upper storey with narrowly placed uprights. Some alterations by *Charles M.C. Armstrong*, 1909.

Immediately E of the church, the OLD RECTORY, 1763. A big square house, stone and very plain. E again, a little green with early C19 HALFORD HOUSE, stuccoed with an iron balcony to the canted bay over the porch. Opposite, chequer brick C18 RESTWAYS. Many stone houses nearby, White Lias, with mullioned windows.

The village lies mainly W of the Fosse, but has roadside buildings on the E and C20 developments off Idlicote Road. On a bank above the Stour S of Idlicote Road is THE FOLLY, a curious three-storeyed Georgian house of grey stone, *c.* 1790. It consists of two octagons placed side by side so that the S front is simply a pair of canted bays. In one of the octagons the drawing room, in the other a room and the staircase. To the N an ashlar addition, also Georgian.

Towards the S, THE HALFORD (previously the Bell, later the Bridge Inn). An C18 stone inn, with carriage arch. The old road descends steeply to the medieval BRIDGE over the Stour. Much repaired, but still with separate narrow pointed arches and stone parapet. The causeway was redesigned by *John Nichol*, County Surveyor, 1832. Alongside, at a higher level, the replacement bridge, 1962, faced in Cotswold stone.

HETHERINGTON HOUSE, ¾ m. E. A large farmhouse in the
Palladian style by *Trevor Edwards* and *William Hawkes*, 1987.
Interior with top-lit stairway.

HAMPTON-IN-ARDEN

2080

Once a large Arden Forest parish that included Knowle, Barston,
Balsall and Nuthurst (Hockley Heath), all now separate. Hampton
was much improved in the second half of the C19 by Sir Frederick
Peel (a younger son of former Prime Minister Sir Robert Peel),
who lived at Hampton Manor from 1855 until his death in 1906.
The village grew in importance after the coming of the London
to Birmingham Railway in 1837 and became very well-to-do in
the later C20. The M42 motorway runs through the parish and
those parts to the W (including Catherine-de-Barnes) are covered
in the *Birmingham and Black Country* volume in this series.

ST MARY AND ST BARTHOLOMEW. The chancel is Norman and
c. 1130, as is shown by the buttresses, three plain round-
headed windows, and the simple N doorway (now inside the
extension) with a tympanum with up-curved base and a cross
incised in it but interfered with by the shape of the base. The
attractive embattled two-storey organ chamber next to it is by
W. Eden Nesfield (*see* below), who restored the church in 1878.
Added link and vestry extension by *W. B. R. Ellender*, 2003.
Perp W tower with stair-turret to middle stage turning round
halfway up. The tower had a spire which fell in 1643. The
embattled clerestory with short twin square-headed windows
probably post-Reformation, the earlier roof-line being visible
on the E face of the tower and in the colour of the stonework
over the chancel arch. The interior tells a different story. The
S arcade of four bays is Norman. The piers are round and may
have been heightened. The abaci are square, the arches with
two slight chamfers pointed. The E respond has waterleaf (i.e.
c. 1170–80) next to inverted scallop-shell palmettes. The
middle capital is different from the others and has had later
heads cut into it. This was probably done when the N arcade
was made, which has round piers and round abaci and normal
double-chamfered arches. One capital (again the middle one)
is surrounded by a ring of crockets; the E respond has curiously
intertwined stiff-leaf. The capitals to the chancel arch have
both crockets and heads. All this looks *c.* 1230–40. Stone
bench seats in the aisles. Fine open timber roof in the chancel,
by *Nesfield*, 1878. E end of S aisle furnished as All Souls chapel,
with stone altar, by *Lawrence King*, 1967–8. – SCREEN and
PULPIT by *Arthur G. Wallace*, 1910. – ORGAN CASE with
carved figures and balustrading, 1884. – TILES. In the chancel
floor, medieval. – STAINED GLASS. Three in chancel by *Powell*:

the E window (*J. W. Brown*) with 'All thy works praise thee' in the form of a Tree of Jesse, 1904, and two side windows, 1905. – Three by *Yoxall & Whitford*, 1952–68 in chancel and N aisle, the latter with an excellent Crucifixion against a background of Coventry in flames with Epstein's St Michael alongside. – E window to S aisle chapel, *John Hayward*, 1968. – Porch window, *H. J. Hobbs & Son*, 1990. – MONUMENTS. Brass to a civilian, *c.* 1500, 14½ in. (37 cm.) figure. – Memorial of a heart burial. Late C13. Demi-figure with a shield under a pointed-trefoiled arch (cf. Coberley, Glos., 1294).

In the CHURCHYARD, E of the church, the base of a CROSS, octagonal with quatrefoiled panels, C15. To the NE, LYCHGATE with shingled roof, 1950.

COPTIC ORTHODOX CHURCH (St Mary and St Anthony), Butcher Street. The former PROVIDENCE CHAPEL, 1836; Congregational until 1985. Red brick, Gothic with lancets.

HAMPTON MANOR HOUSE. By *William Giles* of Derby, 1855, for Frederick Peel (knighted in 1869). Ashlar-faced, Tudor, large and asymmetrical with a castellated skyline. Oriel window over main entrance. Inside arcaded entrance hall and open-well stair with panelling. Peel commissioned various additions in later years. Most notable, *W. Eden Nesfield*'s marvellous clock tower, 1872. An unexpected and lively contrast to the house, with its truncated pyramid roof with a real pyramid at the top and its carvings of the signs of the zodiac. The executed design evolved from Nesfield's initial sketch done in 1869. *Nesfield*'s, too, the LODGE on the High Street and MANOR COTTAGE within the grounds. Both *c.* 1870, yet pretty, intimate and dainty in a later Victorian way with sparing use of stone, tile-hanging, white-painted woodwork and delicate ironwork. Later S extension to the manor by *Bidlake*, 1892. A walled garden with neat Edwardian gateways by *Thomas H. Mawson*, pre-1908. After the Peels the manor eventually became a care home until conversion and restoration as a hotel, 2008–9.

PERAMBULATION. The village begins just W of the church where the ground slopes away towards Solihull. Here is MOAT HOUSE, the original manor, its moated site extending into the churchyard. A fine timber-framed C16 front, but behind it some C15 timbering. The rear irregular, part brick, part stone with hipped roofs. In Solihull Road S of the church and into the High Street E of the church, several timber-framed cottages including the former CHURCH FARM and RING OF BELLS pub. To the S, BELLEVIEW TERRACE, a row of Late Victorian cottages still retaining the blocks for backyard privies. A nice group of early C19 brick-fronted buildings at the junction with Marsh Lane and the WHITE LION with rendered front and C17 woodwork within. Further along the High Street, older properties gave way to Peel estate improvements, beginning with Nos. 3–11, a block of Neo-Tudor COTTAGES, 1853. Then, opposite, *Nesfield*'s delightful row of COTTAGES (Nos. 32–42) with their continuous overhang and their pargetting, built in 1868 but not in the least High Victorian. Shop at one end.

Beyond the lodge, C18 BEECH HOUSE (No. 82) set back from the road; further groups of COTTAGES (Nos. 69–75) by *Nesfield*, 1870, irregular with tile-hanging one end and a black-and-white gable the other; and Nos. 77–79 incorporating an older cottage in similar style with curved tiling over the windows. Opposite, a terrace faintly following the style with tile-hanging in an otherwise bluntly 1960s front. On the corner of Fentham Road a nice corner block, 1840s.

In the road towards the school are the FENTHAM CHARITY buildings – the SCHOOL HOUSE, 1782, and the adjoining classroom (now LIBRARY), *c.* 1820 with round-headed windows and cast-iron glazing bars. Opposite, the present SCHOOL, decent Arts and Crafts Georgian, 1914 by *Willmot, Fowler & Willmot*, with modern extensions. The rest of Fentham Road unmemorable, but on the opposite side of Marsh Lane at the S end is THE BEECHES, probably built for Louisa Simonds *c.* 1830. Neoclassical with stucco facing, slate roof and a porch with Doric fluted half-columns supporting the entablature. The Doric is picked up in the entrance of the adjoining FENTHAM HALL by *G. E. Jenkins* of Coventry, 1913–14. Back up Marsh Lane, THE NOOK is an 1880 Peel estate remodelling of an old cottage among old farm buildings, adapted in 2005 as an apartment development, CROCKETTS COURT.

In Bellemere Road, ¼ m. E, a row of imposing 1880s villas of varied sizes and styles.

Former STATION HOUSE and ticket office, Old Station Road. At the junction of the Stonebridge Railway and the main line, 1839. The present station S of the High Street replaced it in 1884 but has no remaining buildings of that date.

DIDDINGTON HALL, 1¼ m. NE. An Elizabethan brick house with a very condensed E-front, i.e. the three projecting strokes of the E so wide that there is only room for one narrow cross-window each side. Three gables and the porch gable, all with Victorian bargeboarding. Flat stone quoins. (Late C17 staircase with twisted balusters inside.) DIDDINGTON FARMHOUSE, NW of the hall, is very much its brother, though the porch is lacking.

PACKHORSE BRIDGE, on the old Kenilworth road near Bradnocks Marsh, 1½ m. SE towards Berkswell. Stone, of five arches, with the base of a cross on an E pier. C14 or C15.

HAMPTON LUCY

2050

ST PETER AD VINCULA. On a scale to impress, and quite magnificent. Especially fine from the Charlecote side where the church stands proud over the water meadows of the Avon valley. It is the *magnum opus* of *Thomas Rickman & Henry Hutchinson*, built in 1822–6 for the Rev. John Lucy who was rector from 1815 to 1874, and further improved during his lifetime, notably in 1856–8 when *Scott* added the apse. The Lucys and Hammond Lucys were the owners of Charlecote. By 1822 the £900 left in 1778 by Alice Hammond for improving the old church had grown to £9,500, so Lucy embarked on a rebuilding.* The work cost £12,000, to which Lucy contributed £1,700, but by the 1860s further works had brought his total spend to £23,400. *Rickman* seems to have been responsible for the overall design and for the detail of the tower while *Hutchinson* detailed the rest. As Michael Port has observed, it is not an imitation of any one church but has particular features resembling those of many, drawing on Rickman's encyclopaedic knowledge of medieval churches. Writing in *c.* 1840 Glynne thought it 'perhaps one of the best specimens of a modern imitation of the Curvilinear style that exists'.

A splendid skyline with ornate battlements, pinnacles, little turrets and the elaborate high-level work on the apse. Golden ashlar stone from Campden and Postlip. High w tower with elongated pinnacles. Tall two-light bell-openings. Big w doorway. Aisles with high windows and many buttresses. Some of the tracery is cast-iron, in two patterns. All is very profusely decorated, with openwork quatrefoil friezes, etc. The style is Dec throughout. The chancel originally of one short bay the same height as the nave, terminating in a big E window of seven lights. The present polygonal apse with crocketed gables and ornate carving is what *Scott* created for Lucy when he was called in to provide the High Victorian kind of chancel, completed 1856–8. Also very tall, and also highly ornate, only just that much thicker and heavier. Interior restoration followed in 1863–4 under *Scott* who also added the two-storeyed N porch, 1868.

91 Inside, high arcades of very thin members with blank panelling below the rebated clerestory windows. Nave, aisles, and chancel plaster-vaulted with diagonal and ridge ribs. The stone vaulting in the base of the tower must be by Scott, *c.* 1856, and with it the *trumeau* in the tower arch with an ogee-foiled roundel over, like a chapter house entrance. Above it, a rose window. Scott's apse has blank panelling with marble shafts and a lierne-vaulted ceiling. – The WOODWORK and furnishings are largely *Scott*'s. The CHOIR STALLS, 1858, and PULPIT, 1863, were carved by *Rattee & Kett*. The nave seating also 1863. – Stone FONT, 1863. – Brass ALTAR RAIL, choir DESKS of wrought iron and brass, eagle LECTERN and metalwork on the pulpit all by *Skidmore*. – STAINED GLASS. Apse windows rearranged in 1857–8 from the E window made by *Willement* for the original chancel, 1837, hailed at the time as 'the most magnificent window in stained glass that has been produced in modern times, in imitation of the ancient style'. Willement

---

*The Rev. John Lucy (junior) was the builder and not his father of the same name (Alice's son). The elder John laid the foundation stone in July 1822 but died in January 1823.

himself used it as the frontispiece to his book of 1840. Life of St Peter. Restored in 1951 after wartime damage. Some leftover bits by *Willement* in other windows too. – Two chancel side windows by *Hardman*, 1858–9, and another in S aisle, 1866. – One in N aisle by *Clayton & Bell*, 1875. – Interior W rose window and figures of saints in the aisles by *Heaton, Butler & Bayne*, 1860s. – MEMORIALS to Hutchinson †1831, in the churchyard and (a replacement) clergy vestry.

Churchyard RAILINGS of cast iron, *c.* 1825–30.

S of the church, the old RECTORY. *Francis Smith*, 1721–4, of smooth brickwork with raised stone quoins and keystones to the windows. Five bays, two storeys. Doorway with segmental pediment on brackets. Top balustrade around the hipped roof with dormers. The small cartouche in the centre must be C19.

To the E, AVONSIDE was the master's house for the endowed school founded in 1635. Probably also by *Smith c.* 1720; hipped roof. The SCHOOL, N of the church, is a pretty Tudor-style building, said to be 1826 but looking distinctly 1840s with wavy bargeboards and diamond-pane windows. W of the church, facing the little green by the pub, a cottage in the same Tudor style with plain READING ROOM of 1919 attached.

THE LANGLANDS, off Snitterfield Street. A group of austere brick houses by the *Architects Design Group* (Nottingham), 1975, with what Douglas Hickman called barn-like forms. They have distinctive skewed pitched roofs coming low down towards the gardens.

BRIDGE over the Avon. Cast-iron, 1829, from the *Horseley Iron Works* at Tipton, Staffordshire. Paid for again by the Rev. John Lucy. *Thomas Townshend* was the civil engineer and main contractor.

LOWER INGON FARM, 2½ m. W across the Warwick Road, is C16 and has substantial stone chimneys at each end with brick stacks. The house itself timber-framed with brick infill. Good range of early C19 brick farm buildings alongside.

HAMPTON-ON-THE-HILL   2060

ST CHARLES BORROMEO (R.C.). Built for the Dormer family of Grove Park, 1819, re-orientated and enlarged by *John Russell* in 1830. The result is a T-plan, seemingly without a proper chancel. The original part is at the E (i.e. forming the transepts), Regency Gothic with lightly Perp diamond-paned windows and the ceiling at its S end panelled as for the sanctuary. Five-light S window, probably later. The 1830 nave is traditional Perp. Big pinnacles. At the E, a shallow recess for the altar under a panelled four-centred arch, all richly decorated. Family gallery on the N. – ALTAR. Large and beautiful Late Empire piece, white marble, not at all English, perhaps made in Rome. – WALL DECORATION. Sanctuary stencilling and figurework by *T. F. Norman* of Warwick, 1890s. – STAINED GLASS. Three windows by *Hardman*, 1966.

Alongside, the PRESBYTERY, probably 1830s.

In the S end of the village, the former SCHOOL and house, 1854. On the main Henley road, the MISSION CHAPEL (now a house) by *F. H. Moore*, 1895.

GROVE PARK, 1 m. WNW of the village. A medieval park, owned by the Dormer family from 1615. By the C17 there was a sizeable house, replaced in 1833–8 by a stuccoed Neo-Tudor mansion by *C. S. Smith* of Leamington for the 11th Lord Dormer. It contained C17 chimneypieces from Kenilworth Castle and from Eythrop (Bucks.). Demolished in 1976; only the stable block and garden walls remain. The present GROVE PARK, ⅓ m. nearer the village, is by *Francis Pollen* (*Brett & Pollen*), 1962–4. Bungalow-like, with pyramid-roofed pavilions at the corners.

HARBOROUGH MAGNA

ALL SAINTS. Restored in 1868–9 by *Bateman & Corser* who created the W entrance and rebuilt the S aisle. They also refaced the Perp W tower. The rest C13 to early C14. The S windows are Victorian, but their intersecting tracery may represent original evidence. The N aisle is Dec. The N doorway has an ogee head, the E window (renewed) reticulated tracery. SE vestry and organ chamber by *T. W. Willard*, 1903. Inside the C13 begins with the chancel arch, continuing with the S arcade of two bays with standard elements. The two-bay N arcade has a quatrefoil pier, the capital with a fine ring of foliage, the abacus with very dainty wavy tracery. In the N wall an ogee-headed, crocketed tomb recess. – STAINED GLASS. E window, 1873: Christ rising and two angels against a deep blue background. Very elongated figures, tense faces. Who designed it? – W window *Hardman*, 1869. – MONUMENT. Rev. Nathaniel Blake †1712, by *Edward Stanton*.

In Main Street W, the old SCHOOL, 1845, with fish-scale tile roof. The OLD RECTORY, S of the church, may incorporate parts of the house rebuilt by Blake, *c.* 1700; the E wing by *Henry Manning*, 1868, the central section with copper pyramid roof and the W wing altered since that date. Further E, the square Late Georgian MANOR might be the house at Harborough Magna built by *Thomas Lee* for Lady Leigh, 1819.

N of the motorway, ST MARY'S NURSING HOME occupies the isolation hospital built for Rugby Joint Hospital Board, 1912. Present buildings mostly 1933–5 and later, by *H. C. Spicer*, Rugby Borough Engineer.

HARBURY

Harbury is a large village of local White Lias, limestone and marlstone. Quarrying was a major industry here, and later the manufacture of cement.

ALL SAINTS. C13 chancel with a long N lancet and a lowside S lancet. Later C13 the lower stages of the heavily buttressed SW tower – see the arches to N and E and more lancets. The embattled brick top part is Georgian, 1811. Of c. 1300 the S aisle and S arcade (standard elements). All restored and enlarged by C. E. Buckeridge, 1871–3, when the N aisle and organ chamber were added. The geometrical and bar window tracery belongs to the restoration. Through shortage of funds the architect's plans for rebuilding the top stage of the tower and adding a broach spire were not carried out. – Some of the FITTINGS a little later, e.g. PULPIT, 1877. – REREDOS, 1879. Carved stonework, marble shafts and gaudy tiled panels at the sides. – Georgian FONT, moved outside 1990. A tapering pillar. The bowl is very small and just sunk into the top. – COMMUNION RAIL, C18. – STAINED GLASS. E window and another in the chancel, 1873 and two lancets in the tower, 1878, by *Clayton & Bell*. – Two in chancel by *Powell*, 1890 and 1899. – Jubilee window, 1897.

In the churchyard, the LYCHGATE, 1910. Behind the N end of the church is the HAULEY ROOM by *Brown Langstone Matthews*, 1989.

CEMETERY, Park Lane, with simple CHAPEL, 1874. Perhaps designed by *Buckeridge*, although he died in 1873.

Former SCHOOL (now LIBRARY), by *D. G. Squirhill*, 1856. Originally diapered brick and plate tracery. Rather altered. It replaced WAGSTAFFE SCHOOL, N of the church. Founded in 1611. Stone with mullioned and mullioned-and-transomed windows. (In the schoolroom a heavy wooden screen with turned balusters along the top.)

Two principal houses, neither grand. HARBURY HOUSE off Butt Lane is C17/C18. The HALL, N of the church, is an irregular early C19 house, but with quirky stables and clock turret by *Charles M. C. Armstrong* of Warwick, 1905–6.

WINDMILL, off High Street W of the church, with adjoining mill house and outbuildings. A late C18 tower mill without sails, the lower parts stone the rest brick. Now a house.

Many stone houses in the village including two in the Bull Ring, one dated 1616 and another with an obviously later date, 1577 over a horned bull's head. More in Chapel Street, Church Street and Mill Street. Some timber framing, e.g. the SHAKESPEARE INN in Mill Street and an exposed gable-end in High Street. Part stone and part timber frame, the MANOR in Park Lane, a rather pleasing H-plan house of C16 origin. Further W in Temple End is POOL FARM with a long brick frontage and thatched roof. At the far E end of the village facing into Hall

Lane, WESTERN HOUSE, 1688, has Flemish bond red brick and stone quoins.

HARTSHILL

93   HOLY TRINITY, Church Lane. By *T. L. Walker*, designed 1842, begun 1843–5 and completed 1847–8. Neo-Norman in Hartshill stone rubble with sandstone and red and blue brick dressings. Striking w front. Deep super-Norman w portal with six orders of columns and a chamfered shouldered doorway. All the arches of moulded bricks – mainly blue. Above the portal is a wheel window with columns as spokes. Then a vesica-shaped opening below the brick bell-turret which carries a short stone spire. The side is typical of the Commissioners' churches, just long and lean round-headed windows and thin buttresses. Entrances in the first and the last, eighth, bays. Apse at the E end. Interior reordered by *Cachemaille-Day* in 1938–9 with new seating and furnishings. False ceiling 1938 too. w gallery original, with scalloped capitals to the cast-iron columns. – CREED etc., painted on metal, in stone niches in apse. – STAINED GLASS in apse, E and NE by *Hardman*, 1895 and 1907, and SE by *Jones & Willis*, 1905.

Alongside, the OLD VICARAGE. By *Robert Jennings*, 1853. Local stone, gabled with stone window transoms and mullions.

QUAKER MEETING HOUSE, Castle Road. By *Clifford Tee & Gale*, 1972. In the idiom of the time, but the meeting has direct links back to George Fox and Nathaniel Newton in the C17. On the green to the N, the previous meeting house of 1740 (now a house) with the burial ground at the rear. This was built to replace one destroyed by rioters in 1720.

UNITED REFORMED CHURCH, Coleshill Road, Chapel End. Originally Congregational. Built 1840 to replace a chapel of 1807–8, and linked Sunday School added 1853. Rendered front with round-arched windows and pedimental gable with clock, rusticated pilasters with decorated capitals and central doorway.

METHODIST CHURCH (Wesleyan), Grange Road. 1836. Stuccoed front with porch, round-headed windows and pediment.

Former METHODIST CHURCH (Wesleyan), Coleshill Road, Chapel End. 1887, in patterned brick, with apse. Terracotta window arches imported from Italy, but other decoration probably from the Nuneaton works of Reginald Stanley who largely financed the church. Now a house.

MOTTE-AND-BAILEY CASTLE, ¼ m. N of Holy Trinity. On a promontory with moats below the slopes on the E and W. Sections of the C13 curtain walls with sandstone cross-shaped loopholes remain. Traces of C13 chapel stonework also visible. In the NE corner a high brick chimney from the Elizabethan house built within the walls *c.* 1560 but demolished in the 1950s.

Below the escarpment N of the village, *James Brindley*'s COVEN-TRY CANAL, the section to Atherstone opened in 1771 and extensively used to transport stone from the Hartshill quarries. By the Atherstone Road bridge, the CANAL YARD with covered docks, stables, workshops and cottages. All late C18 and early C19, and purple brick. The main building by the road with round-arched windows, hipped roofs and clock tower is 1840. Rebuilt after a fire by *John Sinclair*, Resident Engineer to the Canal Company *c.* 1821–1863, who lived at Hartshill. To the W, CLOCK HOUSE in red brick with shallow porch and hipped roof, mid-C19 and probably the engineer's house.

In Castle Road and overlooking the castle, OLDBURY VIEW, a good block of three-storey flats, 1966–7. Further Atherstone Rural District Council flats in staggered blocks to the N in Trentham Road by *H. N. Jepson & Partners*, 1963, named DRAYTON COURT after the Elizabethan poet Michael Drayton whose birthplace once stood nearby. NE in Grange Road, THE GRANGE, a C16 house altered in 1712, with a late C18 gazebo in the grounds. The house rambling and varied, but with exposed timber framing on two sides.

See also Oldbury.

80

HASELEY

2060

ST MARY. A very attractive little church, little altered by the Victorians. The E end rebuilt in 1867 with a Perp window replacing a Georgian one of 1753. Unfortunate Neo-Norman S porch, 1900. Small Perp W tower of *c.* 1410, embattled with three-light W window. Simple S doorway of about 1200. The nave N and S windows, plain mullioned windows, look C17, and the S view of the chancel is just like that of a cottage: mullioned window under a cross-gable. Sweet, unrestored interior with ceiled wagon roof and BOX PEWS, the family pew with the Throckmorton arms and carved panelling. – FONT. Octagonal, Perp, with quatrefoils. – WALL PAINTING. Creed, in decorative surround, late C16 or early C17. – STAINED GLASS. The W window head complete with a number of figures and an inscription referring to John Aynolph, rector 1406–9. – E window by *William Holland*, 1867. – S chancel window by *Hardman*, 1897. – MONUMENT. Clement Throckmorton †1573 and his wife Catherine (Neville).* Tomb-chest with brasses. The English inscription still in black letter. The fragmentary glass in the window above includes a date, 1573, and

---

*The Throckmortons lived at the Old Hall, N of Haseley Manor. It was built in 1561 and had good Elizabethan features, but was demolished in 1972.

Haseley, Haseley Manor, perspective.
Photo lithograph, 1875

so relates to the original setting of the tomb. The simple iron
CHURCHYARD FENCE, 1873.

A little S, HASELEY HOUSE (former rectory), substantially of
1852 when *John Croft* enlarged a house built in 1825 by *John
Hawkes* of Leek Wootton. Bold window surrounds probably
redone 1867. Outbuildings also by *Croft*, 1853, but now much
altered.

HASELEY MANOR, ⅛ m. SE. A large rock-faced mansion built
in 1873–5 for Alfred Hewlett, a Lancashire mining engineer.
The architect was *William Young*, who trained in Scotland. Its
style is Tudor, from Gothic to Elizabethan. The dominant
feature, however, is a distinctly Scots Baronial tower with a
higher bartizan stair-turret. The published drawings show a
little wooden saddleback shelter (now removed) on the tower
from which visitors could survey the scenery. In front of it is
a deep Gothic porte cochère with an upper storey with oriel.
Another tower at the N end, Baronial with machicolations
below the embattled parapet. Inside, tiled fireplaces of the
greatest variety of designs and patterns. In commercial use
since 1940. Contemporary LODGE on Birmingham Road near
Hatton church (q.v.), again by *Young*.

HASELEY HALL, among trees 1¼ m. N: an existing house
enlarged in the Old English style with embattled canted bays
and half-timbered gables by *Wood & Kendrick* for Sir James
Sawyer, 1892. Once an orphanage, converted into flats in 1997.

HASELOR

Two villages, Haselor (and Upton) on the W and S and Walcote
to the E, with the church on the hill in between. Both have long
streets lined with pretty farms and cottages, mainly timber-
framed and white-painted brick.

ST MARY AND ALL SAINTS. Accessible by paths from each side of the hill. W tower, nave, chancel, S aisle and C19 S porch with reused C15 roof timbers. Odd little gabled pinnacle over the porch. W tower possibly Norman but featureless apart from the arch to the nave and later Dec W window. Top stage rebuilt, 1622, and formerly pinnacled. External masonry shows evidence of a former N chancel chapel, visible inside as a blocked two-bay arcade of *c.* 1190. Round pier with round capital and pointed arches with one slight chamfer. The tower arch and S arcade probably late C12 too. Square piers with chamfered angles to W bays of arcade and single-step pointed arches. The E bay is clearly C13 and may have represented a transept. N of nave, a shallow projecting mausoleum with coffin ledge and window with richly crocketed tracery. By *Lattimer & Son*, 1852–4, in readiness for the vicar, Cornelius Griffin, who died in 1867. Chancel restored by *H. C. Saunders* of Stratford in 1847, the church in 1893 by *A. S. Flower*. – PANELLING in the chancel; Jacobean. – Pretty carved PULPIT, 1893, tucked into blocked arcade. – STAINED GLASS. In N chapel, by *William Holland*, 1857. – Two in chancel. E window, *Powell*, 1893 (designer *Charles Hardgrave*), and N, *Hardman*, 1896.

By the crossroads in Haselor, the SCHOOL, by *Joseph Lattimer*, 1875; gently polychromatic with plate tracery. Good modern extensions. To the S, a single-storey gabled extension by *Holford Associates*, Manchester, 1996. Behind, further additions by *Brown Matthews Architects*, 2003 and 2010. Nearly opposite, the former red brick BAPTIST CHURCH, 1905, converted 1969.

S of these, UPTON HOUSE on the W side of the road has a fine C18 brick front. Further S, MANOR FARM, *c.* 1600 and partially rebuilt 1810, with one jettied and timber-framed gable with various patterns, e.g. lunettes and crosses in circles.

At WALCOTE, facing the church path, the old VICARAGE by *Joseph Lattimer*, 1868. Opposite, but nestling discreetly out of view, HILL HOUSE by *Harry Bloomer & Son* for H.L. Gray-Cheape, 1971: large but traditional. On the street, WALCOTE FARM has a cross-wing with quoins. Outside THE CIDER MILL is a cider press, probably early C19. At the top of the road leading out of the village, WALCOTE MANOR FARM, C17 but refronted early C19, with attractive and varied outbuildings. CRUCK COTTAGE, uninteresting externally, has internal cruck framing dendro-dated to 1384–5.

HASELOR LODGE, at the foot of Redhill on Stratford Road 1¼ m. SE. Three-bay red brick house with a thin Tuscan porch, extended l. and r. by brick walls ending in square pavilions with louvred lanterns. An early C19 model farm built for the Marquess of Hertford, with good farm buildings to the rear.

HOO MILL on the Alne, 1 m. W. The miller's house of brick, mid-C19. Adjoining mill of Lias, 1810. Very notable indeed for its surviving milling machinery.

HATTON

HOLY TRINITY. Late Perp w tower in grey Arden sandstone, its offset w window and the tower arch very high. The window has a transom and a wide hollow for the surround. The rest 1878–80 by *William Young* for the Hewletts of Haseley Manor (q.v.) in place of a church much altered and embellished during the incumbency of Dr Samuel Parr, 1783–1825. Rockfaced, large, but varied in composition with low aisles and tall transept. The clerestory has cross-gables, some with circular windows and quatrefoils. The interior unrewarding. The s aisle and porch partitioned off, 2004. – PAINTINGS. Moses and Aaron from the reredos, provided by Dr Parr, *c.* 1794. – STAINED GLASS. In the w window twelve demi-figures of kings and prophets, German, early c16, set in a N window by *Joseph Hale Miller*, 1811, and re-set here in 1880.* – E window and transept windows by *Lavers & Westlake*, 1892–6. – One N aisle window by *Heaton, Butler & Bayne*, 1898, another, probably by *Burlison & Grylls*, 1903. – s aisle windows by *Mayer & Co.*, 1883 and 1908. – MONUMENTS. Many tablets, e.g. Dr Parr †1825 and his wife Jane †1810, quite plain. – Also Thomas Bree †1778, white and brown marbles, with an obelisk; and John Smitheman †1794, with a big putto head at the foot and an urn and flower garland at the top. – Towards the s edge of the churchyard a plain tombstone to Mrs Maynard †1935, by *Eric Gill*. By the road, a now freestanding LYCHGATE, 1908.

The village lies w of the church, the main street called The Green. Facing the crossroads on Birmingham Road, the VILLAGE HALL: part 1852 (built as the girls' and infants' school), brick, larky Gothic with angle tower; the rest 1924 by Haseley Manor estate staff. In the street, FERNCUMBE SCHOOL, a brick Board School with lancets, 1885; probably by *W. Hawley Lloyd*. Down the lane opposite, the OLD RECTORY, built 1754–7, enlarged in 1785 to accommodate Dr Parr's library and school and altered again in 1825 and for the Rev. John Lynes by *William Parsons* of Leicester, *c.* 1835. Near the crossroads on Hockley Road, c16 GARDENER'S COTTAGE with a stone chimney-breast almost 15 ft (4.6 metres) wide in the centre of the front. Star chimneys of brick. To the l. and r. c17 timber framing and gables. To the E, early c19 HATTON HOUSE: mottled brick with Doric porch, and unidentified improvements by *T. H. Mawson*, 1912.

HATTON PARK, 1 m. E on the site of the former County Lunatic Asylum (later Central Hospital), redeveloped since the hospital closed in 1995. Several of the key buildings survive, although some only as façades. The chapel (*c.* 1862) and the Idiot Asylum (1871–2) have gone, as have the many later additions

---

* The other windows installed by Dr Parr, by *Francis Eginton* and his son, 1794–1815, did not survive the rebuilding.

including those by *Edward Mansell*, 1904. The LODGE, 1851, on Birmingham Road and the main building, 1847–52, are the main survivors of the original asylum by *James Harris* and *F.J. Francis* with *John Croft* as clerk of works. Jacobean-style in brick with mullioned-and-transomed safety windows. Central block with clock tower and cupola, lower wings with corner blocks and projecting ranges. Across the drive in front, EDGE-HILL, *c.* 1895, was the Medical Superintendent's house. On the ridge to the E off Dorsington Close, facing S, LEIGH HOUSE, by *Mansell*, 1891–1904, still Jacobean. Beyond, in Charingworth Drive on Hertford Hill, the symmetrical Neo-Georgian façade of the King Edward VIII Memorial SANATORIUM (later Chest Hospital), by *A. William West*, designed 1914 and built 1922–3.

On the GRAND UNION CANAL, opened in 1799, a flight of twenty-one locks leading down towards Warwick and aligned with the tower of St Mary's church. The engineer for this stretch was *Philip Witton*. The locks were reconstructed and widened in 1929–34. Lock-keepers' COTTAGES at the top and bottom of the flight, *c.* 1800. Beside 1930s concrete BRIDGE (No. 54), the WATERWAYS DEPOT with blue brick engineering workshops and raised tower for the toll-clerk's office, 1899. Opposite, *Gideon Petersen*'s stainless steel dragonfly sculpture, 2006.

See also Beausale and Shrewley.

HAWKESBURY

3080

Hawkesbury straddles the boundaries of Coventry and Nuneaton & Bedworth, but lies N of the M6 motorway where the urban sprawl fades gently into the countryside. Once heavily industrialized – and later disfigured by a huge power station (now gone) whose power lines remain – it has become a waterways refuge around the junction of the Oxford and Coventry canals. The canals were first joined at Longford in 1777. The present junction was made in 1803 and widened in 1836.

Various canal structures around HAWKESBURY JUNCTION (or SUTTON STOP). First, the PUMPING STATION, erected in 1821. Blue brick with chimney. It was built to house a New-comen beam engine of *c.* 1725 used to supply well water to the Coventry Canal* and is probably by *John Sinclair*, the canal company's resident engineer, who designed the cast-iron hump BRIDGE at the junction. This is dated 1837 and was made at the *Britannia Foundry*, Derby. It has a broad trellis pattern to

---

*The engine is preserved in working order at Dartmouth, Newcomen's birth-place.

the parapets. Another iron bridge on the Oxford Canal, and lock-keeper's house, tollhouse (1903) and cottages nearby.

BAPTIST (Particular) CHURCH, Lenton's Lane. 1845, refronted 1921, with round-headed windows. C19 schoolroom at rear with iron-framed windows.

On the road to Bulkington, HAWKESBURY HALL, probably 1760, with pretty Victorian lodge. Beyond, TOLLDISH FARM is heavily plastered but its gables and projections must conceal an essentially C16 core.

HENLEY-IN-ARDEN

Henley-in-Arden and Beaudesert (q.v.) are seemingly one place but are separate administratively. They are divided by the River Alne. Beaudesert, E of the river, is older and originated as a small village at the foot of The Mount with its Norman castle. Henley began as a settlement on an established track through the Arden Forest. It belonged to the ancient ecclesiastical parish of Wootton Wawen until as late as 1914 but grew into a small town in the reign of Henry II, gaining a market charter in 1220. Despite becoming a borough in 1296 Henley was never incorporated. Administration was in the hands of a manorial court which met in the C15 Guildhall. The manorial traditions have been actively maintained and the Guildhall is still used today by the court leet. Another surviving tradition is the annual mop or statute fair which takes place in September.

CHURCHES

29   ST JOHN THE BAPTIST. The whole church later C15, replacing a chapel of 1367. All in the distinctive Perp of northwest War-wickshire with almost triangular arches and window heads, accompanied by bold detailing. Restored by *Street* in 1856, with further restoration by *W. Hawley Lloyd* in 1900. W tower reno-vated by *F. W. B. Yorke*, 1912, when its tall pinnacles were removed. The tower stands right by the High Street, so close indeed that the porch is placed in the W wall of the nave, S of the tower, facing W. It has a four-centred, almost straight-sided arch, as has a little archway N of the tower, set in a wall con-necting the church with the Guildhall (*see* Public Buildings). The tower has tall, two-light, transomed bell-openings. The doorway inside the porch has an arch like the porch entrance and two good headstops, a king and a queen. N aisle of four bays, tall octagonal piers, four-centred arches. Roof with stone corbels, tie-beams, collar-beams and queenposts. – PULPIT. Of wood, Perp, with traceried linenfold panels. – STAINED GLASS. Mostly patterned glass with foliage roundels, *c.* 1856. – E and W windows by *Wailes & Strang*, 1879 and 1882. – E window in

aisle, 1865. – Porch window by *Powell*, 1925. – Millennium window, *Art of Glass*, 2000.

ST NICHOLAS. *See* Beaudesert.

BAPTIST CHURCH, set back from the High Street. *George Ingall*, 1867, with thin steeple. Remodelled by *F. B. Andrews* after a fire in 1936, retaining the shell and modified street front but wholly renewing the interior. Alongside to N (No. 122 and 124), 1688, was the manse of an earlier chapel: brick with moulded string course, central chimney and pyramid roof.

METHODIST CHURCH, by the market cross. By *T. T. Allen*, 1894. Brick with stone dressings, but very humble.

PUBLIC BUILDINGS

GUILDHALL, next to the church on the N side. C15, but much altered when restored in 1915. The ground floor, originally of stone, now has timber framing with brick and tile infill on a stone base. Upper floor with close studding, enlivened with painted shields. The roof trusses have tie-beams with arched braces. C15 stained glass inside, restored by *Camm & Co.* Pleasant courtyard to the rear. ²⁹

HIGH SCHOOL, S end of the town. By *Frederick Gibberd* with *G. R. Barnsley*, the County Architect, 1957. Concrete frame, painted black, brick infillings and glass. Many low-pitched roofs at varied heights.

WARWICKSHIRE COLLEGE, slightly S of the town. The campus centres on WHITE HOUSE, built as a private mental asylum *c.* 1820. Stuccoed brick with Doric porch, much extended. It became Arden House School in 1876, later Ardenhurst and eventually part of the college. An extension by *Guy Pemberton* 1925. Refurbished by *Hitchman Stone Partnership*, 2005. Throughout the C19 Henley was a noted centre for the treatment of mental illness. Other asylum buildings included HURST HOUSE, N of the lane to the college, and GLENDOSSIL (later Riverhouse School), on the E side of Stratford Road, by *W. Hawley Lloyd*, 1882–3, with polygonal bays.

PERAMBULATION

Henley is nearly entirely one HIGH STREET, about a mile long, running N–S, though of course not really straight. The houses are mixed in style, mostly terraced, with few highlights, but hardly any shocks either. Most of the notable buildings are on the E side, fronting burgage plots running down to the river. The timber framing extends the length of the town on both sides of the road, with more concealed or partly visible behind later frontages in brick or stone. The black-and-white results from prettification in the early C20 when it was fashionable to remove rendering to expose the timbers. Yew Trees, The Bluebell and the Guildhall are among the buildings so exposed. The delight of Henley, though, is in its small-scale buildings of the C18 and early C19, ₁ many with pretty doorcases and period detailing. Remarkably, most of the buildings described in the first edition of this guide remain unaltered or in some cases improved. Replacement, for the most part, has been tasteful if unadventurous. While the High Street has survived well, however, there has been intensive infilling behind the frontages and much development between the main road and the railway.

First, the central area between the church and the Market Square to the N. Here the HIGH STREET narrows. Opposite the Guildhall, the WHITE SWAN HOTEL, early C17, restored 1935, of brick, with three canted bay windows and two gables with cusped concave-sided lozenges as the strutting pattern. Facing on the E side, No. 137, re-branded as Ye Olde Bank House in the 1930s, retains a nice early C19 shopfront. YORK HOUSE (Nos. 129–131), late C18, is brick with canted window bays and narrow pediment with urn and festoons.

To the N, the High Street widens to form a small market place and continues wide almost to the N end of the town. LLOYDS BANK (No. 127) is visually important because it closes the view from the N. Its pretty timber-framed gables are perhaps C16, but otherwise the present façade is of 1916. Further altered when it became a bank, 1936. In front, remains of the MARKET CROSS, now just a shaft on a stone base, having lost its elaborate top in the C19.* E of the cross stately mid-C18 STONE HOUSE, looking as if it were a town hall, of ashlar, three bays and three storeys, with a pediment all across and the two main windows as one composition each through the two upper floors: tripartite on the first, lunette on the second. The oddly timber-framed façade of GEORGE HOUSE (No. 119) is largely an inter-war creation.

Opposite, CROMWELL HOUSE (No. 84, formerly the Bear Inn) has timber-framed gables, the l. wing with pretty rainwater goods of 1928. HUNTERS (No. 66 or Neville House), C18 with canted bay windows on first floor and a good Midland Bank stone street frontage, 1914, possibly by *Gotch & Saunders*. At the corner of Station Road, THAI COTTAGE (No. 64), C16 with jettied gable. Former POLICE STATION facing, by *William Kendall*, 1858–9, with the court building behind, 1903.

Back on the E side, THE GABLES (No. 105), with a C15 projecting gabled wing, big stone chimney to one side and Victorian additions with dark corner bricks the other. Then a timber-framed group: No. 97 quite small and gabled, No. 95 with closely set studs, and the BLUEBELL inn (No. 93), C15–C16, with a gable and to its l. also a timbered archway into the coaching yard. Repaired and the framing exposed by *F. W. B. Yorke*, 1920s. Opposite is No. 50, late C17 although much altered, of five bays with giant pilaster-strips probably of c. 1800.

---

*There is a replica in the Heritage Centre.

More timber-framed houses on the E side, Nos. 79–81 gabled, and then ST LOES (No. 77), C15, long, all closely studded, with first-floor overhang and no gables. Late C18 APPLEGARTH (No. 71) has gauged brick window headers and a pretty pedimented doorcase. Nos. 65–69 have been refronted in brick, but are clearly older behind. No. 47 is C16 and has the Wealden arrangement of timbering, i.e. with a recessed centre, braces at right angles to the wall, and an unbroken eaves line. THE LIMES (No. 35), early C19 and three-storey, with pedimented door and fanlight. FORWARD HOUSE (No. 17), an office block by *Cross & Craig Associates*, 2003–4, with stone columns and pediment to entrance. Almost opposite, the FREDERICK JOHNSON ALMSHOUSES by *F.B. Endall*, 1904, extended 1993; ordinary domestic style. Lastly on the E, the former MILL, 1894–5.

From here, return to the town centre, taking in the long tree-lined views towards Lloyds Bank and the church tower beyond. At the corner immediately S of the church, BARCLAYS BANK (No. 143), stuccoed brick, with five bays and two gables in which are oval windows in oblong panels. The most probable date is the late C17. The porch is of course later. Opposite, a Regency pair (Nos. 106–108) with an archway between. Both sides small-scale, mostly brick-fronted, some white-painted, one or two with visible timber framing, until three-storey Late Georgian No. 171 on the E. Alongside, THE WHITE HOUSE (No. 173) with square timber framing and gables. Opposite, the OLD WHITE HORSE (No. 130), C16, with close studding and two gables above. Further S, VINE COTTAGE (No. 140) has a pretty little Adamish doorcase with highlighted decoration. The HERITAGE CENTRE (No. 150) has a cross-wing with crown-post roof dendro-dated to 1345. The main hall rebuilt *c.* 1440. The timber-framed group continues to HENLEY ICE CREAM (No. 152).

Opposite, on No. 185 a MILESTONE dated 1748: 'From London CII miles, from Stratford VIII, from Birmingham XIV'. Nearby, No. 201 is C17 with quoins, string course and keystoned doorway.

Then the former SCHOOL, Gothic, brick, symmetrical with bell-turret, by *W. Hawley Lloyd*, 1883–4. Entrance paired under a centre gable with trefoil hoodmould. After that YEW TREE HOUSE, behind tall, straight-grown yew trees, large, irregular, with, in one gable and also above the entrance, cusped concave-sided lozenge panels. The house is dated 1579. This was the birthplace of William James (1771–1837), the canal and railway pioneer. THE POPLARS (No. 156) is rough-cast, but has unlikely rainwater heads dated 1691.

Yet further S, on the E side, FREEMAN HOUSE (No. 239) with another small Adamish doorcase, this time plain. The rear of No. 257 is timber-framed, as seen from Horsefair, where the street widens. Here No. 261 has another C19 doorcase. On the W, 1960s DE MONTFORT COURT strikes an inappropriate note as the only unashamedly modern building in the long street.

Towards the 1908 RAILWAY VIADUCT in New Road is BROOK END. By *Voysey*, 1909, for the Misses Knight. Roughcast with flush mullioned windows, gabled dormers joined together, spreading slate roof and attenuated brick porch. Single-storey outbuildings attached. Some elements of Voysey's garden design also survive.

WHITLEY PIECE, on top of Blackford Hill towards Warwick. For Colonel W. B. Fletcher, by *Erno Goldfinger*, 1947–8. Mildly modern, in the 1945–55 way, with pitched roof. Concrete floors and columns dividing the recessed centre on the garden front with its large window openings and balcony. Open-plan interiors. The design is an early use of Goldfinger's 2 ft 9 in. (84 cm.) planning grid.

HENLEY GREEN *see* p. 290

HILLFIELDS *see* p. 291

HOLBROOKS *see* p. 292

2070

HONILEY

ST JOHN THE BAPTIST. Approached though GATEPIERS bearing the arms of John Sanders who built this church alongside his house. 1723, with inscription on w front commemorating the donor (†1727). The w tower is exceptionally bold and exceptionally Baroque. It has arched windows and also round windows. The top stage recedes a little, and the mediating is done by volutes, eight altogether – a good sight – terminating in pinnacles. A short spire crowns the little composition in a traditionally English way. The body of the church is of nave and apse. The windows are arched, and the angles, as well as the E angles of the first bay, are stressed by pilasters, of the same kind that clasp the angles of the tower. Inside, the apse has marble pilasters, oddly not carrying anything. Who was the architect? *Sir Christopher Wren* has been suggested, or maybe his son, in view of their ownership of nearby Wroxall from 1713. Terry Friedman gives it to the son. The *Smiths* of Warwick, inevitably, have been named. Another possibility is *Thomas Eayre* of Kettering, designer of the classical church at Stoke Doyle, Northants (1722–5), who cast the Honiley bells in 1731. Sanders's will shows that Wren and Andrew Archer (brother of architect Thomas) were among his trustees, charged with completing the church, while he leased land from Francis Smith. So there are many possibilities, but no answer. Striking, though, is the comparison of the church as it originally appeared, with urns and balustrading, with the broad outline of Archer's Birmingham Cathedral. – WEST GALLERY on marble columns. – BOX PEWS and PULPIT no doubt of 1723 too. – FONT. How Georgian! A little niche in the N wall of the tower arch incorporating a small marble basin with lid. – STAINED GLASS. Apse windows, richly coloured in Arts and Crafts style, by *Theodora Salusbury*, 1924 and 1926. – MEMORIAL. J.L. Osborne †2005, architect and Sanders descendant, by *A. John Poole*.

The OLD HALL, purchased by Sanders in 1707, stood to the immediate N of the church until 1803. Hence the two late C17 service wings in such a position that they seem to form a forecourt to the church. The two wings, known as THE MALTINGS and NORTH LODGE, are of brick and have middle archways and gables over the end bays with oval windows in them. The other windows have wooden mullion-and-transom crosses. Restoration and conversion by *Bateman & Bateman (C. E. Bateman)* for Herbert Wade, 1914.

A little W of the church, three-bay CHURCH FARM, brick-fronted with pilaster-strips at the angles and a steep pediment, also no doubt late C17.

HONILEY HALL, down a long drive E of the church. By *Bateman* for Herbert Wade, 1914. Neo-Elizabethan, patterned brick with square clock tower. *Bateman* also did BLACKCROFT, S of the church, for Charles Wade, 1914. Further S, the OLD RECTORY, by *Osborn, Pemberton & White*, 1923.

HONINGTON

2040

HONINGTON HALL is a gem of a late C17 house. It was built for Henry Parker (later Sir Henry) in 1682. The Parkers were London merchants. Henry became a lawyer and Parliamentarian, acquiring an estate at nearby Talton in 1663 and Honington itself with its old house *c.* 1670. The date 1682 is on a rainwater head, and the E (entrance) side represents that date to perfection. The house is of brick with brown stone dressings. It has to the E a recessed three-bay centre and slightly projecting two-bay wings. Two storeys and a hipped roof. The broad doorway has a broken segmental pediment with a coat of arms and garlands. The pediment rests on Corinthian columns. The one feature which distinguishes the front from that of other such houses of this common late C17 type is the oval recesses with busts of Roman emperors in the spaces between lower and upper windows. It is an irregular motif, and it is doubtful if it is aesthetically justifiable, but it adds individuality. Parker was a collector of rarities whose collection was much admired in 1678 by Anthony Wood. The emperor busts are clearly

shown on the s front too in a Buck engraving of 1731. The s
and w fronts have been altered, but the engraving shows their
original appearance, the w with a recessed centre as on the e.
Steps from the house led down into extensive 'gazebo com-
manded' (Mowl and James) formal gardens with pavilions,
statues, canals and fountains.

While the 1731 engraving records the house in its original
state, three charming views of 1759 by Thomas Robins show
the changes made to the house and grounds between those
dates, when much was altered. In 1741, heavily saddled with
debts, the builder's grandson, also Sir Henry Parker, sold
Honington to Joseph Townsend. He had married Judith Gore
in 1737 and by July 1741 the Townsends were living at Honington. By then building work was in progress, and in a letter
to a friend Judith observed 'we hear nothing, but hammering,
all day long'.

Honington underwent extensive and highly sympathetic restoration under *Benson & Benson* (*Jeremy Benson*) for Sir John
Wiggin, 1974–8, assisted by government grants.

First round the r. corner to see the N side of the house. Here
is a lovely doorway with an apsed hood, richly carved with a
cherub's head, flowers, and leaves. Further N are the late
Tudor STABLES. The surviving block was one of a facing pair.
Its Renaissance-style archway must be c17, with broad fluted
pilasters and a steep gable in which is a niche with a demi-nude
goddess. There is also an octagonal DOVECOTE here and a late
c16 BOTHY in brick with limestone quoins, on brick arches on
staddle-stones.

Townsend's additions to the exterior included several features not shown by the Bucks. The s side of the house has a
deep canted veranda with Tuscan columns. To the l. and r. of
the e front are small rusticated and pedimented gateways into
the garden. Beyond them on the r. is a brick quadrant wall
with pilasters, blank niches, and a triglyph frieze. Its opposite
number on the l. has disappeared, but both are shown by
Robins whose view also shows that the two Roman emperors
displaced from the s front by the addition of the loggia were
repositioned in wide piers with niches at the e end of box
hedges beyond the quadrant walls.* The use of tiny bell-
shaped *guttae* in the frieze identifies the *Woodwards* of Chipping
Campden as the likely authors of this scheme, completed
c. 1745–50. The w front is the old one, except for a wide
canted bay added when alterations were made in 1751–2
(*see* below).

The alterations are most conspicuous in the INTERIOR. The
gorgeous ENTRANCE HALL must indeed be of *c.* 1741. It has
a fireplace, quite likely by *Henry Cheere*, with an intricately
framed mythological stucco relief. Opposite is no fireplace but
a companion relief. The reliefs and their surrounds have been
attributed, convincingly, to *Charles Stanley*. There a stylistic

---

*The two emperors were later moved again. They are now on the w front.

likeness, and a Townsend letter of 1741 mentions Mr Procter
of Langley Park, Norfolk, where Stanley also worked. There
are more stucco panels and a stucco ceiling. The panels
towards the W contained paintings, later removed. As the
arrangement is now, the recesses are simply left open so that
one can look through them towards the staircase. This is
reached by a doorway which leads into a delightful little
PASSAGE, again sumptuously decorated. The ceiling motifs are
Rococo, the spandrel motifs are in the late C17 tradition of
thick garlands. The passage has to the l. and r. two-bay passages with Tuscan columns, lit from above by skylights. That
to the r. leads into a lobby, that to the l. to the STAIRCASE.
This is somewhat pinched in size but has a fine scrolly wrought-
iron balustrade, attributed to *Gardiner*. The lack of space is
due to the centre of the W front having been converted in
1751–2 into an octagonal SALOON with a splendid coffered   61
dome. *John Freeman* of Fawley Court was responsible for the
design, with *William Jones* overseeing the execution. The plasterwork may be by *J. Whitehead* who worked with Jones at
Edgcote, Northants. All the detail is outstanding. Rococo garlands down the angles of the wall, but the doorways and fireplace more classical in the Kentian way. In the middle of the
ceiling a painting of Acis and Galatea by *Luca Giordano* (cf.
Chatsworth), added to on all four sides to fit its frame. Other
rooms include the OAK ROOM, S of the entrance hall. This
contains a doorway which may have been transferred from the
saloon. The rest of the room looks late C17, the original oak
panelling having been rediscovered and reinstated in 1913, the
C18 plaster cornice of Townsend's time being dark-stained to
disguise the mis-match. The fireplace, of curious 1740-ish
details. The SW room (BOUDOIR) has in the ceiling a stucco
relief of Aurora and another fireplace attributed to *Cheere*. On
the first floor the CHINESE CLOSET to the S has preserved its
stucco of *c.* 1682 with an almost detached wreath of flowers.
Small corner chimneypiece, also typical of the late C17. In
panels round the walls, early C18 London-made gilt-leather
hangings depicting Chinese scenes.

Close to the W front is a TEMPLE with Doric columns,
c. 1830. This was attached to the broad canted bay as a portico
until 1875, when it was repositioned against the Victorian
service wing, largely demolished in 1979. Another TEMPLE in
the grounds S of the church, with unfluted Greek Doric
columns and a parapet behind the pediment with a bust on
top. Also a SUNDIAL post. Apart from the two Neptune reclining figures rescued from the cascade in the River Stour, little
remains of the Rococo landscape created by *Sanderson Miller*
for Joseph Townsend in the 1750s and delightfully recorded by
Robins in 1759. There was a Chinese summerhouse and a
grotto, with some features on the opposite side of the river,
which was diverted and altered to form a lake.

Further from the house, a five-arch BRIDGE over the Stour
to the S, with ball finials on the parapet. Is it of *c.* 1682? It

looks a little earlier. At the entrance to the park from the village, GATEPIERS, rather coarse, with much vermiculated rustication, c. 1740–50. Alongside, a LODGE, late C19, imitating features of the hall.

ALL SAINTS, immediately SE of the house and originally brought yet closer to it by the former quadrant brick wall. Simple ironstone W tower of c. 1275–1300 with C17 or C18 parapet and pinnacles. The rest of 1684, when the church was noted as 'pulld downe . . . and rebuilding'. Doubtless financed by Parker and influenced by the London churches rebuilt after the Great Fire. Nave and aisles and small apse. Arched windows with ears. Parapet with flaming urns. Inside four-bay arcades of Doric columns on high plinths and round arches with panelled soffits. Shallow segmental plaster vault. The aisles have simple ceilings. Restored in 1878–9 when a chancel was created within the E end of the church. – FONT. A big stone baluster. – PULPIT. Handsomely decorated along the chief members, horizontal as well as vertical. Staircase with dainty decorated twisted balusters. Also a dove of peace. – COMMUNION RAIL. Also with twisted balusters. – STALLS. The panels with beautiful pierced foliage scrolls are late C17 too. – The BENCHES, which were formerly box pews, are also original. Cut down in 1878–9. – STAINED GLASS. All by *Hardman*, E window 1878, N aisle E 1879, the others 1907. – MONUMENTS. Sir Henry Parker and his son Hugh, †1713 and 1712. Attributed to *William Palmer* (GF). Splendid marble monument of reredos type with the two Parkers standing and elegantly gesticulating. – Joseph Townsend †1763. Large pedimented aedicule with an asymmetrically placed large putto on an odd, heavy Rococo plinth. Oak branches on the l., a skull on the r. A design by *Sir Robert Taylor*, cf. similar ones at St Nicholas, Rochester, and Ludlow. – Lady Elizabeth Townsend †1821. By *Sir Richard Westmacott*. Standing mourning male figure by an urn. Almost identical with the earlier Westmacott tablets at Preston-on-Stour and Ilmington (q.v.). – Gore Townsend †1826. Also by *Westmacott*. At the top, tympanum with a reclining pilgrim at rest, a moving conceit and composition. – Smaller Townsend memorials †1858 and †1865 by *Gardner*, Leamington.

LYCHGATE at the churchyard entrance with Gothic carving but classical gates, c. 1897.

Very pretty and very tidy village. One broad main street and a short spur leading to the church and hall. Mainly stone and mullioned windows. Some thatch. At the W end, C16 MAGPIE HOUSE. Timber-framed. The upper floor with zigzag diagonal bracing. Midway on the S, late C18 HOME FARM, brick with stone plinth, quoins, keystones and flat band. Further E, HONINGTON LODGE, with Arts and Crafts detailing, created from separate cottages in 1910–11 by *Charles M. C. Armstrong* for Sir Grey Skipwith and since subdivided again. Beyond, ROSE COTTAGE with cob walls and thatch.

HUNNINGHAM

St Margaret. Small and low, with a primitive weatherboarded bell-turret carrying a handsome weathercock. The re-set N doorway of *c.* 1200 belongs to the old N wall; very elementary. The mid buttress in the W wall has a long lancet. There is an even more massive buttress off-centre with offsets. Restored by *Fulljames, Waller & Sons* of Gloucester, 1871, when the N aisle was rebuilt. Vestry, 1887. Aisle and vestry adapted as a parish hall, 1996. – FONT. Round, with eight shafts, and in the panels big coarse stiff-leaf patterns. E.E. Or Victorian? – STAINED GLASS. E window by *F. Holt & Co.*, 1898. – W lancet by *Roger Sargent*, 1999. – MONUMENT. Tablet of 1623 with two columns on brackets.

BRIDGE, ¼ m. N. Over the River Leam to Weston. Probably medieval, but in detail mostly of 1651. Three massive arches with cutwaters.

HUNNINGHAM GRANGE, ½ m. E was built as a parsonage by *George Punshon*, 1868, but replaced by the present VICARAGE by *Harold E. Moss* in School Lane, 1924.

At HUNNINGHAM HILL 1 m. SSE, a BRIDGE carrying Ridgeway Lane over a deep railway cutting. By *W. T. Doyne*, 1849–50: at the time, the longest single-span lattice-girder bridge (150 ft (45.7 metres)) yet built. Subsequently reinforced with added columns and tie-bars.

HURLEY
Kingsbury

The largest of the hamlets in Kingsbury parish, although its medieval chapel had fallen into disrepair by the C17. It became a colliery village. The main mine was DEXTER COLLIERY which operated in Dexter Lane from 1927 to 1965. Its buildings were demolished in 1987.

THE RESURRECTION. Erected in 1862 as a combined school and chapel. Timber, of the type prefabricated for export to the colonies. Brick base. Cast-iron frame with dainty Gothic details. Triangular-headed windows. Re-roofed and largely remodelled internally. Interesting in its way, though hardly attractive. – WOODWORK. Low wooden Gothic altar rails of *c.* 1820.

Adjacent, the SCHOOL HOUSE of 1887. The former BOARD SCHOOL of 1895 by *Newton & Cheatle* has been demolished. The present school 1960s, flat-roofed and undistinguished.

ATHERSTONE HOUSE (formerly OLD EAST HOUSE), next to the church. Late C17. Brick with flat stone quoins. Stone cross-windows on ground floor. Four bays with offset doorway with bolection moulding. Half-hipped roof.

HURLEY HALL. Early Georgian, built *c.* 1720 for Waldyve Willington. Brick, of five bays and three storeys, with segment-headed windows. Doorway with fluted pilasters and columns and a triglyph frieze. The windows above with alternating rustication. It is a somewhat gloomy, but heroic façade. (Contemporary woodwork including a staircase with thin twisted balusters. Some very minor painted panels of classical and biblical subjects, Italian and English and bought as well as made for the house.)

2040   IDLICOTE

ST JAMES. Nave with S aisle, chancel, S chapel and shingled bell-turret, with delightful pre-Victorian interior. It is best understood from the inside. Simple N doorway of *c.* 1200. Broad two-bay S arcade late C13 or early C14. Octagonal piers. Chancel rebuilt about 1300 – see the chancel arch, the pointed-trefoiled heads of the stepped E lancets (though poorly reconstructed), and the nicely moulded lowside window. C14 roof to nave, pretty chancel roof with open trefoils at the apex, *c.* 1630. The late C17 Underhill Chapel is divided from the chancel by a two-bay arcade of a Tuscan column and two arches, classical, but in the details not really fully conversant with the new idiom yet. The chapel is barrel-vaulted, its original cornice broken by later window openings. Outside, it was refaced in ashlar *c.* 1810 and big Perp-style windows with Regency Gothic glazing inserted. The interior explains the windows on the W and S of the church too, with simple lancets lighting the WEST GALLERY, the big FAMILY PEW and the vestry (formerly the rectory pew). So the structure matches the use of space inside, suggesting C18 rebuilding of the aisle. The turret carries a splendid boar's head weathervane dated 1707, probably the date of the gallery and alterations at the W end of the church. – Good C17 and C18 FITTINGS throughout, including wainscotting, ALTAR RAILS and STALLS in chancel. – FONT COVER, C17, with ogee-shaped diamond-studded ribs (cf. Binton). – SCREEN. Substantial part of a Jacobean screen which must once have been very handsome. – PULPIT. C17 three-decker with tester. – Wooden CARVING, painted, with the Underhill arms, C17. – WALL PAINTING. Black-letter inscription, early C17. – MONUMENTS. Quite a number of minor tablets, C19, including two by *J.J. Sanders*, †1837 and †1857, and several from the *Patent Works, Westminster*, †1830–1837.

IDLICOTE HOUSE. Probably on the site of a medieval grange of Kenilworth Priory. Remodelled or rebuilt after 1755 for Heneage Legge or by Sir Robert Ladbrooke who bought it in

1759. The form of the three-storey central section of the SW
front belongs to this period but is much altered. Originally with
quoins and balustrading, it has a canted bay with single-storey
bays alongside. Regency tripartite windows with arched surrounds on the second floor, perhaps *c.* 1830. To the l. an older
two-storey service wing with C20 canted bay. On the r, a tall
two-storeyed extension of 1863 with pretty iron veranda facing
the garden. Main entrance on the NE, with pediment and
Diocletian window above. Although used by the Women's
Land Army in the Second World War and as a school from
1954, Idlicote reverted to being a private house in 1972. Some
panelled rooms, and good later C19 drawing room (once
known as the Waterloo Room) with high ceiling and pedimented doorcases.

Beyond the quadrangle of farm buildings N of the house, a
splendid DOVECOTE, octagonal, with Gothic details such as
blind cruciform arrowslits, an ogee-headed window and battlements. Inside 1,002 nesting places. There was a dovecote
here in 1681, but this must be largely *c.* 1760, quite possibly
by *Sanderson Miller* (WH).

To the s on the Honington Road, LODGES. Square, stone,
with pyramid slate roofs, post-1841.

Small hilltop village clustered around a large pond by the drive
to the church and house. s of the pond, C18 thatched cottages,
now combined into one, called BADGERS' COTTAGE.

ILMINGTON   2040

An attractive, large village nestling under the Ilmington Downs
at the N end of the Cotswold Hills. The parish includes Compton
Scorpion and Foxcote (qq.v.).

ST MARY. Encircled by the village and only accessible by footpaths. Basically this is a Norman church. The N and S doorways show it, even if of the latter only a chevron arch survives
above an inserted four-centred one. Also there are Norman
windows to the E of the two doorways. The nave is remarkably
wide. The chancel arch, though much re-cut, is Norman too
(two-step arch). Only a little later lower stages of the ashlar-
faced w tower. Massive with very thick walls. Typical broad
buttresses, the centre ones to w and s with windows cut
through. Puzzling tower arch to the nave: semicircular,
quadruple-chamfered, with continuous chamfers and round
arch. What can the date be? E.E. chancel, see the priest's
doorway and the lancet windows. The w part of the chancel
has niches with pointed arches on both walls. The N transept
is odd, although its opening from the nave with features of
various dates matches Glynne's description of *c.* 1840. It has
a strong E.E. round pier reused as a respond. The masonry is

perhaps of the C15 and the windows are mainly Perp, as are the nave clerestory and the tower top. The near-matching S transept was added when the church was restored in 1846. Further restoration in 1911 and again in 1936–9 under *L.L. Dussault* when the church was re-seated. Over-large and intrusive organ in the S transept, 1990, with casework by *Nigel Gilkes* of Mickleton. – FONT. Curious, perhaps C14. Octagonal, with three tiers of carved ornament beneath the basin. – PULPIT, LECTERN, SEATING, DOORS and MEMORIAL BOARD to Spencer Flower (†1939) all by *Robert Thompson* of Kilburn, 1938–9. – STAINED GLASS. E window by *William Holland*, 1848. – S chancel, probably *Heaton, Butler & Bayne*, 1873. – Others with patterned glass, *c.* 1846. – SCULPTURE. In the S transept part of a C15 or early C16 frieze with a chained bear baited by a dog. – MONUMENTS. Effigy of a priest, *c.* 1400(?), in the tower. Badly defaced. – Francis Canning †1806 and wife. By *(Sir) Richard Westmacott*. Grecian tablet. He stands leaning on an urn, mourning and hiding his face (cf. Preston-on-Stour and Honington). – Several C18 and C19 Canning tablets, all very Roman Catholic in style. One †1824 by *Thomas & James Nelson*, Carlisle. Another †1843 by *Cooke*, Gloucester. – In the churchyard elaborate Georgian Gothic monument erected by Ann Sansom to her husband Samuel, †1750. In the form of a buttressed and embattled tomb-chest structure crowned by a pinnacled tower spire like the Despenser monuments at Tewkesbury. Doubtless, as Howard Colvin suggested, by *Edward Woodward*, who proposed a fanciful steeple of similar design for Preston-on-Stour church in 1752. – Also in the churchyard the base of a CROSS with a panel of the Crucifixion facing towards the church.

ST PHILIP (R.C.). Elevated above the green and picturesquely Victorian Gothic. Built as a Roman Catholic school with teacher's residence attached by *C.A. Buckler*, 1864. Adapted as a church by *E.H. Earp*, 1934–5, with fittings from the Foxcote chapel and from a private chapel at Campden House, Gloucestershire. Closed for worship in 2013 and all fittings removed, the best to Shipston R.C. church (q.v.). Awaiting reuse (2014).

MANOR HOUSE, NE of the church. Handsome, of the familiar Cotswold type. Probably built for Sir Thomas Andrews *c.* 1590–1600 to replace the old manor whose fishponds remain to the w. Best are the gabled SE and SW fronts with mullioned windows and the diamond-shaped chimneystacks on the NE. But much is of *c.* 1920. The house was bought in a sorry state in 1919 by *Spenser Flower* and his wife Ella (*née* Lowndes) who restored and improved it. Flower was his own architect and did much of the woodcarving himself. C17 stonework from the long-demolished house at Weston Park is said to have been reused and local craftsmen were employed (e.g. for the plasterwork ceilings). The Court Leet range with stone slate roof and dormers is especially successful, particularly inside. The house has several resited Tudor and Jacobean fireplaces. The attractive gardens were also laid out by the Flowers, with a hexagonal summerhouse of 1924.

Several worthwhile houses in the village, mostly ironstone and mainly similar, but some in brick. Some thatch too. At the w end of the green CRAB MILL, with a long flat front dated 1711. Still mullioned windows. HOBDAYS in Front Street, 1709, is similar. In Back Street is twin-gabled C17 DOWER HOUSE. Nearby, OLD SCHOOL HOUSE is 1840s Gothic with diamond-pane windows. Behind the Manor House in Middle Street, a simple Wesleyan chapel of 1848 with lancets, now a house. On the green, the Gothic WELL-HEAD, 1864. Off Mickleton Road NW of the village is the OLD RECTORY, Georgian, golden ashlar with bow window, pilasters and stone porch, possibly 1807.

More interesting are the houses by *Robert Harvey* (of *Yorke, Harper & Harvey*) for clients in Ilmington between 1955 and 1965. These begin with his own house, STONECROP, superbly sited on the hillside off the Campden Road, 1955–7, refurbished and extended since Harvey's death by *Barton Hasker Ltd*, 2008. The others are FROG ORCHARD in Frog Lane for Mr Jewsbury, 1959, the ROUND HOUSE in Frog Lane for Miss Hardiman, 1962, and No. 6 Foxcote Hill for Miss Terry, 1965. All different, all novel and all tailored to the individual client's needs, bringing together the ideals of Frank Lloyd Wright and the Arts and Crafts tradition and combining the use of local materials and the up-to-date technologies of their time.

KENILWORTH

INTRODUCTION

Kenilworth became known to generations of readers through the fertile imagination of Sir Walter Scott, whose version of the life and times of Robert Dudley, Earl of Leicester, still permeates historical perceptions of the Tudor age. It is easy to understand how the writer was captivated by the place. Taken together, its castle, ruined abbey and the open landscape of the abbey fields are especially memorable. What is more, the castle and abbey are of common foundation, both owing their origins to Geoffrey de

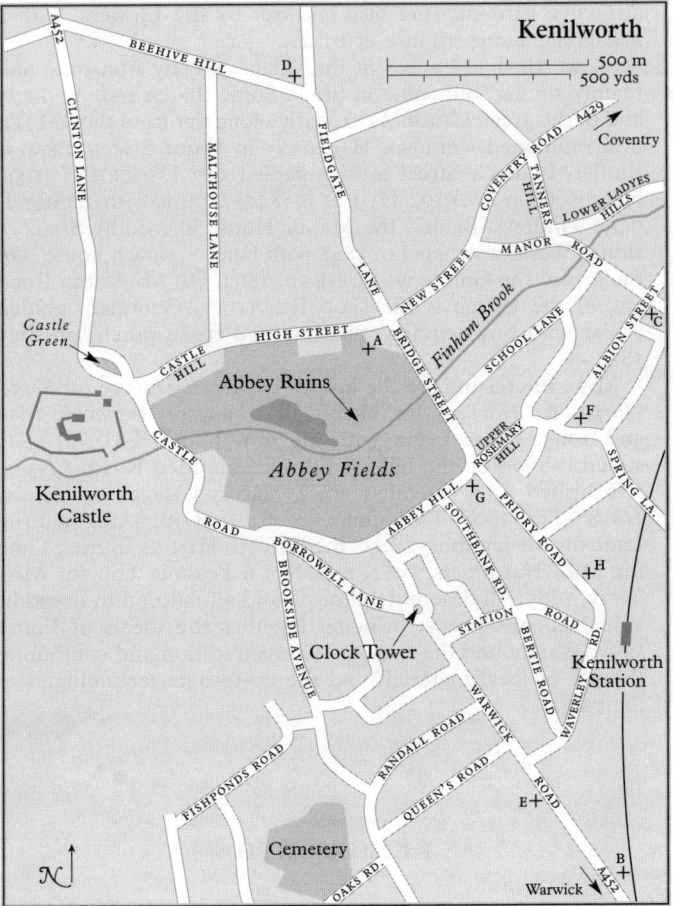

A St Nicholas
B St John
C St Barnabas
D St Augustine (R.C.)
E St Francis of Assisi (R.C.)
F Baptist church (former)
G United Reformed church
   (Congregational)
H Methodist church

Clinton in the time of Henry I. Dudley's additions created a splendid palace. All this eventually became an archetypal 'romantic ruin'.

Of the originally dependent town little need be said, though the place where de Clinton planted his foundations was of pre-Conquest origin. It became a small market town. There was no industry, although from the mid C18 combs of horn and bone were manufactured here. In part due to Scott, whose *Kenilworth* was published in 1821, the town attracted visitors and began to grow. Development was boosted by proximity to fashionable Leamington and, in 1844, by the arrival of the railway. Population increased gradually from 3,149 in 1841 to 5,776 in 1911, with steeper increases after two world wars to 14,449 in 1961. Well placed for commuters travelling to Coventry, Birmingham and Leamington, the town has continued to expand to its current population of 22,413 (2011).

CHURCHES

ST NICHOLAS, High Street. Mostly Perp, but restored and enlarged in 1864–5 by *William Smith* whose additions are entirely Dec. These include the s chancel aisle, s transept and N transept vestry, the latter enlarged in 1893. The Norman w door is re-set, so we can take the rest of the church first. The tower higher up is Dec, turns octagonal, and has a short spire. Externally otherwise the most interesting feature is the N porch, which forms the w bay of the aisle and had entrances (blocked) from w as well as N. Perp N windows, Perp clerestory window. The s wall largely of the drastic restoration of 1864, but retaining one five-light Perp window. The s arcade of five bays is Perp also, the N arcade later Perp with thin piers of four canted shafts. The tower arch has three continuous chamfers. The crudely Dec SEDILIA are re-set. Now the w entrance, which has been much discussed among experts of the Romanesque.* It is agreed that the doorway is a composite and that the elements probably came from the remains of the abbey nearby, but debate continues regarding dates, influences etc. Dates between 1125 and 1150 are proposed for the Norman work, and late C16 or early C17 for its reassembly. It is, nonetheless, undoubtedly the most sumptuous Norman doorway in Warwickshire, albeit with added Renaissance touches (cf. the porch of Leicester's Gatehouse at the castle). An unusual feature is that the doorway itself is framed by a frieze of square leaf, etc., with an outer cable-twist moulding. In the spandrels strange sunk medallions. The doorway has two orders of columns and in the arch beakheads in one moulding, sawtooth and fret in the other. – Caen stone REREDOS of the Last Supper by *Earp*, 1880. – Carved wooden PULPIT by *J. Oldrid Scott*, 1911, and LECTERN in similar style, 1920. – ORGAN CASE, 1902–3, and chancel SCREEN, 1913, by *Harry Quick*. – FONT. By a local mason, 1664. Round, the shallow bowl with flat scallops as a top and bottom band, the date, and four flowers. The stem tapers and is shafted. It has a carved wooden COVER by *Hugh Ledbrook* of Kenilworth, †1914. – LECTERN. Victorian, with the statues of the Evangelists. – Medieval

*The arguments are well summarized by Harry Sunley on the Corpus of Romanesque Sculpture (CRSBI) website.

TILES on S wall in the base of the tower. – STAINED GLASS. E window by *Hardman*, 1867. – Further Hardman windows in the chancel, 1881, N aisle (three), 1883–1910, and S aisle, 1883. – S transept S, an important heraldic window by *David Evans*, 1833. More heraldic glass in another S aisle window, undated, and in the W tower window, 1848, probably by Evans too. – One in the S aisle, *Clayton & Bell*, 1866. – S chapel E, *Burlison & Grylls*, 1878. – Two by *Buckley & Thompson*, 1878–9. – One in chancel by *Lavers, Barraud & Westlake*, 1881. – Chancel N by *Geoffrey Webb*, 1935. – On the S side, fragments of bomb-damaged windows by *Holland* in the S chapel, *c.* 1861, and the five-light S aisle window by *F. Holt*, 1881 and 1889. – Another by *Holt* in the S chapel, 1889. – One other, 1951. – MONU-MENTS. John Bird †1772. By *Nollekens*. Big putto by an urn. – Caroline Gresley †1817. By *(Sir) Richard Westmacott*. Relief of lunette form. She reclines on a couch, her sorrowing family around her. A hovering angel on the r.*

ST JOHN, Warwick Road. By *Ewan Christian*, 1851–2, and more impressive and vigorous than one expects from this often pedestrian architect. Rock-faced with Hartshill stone. Large, with tall SW steeple. Broach spire with alternating tiers of lucarnes. Spacious interior. Nave and five-bay S aisle, the tower standing within the W bay of the aisle. Piers octagonal and round, and a clustered one with carved capitals to the chancel and S chapel. No chancel arch. Plain stone walls with painted texts over the arches. – Chancel FITTINGS already removed, pews going 2015. – REREDOS of Devonshire marble by *Earp*, 1888. – Chunky stone PULPIT, doubtless 1852. – STAINED GLASS. E window, centre light and tracery only, probably *Wailes*, *c.* 1860 (AB). – Three in S aisle, one *Lavers, Barraud & Westlake*, 1877, and two *Lavers & Westlake*, 1897. – One N, *Jones & Willis*, 1907. – Tower S, St John, *c.* 1852.

Originally in a group with vicarage (*Christian*, 1857; dem.) and school (*Christian*, 1854) with diapered brickwork.

ST BARNABAS, Albion Street. A tin tabernacle, originally a mission church for St Nicholas, 1886. Sanctuary added 1905. – MURAL. The Ten Commandments, 1961.

ST AUGUSTINE (R.C.), Fieldgate Lane. By *Pugin*, 1841–2, but so humble that any genius he possessed was certainly not necessary. *George Myers* was the builder. Erected at the cost of Mrs Amherst of Fieldgate House. Red brick, originally aisle-less, with a bellcote and plain, quite severe windows of two pointed-trefoiled lights. The Perp E window may be original or later. N aisle by *Gilbert R. Blount*, 1849–52. Arcade with piers and arches of continuous mouldings. – The carved stone ALTAR looks *Pugin*: five white and gold angels praying. – STAINED GLASS. E window by *Wailes* to a Pugin design, 1841. – Others (four) by *Hardman*, 1848–69. – MEMORIAL BRASSES by *Hardman*. One to William Kerrill Amherst †1835 and wife

---

*ARCHITECTURAL FRAGMENTS mentioned in the first edition of this guide have been moved to the Abbey Barn (q.v.).

Mary Louisa †1871, who donated the church. – Another, George Fortescue Turville †1859, and wife Henrietta †1869.

To the w are the PRESBYTERY and attached schoolroom, also by *Blount*, *c.* 1849. w again, additional SCHOOLS, 1893.

St FRANCIS OF ASSISI (R.C.), Warwick Road. By *Rathbone & Taylor*, 1992–3, with linked parish centre, 2000. Red brick exterior, vaguely Romanesque. Large narthex. Light interior with complex polygonal roof structure and circular baptistery.

Former BAPTIST CHURCH, Albion Street (now the Old Church House). Built as the Albion Chapel, 1829. Red brick. Front with three round-arched bays originally enclosing two tiers of windows (the lower now obscured by a porch extension) with a pedimental gable above.

UNITED REFORMED CHURCH (Congregational), Abbey Hill. *G. & I. Steane*, 1872–3. Brick with stone bands. Geometrical and plate tracery. Light interior with organ gallery at far end and panelled roof. Behind is the former chapel, 1828–9. Brick with two tiers of Gothick windows with delicate leading.

METHODIST CHURCH, Priory Road. *Crouch & Butler*, 1902–3: Gothic, with pretty stone porch. It has glass by *T. W. Camm*, 1903. It is now the church hall. A new church of 1968 and 2002 (*Jacobs Feasey Associates*) alongside.

CEMETERY, Oaks Road. By *Sholto Douglas*, Council Surveyor, for Kenilworth Urban District Council, 1912–13. Plain LODGE set at an angle to the entrance gates. Gothic CHAPEL with short chancel and bellcote.

ABBEY RUINS
sw of St Nicholas

An Augustinian priory was founded here in 1119, according to the C15 chronicler John Strecche, by Geoffrey de Clinton, chamberlain of Henry I. It became an abbey in 1447 and by the time it was dissolved in 1538 it was one of the wealthiest monastic houses in the County. By 1600 most of the buildings had been demolished.

The ruins are of red sandstone and are sited near the parish church in a relationship often to be found (e.g. Westminster Abbey and St Margaret), the abbey crossing being directly s of the church tower. The site is extensive and there are exposed foundations as well as standing remains, now clearly identified and explained with marker plaques and interpretative panels. The Norman s wall of the CHAPTER HOUSE stands to a certain height and can be used as a beacon. It is on its own and protected by railings. The church stood to its N towards the churchyard, the cloisters immediately on its w (i.e. s of the nave) and the monastic buildings to its s in what is now Abbey Fields. The diagonal path to St Nicholas cuts across the crossing of the monastic church, whose chancel lay to the E. To the w of this are remains of the nave and N transept and

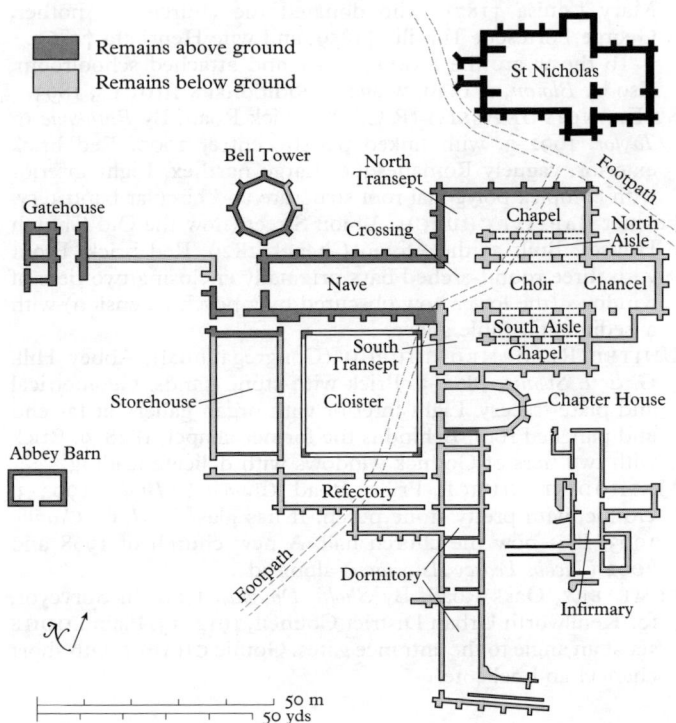

Kenilworth, Kenilworth Abbey.
Plan

the two standing buildings, the abbey barn and the partially surviving gatehouse.

The Norman church was cruciform and the pulpitum ran across the E crossing arch. The form of the E end is known from excavations. The chancel had a straight E wall, something rare (and English) in major Romanesque churches. All this was later changed, with additions on all sides. The eventual plan of the E end included transepts N and S, a choir with narrow aisles plus a wider outer aisle, divided across by partition walls running N–S, and a presbytery (or chancel) 72 ft 6 in. (22 metres) long further E. The E wall of the enlarged chancel was flush all across, with flat buttresses looking early rather than later C13.

W of the path, two of the crossing piers to the N transept can be seen, their mouldings still visible. Shafts with fillets, i.e. later C13 rebuilding. Work was in progress in 1276. The nave was aisleless, and its N and S walls can be followed on the raised area. The C14 W doorway and its jambs are recognizable. To its N was a detached bell-steeple, an octagonal C14 piece with walls nearly 7 ft (2.1 metres) thick and buttresses.

To the S lay the CLOISTER, its N wall (i.e. the S wall of the nave) now inlaid with worked stones. N of the 'beacon' were the SLYPE and apsed CHAPTER HOUSE, both Norman. The slype had seats along its sides. The chapter house was rib-vaulted, and its walls seem to have had tiers of blank arcading much like the Bristol chapter house (also Augustinian) illus-trated in the Bucks' engraving, 1729, but since demolished. The infilling of the vault was by means of tufa from Dursley, for reasons of lightness. Dursley tufa was also used for this purpose at Berkeley Castle and in the chapter house of Much Wenlock. The rest has to be imagined, as the foundations were covered over in 1967. Immediately S of the chapter house were the steps to the DORMITORY. A little further S, the long UNDERCROFT of a Perp enlargement of the dormitory range. This was two-naved, with octagonal piers with concave sides. It was originally and later subdivided across. Across its S end and stretching far out to the E was the REREDORTER or lava-tories and their big drain. The original dormitory must have been much shorter, as it had another drain running towards the infirmary. The INFIRMARY lay E of the dormitory at a distance and was apparently built in the C13. The S range along the cloister starts at its E end with the usual passage. Entrance and exit both have C13 details. There follows W of this the undercroft of the REFECTORY. The excavators attributed the walls to the C13, but the vaulting with the octagonal piers to the later C14. Of the W range only the STOREHOUSE and PARLATORIUM (audience chamber) next to the W front of the church are preserved. It seems to have been early C13 and was vaulted in four bays. One base of the W doorway indicates the date.

The two standing buildings are further W. The ABBEY BARN is supposed to have been the GUESTHOUSE. It is later C14 and has windows with shouldered lintels on ogee corbels. The S front is surprisingly symmetrical. The middle doorway has a basket arch. The upstairs floor was reinstated in the 1990s and the building now serves as a museum for the abbey site. The displays include architectural fragments, carved stones and encaustic tiles previously displayed in St Nicholas' church. The other building is the GATEHOUSE, giving access to the precinct from the NW, i.e. the town's High Street. The Strecche chronicle indicates that it was completed in the time of Prior Bradway (1361–75), and an analysis of the mouldings by Richard Morris suggests that it was commenced earlier and built in three stages. From the outside there is first a big four-centred archway never closed by a door, i.e. forming a porch. This is vaulted with diagonal and ridge-ribs. Then follows a division into carriageway and pedestrian entrance, another vault, not preserved, and another big arch into the priory court.

KENILWORTH CASTLE

31 Of the ruinous castles of England Kenilworth is undoubtedly one of the grandest. It has superb Norman, C14, and Elizabethan work, and where, as from the W, one sees all three together and all three in the strong yet mellow red of their sandstone, the view could not be bettered. Once almost surrounded by water, it must have looked still finer in its prime. When Nathaniel Hawthorne saw the ruins in 1857, he wrote: 'Without the ivy and the shrubbery, this huge Kenilworth would not be a pleasant object.' Since then it has all been successfully conserved. What the picturesque traveller has lost, the traveller eager for knowledge not only of architecture, but also of history, has gained, and the trees in the outer court and the lawns make it a pleasant object, though the mighty cliffs of keep, hall, and Leicester's Building are an object for which the description 'pleasant' seems preposterously feeble.

The BUILDING HISTORY is complex but an outline is necessary.* The castle and nearby priory were established around 1120 by Geoffrey de Clinton, chamberlain to Henry I. The ambitious scale of construction suggests that the castle was subsidized with royal money. Indeed, it was a royal castle for much of its history. Moreover, its history mirrors that of Warwick from its first foundation through to the C17. The Norman KEEP was built 1124–30, i.e. before Clinton fell from grace. By the later C12 there already existed a dam and causeway and waters to the W. The curtain wall and its towers are largely of *c.* 1205–15, in the time of King John, when about £1,100 was spent on the castle. This period also saw the addition of a top storey to the keep and the heightening of the dam to raise the water level of the mere. Simon de Montfort (1244–65) probably created the outer defences at The Brays. After his defeat at Evesham in 1265 Kenilworth Castle withstood a six-month siege, surrendering in 1266. From that time onwards its history mostly follows the Lancastrian succession. Thomas, 2nd Earl of Lancaster (1298–1322) built the Water Tower and erected a collegiate chapel in the outer bailey. It is documented that Henry of Grosmont (1345–60) remodelled an existing great hall in 1347.

The second great period of building at Kenilworth was under John of Gaunt, Earl of Lancaster (1361–99), whose claim to the throne of Portugal gave him a need for a residence appropriate for royal state and ceremony. He transformed the castle into a palace mansion. The magnificent Great Hall (roofed by 1377) and the Strong and Saintlowe towers are all of *c.* 1373–80. The chief mason was *Henry Spenser* and the master carpenter was *William Wintringham*, both previously engaged at Windsor. Work continued into the 1390s, e.g. the state apartments and Gaunt's tower ESE of the Great Hall. *Robert de Skyllington* was the mason

---

*This account draws heavily on the work of the late Richard K. Morris, whose excellent English Heritage guidebook (3rd edn, 2015) combines an analysis of the writings of others with his own research spanning thirty-five years to give a truly up-to-date evaluation of this remarkable site.

in 1389–93. From Gaunt the castle went to his son Henry IV and remained royal. At the far end of the mere, w of the castle, the Pleasance in the Marsh was built for Henry V, c. 1417–18. Henry VIII erected a timber range (using materials from the Pleasance) in the castle grounds and, in 1530–2, rebuilt the E range of the inner court (since dem.). Works undertaken during John Dudley's brief ownership in 1553 included the stables and the tiltyard on the dam. He was executed later that year but his son Robert Dudley gained possession when Elizabeth I gave him Kenilworth in 1563, creating him Earl of Leicester in 1564. The third major phase of building followed in anticipation of the queen's visits in 1572 and 1575. *William Spicer* (in charge in 1571 but elsewhere by 1572) was the principal craftsman here and *Robert Coxe* was master mason. First came the conversion of the C12 forebuilding w of the keep into a loggia, probably in 1569, and then Leicester's Building, the accommodation block erected in 1570–1 and further aggrandized in 1575. The gatehouse followed in 1571–2. There is a stylistic consistency in these works, which were the model for other Midlands 'high houses' (e.g. Hardwick New Hall, Derbys.). Of this time, too, the Elizabethan gardens, recreated by English Heritage in 2009.

In 1588 Kenilworth passed to the earl's brother, Ambrose, Earl of Warwick, but in 1589 it went to Leicester's son Sir Robert Dudley who resided here 1595–1603. The rest of the story is not of architectural interest, except to note that after the Civil War the castle was 'slighted' in 1649–50 – the great tower blasted open with gunpowder, fittings stripped out, the mere drained, etc. Only the stables and the gatehouse were preserved intact, the latter converted by the garrison commander, Col. Joseph Hawkesworth, as a house for his own use. The castle itself ceased to be a residence and the ruins gradually fell to decay. By the early C18 it was a picturesque ruin as depicted by S. and N. Buck in 1729 with trees and ivy on all the standing remains. Kenilworth was made famous by Sir Walter Scott's novel (1821) and gradual restoration began in the 1860s. The castle was placed under public guardianship by the 1st Lord Kenilworth in 1938 and given to the town by his son in 1958. English Heritage has been responsible for it since 1984.

First, the site. The castle stands to the NW of the town and w of de Clinton's contemporary priory. Both lie along the course of the Finham Brook which is joined near the castle by Inchford Brook and its tributaries from the S and w. These natural features were exploited to create large expanses of water above both the castle (the mere) and the abbey (the Abbey Pool). The mere, now drained, was one of the largest man-made water defences in Britain, stretching about ½ m. (800 metres) to the w and some 500 ft (150 metres) across, forming a lake much larger than the whole of Kenilworth, town, priory, and castle. It was completed in c. 1210. Henry V's 'Pleasance in the Marsh' lay at the far end. So in medieval times the castle was surrounded by water, by a moat N and NE, by the lower

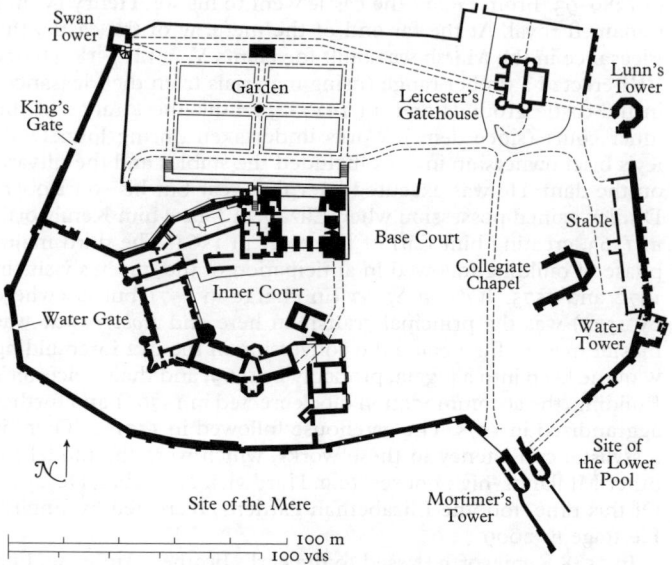

Kenilworth, Kenilworth Castle.
Block plan

pool on the SE, and by the mere S and W. The approach was
by a narrow strip of land at the SE above the dam. The vast
site extended further SE beyond the dam and had outer
defences in The Brays, of which a corner can be seen near
Castle Grove. There is a footpath all round the perimeter, a
walk recommended for anyone wishing to get a feel for the
scale and layout of the site. The perimeter walk takes in the
Water Tower protruding from the curtain wall at the SE angle,
Lunn's Tower at the NE, the deep moat on the N, the oblong
Swan Tower at the NW and the Watergate in the W wall with
its doorway and steps down to the mere.

Visitors enter the castle from The Brays through the ticket office
in the fragmentary remains of the GALLERY TOWER which
guarded the S end of the dam. The modern footbridge crosses
the overflow from the mere which fed the castle mill. The level
top of the dam was used as the TILTYARD, for tournaments
and jousting. At the other end is MORTIMER'S TOWER. It has
two D-shaped towers to the outside. The gateway is flanked by
small guardrooms with cross-shaped arrowslits in the side walls
N and S. This was the main medieval entrance to the castle,
remodelled c. 1210–15. It had a portcullis. Beyond Mortimer's
Tower one is in the OUTER or BASE COURT, with the keep
and state apartments on higher ground in the INNER COURT
to the l.

34

Take the BASE COURT first. To the E the early C13 curtain wall runs first to the Water Tower in the SE corner and then N to Lunn's Tower. Between the towers is the stable range. The WATER TOWER was probably built by Thomas of Lancaster in the early C14. It has a square base with pyramidal corner buttresses. The higher levels are polygonal with windows of two pointed trefoiled lights. Spiral stair in the NW angle with cross-loops to the exterior. Simple rib-vaults behind the single-light windows higher up. Next the STABLES, built for John Dudley, Duke of Northumberland, in 1553. They stand against the outer wall to which broad buttresses were added on the outside. To the courtyard a long front with a projecting porch in the middle. Ashlar base with original mullioned stone windows at one end and later wooden cross-windows at the other. Timber-framed above. The infill of brick, now rendered. Decorative square panelling with ornamental timber braces in the form of ragged staves, an emblem of the Dudleys. Square framing one end, close studding on the other. Inside, an unbroken space with fine open timber roof of eleven bays, shown by dendro-dating to be a reconstruction c. 1665–75. W of the stables are the exposed foundations of the collegiate CHAPEL built for Thomas of Lancaster c. 1320 and demolished c. 1524. It had a polygonal apse (three-eighths). In the stables, a C14

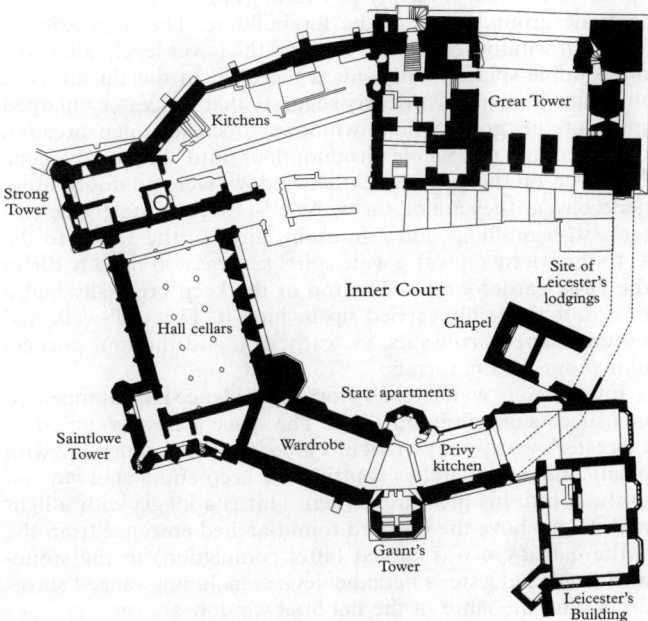

Kenilworth, Kenilworth Castle.
Ground-floor plan

canopied niche probably from the chapel. Then, at the NE corner, LUNN'S TOWER, a wall tower built for King John c. 1210–15. Round with broad pilaster buttresses outside and just polygonal inside. Five (restored) fishtailed arrow loops on the ground floor. Evidence of a sally port low down in the S wall. Within the courtyard a polygonal stair-turret to the upper floors.

Now to the INNER COURT, originally separated from the base court by a ditch and enclosed within its own defensive wall. Its GATEHOUSE was at the SE angle of the keep (or great tower), where the remains can be seen against the side of the corner turret. The position of the portcullis is also visible in the stonework. The sheer and mighty KEEP was begun in the 1120s by Geoffrey de Clinton and its top stage was added by King John c. 1210–15. It is rectangular and has the usual four broad angle turrets. Stepped plinth all round, rising higher between the turrets where the wall is stepped back by about 10 ft (3 metres). Walls of immense thickness. The almost windowless E side is impressive, the S side too, but the N wall was destroyed in 1649 and now allows one to look into the interior from the gardens below. The original entrance was from the W via a forebuilding, now obscured by Leicester's 1570s alterations. Inside, the keep had its lowest 10 ft filled in with earth, and then there were two floors, each with only one big room. The entrance was on the upper one of them, just N of the SW turret. The small doorway to the W from the lower floor led into the ground floor of the forebuilding. The only original Norman window is in the E wall, on the lower level, tall, wide, and double-splayed with only a mere slit in the thickness of the wall. Richard K. Morris suggests that Leicester enlarged most of the ground-floor windows to create open arcades, transforming the whole ground floor into an open loggia. However, on the upper level the windows were no doubt more generous, as they are on the W. As it is, they are mostly Leicester's, with mullions and a transom, three to the S, two to the E. In the NE turret was a wide spiral staircase, in the NW turret the large garderobe pit. The top of the keep originally had a roof, but the walls carried up to hide it. The wall-walk had fishtail-shaped arrowslits, i.e. early C13, and the four corners four rooms in the turrets.

Immediately W, nearly all Norman evidence has disappeared in a succession of remodellings. The space is now occupied by Leicester's FOREBUILDING of 1569–70: a small courtyard with pillars and round arches abutting the keep and a stairway out to the N into his pleasure garden. This is a loggia with a light well. High above the restored round-arched entrance from the S, the date 1570 was carved (after completion) in the stonework, with Leicester's heraldic devices including ragged staves decorating the jamb of the tall oriel window above.

Then, W of the keep, we enter the part remodelled by John of Gaunt from the 1370s, architecturally the most rewarding of the castle. First, a section of the curtain wall to the inner court. Placed against it were the KITCHENS. Only the outer wall survives, with the remains of hearths of four enormous fireplaces, the fourth, to the E, being a C15 addition for a boiling cauldron. The kitchens connected to the larders and storerooms in the Strong Tower and to the Great Hall through what is now an irregular open space in between.

The STRONG TOWER was vaulted on the ground floor, first floor and second floor, the vaults being mostly four-centred rib-vaults with single-chamfered ribs, but also four-centred tunnel-vaults. The ground-floor vaults are intact but only the western rooms survive at the upper levels. On the first floor were no doubt buttery and pantry, for it was the common arrangement of great halls that the portal would lead into a screens passage from which three doors would lead to these service rooms and the middle one into the kitchen, usually a little more distant. This is exactly as it is at Kenilworth, except that the kitchen (as e.g. also at Hampton Court) is on a lower level.

The Strong Tower is at the N end of the Great Hall range which is symmetrical on the exterior, i.e. when seen from the outer court to the W with the Strong Tower on the l. and the Saintlowe Tower to the r. The hall is set between these two angle projections, each with polygonal projections against its own angles and a triangular rib or buttress in the middle between them. This is an early case (though not the earliest) of a domestic building being given what can only be called a façade; for the internal arrangements do not justify the similarity in appearance of the two projecting wings. The SAINTLOWE TOWER contained a wine cellar, but the rest of it was not used for storage. Here the upper levels had a handsome lobby and viewing gallery connecting the hall with the state apartments to the S and lodgings above. Both towers were originally one storey higher than they are now.

Now, the GREAT HALL. Apart from Westminster Hall of the same years there is no late C14 hall to compare with that of Kenilworth, either for architectural quality or for scale.* It occupies the W side of the inner court, standing on the site of an earlier hall built by Thomas, Earl of Lancaster, in 1313–14, remodelled by Henry de Grosmont in 1347. Almost completely rebuilt again by John of Gaunt in 1373–80, following the model of Edward III's new hall at Windsor and raised on cellars. Unsurprising, since craftsmen from Windsor were employed here too. So the Great Hall itself lay on the first floor, above a vaulted undercroft. It has its portal in the N bay and was reached by an outer flight of twenty stairs S of the kitchen and a landing. The front to the courtyard is irregular with the originally square projection for the portal on the r. being balanced by a polygonal bay window on the l. Of the four bays in

35

*After the exceptional roof of Westminster Hall (span 69 ft (21 metres)), Kenilworth (45 ft (13.7 metres)) had the widest roof of any royal hall in medieval and Tudor England. The Kenilworth hall is 90 ft (27.4 metres) long.

between, three have tall two-light Perp windows and the remaining one of solid walling had a fireplace and chimney within. The bays are separated by stepped buttresses, and along the base is a sloping plinth mirroring that on the keep.

The Great Hall UNDERCROFT is of three naves in five bays. The section of the vaulting is again four-centred. The piers start octagonal and then split to repeat the single-chamfer arrangement of transverse arches and diagonal ribs. In the N bay, i.e. below the screens passage, is an entry from the court and an exit to the outer court. The principal PORTAL above this entry has several orders of very fine shafts and in the arch three orders of lively foliage. Morris suggests that the stone-work might have been reused from the 1347 hall. The porch is panelled and the panels are cusped. The HALL has tall windows to the outer as well as the inner court. They are of two lights with two transoms, arched and cusped below the transoms and at the top. The window heads are again four-centred. The tracery is similar to the contemporary Perp windows in the chapter house of St Mary's, Warwick. The windows are deep-set with panelled surrounds and stone seats round the alcoves. There are two large fireplaces facing one another in the middle of the walls. They are panelled in the reveals with one panel for each reveal and an arch bending forward at the top of each panel. The spandrels have pierced tracery. The plain walls above would have been used to display tapestries. The high table was, as always, at the end opposite that of the screens passage, i.e. the S end here. At this end were three smaller fireplaces. Adjoining the high table is a big polygonal bay window to the inner court, and this has, very considerably, a fireplace of its own.

On the opposite side of the hall there is another bay with a lobby facing the outer court. It is entered through an arch smaller than the window arches. This is in the SAINTLOWE TOWER, it and marks the entrance to the passage to the state apartments to the SE. It has large two-light transomed windows in panelled surrounds to the S and W, evidently designed for looking out across the mere. Even in its ruined state, it is easy to see how splendid this all was. It truly expressed Gaunt's wealth, power and hospitality, symbolizing his regal status. Moreover, as Morris observes, Leicester left the Great Hall unaltered when he gave the castle a makeover 200 years later, for this building entirely suited the image he wished to project.

Along the S side of the inner court are the remains of the STATE APARTMENTS, largely dismantled in 1649–50 apart from the lower parts of the walls and GAUNT'S TOWER in the angle on the S which still stands four storeys high on two sides. Less of the living rooms exists, but from the outer court, S of them, one can get a good idea of their bulk. The GREAT CHAMBER and the SECOND CHAMBER were on the upper floor and high in the tower there were private rooms for the duke. There were two ranges separated by an angled joint midway, with the CENTRAL ORIEL containing the direct entrance from the inner court and perhaps intended as a visual echo of the hall oriel. This was rib-vaulted on the ground floor. Leicester refronted the chambers on either side of the oriel, adding canted bay windows to the court. GAUNT'S TOWER also divides the two ranges and projects s into the outer court. It contained garderobes. Just w of Gaunt's Tower on the outside wall is a curious triangular projection, set on a decorated base. This belonged to the 'compass window' lighting the high end of the Great Chamber.

The exposed stone foundations in the grass NE of the state apartments may belong to the C13 CHAPEL. Nearby Henry VIII built a continuous timber-framed range along the E side of the inner court. This range was demolished after the Civil War, but it was barely forty years old and still standing when Leicester added a range of his own, Leicester's Building, E of the range just discussed. It faces E, tall and commanding, and must have been consciously designed as a counterpart to the Norman keep which Leicester also restored. It gains the appearance of great height by having its foundations in the ditch, well below the level of the inner court. The resulting E façade would have had a mighty tower at each end, separated by Henry VIII's lower range in between.

LEICESTER'S BUILDING now stands alone as a striking ruin at the s end of the E front. It abuts the state apartments at the NE corner where the E end was partly rebuilt to accommodate the addition. It was erected in 1571–2 under *William Spicer* to provide accommodation for Queen Elizabeth and her retinue who visited in 1572 and came again in 1575. There were improvements between these dates, the external sw stair-turret being added *c.* 1575. With its basement it has four storeys. The E façade is nearly, but not quite, symmetrical, with three canted bay windows, all with mullions and transoms. To the back the windows are narrower but equally tall. The expanse of glass in the three-storey windows of the principal floor was conspicuously showy and the method of fixing was extremely daring for its date. Inside it is an open shell, but there are internal Tudor doorways and fireplaces and holes in the walls for beams and ceiling plasterwork. The principal state rooms were on the upper two floors on the s. Steel stairs and platforms inserted by English Heritage in 2014 enable visitors to see these features and enjoy the fine views from within.

Leicester also added completely afresh a GATEHOUSE towards Castle Green. This then became the main entrance, but in 1650 it was converted into a private house for Col. Hawkesworth, and the archways were blocked. The gatehouse, though of a substantial size and with a number of sizeable apartments inside, still has the traditional form of castle gatehouse (cf. Warwick and Maxstoke), with turrets to the outside and the inside. The E attachment with its two gables belongs to 1650. But on the w side is Leicester's 1570s porch with his initials, *ex situ,* erected here *c.* 1650.* It has two pairs of pilasters with shell-topped niches between. The doorway is round-arched, and its soffit has a curious transverse ribbing or fluting. A triglyph frieze with decorated metopes follows, and then battlements. Inside, in the SOUTH ROOM on the ground floor, is a splendid and curious stone chimneypiece also with Leicester's initials, dated 1571 and again brought from elsewhere in 1650. Possibly from the Great Chamber in Leicester's Building, for which *Robert Coxe* was making an alabaster chimneypiece in 1571. The opening is flanked by pairs of pilasters with sunk panels and a cusped pointed head, a piece of conscious Gothicism. Above is a wooden overmantel, too large for its location, with beautiful leaf trail in the centre panel and coupled over-decorated colonnettes l. and r. The staircase in Hawkesworth's extension has turned balusters. The spiral stair in the SW turret is entirely of timber, with central post and solid oak treads.

To the W of the gatehouse are the gardens. Immediately alongside, a small KNOT GARDEN with an embattled gateway in the C18 boundary wall on the N. The ELIZABETHAN GARDEN is on the terrace above. This is a reinstatement by *Richard Griffiths Architects* and specialist advisers for English Heritage, 2009, of the long-lost formal garden created by Leicester for Queen Elizabeth. The recreation is based chiefly on a textual description of the original garden by Robert Langham, a minor court official, dated 1575. This has been interpreted using archaeological findings coupled with evidence from contemporary garden illustrations. The grand approach is from a stair leading down from Leicester's forebuilding w of the keep. This leads to a raised terrace with ARBOURS at each end. The garden below is divided into four quarters, each halved by a walkway. In the middle of each quarter is a 15-ft (4.6-metre) mottled pink OBELISK made of oak painted to look like porphyry. The centrepiece of the garden is the white marble FOUNTAIN carved by *Tim Crawley* in the muscular and slightly naïve English Renaissance style of Cornelius Cure of Southwark. It has two Atlantes holding a ball with Leicester's ragged staff above.† Carved panels round the base. Aligned with the stairway and fountain is a Neoclassical two-storeyed AVIARY of painted timber. The recreation has its doubters, but as a foil to the great keep and as a part of Leicester's story it triumphantly succeeds.

Lastly, and w again, is the space in the far NW where Henry VIII relocated portions of the Pleasance buildings in 1524. Nothing remains. Of the original Pleasance created for Henry V *c.* 1417–18, which lay between the edge of the mere and the medieval hunting park, only earthworks remain, ⅝ m. w.

---

*The Renaissance detailing has similarities with the w doorway surround at St Nicholas' Church.

†Some historians have suggested that Langham's 'boll' should have been a bowl rather than a sphere.

These consist of a large double-moated enclosure with a stone-revetted dock or basin towards the mere. Within was a luxurious timber-framed manor house and banqueting house. C15 kings used it as a rural retreat away from the full court.

PERAMBULATIONS

Kenilworth has two distinct parts, divided by the ridge on the southern edge of Abbey Fields. The historic buildings lie to the N, with the modern commercial centre to the S along Warwick Road. The first perambulation takes a circuit round the Abbey Fields with detours N and E. The detours lengthen the route substantially, and visitors may prefer to walk round the fields first and then explore the N and E parts separately.

1. North

Outside the castle is a good place to begin. With one's back to Leicester's Gatehouse CASTLE GREEN is on the l., with a pretty row of houses along its N fringe. Only one pair (Nos. 12–13) a little grander, i.e. of stone with mullioned windows. To the r. a little triangular green known as THE GODCAKE marks the start of CASTLE HILL, which runs E towards the parish church with pleasant brick cottages curving up the slope. They were built from 1803. On the r. is LITTLE VIRGINIA, a large group of thatched cottages around another small green, mainly timber-framed, some with stone infill as well as brick. Restored as a group by *Viner, Barnwell, Hatwood*, 1972. On the r. at the top, WANTAGE (No. 1) by *Buckland & Farmer* for Miss Ethie Gilbert Dennison, 1901. A sturdy house in the Domestic Revival style. Mainly roughcast, partly brick with stone mullion windows. Asymmetrical. Good details, including wrought-iron gutter brackets, decorated rainwater heads and a carved stone block with the name Wantage as a monogram. From here we are in the HIGH STREET, with open views of the ABBEY FIELDS and Abbey Pool on the r. in the gap opposite Nos. 68–80. On the l., CLINTON HOUSE (No. 78) is a large 1840s Tudor-style house in brick with stone-coped gables and clustered chimneys. STONE HOUSE (No. 64), dated 1752 (rainwater head) and supposedly boat-shaped, e.g. the long canted end bays and the roof-line. Angled porch with moulded stepped parapet. Good outbuildings, including former coach house with Venetian window and miniature dovecote above. On the S, No. 35 is low, brick with key-block windows and two angled bays. It adjoins No. 33, built as an extension to the convalescent home by *John Cundall*, 1887, with ornamental stonework above the entrance and in the brickwork of the chimney base alongside. ST NICHOLAS PARISH HALL (No. 26) on the N side is free Gothic-cum-Tudor, brick with dark stone dressings, by *Harry Quick*, 1911. From here the street is lined with pollarded trees and widens out into what was once a small market place. On the S side, just where one turns to the church, is the BANK GALLERY (No. 13), very different front and back. The lively street front is by *Cundall*, 1885, originally for the Leamington Priors and Warwickshire Banking Company. Stone, with rounded corners, pilasters, porch with spandrel carving, and little first-floor oriels, all with Jacobethan ornament. The W end is plain, with shaped gable and tall chimney, but then the rear is charming early Gothic Revival, three bays with a canted bay window in the middle, raised and castellated. Ogee-headed windows and quatrefoil windows. This was THE PRIORY, overlooking the churchyard and abbey fields, built by William Cleeve *c.* 1770.

At the end of the little market place are two fine late C18 three-storey houses separated by New Street and facing W down High Street. The house on the N is FIELDGATE (No. 2 Fieldgate Lane), of five bays, brick and quite simple. It really belongs to Fieldgate Lane. The former ABBOTSFORD SCHOOL (closed in 2010) on the S is the grand Georgian house of Kenilworth, *c.* 1760–70 probably, brick and stone dressings, with two two-storeyed canted bays l. and r., lunette windows over them, and pediments nicely detailed with modillions over the lunettes. The doorway, rather squeezed in, has a broken pediment on Tuscan columns. Abbotsford is in BRIDGE STREET. It is followed soon by KENILWORTH HALL (now flats), a rendered house of the same type, but later. A Venetian window to the street, two canted bays to the S. On the side elevation to Pears Close, a plainer Venetian window and a lunette window over.

Before continuing E, one must explore FIELDGATE LANE which leads to the Roman Catholic church (*see* Churches) and FIELDGATE HOUSE opposite, the latter mainly C18 but with an early C19 Doric stone porch. This was the home of the Amhersts. The Edwardian and inter-war houses make best sense if followed N to S, i.e. back towards the High Street. First in date is QUARRY HOUSE (No. 26), by *Crouch & Butler*, 1907. Brick with stone detailing to offset porch. Hints of Arts and Crafts adventurousness creep in at ARCLID (No. 22) and CAPESTHORNE (No. 16), both *c.* 1910, one roughcast with canted windows to its front bedrooms, the other L-plan with flat-roofed curved overhang above the entrance. Especially delightful, Nos. 33–45 opposite, an attractively varied group, all thatched, by *Crouch, Butler & Savage* after 1924. In contrast, on the E side is FIELDGATE CLOSE (No. 14A), stone gabled centre, brick wings l. and r. and diamond-pane windows, *c.* 1835.

The continuation of the High Street is NEW STREET, and at the top of this is a group of not so small Georgian brick houses. One, LADBROKE HOUSE (No. 46), is datable to *c.* 1761 from a fire insurance plaque. Where they end MANOR ROAD turns r. with the MANOR HOUSE, timber-framed with a projecting porch, late C16 restored. To the r. off Coventry Road, in Water

Tower Lane, the former WINDMILL, built in 1778, heightened as a water tower in 1884 and strikingly converted to a house by *Edward Reynolds Byron*, 1974–5. Sweeping walls and irregular windows, mildly reminiscent of Le Corbusier's church at Ronchamp. Tainter's Hill leads down towards a pleasant terrace of Late Victorian artisan houses in LOWER LADYES HILLS overlooking the allotments along the Finham Brook. Manor Road crosses the brook, and on the r. is another row, ODIBOURNE TERRACE, in School Lane. Red brick with blue bands and alternating headers, double porches and barge-boarded gables with iron finials, *c.* 1865, by Kenilworth builder *John Swain*.

Park Road leads to ALBION STREET. Opposite St Barnabas (*see* Churches), the former POLICE STATION (Copper House Club), by *William Kendall*, County Surveyor, 1857. In Albion Street, and in Hyde Road and School Lane to the N, Kenilworth UDC COUNCIL HOUSING by their architect and surveyor, *Sholto Douglas*, 1920–5. Head W past the former Baptist church (*see* Churches) and along Upper Rosemary Hill, where a footpath on the r. provides a shortcut to School Lane. On the r. towards the end, the former ST NICHOLAS NATIONAL SCHOOL, 1836, two-storeyed and looking more like a Nonconformist chapel than a school.

From here we resume our circuit of the Abbey Fields. On the corner, Nos. 2–4 Bridge Street, the so-called MARKET HOUSE, stone with arched opening at the front and a mullioned side window. In Rosemary Hill, ROSEMARY LODGE (No. 8) is a fanciful half-timbered concoction (1920s?) and No. 2 of the 1880s has a tourelle-like corner chimney. At the top of the hill, the former ABBEY HOTEL (now flats) at the corner of Priory Road. Big, brick with painted stone dressings and half-timbered gables. Gothic castellated corner tower. It is by *James P. Norrington* of Birmingham, whose designs were published (under the previous name of the Bowling Green Hotel) in *Building News*, 1885. In all of these there are historical echoes.

Turn r., i.e. W, and follow ABBEY HILL. A modest parade, as one expects in such a setting, with superb views over the park towards the church, abbey pool and castle. In it three Georgian brick houses. The first, past the Congregational church (*see* Churches), is ABBEY HOUSE (No. 9), of four bays with a doorway with squashed columns and a triglyph frieze. DUDLEY HOUSE (No. 12) is earlier, with angle pilaster strips. A pity the doorway has been treated so incongruously. CUMNOR HOUSE (No. 18) is a straightforward five-bay job. Among them, some striking Victorian houses. MONTPELIER HOUSE (No. 10) is double-fronted, brick with canted bays of stone and a Gothic doorway, 1870s. BELMONT (No. 16), stone with steep gables and a Gothic porch in the angle to the projecting l. wing, probably 1860s. Several others of passing interest, one C18 (No. 15), one mid-Victorian Gothic (No. 14) and another verging on the Italianate (No. 12A).

Beyond the WAR MEMORIAL, a Portland stone obelisk of 1922, the road round the park becomes FORREST ROAD. On the l., a large house with tile-hung gables (originally HILL CREST, but part since subdivided as MAX GATE), by *William de Lacy Aherne*, whose designs were published (as 'Drishane') in *Building News*, 1898. Then ROBIN HILL, by *Robert Harvey*, 1960. Bungalow, open-plan with large intercommunicating reception rooms under deep but low pitched roofs. After the brook the road leads back to the castle. Of note only the out-lying castle defences by the bend near Castle Grove and, off Castle Road to the r. opposite the car park entrance, FORD HOUSE. On an eminence with views towards the castle and abbey. Built as The Bungalow (although always two-storeyed), also by *Aherne*, for James and Ada Whittindale, 1895–6. Half-timbered and brick, with veranda facing the Abbey Pool.

2. South

From the war memorial on Abbey Hill, head s towards ABBEY END. The area suffered a devastating landmine explosion in 1940 and its redevelopment in the 1960s was clearly influenced by the new start made in the centre of nearby Coventry. It has a large open space, triangular with a traffic island, dominated by the HOLIDAY INN (originally the De Montfort Hotel), 1967. At the s facing down Warwick Road is the CLOCK TOWER, by *Harry Quick*, 1906, with its crown steeple (destroyed in 1940) restored in 1973–4. To the w on Smalley Place are the public buildings, the LIBRARY, by County Architect *Eric Davies*, 1967, and the former police station (now JUBILEE HOUSE). A little N, fronting Barrowfield Lane, is the OLD SCHOOL HOUSE, dated 1724. On the e side, a bus pull-in and shops with flats above, again 1960s although THE GALLERY at the N end, by *Robothams*, 2007, belongs to a regeneration scheme. It has THE ALMANACK bar on the ground floor, flats above and a cylindrical corner feature.

To the s, there is very little of note. The frontage on the w side of THE SQUARE is all new but this was the site of de Clinton's early C12 burh. On the l., the former KING'S ARMS AND CASTLE HOTEL has a handsome 1830s-looking front with dark stone unfluted Doric columns, but it is a copy, 1986–7. To the rear in Station Road, a bar created as an assembly room for the King's Arms after 1884 using the sandstone front of the original railway station building, 1844.* To the e on STATION ROAD nearer the railway, good later C19 villas, e.g. HYDE HOUSE (No. 34), double-fronted with decorative stone carving to doorway, canted bays with railings and wavy bargeboards to the gables. In SOUTHBANK ROAD, several of the 1880s villas are by *E. H. Lingen Barker* including WAVERLEY HOUSE,

---

*The station was demolished in the 1960s, but a new one, similar in form to the 1884 station, is due to open in 2016.

at the corner of Station Road, 1884–5, with half-hipped roof and decorative brickwork.

CASTLE END is the name for the lower (S) end of WARWICK ROAD, roughly S of Station Road. A few surviving timber-framed and C18 or C19 buildings – those in narrower parts of the street – serve as a reminder that the commercial centre of the town had already moved from the High Street to the S by the early C19. However, it was commerce without architectural pretension, as subsequent rebuilding has been too. Beyond Waverley Road, the CHRISTADELPHIAN HALL (No. 111) occupies the former Methodist church, 1844. Off to the l. a little further S, a long terrace of three-storeyed houses in CLARENDON ROAD, 1851. Little else until St John's church (*see* Churches) and a few older houses nearby, e.g. Nos. 190–192, early C19 Georgian.

Just beyond the S end of the town, two houses of note. Just E of Leamington Road, KENILWORTH LODGE (originally The Lodge), by *James Murray* for Thomas Hennell, 1861. Classical. To the E, approached via Birches Lane, THICKTHORN (now Kenilworth Manor Nursing Home). A large Neo-Tudor house of 1811. Ashlar, castellated, with polygonal turrets and canted bay windows. Central tower and pinnacled porch on W side. An added Victorian wing was demolished in the 1950s, but the building was restored to its former size with a new three-storey E wing in matching style, 1987. To the E, an even larger stable range, also castellated, with a four-centred archway to the gatehouse on S front. For 1907, extraordinary.

WOODSIDE, off Glasshouse Lane, ⅞ m. NE of Thickthorn. Now a hotel. A brick house of *c.* 1872 with kneelered gables, apparently built for William Sands Cox, a surgeon. Enlarged and refronted for Albert and Annie Cay by *Harry Quick*, 1906, with a striking porch tower with Tudor-arched doorway with coats of arms in the spandrels.

RUDFYN MANOR, Chase Lane, 2¼ m. NW of the clock tower. Timber-framed, of two storeys with attic. Oblong panel framing. Jettied front to cross-wing. Brick nogging. C19 diamond-pane windows, and a wooden oriel at the back. Extensively but attractively restored. (REDFERN MANOR nearby, on Birmingham Road, is early C16, again timber-framed, with an C18 rear addition in brick.)

KERESLEY *see* p. 293

KINETON

3050

A large village and former market town which gained its charter in 1227. The Battle of Edgehill in the English Civil War in 1642 is the most significant event in its history. The main centre is N of the River Dene, with Little Kineton to the s and Brookhampton to the w.

St Peter. Toffee-coloured Hornton stone. The w tower is of the late C13 to C15. Splendid late C13 w doorway of rich shafting and moulding (with fillets). The small window above is early C14. The rest of the church represents a remodelling by *J. & J. Belcher* of the nave, n aisle and transepts built by *Sanderson Miller* for the Rev. William Talbot, 1755–6. Carried out 1877–82 and subsequently. The Belchers also rebuilt the *c.* 1535 chancel on a grander scale. The Victorians, of course, regarded Miller's work as 'the lowest form of debased Gothic' and sought to improve it. The result is monumental and convincingly 'correct', yet also fanciful with openwork parapets and pinnacles, features also applied to the tower top, which has a zigzag frieze below the battlements. One enters through a curious pointed-tunnel-vaulted passage under the tower. It is of smooth speckled stonework, with transverse arches. On one side the stair to the ringing room, on the other a store. It is not medieval. Can it be of Miller's time or is it Victorian? Opinions differ. Inside, the arcade piers are the only detail which looks strange and the same question arises. The piers are as described by Glynne (*c.* 1840) but then they carried Tudor arches, evidently heightened at the restoration. – Plain WEST GALLERY. – ORGAN CASE and SCREEN by *John Belcher*,

Kineton, St Peter, view showing alterations by Sanderson Miller.
Drawing by Captain James Saunders, early C19

1905. Good, in a freely mixed classical style between Jacobean and Dixhuitième. – ROYAL ARMS, 1724. – PROCESSIONAL CROSS, of beaten copper. Given in 1924 and at that time said to be 'of ancient Italian workmanship'. – STAINED GLASS. Three by *Powell*: E, 1892 (designer *J.W. Brown*), chancel S, 1907, and chancel N, 1922. – Over vestry door also *Powell* (*J.D. Egan*), 1898, with inscription on copper *repoussé* panel below. – Transepts by *F. Holt & Co.*, 1894 and 1896. – MONUMENTS. Late C14 stone effigy, defaced. – Engraved brass plaque to John Venour †1730. – Charles Bentley, †1727, and others. Large tablet with pilasters, broken segmental pediment and a mermaid in the predella. – Several C18 to C19 tablets in chancel and transepts.

ST FRANCIS OF ASSISI (R.C.), Southam Street. *Brian A. Rush & Associates*, 1974–5. Rectangular with a long clerestory over the worship area. Open timber roof. Some fittings from the previous chapel in Bridge Street. – Victorian Gothic REREDOS.

METHODIST CHURCH, Southam Road. *T.T. Allen* of Stratford, 1893. Brick with stone dressing, plate tracery, slate roof and iron gable finial.

Former SCHOOL (now a SURGERY) SW of Market Place. By *Francis Trepess* of Warwick, 1892, brick with stone dressings, faintly Jacobean with characterful shaped gables.

PERAMBULATION. Kineton, although pleasant and attractive, is generally small-scale and even timid architecturally. Mostly the town is of Grey Lias and brown ironstone. The MARKET SQUARE is N of the church, quite secluded. In the middle, the single-storey brick former SCHOOL that replaced the Market Hall in 1840. On the S, the former ROSE & CROWN dated 1664: mullioned windows with hoodmoulds and still a four-centred head to the doorway. On the E the chequerwork front of BOX TREE COTTAGE disguises an entirely timber-framed property within. Along the N a row of five stone houses built by the tenants on building leases granted in 1671. Lias with ironstone dressings. The details much like the Rose & Crown. One is discreetly dated 1674.

To the E fronting Southam Road, the former SCHOOL of 1866. On SOUTHAM ROAD by the Methodist church (*see* above) is a small green, with chequer brick ODDFELLOWS COTTAGES, *c.* 1830, on the E. WOODFIELDS alongside is another typical C17 Kineton Lias house with ironstone mullions and dressings. S again, facing the junction in the village centre, a good resited Victorian shopfront with iron cresting. On the opposite corner by the church, a nice Early Georgian house, THE CHESTNUTS, red and yellow chequer with a blind Venetian opening facing the churchyard. Into BANBURY STREET where a small green has the WAR MEMORIAL by *F.W.B. Yorke*, 1920, its design based on the medieval cross at Brigstock, Northants. Beyond, the Victorian POST OFFICE with polychromatic headers to the windows (*see* below).

Back to the green, and down Manor Lane past the CHURCH
HOUSES and the MANOR (now a nursing home) to the bottom
of Bridge Street, which runs s from the church down to the
river. CLARENDON HOUSE of *c.* 1865 has a handsome stone
front with two-storey square bays. Higher up, mid-C18 DENE
HOUSE has a curious ironstone porch, added after 1915.
Across the road low brick ST FRANCIS CHAPEL with stone
hoodmoulds was the Roman Catholic church from 1927 to
1975. Higher again, PRESCOTT HOUSE has a Venetian
window. Then towards the junction, the COURT HOUSE,
1807–8 with later extension on Warwick Road, has a wide
limestone frontage with a presumably re-set ironstone doorway
with late C17 bolection mouldings and broken pediment.

In WARWICK ROAD, a run of minor semi-public buildings.
On the N, the PUBLIC HALL, by *T. T. Allen*, 1894, with stone
at street level and brick above. Beyond WESLEY MANSE, the
former POLICE STATION by *William Kendall*, County Sur-
veyor, 1857–8. Opposite, ROXBURGH HOUSE was built by
Lady Willoughby de Broke as the Middle Class School. By
William Lait, the Compton Verney estate architect (and also
County Surveyor), 1863. In the distinctive Kineton style in
Lias with plate tracery, yellow brick dressings and red, blue
and yellow brick patterning to the window headers (cf. the Post
Office, above). Further w, more polychromatic ESTATE COT-
TAGES in the same manner.

In a woodland off Castle Road, s of Warwick Road, the remains
of a late C12 or early C13 MOTTE-AND-BAILEY CASTLE.
Motte, 125 ft (38 metres) in diameter at the base, and evidence
of the bailey wall NE of it.

LONGBOURN FARM, N of Brookhampton Lane. A mid-C19
model farm, originally on the Compton Verney estate. Barns
and covered yards in six units under one roof.

p. 74 PITTERN HILL HOUSE, ½ m. w of the church. By *E. Guy
Dawber*, 1901. Roughcast Arts and Crafts. Still further out on
the other side of the road, WINDMILL FARM has a sail-less
stone TOWER MILL. Described as 'new erected' in 1794. The
woodwork of the rotating cap remains, but the machinery
has gone.

LITTLE KINETON, s of the River Dene, has several stone cottages round a spacious green. DIANA LODGE is the only
notable house s of the green, 1840s with ironstone dressings,
irregular gables and diamond-pane windows. Used as a school
in the 1850s to 1880s. Large early C20 extensions by *Charles
M. C. Armstrong*. N of the green is the NORTON GRANGE
ESTATE, clustered round the mansion (sometime KINETON
HOUSE), built after 1823 on the site of the old seat of the
Bentleys (cf. the mermaid memorials in the church). The house
much altered and plain. To the w, the STABLES and KENNELS
built for the Warwickshire Hunt by *Hugh Williams*, 1839. Williams was a hunt member, related to the Willoughby de Broke
and Lucy families. House and stable-kennel range, quite grand.
Brick, Flemish bond with stucco dressings and slate roof.

· Henley-in-Arden, High Street (p. 361)
· Atherstone, Long Street (p. 123)

3	5
4	6

7. Halford, St Mary, tympanum, *c.* 1125–30 (p. 345)
8. Berkswell, St John the Baptist, crypt, *c.* 1170–80 (p. 150)

9. Billesley, All Saints, remnant of tympanum, *c.* 1140–50 (p. 154)
10. Berkswell, St John the Baptist, chancel, *c.* 1170–80 (p. 150)

11. Temple Balsall, St Mary, sw window, late C13 (p. 626)
12. Pillerton Hersey, St Mary, priest's doorway, mid-C13 (p. 504)
13. Burton Dassett, All Saints, N aisle, detail of capital, C13 (p. 173)
14. Austrey, St Nicholas, tower and spire, late C13 (p. 125)

11 12
13   14

23. Coventry, Holy Trinity, nave, begun *c.* 1360, interior view W (p. 240)
24. Guy's Cliffe, Chapel of St Mary Magdalene, mostly *c.* 1454–5, interior (p. 344)

19. Kinwarton, St Mary the Virgin, chancel s window, stained glass, *c.* 1316 (p. 400)
20. Astley, St Mary the Virgin, stall backs, *c.* 1365–90 (p. 116)
21. Coventry, Holy Trinity, Doom wall painting, *c.* 1430–40 (p. 243)
22. Warwick, St Mary, Beauchamp Chapel, E window, figure sculpture, *c.* 1445–9 (p. 655); stained glass by John Prudde, 1447 (p. 656)

| 19 | 21 |
| 20 | 22 |

23. Coventry, Holy Trinity, nave, begun *c.* 1360, interior view w (p. 240)
24. Guy's Cliffe, Chapel of St Mary Magdalene, mostly *c.* 1454–5, interior (p. 344)

25. Warwick, St Mary, Beauchamp Chapel, 1443–9, interior, furnishings completed 1464 (pp. 654–5)
26. Warwick, St Mary, monument to Richard Beauchamp, Earl of Warwick (†1439), made *c.* 1448–53 (p. 656)

| 27 | 29 |
| 28 | 30 |

31. Kenilworth Castle, aerial view; keep *c.* 1124–30, extended *c.* 1205–15 and
    c. 1361–93; Leicester's Building and gatehouse, 1570s (p. 380)
32. Warwick Castle, view from s, mostly 1330s–90s (p. 661)
33. Maxstoke Castle, aerial view, mid-C14 (p. 450)

<table>
<tr><td rowspan="2">31</td><td>32</td></tr>
<tr><td>33</td></tr>
</table>

34. Kenilworth Castle,
Inner Court facing SE
(p. 384); Leicester's
Building (l., p. 387),
1570–1 and 1575, State
Apartments (p. 386)
and Gaunt's Tower
(r.), late C14 (p. 387)
35. Kenilworth Castle,
Great Hall, c. 1373–80,
interior (pp. 385–6)
36. Coughton Court,
gatehouse, c. 1510–20
(p. 214)

34
35 | 36

37 | 39
38 | 40
   | 41

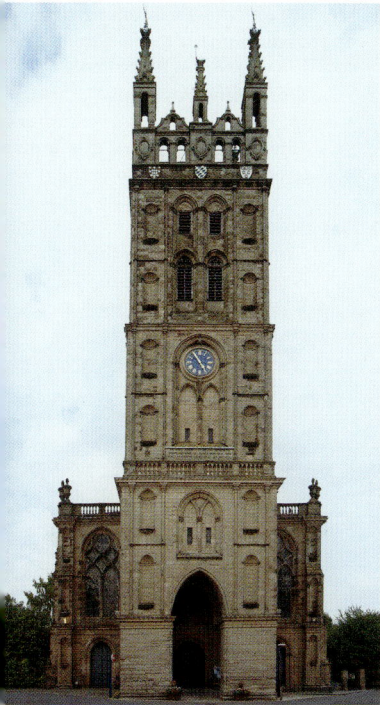

50
51 52

53. Arbury Hall, chapel, 1678, plasterwork by Edward Martin (p. 107)

58. Ragley Hall, 1679–83, built by William Hurlbutt, E front; portico by James Wyatt, *c*. 1780 (p. 523)
59. Ragley Hall, Great Hall, by James Gibbs, 1749–56 (p. 523)

60. Farnborough Hall, Drawing Room (former Dining Room), plasterwork by William Perritt of York and others, *c.* 1750 (p. 326)

61. Honington Hall, Saloon, designed by John Freeman of Fawley Court, executed by William Jones, 1751–2 (p. 367)

62. Arbury Hall,
s front centrepiece,
by Henry Keene,
1769–73 (p. 107)

63. Alscot Park,
Drawing Room,
ceiling by Thomas
Bromwich, 1765
(p. 100)

4. Great Packington, Packington Hall, by Matthew Brettingham the elder and Henry Couchman, 1766–72, w front (p. 338)
5. Great Packington, Packington Hall, Pompeian Room, decoration by Joseph Bonomi after 1782 (p. 339)

66. Farnborough Hall, Oval Pavilion, attributed to Sanderson Miller and William Hiorne (builder), *c.* 1750 (p. 327)
67. Radway, Edgehill, The Castle, by Sanderson Miller, completed 1745–5 (p. 521)
68. Walton, Bath House, by Sanderson Miller, 1749, interior (p. 643)

9. Napton-on-the-Hill, St Lawrence, tower, 1731 (p. 468)
0. Brailes, St Peter and St Paul (R.C.), 1726, interior (p. 165)

71. Over Whitacre, St Leonard, by Francis Hiorne, 1765–6, spire 1850 (p. 498)

2. Coventry, Binley, St Bartholomew, probably by Henry Couchman and Capability Brown, 1771–3, interior (p. 282)

3. Great Packington, St James, by Joseph Bonomi, 1789–90, nave interior (p. 337)

78	80
79	81

86. Studley Castle, by Samuel Beazley, 1834–7, principal front (p. 619)
87. Studley Castle, by Samuel Beazley, 1834–7, drawing room (p. 620)

88.   Merevale Hall, by Edward Blore, 1838–44, principal front (p. 457)

SACRED TO THE MEMORY OF
ELIZABETH EMMA,
WIFE OF JOHN EARDLEY-EARDLEY-WILMOT, ESQ.RE OF BERKSWELL HALL, IN THIS PARISH,
AND DAUGHTER OF C.H. PARRY, M.D.
OF THE CITY OF BATH.
ON THE 12.TH OF MAR.CH 1838, SHE GAVE BIRTH TO A SON AND A DAUGHTER,
AND, ON THE 22.ND OF THE SAME MONTH, AGED 29,
LEAVING HER HUSBAND AND EIGHT CHILDREN TO DEPLORE HER UNTIMELY LOSS,
HER BLESSED SPIRIT
WAS SUMMONED TO THE TRIBUNAL OF HER ALMIGHTY FATHER,
IN THE WELL GROUNDED HOPE
OF BEING RECEIVED, THROUGH THE MERITS OF HER REDEEMER,
INTO THE MANSIONS OF ETERNAL LIFE,
AND OF ENDLESS HAPPINESS AND GLORY.

89. Berkswell, St John the Baptist, monument to Elizabeth Emma Eardley-Wilmot (†1818), by Sir Richard Westmacott (p. 151)

90. Bidford-on-Avon, St Laurence, nave N arcade, by John Lattimer, 1835 (p. 153)

91. Hampton Lucy, St Peter ad Vincula, by Thomas Rickman and Henry Hutchinson, 1822–6, nave interior (p. 350)

89
90 | 91

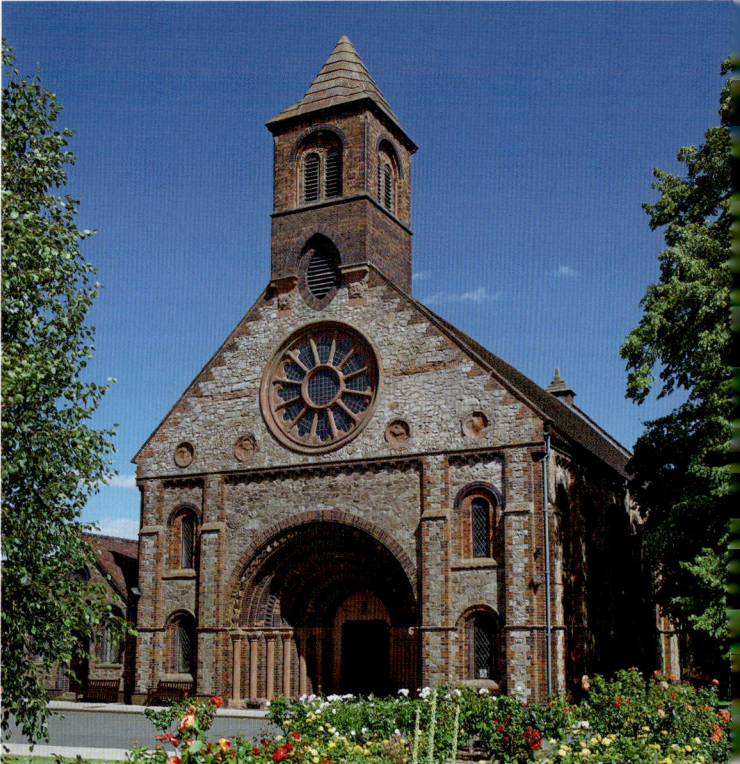

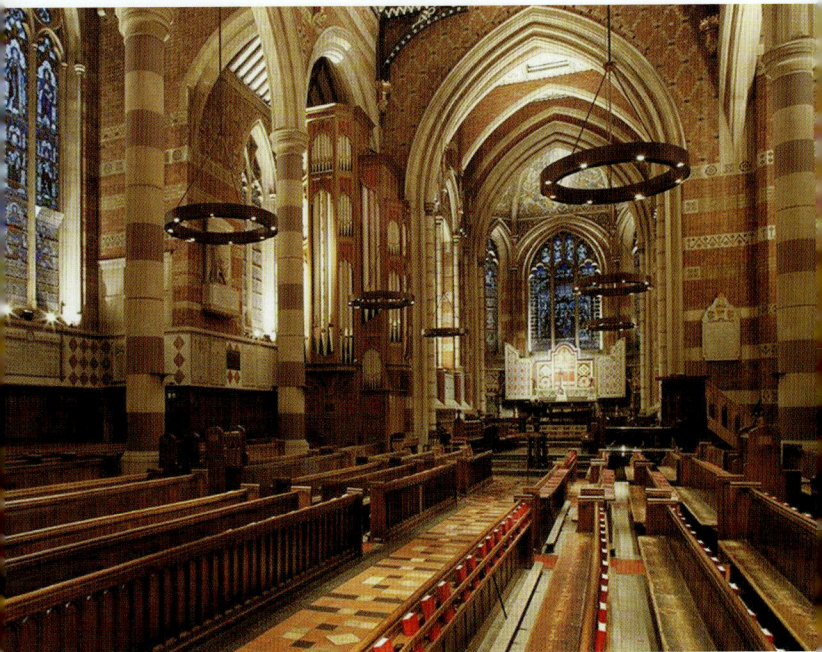

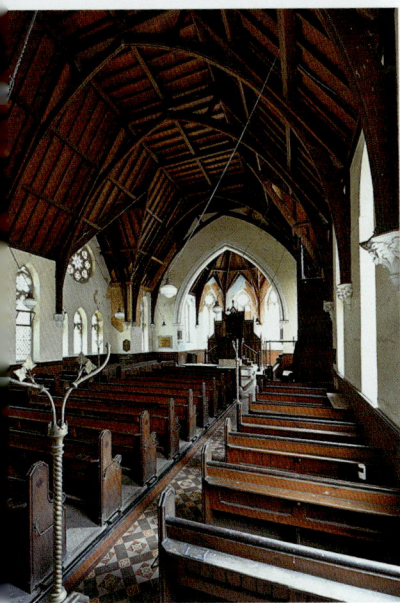

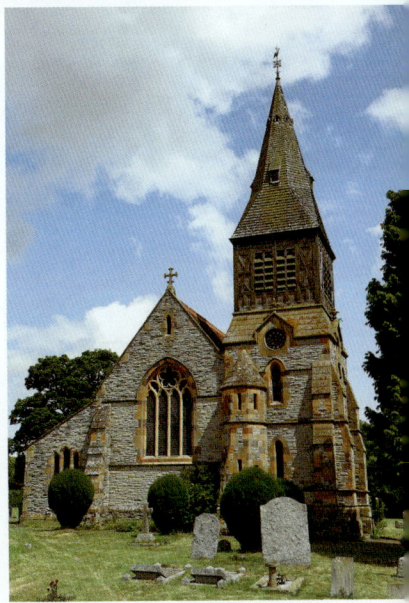

96. Rugby, St Marie (R.C.), by A.W.N. Pugin, 1845–7; tower and spire by Bernard Whelan, 1872 (p. 533)
97. Lower Shuckburgh, St John the Baptist, by John Croft, 1863–4, nave interior (p. 443)
98. Umberslade Baptist Church, by George Ingall, 1877, nave interior (p. 638)
99. Temple Grafton, St Andrew, chancel and tower, by Frederick Preedy, 1875 (p. 628)

104. Hampton-in-Arden, cottages, by W. E. Nesfield, 1868 (p. 348)

105. Hampton-in-Arden, Hampton Manor, clock tower, by W. E. Nesfield, 1872 (p. 348)

106. Nuneaton, King Edward VI College, by Clapton Crabb Rolfe, 1880 (p. 485)

107. Leamington Spa, Town Hall, by John Cundall, 1882–4 (p. 418)

108. Nether Whitacre, Whitacre Waterworks, by Martin & Chamberlain, 1872 and later (p. 470)
109. Alcester, Minerva Mill, c. 1878 (p. 97)

110. Stratford-upon-Avon, American Fountain, by Jethro Cossins, with carvings by Robert Bridgeman, 1887 (p. 608)

111. Nuneaton, United Reformed church (former Congregational), by Ingall & Son, 1903–4 (p. 483)

112. Wolverton Court, C16 (r.), C18 (l.), and 1912 (centre), by Clough Williams-Ellis (p. 719)

113. Ansley, St Laurence, w window, by Karl Parsons, 1931 (p. 104)
114. Coventry, Coundon, St George, by N.F. Cachemaille-Day, 1938 (p. 286)
115. Nuneaton, St Thomas More R.C. School, by H.N. Jepson, 1937 (p. 485)
116. Leamington Spa, Lillington, Our Lady (R.C.), by Rayner & Fedeski (Henry Fedeski) 1962–3; stained glass by Dom Charles Norris of Buckfast (p. 429)
117. Coventry, Lower Precinct, tile mural by Gordon Cullen, 1958, detail (p. 259)

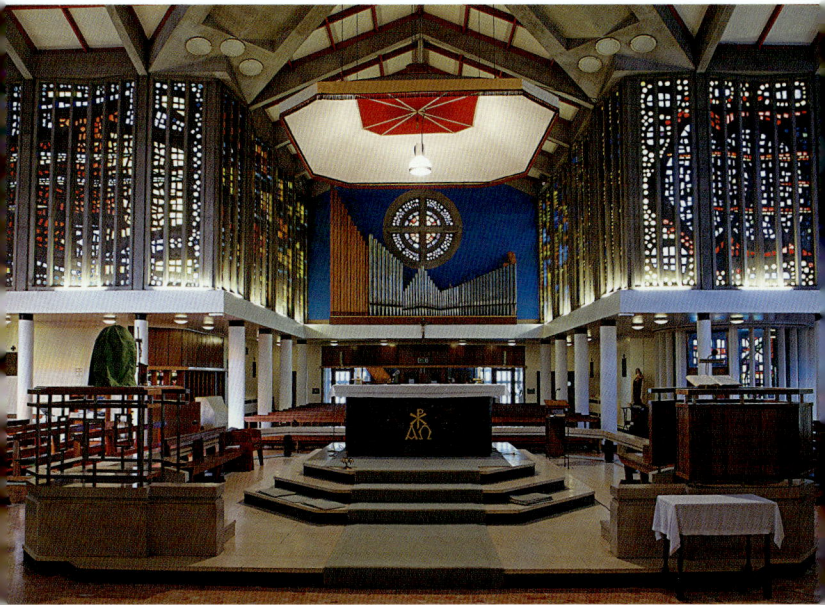

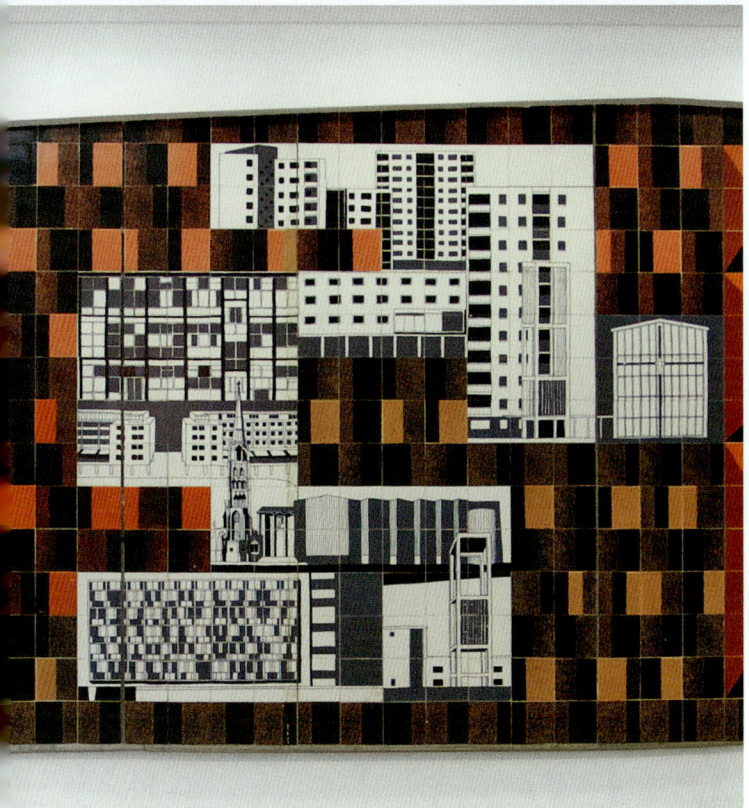

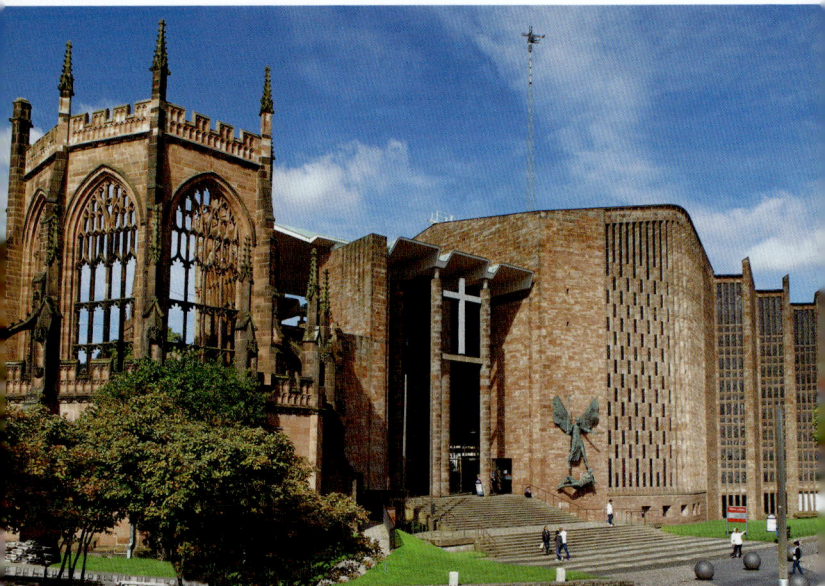

118. Coventry Cathedral, by Sir Basil Spence, 1956–62, with St Michael's church, C15, l. (p. 224)
119. Coventry Cathedral, baptistery, font and stained glass by John Piper and Patrick Reyntiens, 1957–61 (p. 229)

20. Coventry Cathedral, 1951–62, view towards Lady Chapel (p. 228); tapestry by Graham Sutherland, 1957–62 (p. 231)

121. Coventry, Warwick University, Maths House, by Howell, Killick, Partridge & Amis, 1968–70 (p. 301)
122. Barford, Debden Hollow, by Yorke, Harper & Harvey (Robert Harvey), 1969 (p. 138)

23. Coventry, Leisure Centre (The Elephant), City Architect's Department, 1974–6 (p. 251)

24. Stratford-upon-Avon, Royal Shakespeare Theatre, N front, by Scott, Chesterton & Shepherd, 1928–32; refurbished and extended by Bennetts Associates, 2005–11 (p. 595)

125. Coventry University, Engineering & Computing Building, by Arup Associates, 2009–12 (p. 253)

KINGSBURY

A very large ancient parish which included Hurley, Whateley and
Wood End (qq.v.) and Dosthill (Staffs.). Industrialization came
with the opening of the brickworks in the later C19 and the colliery in 1897. These operated until 1968–9. There was large-scale
gravel extraction in the Tame valley from 1936/7 into the 1970s,
and the giant oil terminal dominating the NE side of the village
was begun in the late 1960s.

ST PETER AND ST PAUL. The nave is essentially Norman. This
is shown by the arcade piers, N and S. They are round, with
decorated scallop capitals and square abaci. But the arches are
pointed, double-chamfered, and much too wide. Probably the
intermediate piers were removed and the arcades remodelled
with wider and taller arches c. 1300. Further Norman work in
the responds of the chancel arch, itself redone in 1887. In the
N chancel wall a trace of a C12 window r. of the arch into the
chapel. Everything was remodelled about 1300, namely the W
tower, the S aisle, the N transept (or Bracebridge Chapel), the
N aisle, and the chancel (E window, SEDILIA, and combined
PISCINA and CREDENCE SHELF with ballflower ornament).
C13 windows, several with intersecting tracery, some cusped,
and one in the N transept with trefoiled lights. Good figured
corbels to the arch from the N aisle into the transept. One is a
Green Man, the other puts his tongue out, holds his head, and
has a monkey by his side. The sandstone porch with its timber
roof is a fine C15 piece with cusped wind-braces. The W tower
largely rebuilt and heightened in 1610 as shown by an inscription over the W window. Of three stages, with Y-tracery in the
W window and belfry windows – no hint of Renaissance influences. The aisle roofs are Perp with carved bosses. The nave
has a flat plaster ceiling, C18, and stubby clerestory windows.
Restoration by *Bidlake* in 1907–8 – his, the pretty rainwater
heads of 1908. Tower repairs by *W.H.D. Caple*, 1928, and
restoration of the porch by *P.B. & A.B. Chatwin*, 1938, all
discreet and conservative. – PULPIT. A bold Victorian piece,
†1889, stone with marble shafts and baubles. – PEWS in nave
and aisles from a re-seating by *Richard Bennett* of Tamworth
in 1821–2. Intact, with curved fronts towards the E where the
triple-decker pulpit once stood. – (WALL PAINTING, C14
depiction of Christ in Majesty flanked by angels, concealed in
the roofspace over the E window.) – STAINED GLASS. Medieval
heraldic fragments in E window of N chapel. – E window by
Alexander Gibbs, 1883. – Two in chancel and one in S aisle by
Camm Bros, 1882. – Others by *T.W. Camm* for *R.W. Winfield
& Co.*, 1885–8. – Five by *Swaine Bourne*, 1878–89, two as
memorials to the artist's relatives. – In N aisle, by *A.N. Yoxall*
and *E.M. Whitford*, 1934. Excellent. – N aisle clerestory window
by *Terence Randall*, 1955. – MONUMENTS. In the N transept
three badly defaced effigies, one a slab with a bust in a

quatrefoil, the other two early to mid-C14. Dugdale gives an illustration of the effigy of Sir John de Bracebridge in its unmutilated state. It is said to be the earliest alabaster monument in the county. – Tablet in chancel to Ann Thirkell †1738, by *Samuel Huskinson*. – Simon Luttrell †1788. By *E. Grubb*. Large tablet, with a cherub by an urn in front of an obelisk. – James Luttrell, also †1788, unsigned, but similar.

KINGSBURY HALL. On a bluff above the river and separated from the church by a deep gulley. This really was a fortified site and house. The manor belonged to the Bracebridge family from the C12 until 1585. Parts of a C14 curtain wall remain, with a polygonal SE tower and an E archway. The house itself is of stone, largely C15, of three ranges, two of them irregularly attached to the longest, which runs along the S side. There was an extensive refurbishment *c.* 1565, as indicated by dendro-dating of roof timbers and floor frames in the E and S wings. The features are not very telling any longer, but there was a C17 shaped gable on the stone central section of the W front where the two side portions were rebuilt in brick in the C18. Inside a Tudor stone fireplace in the Great Hall on the first floor. Some lime-ash floors. Abandoned and ruinous since the 1970s, but restoration commenced under *Acanthus Clews*, 2009.

Down Church Lane running E from the church, the TEACHER'S HOUSE of Thomas Coton's original school endowment of 1686. Late C17. Of brick, five bays and two storeys. Hipped roof with dormer windows. Giant angle pilasters of stone and a stone string course which links up with the big segmental pediment of the doorway. Sundial over the door. Adjacent, the former BOARD SCHOOL (now residential) by *Charles Starkey*, 1884, with an extension by *J. W. Godderidge*, 1900. Red brick (now painted) with minimal stone dressings. Recessed centre with bellcote.

CORNFORTH ALMSHOUSES, Trinity Road, by *A. W. B. Macer-Wright*, 1926. A small group in domestic style, but in the spirit of the almshouse tradition.

Down by the river, the MILL (converted to apartments in 2008), 1747, and what remains of HEMLINGFORD BRIDGE, 1783, partly destroyed in 1982, since reconstructed as a footbridge.

TAMEHURST HOUSE, ½ m. S, Coventry Road. 1803, with fretwork timber porch and moulded plaster surrounds to the windows with rosettes frieze and cornice.

FLANDERS HALL, 1½ m. SE. Of *c.* 1700; H-shaped. Brick with stone quoins. Doorway with bolection moulding, narrow windows l. and r. Hipped roof. Rainwater heads dated 1854 with the initials of Kelyng Greenway. Of that date probably the windows with gauged brick flat arches with keystones, those on the main front with acanthus decoration.

BODYMOOR HEATH, 2½ m. W, has a former METHODIST CHAPEL, 1844: brick with pointed windows, gabled front and two short windows to gallery. Pleasant CANALSIDE buildings nearby. Near a lock, the DOG AND DOUBLET pub, *c.* 1800.

Further W, the Aston Villa Football Club TRAINING GROUND by *HB Architects*, 2006.

KINGS COUGHTON
Alcester

0050

BEAUCHAMP COURT, N of Arden Road, is an early C19 double-depth brick house of three storeys with round-arched ground-floor windows and slate hipped roof. It stands near the moated site of the manor house for which Giles de Beauchamp obtained a licence to crenellate in 1341.

KING'S NEWNHAM
Church Lawford

4070

The CHURCH was last used *c.* 1785 and had been demolished by 1795.* Only the tower and part of the roadside wall remain. The tower unbuttressed with tiled pyramid roof. Limestone rubble. Lower stage C12 with one Norman S window. Upper stages rebuilt with red sandstone quoins and mullioned two-light bell-openings, probably C16. – Slate slab for BRASS, 1852. – FONT and PISCINA preserved in the garden at the hall.

NEWNHAM HALL, S of the tower, is a three-bay Georgian brick house with a mansard roof, 1781. Next to it stands a stone building with mullioned windows in the gable-ends, said to have been a dovecote, now a house.

MONUMENT COMPLEX. In the fields ¼ m. E of Bretford and N of the road to King's Newnham a remarkable group of Neolithic ring-ditches revealed by aerial photography. A linear arrangement of four mounds connected by an oblong enclosure. The only relief feature, now barely visible, lies just N of the road in the third field E of the Fosse Way. Excavations have revealed a Mesolithic–Neolithic transitional flint tool scatter pre-dating the ring-ditches. No burials were found.

KINWARTON

1050

ST MARY THE VIRGIN. The church is small, of nave and chancel, with a weatherboarded bell-turret. A consecration date of 1316

*The village was depopulated in the late C16.

is recorded but the shell of the building (see the two N lancet windows) is C13. On the S two Dec windows. One in the chancel with the SEDILIA cutting into it, the other in the nave window of wood, with cusped Y-tracery. Restoration by *Butterfield*, 1847, when the internal division between nave and chancel was moved one bay E. The fine C14 roof maintains the old plan. Further work on porch and turret, 1850, including rebuilding the W wall. Inside the turret stands on excellent sturdy posts with arched bracing. This is perhaps C16 to C17. Two nave windows redone by *W. J. Hopkins* to receive new glass, 1866. – FITTINGS. Mainly by *Butterfield*, 1847. – Cup-shaped FONT on tapering cylindrical stem. Possibly 1316, with plain wooden cover secured with C16 metal bar and staples and a *Butterfield* corona above. – CHANDELIER. Of brass; C18, with three tiers of arms. – SCULPTURE. Alabaster panel of the Virgin in the Temple, typical work of the C15. Acquired in 1933. – STAINED GLASS. In a chancel S window an excellent early C14 Virgin and two praying donors. The inscription refers to Wili atte ye wode, i.e. William at Wood or de Bosco, and his wife, Leticie. William acquired land at nearby Great Alne from his brother John, a priest, in 1316. – Fine E window by *O'Connor*, 1847. – Maybe his too the quarry glass W window, *c.* 1850. – Bright N and S nave windows by *Alexander Gibbs*, 1866, both with later added inscriptions. Rich colours and mosaic style, doubtless under *Butterfield*'s influence. – Two lancets in nave, *Hardman*, 1867 and 1871. – Chancel N, *Kempe & Co.*, 1911. – In the churchyard a CROSS-SHAFT, Anglo-Danish, with defaced interlace, incorporated in a monument to Fanny Seymour, †1871, by *Preedy*.

The church, the former RECTORY and a huge beech tree form a happy group. The house, 1788; red brick of three bays and two and a half storeys. Drawing room enlarged 1836. New room alongside dining room, 1843. Later coach house and outbuildings, 1838 and (by *Joseph Lattimer*) 1868. Further S, timber-framed GLEBE FARM, with barns and cartshed with brick infill and weatherboarding. An excellent group.

DOVECOTE. In a field NE of the church. A relic of a long-vanished moated grange of Evesham Abbey. In the care of the National Trust since 1957. Round with conical roof, and from the ogee head of the small doorway to be dated early or mid-C14. There are over 580 nesting holes in 17 tiers, complete with a potence – a central rotating beam with an attached ladder from which any nest can be reached.

On the main road W of the church, a brick house (now two cottages and much altered) with Gothick details, built as a TOLLHOUSE on the Alcester to Wootton Wawen road, turnpiked in 1814.

Towards Alcester, KINWARTON HOUSE on a ridge overlooking the Arrow valley. A substantial but plain house, 'new erected' in 1823–4 for Thomas Brown and enlarged for Frederick Gerard, who bought it in 1877. The older part at the rear, the S front of *c.* 1880, wider than the main house and symmetrical with a canted bay. Once a school but now converted to commercial use.

KNIGHTCOTE

Burton Dassett

METHODIST CHURCH. Chequered brick with three-bay gabled front dated 1837. Porch added 1914. Plain interior with raised desk, later C19 iron rails and pews. Alongside, a good group of ironstone COTTAGES with thatched roofs. KNIGHTCOTE MANOR is H-plan, C17 with mullioned windows. To the S, STOCKWELL FARMHOUSE has an ironstone range dated 1698, still with mullioned windows.

KNOWLE

Knowle was originally a chapelry in Hampton-in-Arden, only becoming a separate ecclesiastical parish in 1859 (and civil parish in 1866). By then it was a substantial village, on the main Warwick–Birmingham road. It had a wharf on the Grand Union Canal, opened in 1800, and from 1852 Knowle had access to the railway at nearby Dorridge. Rapid expansion came after the Second World War when proximity to Birmingham and the Warwickshire countryside made Knowle attractive for residential development. It is now a small town but urbanization of the central area has been restrained and a village character is maintained.

Parts of the pre-1974 parish have now been taken into Dorridge, Packwood and Temple Balsall (qq.v.).

CHURCHES

ST JOHN THE BAPTIST, ST LAWRENCE AND ST ANNE, Kenilworth Road. A Perp church of some ambition. Dates refer to the foundation of a chapel in 1396, a consecration in 1403, and the foundation of a chantry college in the church in 1416. Often cited as a church of one period, it was clearly built in stages over several decades in the early C15 with changes of plan along the way. The use of different stone helps to differentiate between the stages, the older parts being in soft white Arden stone while red Kenilworth sandstone was used later on. First, a chancel (originally three bays) with nave and N aisle (four bays). Soon after came the S aisle and arcade of five bays, initially overlapping the chancel. Later the chancel was extended E over a processional way and the nave and N aisle altered with added N chapel. The stonework of the tower indicates at least two phases, the lower part in grey sandstone and the top in white stone. Its date is unclear but it was clearly built on to the existing nave. With the clerestory and unifying parapets the church was complete by *c.* 1440. The clerestory has three-light windows and battlements and pinnacles to the S. The S aisle has battlements and pinnacles too. High chancel with canted E end over a processional subway (blocked since *c.* 1745) from N to S, apparently because there was no room to build E of the chancel. The interior is without a chancel arch. Five-bay arcades of standard elements, but differing N from S. The last bay on the N side is later and lower. It opens into a transeptal N chapel, also later. The chapel has a specially good ceiling with bosses.

Just inside the chancel, remains of SEDILIA and PISCINA of a time when the chancel was shorter. In the sanctuary the later SEDILIA and PISCINA, now skied because the floor was lowered after the subway ceased to function. Main interior restoration and re-seating by *Joseph Nevill* of Coventry, 1859–60. The exterior done by *J.A. Chatwin*, 1877, and the roof, 1891. Also by *Chatwin* the vestry and organ chamber on the N side, 1899–1900, when the chancel was rearranged. The N chapel was delightfully reworked as the Soldiers Chapel in 1921 by *W.H. Bidlake*, with an elaborate carved stone screen at the entrance and stencilled wall decoration within. Other work by *Bidlake*, 1909–32. – FONT. Octagonal, Perp, with awkward quatrefoils. – REREDOS. Oak, *Jones & Willis*, 1890. – STALLS. With MISERICORDS which have mostly foliage, early C15 – SCREEN. The best in the county. High, Perp, with bressumer, carved trails, lierne-vaulting and unusual pendant arches; dado has exuberantly carved double middle rail; E face much restored. – PULPIT. An excellent Arts and Crafts piece. Designed by *Bidlake* and carved in oak by *Alec Miller* (of *J.W. Pyment & Sons*) of Chipping Campden, 1929–30. – CHESTS. Two dugouts, one of them 7 ft 7 in. (2.31 metres) long. – STAINED GLASS. A full scheme, mostly of good quality. Five by *Lavers, Barraud & Westlake*, the E window 1871 and others in chancel and S aisle 1876–90. – Four by *Heaton, Butler & Bayne*, in N and S aisles, 1902–10. – Two by *Hardman*, S aisle, 1864 and 1896. – Two by *Clayton & Bell*, W tower, 1893, and N chapel, 1904. – Then in chancel S one by *James Ballantine & Co.*, 1871. – Finally, Arts and Crafts windows from three different artists, all excellent. In the N chapel E, war memorial window by *Harvey & Ashby* to a design by *C.E. Bateman* with advice from *Arthur Orr* and *Bidlake*, 1920. In the N aisle, a delightfully rich Christ blessing children by *Theodora Salusbury*, 1933. Last, the S aisle window by *Veronica Whall*, 1948. – MONUMENTS to Grimshaws, Wilsons and others, but nothing remarkable except a mural tablet on the N arcade to local schoolmaster Thomas Trehern †1800 and his parents. By *W. Thompson*, Birmingham, with a lifelike skull. – Bronze

MEMORIAL tablet to Walter Cook †1423, by *Bidlake*, 1926, and based on the design of a brass at Flamstead, Herts.

In the churchyard, *Bidlake*'s Hollington stone CHURCH-YARD CROSS, 1921.

UNITED REFORMED CHURCH (Congregational), Station Road. By *John W. Wilson* of Birmingham, 1932. Exterior with curvaceous doorway, window and gable shapes and curiously patterned roughcasting. The curves are echoed in the internal arch towards the front. Interesting in an unusual way. Probably influenced by styles illustrated in German magazines of the 1920s, but also reminiscent of the work of Ragnar Östberg, the Swedish architect, and his Stockholm City Hall, completed 1923.

PERAMBULATION

Begin immediately W of the church with the GUILD HOUSE. Heavily timber-framed. Built for the Guild of St Anne founded by Walter Cook in 1412–13* and dissolved in 1547, along with Cook's College established in 1416. Recovered from private ownership with the adjoining ST ANNE'S COTTAGE by George Jackson and restored for church use by *Bidlake* in 1911–12. Two-storey. Close studding to the E side with diagonal bracing on the ground floor and coving under the eaves. The S end rendered with timber-framed gable, all *Bidlake*'s, with carved stone seals of the Guild and College of St Anne, probably by *H.C. Mitchell* of Tamworth. An in-line bay to the N has gone, and Stanley Jones suggests that coving on the W side was removed when the cottage was added in the early C16. Inside, later C15 posts support the added upper floor. On the ground floor, two good Arts and Crafts fireplaces and the Guild and College arms in stained glass. To the N, ST LAWRENCE HOUSE, built for church offices, 1981, and blending well into its surrounding. Further N, ST JOHN'S HALL, by *Associated Architects*, 1995. Discreetly modern.

Then the triangle S of the church where the buildings N and S once faced an open space. On the E, in KENILWORTH ROAD, a group with polychromatic and patterned brickwork. The former SCHOOL by *J.A. Chatwin*, 1871, and block of 1870s cottages (Nos. 3–11) alongside. On the S in WILSON'S ROAD, a neat row of cottages (Nos. 12–24) dated 1841 with the initials of William Henry Wilson. Then comes MILVERTON CRES-CENT, a rendered Jacobean-style terrace of *c.* 1870 with curvilinear gables. These adjoin MILVERTON HOUSE, a multi-gabled and big-chimneyed C16 timber-framed house in plum position at the Warwick Road crossroads with extravagant patterns of diagonal and curved bracing. In the 1860s these belonged to William Berrow of Milverton near Leamington.

*Westminster Abbey sold twelve oak trees from their park in Knowle for its building in 1412.

On the former green itself are the BERROW COTTAGE HOMES, built by Sarah Berrow in memory of her parents. The original block facing the High Street is by *W. Hawley Lloyd*, 1885–6. Queen Anne revival style with moulded brick dressings forming tracery-like patterns in the gables. Another block in Kenilworth Road, 1891, and a further twenty-two homes added in 1977.

Briefly s, and the PARADE at the corner of Warwick Road and Station Road. By *Satchwell & Roberts*, 1932. Shops on three sides of the block. The twin-gabled middle section (THE LLOYDS) in mock-Tudor has impish carved figures on the brackets to the coving.

Back to the Cottage Homes and N along the HIGH STREET. First, the RED LION, brick and timber-framed, nicely redone and enlarged by *Batemans*, 1935. On the front, an inn sign and wrought-iron bracket. This was from the White Swan (dem. 1939) on whose site stands the NATWEST BANK, a three-storey block, built as shops by *Ewen Harper & Brother*, 1939. On the front, carvings and inscriptions referring to the lost pub. On the same side, a block of four shops (Nos. 1646–1654) by *Warr, Barnett & Sadler*, 1962–3, with first-floor balconies and mansard roof. This style of redevelopment met with local opposition as being inappropriate for the old village centre and its timber-framed buildings. Of these, the best example is CHESTER HOUSE (Nos. 1667–1669). Originally two timber-framed houses with similar gabled wings and jettied fronts. The s house of *c.* 1400 and the other of *c.* 1500. They were joined by the middle hall and combined into a single dwelling in the C16. Restored and converted to a LIBRARY by *F. W. B. Charles*, 1975. Behind, an attractive KNOT GARDEN created in 1989.

Almost opposite Chester House is HSBC (formerly Midland) (No. 1630), half-timbered to suit the location. It is by *T.B. Whinney*, 1922. Beyond, No. 1622, a curious single-storey building with Queen Anne details, built as the MEN'S INSTITUTE, 1886. Then, back on the other side, the GRESWOLDE ARMS in three distinct parts, the centre with 1830s barge-boarded gables and the sides simple Georgian. Much further N, at the edge of the old village, a good group with timber framing and brick nogging at ARTILLERY COTTAGES (Nos. 1587–1591).

In LADY BYRON LANE, s of the road towards Solihull, several inter-war houses of some quality, e.g. No. 67, a late Arts and Crafts residence by *Baron Underhill*, 1935. Big chimneys, slate-hung gables and broad rounded porch with conical roof. The porch is reminiscent of the style of *Oliver Hill*, whose THATCHED HOUSE of 1924 was nearby but stood in the path of the M42 motorway and was demolished.

44 GRIMSHAW HALL, ½ m. N. One of the most attractive of Warwickshire's older houses, Elizabethan, *c.* 1560. The Grimshaws lived here from the C17 until the C18, the names of Nancy and

Fanny Grimshaw being scratched on a window pane associated with a charming story about the two young girls and their
horses in 1718. Many-gabled, timber-framed, of two storeys.
Centre and two wings plus a central porch projection with
gables in three directions. Closely set studs on the ground
floor. Herringbone, lozenge, and concave-sided lozenge patterns above, their variety noteworthy. Balusters in the sides of
the porch, brackets to support its upper overhang. Genuine
oriel windows on brackets. Many of the other windows are
restoration. Having been subdivided into cottages it was
bought by Joseph Gillott of Berry Hall and restored in 1886
by *J.A. Chatwin* who removed the rendering and exposed
the timber framing to view. Further interior restoration by
W. Alexander Harvey for J.W. Murray in 1913. Relatively plain
panelled interior.

MANOR HOUSE, Kenilworth Road. ¼ m. E. Built as a lodge to
Knowle Hall further E. Never a manor, but a good late C16
house altered *c.* 1900 with timber framing concealed under
colour washed roughcast. In the garden, a pair of gatepiers to
Knowle Hall.

KNOWLE HALL, ¾ m. E. Archaeological remains of an early
moated manor here have been dated to *c.* 1194. A later house
was built in the C16 and enlarged in the 1660s for Fulke Greville, later 5th Lord Brooke. It was a well-documented and
impressive house which remained in the possession of the
family until 1743 when it was bought by William Smith, the
Warwick builder and architect, whose family sold it in 1754.
The house had been leased out since the 1720s and gradually
fell into ruin, and in 1834 its owner William 'Gumley' Wilson
commissioned plans for a new house from *Edward Blore*.
Although the old house was mostly demolished, the new one
remained unbuilt owing to Wilson's other extravagances. A
new owner, Robert Emilius Wilson (no relation of 'Gumley'),
had the present house built in 1849. Italian Renaissance-style,
rendered brick, of five bays now reduced to two storeys with
balustrading. Rusticated porch. A C20 chapel in the grounds.

SPRINGFIELD HALL. *See* Temple Balsall.

LADBROKE

ALL SAINTS. Tall W tower of the early C14, crowned by a later
recessed spire. The spire is grey, the tower has alternate stripes
of White Lias and brown ironstone. Later C13 chancel with
pairs of lancets to the N, three stepped lancet lights under one
arch to the E. Gabled buttresses. The nave clerestory is of
course Perp. Exceptionally lofty interior, the chancel heightened in the C15 too. Early C14 three-bay arcades and chancel
arch. Also early C14 the lower parts of the SEDILIA and the
elementary EASTER SEPULCHRE. The S chancel doorway

typically Dec. Good ogee head above it. All expensively restored
by *Sir G. G. Scott* for the Rev. J. R. Errington, 1876. N extension
by *Brown Matthews*, 2003. – The FITTINGS mostly of *Scott*'s
1876 restoration, and a fine ensemble of the time. – ORGAN
CASE. *Farmer & Brindley*, 1876. – SCULPTURE. In the porch,
four more heads, C15, one of them with a liripipe. They are
roof corbels, said to be from the former church at Radbourne. – STAINED GLASS. In a chancel S clerestory window
parts of three original figures, probably C16. – Alongside, one
by *William Holland*, 1862. – The E window, representing All
Saints, by *Hardman*, 1876. – Four more by *Hardman*: aisle E
windows 1876 (two), one in chancel 1886, and tower †1902.
– S chancel window with heraldic panels, 1877, and old quarries. – Two chancel N windows by *Kempe & Co.*, 1912 and 1914.
– Good early work by *Geoffrey Webb*, 1911, in N aisle, with
attractively painted MEMORIAL BOARD of the same date
alongside. – S aisle, *Heaton, Butler & Bayne*, 1910. – MONU-
MENTS. Badly preserved effigy of a priest, early C14 (S aisle).
– Elisabeth Skrymsher †1712. By *Edward Stanton*. Oval tablet
with floral surround. – Mrs Eleanor Hewitt †1716 (in the
tower), of aedicule type with pilasters. – William Palmer †1720
and wife Mary †1729. Architectural tablet. Black Ionic pilasters, broken segmental pediment with coat of arms. Both
attributed by Andor Gomme to *Francis Smith*.
　　Open timber LYCHGATE, by *J. T. Irvine*, 1884.
OLD RECTORY, W of the church. A fine house of *c.* 1700. Square,
with hipped roof. Brick with stone quoins, but with C19 rendering and porch.
LADBROKE HALL. A house of 1598 enlarged and refronted for
William Palmer, *c.* 1670. Alternating courses of White Lias
and Rugby limestone and quoins of Warwick sandstone.
Seven bays, two storeys, the usual recessed three-bay centre
and hipped roof. Doorway with open segmental pediment.
Staircase with three balusters to the tread, one fluted, the
other two of different twistings, probably by *Francis Smith*,
c. 1711. A standard house, but a very pleasing one. Subdivided
as flats, 1973.
On Banbury Road, THE CROFT has a fine display of timber
framing with circular braces, herringbone and close studding;
C16, although restored.

LANGLEY
Claverdon

ST MARY. *W. Davis* of Birmingham, 1890. Brick with trefoiled
windows, apse and bellcote. Plain interior with boldly pointed
chancel arch. – STAINED GLASS. Adoration by *Bernard Lamp-
lugh*, 1907.

LAPWORTH

St Mary the Virgin. A splendid-looking but problematic church. The general impression of the exterior from the w is Perp and very ambitious and compact. Short but high nave with clerestory, aisles embattled and with pinnacles like the nave, a w chapel, and almost free-standing n steeple. The steeple was no doubt placed thus because the ground falls away w of the nave and the street runs close to the church. However, offset to the s of the w front and projecting a little into the street is a c15 two-storey annexe. It has openings n and s for processions to get round the church and remains of vaulting over the passage. In its w wall two spiral staircases lead into an upper room lit on three sides by Perp windows but originally closed off from the church. This must have been a pilgrim chapel, probably with relics. Such a relic chamber could have been provided in some other way but this arrangement is like a wayside chapel. The stately n tower is Dec, except for the recessed spire, which may be later. Its top was rebuilt by *J.A. Chatwin*, 1884. But the history of the church goes further back. The first indication of this is the s aisle w window with Y-tracery, i.e. of *c.* 1300. The second is the chancel s windows of the Wroxall type, i.e. also of *c.* 1310–15. The third is again a Y-window with cusping, in the n chapel. The interior reveals an even more complicated history. It starts with one Norman window in the n arcade belonging to the first aisleless church. After that comes the c13. It gave aisles to the church. First comes the n, then the s arcade, both with double-chamfered arches. The n arcade with round piers is irregular and of several dates. Its w bay has what Simon Jenkins calls 'an endearing distortion'. The e arch, which cuts into the Norman window, is wider than the others, its chamfers slighter, so probably earlier too. The s arcade of one build has slimmer piers, one round, the rest octagonal. The n chapel must be earlier still, for its double-chamfered arch to the chancel is round, and to the aisle it has a positively Norman arch. This must have been given pointed voussoirs by an easy adjustment and must in any case be re-set. So was there a Norman chancel and a Norman transept, off which the n chapel was built? There are other teasing details, notably the two much too low windows at the w end of the s aisle s wall and the two blank recesses below two others inside. The Perp clerestory has very lively figurework, and the timber roof is uncommonly good with carved spandrels to the braces. Chancel restoration by *Street*, 1860, followed by the rest of the church, 1872. N chapel of St Katharine partially rebuilt and furnished as a war memorial chapel by *E.F. Reynolds*, 1923. – Carved stone reredos by *Earp*, 1860. – font. Octagonal, early c14, with small heads projecting from the underside. – stalls. With some re-set Perp tracery panels. – screen and pulpit, 1925, and altar rails, 1935, all by *Reynolds*. – Later woodwork, including chapel stairs, by *A.B. Chatwin* (carved by *Hugh Birkett*), 1960s.

– WALL PAINTINGS. On the N chapel W wall some C13 red roses and tendrils. – STAINED GLASS. By *Powell* (designer *H.E. Wooldridge*) and typical of the firm, the E window, and two smaller windows in aisles, 1872. – By *Powell* also, the quarry glass in one W window, and probably the S aisle E window, †1867. – Two chancel S windows by *Clayton & Bell*, 1861. – W window with heraldic glass, medieval to late C19, and bright C18 coloured borders. – N chapel window, sombre and busy, by *Richard Stubbington*, 1922. – MONUMENT. Florence Bradshaw, a Mater Amabilis, by *Eric Gill*, 1928; a very good example of his tender Expressionism. – SCULPTURE. Madonna and Child by *John Poole*, 2001. – ORGAN CASE by *Christopher Thomas*, 1997.

SE of church, former SCHOOL with residences for the schoolmaster and parish clerk, 1825–6, by *Thomas Harborne* of Solihull. Brick with quoined window surrounds and bargeboards. Enlarged by *E. Llewellyn Edwards*, 1911. Restored and extended as a CHURCH HALL, by *APEC*, 2001.

In Station Road at Kingswood, 1½ m. E, the LEES CHAPEL, built as Kingswood Mission Room, 1886, and now used by an Evangelical congregation. Brick with lancets and dormers, and terracotta decoration. Set among 1880s middle-class houses by the railway.

There is no village centre, and this was once a parish of isolated farmhouses and small settlements. Lapworth and Kingswood are characterized by large late C19 and early C20 houses designed and built for the well-to-do. The concentrations are along Old Warwick Road and off Lapworth Street.

At Kingswood, the junction of the Grand Union and the Stratford-upon-Avon CANALS. The connecting branch first opened in 1802. From the canal bridge on the road just W of the railway, the basin and its canal architecture can be seen and are worth seeing. There are offices, lock-keeper's cottages and C19 workshops, and, on the Stratford Canal, several split bridges with cast-iron trellis parapets.

LEA MARSTON

ST JOHN THE BAPTIST. Isolated down Church Lane at the far S end of the village. The nave is C14 and much renewed, but the S door and two S windows have original wave-moulded surrounds. The rest mainly of 1876–7 when *Frederick Preedy* rebuilt the chancel, restored the nave and added a NW tower to replace one that stood within the W end of the nave. The tower is in light and pink sandstone, in three stages with a pyramidical roof. Inside, the chancel arch and chancel are typically *Preedy*'s and good, the ensemble of 1876–7 furnishings complemented by gifts from Lord Norton and the Adderley family from 1870. – REREDOS. By *C. Ford Whitcombe*, 1907, with delicate tracery and painted panels, set against the background of an earlier tiled reredos by *Mintons*, 1870. Pretty painted board alongside, 1907. – Oak PULPIT carved by the Misses Adderley in 1874. – Alabaster CARVING of lamb and flag on W wall behind the FONT, probably 1877. – STAINED GLASS, mostly by *Burlison & Grylls* from †1869, the best the S nave window of †1903. – W window by *Powell*, 1906. – One in chancel by *Swaine Bourne & Son*, 1908. – Good memorial by *Paul Woodroffe*, †1917, of a medieval soldier kneeling before a crucifix. – N nave window by *T.F. Curtis, Ward & Hughes*, 1920. – MONUMENTS. Many to the Adderleys of Hams Hall,* notably Sir Charles †1682 (with an open curly pediment) and Mrs Lettice Adderley †1784, a *Coade* stone piece, with a roundel on the sarcophagus containing a seated woman, and, at the top, an urn. – In chancel S, a group of three by *Hollins*, †1826 to †1848. – WAR MEMORIAL. Painted board by *Geoffrey Webb*, 1923, with inset figure of St John the Baptist.

Outside the churchyard, a tall floriated CROSS on a tapering octagonal column on a moulded base, erected by Lord Norton to commemorate the visit of W.E. Gladstone to Hams Hall in 1895.

The village consists of two settlements, Lea and Marston. At the former, only a few buildings of interest. N of the church is WOODHOUSE FARM, late C18 with an extraordinary brick façade with full-height pilasters and windows under segmental arches within semicircular blind openings. In the village, the OLD SCHOOL HOUSE of c. 1840 – Tudor with hoodmoulds and buttresses – remains. Then the string of blue brick bridges across the Tame valley, first LEA BRIDGE reconstructed by *John Willmot*, the Bridgemaster and County Surveyor, in 1899, then the seven arches over the flood plain and the railway bridge on the Water Orton to Kingsbury link of 1909.

At Marston in the N, a small green near early C19 HOLLIES FARM. On Kingsbury Road, sheltered by cedars, is OAKWOOD, a farmhouse refronted in 1840s Tudor style in plum brick with big chimneys and latticed windows, with contemporary outbuildings alongside.

LEAMINGTON HASTINGS

4060

ALL SAINTS. A grand church. C13 onwards, restored 1875 with further work by *A.E. Lloyd Oswell*, 1887. Perp W tower of red

---

*Hams Hall, a Palladian house built in 1760–6 for Sir Charles Adderley and probably by *Joseph Pickford* of Derby, was demolished c. 1920, and the power station built on its site is also now demolished. The upper stages of the façade of Hams Hall are now at Bledisloe Lodge, Glos.

ashlar. Twin two-light bell-openings with traceried panels, W doorway with ogee gable and thin buttress-shafts. Dec N doorway, projecting, gabled, and of specially attractive details. Two orders of columns. In the outer order of the arch grows a vine trail. It issues from the mouth of a headstop, passes the mouth of a head at the apex, and ends in the other headstop. The N aisle is a little above the ordinary altogether. All the buttresses are gabled, and there is a series of heads along the corbel table. In the church also a doorway, projecting and gabled. The interior is rather more complex. The S arcade is E.E. in its three E bays – see the nailhead enrichment and the arch mouldings. The next move was to add a N transept to the preceding aisleless church. Of this transept one small N window remains. After that the S aisle was extended by two bays to the W and a N arcade of three wider bays was built. All these stages must have followed each other quickly, as there is little stylistic development. It is different with the chancel, extraordinarily long. This has the date 1677 above the E window. The window shows it, also the N and S windows. The proportions of the chancel inside are indeed curiously like those of a drawing room. The nave clerestory windows are also post-Reformation and could be C17, though different. Those on the S look rather C16. Date 1703 on S porch probably refers to repairs. No chancel arch. Just a light wooden arch with panelling above. Ringing gallery in the tower by *John D. Holmes*, 2000. S aisle restored by *Mark Evans Architects*, 2009–10, after fire damage. – FONT. Hexagonal, Perp, with angel busts. – PULPIT. With Perp panels. – READING DESK. The traceried panel was probably the pulpit door. – Jacobean PANELLING as screen to NW vestry. – STAINED GLASS. C18 heraldic glass in tower window, originally in the chancel. – E window, probably *Burlison & Grylls*, †1874. – N window, †1887. – MONUMENTS. Sir Thomas Trevor †1656. Black-and-white marble. Bust not strictly frontal, like that of a doge. Big cartouche below. Attributed by Mrs Esdaile to *Bushnell*. – She also attributed to him Sir Thomas Trevor †1676 and wife Mary †1695. Two busts, facing each other, also not frontal. Also black and white marble. The decoration is somewhat bald. – John Allington †1682. Marble pedestal in arched recess. – Lady Wheler †1800, by *Coulman* of London.

The MANOR HOUSE, W of the church, C17 with mullioned-and-transomed windows, the front remodelled in the 1840s. S wing added 1827.

ALMSHOUSES. Founded in 1633 and enlarged on the l. in 1696. They are one range, and the only difference is in the mullioned windows. The earlier mullions are chamfered, the later round with a fillet. Now only the outer walls remain, the rest having been entirely renewed by *Christopher Martindale*, 1980–1, with additional accommodation behind.

LESSINGHAM HOUSE (former vicarage), behind the almshouses. *William Slater* of Sudbury, Derbyshire, for the Rev. Hervey Wilmot-Sitwell, 1822. Red brick with hipped slate roof.

At HILL, ¼ m. ESE, a group of Swedish prefabricated timber houses, 1946–7.

MANOR FARMHOUSE, Kites Hardwick, ¾ m. E, has a three-storey C18 range with rusticated quoins, string courses and doorway with segmental pediment.

At BROADWELL, 1 m. SSE, the GOOD SHEPHERD, a plain mission church, 1871. Plum brick METHODIST CHAPEL, 1962, attached to previous chapel, 1871.

LEAMINGTON SPA

INTRODUCTION

Leamington owes its architectural character to its mineral springs. The well is first mentioned by Camden in 1586, but came into its own only in the late C18. The C19 was the golden age for Leamington when taking the waters was highly fashionable. The old village was transformed. Building the New Town N of the river started in 1808 and had reached Warwick Street by 1822 and Beauchamp Square and even Binswood Avenue by 1834. The extent of development is shown on D. G. Squirhill's 1838 plan, including New Milverton to the NW of the main area. The population was 315 in 1801, 15,700 in 1841, and 23,000 in 1881. Lillington, parts of which had already been heavily developed as North Leamington, was taken into the borough in 1890. In 2011 the population was about 49,500, only slightly larger than fifty years ago. Originally known as Leamington Priors, the town was renamed Royal Leamington Spa under authorization from Queen Victoria in 1838.

Architecturally the high point for secular building was between 1820 and 1840. However, the Leamington banking crash in 1838 brought an abrupt end to the building boom and forced many

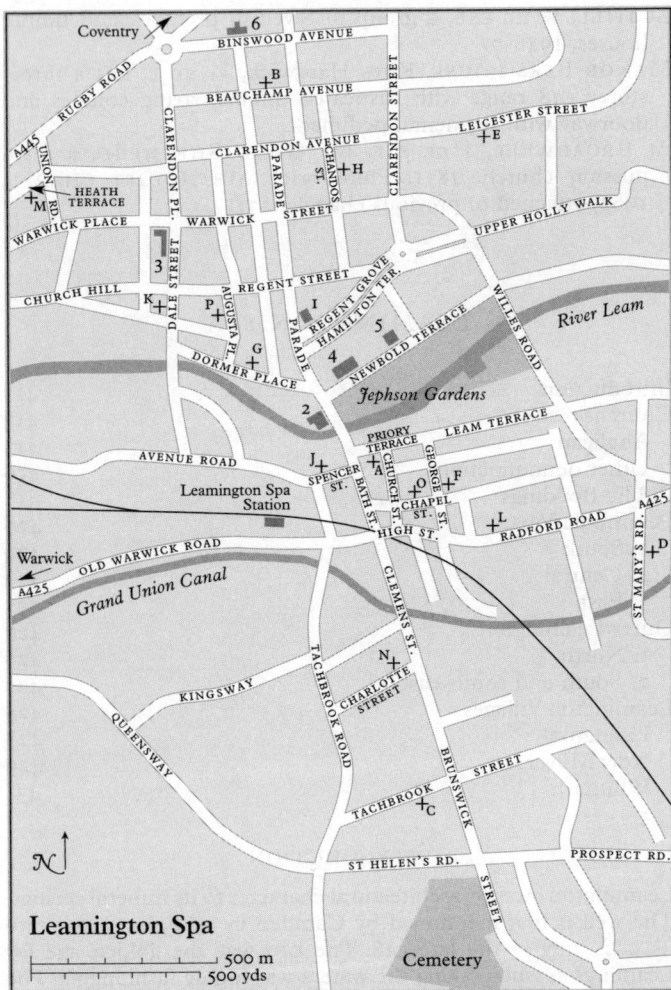

Leamington Spa

A   All Saints
B   Holy Trinity
C   St John the Baptist
D   St Mary
E   St Paul
F   Leamington Spa Mission
G   St Peter (R.C.)
H   Baptist chapel
J   Congregational chapel (former)
K   Methodist church
L   Radford Road Church
     (Methodist and United
     Reformed)

M   Emmanuel Evangelical
     Church
N   Life Community Church
O   Salvation Army
P   First Church of Christ
     Scientist

1   Town hall
2   Royal Pump Rooms and
     Baths
3   Fire station
4   Southern Justice Centre
5   Royal Spa Centre
6   Leamington College
     (former)

local builders into bankruptcy. The Regency style had prevailed, of course, and the classical terraces of Leamington derive from Regent's Park, Brighton and even Cheltenham. The norm was for 'typical Leamington stucco terraces of four storeys', as Pevsner observed fifty years ago. But he also concurred with the view of Ross Williamson who had written that 'It is in Leamington's villas that her peculiar glory lies.'

Even by the time of the banking crisis, a degree of stylistic freedom had crept in. Indeed, the *cottage orné* style had been introduced by *P. F. Robinson* as early as 1824 and mimicked by others. By the mid 1830s *William Thomas* was experimenting in a range of styles, best seen around Willes Road and Upper Holly Walk where contemporary Gothic and Jacobean works stand alongside the architect's fine Regency buildings. 'So that amount of freedom of choice had been reached as early as this', observed Pevsner.

The main period for chapel building came early, between 1825 and 1860, and rather later, from 1840 to 1890, for churches. The best public architecture belongs to the 1860s to 1880s, including the ambitious town hall of 1882–4 and the revamped Pump Rooms. The post-war period saw some redevelopment – and significant losses of older buildings[*] – but fifty years ago Pevsner thought little of the then recent architecture and noted that 'what has come of high blocks of flats is entirely undistinguished'. Since then, there have been many noteworthy additions (e.g. housing schemes and public buildings), coupled with greater respect for the town's Regency heritage.

As to architectural practices, Lyndon F. Cave has given a thorough account of the individuals who set up as architects in Leamington during the C19 – and of others, like *John Nash, Samuel Beazley, Henry Hakewill* and *P. F. Robinson,* whose influence was felt in the town. The names include *C. S. Smith, John Russell, Samuel Nicklin, William Thomas, John George Jackson, Daniel Goodman Squirhill, Edmund Mitchell* – and the *Cundalls* father and son, *John* (†1889) and *Frederick George* (1866–1947). Mention should also be made of *William de Normanville,* the Borough Engineer from 1882 until 1917. In the later C20, *Frederick Gibberd*'s strong associations with the town should be noted, together with the distinguished local work of *Rayner & Fedeski.*

CHURCHES

Anglican[†]

ALL SAINTS, Priory Terrace. The parish church and one as out of the ordinary for scale as for style. On the site of the old

---

[*]These are mostly noted in the text and do not need separate identification here.
[†]CHRIST CHURCH, Beauchamp Square (*P. F. Robinson,* Neo-Norman, 1825) was included in the first edition even though it had already been demolished. It went in 1959. ST ALBAN'S (dedicated to St Michael and All Angels when first built), Warwick Street (*Cundall,* 1877–87), was demolished in 1968. Both had been proprietary chapels when built.

village church,* it was begun in 1843 on the initiative of Dr
John Craig (vicar 1839–77). Largely his own architect, Craig
worked first with *J. G. Jackson* but they fell out over the dimensions of the crossing piers.† By the time work began in 1843
Edmund Mitchell had become Craig's professional assistant and
oversaw the early stages. It was a complete rebuilding. First,
the four-bay aisled nave and the crossing piers, completed to
roof level in 1843–4. Then the chancel, opened in July 1845.
The N transept and Angel tower followed in 1846–9 and the
chancel was enlarged in 1851. By then the vicar was embroiled
in a bitter dispute with the vestry and work came to a standstill.
The S transept remained unfinished until completed under
T. D. Barry of Liverpool, still to Craig's design concept, in
1867–9. Shortly afterwards Craig was forced to give up his
hopes of erecting a lantern tower over the crossing which was
levelled off and roofed over in 1871. A change of vicar saw
chancel improvements and the addition of new vestries by
Cundall in 1879. Finally two nave bays to a different plan and
a proud SW porch tower were added by *Sir Arthur Blomfield*
(†1899). Construction began in 1898, the nave being finished
in 1900 and the tower in 1902.

Craig's work is in a Continental Gothic style, not correct in
the details and a little bald. It can be best appreciated from
the SE on Church Street. Polygonal apse; N transept with a
large wheel window patterned on Rouen Cathedral; side
entrance into a transept W aisle; thin Angel tower with spire E
of the transept; a different S transept with a flamboyant rose
window taken from St Ouen at Rouen, and a triple gabled
porch, oddly low to fit in below the rose and flanked by tall
pinnacles. The nave is high with five-light Perp clerestory
windows and flying buttresses to the outer walls of the aisles.
Blomfield made his bays wider and altered the rhythm of the
upper parts. This and the SW tower are of course far more
knowledgeable, but lack Craig's improvident zest.

Inside the view from the W gallery is best. From under the
crossing, too, the ambitious scale is especially evident. The
church is 172 ft (52.4 metres) long and 80 ft (24.4 metres)
high. All the piers quite thin. In the nave, the blind panelling
and triforium-like arcading between the arches and clerestory
recall Continental models. The W end partitioned off as the
Urquhart Room, separated from the nave by a wooden screen
from Holy Trinity, Rugby. Gallery above. All by *Rayner &
Fedeski*, 1986. – Caen stone REREDOS of the Last Supper
carved by *R. L. Boulton*, 1879. Also the SEDILIA and other
stone carving in the apse. – Chancel ORGAN CASE by *Bodley*

---

*It stood between the apse and the crossing of the present church. Originally
consisting of chancel, nave and W tower, it was several times altered and enlarged
between 1781 and 1834.
†Jackson, who had undertaken improvements to the old church for the previous
vicar in 1833–4, was responsible for drawings prepared in 1841–2. He also published
his own perspective view of the proposed additions, showing a cruciform church
with central tower and spire clearly modelled on Rotherham.

(1886) also from Rugby, 1982. – SCREEN. Of iron, by *Blomfield*, 1898–9. – Bath stone PULPIT carved by *Miss Bonham* (cf. Whitnash, p. 431, and Bangor Cathedral) and fixed by Messrs *Cox* of London, 1879. – STAINED GLASS. Apse windows by *Chance* of Birmingham, 1851. Very beautiful, deeply glowing. – Two in N transept W clerestory by *Holland*, 1849. Pictorial. – The rest numerous and varied. They can only be summarized. Artists represented (in date order by first commission) include *William Holland & Son*, 1871; *Holland & Holt*, 1879–82; *F. Holt & Co.*, 1882–1903; *Heaton, Butler & Bayne*, 1883; *Clayton & Bell*, †1887; *Hardman*, 1889; *Cox, Buckley & Co.*, 1890; *Powell*, 1896 and 1909; *Herbert W. Bryans*, 1902–5, one (†1895) very much in the Kempe style; and *Percy Bacon*, 1918.

HOLY TRINITY, Beauchamp Avenue. Begun by *Edmund Mitchell*, 1847. It was a proprietary chapel until 1899. Cruciform. Mitchell's transepts and chancel remain, though altered. They have added low projections, those to the transepts by *Cundall*, 1881, that at the E end by *Jethro Cossins*, 1891. Infill in the NE and SE corners too, including the former SE porch with chamber above, 1901–2. The result is somewhat confused. Site enlarged in 1913, after which the original nave was rebuilt. Present aisled five-bay nave and stump of SW porch tower by *W. Hawley Lloyd*, 1913–14. Inside, wide nave with slender piers. Crossing with vaulted ceiling. The added ends of the transepts have triple arches and pairs of marble columns, 1902. Chancel E wall with diapering, statues and Ten Commandments carved in stone. Side-lit alcove at E end with REREDOS by *Cossins*, 1891, carved by *Bridgeman*. – Alabaster FONT, 1899, with carved oak cover by *Bridgeman*, 1900. – STAINED GLASS. E window *Heaton, Butler & Bayne*, 1891. – Main S transept window by *Cottier & Co.*, 1891. – Narrow windows in end bay by *Cox, Sons, Buckley & Co.*, 1882, *Heaton, Butler & Bayne*, 1891, and *G. Maile & Son Ltd* (designer *Vernon Spreadbury*), 1934. – Others by *Heaton, Butler & Bayne* in S chapel and N transept, 1901–2. – Main N transept window by *Caroline Townshend* and *Joan Howson*, 1935; excellent. – W window (war memorial) of 1919 by *Percy Bacon*. – N transept, 1927, and S aisle, 1930, also by *Bacon*.

ST JOHN THE BAPTIST, Tachbrook Street, South Leamington. By *John Cundall* of Leamington. His best church, built in stages 1877–88 beginning with the aisled nave and ending with the prominent NE steeple. Chancel and N vestry 1882. S transept and vestry 1884. Large, of brick with stone dressings. Lancets and bar tracery. In the apse and clerestory stepped triplets of lancets. Good W end with three stepped above four longer even lancets. Fine detailing to the N porch, belfry stage of the tower and lower section of the spire. Brick-faced interior. Long tall nave with six-bay arcades. W baptistery with trefoiled alcove. Chancel with encaustic tiles, stencilled decoration and panelled roof. – REREDOS, 1908 with later statuary. – ROOD SCREEN and WAR MEMORIAL board, 1921. – Stone PULPIT, *Jones & Willis*, 1882. – STAINED GLASS in apse by *Hardman*,

1882–4. – In aisles, windows of British saints, by *Frank Holt & Co.*, 1884–99. One in N aisle commemorates John Cundall †1889. – N aisle W, 1908. – WALL PAINTING in baptistery, *c.* 1885, and canvas memorial PAINTING in chancel alcove, 1906, also by *Holt*. Immediately S, HITCHMAN COURT (the former vicarage), also by *Cundall*.

ST MARK, Rugby Road. *See* New Milverton below (p. 430).

ST MARY, St Mary's Road. *J. G. Jackson*, 1838–9. Cemented. Short W tower, originally pinnacled. Long Perp windows, many buttresses. Nave and aisles of the same height. Six bays. Four-centred arcade arches. Galleries on three sides, with staircases each side of the tower. Added chancel by *J. Harold Gibbons*, 1930. Attached hall on the N, 1996, by *Clews Architects*. Re-seated with chairs 2012. – Heavy carved wooden REREDOS with inset carving of the Last Supper, 1930. – PAINTINGS of the Easter story in lancets either side of the reredos by *Mo Enright*, 2001–2. – STAINED GLASS. E window, *M. E. Aldrich Rope*, 1930. – In S aisle four, 1923–34, probably *Camm & Co.* (AB), and one by *Florence & Walter Camm*, 1951.

ST PAUL, Leicester Street. *John Cundall*, 1873–4, but less ambitious than St John's (*see* above). Brick and stone, with two spires. The spirelet at the NE angle of the N transept belongs to the original build. The much larger N porch steeple added 1875, i.e. soon afterwards. E.E. in style; lancets and plate tracery. Inside, polished Aberdeen red granite columns to arcades. Patterned brickwork high up all round the nave and above the chancel arch and W window. Transepts galleried. Internal reordering by *John D. Holmes*, 1980s. Improvement of W end facilities and new external entrance by *Robothams*, 2012. – PULPIT and READING DESK of Bath stone with Devonshire marble shafts and inlaid decoration, 1874. – STAINED GLASS. Patterned glass in chancel windows, E (possibly *Powell*) †1878, and sides by *F. Holt & Co.*, 1887. – W window also by *Holt*, 1885. – S chapel E by *Jones & Willis*, 1913.

Immediately W, the PAROCHIAL ROOMS and CHURCH HOUSE; *W. Hawley Lloyd* (a parishioner), 1887–8. The main hall Gothic with ogee surrounds to ground-floor windows and full tracery above.

*Other denominations**

LEAMINGTON SPA MISSION (Seventh Day Adventist), George Street. Built by *John Russell* as the Roman Catholic chapel, 1828. Three bays, stuccoed with attached Ionic columns and pediment. Statue of St Peter above the door by *Clarke* of Birmingham, 1828. After St Peter's church (*see* below) opened

---

* Former churches are included here – rather than in the perambulations – to retain an overview of the range of provision for public worship in the Spa era.

in 1864 it found alternative uses, latterly as a youth mission and social club. Restored for the Adventists 1993–9 with new STAINED GLASS by *Dagmar Kraus*.

ST PETER (R.C.), Dormer Place. Replaced the George Street chapel (above). By *Henry Clutton*, 1861–4, with slender SW tower of 1877–8. Gutted by fire in 1883 and afterwards restored by *G.H. Cox*, 1884. N Sacred Heart chapel added by *A.J. Pilkington*, 1894. A noble building in a C13 French style. Brick with stone bands. On the W front an ornate double entrance under a rose window. Nobbly ballflower decoration round the transept windows. Aisled nave with narrow windows and clerestory. Broad apse with bar tracery and cinquefoils. Rose windows in transepts and at W end. Almost free-standing tower, so tall and thin it seems scarcely believable that it once carried a pyramid spire, removed in 1950. High interior with wagon roof. Arcades with double-shafted columns and foliate capitals (cf. Clutton's church at Woburn, Beds., 1865–8). W organ gallery. Lavish sanctuary decoration by *John Hardman & Co.* (*Dunstan Powell*), 1901. – Main ALTAR and REREDOS with statues of St Peter and St Paul designed by *A.B. Wall* of Cheltenham, 1884. – S chapel altar from the George Street church and by *Pugin*, 1845. – N chapel ALTAR and REREDOS ensemble carved by *Boulton* to a design by *Pilkington*, 1894. – STAINED GLASS. In nave, four figures of saints, by *Tony Dury*, 1864–5. – The rest by *Hardman*, 1878–1933. – MEMORIAL BRASSES by *Hardman* in vestibule, Patrick Bisshop †1846 and Elizabeth Bisshop †1859.

The PRESBYTERY, SE of the church, also by *Clutton*, 1861–6.

BAPTIST CHAPEL, Chandos Street. *Brown Matthews*, 1995–6. Two-storey, brick, with low pyramid roof and glazed spike. Tall top-lit galleried worship area. It replaces Warwick Street Chapel (*William Thomas*, 1833; cemented, gabled front with lancets) which stood at the N end of the Royal Priors shopping centre site.

Former CONGREGATIONAL CHAPEL, Spencer Street. 1836 by *John Russell*, a church member. Stuccoed. With a pedimented portico of four unfluted Ionic columns. Windows with Lombardic tracery. Closed in the 1980s and currently (2014) awaiting new use. – Another CONGREGATIONAL CHAPEL (now offices), Holly Walk, by *Squirhill*, 1849: Tudor with diapered brickwork. Gothic schoolroom behind, in William Street, by *Henry Fuller*, 1868. Used as St Luke's Episcopal Church 1895–1947.

METHODIST CHURCH, Dale Street. *Cripps & Stewart*, 1971, replacing the Italianate chapel of 1869–70 by *George Woodhouse*. Light blockwork with oblong windows and flimsy spike. Neoclassical Sunday Schools alongside, by *F.W.H. Lee*, 1928.

RADFORD ROAD CHURCH (Methodist and United Reformed, originally Wesleyan). *Cundall*, 1876–7. Brick with stone dressings. Geometrical detailing, originally with tall pinnacles and central spirelet on main front. Refronted after amalgamation in 1992. Arcades with light iron columns. w gallery. – STAINED GLASS. Rose window behind organ, probably 1877.

EMMANUEL EVANGELICAL CHURCH (formerly St Saviour's), Heath Terrace. Designed and built as a children's church for New Milverton by *G.F. Smith* for Frances, Lady Wheler, 1872. Simple Dec. Brick with stone dressings and fish-scale slate roof. Nave, chancel porch and w bell-turret. Later used as St Mark's Church Hall and sold to Emmanuel Church in 1984.

LIFE COMMUNITY CHURCH, Charlotte Street. *F.G. Cundall*, 1925. Brick and terracotta. Built as the chapel for the Anglican nuns of St Michael's Home.

SALVATION ARMY, Chapel Street. A low brick building with gables and slate roof, 1986. It replaces the old Citadel (*Edmund Sherwood*, 1884–5) in Park Street.

FIRST CHURCH OF CHRIST SCIENTIST, Augusta Place. *Symington, Prince & Pike* of Leicester, 1958. Simple, yellow brick with grid of concrete windows. On the site of St Luke's Episcopal Church (*Squirhill*, 1850) whose two-storey schoolroom with lancets (now AUGUSTA HOUSE) stands alongside. The schools by *Mitchell*, 1851.

CEMETERY, Brunswick Street. Commenced in 1852, the date of the lodge at the middle entrance. It is by *Squirhill* whose substantial spired chapel, also 1852, was demolished in 1978. The N lodge and the two remaining chapels by *Cundall*, 1868. The chapels are apsed and have similar fronts. The N (Nonconformist) chapel entirely Neo-Norman with bellcote, the s (Anglican) with plate tracery and bristling Gothic stone bell-turret.

PUBLIC BUILDINGS

107 TOWN HALL, The Parade. 1882–4 by *John Cundall*, a very large and proud building, quite out of keeping with Leamington. Red brick and brown Camden stone. Tudor, Baroque and Italian Renaissance features. Symmetrical, or nearly symmetrical, w front, with an elaborate centrepiece above the porch including a mosaic representing Hygeia below the pediment. The s entrance similar, but on a smaller scale. But the very commanding campanile tower with its domed stone cap is placed asymmetrically. Behind the centrepiece of the main façade, a Second Empire mansard roof with fish-scale slates and ironwork. This is over the grand staircase leading to the main rooms on the first floor, the council chamber on the s and an assembly hall on the N. Carving by *R.L. Boulton* of Cheltenham and stained glass by *Frank Holt* of Warwick including a six-light window of *As You Like It* in the council chamber. Below is a fine carved chimneypiece. STATUE of Queen Victoria outside and BUST of Edward VII inside, both by *Albert Toft*, 1902.

ROYAL PUMP ROOMS AND BATHS (Library, Art Gallery and Museum), The Parade. Originally built in 1813–14 by *C.S.*

Smith, following discovery of the spring here in 1811. But of that only the stone colonnaded façade survives. As to alterations, *Cundall* rearranged the columns and lowered the original roof behind the balustrade in 1861–3, also adding a corner tower, since removed. Rear additions including former public baths, first added in 1864. Flanking glass-roofed pavilions added in 1910 and 1926. Refurbished as the town Library, Art Gallery and Museum by *Capita Property Services*, 1999. The museum area includes the splendidly restored Turkish Baths of 1863, an octagonal room, domed with Islamic arches. Decorative brickwork and tiling. The library is under the iron and glass roof of the 1890 swimming bath by *William de Normanville*.

In the PUMP ROOM GARDENS, which extend w along the N bank of the River Leam, is a BANDSTAND, 1889, and the YORK BRIDGE, 1893, both also by *de Normanville*.

The JEPHSON GARDENS to the E of the Pump Rooms along the river were originally landscaped privately by *J.G. Jackson*, 1834, and developed into public gardens in the 1840s. The Italianate LODGES opposite the Pump Room are by *Squirhill*, 1846, when the gardens were renamed in honour of Dr Henry Jephson, the town's physician. A later cottage-style lodge by *Jackson* at the Willes Road end of the gardens. Also *Squirhill*'s the circular Corinthian TEMPLE containing a statue of Jephson by *Peter Hollins*, 1848–9. The HITCHMAN FOUNTAIN, rather hilarious E.E., is by *Cundall*, 1869. WILLES OBELISK also by *Cundall*, 1875. In the middle of the gardens, MILL BRIDGE connects the two sides of the town via a sunken footpath, allowing N–S access when the gardens are closed. It is a small suspension bridge over a weir, built in 1903 by *de Normanville*. Facing Newbold Street, the DAVIS CLOCK TOWER, by *F.W.H. Lee*, 1925. In the middle, the AVIARY CAFÉ with pretty ironwork, 1899, and the GLASSHOUSE by *Architecture PLB*, 2003, the sub-tropical enclosure with linked valley roof glazing.

FIRE STATION, Warwick Street, by *Eric Davies*, County Architect, 1962. Brick with stone panels to the office block and tiled square columns on the engine bays.

SOUTHERN JUSTICE CENTRE (cf. Nuneaton), Newbold Terrace. *HLM Architects*, 2009–10. Purpose-built to house the courts, police and related agencies. Imposing façade with raised entrance.

ROYAL SPA CENTRE, Newbold Terrace. By *Frederick Gibberd*, 1970–2. Theatre and cinema complex. Low with shallow-pitched roofs. On the site of *E.W. Pugin*'s demolished HARRINGTON HOUSE, 1869, described by Pevsner as 'symmetrical, but a dissolute Gothic-cum-Italian-cum-French'.

Former LEAMINGTON COLLEGE, Binswood Avenue. Now BINSWOOD HALL, the centrepiece of the Audley Binswood Retirement Village. By *Squirhill*, 1847–8. Grand Collegiate Tudor front in diapered brick with pale stone dressings. Large Perp windows, battlements, ogee-domed turrets l. and r. and

outer gabled bays. Central porch with carved coat of arms.
Good carved details. Inside, the hall and roof redecorated in
pastel colours. One half open full-height, the other subdivided
with swimming pool beneath a dining gallery. At right angles
behind, the former chapel by *Cundall*, 1876. In the apse of
what has become the fitness centre, STAINED GLASS by
Holland, 1858, and *Hardman*, 1883 and 1889. Side window,
1898. Side range on the s, with high-level balcony and Gothic
turret at the end, after 1903 when (until 1922) the buildings
were used as a Roman Catholic convent school. Behind, the
former gymnasium by *W. Hawley Lloyd*, 1891–2. Restored by
Quad Architects (*Martin Cummins*, project architect) in
2011–14.

RAILWAY STATION, Old Warwick Road. On the site of the GWR
station of 1852, but entirely rebuilt by *P.E. Culverhouse*, 1939.
Wide Regency-style front in Portland stone blocks. Art Deco
detailing to the buffet, waiting rooms and booking hall.

The COLLEGE and some of the SCHOOLS are described in their
locations, i.e. in the perambulations or under the villages.

PERAMBULATIONS

Leamington divides into a series of short perambulations: 1)
south of the River Leam, covering the old village and the first
phases of spa development; 2) New Town with The Parade
and the streets either side; and 3) the east from Holly Walk.

1. South

The original village lay between the river and the High Street,
the Southam–Warwick road. The perambulation covers the
redeveloped village centre and the areas of early development
E, W and S.

The natural start is in the square outside the parish church (*see*
above). Here stood Lord Aylesford's well (dem. 1961) over the
original spring, and a row of shops which blocked the western
extension of the church until removed in 1890. The typical
Leamington stucco terraces of four storeys begin right here
in all directions. First, opposite the church is VICTORIA
TERRACE of 1836–8, a palace-front terrace of twenty-two bays
by *William Thomas* with giant Corinthian columns and pilasters as main and subsidiary accents – on the pattern of Brighton,
needless to say. The quadrant s corner to SPENCER STREET
originally had a Greek Doric porch. Continuous cast-iron
balcony above the shops and around the N end which has a
quadrant corner and a nice Tuscan colonnade facing the river
and originally housed the Victoria Baths. The VICTORIA
BRIDGE, crossing the river towards the Pump Rooms, is of
1808–9 and by *H. Couchman Jun.* Three stone arches and bal-
ustrades. It was widened by *Jackson*, 1840.

s of Victoria Terrace, at the road junction good corner blocks on three sides, including the JUG & JESTER of *c*. 1814–15, possibly by *Henry Hakewill*, although altered. Continuing s down BATH STREET, which has suffered from insensitive commercial development and neglect, but towards the s one can still see here and there giant pilaster-strips with sunk panels, and also Grecian cast-iron balconies. Two good astylar blocks on the E, either side of Regent Place, the larger (Nos. 35–49) stretching to the High Street and turning back again into Church Street. It is by *William Thomas*, *c*. 1836. Opposite, WATERLOO HOUSE (Nos. 44–48), classical but restored with Gothic glazing to top-floor window lights, and the PARTHE-NON (Nos. 50–54), retaining the restored façade of *Samuel Beazley*'s Royal Assembly Rooms and Music Hall, 1821. Corinthian pilasters to middle floors of the remaining terrace (Nos. 60–64) before the High Street intersection. Here the railway cut through the heart of the old town with characteristic Victorian ruthlessness and ingenuity. Two BRIDGES crossed the intersection diagonally. One (demolished 1968) belonged to the Leamington–Rugby line and opened in 1851. The surviving girder bridge was built alongside for the GWR's Birmingham–Oxford line in 1852 but rebuilt in 1907.

The coming of the railway necessitated the removal of some of the most prestigious and grandest buildings of the spa town's early days, and sounded the death knell for the once-fashionable HIGH STREET, leaving little to see. To the E, at the corner of Althorpe Street, *John Russell*'s OLD TOWN HALL, 1831 (now the Polish Club). Stuccoed brick. Very modest in size, but with two giant fluted Ionic columns *in antis*. w of the railway bridge the former CROWN HOTEL (No. 10), built as the vicarage, 1808, and opened as a hotel in 1814. Now much altered. The r. hand addition of six bays with arched windows and balconies on the first floor is the former assembly room. Grecian decoration in the window arches.*

Bath Street is continued s in CLEMENS STREET. Easily missed, near the bridge, the APOLLO ROOMS (No. 6) on the w, *c*. 1816, originally the Marble Baths, with segmental-arched recesses, pilasters and pediment. Nicely restored 2001–2. Little else of note survives here – the odd Doric porch and the odd cast-iron balcony.

Now w towards the crossroads on High Street near the station. At the N end of TACHBROOK ROAD is EASTNOR TERRACE, two-storey houses on rising ground with a stepped parapet, *c*. 1852. Opposite is STATION HOUSE, a handsome Neo-Regency student accommodation block with leaded mansard roof, by *AT Architects*, 2010.

N beyond the railway is AVENUE ROAD, lined with trees and 1850s detached and semi-detached villas, especially good the

---

*Identical decoration can be seen at Warwick Market Place at Nos. 3–4 (former Lloyds Bank of 1826).

group w of Park Road on the N side (Nos. 12–26), of similar design with slate hipped roofs and cast-iron verandas. They were near the Avenue Road station, opened 1851. Before these on the N side, the old LIBRARY and TECHNICAL SCHOOL (now apartments). By *J. Mitchell Bottomley* of Middlesbrough, 1900–2. Red brick and terracotta, with straight and curved gables. Octagonal corner towers on the rear elevation. The single-storey gallery extension on the r., cruciform with a central dome, is by *A.C. Bunch*, 1928. In an alcove, a female nude by *W.J. Bloye*, 1929. Then the MANOR HOUSE (apartments too), possibly 1871. High Victorian Gothic, of brick, and rather grim. E is SPENCER STREET and a pair of curly barge-boarded Neo-Tudor villas (Nos. 1–3) of 1842, next to the former Congregational chapel (*see* Churches). Opposite, *Horace G. Bradley*'s Art Deco BATH CINEMA, 1925, and BATH ASSEMBLY HALL, 1926, a *palais de danse*. In Georgian vein with quirky details, e.g. the three wheel-headed windows to the cinema and, on the hall, the big Adamesque window and triumphal arch with goddess statue and ball above. The main hall décor sympathetically restored under *Laurence Llewelyn-Bowen*, 2008.

A short walk brings us back to the church, from where we head E along PRIORY TERRACE. On the corner, the Italianate stone POST OFFICE (disused, 2015), by the *Office of Works* (*James Williams*), 1870, extended by *Edward Cropper*, 1911, and continuing with the sorting office, 1975–8. E of the church is *John Cundall*'s PRIORY HOUSE, built for Signor Aspa, 1864, alongside the remains of Rev. John Craig's short-lived Vicar's Grammar School. Now used by CHRIST CHURCH, the hall with huge lancets and carved stone parapet is by *Squirhill*, 1847. After the former URQUHART HALL (*F.G. Cundall*, 1905) we are in the Willes estate, where development began in 1824. Mostly classical in LEAM TERRACE, including two fine three-storey balconied terraces (Nos. 30–42 and 48–52) on the s, both *c.* 1831, and Florence House (No. 39) on the N with Corinthian porch, *c.* 1838. Also on the N, a charming little group of Gothic villas (Nos. 9–13), 1833–6, possibly by *John Mair* of London. Further E a long run of later two-storey houses to Willes Road. A few villas beyond and in St Mary's Road, but here they peter out. The area is mostly infilled with later C19 terraced housing. At Willes Road, turn s into Farley Street and head back via RUSSELL TERRACE, laid out *c.* 1828–36. Towards the W end, something of the classical style appears still; but mostly gables and Gothic to Tudor details. A short walk up George Street past the first Roman Catholic church (*see* Churches), l. into Church Terrace with its attractive corner group round the TOWN HOUSE pub, brings us back to the parish church. Facing the churchyard s is the old COM-MONWEALTH CLUB in Church Street (No. 3), *c.* 1825, with unorthodox Corinthian columns to the balcony level of its pedimented two-storeyed porch.

2. Central

The Parade forms the central spine to the New Town, begun N of the river in 1808. This perambulation takes in The Parade itself up to Beauchamp Square, then continues via Clarendon Avenue (and Square) into Clarendon Place, and then takes Dale Street back to Dormer Place. This route makes little mention of the two E–W streets leading off The Parade, i.e. Regent Street and Warwick Street. In these, the buildings were significantly less grand, and in the N–S streets crossing them more so still.

We start at the lower end of THE PARADE, ignoring Euston Place (*see* Perambulation 3) on the E. The Parade starts with a long terrace on the curve with giant coupled pilasters – Ionic on the wedge-shaped corner block (on Dormer Place, No. 168) and Corinthian beyond (Nos. 152–164). Here the line of the street straightens out, and the gentle rise of the Regency Parade once terminated with the centrally placed Neo-Norman tower of Christ Church. A few fronts of stone and brick bring a little colour to the prevailing whiteness. The former BARCLAYS BANK (Nos. 148–150) has a stone ground-floor façade with an arcade of Ionic columns and horizontal rustication, added *c.* 1903. In its segmental pediment the beehive emblem of the Refuge Assurance Company. Nos. 140–142 has a classic Montague Burton Art Deco front, 1931, doubtless by *Harry Wilson*. No. 130 is half-timbered and looks extraordinarily out of place here. At HSBC (No. 126) a good Italianate palazzo front to a former hotel by *Joseph Bateman* for the Leamington Priors & Warwickshire Bank, 1856. Rusticated arches and columns with blocking. Opposite, immediately beyond the TOWN HALL (*see* Public Buildings), *C.S. Smith*'s REGENT HOTEL, 1818–19, then one of the largest hotels in Europe. It has a side porch of two pairs of Greek Doric columns topped by the Regent's stucco coat of arms. The front porch with plain Greek columns was added in 1849. Façades restored and interior remodelled 2003–5. To the N, 1970s REGENT SQUARE HOUSE occupies what was once an open space.

A good group at The Parade's intersection with Regent Street: OLD BANK (Lloyds) (No. 73) NE, the large Late Victorian department store (Nos. 94–96; River Island in 2015) SW, running W along Regent Street, and Thornton's (No. 92) at NW with especially ornate Grecian classical details above street level, including pilasters with Temple of the Winds capitals. Between Regent Street and Warwick Street, parallel to The Parade, the ROYAL PRIORS shopping centre, by *Chapman Taylor & Partners*, 1985–6, with a tinted glazed barrel vault to its central colonnaded mall. N of this more Doric porches and giant pilasters, always much interfered with by shopfronts. The climax is the end, i.e. the last blocks before Beauchamp Square. On the E side the former CLARENDON HOTEL (Nos. 1–3), of 1830, giant Ionic pilasters, continuous balcony with lacy ironwork, Doric porches. In this run, divisions of three bays, Adam-type doorways (e.g. Nos. 7–9) and railed basements. The same in the preserved façade opposite, with Ionic porches at its s end, and again at the se corner of Beauchamp Square (once Guy's Hotel), again of three bays.

BEAUCHAMP SQUARE was laid out by *P. F. Robinson* for Edward Willes in 1825 and had his Neo-Norman CHRIST CHURCH as its centre from 1825. It went in 1959. The area to the N will be dealt with later (*see* p. 426). We head w along Clarendon Avenue, which opens up into CLARENDON SQUARE, the finest of Leamington's squares. Built *c.* 1828–32 and largely complete, especially on the three main sides. Greek Doric porches again. The e side is a standard palace front, four storeys with the six-bay end and centre projected. The w side, however, separated by a through road but also set back with its own road closed by gatepiers N and s, is a little out of the ordinary. It comprises a nine-bay four-storey centre block of three-bay houses flanked by seven-bay and three-storey side blocks and at each end three-bay two-storey cottage villas. The centre houses in each terrace have Greek Doric porches but the entrances to their neighbours are at the side and set back behind Doric screens that link the three blocks. Tent-roofed cast-iron balconies on the first floor and verandas to the cottages. A little N, facing Beauchamp Terrace, is MAGNOLIA HOUSE (No. 22a), gabled, of the cottage type and by *Robinson*, 1824.

Clarendon Place leads s, with a good group of ornate houses (Nos. 2–10) with two-storey canted bays on the w. These are by *Thomas Mason*, 1869. Then in WARWICK STREET going e, two specially extensive terraces face one another, WATERLOO PLACE on the N and CLARENCE TERRACE opposite. The former, *c.* 1828–32, with Ionic porches, thirty-five bays and broadly similar to the e side of Clarendon Square. Clarence Terrace by *Joseph Nevill*, *c.* 1836, with Greek Doric porches, is half the length and has no central emphasis. The curved bays at the rear, five storeys with the fall of the land, look well from DALE STREET, which continues s opposite the fire station (*see* Public Buildings) with more balconied fronts. Behind and parallel to the e is PORTLAND STREET which has a few classical villas (Nos. 2–10) with pilasters and balconied single-storey curved bays. Also (Nos. 17–19) the former Wesleyan chapel, 1825. This street is rewarding above and below Regent Street, with PORTLAND HOUSE (street address Nos. 20A–30 Regent Street, side on Portland Street) at the intersection.

At the bottom of Portland Street, in Portland Place East, the remains of the former REGAL CINEMA (now VUE); Art Deco by *Horace G. Bradley*, 1931, with sympathetic additions 1996–2000. To the e, the ST PETER'S CAR PARK by *Smith & Way*, 1990, harmonizing unexpectedly with the architecture of the nearby Roman Catholic church. Nearby, the REAL TENNIS CLUB in BEDFORD STREET by *Jackson*, 1846, its club house of 1847–54 and Racquets Court, 1858.

Across Dale Street, Portland Place West has further Regency housing and leads to the lower end of New Milverton (*see* Leamington Villages). A little s, the ADELAIDE BRIDGE was rebuilt in wrought iron with elaborate cast-iron parapets by *William de Normanville*, 1891. Stay N of the Leam and return to the Parade via Dormer Place, with the Pump Room gardens (*see* Public Buildings) on the r.

3. East

Back to our start at the town hall on The Parade. The perambulation begins with the string of separately named streets collectively known as Holly Walk. REGENT GROVE (N) and HAMILTON TERRACE (S) are the two sides of one wide street in the centre of which are two lines of trees and a walk – as in French towns. In Regent Grove immediately E of the town hall, DENBY BUILDINGS, 1885, a symmetrical group in brick and stone with lively details of corner turrets, stepped gables and Gothic centre block. Further E, the ANGEL HOTEL, *c.* 1813. Little opposite except for the rear of the new Justice Centre (*see* Public Buildings) and balconied HAMILTON HOUSE, 1833–4, with alternating recessed blocks. On the r. NEWBOLD STREET, pleasantly lined with post-1826 smaller-scale housing and the Davis Clock Tower (*see* Public Buildings) at the S end. Then HOLLY WALK (N) itself, the direct continuation, once lined with villas but now mostly commercial and extensively redeveloped. KINGSLEY HOUSE (No. 63) is a Regency survivor, *c.* 1833, squeezed between a turreted High Victorian corner block and *W. Hawley Lloyd*'s brick and stone-banded ST PAUL'S SCHOOLS (now offices) of 1911. On the S, the former Congregational chapel (*see* Churches), a Gothic pair at Nos. 56–58 BRANDON PARADE, and No. 60, still classical.

Across Willes Road, a large and varied group of 1830s developments, all by *William Thomas*. At the corner is VICTORIA HOUSE (No. 59 Willes Road), 1835: a fine late classical villa with giant pilasters carrying rich Corinthianesque capitals. One-storeyed Ionic portico with pediment. Then in UPPER HOLLY WALK a key-piece, Nos. 79–81, one occupied by *Thomas* himself: dated in the openwork parapet 1836, ornately Jacobean. In contrast, No. 87, the OAK HOUSE CLUB, *c.* 1838, is in fanciful Gothick. On the S side, COMYN VILLA (No. 66) is the survivor of three Gothic villas. N of all these, approached through narrow entrances S and W, is LANSDOWNE CIRCUS, 84 a tucked-away square of sweet cottages in pairs with tent-roofed and ornate cast-iron verandas, *c.* 1834–8. Entrances set back in the end bays. But even here, in a corner, a gabled Gothic villa (No. 18). Delightful as it is, the Circus is only an adjunct to the principal group, LANSDOWNE CRESCENT, 83 1838, which curves gracefully round Willes Road to the NW. Entirely classical, of course, and surely the finest of

Leamington's crescents and terraces. Three storeys (not four) over a basement, with attic. Twenty-one blocks of two bays (2–7–3–7–2). Continuous ground-floor veranda with uprights of Greek key decoration. Pedimented first-floor windows. Simple pilasters at the ends but Corinthian at the centre

Behind it in Thomas Street and stretching N to Leicester Street some housing by *F. Gibberd*, 1963–4: KENNEDY SQUARE, with shops behind a colonnade on the Lansdowne Street frontage. Four-storey, rather severe, but enlivened by balconies and pleasantly grouped around courtyards within.

Then s to NEWBOLD TERRACE which runs N of the Jephson Gardens. Two fine Italianate villas (Nos. 26–27) of *c.* 1860 at the start of Newbold Terrace East, and pretty mid-C19 brick (No. 34) and stuccoed (Nos. 37–38) houses beyond. The main terrace faces the gardens, beginning with a handsome four-storey corner block (Nos. 23–25) with continuous wrought-iron balcony. Next, REGENCY HOUSE, a large block of sixty apartments by *Redgrave & Clarke*, 1970–1: unashamedly Modernist, but sympathetic in scale and texture. After that a group of Italianate villas (Nos. 14–17). Between the Royal Spa Centre and the Justice Centre (*see* Public Buildings), ROSSMORE HOUSE preserves the fronts of three villas of five bays each with Corinthian columns. Then at the corner, AGRICULTURE HOUSE (No. 1) with a porch of two pairs of fluted Ionic columns, and similar columns of trellis-work above. This belongs with EUSTON PLACE on the E side of The Parade. Of 1832–5, rebuilt after a fire in 1839. Fronts at s end altered but N end still has Greek Doric porches side by side. In front, facing The Parade, the WAR MEMORIAL by *Albert Toft*, 1922, with bronze statues of infantryman with bowed head and rifle pointing to the ground. Further N, by the town hall, an OBELISK by *John Cundall*, 1880, in memory of Alderman Henry Bright.

OUTER LEAMINGTON

There are two areas to consider: 1) N towards Kenilworth and Lillington, and 2) the s and se towards Whitnash and Radford Semele.

1. North

N of Beauchamp Square, the streets are regular and the houses predictable. The main W–E streets are wide and tree-lined. Plenty of cast-iron verandas or balconies. Villas mainly, developing from Regency to Gothic and then Italianate with the outward march of development. These stretch far up the Kenilworth Road, which is lined with 1860s and 1870s housing, and also along the road to Lillington (*see* Leamington Villages) where there are further Leamington residences.

In Beauchamp Avenue, N of the square, are HOLY TRINITY church (*see* Churches) and the BEAUCHAMP HALL of Kingsley School, built 1862–3 as a private house for Robert Hobson. Stone-faced with mullioned-and-transomed windows and a Frenchy turret. Providing the visual focus at the head of Beauchamp Avenue is Binswood Hall (*see* former Leamington College, p. 419) on BINSWOOD AVENUE, flanked by a shallow crescent of good late Regency villas with balconies and verandas, and an especially good terrace at the W end of Binswood Avenue.

Further N in LILLINGTON AVENUE is the redeveloped LEAMINGTON BREWERY, retaining part of the main block, the brewer's house and ornamental iron gates in a housing complex. The main building originally by *Robert Davison* for Lucas & Co., 1861. Of brick with a steep French hipped roof, its details perhaps Quattrocento, perhaps Romanesque.*

On KENILWORTH ROAD, 1860s THORNCLIFFE HOUSE (No. 14) with entrance tower and Gothic porch differs from the norm. Since the 1960s, small-scale blocks of flats have replaced the villas or filled gaps. On a larger scale is NORTHUMBERLAND COURT at the corner of Northumberland Road, by *Gibberd*, 1962. Mixed height blocks, linked.

Among the 1930s stockbroker Tudor of NORTHUMBERLAND ROAD, TURRET HOUSE (No. 39) stands out: *moderne*, circular tower flanked by canted wings. Here a fine avenue of trees leads W along Beverley Road to Navonhill (replaced by flats) and THE GRANGE, the largest of the surviving Late Victorian houses in Guy's Cliffe Avenue.

2. South and south-east

Beyond the canal in BRUNSWICK STREET a restored Regency terrace (Nos. 15–27), *c.* 1818–28. Then extensive 1960s redevelopment with flats and two eleven-storey tower blocks. Off Brunswick Street at the end of Ranelagh Street is the RANGEMASTER or EAGLE WORKS on a site occupied by Flavel's since 1856. The firm manufactured cooking stoves and kitchen ranges. To the rear, at right angles to the canal and facing towards Eagle Park on the E, is the late Art Deco office block by company architect *R.W. Willcocks*, 1946-7. In Shrubland Street, the SCHOOLS (originally Board Schools), partly by *G.B. Nichols & Son*, 1884, and partly (the block facing Eagle Street) to a Nichols design modified by *Frederick Foster*, 1891; a group, little altered. Off the W side of Shrubland Street in CHARLES GARDENER ROAD, housing for old people by *Denys Hinton & Associates*, 1962-4. One five-storey block, the rest two-storeyed with monopitch roofs. W of Tachbrook Road the SHRUBLAND HALL Housing Estate of

---

* Significant additions by *Scamell & Colyer*, 1896, were lost in the redevelopment.

1939, a typical low-density cottage estate on the garden suburb model.

Returning to the bridges, next E along RADFORD ROAD past the redeveloped Warneford Hospital site.* Later Victorian housing on Radford Road and in the side streets. CLAPHAM TERRACE has the BOARD SCHOOL by *Frederick Foster*, 1889–90, Gothic-cum-Queen Anne style with spirelet and gabled and half-hipped roofs. Opposite, two side wings of the former MILITIA BARRACKS: classical, by *William Kendall*, County Surveyor, 1856–7. The once-pedimented centre cruelly cut away to create access to a back street.

Further E, the ST MARY'S district was sparsely populated when the church was built. It was developed from 1838. Decent mid-C19 brick-fronted villas in St Mary's Road (e.g. Nos. 15–17). Others stuccoed with verandas. EATON VILLA (No. 13) on the corner of Radford Road has Jacobean gables. More on Radford Road and in the outer parts of Willes Road and Leam Terrace.

SE of these, over the canal, is the SYDENHAM FARM ESTATE. Laid out and built by *Gibberd* on the Radburn plan with green space and short closes radiating from Gainsborough Drive. In four main phases, 1964–72.

LEAMINGTON VILLAGES

LILLINGTON

Part of Leamington since 1890, before which much of north Leamington was already in Lillington parish.

ST MARY MAGDALENE, Church Lane. Norman origins, some C14 evidence in the chancel, and a Perp W tower. Otherwise all is Victorian, beginning with a restoration by *J.G. Jackson*, 1847. N aisle added by *William Ballard*, 1858, followed by the S aisle and porch in 1868, also by Ballard. Chancel extended E by *Cundall*, 1884, with vestry alongside. Additional N vestry by *Edward P. Warren*, 1914. N chapel created in 1936 when the organ was removed to the back of the church. The nave is low and has dormers. – REREDOS. *Jones & Willis*, 1890. – CHANCEL FURNISHINGS by Warren, 1908. – FONT. Octagonal, Perp, with shields in pointed quatrefoils. – STAINED GLASS. By *Clayton & Bell* the E window, 1885, and W window, 1870. – One in S aisle by *Ward & Hughes*, 1876. – *Hardman* glass (four windows) in aisles, 1883–96. – By *Kempe* S aisle E, 1896, and two in N aisle, 1907 and 1920.

In the angle outside between S aisle and tower, a WAR MEMORIAL, by *Warren*, 1920. To the S, the OCTAGON ROOM, locally designed, 1987.

---

*It was late classical, by *Joseph Bateman*, 1832–4, with substantial additions of 1892–1900 by *Keith D. Young*.

OUR LADY'S (R.C.), Valley Road. *Rayner & Fedeski* (project architect *Henry Fedeski*), 1962–3. An exceptional church, especially the interior. Much influenced by the Liturgical Movement and Gerard Goalen's church of Our Lady at Harlow, Essex (1953–60). Brick with thin concrete mullions to the windows and tall copper spire. Cruciform, with central altar on raised dais. Lady Chapel and children's chapel on one side. Cylindrical room designed as a baptistery on the other. The whole with brilliant *dalle-de-verre* STAINED GLASS designed by *Dom Charles Norris* of Buckfast and made at Prinknash. Mainly abstract, but figures of the Archangel Gabriel and Our Lady in the transepts. – MOSAIC on E wall by *Steven Sykes*, 1963.

FREE CHURCH, Cubbington Road. *Cecil E.M. Fillmore & Partners* (project architect *Geoffrey Cox*), 1965–6. Brick with concrete ribs and light steel flèche. Aisled interior.

SCHOOLS in Telford Avenue by *Jackson & Edmonds*, 1950. In Sandy Lane, NORTH LEAMINGTON SCHOOL, by *Robothams*, 2009. Timber-clad with sedum roofs.

The old village was on the hilltop, clustered around the church. THE MANOR opposite was largely rebuilt in 1741–2 by *William Smith* the younger for Barkinsdale Robbins, but incorporates C16 and C17 elements. From the mid 1930s there was expansion to the NE between the Lillington and Cubbington roads. The major change came in the late 1950s with the creation of a new village centre and Leamington Borough Council Estate SE of the Cubbington Road. CROWN WAY has low-rise flats and an attractive shopping precinct, all by the *Borough Architect*, 1957. At the junction with Valley Road the flats are taller. Here too, the Four Ways care home by the *County Architect* (*Eric Davies*), 1963. On a bank above the roundabout and alongside the Roman Catholic church, the LIBRARY, by *Rayner & Fedeski* for the borough council, 1959–60, designed as a colourful centrepiece to the estate. To the S, COUNCIL HOUSING, with one high block, EDEN COURT.

On Cubbington Road, the former LOCAL BOARD OFFICES with broad shaped gable, by *John Cundall*, 1882. A little E and opposite at Nos. 43–49, a group of four steel-framed HEXAGONAL HOUSES, 1964; two-storeyed, serrated tile-hanging. A modular design by *Thorne & Barton* (*John B. Thorne*) patented by Formula Housing Research Ltd in 1967 but never commercially developed.

Along LILLINGTON ROAD (*see also* Outer Leamington: North) N of the roundabout, several attractive red brick villas of the 1860s, some late Neoclassical, some Gothic. On the l., CASTELL FROMA, a large Italianate house of 1870 for George Unett, now rather engulfed in a care home.

NEW MILVERTON

An area immediately to the NW of the New Town developed on land belonging to the Willes and Greatheed families straddling the boundary between Leamington and Milverton on either side of the Bins brook. A town map of 1838 by Squirhill shows the street layout for an extensive suburb already partly developed. By 1887 housing in New Milverton stretched to the Rugby Road and well towards Warwick.

100   ST MARK, Rugby Road. The successor of *J. G. Jackson*'s 1835 'Pepperpot' chapel on Milverton Hill. On a new site. Built in memory of Lady Frances Wheler by her brothers E. S. and the Rev. C. Carus-Wilson. By *George Gilbert Scott Jun.*, 1876–9, and the principal surviving work of this excellent architect. Large, of brick with Box stone banding and dressings, very lively in the external details, especially the top of the w tower. Aisled nave, chancel, transepts. Dec details. The interior has Scott's typical lozenge-shaped piers into which the arches die. Tall three-light clerestory windows with mullions descending lower down into a blank continuation. Pier bases and side walls of aisles with high wooden panelling. Three-bay chancel with fine verticals. Wooden lierne-vault. In the transepts wooden tierceron vaults. The nave roof boarded, of four-centred section on a coving *à la* S. Zeno, Verona. Reordering by *Kenneth C. White*, 1979, and in 2010. – Some original furnishings designed by Scott. – Oak PULPIT carved by *Farmer & Brindley*, under a small stone canopy (like a tester) in the wall behind. – Alabaster FONT with shafts of Frosterley marble and elaborate wooden canopy, also worked by *Farmer & Brindley*. – ORGAN CASE. Delightful, Gothic. 1879 by *John Hardman Powell*. – Later furnishings. – Carved oak REREDOS by *Plucknett* of Warwick, 1902. – SCREEN by *Bodley*, 1904, resited at the back of the nave, 2010. – STAINED GLASS. E window by *Cox, Buckley & Son*, 1881. – Chancel side windows by *Kempe*, 1892 and 1906. – In S transept one by *A. O. Hemming*, 1890 – The rest all by *Hardman*, 1882–1934. – CHANCEL ROOF DECORATION by *C. J. Blomfield*, 1904, executed by *Powell & Sons*. – The CHURCH ROOM on the N is contemporary with the church and also by Scott. It was subdivided into two floors by *K. White*, 1979. CHURCHYARD boundary wall original too, with memorial GATEWAY by *Philip B. Chatwin*, 1939.

The former vicarage (LEAMINGTON HOUSE) N of the church is also by *Scott Jun.*, 1873–6, originally with interior decoration by *Watts & Co.* and a heraldic glass skylight (sold 1990) over the staircase by *Burlison & Grylls*, 1875. Queen Anne revival. Banded brickwork with ashlar dressings. Dutch gables and dormers. Tall chimneys. Garden front with rectangular bays finished with pairs of segmental pediments and balustrading.

In Rugby Road, a good Queen Anne BOARD SCHOOL, 1887–92 by *F. H. Moore* of Warwick.

CLARENDON CRESCENT, off Beauchamp Hill, was laid out on Willes land and developed between 1830 and 1839. On wedge-shaped plots backing onto an enclosed private garden. Original plans by *Samuel Nicklin* whose rear elevation with double bow-fronts was followed. More variety on the street side but several houses have extended porches with classical fronts while Nos. 1 and 2 are more open and traditional. Regency again in BERTIE TERRACE, Warwick Place, by *Jackson*, 1836. Early Gothic is to be seen in Warwick Place at EATON LODGE (No. 44): bargeboarded, with fancy bay window and pinnacled side porch. Grander still, though diminished by alterations, two pairs of Gothic villas (Nos. 34–40) with parapets and battlements, *c.* 1840. High Victorian steep gables and porches with chunky columns and carved capitals in BEAUCHAMP HILL, 1850s. Polychromatic window headers to the corner house in Heath Terrace laid out by *Joseph Nevill*, *c.* 1853. On the N side of Heath Terrace is STANFORD PLACE with half-timbered gables by *T. R. Donnelly*, 1885. On RUGBY ROAD, terraces and blocks of houses in a wide range of later Victorian styles.

Further S, off WARWICK NEW ROAD, is SUNSHINE HOUSE (No. 15), now surrounded by housing off Copps Road. Built as Milverton Lawn by *G. T. Robinson*, 1863, for Hubert Lloyd, in the late classical style with Grecian decorative motifs. Once one of several large houses in this area, now mostly replaced. The largest was Thornbank, whose site is now occupied by ROYAL LEAMINGTON SPA COLLEGE. Its main block with grey walls and coloured panels was completed in 2014. Other buildings on site by *Robothams*, 2006 and 2009.

WHITNASH

Once noted as a picturesque village, 1¼ m. SSE. of Leamington, Whitnash changed dramatically in the post-war period. Development came in the rush of the 1950s and the results here compare unfavourably with Lillington, where greater attention was paid to design and planning. By the mid 1960s the gap between Leamington and the village had been filled and there was also substantial expansion to the SW and SE.

ST MARGARET. A small village church quite lavishly improved under Canon Young (rector 1846–84) and enlarged in 1989 for its much expanded community. Ashlar-faced W tower; probably Perp. Parts by *G. G. Scott*: chancel 1855, S aisle and porch 1867. Nave after Scott's death by *J. D. Wyatt*, 1880. As Scott liked it, there is extremely lush foliage on capitals, etc. Much of the stone carving is by *Agnes Bonham* of Leamington whose name deserves to be here perpetuated. To this decent Victorian ensemble *John D. Holmes* has added an extension to the N aisle and a new chapter house SE of the church. The extension is a demi-octagon, reusing a C19 window and exterior stonework. The chapter house is an elongated octagon in brick with gabled roof-lights. – Good Victorian FURNISHINGS, especially in the chancel, e.g. the STALLS, *Minton* TILES, etc. – FONT. Caen stone, by *Squirhill*, 1848.* Cover by *Skidmore*, 1863. – PULPIT, 1861–2, and REREDOS of carved reliefs either side of the E window, 1864, both by *G.T. Robinson*, carved by Bonham. – STAINED GLASS. Several by *Holland*, including the E window, 1856, and others in the chancel, nave, s chapel, vestry and porch *c.* 1854–70. – One chancel N window by *N.W. Lavers* (designed by *Alfred Bell*, later of Clayton & Bell), 1857. – Two by *Hardman*, 1856 and 1870. – One each by *Wailes*, 1868, *Ward & Hughes*, 1873, and *Buckley & Co.*, 1876. – One N window by *F.C. Eden*, 1937. – BRASSES. Benedict Medley †1503 and wife, 2 ft (61 cm.) figures. – Richard Bennet, rector, †1532, 17 in. (43 cm.) figure.

ST JOSEPH (R.C.), Murcott Road. *Brian A. Rush & Associates*, 1971. Buff brick. Fan-shaped with curved end to sanctuary and long slit windows. – SCULPTURE. Bas relief in lobby brick-work. The flight into Egypt, by *Walter Ritchie*, presumably 1971.

METHODIST CHURCH, Murcott Road. *L. Cripps* of Headington, 1968. A plain hall with Cotswold stone facing and cross on E wall, spike above.

Timber-framed cottages remain along Whitnash Road, some thatched. All hemmed in by bungalows and modern housing. The best are No. 33, formerly HOME FARM, and the PLOUGH & HARROW pub.

LEEK WOOTTON

ALL SAINTS. Rebuilt for Lady Mary Leigh by *Joseph Eglington*, 1790–2, but much altered. In 1843 *J.G. Jackson* rebuilt the chancel. *John Gibson* re-roofed the nave and inserted a rose window, 1864–5. Then in 1889–90 *W.D. Caröe* remodelled the church, extending the nave by one Perp bay, rebuilding the chancel and adding the N vestry. He reworked Gibson's ham-merbeam nave roof and moved Jackson's E window to the vestry. Of 1792, the shell of the w end of the nave and the w tower remain intact. The nave has *ingénu* cusped Y-traceried windows. Embattled and pinnacled tower with characteristic Georgian Gothic quatrefoils within roundels. On the N (and formerly s), a blind panel like the nave windows. Caröe redid the w window and added the stair-turret, but all with impres-sive care to match stonework and finishes. Inside, harsh point-ing. Reordering at the w end, 1999, with rooms under tower and gallery. – FONTS. C12 tub font outside, and octagonal panelled stone font inside, 1845. This replaced a Derbyshire marble font by *Eglington*, 1793. – WOODWORK. Elaborate chancel STALLS, ALTAR RAILS and LECTERN by *Caröe*, 1897,

---

* Squirhill had designed a new rectory (demolished) in 1846.

later complemented by REREDOS, 1923, and SCREEN, 1929. – C18 PULPIT, reconstructed 1938. – STAINED GLASS. E window and one chancel S by *Powell*, 1890, the latter designed by *H. Holiday*. – The rest by *Holland*, mostly 1840s, the rose window 1864.

WOOTTON PADDOX (former vicarage), W of the church, by *John Bradford*, 1824. Five bays and three storeys, with balustrading on the top storey whose brickwork differs from the lower stages yet matches the architect's design. N of the church, STONE HOUSE, 1860. Built for the Woodcote agent yet looking like a Victorian parsonage. W of the main road to the S, STONE EDGE by *H.B. Creswell*, dated 1909; Tudor-style, with none of his usual adventurousness.

A long village on the Warwick–Kenilworth road, with a good mixture of timber-framed, stone and brick buildings, some thatched, especially around the junction with Woodcote Lane. N of the Anchor Inn, ROCK COTTAGES by *Armstrong & Gardner*, 1934. Beyond, the former SCHOOL, 1874–5, and a pair of Woodcote ESTATE COTTAGES, 1866. YEW TREES cottage with porthole windows and diapered brickwork is by *H.W. Hobbiss*, 1910, greatly extended. Off Woodcote Lane, more estate cottages by *Armstrong*, 1912 and 1926.

WOODCOTE, ½ m. W. By *John Gibson* for H.C. Wise, 1861–2, extended 1869. Stone, two-storeyed, with small dormers, canted bays and openwork parapets. The whole somewhat lumpy. From 1949 until 2012 it was the headquarters of Warwickshire Police and part of the house was demolished and replaced by an office extension, 1969. Many additions in the grounds.

GOODREST FARM beyond Woodcote is a big square house of 1784, altered in 1821. WOOTTON GRANGE FARM, 1777–8, on the Kenilworth Road, has Gothick elements.

CHESFORD GRANGE, 1¼ m. ENE. By *Frederick Foster* for Joseph Hinks, 1900. Applied half-timbering and a corner turret. Developed as a hotel since 1956 and surrounded by later additions.

HILL WOOTTON is an elevated hamlet of farms and cottages, 1 m. E. HILL WOOTTON HOUSE has minor additions by *P. Morley Horder*, 1895–8, and *Charles M.C. Armstrong*, 1924. Red brick TOWER HOUSE, by *Crouch, Butler & Savage*, 1920 with later additions, has conical turrets.

See also Beausale and Guy's Cliffe.

LIGHTHORNE

3050

ST LAURENCE. The W tower is 1773–4, when the entire church was rebuilt. It is in three stepped stages with an embattled parapet. It has the blank quatrefoils and bell-openings with

Y-tracery typical of the C18 Gothic. The architect was *Thomas Squirrell* (a forebear of D.G. Squirhill), who was paid four guineas for a plan and estimate, while *Samuel Eglington*, to whom it has been attributed hitherto, was the mason. *John Mantun* was Eglington's co-contractor. The rest a later rebuilding by *John Gibson*, 1875–6. Chancel, nave, N aisle, N mortuary chapel and S porch, all rock-faced, with early C14 details. Unadventurous, but given a distinctive character by subtle use of varied materials and colours. Striking twin balcony window above the doorway from nave to tower. – FITTINGS, mostly original, 1875–6, with mosaic REREDOS by *Powell* and elaborate carved FONT. – Later Perp-style PULPIT, 1913. – STAINED GLASS. Medieval shields in S chancel, one dated 1413. – Heraldic glass of the Verney family in N aisle, possibly from Compton Verney, the lower C16 and probably by *Nicholas Eyffeler*, and the rest C17. – Two adjacent S nave windows contemporary with the 1876 rebuilding, one (l.) given by *Gibson*, the other (r.) by William Wilkins of Lighthorne, the contractor. The r. window by *Holland & Holt* incorporates a C16 St Sebastian from the former E window. Aidan McRae Thomson has shown that it matches a figure at Fairford and might be from the Southwark workshops of *Barnard Flower*, *c*. 1510, with repairs of *c*. 1600, all re-set, 1876. – Several by *Powell*, the N chapel E, 1876 (*H.E. Wooldridge*), chapel N windows, 1879 and 1897 (*Ada Currey*), and E window, 1886 (*J.W. Brown*). – One in N aisle by *Florence Camm*, 1946. – Tower window (internal) by *Christopher Lund*, 1996.

LYCHGATE, by *Gibson*, 1883.

OLD RECTORY, E of the church, C17 house with an C18 front. Five bays, the outer ones in gabled cross-wings. Flatly framed windows. Brick arch to former stables, now residential, to the E. Its successor (now NORTHBROOK HOUSE), S of Moreton Morrell Lane, is an inventive and attractive design by *Coleridge, Jennings & Soimenow* of Westminster, 1929–30. Also near the church, CHURCH HILL FARM, C16 and later, irregular and rambling, with tall brick chimneys.

A compact Compton Verney estate village in a steep-sided valley. Terraces of cottages on each side, many originally thatched. Mostly stone, but FAIRFIELD in Church Lane is timber-framed. Opposite, a long row of cottages still with eyebrow dormers to the first-floor windows even though the thatch has been replaced with tiles. Towards the green, the well-head built into the hillside with an C18 stone surround with shaped gable. Nearby, C18 SMITHY COTTAGE, thatched, and the former smithy. On the S bank above the small green, the C18 ANTE-LOPE pub with hipped roof, cross-windows and dormers. To the E in Old School Lane, DENE HOLLOW is a large late C16 or early C17 stone house with ironstone quoins and mullioned windows with hoodmoulds. Above the village on the N, the former SCHOOL by *William Lait*, 1871–2, now a house, as is an earlier school of 1781 in Old School Lane. This is in coursed limestone with a timber-framed wing behind.

LITTLE COMPTON

St Denys. C13 origins – see the reused E.E. windows in the chancel s wall. Rugged C14(?) s tower with saddleback roof. The rest of 1863–4 by *E.G. Bruton* of Oxford, including the rebuilt Perp s chapel aisle. Severe plate tracery. Plain interior, with inbuilt stone PULPIT in SE angle of nave. – FONT. C13, round. – REREDOS of gesso work, by the *Rev. John Rivington*, 1916. – STAINED GLASS. E window by *Jones & Willis*, 1899. – S chancel with C16–C17 fragments rescued by *Oswald Mace* (a glazier) from a war-damaged church at Villers-Bretonneux, France, 1918. – Two s chapel windows by *Hugh Easton*, 1934. One depicting Bishop Juxon and the last days of King Charles I. – Churchyard MEMORIAL to Gertrude Leverton Harris, †1938, by *Eric Gill*.

Little Compton Manor, immediately w of the church. Now the Reed Business School, but once the home of Archbishop William Juxon whose brother bought the property in 1641. The house is a composite affair. Its E range is pre-Reformation, but the s part of the range was incorporated into a remodelling of 1620 (lead rainwater heads on three sides). This made the s front of the house regular, with two projecting wings. However, the w side of the w wing also looks as if it contained earlier work. In the centre of the s front an C18 doorway with pediment. Rear extension, 1927, for Gertrude Leverton Harris, who personally supervised repairs to the house after a fire in the centre and w wing in 1928. In the pre-Reformation E range the principal room has moulded ceiling beams. Of *c.* 1620 one room remains, facing E. This has panelling with pretty pilasters and frieze. In the main hall a chimneypiece with coat of arms. – DOVECOTE. With four steep gables, also probably Jacobean. – Perimeter wall with good C17 GATEPIERS.

A village of golden stone cottages, many with stone slate roofs, including BLACKSMITH'S COTTAGE in Pinchester Close, dated 1794. In Brewery Row, the former BAPTIST CHAPEL, 1888: Italianate, with keystones in round-headed windows and a clock in the pediment. On the main Oxford road, the old SCHOOL and teacher's house, 1862: Tudorish, but with Victorian Gothic end window to schoolroom.

At the w edge of the parish, C18 FOUR SHIRE STONE: a square limestone pillar at the spot where Warwickshire once converged with Oxfordshire, Gloucestershire and Worcestershire.

LITTLE LAWFORD

Newbold-on-Avon

The HALL is really the stable block of Lawford Hall, the home of the Boughton family, pulled down *c.* 1790. What seems to have happened is that the stables were then made habitable. The date 1604 over the door refers to the main structure, of stone. The stuccoed hoodmoulds and Gothicky windows look *c.* 1800.

LITTLE LAWFORD MILL, by the Avon, is mentioned in Domesday. The present mill and adjoining mill house are mainly brick and late C18 onwards, incorporating parts of an older stone building. Converted into a house, 1997–2000, but retaining C19 machinery on three floors in the mill.

LITTLE PACKINGTON

ST BARTHOLOMEW. Closed in 1966 and after many years of disuse adapted for residential use in 1997–8 by *Panter Hudspith Architects* for John Shepherd.[*] In the conversion a floor has been inserted in the W end of the nave but the chancel and E end have been left open. Outside, the general impression is Victorian, with the distinctive timber-framed gable and the timber-framed bell-turret. These belong to *Preedy*'s restoration of the nave and tower in 1878–9, but the lower part of the timberwork is medieval. The chancel had been previously restored in 1863. N vestry added 1924, possibly by *E. F. Reynolds*. But it is essentially a Norman church. The N and S doorways are of the C12, and the carvings on the corbel tables of the nave walls are original too – repositioned *in situ* when the walls were rebuilt. The chancel windows tell of late C13 improvements. The E window has intersecting tracery with trefoil-headed lights, *c.* 1290. Other windows Dec and Perp. The chancel arch and S porch by *Preedy*, 1878–9. – FONT. C16 or C17, plain.[†]

In the CHURCHYARD, a headstone to Joseph Todd †1788, with carved representation of the Good Samaritan in an oval cartouche, by *Waring* of Fazeley.

Former RECTORY, N of the church, with a Georgian front of five bays and an older gabled rear. In several stages, confused and confusing. Inside, C19 staircase with curving rail and slender vase-shaped balusters.

PARK FARM, ⅓ m. SW on the other side of the A452. Symmetrical, rendered, with stepped gables and rugged pinnacles, coarse Gothic windows, and a general Scottish Baronial air. Probably *c.* 1830.

---

[*]This account owes much to his researches.
[†]The fittings were mostly removed or vandalized while the church was disused, and all the stained glass was smashed or stolen. Losses include the C17 pulpit and panelling, and heraldic glass (possibly from Great Packington) re-set in the head of *Preedy*'s E window, 1879.

LITTLE WOLFORD MANOR. Built for the Ingram family who retained possession until the early C19. Restored and enlarged by *Norman Jewson* for Sir Robert Hilton, 1934–9. L-shaped, but originally U-plan, the E wing now lost. The N hall range is early Tudor, of stone. The W wing is stone below and timber-framed above. This is probably a little later. Its projecting upper has thin buttress-shafts. The ground-floor canted bay window is probably of *c.* 1670. The main entrance was on the S through a gabled porch dated 1671. The inner doorway has a Tudor arch and traceried door. The screens passage in the hall has carved spandrels to the arched openings. The hall windows are straight-headed with depressed arches as heads of the lights. Between the two rooms, to the S, is a stair-turret. The masonry of its E wall is disturbed, showing that the E wing projected here. The windows have some heraldic stained glass, among it the date 1557. Stone chimneypiece with two small caryatids, 1628. The hall roof is C20. To the E of the hall is the parlour, with a splendid chimneypiece with stucco overmantel. This is Elizabethan and comes from Bideford in Devon, and is one of several pieces introduced by Hilton in the 1930s, including balustrading in the hall. From the passage on the upper floor a peephole looks into the hall. This is a C15 two-light window, also from Bideford. W of the hall and screens passage, a lobby with linenfold panelling, part original and part 1930s. The ceiling of the dining room beyond, once the kitchen, has heavy painted beams. The W wing is longer now than it was, having been joined up in 1935 to a building at its S end previously separated by a small courtyard. Added W of the kitchen is a two-storey gabled range by Jewson with a drawing room inside. In the S face is a small re-set C15 window. Jewson's Arts and Crafts style excellently complements the original house. In the grounds, a COTTAGE also by *Jewson*, *c.* 1935, and wrought-iron entrance GATES, also from elsewhere.

Little Wolford lay between Weston and Great Wolford (qq.v.), which belonged to the Redesdale (Batsford Park) estate. Sir George Philips of Weston acquired it in 1845, embarking on a programme of farm improvements and rebuilding under *Thomas Johnson*. BIRD'S LODGE at the W end of the village, 1848, is his. In a recess in the wall by the manor, the WELL-HEAD with lion's head fountain, 1847, with reused C16 armorial and decorative fragments from Weston. *Johnson*'s plans for a more lavish ornamental well-house were unexecuted. There are ESTATE COTTAGES of 1858 and 1896, and decent 1950s COUNCIL HOUSES on the green.

The Weston estate LODGES on the main Stratford–Oxford road, re-routed in the 1830s, preceded these works. WESTON LODGE (or MOLLY'S LODGE), at the top of the hill from Long Compton, and BROADMOOR LODGE, at the junction with the Cherington road, are both by *Blore*, *c.* 1835. Both Tudor, stone with embattled parapets and gargoyles. Broadmoor is polygonal whereas Weston Lodge is square. Between them, BEDLAM LODGE by *James Deason*, 1849. On the w side of the road DOUBLE LODGES with shaped gables, probably by *Blore*, 1830s.

Further N, chunky rock-faced WOLFORDS FIELDS FARM and outbuildings, by *George Hunt*, 1876.

LONG COMPTON

ST PETER AND ST PAUL. Finely positioned in a valley surrounded by hills. C13 and later, extensively restored by *Henry Woodyer*, 1862–3. The nave is early C13 – see the broad s doorway with a trefoil arch and a roll-moulded round hoodmould. Of the same date the plain N doorway. A little later the parts of the W tower up to the blocked former bell-chamber windows. The tower was heightened in the C15 and has twin bell-openings with a dividing shaft. The embattled parapet has cross-loops. Gargoyles too, N and S. The chancel represents the late C13, although now largely of Woodyer's restoration. Projecting to the S a delightful little two-bay chapel or annexe of the C15 (6 ft by 8½ ft (1.83 by 2.59 metres)). It has a lean-to stone roof and straight-headed Perp windows with panel tracery. The clerestory has similar windows. Over the chancel arch a pretty bellcote with ogee-headed openings, crocketing and tall pinnacle with finial. Inside, the tower arch to the nave is triple-chamfered and has an original stiff-leaf corbel. About 1300 a four-bay N aisle was built. Slim octagonal piers, double-chamfered stilted arches. Also *c.* 1300 the nave received new s windows. It is curious that the clerestory windows were given pointed rere-arches. These may be by Woodyer, who also added scalloped plaster surrounds to the windows and arches. Further restoration by *Cossins, Peacock & Bewlay*, 1900, and tower repairs by *William Weir*, 1930. Meeting rooms within the W end of the nave by *Christopher Langstone*, 2004. – Rich Victorian FITTINGS, by *Woodyer*, complemented by *Minton* tiles. They include the carved alabaster REREDOS with rich colouring, the open wooden SCREEN with angels, CHOIR STALLS, elaborately carved FONT with flowing tracery and nave SEATING fronted with light iron RAILS. – Stone PULPIT with reused Perp stonework with ogee-headed gables against blank transomed panels. – DOORS to s porch, 1620. – STAINED GLASS. E window, 1863, and another in chancel, *Hardman*, 1876. – Small W tower window by *Donald Brooke* of Long Compton, mid-C20. – MONUMENT. In the porch an early C14 female effigy, almost completely defaced.

LYCHGATE. Of *c.* 1600. Two-storeyed with a pitched roof. Limestone side walls, the others timber-framed with brick and rendered infill. It is really a cottage with the ground storey removed. Originally at the end of a row, it had been converted as a churchyard entrance by the late C19.

Nonconformity of most persuasions here. In use, the CONGREGATIONAL (Ebenezer) CHAPEL in Butlers Lane, 1824–5. Classical, brick and stucco, with stone finials. MANSE alongside. The rest in varying states of survival and conversion, the former QUAKER MEETING in Malthouse Lane, founded 1670, and two old METHODIST CHAPELS, WESLEYAN, 1807, in East Street and PRIMITIVE, 1881, on the corner of Broad Lane.

Rambling SCHOOL and residence, School Close. A plain early C19 two-storey house with Y-tracery in the end window of the added schoolroom, 1866. Enlarged by *Willmot, Fowler & Willmot*, 1913, and again in 1996. Disparate elements unified by use of stone.

Stone village of Cotswold character. The grandest houses are the former VICARAGE, SE of the church, with stately C18 N wing with rusticated quoins, pediment and bits from other periods and styles, and C19 COLLEGE FARM (the Manor House), E of the main road, with a full range of two-light Gothic casement windows. It is said to have 1830s heraldic glass from Weston House (dem.). Large farmhouses include NORTHDOWN HOUSE in Malthouse Lane, 1688, and BUTLERS HOUSE, Butlers Road, 1663, both with square-headed mullioned windows with hoodmoulds and label stops. On the main road, several dated C18 houses, including the RED LION, 1748, and WHITE HART COTTAGES, 1766. Towards the church, the old FORGE (now the garage), for Sir George Philips, 1838. This, with YERDLEY HOUSE in Back Lane, 1839, is perhaps by *James Trubshaw*. Later, the High Victorian VILLAGE STORE, 1865: painted brick, with relieving arches on the front, segmental over the side windows and pointed above the door, and hipped roof with iron finials. Nearby, the base of the medieval village cross, converted to a well. In a garden at the corner of Butlers Lane, the Millennium CHRONOLOG with cross and sundial, a community design realized by *Richard Podd* of Todenham, 2000.

KING'S STONE, 1½ m. SE. A large standing stone, 8 ft (2.44 metres) high and 5 ft (1.52 metres) wide, with a large semicircular notch on its E edge. The stone is undated but forms part of the Rollright Stones complex, which includes an early Neolithic portal dolmen known as the Whispering Knights and a later Neolithic or early Bronze Age stone circle known as the King's Men across the county boundary in Oxfordshire.

LONGFORD *see* p. 294

LONG ITCHINGTON

4060

HOLY TRINITY. White and Blue Lias with quoins and buttresses of red Warwick sandstone. W tower with the stump of a spire blown down in 1762. Perp two-light bell-openings with transoms. Frieze of blank pointed quatrefoils on two sides, and also above the tower arch inside the nave. The earliest surviving part of the church is the s aisle. The doorway has a waterleaf capital and a round arch with keeled roll mouldings. That can hardly be later than 1190. The w and s lancets are a little later. But the arcade was rebuilt in the C15, when the clerestory was added. It has curious carved corbels supporting nave and aisle roofs. The best work at Long Itchington, however, is of *c.* 1300: the chancel N and S windows of three stepped lancet lights under one arch, cusped as well as uncusped, the S aisle E window of the same kind, and originally probably the two nave N windows which have now just two (C17?) mullions running into the arch. Inside the S aisle are two fine TOMB RECESSES with elegantly long and slender trefoil cusping. Equally fine the chancel SEDILIA, each seat cinquecusped with a crocketed gable, the DOUBLE PISCINA with a trefoil in the tympanum and the EASTER SEPULCHRE. The responds of the chancel arch have three shafts connected by shallow continuous hollows and there are carved heads facing into the chancel. Restoration by *G.T. Robinson* in 1865–6, when the roofs were much heightened and the nave re-pewed. N vestry rebuilt 1876. – SCREEN. C14, with unusual bold tracery of round arches above shafts with rings. – COMMUNION RAIL. Later C17. – Stone and marble PULPIT by *Robinson*, 1866. – STAINED GLASS. One N window, †1919. – Panels in S aisle, of St Wulstan by *H.R. Hosking*, 1964, and heraldic roundels, 1967. – MONUMENT. John Bosworth †1674. Brass inscription with small figures of husband and two wives and cross-bones below. Framework of two coarse columns and an equally coarse segmental pediment.

CONGREGATIONAL CHAPEL, Church Road: brick, 1827–8, with plain stone extension, 1863–4.

An attractive village, with a large tree-lined pond on the green by the Southam–Coventry road and a pretty little square E of the church. Despite extensive redevelopment some thatched and timber-framed cottages remain. There are groups of C19 brick cottages too, some with chequered brickwork. Opposite the church, the former SCHOOL: by *William Hey Dykes* of York, 1855–6, with long schoolroom fronting the street and teacher's house behind. In the SQUARE E of the churchyard, No. 8 is timber-framed with curved wind-braces, C16. S between church and River Itchen, C18 MANOR FARM with good staircase and panelling inside.

The remaining noteworthy buildings are on the extremities. DEVON HOUSE, w on Church Road. A large timber-framed house of *c.* 1600, now three cottages. The l. and r. gables with nicely alternating diagonal struts, the centre with herringbone strutting, also nicely alternating. At the w end of the village – but once in a central position when Long Itchington was longer, as earthworks beyond indicate – WHITE HALL FARM is the manor house, with remains inside of the C15 hall with moulded timbers and two bosses. Two C15 windows also survive and a door with moulded timber surround and foliage carving in the spandrels of the arch.

TUDOR HOUSE, on Southam Road at the E end of the village. Also *c.* 1600, also timber-framed with vertical studs only, placed close together, and a mid-rail. Five equal gables on jetties.

RED HOUSE, on Marton Road N of The Green. Of brick. Probably *c.* 1700. The house must have been a normal five-bay house, but the l. side now has a big Georgian canted bay window. The steep, gable-like pediment suggests the early date. Nearby, the DUCK ON THE POND by *F. P. Trepess & Son*, 1930, Brewer's Tudor.

On Leamington Road, the OLD VICARAGE by *Robinson*, 1862: astonishingly plain and un-Victorian.

½ m. S beyond the canal towards Southam, the MODEL VILLAGE, originally laid out by *Charles M. C. Armstrong*, 1912–13. A small housing development for workers at Kaye & Co.'s nearby cement works. The houses had external walls of concrete on the Calway patent cavity system.

LONG LAWFORD

ST JOHN. 1839 by *William Walker* for John Caldecott of Holbrook Grange as a chapel of ease to Newbold-on-Avon. Closed in 1995 and now (2013) perilously neglected. Of yellow brick with lancets, stumpy bell-turret and short chancel, never lengthened. The interior has the quite rare survival of furnishings of *c.* 1840: PEWS, PULPIT, etc., all as they were from the beginning. – STAINED GLASS. E window clear except for one heraldic shield and a number of foliage bosses. An early work by *William Holland*, 1839, yet markedly C18 in character.

The CHURCH HALL alongside by *S. J. Oldham*, 1936, was adapted as a church in 1995.

METHODIST CHURCH, School Street. 1955, replacing two previous chapels in Chapel Street, both converted into houses. The OLD CHAPEL (former Primitive Methodist), 1872, has a gabled frontage in yellow and red brick with circular window above the entrance and tall side windows.

Also adapted for housing, the former BOARD SCHOOLS and teacher's house in School Street, 1878: polychromatic brickwork, lancets with banded headers.

In Main Street, the CALDECOTT ARMS, built as the New Inn by *Herbert Norman* for the Northampton Brewery Company, 1922. A good inter-war pub, with box dormer between rendered gables and extended tiled canopy to the porch.

LIVINGSTONE AVENUE between the railway and the Coventry road was laid out for the Land Settlement Association by *A. G.*

Sheppard Fidler with plans for forty detached houses on spacious plots, 1936–7.

In parkland N of the village, Neoclassical HOLBROOK GRANGE. Built in 1804 for John Caldecott, extended on the N in 1847. Grey sandstone ashlar. Porch with Greek Doric columns *in antis* and fanlight above the door.

LONG MARSTON

1040

Also known as Marston Sicca.

ST JAMES. A pretty church with a good aspect across the field from the S. Soft-coloured stone with timber-framed bell-turret and N porch. The porch C15, the top of the turret by *Cossins, Peacock & Bewlay*, 1897, in place of a Georgian weatherboarded affair. Nave and chancel Dec. Inside, the C16 framing of the bell-turret stands within the building, an arch to the nave being filled above by two tiers of close timber studding. The sides partitioned off to the nave. Inside the N and S sides have old wooden panelling. Queenpost roof in chancel. Restoration and re-seating by *William Thompson* of Stratford in 1867–8, and re-roofing and repairs by *Osborn, Pemberton & White* (*Guy Pemberton*) in 1912. – Circular FONT, perhaps Norman, on a C15 panelled octagonal stem. – PULPIT. Jacobean, with high blank arches. – BIER. C17. – STAINED GLASS. Jumbled medieval bits in the E window head. – Nice Victorian CANDLE STANDARDS, probably 1868.

Good open timber LYCHGATE on N side of church, 1919. By *J. W. Pyment & Son*, who had re-roofed the church in 1912. Restored by the Royal Engineers, 1996.

One long street, as the name implies, the church towards the S end. The older houses mainly on the W side, set back, with clusters of timber-framed cottages at intervals between the larger properties. From the S, begin at KING'S LODGE, where Charles II hid in disguise after his defeat at Worcester in 1651. Early C17 and stone, with additions including 1896 wing to N. At the end of the road E of the church, the former SCHOOL, 1840s Tudor. Further N set back across a field, ORCHARD COTTAGES. Timber-framed, but with a two-light C14 church window re-set in the S wing gable-end. Then several bigger houses. THE GRANGE, an C18 three-storey farmhouse, rendered. Next door, the OLD RECTORY with an imposing rendered H-plan façade with Regency details and a big pillared porch on the S side, but all concealing older fabric within. CHURCH FARM was the grammar school founded by John Cooper in 1643 until it closed in 1910. The front *c.* 1800, but the C17 rear wing with quoins and cornice may have been the schoolroom. Tucked away behind brick cottages on the main street, THE GREEN has several timber-framed cottages. Past

THE ROSARY, two cottages (one dated 1672) conjoined with a stone front, *c.* 1990, is the former METHODIST CHAPEL, 1927.

Down Wyre Lane E of the Welford Road, two significant houses. HOPKINS is a Lias and brick house with bold chimneystacks, apparently C17 and later, but with a two-bay open hall with base crucks and crown-post roof tree-ring-dated to 1339/40. Further E, THE GOODWINS, with a C17 stone front with three even gabled dormers and mullioned windows.

LOWER EASTERN GREEN *see* p. 295

LOWER SHUCKBURGH

4060

ST JOHN THE BAPTIST. One of the most extraordinary and wayward churches of the High Victorian era, full of curiosities, shocks and delights. A rebuild on the site of a previous church. By *John Croft* of Islington, 1863–4, but with Moorish design influences attributable to Major George Shuckburgh, who had fought in the Crimea.* The *Leamington Spa Courier* described the styles as 'Early Pointed' on the S and 'Byzantine' for the N nave windows and interior. For this, and for his Cold Hanworth (1861–2) in Lincolnshire, Croft stands with Goodhart-Rendel's so-called rogue-architects. But neither Lamb nor Teulon nor Keeling ever built more originally or more larkily than Croft did here. Nor is it easy to find much in the Gothic C19 to match the sheer ugliness of Croft's tracery, flat-membered, but with stop-chamfers and of wildly improbable combinations of forms. Yet the exterior of the church, as seen from the road, is first of all lively, rich, enterprising. Dark and light stone. Hexagonal SW tower with six steep gables around the base of a ribbed and perforated spire. To the S further E two cross-gables of different height and width. A number of these gables are faced with purple gravel, described in the *Courier* as Harts-hill patchwork, also found in some arch spandrels. Twin W porch (rebuilt without its patchwork in 1906).

The interior knocks you out with the contrast of stone and particularly flaming brick with crisp white joints. Don't be taken in. The joints are mortarless and the lines are just puttied into shallow incisions in what seem to be terracotta blocks. The piers sound hollow. They are of elongated form in depth with chamfered edges, and they divide the nave from the narrow aisles. On the S side there is in addition an outer yet narrower aisle with a passage to the belfry entrance (once the

97

* George held the advowson from 1860 and he was treasurer of the Restoration Fund. It seems that he was largely responsible, his father (Sir Francis Shuckburgh †1876) playing little part in the scheme.

baptistery). With its Moorish vault, this is a specially haunting area. The chancel is rib-vaulted in two bays, with a further half-bay to the w. The vaulting is faced in tiny terracotta tiles of varied designs,* and all the arches are of brick with jagged, sawtooth edges. The brickwork and tiling add a pinch of Alhambra. Shallow transepts, one with a dummy tomb recess. Hammerbeam nave roof. One Dec window head from the old church smuggled into the E wall of the organ chamber. Buttresses added and strengthened and walls tied together under *J. B. Williams* of Daventry, 1906. – FURNISHINGS largely contemporary, including the stone REREDOS with intersecting arcading, the wooden PULPIT and DESK with serrated carving, and the PEWS with chunky bench ends, those at front and back with elongated Eastern finials. – FONT. C13, round, with elementary flat blank arches.

Former VICARAGE, 250 yds S. Also by *Croft*, 1862–3, though larky only in details. Brick with stone dressings and polychromatic window headers, some with Hartshill patchwork again.

An estate village. Along Daventry Road there are COTTAGES of 1895 in brick and stone with diamond-paned windows and half-timbered gables (1895) and plain ironstone (1906). More (*c.* 1880 and 1913) in Park Lane, where there is a stone WELL-HEAD dated 1856. Also on Daventry Road, the former SCHOOL, square with low pyramid roof, *c.* 1860. Alongside, RED HOUSE FARM. C18, brick, two and a half storeys, with a Roman Doric doorcase and fanlight.

LOWSONFORD
Rowington

ST LUKE. *Payne & Talbot*, 1877. Built as 'the School Chapel at Lonesome Ford'. Brick, with grouped lancets E and W, segmental-headed side windows and substantial tiled buttresses. – STAINED GLASS. E window possibly by *Francis Skeat*, 1945. – W window similar, 1954.

CHAPELHAVEN, Narrow Lane. Originally an Independent chapel (Congregational), 1842, but converted to a house in 1933 and imaginatively refronted and extended in 2004–8 by *Barton Hasker*. Brick with round-headed windows and careful detailing.

The Stratford-upon-Avon Canal passes through Lowsonford. Good canalside group, including the LENGTHMAN'S COTTAGE at Lock 31, the best preserved of the barrel-roofed cottages on the section completed by *William Whitmore*,

---

*In all 5,530 of these were used. They were made of Shuckburgh clay by local brickmaker *John Tomlin*.

1812–13. Restored in 2005 for the Landmark Trust, who acquired it in 1992. At Yarningale, 1½ m. sww, a short cast-iron AQUEDUCT of 1834 by the *Horseley Iron Company*, replacing an earlier bridge destroyed in a flood.

LOXLEY

St NICHOLAS. There are dates – foundation in 760, and a re-dedication in 1286. The extensive herringbone masonry in the chancel S (outside) and N (inside) must be early, perhaps C11. Of the C13, a lancet window in the chancel and the E window surround. Also the remains of a S arcade by the SW tower. The lower stages of the tower ironstone S and E and Lias W and N. It stands within a former aisle and must be a reconstruction, but parts are C13. The battlemented top probably *c.* 1800. The rest dates from the C18, stylistically *c.* 1740 with arched windows, arched W doorway with an oculus over. S vestry,* its front all bits and pieces from early C18 memorials and with balusters to window surround. Inside, the vestry gives access to the raised pulpit. The wide chancel arch, round and double-chamfered both sides, is neither Norman nor Georgian, so when was it done? Good interior retained through sensitive C20 restorations, with BOX PEWS in nave and panelling in chancel. – Norman PILLAR PISCINA with scallop capitals. – COMMUNION RAIL, *c.* 1680. – EMBROIDERY on lectern. St Nicholas in pyjamas and slippers, by *Anthony Green*, 1972, accompanied by his framed drawing and artist's notes. – STAINED GLASS in chancel S, by *Donald Brooke*, *c.* 1950. – MONUMENT. George Huddesford †1809, by *(Sir) Richard Westmacott*; plain tablet.

LOXLEY HALL, immediately N of the church. A plain Georgian stuccoed house of five bays and two storeys, enlarged to N and E for James Cove Jones by *T. T. Allen*, 1868. The additions in polychromatic brick, Gothic. A little later, the astoundingly fanciful porch in no definite style. The Gregory-Hood family acquired the hall in 1928, bringing with them a chimneypiece by *Richard Hayward*, *c.* 1775, from demolished Stivichall Hall (*see* p. 296).

Former VICARAGE, SE of the church. Double-depth plan, hipped roof and stuccoed, but with square-headed windows and hoodmoulds. By *John Nichol* of Wellesbourne, 1833.

---

*The vestry is not shown on an illustration of *c.* 1790, although the memorials (1681 to 1726) suggest a *terminus post quem* for it; similarly, documentary sources indicate a date later than 1740 for the main rebuilding, the need for major repairs being noted in 1757 and *c.* 1782. So dates are a puzzle. Thanks to Peter Bolton for insightful observations on this church.

LUDDINGTON

ALL SAINTS. A chapelry of Holy Trinity, Stratford. 1871–2 by *John Cotton*. The architectural style is *c.* 1300. Lias with Bath stone dressings and curious brick wedges in the buttress set-offs. Very Victorian open timber porch with pierced barge-boards and fascias. Turret with spire at the E end of the N side of the nave. Inside, carved angel corbels to chancel arch, painted texts on steps. – C15 FONT from the old church (*see* below). On the base of a churchyard cross, it seems, with a quatrefoil frieze. – STAINED GLASS. A complete scheme of 1871–2, in chancel by *Lavers, Barraud & Westlake*, in nave by *William Holland & Son*.

THE MANOR stands by a small green at whose N end was the old church, abandoned in the mid C18 and in ruins by 1806. Several timber-framed houses along the street near the new church.

MANCETTER

On Watling Street and at the county boundary with Leicester-shire, Mancetter was a place of importance from Roman times. The parish anciently included Hartshill and Oldbury (qq.v.) as well as what is now the town of Atherstone (q.v.).

ST PETER. Evidence of a substantial early C13 church on the site is the enormously tall lancet window in the nave W wall to the tower, which is now hidden by the organ. The first additions to this C13 nave were the N arcade and N aisle, which has been partitioned off as the Bracebridge Chapel. The arcade of three bays has standard elements, the aisle window tracery ranging from cusped intersected to curvilinear and to the grand display of the reticulations of the five-light E window. The chancel also is Dec, with side windows probably late C14 (cf. Atherstone) and ogee-headed PISCINA. The E window is partly Victorian, by *C. C. Rolfe*, 1875–6, as is the chancel arch with its very thin and long shafts to the nave. Niches with canopies l. and r. of the E window. The S arcade with transversely elongated octag-onal piers is Perp; the aisle windows are Dec like the chancel side windows. C15 clerestory and nave roof, and Perp also the upper stages of the W tower. There was no space for proces-sions W of the church in the Middle Ages and so the tower had a passage from N to S through tall openings with pointed arches. Late C17 S porch, brick on older stone foundations. – FONT. Very big. Fat ribs rise up at the angles and fatter ones still up the middles of the diagonals. Probably Perp. – MEMORIAL BOARDS to the Marian martyrs of Mancetter,

Robert Glover †1553 and Joyce Lewis †1557. Of wood, very handsomely inscribed, and dating from 1833. The martyrs also commemorated on painted stone tablets in s aisle. – STAINED GLASS. In the E window are some very fine parts of various windows, including three figures which may belong to the Merevale Tree of Jesse (*see* p. 456), and others of the C14 (in pointed quatrefoils) and later. Restored by the *York Glaziers Trust*, 1989. – Figure of St James the Less, C15, in a chancel N window and fragments and quarries in other windows. – s aisle E by *Hardman*, 1877. – MONUMENTS. John Blise †1633 (s porch outside). Strapwork plaque. – Edward Hinton †1689. Bust with wig in front of an oval recess decorated with cherubs' heads. – Bracebridge memorials in N aisle, including Abraham †1743 and Mary †1745 in coloured marble with shaped panel above, and another to Theodosia †1742 with obelisk panel. – George Mitchell †1846 by *Edgar George Papworth*.

Built on to N side of church, the CHURCH SCHOOLROOM and LINK, by *Wood, Kendrick & Williams*, 1997.

In the churchyard the ALMSHOUSES founded under the will of James Gramer (†1727), a London goldsmith born at Mancetter. Of 1728, plain, one-storeyed, white, with a central inscription in a column-and-pediment frame. Across the road E of the church another range of ALMSHOUSES, called Gramer Cottages. They are of 1822 and no less modest. In front an iron veranda with traceried spandrels and mock battlements above.

MANOR HOUSE, s of the church. A large timber-framed house of about 1330. Its centre is a hall about 40 ft (12 metres) long. The screens passage is at the N end, and to the N of this is a projecting service wing of the same date. The corresponding s wing was added only about 1580. The timber trusses of hall and office wing are remarkably well preserved, though they must now of course be sought out from later insertions and alterations. The trusses N and s of the screens passage and the s truss of the hall have pointed-trefoiled braces on posts forming aisles and carry collar-beams. The central truss of the hall is a base cruck, also of pointed-trefoiled type, with a highly cambered collar carrying a collar purlin. From the arcade posts similar trefoiled braces rise to the plates. In the s part of the hall a ceiling was put in as early as the late C15 to form an upper room. The ceiling beams are moulded. The trusses of the N wing have normal arched braces to support tie-beams. Forecourt with rendered C18 gatepiers and PAVILIONS at each end of the curtain wall.

In Quarry Lane, just s of the green, the old VICARAGE, 1816, but the plans are unsigned. Rendered, two storeys with hipped roof and bellcote. Further s, the old CROSSING-KEEPER'S COTTAGE on the railway, Jacobean-style with shaped gables, by *J. W. Livock* for the Trent Valley Railway, *c.* 1847.

On the w side of WATLING STREET, some early C19 Late Georgian three-bay houses, including OLD HOUSE (No. 30) with ogee-headed Gothick windows. Also, w towards Atherstone on the s side, mid-C19 ARBOUR COTTAGES (Nos. 1–15), a row of eight with Tudor windows, shallow porches and steep roofs with ridge stacks.

MANDUESSEDUM, a Roman vexillation fortress and small fortified town mentioned in the Antonine Itinerary. The fortress site was on high ground s of the village. It was first constructed in the late A.D. 40s and remodelled over the next four decades. Excavations have identified a possible headquarters building, a barrack block and an external annexe to the N. The town site straddles Watling Street, SE of the River Anker, and part of the settlement lies across the Leicestershire boundary. It is marked by a rectangular EARTHWORK, 350 ft by 600 ft (107 by 183 metres), enclosing an area of 6 acres (2.4 ha). Excavations across the NE corner of the defences showed a ditch with a wide berm and a stone wall wide with clay backing behind. Post-holes and clay floors within the earthworks indicate two settlement phases in the C1 and C2 A.D. There is evidence of glass-making and of a significant pottery industry in an area s of the town.

MAPPLEBOROUGH GREEN

HOLY ASCENSION. 1888 by *J. A. Chatwin* for William Jaffray. W tower, aisled nave, s porch and chancel with s chapel and N organ chamber. Rock-faced outside, with bar tracery in limestone. The E end with three stepped lancets. Four-bay nave broad and high with narrow aisles. Vaulted s chapel connecting to the chancel through paired arches under a blank super-arch. The chapel is an intimate memorial to Mabel Augusta Jaffray, †1886. Ian Nairn called it 'an absolute masterpiece of Victorian religious feeling', but H. S. Goodhart-Rendel thought it 'expensive, correctly detailed, and very weakly designed'. – FONT. A life-size, nobly draped kneeling alabaster angel holding the bowl, 1888. – STAINED GLASS. All by *Hardman*. Chancel and s chapel windows designed by *John Hardman Powell*, 1888. – Three more (*Dunstan Powell*), w window, 1901, N aisle (moved from s in 1925), 1906, and s aisle, 1925.

On the main road near the church, the former SCHOOL (now ANKCORN HOUSE and cottages adjoining). Georgian Gothick, *c.* 1750, with ogee-arched windows and hipped roofs. Brick, painted white. The single-storey schoolroom attractively restored as a church hall by *Graham J. Masefield*, 1987, and the house now divided into two.

GORCOTT HALL, ½ m. N. A delightful and once well-situated house, but rather cruelly treated by the road planners and their Coventry Highway. Rescued and restored since 2004. Brick and timber-framed. C15 in origin. The s front has a two-storeyed brick porch of *c.* 1540 with blue brick diapering and a mullioned upper window in stone with arched lights without cusping. The hall was on the l., but its original stone mullions have been replaced in wood. Further l. a timber-framed gable with close studs. To the N two such gables of equal size and then more brick and more gables. Big chimney-breast on the w side. Interior with exposed framing and panelling, and painted wainscoting in sitting room. Curtain wall to s and E with stone-capped gatepiers.

At SKILTS, two houses, old and new. The original house at LOWER SKILTS (¾ m. E of the church) was built for William Sheldon of Beoley after 1561. It became a farmhouse, of which some parts survive. Later owners built at UPPER SKILTS (¼ m. NNW) on a superb site with wide views. The Moilliet family lived there, followed by the Jaffrays. In the 1880s, Sir John Jaffray employed *J. A. Chatwin* to build a modest new house with timber-framed gables. Later much extended on the E in a Tudor Free Style by *Chatwin & Son* for Sir William Jaffray in 1900. The exterior with gables, turret and sundial intact, but now painted white. *Thomas H. Mawson* did the gardens, *c.* 1909, and a rather charming brick gateway survives. It has been a Birmingham Corporation special school since 1958.

MARTON

4060

ST ESPRIT. A very exceptional dedication. w tower, the lower stages red sandstone, C13, and the upper part limestone ashlar and later. Early C13 s doorway. Perp s arcade of two bays with standard elements. Otherwise rebuilt by *G. Punshon*, 1871. Trefoiled lights in nave. Reticulated tracery in chancel. Inside, arch to organ chamber with stiff-leaf capitals. – Of 1871, the stone PULPIT and AMBO. – Carved wooden REREDOS. *Holland & Co.*, 1879. – STAINED GLASS. E window, *Holland, Son & Holt*, 1873. – Another, *Camm & Co.*, †1945. – PAINTED METAL texts on tower wall and in sw corner.

BRIDGE across the Leam. Built by John Middleton in 1414. Two depressed-pointed, double-chamfered arches. The arches die against the abutments and the cutwaters. Also flood arches. Widened in 1926 and in use until 2000 when a new road bridge was built alongside. Another BRIDGE over the Itchen, w of the church. Late C18 with brick vault, rusticated stone arches and circular flood openings.

OLD VICARAGE opposite the church, brick with hoodmoulded windows, two-storey porch, 1840s. The 1866 CONGREGA-TIONAL CHURCH, High Street, also adapted for residential use, but its Gothic gabled front remains. On the main road some C18 houses: the best is MANOR FARMHOUSE at the corner of Birdingbury Road.

2080

MAXSTOKE

In flat country E of Coleshill, but with rising ground towards Fillongley on the E. Remarkable in possessing a church, priory and castle all of C14 foundation, all established by one man and all with substantial remains. The founder was William de Clinton who was born at Maxstoke and became Earl of Huntingdon in 1337. The essential dates are all between 1330 and 1345, suggesting a building spree symbolical of his elevation to the earldom. The church and priory are close together in the S of the parish near the site of the old manor. The castle, 1½ m. N, became the new centre of de Clinton's very considerable power and influence. After the Reformation the southern half of the parish, including the priory site, belonged to the Leighs of Stoneleigh. Thereafter it followed a different history from the castle estate, owned by the Dilkes and their descendants since 1599.

33 MAXSTOKE CASTLE. Architecturally speaking, the type of castle which Maxstoke represents was established in Britain by the 1190s, its development culminating with Harlech in 1283–9. The form is quadrangular and characterized by strict symmetry: a rectangle with four corner towers and in the middle of one side the mighty gatehouse. Other buildings as needed would lean against the high wall and be made of stone or wood. In the course of the C14, the type was fundamentally revised and improved as domestic considerations gained greater emphasis. Bolton Castle or Bodiam may at first glance look like Harlech. But, if one were asked to define them, one would have to call them buildings of four ranges round an inner courtyard, even if the ranges still include angle towers and gate towers. Bolton was licensed in 1379 and Bodiam in 1385. Maxstoke, licensed in 1345, is a transition from the Harlech to the Bolton and Bodiam type. Marcus Binney has suggested that it marks a key point in the development of the quadrilateral castle into the moated manor house. But to its builders there can have been no doubt that this was still a castle. Demonstrating 'aristocratic pretension over defensive pragmatism', as George Fetherston-Dilke remarks,* it is sensibly and seriously fortified, though not intended to withstand a full-on attack. Despite its many defensive features, it lacks internal security and its big external windows make it vulnerable. Yet it is meticulously planned and carefully designed, not only to achieve precise symmetry in plan but also in the use of space to provide the accommodation required, especially in the towers. As Alcock et al. observed, Maxstoke 'reveals at every point the skilled hand of a master architect, working with the highest possible skill'. Who was he? On the basis of a comparison with the near contemporary castle at Stafford (1347), Malcolm

---

*Dissertation by George Fetherston-Dilke, *Maxstoke Castle and the Clinton family in the later Middle Ages* (2008).

Hislop has suggested that both may be the work of master mason *John de Burcestre*.*

Maxstoke, then, is an excellent example of one of the smaller castles of the mid C14. It was begun soon after 1337 and virtually complete by 1344.† It is of a distinctly Midlands type, notable for the use of polygonal towers where different forms (e.g. square in the north) developed in other regions. Moreover, in elevation the Lady Tower is larger than its neighbours and gives a classic castle asymmetry to the whole design. Also important, the decorative features, including gargoyles and the splendid chimney pots ornamented with two levels of miniature battlements. John Goodall suggests that these are at once symbols of wealth and architectural flattery, looking like models of Caesar's Tower at near contemporary Warwick Castle. The detailing of the gatehouse here has many similarities with Warwick too.

Of its original form, much remains. It has the gatehouse on the E side, a stone range against the W side and a timber-framed range against the W half of the N side. According to visible evidence (corbels, fireplaces and beam holes) it once had a continuation of the latter along the rest of the N side and a range against the S side as well.‡ The E side seems always to have been wall only, although the existence of two garderobes S of the gatehouse proves that some shelter was provided here as well. The Great Hall was in the W range, on an axis with the gatehouse, and its crown-post roof has been tree-ring-dated to *c.* 1345. Surveys of 1521 and 1582 both refer to an outer or base court N of the present castle site. No traces remain.

According to Christine Carpenter, the de Clintons were 'the most important of the minor nobility of north Warwickshire'.§ Maxstoke was their principal seat. But they built and lost it in less than a century. Ownership transferred in 1437 to Humphrey Stafford, Duke of Buckingham (†1460), whose favourite residence it became. He remodelled it in parts and decorated it with his family insignia, the Stafford knot, which occurs on the sheet iron cladding the medieval gates. In early Tudor times the N range was partially rebuilt but left unfinished. After the Buckinghams came the Comptons, who neglected Maxstoke. By the time of a survey in 1582 it was in poor condition. Sir Thomas Egerton may have embarked on improvements

---

* M.J.B. Hislop, 'Master John of Burcestre and the Castles of Stafford and Maxstoke' in *Transactions of the South Staffordshire Archaeological and Historical Society* (1993) vol. 33.

† Crenellation was licensed in 1345, but as Clinton was able to grant away the old manor house (to his priory) in 1344 this suggests that the castle was by then nearing completion and habitable.

‡ In 1485 Richard III ordered parts of the building to be dismantled and taken to Nottingham to improve the castle there. But events overtook him, and it is unclear whether this explains the removal of some of Maxstoke's timber-framed fabric.

§ Cited in Fetherstone-Dilke *op cit.*

when he acquired the castle in 1597 but he sold it again almost immediately.

In 1599 it came to Sir Thomas Dilke, in whose family (now Fetherston-Dilke) it remains. Dilke completed the unfinished C15 N range and divided the hall horizontally. Although relatively little altered since *c.* 1600, there have been changes. A panel in the NW corner refers to repairs in 1698. A fire in the kitchen in 1762 burnt out the top of the W range. It was never fully replaced, although a single-storey structure was afterwards built in the centre part. The two-storey bay towards the r. on the W side, brick with simple Gothic windows, is of about 1820. It projects into the courtyard on the E and peeks over the castle wall to the W, providing a new dining room and bedrooms for the family. The main rooms were refurbished in the medieval style for Charles Fetherston-Dilke *c.* 1870, with splendid High Victorian fireplaces in the Banqueting Hall and Lady Tower. Although alien to his usual style, these may be by *W. H. Ward*, who certainly worked here at about that time. The removal of the rendering on the N range in 1964 uncovered the timber framing and in the 1970s the Banqueting Hall was restored and its fine timber roof again revealed to view. More recently, there has been some internal reordering of the private apartments by *Graham Winteringham* in 1989, including the creation of a hallway and the erection of a new staircase in the position it occupied before the 1820s additions.

EXTERIOR. The castle is surrounded by a perfect moat.* The curtain wall and the four corner towers are embattled. The towers are polygonal, the Lady Tower (NW) belonging to the house being higher than the others. There is a walkway round the battlements leading through the other towers but not into them. There are grooves for protective shutters in the merlons of the parapet. Windows are either ogee-headed single lights, or twins with a transom and ogee-headed lights. The only exception is one very large traceried window in the W range facing W. This can only have belonged to the chapel and, for a chapel W window looking out of the castle, it is surprisingly large. The window lies immediately N of where the Great Hall must have been. The location of the hall is marked by the two tall windows in the W wall (i.e. as visible from outside) and by the two buttresses to the courtyard – one with a big carved head comically perched on top – representing the positions of the inner roof trusses. The hall was full-height with an open truss roof. To its S lay the kitchen, etc. There is a C15 doorway there and also a doorway out of the courtyard. The windows here are Elizabethan. The relation in plan of hall to chapel is strange too. How would the main living rooms have been reached? Or would they have been above the kitchen and offices? The arrangements N of the hall are obscured by the 1820s additions. There is, however, behind it, i.e. in the NW

---

*The C16 surveys suggest that there was once an embattled wall on the inner side of the moat.

corner, a large BANQUETING HALL on the first floor with tie-beams on arched braces and kingposts with four-way struts. Its windows are Elizabethan and square-headed. The NW tower has an octagonal rib-vault on the ground floor and on the first floor an original floor with C15 Coventry tiles and one of the High Victorian fireplaces.

The timber-framed N range is late C16, probably of *c.* 1595 and shortly before Dilke acquired the castle. It has a spacious polygonal projection to the courtyard. Inside this range is the OAK DRAWING ROOM, a large room with a sumptuous Elizabethan overmantel with carvings. At its entrance the WHISPERING DOOR, an internal porch, in the same style. This was brought from Kenilworth Castle. The panelling of the room is articulated by pilasters.

The GATEHOUSE has polygonal turrets to the outside, but not to the inside. It is vaulted inside by a two-bay tierceron vault with splendid big bosses. The DOORS are mid-C15 with original ironwork including the Stafford knot of the Dukes of Buckingham. Inside, the defences include the grooves for a portcullis and murder holes over the entrance. On the first floor, the Constables' Chamber with fireplace and window seats and a prison pit. On the floor above, a pigeon loft with about 230 nesting boxes.

The COACH HOUSE and STABLES to the NE of the castle are probably by *W. H. Ward, c.* 1865. At the Castle Lane entrance to the drive, a small lodge by *C. M. C. Armstrong,* 1904. There is a further contemporary cottage by Armstrong off the drive.

MAXSTOKE PRIORY. Near the site of the ancient manor.*
Founded by the same William de Clinton who built the castle, initially as a college of priests in 1330. It was re-founded as an Augustinian priory in 1336–7 and consecrated in 1342. This is a late foundation for the Augustinians in England. It was laid out and built on a grand scale. All that stands clearly recognizable above ground are the two gatehouses, remains of the crossing tower of the church and the W wall of the infirmary. But excavations, unfortunately not allowed to remain uncovered, have disclosed almost the whole plan. The OUTER GATEHOUSE has broad polygonal angle turrets to outside and inside, a large double-chamfered segmental arch to outside and inside, a division between carriages and pedestrians beyond the middle, i.e. with two bays of vaulting (diagonal and ridge ribs) to the outside, and only one very narrow one to the inside. There is a Dec upper window of two lights both sides but, on the outside, there are canopied niches l. and r. too. The INNER GATEHOUSE is no longer recognizable as such. The archways are blocked on both sides and on the E side is now an Elizabethan house with mullioned and mullioned-and-transomed windows. The house is stone below with timber framing and brick infill above.

---

*The de Clintons' manor house was given to the Augustinians in 1344. It was near the mill.

All that remains of the church is the CROSSING TOWER, sadly diminished by a partial collapse in 1988. Even now it is a most interesting piece of architecture, for it can be related to other important mid-C14 churches in the area. Moreover, as Richard Morris observed, it shows that the design here imitated the fashionable plans of the friars. The tower starts square but continues octagonal, externally by very high broaches, internally by squinches – a friars' rather than a canons' motif. The crossing arches to N and S were oddly narrow. The arches died into the imposts. On the E of the NE crossing pier is the jamb of a large chancel window. The chancel was straight-headed and had no aisles. The nave was aisleless too. The E range of the cloister did not continue the line of the N transept. It was pushed further E. Refectory and dormitory were in the normal places. The INFIRMARY lay E of the E range, as customary. It was aisled and what remains is the wall with the main W entrance and a smaller entrance on its l. Much of the precinct wall is also preserved and at the extreme N end the two arches represent the place where the mill race left the MILL.

ST MICHAEL. Of the same period as priory and castle, but it is a surprising building for William de Clinton to have provided. Immediately E of the old manor site and later priory, it looks as if it were the very proud chancel to a church never built. It is now believed to have originated as the chantry founded in 1333 rather than as the chapel *ante portas* of the priory. It is oblong, unbuttressed on W and E, and has no division between nave and chancel. The liturgical division is indicated by the ogee-headed lowside S window. The Dec E window has flowing tracery with some oddly shaped motifs. The other windows are standard. The side doorways are normal, the W doorway a Perp insertion. The mean bell-turret is Georgian and faintly Gothic. There was a remodelling in 1773–4. The builders were *Thomas Shuttleworth* and *John Cheshire*. Faculty papers of 1773 include sketch designs for the turret and the W gallery, which stands on short stone Tuscan columns. Internally the C18 cornice and coved ceiling survive, though reconstructed in 2004–6. – On the gallery, painting of Raphael's St Michael from the former ALTARPIECE. – Carved oak ALTAR TABLE, *c.* 1750 but in Elizabethan style. – FONTS. One Georgian and plain, the other of Caen stone with serpentine marble shafts, 1887. – PULPIT. Georgian, with handsome inlay, 1773. – ROYAL ARMS. Two, one of Queen Anne's reign, repainted by *Allport*, Birmingham, 1774. – Some TILES with geometrical patterns, probably C15 and of Coventry manufacture.

SE of the church, C14 CHURCHYARD CROSS, restored in 1886.

Immediately W of the priory, the former RECTORY, 1848–9. Rock-faced with stone window mullions and transoms. In the grounds, remains of the monastic granary and fishponds.

BRIDGE over the Blythe on Coleshill Road at Duke End. *Thomas Sheasby Sen.*, 1780. Sandstone, five arches with coped parapet.

Two noteworthy farms. Across fields E of Castle Lane, DUMBLE FARM. Timber-framed H-shaped farmhouse, with chimney-stack dated 1595 with initials WP, FP and AP, thought to represent William Phipps and his family. In Fillongley Road ½ m. E of the village centre, MAXSTOKE HALL FARMHOUSE, c. 1632 and mid-C18.

WOODBINE COTTAGE, Duke End, 1⅛ m. NW of the church. A C15 cruck cottage with exposed crucks.

MEREVALE

2090

Merevale is most fortunate in its landscape. The parish covers a wooded area to the SW of Atherstone, with Merevale Hall on a high ridge with wide views into Leicestershire to the N. The abbey and church are to the NW, separated by a wide valley with pools and on a gently rising slope along Merevale Lane. In contrast, the high ground to the W towards Baxterley and Baddesley Ensor was mining country – altogether different from the quiet natural beauty of Merevale itself.

MEREVALE ABBEY was a Cistercian house, founded in 1148 by Robert, Earl Ferrers. What little of it remains above ground is S and E of ABBEY FARMHOUSE, E of the parish church. The farmhouse itself, refronted and altered with pointed windows in the late C18 or early C19, may also incorporate masonry from the abbey. There are two fragments, one of the highest architectural interest, the other just a piece of walling. The latter is part of the S aisle at its W end and is now the N wall of a farm outbuilding. The former is the N and S wall of the REFECTORY. The N wall stands to a considerable height and has to the inside on a high dado a row of very closely set attached shafts, their bases and the fillets running up them dating them firmly to the C13. To the outside chamfered buttresses are placed about as closely as the shafts inside. Can these buttresses have projected into a cloister walk? Or did the abbey have no cloister walks? The area of the cloister is clearly defined. Refectories lay in the range opposite the churches. Cistercian refectories admittedly usually projected from them at right angles, i.e. ran N–S, but those of the Benedictines were placed as that of Merevale is. The excavations carried out as far back as 1849 show no cloister walk in their drawn plan of results. The S wall of the refectory contains the reading pulpit, with its staircase slightly projecting to the outside, i.e. the S. The doorway exists, the steps, and two quatrefoil peepholes. The wall articulation of the rest of the wall seems to have been as on the other side. According to the excavators of 1849 the church was 240 ft (73 metres) long and had aisles, transepts and a straight chancel end, but not the usual straight-ended chapels E of the transept.

Preserved apart from what has already been described the richly moulded main portal into the refectory at its W end, and beyond a simply double-chamfered archway parallel with it.

OUR LADY. The parish church strikes the experienced church visitor as very odd. It has a nave and had aisles, but they are only of two bays, while the aisled chancel is of four. It results in something quite lopsided, and one first speculates whether the nave might not have been longer to the W or the E. But neither is possible. The W wall with its doorway and the window of three stepped lancet lights is late C13; so are the octagonal piers of the wide arcade openings; so clearly is the chancel arch. There would not be anything puzzling if it were not for the considerable width of this short nave. The answer is probably that this was not a normal parish church but a *capella ante portas* of the abbey. It sits on higher ground above the main site, the E end with its five-light Perp window facing the abbey and the pinnacled N chancel aisle fronting the road. The tiled belfry over the middle of the church is of 1893 when the whole church underwent a thorough restoration by *Alfred Bickerdike* who had previously supervised work in the N and S aisles in 1875 and 1884 respectively. On the S, the vestry built at the time of repairs by *Henry Clutton* in 1845–7 nestles within the space once occupied by the nave aisle. The nave arcade arches are double-chamfered, starting with vertical pieces (i.e. stilted). The windows of the S chancel aisle are Dec, the pattern of tracery being exactly like the more complex of the two at Astley nearby. The chancel at that time must have had aisles already, for the W arch from the S aisle into the S chancel aisle is Dec as well. It has figured hoodmould stops. The arch corresponding on the N side is Perp. The chancel was remodelled internally about 1500. It has very slim piers, very thinly moulded, and arches – almost triangular – to go with them. On the abaci rise thin shafts connecting with a horizontal course at eaves level forming framed panels. All very delicate and quite unlike anything else in the locality, but in a style more familiar in Oxfordshire. – SCREEN. This is a Perp screen so unusual that it has been assumed that it was originally in the abbey church. Such a screen from the abbey was confiscated and sold in 1538. But the measurements fit this church, not the abbey. It is shown *in situ* against the W wall of the chancel in Buckler's sketch of 1820 but now stands at the W end of the nave. It is of wood, of the veranda type, open to the front without any dado, and also without any subdivisions other than the doorway and the two wide, straight-topped side-pieces. There is pierced tracery in the spandrels. The loft and its plainly panelled parapet is also preserved and has a square, balcony-like projection in the middle. – Chamber ORGAN and contemporary case, by *John Snetzler*, 1777. – TILES. Thirteen patterned tiles of Nottingham type, later C14, some of them heraldic. – STAINED GLASS.* Tree of Jesse, in the E

---

*The stained glass, monuments and other artefacts are described in detail in John D. Austin's *Merevale Church and Abbey* (1998).

window, thought to have been painted *c.* 1320–40 by the same workshop that made glass for the Latin Chapel at Christ Church Cathedral, Oxford. It probably comes from the abbey. It does not fit the present window, as will at once be admitted, when one notices that both Jesse and the Virgin are missing. It was discovered in the grounds of Merevale Hall in the early C19, re-erected under the supervision of *Clutton* in 1850 and restored by *Ward & Hughes* in 1872. Beautiful ruby and blue grounds to the figures and lush green vine trails. Borders of charming details. Much here and in the figures is good C19 replacement. In the tracery lights two C15 figures and some late C14 heads. – In two s windows more C14 glass and in two N aisle windows glass of *c.* 1520–30 with canopies and saints. – Several Victorian windows, starting with a s window in the chancel aisle by *Ward & Hughes* (signed *H. Hughes*), 1872. – In the N aisle, one by *Clayton & Bell* in memory of the architect Robert Jennings of Atherstone, †1874. – Two by *Burlison & Grylls*, one on the N †1879 and another on the s 1885. – w window of s aisle, high up, by *Wailes & Strang*, 1865: excellent colouring. – MONUMENTS. Effigy of a knight, more than life-size, unfortunately headless and footless, but of the very highest quality. It is second half of the C13, and thus a very early case of crossed legs. Chain-mail, the drapery wind-swept. Possibly William, Earl Ferrers of Chartley, †1248. – Brasses to Robert, Earl Ferrers, †1412 and his wife Margaret. Of excellent quality, the figures 5 ft 3 in. (1.6 metres) long. – Alabaster effigies of a knight and lady, *c.* 1440. The angels against the tomb-chest very similar to those at Lowick (Northants) and Aston (Birmingham). The effigies should be compared with those at Willoughby-on-the-Wolds (Notts.), †1448, Ashbourne (Derbys.), †1447, and East Shefford (Berks.), *c.* 1440. – Large Gothic monument to Dugdale Stratford Dugdale †1836 and other members of the family, by *S. Hills*.

The church is approached through a gatehouse so intensely medieval that it is at once recognized as Victorian. With the adjacent Gate House (i.e. house by the gate) and its associated coach house, it was built for William Stratford Dugdale of Merevale Hall by *Clutton* in 1848–9. The GATEHOUSE has a large vaulted entry arch with continuous mouldings and a large plain gable. On the N side, an octagonal stair-turret and short spire. The GATE HOUSE on the w is stately and has a varied s front with a steep pyramidal roof to the canted bay on the side nearest the church. Although ecclesiastical in style and location, these are estate buildings – the gatehouse is a lodge, and the Gate House a house (never a parsonage as often claimed) – designed as landscape features for the northern view from the hall as well as to enhance the setting of the church.

MEREVALE HALL, SE of the abbey. On top of a hill in spacious grounds surrounded by ancient oaks and other trees. Although called Hall, it looks like a castle with its embattled tower and walls when seen from the N and W. It is prominent from a distance from nearly all sides, and every time appears to advantage. That is something. It is also from nearby the most monumentally and dramatically composed of all the houses in Warwickshire. It is Victorian, as no one would doubt. It is in fact remarkably early, built in 1838–44 for William Stratford Dugdale, whose family wealth came from mining. It was designed by *Edward Blore*, assisted first by *Robert Jennings* and afterwards by *Henry Clutton*, who was working at Merevale by 1842 and later took over. It took the place of an earlier seven-bay house with a hipped roof dating from the later C17, the home of the Stratford family. What started as a programme of improvements turned into a virtual rebuilding – the eventual cost £35,000 rather than the £5,000 originally intended. In consequence, little of the earlier structure now remains. The grand E front is entirely symmetrical – Neo-Jacobean (although *Blore* would have called it Elizabethan), with mullioned-and-transomed windows, shaped gables, and a semicircular oriel above the central doorway which was the original main entrance. There is a high tower near the NW corner, a smaller one near the SW corner. To the S and W an extra service wing and a stable court with clock tower, Gothic and built ruggedly in rough stone. Entirely different in character and almost Scottish Baronial in style, these portions are crenellated and have low towers with distinctive coped parapets with ball finials. Begun after 1842, they were perhaps designed by the young *Clutton* rather than by *Blore*. The main entrance to the hall is now in the SE corner, altered by *Blore* in 1842 at the insistence of Mrs Dugdale and remodelled by *Clutton* in 1853. This leads to a wide corridor or long gallery giving access to the main apartments. Here the ceiling is a direct copy of a design by *Serlio*. Throughout, the house has fine Neo-Jacobean plaster ceilings and ornate classical fireplaces done in marbleized slate. The staircase hall, lit by windows with Venetian tracery high up on two sides, is at the centre of the house, separated from the organ hall (the original entrance) by an arcade of three rounded arches. The staircase balustrade is mid-C17 in style. To the r., the octagonal saloon with skylight opens to the drawing room running the length of the N side, the L-shaped library and the dining room. Fittings largely unaltered, including those in the dining room furnished by *W. & E. Snell* of Albemarle Street, London, in 1844 with built-in servery with carved canopy and mirrors.

The garden terraces to the E of the house were landscaped by *W. A. Nesfield* c. 1850. *Nesfield*'s scheme remains largely intact. The stone vases came from Drayton Manor (Staffs.) c. 1926.

There are LODGES at all the main entrances to the park. On the Coleshill Road is the BEEHIVE, an early C19 octagonal thatched building in the *cottage orné* style, with two octagonal wings added by *F. W. B. Charles* in 1962. To the N towards Atherstone and on Watling Street, a pair of classical lodges, more likely of c. 1830 than of the time of *Blore*'s rebuilding of the hall. To the NW by the church, *Clutton*'s GATEHOUSE already described.

MERIDEN

Meriden, formerly called Alspath, is supposedly at the centre of England. It was once a staging post on the Holyhead Road, noted for its inns. The village is in three distinct parts, now linked along the main road. The church is on a hill at the E. At the W is Meriden Green. Between them, a settlement in the hollow alongside Meriden Pool. Later C20 development has involved some notable losses, including C18 Darlaston Hall (the original Bull's Head), replaced by 1960s flats. It stood alongside the manor which, between 1872 and 1883, was the home and manufactory of *Francis Skidmore*, the art metal worker. In the mid C20 Meriden became known as a centre for the manufacture of motor cycles.

ST LAWRENCE. The chancel is Norman: see the deeply splayed N window and the remains of a corresponding one on the S. Inside in the SEDILE a re-set voussoir stone with chevron. Norman remains at the W end of the nave too, between the arcades and tower. The chancel lengthened with E.E. windows in the sides. Also in the C13 the chancel arch was renewed and given its elementary leaf capitals. Only the E window is Perp. Aisled nave. Both arcades have the standard elements, but the difference in date is clearly visible, the S C14* and the N C15. The outer aisle walls with high transomed three-light windows designed to light galleries date from a rebuilding by *John Bradford* of Coventry, 1826–7. S porch also by *Bradford*. Galleries removed during restoration by *J. T. Micklethwaite*, 1883. Further restoration under *Guy Pemberton*, 1924. Meeting room and gallery in W end of church and tower, 1989. The W tower is Perp, but its W window has tracery very probably of the C17. – Brass LECTERN, 1884, by *Skidmore*. – ROYAL ARMS, 1704. – STAINED GLASS. E, *Heaton, Butler & Bayne*, 1886. – Tower window, †1897, probably *Lavers & Westlake*. – Two in S aisle by *Powell*, 1900 and 1909. – Also in aisle, a marvellous Great War memorial window by *Florence, Robert & Walter Camm*, 1921, rich in colour and symbolism. – MONUMENTS. Alabaster effigy of a knight, *c.* 1400, angels by his head. – Stone effigy of a knight, *c.* 1450–60, also with angels. – In the chancel, two memorials by *Alcott* of Coventry, †1830s.

METHODIST CHURCH, Main Road. *C. F. Redgrave & Partners*, 1955, extended in 1967 by *Cripps & Stewart*; with asymmetrical façade, part stone-clad, part rendered, with brick corner turret and cross.

MERIDEN HALL, S of the main street, a little elevated and in landscaped grounds. By *Francis Smith*, 1721–4, for Martin Baldwin (†1725) (now offices). Stone-built, of seven bays and two and a half storeys. Three-bay pediment, moulded window surrounds. The large E room is tripartite by screens of two columns and has a ceiling of the late C18. The *Hiornes* worked

---

*Or just after 1400, as a chapel was founded in the S aisle in 1404.

here in 1757–8 and *Thomas Gardner* in 1785. To the W, C18 brick stables with quoins. Between the two, the base of the earlier stone house with mullioned windows and later upper storeys. In the grounds S, an C18 ICE HOUSE with egg-shaped brick dome.

Round the church a cluster of old buildings. MOAT HOUSE, E, is timber-framed, with symmetrical side gables and brick infilling. Supposedly dated 1609 but largely older. Traces of fleur-de-lys decoration on plaster under one gable. The old VICARAGE, SW, has a garden front of 1761. To the N, early C19 MERIDEN HOUSE with Doric porch.

Off Main Road below the hill, set back to the S, the former SCHOOL (No. 200); Tudor, brick, *c.* 1843. Further W, some decent Georgian houses, C18 MERIDEN HOTEL (No. 155) and early C19 BROOKLYN near the Methodist church. What remains of the MANOR, 1745, has been all but engulfed by the vast Neo-Georgian MANOR HOTEL (No. 127), the added blocks of 1964, 1969 and 1987 by *G. R. Stone* and another by *Temple Cox*, 1996. Further W, the C19 front of the 'new' BULL'S HEAD, created from older properties *c.* 1835, retains a good wrought-iron bracket for its inn sign.

On the green at the W end of the village, a C15 CROSS with tapering octagonal shaft and the CYCLISTS' MEMORIAL, an obelisk, 1921. Nothing much on the green itself, but there is a pretty pair of thatched cottages with eyebrow windows in Maxstoke Lane. By the roundabout at the junction with Hampton Lane, double-fronted CORNER HOUSE has early C19 pointed arched casement windows. Opposite, a striking circular SPORTS PAVILION with conical roof, by *Solihull MBC* architects, 2011. HEATH FARM in Hampton Lane has a large sandstone stable range, C18 with Diocletian windows, once belonging to the Packington estate and perhaps by *Joseph Bonomi*.

FOREST HALL, ¼ m. W of the green. Headquarters of the Woodmen of Arden, a gentlemen's archery club founded by the 4th Earl of Aylesford in 1785. The Ascham Room is the original hall, erected by *Bonomi* in 1787–8: oblong with chamfered corners, with a wreath and the device of the Woodmen in the centre of the ceiling. The panelled walls incorporate individual aschams for storing bows and arrows and boards recording competition awards from 1786. At one end is the bust of the 4th Earl, bare-chested and with the Woodmen's emblem on his belt, successfully caught in action: by *Thomas Banks*, 1795. A ballroom was added by *J. L. Akroyd* in 1845: the same shape, but top-lit. At the far end, the bust of Wriothesley Digby, secretary of the Woodmen, by *Nollekens*, *c.* 1811. Inside the two main rooms are linked. Outside, they are of uniform appearance: red sandstone, round-arched windows and angular projections for the offices. Overlooking the archery ground, a 1930s Neoclassical pavilion with colonnade and pediment. The group of buildings also includes a lodge or workshop and an early C19 cottage for the bowmaker.

WALSH HALL, ¾ m. N across the by-pass. Excellent timber-framed C15 to C16 house with additions of 1938 and a C16 chimneypiece with a lozenge frieze on the lintel (brought in).

MIDDLETON

1090

ST JOHN THE BAPTIST. Norman S doorway with lateral chevron mouldings to the arch. Remains of C12 lancets in N and S walls of chancel. The lower walls of nave and chancel in buff sandstone, the later work above in red. Perp the big upper windows on S side. Perp too the fine W tower. Red sandstone and with typical North Warwickshire details and heavily crocketed gables over doorway and windows.* The NW vestry with its intersecting tracery is of 1784, used as a school until *c.* 1875. Georgian S porch, brick with stone dressings. Inside, the N arcade of four bays with standard elements, *c.* 1300. The humble N aisle almost barn-like in its simplicity. Restoration by *Farmer & Brindley*, 1875–6. Theirs the nave seating with good traceried end-panels and the floor tiling. – FONTS. Plain C18 baluster (disused) and octagonal font with carved panels, 1848. – SCREEN. In specially good condition. Single-light divisions with ogee heads and fine tracery over. – PULPIT. Only sparsely decorated, but with winged cherubs and barley-sugar twist half-columns. Perhaps late C17. – WALL PAINTINGS. Remains in the N aisle, C13, and more – later – over the chancel arch and in the nave. – STAINED GLASS. Several by *Hardman*: the E window 1867, S chancel 1885, tower 1876 and one in S aisle 1872. Another there by *Kempe*, 1888. – MONUMENTS. Very good brasses of Sir Richard Bingham †1476 and wife. The figures are 3 ft 2 in. (97 cm.) long. He stands elevated. The drapery of his mantle is in the angular style of the later C15. – Lord Edward Ridgway, second son of the Earl of Londonderry, †1638, with kneeling figure between Corinthian columns. – His HELM and GAUNTLETS are suspended l. and r. – Willoughby family, †1665–88. Attributed to *James Hardy* *52* (GF). A large and stylistically important monument, done with considerable swagger. Very tall tablet of white and black marble, on a black marble background. Rich in detail, including cartouches at the foot, skulls in the capitals, flaming urns and three interlocked oval inscription plates. Three distinctly individual putti. Above the top one, who holds an hourglass, an urn and two laurel-like garlands. At the foot three putto heads; identical triplets. – Benjamin and Samuel White †1685 and 1688. Two grotesquely stolid busts in an architectural surround with segmental pediment and skulls in linen drapes below.

---

* In the tower the bell-frame is probably contemporary with the tower. An exceptional and very rare survival.

MIDDLETON HALL. An important house with a highly complex building history from *c.* 1100. It is the oldest domestic building in the county still in use. The site is moated. Previously occupied by the de Marmion and the de Freville families, Middleton belonged to the Willoughbys of Willoughby-on-the-Wolds and Wollaton, Notts., from the C15 until 1924. It was inhabited until 1966. Left abandoned among gravel workings it was endangered for some time, but since 1980 it has been gradually restored and opened to the public by the Middleton Hall Trust. The restoration was initially supervised by *Lyndon F. Cave* of Leamington, beginning with the w wing, 1981–8. Later phases include the Great Hall, 1992–4, the timber-framed building on the N front, 2000–3, and the E side in two stages ending with the oldest part, the Stone Building, in 2007–10. This must be one of the very best examples of what can be achieved in bringing historic buildings back from the brink of destruction, all the more so for having been undertaken largely by volunteers.

The house has a stately Early Georgian w front of eight bays, scanned by fluted giant pilasters. A three-bay addition on the r., 1824. Round the corner to the N three more bays with giant pilasters and then a quite irregular part including the opening into a courtyard, and to the l. of that a timber-framed range with an overhang on big scrolls. The E range completely irregular too, continuing round to the kitchen range on the s. On entering the courtyard, the reason for the disjointed appearance becomes clear. This was never a unified design, but always a series of linked buildings round a quadrangle. The story begins in the sw corner where there is a Norman window in the inner wall of the STONE BUILDING, itself a reconstruction of *c.* 1285 with fine ashlar walling inside. It also has a trussed collar barrel roof. Alongside on the E front, the JOHN RAY BUILDING, timber-framed, 1647. In the NE corner the splendid JETTIED BUILDING, dendro-dated *c.* 1530–50, now restored with oriel windows to the exterior. The demolished building in the gap had a fragment of a C14 roof with trefoiled bracing. Then the GREAT HALL, originally built *c.* 1491–7, although of that date nothing is discernible. Inside, a fine early C18 staircase with delicately carved balusters and square fluted columns to the landing in the entrance hall. This belongs with the additions (i.e. the w range) for Lord Middleton around the time he was raised to the peerage in 1712. The work has been dendro-dated to 1708–18. The rooms in the w wing retain such period features as survived the period of neglect.

Across the moat to the E of the house, the TUDOR BARN, a timber-framed range later used as a barn. The dendro-date is 1591, and 1604 is carved on a beam. This still awaits restoration.

To the N, a large walled garden originally laid out by Lord Middleton in 1717, with restored two-storey GAZEBO in the NE corner.

In the village, the former SCHOOL, w of the church, *c.* 1874 in red brick with blue brick bands, moulded window heads and bold Victorian details. s extension of 1886 with excessively tall sash windows breaking the eaves on the s side. Later additions. Opposite the church, C18 SCHOOL HOUSE for the master of the charity school. The former VICARAGE in Vicarage Hill – mid-C18, with major additions of *c.* 1800 but all much altered.

MONKS KIRBY

ST EDITH. A grand but rather puzzling church, oddly mis-matched outside and in. There was a priory here, founded in 971. It was re-endowed in 1077 for the Benedictines of St Nicholas at Angers and later held in 1397–9 and from 1415 to 1538 by the Carthusians of Epworth in Lincolnshire. Of the priory buildings not one stone survives and the church refers to its monastic origins only in a few minor ways. Some N aisle windows are placed high enough to allow for a cloister beneath, and in the chancel are remains of doorways and windows into some monastic annexe not of a familiar kind. So architecturally one can treat it as a parish church, albeit the grandest in its region. It is mostly Dec and Perp, but the largely featureless chancel shows signs of E.E. work. There is a high lancet (originally external) on the N and on the s are C13 PISCINA with SEDILIA set in modern walling jutting awkwardly into the first bay of the arcade. Perhaps they were discovered and re-set during *Street's* extensive restoration in 1868–9. At that date, the whole church was re-roofed and re-seated and several of the windows 'corrected'. The geometrical E window is one of Street's amendments.

The Dec portions are on the s and w. The mighty sw tower is of red sandstone below, of beige stone (Bromsgrove sand-stone) above. Flowing tracery in the w and s windows in the lower stage and the plainer windows above are Dec too. But the top is evidently later and belongs to a rebuilding after the fall of the spire in 1701. The parapet has shaped gables and the pinnacles look Gothick, reminiscent of St Mary's Warwick of the same date. The accounts show it was done by *Edward Lythall*, a Warwick stonemason, in 1709. Dec also seems the proud two-storeyed s porch of red sandstone. It has a tierceron star-vault inside, as has the tower. Then the s aisle whose window tracery, although probably Victorian, resembles what was there before, described by Glynne (1861) as 'having some-thing of [the] Flamboyant about it'. The w window of the nave is 'advanced' Dec (Glynne again) too. Externally the N aisle, the NE chapel, the low SE vestry and the windows above are all Perp.

How is all this matched by the interior? Unexpectedly, the nave and chancel form one undivided space, separated from the aisles by identical arcades of six bays running almost the full length of the church. The N arcade ends at the NE chapel.

That on the s encroaches on the former chancel on the E (cf. the present position of the sedilia) and ends at the W in a wall built into the E arch of the tower. The arcades are of red stone with moulded lozenge shape for the piers and finely moulded arches dying into them. The church was described as in danger of collapse in 1360 and this internal reconstruction must have followed *c*. 1375. An earlier roof-line is visible on the E face of the tower. Evidently the nave was widened at the expense of the aisle, the new arcade being set further s. In the NE chapel l. and r. of the E window are high image niches with elaborate canopies. – FURNISHINGS. Complete ensemble by *Street*, 1868–9, including *Minton* FLOOR TILES and good brass ALTAR RAILS. – STAINED GLASS, E window by *Lavers & Barraud* (designer *R. R. Holmes*), 1869. – s chapel E window, *Ward & Hughes*, 1868. – Others by *Hardman*: two W windows 1869, s chapel 1877 and tower (two) 1884. – ROYAL ARMS. 1660. – MONUMENTS. Upper half of a defaced C14 effigy (N aisle). – Sir William Feilding †1547 and wife Elizabeth †1539. Alabaster. By *Garrat Hollemans* of Burton upon Trent (JB). Two recumbent effigies. Tomb-chest with semi-Gothic pilasters and shields. – Basil Feilding and his wife 'Gooddethe', †1580. Alabaster. Also by *Hollemans*. Two recumbent effigies. Against her skirts two puppies, one at rest, the other playful. His feet pressed against the tail of a lion. Tomb-chest with elementary balusters, 'mourners' stiffly against the sides, holding shields, and two ugly cherubs with a shield at the head end. – Lady Augusta Feilding †1848, reclining effigy on a couch. – William, 7th Earl of Denbigh, †1865, and his countess, †1842, recumbent in relief on a tomb-chest. Both monuments signed *Mary Grant* 1881.

ST JOSEPH (R.C.), Brockhurst Lane. Alongside the former CONVENT, whose chapel was used for public worship from 1952, services having previously taken place in the private chapel at Newnham Paddox. By *John D. Holmes*, 1991–2. Brick with simple pointed windows, slate roof and thin bell-turret. Laminated roof trusses and wooden ceiling. Short chancel with plain E wall. – STAINED GLASS. Two of 1977 by *Hardman* from previous chapel.

ROMAN CATHOLIC CEMETERY, Sandy Lane, with MORTUARY CHAPEL in the French Baroque style by *F. A. Walters* for the Earl of Denbigh, 1897–8. Delightful though badly vandalized, especially inside. Roughcast brick with limestone dressings. Heavy stone buttresses with curled tops. Dormers and copper-covered spirelet. Timber canopied porch. Apsed sanctuary with tiled and painted decoration.

In the village, a mix of timber-framed cottages and ESTATE HOUSING (dated 1877–96). In ST EDITH'S CLOSE, E of the church, a distinctive small development of houses by *Kendrick Findlay & Partners*, 1974. Opposite the SCHOOL at Brockhurst, a small group of 1860s ALMSHOUSES. Up the hill W of the church, the old VICARAGE with diapered brickwork, stone dressings, fish-scale tiling and big chimneys, by *Scott & Moffatt*,

1842–3. Further w, MANOR FARMHOUSE is of similar date with similar details, Tudor-style with diapering in the roof and walls and iron latticed casement windows.

NEWNHAM PADDOX, 1¼ m. NE. Acquired in 1433 by the Feilding family, Earls of Denbigh since 1622. Already a grand mansion in landscaped grounds by the time of Kip (1707), the house and park were improved for the 5th and 6th Earls by *Capability Brown* from 1746. The house itself was largely rebuilt by Brown in 1753–5, but again remodelled and enlarged in the French Renaissance style for the 8th Earl of Denbigh by *T. H. Wyatt* in 1875. A Roman Catholic chapel was built alongside in 1878–80, again by Wyatt. It was all pulled down in 1952 but a much smaller clapboarded house by *Garnett Cloughley Blakemore* was built on the site in the 1980s, aligned with the ornamental entrance GATES to the s. There are five gates, of cast and wrought iron. The inner piers are of iron too. The style is clearly C18, and the gates have been variously attributed to English and Welsh craftsmen of the period. In fact, they came originally from a Spanish monastery and were brought here from Berwick House, Shrewsbury, by the 8th Earl in 1873. The C18 STABLES survive as does the WALLED GARDEN of 1770–2. In the park, elements of Brown's C18 planting and later landscaping by *John Webb*, 1818–21, and *John Fleming*, c. 1870, also remain. Since 2003 Newnham Paddox has been developed by the 12th Earl and his wife as a SCULPTURE GARDEN and ART PARK.

MORETON MORRELL

HOLY CROSS. A 'Churchwarden Gothic' survival. Wide pointed windows without tracery in the nave N and S, all from a remodelling of c. 1810. Gone, though, the near contemporary Late Georgian brick tower top, rebuilt plainly in stone by *W. S. Hattrell & Partners*, 1966–7. The lower part of the tower C15. The nave walls are still medieval, the N doorway Perp. The chancel side windows have wooden lintels, probably C16. Some restoration in 1886 by *C. R. Baker King* whose proposals were only partially implemented. The nave was re-seated and the chancel arch rebuilt. The E window tracery was renewed to his designs in 1896. N porch also 1895–6. – PULPIT. With a few minor C17 lozenge panels. – SCULPTURE. Inside the church a Norman lintel and incomplete tympanum are kept. It was found outside in 1886. The tympanum is plain, the lintel has a cross oddly laid horizontally and Romanesque saltire crosses. – MONUMENT. Richard Murden †1635 and wife Maria. Large alabaster wall monument with the two figures kneeling under arches and facing one another across a prayer-desk. They are too big to be kneeling thus, and actually cannot see one another. At the top in a broken pediment an angel holding two shields. Two tough putti lower down l. and r., one with hourglass the other with skull.

MANOR HOUSE, N of the church. One wing with mullioned-and-transomed windows; C17. The gatepiers also C17; rusticated with ball finials.

In the village, C18 MORETON HOUSE with wide pediment, Doric doorcase and Gothic chimneys. Stables alongside, square with blind window openings and pyramid roof with ball finial. By the pub, a pretty Victorian cottage with polychromatic brick-work and diamond-pane windows. Nearby, the VILLAGE HALL built as the school, 1869. The present SCHOOL, opposite, by *Dallas & Lloyd* of Birmingham, 1914, but obscured by later additions.

Beyond the church, the 1905 LODGE and entrance gates to MORETON HALL, ⅜ m. SW. The hall was built in 1905–8 for Charles Tuller Garland (cf. Ashorne Hill House) by *W. H. Romaine-Walker*. C18 Palladian in the style of Wilton House. Thirteen-bay front of Bath stone with pediment above the first two and the last two bays. Doorway with foliage frieze and open scrolly pediment. Similar garden front but of eight bays and with Venetian windows in the first and last. It had rich Edwardian interiors, badly damaged by fire in 2008 and not yet restored (2013). Landscaped gardens, including a *Bromsgrove Guild* statue of Diana and the nymphs. The Moreton Hall estate became an agricultural college in 1948 and it is now part of Warwickshire College. The college uses Garland's fine STABLES and RIDING SCHOOL of 1905–7, also by *Romaine-Walker*. The POLO SCHOOL was converted into a LEARNING RESOURCE CENTRE for the college by *Robothams*, 2000.

The indoor TENNIS COURTS opposite the lodge were also built for Garland, 1905. The court itself was plastered in black by *Joseph Bickley*.

MORETON PADDOX, 1 m. S, was pulled down in 1959. It was built in 1909 by *Romaine-Walker* for Major Robert Emmett, whose wife was Garland's sister. Its N lodge, water tower, the fine Edwardian stables and some parts of the gardens remain. The two drives, one originally from the lodge to the house and a parallel one to the stables a little further E, have large houses from the 1960s onwards, some quite striking. The most adventurous architecturally are MCGOVERN HOUSE on the ridge and ROOFTOPS above the former Long Terrace of the garden.

MORTON BAGOT

HOLY TRINITY. Unrestored and un-neglected until insensitive repairs to the chancel in 1972 left its walls bare and the roof open as they were never intended to be. Less damaging, but a major change nonetheless, was the total replacement of the

Victorian nave seating with C20 pews from nearby Spernall when that church was converted, *c.* 1982. The fabric, though, is little altered since the early C19 despite partial restorations in 1844 and 1877. Grey stone and red trimmings.* Nave and chancel, s porch and timber-framed bell-turret. A high-up Norman window in the N wall. The others mostly of *c.* 1300, one with cusped intersecting tracery and a single light with thin trefoil piercing in the head. On the capitals of the chancel arch and below the PISCINA, simple leaf carving in shallow relief. Perp E window of three lights. Queenpost roof and big beams across the W end of the nave, supporting the belfry. – PRAYER-DESK. A rare, complete piece with two poppyheads, and open-work front panels, *c.* 1500. On the ends, circles with mouchette wheels. It is said to have come from a Catholic chapel on the Avon Carrow estate at Avon Dassett. – COMMUNION RAIL with open traceried panels from a C15 screen. – STAINED GLASS. E window by *Hardman*, 1963.

The church is memorable for its hillside setting. It stands on a mound approached through a simple LYCHGATE of 1936, with the fine timber-framed barns (adapted for housing) and farm-house alongside. CHURCH FARM, *c.* 1580, restored with timber-framed additions by *Richard Crook*, 2006. Close studding to the ground floor, then square-framed above and gable dormers on the N side facing the church. Higher up to the SE, a RING MOTTE represents the site of earlier occupation.

NETHERSTEAD, ¾ m. SW, part timber-framed and part brick and on a moated site with a reconstructed medieval bridge. Netherstead was the home of the Holyoak family, and Nat Alcock has shown that the remaining C16 wing of an earlier house was enlarged and given its present S front for John Holyoak between 1649 and 1653. Especially fine, the two-storey jettied and gabled porch, giving a lobby-entry plan with a central stack and fireplaces to the five principal rooms. The parlour fireplace retains an original scheme of painted decoration and there are distinctive mouldings and carpenters' marks throughout. Restored by *Richard Crook* for Mr and Mrs Paul Harvey in 2004–6.

To the NW, model farm buildings, *c.* 1896, now converted to housing as NETHERSTEAD COURT.

NAPTON-ON-THE-HILL

4060

St LAWRENCE. Quite a large church, low, on the brow of the hill. The chancel is Norman – see the three widely spaced N windows. The main S doorway must also be of *c.* 1200, i.e. it

---

*Inside the chancel a large area of tufa-like limestone, found in C12 churches in W Worcestershire but not local to the Morton Bagot area. Was it brought from a building elsewhere as the VCH suggests?

still has a round arch with roll mouldings, but also early stiff-leaf capitals. Then there is impressive work of *c.* 1275, namely both transepts. The much restored s transept s window is of three stepped pointed-trefoiled lancets, the N transept N window is the same but has a shafted outer surround with a round super-arch. The inner shafting is probably Victorian. Of the two the N transept comes first – the mouldings of the super-arch show that, but even more the nave N arcade inside and the way it joins the transept. The arcade piers are octagonal, but the joining pier has a round abacus, made as one piece with the smaller round abacus of the arch from aisle into transept. The corresponding junction on the s side is managed without round abaci. The N transept has good E windows too: one lancet and one triplet of stepped lancets. Again in the N transept a pair of large round-arched tomb recesses. In the s transept one smaller and lower one, with a segmental arch. Chancel E wall and window Perp. The buttresses are gabled. The arch between nave and tower is of *c.* 1300 (see the three continuous chamfers both sides). The s porch is puzzling. It has blank arcading l. and r., made up of C12 or early C13 round shafts and coarse Perp tracery. The tower abuts the w wall but is wholly of 1731, and very like that of 1721 at Priors Marston (q.v.). Both have quirky pilaster buttresses and round-arched bell-openings with Y-tracery. The nave and transepts were restored in 1860–1 by *John Croft. William Watson* of Napton was the builder. May one discover their hands in the s porch? The nave clerestory is of 1861. *E. B. Ferrey* restored the chancel, 1876. N meeting room extension by *Acanthus Clews*, 2013. – Plain FONT by *Cox & Sons* with wooden cover by *Charles Watson* of Napton, 1872. – SCULPTURE. Some Norman carving at the foot of the s respond of the chancel arch. – STAINED GLASS. Two s chancel windows with roundels in patterned glass, *J. B. Cottier*, 1876. – In N transept, mainly 1861, possibly by *Holland*, but with a small C18 piece in the lancet. – N window by *F. Holt & Co.*, 1898. – One s window †1885, possibly by *Holt* too. – Another by *Hardman*, 1906.

CHRISTADELPHIAN HALL, Howcombe Lane, *c.* 1900. Very plain, but strikingly situated alone on the green.

SCHOOL, Vicarage Road. Girls National School building, 1843. Low, yellow brick, with slate roof. On the street frontage, with newer buildings behind.

WINDMILL. On the hill and conspicuous from all around. An early C19 brick tower on stone foundations. Now a house, but with domed aluminium cap and complete non-operational sails.

A large and attractive village, with a pleasant mix of ironstone, thatch and locally made bricks. But it is disappointing architecturally, partly owing to the loss or conversion of the C19 schools and chapels. The greatest loss was the old VICARAGE, demolished in 1968: a medieval house rather charmingly enlarged by *D. G. Squirhill* in 1849 and *William Watson* in 1865.

The main settlement is on the s side of the hill, where houses in School Hill and Vicarage Road hug the hillside. The High Street forms a broad green, with chequer brick Leeson House, c. 1835, on the w. Lower down, in New Street is HOME FARM with a quoined two-storey front and Doric doorcase. The former brickworks (*fl.* mid C19 to 1970s) was to the w, near the Oxford Canal which curves round the w side of the hill, joining the Grand Union NE of the village. Some minor C19 CANAL buildings at Napton Bottom Lock in Folly Lane. Further s, CHAPEL GREEN FARMHOUSE, 1637, has mullioned windows and a chimneystack with four clustered shafts diagonally.

Further C17 and C18 ironstone buildings N of the hill and along the Southam–Daventry road. Also on the main road, the KINGS HEAD, by *Francis P. Trepess & Son*, 1923.

NETHER WHITACRE

2090

ST GILES. Heavily buttressed w tower of red ashlar with Y-tracery in the windows and old carvings re-set in the masonry. Hard to date, but perhaps C16. Otherwise mostly of 1870 and by *Robert Jennings*, though the E window with its flowing tracery may represent the original. The s side grimly rock-faced, with rather glaring window surrounds – those on the N set in sandstone and even more so. The N vestry houses the Jennens monument. Inside, the walls all cement-rendered and the fittings mostly pitch-pine. – STAINED GLASS. Fine early C14 censing angel (chancel s). – E window and patterned glass in nave and tower mostly by *Swaine Bourne*, 1870, with one N window completed in 1876. Poor. – s nave window with angels in a vesica surround by *Claude Price*, 1979. – s porch window by *G. Howell*, 2000. – MONUMENT. Charles Jennens †1773. Lengthy inscription extolling his virtues and charitable gifts – including the endowment of the village school – but saying nothing of his musical interests and association with Handel for which he is chiefly noted. By *Richard Hayward*, 1775. Large tablet. Mourning woman, her handkerchief held over her eyes, standing by a sarcophagus set diagonally. Behind, a collapsing pyramid. The style is still that of Roubiliac, not yet that of, say, Wilton. Hayward, who could be so delicate on a small scale, has here undertaken more than he could cope with.

75

METHODIST CHURCH, in Station Road at Whitacre Heath. 1914 by *A. McKewan*, who enlarged it in 1929. Brick and tile, with large Diocletian window in a tiled surround on the street front. It replaced an earlier Wesleyan chapel of 1836 in Birmingham Road, now CHAPEL COTTAGE, with a pointed Gothic window.

E of the churchyard is the former JENNENS SCHOOL, founded in 1773 and enlarged in 1878. The two long ranges with a raised central section look c. 1840s. NW of the church, the OLD RECTORY. Of plum brick, and by *Robert Jennings*, 1873. E of these, the DOG INN, with features of 1900 by *A. G. Latham* whose attractive remodelling with timber framing has since been spoiled.

HALLOUGHTON GRANGE, ¾ m. N, is an 1860s gabled farmhouse with model farm buildings to the rear.

In Hoggrill's End Lane, S of the church, THE OLD HOUSE dated 1593 but much enlarged by *C. S. Archer* for Walter Collins in 1908. About ¾ m. E, C18 red brick HILL FARMHOUSE has good blue and red brick farm buildings (now residential) alongside.

WHITACRE HEATH, ¾ m. W, grew up alongside the Birmingham and Derby Railway, opened in 1839. The pubs, two good stone road bridges of c. 1841 and a long row of terraced cottages in Station Road are all associated with the development. At the far S, towards Shustoke Reservoir, an isolated rock-faced Gothic LODGE of c. 1870 to the old drive to the Hams Hall estate, and timber-framed PEGG'S BARN, dendro-dated 1668–9, moved from the Daw Mill Colliery site.

WHITACRE HALL, ¾ m. NE. Once the home of Charles Jennens, who also owned Gopsal Park in Leicestershire. The house is surrounded by a sandstone wall which rises directly as the inner wall of the moat. Remains of corner towers. Miniature Jacobean brick gatehouse with a shaped gable. The house partly C17, but mainly C19 in roughcast brick.

108   WHITACRE WATERWORKS. An impressive Ruskinian Gothic complex in red brick with stone dressings and tiled roofs. By *Martin & Chamberlain* for the Birmingham Corporation Water Committee. The W pumphouse, 1872, the one to the E larger and later.* Soaring cathedral-like structures with high-pitched roofs, steep gables and Venetian Gothic details. The tall centre section of the E pumphouse is flanked by lower aisles with apsidal ends with semi-conical roofs. Along the side facing the railway the pumphouses are linked by a covered range with seven gables. There is also a superintendent's house in the same style, with Gothic relieving arches, and a circular well with a conical roof – both reminiscent of Philip Webb's Red House, London.

BOTTS GREEN HOUSE. *See* Botts Green.

NEW ARLEY

New Arley is a mining village that grew up around the Arley Colliery (1901–68).

---

*Parts of its James Watt beam engine of 1885 are now in the Birmingham City Museums.

St Michael and All Angels. By *Tanner & Horsburgh*, 1927–8, replacing an iron mission room. Cruciform, brick and tile with hardwood windows. Sweeping roofs (their dormer windows removed 1976), and a semi-classical stone-dressed w front with bellcote and cross. Sympathetically enlarged in 2009 by *Vagdia & Holmes* with a community centre to the rear.

St Joseph (R.C.), Spring Hill. *John D. Holmes*, 1996, on the site of a church (1926) and hall (1950). Cruciform with arms of equal length and steeply pitched roofs. – stained glass. Triangular gable window by *Aidan McRae Thomson*, 2005.

Gun Hill Infant School. A typical *County Architect's Department* school, 1926. Low classroom blocks with tall windows and hipped roofs.

The Fir Tree, a large pub with sweeping roofs and big chimneys, by *Tanner & Horsburgh*, 1927. It belongs – like the now demolished Miners' Welfare Hall of *c*. 1930 – with a phase of village development around George Street financed by the Ransome family and by the same architects.

NEWBOLD PACEY

2050

St George. 1880–1 by *J. L. Pearson*, perhaps influenced by a previous scheme of 1870 by his friend *C. E. Buckeridge*. In the E.E. style, mostly with lancets. Excellent w front, very ingeniously balanced. NW porch tower with saddleback roof. Four lancets with a sexfoiled oculus over to represent the nave, and a small two-light window to represent the S aisle. The roof also changes its pitch slightly and the sill course of the windows climbs down. The E end treated similarly. On the nave N side groups of three stepped lancet lights under one arch. On the S side a transept and a two-bay chapel. Continuous string course all round at varying heights. The roofs of nave and chancel differ in construction, the nave with pretty curved braces. Pearson reused two Norman doorways. The N door has one order of columns and unusual capitals with volutes. The l. capital has a pattern of lozenges set in. The r. capital with triple cable and looped ribbons. – Heavy Gothic altar and reredos with painted panels: *Bromsgrove Guild*, 1926. – stained glass. E window by *Hardman*, 1881 and 1892. – w window probably by *A. O. Hemming*, †1890 (AB). – monuments. Edward Carew †1668 and his infant daughter Felicia. Attributed to *Thomas Stanton* (GF). Frontal demi-figure in an oval recess. His hand on his heart. The baby lies on a ledge in front of him. Good architectural setting. – William Little †1834. With a small, quite sensitive relief of charity given. The style still in the Grecian tradition.

Immediately w of the church, the old vicarage has a late C17 S front of two storeys plus attic with hipped roof and dormers. The E side elevation, a refronting of *c*. 1720, is altogether grander with rusticated quoins and windows with keystones and aprons: attractive yet absurd in its relationship with the older parts of the house, especially above the roof.

In the village, NEWBOLD PACEY HALL on the site of a C17 manor house. Built in the late C18 for Thomas or William Little who inherited in 1789 and 1791 respectively. Plain stuccoed entrance front with Doric porch. Garden front with central pediment and Venetian ground-floor windows. To the N, a good range of brick stables and outbuildings with clock turret, probably 1814.

For Ashorne, *see* p. 113.

NEWBOLD REVEL
Stretton-under-Fosse

The Newbold Revel estate (once known as Fenny Newbold) belonged to the Mallory family in the C17 and passed into the hands of the Skipwiths in 1659. They built the main house. By 1862 it was owned by Edward Wood, a Staffordshire financier and railway promoter with further estates in Scotland. Wood and his grandson Arthur, who succeeded in 1886, transformed the house (as Geoffrey Tyack observes) into a luxurious late Victorian country seat. By 1868 Edward had revamped the house and in 1871 employed *Joseph Goddard* to build a lodge and cottages at Easenhall (q.v.). Arthur Wood spent nearly £33,000 on works in 1891–3. Arthur Heath, the owner from 1898 to 1911, made further improvements. Since 1931 it has been in institutional use, as a Seventh Day Adventist theological college 1931–41, a Roman Catholic teacher training college (St Paul's College) 1946–78, and since 1986 as a Prison Service college.

An earlier mansion was remodelled for Sir Fulwar Skipwith in 1716 and illustrated in *Vitruvius Britannicus* in 1717. The external appearance is still of that date. Preserved rainwater heads on the S front say 1673 but this can apply to nothing now visible. Inside, however, the irregular planning confirms a reworking of an older house. On the strength of style *Francis Smith* of Warwick is assumed to have been the designer. The entrance (NW) side is of eleven bays. The first and last three are slightly projecting wings. The recessed centre was filled in at ground level in the late C19 but the original doorway was moved forward. The house is of red brick with stone dressings and three storeys high. The quoins are of even length, a motif typical of the first quarter of the C18. The doorway has Roman Doric columns against rustication and a triglyph frieze at the top. The windows have busy surrounds and brick aprons. The urns are of original form too. The SW side is of seven bays, the SE garden side again of eleven, but of a different rhythm: 2–7–2. Also, it has a three-bay pediment and a special accent on the top-floor middle window, which is made round-arched. The colonnade was added after 1887, probably for Wood.

The first room inside is the STAIRCASE HALL. The staircase is of wood, with some inlay, three turned balusters to each step, and carved tread-ends. The door surrounds are ornamented, but the ceiling is plain. Some of the upper details – two doorways and some garlands – could be original, as is an overmantel in the HAYWOOD ROOM upstairs with genuine garlands in the Gibbons tradition. In other rooms Adamish fireplaces. But the finest chimneypiece is in the BLUE ROOM, a galleried saloon on the SE front created after 1887. It is of white marble and has two large bearded men as Atlantes l. and r. and a dainty relief in the middle. The centre room on the SW side has a chimneypiece of about the same date and style, i.e. Chambers rather than Adam.

Large NE extension with corner tower, the 'Cricketers' wing' added for Arthur Wood 1891–3, and the contemporary gymnasium block. Numerous additions in the grounds, mainly for St Paul's College including a CHAPEL by *Harrison & Cox* (*G. B. Cox*), 1951. Originally barrel-roofed but since given a clerestory and pitched roof. Further developments for the Prison College.

The altered C18 STABLES are of brick, one-storeyed, and with the customary cupola.

Of the formal gardens S of the house, there remain the balustrading, urns and a cast-iron FOUNTAIN to a design shown at the Great Exhibition, 1851. Also a series of ponds with cascade, boathouse and ornamental iron bridge.

Newbold Revel, elevation and plan.
Engraving by Colen Campbell, 1717

NEWBOLD-ON-STOUR

St David. *William Walker*, 1833–5. Typical of its date, with lancets and thin buttresses along the sides. Limestone but stucco mouldings. Chancel, nave, N vestry and an unusually ambitious NW porch tower which originally carried a splay-foot spire, removed in 1948. Chancel lengthened in 1884. Inside, the chancel arch was replaced in stone by *R. A. Briggs*, 1889. Good nave roof with Gothic detailing between the posts. Most fittings renewed, 1874 and 1884. – STAINED GLASS. Patterned glass with borders in nave. – E window and two chancel side windows, by *Lavers & Co.*, 1884. – Two more, *Lavers, Westlake & Co.*, 1886. – Centre light in w window, *Derek Hunt*, 2006.

Nearby, the Cotswold-style SCHOOL with mullioned windows: 1848 and 1865 with later extensions. On the green to the N, a tiny thatched cob building. Cob across the main road too in the garden wall of early C19 COTSWOLDS HOUSE, fronted in brick and Cotswold stone but with limestone sides. A little N, THE GRANGE, built as a rectory for the Rev. Richard Prichard, and by his brother, *John Prichard*, 1867–8: Muscular Gothic, with big polygonal bay facing the street. Past the (partly) C16 WHITE HART, the former METHODIST CHAPEL AND INSTITUTE by *Henry Harper* of Nottingham, 1910: in brick with free Perp-ish window in stone, the style described as 'oriental gothic' in a contemporary report. Down the lane alongside, PARK VIEW HOUSE dated 1714 still has mullioned-and-transomed windows, even if they are arranged symmetrically.

Just N towards Stratford, SOUTH LODGE at the former entrance to Ettington Park (q.v.): *Prichard*, 1862, and in the same style as the house. Excellent extensions in the original style by *Impact Design* (*Tony Brandon*), 2008–10. Opposite, a Gothic MILESTONE, 1871.

Talton House, 1 m. NNW. Mixed styles and dates, C17 and later. Attractively landscaped grounds with mid-C19 walls and railings and wide entrance with brick piers. LODGE opposite with Italianate extension, also mid-C19. To the E, two similar BRIDGES near the site of the demolished mill. Both ashlar, single-arched with keystones, one on the mill bridge dated 1746.

NEWTON REGIS

St Mary. Built in the C12 as a chapelry of Seckington and gradually rebuilt and enlarged from the C13 to the C15. The w tower was probably begun early in the C13. The arch from tower to nave has only one step and one slight chamfer. Nothing else is as early as this. The bell-openings of the tower are Dec. The spire was completed later still. It is of different stone and has two tiers of lucarnes. The chancel was rebuilt *c.* 1320. Its five-light E window of *c.* 1320 has cusped interlocking lights with a big pointed quatrefoil in place of the intersections at the top. One S window has ogee details and must be of slightly later date (cf. the E window and ogee-headed work at Seckington), perhaps contemporary with the nave of *c.* 1330–40. Both chancel and nave are Dec below and Perp above, the chancel clerestory late C14 and the nave clerestory with its embattled parapet later. In the nave, Dec windows of two types, identical ones in corresponding positions N and S (although the S tracery was only reinstated in 1927) and Perp above. The C15 S porch has a pointed tunnel-vault with transverse ribs, a type more familiar in Nottinghamshire and Derbyshire than in Warwickshire. Inside the chancel a charming little PISCINA, with four open-work cusps and at the top a Kentish barb. Also in the N wall a tomb or EASTER SEPULCHRE recess. It should be noted as a curiosity that the NE buttress of the tower is pierced by a squint, allowing a person outside the tower to look into the nave.

Restoration under *C. Ford Whitcombe*, the exterior in 1905 and the interior in 1907. Of Whitcombe's time, the delightful Arts and Crafts leading on most of the windows on the N side of the church; the S door with fine ironwork and an ingenious grille to let air in and keep birds out; and the parquet floor and nave seating. – PULPIT. Simple, with tester and probably a survivor from alterations carried out in 1825. – WALL PAINT-ING. In the nave NE window some old paint of chevrons, in the NW window of foliage trails – who can say what date? – STAINED GLASS. In the E window a C14 heraldic panel set in clear glass. Further C14 and C15 fragments in the W window and in the nave clerestory. – Two good windows by *Roger Fifield*, nave S of 1988 and chancel N of 1990. – MONUMENTS. In the Easter sepulchre, an uncommonly complexly carved coffin-lid of the early C14, the date being fixed by the rim of ballflower. At the foot of the lid the Lamb carrying a high cross ending in a rounded quatrefoil, the lowest lobe being shallower than the others. In the quatrefoil the bust of a priest. In the l. and r. lobes the chalice and the book. To the sides of the cross-shaft two kneeling acolytes with tapers. Above the side lobes two censing angels, and above the top lobe the priest's soul carried up in a napkin by angels and the dove of the Holy Spirit. – Alabaster slab with C15 figure of priest in Mass vestments and an illegible inscription. – Monument to Rev. John Guest †1832 and his family, by *Birkenhead* of Ashby and in C17 style although of *c.* 1835.

At the entrance to the CHURCHYARD, a war memorial LYCHGATE of 1928 by *Bridgeman & Sons* of Lichfield.

To the S, the former SCHOOL of 1848. Very plain and with
segment-headed windows and no Gothic details at all. Its successor, of 1995, stands E of the church.

NEWTON HOUSE, set back behind houses in St Mary's Grove,
N of the church, is a grey ashlar house of *c.* 1830 on the double-
pile plan with symmetrical front and open porch. The approach
to the house passes thatched and timber-framed POOL
COTTAGE by the village pond and pump and the SCHOOL
HOUSE of 1897.

MANOR FARMHOUSE, near the church, is dated 1718 and built
for Robert Spencer, brick in typical Early Georgian style with
moulded wood modillion cornice and doorcase.

At the corner of Hames Lane, the former INSTITUTE (now a
house) of 1883, in the Queen Anne style in brick and stone
with tile-hung gables and bench seating in the porch. Originally given by trustees of William Frederick Inge as a reading
room and lecture room with a cottage attached for the
caretaker.

NO MANS HEATH
Newton Regis

2000

At the junction of four counties and originally extra-parochial,
No Mans Heath was an area of open common notorious in the
C18 for squatters and for prize-fighting. The village grew up in
the later C19 and is partly in Staffordshire.

ST MARY THE VIRGIN. In the care of a local trust since 2003.
High Victorian Gothic of 1863 in red brick with stone dressings
and banded slate roofs.* Chancel, nave and S porch, with N
vestry added by *F. T. Beck* in 1900–1. Thin iron gable cross over
E end. W bellcote. Nave details mainly Perp, but chancel has N
and S lancets and circular E window with sexfoil stone tracery.
Moulded stone chancel arch with polychromatic extrados.
Open roofs. – FONT. Circular with carved shields, on a clustered pier. – STAINED GLASS. E window by *Clayton & Bell*,
1866. – S windows by *G. J. Baguley*, nave 1901 and chancel
1908.

NORTHEND
Burton Dassett

3050

Little Dassett and Northend form a continuous settlement
wrapped round the north end of the Dassett Hills.

*Said to be by *G. E. Street*, but no firm evidence has been found.

ALL SAINTS, built as a school and chapel by *William Kendall*, 1851. Chancel and nave with lancets, and formerly a bellcote. Reordered internally and liturgical orientation reversed by *Trepess, Harley-Smith & Steel*, 1971.

The former SCHOOL, S of the church, 1886. L-shaped. Stone front with castellated door surround. Side walls brick.

METHODIST CHURCH (Wesleyan), Bottom Street. Gabled brick front with arched windows and datestone, 1831. On rising ground above a small green, making a pleasant group with the adjoining Sunday School of 1900 and neighbouring ironstone cottages. Down Top Street past the village hall, OLD CHAPEL COTTAGE is the former Primitive Methodist chapel, dated 1855.

GREEN FARM HOUSE, Bottom End. Dated 1654. Ironstone with mullioned windows. Symmetrical, with two gables.

The MANOR HOUSE, part 1664 with two symmetrical gables. Sympathetic additions l. of the main front and new raised entrance by *W. T. Loveday* for Mrs Rosselli, 1938. Further minor work (after a fire) by *Loveday & Davis*, 1940. C18 gate-piers with ball finials.

CHAPEL GROUNDS at Little Dassett, S of the manor. A former chapel with house attached. The chapel was late C13 and had remains of a Dec W window until 1943. On the E was a two-storeyed addition, adapted in 1632 as a house for a recusant priest. After decades of agricultural use and neglect, it was converted to a house by *Clews Architects*, 1998. Few distinguishing features remain.

NORTON LINDSEY

2060

HOLY TRINITY. Small. A date is recorded, 1208. In the chancel small early C13 lancets. Of the same date the S doorway. Reconstructed Dec E window. Restored by *Ewan Christian*, 1872–5, when the N aisle and double bellcote were added. Embattled N vestry, 1880. – PULPIT incorporating Jacobean panels and one dated 1682. – STAINED GLASS. E window by *Hardman*, 1890, the rest by *F. Holt & Co.*, 1892–7. All donated by the Rev. H.J. Torre of Norton Curlieu, also said to have been the designer.

At the churchyard gate, the old SCHOOLROOM, 1851: brick with round-headed windows.

Where Main Street joins Wolverton Road, a Diamond Jubilee SIGNPOST, 1897: triangular stone pedestal and fanciful ironwork.

The WINDMILL, ¼ m. NW of the church, 1802–3, with nearby miller's cottage, 1804 but much altered. A well-preserved tower mill with boat cap and remains of two common sails. The tower designed with offset windows for maximum strength.

NORTON LODGE, at Norton Curlieu, N towards the Warwick
Road. Italianate, with bracketed eaves and portico, late 1850s.
Probably built for the Rev. H. J. Torre.

3090

NUNEATON

INTRODUCTION

The town, originally Eaton or Etone, takes its name from the
abbey, a Benedictine nunnery founded here *c.* 1155. The conventual remains are incorporated into the late Victorian church (St
Mary's) on part of the site. The town grew up nearby with a
market place at the convergence of the main roads and near the
River Anker with its crossing in Bridge Street. Nuneaton gained
a market charter in 1233. As early as the C17, however, proximity
to the Warwickshire coalfields brought industry and expansion.
The Coventry Canal, passing through Nuneaton, was completed
between Coventry and Atherstone in 1769. By 1800 Nuneaton
was a place of some size and importance, with an economy based
on weaving, brickmaking and tile-making, and quarrying as well
as coal mining. Mount Judd, a tall slag heap w of the town, is
the most prominent reminder of Nuneaton's former extractive
industries. The Trent Valley Railway (West Coast main line)
arrived in 1847, with later connections to Coventry, Leicester and
Birmingham. The population in 2011 was 70,721. It remained
fairly stable through the middle years of the C19, but increased
sharply from 8,465 in 1881 to 26,581 in 1911 and 41,875 in 1921.
This was a period of much building activity, leaving a great many
good buildings of the Victorian, Edwardian and post-war periods.
Nuneaton gained municipal borough status in 1907, having
become an urban district in 1894. Primarily associated with
Chilvers Coton (*see* Suburbs, below), the novelist George Eliot
(1819–80) spent her early life in Nuneaton and the town is represented by Milby in her novels.

In the later decades of the C19, many buildings in the town
were designed by *F. J. Yates* of Birmingham, who enjoyed the

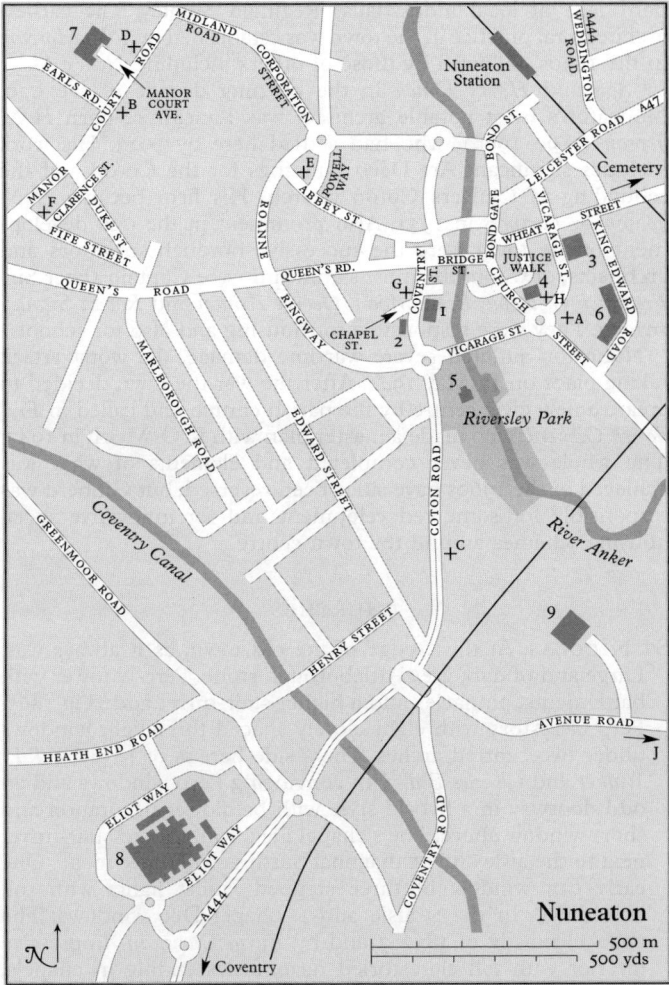

Nuneaton

500 m
500 yds

A	St Nicholas	I	Town hall
B	St Mary (Abbey Church)	2	Police station and
C	Our Lady of the Angels (R.C.)		courthouse (former)
D	Baptist church	3	Northern Justice Centre
E	St. John's Methodist Church	4	Library
F	Free Methodist church	5	Museum and Art Gallery
G	United Reformed church	6	King Edward VI College
H	Christadelphian Hall	7	Manor Medical Centre
J	Heart of England	8	George Eliot Hospital
	Crematorium	9	Pingles Leisure Centre
			and Swimming Pool

patronage of local industrialist Reginald Stanley. The earliest architectural practice in the town was established by *John Moreton* in the 1890s, followed by those of others including *Henry Mayo & Son* and *Harry Quick* in the opening decade of the C20. Nuneaton's most notable architect was Lancashire-born *H. N. Jepson* (1890–1966), who had settled here by 1923. His work includes significant Art Deco buildings for the Co-op and the rebuilding of Chilvers Coton church. His firm became *H. N. Jepson & Partners* in 1951. Also prominent in the C20 development of the town were the successive borough surveyors and architects, of whom the most significant were Captain (later Sir) *Frederick C. Cook*, *R. C. Moon*, *George Ashton* and *Robert Stanley Ireland*. They were responsible for housing and also for schools.

Nuneaton suffered severe wartime damage, the worst attack taking place on 17 May 1941. After the war the town decided to create a new civic centre by the parish church and called in *Frederick Gibberd*, who made a master plan with R. C. Moon in 1947. The whole was never completed and elements of what was achieved in the 1960s have since been reversed, but Gibberd was responsible for some redevelopment and for innovative social housing schemes around the town centre.

CHURCHES

St Nicolas. At the E edge of the old town, as it always was. Large and of dark grey Attleborough stone. Perp W tower with battlements, pinnacles and a higher stair-turret added in 1865. Perp clerestory with eight closely spaced three-light windows under two-centred arches. The s side here is of 1838 by *T. L. Walker* and *Charles Ball* with convincing Perp windows and an odd doorway in a hybrid style with ballflower decoration and short window above. The s chapel Dec, with canted stair-turret next to the aisle and SE diagonal buttress with ogee niche. One early C14 window of three stepped lancet lights with roll mouldings. In the N aisle and N chapel Dec windows. The chancel mostly of 1852–3 and by *Ewan Christian*. Impressive interior with tall clerestoried nave, aisles ending in chapels, Victorian chancel arch with pierced tracery in the spandrels and Christian's long chancel with five-light E window of reticulated tracery. Good ceiled nave and aisle roofs with bosses. The N chapel (now the organ chamber) was St Katherine's Chapel, part 'newe' in 1525, and the arches to the chancel must be of that date. The C14 Lady Chapel on the s was 're-edified' as a chantry (the Leeke chapel) before 1507 and had a two-bay Dec arcade extended by Christian, his E bay with big capitals and the others with none. In this chapel a Dec vaulted SEDILE with nodding ogee arch and a PISCINA combined with a CREDENCE SHELF. Big corbel head l. of the E window. The nave arcades are a puzzle and may not be simple late Perp as they seem. The arcades are slightly offset. They have a typical Perp section and small capitals, their abaci curving forward and backward. Above, the wall is panelled and connects with the clerestory. The E face of the tower shows the roof-line of the nave before there was a clerestory. So what was the arcade like then? Why should the piers start from high plinths of chamfered lozenge shape, just as the shape of the early C16 piers of the N chapel still is? The mouldings of the chapel arches are indeed earlier than those of the aisle arcades. Were the piers re-cut with the panels when the clerestory was added? And when? There is an evenness and smoothness about it all that makes one think of the C17. Internal reordering in 1965 when the C18 N and S galleries were removed, and again in 2010 when seating replaced pews. C15 N vestry at W end of N aisle, extended in 1913 and later opened out to link with the ST NICOLAS HALL AND COMMUNITY CENTRE between the church and old school, by *Kenneth Holmes*, 2009. – Carved oak PULPIT by *Bodley*, 1902. – STAINED GLASS. Surviving fragments of Victorian windows destroyed in 1941, mostly by *Burlison & Grylls*. Theirs the incomplete S chapel S window, 1921. – MONUMENTS. Sir Marmaduke Constable †1560, by *Richard Parker* of Burton upon Trent (JB) and restored in 1854 by *Edward Richardson*. Sir Marmaduke obtained the lands of the dissolved priory in 1540. Alabaster. Recumbent effigy, bearded. His head rests on a helmet. The crest on the helmet is a boat fully rigged. The inscription on the tomb-chest is in black letter. – Antony Trotman †1703 and wife Abigail †1705. Two frontal busts, flatly carved. In the predella, a corpse in a winding sheet. The sheet is tied to the architectural framework. It is a rustic job but quite impressive. – William Craddock †1833. By the *Patent Works, Westminster*. Urn at the top.

Immediately N of the church, now linked by the hall, the OLD GRAMMAR SCHOOL dated 1696. Small but with a middle tower with a hexagonal cupola and ornamental weathervane; largely rebuilt after bomb damage of 1941. To the E, the former VICARAGE (now offices), a mid-C17 building with shaped gables. Moulded surrounds to the windows. Major alterations here by *T. L. Walker* for the Rev. Robert Savage, 1845–6, including the added garden wing in a delightfully sympathetic style.

ST MARY (abbey church), Manor Court Road. A church created since 1876–7 among the ruins of the Benedictine nunnery founded here *c.* 1155–60. The lower nave walls are all that is left of the first church, and the chancel and N transept were apparently rebuilt after the central tower had fallen early in the C13. In 1236–8 the nuns were busy rebuilding their church. The nunnery was dissolved in 1539 and converted into a manor house for the Constable family; it later fell to ruin until conveniently revived by the Victorians to meet the needs of Nuneaton's expanding western suburbs. As Lingen Barker commented in 1890, 'A spirited attempt has been made here . . . to reproduce the old Abbey . . . instead of building an ordinary new church.' Mangled, yet in parts powerful, the result hardly succeeds in preserving the monastic remains, nor does it afford an entirely satisfactory setting for worship. Outside the rock-facing is hard and unlovable. Inside the effect is marred by makeshift roofing. Jagged stones and temporary brickwork without, more jagged bits within. The additions, moreover, were designed primarily for archae-ological correctness – complementing the remains, maybe, but decidedly second-rate as Victorian architecture. They can be quickly summarized. First *Clapton Crabb Rolfe*'s nave and temporary chancel, later replaced, of 1876–7. Next came *Harold Brakspear*'s E.E.-style chancel, 1906, followed by the lean-to S vestry, 1903. Lastly, the N transept, also by *Brak-spear*, 1929–31. The S transept was never rebuilt, and the proposed central tower got no further than the illustrative scheme produced by *Brakspear* in 1904.

One enters the site from the W past the ruins of the last three bays of the aisleless nave. The walls have shallow buttresses. There was no W doorway. Rolfe's nave has a deplorably per-functory brick W wall and porch and tiny bellcote, but stepping in, one senses what the restorers hoped to achieve – a cruci-form church of some dignity enhanced by the antiquity of its parts. Four-bay nave, with Neo-Norman triforium windows high up, not only on the former cloister side, but also on the N side. Blind intersecting arcading below with dogtooth, on shafts with waterleaf interrupted by the slender wall-shafts. Then the crossing, the one place where one becomes aware of the aesthetic loss suffered by the disappearance of the church. It never had aisles or chancel aisles. Yet the crossing piers are overwhelmingly mighty. They stand high up, though to differ-ing heights. They consist of responds to two sides each; and each respond of four orders. On the SW pier two late C12 capi-tals can still be seen, and also the springing of the vault. The E piers differ considerably from the W piers. They must be of after the fall of the tower and are fully E.E., with detached in front of attached shafts. In rebuilding the chancel and N tran-sept *Brakspear* had the foundations to go by, and in the case of the transept more, e.g. the SE triple vaulting-shaft standing on a corbel and capital. The transept had a W porch whose foundations survive. So this was probably the congregational part of the church. The S transept was never restored, and bricked up instead, but the ruin outside shows the jamb of a big E window. The S wall stands up high. – ROOD SCREEN by *Brakspear*, 1912. – FONT from Godstow Priory, Oxon: octag-onal, on four clustered columns with fillets. – TILES. Quite a number of medieval tiles representing the wheel of life are laid in the floor, but now covered by carpeting. – STAINED GLASS. E window by *Powell*, 1919. – Figures of saints in chancel windows mostly by *Powell*, 1920s to 1956, and two more similar, but anonymous, 1978–9. – N transept, 1931. – Abstract Resurrection window in S transept by *Roger Sargent*, 2006.

The CLOISTER was S of the nave, as usual, and the one baf-fling detail is a double shaft in the angle between nave and S transept, rather too high and too big to be inside a cloister or connected with the customary doorways from nave and transept into the cloister. Otherwise there is something recognizable of the monastic E range, including the excavated lowest courses of the jambs of the chapter house entrance. The range went a good deal further S than the S range of the cloister. Of outbuildings, one was the brewhouse and has a rounded projection for the vat. It stands S of the former VICARAGE, which is by *Rolfe*, 1885: Arts and Crafts, with medieval detailing and mullioned windows, interestingly combined as if to suggest that the house had evolved over several centuries.

OUR LADY OF THE ANGELS (R.C.), Coton Road. 1838 and by *J. A. Hansom*, then living at Caldecote. Originally a plain aisleless brick building with lancet windows. Enlarged with transepts, aisled and clerestoried nave of three bays by *Thomas Ignatius McCarthy* of Coalville, 1910–11. Nave and aisles remodelled and extended with solid W tower with extreme lancet openings by *McCarthy & Collings*, 1936. Good open interior, with side altars in transepts. – STAINED GLASS. Two spherical triangle windows by *Hardman*, 1909–10. – N aisle, *Hardman*, 1980. – The rest probably by *G. E. Sheedy*, from 1947 to late 1950s. Adjoining PRESBYTERY, after 1855.

BAPTIST CHURCH, Manor Court Road. *John Wills* of Derby, 1899. Gothic, with lancets and plate tracery. Inside, galleried with hammerbeam roof partly supported on iron columns through the galleries. The adjoining school of the same date replaced by present hall, 1987. – STAINED GLASS. War memorial window by *Abbot & Co.*, †1919.

ST JOHN'S METHODIST CHURCH, Abbey Street.* *A. H. Gardner*, 1966, with a boxy, un-ecclesiastical exterior. Walnut FONT by *Gardner*.

FREE METHODIST CHURCH, Fife Street at the corner of Clarence Street. *George Baines & Son*, 1905, in their unmistakable free Gothic, brick with white-painted stone dressings, big Perp-style window and side turrets with cinquefoiled tops and thin rods with vanes.

UNITED REFORMED CHURCH (originally Congregational), junction of Coventry Street and Chapel Street. By *Ingall & Son* of Birmingham, 1903–4. Wild pinnacled front and prominent ventilator turret. Brick and terracotta in a free Gothic style. CHAPEL HOUSE alongside, same style and date.

CHRISTADELPHIAN HALL, in Vicarage Street, facing the parish church; *H. Mayo & Son*, 1907, an ordinary church room.

CEMETERY, Oaston Road. Laid out by *Richard Ashwell* of Coventry for the Burial Board, 1874–5. Chapels, 1874, originally separated by a covered passage, its openings blocked on conversion to a crematorium in 1957. Simple Gothic. Clumsy window tracery in the ends, serrated brickwork in the sides. At the entrance, a lodge or keeper's house, 1936, probably by *R. C. Moon*, Borough Surveyor.

---

*Replacing a chapel by *W. S. Burton* of Leicester, 1872–3, enlarged and refronted with the addition of a tower and spire by *F. J. Yates* of Birmingham in 1891. It was destroyed by fire in 1941.

HEART OF ENGLAND CREMATORIUM, Heart of England Way, 1½ m. SE. *Critchell Harrington & Partners* of Chichester, 1995. Brick and hardwood with wide-sweeping roofs. Porte cochère with twisted brick columns.

PUBLIC BUILDINGS

TOWN HALL, Coventry Street. By *Peacock & Bewlay* of Birmingham, 1934. Large and dully Neo-Georgian, but on its own and a dominating presence. Grand colonnaded front with copper-covered cupola above. Inside, a pillared and panelled top-lit council chamber. Alongside to the S in Coton Road, the COUNCIL HOUSE, 1988. Brick, with projecting second floor and entrance front.

Former POLICE STATION AND COURTHOUSE, Coton Road, opposite the town hall. Now Yorkshire Bank. 1896–7 by *John Willmot*, the County Surveyor, in 'a judicious mixture of Italian and Gothic'. The Mining School occupied the central portion of the building until 1923. Behind in Chapel Street, the old cells and separate superintendent's residence, also 1896.

NORTHERN JUSTICE CENTRE, Vicarage Street. *Frank Shaw Associates Ltd*, of Chesterfield, 2005. The first project of its kind in England and Wales, housing all police, criminal justice, probation and support services in one place. Three storeys in different colours. Raised glass-fronted centre with segmental roof and porch canopy. It replaces the now demolished 1960s police station and courts by *Eric Davies*, the County Architect.

LIBRARY, Justice Walk. The one remnant of the 1960s civic buildings for the town. By *Frederick Gibberd*, 1961–2. Pevsner thought it 'a strange building, impressive, monumental, but undeniably part of that revival of historicism which has lately become an alarming feature of the architectural scene'. It has a single-storeyed block, of chalk ashlar below, of blueish-grey rendering above, arched throughout and arched so that lintels separate the oblong lower part of the openings from the arches. This and the absence of all mouldings Pevsner saw as 'pure Ledoux or even more Gilly, i.e. Neoclassical of the end of the C18'. The porch, although also triple-arched, is the only less formal element. At the back a two-storey administration block, all ashlar. Inside, one big open space, the vast roof supported only by light and almost invisible columns.

MUSEUM AND ART GALLERY, Riversley Park. By *Horace J. Ash*, 1916–17. Modest, classical, in red brick with stone quoins and doorcase under a segmental pediment in the middle projection. Central Venetian window, the upper floors otherwise blank. Parapet. Sympathetically enlarged 1990 with accommodation for the register office on lower floors.

The museum stands in RIVERSLEY PARK, given by Alderman Melly and opened in 1907. Features include the River Anker bridges, bandstand, ornamental entrance gates, war memorials etc. At the edge, RIVERSLEY PARK CLINIC,

1931. In front of the museum the BOER WAR MEMORIAL, 1905, the original figure by *Adolphus E. L. Rost* stolen and replicated in 2008 by *Allan Beattie Heriot*. First erected in Bond Gate.

KING EDWARD VI COLLEGE, King Edward Road. Formerly the grammar school, founded in 1552 by the parish church but on its present site from 1880. The main block is of that date by *Clapton Crabb Rolfe*, still with the Gothic motifs of Street and Butterfield schools but also with the tile-hanging of Norman Shaw. Carving by *Harry Hems*. Later additions include a block of 1903, and the successfully placed crescent by *Essex, Goodman & Suggitt* of Birmingham, 1959, containing assembly hall, gymnasium, and laboratory. Library and administration block, 1975. This is concave towards the church and vertically weatherboarded all along the first floor. Neatly extended by *Alan C. Riley Associates*, 2007.

Of SCHOOLS generally, there is a good mix of types and styles. At ABBEY SCHOOL, Aston Road, part of the original 1848 school remains: patterned brick with heavy mullioned-and-transomed windows in blue brick. Sympathetic additions of 1996 and 2009 as infill between the 1848 range and a large block of 1896. From 1902 to 1974 elementary education came under the borough council. New schools of the early C20 include QUEEN'S ROAD, 1904–5, with two-storey towers with pavilion roofs, and PARK AVENUE in Attleborough, 1907–8, in brick with stone bands and Tudor details, both by *Harry Quick*. The county council, responsible for higher education, built the Girls' High School (now ETONE COMMUNITY SCHOOL), in Leicester Road. By *F. P. Trepess* of Warwick, 1909–10. Scholastic Jacobethan. Its sixth form centre facing the railway by *BBLB* architects opened in 2011.

Of the inter-war schools MANOR PARK, Beaumont Road, 1927–8, has a two-storey hipped roof block flanked by long single-storey ranges with covered walkways, veranda style. HIGHAM LANE, however, of 1938–9, is modernistic, with off-centre rounded tower. ST THOMAS MORE ROMAN CATHOLIC SCHOOL (originally Arbury Secondary School), Greenmoor Road, by *H. N. Jepson*, 1937, is a distinguished low two-storey design in the brick style of contemporary Holland with streamlined corners, brick fins and emphatic Art Deco tower at the centre over the entrance. *Ashton*, the Borough Surveyor, was responsible for some rather economical post-war schools, including MIDDLEMARCH, College Street, 1950–2, and GEORGE ELIOT (Caldwell Junior), 1951, and secondary, 1961.

MANOR MEDICAL CENTRE, Manor Court Avenue. At the core is the former COTTAGE HOSPITAL by *Yates*, 1893. Central block with hipped roof, linked by covered walkways to separate blocks l. and r. with moulded brick and stone aedicules to the gables. Much extended, 1899 and 1920, and then with various additions by *Jepson* until the 1950s, including Neo-Georgian JEPSON HOUSE, at the head of Manor Court Avenue.

Refurbished for its present use in 1993 by the *Design Büro* of
Leamington.

GEORGE ELIOT HOSPITAL, 1 m. SW, on the site of the 1809
workhouse (Coton Lodge) which became a hospital in 1948.
Largely new buildings, 1991–4, but retaining the maternity
hospital built for the Birmingham Regional Hospital Board
(principal architect *G. E. Gott*), 1966–7. Inside, a portrait bust
of the Queen by *J. B. Letts*, 1994. Outside, George Eliot statue
by *Letts*, 1996, and big hospital sign on a brick base with a
figurative sculpture of a family group by *John McKenna*, 1990s.

PINGLES LEISURE CENTRE AND SWIMMING POOL, off The
Avenue, by *FaulknerBrowns* of Newcastle, 2003, replacing the
previous pool, 1965. Glass and silver cladding, with bright red
painted trimmings. Wide segmental roof and thin tower above
the entrance.

RAILWAY STATION. The railway came in 1847. The first station
by *J. W. Livock* (cf. Atherstone) was replaced in 1875 and again
in 1915 by *Ernest C. Trench*, LNWR Chief Engineer. The clock
tower with its swag decoration clearly influenced by G.C.
Horsley's Harrow & Wealdstone Station of 1910. New platforms and overbridge by *Railtrack Plc*, 2004, with plain lift
tower.

In Oaston Road, SE of the station, the Power SIGNAL BOX
on the West Coast main line is by *Paul Hamilton c.* 1964.

PERAMBULATIONS

Neither the parish church nor the abbey developed into urban
nuclei and Nuneaton centres instead on its market place. The
ring road, although it breaks the visual continuity of all the main
roads leading out of the town, encloses a natural area for the
first perambulation. A second perambulation deals with outer
Nuneaton.

1. Town centre

This perambulation begins in the central market area, by the C12
a large open space at the E end of Abbey Street, infilled in
medieval times to create a rectangle of streets, now pedestrianized, of which the MARKET PLACE provides the S side. In the
centre of its N side is its landmark, the CLOCK TOWER, facing
down Coventry Street, the clock on a tapered leaded base with
spike and weathervane, by *Wood & Kendrick*, 1901. Adjacent
SANTANDER (No. 25), decent but traditional, by *S. N. Cooke*,
1925. The liveliest building however is BARCLAYS BANK, at
the corner of Coventry Street, also by *Wood & Kendrick* for
the Birmingham Dudley & District Banking Co., 1896.
Renaissance-style in brick and terracotta, with lavish detail on
the balconies and around the entrance. On the S, No. 11
(originally Boots) in buff terracotta with ornate pinnacled
gable, 1907, very characteristic of their usual architect *Albert*

Bromley of Nottingham. Towards Abbey Gate, CLINTON CARDS (Nos. 19–20) was originally Burton's the tailor, and by *Harry Wilson*, their architect, 1929.

Down COVENTRY STREET, s of the bank, at the corner of Mill Walk is GEORGE ELIOT HOUSE by *Horace G. Bradley*, 1926. Brick with a canted corner topped by faience parapet on fat consoles. Opposite the town hall (*see* Public Buildings) and across Coton Road the former police station and courthouse (*see* Public Buildings), entirely on their own.

E of Market Place is BRIDGE STREET. At the junction with Newdegate Street, the handsome SANTANDER BANK, originally for the Union of London and Smiths Bank by *Bateman & Bateman*, 1909. English Renaissance-style, in stone and brick with arched hoods with shell tympana, prominent dormers and ornamental chimneys. Then the GEORGE ELIOT HOTEL (once the Bull Hotel) on the N, retaining elements of an 1820s refronting above street level. The s side all rebuilt without distinction since 1960 when the road was widened. At the far end is CHURCH STREET, and of the same era of rebuilding is the former POST OFFICE (1967–9), alongside plain two-storeyed POWELL HOUSE, built as the Crown Offices by the *Ministry of Works*, 1961. This faces the library (*see* Public Buildings). N, where Bridge Street joins BOND GATE, the former CONSERVATIVE CLUB on the corner, by *Charles W. Smith*, 1898–9; red brick with stone dressings. It has been shorn of its corner turret and gable but to Newdegate Street at first floor a recessed loggia with ogee arches and iron balconies. Some nice carved Free Style decoration. Further out on LEICESTER ROAD, by the ring road, the former Empire Hall and skating rink, later a cinema, nightclub etc., by *Owen & Ward*, 1909. Free Baroque.

NEWDEGATE STREET leads back to the centre over the river into a square at the crossing with Harefield Road. Former HSBC (empty in 2011) at No. 20, by *Goddard & Co.*, for the Leicestershire Banking Company, 1898–1900. Baroque, with rusticated ground floor and projecting pavilions at the corners. Alterations and matching side extensions for Midland Bank by *Whinney, Son & Austen Hall*, 1953 and 1961. Opposite, on the square's W side, HAWKINS (Kathleen House), by *James & Lister Lea* for Lloyds Bank, 1911; stone front, Baroque Revival style. Alongside, the former premises of J.C. Smiths of Stratford, 1935, probably by *Healing & Overbury*. In the square, the George Eliot statue by *John Barry Letts*, 1986. Up HAREFIELD ROAD is the 1956 BUS STATION, in the Festival style with clock tower and, opposite, the TELEPHONE EXCHANGE by the *Office of Works*, 1938, cubic brick Modernism. w of Harefield Road the ABBEYGATE shopping centre, built in 1966–8 as the Heron Way precinct forming part of a major redevelopment of the area by *E.S. Boyer & Partners*. Two-storey outer ranges with boxy oriels. Refurbished with an atrium roof by *Crampin Pring*, 1989. At the s entrance HERON HOUSE fronts Newdegate Street: a robust office block in the same style as

the rest but with upper storeys oversailing. Facing, at the
corner with Abbey Gate, the former GATE TEMPERANCE
HOTEL (now the Schoolwear Centre) built for Reginald
Stanley (*see* Manor Court, p. 489) by *Yates*, 1898. Old English
style of the West Midlands variety; the picturesquely composed
upper storeys have big ribbed chimneys and exuberant half-
timbered and jettied gables with sculpture panels, barley-twist
columns and a delightful domed balcony on the street corner.
Also by *Yates*, on ABBEY STREET which continues w out of
the centre, is the old LIBERAL CLUB, at the corner of Stratford
Street; of 1893–4, with shaped gables and an octagonal turret.
Very little of note except, on the N side, the Neoclassical former
SCALA THEATRE, 1914, built as the Grand Theatre but
quickly adapted as a cinema and renamed in 1915. By *H. Mayo
& Son*. Opposite and further out, a long row of NUNEATON
CO-OPERATIVE SOCIETY buildings. The three-storey block
of 1903 (originally Wilkinson & Son), possibly by *T. F. Tickner*,
was taken over by the Co-op and refurbished in the 1920s and
has a good Art Deco first-floor interior, probably by *Jepson*. To
the r. a block of 1913, then a long two-storey range (No. 22)
with an arcade, *c.* 1905, all originally with cresting and gables,
and *Jepson*'s 1928 extension with short columns *in antis* at
each floor. 100 yds further W by the Ringway, the former
RITZ CINEMA, by *Verity & Beverley* for the Union Cinema
group, in their streamlined *moderne* style, 1937. Big, brick with
thin courses projecting and severe outside (disused in 2011),
but said to retain well-preserved and colourful Art Deco
interiors.

s of Abbey Street is QUEENS ROAD. On the N side, the outstanding Art Deco front of the former NUNEATON CO-OPERATIVE
STORE by *Jepson*, 1938. Brick with faience dressings and steel
windows, the façade curving inward to a central fin with
faience lettering. Opposite is the ROPEWALK SHOPPING
CENTRE, by *Corstorphine & Wright*, 2005, replacing *Gibberd*'s
1969 Queen's Arcade. Generally well handled, especially the
entrances from Queens Road and Chapel Street and the high
glass skylight at the corner by Dugdale Street. Curved covered
walkways with pillared divisions between the shopfronts and
varied wall finishes. Less successful the gimmicky corner tower
and the open cage car park, both fronting the Ringway.

2. Outer Nuneaton

This perambulation takes in housing developments, public and
private.

From 1907 until well after the Second World War, Nuneaton
Borough Council ran an extensive housing programme. Of the
pre-war period, the BLACK-A-TREE ESTATE of 1937 towards
Stockingford is especially notable, its two-storey semi-detached
brick-and-pebbledash houses on a radial street plan. Post-war

building began in the SE part of the estate with housing in
WOOD STREET and VERNONS LANE, 1946. Under *Moon* and
Ashton as Borough Surveyors and *Robert Stanley Ireland* as
Borough Architect progress was rapid, with the 1,000th post-
war house completed in 1949, the 2,000th in 1953 and 3,000th
in 1956.

Some of these are close to the town centre. Just outside the ring
road there are blocks of flats and social housing, with major
concentrations E, S and W of the town. The three-storey
DEMPSTER COURT flats SW of the church are by *Gibberd*,
1950–1, and in his familiar low-key and intimate style, three
brick blocks informally arranged within green spaces planted
with trees. Some diaper patterns on the gable-ends. Those
along the W side of Coton Road, including forty-six flats at
TEMPLAR COURT, Prince's Street, are by *Jepson & Partners*,
1971. Further out to the SE, off Attleborough Road, ASHBY
COURT also by *Jepson & Partners*, 1972, of three block set
diagonally with linking ranges of garages. The same palette of
brown serrated-edge tile-hanging but with blue engineering
brick as the base. NW of the centre, between ABBEY STREET
and BURGAGE WALK, more by *Gibberd*, 1960, including some
long three-storey rows of flats and maisonettes with the concrete floor bands forming arches over the windows and to the
access balconies behind. On the other side of Abbey Street is
EDYVEAN-WALKER COURT, by *Gibberd & Associates*, 1973,
similar but less interesting.

Of private housing, the most notable area is the MANOR COURT
ESTATE W of the town centre. This is a middle-class residential
suburb laid out in 1891–2 for the industrialist Reginald Stanley
and the Tomkinson family who owned much of the priory
land. It has the best of Nuneaton's late Victorian and Edwardian housing, chiefly around Earls Road, Manor Park Road and
Manor Court Road itself. Nearby, the Pool Bank Street recreation ground, laid out in 1892. Many of the earlier buildings are
by *Yates*, who did Stanley's own house, MANOR COURT
(1894–5, now a care home), with corner turret and conical
roof, opposite the priory ruins in MANOR COURT ROAD, as
well as the cottage hospital, Manor Medical Centre (*see* Public
Buildings), nearby. Others by *Yates* on MANOR COURT ROAD
include two standard Arts and Crafts designs, MARDALE (No.
123, corner of Earls Road, 1893) and GAYTON HOUSE (No.
115, 1893), but also others of a more distinctively West Midlands character: LANSDOWNE TERRACE (1896), Nos. 108–116
with alternating gables in Jacobean style and half-timbering
between, and Nos. 118–124 taller with big timbered gables,
jettied over canted bays. Other architects represented include
T. J. Gordon of Leicester at BADEN HOUSE (No. 140, 1900),
and Nuneaton architects *R. H. Smith* at Nos. 102–104, *c.* 1905,
Arthur Moreton at Nos. 144–150, *c.* 1906, and *Henry Mayo &
Son* at Nos. 5–7 and 6–8 in 1909. Development of EARLS
ROAD on a double curve NW of Manor Court Road came after
1908, the earliest houses being again by *Mayo & Son*, 1909–11.

The later houses are decent, but lacking the architectural
assurance of those of the mid 1890s. *Ernest E. Shepherd* also
built here before the Great War, and some of the better inter-
war houses are by *J. B. Hingley* in the 1920s and *Jepson* from
the 1930s.

SUBURBS

ATTLEBOROUGH

HOLY TRINITY. By *Thomas Larkins Walker*, 1841–2. On a site
given by the Earl of Harrowby. The cost was £2,629 including
a Commissioners' grant. Brick, with lancets and closely set
buttresses. Tall apse with lancets, SW tower with later top and
spire rebuilt after lightning damage in 1936. Internally the
charm of the church is the tripartite arched, slightly stepped
division W of the apse and its slender shafts. The W window
echoes this by being of three stepped lancet lights. Gallery
access by tower stairs. Restored in 1889 and after bomb
damage in 1940. Reordering, gallery enlargement and NW
extension to church by *John D. Holmes*, 1992. – STAINED
GLASS. One S window by *G. Maile & Son Ltd*, 1929. – Bright
E apse window, *Lawrence Lee*, 1960.
The church forms a group with what remains to the W of the
much altered SCHOOL, 1848, and the old VICARAGE, by *Ewan
Christian*, 1855.
BAPTIST CHURCH, The Green. By *John Wills & Sons*, 1930, in
period chapel Gothic, with schoolroom behind. Old chapel
(now a warehouse) alongside, still with 'Baptist Chapel &
Schools' over the door.
DEVALL'S FUNERAL PARLOUR, The Green. On a corner site
with clock tower. By *Alan C. Riley Associates*, 2010, with back-
lit STAINED GLASS by *Aidan McRae Thomson* in the foyer and
in the seven chapels of rest.
ALBION BUILDINGS, Attleborough Road. Terrace of thirty
weavers' cottages, 1858. Originally three-storeyed with windows
lighting the 'top-shop' where the looms stood but reduced in
height in 1968 and savagely remodelled. Long frontage with
faintly Gothic ground-floor detailing. Opposite the RUGGER
TAVERN (previously New Inn), by *Seale & Riley*, 1911.

CAMP HILL

On the ridge NW of the town, overlooking the Anker valley and
Watling Street to the N and the steep valley towards Stockingford
on the S.

ST MARY AND ST JOHN, Cedar Road. *H. N. Jepson & Partners*,
1966–7. Steel-framed, with glazing between the walls and roof.
Tapering side towards the top-lit sanctuary with side walls
carried upwards externally as a tower. Finished outside with a
girder cross. Alongside, the original church, now the HALL, by
H. Mayo & Son, 1952.

St Anne (R.C.), Camp Hill Road. *Peter Thompson*, 1999–2000, replacing a prefabricated building of 1949. Square with angled corners, shallow-pitched roof and triangular-headed windows. – STAINED GLASS. A bright and thoughtful scheme by *Aidan McRae Thomson*, 2000–8.

Early C20 ribbon development along Tuttle Hill towards the WINDMILL, whose tower remains. More up Camp Hill Road towards Chapel End. C19 Camp Hill House was demolished in 1934. Borough council housing began with the GREEN LANE ESTATE, 1934, mainly for an influx of miners from northern England. On CAMP HILL ESTATE, 1950–8, some 370 homes built of 'no-fines' concrete. Further development and regeneration since 2005. The COMMUNITY CENTRE, including library, education centre and youth centre, is by *Brown Matthews Architects* of Warwick, 2008.

CHILVERS COTON

An extensive parish originally covering Griff, Bermuda, Stockingford and Arbury. Chilvers Coton is the Shepperton of the novels of George Eliot (Mary Ann Evans) who was baptized here in 1819. Her father, Robert Evans, was the land agent on the Arbury estate. Mary Ann would have difficulty recognizing her old village today. Still picturesque even in the later C19, it is now absorbed in the sprawl s of Nuneaton. Of the houses illustrated on a map of 1684 all have gone.*

ALL SAINTS, Avenue Road. Mostly of 1944–7, by *H. N. Jepson*, after the church had been destroyed by bombing in 1941. Built by German prisoners of war, and decorated by them, naïvely, including the MONUMENT in the churchyard which, stylistically, looks 1910 rather than 1950. Extended by *Jepson* in 1957–8. Broad, with wide flat-roofed aisles and large s transept. Vestry flanking N side of tower. The W tower is Perp and has a base frieze of quatrefoils. It has clasping buttresses up to the hoodmould over the W window and diagonal buttresses above. The shell of the chancel is old, the E window with intersecting tracery. The N transept (now the organ chamber) by *F. C. Penrose*, 1890. His, too, the chancel arch inside. In the nave, square brick piers to arcades with shallow segmental arches. Parquet flooring.

W of the church, the CHURCH HALL, 1932, brick with stone banding and Tudorish doorways to main entrance. To its s, the VICARAGE, in similar style, 1934. Both by *Jepson*.

METHODIST CHURCH, Edward Street. Big brick church, 1957–8, replacing one of 1904 bombed in 1941. – STAINED GLASS. Three apse windows by *Abbott & Co. Ltd*, 1958.

METHODIST CHURCH, Heath End. Disused in 2010. By *F. J. Yates*, 1903. Brick and Bath stone. Free Style with fussy

---

* Coton House, described in the first edition of this guide, has been replaced by an old people's complex, SHEPPERTON COURT.

detailing to the street façade. Opposite, the HEATH END CHURCH, built as a Methodist school by *J. B. Hingley*, 1932.

Former FREE SCHOOL, Avenue Road, NE of the church (now Heritage Centre). Founded by Lady Elizabeth Newdigate in 1735. Much altered, but the main building based on a design of *c.* 1766 by *Sir Roger Newdigate* with 1846 and later C19 extensions. Not Gothick, but entirely classical. Tall hip-roofed central block with a segmental-headed archway, two-storey range to S and linked pavilions. Grey Attleborough sandstone ashlar, with hipped roofs.

The centre of Chilvers Coton is dominated by the COTON ARCHES, a railway viaduct built in the 1860s to replace the temporary bridge on the Nuneaton to Coventry line, opened in 1850. Its piers once crowded by small buildings, it now strides clear over a traffic island since road improvements in 1974. To the NW, a network of Late Victorian streets off Edward Street remains substantially intact. In Edward Street itself, the former MISSION CHURCH by *F. C. Penrose*, 1899 (now a day centre). Off Fitton Street CHILVERS COTON COMMUNITY INFANT SCHOOL is by *E. E. Shepherd*, 1910, with shaped gables, brick striped with stone and a central hall. In Prince's Avenue, a plum brick building with Diocletian window and twin turrets (originally the ST JOHN'S AMBULANCE HEAD-QUARTERS), by *H. N. Jepson*, 1923. In Marlborough Road, remnants of the massive COURTAULD factory by *Harry Quick*, 1920, originally a five-storeyed block with a clock tower at one corner. Preserved are the entrance, dated 1920, and ground-floor walls to the OLD MILL SURGERY.

In the Bull Ring, at the NE edge of the George Eliot Hospital site (*see* p. 486), early C19 MERCHANT HOUSE, restored as apart-ments since 2005. Brick, three bays with pretty glazing. Attached rear workshop section, two storeys with large round-arched iron windows.

S of the village, large areas of Nuneaton Borough COUNCIL HOUSING. The earliest, the Middlemarch Road Estate, 1931. Then at Hill Top, above the canal, 1947, and below, 1949.

At BERMUDA, ¾ m. SW, a colliery village of ninety cottages, 1893. Built in just twelve working weeks for the Griff Colliery Company to house workers for their New Winnings (later known as Griff 'Clara') mine. A distinct entity, surprisingly intact, but now surrounded by late C20 industrial and housing development.

GRIFF HOUSE, 1 m. S of the church. The Evans family home 1820–41. C17 farmhouse with five-bay front of *c.* 1800, now part of a large hotel complex.

STOCKINGFORD

Stockingford was Paddiford Common in the novels of George Eliot and her Mr Tryan (based on the Rev. John Edward Jones †1831) was its parson. Coal has been dug here since at least the C14, with considerable expansion in the later C19. The last pit closed in 1928 but brick and tile-making, Stockingford's other major industry, continued until 1969.

ST PAUL. By *John Russell*, 1822–3, and a rare example of a provincial Commissioners' church not in the Gothic style. Termed Grecian in contemporary sources. It cost £2,340. Red brick with deep eaves, low-pitched roof and large round-arched windows in blank arches. Painted wooden tracery of the Lombardic type, probably 1870. The original chancel was similar and in scale like the present vestries. w tower with blind louvred openings, round belfry windows – later filled with clock dials – and a balustrade. Mean Gothic chancel by *J. R. Veall* of Wolverhampton, 1897. w gallery. Internal reordering by *Inclusive Design Ltd* (*Mark Goodwill-Hodgson*), 2008. Church Centre and porch on s by *J. D. Holmes*, 1994–5. The centre octagonal with projecting wings and an open pyramid lantern. – STAINED GLASS. War memorial e window by *R. Anning Bell*, 1921.

NUNEATON COMMUNITY CHURCH (originally Wesleyan), Church Road. Built with schoolroom. By *F. J. Yates*, 1899; Free Style Gothic.

CONGREGATIONAL CHURCH, Croft Road. Built as Independent Methodist church, 1897, for congregation established in 1833. Mixed style. Façade with large shaped gable and round window above a Gothic door and windows with Y-tracery.

METHODIST CHURCH, Arbury Road. 1881. Late and debased Ruskinian Gothic with wheel window in gable. Speckled brick with red and blue brick and local terracotta dressings. Schoolroom and offices behind originally 1888, rebuilt in yellow brick.

CEMETERY, Bucks Hill. 1912, with lodge, chapel and boundary walls. All by *Frederick C. Cook*, Borough Surveyor.

Stockingford is a sprawl of later C19 and early C20 terraced houses, many dated, built for the miners and brick and tile workers. Many are ornamented with local terracotta. This is at the edge of the Arbury Hall estate (*see* p. 106), whose towered gatehouse faces the s end of Church Road on Arbury Road. The pit and kilns were at the other end at Whittleford. Since the closure of the tile works in 1969 the area has been redeveloped for housing, with part of the Whittleford site being cleared as an open space.

Few buildings of special note, but at the e end of ARBURY ROAD No. 14 (s side) is a former Nuneaton Co-operative Society building with a good faience-decorated Art Deco front, by *H. N. Jepson*, 1931.

WEDDINGTON

Originally a separate parish, brought into Nuneaton in 1931.

ST JAMES. Norman origins; largely rebuilt for Gilbert Adderley of Weddington Hall in 1733 after an earlier fire. The shell is

Georgian, but the character is wholly of *A. W. Blomfield*'s restoration, 1880–1. The windows Gothicized in a style of *c.* 1300,
handled without zest. Brick on older sandstone foundations.
Nave, chancel, w tower and s porch. Tower has brick pyramid
roof with awkward lucarnes and Star of David tracery in one
belfry window. C14 N vestry of stone with blocked N window
flanked by quatrefoil openings. Reordering and NW extension
by *J. D. Holmes*, 2000. – Oak REREDOS with carved panels and
screen (resited to w wall), 1909. – FONT. Norman, tub-shaped.
Interlacing round-headed arches and, above them, a band of
rosettes. – STAINED GLASS. E window by *Burlison & Grylls*,
1883. – S nave windows by *Kempe & Co.*, 1916, and *Jane
Gray*, 1990. – Another probably by *T. W. Camm*, 1905. –
MONUMENT in vestry to Humphrey Adderley Sen. (†1598)
and Jun. (†1637), 1639. Panelled pilasters, steep pediment and
shields.

Residential development began in the 1930s around CASTLE
ROAD and SHAWE AVENUE on the site of Weddington
Hall (*Robert Lugar* for Lionel Place, *c.* 1805; demolished 1928).
This was followed by *Wimpey* housing, 1959–60, E of the
main road.

NUTHURST

An ancient chapelry of Hampton-in-Arden, 7 m. to the NNE. The
ecclesiastical parish is Nuthurst but the village is better known
as HOCKLEY HEATH. The settlement grew up from the early
C19 where the Birmingham to Stratford road crosses the Stratford-
upon-Avon Canal.

ST THOMAS, Hockley Heath. 1879–80 by *John Cotton*. Built
shortly after the Baptist church at nearby Umberslade (q.v.).
Red brick with some blue brick patterns. Style of *c.* 1300. N
tower with the bell-openings in steep gables reaching up into
the spire. The spire is of yellow brick with decorative patterns
in red. Inside yellow brick facing too, with red patterns and
carved stonework. The carving by *Roddis* of Birmingham. Odd
w wall with three widely spaced veritable arrowslit lancets and
a rose. The tower also has such lancets. w end partitioned off
with wooden screen to nave, 1999. – STAINED GLASS. Mostly
by *William Pearce Ltd*, E and one N window 1907, another S,
1912. – One by *Jones & Willis*, †1918. – Good S window by
Theodora Salusbury, †1933.

Former Nuthurst MORTUARY CHAPEL (privately owned and
semi-derelict in 2011), ½ m. SSW. By *J. B. Harper*, 1834–5. Red
brick, stuccoed, with lancets and short chancel with wooden
Y-tracery in E window. Used as the parish church until 1880.
It replaced a medieval chapel on the site.

VICARAGE, immediately s of church, by *W.H. Bidlake*, 1896. The INSTITUTE on Stratford Road by *Ingall & Son*, 1892, with the GEORGE V MEMORIAL HALL by *Bidlake*, 1912. Further s on Stratford Road, the ROYAL OAK, 1937, is recognizably by *F. W.B. Yorke*, although much altered.

In School Road, the two-storey SCHOOL (Hockley Heath Academy) of 1913 by *Willmot, Fowler & Willmot* with low classroom blocks on each side, extended in 1934 by *A. C. Bunch*, County Architect, and subsequently.

OFFCHURCH

3060

ST GREGORY. Norman and E.E. with Perp w tower. Some restoration in 1866–8. N vestry and organ chamber added 1898. These are the certainties. But most of the windows are altered and thus unreliable for dating. Norman, then, the nave masonry. A blocked s window visible inside. N doorway with one order of columns and, in the hoodmould, saltire crosses, stars, etc. The chancel Norman too: one s window has an arched headstone decorated with a serpent (cf. Stoneleigh). Its N windows, if at all original, are completely redone. Late C13 chancel alterations include E window with cusped intersecting tracery and priest's doorway with nailhead decoration on the imposts. The C13 s porch, either re-set or remodelled, has clustered shafts and an ill-fitting arch under a steep gable. Good C15 w tower in grey ashlar. Inside the imposts of the wonky chancel arch repeat the earlier C12 motifs of the N door, though the arch itself was rebuilt later. – PULPIT. C18, with some marquetry. – Stone FONT and carved wooden CLERGY DESK and LECTERN by *Wood & Kendrick and E. F. Reynolds*, 1947. – STAINED GLASS. Mostly by *Wailes*, †1861 to 1868. – Three by *Hardman*, 1868–83. – E window by *Clayton & Bell*, †1874. – Abstract nave window by *Roger Sargent*, 2002. – MONUMENTS. Sir John Knightley †1688 and his wife Dame Mercy †1686. Tablet with broken pediment and pretty floral trails down the wings. – One blank tablet in chancel with pilasters and cherub in full-bottomed wig, probably by *Thomas Burman*, c. 1660 (GF). – John Wightwick Knightley †1814, by *Green*, Warwick. – Lady Aylesford †1911, by *H. S. Goodhart-Rendel*, 1914. Plain, but nicely lettered.

Former VICARAGE, w of the church. Of the early C18. Brick, small-scale. Five windows and two storeys plus attic. Altered roof-line. Quoins. Brick aprons to the windows. To the s side a big later bow shown in an 1819 engraving. Rear extensions after 1962 when the house became a diocesan retreat (closed in 2013). Victorian LODGE at entrance from the road.

Thatched cottages in School Hill and in Welsh Road below – the old drover's route which enters Offchurch over a sandstone ashlar BRIDGE across the Leam, 1785. Opposite the pub, TUDOR COTTAGE and WISTERIA COTTAGE adjoining are probably a late C15 hall house with C17 cross-wing behind.

OFFCHURCH BURY, 1 m. NW. Once a large and rambling house built around a medieval grange belonging to Coventry Priory, enlarged for the Knightleys in the 1560s and 1660s. Much reduced in size in 1954. Of the C17 building only the re-erected porch arches remain. The extant portion has the S front as rebuilt for John Wightwick Knightley *c.* 1792–4. The castellated façade is Gothick, ashlar, seven bays, the windows with four-centred heads. Doorway with clustered Gothick shafts. A *Mr Eglington* (i.e. Samuel or Joseph) supplied a cornice and chimneypiece in 1794. In extensive parkland with C18 STABLES and DOVECOTE. At the SE entrance to the park a *cottage orné* LODGE, 1822.

OLDBERROW

ST MARY. Rebuilt by *Bodley & Garner*, 1875–6. Sandstone. Nave and chancel in one, and timber bell-turret with shingled spirelet. Small mixed windows re-set. In the chancel one Norman S window, also a tiny C13 N window and a trefoil-pointed C13 S window. Plain C14 S doorway; blocked C15 N doorway with decoration on its solid stone lintel. Added S porch with pretty carved bargeboards and side panels, by *Thomas Garner*, 1881. – FONT. Of cup-shape, but turning vaguely polygonal. Big coarse stiff-leaf motifs. – SCULPTURE. C12 pillar piscina. – STAINED GLASS. E by *Hardman*, 1876, incorporating a small medieval panel with the arms of Evesham Abbey. – W by *Clive Sinclair*, 1988.

W of the church, OLDBERROW HOUSE (the former rectory). For the Peshall family, who were rectors for over 150 years and rebuilt the church. Big and rather bleak, in cream brick with tall chimneys. By *R. Bradshaw* of Leamington, 1878.

OLDBERROW COURT, on a moated site E of church. Mid-C16 or earlier, incorporating the cruck truss of a medieval hall. Timber-framed and gabled with brick infill. Close studding to E wing, but box framing with lath and plaster to N. Broad chimneys with stone bases and brick tops. Pretty plaster decoration and stone window mullions on the C19 W wing. Restored by *Richard Crook* for Mr and Mrs Paul Harvey from 1992 (cf. Netherstead, Morton Bagot). C19 brick farm buildings and timber-framed additions for an equestrian centre since 1997, including a pyramid-roofed three-storey corner tower.

OLDBURY

Oldbury is on a high point (580 ft (177 metres) above sea level) on the ridge above the Anker valley, with wide views to the N over Leicestershire and Derbyshire. Originally in the parish of Mancetter, now part of Hartshill. Oldbury Hall, the C18 classical villa of the Okeover family, has gone, although a few outbuildings remain W of the Hartshill Hayes Country Park. The hall stood close to two significant monuments from earlier periods of occupation.

OLDBURY CAMP, 2 m. S, just N of Oldbury village. A small rectangular Iron Age hillfort of 7 acres (2.8 ha) marked by a single bank and ditch, the latter still 6 ft (1.8 metres) high in places but elsewhere, particularly on the SE, levelled by ploughing.

ROUND BARROW, ¼ m. SE of the camp and in woods just N of the road to Hartshill. The barrow is approximately 65 ft (19.8 metres) in diameter and 7 ft (2.1 metres) high. It contained two Bronze Age cremation burials and a later Anglo-Saxon burial. Evidence of a buried ditch has been reported.

OLD MILVERTON

St JAMES. 1879–80 by *John Gibson* for Lady Charles Bertie Percy of Guy's Cliffe, incorporating the lower part of the tower rebuilt in ashlar by *G. T. Robinson* in 1863. Gibson heightened the tower by inserting a middle stage with E.E. blank arcading and raising Robinson's timber belfry stage and pyramid roof. The rest rock-faced. Late C13 style. Organ chamber and vestry 1886. – FONT carved by *Mabey & Co.* to Gibson's designs, 1880. – STAINED GLASS. In chancel and nave, four by *Burlison & Grylls*, 1880 (three) and 1885 (N). – Also in chancel, one by *Powell (James Hogan)*, 1924. – In N aisle, one by *Frank Holt*, 1880, another by *A. L. Moore & Co.* to a design by *George Harris* (cf. Warwick, St Mary), also 1880, and the W widow by *Swaine Bourne*, 1902. – Nave S probably *Lavers & Westlake*, 1880. – MONUMENTS repositioned on W wall, some good. Two by *Gardner*, Leamington, †1850 and †1859. – One by *Tyley*, Bristol, †1854.

Former VICARAGE and outbuildings, immediately SE. Also 1880 and rock-faced too. Nearby the READING ROOM (now VILLAGE HALL), 1891: gault brick with Bath stone dressings. Steep gables carried on heavy corbels. On the green, a few later Victorian estate cottages.

ROCK MILLS, 1m. S, on the Avon. Built as a cotton spinning mill, 1792, later adapted as a corn mill and eventually converted to housing. It retains some mid-C19 mill gear by *Lampitts* of Todenham. Impressive frontage of three storeys plus attic, with restored lucam and hoist. Brick with stone bands. Late C18 Mill House alongside.

See also Blackdown.

OVER WHITACRE

71   St Leonard. In an elevated position above the road with wide views towards Birmingham punctuated by the steeples of Shustoke and Coleshill. High w steeple, Baroque and dramatic. Dated 1765–6, but it looks earlier. On stylistic grounds an attribution to the Hiornes of Warwick has been suggested. It is perhaps an early work by *Francis Hiorne*, since it is very like his church of 1776–7 at Tardebigge (Worcs.). w doorway still flanked by volutes. A tripartite lunette over. The bell-openings large, with Gibbs surrounds and rising up into broken pediments. The outline then recedes a little and on the corners are big globes. The outline is further enriched by the pedimented oval lucarnes of the spire. Actually this spire is an amendment of 1850 and astonishingly sympathetic for the date. Who did it we do not know. Originally the tower ended in a dome which can be seen in the scale model in the church. Plain three-bay nave with arched windows. One blind window on the n where memorials were repositioned within, and another on the s of the short chancel which has a Venetian e window. Plain, rather disappointing interior, where ordinary

Over Whitacre, St Leonard.
Drawing by Henry Jeayes, *c.* 1790

seating replaced the original box pews in the reordering by
Batemans in 1927–8, but the W gallery remains. – Some original
fittings of 1766 including the ALTAR RAILS and the PULPIT
with inlaid panels. – C19 marble FONT on a fluted column, the
bowl with gadrooning on the underside.* – STAINED GLASS.
Three by *Hardman*, the E window of 1853–4, the oculus in the
tower of 1855 and a N window of 1892. The unattractive S
window of 1912 by *Jones & Willis* mirrors the heavy foliage of
the one on the N. – MONUMENTS. Several C17 and C18 mural
tablets, and one large black Gothic memorial to Arthur
Grammer Miller †1831 by *Allcott* of Coventry.

A rewarding churchyard, full of good C18 and C19 memorials
in slate and stone, some of the latter with cherubs' heads.
Among them a plain headstone to *John Cheshire* †1812, the
noted Warwickshire steeple-mender who lived at Over Whitacre. Also the base of a CHURCHYARD CROSS supporting an
octagonal bowl with quatrefoils alternating with Symbols of
the Evangelists.

By the NW churchyard gate, the former SCHOOL (now fronting
the VILLAGE HALL of 1929). 1840s Tudor in stone with hipped
slate roof and central gable with cross.

OVER WHITACRE HOUSE, ½ m. E. A small country house built
after 1837 with extensive outbuildings including a pretty 1860s
lodge by the main road.

Further E, only ¼ m. apart, two large farmhouses with similar
fronts. First MONWODE HOUSE FARM and, further E,
MONWODE LEA FARM. Both Late Georgian, both three bays
and both with quoins and doorways with broken pediments.
Near Monwode Lea is a free-standing brick chimney with
brick stacks to a two-storey house of *c.* 1600, now demolished.
Back towards Monwode House is red sandstone TOLLGATE
COTTAGE (formerly Monwode Stone Cottage). 1769, with
Strawberry Hill Gothick details – an ogee-shaped gable with a
finial and a large cinquefoiled oculus window. Other windows
with cinquefoiled heads.

The parish has several other good farmhouses, the best HOAR
HALL FARM, set in a valley with pools. Double-pile plan with
S façade of five bays and a rainwater head dated 1732. Built
for Edward Weston whose family lived here from 1692 until
the 1890s.

The main settlement is by the crossroads at FURNACE END. Set
back on the bank above is early C19 MILL FARM HOUSE,
two-storey with hipped roof and front of three bays. Looking
down on the village from the N is the OLD RECTORY in Pound
Lane, partly of 1884.

See also Botts Green.

---

*A fine carved Romanesque font was apparently ejected in 1765–6. It is now at
Holy Trinity, Sutton Coldfield, to which it was given in 1856 after it had been
rediscovered.

OXHILL

St Lawrence. Norman nave and chancel. On the N side, two mid-C12 chancel windows. On the nave, pilaster buttresses and a window with a chevron hoodmould. N and S doorways Norman too, both with two orders of columns and Green Man foliate capitals. Over the apex of the N doorway a head with a thin hand at the mouth. The S doorway has chevrons to face and soffit in the second order, and chevrons with inset rosettes in the outer order. Above the doorway a re-set corbel table with seven heads linked by round arches with end-facing billet in the middle. One three-light Dec window with reticulated tracery in nave, used as a pattern for the E window when *Thomas Garner* restored the chancel, 1865. Perp W tower, clerestory (altered) and N porch; also two S chancel windows. Inside the two Norman N chancel windows have chevron hoodmoulds. The lower part of the chancel arch Norman too, with shafts and scallop capitals, but the arch itself is C13 with one step and continuous chamfer. Tall C15 arch between tower and nave with hollow chamfers and even polygonal concave-sided responds. Restoration of nave by *Bodley & Garner*, 1877–8 when the S clerestory was remodelled. – FONT. Norman, tub-shaped. Intersecting arches and in the spaces between the supports scrolls, flowers, and also Adam and Eve, very thin and pitiable. The base 1879. – SCREEN. Acquired from elsewhere in 1878, but removed from the chancel arch in 1908. Parts reused in the tower screen. – At the back of the nave, C15 BENCHES with traceried ends.

Methodist chapel (Wesleyan). 1814 and 1878, with Gothic Y-tracery in the side windows.

Some decent C16 to C18 Hornton stone houses, including the Old Rectory and Fexloe House N of the church, and Oxhill House, 1706, at the W end of the village.

PACKWOOD
Lapworth

A last breath of rural Warwickshire at the edge of the West Midlands conurbation.

St Giles. Nave and chancel of *c.* 1300, with easily recognizable elements, including Y-tracery and the corbels of the chancel arch with pretty tails tied like knots. Perp W tower of grey stone. Money was given for it by Nicholas Brome (†1517) as at nearby Baddesley Clinton. W doorway with decorated spandrels and big diamond-shaped hoodmould stops. In 1704 a N transept was built as a Fetherston family pew. It is of brick and has angle pilasters, a boldly moulded brick cornice, and a large arched window with moulded surround. A pity someone later felt compelled to add the intersecting tracery to re-establish some Gothic decency. It was done earlier than the restoration by *Gordon Macdonald Hills*, 1885–6. Organ chamber, 1902. – SCREEN. Perp, of one-light divisions, Tudor-arched with spandrels. – BENCHES. Two with very primitive Perp ends. – WALL PAINTING. Above the chancel arch the remains of the Three Quick and the Three Dead, early C14. On the l. the figures of the Quick are very good, but the Dead on the r. have almost disappeared. – STAINED GLASS. In the N transept window an early C14 Crucifixion. In the same window, a heraldic shield and an C18 panel of the Deposition. – Smaller medieval fragments in the chancel N and S windows. – Striking E window by *Richard Stubbington*, 1914, in the Arts and Crafts tradition, deep-coloured and full of events. – Two by *Hardman*, in the nave, 1884, and tower, 1895. – One by *Heaton, Butler & Bayne*, 1919. – Presentation by *Theodora Salusbury*, with her usual peacock, 1935. – St Giles, by *Claude Price*, 1969. – MONUMENTS. Many tablets to the Fetherstons and Dilkes. The best is John Fetherston †1670, classical, white marble with black columns and achievement. Attributed to *Joshua Marshall* (GF). – Thomas Fetherston †1714, the builder of the transept. Black columns with Ionic capitals, drapes, flaming urns and skulls. – Thomas Fetherston Leigh †1755. Fluted pilasters with Corinthian capitals, broken pediment and an expressive cherub. – Mrs Mary Dilke †1768. Astonishingly conservative cartouche, with drapery and death's head.

PACKWOOD HALL, W of the church and surrounded by a moat. C16, H-plan with exposed timber framing to rear. The front has Victorian bargeboards, diamond-pane windows and clustered chimneys. Along the S of the churchyard, a long timber-framed BARN belonging to Church Farm.

The main village is to the N, with former VICARAGE (now WINDMILL HOUSE), *c.* 1838, and much altered 1862 SCHOOL, enlarged in 1910, on the ridge. Windmill Lane leading NW towards Dorridge (q.v.) has several large Late Victorian and Edwardian houses. First, PACKWOOD MOOR, by *J. P. Osborne* for J. H. James, 1913. Next, PACKWOOD TOWER, by *W. H. Bidlake* for Christopher Lewis, 1897. Behind, a C20 house around the stump of the C18 WINDMILL TOWER. Lastly, after a gap, BARN CLOSE, by *E. F. Reynolds* for H. A. Dugard, 1912. S towards Lapworth, another is FETHERSTON HOUSE, Glasshouse Lane, by *Alfred Holt* for Richard Mealings, 1910.

PACKWOOD HOUSE, ½ m. SE. Quite a stately timber-framed house of about the third quarter of the C16. Probably built for William Fetherston (†1601) whose descendants owned Packwood until 1869. It was much altered after 1905 by Arthur Ash (a Midlands industrialist) and his son, Graham Baron Ash, as their ideal of an Old English house. Baron Ash presented it to the National Trust in 1941. The house is rendered,

concealing elaborate timber framing known from pre-C19 illustrations. These also show the earlier form of the three gables
on each of the E and S fronts, those on the garden side symmetrically arranged, and transomed windows, all subtly altered.
Square plan, two-storey with an attic in the gables and four
main rooms on each floor. The porch on the E leads to a
screens passage flanked r. by galleried hall, lit by a window
with three transoms which is not original, and l. by the dining
room. The brick range along the N side of the forecourt was
added by John Fetherston in the 1660s (*see* below). Significant
additions of 1924–31 N of the old house by *Wood, Kendrick &
Williams* (i.e. *E. F. Reynolds*) for Baron Ash. Their brick exterior
looks rather like part of an inter-war grammar school. First,
reusing salvaged timbers, Ash created the GREAT HALL in a
detached barn in 1924–7, adding an oriel window and gallery
and bringing in an Elizabethan stone chimneypiece from an
inn at Stratford-upon-Avon. Then in 1931–2 came the Tudor-
style LONG GALLERY, with panelled ceiling, brilliantly linking
the Great Hall with the main building. The staircase in the
angle N of the house also 1931–2, rendered and discreet. Alongside the extensions went extensive remodelling of the interior.
The Jacobean panelling of the DINING ROOM and the STUDY
is original but *ex situ*. So are the DRAWING ROOM panelling
and the fireplace. The panelling and the elaborate overmantel
upstairs in the IRETON ROOM however are *in situ*. Among the
more lavish additions, the Delft tiled bathroom upstairs and
the tapestry wall hangings. All this typifies the provision of new
period exteriors in this way at a time when there was a fashion
for architectural salvages in England and America.*

The STABLE RANGE extends N from the forecourt. The
stables are of the 1660s and architecturally much more rewarding than the house. Artisan Mannerist, by *Roger Hurlbutt* for
John Fetherston who died in 1670. Red brick with blue brick
chequer and other patterns. They have pilasters of brick,
moulded cornices, and blank ovals and roundels. The mullioned windows are set in raised, flat surrounds. To the forecourt of the house, a pedimented sundial and an end gable
with clock dial and turret. The forecourt is walled with a pair
of brick gatepiers at the entrance.

Over the road E of the house, an early C17 red brick barn or
stables, to which *Reynolds* added a MOTOR HOUSE with clock
turret for Arthur Ash in 1914.

To the S of the house, a Carolean walled garden with a
GAZEBO in each of the four corners, the NE one of *c.* 1680, the
SW one perhaps early C18, the others recent. The S wall has a
TERRACE WALK between the gazebos, approached by an ellip-
tical flight of steps from each side. In the middle, a pair of C18
iron gates. The S face of the wall has thirty round-headed

*Although Pevsner in the first edition of this guide considered it 'more appropriate
in America, where the real houses don't exist, than in England'.

niches or bee boles for straw beehives or skeps. Beyond it is the celebrated Yew Garden, supposedly representing the Sermon on the Mount, with an avenue called the Multitude Walk, then twelve larger Apostles, the four yet larger Evangelists, and finally one gigantic yew meant as Christ. The planting is C19, but the Mount at the far s does belong to the garden laid out for John Fetherston in the 1660s. NW of the house, a PLUNGE POOL with ashlar-fronted column for the water faucet, again 1660s.

At CHESSETS WOOD, 1 m. ENE, the former lancet-windowed Mission church adapted from a mid-C19 Wesleyan chapel in 1890 and extended by *Bidlake*, 1925.

RISING SUN HOUSE, Bakers Lane, N of the above. A very pretty timber-framed house, partly early, partly late C16.

HERONFIELD HOUSE, Baker's Lane, a little E. C18, with Venetian windows on the top floor.

A little N towards Knowle, on the E side of Warwick Road, THE DIAL HOUSE, dendro-dated to 1651. Somewhat restored, with close studding and frieze windows.

PAILTON

Originally a hamlet of Monks Kirby, and in the curtilage of the Denbigh estate at Newnham Paddox.

ST DENIS. 1883–4 by *William Chick*, County Surveyor for Herefordshire, by then calling himself Cheiake. Neo-Norman, clearly inspired by the Romanesque church at Kilpeck, Herefordshire, near the home of Lady Katherine Clive (†1882), a younger sister of the 8th Earl of Denbigh. Brick with polychrome dressings of Camden and Hollington stone. Nave and apsidal chancel, originally with a high bellcote over the chancel arch. Carvings of heads, animals and foliage round the corbel table of the apse. The interior has the brickwork exposed. – Contemporary stone PULPIT with Norman interlaced arcading and FONT with Kilpeck-like dragons on the underside. – TILES by *Godwin*. – METALWORK by *Skidmore*.

VILLAGE HALL, built as a reading room by Mrs Louisa Daniell (cf. Hillmorton, p. 552), 1860. Colourful Italianate façade.

PAILTON HALL, in the village centre by the war memorial, has a pretty C17 timber-framed and jettied gable with curved braces and wooden porch with C19 classical detailing. PAILTON HOUSE, Coventry Road, C19 stuccoed, with hipped roof and Doric porch.

PASTURES FARM, 1 m. ENE. A model farmstead on land then owned by Trinity College, Cambridge, 1854–6. Farmhouse with diapered brickwork. Extensive outbuildings.

2040

PILLERTON HERSEY

St Mary. The church has an uncommonly fine mid-C13 chancel. Well profiled lancets and an E window of three lancets, the middle one wider,* all under a shafted blank arch with a cusped quatrefoil in a circle, i.e. plate tracery. Inside the window is shafted and at the outsides of the group double-shafted. Stiff-leaf capitals. The priest's doorway is of a design which may well be unique, with the inner order enriched by a shaft at the angle, two more side by side to the outside, and two more side by side to the reveal, i.e. five in all. The outer orders are continuous. DOUBLE PISCINA with one shaft. DOUBLE AUMBRY with trefoil arches. Unfortunately the rest of the church is not up to the chancel. The N aisle is by *William Kendall*, 1845, with N lancets, an arcade of quatrefoil piers, and a hefty two-light W window. The S arcade also rebuilt, probably 1845 too. The chancel arch is something of a puzzle. The shafts, connected in one curve by deep hollows, are typical of *c.* 1300 and after and do not go with the chancel nor with anything of the nave. Nice low-pitched Perp nave roof with many carved bosses. Rough chancel hammerbeam roof, probably C17. Lower stages of the W tower limestone and C13, the upper stages of brown ironstone and Perp. S aisle early C15 but the big Perp S window is a Victorian insertion. – FONT COVER. High and with long, thin shafts. Made by Canon *Vernon Staley* of Ickford (Bucks.) and presented in 1927. – ROYAL ARMS of George III, restored 1956. – STAINED GLASS. Quatrefoil dated 1574, set in clear glass in S aisle E window.

A small village with Lias farms and cottages. S of the church, the stone vicarage is by *William Allibone* of Pillerton, 1818–19, later extended in brick with gabled ends fronting the street. Further S beyond the war memorial, C18 FLAXLANDS has ironstone quoins and lintels.

Tucked away E of the church, THE MANOR. C17, but much enlarged for the Rev. Francis Mills with a wing of 1850 in the Cotswold style, further extensions dated 1860 and an open Gothic arcade from a demolished later Victorian N wing.

2040

PILLERTON PRIORS

The church was destroyed by fire in 1666 and never rebuilt. Its CHURCHYARD remains down a lane S of the Banbury Road, with good early C18 headstones. Nearby, C17 limestone farm-houses in the older part of the village. Newer houses across the main road towards Pillerton Hersey. The most dominant

---

*Illustrations indicate that the centre light is an insertion and the itemized bills for stonework show extensive remodelling of this window in 1845–6.

is red brick CADBOLD FARM, c. 1800. Tucked away down
Priory Lane, the former WESLEYAN CHAPEL, 1861: short,
with lancets. STAMFORD HALL FARM, 1 m. NNW, late C18,
has a lunette in the pediment and a fanlight above the door.

PINLEY ABBEY
Claverdon

2060

Pinley was a Cistercian nunnery founded *temp*. Henry I, i.e.
remarkably early. All that survives has been interpreted as part
of the w wall of the nave with a small Perp doorway with four-
centred head, and the outline of a very large window above,
part of the N wall with the shape of another window, and the
walls of the s chapel. Inside a Tudor-arched blocked doorway
with carved spandrels. Everything quite small. At the Dissolution in 1536 the Commissioners found a small community and
noted 'The house in metely good Reparation and most parte
of ytt old.' Adjoining the w front and at right angles to it,
projecting to the w, is timber-framed ABBEY FARM HOUSE
of c. 1500, with close studding, a jettied porch, and the stone
chimney-breasts of hall, chamber, and kitchen. This may have
been the refectory – or perhaps the house of the prioress. A
COTTAGE, to the N, may have been the guesthouse. To the SE,
the site is moated.

POLESWORTH

2000

A large parish in the Anker valley, originally including Warton,
Dordon, Freasley (qq.v.) and Birchmoor. The Coventry Canal
and the West Coast main railway line pass through the valley.
Coal was mined here from early times but mining grew into a
major industry by the 1840s. Pooley Hall Colliery, worked from
1897 to 1965, was the main mine in the village and near the
Polesworth Basin in Tamworth Road there was a brick and tile
works.

ST EDITHA (Polesworth Abbey).* A Benedictine nunnery had
been established at Polesworth by the C10, and possibly in 827.
Soon after the Conquest the nuns were expelled but they
returned in about 1130 and remained until the Dissolution in
1539. Much that is strange about the building is explained by
the fact that this was part of a nunnery church. A harsh and

---

* Fr Philip Wells kindly contributed much to this account of the church and monastic remains.

undistinguished restoration by *G. E. Street* in 1868–9 also altered its character. *Street*'s the chancel, the W side windows of the nave, the N porch, much of the N side and the pitched roofs to the nave and aisle. To make sense of what remains it is best to start in the gardens on the S. Here is a low wall against the Victorian chancel with a blocked Norman doorway. This extends E to a wall at right angles to the S. W of the Norman doorway the three windows in the nave are set high in the wall. Together these features indicate the position of the cloister, terminating at a buttress dated 1591 to the W and at a small doorway in the E wall which must have given access to the monastic apartments. The W front is very plain. Perp W window to nave. Two-light W window with cusped Y-tracery to aisle. Between them a big buttress set at a slight angle, and alongside an early C13 aisle doorway placed asymmetrically. The N side largely Victorian. Then the mighty NE tower, oddly placed and odd in its details. The N side clearly original with its tall Dec window with a transom. The low N and W belfry windows are C14 too. Heavy diagonal buttresses on three corners, but not at the SE. On the S and E sides, tall oblong slit windows. The top with lower slits and shields below the battlements. This cannot represent the original state as Pevsner suggested. The nature of the masonry, and visible traces of an E belfry window in the same C14 form as the others, suggest a massive collapse of the SE corner and a later rebuilding. The accounts show that it was done in 1711–12 under the supervision of the church-wardens using direct labour, perhaps explaining the plainness and severity of the work. Only the moulded string courses on the S and E sides have any architectural character. The records also show that there was previously a spire and that a breach in the hall garden wall on the S had to be made good.

The entrance is through a narthex by *Michael Potter & Associates* in 2005 linking the church with the hall (now known as the Refectory – *see* below) to the S. Interior dominated by the long Norman arcade between nave and N aisle. This is eight bays, of round piers with shallow scalloped capitals, square abaci and unmoulded arches, of *c.* 1130. Only the two E bays and the W end are original. The remainder rebuilt by *Street* in 1868–9. The W respond is a whole pier embedded in the wall, suggesting – if it is *in situ* – that the nave was once longer still. The massive buttress W of the arcade outside may also indicate a shortening. The arcade has a clerestory, the splays establishing the S side as the nave and the N as the aisle. The aisle may have been narrow originally, as implied by the position of the C13 W door close to the arcade. High up in the E angles above the arcade in nave and aisle, splendid carvings of the Green Man. The chancel arch marked the E end of the church until *Street* added the present chancel in 1869, sweeping away improvements to the E wall and sanctuary within the first two bays of the nave done by *W. H. Crompton* in 1859. *Street*'s chancel is E.E. with an E window of five stepped lancets in a blank arch.

Carved wooden chancel SCREEN by *George Ostrehan*, 1902.
– Alabaster PULPIT on stone base, by *Earp*, 1869. – FONT.
Octagonal with trefoiled blind arches and simple shafts, C14.
– SCULPTURE. In the N aisle a head corbel with a Crucifixus
and two small damaged figures placed as though they were
standing against drapery. What was it? The date seems to be
C14. – TILES set in E wall at end of N aisle. – STAINED GLASS.
Several by *Clayton & Bell*, the E window 1869–72, St Editha
in N aisle 1869, the bellringer window in the nave †1871 and
adjacent window 1902 (designer *George Daniels*). – S chancel
window by *Ostrehan*, 1902. – W window by *Burlison & Grylls*,
†1916, and also S nave window, 1935. – One in nave by *Camm
& Co.*, 1951. – Three in N aisle, the first †1884 probably by
T. W. Camm for *R. W. Winfield & Co.*, the next *Clayton & Bell*
1869, and one by *Swaine Bourne*, 1884. At W end of aisle,
Hardman, 1875. – MONUMENTS. Effigy of an abbess, C12.
Carved in shallow relief and clothed in drapery hanging in
straight folds. She holds a crozier in one hand and a book in
the other. She has a head-dress and there is a shallow trefoil
around her head. Possibly Osanna, †c. 1135. On a Perp tomb-
chest with shields in quatrefoils, said to have been prepared
for Sir Richard Herthill †1389 who built the tower. – Another
tomb-chest with early C15 alabaster effigy of Elizabeth
Cockayne †1418. She has side-pads to her coiffure, two angels
by her pillow and dogs at her feet. – Lucy, Lady Nethersole,
†1652, signed by *Edward Marshall*. – Memorial to Sir Francis
Nethersole †1659, by *W. H. Crompton*, 1859, and originally
against the E wall.

Next the remaining monastic buildings. To the S of the
church stood the abbess's house, converted into a manor house
in Elizabethan times by Henry Goodere whose father Francis
acquired the site in 1544. This was known as Polesworth Hall.
The Nethersoles lived here from 1627. The property was
acquired as a VICARAGE in 1876, and *John Douglas* created a
characterful house incorporating the remains of the earlier
buildings. Arts and Crafts style in diapered brick with pretty

Polesworth, vicarage, perspective.
Photo lithograph, 1881

timber-framed gables. The N wing nearest the church is a hall (the Refectory) with a big Elizabethan stone fireplace. The roof, partially original, has arched braces right up to the ridge beam. In the vicarage grounds a C17 stone column, probably for a sundial.

The church is approached from the N through the ABBEY GATEHOUSE, of stone with a carriage and a pedestrian entrance. The archway was not vaulted. The upper floor is timber-framed with brick infilling, and the upper room has a roof with tie-beams and crown-posts dendro-dated to 1336–42. To the w of the abbey gatehouse the stone wall continues two-storeyed. In Hall Court behind, an C18 DOVECOTE and the TITHE BARN, restored in 1995. In the churchyard, the granite WAR MEMORIAL cross by *Henry Charles Mitchell*, 1921.

BAPTIST CHAPEL, The Gullett. Built in 1828. Rendered brick with two tiers of round-arched windows with keystones and impost blocks. Gallery on cast-iron columns inside.

CONGREGATIONAL CHAPEL, High Street. Also 1828, red brick, of three bays, with arched windows and a steep pediment.

Former NETHERSOLE FOUNDATION SCHOOL, High Street and Station Road. Founded in 1638 and rebuilt in 1818 by *Joseph Potter* in the Tudor Gothic style. Remarkably stately. Chequer brick, of five large bays with mullioned-and-transomed windows. Stone centre with angle turrets ending in bulbous caps and a big stone cupola with ogee lead roof. Two-storey ranges flanking yard at rear. To the E on the S side of High Street, the old INFANT SCHOOL and teacher's house of 1848 by *Robert Jennings* dwarfed by *A. S. Dixon*'s 1912 additions. Both schools now disused.

POLESWORTH SCHOOL, High Street, up the hill towards Dordon. The big Victorian Board School of 1881 by *George Taylor*. Reddish brown brick with blue bands and patterning. Apsed lobbies l. and r. of front. Detached teacher's house alongside.

In HIGH STREET, to the E of the abbey gatehouse a handsome timber-framed house with gable and overhang, and next to this two cottages (Nos. 32 and 34 High Street) with an exposed cruck truss to the E on No. 34. No. 63, further E, is also of cruck construction, dendro-dated to 1508–9.

On STATION ROAD, facing the Nethersole School, the former POLICE STATION and lock-up of 1858 (now a house), by *William Kendall*, County Surveyor. Further out towards the railway some large late Victorian houses. In BRIDGE STREET, some old cottages nestling alongside Victorian and C20 shops and houses. On the E side, on an awkward plot in the angle between Bridge Street and a lane towards the church, CHURCH WALK of 1908. Near the bridge on the w side, the former METHODIST CHURCH of 1850 and a 1938 extension by *Leeson & Snow*, now confused by a modern shopfront. Next the BRIDGE over the Anker, by *Thomas Sheasby*, 1776–9. Brick with nine stone arches and parapet. Widened in concrete, 1924. Immediately S of the river the former COFFEE HOUSE of 1880, in blue brick and now largely concealed by later additions. In Market Street and Tamworth Road, some remaining industrial buildings alongside the canal. In a field off GRENDON ROAD, the stone OBELISK erected in 1846 by Sir George Chetwynd to mark the site of Dordon's medieval chapel of St Leonard, discovered during the construction of the railway but moved here in 1901.

POOLEY HALL, ½ m. NW. On a steep bank overlooking the village with the canal and River Anker below. Said to have been built in 1509 by Sir Thomas Cokayne, but on the site of an earlier house. As the embattled river front (E) shows, the character is still that of a fortified manor. The form, however, was of an early Tudor gentry house. It is of brick and the windows are of uniform type, stone with four-centred arched lights. There are three independent ranges, now linked. The southernmost was the chapel, with a W doorway, a stair-turret on the N side, and an E window of three lights under a four-centred head. The turret turns octagonal at the top. The next range has near its S end a big two-storeyed bay window to the E and near its N end a garderobe projection. This range is T-shaped, and the wing projecting to the W contained the great hall to which belongs a blocked three-light window on the S side. The W end was rebuilt in 1692 (dated rainwater head). The third (N) range is now POOLEY HALL FARM. It has at its E end a sturdy tower of three storeys with more three-light windows. The spiral stair is in the NE angle. W of the tower is a later block with black brick diapering. It is difficult to make sense of the relation of the various parts to each other. There was once a gatehouse, mentioned in 1683, and perhaps a courtyard. What remains, certainly, is 'oddly grouped' and 'the plan even less coherent than it was' (Anthony Emery).

BRAMCOTE HALL, 1½ m. NE. Once the home of the Burdett family, later of Foremarke Hall (Derbys.). In an isolated position with fine views to the N. Early Georgian, of brick, nine by five exceedingly closely set windows in two storeys. The house is now derelict and the distinctive attic storey with concave sides rising from the cornice has almost gone.

POTTER'S GREEN see p. 295

PRESTON BAGOT   1060

ALL SAINTS. A hilltop church. Nave and chancel, mainly mid-C12 although restored by J. A. Chatwin, 1878–9. Chatwin lengthened the chancel, added the chancel arch, heightened the walls, and re-roofed with a pretty timber bell-turret with spire at the W end. Porch and vestry also 1879. Norman nave: see the S windows and the simple S doorway. The N side is better still, a complete Norman wall with three windows and doorway, especially impressive and instructive inside. All very plain and simple. Trefoil-headed lancets characterize C13 enlargement and improvement. Chunky Victorian chancel arch with zigzag moulding to nave and waterleaf capitals on the columns. Carved by *Roddis* of Birmingham, who also did the heads above the rainwater pipes outside. – ORGAN. Reform type case by *Kenneth Tickell & Co.*, 1986. – STAINED GLASS. Figures by *Burne-Jones* in clear glass in several windows, all *c.* 1910–15 and from the Old Meeting in Birmingham. Installed here 1964–8. – Nave S and two small N windows by *Hardman*, 1870 and 1879. – Chancel S has roundels from the former E window, possibly by *Holland*, †1856.

OLD RECTORY, W of the church. Brick with stone window surrounds and square hoodmoulds, kneelered gables with stone finials and big chimneys. Possibly by *J. B. Harper*, *c.* 1830 (cf. his vicarage at Tanworth).

MANOR HOUSE, ⅜ m. S of the church. Built *c.* 1550, with two equal gables. Timber framing and brick infilling. Closely spaced struts. Divided into two houses *c.* 1980 and the dual ownership very evident in the differing treatment of the restored timberwork.

The Manor House is by the STRATFORD CANAL, with typical SPLIT BRIDGES with cantilevered decks and cast-iron handrails, and a much extended LOCK-KEEPER'S COTTAGE with barrel roof, all *c.* 1810.

PRESTON-ON-STOUR

An estate village SW of Alscot Park (q.v.), owned by the West family (later Roberts West and Alston Roberts West) since 1747.

ST MARY. On a sloping site above the green, the S side of the nave dug into the churchyard and the E end perched high above the ground. Remodelled in 1753–7 by *Edward Woodward* of Chipping Campden for James West of Alscot. The original, p. 43 very elaborate Gothic drawing of 1752 was not followed. The rebuilt church would have had a three-bay chancel, a five-bay nave and a W tower modelled on Chipping Campden carrying a crown steeple like Newcastle upon Tyne. Instead, the old church was adapted. The Perp tower was allowed to remain but with alterations, the W window and entrance attractively redone and the belfry stage perhaps rebuilt (cf. Fladbury, Worcs., where the Woodwards' 1752 tower top has very similar belfry windows). The nave N wall rebuilt. New window tracery in the medieval S wall. Only the chancel was entirely rebuilt. The remarkable thing about Woodward's work is the nave windows which, with their cusped intersected tracery and hoodmoulds, are not at all Rococo-Gothic, like Alscot, but archaeologically very creditable indeed. Superb workmanship too. Inside, the C15 nave ceiling, oddly enough, was also preserved: low pitch, bosses. The chancel ceiling, on the other hand, gently arched and panelled, is typical of 1750–60, as are the wall panelling, cornices and coving in the chancel. Chancel restored internally, 1904, with marble floor and Art Nouveau furnishings by *Powell*. – FONT. A stone baluster, said to be 1749. – SCREEN, STALLS and oak PANELLING in the chancel. Solid Georgian woodwork with ogees and quatrefoils, by *John Phillips* and *George Shakespear*, 1754. (cf. Alscot Park). The screen has iron spikes and gates, the ironwork by *Phillips*, 1755. – DECALOGUE, CREED etc. Closely resembling *Woodward*'s drawing, 1756. – PULPIT and LECTERN to designs by *Bidlake*, 1923. – WEST GALLERY, *c.* 1760, by *Salmon* of Stratford who also did the original nave pews. Two small rooms created under the gallery in 1988–9. – STAINED GLASS. A scheme of 1754 by *William Price*, who was paid £265 for his work including the E and W windows and who seems to have been introduced to West by Sanderson Miller in 1750. In the W window some English early C16 parts and C17 heraldic glass. – The E window was given by West in 1754. It consists of mostly C17 Flemish pieces (dates are 1605 and 1632), some almost certainly recoloured by Price for their new setting (cf. Strawberry Hill). Old and New Testament scenes, many concerned with death. A Salvator Mundi panel by *Powell* (designer *J. W. Brown*), 1904, now fills much of the centre light. – Two chancel N and S windows with heads set in background of crude colours, by Price, 1754. – MONUMENTS. In the sanctuary, Sir Nicholas Kempe †1624, flanked by two wives. He kneels frontally, the two wives in profile. Corinthian columns between. By *Gerard Christmas* (GF) and possibly brought from Islington. – Opposite, two decent early C18 memorials in chancel to Marietts of Alscot. – Then the main assembly, set within ogee-crocketed Gothic panelling on N and S sides of the chancel, three each side. In date order, first Thomas Steavens †1759, erected by his sister Sarah West, after 1772. Designed by *James Stuart*, executed by *Thomas Scheemakers*. Of coloured marbles. Sarcophagus and medallion with profile in front of an obelisk. – James West †1797. By *Richard Westmacott* (later Sir Richard). Grecian in style. Standing mourner by an urn hiding his face. – James West †1772 and wife Sarah †1799. Erected in 1800 and by *Peter Matthias Vangelder*. Decidedly conservative if one compares it with the preceding. Two urns in relief, one a little in front of the other – A plain tablet to Harriett West †1815, also by *Westmacott*. – James Roberts West †1838. By *R. Westmacott Jun.* Hope and Faith, two standing Grecian women. – In the nave, a crucifix in driftwood and polished copper by *Peter Eugene Ball* above a tablet to Sir Michael West, †1978. Good rusticated churchyard GATEPIERS and iron GATES immediately W of the church and NE towards the village. The ironwork possibly by *Paris* of Warwick, *c.* 1750.

PERAMBULATION. The village is very rewarding, with a pleasant mix of building materials and styles. Beginning on the green E of the church, a three-gabled timber-framed house (Nos. 46–48 or LOCKE'S FARM) with very lively decoration in the gables. The ground floor of closely set vertical studding. The house is probably of the late C16, its rendering removed to reveal the framing c. 1830, the date of its stone chimneys. Opposite, by the church, the OLD BAKERY, a two-storeyed early C18 brick house with wooden cross-windows widely spaced, and separated bay from bay by lesenes. Further N, tiny black-and-white PRIEST COTTAGE, with jettied first floor, facing brick and timber PARK FARM with a curious C17 added porch. Up the lane, the former TOP LODGE to Alscot Park, Italianate, red brick with blue bands and round-headed windows, 1860s.

Back down past Park Farm, ROSEHIP COTTAGE (No. 36), restored since being sold from the estate in 1978. At the bottom, the OLD VICARAGE, its rear lowlier and lower than its C18 garden front. Then THE COTTAGE, 1860s, but fronting an older black-and-white building with bow windows projecting from a stone base on the hillside. Round the corner, the OLD MISSION, a former Baptist chapel by *T. T. Allen*, 1885. Tucked away, LOWER FARM, perhaps 1830s, with associated farm buildings. Then three black-and-white houses all close together, THE DELL and THE GABLES, with similar timbering, and the OLD MANOR (supposedly 1659), with gable decoration and stone chimneys of c. 1830 like Locke's Farm.

Then the former school, 1848, and C19 model ESTATE HOUSING at the S end of the street. The COTTAGES dated on the ends, 1852–5. Built for James Roberts West. Red brick, gabled, Tudor, fish-scale tiling and cresting, varied chimneys and windows with diamond leading. Four pairs of cottages on each side of the street. A symmetrical composition.

PRINCETHORPE

92   PRINCETHORPE COLLEGE occupies the buildings of ST MARY'S PRIORY, begun in 1833 for French Benedictine nuns from Montargis. They had escaped from the Revolution in 1792, been given asylum by the Prince Regent and Mrs Fitzherbert, and had moved to Norfolk, then to the West Riding, then to Lancashire, and finally to Princethorpe in 1835. The original buildings included a school as well as the convent. After the nuns left in 1965–6 Princethorpe became an independent school, run since 2001 by the Princethorpe Foundation.

Architecturally the first phase belongs to *John Russell* of Leamington (*Russell & Mitchell*) who designed the original buildings, 1832–5, and was being paid up to the time of his death in 1840. *John Craven*, once thought to have been the architect, helped the nuns find and purchase the site, and later became their builder and clerk of works. Craven is said to have been experienced in building religious houses and to have worked in Spain.

The shell was thrown up very quickly. By January 1834 it had a 'towering appearance', already 'a landmark for a great extent of country'. Most of the convent buildings were complete by mid 1835 when the nuns and pupils moved in, even though much remained unfinished internally. In 1841 Pugin thought it 'a miserable specimen of the tawdry trashy taste of the Modern religious'. It is pre-Puginesque, certainly, but Russell had to follow a model based on recollections of Montargis prepared by the nuns themselves.

Completion was left to *Joseph Aloysius Hansom* who was involved by 1837 and made improvements to Russell's designs as work progressed to about 1844. He and his son *Joseph Stanislaus Hansom* continued to work at Princethorpe until 1892. Then came works by *T. R. Donnelly* and by *Pugin & Pugin* in the 1890s.

One arrives via *Russell*'s WEST LODGE, colonnaded and gabled, with Gothicky details, 1834–5. At the top of the drive is the GUEST HOUSE or Strangers' Building, started in 1834 and completed in 1840, probably by *Hansom*. It is of brick, symmetrical, with a kind of gatehouse centre (the nuns also called it les Tours) and plaster-vaulted porch. Georgian-type windows with pretty Rococo-Gothick glazing and, over the door, a panel of Virgin and Child by *Willement*, 1838. Behind is the enclosure, best considered from the N (*see* below). The buildings are described anti-clockwise from the Guest House.

First, the OLD CHURCH, with a square turret over the S (ritually E) end. The church dates from 1835–7. The turret has simple Y-tracery in the belfry windows and naïve parapet and pinnacles. The original side windows were probably lancets, like those at the S end (concealed from within) but cusped tracery was inserted by *Hansom* in 1862. *Pugin* designed a new sanctuary window in 1842 but the present thin Gothic tracery can hardly be his. Hansom also made internal improvements to the chapel between its opening in 1837 and consecration in 1843. The organ chamber on the side was added by *J. S. Hansom* in 1892. Inside, the space was subdivided in 1968 with a theatre on the ground floor and a library above. In the library a Tudor ceiling, part timber and part plaster. The sanctuary end plaster-vaulted with painted decoration. – STAINED GLASS. In the main window, parts of the original glass by *Wailes* to a design by *Pugin*, 1845. – What remains in the side windows is by *Hardman*, 1862. – MURAL. Martyrdom of St Benedict by *Pippet*, 1892.

Back outside, the ROUNDHOUSE was the nuns' cemetery, begun in 1835–6 and completed by *Hansom*, 1843. Inside, it had a round cloister with pointed arches to the centre which was once turfed and open to the sky. Memorials are fixed to the pillars. Sensitively roofed and refurbished as a music room by *AT Architects*, 2012. Adjoining to the N, *Hansom*'s MORTU-ARY CHAPEL, finished in 1843. This is Neo-Norman, a fashion of the 1840s, with plaster groin-vaults and an apse.

To the E, the original SCHOOL buildings of 1833–5 with an added block of three storeys with gables by *J. A. Hansom & Son*, 1875–6. Behind, the LAUNDRY and KITCHEN, by *Peter Paul Pugin*, 1897. Top-lit by traceried wooden panels in the gables.

Then the N side, and the main block of the original convent building, 1833–5. It is three-storey and has an irregular group-ing of fifteen bays. Plain, but with gables on the projecting bays. On an upper floor, the former MERE DIEU CHAPEL with *Hansom*'s plaster ceiling with ribs and pendants, 1845. It housed the refectory, dormitories and living accommodation of the enclosure. On the W end a little oriel to back-light a statue of the Virgin and child in the cloister. The adjoining W range completed later, 1841–2.

The NEW CHURCH stands at the SW corner of the site, its tall steeple at its SW. It is so big and so red in its imperishable bricks that it squashes the rest. Begun in 1898, it was designed by *P. P. Pugin* and consecrated in 1901. Much of the money came from Hilda de Trafford, for whose family E.W. Pugin had built extensively in Manchester. Ruabon brick, Grinshill stone and Westmorland slate. Dec. High and broad tower with higher stair-turret, placed SW of the S aisle. Nave, transepts, and a polygonal apse with ambulatory. While the exterior is perhaps awkward and reactionary for its date, the interior is altogether more rewarding. W gallery, canopied stalls to nave and stone screens to the side chapels. In the sanctuary, rich FITTINGS mostly to the architect's designs. – An enormously lavish white marble ALTAR with winged angels, under a tower-ing BALDACCHINO with carved painted and gilt figures. Both were made by *Boulton* of Cheltenham. – Side ALTARS, in wood, also by *Boulton*. – Iron SCREEN by *Hardman Powell & Co.* – FRESCOES by *J. Alphonse Pippet*, those in the N chapel 1901.[*] – STAINED GLASS all by *Hardman*, mainly 1899–1902, but odd ones to 1916.

For the college, *Peter Manning Associates* did the SIXTH FORM CENTRE, N of the church, 2007. At the NE side, the 1981 SPORTS HALL extended by *Manning* as a SPORTS HALL, 2005. Alongside, a new CLASSROOM BLOCK by *AT Architects*, 2013–14.

On the Coventry Road to the E, the SISTERS OF MERCY CONVENT by *T. R. Donnelly*, 1897. The lodge alongside also by *Donnelly*, 1899.

The village is at the crossing of three major roads, the Roman Fosse Way and the Coventry–Oxford and Rugby–Leamington

[*] *T. F. Norman* of Warwick also worked here but his work is not immediately dis-tinguishable from Pippet's.

roads. Of note only ST CUTHBERT'S, built as a school in 1844 and adapted as a church in 1959. Brick with stone quoins, hoodmoulded windows and slate roof. THE MANOR, much restored and enlarged, has a timber-framed wing dated 1636.

PRIORS HARDWICK   *4050*

Priors Hardwick lies in an area of deserted villages and sparse population. To its w Hodnell, Radbourne, Watergall, and Wills Pastures have virtually disappeared, as has Stoneton to the s.

ST MARY. Restored and the nave rebuilt by *Slater & Carpenter*, 1868–9. Of Hornton stone. Stunted w tower, high nave, high chancel and no aisles. The lower part of the tower late C13, the parapet later. Late C13 also the chancel. The windows deserve to be remembered. Three N and one s with Y-tracery. E window of three lights with three spherical triangles over. On the s, a high window of four lights with two circles over and a third bigger one at the top. Mostly cusped internally. Excellent, spacious SEDILIA and PISCINA, with the naturalistic foliage which is characteristic of the late C13. The chancel arch is Victorian, as is the nave with its uniform tracery, all of 1868–9. Flat-roofed N vestry added 1891. – COMMUNION RAIL. Of *c.* 1700. – Carved wooden PULPIT by *J. E. K. & J. P. Cutts*, 1904. – MONUMENT. Bottom part of an incised alabaster slab of the mid C15. Legs and pointed shoes of a knight, the shoes on a dog. In the CHURCHYARD, good C17 and C18 tomb-chests and headstones.

An ironstone village, with cottages round the green at Church End. At London End, C17 HILL FARMHOUSE and the OLD VICARAGE, rebuilt in 1915 after a fire in 1907.

PRIORS MARSTON   *4050*

Under the long ridge marking the boundary with Northamptonshire and one of the most rewarding villages in this part of the county. A compact settlement with mostly ironstone buildings.

ST LEONARD. Accessible only by footpaths. Early Georgian w tower with clasping pilasters and Y-tracery in the round-arched bell-openings; probably 1721.* The rest ostensibly Victorian: the chancel restored for Earl Spencer, 1861, and the nave by *Nicholas Joyce* of Burton upon Trent, 1863. Chancel windows geometrical. Plate tracery to the nave. C14 two-light straight-headed Dec windows to N aisle. C15 s doorway with fleurons.

* Date of bells. Napton-on-the-Hill tower (bells 1731) is very similar.

Late C13 N arcade of four bays, extended W 1863. Kitchen and toilet in N aisle and glass screen to tower arch by *Bryan Martin*, 2011–12. – FURNISHINGS mostly post-1863, including *Minton* tiles in sanctuary, 1866. – SCULPTURE. C14 cross-head with broken figures, found near the churchyard. – STAINED GLASS. One in chancel by *Lavers & Barraud*, 1866. Others mostly by *Lavers, Barraud & Westlake*, 1875–7, including the E window. – Nave S, 1892, probably *Burlison & Grylls*. – Alongside, one by *F. Holt & Co.*, 1906. – Two abstract windows by *Henry Haig*, 1993. – Bradshaw MONUMENT (†1770 to †1848), by *William Blundell* of Daventry, *c.* 1830.

NE of the church, the OLD VICARAGE is C17, the entrance front an addition of 1879. In Keys Lane behind, mullioned-windowed COURT LEET MANOR (or Westfield) has a datestone 1663. Alongside, the MORAVIAN CHAPEL (disused) of 1862 and its MANSE, 1864. The chapel has cast-iron window frames with intersecting glazing bars. Nearby, KEYS HOUSE, its front section dated 1660 with mullioned windows.

In the middle of the village, the humble bellcoted SCHOOL: 1847, with rear extension 1879. In Holly Bush Lane, the former WESLEYAN CHAPEL, 1858, converted into a house in 1973.

The best houses are around the war memorial by the main crossing. HIGH HOUSE, *c.* 1700, symmetrical, of three bays and two and a half storeys. All windows in thick moulded frames. So are also the two horizontally placed ovals, one on top of the other. SWISS COTTAGE, 1771, with Gothick windows. On the corner of Hellidon Road, C17 CEDARS FARM has a C19 porch with columns, domed hood and shell moulding and canted bays facing the green. Behind, the 1820s brick walls with embattled gateway and corner folly belonged to its garden, and the covered entrance to PRIORY COURT on the S led to its farm buildings, one dated 1690. Opposite, THE MANOR is a large double-depth house with a plain Georgian W front of 1804 (datestone on the chimney). Built for the Wells family. Good early C21 additions by *Johnston Cave Associates*.

In Hardwick Road, a good cluster of Althorp estate houses, GRANGE COTTAGES, by *William Tomlinson* for Earl Spencer, 1866.

QUINTON

ST SWITHIN. The interior is earlier than the exterior. Norman S arcade of two bays, with round piers, multi-scalloped capitals, and square abaci. One-stepped arches. The N arcade is late C12, four bays, with round piers and round abaci. But the E and W responds still have trumpet-scallop capitals. The arches are steeply pointed and also still one-stepped. At about the same time the S arcade was lengthened by one round-arched bay to the W. The chancel is E.E. – see the N lancets. The five-light E window is Victorian, the continuous chancel arch early C14 (sunk-quadrant mouldings). Early C14 also the lowest part of the big W tower (the same mouldings) and the aisle walls and windows. In the S aisle SEDILIA and DOUBLE PISCINA. The N aisle W and E windows have reticulated tracery. Perp clerestory and top of the steeple. Tall two-light bell-openings with transoms and stone slate louvres. Recessed spire behind battlements and pinnacles. At the foot of the spire another set of bigger square pinnacles close to the spire. The spire has rolls up the edges and a decorated collar. Restoration by *Preedy*, 1864, praised by *The Ecclesiologist* but partly undone in 1923–6 when the interior was gently reworked under *Gerald Cogswell*, with new fittings by *J. W. Pyment* and *Geoffrey Webb*. The LADY CHAPEL fittings and SCREENS are of that scheme, 1922–6. – FONT. Circular, Norman, with scallops against the underside. – BENCH END. One traceried end, reused in a side-table. Others in N aisle. – PULPIT. By *Cogswell*, 1926. – SCULPTURE. Virgin and Child in niche, by *Webb*, and smaller C15 German female saint alongside, added to the Lady Chapel ensemble, 1930. – PAINTING. Elizabethan royal arms above the chancel arch. Also cartouche with inscriptions in S aisle. – STAINED GLASS. Bits assembled in the N chapel and aisle. – E window by *Preedy*, 1871. – Royal Engineers' window by *Norgrove Studios*, 1998. – Otherwise by *Geoffrey Webb*, 1921–39, mostly heraldic. – MONUMENTS. Recumbent effigy of Sir William Clopton †1419, in armour, with a small dog at his feet. – Lady Joanna Clopton †1430. Tomb-chest with plain panelling and on it a very fine brass effigy complete with canopy and inscription frame. The figure is 3 ft (0.9 metres) long. – Thomas Lingen of Radbrook †1742. Big tablet of black-and-white marble. On top putto heads and two small putti. – In the churchyard, remains of a CROSS with part of the reeded shaft. Also the WAR MEMORIAL by *Gerald Cogswell*, 1920.

LOWER QUINTON is a handsome village, with a variety of older buildings round the church, stone, timber-framed, brick and thatched. W of the church the OLD VICARAGE, red brick, late C17, seven bays, wooden cross-windows, hipped roof with dormers. The house was originally of five bays only. The additional two bays on the l. have plain pilasters in two tiers. QUINTON GRANGE, E of the church, built as a replacement vicarage, 1880–1, by *Medland & Powell*, i.e. *C. E. Powell*, cousin of the vicar and also of J. O. Scott. Stone with shingled gables. Off to the N in Friday Street, timber-framed GABLE COTTAGE is C16, with overhang, gable and big stone chimney. Nearby, the WELLBEING CENTRE (former Primitive Methodist chapel), 1885. Next door, a pair of Magdalen College estate cottages, 1913. In Back Lane, more College COTTAGES, also 1913, built with rusticated concrete blocks. On Main Road, the OLD SCHOOL is by *Preedy*, 1864, and Butterfieldian: brick with stone bands and carved text. Also a nice eaves gable bellcote.

The W end of the village heavily developed since the Second World War, beginning with 1950s council housing off Goose Lane by *F. W. B. Yorke*. Further development to accommodate

families at the Royal Engineers Depot at Long Marston. Late
c20 estates with the now obligatory feigned variety in design
and texture. w of these, QUINTON HOUSE, a big square blue
brick late classical house with quoins and stone dressings, built
for John Hiatt, *c.* 1840.

MANOR HOUSE, Upper Quinton. c16, with a part of the front
picturesquely timber-framed, mostly close vertical studs. The
s part of the front is symmetrical, with two tall dormers.

IRON AGE HILLFORT, 1 m. s, on Meon Hill. The remains of a
multivallate fort are visible on the hill, enclosing some 24 acres
(9.7 ha). The site has been considerably damaged by ploughing, and the best preserved portion of the ramparts is on the
sw. A large hoard of iron currency bars was found in its
interior in 1824 and a Bronze Age chisel has also been found
here.

LOWER CLOPTON, Nestling under the w side of Meon Hill.
Farmhouse and model farm building of 1858 by *J. Bailey
Denton*, with clock tower on stables.

RADBROOK MANOR, 1 m. NE of the church. Remodelled for
Thomas Lingen in the 1720s, doubtless by the *Woodwards*
of Chipping Campden. Impressive Baroque front of 2+3+2
bays with central pediment, giant pilasters and the bell-
shaped *guttae* identified by Colvin as characteristic of the
Woodwards.

RADFORD *see* p. 295

RADFORD *see* p. 295

RADFORD SEMELE

3060

ST NICHOLAS. In the nave one Norman s window. Perp ashlar-
faced w tower. Restored with new N aisle by *Rowe & Son* of
Worcester, 1889.* Gutted by fire in 2008. Successfully reconstructed and reordered by *Caroe & Partners* (project architect
Alex Veal), 2012–13. N orientation made possible by the
removal of part of the former arcade. Roof of Douglas fir with
flitched beams, forming crosses leading the eye to the N. Of
1889, the chancel arch and stone REREDOS. New top-lit NW
toilet block and NE vestry, faced externally with thin blocks of
Warwickshire stone. – STAINED GLASS all by *Emma Blount*,
2012–13, except for the replacement Millennial rose window
over the main door by *Aidan McRae Thomson*, remade 2013.
The *Blount* glass is of several types, the E window and St
Nicholas window traditional and brightly coloured. Plain
memorial glass in chancel. Etched window in the big gable and
fused glass to be installed in the prayer corner (2014). – JUBILEE

---

*The aisle replaced one created by *William Thomas* in 1837–8 using materials from
the demolished church at Stretton-on-Dunsmore.

PLAQUES. One of 1897 and the other by *Charnley Memorials*, 2012.

BAPTIST CHURCH, Lewis Road. *John Cundall*, 1874. C14-style, with clock tower to r. of entrance front. Inside, buff brick with red bands. – STAINED GLASS, probably by *Holland*, c. 1875.

Off the main road W of the church, GLEBE HOUSE: the former vicarage, by *Robert Ebbels*, 1838. To the N, Jacobean-style RADFORD HALL. Early C17, but remodelled by *William Thomas* for Henry Greswolde, 1835–7. The long brick façade is almost symmetrical: wholly of the 1830s, but retaining the stonework of the C17 two-storey centre porch and its four-centred door. Mullioned-and-transomed windows. Two end gables with odd finials. Inside, woodwork of 1622. Now apartments.

At the junction of Offchurch Lane, a group of buildings clustered around a twelve-sided brick tower with machicolations below the embattled parapet. The Gothick tower belongs to the MANOR, built for Henry Greswolde Lewis as a 'neat little country box, fitted up in the most tasty style' in 1809. Inside, plaster ceilings dated 1809 with the initials HGL. The circular bay to the garden with balustraded parapet is of 1823. Opposite, two thatched cottages with eyebrow dormers, one (No. 68) with C18 Gothick chimney and windows.

RADWAY

3040

ST PETER. By *C. E. Buckeridge*, 1865–6, to replace the former church in the old graveyard in West End. One genuine two-light window head from the predecessor church built into the coal-shed W of the church. Hornton stone with W tower and broach spire. Plate tracery to belfry windows. The rest in a mixed style (cf. the historicism of Buckeridge's later church at Avon Dassett) replicating window patterns from the old church and creating an impression of phased development. Inside, E.E.-style chancel arch and arcades. – FURNISHINGS mainly 1866, including alabaster REREDOS with marble columns, FONT carved by *Boulton* and wooden PULPIT worked by *Mrs Noyes*. – STAINED GLASS. Netherlandish biblical scenes, C17. From a Dorset farmhouse. Given to Sanderson Miller for his Edgehill Tower (*see* Radway Grange, below) in 1747. Placed in a N chancel window of the new church in the C19. Moved to the S aisle E window and restored by *G. King & Son*, 1975. – One in chancel, *Clutterbuck*, †1855. – E window, *Ward & Hughes*, 1868. – Good Arts and Crafts S aisle window, *Arild Rosenkrantz*, †1905. – In N aisle, three modern windows. One, incorporating panels of Victorian glass, by *David Sear* and *Michael Coles*, 1990. Another by *Michael Coles* with *Roy & Holly Bowles*, 2002. The last by *William Nichol*, †2004. – MONUMENTS. In a recess in the chancel. Effigy of a priest, mid-C15.

– Under the tower, Captain Henry Kingsmill, a Royalist soldier killed at Edgehill 1642. Tablet and semi-reclining stone figure. Erected 1670. Probably by *William Stanton*, who did a memorial to Henry's parents at Kingsclere (Hants), also 1670 (GF). – On the N wall of the tower the plain tablet to Sanderson Miller †1780, by *William Cox* of Northampton. – Fiennes Sanderson Miller †1817, by *George Cakebread* of Bloxham. – Charles Chambers, R.N., †1854. In the predella, a panel depicting his naval victory at Fredericksham (Gulf of Finland).

METHODIST CHAPEL (Primitive), West End. 1866.

Former SCHOOL and teacher's house, immediately s of the church, by *D. G. Squirhill*, 1851. Built at the expense of Charles Chambers. Gothic with decorated bargeboards and ornamental tiled roof. The READING ROOM in the village centre, given by Chambers and his brother, doubtless by *Squirhill* too, 1852. In the village, pleasant ironstone houses, some thatched. On the green, good Southam RDC COUNCIL HOUSING by *Quick & Lee* (*Guy Silk*), 1951–2.

RADWAY GRANGE. Radway Grange was once a square Elizabethan house with two steep gables to each side and mullioned windows. On the N it is essentially still like that, on the w also. But what makes Radway especial – a key building in the early Gothic Revival – is the work of *Sanderson Miller*, that pioneer of the Rococo-Gothic or Gothick. His father, also Sanderson Miller, had bought the property in 1715. Sanderson Miller Jun. was twenty when he succeeded in 1737. His initial interest was in landscaping. But six or seven years later, *c.* 1745, i.e. about three or four years before Horace Walpole started at Strawberry Hill, he began his architectural improvements. On the s side in 1746 he added two symmetrical canted bay windows

Radway, Radway Grange, south front.
Drawing by Sanderson Miller, *c.* 1740

and a doorway between. The details are decidedly fanciful: e.g. the doorway has a lacy cresting, the bay windows broad quat-refoil panels, and in the infill between the Tudor gables is a curvy star, a motif he also used at Lacock, Wilts. Miller also added a new E front, one bay deep, with a central loggia and a three-window group above – all arches being four-centred and ogee canopied. It has lost its short polygonal turrets. The wing on the NE of this front is of 1923 by *P. Morley Horder*, and E again is an orangery by *David Robotham Ltd*, 1998. On the W front the loggia is *Miller*'s. He gave it a gable taken from the Elizabethan E side. Inside the house, not much needs special attention. In the DINING ROOM is a pretty alcove. In other rooms there are chimneypieces. One is Gothick, and clearly of Miller's own design.

In the garden is a STATUE of Caractacus enchained, designed by *Miller* and carved by *James Lovell, c.* 1750. It was made to stand inside the Edgehill Tower, but was found to be too large for its niche.

On Edgehill to the SE are an OBELISK of 1854 and, historically of considerable interest, *Sanderson Miller*'s Cottage and Castle. EGGE COTTAGE is completely asymmetrical, with pointed windows and a steep roof, originally thatched. It dates from 1744 and Swift mentions it in a letter of 1745. It was *Miller*'s first essay in the Picturesque, a sort-of *cottage orné*. The CASTLE (or Edgehill Tower) was begun in 1745 and fully completed in 1750. It served both as an eyecatcher and as a lodge at the head of a drive leading down to the Grange. It is irregular in composition and consists of a gateway with one low tower by the road, a bridge (rebuilt 1992), and the tower proper on the hillside. Topped with machicolations and strangely high battlements, it is loosely based on Guy's Tower at Warwick Castle. Inside, the octagon room at the top has Gothic plasterwork by *Robert Moore*. There are alternately four windows and four fireplaces. The CASTLE INN adjoining the SW side of the tower is complementary but later, probably earlier C19, and has a 1994 extension. Opposite were the medieval RUINS of Ratley Grange, completing the group. Having bought the property in 1743 *Miller* later adapted the ruins picturesquely to form stables for his dining guests at the Castle. Already plundered, the remains were demolished in the 1960s.

67

RAGLEY HALL
2 m. SW of Alcester

0050

Ragley was designed to impress. It stands impractically on a hill whose top was levelled to receive it. Viewed from below up the main drive, seen down the long avenue at the back or fleetingly glimpsed from the Ridgeway to the W, it has an imposing presence. Inside, the main floor is elevated like a floating platform from which one can enjoy splendid views of the attractive countryside around. All this emphasizes both the status of the house and the scale of the park. Here, as Geoffrey Tyack has commented, was 'a completely controlled environment proclaiming man's mastery over nature and the nobleman's mastery over the landscape'.

One of the most ambitious new builds of the later C17, Ragley was the creation of Edward, 3rd Viscount and (from 1679) 1st Earl of Conway, whose great-grandfather had bought the estate in 1591. Take away the later portico and Conway's house looks almost the same today as it did when first built in 1679–83. It has long been attributed to *Robert Hooke* on the basis of surviving correspondence and diary entries. Of Hooke's involvement there is no doubt, but the extent of his hand in the built design is less certain. Peter Leach has shown that Hooke was not the main designer, pointing out that construction had begun before Conway consulted him for advice about the 'modell' already prepared, and his observation that Hooke's suggestions were largely ignored is confirmed by Patricia Smith.* Indeed, Smith asserts that none were carried out. Odd, since Hooke was generously paid for his work.

So who was the designer? Was it, as Smith suggests, a collaborative effort? One name is definite, that of *William Hurlbutt*, described (with his brother Roger) by Colvin as 'among the more important provincial builder-architects of late seventeenth-century England'. Hurlbutt had designed stables in Ireland for Conway in 1670 and the Hooke letters make it clear that he built Ragley. He could have been its designer too, especially if he provided the 'modell' as Leach infers. But who made it is unclear and Smith rightly urges caution in attributing it. What is now clear is that the built design owes much to the work of Roger Pratt and, in particular, to his short-lived Clarendon House, London, of 1664–6 (demolished 1683), and Kingston Lacy, Dorset, of 1663–5, which Hurlbutt is known to have visited in 1670. Hooke's drawings for Ragley, on the other hand, relate more closely to Tring Park in Hertfordshire, built for Henry Guy in the 1680s and hitherto attributed to Wren.

Whoever its author, Ragley ultimately owes all to Conway himself, who clearly had a controlling hand. Distinctive are the French-influenced projecting corner pavilions, originally housing self-contained apartments. The generous double staircases N and S (both rebuilt) must relate to these rooms, and especially to those on the upper floors. Mentioned by Jeremiah Milles in 1743 and marked on a James Gibbs plan of *c.* 1750, they belong to the original plan. Then the double-height Great Hall, originally galleried. Also the basement at ground level. There are features here anticipating by some decades, as Leach observed, the emergence of the English Baroque.

Ragley was incomplete at the time of the 1st Earl's death in 1683, but he left instructions for the building to be finished. The

---

*Patricia Smith, '"Contriving Lord Conway's house": who really designed Ragley Hall?' in *Georgian Group Journal* Vol.21 (2013).

exterior must have been complete when it was engraved by Kip
c. 1698 but the interior remained unfinished. In 1743 Milles
found the Great Hall 'had nothing except bare walls'. The full
fitting-out came later. This was in two main phases, both in the
lifetime of Francis Seymour, the 2nd Lord Conway of the second
creation, who became Earl of Hertford in 1750 and Marquess in
1793, the year before his death. Horace Walpole, whose letters
refer to the works, was his cousin. First, there was work under
James Gibbs (†1754) from 1749 until 1756. His the Great Hall,
the adjoining rooms N and S and one room on the W, as we shall
see. Then, after a pause, Lord Hertford embarked on a second
phase in 1778, engaging *James Wyatt* as his architect. Wyatt's
work is mainly of 1778–83 although he was employed at Ragley
for two decades into the 1790s. He did the grand portico, stables
and probably the lodges. Inside, he was responsible for the dining
room and the interiors along the W side of the house. Later came
restorations by *William Tasker*, 1871–3, for the 5th Marquess, and
again for the 8th Marquess of Hertford from 1956 until 1964.
Ragley opened to the public in 1958, Lord Hertford being one
of the first owners to develop his house as a visitor attraction.

Ragley presents a monumental front of fifteen bays, Lias and
  white oölite, a basement, two upper storeys, a balustrade, and
  a hipped roof. The centre of the E façade is a grand giant portico   58
  of four unfluted Ionic columns carrying a pediment and reached
  by a two-armed outer staircase with a wrought-iron balustrade.
  This addition is *Wyatt, c.* 1780. Also alien to the original house
  are the basement windows with Gibbs surrounds, which must
  represent an alteration by *Gibbs* himself *c.* 1750. They continue
  all round. On the W side the upper windows are primary, tall
  and narrow. *Wyatt* did only the square attic above the three
  middle bays with its three round windows linked by garlands.
  The complicated terrace and steps to the garden are in the same
  style but by *Tasker*, 1871–3. To the N and S are façades of curious
  design: three bays, then two pairs of high arched windows, and
  then again three bays.
As one enters, one finds oneself at once in the GREAT HALL, a   59
  room so large and so high that even in a house on the scale of
  Ragley the effect is sensational. The room was made and decorated by *Gibbs*, noted as 'new modelled, and embellished with
  ornaments of stucco' when Bishop Pococke visited in 1756.
  The hall is 70 by 40 by 40 ft (21.3 by 12.2 by 12.2 metres) and
  its longer axis is at right angles to the façade. It reaches up into
  the roof. The walls are articulated by coupled pilasters. Above
  them the high coving is managed with penetrations, and the
  ceiling is flat. There are two fireplaces with bearded termini
  Atlantes. Above the fireplaces are stucco figures of War and
  Peace in rich Rococo frames. The stucco motifs in the other
  spaces between the pilasters are smaller. In the spandrels of
  the coving are trophies, in the wall at the back of the penetrations busts and vases on brackets. The centre motif of the
  ceiling is Britannia in a lion-drawn chariot. The plasterwork is

now attributed to Gibbs's associate *Giuseppe Artari*, perhaps with *Giovanni Bagutti*, 1756–60. *Francesco Vassalli*, employed at Ditchley (Oxon) and Hagley (Worcs.) at about the same time, is another candidate. The present colour scheme was suggested by *John Fowler* during the 1970s restoration.

The rest of the house is best described in three parts. First, N of the Great Hall, is the MUSIC ROOM, also by *Gibbs*. Charming bacchic children in the overmantel. Ceiling with putti. Next, i.e. in the NE corner, follows the BREAKFAST ROOM (or small dining room) with an exuberant Rococo overmantel. Of pearwood, 1756, restored by *Thomas Kendall* of Warwick, 1872. The dragons holding sconces are admirable. The GREAT DINING ROOM faces N. It is probably one of *Wyatt*'s later works, perhaps 1790s, and has grisaille overdoors. The room W of this is one of the two symmetrically placed STAIRCASES. They are both ample in scale and obviously Victorian, and must be by *Tasker*.

Returning through the Great Hall to the SE part of the house, one comes to the STUDY to the S. This has a Gibbs ceiling with putti and an Adamish chimneypiece. S of the Study, in the SE corner, is the FAMILY DINING ROOM and W of this, facing S, the LIBRARY. The Gibbs plan shows that this was originally the chapel. The simple bookcases and decoration are probably C19, but over the doors are Gibbonsish swags preserved from the 1680s build. After that comes the SOUTH STAIRCASE HALL, with *Graham Rust*'s mural of 'The Temptation' commissioned by the 8th Marquess and completed between 1969 and 1983. This covers the whole height of the staircase, with Christ and the Devil in the centre of the ceiling in *trompe l'œil*. The design is partly architectural, combining features in the classical and light Rococo styles. At the higher level, family members look down enjoying the enthralling landscapes.

From the South Staircase Hall into the procession of rooms along the W front. The first, towards the S, is now a family room but formerly housed the Prince Regent's bed (*see* below). The details here are Wyatt's. Immediately N, the GREEN DRAWING ROOM, where the ceiling offers a parting glance at *Gibbs*. Fine Rococo mirrors in Chinese Chippendale manner. Then a suite of rooms with 1780s interiors. In the centre is the RED SALOON adjoining the Great Hall, with typical Wyatt chimneypiece and delicate ceiling. N again, the MAUVE DRAWING ROOM, with a very graceful coved Wyatt ceiling, to the S. Lastly, in the NW corner, the PRINCE REGENT'S BEDROOM, again Wyatt, with the bed surmounted by the Prince of Wales's badge of feathers specially built for his first visit to Ragley in 1796.

Finally, the basement. The whole house stands on a vaulted undercroft at ground level, evidently of *c.* 1679–80.

The STABLES originally stood in front of the house, occupying one of the detached wings of *c.* 1679 illustrated by Kip. They were removed to the N *c.* 1750. The present stables are low and hidden. The S court in limestone ashlar has an oblong yard whose end wall is a Tuscan colonnade. Although altered, this block may be by Gibbs. The N court is by *Wyatt, c.* 1780, one-storeyed and semicircular in plan. Lias ashlar with limestone dressings. Over the archway between the two courts a low octagonal chamber for the clock bell (1748) with oval openings and shallow dome. Vane referring to restorations dated 1873 and 1991.

ICE HOUSE, by the stables. Probably *Wyatt*.

Walled KITCHEN GARDEN, in the park NNE of the house. With a fine wrought-iron gate* and, at the far end, in the centre, the three-bay C18 GARDENER'S HOUSE, built of brick.

The one-storeyed LODGES at Arrow are set back symmetrically with curved flanking walls. Probably by *Wyatt, c.* 1785.

Evesham Road LODGE, 1872, doubtless by *Tasker: cottage orné* style with half-timbering.

The lavish formal GARDENS shown by Kip were probably never completed. The gardens around the house are now as laid out by *Robert Marnock*, 1871–2. Horace Walpole's letters suggest that the PARK was landscaped about 1757 by 'Browne' (i.e. *Capability Brown*), who 'improved both the ground and the water'. Of Brown's planting a shelterbelt to the S still exists.

High on a steep bank on the far side of the Arrow valley is OVERSLEY CASTLE, an eyecatcher in the direct line of vision from Ragley. Said to have been built at the suggestion of the Prince Regent. Possibly 1810–12. A white tower with battlements and, attached to it, a house built for David Greig, 1932 (undergoing conversion to apartments, 2014).

RATLEY

On the E slope of Edgehill, the church in a hollow at the bottom of the street. Much use of Hornton stone, quarried in the village. C16 and C17 buildings with the usual details, e.g. coped gables, mullioned windows, etc.

ST PETER AD VINCULA. Of Hornton stone, grey with lichen. Chancel, S chapel and aisle, and W tower. Almost entirely Dec and very handsome. *Sanderson Miller* (cf. Radway) worked here in 1758 and doubtless admired it. Respectful restorations by *Bateman & Corser*, 1872–3, and *Philip Chatwin*, 1935–8. Outside, a good variety of Dec tracery patterns: ogee-headed on the N, reticulated, daggers and mouchettes, cusped intersecting in the chancel S and a mouchette wheel in the S chapel. A big reticulated S window and an early Perp one alongside. Internally, the three-bay S arcade, chancel arch, and one-bay chapel arches, all without capitals, have identical continuous

*Probably the C17 gates shown in the main forecourt in Kip's engraving.

mouldings. These are typically Dec, as is the absence of capitals. Perp tower top with NW corner turret. Later N porch. – Chancel FURNISHINGS 1872–3, including richly coloured tiling in the sanctuary. – Stone REREDOS by *Bateman & Corser*, 1875, with crocketed arches and gables, polished granite shafts and diapering. – C14 octagonal FONT, with wooden cover by local carvers, 2002. – STAINED GLASS. One N chancel window by *Ward & Hughes*, 1884.

CHURCHYARD CROSS. The shaft is complete and fragmentary remains of the head survive too.

N of the church, RATLEY HOUSE was the vicarage, rebuilt *c.* 1845: rock-faced, with steep roofs and trefoil windows in the gables. Minor extension by *William Lait*, 1864.

Former WESLEYAN CHAPEL, perched on a bank in Chapel Lane. 1865. Churchy Gothic windows with banded stone surrounds.

The old SCHOOL off the Town Hill green is Tudor-style, 1849. Also on the green, the VILLAGE HALL created from a barn by *Guy Pemberton*, 1935. Three good ESTATE COTTAGES, 1874, at the top of the High Street, and lower down a COACH HOUSE dated 1884 with a splendid eaves corbel course with carved heads etc.

W of the High Street, a motte-and-bailey CASTLE: well preserved.

NADBURY CAMP, ¾ m. NE on a commanding site in Camp Lane. Iron Age hillfort enclosing 17 acres (6.9 ha) with entrances E and W. Originally multivallate but much damaged by ploughing. Only the outer bank is now visible, its best preserved portion being along the wood on the S. On the N the ditch runs alongside the ridge road to Warmington.

See also Upton House.

ROWINGTON

ST LAURENCE. An unusual and rather puzzling church, although its oddities and complexities long pre-date the respectful restoration by *Bodley & Garner* in 1872. It has a Norman N wall: see the one remaining shallow buttress by the N door. The width of that Norman church is not known, but in the late C13 the nave had the present width. The two S windows are of *c.* 1280 (three lights, intersecting tracery – also one blocked W lancet). About 1300 a crossing tower was set into this nave. The date is indicated by the Y-tracery of the bell-openings, the mouldings of the shafted crossing piers (continuous shallow curves connecting the shafts), and the odd procedure of building inside the nave walls. That this was done can be deduced from the position of the two S windows just referred to. Altogether the interior of the church is most odd. The crossing continues by an extra bay before the chancel arch is reached.

The chancel is Dec – see the relatively simple flowing tracery of the E window. Moreover, to confuse the interior more, the Norman nave was divided into nave and aisles about 1400 by arcades with standard elements though differing details, creating abnormally narrow aisles. Perhaps a more ambitious rebuilding with wider aisles was begun but never completed. In the nave W wall are a Perp doorway and five-light window, maybe representing completion to a modified plan. As late as 1554 a NE aisle or chapel was built, not along the old N aisle but along crossing and chancel. The windows are of the plain, mullioned type without arches to the lights, but early C16 straight-headed windows were also reused. Nice Perp ceiled wagon roof with bosses in the nave. At least as nice the stencilling of the N chapel ceiling, belonging to the 1872 restoration, as does the chancel roof with gilded sun and stars. Further work by *Wood & Kendrick*, 1905–6, including the present S porch. Internal reordering in 1967–9 when the N chapel was adapted as a vestry and Lady Chapel. – PULPIT. Of stone; Perp. Iron rail by *Bodley & Garner*, 1890. – SCREEN. To the N chapel (originally in the far chancel arch), one-light divisions with quatrefoils in the spandrels. – COMMUNION RAIL with turned balusters. Brought from Studley in 1906. Made in 1682 by *Edward Elvins* – C18 in appearance. – DECALOGUE. Two marble tablets with gilded edges, 1750. – STAINED GLASS. C14 fragments in a chancel S window. – Some also in E window, but this is largely of 1872 by *Burlison & Grylls* who also did another chancel window 1874. – Two by *Kempe*, 1899, one in the chancel and one in the crossing. – One N chapel window by *Heaton & Butler*, 1897. – Another by *Florence, Robert & Walter Camm*, 1937. – Millennium W window by *Graeme Wilson*, 2003. – MONUMENT. Tablets to Thomas Reeve †1612 and John Wollaston †1615; no figures. Both restored by *S. Dykes Bower*, c. 1967. – Samuel Aston †1820 by *William Hollins*, with weeping urn.

Near the church, on the N the OLD RECTORY with shaped gables; by *Horace Francis*, 1850. Over the main road S, the HALL: plain late C18 E front of six bays in locally quarried Arden stone, facing landscaped grounds with pool. Immediately W, the old SCHOOL by *G. T. Robinson*, 1859–60, with roguish features: rather savagely converted to housing, c. 1989.

Of the two main settlements, W and NW of the church, TURNERS GREEN has the older properties, especially in Mill Lane and beyond the canal bridge. These include THE OLD MANOR, C16 with pretty timber framing, especially in the front gable. Off Finwood Road, WINDMILL HOUSE has a red brick C18 front with Gothick glazing. W towards Kingswood on Old Warwick Road timber-framed EASTFIELD MANOR by *Rajkowski*, 2006, is in the vernacular idiom with red brick lozenge piers in the boundary wall.

E of Old Warwick Road is ROWINGTON GREEN. SHAKESPEARE HALL, ½ m. N of the church, has a handsome front with an early C16 centre and projecting porch; close studding. A gabled dormer dated 1682 TS IS (i.e. the Shakespeares). Restored in

1873 by *Payne & Talbot*, who added a block to the l. Enlarged
again in 1901 by *F. B. Endall* of Solihull with a further addition
on the l. and rear infill. The extensions timber-framed with
brick infilling. Immediately E, ROWINGTON MILL has a
cluster of low buildings erected in 1978 by *D. H. Robotham*
around the brick mill tower of *c.* 1780, the roofs being all
jauntily truncated at varied angles: an interesting group, prettily set among tall conifers.

In Queen's Drive, ½ m. NNW of the church, LYNTON HOUSE
is by *F. P. Trepess* of Warwick, 1897–1904, with additions of
1911–15 by *E. Llewellyn Edwards* and enlarged by *Robothams*,
2012; brick with half-timbered gables. Edwards lived at THE
CROFT, Rowington Green, by *Grew & Edwards*, 1905. His
firm also did the nearby CLUB HOUSE, 1906, and the rather
altered ALMSHOUSES in The Avenue, 1907. *Edwards*'s solo
work includes CORNERWAYS in Mill Lane, 1912, and BELL
HOUSE on Old Warwick Road, 1926. The Cottage (now
HICKECROFT) in Mill Lane is a C16 house enlarged by another
Birmingham architect, *E. F. Reynolds, c.* 1914: he lived here
from 1913 until 1925. Also by *Reynolds*, FIVE ELMS on Old
Warwick Road, 1926, extended 1934.

OLD FARM, Mousley End, ⅝ m. E. Late C16. Timber-framed
with especially elaborate gable above the porch with herringbone bracing and concave-sided lozenges.

HIGH HOUSE, ⅞ m. SE. A big square house of *c.* 1700: red and
black brick chequer, pilaster-strips, hipped roof and two groups
of high chimneys. The curiosity is the two stair-turrets at the
base of the chimneys, originally giving access to a fenced
viewing platform on the roof.

See also Lowsonford, Pinley Abbey and Shrewley.

RUGBY

INTRODUCTION

First views of Rugby from the railway are unprepossessing, with derelict factory sites near the track and monotonous lines of housing on the slope leading up to the town. The approach is no less flattering by road from the N through modern commercial sprawl. The distant steeples, however, remind one that Rugby is Butterfield-town on account of the dominant presence of Rugby School and the parish church. It is certainly no mere industrial town architecturally speaking.

At the start of the C19 Rugby was a small market town with a population of only 1,487. By 1901 this had grown to 16,830, the biggest change taking place in the 1890s with an increase of 5,568 accompanied by the erection of 1,137 new houses. There were three main causes of this rapid expansion. First, the enhanced reputation of Rugby School under Dr Thomas Arnold (headmaster 1828–42) brought a number of respectable families to the town. Then came the railway in 1838, followed by heavy industry in the closing decades of the century. Heavy industry has largely come and gone, with the main factories north of the railway demolished only recently. The canal arrived in 1773, but it was the coming of the railway in 1838 that made Rugby a place for industrial development. As a hub – eventually with services from nine different directions operated by three different companies – the town became first a centre for the railway industry itself. Most notable were the LNWR works and Thomas Hunter's wagon works just N of the present station. A corset factory was established in 1882. The former British Thomson-Houston works in Mill Road opened in 1900–2. Another factory of the period, the Willans works (1899), remains. Rich deposits of Lias limestone gave birth to the cement industry in the 1860s, its growth aided by access to the rail network. Deep excavations can be seen between the railway and Lawford Road and the 377-ft (115-metre) chimney of the modern Cemex works dominates the western side of the town.

So to the town itself. While Butterfield's buildings are the most striking, his work came after several previous phases of building activity. *Scott* and *Pugin* were here immediately before Butterfield first appeared and their use of patterned brickwork was much imitated around the town in the 1850s. Previously Rugby had seen considerable residential expansion, and houses of the 1830s and 1840s exist in some numbers, especially along the main roads radiating out of the town. Earlier still, there are decent Late Georgian and Regency buildings in the town centre and in the residential areas. Add to this what came later with the creation of Regent Street in 1900 and early C20 rebuilding in the town, and then one can see Rugby as a town with much architectural variety and character.*

* There have been losses since the first edition of this guide – notably *Scott*'s Holy Trinity (1852–4), an early work demolished in 1983 after much controversy. It was built as 'an Anglican counter-blast to the building of St Marie's Roman Catholic church in 1847' (John Maddison). Also good Georgian buildings W and E of the clock tower, significant railway and factory buildings, cinemas (e.g. the Art Deco Granada (originally Plaza) of 1933), the 1852 water tower, etc.

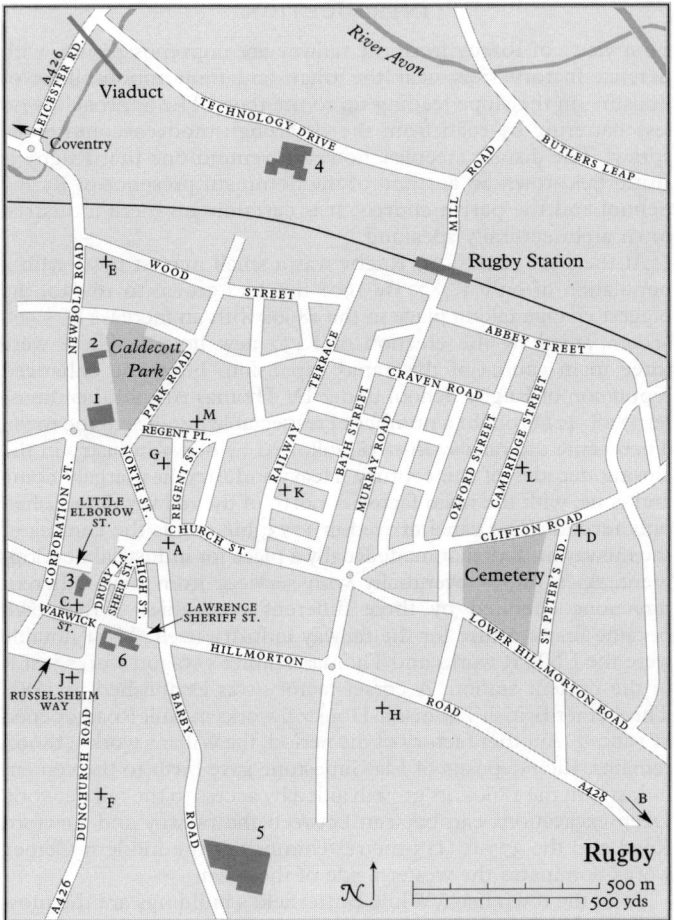

Rugby

A St Andrew
B St George
C St Matthew (former)
D St Peter & St John
E St Philip
F St Marie (R.C.)
G Baptist church and Regent Rooms
   (the Sunday School)
H United Reformed church
J Methodist Church Centre
K Evangelical Free Church
L Christian Fellowship
M Quaker Meeting

I Town hall
2 Magistrates' Court and
   Police Headquarters
3 Public library
4 Warwickshire College
5 Hospital of St Cross
6 Rugby School

Rugby had no architectural practice of any note until the 1890s and perhaps looked to nearby Leamington Spa, some 14 miles to the SW, for designers for its more fashionable early C19 houses. Even in the 1870s and 1880s commissions generally went to London architects or established provincial firms. Rugby-born *Thomas Webb Willard* (1862–1940) was the first local architect of any note, established in practice by 1888 and responsible for several major projects. From 1922 the practice continued under his son *James Donald Willard* (1897–1977) and *Ernest J. Ellingham* (1888–1948) as *Willard Son & Ellingham*. Rather more adventurous as a designer was *John Thomas Franklin* (1852–1906), a Lincolnshire-born carpenter-turned-architect who was in practice in Rugby by 1891. His best work was in Regent Street, begun in 1900 and continued by his pupil and partner *C. J. Newman* who carried on as *Franklin & Newman*. Another local architect of note was Northampton-trained *John Herbert Liddington* (b. 1878) who was established in the town by 1901 and later took his younger brother Ralph into partnership after the Great War as *J. H. & R. B. Liddington*. *H. B. Creswell* had a Rugby office from about 1900 too. Everyday commercial and residential work apart, these local architects also produced a number of significant buildings.

CHURCHES

ST ANDREW. Rugby's ancient parish church, but mostly by *Butterfield*. Largely rebuilt 1877–9, the sanctuary completed 1885 and the NE steeple added in 1895–6. The church cost £18,000 and the steeple an extra £8,000. Here Butterfield is not at his strongest and most aggressive. The colouring inside is restrained; the exterior buff and calm. Yet it is a building of much character externally and internally. It started from an existing C14–C15 church with plain W tower, nave, N aisle, and chancel. They remain, but became for Butterfield a subsidiary tower and an inner N aisle with N chapel. He provided a new nave* and further aisle to the S and made the old N aisle his outer N aisle. Finally, he added the grand steeple to the E of the old aisle, 182 ft (55.5 metres) high. Butterfield's style is Second Pointed, i.e. late C13 to early C14, as the Ecclesiologists (whose favourite he was) recommended. So the steeple has bell-openings with bar tracery, a trellis pattern above, and then short, squat pinnacles and a spire with broad bands of fish-scale patterning. Butterfield also created a two-storeyed N porch, thus achieving a maximum of variety in the volumes as seen from Church Street. Inside the old arcade has octagonal piers; Butterfield's new arcades S of the old nave and S of his new nave have round piers. He uses throughout an alternation of pink and cream stone and in addition some grey marble for shafts. Butterfield was fond of internal polychromy. Shafts run up from the piers to the principals of the ceiled roof. Nave and

*In place of the S aisle added by *Rickman* in 1831.

chancel are continuous, the division marked by a rood screen in the form of a flying arch carrying a large stone cross. The arch has leaf capitals standing on large brackets with eagles. The chancel is much busier than the nave. There is e.g. some red and cream chequerwork, marble and polished stone and a good deal of clashing between arch forms and sizes. The outer N aisle partitioned off and seating removed from the back of the nave and aisles, late 1980s. – Good *Butterfield* furnishings, including ALTAR RAILS, brass CANDESTICKS in sanctuary, 1885, wooden PULPIT and FONT with coloured marbles, 1879. – REREDOS of alabaster and Devonshire marble, 1879, modified by the insertion of *Alec Miller*'s 1909 adaptation of Fra Angelico's Transfiguration, set in *Butterfield*'s stonework. – Wrought-iron SCREENS also by *Miller* and the Chipping Campden *Guild of Handicraft*, 1914. Arts and Crafts. The one at the entrance to the chancel has vine trails and coloured enamelled shields. – A fine CHEST with iron scrolls, the ironwork late C12. – STAINED GLASS. E window by *Clayton & Bell* to *Butterfield*'s designs, 1881. – N and S chancel windows by *Clayton & Bell*, 1895 and 1885, and W window too, 1900. – The rest by *Burlison & Grylls*, 1879–1912. – MEMORIALS all re-set at the W end, including one to Thomas Crossfield (†1744) by *William Hiorne*.

ST GEORGE, St John's Avenue. By *Denys Hinton & Associates*, 1961–2. For its time up to the standard of the best ecclesiastical buildings in the county. From the outside one sees a plain curved brick wall (rather dead brick unfortunately) without any windows, a portal-like glass opening to the baptistery and then a straight windowless brick wall with just a square cut in to hang a bell. These brick walls curve into the baptistery opening and rise towards the bell end. The entry is through a porch further W and then past a planted inner courtyard to the church. The porch links the church with its 1940 predecessor, now the hall. Inside, not quite so convincing. The altar wall is plain and the roof has light metal beams. – Contemporary FURNISHINGS including the altar, lectern and pulpit. – FONT with angel carvings by *John Bridgeman*, set on a watery blue-green mosaic pavement extending beyond the window to the ground outside: a striking feature. – No stained glass.

ST MATTHEW, Warwick Street (closed in 2012). 1841 by *R. C. Hussey*, enlarged by *Ewan Christian* in 1860–1 and the chancel and ancillary rooms added by *C. H. Samson*, 1914. The church is ashlar-faced and in the lancet style. Originally nave and narrow aisles and no chancel; the outline preserved in the gables of the W wall. Oddly pre-archaeological for Rickman's partner, especially given the influence of the antiquary M. H. Bloxam whose father gave the site. *Christian* widened the aisles and added the low W porch and lean-to narthex. Here is the only external decoration, with four quatrefoils in a circle and spandrel carvings over the double doors. Pointed-trefoiled lancets to the narthex and aisles. The sides of the aisles are gabled and have tall lancets to light the deep galleries within.

Inside, curious cross roofing or penetrations for the upper windows. Slender piers, alternatingly round and octagonal, carrying pointed arches to the nave and aisles. N and S galleries *c.* 1846. The added chancel retains the original E wall and window. – STAINED GLASS. E window probably *Lavers & Barraud*, 1865. – The rest mostly by *John Hall & Sons Ltd*, 1917–40.

ST MATTHEW AND ST OSWALD, Lawford Road. *See* New Bilton (p. 552).

ST PETER AND ST JOHN, Clifton Road. 1909 by *C. Ford Whitcombe*. The chancel by *W.A. Forsyth*, 1933. Brick, with an apsed baptistery, the tracery just a little fanciful in detail. The Gothic windows set in blank segmental arches. Piers oblong, chamfered, and set diagonally. No capitals. Narrow, high aisles. The W end remodelled as a church hall by *Kellett & Thompson*, 1984–5 with gallery above and a small chapel in the upper part of the apse. – STAINED GLASS. E window by *Francis Stephens*, 1955.

ST PHILIP, Wood Street. By *H.B. Creswell*, 1914. Closed in 2003. Arts and Crafts brick with pantile roof. The style is Romanesque, though all the arches are very slightly pointed and the motif of the tripartite lunette used for the nave S and N aisle windows is of Palladian descent. The bellcote is set transversely and helps to form a picturesque group. Celtic decorations in stone panels above the porch. The interior all tunnel-vaulted. – FURNISHINGS mainly contemporary and by *Alec Miller* and *Jim Pyment*, of the *Guild of Handicraft*. – STAINED GLASS. *Arild Rosenkrantz*, 1914.

ST MARIE (R.C.), Dunchurch Road. 1845–7 by *Pugin*, paid for   96
by Captain J.W. Hibbert of Bilton Grange (q.v.). His however only the SW saddleback tower with its nave (now S aisle) and chancel (now Hibbert Chapel) behind. In 1864–7 *E.W. Pugin* enlarged the church and gave it its present nave and chancel. The steeple, the most impressive feature of the church, came yet later, along with the baptistery, in 1872. It was designed by *Bernard Whelan*. It is E.E., with an extremely tall and slender broach spire. At the foot of the spire trumpeting angels with big wings stand in elaborate niches. The statues of the Virgin and St John either side of the main entrance are by *Theodore Phyffers*. The interior with its arcades and polygonal apse is humble architecturally, but the sanctuary and Hibbert Chapel are richly decorated. Brightly painted ceilings. – HIGH ALTAR and REREDOS by *T.R. Donnelly*, carved by *Boulton*, 1897–8. Painted panels of saints above by *Hardman* (designer *J.A. Pippet*), 1908. – Chancel STALLS by *Boulton*, 1904. – N aisle ALTAR, 1901. – STAINED GLASS in apse and chancel by *Hardman*, 1865; other N windows theirs too, to 1935. – Two on S probably by *Mayer & Co.*, one signed, *c.* 1890, another unsigned, †1904. – Hibbert Chapel and SW tower windows by *J.E. Nuttgens*, *c.* 1946–7. – Under the Pugin tower, small windows by *Aidan McRae Thomson*, 1997. – Hibbert MEMORIAL BRASS, by *Hardman*, 1856.

St Marie's is at the centre of a group comprising the church with burial ground complete with lychgate and churchyard cross, the Rosiminian Novitiate college (1850–1) to the E, the boys' school (1851) in the NW corner of the churchyard, the turreted convent and girls' school (1853–4) towards Oak Street and a presbytery (1865) linked to the college; also Hibbert's coach house near the road. Mostly by *Pugin* in origin, but completed by others – the college by *Myers* and the schools and convent by *Charles Hansom*. Gabled additions to the convent buildings by *Hawksley* in 1911, by when it was an infants' school. The buildings N of the church are now (2015) used as a primary school, nursery and convent. The College became Bishop Wulstan's Roman Catholic secondary school which closed in 2007. Its buildings were converted for Rugby School as the Collingwood Centre by *HLN Architects*, 2011–13.

BAPTIST CHURCH and REGENT ROOMS (the Sunday School), Regent Place. *G. & R. P. Baines*, 1905–6. Their usual Arts and Crafts Perp with attractive detailing. Brick with stone bands. Tower with lantern and thin leaded spire.

UNITED REFORMED CHURCH, Hillmorton Road. A utilitarian building, originally Presbyterian, 1954–5, with stained glass by *Goddard & Gibbs*.*

METHODIST CHURCH CENTRE, Russelsheim Way. *Peter Thimbleby*, 1983–4. A combined church and hall with classrooms and meeting rooms, successor to the Market Place church (*C. O. Ellison*, 1868–9), and others. Brick with aluminium windows. Flèche on roof. Aisled interior with slate panels between concrete ribs behind the altar and abstract STAINED GLASS above. – Also a window panel from the old chapel in the vestibule.

EVANGELICAL FREE CHURCH, Railway Terrace (formerly Primitive Methodist), by *James Kerridge & Sons* of Wisbech, 1877. Pedimented front with rusticated stone pilasters and window headers.

CHRISTIAN FELLOWSHIP, Cambridge Street (formerly Wesleyan Methodist). Begun in 1883, but the chapel fronting the street added by *John Wills* of Derby, 1898. Tired Gothic, with plate tracery and thin brick pinnacles.

QUAKER MEETING, Regent Place. By *H. Bedford Tylor* of Bournville, 1909. Plain, but with a timber-framed porch – suitably Quaker, very Bournville.

CEMETERY, Clifton Road. Lodge, gates and surviving chapel (now used by the ORTHODOX CHURCH) by *George Bidlake*, 1863. Chapel stone with slate roof, geometric tracery and spiky turret with sandstone columns and fussy capitals. – SCREEN, with ICONS by *Aidan Hart*.

---

*The Gothic Congregational chapel in Albert Street by *Joseph James*, 1865–7, has been demolished.

PUBLIC BUILDINGS

TOWN HALL, Caldecott Park, i.e. out of the centre, and hence spacious. Alas it is quite dead architecturally, with its façade of a rigid portico of square stone piers and Neo-Georgian light brick wings each side. By *J. C. Prestwich & Sons*, 1959–61. The BENN HALL attached, contemporary.

MAGISTRATES' COURT and POLICE HEADQUARTERS, Newbold Road. 1974–6 by the *County Architect*. Wide two-storeyed front, with higher internal block to the N. Plain brickwork. Pretty functional.

PUBLIC LIBRARY, Little Elborow Street. *Crampin Pring McCartney Gatt*, 2000, with symmetrical façade and a reverse-apse entrance in glass.

WARWICKSHIRE COLLEGE, Technology Drive. The *Hitchman Stone Partnership*, 2010. Green curved roofs and walls of white artificial stone with red bands.

Of SCHOOLS, the best is LAWRENCE SHERIFF (the Lower School) in Clifton Road, with the founder's statue on the façade. The main building by *Joseph Clarke*, 1875–8, with plate tracery and shingled bell-turret. Single-storey side extensions by *J. D. & T. L. Hoper*, 1907–9, raised to two storeys on the r. with rear extension by *Loveday*, 1931. Behind, a classroom block by *Loveday*, 1926. Recent additions include the GRIFFIN CENTRE, 1996, and the LEARNING RESOURCE CENTRE, 2009, both by *HB Architects*.

Other schools by successive *County Architects* with the usual economy in design, but with contemporary brickwork sculpture at BILTON, *c.* 1938, and artworks at ROKEBY, 1953, and ABBOTS FARM, 1961–2, all by *Walter Ritchie*; another by *John Skeaping* at BAWNMORE, *c.* 1958.

Of former schools still extant, yellow brick lancet-windowed St Matthew's School, Pennington Street (now INTEC BUSINESS COLLEGE), is by *Frederick Wood* of Rugby, 1845 and 1852, enlarged by *Ward & Hall*, 1890. Conversion by *HB Architects*, 2009. EASTLANDS in St Peter's Road is a good Edwardian example: the original building by *John Willmot*, County Surveyor, 1905–7, and the adjacent boys' school by *Willmot, Fowler & Willmot*, 1911–12.

HOSPITAL OF ST CROSS, Barby Road. The core is of 1884 by *Henry Wilson*. Long front, red brick with black brick patterns; Tudor. E wing and chapel by *Wilson*, 1897–9, with STAINED GLASS by *Powell* in the chapel. Additions included a children's wing by *J. D. Hoper*, 1907, and an outpatients' department by *Young & Hall*, 1928–9. Hugely extended to the S.

VIADUCT, 'the eleven arches', over the Avon by *C. B. Vignoles* for the Midland Railway, 1839–40. The first STATION was near the viaduct and the older buildings on the present site in Railway Terrace are those of Rugby's third station, 1885: one of the island platforms and its offices. Otherwise the station was rebuilt in 2002 and again remodelled 2006–8. SE of the station, RUGBY POWER SIGNAL BOX by *Bicknell & Hamilton*, 1962–4 (superseded for signalling, 2004). Good, in the 1960s way. Broad bands of concrete and blue engineering bricks, with corner tower and projecting top storey.

RUGBY SCHOOL

Founded in 1567 by Lawrence Sheriff, a London grocer, Rugby was one of the many post-Reformation grammar schools. Originally in premises N of the church, it moved to its present site in 1748–50 when *William Hiorne* remodelled the old manor house for the purpose. By the early C19 the buildings had become inadequate. Samuel Wyatt prepared plans for a new school but died in 1807. *Henry Hakewill* picked up the commission and undertook a complete rebuilding of the main block, which remains substantially intact complete with the old school house, schoolroom, courtyard and clock tower, all of 1809–14. Hakewill also designed the original chapel, built in 1818–21. It was Georgian Gothic with a collegiate-style interior. School and chapel face S. Seen across the spacious playing fields and partly screened by a few well placed trees the various Gothic buildings are picturesque and one can get attached to the view.

The middle years of the C19 brought expansion, especially under Thomas Arnold, headmaster from 1828 to 1842, and Dr Frederick Temple, 1857–69. Architecturally Arnold did little, Temple did much. Nevertheless, under Arnold and his successors Hakewill's buildings were seamlessly heightened and enlarged on the street side. Hakewill's own later works include the oriel windowed Sixth School over the gateway (1827–8). Other architects involved included *R. C. Hussey* who did the Arnold Library (1846–7) and *F. C. Penrose* (Arnold's nephew) who added a transept to the old chapel (1847).

While Hakewill set the style for three decades of building, the real spirit of Rugger is *Butterfield*. First approached by the head boy to design the racquets courts in 1859, Butterfield did a few minor things in 1860–5.* Yet on the strength of these he was engaged in 1867 to design New Quad in his own distinctive style. The rebuilding of the chapel followed, giving the school a statement of its identity. That was what just Temple wanted when he commissioned it, in the face of strong opposition from the trustees, shortly before his elevation to the bishopric of Exeter in 1869. Butterfield continued to work for the school into old age, assisting *T. G. Jackson* with the completion of the chapel in 1897–8.

Turning to the buildings, it is best to begin with the main block around the old school and the chapel, first from outside and then from within the grounds, before exploring the full extent of the now greatly expanded school.

*Including a chapel window commissioned in 1859, which led to a bitter dispute with Hardman and ended any future collaboration.

From the town, one glimpses the gateway at the s end of the
High Street and the polychromatic brickwork of New Quad
down Sheep Street; hardly impressive, and hardly cheering.
From the w, however, the school is at its most imposing. On
the corner of Lawrence Sheriff Street are *Butterfield*'s NEW   103
SCHOOLS of 1867 (extended to the s, 1885), a short cloister,
then the CHAPEL (*see below*) with Butterfield's octagonal tower
of 1872 standing high over *Jackson*'s 1897 w front and the
flamboyant Gothic narthex of 1856. Then another short link
to *Sir Charles Nicholson*'s 1922 MEMORIAL CHAPEL (p. 539).

To the street, the NEW SCHOOLS are a masterpiece of *Butterfield*'s personal, inventive Neo-Gothic, totally unconcerned
with symmetry and regularity. It is of red and yellow and black
brick, with fleuron-friezes which Butterfield repeated in his
other Rugby buildings, and the composition is ruthlessly
varied, with unexpected accents. The corner is chamfered,
except for the top floor, where it is rectangular. Into Lawrence
Sheriff Street the controlled riot carries on, with the only real
large window somewhere on the top floor close to the corner.
Then three bays of 1858 link New Quad to Hakewill's Old
Buildings of 1809–14, originally single-storey here but heightened; the ARNOLD LIBRARY with a small oriel and five Perp
windows by *Hussey*, 1846–7, and the upper part of the gateway
by *Hakewill* himself, 1827–8. Here a rainwater head dated
1809. The cheeky Gothic gable l. of the gateway belongs to a
library extension by *Cossins & Peacock*, 1893. Beyond, SCHOOL
HOUSE with its angle tower and porch across. The character
here, both the original buildings and the additions, is pale brick
and castellated, Gothic to Tudor, much as Cambridge college
buildings might be during the same years. Apart from minor
alterations by the insertion of a third floor and addition of a
projecting e wing to SCHOOL HOUSE, the varied s front of
Hakewill's OLD BUILDINGS is virtually unaltered.

On entering the school through the archway one is in
Hakewill's cloister, OLD QUAD, with its ranges of four-centred
arcading. Opposite the entrance a higher arch and the clock
turret. On the w, the school pump dated 1814 in a recess. To
the r. of the passageway, the OLD BIG SCHOOL, a Georgian
double cube inside with wood-panelled walls. Beyond, the
passage leads into NEW QUAD with the chapel on the s and
Butterfield's L-shaped NEW SCHOOLS N and w. They were   103
completed 1867–72, but the end nearest the chapel is a matching addition, 1884–5. Much more reasonable than the façade
towards the street. In the angle, a stair tower with pyramid
roof.

Then, *Butterfield*'s CHAPEL. It stands on the extended footprint   94
of the *Hakewill* chapel and retains the old w door, dated 1820.
The enlargement and rebuilding took place in stages, which
explains some quirks in the plan. It is mainly of 1872 and
amazingly resourceful. The polychromy is as pronounced as
before. The climax of the composition is the octagonal central

tower with steep pyramid roof* and big gargoyles sparring out. Big broaches mediate between square and octagon. The whole is as multiform and as stepped as possible. The apse is polygonal. To the sides three bays project transeptally, one slightly, the others more boldly and with steep cross-gables. That leaves little length to the nave and the very low aisles. Here Hakewill's work remained intact until *Jackson* completed the rebuilding in 1897–8. The interior is very striking, and as a college chapel entirely convincing. It is soaring all right, yet the transeptal spaces bring the worshippers closer to the service than the normal nave and aisle arrangement would make possible. Two-bay nave, three-bay transepts with very tall, round, red and white striped piers. Open timber roofs (strikingly painted by *Stephen Dykes Bower*, 1958–61) and only in the chancel transverse brick arches. The transept roofs are remarkably intricate, in an alternating rhythm of tie-beams and hammerbeams. Butterfield's walls are red and white too and have in addition black sgraffito patterns. In the vaulting of the apse, stylized MOSAICS by *Salviati* of Venice, begun in 1872 and completed 1882. – Mixed FURNISHINGS, not all by *Butterfield*; the nave SEATING partly of 1821. – CANDLESTICKS by *Butterfield*, 1885. – ORGAN CASE by *Kenneth Jones*, 2003. – Exceptional STAINED GLASS, best treated chronologically beginning with windows from the old chapel. The E window has C16 Flemish glass from Aerschot near Louvain, given in 1834. The Adoration of the Magi. More Aerschot glass (Christ appearing to Mary Magdalene) in a N clerestory window. – In the S transept another C16 piece (the Presentation) said to come from Rouen. – This ancient glass successfully imitated in 1842 by *Thomas Willement*: a window in the N transept, and perhaps another in the S clerestory with some C16 German glass. – Then *Hardman* from 1853, although the Crimea memorial window, 1856, is the only complete survivor; fragments in a N transept window too. – In the narthex, four by a French artist in spherical triangle windows, *c.* 1856. – Next, the *Butterfield*-designed *Hardman* window in the S clerestory, 1859–64. – All these re-set at the rebuilding, 1872, when *Alexander Gibbs* provided the side windows in the apse, probably designed by *Butterfield*. – Soon afterwards, two facing pairs of three-light transept windows by *Gibbs*, 1873 on the S and 1877–8 on the N. Clean, light colours, sharp outlines and just the effect that *Butterfield* wished for. – *Kempe* did the S transept W window when the chapel was completed, 1898. – Then the W window and seven in the aisles, chancel and porch by *Morris & Co.*, 1900–27, some using cartoons by *Burne-Jones* and others designed by *J. H. Dearle*. The W window of the Last Judgment, 1902, was *Dearle*'s first independent large-scale work. – Lastly, single N aisle windows by *Powell* (*J. W. Brown*), 1911, *Edward Woore*, 1924, and *Walter Camm*, 1947. – MONUMENTS. Dr Thomas James †1804 by *Sir Francis Chantrey*, 1824.

---

* Originally timber and slate, rebuilt in stone 1882.

White marble. Very fine, with the seated figure and the two busts of Homer and Virgil in shallow relief, one frontal, the other in profile. The motif was taken over by *Chantrey* from Flaxman's 1801 Warton memorial at Winchester Cathedral. – Opposite Dr John Wooll, by *R. Westmacott Jun.*, 1833. Also seated white figure, but looser in composition. – Dr Thomas Arnold †1842. Stone. Recumbent effigy under a rich Gothic canopy. 1844 by *John Thomas*. – Arthur P. Stanley, Arnold's biographer and later Dean of Westminster, by *J. E. Boehm*, 1884. Recumbent marble effigy. – Marble medallions of A. H. Clough and Matthew Arnold by *Lilian Morris*, 1901, in a setting designed by *Jackson*.

Immediately s is the MEMORIAL CHAPEL, 1922 by *Sir Charles Nicholson*. Very anaemic after Butterfield – but what else could it be? Yet it has a quiet beauty. The style is French flamboyant. Inside, plain walls and simplified mouldings. Cruciform, Gothic, ashlar-faced, with a rib-vault in the centre and pointed tunnel-vaults in the arms. – Canopied REREDOS with statues, a Second World War memorial. – FONT. By *Fabio Barraclough*, 1957, with four female figures *à la* Dobson. – LECTERNS with marquetry inlay for the books of memorial. – STAINED GLASS in the cloister, ante-chapel and chapel, all by *Burlison & Grylls*, 1923. The cloister windows have moving scenes depicting tanks, dreadnoughts and trench warfare.

More buildings along the periphery of the main site and in the adjoining streets, s of the Memorial Chapel along Dunchurch Road. First *Butterfield*'s former SWIMMING BATH, 1876, with glass roof but a group of stepped lancets above the N doorway. Then the GYMNASIUM, also *Butterfield*, 1872, varied brick, with a varied front but utilitarian sides 'just like a Methodist chapel with a belfry' (Peter Howell). The balconied JAMES MEMORIAL PAVILION is by *Knapp-Fisher, Powell & Russell*, 1936. Along Barby Road (from the s) the RACQUETS COURTS of 1860 and 1885, both by *Butterfield*. Glass roof; simple, heavy brickwork. The OLD PAVILION (now a classroom), 1869. The DESIGN CENTRE tucked in between and behind the racquets courts, by the *Stillman Eastwick-Field Partnership*, 1992. N of this SCHOOL FIELD, a big house, red brick and black diapers, steep dormers originally with tall chimneys in between,* an asymmetrical composition. This is by *G. G. Scott*, 1852 – the same year as Holy Trinity church. Rear extension in paler brick with diapered end facing Barby Road, by *Farmer & Dark*, 1956.

Opposite this, across Barby Road, is the OLD SANATORIUM, by *Penrose*, 1857–9, also brick, also diapers, but a free composition with a round tower containing a wide spiral stair. Remarkably light of touch. Matching rear extension by *Penrose*, 1892, and further additions by *Franklin*, 1897. E of this TUDOR HOUSE, brick and bleak, by *John Sander* of Nottingham, 1891 – just Gothic shaped windows. Opposite, the OBSERVATORY and OBSERVATORY HOUSE, 1877. S of the Old Sanatorium

*These have been removed.

BRADLEY HOUSE, 1830. Ashlar, with castellated angle turrets and token castellation to the porch and parapets. Influenced by *Hakewill*, though probably not by him. Then SHERIFF HOUSE, with hipped roof and dormers, by *W. A. Forsyth*, 1930; the hammerbeam-roofed dining room has stained glass by *A. J. Davies*. Opposite, *Henman & Cooper*'s 1902–3 SCIENCE SCHOOL, originally single-storey with a colonnaded entrance and turret retained when it was heightened by *W. T. Loveday*, 1939; atrium added by *EllisWilliams Architects*, 2008. A good deal further s KILBRACKEN, built in 1865–7 by *Butterfield* as a preparatory school (Hillbrow). Again Gothic, again with typical Butterfield windows. The big boarding house behind is by *W. T. Loveday*, 1939.

Back to Horton Crescent, and STANLEY HOUSE, 1824, with canted bays and odd parapet; the front EXTENSION by *W. Henman*, 1892, has curious ornamental chimneys. Alongside is *Butterfield*'s TEMPLE READING ROOM, 1878, now the library. Paul Thompson thought it Butterfield's best non-ecclesiastical interior. The upper room is still entirely Butterfield's, with open timber roof and a large Gothic window for the staircase, but the ground-floor room – still memorable – has been softened by the removal of the stained glass and painted decoration. Outside, the TOM BROWN STATUE by *Thomas Brock*, 1899.

At the corner of Barby Road and Hillmorton Road is the TEMPLE SPEECH ROOM, 1908–9 by *T. G. Jackson*. It is placed diagonally so that the Tudor turret and the porch l. and r. of it with its classical Tuscan columns face the corner. Typically Jacksonian mixture of Tudor and Baroque. The two transepts have Venetian windows under Baroque pediments. Tunnel-vaulted interior with the crossing emphasized by a fancy rib-vault. STAINED GLASS in transept windows by *Powell*, 1909. Across the road, i.e. at the corner of Little Church Street and Lawrence Sheriff Street, NEW BIG SCHOOL, by *Butterfield*, 1885, at once recognizable but not distinguished. Originally classrooms below a big hall, but converted as the MACREADY THEATRE in 1975. Then the BURSARY: 1850s with diapered brickwork and an oriel with a fan-vaulted underside. Into Hillmorton Road, there are more school buildings beyond the Temple Speech Room. Immediately E, the MUSIC SCHOOL, brick with embattled parapet with stone mullioned-and-transomed windows, by *Sir Charles Nicholson*, 1925 and 1939; extension with curved walls, 2011. Over the road, set well back, is Queen Anne-style MICHELL HOUSE, red brick with gables and tile infill in the window heads, 1882–3. Back on the s, the new SANATORIUM by *Pite, Son & Fairweather*, 1934, and adjacent DEAN HOUSE. Then WHITELAW HOUSE, Rugby's first boarding house of 1790, with a bold addition of 1887. COTTON HOUSE (No. 10) was also formerly private: early C19, of five bays with giant pilasters; frontage altered in Queen Anne style by *Nicholson & Corlette*, 1895.

In Horton Crescent, the L-shaped MODERN LANGUAGES
BUILDING is by *HLN Architects*, 2012, constructed to very
high environmental and sustainability standards. Opposite a
group of four 1860s Gothic houses with diapered brickwork,
originally private but now linked to form RUPERT BROOKE
HOUSE. Other boarding houses in Horton Crescent also
occupy later C19 private houses; some late classical, some
Gothic.

PERAMBULATIONS

The centre of Rugby is quite compact and these three routes all
begin and end near the clock tower. Perambulation 1 takes in the
historic heart of the old market town and the heavily redeveloped
western periphery. The second tours the Victorian and Edwardian areas and the third covers the residential areas close to the
town centre. The scale in the town centre is all modest, three or
even two storeys.

1. Central south-west

In the MARKET PLACE, *R. J. & J. Goodacre*'s CLOCK TOWER,
1888–9. On the E, featureless shops of 1953 stand in place of the
GEORGE INN, but the w side has fared better. At the N end
THE CROWN (No. 25) with half-timbering and pargetting; by
Harry Percival, 1896–7. SANTANDER BANK alongside (No.
23–24), mid-C19 Italianate with C20 corporate façade at street
level. Plain Georgian frontages remain above the colonnaded
entrance to CLOCK TOWERS SHOPPING CENTRE, 1980. The
CARD FACTORY (No. 20–20A) was the Eagle Hotel, built
c. 1820: stuccoed with upper unfluted giant Ionic pilasters.
Jutting out into the street, No. 19, with polished granite columns
at the entrance and a spiky pinnacle above, is by *Willard*, 1893.
Here the street narrows. Rounded corners to three of the buildings at the junction with Chapel Street, MCDONALD'S (No. 4)
with carved and painted arms below the parapet; it was previously the WINE BARREL pub. Down CHAPEL STREET one
humble and very restored C16 timber-framed and gabled
cottage survives (No. 1). Where the Market Place widens out
again the open space has decent shops on all sides. On the w,
No. 11–12 is early C19 with Doric pilasters but dated 1893 on
the cornice. No. 14 has 1860s Ruskinian Gothic details. On the
E, MONSOON (No. 6) is Neo-Georgian with a stone canted bay
in the centre; by *Cossins, Peacock & Bewlay* for the United
Counties Bank, 1912. Next door BURTON'S (No. 7), 1938; a
typical company job, probably by *Nathaniel Martin*. At the far
s, No. 42 High Street marks the end of the Market Place: again
with Doric pilasters, probably 1824.

Here the road divides, with the High Street on the l. terminating opposite the entrance gateway to Rugby School and

Sheep Street to the r. leading towards the New Schools. The buildings between them represent infill in the originally funnel-shaped market place which opened out to the S. The long run of shallow buildings in SHEEP STREET (Nos. 1–10) developed from the old Shambles, including MANOR BUILDINGS, 1890. Also in Sheep Street, the plain Late Georgian RUGBY HOTEL of five widely spaced bays.

The better buildings are in the HIGH STREET. No. 4 retains the Baroque upper frontage of the municipal offices (known as the Benn Building) by *North & Hawke*, 1897–1901, originally converted for MARKS & SPENCER by *Albert E. Batzer*, 1936–7. Opposite, late C19 No. 37 rises awkwardly to four storeys. Of *c.* 1810, SALTERS (No. 6–7) on the E typifies the plain Late Georgian of the period before the town's early C19 expansion. Further S, nothing remains of *James Murray*'s original town hall and Corn Exchange of 1858, whose site extending through to Sheep Street was redeveloped for Woolworths (now FAMILY BARGAINS) in the 1960s; concrete slab façade with blue mosaic decoration. Alongside, the concrete classical upper parts of No. 31–32 belong to *Warren Hawksley*'s town hall extension, 1911. The lively front of the SUMMERSAULT café (No. 27) is by *Albert Bromley* of Nottingham for Boots, 1912; richly Baroque upper storey in light faience and Art Nouveau doors to the shopfront. The adjoining building (LAWRENCE SHERIFF pub) is its Art Deco extension of 1935 by Boots' architect *Percy Bartlett*, with a pharmaceutical sculpture above the first-floor balcony. Opposite, at the end facing the school, PIZZA EXPRESS (No. 23–24) with simplified Tudor details and red brick mullions, 1934–5. Opposite, an 1840s shop (No. 25) with brick pilasters and rounded corner.

Along LAWRENCE SHERIFF STREET to the W, the former Red Lion pub (now Nipa Thai) by *Warren Hawksley*, 1926, with Arts and Crafts rainwater goods and an octagonal room over the entrance. W again, facing the traffic below the Butterfield façade of the school where Rugger originated, is *Graham Ibbeson*'s 1997 statue of William Webb Ellis, traditionally credited with inventing the game in 1823. Nearby in ST MATTHEW'S STREET the Webb Ellis Rugby Football Museum – William Gilbert's shop where rugby balls were made – in a row of early C19 yellow brick classical houses. Behind St Matthew's church in walled grounds is the PERCIVAL GUILDHOUSE (originally St Matthew's Place), a rather gaunt 1840s house with a turret reminiscent of Pugin. It was the home of solicitor and antiquary Matthew Holbeche Bloxam, whose *Principles of Gothic Architecture* (1829) ran to ten editions. W of the church, more 1840s houses in WARWICK STREET, ADDISON ROW on the N (Nos. 22–24) and ADDISON PLACE (Nos. 16–18) opposite with Doric pilasters and a triglyph frieze round the doorway.

At the junction turn into CORPORATION STREET, Rugby's 1958 relief road, now lined with late C20 and early C21 buildings.

BLOXAM COURT on the corner of Lawford Road lightly complements the style of Rugby School; by *HB Architects*, 1993. Further N, brutalist MILLER HOUSE, 1972, and *HB*'s HILTON HOUSE medical centre, 2004, stand opposite the ASDA supermarket by *WCEC Architects*, 2009. ASDA is linked to the SWAN CENTRE in Chapel Street and faces the library. Further N, the severe concrete car park of CLOCK TOWERS SHOPPING CENTRE now has softening vertical aluminium bars. Towards the roundabout, the 1966 FIRE STATION faces the dominant CEMEX HOUSE (formerly Crown House) at the corner of Evreux Way: by *T. P. Bennett & Son* for the Portland Cement Company, 1964–5, a straightforward curtain-wall job, ten triple-window units in width and eight storeys in height plus a recessed ninth set back in the unrecessed framework. On the corner of Oliver Street and Newbold Road, THE ELMS: plum brick with white-painted stonework, 1840s. Behind the town hall two 1840s villas, THE LAWN and THE RETREAT, the former with a roof tower. In St John Street off Newbold Road, the ELBOROW ALMSHOUSES, 1878. Continue up Newbold Road past the police station and right into LANCASTER ROAD to CALDECOTT PARK, laid out in 1904 with its bandstand and modern sculptures, including Echo, 2009 by *Hilary Cartmel*.

In NORTH STREET, first the COURTHOUSE pub (previously the SARACEN'S HEAD) by *Forshaw & Palmer* of Burton upon Trent for Ind Coope Ltd, 1931, half-timbered with brick nogging. Alongside, 1950s Neo-Georgian CHESTNUT HOUSE, the public TOILETS by *HB Architects*, 1999, in brick with a carved brick mural by *John McKenna* depicting aspects of Rugby's industrial past. Past the N entrance of the shopping centre, NATWEST BANK (No. 9) at the base of a *moderne* office block with rounded corner. Horizontal bands of windows and vertical fins above the entrance; by *S. N. Cooke* for the Rugby Portland Cement Co., 1936. Then IMPERIAL BUILDINGS: two storeys plus attic above shops, by *T. W. Willard*, dated 1897 on its rich plasterwork coved cornice. Opposite, No. 35, built for the Rugby Club, 1866: classical with porch of a rusticated arch within Doric pilasters and entablature.

From here, continue directly to Perambulation 2.

2. Central north

A bland beginning to CHURCH STREET, E of the clock tower, with a very ordinary range (Nos. 1–10) of 1961 round the corner from North Street: disappointing replacements for the C19 almshouses and 1729 Boughton House. At the corner of Regent Street, the curved front of Lennards (No. 13) by *Bridgman & Bridgman* of Torquay, 1914. Then Church Street's most striking building: LLOYDS BANK (No. 14) on the opposite corner, by *J. A. Chatwin*, 1904: free classical with Renaissance motifs, still with its original plaster ceiling in the main banking hall. In contrast, adjacent HSBC (No. 15) has a plain Modernist façade by *Douglas J. Oliver & Partners*, 1964, with contemporary abstract sculpture by *Don Foster*. Next is No. 16, built for Count Wratislaw *c.* 1790. Gault brick with pilasters, shallow curved bow with three tiers of segmental-headed windows. In contrast again, RBS alongside is in red brick. Built for the National Provincial Bank by *John Gibson*, 1877, with five-bay front and round-headed dormer windows. Facing back towards the church, early C19 CHURCH VIEW APARTMENTS (No. 18), stucco with Ionic pilasters and slate roof.

Round the corner in CASTLE STREET, a handsome block of six shops, CASTLE BUILDINGS (Nos. 3–13), by *J. T. Franklin*, 1898. Beyond in GAS STREET, BROTHERHOOD HOUSE (former Baptist chapel) by *Mr Whorwood*, 1881, described as 'in the Italian style' with white-painted window surrounds. Back to ALBERT STREET, the sharply angled corner building is the RUGBY ADVERTISER newspaper office, *c.* 1850, with the former printing works on the Castle Street side; originally plain brickwork, now stuccoed. After the Gothic frontage of the 1872–3 court building (Nos. 10–12), the grand Neoclassical corner building at the junction of Bank Street was built as a CONSERVATIVE CLUB, by *Tollit & Lee* of Oxford, 1904. Opposite, white terracotta ESTATE OFFICES (Nos. 11–13) with delicate classical details: by *Franklin & Newman*, 1923, heightened to three storeys, 1928. Adjoining in BANK STREET, another block of shops (Nos. 13–17) by *Franklin*, 1903. *Willard*'s Regent Cinema in Bank Street, 1920, is now BANK RESTAURANT. Albert Street itself was laid out in 1851 as a route to the railway station. Of this date, ALMA LODGE (No. 30) whose patterned brickwork is picked up in the walling of the multi-storey car park in James Street behind by *Keltecs*, 1989. Beyond, the 1930s *Office of Works* TELEPHONE EXCHANGE and 1975 government offices, KINGSFORTH HOUSE, and JOBCENTRE.

Back at the corner of HENRY STREET, the four-storey former SAM ROBBINS department store, by *Willard Son & Ellingham*, 1936. Opposite (Nos. 14–22 Henry Street) a row of five low lock-up shops on a narrow site, by *Franklin & Newman*, 1908. Facing each other in Henry Street, RUGBY THEATRE by *Eames & Jackson*, 1913, and (used by the theatre since 1955) the CENTRAL HALL by *J H. & R. B. Liddington*, 1929: white terracotta, lugged architraves to the windows and big chimney pinnacles above the entrance.

From Henry Street turn r. and head N to REGENT PLACE and the small open space, with sculptures. Turn back, and the date 1901 boldly above a shopfront marks the start – chronologically and physically – of Rugby's Edwardian showpiece: REGENT STREET. It was laid out by *Franklin* on the old Moat estate in 1901 and is a delight, especially looking s to the spire of St Andrew's (*see* Churches). All the frontages, for which most of the shopfronts have survived, are of 1901–5 and mainly by *Franklin* but with a most pleasing variety of style and texture, drawn from the Domestic Revival. Towards the N end, a former furniture warehouse (Nos. 18–20) has plate glass windows separated by thin iron columns. Netherlandish gables on No. 16. Opposite, a rock-faced pair (Nos. 23–25) also gabled with odd motifs. Opposite, No. 10 has a big semicircular opening to the first-floor balcony with bay window set inside the archway and a triangular gable with round window above. No. 8 in Art Nouveau style with balconies and curved gable. Nos. 5–7 opposite is by *Liddington*, 1901, with roughcast gable and serrated window surrounds.

3. Central south-east

In LITTLE CHURCH STREET is the former RECTORY (latterly HERBERT GREY COLLEGE but currently (2015) awaiting redevelopment). Immediately s of the parish church, it may stand on the site of the manor of the de Rokeby family which had been given over for the parsonage by the C13. The earliest parts of the present house are C18, with alterations by *John Russell* in 1827 – probably the bargeboarded garden front – and subsequent extensions, chiefly those by *Christian E. Eliot*, 1899.

Beyond in EASTFIELD PLACE is THE ARNOLD HOUSE, early C19 with Doric pilasters and attic dormers between chimneys. Alongside on the N, the almost windowless MASONIC HALL by *Loveday*, 1935. Heading s, off Church Walk to the E are ARNOLD VILLAS, six cottages in gault brick with small Gothic windows and fish-scale tiled roofs, the garden wall dated 1851.

On reaching HILLMORTON ROAD, one is among the boarding houses of Rugby School (*see* above). At the corner of Church Walk, No. 5 (the birthplace of Rupert Brooke) is plain mid-C19 with simple Gothic details, and No. 7 has attractive details to the projecting bay windows. Then (Nos. 9–15) a block of four slate-roofed gault brick houses, 1840s: three-storey with basement, raised entrances approached by stairs and first-floor iron balconies. Opposite, HORTON HOUSE (No. 6), a private house built for William Sharp *c.* 1850: clearly influenced by Scott's School Field (*see* Rugby School, above), with black brick diapering and steep bargeboards. HILLMORTON LODGE (No. 17), *c.* 1835, has curious Neoclassical detail and a large square turret to the rear.

Further out, more Early Victorian yellow brick houses (between No. 12 and No. 38) including ARNOLD PLACE (Nos. 20–26). Beyond the park, with WAR MEMORIAL GATES of 1922 by *H. S. Goodhart-Rendel*, is ELMHURST (No. 42) by *W. Sugden & Son* of Leek for Thomas Hunter, 1896–1900: free Renaissance-style, with curvilinear gables and a central octagonal tower.

Then back to Whitehall Road and around Lawrence Sheriff School (*see* Public Buildings) into tree-lined CLIFTON ROAD. Nothing remarkable, but towards the town centre TRINITY COURT, 1983–4, stands on the site of demolished Holy Trinity, retaining the curtain wall and *Comper*'s very ordinary lychgate, 1922. Then back to MOULTRIE ROAD for Rugby's best Edwardian houses, built on the Rectory Estate from 1901. The corner house (No. 1 Clifton Road, taken into the campus of Lawrence Sheriff School) has a stone-clad entrance with semicircular rusticated arch, iron balustrading round a circular corner turret and baubles on top of the coping of the dormer above the entrance. It is by *Liddington*, 1903. No. 5, with a catslide roof each side of a central gabled dormer, is by *Unwin & Parker*, 1904. Opposite, No. 6 with angled window bay and sloping-sided chimneys: 1905, by *H. H. Thomson* of Leicester. Next door, THE COTTAGE (No. 8) by *Creswell*, 1910. No. 15, with canted bays and porch in angle, is by *Liddington*, 1910. At the junction with Hillmorton Road, *John W. Simpson*'s Arts and Crafts TE HIRA (No. 21–23), 1903–4: roughcast and tile-hung, with half-timbering above the colonnaded entrance and turreted roof-line above the stair enclosure. Leading W, ELSEE ROAD belongs to the same development on the Rectory Estate but its *c.* 1900 houses are less grand, closely packed and more commonplace in appearance. A short step N up Church Walk leads back to Church Street past 1840s MARJORY HUME HOUSE and, facing the E end of the church, ST ANDREW'S CHURCH HOUSE, Neo-Byzantine, by *G. A. Steane*, 1934–6.

Rugby, Te Hira, perspective.
Photo lithograph, 1905

OUTER RUGBY

On the main roads out of Rugby early C19 to Early Victorian, i.e. late classical, housing spreads, e.g. as already noted in HILL-MORTON ROAD (*see* Perambulation 3), NEWBOLD ROAD and WARWICK STREET (Perambulation 1). The best and most varied are along BILTON ROAD to the SW, beginning at the junction with Warwick Street. All 1830s, mostly in yellow brick and generally with Doric porches or pilasters, sometimes with stucco details. On the E side, two handsome blocks (Nos. 3–7 and 9–11). Opposite, SHAFTO HOUSE (No. 6), refronted in 1902 with Venetian windows and quirky details. STARBOR-OUGH HOUSE (No. 10, originally The Elms) has attic dormers between chimneys on the W side like The Arnold House. GATEWAY HOUSE (No. 14) is red brick and later, with Vene-tian doorway. Beyond, three Regency pairs (Nos. 18–28), one rather cruelly rock-faced. Another yellow brick block opposite (No. 17–23) with pilasters between each house. Then Gothic WALTON HOUSE (No. 25): typical Rugby 1850s, red brick, diapering, bargeboards. Across Merttens Drive, RICHMOND LODGE (No. 27) with good recessed Doric porch. TOWER LODGE (No. 29–31) has awkward brick towers at each end. OAKFIELD (No. 32) opposite, a substantial house set back in grounds, has been a school, club and offices since 1859. The early C19 houses end here.

To the E and NE, HILLMORTON ROAD and CLIFTON ROAD are lined with later C19 houses, of the 1880s onwards. N of Clifton Road, streets of terraced housing leading down to the railway.

Leading S, DUNCHURCH ROAD has the replacement LAW-RENCE SHERIFF ALMSHOUSES, 1961, on the island facing Rugby School playing fields, and some small-scale mid-C19 housing towards the Roman Catholic church. Further down, immediately alongside blocks of flats on the site of BROOK-SIDE, a house by *Rickman*, 1833, is No. 116: an 'Early-Modern', white, cubic house, built in 1934 for Mrs Shann, the wife of a biology master at Rugby School. Compact, two-storey, the windows flush with the concrete walls and three-quarter circle balcony at one corner, also for access to the roof, its form echoed by the curved terrace below. The architect was *Serge Chermayeff*. Also in Dunchurch Road, SHEPHERD'S HEY (No. 279): a large thatched house by *J. H. & R. B. Liddington* for G.A. Frost, 1936.

Lastly, the industrial buildings to the N. On Newbold Road, S of the railway, the WILLANS WORKS (originally the VICTORIA WORKS and now ALSTOM) was built by *Willard*, 1894–5, and in full production by 1898. An office building and the original works with substantial brick clock tower remain.

Much of the former British Thomson-Houston site (later AEI and GEC) in Mill Road and Boughton Road has been re-developed for housing, but the AEI Research Laboratory in Projects Drive remains. By *W. S. Hattrell & Partners*, 1958–60. GE Energy now occupies old factory buildings in Technology

Drive, alongside the BTH war memorial by *Lutyens*, 1921, relocated from Mill Road in 2010.

W of Leicester Road, in the Swift valley between Newbold and Brownsover, extensive late C20 and early C21 commercial developments. Glass-fronted LUMONICS HOUSE, Cosford Drive, is by *HB Architects*, 1986. The HAFELE warehouse by the same, 1996.

SUBURBS

BILTON

On the road SW towards Leamington. Originally a linear settlement with a small green, the church and hall standing NE of the main village. Now linked to Rugby with continuous development along the main road and large areas of post-war housing N and E, especially towards the Dunchurch Road.

ST MARK. Red sandstone, originally aisleless and all Dec. Probably built for Sir Nicholas de Charnels whose family arms are on the tower. Restored in 1871–2 for the Rev. Richard Orme Assheton, rector 1862–95. Himself an amateur architect and stained glass artist, Assheton was the guiding influence for the later C19 embellishments. *Bodley & Garner* were his architects. Their work included the restoration of the chancel with its grand E window. They also added the N aisle, repositioning the old chancel E window (said to be an 1821 replacement for one of 1609) at its W end. The S aisle came much later, added by *J. A. Chatwin & Son*, 1961–2. The nave walls were both moved outwards and so the bold flowing and reticulated tracery of the windows is basically original Dec. The tower with recessed spire has Dec details too, including the arch to the nave with three continuous chamfers. Dec also the chancel side windows and the large, ogee-headed EASTER SEPULCHRE. This has a cusped and subcusped arch with leafy spandrels and crockets along the outside of the arch. SEDILIA and PISCINA only partly old. Typically *Bodley* is the stencilling around the organ and the painting of the chancel roof, executed by *F. R. Leach*. In the nave the Victorian N arcade has continuous mouldings without capitals, a style repeated with the facing C20 arcade. Timber-framed N porch extension by *William Assheton*, 2011. – Memorable FURNISHINGS by *Bodley & Garner*, including the N aisle E SCREEN, 1877, the chancel REREDOS and panelling, 1880, and the excellent CHOIR STALLS, 1885. – FOLDING PANELS with musical angels above the N door, by *F. H. Sutton*, pre-1866. Made for the previous organ and adapted as a diptych after 1872. – FONT, C14. Octagonal, with two flatly carved tracery patterns repeating. – ORGAN CASE. From St John's College Chapel, Cambridge; by *Thomas*

Thamar, 1661,* with overhang and pinnacles designed by *F. H. Sutton* when it was resited here in 1872. – COMMUNION RAIL. Late C17; from Great St Mary at Cambridge. – CHANDE-LIERS. Pair of C17 brass chandeliers, from the Netherlands. – STAINED GLASS. E window by *Burlison & Grylls*, 1879. – Theirs also the w window, 1872, and two in the s aisle, 1883–4. – By *Powell*, 1857, the N aisle w window, moved with the stone-work in 1872. – Another *Powell* window in chancel s, 1853. – N window by *Heaton, Butler & Bayne*, 1885. – The rest made up at the rectory by *Assheton* and his brother Ralph: the E window in the N aisle 1874–5, and the N chancel window 1887 contain-ing fragments of C14 glass from Bilton and elsewhere. – s aisle E window, 1878–82, by the *Asshetons* in a convincing C14 style.

SACRED HEART (R.C.), Alwyn Road. By *E. Bower Norris*, 1959. Brick with porch tower. Enlarged and reordered in 1991–3. – Immersion FONT, with mosaic by *Lucy Thackeray*. – STAINED GLASS. Some of *c.* 1959. – Windows in Blessed Sacrament chapel by *Chris Lund Studios* to designs by *Fr Paul Chamberlain*, 1993. – Creation windows by *Aidan McRae Thomson*, 1998–9.

METHODIST CHURCH (Wesleyan), Main Street. *Ewen Harper*, 1893. Brick with lancets.

Immediately s of the parish church, the OLD RECTORY by *R. C. Hussey*, 1853: gault brick with red window headers and attrac-tive doorcase.

BILTON HALL, s again. An old house bought by Edward Boughton of Lawford (cf. Newbold-on-Avon, p. 553) in 1610 and settled on his younger son Thomas. He built the three-storied porch dated 1623 and the gabled block alongside. Brick, with mullioned-and-transomed windows. The rest plainer and lower, mid-C17. Joseph Addison, the essayist and poet, bought the estate in 1711. He probably built the early C18 range on the garden side; brick, with flat quoins. Of the same date the staircase with two gauges of twisted balusters to each tread and carved tread-ends. The old part towards the garden was Tudorized in 1831. Now flats.

LONG BARN, Church Walk. A thatched timber-framed house of *c.* 1600, perhaps originally a barn.

On the green, the medieval CROSS and C18 STOCKS with the white gabled MANOR in the lane leading SE and early C19 GEORGE INN on the N. On Bilton Road towards Rugby, CHURCH HOUSE by *H. B. Creswell*, 1911; a village hall with eyebrow dormers and big chimneys. w on Main Street, the former SCHOOL, 1841, with late C20 matching additions. In Magnet Lane, the former NUNC DIMITTIS CHAPEL, by *Bucknall & Comper*, 1893, for Assheton as a memorial to his

---

*Earlier accounts credit this to *Robert Dallam* who did the original organ in 1635, but these parts are now believed to belong to Thamar's post-Restoration work. Further parts of the Cambridge organ are at Brownsover (q.v.).

wife. Tower added 1905, probably by *Assheton*. Converted to a dwelling 1980–1. – STAINED GLASS of 1893 remains. *See also* Bilton Grange.

BROWNSOVER

On the N side of the Avon, with views towards Rugby across the valley and its railway viaduct (p. 535). Much altered by late C20 retail development, an industrial estate in the Swift valley and a large residential area E of Leicester Road. The old village round the church and the hall has been protected from serious encroachment.

ST MICHAEL AND ALL ANGELS. Originally a chapel of ease to Clifton-on-Dunsmore and once larger. The tower fell in the Civil War and the church was repaired in 1701. What remains is largely C13: the doorway now in the W front, the chancel arch, the two N windows with Y-tracery and a lozenge in the spandrel, and the paired lancets in the chancel, all retained in a careful rebuilding by *G. G. Scott*, 1875–6. In the care of the Churches Conservation Trust since 1987. – WOODWORK, evidently collected by the Ward-Boughton-Leighs and used in a haphazard way, e.g. in the screen dado (Jacobean), some panelling behind the pulpit (Perp), and also the ORGAN. The woodwork around the keyboard is from various sources but the upper casework, early C18, comes from St John's College, Cambridge, re-erected here under *F. H. Sutton*, 1876.* – PULPIT. Flemish; C18, with a medallion of Christ in profile, two religious trophies, and a thin tester. – STAINED GLASS. E window by *Frank Holt*, 1881, given by M.H. Bloxam in memory of Lawrence Sheriff, the founder of Rugby School, supposedly born at Brownsover.

CHRIST CHURCH, Helvellyn Way. An ecumenical church, built to serve the new housing estates. By *Kellett, Thompson & Byrne* of Rugby, 1990: octagonal with open roof and lantern.

BROWNSOVER HALL. By *Scott* for John Ward-Boughton-Leigh, 1857, but wrapped round an earlier house of *c.* 1787. Red brick, with blue patterns. Middle Pointed, Scott's favoured style of the period. A well-composed, asymmetrical front in which one bay plus a bay window balance a porch tower which rises to some height and ends in a French steep hipped roof plus a yet higher polygonal stair-turret with a spire – a weird sight from a distance. Lively roof-line with dormers and stone chimneys on polychromatic bases. Good restored interiors, especially the inner hall, staircase and dining room, with dark-hued patterned wallpapers recreating a High Victorian feel. Of Scott's time, several carved stone fireplaces, marble pillars in the staircase gallery and a passageway with arches. After use as a research centre by Sir Frank Whittle in the Second World War, the hall was used by GEC until 1965. It has been a hotel since 1973.

---

*Other parts of the Cambridge organ were used at Bilton (*see* above).

C18 stables behind and added mid-C19 ranges with diapered brickwork and steep gables, doubtless by *Scott*.

In Brownsover Lane, a much restored C16 timber-framed cottage, Lawrence Sheriff's birthplace. The OXFORD CANAL runs round the hill below the village with a single-span cast-iron AQUEDUCT over the Old Leicester Road, built when the canal was improved under *William Cubitt*, 1831–4.

HILLMORTON

Approached by two roads ESE from Rugby. Hillmorton Road leads to the High Street and its long, broad green. This had become the main settlement by the early C18. Lower Hillmorton Road, to the N, goes to the older settlement in the valley. Here the tall embankment of the original London to Birmingham railway, constructed by *Stephenson* in 1835–8, separates Hillmorton from its church, which lies to the N.

ST JOHN THE BAPTIST. Unrestored and still delightfully patched with brick, stucco rendering and pre-Ecclesiological work. Recorded datestones (now eroded) refer to repairs, the N aisle *c.* 1609, the E end 1640 and the tower 1655. Mostly otherwise of *c.* 1300. Of that date the red ashlar W tower, the five-bay arcades of standard elements, the tomb recess in the N aisle, and the chancel and N aisle windows. There have however been later adjustments. The clerestory looks mid-C16, and the E window, quite convincing with its intersecting tracery, is partly of 1640. The S aisle windows also look as if their stouter mid-mullions are later. S porch early C19. Good nave roof, C16, with tie-beams on curved braces and diagonal braces to the rafter and ridge. – PULPIT. Simple, 1777–8. By *Samuel Thomson* of Kilsby. – BOX PEWS in NW corner, surviving from a re-pewing of 1777–8, also by *Thomson*. – WEST GALLERY. Early C19, with thin classical columns and Gothic front. Curved wooden stair in base of tower, and Gothic infill to tower arch. – ORGAN on the gallery with pretty Gothic case, 1842. – STAINED GLASS by *Frank Holt & Co.* in S aisle E window, 1885, and two lights of composite S window, 1889–94. Other two lights †1911. – Chancel lancet window, *Jones & Willis*, 1927. – MONUMENTS. Early C14 knight, possibly Thomas de Astley, *c.* 1345; defaced. – Excellent early C14 lady, said to be Margaret de Astley, over-life-size, with a big canopy. The canopy corbels are formed of two little male figures, and on it are carved two slender saints. The drapery of the lady must once have been very fine. – Effigy of a priest, William de Walton, *c.* 1348, defaced (N aisle). – Brass of a lady, early C15, a good 4-ft 5-in. (1.35-metre) figure (S of the effigy of the lady).

Beyond the church, a good assembly of CANAL BUILDINGS including *c.* 1800 workshops, C19 Gothic cottages and a former pub by the bridge.

ENGLISH MARTYRS (R.C.), High Street. *Sandy & Norris* (*E. Bower Norris*), 1965–6. The first part of an intended cruciform church. Square with triangular gables and spike. Gable windows originally filled with abstract *dalle-de-verre* by *Leonard Jonah Jones*, sadly replaced by clear glass after materials failure, 2011. Plain interior, enlivened in 2015 with painted panels depicting the English Martyrs by *Aidan McRae Thomson* on the altar wall.

At the w end of the green, N of the Roman Catholic church, THE ELMS is a large early C19 house marking the start of the HIGH STREET. Facing the green, the OLD VICARAGE (No. 16 Hoskyn Close), 1865, and the GRAPEVINE CHURCH (No. 9 High Street), built as a mission hall for Mrs Louisa Daniell (cf. Pailton), 1861; brick with pale diapering. On the s side of the wide High Street, decent C18 (No. 88) and C19 (No. 42) houses, and on the N a large Regency stuccoed one (No. 81). Nearby, opposite Fenwick Drive, the plinth and shaft of the medieval MARKET CROSS.

HILLMORTON PADDOX, off Dunsmore Avenue, hemmed in tight by later housing. Late Georgian with thin porch on columns with Ionic capitals, and a rear extension by *Waterhouse*, 1889.

NEW BILTON

Along the Lawford Road w towards the cement works. Late C19 development N of the main road and housing fronting the street w of the church. Inter-war housing s of the main road including Glebe Crescent and around Pendred Road.

ST MATTHEW AND ST OSWALD (originally St Oswald's). N aisle with its E rose window 1867–8 by *Street*, the rest 1881 by *Bodley & Garner*. In spite of the great names a church of little interest. Group of five stepped lancet E windows. Piers inside for a future s aisle; N piers also, presumably for a planned replacement of Street's building. – SCREEN and rood. Designed by *Bodley*; 1900. – Carved wooden CRUCIFIX and figures brought from Holy Trinity, 1978; probably by *Bodley*, *c.* 1886. – STAINED GLASS. Two in N aisle by *Morris & Co.*: the rose window (designer *Philip Webb*), 1867, and another (*J. H. Dearle*), 1922. – E window, *Powell*, 1919.

CHURCH HALL, alongside: 1913. Venetian window, shaped gable and Arts and Crafts pinnacles with rounded tops.

Set back s of Lawford Road, No. 103 is the former vicarage: *Ewan Christian*, 1868.

NEWBOLD-ON-AVON

A village suburb.

ST BOTOLPH. Mostly Perp and mostly in a soft blend of sandstone and limestone. Just red sandstone the w tower and the porches. The N porch has rows of big canopied niches l. and r. of the entrance and decorated buttresses. The s porch, groined within, has a canopied niche under a raised parapet flanked by pinnacles. Clerestoried nave and aisles also C15. Inside, the arcades evidently Perp too. The piers have lozenge-shaped bases and finely moulded sections with shafts and chamfers and two-centred arches. The shafts in the nave are continued up into the clerestory. In the aisles they carry roof corbels. Early Victorian chancel, probably 1840s. Restorations in 1901–9 including roofs and seating. – COMMUNION RAIL. Jacobean. – TILES. Original tiles in the S aisle at the E end, and more said to be below the present pavement. – NORTH DOOR. C15. With small plaques carrying black-letter inscriptions. – TOWER SCREEN. Of wrought iron, early C18. Originally in front of the monument to Sir William Boughton and now raised to form a balcony to the ringing gallery. – HELM and SWORD, chancel S, probably C17. – ROYAL ARMS, 1796. – STAINED GLASS. In N aisle, three by *Heaton, Butler & Bayne*, one (E) 1895, the others 1907. – S aisle E window, *Burlison & Grylls*, 1905. – Uncommonly plentiful funerary MONUMENTS, chiefly of Boughtons of Lawford Hall, Little Lawford. – Geoffrey Allesley Boughton †1441 and his wife Eleanor. Incised alabaster slab on a tomb-chest with trefoil-headed panels. – Thomas Boughton †1454 and Elizabeth. Incised slab with all the carved details outlined in black. Redis-covered in 1905 and especially well preserved. Also on a pan-elled tomb-chest with figures holding shields. – Edward Boughton †1548 and Elizabeth †1583. Attributed to *Garrat Hollemans*, 1583 (JB). Alabaster. Two tiers of figures. Family group above, the parents kneeling. Below are standing figures with shields and scrolls. Decidedly Mannerist in detail and rather crudely done, especially the figures holding shields. – Edward Boughton †1625 and Elizabeth, and their son William †1635 and his wife Abigail †1636. Two kneeling couples each facing one another across a prayer-desk, one couple above the other. Also children; also crude. – In the chancel, Sir William Boughton †1716. Signed by *John Hunt* of Northampton. Pompous. White and black marble. Two life-size standing figures, a hand on the heart. Urn on pedestal between them. Baldacchino and cherubs above. Black pilasters and broken scrolly pediment. – Sir Egerton Leigh †1818. By *John Bacon Jun*. Relief, white. He lies on a couch and a woman by his head points upwards to a cross. Obelisk background. – John Ward-Boughton-Leigh †1868. Standing woman and standing angel. In a Gothic stone surround with black marble columns. – Mrs Elizabeth Ward-Boughton-Leigh †1897. Bust. The inscription mentions that she was the 'daughter and heiress of Thomas Cotterell of 50 Eaton Square'.

E of the church, the OLD VICARAGE. Unsigned plans of 1745 show a square house with a five-bay front, i.e. the present l. side. Much altered and enlarged in the C19.

Down the hill, the METHODIST CHURCH, 1879. Faintly poly-chromatic. Lancets. Beyond and opposite, the OLD SCHOOL

HOUSE and schoolroom (now VILLAGE HALL), 1878. Diapered brick nogging above the segmental-headed windows. Tile-hung gables.

On the OXFORD CANAL, N of the church, a tunnel with double towpaths. Constructed when the canal was re-routed in 1831–4.

RYTON-ON-DUNSMORE

ST LEONARD. An early Norman church of red sandstone, with a handsome Perp W tower in grey ashlar. Both nave and chancel are of before 1100, a date exemplified by the heavy proportions of the S doorway, the two strange tendrils on a capital of the blocked N doorway, and the early window outlines in the masonry in the nave and chancel S. Also early, one narrow N chancel window with an order of shafts, cushion capitals, and a thick roll. One E.E. lowside lancet window in the chancel. Perp replacement windows in nave and chancel. The lunette windows in the nave relate to the installation of a W gallery in 1794. Brick S porch of similar date. The N vestry with 'Churchwarden Gothic' windows and nice panelled N gallery began as an attached schoolroom, before 1803, and the interior was re-pewed by *John Bradford* of Coventry in 1812. The chancel arch belongs to a restoration by *Ewan Christian*, 1885–6, and there were roof repairs and internal improvements by *W.H. Wood* of Newcastle upon Tyne, 1913. The attached CHURCH HALL was added 1975–6. – PULPIT. Jacobean. – COMMUNION RAIL. Late C17, with twisted balusters. – STALLS. Two traceried panels, probably from the screen. – STAINED GLASS. Chancel N, †1850, possibly *C.A. Gibbs* (AB). – Nave S, St Leonard, 1999. – MONUMENT. Edward Bonham †1679. By *William Beard*, 1680.

The church is separated from the village by the busy London Road and from 1940 to 2007 there was a large car-manufacturing plant (Rootes, later Chrysler and eventually Peugeot Citroën) on the S side of the road towards Coventry; currently (2014) being redeveloped as a distribution centre. At the boundary is RYTON BRIDGE over the Avon, the S side still largely by *Henry Couchman*, County Bridgemaster, 1786–7.

Off Leamington Road is what remains of RYTON HOUSE, a small classical villa by *Edward Gyfford* for Stephen Freeman, 1806–7. It was altered in 1850 by *J.L. Akroyd* who raised the wings to two storeys, and underwent further alterations after 1945. Now (2014) semi-derelict. The Lodge is by *Akroyd*, 1850.

On the road to Wolston, GARDEN ORGANIC CENTRE is the headquarters of the Henry Doubleday Research organization which is dedicated to promoting organic growing and food.

The buildings, with a green oak frame, were designed to an eco-friendly specification by *HB Architects*, 2003–7.

SALFORD PRIORS

0050

St Matthew. An interesting if rather awkwardly proportioned and gloomy church, with substantial C12 elements. The lower stages of the w tower are Norman – see the w window with a little decoration, the window above it and also the clasping buttresses. Norman also the elaborate n doorway. One order of columns with capitals, decorated scallops r. and interlacing and spirals l. Arch with four rows of chevron lateral to the face. Tympanum of two stones with bands of scales, eight-point stars and rosettes. The Norman nave must originally have been very narrow and long, i.e. of Saxon proportions. Then in the later C12 a three-bay s arcade was made rather primitively. The wall was left standing in chunks and responds were formed with multi-scalloped capitals of the trumpet type. The arches are single-stepped, but pointed. In the C13 the arcade was extended by a bay to form a s chapel and the chancel was rebuilt further E. The chancel details all E.E, with lancets in the n wall, one of them with a separate oblong lowside window under. The e wall has three stepped individual lancets, shafted inside. The chancel arch is also E.E. Moreover, in the nave two lancets were made, but between them is one of the major Dec windows of Warwickshire, of three lights only, but with wild flowing tracery. All the lancets in the church have rere-arches. Dec, but simple, the s aisle windows and s doorway. The aisle is wider than the nave. On the s aisle an octagonal stair-turret, elaborately decorated outside with image niche, gargoyles and battlements. It reaches above the aisle roof (cf. Aston Cantlow) and seems to have carried a beacon to guide travellers crossing the ford over the Avon. Then at some date the tower was widened, made oblong and heightened. When? The arch standing forward into the nave is of the early C13: double-chamfered, pointed, with pellet moulding to the sur-round. The tower top, with its tall Perp bell-openings, pin-nacles and more gargoyles looks straightforwardly C15, but the VCH argues strongly for a major remodelling by Sir Simon Clarke in the C17. There is a date 1633 on the section of the w wall that has been thickened. What of the w end of the s aisle and its relationship with the widened tower? The w wall here is very curious with, l. and r. of a two-light Dec window and a little higher up, two straight-headed two-light windows, blank except for a recess like a bit of wall passage behind them. Were they for images? In the s side, a square-headed two-light window directly above a Tudor-arched doorway. It remains baffling. Restoration by *T. D. Barry & Sons* of Liverpool, 1873–4: the nave n wall rebuilt, the s clerestory added, the roof raised and new n porch. s organ chamber added in 1893–4 by

p. 20

J. A. Chatwin who also refurnished the chancel. – PULPIT. C19, deal, with carvings set in panels.* – STAINED GLASS. Three in chancel by *Paul Woodroffe*, two side windows, 1910, and E window, 1937. – Another in chancel by *Powell*, 1854. – In N nave, one by *Clayton & Bell*, †1864, and one by *F. Holt & Co.*, 1891. – In S aisle, one by *Cox & Son*, †1872, and another †1869, probably by *Cakebread & Robey*, 1890s. – Worked into vestry and tower screens, panels from the demolished church of All Saints, Emscote, Warwick, in 1967, all by *Hardman*, 1884–5. – MONUMENTS of the Clarkes of Park Hall and, later, Broom Court. Mainly erected by Sir Simon Clarke (†1652), antiquary and friend of Dugdale. Large tablet of 1631 to Dame Margaret †1617, and two boys, Walter †1607 and Thomas 1616. In the centre one of the little boys, propped up on an elbow. A toy sword hangs from his shoulder. Around the figure eighteen coats of arms, all with inscriptions. Two broad pilasters. – Margaret †1640, aged 3½. Small, very flat standing child figure in a shell niche. – Dorothy, widow of Sir Simon, †1669, and very reactionary for the date. Semi-reclining figure, black columns, big plain pediment.

PARK HALL, ¾ m. NW. About 1880 by *William Tasker* and on the site of a manor, destroyed by fire in 1879 just as enlargement as a seat for Lord Yarmouth was nearing completion. 'Queen Anne', handled rather wildly, i.e. red brick with stone dressings. Hipped roof, windows with aprons, one Venetian window, etc. – but all restless, especially the porches and the dormers. Now at the centre of a small housing estate and shielded by small-scale look-alikes by *David H. Robotham Ltd*, 1989.

PRIMARY SCHOOL, founded by William Perkins in 1656. Main building by *Solomon Hunt*, 1861. Originally red and blue brick, now painted cream, with round-headed windows. Later extensions, including copper-roofed entrance block, 2000.

Many black-and-white cottages along Evesham Road, and some decent C18 HOUSES in the village centre. CHURCH HOUSE, opposite the church, with Ionic columns, *c.* 1800. To the E, SALFORD HALL, a plain C18 double-plan with added C19 Italianate porch and conservatory. On the S side opposite, the old RECTORY, *c.* 1820, with almost separate Victorian additions. Further E, three-storey ARROWBANK, dated 1796.

PITCHILL, 1½ m. NW of Salford Priors church. The best of several sizeable farmhouses at Rushford and Iron Cross. Once associated with the Bomford family, notable C19 and C20 agriculturalists and manufacturers. Now a care home. C18. Three bays, three storeys with round-headed window in the pediment in the middle bay. ¾ m. NE, BURLEIGH HOUSE, *c.* 1810: two storeys, rendered, with light Gothic details in the tops of the square-headed windows.

The parish includes Abbots Salford and Dunnington (qq.v.).

---

* Further carved panels, said to be from the pulpit and described in the first edition, are no longer to be seen. They were of a secular character (hunting, monsters, foliage), possibly C15. Also three shields with the arms of Sir Simon Clarke.

SAMBOURNE

MISSION CHURCH. 1892. Brick, with stone dressings. Lancet windows made more interesting by nailhead along the edges of the arch, a sawtooth effect. Dual-purpose church and hall. Inside, wooden shutters can partition off the apsidal sanctuary. – STAINED GLASS. Sanctuary window by *Noel Sinclair*, 1992, and a commemorative panel, †1993.

A small village around a green, with outlying farms. Also extending E towards Spernall Ash and along the Roman Icknield Street (called Haydon Way) towards Coughton.

THE JUBILEE, Bromsgrove Road, ¾ m. NE. By *Hawkes & McFarlane* of Birmingham for Ind, Coope & Allsopp, 1936. It has sweeping roofs and mullioned-and-transomed windows.

HAYDONWAY FARM, Haydon Way, I m. E. One of several in the locality with outbuildings in brick or timber-framed with brick infill, probably C18. Also a C17 weatherboarded barn.

SAWBRIDGE

Wolfhampcote

A settlement of houses clustered round a long green. Ironstone MANOR FARM has a datestone, 1654, on a gable. LEAM FARM in Wolfhampcote Lane is partly of 1665. On the E side of the green, two low timber-framed buildings. OLD HOUSE is timber-framed and thatched, with one C15 cruck inside and a C17 cross-wing. Unassuming yet much more interesting is HALL HOUSE, once used as a poor house and only recently rescued from dereliction. It retains the hall range of a house of sophisticated construction that originally had additional ranges at both ends. It has been tree-ring-dated to 1449 and research by Nat Alcock and Paul Woodfield* has shown that it was built for John Andrewe, whose family lived there until 1556.

SECKINGTON

ALL SAINTS. A fine church of the C13 and C14, but thoroughly restored – the chancel in 1869 by *G. E. Street* and the rest by *A. W. Blomfield* in 1883 when the tower and spire were rebuilt from the ground on new foundations. The tower and spire are faithful copies, with many stones replaced in their original

---

*N.W. Alcock and C.T.P. Woodfield on 'Hall House, Sawbridge, and the Andrewe family' in *Antiquaries Journal* 76 (1996).

positions. The tower is mid- to late C13 with lancets in the s and w walls of the middle stage, but the w window is Dec with an ogee head. The bell-openings are E.E. twins with a lozenge as tracery. The tower buttresses are diagonal and chamfered so as to form sharp angles. Perp parapet with blind arcading and spire with two tiers of lucarnes. Nave and chancel all Dec but with largely renewed window tracery, some ogee-headed as are the s and n doorways of the nave. The ogees are all very understated. The chancel E window of five lights with cusped and intersecting tracery and a large quatrefoil at the top (cf. Newton Regis). Ogee-headed DOUBLE PISCINA. Low tomb recess on n side of sanctuary. – REREDOS of alabaster, by *Bridgeman* of Lichfield, 1888. Dull. – SCREEN. Four dado panels with tracery, now open. The outline of the former rood screen and loft still visible as scars in the masonry. – STAINED GLASS. Fragments of C14 glass in the heads of the nave n and s windows. – E window by *Hardman*, 1899, and also by *Hardman* a chancel s window, 1876. – MONUMENTS. In the blocked n door of the nave, the defaced effigy of a lady, early C14. – In the chancel, Robert Burdett †1603 and his wife Mary. Attributed to *Jasper Hollemans* of Burton upon Trent, 1599 (JB). Alabaster. Kneeling figures facing each other across a prayer-desk: three male, five female, but arranged in two rows in depth, the back ones in relief. – CORONAS. Two in the nave, C19 and good.

MOTTE-AND-BAILEY CASTLE, 150 yds NW of the church. Begun in the C11 by the Earl of Mellant or his son Robert, Earl of Leicester. Substantial earthworks but no standing remains. It covers an area of *c.* 2½ acres (1 ha). The motte is *c.* 30 ft (9 metres) high and *c.* 150 ft (48 metres) in diameter at the base. The bailey lies to the E and S.

Former RECTORY, N of the church. Probably C18, but altered and enlarged by *J. A. Chatwin*, 1866. Sandstone ashlar with groups of square-headed windows to the lower floors and two segmental-pointed lancets in the gabled attic storey. High Victorian detail in the polychromatic brickwork of the E range and chimneys.

In the village several decent farmhouses of the C18 and C19, the best being CHURCH FARMHOUSE in Hangman's Lane. Only three bays, but the main frontage of *c.* 1810 quite grand with a fanlight and moulded surround to the entrance.

SHERBOURNE

ALL SAINTS. On the site of a medieval church, largely rebuilt 1747 and further altered in 1802 and 1837. The present church of 1862–4 is by *George Gilbert Scott*, with *Thomas Garner* as 'sub-architect'. Built for Miss Louisa Ann Ryland of Barford Hill, whose family purchased the Sherbourne estate in 1830.

The Rylands were Birmingham industrialists whose money came from wire-drawing works. Louisa bestowed a large part of her inheritance on charitable and philanthropic works, especially in Birmingham. It is a generous and expensive estate church, lavish in every detail. It cost £20,898 including additions and improvements in 1883–4. Geometrical Dec. Ashlarfaced. Very prominent NW steeple with a thin and high spire. The bell-stage is flanked by detached polygonal pinnacles growing out of the buttresses. The bell-openings themselves have gables and thus reach up to the spire. The composition is engagingly varied, e.g. the w front with long vestry terminating with a tall chimney on the s and short porch under the tower on the N. On the s, the heavy buttressing of the Ryland Chapel contrasts with the easy lines of the nave and aisle. The outer wall of the N organ chamber, added by *J. Oldrid Scott* in 1883–4, is enhanced by *Farmer & Brindley* statues of David and two angels under canopies. Inside, natural foliage carving and the use of two-colour marbles (Ipplepen and *verde antico*) in the arcades and window columns. The richly cinquefoiled circular clerestory windows have detached two-light openings to the inside. The major carving was all done by *Farmer* of *Farmer & Brindley*, including the reworking of the chancel under *J. O. Scott* in 1883–4. The tower is vaulted, as are the Ryland Chapel on the s side and the added organ chamber, all differently. – REREDOS by *Farmer* to *Scott*'s design, 1864, with statues under canopies and flanking reliefs.* – FONT. White marble inlaid with big polished coloured stones, with marble columns on the base. – METALWORK. By *Skidmore* of Coventry, including pulpit stair, screen to Ryland Chapel and organ chamber. – STAINED GLASS. Much by *Clayton & Bell*: the chancel windows, 1864, the w window and two others, one 1885. – In the Ryland Chapel by *Hardman*, 1864. – In the s aisle, four by *Heaton, Butler & Bayne*, †1901 to 1933. – One in N aisle by *F. C. Eden* (designer *George Daniels*), 1923. – MONUMENT. In the s transeptal chapel the Ryland tomb-chest by *Pugin*, 1845, originally erected by Miss Ryland to commemorate her father Samuel (†1843) and grandparents John and Martha. Caen stone with marble and inlaid brass quatrefoils by *Hardman* to a *Pugin* design. – In the nave, Webb family monuments, including John Webb †1827 by *Samuel Cakebread* of Warwick. – Good C20 memorials to the Smith-Rylands of Sherbourne Park.

At the churchyard entrance, a lychgate by *Armstrong & Gardner*, 1936. Within, a fragment of churchyard cross, early C15. *W. A. Nesfield* did a scheme for the CHURCHYARD layout, 1862.

In the village mid-C19 Ryland ESTATE HOUSING in Church Lane, brick, with bargeboards and Tudor chimneys. Being later, *John Cundall*'s former SCHOOL of 1881 is characteristically different, with tile-hanging in the gables. In Watery Lane

---

*Not by *F. W. Pomeroy* as stated in the *Shell Guide* and National Heritage List for England.

gaunt 'Elizabethan' SHERBOURNE PRIORS was built as a vicarage for Miss Ryland by *Yeoville Thomason*, 1863. SHERBOURNE HOUSE (now apartments) at the N end of Vicarage Lane, a large C18 red brick house with rusticated quoins and with lunettes on the three-bay N front. Converted DOVECOTE among former farm buildings to the S.

SHERBOURNE MANOR (formerly called Morville), at the corner of Vicarage Lane, was the family home of Warwick architect Charles Armstrong (1874–1959). Early C19, stucco-faced with Ionic columns to porch, but much enlarged.

SHERBOURNE PARK. Built for John Webb, 1754–8, and perhaps by *David Hiorne* of Warwick and whose associated craftsmen were employed here. A house of five bays and two and a half storeys with giant pilasters and a hipped roof. Rather traditional for its date. The mid-C18 staircase has two turned balusters to the step and carved tread-ends, and the staircase hall has Rococo plasterwork by *Robert Moore*. *William Hiorne* supplied the chimneypieces and *Thomas Blockley* was the locksmith.

SHILTON

ST ANDREW. Right by the road, and of sooty stone. C13 onwards with windows of different periods: a chancel lancet, Y-tracery in S windows and reticulated tracery in the N aisle E window. The W tower is Perp, and so is the timber S porch. Restored in 1865–6 by *G. G. Scott* who added an outer N aisle, there being no room for one on the S. *J. Oldrid Scott* supervised further work in 1879 including the carving of the unfinished stonework. Beyond Scott's aisle, a porch-like toilet extension by *GSS Architecture*, 2013. Inside, the N arcade is Perp, of standard elements, but the W bay of the aisle (containing the organ) is separated from the next by a transverse arch (of two continuous chamfers) and the W pier of the arcade is stronger than the others. The strength of the pier and the arch inside the aisle perhaps suggests that a NW belfry was intended before the W tower was decided on. Why the chamfered respond on the S of the strengthened pier? These features are beyond easy explanation. In the nave, an ANGLE PISCINA. Traces of stencilling round the E window by *A. Welch* of Bovey Tracey, 1871. – Panels of uncommonly imaginative C15 tracery are preserved in the SCREEN. – Excellent ensemble of Victorian FURNISHINGS, accumulated piecemeal after 1865–6. – Woodwork including internal SCREENS, 1867. – PULPIT and FONT by *J. Oldrid Scott*, 1878. – Iron LECTERN, painted. – Set of CANDLESTANDS by *Skidmore*, 1868, and a pair of more elaborate CANDELABRA in the chancel, 1872. – STAINED GLASS. C15 fragments in two windows, S and W. In the S clerestory, the arms of Essex and Babthorpe. – E window by *Clayton & Bell*, 1865. – N aisle E window by *Hardman* (probably *J. H. Powell*), 1873. – Others in nave and chancel by *Hardman*, 1869–70.

BAPTIST CHAPEL, 150 yds sw. 1867. Plain brick, but with blue and read headers to door and window surrounds, the windows with light Gothic glazing bars.

Opposite the chapel, the SCHOOL, 1849: Tudor-style with brick hoodmoulds, diamond-pane windows and bargeboards. Extensions of 1887, by *T. F. Tickner* (1901) and *W. T. Loveday* (1927).

SHILTON HOUSE, Leicester Road. Drawings exist by *Richard Booth*, dated 1824. Plain Late Georgian box with pretty doorcase and hipped slate roof. Further E, WHITE STACKS near the Withybrook Road, by *John W. Grindal*, 1937, featured in a 1939 book by Alan Hastings on weekend houses. Roughcast and tile-hung.

OLD VICARAGE, Barnacle Lane, beyond the railway. By *R. D. Oliver*, 1906. Plum brick with red brick dressings.

BARNACLE HALL, 1 m. W. A C16 timber-framed house with an added stone S front. This front is completely symmetrical, with squat mullioned windows and a string course broken by the doorway. The odd rhomboid top has short pinnacles on kneelers, slightly North Country in character. The relationship between the pediment and its triple-ridged roof behind and the placing of the pinnacles suggests a composition of one date. One would guess 1660 or 1670 but 'D P / 1745' is inscribed in an oval in the centre of the top (referring to the owner Dormer Parkhurst who had connections in County Durham) and 1628 on the E side lower down. Neither seems right.

SHIPSTON-ON-STOUR

2040

Shipston was in Worcestershire until 1931. It is a small town of Saxon origin and gained its right to hold markets and fairs by charter in 1268. High Street and Sheep Street were the principal streets in a new town laid out by the lords of the manor at that time. There was a major fire here in 1478 but the town quickly recovered. It was at the centre of an agricultural district noted for its sheep fairs and, by association, its cloth trade. The principal trade was in shag and plush, which brought prosperity in the C17 and C18. The best buildings are of that time. In the C18 Shipston became a calling point for stagecoaches on the main Oxford to Birmingham road. Originally by-passed by the Stratford–Moreton tramway (opened in 1826), Shipston was connected by a branch line in 1836. The town became the centre for a Poor Law Union in 1836 and, later, for a Rural District Council from 1894 to 1974.

CHURCHES

ST EDMUND. Brown stone w tower of the C15, the rest 1854–5 by *Street*, and, considering what he was capable of, very disappointing. Long, low, with wide aisles, and weak round piers. Early C14 style, the tracery patterns all different. Unpainted plaster with texts over some arches. Reordered at w end, organ gallery 1961, partitions across whole church, 1995. – PULPIT. The 1824 sounding-board of the former pulpit is now an octagonal table. – Thinly detailed stone FONT and PULPIT, both 1855, as are the wooden CHOIR STALLS. – STAINED GLASS. E window, *Clayton & Bell*, 1880. – One in chancel, 1955. – S aisle E window, *Nora Yoxall & Elsie Whitford*, 1960. – MONUMENT. John Hart †1747. 'A considerable Improver and Promoter of Manufacture in this his Native Town.' Small bust, not dead-frontal, in front of the usual obelisk. – On the churchyard wall outside, the WAR MEMORIAL with Arts and Crafts stonework and bronze plates, by *Edward Adams*, 1920.

OUR LADY AND ST MICHAEL (R.C.), Darlingscote Road. Brick, lancets, with short chancel and w bellcote. Built as the workhouse chapel, 1847, with porch added 1858. Good carved corbels to roof. Acquired in a derelict state by the Roman Catholics in 1978 and restored by *Brian A. Rush*. – Some FURNISHINGS from Foxcote, Ilmington and Newbold Revel. – Gothic stone REREDOS by *Charles Hansom*, 1853, originally at Campden House and later at Ilmington (1935–2013). – STAINED GLASS. Two *Hardman* lancets (designed by *A. W. Pugin*) of 1851, again from Campden via Ilmington. – E window, 1980, and replacement porch windows 2006, by *Anthony Naylor* of Birmingham. – SCULPTURE. Angel stoup in the porch, also *Hansom*, 1853.

The PARISH CENTRE by *Rush*, 1979, extended by *Laurie Day* in 2011, has an external metal SCULPTURE of St Michael overcoming the dragon, by *Judy Brown* of Shipston, *c.* 1980.

METHODIST CHURCH (Wesleyan), New Road. 1880. *John Wills* of Derby. Rather sparse Geometric, with a lonely pinnacle on the w front. Apsed end to Old Road. New entrance and vestibule by *E. N. Sandiford*, 1990.

CEMETERY, on the S edge of the town. By *W. H. Knight* of Cheltenham, 1864–5. Chapels, lodge and boundary wall. Dec. Imaginatively done with chapels of different sizes in opposite directions from the linking tower. Ballflower ornament round the top of the tower and beasts around the broaches of the spire.

PUBLIC BUILDINGS

BRIDGE over the Stour. Six pointed stone arches and a date, 1698, on the downstream side. Widened in 1826 and much repaired in brick.

ELLEN BADGER MEMORIAL HOSPITAL, Stratford Road. 1896, by *E. W. Mountford*, a native of Shipston. Rather engulfed by

Shipston-on-Stour, Ellen Badger Memorial Hospital, perspective.
Photo lithograph, 1897

later additions, but Mountford's cottagey core remains, the centre brick with stone windows below, roughcast and half-timbered above, with a timber oriel. Good boundary wall with curved sections between the piers and gatepiers with beasts holding shields.

PERAMBULATION

Begin at the S, near the Bridge, and the C18 MILL (now a hotel) with some remaining machinery. In MILL STREET, N, Lias cottages (Nos. 1–3) with mullioned windows. To the N, the road widens and becomes Church Street. The HORSESHOE INN (No. 6) with timber-framed upper floor: upright and parallel diagonal struts making herringbone patterns. The former FRIENDS' MEETING HOUSE (No. 12), of c. 1689, used as SHIPSTON LIBRARY since 1956 and rather shockingly extended on the E, 1995. Just one mullioned window in the limestone wall facing the street, and another in the Lias N wall. Inside, two turned wooden columns originally supporting a gallery. Between the meeting house and the church, a group of C18 Lias cottages (Nos. 14–16). Further N, early C19 VANE HOUSE (No. 26) facing the Market Place, is brick with stone band and cornice and shaped gable with weathervane. Down an alley by No. 32, the former BAPTIST CHURCH, 1866, with Y-tracery and banded headers. Then, on the E side, a number of three-storeyed Georgian brick houses. The best are PARK HOUSE (No. 40) with a Greek Doric porch and the centre of its three bays taller with an attic, and CEDAR LAWN (No. 38) with ground-floor windows in blank arches. Beyond, it becomes STRATFORD ROAD. On the W, the former BOARD SCHOOL, by *Bland & Cossins* of Birmingham, 1874–6. Armscote stone.

Lancets and some plate tracery. Turrets removed but dormers added when it was converted for housing by *John Bradley*, 1983. Further out, the BAPTIST MANSE (No. 32) with frieze of floral tiles and central gable, 1906.

Return to the town and into the MARKET PLACE which opens off Church Street near THE FALCON and then divides, with Sheep Street (below) leading off to the r. All small-scale and mixed, but the Market Place leads to the High Street in the heart of the town. It runs N, parallel with Church Street: a very handsome short, wide street, closed at both ends. The best houses are THE GEORGE, Early Georgian, brick, five bays, three storeys, with segment-headed windows; plainer five-bay brick GRANVILLE HOUSE to its S; and some with nice shopfronts. At the NE corner, a group (Nos. 12–14) with quoins and keystoned windows, dated 1731 with the initials of John Hart, whose monument is in the church. The W side has been partly rebuilt, but to the N a decent group of early C19 three-storey shops. The S closure of the street is the OLD COUNCIL HOUSE (previously the rectory, now flats); mainly 1799, its pretty Victorian-Italianate addition with large triparte window facing the High Street by *Foster & Wood* of Bristol, 1883. The N end has LLOYDS BANK with early C19 stuccoed front.

From here a short passage leads back to SHEEP STREET, which begins to the E with SHELDON HOUSE on the N side; a 1960s intrusion with exposed concrete framing. The start of the street is, indeed, unpromising, but to the W are Shipston's best houses. Several have date-plates, and those of 1700 and even 1714 are Jacobean rather than Queen Anne in style. The houses are two-storeyed, some with an attic storey, and on the N side form one long terrace. BELL HOUSE is a plain Georgian brick house of five bays with a central archway. Then the MANOR HOUSE, more ambitious. Early Georgian, of six bays, with a pedimented two-bay projection and quoins of even length. To its l. the embattled stables entrance, dated 1876. Opposite STOKES HOUSE, dated 1715, also stone, with moulded eaves cornice and parapet with ball finials. No. 17, again stone, is dated 1714 and still has one mullioned window preserved. No. 19 has two nice ground-floor bows. The old POLICE STATION and COURT (No. 21) breaks the rhythm, being detached, lying back, and Neo-Elizabethan of 1874, by *Medland & Son* of Gloucester. Opposite, TOWNSEND HALL, stone, brick, and cream wash, of 1960–1, by *Earp, Badger & Harrison*, not quite comfortable here. No. 31 is an elegant Early Victorian house of stone, a little higher than the others, with a columned porch, two very shallow two-storey bows and moulded cornice. Alongside, FALSTAFF HOUSE (No. 33) has stuccoed hoodmoulds and a re-set datestone, 1683. The whole street is extremely varied and pleasing.

Just off the W end of Sheep Street, in DARLINGSCOTE ROAD, is SUNDOWN HOUSE, with a date-plate 1678 re-set on a modern porch. Originally symmetrical, with mullioned windows. Nearby, one of two granite DRINKING TROUGHS given by Richard Badger, 1902.* To the r. in Telegraph Street, a good Poundbury-style development by *John Bradley Associates*, 1998. Further out to the NW, the former WORKHOUSE (Shipston House), by *John Plowman* of Oxford, 1837–9, of brick, latest classical. The entrance block survives and the chapel (now the Roman Catholic church – *see* Churches), but the rest of the site has been redeveloped for housing.

A short walk from the s end of Darlingscote Road leads back to the High Street, from where NEW STREET runs s. Opposite the Old Council House, a chequer brick house (No. 1) with a rounded corner. No. 3 is timber-framed and L-shaped, only the framing of the cross-wing's gable exposed. Opposite a picturesque brick and stone group, SHELDON'S WINE MER-CHANTS, which was established in 1842. New vaults with the present open courtyard were completed in 1863. The façade is 1892 (date on chimney). Irregular, with pyramid roof one end, gable with Diocletian window, archway and a coped shaped gable with oval window. Brick with stone quoins and heavy blocking. Also in the group are LITTLE SHELDON HOUSE (No. 12) with tile-hung gables, and Sheldon's own house, WEST CROFT, which actually fronts Old Road. Some way s, at the road junction, the OLD SCHOOL ROOM, 1841: brick with slate roof, pedimented gable-ends and stone ogee-headed windows. In Old Road, N of the Methodist church, Nos. 17–19 also with ogee windows and hoodmoulds; originally a police station and lock-up, built *c.* 1840.

SHOTTESWELL

4040

ST LAURENCE. Small, of Hornton stone, with w tower with recessed spire. Tower seemingly C13 with later spire, but largely rebuilt by *John Pullinger* of Banbury, 1807. Light-handed general restoration in 1875, and nave and s aisle roofs renewed by *Temple Moore*, 1902. The windows of the church are mixed. The nicest are those in the chancel N and s with pretty, unusual tracery; late C14. Small Perp clerestory. But inside one is faced with a Norman N arcade of three bays. Round piers, multi-scalloped capitals, square abaci, unmoulded arches (as at Warmington). The s arcade is C13: round piers, round abaci, double-chamfered arches. The tower arch is triple-chamfered and dies into the imposts. C13 chancel arch. Ogee-headed, i.e. Dec, doorway to the NE vestry. – Plain tub FONT. One of the supports is a short Norman turned baluster. – WOODWORK. An interesting assembly. – SCREEN to the N chapel, C14, i.e. still with shafts (though renewed) instead of mullions. The tracery is cusped semicircles and on top reversed cusped semicircles. – STALLS. Fronts with panels with most

*The other is outside the Black Horse in Station Road.

unusual Perp tracery, e.g. a complete close trellis, reticulation etc. – The PULPIT has some of these panels too. – BENCHES and TOWER SCREEN with more of them. – COMMUNION RAIL. Late C17, with twisted balusters. – REREDOS with eleven carved panels from more than one source, some scenes religious but others avowedly secular. Flemish, early C17.

Hillside village, sloping steeply towards a tributary of the Cherwell, with narrow streets and ironstone buildings, some thatched. The best are early C17 COLLEGE FARMHOUSE in Middle Lane and THE MANOR in Mollington Road. Victorian only the former WESLEYAN CHAPEL in Chapel Lane, 1854, and VILLAGE HALL (former school), 1868. Of the C20, the post-war ironstone COUNCIL HOUSES in New Road, and CHERRY LODGE built for Miss Profumo, c. 1965, with cupola on the range linking the two wings.

SHREWLEY
Hatton

2060

Long street of mainly later C19 houses on Shrewley Common, with polychromatic former CONGREGATIONAL CHAPEL, 1866. Down tracks s of the chapel, CANAL TUNNEL of the Grand Union Canal. On the N side there is a separate sloping HORSE TUNNEL between the road and the towpath – a rare arrangement. There being no towpath through the tunnel, this enabled the horses to be led overground to the other end while the bargees legged their vessel through the tunnel. Probably by *Philip Witton* for Warwick and Birmingham Canal Company, c. 1799.

SHUSTOKE

2090

ST CUTHBERT. Red sandstone, and looking almost entirely of the early C14. The chancel and s porch, however, were rebuilt at *Preedy*'s restoration in 1872–3 and the whole church was redone by *Bodley & Garner* in 1886–7 after a fire that left nave and chancel a roofless shell. Of the C14 the tower arch and w window (continuous chamfers and Y-tracery), the width of the nave, its s doorway, its windows with ballflowers as hoodmould stops, and the chancel with its pretty DOUBLE PISCINA of pointed-trefoiled arches and a quatrefoil over. In the N organ chamber is a re-set Norman window. The top stage of the tower is typical Warwickshire Perp. The spire was damaged by lightning in 1777 and 1801 and twice repaired by *John Cheshire*, but escaped harm in 1886. Inside, only the tracery of the older windows detracts from the over-riding impression that this is a church of 1886–7 – the E window alone being altered at the restoration. The smooth sandstone walls, the high roof with a

Blyth Hall, aerial perspective.
Engraving by Henry Beighton, 1728

carved wall-plate, and the ensemble of Late Victorian fittings are all entirely typical. – FONT. 1887, but said to be an exact copy of the Norman font damaged in the fire. – ARCHITECTURAL FRAGMENTS. A Norman capital and a short length of dogtooth re-set in the porch. – STAINED GLASS all by *Burlison & Grylls*, 1887–95. – MONUMENT. Sir William Dugdale †1685, the antiquary (of Blyth Hall), partly by *William Langley*, 1681. Plain tomb-chest with a shield and garlands. Back panel with open segmental pediment.

BLYTH HALL, 2 m. WSW. In parkland alongside the river Blyth. Sir William Dugdale bought the Hall in 1625 and it remains in the same family today. Of the antiquary's time there is a stone chimney dated 1629. The roof-line suggests that the C17 house must have been originally of five gabled bays of equal depth. Nobly refronted for Sir John Dugdale in 1692, possibly by *William Smith* the elder (Andor Gomme). Eleven bays, the first and last two slightly projecting. Brick, two storeys and a hipped roof with pedimented dormers. Only the middle one is segmental, so as to match the segmental pediment of the doorway. The doorway has also a bolection moulded surround and pulvinated frieze. This is as shown on Beighton's engraving of 1728. Six rainwater heads dated 1833 indicate later work and there are extensions at the rear. Inside there is no entrance hall, just a low passage between two chimneys. One mighty C17 staircase in the Jacobean tradition. Another typically early C18 with alternating plain and twisted balusters. Behind are outbuildings, mainly later C17, also little altered since Beighton's time.* Rectangular DOVECOTE and a stable range. The STABLES with shaped gables (one with a vertically placed oval), the block with a cupola nearest the house a later addition with

---

*The chief difference is that the engraving shows a long range to the r. of the main front of the house, no longer there by the late C19. It may have been an elaboration by the artist. However, a transverse gable on the stables suggests a demolished (or intended) range in this position.

the date 1709 on the clock (internally). In the courtyard, a hexagonal GAME LARDER, *c.* 1830.

Church End is at the E of the parish. The buildings S and W of the church include the CHURCH COTTAGES, originally built as a school and almshouses founded by Thomas Huntbach in 1699. C19 alterations. Here too is H-shaped CHURCH FARM, C16 with a cross-wing of 1699 and C18 additions – an enjoyable jumble. More refined, the former VICARAGE by *John Dumolo* of Dunton, 1833–5. This replaced the OLD RECTORY in Shawbury Lane, a C14 house where Sir William Dugdale was born in 1605. Cruck-built but much disguised externally by tasteless accretions.

The main settlement is 1 m. further W. Mid-C18 Shustoke House, the seat of the Croxalls, formerly stood here (demolished 1947). C15 PRIORY FARM at the corner of Bixhill Lane has an open hall of cruck construction at the core. The E wing dated 1620 has lunette windows and there are gatepiers of *c.* 1700 in the sandstone garden wall. At the road junction in the village centre, the PARISH HALL by *Harrison & Cox*, 1923, is typical of its date.

To the N is SHUSTOKE RESERVOIR with a staff house (FERN COTTAGE) of *c.* 1880, but the Gothic Boat House in the style of Whitacre Waterworks (*see* Nether Whitacre) has gone.

Of the farms, the best is SHUSTOKE HALL, off Moat House Lane to the S. On a moated site. Built *c.* 1686 for Thomas Huntbach. Double-pile plan with front of six bays with modillion cornice and hipped roof. (Inside, a moulded fireplace with a painted overmantel depicting a hunter offering a boar's head to a woman.) N of this, late C16 MOAT HOUSE FARM with striking chimney to one side, stone base with sundial and three tall brick stacks. On the main road, HOLLIARS FARM of 1641 with gabled front and timber-framed early C17 YEW TREE FARM are good.

To the W on Coleshill Road is BLYTH FARMHOUSE, red brick with three-bay façade with pedimented and slightly projecting centre bay, *c.* 1800. Nearby, rock-faced BLYTHE LODGE was built *c.* 1839 as a crossing-keeper's house for the Stonebridge Junction Railway Company.

SHUTTINGTON

ST MATTHEW. Small, on a hilltop site overlooking a wide valley with large lakes created by mining subsidence. Promising at first glance, but disappointing on closer inspection. Chancel and nave with weatherboarded W bell-turret. Masonry irregular and disturbed but incorporating some original Norman features. Chancel perhaps C13. Notable the W doorway with chevrons in two planes, point-to-point with edge chevrons flanking a keeled roll. Possibly brought from Alvecote Priory (q.v.). In the S wall, part of the archway to a blocked doorway revealed by a recess in the masonry. In the w wall are CI5 trefoiled lights with pointed heads, and a two-light window above the door. On the s side of the chancel the remains of a CI3 window and a CI4 window of two narrow ogee-headed lights under a square head. The main windows Neo-Norman and by *W.H. Bidlake*, 1908–9, copying windows of the previous restoration in 1844. His also the big Neo-Norman chancel arch – all in a very unfamiliar style for an architect best known for his Arts and Crafts version of Gothic. – PULPIT. CI8; plain.

In the CHURCHYARD, several slate headstones CI9 and C20, many signed 'Mitchell Tamworth'.

See also Alvecote.

SNITTERFIELD

2050

ST JAMES. Of oölite limestone. Substantial w tower, quite clearly built in stages from the early CI4 to the CI5 with changes in style and construction on the way. There is a break midway up the w window, and what start as angle buttresses turn diagonal. Bell-openings of two twins with transoms. Early CI4 nave and aisles. The chancel structurally of *c.* 1300 with big E window of intersecting tracery. The aisle windows have nicely moulded surrounds and Y-tracery. Inside, a very high arch between tower and nave, triple-chamfered. The arcades differ. The N arcade has octagonal piers and double-chamfered arches, conventional except that the arches are stilted. The s arcade is unusual and quite striking. It has typical early CI4 piers of eight shafts connected by continuous hollows rising into funnel-shaped capitals, with hollow-chamfered arches above. The CI5 clerestory is Perp and has windows with basket arches. The heightening is visible on both sides, though less so on the s than the N where there is a clumsy overhang towards the w. Open chancel roof said to be Georgian, but looks mostly of after 1858. Additions include the sw vestry by the tower, probably belonging to major alterations of 1841 (though looking earlier), and the N organ chamber of 1881–2 and *J.A. Chatwin*'s restoration. Also of Chatwin's time the lavish tiled floors by *Craven Dunnill & Co.* – COMMUNION RAIL. Jacobean, with some carving. – Two sets of STALLS in the chancel by *Bridgeman* of Lichfield, 1881–2, but based on and incorporating superb carved work of *c.* 1530. The E ends of the longer range and the facing fronts of the shorter run are original. They have Renaissance touches yet are otherwise still entirely Gothic. The balusters with turned shafts; the tiny figures and the ends with tracery and a coat of arms are very well done. – PULPIT with early CI8 panels (oval, and still pre-classical) from a three-decker arrangement of 1730. – FONT. Dec, octagonal, with good strong heads coming forward from the underside. – PAINTING of St James the Great in blocked window in s aisle, by *Hardman & Co.*, 1882. – STAINED GLASS. In the chancel three by *Edward Frampton*, †1899 to 1910, and one of 1887 on s by *Heaton, Butler & Bayne* who also did one in the N aisle, 1884. – In aisles, three by *William Holland (& Son)*, †1846, †1855 and, brightly coloured, 1870. – Lastly, one by *F. Holt & Co.*, 1899. – MEMORIALS to Warwickshire antiquary the Rev. Thomas Warde by *Bourgès* the elder of Paris, 1850, typically French. – Adjacent mural to his reprobate son, C.T. Warde †1865. – Others to the Lloyds and Philips of Welcombe and the Attyes of Ingon, one by *Thomas Denman* †1831.

METHODIST CHAPEL, The Square. 1883, dull Gothic with lancets and spindly turret. Designed and built by *J. Smallwood* of Wootton Wawen. Church Hall extension in matching style, 1981. Gothic EPWORTH COTTAGE in The Green may be the previous chapel of 1840.

Opposite, the SCHOOL. Plain Tudor and brick with golden stone dressings, 1839 with later extensions including a sympathetic addition, 2004.

SNITTERFIELD HOUSE. The house of the Hales family and then the Earls of Coventry s of the church was demolished in the 1830s. Of the 1670s, it has been attributed to *Robert Hooke*. What survives is the high garden wall w of the church and PARK COTTAGES to the s, a late C17 range with a Dutch gable at the w end. This appears in illustrations as early as *c.* 1700 but the original function of the building is unclear. Substantial C17 red brick DOWER HOUSE in Church Lane to the N is associated with the house too.

Snitterfield was an estate village owing its character and appearance to wealth from the Manchester cotton trade. The Philips family (later at Welcombe, q.v.), who bought the estate in 1816, systematically rebuilt the farms and cottages over several decades from the 1830s, and especially in the time of Mark Philips (†1873) and his brother Robert Needham Philips (†1890). Neo-Tudor everywhere, but with sufficient variety and quality to maintain visual interest. Key elements include chimneys, steep gables, pretty bargeboards with spikes, and diamond window glazing. Mainly brick with stone dressings: the best are in Church Road, Smiths Lane, Park Lane and School Lane. Mostly 1840s but none precisely dated. In contrast STABLE COTTAGE in The Green initialled 'RNP 1877' exemplifies the humbler estate dwellings in a village where buildings defined the hierarchies of the social order. THE GABLES in Smiths Lane was the village Institute and Reading Room, 1873, with billiard room behind, 1887.

For themselves, the Philips family remodelled PARK VIEW in Church Road, an older house with timber framing, a pretty Gothick extension with an embattled turret and ogee mouldings, and a decent 1840s gabled wing on the E. At the far w end of the road, Mark Philips created PARK HOUSE (now subdivided) around a courtyard. The garden front incorporates a C17 timber-framed cottage at the SE end and there is an octagonal corner tower at the NE. *J. L. Akroyd* did the NW range with clock and turret in 1844 and may have done other work for the estate as well as the flanking Neo-Tudor ranges here.

Among the Victorian improvements, older houses and farm buildings survive, some good. In Smiths Lane brick and timber FERN COTTAGE has a thatched roof with eyebrow windows. C17 OLD COTTAGE in Brookside is another. Along The Green, where building was less ordered, the result is an attractively varied jumble of smaller cottages leading S towards THE WOLDS, one of the larger former estate houses in the village.

Of newer buildings, the old VICARAGE opposite the church is by *Francis Trepess* of Warwick, 1900. The front has varied gables, one half-timbered, one tiled and one over the entrance with vertical slots. In Church Lane, DAWN EDGE is a large thatched house with a curved range in walled grounds, by *Yorke & Barker*, 1952. On the old village GAS WORKS site in Brookside – where the little office building survives – ROBOTHAMS, 1966–7, by *D. H. Robotham* for himself, with later extensions. White-painted with vertical glass panels in the roof to light the stairwell built round a C-shaped brick column.

The WAR MEMORIAL in Kings Lane overlooks a wide view of the Avon valley. The present cross of 1948 replaces the 1920 memorial by *Guy Pemberton* damaged in 1946–7.

At the E edge of the parish towards Warwick, MARRAWAY FARMHOUSE, a double-plan brick house with a handsome 1830s brick front and Tuscan porch.

SOUTHAM

At the junction of several main roads and also on the Welsh drovers' route to London. King Henry III granted a market charter in 1227 and there was also an annual fair. Travel and commerce accounted for the extraordinarily large number of inns and public houses here, now mainly closed and adapted to other uses. Southam was also an administrative centre with a Poor Law Union,* magistrates' court and rural district council.

CHURCHES

ST JAMES. Red sandstone and White Lias. Prominent W tower with broach spire. Pinnacles on the broaches. Two tiers of lucarnes in alternating directions; collars. In fact, if it were not for the red stone, a Northamptonshire sight. The tower is C14

*The 1837 WORKHOUSE by *John Plowman* of Oxford in Welsh Road West was demolished in 1960.

(see the ogee-headed W window), the spire probably C15. Yet a little later the splendid clerestory (eight two-light windows with panel tracery, set closely) and the nave roof (low pitch, tie-beams and arched braces with tracery). Otherwise arcades of four bays with standard elements, N before S, which has hollow chamfers. In the S aisle two tomb recesses. Most of the other details to the nave and aisles are Victorian, from the restoration begun by *D. G. Squirhill*, 1854, and completed under *William Watson* of Napton, 1861, when the N aisle was widened. The chancel was restored and N chancel aisle added by *Scott*, 1853–4. The windows with their big flowing tracery copy original Dec work. Nave and aisles reordered 2004 with nave altar, chairs and York stone paving. – REREDOS and FONT, 1866. – SCREEN. *F. H. Crossley*, 1938, in the style of the former Southam screen moved to Wormleighton (q.v.) after the Civil Wars. – PULPIT. Returned from Wormleighton in 1841. Probably C16, of wood, with some unusual tracery motifs, especially one of close trellis. – ROYAL ARMS of Charles I from St Ewen, Bristol (dem. 1779), presented by the Bristol Tailors' Guild, 1936. – WALL PAINTINGS. Traces of C16 texts on nave W wall. – STAINED GLASS. Mostly by *Wailes*, the E window dated 1854, the others with dates †1849–61. – S aisle E by *Holland*, 1856. – Tower window 1935, probably *Percy Bacon* (AB). – Panel depicting the church, *Helen Ashman*, 1994.

At the S entrance to the CHURCHYARD, pretty 1870s cast-iron gates at the top of a steep flight of steps. On the N the church is approached by an avenue of limes, originally set in 1816 to celebrate victory at Waterloo and replanted in 2000. – WAR MEMORIAL. W of the tower, by *F. P. Trepess*, 1920.

OUR LADY AND ST WULSTAN (R.C.), by *Sandy & Norris* (*E. Bower Norris*) of Stafford, 1925. Simple Byzantine in brick with plain vaulted interior.* S Lady Chapel. W narthex with gallery above. – Alabaster HIGH ALTAR, 1952. – Patterned STAINED GLASS, probably 1925.

The church goes with the CONVENT established by fugitive nuns from Germany in 1876. They began in the OLD RETREAT HOUSE fronting Wood Street, afterwards adding an orphanage (1880), school and temporary church. The PRESBYTERY dates from 1886. In 1892 the nuns moved to a rather gaunt Gothic convent 'by a German architect' (demolished 1987) on part of the site near Daventry Road since redeveloped for housing. In the 1980s the novitiate (*Sandy & Norris*, 1931) beyond the church became the convent. This remains as the backdrop to the 1980s school but there are proposals (2013) for redevelopment leaving the exterior unaltered. The nuns now (2016) occupy a small building alongside the W front of the church, begun in 1925 and completed as a link between the novitiate and original convent in 1959 (*Sandy & Norris* again).

---

* Until 1976 the sanctuary and Lady Chapel were adorned with wall paintings by *Sr. Mary Sales*.

CONGREGATIONAL CHAPEL, Wood Street. 1839. Rendered front with fancy Gothick detailing. Brick sides with tall narrow windows. Decorated-style cast-iron tracery. Plaster cornice and decorative ceiling rosettes. Alterations and interior reordering by *John D. Holmes*, 1993.

SOUTHAM COMMUNITY CHURCH, behind Nos. 47–48 Coventry Street. Also by *Holmes*, 2003.

PUBLIC BUILDINGS

In High Street, the former magistrates' court, later used as a POLICE STATION (closed in 2011). Doubtless by the *County Architect*, 1960s, with pillared entrance and pantile roofs.

Immediately S, a new LIBRARY with community space is being built within the TITHE LODGE residential development, by *Walker Troup Architects*, 2014.

Off Stowe Drive, the unashamedly contemporary SURGERY by *Denton Scott*, 1992–3.

PERAMBULATION

The centre of the town is MARKET HILL. Its best buildings are on the E side, beginning with the C16 MANOR HOUSE at the corner of Daventry Street. L-plan. Banded base of Lias and limestone with mullioned-and-transomed windows. Elaborate timber framing above, with large and small gables on the front, two on the side and one at the back. Herringbone on the jettied first floor, supported on carved brackets (mostly replacements). This floor has timber oriels and originally had a continuous band of windows below the eaves. On the front, a canted and pedimented oriel, with decoration on the front. Intricate decorative framing in the attic gables, also jettied. Motifs include patterns of hearts and arrows piercing the circles and squares of the gables and cusped quatrefoils in squares. Pretty carved bargeboards on the front gables. Restoration supervised by *Malcolm J. Peters*, 2006–7.

HSBC Bank is C18, but with street level frontage by *Whinney, Son & Austen Hall* for Midland Bank, 1924. Adjoining early C19 house has Italianate details. The W side has a long range of plain brick buildings, raised above street level. Noteworthy only stuccoed VIVIAN HOUSE (No. 21) at the corner of Park Lane, with large Ionic door surround.

The short High Street continues N into Coventry Street with the OLDE MINT on the E. C16, stone, L-plan with full-height porch in the angle, mullioned windows, not regular. C17 open-well staircase inside. At ARUNDEL HOUSE (No. 50) a C19 rendered front, with giant pilasters and windows linked vertically by moulded surrounds, conceals an early C17 house.

DAVENTRY STREET has little but leads to SCHOOL ROAD, with the former NATIONAL SCHOOL of 1816, still with traces of

Gothick pointed windows but refronted with diapered brick-work in 1859. Opposite the former BOARD SCHOOL, 1875.

A little s from Market Hill, in OXFORD STREET, Late Georgian three-bay brick VERNON HOUSE (No. 24) with a one-bay pediment and minimum Venetian windows.

On WARWICK ROAD, down a dip and over the river, a small green with an attractive group of houses, including THE ABBEY, SW of the green, which has Jacobean-style shaped gables, copied in brick on an added wing and C20 garage block. Opposite, early C19 HILL HOUSE and the former EYE & EAR INFIRMARY (later a parish institute and now WARWICK HOUSE hotel) of 1818, white, with Gothick pointed windows and two-storey canted bay. It was built for Dr Henry Lilley Smith who also founded the first provident dispensary in the country here in 1823, commemorated by the DISPENSARY URN, 1889, on a short granite pedestal. Nearby are mid-C19 gault brick BEECH HURST, and cottages (Nos. 24–26) with internal cruck construction dated to 1418–19.

STONEYTHORPE HALL, in a wooded park ⅞ m. WNW. Originally built for the Hanslap family in the C16, with internal woodwork dendro-dated to 1548/9. The cement-rendered façade has a C17 porch (said to be dated 1623), mullioned-and-transomed windows, and gables. Much of the evidence belongs to restorations, including rainwater heads dated 1875. (Inside a C16 carved chimneypiece.)

On the Stoneythorpe estate to the w is the DALLAS BURSTON POLO CLUB, established in 1999. With six neatly railed pitches, it has a lavish colonial-style clubhouse pavilion, the Golden Jubilee QE2 pavilion of 2002 and the IXL event centre, 2013.

SPERNALL

ST LEONARD (Friends of Friendless Churches). Close by the River Arrow and the former rectory. Blue Lias and sandstone. Small Norman and medieval church of nave and chancel. The chancel Neo-Norman, by *Harvey Eginton*, 1844, and much like his contemporary church at Trimpley (Worcs.). Crazy wheel window with radiating colonnettes has hoodmould with beakheads. Nook-columns in the outer E angles. Probably Eginton's too, the w bellcote replacing an enclosed timber turret. The nave has a late C13 w window (Y-tracery with a trefoil in the spandrel), Dec side windows, and some Victorian replacements. Brick patching to the w end of the N wall, probably 1802. Georgian-style s porch, rebuilt 1997. Inside, a C12 chancel arch, heavily reworked. – WOODWORK. Good N door with applied ribs and traceried panels of c. 1535 (vandalized 1994). – STAINED GLASS. In a N window C15 fragments.

– MONUMENT. Thomas Chambers †1836, by *M. Allen* of Birmingham.

OLD RECTORY, immediately N of the church. C18 but improved in 1800. Brick, but the front has rendered quoins, string course band and hoodmoulds.

Spernall belonged to the Throckmortons of Coughton. The best estate farm is SPERNALL HALL FARM, down a drive opposite the Old Rectory. 1840s Tudor, with gables and big chimneys. Also Tudor-style cottages. The Throckmortons were not great improvers and many estate farms are older, like UPPER SPER-NALL FARM, 1 m. E, which has a C17 L-plan house sandwiched between connecting outbuildings and a C19 front.

STIVICHALL *see* p. 296

STOCKTON

4060

ST MICHAEL. Perp w tower of red sandstone. The bell-openings are of two lights with a transom. Shields on the battlements and faces below. Dec chancel restored in 1847. The rest by *William Slater*. Blue Lias, quarried in the immediate neighbourhood, with sandstone bands. Nave rebuilt and N aisle added, 1863, and the now ill-fitting C13 porch restored and moved outwards. S aisle rebuilt 1873. SW toilet extension and internal reordering by *Acanthus Clews*, 2008. Inside, Perp chancel arch. Hammerbeam roof in chancel, 1847. – STAINED GLASS. E window and patterned glass in chancel by *Holland*, 1847. – Tower window, 1874. – N aisle w, †1901. – Two in S aisle 1876, possibly *Holland & Holt*. – One by *Powell* (designer *Hardgrave*), 1885. – Another *Jones & Willis*, 1938. – War memorial window, *Camm & Co.*, 1955.

Several phases of SCHOOL building. School house, NW of the church, dated 1843. Altered schoolroom by *William Watson* c. 1850. New school of 1883 with large extension by *Willmot, Fowler & Willmot*, 1908.

MANOR FARMHOUSE, E of the church, C17, with garden front of c. 1720 in stone with banded headers. Quoins on sides where the walls are of brick. A staircase inside, the balusters with diminishing twist.

Aided by the convenience of the Grand Union Canal, an extensive lime and cement industry developed at Stockton in the mid C19. The works and quarries were N of the village. In 1898 a large fossil of an ichthyosaurus was found here. Messrs Nelson provided workers' cottages. The earliest in ELM ROW are pre-1887, GEORGE STREET and VICTORIA TERRACE a little later. Also the NELSON CLUB, 1914.

NW of the village, a flight of eight locks on the CANAL and C19 canalside buildings.

STOKE *see* p. 297

STONELEIGH

3070

ST MARY. Alongside fields by the River Sowe. Red sandstone quarried nearby. Essentially the church is Norman and very ambitious for its date. The oblong w tower has a blocked N window and an arch to the nave with double responds and multi-scallop capitals; sober, compared with the rest, and partly concealed. The blocked nave N doorway is of three orders with decorated scallops and in the arch double cones, in the hoodmould raised discs. Exciting if barbaric tympanum. Two dragons, their necks interlocked, biting their own tails. Above, a little panel where two snakes do the same. The nave is very wide for a Norman nave. The chancel arch is rich indeed: its decoration includes horizontal clasps from the imposts to the responds, tapering and inlaid with discs. Chevron carving lavishly applied, even up responds and columns. Carved into the main responds are a tiny bird and a tiny snake. To the main arch the N base is rectangular with three-stranded interlace; the one on the S is bulbous with trellis ornament. The chancel itself is of two bays, and the responds in the centre of the N and S walls show that it was meant to be vaulted. Also, it has against the E and S wall blind arcading on clustered shafts. The pointed arches with lateral chevrons are basically original, although the similar door to the vestry is C19.* In the responds for vaulting and blind arcading there is a great similarity to the chancels of the two parish churches of Devizes (Wilts.).

Of later medieval work, there is the nave N window nearest the chancel of *c.* 1300 with intersecting tracery finely moulded, the S arcade – at least the arches – probably of the C14, and the rather peculiar tower, which seems to have been made oblong by C14 rebuilding. Its mean Perp top is oddly set back from the walling below. Now a surprise, the S VESTRY, raised to the outside and with obelisk pinnacles. An inscription records that Thomas Lord Leigh built the vestry and vault under it in 1665, 'the one for the use of the parishowners and the other for a burying place for himselfe his lady and their desendents'. The S window tracery seems quite correctly Perp and inside the vault looks convincingly medieval. However, *Charles Hanbury Tracy* of Toddington Manor, Glos., subtly reworked it in 1823 when he was also advising at Stoneleigh Abbey, and elements are his, e.g. the tracery over the E doorway, the angel-stops of the hoodmoulds and the vault. At

---

*During conservation work to the Dudley monument in 2003 traces of arcading were found on the N wall behind it, proving it to be an early feature and showing that it originally extended round three sides of the chancel. It is often described as 'heavily restored', but it appears in its present form in measured drawings by C. Jones dated 1826 and in a published illustration by Bloxam (1845). Glynne (*c.* 1840) thought this 'a remarkable feature'.

the same time, *c.* 1823, a Gothic MAUSOLEUM was built on
the N side of the chancel for the Leighs, the design being by
C. S. Smith as improved by Hanbury Tracy in 1823. The N
window is Dec like those to the nave, the side windows Perp.
Inside, a plaster tierceron star-vault. Early C19 improvements
to the rest of the church began with alterations in 1810–11
when the once irregular S side was smoothed out,* its porch
removed and the church re-roofed by *John Bradford*. Not all
the works authorized by faculty in 1814 were done immediately, but soon afterwards the two western windows on the N
side were given Dec tracery, the tower arch was bricked up and
part of the gallery erected. The scheme was completed in
1820–1, the pews and gallery extension being executed to
Smith's designs by *John Whitehead*. E window tracery also
renewed and a barrel organ installed (since replaced), 1821.

This early C19 ensemble remains largely intact, with PULPIT,
BOX PEWS, and continuous WEST GALLERY supported on
cast-iron columns with Neo-Norman capitals of varied designs.
Across the front it has inscriptions in gold done by *James
Cherry*, 1821, and early C19 painted cast-iron ROYAL ARMS.
– FONT. Norman, with tight arcading and the twelve Apostles
tightly in them, ruthlessly stylized figurines, the restless drapery
with much of the Anglo-Saxon. In the spandrels small heads.[†]
– COMMUNION RAIL. Thin balusters; C18. – STAINED GLASS.
E window by *Clayton & Bell*, 1885. – In the N chapel, heraldic
glass, *c.* 1823–6, possibly by *Charles Pemberton* of Birmingham,
with heraldry based on sketches provided by Sir George Nayler
of the College of Arms. – MONUMENTS. Effigy, almost totally
defaced, under the tower, probably C14. – Effigy of a priest,
C15 (chancel N). – Alice, Duchess Dudley, †1668/9. By *William
Wright*, *c.* 1648, with inscriptions added by *Thomas Stanton*
(GF) under the direction of William Dugdale, 1669. A large and
noble piece of black-and-white marble, too large for its position. Recumbent effigy in a shroud and below and in front the
effigy of the duchess's daughter also in a shroud. Two cherubs
between pairs of black columns blow trumpets and hold open
a white drapery. Big flat black top with a gold fringe of tassels
(chancel N). – Humphrey How, porter to Lord Leigh, †1669.
Outside, in the blocked S doorway. The inscription ought to be
read. – Edward, 5th Lord Leigh, †1786, and the Hon. Mary
Leigh †1806, both by *Joseph Nollekens*. Plain tablets. – Chandos,
1st Baron Leigh, 1850. Possibly by *G. G. Scott*.[‡] Alabaster tomb-
chest with vine and oak branches. Placed in a vaulted polygonal recess, all in the late C13 Gothic style (leaves etc. derived
from Southwell, Notts.). – Margarette, Lady Leigh, †1860,

---

* *John Alcott* of Coventry inserted the Perp-style windows on this side, but the wall
was redone again in 1869.
† The font is supposed to have come from Maxstoke *c.* 1865, having been found in
the priory farmyard there. However, Maxstoke Priory was founded in the mid C14
and Glynne describes the font at Stoneleigh *c.* 1840.
‡ *Scott & Moffatt* designed the daughter church at Westwood Heath (p. 304) for the
Leighs, 1842–4.

depicted visiting the sick. Carved alabaster relief by *J. Birnie Philip*, in a Gothic stone surround by *Scott*, 1861. – In the family chapel further tablets, e.g. the Hon. Julia Judith Leigh †1843. By *Forsyth* of Worcester, 1867. Bold architectural tablet with serpentine columns and chunky carving, supported on a broad-winged angel with hands crossed. – Harry Richard Leigh †1862, by *Butterfield*, 1863. Small tablet of coloured marble with inlays. – G.H.C. Leigh †1884. Entirely in the Quattrocento taste, and signed by *E. Orlandini* of Florence, 1886. – Frances, Lady Leigh, †1909. Signed by *A. Apolloni*. Very Edwardian, with white figures in very shallow relief.

Despite its proximity to Coventry and three other towns, Stoneleigh retains its rural appearance and charm. Until as recently as the 1980s it was still an estate village whose owners, the Leighs, were keen to preserve its character. Thus it retains many TIMBER-FRAMED HOUSES.* In the village area there are some twenty-six timber-framed houses datable from *c.* 1450 to the later C17. Many have brick infilling, and brick houses commence *c.* 1700. Only a few examples can be highlighted here. The best of the early cruck houses is No. 1 Birmingham Road (Phoenix Cottage), of three bays, thatched, *c.* 1480. Another in Vicarage Road (Nos. 8–9) has similar crucks, *c.* 1500. Part of MOTSLOW COTTAGE, across the river 200 yds w, has been dendro-dated to 1537. It has square framing with curved braces. Thatched, with eyebrow windows. Nos. 11–12 Coventry Road also have curved braces to the wall-plates. A complex group with a gabled cross-wing at Nos. 6–9 The Bank illustrates stages of development from the C15 to the late C17. Only C16–C17 MANOR FARM, Vicarage Road, is black-and-white, with closely spaced studs, and three symmetrical gables, the outer two jettied with diagonal struts. Big stone chimney at one end. On The Bank, a pair of estate cottages (Nos. 4–5) with square framing, brick infill and stone plinths, are datable to 1727 and 1732. No. 16 Birmingham Road, 1767, is brick with raised platband and segmental windows, with later slate roof and rebuilt chimneys, *c.* 1840.

For the rest, begin on THE GREEN with the old SMITHY, dated 1851. To the w, Nos. 10–13 The Bank were built as the NEW ALMSHOUSES by *James Murray*, 1855. Red sandstone with half-timbered projecting porch and canted end-bays. The OLD ALMSHOUSES line the SE side of The Green. There are ten in all. They are of 1576, originally timber-framed, but dated 1594 when they were re-cased in red sandstone. Long frontage with five Tudor-arched doors, small windows with timber lintels, five tall, prominent single chimneystacks alternating with dormers. The same arrangement was repeated to the garden where late C20 amenity blocks have been added. w, at the corner of Church Lane, the SCHOOL HOUSE (now flats), *c.* 1740. A plain rectangle, brick with hipped tile roof

---

*These are especially well understood thanks to the researches of Dr N.W. Alcock, published in *People at Home: Living in a Warwickshire Village 1500–1800* (1993).

and segmental window arches. Opposite in Vicarage Road (Nos. 1–4) are READING ROOM COTTAGES, 1850s. Sandstone fronted, Neo-Tudor with close-set kneelered gables and intermediate dormers. The CLUB ROOM (i.e. former reading room) in similar style, 1856, adjoins on the E end. At the far w end of Vicarage Road is WENTWORTH HOUSE, built as the parish workhouse by *Robert Johnson*, 1787, used as the vicarage from 1817 until 1948 and now a house. Much altered. By the churchyard gates, THE OLD PARSONAGE of *c.* 1700; brick with gabled front of eight bays (3–2–3) to Church Lane, the l. side an addition.

Towards the edge of the village on the W side of Birmingham Road, a pair of Swedish prefabricated timber houses, *c.* 1947 (cf. Leamington Hastings).

Leaving the village to the E one crosses the SOWE BRIDGE of eight elegant segmental arches, of the early C19. ¾ m. S is the STARE BRIDGE, an excellent late medieval piece of nine stepped arches of divers forms and with cutwaters in between. It has a long causeway. The road now crosses the Avon by a replacement bridge to the E by *D. H. Brown* (*County Surveyor*), 1928–9.

At STARETON, ⅞ m. SSE, Nos. 1–2 have a brick front of *c.* 1770, concealing a timber-framed cottage of *c.* 1680 within. The brickwork and segmental-headed windows are as already seen in Stoneleigh, and PARK FARM is the same. Other buildings here are described with the Abbey deer park (p. 586) or Abbey Park (p. 587).

STONE HOUSE (or New House), Cubbington Heath, 1½ m. S. By *Francis Smith*, 1716. Square, smooth ashlar with quoins, moulded eaves cornice and cross-windows. Five-window façade. Doorway with moulded architrave and key block.

STONELEIGH ABBEY AND PARK
1 m. SSW

Stoneleigh Abbey is the grandest, most dramatic Georgian mansion of Warwickshire. But it was an abbey originally, and one of the great attractions of the house is the interlocking of periods. It has this in common with Combe Abbey, but, whereas Combe was mighty in the Middle Ages and Stoneleigh small, as an adventure in piecing together architectural evidence, Stoneleigh wins. That adventure is not easy now, as the house has been subdivided into sixteen apartments in separate ownership.*

The abbey was Cistercian, and the monks moved to the present site in 1155 or 1156. The plan of the church was Cistercian standard: a nave and aisles, transepts, a crossing and a chancel. The inner courtyard of the house was the cloister. The cloister, as usual, lay to the S of the church, with the familiar arrangement of the accommodation. Along the E side were the chapter house,

*This revised account therefore takes account of what the visitor can and cannot normally see.

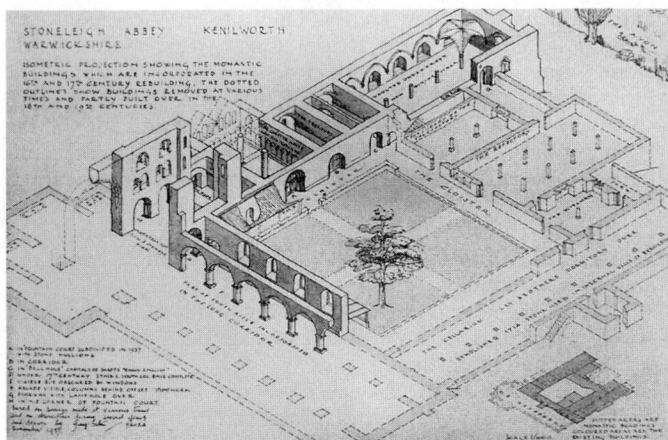

Stoneleigh, Stoneleigh Abbey.
Isometric drawing by Guy Silk, 1957

slype and domestic range with an impressive vaulted undercroft, and more (almost entirely gone) to the s and w of the cloister. To the n still stand the gatehouse and hospitium. After the Dissolution the abbey was granted in 1538 to Charles Brandon, Duke of Suffolk, and then sold by one of his heirs in 1561 to Sir Rowland Hill and Sir Thomas Leigh, two London merchants, jointly. Leigh married Hill's niece and heiress, Alice Barker, and became Lord Mayor of London in 1558.

Leighs remained at Stoneleigh until 1996 and so the abbey is their creation. Dates are uncertain, but work must have begun under the first Sir Thomas (†1571) and was no doubt continued by his widow Alice (†1603) and their son (†1626) and maybe even by the third Sir Thomas, the grandson.* Certainly by the early c17 Stoneleigh was a large house around a central courtyard. The first major development came after 1714 when Edward, 3rd Lord Leigh, obtained an estimate from *Francis Smith* for adding a new front to the existing w range. This turned into a rebuilding, completed in 1720–6 at a cost of £3,300. Fitting out proceeded more slowly and only some of the principal rooms were finished immediately. For the 4th Lord Leigh, *George Eborall* fitted out the chapel in 1743–4, aided by the plasterer *John Wright* of Worcester and Warwick carver *Benjamin King*. Schemes for the saloon by *William Smith* in the 1740s went unexecuted. Then, between 1763 and 1765, came a flurry of activity as *William Hiorne* and (principally) *Timothy Lightoler* lavishly adorned the unfinished parts of the w wing for Edward, 5th Lord Leigh. The spectacular saloon with its remarkable plasterwork attributed to *Vassalli*, the staircase landing ornamented by *Robert Moore*, and

---

*Tree-ring dating has recently shown that the roof of the n end of the e range dates from *c.* 1568–70, suggesting that substantial parts are earlier than the date of *c.* 1600 often given.

the parlour are the chief works of these years. More might have been done, but Edward was declared insane in 1774 and on his death in 1786 he was succeeded by his sister, Mary. When she died in 1806 the estate passed to the Rev. Thomas Leigh of the Adlestrop branch of the family. He commissioned *Humphry Repton* to suggest improvements to the landscape and initiated a major building programme continued after his death in 1813 by his collateral descendants and successors. Under James Henry Leigh (†1823) and his widow, Julia Judith (†1843), work continued into the late 1830s, mostly under *C. S. Smith*. He was assisted on site by the Stoneleigh agent, *George Jones*, who had been a civil engineer in the army. By Smith, the stables and riding house, the lodges and alterations to the N range. Others were brought in, such as *John Rennie* for the Park Bridge, while *Charles Hanbury Tracy* of Toddington Manor makes a surprise appearance as Gothic adviser in 1823 (cf. St Mary, above). Very little building took place after 1840, *William Burn*'s conservatory of 1851 being the main exception. A fire badly damaged the W wing in 1960, and initial repairs were limited to re-roofing and re-glazing. It was only after a sale of furniture, paintings and books that the state rooms could be restored. This was completed under *William Hawkes* in 1982–4.

The transfer in 1996 of the abbey and its 780-acre (316-ha) estate to a new preservation trust, Stoneleigh Abbey Limited, offered a radical solution to long-standing financial problems that had left it in poor repair. *Kit Martin* devised a scheme to subdivide the house and for related developments in the estate to establish a financially sustainable future for the building, which was restored and converted under *Rodney Melville & Partners* of Leamington (*Andrew Brookes*, project architect), 1997–2002. In 2013 the trustees embarked on the restoration of Repton's landscape and its associated buildings.

One enters through the GATEHOUSE on the N. It is the most complete surviving structure from the abbey, belonging to a reconstruction of the previous guest range at the time of Robert de Hockele, abbot from 1308 to 1349. The gatehouse is of *c.* 1342–5. It has an archway with a depressed-pointed arch, buttresses, a gable, and above the archway to outside and inside a two-light window with flowing tracery. Adjoining on the E is the HOSPITIUM, rebuilt *c.* 1349–50. Its porch, facing the abbey, has a small blocked spiral stair and a later outer staircase to its upper room. A vaulted walkway links the stairs to the upper floor of the gatehouse. The porch has another two-light window with flowing tracery. The upper hall of the hospitium has two more of these to the outside and a blocked E window. What is not C14 is Elizabethan, e.g. the mullioned windows and the coped gables and dormers with ball finials.

Turning S, one faces the house. The W range is utterly dominant, but to follow the adventure it must be ignored until the N and E ranges have been viewed from outside. The N range was developed by the Leighs from the S aisle of the monastic church, whose nave, N transept and chancel have been

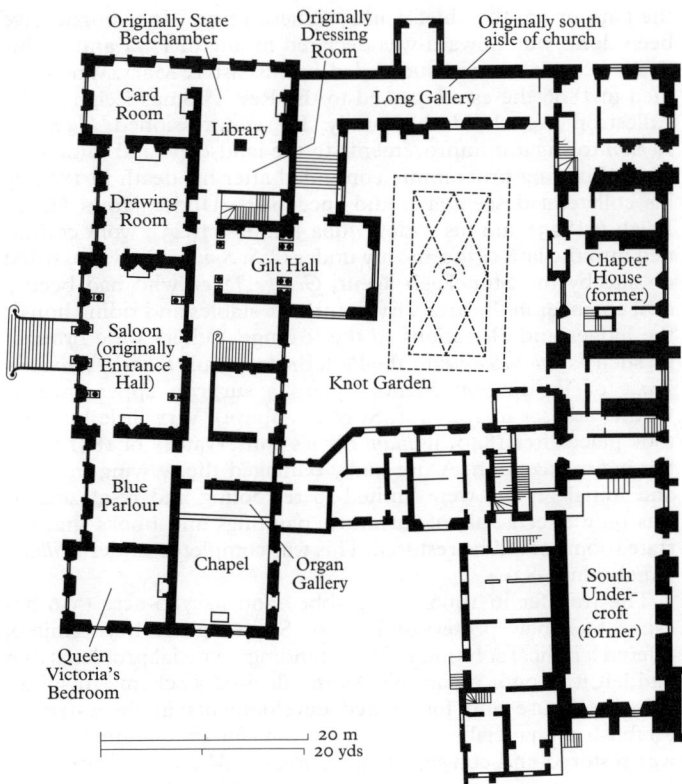

Originally State Bedchamber

Originally Dressing Room

Originally south aisle of church

Card Room

Library

Long Gallery

Drawing Room

Gilt Hall

Chapter House (former)

Saloon (originally Entrance Hall)

Knot Garden

Blue Parlour

Chapel

Organ Gallery

South Under-croft (former)

Queen Victoria's Bedroom

20 m
20 yds

Stoneleigh, Stoneleigh Abbey.
Plan

removed. It has two storeys and an attic. In the N wall there are four high blocked arches, and they represent the s arcade of the church. The two-storey porch in the centre of this front, however, is by *C. S. Smith*, 1836, replacing a classical mid-C17 entrance with sweeping double stairs and balcony. Also classical, the blocked arches l. and r. of the porch at the ground floor. E of the porch is a rainwater head with the date 1655. The gables and windows here must be *c.* 1570–1600.

The Leighs also created the three-storey and attic accommodation block at the E end within the s transept of the church, apparently *c.* 1570. This block, at the NE corner of the house, is taller than the ranges either side. The monastic evidence is mainly inside, but outside on the N there is a cone-shaped corbel to the former E crossing arch. Round the corner, the thick s wall of the transept is clearly noticeable in the E front, and low down, arches of two chapels on the E end of the transept can be seen. The C19 Neo-Norman door now in the s bay has real Norman capitals, reused, and links to a passageway within. As remodelled, the details of this N range are as in the gatehouse, i.e. mullioned and cross-windows, gables with flat coping stones and ball finials. The windows to the N regularly arranged, those on the E not. The E range continues S with seven even gables. Mullioned or cross windows again, but with some Norman and medieval openings all along the ground floor. The range ends with a taller block with hipped roof, the lower stage with a C13 two-light window with bar tracery facing E and big buttresses on the S. This is part of the former dormitory and undercroft in the monastic E range. The whole E front is pleasing, but distinctly conservative when compared with work of similar date at Kenilworth Castle or the great Midlands 'high houses' (e.g. Hardwick New Hall, Derbys.) at the forefront of Elizabethan architectural fashion.

The S range of the house is irregular and hard to date. Set back from the end of the two ranges either side, it is indicated on an estate map of 1749 but seems to have been rebuilt in 1838 (dated rainwater heads). In the SE corner are other additions of little interest, but on slightly lower ground towards the river is the CONSERVATORY, by *William Burn*, 1851. Ashlar, of seven bays with three-bay gabled ends, Doric pilasters, arched windows, and urns. Light cast-iron roof structure.

The towering WEST RANGE was built in 1720–6 by *Francis Smith* of Warwick for Edward, 3rd Lord Leigh, and is unquestionably his *chef d'œuvre*. It is English Baroque emphatically, and, like so much of the English Baroque, mighty rather than festive. The stone is dark grey. The windows are high, on the narrow side, and kept close together. There are a basement with banded rustication, two principal storeys, an attic, and a balustrade. The façade is fifteen bays long, grouped as 2–3–5–3–2, with the two and the five jumping forward and flanked by giant fluted Ionic pilasters or rather square pillars. The ground-floor windows all have segmental pediments on pilasters with fluted capitals. The doorway is reached by an open stair with a wrought-iron balustrade and has a bigger segmental pediment. The upper-floor windows have normal pediments. So there are thirty pediments crowded into the façade. The middle window is given volutes rising up its sides. Finally the attic windows reach up into the zone of the entablature above the pillars. The sides of the W block are four bays deep, divided into two plus two, i.e. with an awkward total of three giant pilasters.

56

If one enters through the N porch, rather than by the grand entrance on the W front, the monastic adventure can be continued. Here is the LONG GALLERY in the S aisle of the church. The C17 gallery was on an upper floor, now removed. As remodelled by *C. S. Smith* in 1836 the gallery runs the length of the N range, double-height. The plaster vaulting is Smith's. The panelling is by *James Willcox* of Warwick and incorporates a wooden C16 chimneypiece from the Leighs' nearby Fletchamstead Hall, then recently demolished. As well as fine medieval stained glass there is a sequence of eleven heraldic windows by *Willement* 'containing the various alliances of the family' presented by the Hon. Mrs Leigh in 1837.

Towards the E end of the gallery a doorway on the S led to the cloister, again a usual feature in the usual position, i.e. the E bay. Through the end door into the Tudor NE corner block is a Norman arch facing E and W. This was from the aisle to the S transept. It has strong responds and scalloped capitals. In this range, but still inside the transept, is a Neo-Norman passage to the external door in the E front already noted. There are four re-set Norman capitals with decorated scallops. Also in this part, a fine mid-C17 STAIRCASE with openwork balustrade of foliage and urns. The staircase leads to the first and the second floors. The ceiling has some stucco decoration typical of c. 1660, and in one room is panelling of about the same date.

From within the open courtyard at the heart of the house more of the medieval cloister can be seen.* At one end of the S wall of the N range, i.e. the former S aisle, is an outdoor fireplace with a pediment on the main chimney. At the other, the Norman doorway from the cloister into the S aisle. It has a roll moulding with chevrons at right angles (i.e. across the roll). Along the E side, the monastic buildings are surprisingly complete at ground level although the original uses of some rooms are uncertain. Moving S are a vaulted room (possibly a SACRISTY), without any telling details, and then the CHAPTER HOUSE. Its doorway from the inner courtyard is again Norman, with three orders of shafts with waterleaf capitals and roll mouldings in the arch. Inside there is a central round pier. It has no capital, and no vault survives. (After that a room with a tunnel-vault and a doorway from the cloister and a passage, also tunnel-vaulted, with a round-headed doorway to the E. In its N wall is a very large blocked arch with a depressed-pointed head.) The day stairs and the slype were in this area. The SE end of the range has a vaulted undercroft of five bays in two naves. Its function is uncertain. The piers are octagonal, the first big, the other three thinner. The ribs are single-chamfered and rest against the wall on corbels. It must be late C13 or early C14. In the W wall is one small blocked Norman window and another opening.

Protruding into the courtyard's W side is the GILT HALL, an addition by *C. S. Smith*, 1836, which is reached from the W end of the long gallery by a short stair. It chiefly serves to connect the C18 W wing to the N entrance created by Smith. The space is subdivided by two sets of columns. In the S window, medieval heraldic glass from Brereton Hall, Cheshire, given to Lord Leigh in 1872. From here one would ideally explore the state rooms of the W range from the N. The three rooms in the NW corner of the house all have Early Georgian dark wooden panelling with noble giant pilasters and full

---

*There is also a good view from the end window of the Gilt Hall inside the house.

entablature. This is of *c.* 1726–35, and probably by *Thomas Eborall*, one of Francis Smith's regular collaborators. In the centre of the range is the SALOON, built as the principal entrance hall. It is the showpiece of the house, finished internally for the 5th Lord Leigh by *Hiorne* and *Lightoler*, 1763–5. It has giant yellow demi-columns in an arrangement which divides the room into 1–3–1 bays. Stucco wall panels, rich door surrounds, chimneypieces, one with two caryatids, the other with two Atlantes. The plasterwork, attributed to *Vassalli*, depicts scenes from the Greek myth of Hercules. Six of the labours in roundels, probably The Choice and The Sacrifice in the overmantels and The Apotheosis on the ceiling. The first room to the S, the BLUE PARLOUR, was also finished by *Lightoler*, its lightness reflecting the change of taste from the dark panelling of the earlier rooms. At the S end is QUEEN VICTORIA'S BEDROOM, originally created upstairs for the royal visit in 1858, but relocated in 1982–4 when the rooms above were adapted for commercial letting. All here is white and gold and essentially Louis XVI.

The STAIRCASE lies immediately behind the saloon. Each step has two twisted and one fluted baluster, i.e. details of the Smith period. Probably by *Thomas Eborall*, along with the panelling and doorway pilasters and capitals around the lower flight. But the decorated wall panels and the ceiling to the top flight and landing are of the 1760s, the plasterwork by *Robert Moore* of Warwick. The ceiling is characteristically more classical than that of the saloon. The window of the staircase is of the Venetian type, and, seen from outside, patently a later insertion. The opening from the landing towards the rooms in the W front is Venetian too. There are drawings by *Lightoler* for these.

Reached by a passage from the bottom of the stairs, the CHAPEL stands to the height of two floors in the SW corner of the house. It is *Francis Smith*'s, but the fitting out was completed under *George Eborall* for the 4th Lord Leigh in 1743–4 with fine plasterwork by *John Wright* of Worcester. The centrepiece in the ceiling has a sunburst with cherubs' heads in the clouds. Original pews, communion rail, gallery and also the pulpit, mostly by *Eborall*. The reredos by *Benjamin King* is flanked by two columns with rising volutes l. and r., flaming urns, and more cherubs in the pediment. The mahogany communion table is by *William Gomm & Son* to a design by *Lightoler*, 1764, again with cherubs. The organ on the gallery, in a case based on a design by William Kent, is by *John Crang* of London, 1761.

In the basement under the Saloon, in the middle of the W front, is the vaulted SERVANTS' HALL.

Of the Victorian GARDENS around the house, little remains. *W.A. Nesfield* was working here in the 1840s and in 1858 created an Italian Garden on the W front for Queen Victoria's visit. Of *Repton*'s landscape, currently under restoration, there is much to see. He visited in 1808 and his Red Book is dated

1809. His chief work was the widening of the River Avon to create a lake and bring the water closer to the s front. Along the river to the E, the restored gazebo and bridges. On the riverside lawns SE of the house, a delightful rustic SUMMER-HOUSE, evidently Repton's. Low-pitched conical thatched roof on a central timber post. Open fronted with a ring of posts. Brick wall at the back with a bench. Charming ceiling with shallow ribbed vault made from bark-covered branches, artfully arranged.

Repton also suggested the erection of buildings all over the park to enhance the landscape. Although not erected to his designs or under his supervision, they belong to his scheme. Among them are the new approaches to the house. To the w, at the Warwick Road (B4115) entrance, a pair of Grecian LODGES, probably by *C. S. Smith*, 1814. The straight drive to the abbey crosses the river over the PARK BRIDGE by *John Rennie*, 1813–14, supervised by *George Jones*. They had worked together on the Grand Military Canal. Heavily rusticated with balustraded parapet. One main span, side arches and round-headed niches.

To the Stoneleigh Road on the E towards Stareton, two plain LODGES, again probably by *Smith*. Both sandstone, Neo-Tudor. EAST LODGE, to the N towards Stare Bridge, was under construction in 1822–3. MARY LODGE, *c.* 1815–20, is on the southern drive nearer Leamington. Off this drive are the detached houses in THE CUNNERY and GROVEHURST PARK built in 2002 to fund the Stoneleigh Abbey restoration scheme.

Closer to the house are the STABLES, for which *C. S. Smith*'s drawing is dated 1813. They are of red sandstone, symmetrical and castellated, with a raised entrance arch. The inner court-yard is spacious, seemingly curved on the N side but actually of seven sides of a dodecagon. In the first two bays, stalls for horses restored to their original form. The adjoining RIDING SCHOOL is dated 1820 on a drawing. It is of three by ten bays, of which one is a gallery with stair-turret. All Tudor-Gothic, the windows with four-centred arches. All restored 1997–2002. The whole group was originally connected with the house by a covered way. Of this only the gateway across the drive along the E side of the house remains.

The DEER PARK created after 1640 lay E of the Coventry–Leamington road on both sides of the Avon. In the centre was a hunting lodge and, nearby, a C17 bridge of two arches with cutwater across the river. C19 additions include the TANTARA LODGE (or London Lodge) at the far side of the park towards Bubbenhall, suggested by *Repton* and built in 1818. In the style of a monastic gatehouse (cf. Maxstoke Priory), stone with vaulted archway, gables with medieval windows and octagonal turret on the park side. At the N entrance, a plain sandstone lodge with bargeboarded gables, but from Stareton the park gate was a picturesque cottage, 1818, in the manner of P. F. Robinson or Nash. This is BEEHIVE COTTAGE, once called

Park Cottage or Stareton Gate. Originally thatched with tree-trunk columns. There are drawings for a cottage of this type at 'Stoneleigh, labelled 'Pooley Lane Cottage' (amended to 'Thickthorn Cottage'), signed by *C.S. Smith*, 1817 and 1818. ABBEY PARK business centre is in the SE corner of the old deer park. It has curved office blocks by *Robothams*, 2008, and the single-storey headquarters of the British Horse Society by *Archial Architects*, 2011. Oak cladding and sedum roof. Doughnut-shaped around an existing tree. *Buckley Gray Yeoman* have prepared a masterplan for a park extension with timber-clad pavilions, 2013.

STONELEIGH PARK (formerly the National Agricultural Centre) occupies a 800-acre (324-ha) site NE of the abbey. It was created in 1963 on a grid plan with offices for agriculture-related organizations, indoor arenas and grassed areas for outdoor events. Until 2009 it was the venue for the Royal Show. It has, however, no buildings of note.

STOURTON

2030

Mainly stone houses, including C17 STOURTON MANOR, triple gabled, on the S side of the bend in Main Road. Opposite STOURTON FARMHOUSE, also C17, has a C19 ashlar front with coped gables and end stacks. Down the track to its N, the former METHODIST CHAPEL, 1809. Brick with gabled front and Gothick casement windows. Elsewhere in the village, other buildings with attractive initialled datestones, 1707 to 1832. Facing the S end of Featherbed Lane, the former Cherington and Stourton NATIONAL SCHOOL, by *William Thompson*, 1871. Brick with stone mullions and dressings.

STRATFORD-UPON-AVON

2050

INTRODUCTION

To appreciate Stratford-upon-Avon one has to make the gigantic effort of forgetting Shakespeare and the pilgrims and the trippers – there were 805,000 visits to the Birthplace Trust sites in 2013. Shakespeare was born and died at Stratford. He went in all probability to the local grammar school, and he married Anne Hathaway when only eighteen years old. From 1587 he was in London acting and writing. From about 1595 he re-visited Stratford. He bought New Place in 1597, and retired there five years before he died. The houses you are shown are the birthplace, that is the house of his father, a glover and wool-dealer who was bailiff (i.e. mayor) of the borough in 1568, the New Place Museum, that is the house of Thomas Nash, who married Shakespeare's granddaughter, Hall's Croft, the house of Dr John Hall, who married Shakespeare's daughter, and the cottage at Shottery of the Hathaway family. The architectural value of these houses is minor; so is the biographical value. But for mass enjoyment they are first-class, and they are for that purpose extremely well managed, with their pretty gardens. Once Shakespeare is out of the way and once you can see Stratford out of season, you can still visualize the thriving Midland market town with the comfortable, staid, minor Georgian town superimposed on it.

So wrote Pevsner in 1965, and (apart from an update to his figure for visitor numbers) it remains entirely valid now. The town, however, needs a little more by way of introduction. It began as a settlement by an ancient river crossing and so-called Old Town near the church probably marks the original centre. Change came with the planning of a new town in 1196 resulting in broad, straight streets forming a grid, with two market areas, one in Bridge Street and the other in Rother Street by the present American Fountain. Much rebuilding followed the disastrous fires which occurred in 1594, 1595, 1614 and 1641. Regulations of 1650 encouraged the use of brick for building, and C19 views and photographs show a largely Georgian and Regency town. A fashion in the early C20 for exposing concealed timber framing brought a dramatic transformation to the townscape to recreate Stratford as Shakespeare's Tudor town.

Economically, Stratford enjoyed the prosperity of a well-situated market town without any single dominant industry. Being on an E–W route of Roman origin, close to the N–S Fosse Way, and on the main road from Oxford to Birmingham, Stratford had good land communications. In 1817 twenty-four coaches a day called at the town. In addition the River Avon was made navigable from the Severn estuary in 1635 and the canal to Birmingham opened in 1816. The Moreton tramway opened in 1826 and other railway connections from 1859–60.

Stratford's first local architectural practices were established in the 1820s and 1830s when the town first began to expand. Most notable in the early period were *John Lattimer* (†1858) and his son *Joseph* (†1883), and *Edward Gibbs* (*fl.* 1840s–1870s). Of some significance locally was *Thomas Taylor Allen* (†1913),

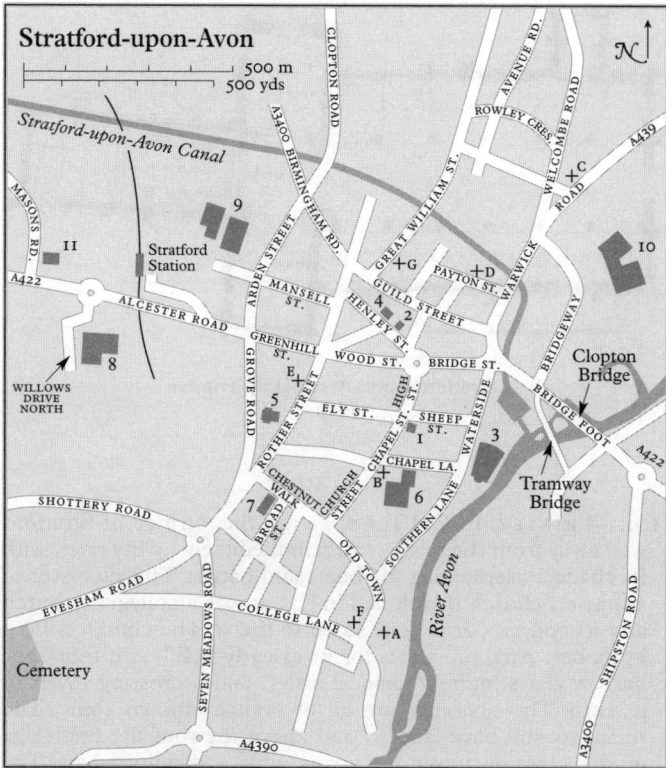

Stratford-upon-Avon

| 500 m |
| 500 yds |

Stratford-upon-Avon Canal

CLOPTON ROAD

A3400 BIRMINGHAM RD.

AVENUE RD.

ROWLEY CRES.

WELCOMBE ROAD

A439

MASONS RD.

11

Stratford Station

9

A422

ALCESTER ROAD

ARDEN STREET

MANSELL ST.

GREAT WILLIAM ST.

GUILD STREET

PAYTON ST.

G

D

C

WARWICK ROAD

10

GREENHILL

HENLEY ST.

4

2

BRIDGEWAY

Clopton Bridge

8

WILLOWS DRIVE NORTH

GROVE ROAD

WOOD ST.

BRIDGE ST.

BRIDGE FOOT

A422

E

5

ELY ST.

HIGH ST.

SHEEP ST.

WATERSIDE

3

Tramway Bridge

ROTHER STREET

1

SHOTTERY ROAD

CHESTNUT WALK

BROAD ST.

CHURCH STREET

CHAPEL ST.

CHAPEL LA.

B

6

SOUTHERN LANE

7

OLD TOWN

EVESHAM ROAD

SEVEN MEADOWS ROAD

COLLEGE LANE

F

A

River Avon

SHIPSTON ROAD

A3400

Cemetery

A4390

A	Holy Trinity	1 Town hall
B	Guild Chapel	2 Library
C	St Gregory (RC.)	3 Royal Shakespeare Theatre
D	Baptist chapel	4 Shakespeare's Birthplace
E	United Reformed church	and the Shakespeare Centre
	(Congregational)	5 Magistrates' court and
F	Methodist church	police station
G	Primitive Methodist	6 King Edward VI School
	chapel (former)	7 Stratford County Primary
		School
		8 Stratford-upon-Avon College
		9 Stratford Hospital
		10 Leisure Centre and
		Swimming Pool
		11 Fire station

especially as architect for Methodist chapels. More notable were father *F. W. B. Yorke* (1879–1957) and his son *F. R. S. Yorke* (1906–62), whose careers linked the Arts and Crafts and Modern movements. Robert Harvey took on the practice (*Yorke, Harper & Harvey*) in 1954, retiring in 1987. He specialized in free-thinking domestic commissions. *Guy Pemberton* (1884–1959) also had an office in Stratford for some years.

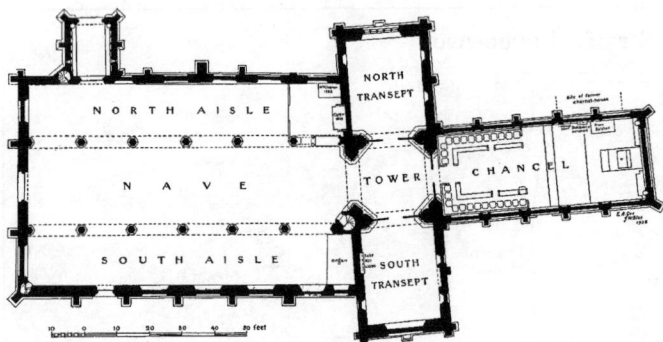

Stratford-upon-Avon, Holy Trinity.
Plan

CHURCHES*

HOLY TRINITY. In Old Town, i.e. on the s fringe of Stratford
well away from the town centre, immediately by the river, with
its chancel overlooking the boats and barges. The successor of
a minster church mentioned in 845, it was a collegiate church
and its college (*see* p. 607) stood to the w. The church is Perp
in its best part, but starts for us as early E.E., with transepts,
narrow aisles, narrow chancel aisles, and a crossing tower of
c. 1210. The dressings are all of orangey brown stone. The
transepts still have lancets, and above the roof the first stage
of the crossing tower has twins with a dividing shaft. The
lancets are not shafted but have roll-hoodmoulds inside. The
narrow aisles and chancel aisles can be deduced from the
exposed shafts and half-arches in the N transept. In the W wall
of the N transept must have been a window larger than the
lancets, perhaps a group of three, stepped. The crossing tower
had its arches remodelled early in the C14, as the typical filleted
shafts connected by continuous hollows show. Possibly at the
same time the tower was heightened and received its unusual
and distinctive rose windows. The recessed spire was probably
later still. It was of timber by the time *William Hiorne* of
Warwick rebuilt it in 1763 to a Gothic design by *Timothy Lightoler*. The nave and aisles are askew from the E parts. The aisles
are Dec, their arcades of six bays with hexagonal piers and
double-chamfered arches uneventful, but their windows nicely
varied, from a stepped group of pointed-trefoiled lancet lights
to reticulated and fully Dec. The S aisle is connected with the
foundation of a college by John de Stratford, later Bishop of
Winchester, in 1331 and has its original ceiling with bosses and
the rebuilt SEDILIA incorporating fragments of the original,
with richly gabled canopies. The Perp contributions are as

---

*St James's Church, Guild Street, by *James Murray*, 1853–5, with later tower (1875)
and spire (1893), was demolished in 1968–9.

follows: a clerestory of twelve windows, quite large, of three lights, a truly splendid chancel of five bays with giant four-light windows, an E window of seven lights and a four-centred arch, decorated buttresses, and panelled battlements, and the two-storeyed N porch. This has niches l. and r. of the upper window, handsome blank arcading above benches inside, and a vault with ridge ribs as well as diagonal ribs, bosses, and small corner figures as supports. The central boss is a defaced Christ in Majesty. In the chancel are rich SEDILIA with nodding ogee arches under pinnacles and a row of angel busts in front of the seats. Under the r. canopy, a carved head of Christ (r.). The same motifs are used for the PISCINA. Between the windows are big blank panels (cf. Guild Chapel). The S side doorway has an ogee arch, the N door a stilted pointed arch with large carved stops. The E window is flanked inside by spectacular tall niches for images. The brackets have frightening giant flying insects. The nave clerestory zone is treated inside as sumptuously. Shafts on angels start on top of the Dec capitals, and the wall has blank panelling with mullions descending from the windows. The W window of the nave was redone at the same time. It is of nine lights with canopied niches to the three centre lights inside and out. All this is not actually datable, but the chancel was built by Dean Balshall who died in 1491 (*see* below), and the clerestory and N porch probably by his successor, Dean Collingwood, who died in 1521 or 1522. The church was first 'restored' by *Harvey Eginton*, 1839–40. Much of that phase has been swept away, but Eginton's hand is still visible in the external appearance of the transepts and S aisle. Later restoration under *Bodley & Garner*, the exterior in 1885–6 (the galleries were also removed), the chancel in 1890–2 and the rest in 1897–8. Here William Morris protested against the excessive zeal of his very earliest patron, Bodley.

– FURNISHINGS. FONT. In the chancel the former font bowl, Perp, relatively shallow, with quatrefoils. The font in use is a replica, 1885. – PULPIT. Dark green Italian marble with figures in white alabaster. *Bodley & Garner*, 1900. – SCREENS. Of the tall chancel screen little is original. Better preserved the screen to the N transept. – STALLS. New backs by *Bodley & Garner*, 1892. Original the seats with angels on the arms, the fronts with poppyheads on the ends, and the MISERICORDS. They date from the late C15 and are most entertaining even if no great shakes as sculpture, S from W: birds, unicorn and virgin, two bears and the ragged staff, St George, angels, a husband birching his wife, holding her rather obscenely, the same husband quarrelling with his wife, leaves, heads, etc. N from E: a dromedary, a naked woman on a stag, a merman and mermaid, an eagle and an infant (Ganymede), two figures growing out of whelks. – ORGAN CASE. By *Bodley*, 1898. Gothic, high up above the W arch of the crossing and incorporating the rood, with vaulting below. – DOORS. Perp N door with re-set SANCTUARY KNOCKER and the tower door from the crossing, both with some tracery. – CHANDELIER. Brass, given in 1720. Three tiers of scrolly arms, and an equally scrolly iron support. – SWORD RESTS. One is *temp*. George III, the other, also in the C18 style, is of 1920. – SCULPTURE. In the niches of the chancel E wall, statues carved by *Farmer & Brindley* to designs by *Bodley & Garner*, 1893. – PROCESSIONAL CROSS. Silver, by *Barkentin & Krall*, 1901. – STAINED GLASS. Within the later Clopton Chapel N window small fragments of original glass. – More fragments in tracery lights of window S of the high altar. – The rest (thirty-four in all) topographically arranged. – E window, *Heaton, Butler & Bayne*, 1895. – In the chancel N, four by *Lavers, Barraud & Westlake* (later *Lavers & Westlake*), and three more on the S, 1873–91. – The remaining N window by *Heaton, Butler & Bayne*, 1891, and the first two on the S by *William Holland*, 1862 and 1865. – In the transepts more by *Holland*, including his 1855–9 E window re-erected in the N transept after 1895. – In the N transept one by *Lavers & Westlake*, 1893. – Main S transept window, *Heaton, Butler & Bayne*, 1896. – Nave W window by *Holland*, 1860. – In the N aisle, five by *Heaton, Butler & Bayne*, 1897–1910, and aisle W by *Kempe & Co.*, 1910. – In the S aisle, a hidden window by *Holland* (possibly designed by *Clement Heaton*), 1850. – Others include two by *Kempe*, 1901 and 1905, one by *Herbert W. Bryans*, 1904, one by *Clayton & Bell*, 1907, and the aisle W window by *T. F. Curtis, Ward & Hughes*, 1904. – N porch windows by *Lavers, Barraud & Westlake*, 1870 and 1879.

– MONUMENTS (topographically arranged again). In the chancel, Dean Balshall †1491, erected before. Big tomb-chest with frantically ill-treated scenes under nodding ogee arches. The brass is lost. – Rev. James Davenport †1841. Elaborate and Gothic. By *Wm Moysen* of Birmingham. – James Aldborough Dennis †1838. White, with kneeling young woman. By *Sir Richard Westmacott*. – William Shakespeare †1616, alabaster, attributed to *Gheerart Jansen* the younger (Anglicized as *Gerard Johnson*), who succeeded in making the bard look like a self-satisfied schoolmaster. What is however extremely interesting is that the iconographical type chosen is that of the scholar or divine. Frontal demi-figure with paper and quill. The inscription reads:

IVDICIO PYLIVM GENIO SOCRATEM ARTE MARONEM
TERRA TEGIT POPVLVS MAERET OLYMPVS HABET
Stay Passenger, why goest thou by so fast,
Read if thou canst, whom envious death has plast,
Within this monument Shakespeare: with whome,
Quick nature dide: whose name doth deck Ys tombe,
Far more, then cost: Sieh all, Yt he hath Writt
Leaves living art, but page, to serve his Witt.

– Judith Combe and her betrothed Richard. She died in 1649. Two demi-figures under a double arch. They are holding hands. The other hand is on a skull. Black columns l. and r., garlands above. Alabaster. The monument is by *Thomas Stanton*. – John Combe †1614, also attributed to *Jansen*, and for the construction of which Combe left £60 in his will. Recumbent effigy, two columns, flat arch, two obelisks. Alabaster. – Will Combe †1666/7 and wife, attributed to *Thomas Stanton* (GF). – Elizabeth Rawlins, n.d. (†1658), by *Thomas Burman* (GF). – James Kendall †1751 and wife Jane †1769. By *Michael Rysbrack*, 1756. Dull full-round bust in Roman attire, but l. and r. two excellent putti, asymmetrically composed, the l. one standing and holding a medallion portrait of Mrs Kendall, the r. one seated with a snake as the sign of eternity. – In the s transept, the front of a tomb-chest: Richard Hill †1593. With crude, fluted pilasters. He was a grazier, but the inscription begins in Hebrew and then turns Greek before settling down to Latin and English. – In the Clopton Chapel (N aisle E), Hugh Clopton (Lord Mayor of London in 1492),* †1496 (cenotaph, much restored). Tomb-chest under an arch between chapel and nave. To its w a narrower passage arch. Both arches are four-centred. The piers are concave-sided. Between the two E piers, a bracket for an image. The arches are panelled inside. Cresting at the top. – William Clopton †1592. Alabaster, by *Garrat Hollemans* of Burton upon Trent (JB). Two recumbent effigies holding little prayer-books. Tomb-chest still with Gothic script. Against the wall the children. – George Carew, Earl of Totnes and Lord Clopton, and his wife Joyce Clopton. He died in 1629. Alabaster. Tomb-chest with recumbent effigies. Coffered arch. Five slender angels on top and against the back wall. On the chest front splendid still-life of powder barrels, cannon balls, guns, and flags. On the side walls trophies, one with drum and trumpet. It is by *Edward Marshall*, and one of his earliest works. – Sir Edward Walker †1676/7, attributed to *Joshua Marshall*.

GUILD CHAPEL, at the s end of Chapel Street. Owned by the corporation since 1553, but originally the chapel of the Guild of the Holy Cross (*see* Guildhall, p. 598), founded before 1269, amalgamated with the guilds of Our Lady and St John Baptist in 1403, and the ruling body of Stratford to the time of the Dissolution. Among C15 members were Edward, Prince of Wales (i.e. later Edward V), the Duke of Clarence, and his son Edward, Earl of Warwick. A new, ambitious nave was built by Hugh Clopton in the late C15 and building was still in progress when he died in 1496. Four bays. Large four-light Perp transomed windows, battlements and pinnacles. The chancel, re-consecrated 1452/3, is much humbler and its rubble s wall survives from earlier times. The w tower again late C15. Proud N porch in typical local Perp with gargoyles and chunky carvings. Restoration by *Stephen Dykes Bower*, 1954–83, including refacing the nave, porch and tower with Hollington stone instead of the original Arden stone. Inside, blind panels between the windows (cf. Holy Trinity) and more chunky

39

---

*He was actually buried in London.

moulding over the N door whose W door stop has a shield. Interior scraped and refurnished by Dykes Bower. Panelled nave with chaste collegiate-style seating in place of former box pews. – FONT. C18. Marble, with baluster stem and fluted basin. – ORGAN CASE, filling the narrow tower arch. *Dykes Bower*, 1955. – WALL PAINTINGS. A once extensive set, uncovered in 1804 and vividly recorded in a set of contemporary watercolours but 'afterwards again obliterated' (Bloxam). Faded remains left exposed in 1955.* Over the chancel arch a Doom, *c.* 1500, quite recognizable and full of incident. Christ in Majesty with the Virgin and St John at the top. Hell on the r., a very architectural Heaven with St Peter on the l. Many little figures climbing out of their graves, including a king, a bishop, and an abbot. Also remains of paintings at the W end (St George, St Thomas Becket, etc.). – STAINED GLASS in chancel by *H. Vernon Spreadbury*, 1962–70, representing people and events in Stratford's history. – MONUMENT. Tablet commemorating the life and good works of Hugh Clopton, †1496, by *Edward Stanton*, 1708.

See Villages below for St Andrew, Shottery (p. 614), and St Peter, Bridgetown (p. 613).

ST GREGORY (R.C.), Warwick Road. By *E. W. Pugin*, 1865–6, except for the W (ritually W) front and porch remodelled by *Healing & Overbury*, 1957. Aisles and apse, the aisle windows groups of three thin lancets. A poor interior. – REREDOS and other carved stone decoration by *Boulton* of Worcester, 1866. – STAINED GLASS. Mostly by *Tony Dury*, 1866. – S aisle, 1871. – One by *Hardman*, 1924.

Adjoining PRESBYTERY by *G. H. Cox*, 1889.

BAPTIST CHAPEL, Payton Street. 1835. Greek Revival style. Portico with two pairs of Tuscan columns and dated pediment. Channelled rustication. Battered windows in side walls. Schoolrooms alongside by *Joseph Lattimer* 'after a Grecian style' to harmonize, 1861.

UNITED REFORMED CHURCH (Congregational), Rother Street. *H. J. Paull*, 1878–80, on a new site for a meeting founded in 1662. Lias with limestone dressings. Rather deplorable Gothic. Diminished by the loss of its corner spire. Interior with W gallery and hammerbeam-style roof, partially supported on cast-iron columns. Sunday School rooms behind by *Allen*, 1888. The previous chapel became the Public Hall and was demolished in 1976. On its site the CHRISTADELPHIAN HALL by *Butler Jones & Partners*, 1979.

METHODIST CHURCH, opposite Holy Trinity. *Cripps & Stewart* of Oxford, 1962–4. Brick with Cotswold stone cladding on the front. As built, it had an open wooden spire and cross over the main entrance. Portico removed and entrance remodelled by *Vagdia & Holmes*, 2013–14, along with internal reordering and improved facilities.

---

* Others on the N and S walls are now concealed behind panelling.

Former PRIMITIVE METHODIST CHAPEL, Great William Street. Now the MASONIC HALL. By *T. T. Allen*, 1865–6. Red brick with pilasters and pediment boldly outlined in blue brick, the window arches in yellow.

CEMETERY, Evesham Road, 1881. Ground layout by *Wood & Kendrick*, winners of the design competition. Buildings by *T. T. Allen* instead, also 1881. The CHAPEL has a tower with a tiled pyramid spire and an apsed vestry. Left open at both ends since a fire in 1994. LODGE with mullioned-and-transomed windows and fish-scale tile roofs. BOUNDARY WALLS with good railings and gates. Allen †1913 is buried near the entrance.

PUBLIC BUILDINGS

TOWN HALL, Sheep Street. 1767–8 by *Robert Newman* of Whittington (Glos.), builder and mason. But did he design it? A civilized, urban, Palladian job. Fine-grained light cream-coloured Cotswold stone. Three bays to Sheep Street and five to Chapel Street. The ground floor originally open, now with segmental-headed windows in blank arches of 1863–4 when improvements were undertaken by *J. H. & G. F. Hawkes* of Birmingham. Facing Sheep Street, in an alcove designed for it by *Timothy Lightoler*, a lead STATUE of Shakespeare by *John Cheere*, presented by David Garrick *c.* 1769, to coincide with the first festival (*see* Royal Shakespeare Theatre). In the principal upper room sparse stucco panels on the walls, all identical except for the heads at the bottom. The decoration had to be redone after a fire in 1946. The architect for the restoration was *F. W. B. Yorke*.

LIBRARY, Henley Street. Funded by Carnegie. Early C16 timber-framed house, but partly restored and part new by *E. G. Holtom*, 1903–5.

ROYAL SHAKESPEARE THEATRE, Bancroft Gardens/Waterside. The story starts with the octagon built for 1,000 people on the occasion of Garrick's festival of 1769. It was a great success, but it strikes us as odd that no performance of a play was part of it. The first permanent theatre was built in 1827. It was a very modest affair. Then, thanks to the enthusiasm and wealth of the brewer C. E. Flower and the Shakespeare Memorial Association (founded 1875), a more ambitious theatre was built in 1877–9 and called the SHAKESPEARE MEMORIAL THEATRE. It was very Gothic and had an asymmetrically placed high tower. The library and art gallery, added in 1881 as an independent building connected to the theatre by a bridge, remains to this day. The architects selected by competition were *Dodgshun & Unsworth*, *W. F. Unsworth* being a pupil of Burges. As a whole, the building had a wildly Romantic appearance, much influenced by Continental styles. From 1886 to 1916 Sir Frank Benson managed the Shakespearean Festival, his company being referred to as the Bensonians.

The main theatre was destroyed by fire in 1926. A design competition held in 1928 for rebuilding on the adjacent site

124

p. 72

was won by *Elizabeth Scott*, a cousin of Sir Giles. The new theatre by *Scott, Chesterton & Shepherd* was completed in 1932, partly wrapping around the ruins of its predecessor which was reused for a conference centre, and later rehearsal rooms etc. Scott's firm (by then *Scott, Shepherd & Breakwell*) added the restaurant on the river side in 1938. The theatre was granted the title of the Royal Shakespeare Theatre in 1961. In 1984–6 the Swan Theatre was created by *Michael Reardon & Associates* in the shell of the original theatre. Then, after a number of failed schemes from the 1970s onwards, came the latest remodelling of the entire complex, initiated in 1998 (when total demolition of the 1930s building and replacement to a design by *Erick van Egeraat* was proposed) but following intervention by English Heritage a compromise was reached in the present design, won in competition by *Bennetts Associates* and completed 2005–11.

So the building as we see it is a composite of four main phases. Of *Dodgshun & Unsworth*'s 1877–9 Memorial Theatre the s end remains, with its rounded end. Red brick with thin courses of stone and Gothic windows. This has an upper storey jettied on corbels, *donjon* style, which was originally timber-framed, redone less interestingly in brick in the 1930s remodelling. The brilliant restoration and conversion in 1984–6 by *Reardon* as the SWAN THEATRE reinstated the tent-like roof with big vanes recreating the original (itself recalling Garrick's festival theatre) destroyed in 1926, but omitting the flèche of its predecessor. Abutting this is the stump of the great tower also destroyed in the fire but again with a plain brick top stage. To the w, fronting Waterside, and still linked to the theatre by a bridge, is the former LIBRARY AND ART GALLERY building (SWAN WING) of 1880–1, wholly intact. Lavishly Gothic but like the theatre European rather than English with a recessed centre and matching wings that have steep Burgesian slate roofs behind chequerboard parapets. The s wing has an open loggia at the first floor. In the centre gabled arches of rich blind tracery and three terracotta panels on Shakespearean themes of history, tragedy and comedy by *Paul Kummer*, 1886. Carved gargoyles by *Gilbert W. Seale*.

The theatre as designed by Scott faces N to the Bancroft Gardens and much of its main façade and riverside frontage has been preserved although spoiled by the alterations of 2011. What remains is impressive but Pevsner's assessment of 1966 is worth recording: 'The building strikes us now as very dated, in its blocky brick shape and its playing with bricks as the chief decorative element – the one inspired by Holland, the other by North Germany. At the time of its building it was a radical statement in England, very remarkable in a place of such strong and live traditions. This is what made Maxwell Fry and F. R. S. Yorke write with conviction of it in *The Architectural Review*. Modern-minded members of the Design and Industries Association from Birmingham showed it proudly to

Gropius one day in 1934 or 1935, and it was embarrassing to see his embarrassment. Taken in its English context of 1930, however, it can surely be appreciated, and it has aged well – better than *béton brut* will.' The last is a reference to the exposed rough concrete finishes of the contemporary (i.e. 1960s) brutalists.

The front is curved with vertical fins dividing the bays and has a copper-clad canopy with balconied vertical windows above. Below the parapet, sculpture by *Eric Kennington*, Expressionist, allegorical, and all in cut brick. At the river corner, a polygonal stair tower. Scott's auditorium had tapering sides and the stage-house, also with fins to the four sides, rose high and square at the far end abutting the old theatre, but the elevation which tells the plan frankly has been lost in the remodelling that has imposed a completely new glass storey with canopy at roof level. The river frontage has also been altered by removing the tiers of restaurants etc. added since the 1930s, revealing Scott's original façade to restaurant and terrace, and at the S end steel-framed additions (for offices etc.) have been plugged into the monumental sheer walling of the 1930s. So the composite is a bit of a hotch-potch and on Waterside at the entrance to the main foyer of 2011 is a gimmicky 120-ft (36.6-metre) viewing tower, brick with chamfered corners and better suited to a fire station than an internationally renowned theatre.

Inside, the central FOYER of the 1930s theatre is largely preserved. This has plain brick walls, marble flooring and brass and chrome-plated fixtures. Large spiral stair in the corner, its stair balustrade faced with green marble. Star-shaped ceiling over. Above the foyer and along the river frontage other largely unaltered interiors of this period, with inlaid doors and panelling.

The AUDITORIUM was first altered 1950–1 by *E. Brian O'Rorke*, replacing the proscenium arch of the 1930s with an apron stage bringing performers into the audience. There were numerous small revisions thereafter before the remodelling of 2011 completely removed the auditorium and inserted a brick horseshoe within the space, containing a thrust stage with audience on three sides – the experience of course as it had been in the C16 theatres like the Globe and the Rose. This followed the precedent set by the interior of the SWAN THEATRE, which has a three-tier U-shaped auditorium with timber staging and specifically balconies designed as a venue for C16 and C17 plays. In the glazed FOYER between the entrance of 2011 and The Swan are SLATE PANELS carved by *John Skelton*, originally for the Flowers Brewery, 1966 (dem. 1972). In the SWAN WING (i.e. the former library and art gallery), refurbished in 2015, much STAINED GLASS. On the stairs, Seven Ages of Man, probably 1881; war memorial window, 1925; oriel window with members of the Old Bensonians in character roles, a composite by *William Pearce Ltd*, 1905, *F. E. Osborne* and the *Stratford-upon-Avon Guild*, 1925 and

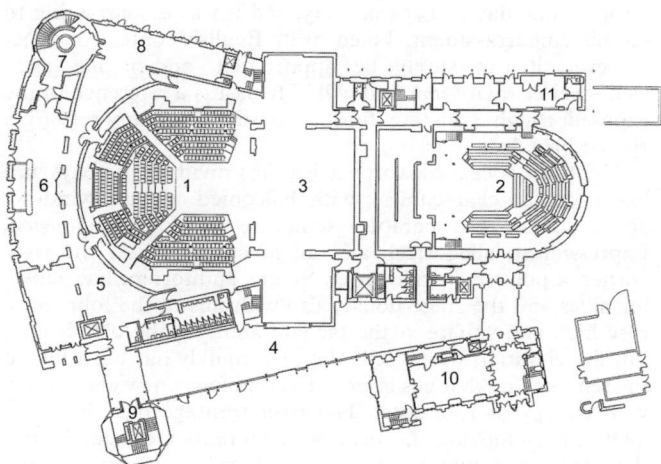

1. Royal Shakespeare Theatre
2. Swan Theatre
3. Stage and wing spaces
4. Colonnade
5. Foyer void
6. Scott Foyer
7. Fountain Staircase
8. Café
9. Theatre Tower
10. Library and Reading Room
11. Stage door

Stratford-upon-Avon, Shakespeare Memorial Theatre.
Plan

H. Vernon Spreadbury, 1950; two similar three-light windows by *Spreadbury*, 1932.

Opposite the theatre, on the w side of Waterside, the former LECTURE HALL AND SCENERY DOCK, 1887 by *A. S. Flower*, with a big half-timbered gable. For the RSC offices *see* p. 601.

SHAKESPEARE'S BIRTHPLACE and SHAKESPEARE CENTRE, Henley Street. *See* pp. 609–10.

MAGISTRATES' COURT and POLICE STATION, Rother Street. By the *County Architect*'s *Department*, 1978. An overbearing red brick fortress, mercifully set back from the street.

39 KING EDWARD VI SCHOOL, Chapel Street. The school was established in the C13 (re-founded 1553) and occupied the upper room (or Over Hall) of the GUILDHALL in Church Street, built *c.* 1417, from 1553 when the Guild of the Holy Cross was suppressed by Edward VI and its properties given to the town; the corporation met in the Guildhall proper on the ground floor until 1864, since when the whole building has

been part of the school. From the s end to the e projects a
wing, also *c.* 1417. Historically the council chamber occupied
its ground floor. To Church Street the main range has close
vertical studding. The main posts on the ground floor have
attached shafts and curved brackets for the overhang. Moulded
ceiling beams in the ground-floor hall of the main range and
in the wing. The Over Hall has the roof open with original
trusses. Original windows in the e wall of the main range on
the ground floor. In the s wall between the studs traces of wall
paintings and inscriptions. More painted decorations in the
upstairs chamber. The Guildhall and the Guild Chapel (*see*
Churches) enclose three sides of a small courtyard. On the s
side are the PEDAGOGUE'S HOUSE, timber-framed, of *c.* 1500
and the former VICARAGE (headmaster's house since the
1870s), almost touching the s side of the Guild Chapel. By
Francis Smith, 1702–3. Red brick with wooden cross-windows
and dormers. The rest of the school buildings, arranged around
two larger courtyards, include the timber-framed MEMORIAL
LIBRARY, 1923, and LEVI FOX HALL, by *Hawkes, Edwards &
Cave*, 1997. Brick front with glazed gables, wide and low. Roof
with side dormers. Galleried interior with exposed steel roof
structure.

GIRLS' GRAMMAR SCHOOL. *See* Shottery (p. 615).

STRATFORD COUNTY PRIMARY SCHOOL, Broad Street. The
BOARD SCHOOL by *William O. Milne*, 1883, in Old English
style. Enlarged in 1895, with sympathetic but contemporary
extension by *MRT*, 2005. No. 41 Broad Street is the teacher's
house by *Allen*, 1901.

STRATFORD-UPON-AVON COLLEGE, The Willows North,
Alcester Road. Commenced on this site in buildings designed
by the *County Architect's Department*, 1968. New academic
buildings by *D5 Architects*, 2005–6, and an accommodation
block with wooden cladding.

STRATFORD HOSPITAL, Arden Street. Undergoing redevelopment (2015), with a new hospital by *AFL Architects* due to open
in 2016–17. It will complement the existing early C21 buildings.
The site was previously occupied by the UNION WORK-
HOUSE (*Bateman and Drury*, 1837), whose buildings were
replaced piecemeal in the C20. Towards Alcester Road on the
s stood the original HOSPITAL (by *E. W. Mountford*, 1883–4),
also demolished although its LODGE on Arden Street (by *T. T.
Allen*, 1899) survives. The clock turret of Mountford's hospital
is incorporated into the STRATFORD VICTORIA HOTEL, by
Brown Matthews, 1997.

LEISURE CENTRE and SWIMMING POOL, Bridgeway. By the
County Architect, *J. C. E. Tainsh*, 1973–4. Low, with angled
wings and a tower with octagonal top. Under refurbishment
2014–15.

FIRE STATION, Mason Road. Plain and functional, but with a
carving of a fireman in the brickwork by *Walter Ritchie*, 1951.
Also memorial garden with firefighter statue by *Allan Scott*,
2008.

RAILWAY STATION, Alcester Road. 1865, altered 1906. Platform buildings remain on the E side only. Red brick with yellow surrounds to round-headed windows and doorways. Canopy and awnings. GWR footbridge, 1891.

PERAMBULATIONS

There are four. The first takes in Stratford's historic spine, from the bridge to the centre of the town and then along High Street and Chapel Street to the Guild Chapel. The second continues along Church Street and looks at the Old Town. The third deals with the western side from the middle of the town out to the railway. The fourth covers New Town and the angle between the Birmingham and Warwick roads.

1. Bancroft Gardens and the historic spine

The CLOPTON BRIDGE might make the best start. It is of fourteen depressed-pointed arches of Arden stone and was built by Hugh Clopton c. 1480–90. Originally there were five flood arches in the direction of the town. Cast-iron footbridge on the N (*Eagle Foundry*, Birmingham) added by *John Nichol*, 1827. The little castellated TOWER at the W end was a tollhouse and was built in 1814 when the bridge had been widened (*Hugh McIntosh*, contractor). The brick BRIDGE of nine arches a little to the S dates from 1823. It is now for pedestrians but originally carried the horse tramway from the Stratford wharf to Moreton-in-Marsh (1826) and by branch line to Shipston-on-Stour (1836). *John Urpeth Raistrick* was the engineer and William James was the chief promoter. A wagon is preserved on a short length of track.

The tramway connected with the STRATFORD CANAL (William James, again), opened in 1816 to provide a route to Birmingham from the River Avon which was navigable to the Severn estuary. Between the two bridges on the W bank is COX'S YARD, with a timber-framed and weatherboarded former WAREHOUSE (now Attic Theatre), brick buildings and a tall CHIMNEY, 1830s survivors of Cox's once extensive timber yard, one of the first industries once associated with this area and its transport links. S of these one of the former CANAL BASINS is now a marina, and the space between the Avon and Waterside on the W was pleasantly laid out as BANCROFT GARDENS from 1902. It is pretty and, for Stratford, right. Here, with the theatre in the distance, one is right away from the Old Town. This is all for visitors, and could not be more appropriate. Several public sculptures, notably the SHAKESPEARE MEMORIAL (moved from its original site near the theatre in 1933), 1888, with bronze statue seated on high pedestal decorated with bronze wreaths and masks, and detached corner statues of Lady Macbeth, Hamlet, Prince Henry and Falstaff. The statues by the donor *Lord Ronald*

Gower, the pedestal by his associates *Peignet & Marnay*, architects of Paris. Others include *J. H. Foley*'s HERMAPHRODITUS, 1844/51, *Christine Lee*'s COUNTRY ARTISTS FOUNTAIN with rising swans in stainless steel, 1996, and the Hornton stone PEACE MEMORIAL, 1995, by *Brent Hayward*, to a design by High School pupils *Naomi Hamer* and *Trevor Burn*. Most recent, the Firefighters' Memorial SUNDIAL by *Richard Kindersley*, 2008–9.

WATERSIDE itself is lined by small-scale C19 cottages, of various classes e.g. Nos. 26–35 and Nos. 41–43 with the interruption of the 1887 lecture theatre (now the scenery dock for the theatre – *see* p. 598) between them. Just beyond is the C18 ARDEN HOTEL and set back behind, and now part of it, a substantial three-storey house by *Albert Callaway* for Annie Justins, proprietor of the Shakespeare Hotel, 1915, half-timbered with gables and square bays below oriels on the front. Up CHAPEL LANE at this point the offices of the ROYAL SHAKESPEARE COMPANY with pedimented gables over the centre and two wings. The central section is of 1838, when the Stratford Dispensary took over and adapted the gas works building of 1834. It became the Union Club in 1884. RSC offices since 2000; the large rear extension by *Bennetts Associates*, 2006, with outer skin of thin timbers detached from the structure.

Then into the town and BRIDGE STREET with its long rising view. It was originally the main thoroughfare and principal market place, hence the width, and at its head is the former market house with its clock tower (*see* below). From the medieval period until the C19 the top two thirds of the street were divided by Middle Row, which was demolished in stages between *c.* 1810 and the late 1850s. So the wide street now makes a grand sight from the E, though disappointing in detail and homogenized since the numerous former inns have become chain stores. First, on the r., a tall cedar stands alongside the MULBERY TREE CENTRE. By *Building Design Partnership*, Sheffield, 1988–9, to complement No. 34 (the Mulbery Tree) with its charming late C19 two-storey cast-iron veranda. The house, *c.* 1777, is brick, almost alone defying the blandness of a street otherwise dressed all in cream and white, with the exception of Nos. 8–9 (S side) behind a modernistic polished black marble front, for Burton's, 1937. On the N, the four gables over Nos. 29–30 belong to what was the GOLDEN LION. To its l. MARKS & SPENCER's frontage (all is new behind) was until the 1970s the Red Horse, whose Greek Doric portico came in 1920 from the Shakespeare Hotel in Chapel Street (*see* below). Little else, although the 1832 front of Nos. 17–18 with stucco Ionic pilasters is grander than the other Regency and Early Victorian fronts. On the N, nice 1860s details to the upper floors of No. 28.

At the top, a roundabout at the junction of five streets. Pointing down Bridge Street in the centre is the former MARKET HOUSE, built in 1821 and used as a bank since 1908. The building contract and unsigned drawings exist but the architect

Stratford-upon-Avon, Market House and surrounding buildings.
Engraving by Rock & Co., 1864

is unknown. Stuccoed white with curved front, pedimented doorway and domed octagonal clock turret. Banks take up the other significant corner sites too. On the N side at the corner with Union Street, the former National Provincial Bank (now COSTA) by *F.C.R. Palmer*, 1924. Wholly in the Tudor idiom. Close studding with brick nogging to ground floor, varied timber framing above, two gables and good carved details of impish figures. Opposite, three-storey LLOYDS BANK by *J.A. Chatwin*, 1898–9. Ashlar-faced. Classical but with Renaissance and Gothic details to the oriel and turret over the entrance.

Now the HIGH STREET, where Stratford as an old town starts seriously. Several timber-framed houses – interspersed, of course, with some of later periods and some in pastiche. On the E corner of the High Street (No. 1) roughcast of 1923 conceals a substantial town house of the 1440s, while the Wood Street corner opposite (No. 40) has a late classical house of 1840–1, stuccoed with rounded corner and Ionic columns to the shopfront. On the E, No. 3 (formerly Loggin's chemists) has an attractive shopfront of *c.* 1843. Next, W.H. SMITH, designed for the company by *Osborn, Pemberton & White* (*Guy Pemberton*), 1920–1, and again quasi-Tudor, with square oriels supporting the deeply jettied top floor with bargeboarded gables. Inset above the shopfront a panel quoting Shakespeare's Titus Andronicus: 'Come and take choice of all my library and so beguile thy sorrow.' Inside, stained glass roundels of Shakespeare, Chaucer, Dickens, etc. Nos. 6–7 similar but of 1937 by the in-house designers for Timothy Whites & Taylors. Then an early 1840s Regency block (Nos. 8–9), a tiny property (No. 10) squeezed into a burgage passageway, and a plain Georgian group of *c.* 1790 (Nos. 11–13). This was the norm until the early C20 enthusiasm for uncovering the timber-framed houses began. Opposite, similar until the rather bland Neo-Georgian Debenhams front of 1960–1 by *Healing & Overbury* for J.C. Smith's department store (cf. Nuneaton). Here is the entrance (No. 32) to Town Square (p. 609). So, on both sides, a very good show of exposed and genuine C16 timber framing. This is all attributable to rebuilding after the fires of 1594–5. Nos. 17–18 and 19–21 on the E side are especially impressive, three-storey with attics, with close-studded framing, jetties and gables. No. 19 is a tearoom and the interior is accessible to view. On the W, No. 29 and No. 30 of *c.* 1600 with stout square framing. No. 30 has partially lost its gables (truncated and infilled) and the upper bressumer is carved. Restoration in 1917 brought these features to light. HARVARD HOUSE (No. 26, open to the public) is dated 1596 and was never plastered over, nor have the timbers been painted black. A one-bay front, but very ornate. Decorated friezes, bressumers, corbels for the oriel windows. The panels decorated by crosses of struts. Restored in 1909 under the influence of the novelist Marie Corelli, who put much energy into the restoration of Stratford's early buildings, the house was then purchased by Harvard University.* Inside a mid-C17 staircase, repositioned *c.* 1700, with turned balusters and an original upper room with pilastered panelling and a very elementary stucco overmantel with shields. In the attic bedroom also two original fragments of painted fictive panelling to dado. Next door the double-gabled GARRICK INN (No. 25) of about the same time, though reconstructed in 1912 after the removal of a brick façade. The panels here have concave-sided lozenges formed of struts. At the corner of Ely Street, TUDOR HOUSE (Nos. 23–24) with ogee-shaped struts at the top. The framing here, and the fine carved corner post with gryphon and masked human face, were exposed when the building was restored in 1903 by *Holtom & Yorke*, again at Marie Corelli's expense.

Before continuing into Chapel Street, turn l. to explore SHEEP STREET. At the corner, shops and offices by *Frederick Gibberd*, 1963–4. Concrete frame, painted black like oak beams, and brick infill. An overhang and gables in the Stratford tradition, but all in entirely C20 forms. The attached SCULPTURE of 'Everyman' is by *Fred Kormis*. More timber-framed houses of *c.* 1600 opposite but only two-storey and some reconstruction too, e.g. No. 4 with gable amusingly lettered 'Built 1490, restored 1910 by Wm Jaggard', a bibliophile and publisher at this address from 1909. The best is the SHRIEVE'S HOUSE (No. 40), probably after 1614, restored in 1908 and still in domestic use. It has discreet vernacular extensions by *F. W. B. Yorke*, 1947, and an unusually good range of surviving outbuildings behind at an angle to the street. Much lower down on the same side (No. 31), a small single-bay hall house of

*John Harvard, founder of the university, was the grandson of Thomas Rogers, for whom the house was built.

medieval type, with single-storey hall and two-storeyed wing. Probably C15. The rest small-scale, pleasant and varied, C17 to C20, but nothing exceptional.

Back at the top in CHAPEL STREET, facing the town hall, is Stratford's best Victorian building, the HSBC BANK of 1883. By Birmingham architects *Harris, Martin & Harris* for the Birmingham Banking Co. and reminiscent of the commercial heart of that city. Red brick and terracotta, Gothic, with an angle turret with pyramid roof. Exquisite details of foliage, many small reliefs of scenes from Shakespeare's plays (by *Samuel Barfield* of Leicester) and mosaic over the door after the poet's monument in Holy Trinity. Opposite, the SHAKE-SPEARE HOTEL: big (formed from two or three houses), timber-framed, over-restored but still with exposed beams and authentic features inside. Long range of two parts; only the impressive S part of five gables on a continuous jetty is C17. The N part is timber-framed internally but the façade with four gables was recreated by *Albert Callaway* in 1919–20 for Annie Justins, following removal of a Georgian façade of 1830; the porch is now in High Street (*see* above). The timber framing of No. 20 was covered with rendering during alterations in 1646 and re-exposed in 1885. No. 21 was remodelled in 1790: three bays, brick, with a nice, not very correct C19 doorway with blocking. Finally NASH'S HOUSE (a Birthplace Trust museum), again timber-framed within, has a double-gabled and close-studded front by *Guy Pemberton*, 1912. Long ranges behind. Inside, a staircase of *c.* 1630–40 with twisted balusters. It was acquired by public subscription as a national memorial in 1862 along with the site of Shakespeare's home, NEW PLACE, which stood alongside. Demolished *c.* 1700, New Place had been one of the grandest houses in Stratford. In its garden at the end nearest the theatre a RELIEF of Shakespeare between the dramatic muse and the genius of fine art. This is by *Thomas Banks*, 1789, and was originally at Alderman John Boydell's Shakespeare Gallery in Pall Mall. It was erected here on a new plinth in 1871. Also in the garden, a column from the old town hall, 1633–4, and a series of Shakespearean statues by *Greg Wyatt*, 1999–2008. Across the road again, a pleasant Georgian house of *c.* 1810 (No. 4), sandwiched between the Falcon Hotel and No. 5, which is dated 1673 and one of the earliest brick buildings in the town. The brickwork is painted but the pilasters with moulded caps can be seen on the first floor above the later shopfronts. Finally the FALCON HOTEL, large again like the Shakespeare, essentially of *c.* 1500, but with an obviously added top storey, of *c.* 1645. The culmination is the Guild Chapel (*see* Churches).

2. Church Street towards Old Town

The Guild Chapel marks the end of Chapel Street and the start of CHURCH STREET. Immediately adjoining the chapel to the s is the timber-framed GUILDHALL of the Guild of the Holy Cross, built *c*. 1417 but after 1553 shared by the corporation and the grammar school and still part of King Edward VI School (*see* Public Buildings). The building next to it looks like an infill, squeezed between the blocks on either side. It was the original school house, built in 1426–7, the date confirmed by dendro-dating. In appearance it is consistent with the GUILD COTTAGES (or ALMSHOUSES) that follow. They probably date from after 1502 when John Hannys left a bequest for 'newe building and setting up of the almeshowses', replacing others which the guild had managed since the early C15. A row of sixteen with a frontage of *c*. 150 ft (48 metres), originally rendered but now with their framing exposed. All with upper overhang and no gables. On the ground floor, buttress-shafts and curved braces to support the overhang. The walls all have close studding. Original door arches but restored windows. On the upper floor, open roof with original trusses. Most recent restoration, 1981–4 by *Badger, Harrison & Cross*.

On the w side, opposite the Guild Chapel, CHURCH STREET TOWNHOUSE (No. 16) displays timber framing to Scholars Lane but the front of three double bays is roughcast and Gothick. The ogee-headed windows represent Gothicizing of 1758 while the small battlements belong to a further remodelling in 1840. Between those dates the front had pilasters, cornice and a fancy Gothick door surround doubtless influenced by West's enhancements at Alscot. On the same side the STRATFORD-ON-AVON DISTRICT COUNCIL OFFICES, originally built for the National Farmers' Union Mutual Insurance Co. who moved to Tiddington (q.v.) in 1984. A long stone front beginning at the N with No. 15, a William and Mary style house by *Albert Callaway* for Dr Henry Ross, 1911. The NFU

Stratford-upon-Avon, Church Street Townhouse.
Drawing by Robert Bell Wheler, 1800

acquired it *c.* 1920 and followed its style as they expanded the frontage, beginning with the first phase (now the centre) by *F. W. B. Yorke*, 1927–9, and then the S by *Yorke, Harper & Harvey*, 1954–9. Canted stone bays of two storeys. Roughcast walls. It is sufficiently varied (e.g. the entrances, dormers and spacing) not to crush anything. On the other side a variety of early to mid-C19 styles – a Georgian pair of 1856 sharing an archway (Nos. 17–18), a Regency pair (Nos. 19–20) with naïve giant Ionic pilasters, 1831, and stuccoed Georgian WINTON HOUSE (No. 23), 1836. Back on the w, Nos. 6–7, Old English, again by *Callaway*, 1900. Then MASON CROFT, a seven-bay brick front of two storeys, with raised quoins, modillion cornice and door with lugged architrave. Inside, staircase with twisted balusters. It was built for Nathaniel Mason, probably to the designs of *Francis Smith*, 1724, and extended on the l. in 1735 and to the rear in 1745. It was Marie Corelli's house from 1901 to 1924 (currently the Shakespeare Institute). In the garden a lonely C17 stone archway with pediment and a square brick garden house of two storeys with ogee cap. At the SW end No. 2, *c.* 1720, of nine bays, heightened to three storeys in 1872 as Trinity College School, when the three-bay pediment was raised. Quoins of even length. Windows with aprons and key blocks.

The view is closed at the S by the STRATFORD PREPARA-TORY SCHOOL (No. 1), 1697, originally five bays with raised quoins and dormers. Extended to seven bays and porch added, 1836.

3. Old Town, inner Stratford south and west

Here, one turns l. into OLD TOWN and towards the church. On the corner, a three-storey gabled block (Nos. 17–19) in an Elizabethan style, 1841–2 (*Joseph Holtom*, builder). Chequer brick, with stone dressings, hoodmoulds and pretty barge-boards. No. 6 similar but smaller, also 1842. These may be by *George Hamilton* who briefly practised in the town (cf. Warwick Road, Perambulation 4). On the w side, several fine Georgian fronts including No. 1 with Diocletian window in the pedi-ment. The best is No. 5. It has a handsome five-bay front, two storeys with attic, dentil cornice, window aprons and centre breaking forward with fine doorcase of robust consoles. Attrib-uted to *Francis Smith*, *c.* 1720s (Andor Gomme), although documentary evidence suggests a date of 1760–1. Opposite is HALL'S CROFT, acquired by the Birthplace Trust in 1949 because Shakespeare's daughter may have lived here with her husband Dr John Hall until 1616. The timber framing was exposed in the early C20, and later bay windows and a central porch were removed at a further restoration in 1950–1. Timber-framed, cement render infill. Close studding to ground floor. Gables on all sides, one on the N with patterned framing. Prominent from the street side, a massive chimneystack of four brick shafts on a Lias base. This serves the central hall range (dendro-dated 1612–13). Inside, there is a passage behind the ground-floor parlour to the l. In the angle between the front range and the kitchen range (dendro-dated 1632) at the rear is the mid-C17 staircase with long turned balusters and shaped finials to the newels. Then OLD TOWN CROFT, late C16 (partly by *Callaway*, 1916), and the inconspicuous roughcast C16 DOWER HOUSE and AVON CROFT. This had its original entrance to the S, with two gables and a gabled porch.

Opposite is the WAR MEMORIAL GARDEN, laid out in 1954. It contains the CROSS (1914–18) of 1922 and MEMORIAL WALL (1939–45) with inscription from *Henry V*, 'We Few We Happy Few . . .' The cross, by *Guy Pemberton*, was originally at the head of Bridge Street and afterwards in Bancroft Gardens from the 1930s until 1954.

Across Southern Lane is AVONBANK GARDEN. Avonbank itself was demolished *c.* 1955. It was built for Charles Flower in 1866–7 by *F. C. Penrose*, replacing an extended house of C16 origin. Its fine riverside gardens are now public. In one corner is the C18 ORANGERY to which the oval conservatory by *Henry Hakewill*, *c.* 1820, from the old house was attached in 1866. The orangery was built with materials from the nearby college that originally housed priests serving Holy Trinity (*see* Churches). After the Reformation it became a private house, demolished in the late C18. The land was sold off for development from the 1820s, resulting in a network of streets of small-scale artisan dwellings of varied and pleasant design. Some in chequer brick. These are in COLLEGE STREET from the 1820s (Nos. 1–2 especially), COLLEGE LANE, NEW STREET from 1837, RYLAND STREET from 1840 (Nos. 26–27) and TRINITY STREET from 1841 (No. 3). The character well preserved, although COLLEGE MEWS by the *Wallace & Hoblyn Partnership*, 1985, is incongruous in some details while sympathetic in scale.

Returning N and W to the foot of Church Street, Chestnut Walk leads to ROTHER STREET. To begin with on the W side, wedge-shaped gardens formerly of THE FIRS (dem. 1976), the home of Joseph Hunt until 1720. On the Grove Road side, a brick DOVECOTE with pyramid roof and turret, with Hunt's initials and the date 1684 on the weathervane. The site is now occupied by the police station and magistrates' court (*see* Public Buildings). Just to the W, ST JOSEPH'S HOMESTEAD, Albany Road. A small group of roughcast gabled cottage almshouses with balconies and pentice roofs over the paired porches, battered buttressing and Arts and Crafts detailing; by *John Brearley*, 1911.

Back in Rother Street, on the l. is MASON'S COURT (Nos. 1–4), a single build of *c.* 1490 with wings projecting to the rear at both ends. The front of Wealden type, the l. bay jettied and the r. side underbuilt. Opposite No. 47, also timber-framed. Then KNIGHT COURT at the corner of ELY STREET, a court-yard housing development of 1976–8 by the *County Architect*

(*J. C. E. Tainsh*) for the Stratford Borough and District Coun-
cils, following the restoration of timber-framed cottages in Ely
Street (Nos. 30–35, 39–40, rebuilding of Nos. 37–38), 1969–70
(cf. Malt Mill Lane, Alcester). Also in Ely Street, No. 26 (First
Church of Christ Scientist) of *c.* 1600, remodelled in a fancy
Elizabethan style by *Edward Gibbs*, *c.* 1849. Alongside, a strikingly Modernist dental surgery by *Corstorphine & Wright*,
2011–2. The rest of Ely Street unremarkable.

After this Rother Street becomes the funnel-shaped market
place of Stratford. It was the cattle market. Along the w side
a Late Georgian brick pair of six bays (Nos. 7–8). Next to the
Congregational church (*see* Churches) two brick cottages with
exposed timber framing (Nos. 11–12), a narrow Georgian town
house (No. 13) and the white stuccoed ARTSHOUSE with
Greek Doric porch. Built 1829–30 as two houses (Nos. 14–15)
with central archway behind the porch. Converted into a
nursing home by *Joseph Lattimer*, 1876. Former civic hall
behind. At the corner the OLD THATCH TAVERN, one of the
town's few thatched buildings. This brings us to the N end
facing the WHITE SWAN HOTEL, a C15 timber-framed building of central former hall and two projecting wings. The attractive Neo-Tudor frontage and brick archway to the courtyard
are by *S. W. Davis*, the Trust House architect, 1927. Inside,
three painted scenes from the apocryphal book of Tobit. Also
exceedingly big flowers. All very rustic; second half of the C16.
At the top of the market place opposite, the AMERICAN
FOUNTAIN, a kind of Gothic market cross with horse and
cattle troughs round the base and buttresses with pinnacles
framing one large pinnacle over a clock stage. York stone. By
Jethro Cossins, with decorative carvings by *Robert Bridgeman*
and Shakespearean quotations. It was donated by George W.
Childs of Philadelphia to mark the 1887 Jubilee and dedicated
by Sir Henry Irving.

Next, w into GREENHILL STREET, with the westernmost of
Stratford's timber-framed buildings next to a fine block of
shops (Nos. 14–17) with angled fronts under an overhang, by
Yorke, Harper & Harvey (*Robert Harvey*), 1954–6.

A brief circular detour can continue N into ARDEN STREET,
which begins with a vigorous High Victorian terrace called
Glencoe (Nos. 2–7), 1866, by *J. H. & G. F. Hawkes* of Birmingham. Nearby are two terraces of labourers' cottages (Nos.
8–17 Arden Street and 12–28 Mansell Street) of 1876–7 erected
for the Labourers' Dwelling Company to provide better
housing. Mansell Street leads back to WINDSOR STREET and
the PICTUREHOUSE cinema, converted from the Art Deco
Guyver's motor showroom. The ground floor and ends by *S. J.
Oldham* of Coventry, 1946, altered and heightened in matching
style by *J. H. Knight & H. W. Carter* of Stratford, 1954.

Back in Rother Street one faces NATIONAL WESTMINSTER
HOUSE (No. 31) by *J. Seymour Harris & Partners* 1964–7,
modern yet well-considered for its site. Then into WOOD
STREET, which begins on the opposite corner (Nos. 26–28),

a timber-framed, early C16 building with close studding. Otherwise all routine until Nos. 38–39 (formerly the Horse & Jockey), double-fronted with half-timbering, gables and remains of its pub frontage by *Owen & Ward*, 1898. No. 41 (Coventry Building Society) again half-timbered, this time by *William Leah* of Gloucester, 1935. Between the two is BARD'S WALK, a galleried mall linking to Henley Street, by *The Hitchman Stone Partnership* (Warwick), 1989. Opposite, the entrance to *Frederick Gibberd*'s TOWN SQUARE, 1969–71, a large scheme to clear the backlands from here to Ely Street and originally envisioning a six-storey point block, but never commercially or architecturally successful. Several times revamped and due for further refurbishment in 2015. Also accessible from the High Street. Back on Wood Street, Pragnells (Nos. 5–6, once the Unicorn Inn), refronted in brick in 1815, dates from after the 1595 fire, and No. 6 has a Jacobean plaster ceiling frieze inside. To end, a long Regency range ending at the High Street corner with Nos. 1–2 of 1840 (i.e. No. 40 High Street – *see* p. 602). Opposite, No. 44 is Georgian, *c.* 1760, five bays, extended in like style in the 1930s round Cook's Alley and into Henley Street. Then a fine timber-framed group, with No. 45A, restored by *F. W. B. Yorke*, 1915, right through into Henley Street. Lastly a Dutch gabled brick front (No. 47) to the building behind the bank (Market Hall) bringing us back to Bridge Street.

Finally up HENLEY STREET NW from the former Market House. It begins with a pleasant variety of small-scale shops. After Cook's Alley comes Bard's Walk (*see* above) and two blocks (Nos. 57–60) with half-timbered gables by *E. G. Holtom*, 1901–2. Opposite, the PUBLIC LIBRARY (*see* Public Buildings). In MEER STREET on the l., widened in the 1930s, a good curved range by *Robert Harvey*, 1955–6, with overhanging upper storey.

Now we are in the prime tourist area and at the BIRTHPLACE, i.e. the house in which in all probability Shakespeare was born. It was acquired for the nation by public subscription in 1847 and it is now in the care of the Shakespeare Birthplace Trust, formally established in 1891. Restored in 1858 by *Edward Gibbs* to what it looked like on a drawing of 1769.* It was originally two houses, one of three bays with a single-bay house to the NW. Behind the former is an over-restored back wing, set at a slight angle. Close studding on the ground floor, and rectangular panels on the upper floor. On the upper floor there are original roof trusses with tie-beams, queenposts and collar-beams. The houses either side were demolished as a fire precaution when it was restored, helping to create the fine garden in which it now stands. The gift shop or HORNBY COTTAGE to the SE has a brick front but the internal structure belongs to a house of the C15 Wealden type.

---

*Published in the *Gentleman's Magazine*.

Then the SHAKESPEARE CENTRE, 1963–4 by *Laurence Williams*, a very handsome job and highly praiseworthy, because so entirely uncompromising in so hallowed a spot. Concrete and brick. Artworks commissioned in 1964. The abstract relief by the entrance is by *Douglas Wain Hobson*, the statue of Shakespeare inside by the same. The figures engraved in the glass doors are the work of *John Hutton* (cf. Coventry Cathedral). Inside, a relief of Harry the King by *Angela Conner* and a decorative wall panel by *Nicolete Gray*. Later, a commemorative plaque to Levi Fox, the Director 1945–89, by *Richard Kindersley* and *Paul Vincze*, 1989. Immediately N, the gabled extension with open arches at ground level, also by *Williams*, 1979–80. The Shakespeare Coat of Arms by *Skelton*, and (inside) a tile collage of Shakespeare's Stratford by *Christina Sheppard*.

Over the road, some minor Georgian houses, but behind the plain C19 front for No. 41 is the internal structure of a late C15 timber-framed house with hall and cross-wing, visible inside the shop. At the Windsor Street corner the former Roman Catholic school, by *G. H. Cox*, 1883. In the street, a SCULPTURE, the Stratford Jester, by *James Walter Butler*, 1994. On the E is CONRAD HOUSE, an Art Deco block curving round the corner into Guild Street, by *A. Macer-Wright*, 1933.

From here, a short extension N into BIRMINGHAM ROAD. On the W side the former WESLEYAN CHAPEL (now a bar), 1834–5, refronted in grand classical style by *Frederick Foster* of Leamington, 1883. Former Sunday School behind in Shakespeare Street by *Gibbs*, 1858, and red brick gabled schoolroom on street front by *J. Jameson Green*, 1903.

Opposite, a group of cottages of 1815 (Nos. 9–19, once called Birmingham Row). The next block (Nos. 21–31) later, 1829–30, with delicate gauged brickwork over the arch to Wheelwright Court and an ogee-headed door (Nos. 23–23A). More early C19 cottages beyond, WELLINGTON TERRACE (Nos. 37–43), 1826–7, and opposite.

200 yds N on the Birmingham Road, beyond the junction and past the canal bridge, MAYFLOWER GREEN (Nos. 60–72) is a row of cottages at right angles to the E side of the road. Yellow brick with stone gable-ends and a shallow monopitch roof with deeply projecting eaves. Built for workers at the Flower's Brewery (dem. 1972) by *F. R. S. Yorke*, 1938–9, i.e. a comparatively early date for cottages in this Scandinavian style, which became very prevalent in the early post-war housing estates.

4. Union Street, New Town and northern suburbs

UNION STREET, starting at the W end of Bridge Street, was created *c.* 1830 as a link to a developing suburb to the N. The first buildings were erected *c.* 1833. On the l, a long range of Italianate warehouse buildings built for Ashwin & Co. from 1861. The first section with the arch by *Joseph Lattimer*, 1861.

Then came the second section with the tower in 1868, also *Lattimer*, and the continuation to Guild Street by *Allen*, 1898. At the N end is GUILD STREET, the main road and much spoiled by traffic. On the N side, however, two fine terraces of 1837. Both chequer brick, three storeys and similar, but with subtly differing detail. Different builder-developers were responsible for Nos. 9–11 (*Joseph Mills*) and Nos. 12–14 (*William Martin*). The doorways have pilasters (Corinthian l. and Ionic r.). The grander block (Nos. 12–14) has giant pilasters for the whole façade. Opposite, the rear of WINTERS (in Henley Street), by *Robothams*, 1999. E past the end of Union Street, on the s side two surprises: a timber-framed cottage standing back from the road, and an odd little archway at the rear of 28 Bridge Street by *Lattimer*, 1868. On the N side again, the Newland Alms-houses (Nos. 23–26), 1857 and institutional Gothic.

The side streets here are New Town proper, a residential devel-opment commenced in 1818 on land sold for building by John Payton of the White Lion Inn. The plots were large enough for 'Leamington style' villas, e.g. pair of stuccoed houses in PAYTON STREET, next to the Baptist chapel, with Greek Doric porches *in antis*: built between 1818 and 1826. The buildings erected were mostly smaller and plainer, but John Street, Payton Street and Tyler Street have pleasant Late Georgian houses, e.g. a handsome pair in TYLER STREET (Nos. 4–5) of 1839.

Warwick Road comes next, but beyond the canal in BRIDGEWAY is the HOLIDAY INN (originally Hilton Hotel), 1972–3 by *Sidney Kaye, Eric Firmin & Partners*. Lumpish but low. Clad in Wrekin brick and Hornton stone. It was built with its own marina on a newly dug channel from the river. Return past BRIDGEWAY HOUSE (*Robothams*, 2006) and the leisure centre (*see* Public Buildings).

Immediately facing Bridgeway in WARWICK ROAD, a striking run of early C19 houses on a raised bank above the road. The GROSVENOR HOTEL (No. 12–13) is part Regency classical with Doric details 1832–4 and *c*. 1840, and part (No. 14–15) fancy Tudor (cf. Old Town), 1842–3 and perhaps by *George Hamilton*. No. 16 plainer and conventional for 1857, and No. 17 classical again, 1833–4.

From WELCOMBE ROAD on the l. into the smarter suburb com-menced in the mid 1880s. The Late Victorian houses mostly large and dull, e.g. THE BEECHES (No. 11) on Welcombe Road by *Tasker*, 1884, and a pair at 2–4 Rowley Crescent (ROWLEY LODGE and HIGH VIEW) of 1881 by *John Smallwood* who developed this area. But Avenue Road (turning N from Rowley Crescent) has some later houses of interest, with Arts and Crafts at HELSTON (No. 14) by *Pemberton*, 1913–14, and THE HOLTE (No. 12) by *S. N. Cooke*, 1924. At the corner of Benson Road is COTSWOLD LODGE (No. 18), a Voyseyesque house by an unidentified architect for T. J. Daniel, 1925. Opposite, No. 23 by *Denys Hinton* for Tibor Reich, the textile designer, 1956–8. At the far N of Avenue Road, No. 30

by *H. W. Simister* for the industrialist Barney Joseph, 1934. International modern style and flat-roofed, although its chequered parapet and projecting stairwell recall a Tudor castle too.

W of here and N of the Birmingham road, a large area of post-war housing at the top of Clopton Road encroaching on the parkland of Clopton House (q.v.).

THE HILL, ¾ m. NE from the centre off Warwick Road. Large Gothic house by *James Murray* with canted bays, quirky oriel and steep roofs, built for the Flower brewing family, 1856–7. Lodge at the entrance.

VILLAGES

BISHOPTON

An outlying hamlet with its own chapel, a failed early Victorian spa, then a secluded community of genteel villas and now a Stratford suburb of mainly late C20 and subsequent development. The old settlement was by Manor Farm NW of the 1987 by-pass, but its chapel was superseded by a new one in The Avenue in 1842–3. The Victorian chapel was demolished in 1969* but its overgrown graveyard remains.

Immediately S of the graveyard is BISHOPTON HOUSE, a decent Italianate villa, *c.* 1855. Further S, THE AVENUE turns E, where stuccoed LINDEN HOUSE of *c.* 1845 once stood alone. This now stands among the late C20 villas of BISHOPTON PARK. At the end of The Avenue on Birmingham Road, a pretty LODGE (No. 367) in *cottage orné* style, *c.* 1841, with pointed windows, scalloped bargeboards with finials and fish-scale tile roof. Immediately N, THE LIMES (No. 369) in a fancy Tudor style with pretty decorative glazing. Built for Diana Salmon, 1848. Opposite, BISHOPTON LODGE (Nos. 346–348), 1842, with Doric columns to the veranda.

Returning down The Avenue, the long drive leads to AVENUE HOUSE at the far end. A large but dull house with brick and timber framing by *G. H. Hunt* of Evesham for T.P. Potts, 1880. It had its own LODGE at the approach from The Avenue.

Alongside the Stratford-upon-Avon Canal to the NW of the foregoing is the VICTORIA SPA (chalybeate) started in 1837. Two buildings by the canal, the SPA LODGE by the road and the PUMP HOUSE further N. Apparently by *S. W. Daukes* and *J. R. Hamilton*, *c.* 1837 (AB), although costly improvements were undertaken by *Joseph Lattimer* after Charles Ford revived the spa in 1868. Gabled and bargeboarded. According to an early illustration the whole looked like a villa and very pretty.

Wrapped round the Victorian village, ST PETER'S WAY is a decent early C21 development of mixed housing, while on

---

* It was by *Henry Caulfield Saunders* of Stratford, 1842–3, and not Joseph Lattimore, 1836.

Stratford-upon-Avon, Bishopton, Victoria Spa, perspective.
Engraving by Rock & Co., C19

TIMOTHY'S BRIDGE ROAD backing onto the canal is a tidy industrial estate with some good modern buildings.

BRIDGETOWN

On the E side of the River Avon, extending S along Shipton Road, E on Banbury Road and hugging the river bank on the N. Originally in Alveston until brought within the old borough boundary in 1924. The drive to Rayford Caravan Park makes a convenient boundary with Tiddington (q.v.).

ST PETER, Manor Road. *Hinton Brown Langstone*, 1986–8, replacing an Alveston mission church of 1951–2. Hexagonal with porch and bell-turret.

Immediately over the river is a pretty brick SUMMERHOUSE of the early C18, now isolated on a traffic island. It belonged to ALVESTON MANOR, now a hotel and very much restored. Timber-framed with brick infilling. The three-gabled centre is of *c.* 1500, the wings later. In the hall, close linenfold panelling and also a row of panels with flamboyant tracery. The panels with Early Renaissance heads are a little later. The staircase next to the hall has square balusters and is probably of *c.* 1600.

Also right by the bridge, S of the road, the SWAN'S NEST HOTEL, in brick with stone quoins, 1673.* Close by are the BOAT CLUB BOATHOUSE, 1897, and the THAI BOATHOUSE, pre-1905. In the recreation ground beyond, copper-roofed BANDSTAND by *AMEC Design & Management* in partnership with the Royal Engineers from Long Marston, 1995.

Briefly into Shipston Road, which has a fair range of C19 styles, including VICTORIA COTTAGES, a terrace of ten, 1836;

*This date marks the introduction of brick into Stratford; cf. No. 5 CHAPEL STREET, also 1673.

EASTNOR HOUSE (No. 33), by *T. T. Allen*, 1896; a good group of three (Nos. 51–55) with pretty panelled decoration on their canted bays; the TRAMWAY INN, 1856–7; and a well-preserved section of the TRAMWAY embankment with a brick bridge, 1826.

Off the Banbury Road are several housing estates, beginning with the Bridgetown Estate commenced in 1957. TRINITY MEAD, 2002–5, is one of the later developments, now encircling a Victorian farmhouse off Betjeman Road. This is BRIDGETOWN HOUSE, by *H. R. Yeoville Thomason* for Miss Ryland, 1863. Yellow brick with coloured bands, steeply pitched slate roofs.

On the playing fields of King Edward VI School off Manor Drive, a SPORTS PAVILION by *Robert Harvey* of *Yorke, Harper and Harvey*, 1971. Set against a man-made grassed bank with a stepped terrace. Plain brickwork with timber and plate glass superstructure, metal-clad roof with central gutter and a projecting score booth on one side.

In TIDDINGTON ROAD, well-to-do houses on large plots. One of the earliest is Italianate AVONDALE in wooded grounds on the N side, probably 1860s. BRADLEY LODGE (No. 77), built in 1924 by Major *Kenneth Hutchinson Smith*, incorporates substantial elements from Bradley Hall, Kingswinford, Staffs., including a splendid three-storey porch of 1596. Other houses nearby also include reused materials from older houses. By 1938 the E side of the road had been extensively developed. The inter-war houses, though large, are not especially distinguished. Many are Neo-Tudor, e.g. No. 73 by *L.L. Dussault*, 1924. Stratford architects are represented, including *Robert Harvey* who designed three houses for clients in Tiddington Road in the 1950s.

In Riverside, off Tiddington Road, is NEWSTEAD: a house on stilts in the Avon flood meadows, initiated by *Corstorphine & Wright* and completed under *Fowkes McIntyre Architects*, 2003–4. Seen best from the Warwick Road on the other side of the river.

SHOTTERY

ST ANDREW. By *Joseph Lattimer* of Stratford. Built in 1870 as a dual-purpose building with nave and chancel unsubdivided. Adapted as a church with added apse and bellcote in 1871 after a separate school was provided. Light brick and stone dressings, C13 style (plate tracery). Parish Centre at the E by *J. D. Holmes*, 1997. Internal reordering and new S aisle also by Holmes, 2005. – FONT, 1872. Bowl supported on three fishes with tails entwined. – STAINED GLASS. Apse windows, *James Plucknett* of Warwick, 1889. – N aisle, *G. E. R. Smith*, c. 1960. – W window, *Heaton, Butler & Bayne*, 1932. – SCULPTURE. Tree of Life, *Caroline Barnett*, 2013.

OUR LADY OF PEACE AND BLESSED ROBERT DIBDALE (R.C.), Church Lane, 200 yds N. *Radford Harper Associates*, 1972–3.

A plain rectangle with sloping roof and a raised light over the sanctuary.

GIRLS' GRAMMAR SCHOOL, Shottery Road. The nucleus is a stone range of the C14 or C15 manor house. Late C17 wooden cross-windows. Inside a good hammerbeam roof. Restored and extended with an added NE wing by *F. W. B. & F. R. S. Yorke* for Fordham Flower, 1939. Behind, across a broad lawn, are the three main blocks erected by the *County Architect* for the school, which opened in 1958. Recent additions and further development planned (2014) by the *Brown Matthews Architects*. To the NE a C17 square stone DOVECOTE.

SCHOOL, Hathaway Lane. An early instance of the relocation of a timber-framed barn, brought from Worcestershire and re-erected as a school by *William Thompson*, 1870–1. Probably C17. Prettily adapted, with the brick, stone, tile and rubble infill giving a varied appearance.

A village of pretty timber-framed cottages, some thatched. The best are in Cottage Lane and Tavern Lane and include of course ANNE HATHAWAY'S COTTAGE, acquired by the Shakespeare Birthplace Trust in 1892 because it was the home of the poet's wife, Anne Hathaway, whom he married in 1582. It is furnished as a museum of life in Shakespearean times. The lower part of the house by the road has been dendro-dated to 1462–3. It is a three-bay cruck house and the crucks are visible in the hall area l. of the visitor entrance on the S and upstairs. The W part is of *c.* 1600 and higher. All thatched. In the gardens, a late C20 SCULPTURE TRAIL.

To the S and E, decent suburban housing, some in overblown cottage style. Particularly striking are the four similar cottages on SHOTTERY ROAD (e.g. Blue Cedars, The Lea, etc.) by *Osborn, Pemberton & White*, 1921–2. On the N, a large 1950s council estate. On the S side of Alcester Road, the entrance to demolished Shottery Hall with Gothic stone LODGE, 1873, probably by *John Cotton*.

STRETTON-ON-DUNSMORE

4070

ALL SAINTS. By *Thomas Rickman*, 1835–7, and a capital work of its date. The outline admittedly is still that of the first third of the century, i.e. the so-called Commissioners' churches, decidedly high and decidedly narrow, and with a short chancel. The ashlar walls also are smoother than the archaeologically minded architects of Pugin's and Scott's generation would have liked. But the details are remarkably accurate, especially the window tracery: Geometrical and Dec motifs, familiar to Rickman from his study of English medieval churches. The clerestory e.g. has round windows, and Rickman filled them with four foiled circles, three foiled circles, a wheel of three mouchettes, *p. 54* and a wheel of four mouchettes. The interior also has late Perp piers of well-informed section and the curious but quite convincing motif of blank Perp tracery panels below the clerestory oculi. The stone-fronted WEST GALLERY remains. The ceilings have plaster rib-vaults with bosses. Decorated stone panelling in the E wall of the sanctuary and canopied panels in the angles with paintings of 1918 and 1920. SE vestry added 1908. Stonework repairs by *H. B. Creswell*, 1913. – Rickman's chunky Gothic PULPIT and AMBO, fortified by castellated turrets, are entirely unarchaeological. – The WEST DOOR has excellent pierced Gothic cast-iron tracery, complementing the decorated stonework of the portal. – STAINED GLASS. In the chancel S window C17 Christ at Emmaus, given to the old church *c.* 1830. – E window by *Hardman* (designer *Donald B. Taunton*), 1936. – MONUMENT. William Daniel †1817, the vicar who generously left funds 'for the reconstruction of the church'. By *J. Bacon Jun.* and *S. Manning*. Sarcophagus with a religious still-life on top.

Facing the churchyard's N side, STRETTON HOUSE: 'the new vicarage' built for William Daniel, *c.* 1770, and mentioned on his monument in the church. Flemish bond with keystoned windows and pretty Tuscan doorcase. In the wall between the vicarage and manor, a stone pier from the old church.

E of the church a stream flows through a small green with cottages either side. At the N end, MOOR FARMHOUSE. Timber-framed with two gables. The front garden is entered by a low C17 stone archway with four-centred head and pediment.

SW of the village, THE CASTLE off Fineacre Lane. A castellated folly house for the Wilcox family by *Willard Son & Ellingham* with Miss Marjorie Wilcox as honorary architect, 1931–4.

At the junction of the Fosse Way and the London Road, a prominent obelisk WAR MEMORIAL to the XXIXth Division, by *Robert Bridgeman & Sons*, 1921.

STRETTON-ON-FOSSE

ST PETER. 1841–2 by *Thomas Johnson*. Ashlar and Dec. Aisleless, with short chancel and thin W tower with octagonal top and spire. Lean-to compartments each side of tower entrance, with small baptistery N and gallery access S. Jacobean-style W gallery. Hammerbeam roof. – FITTINGS, mainly 1841–2. – Stone ALTAR and painted REREDOS. – STAINED GLASS. The E window probably of *c.* 1845–50 (AB). – Two by *Powell*, 1902.

In the CHURCHYARD, memorials pre-dating the present church. Good group W of the church, one tomb-chest of 1748 with skull, skeleton and putti.

COURT HOUSE, immediately to the S. A Late Georgian three-bay block and a C17 wing with mullioned windows and gables. The C18 block has a stone front and central doorway with open pediment and Doric columns. The garden front is brick.

OLD RECTORY, across the road E of the church. C16 and later, with rear block dated 1690 and a striking C18 E front of five bays with a three-bay pediment. This front has parapet and quoins. The Tuscan porch is later.

STRETTON HOUSE, to the SW. In a loosely C17 style but said to be largely of 1836, and if so an early case of imitation Cotswold style. The real date is recognized by small solecisms. It is extraordinary. Some of the details are almost Queen Anne revival style, e.g. the long runs of mullioned windows on two levels with, in each case, a round-headed light in the middle. In the gables, bullseye windows. Coped gables with stone finials on the corners. Down the adjoining lane, THE MALT-HOUSE shows similar influences.

Tightly clustered village with stone cottages, some thatched. TOWN FARMHOUSE is dated 1668 on a gable. Set back, almost opposite, the simple three-bay former SCHOOL, 1879. Down Belcony is HOME FARM, part C17 stone and part C19 chequered brick, with unusual canted first-floor projections.

DITCHFORD FRIARY, 1 m. SE. At the E end of a string of deserted villages along the Knee Brook, mostly in Gloucestershire (see The Buildings of England: Gloucestershire I: The Cotswolds, p. 147). Of the ancient village, depopulated in the late C15, nothing remains but earthworks. The chapel of St Giles was ruinous by 1642 when the living was united with Stretton.

STRETTON-UNDER-FOSSE

A linear village close by the Newbold Revel estate (q.v.).

Former CHAPEL, originally Presbyterian and later Congregational. First registered as 'new erected' 1781. Closed c. 1965 and now (2014) used as a workshop. English bond brick with pyramid Swithland slate roof. Semicircular ground-floor windows and circular openings above.*

In the village centre, THE MANOR is twin-gabled with mid-Victorian half-timbering, bargeboards and banded tile roof. On the S side of the road at the E of the village, HOME FARM has good 1870s model farm buildings. Three parallel blocks. Arches and windows in gault brick. Long street frontage in red brick with pilasters and gable in mauve.

---

*In 1986 the interior retained a gallery and some original box pews.

STUDLEY

In the Arrow valley, close to Worcestershire and Redditch. The main street follows the Roman Icknield (or Ryknield) Street towards Alcester. The church and old castle are on their own ½ m. E of the river. Studley grew with the rise of needle-making. Needles were made here as early as 1695 and the use of steam power from about 1800 led to expansion of the village, especially from the 1830s. White's *Directory* noted in 1874 that 'upwards of 800 hands' were employed in the trade and that the increase had 'caused a considerable quantity of houses to be erected during the last 20 years'. By the later C19 Redditch had become firmly established as the centre of the industry but needle-making continued at Studley until 1977.

NATIVITY OF THE BLESSED VIRGIN MARY. The limestone N wall of the nave Norman, with herringbone masonry and one small window high up. N doorway with one order of shafts. One capital (r.) has double scallops, the other interlacing bands (cf. Salford Priors). The arch has two rolls of chevrons lateral to the face and the hoodmould has a band of eight-point stars within squares. In the apex a worn beast-head with long snout and pointed ears. The S doorway E.E. with one order of shafts and stiff-leaf capitals. The S windows early C14 (cusped intersecting as well as reticulated tracery). The arcade may be E.E. or early C14. The elements are standard. The N windows of the nave like the S windows. The chancel is Dec too, but of red sandstone. Perp E window. Strange C14 PISCINA with a cusped pierced trefoil in a round arch. Perp W tower, the lower stages grey Lias like the S aisle but the top in darker limestone. Panelled barrel vault ceiling in chancel, 1862. Restoration by the vicar (Rev. T.S. Turner) 'without the employment of either architect or builder' in 1888, and interior improvements in 1935. Base of the tower refurbished as the Millennium Room, 2002. S porch extension by *John C. Goom*, 2010. – C18 baluster FONT with a fluted bowl. – PULPIT. Jacobean, on a carved stone base, 1909. – COMMUNION RAIL. C17.[*] – SCULPTURE. Square panel with a Norman-looking Lamb and Cross and very coarse leaves in the corners (cf. Tysoe and Whitchurch), found in 1888 and re-set in the chancel arch. – PAINTING, C13 tendrils in the reveal of the Norman N window. – METALWORK. Scrolled wrought iron in N door, with oval brass plate, from a former altar given by Court Dewes, 1738. – MONUMENTS. Large C13 coffin-lid with an exquisite foliated cross, foliage also sprouting out l. and r. below the cross. It was found on the priory site. Its charming Latin inscription in Gothic lettering commemorates a much-loved prior. – Many tablets, e.g. Mercy Chambers †1702 above the pulpit, dark with swan-necked pediment and acanthus capitals.

---

[*]The rails made by *Edward Elvins* in 1682 are now at Rowington.

– George Petre †1759 by *Peter Scheemakers*. Small, white, the inscription on a draped cloth, a still-life below. – STAINED GLASS. E window by *Holland*, 1847, and stamped quarries in adjacent N and S windows probably contemporary. –Two by *Hardman* in S aisle, 1873 and 1915. – S aisle E window, 1924, and N chancel window, †1914, unidentified. – Commemorative panel inserted in S aisle window by *Norgrove Studios*, 1991.

Immediately N, the GOODRICKE VAULT, 1837. A stepped pyramid topped with moulded cornice and round-arched corner finials.

ST MARY (R.C.), Alcester Road. 1853 by *Charles Hansom* of Clifton with money from the Throckmortons of Coughton. Grey Lias. Plate tracery. Aisleless, with two-storey S porch and matching bay on N. W front with the stump of bellcote and a middle buttress incorporating a spiral stair leading to the gallery. Painted and stencilled panelled chancel roof. – CHANCEL FITTINGS later, the ALTAR and REREDOS by *A. B. Wall*, 1882. – Two STATUES on the chancel arch and a third (Sacred Heart) now in the presbytery, 1885. – STAINED GLASS. E window by *Hardman*, 1870. Linked to the church, the Gothic PRESBYTERY, 1865. Gables with bargeboards and a bay window with a crenellated parapet. In the corridor to the church, STAINED GLASS by *Paul Woodroffe*, c. 1910.

BAPTIST CHAPEL, New Road. 1847. Brick with plain arched windows, originally with cast-iron frames. Three-bay front with a three-bay pediment. Refurbished internally in 1988, and now on two levels with meeting rooms. – STAINED GLASS in worship area, 1988, and a Jesus window in the vestibule, 1998.

METHODIST CHURCH (Wesleyan), Alcester Road. *E. Axten* of Redditch, 1872. Round-arched brick chapel, but with quite a grand façade with foliated stone capitals to the windows and big stone porch. The pediment window glazed to look like a double one.

OLD CASTLE, N of the church and on the site of Studley's medieval castle. Very picturesque and the NE part quite striking. The low, creeper-clad W front gives little idea of what is to be seen to the rear, where a large C16 timber-framed house stands hidden by the later additions. The N side has three equal gables with wavy braces. Closely studded ground floor, first floor jutting. The E side with four unequal gables, all with different patterns.

STUDLEY CASTLE (Best Western Hotel). Built in 1834–7 for Sir Francis Goodricke and no doubt far more impressive than the real castle ever was. It is by *Samuel Beazley*, the theatre specialist. Showy it is – and fun. Large and entirely symmetrical, with a big keep tower as its centre. Square, with mighty round angle projections and an octagonal Norman lantern. There is nothing else Norman. The rest is Gothic from lancets to Perp – an irresponsible hotchpotch of motifs. The entrance front has a porte cochère. The garden front is wider than the entrance and has two projecting wings. Octagonal angle turrets, machicolation, oriel windows and mock loopholes all round. The keep is a hall inside open to the top, with a wooden balcony round. At the top, armorial stained glass panels in the windows and ceiling. The hall has a fireplace with a low Norman arch and blind arcading of round arches above. To the l. the drawing room with low rib-vaulted ceiling and bay windows. To the r., the dining room has a false hammerbeam roof with pendants.

Goodricke sold the castle to the Walkers in 1863. In 1903 it became the home of an agricultural training college for women, which became Studley College in 1908 and finally closed in 1969. During the college years, the large five-storey s wing with laboratories and student accommodation was added by *Holland W. Hobbiss*, 1936–8. After the college closed, the castle became a conference centre for the motor industry and in 2004 it opened as a hotel.

Gothic GATE LODGES, *c.* 1835. Octagonal and castellated, with castellated tops to the iron gates. NE of the castle is CASTLE FARM. The house, *c.* 1835 and Gothic, must have been built with the castle. The rainwater heads are the same. The sides are plain, but the front facing the castle has projecting wings with finials on the gables, a shaped central gable and castellations on the porch and window bays. Behind, an extensive range of model farm buildings put up for Thomas Walker in 1880.

PERAMBULATION. The village centre is a mess architecturally. Phases of partial redevelopment and lacklustre intrusions have removed what little character there was.

By the roundabout (Priory Square) where the main roads meet, C17 timber-framed PRIORY COURT survives almost alone. It deserves a better setting. Opposite, the much altered BARLEY MOW. Nearby in Redditch Road there are two C17 cottages (Nos. 29–31) which also represent the pre-industrial past.

PRIORY FARM, E of the roundabout, stands in the locality of the Augustinian priory founded by Peter Corbizun in the C12. The farmhouse is largely C19 with hoodmoulded windows with pretty glazing, but incorporates a large fragment of a large C14 window, possibly of *c.* 1309 when the priory church was re-consecrated. Of the tracery only short stumps remain. The window faces w. In 1539 (date on chimneystack) a big chimney was placed in front of it, part of the secularization by Sir Edmund Knightley after the suppression of the priory.

To the N on Birmingham Road, the ARROW WORKS (now Ricor Ltd), by *S. N. Cooke & Partners* for Needle Industries Ltd, 1950. Long, low brick façade with projecting centre bay and columns at the sides of the main entrance.

By the River Arrow ¼ m. N, WASHFORD MILL. An C18 needle mill, now pub, with the low breast-shot waterwheel retained in the bar.

The best buildings are in ALCESTER ROAD. By the roundabout, two pairs of 1880s houses, THE AVENUE and PRIORY VIEW, with pretty terracotta details (SWAN VILLAS, in the High Street, is another). Next, the former POLICE STATION, Tudor, with rendered gables and single-storey bay fronts in stone, 1894. Nothing else until the junction with Castle Road, where CLAREMONT HOUSE with its soaring C16 stone and brick chimneys nestles beneath the side of the Methodist church. Further S, ALEXANDRA BUILDINGS (Nos. 57–63), a block of four 1840s houses, two and a half storeys with bargeboards and pointed windows in the gables of the taller projecting end bays. On the W side, ALBION HOUSE (No. 14), 1830s, in red brick with gauged brick arches and fanlight. No. 83 (opposite) is similar.

The best house, however, is No. 101 on the E side, now called MOUNTBATTEN HOUSE (formerly The Manor). A beautiful brick house of five bays and two storeys, with giant Ionic stone angle pilasters, and a parapet with balustrading and urns at the angles. Doorway with Tuscan columns and segmental pediment. The staircase has three slim turned balusters to the tread. Professor Gomme has shown that it is almost certainly by *Francis Smith*, *c.* 1725, for Thomas Chambers, whose initials appear on the scrollwork overthrow of the excellent wrought-iron gates. Chambers is associated with the house on Beighton's map of *c.* 1725 and his will describing him as 'of New Hall, Studley, esquire' was proved in 1728. The gatepiers and gates, perhaps by *Thomas Paris* of Warwick, are doubtless contemporary. Apart from a small side extension and a C19 stable block on the N the house is little altered.

From here on the W side as far out as Toms Town Lane there are several pleasant houses of the middle decades of the C19, some Greek Revival and some Italianate. Opposite St Mary's church, No. 56 with extensive factory premises in Church Street behind. Two noteworthy surprises are a humble pair of 1840s cottages at VIVIAN PLACE, and PARK WORKS (No. 98), a three-storey former factory, mid C19, set back from the road.

HOLT FARMHOUSE, Alcester Road, ¼ m. S. 1840s, with extensive model farm buildings alongside.

SUTTON-UNDER-BRAILES

2030

ST THOMAS BECKET. The oldest piece is the simple late C12 N doorway. After that the C13 chancel, the W end early with lancets and the E part later with bar tracery. In both, eaves cornice with heads etc. The E window is of three lights, with three circles over. The SE window is oddly distorted. Nicely moulded rere-arches in this E part. Inside to the l. of the E window a C13 capital used as an image bracket. The PISCINA with its trefoil head and the attractive way it is tied into the roll moulding at the sill level of the window shows it to be part of the C13 composition. In the C14 a s porch tower was added to the church. This alone is ashlar-faced. Perp three-light nave w window. On the N side of the nave a shallow projection with stone slate roof, and three-light square-headed window, *c.* 1500. The interior is spoiled by scraped stonework with harsh pointing, a feature of *William Smith*'s restoration, 1878–9. The FITTINGS are mainly of that restoration too. – STAINED GLASS. One †1862, probably *Clayton & Bell*, another by *Jones & Willis*, 1930.

In the CHURCHYARD, several good tomb-chests, including one s of the church of 1675 with big cornucopia, rustic but very likeable.

A village round a broad green with substantial stone houses on all sides and obelisk WAR MEMORIAL, *c.* 1920, in the middle. On the N, the OLD RECTORY, 1825: a pleasant two-storey Regency house with slated hipped roof. To its E, a stone farm-house, 1720, re-styled SUTTON BRAILES MANOR, restored and much enlarged for Robert Allen, 1932–7. The big N wing is by *Guy Pemberton*, 1936: garage at one end with oriel above, semicircular stair-turret on the side and first-floor gallery on the garden end. Outbuildings to the N charmingly adapted as domestic accommodation by *Norman Jewson*, 1937. The best on the s side of the green is GREEN FARMHOUSE, with date-stones of 1721 and 1840. Coped gables and gabled dormers. Round the corner by the church, SADLERS (former school), 1852, with fish-scale roof and inscription from the psalms.

On the Stour ¾ m. SE, SUTTON MILL has a stone house, a brick mill building, 1841, and working machinery with iron breast-shot waterwheel.

TANWORTH-IN-ARDEN

On high ground at the southern edge of the Birmingham plateau and at the head of the Alne valley. Once an Arden Forest parish. The arrival of the railway in 1908 began the spread of Birming-ham villas and housing around the three stations (The Lakes, Wood End and Danzey) and in the old village. In spite of having become a wealthy dormitory village Tanworth retains a rural air.*

ST MARY MAGDALENE. Nearly everything is of *c.* 1300–40, yet this is a puzzling church. The puzzle is in the plan, which is odd and hard to explain. At first sight the church seems par-ticularly easy, because it is largely Dec. *G. E. Street*'s restoration of 1880–1 made only minor alterations to the exterior and

---

*Earlswood and Salter Street – beyond the motorway – will be covered in the *Birmingham and Black Country* volume.

(although the interior underwent drastic alterations in 1789–
90) it is clear that the C14 shell remained largely undisturbed.
So what is odd cannot simply be explained by later events. The
church is of grey Umberslade sandstone and has a W tower
with a blunt parapet and a bluntly recessed spire. The nave S
windows and N aisle windows, mostly original, include some
with reticulated tracery and others of the Wroxall type, i.e. of
c. 1310–15. The same is true of the chancel, but the E window
is of five lights, with cusped intersections and infillings by
pointed trefoils. Here, though, is the oddness. First, the
chancel is totally out of line with the nave. Second, the W and
E windows of the nave seem remarkably close to its S wall.
Third, the N aisle E window is cut into by the chancel N wall.
So the chancel must have come after the aisle, even if only by
a few years. The effects are more clearly visible inside. The
tower arch and chancel arch, the latter widened, are both of
an accepted type of c. 1300 and the two are in line, as one
would expect. But while the N aisle is perfectly normally
placed, there is no S aisle. The absence makes the whole interior lopsided and, as noted, the E and W windows on the S are
unusually close to the outside wall. Might the whole S wall
have been set back at some time? Hardly. Perhaps one is over-
worried about the problems here indicated. Perhaps it was all
a matter of bad calculation or bad setting-out? Maybe the
scheme just became more ambitious as the church was built.
It may have begun with a tower, wide aisleless nave and modest
chancel, with first the N aisle and then a larger chancel representing later developments to the original plan. The S wall
remained, but the next logical development – a proper S aisle
(i.e. wider, and separated from the nave by an arcade) – never
took place. But this still does not fully explain the alignment
of the chancel arch and chancel. The N arcade is a reinstatement by Street, having been removed in 1790 when the whole
interior – re-roofed with a huge single span – was adapted as
a preaching house, with central pulpit and desk l. of the chancel
arch and a wide W gallery.* By the tower, exposed, is the
original W respond of the arcade. Its section with four shafts
and four set-back diagonals is a possible one for Dec, even if
more usually Perp. The solid wall in the W bay of the arcade
is of 1880–1. It shields the church rooms (*S. T. Walker & Partners*, 1993) in the NW corner with limed oak and glazed screens
with mezzanine floor above. Porches rebuilt, N by *Street*,
1880–1, and S by *P.B. Chatwin*, 1936. N chapel and chancel
reordered with English altars, both by *Faithcraft*, 1932 and
1946. Nave re-pewed, with good carving by *J. W. Pyment &
Sons* on the front row, 1960. – FONT. A big C18 baluster.
– CHEST. A tremendous 8-ft 2-in. (2.49-metre) piece of c. 1300
with iron bands, scrolls and remains of hinges. – Two splendid

*The names of Mr *Standbridge* (i.e. John Standbridge of Warwick) and Mr *Couchman* (Henry) are mentioned in the accounts, but it is not clear if either was responsible. Bloxam described the scheme as a 'barbarous and wanton mutilation'.

big CORBELS for images l. and r. of the E window inside. Perp, with traces of colouring. – Medieval TILES just below them. – ORGAN CASE. Ornately Gothic. By *Horace G. Bradley*, 1907. – Good carved, gilded and painted WAR MEMORIAL by *Faith-craft*, 1946. Central figure of Christ in Glory. – STAINED GLASS. Mostly by *William Pearce Ltd*, †1885–1920, and *W. Pearce & E. Cutler Ltd*, 1920–46. – One in N aisle, by *Benjamin J. Warren*, 1947. – Another, *Art of Glass* (designer *Judith Allen*), 2002. – MONUMENTS. Ten small figures of children from an early C16 brass. – Two unusual engraved brass plates in carved wooden surrounds, one Margaret Archer †1614, the other John Chambers, signed 'E.C. Sculpsit', †1650. – Thomas Archer and wife Anne, both †1685, and Elizabeth †1703, wife of Andrew Archer of Umberslade Park (q.v.) who erected the monument. Perhaps designed by *Thomas Archer*, son of Thomas and Anne and brother of Andrew. Very big standing monument with an uncommonly large obelisk behind, two weeping putti, and the cartouches for arms and inscription very Baroquely carved, with wilfully wavy outlines. – Lord Archer †1778. By *John Hickey*. Also a standing monument, but smaller. Young woman standing over a curved pedestal with a portrait medallion. – In the churchyard by the S door, monument to Richard Lea †1818. With four columns round a square core and an urn at the top.

SCHOOL, NE of the church. By *J. A. Chatwin*, 1875. Queen Anne style with half-timbered gables, segmental-headed windows with stone mullions and elaborate chimney-cum-bellcote. Substantial 1980s gabled additions to rear. Curtain wall with star-shaped openings.

From the W, the village street funnels out towards the church. Where it is widest, a chestnut tree and WAR MEMORIAL cross by *F. H. Thomason*, 1922. Nice old houses l. and r. round the green, mainly brick but probably timber-framed behind the fronts. On the S two decent brick houses, OLD BANK HOUSE and BANK HOUSE, built as a pair by Thomas Mortiboys, 1730s. Set back S of the church, a bigger Late Georgian one, ASPLEY HOUSE, built *c.* 1808 for John Burman. Prominent Doric porch with decorated frieze. Opposite the school, C18 OLD HOUSE. Further N, OLD BELL COTTAGE is a refronted Wealden house of four bays dendro-dated to 1447–9. N again, the DOCTOR'S HOUSE, late C18, of five bays with recessed centre, canted break-forwards and scooped parapets above moulded brick cornice.

In Vicarage Hill, W from the green, are WHALEBONE COTTAGE, 1870s, its windows mimicking the bone-like arch at the gate, and the Tudor-style old VICARAGE. By *J. B. Harper*, 1835, with bay window to drawing room by *Street*, 1868. In Bates Lane, the VILLAGE HALL, by *George Bernard Cox (Harrison & Cox)*, 1927. Side entrance with donor's plaque and prettily detailed brickwork. Further W, WHITEHEAD'S ALMSHOUSES, 1871, look out of place among their showy neighbours. Two pairs, Arts and Crafts, with double-pitched roofs, pierced bargeboards and tile-hanging. Additional blocks behind, 1987, with similar detailing.

WOOD END, 1 m. NW. Around the station, substantial early C20 residences in Broad Lane, Poolhead Lane and Wood End Lane. Birmingham architects such as *L. L. Dussault's*, *Horace G. Bradley* and *A. Macer-Wright* designed some of the earlier ones, mostly aggrandized or replaced since. LADBROOK PARK GOLF CLUB, Poolhead Lane. Established in 1908. *Dussault's* CLUBHOUSE of 1909 has been replaced. The original course was planned by golf architect *Harry S. Colt*.

PINE WINDS, Penn Lane. 1954. By *Robert Harvey* of *Yorke, Harper & Harvey* for K.B.L. Bailey, 1954. An early work, clearly influenced by the Prairie Houses of Frank Lloyd Wright. L-plan, brick with cedar finishes and shingled roof. Open-plan living area and much use of glass. Designed, as Louise Campbell comments, for the 'ideal of family life in the 1950s'. Subsequent extensions to side and rear, 1992–3, follow the original style.

Further NW, LADBROOKE HALL, a castellated rock-faced house built for Oscar W. Bowen, 1893. Enlargements by *Thomas Heald*, 1894 and 1897, and LADBROOK COTTAGE behind, 1895, with clock turret.

DANZEY GREEN, 1¼ m. SE. More distinctive C20 houses near the station and DANZEY GREEN FARM, with C18 front and chequered tile roof.* TANWORTH MILL. C17 and later mill house and watermill, still with machinery by Tanworth millwright, *Robert Summers*, 1867.

TEMPLE BALSALL   2070

The place takes its name from the preceptory of the Templars founded here *c.* 1150. After the order was disbanded in 1312 the estate passed to the Hospitallers who retained it until the dissolution in 1541. On an amazingly grand scale, the chapel remains. But Temple Balsall's special character derives from the munificence of two sisters, the granddaughters of Robert Dudley, Earl of Leicester. Lady Anne Holbourne (†1663) left money for the repair of the church and an endowment for a minister. Lady Katherine Leveson (†1674) endowed the hospital and the school. The restored church then served as both a parochial chapelry[†] and also as a chapel for the hospital almswomen. The associated buildings not only form an attractive group architecturally, they are also still in use for much the same purposes as the C17 founders intended.

---

*The early C19 WINDMILL at Danzey Green noted in the first edition was moved to Avoncroft Museum of Buildings, in 1969 (*see The Buildings of England: Worcestershire*, p. 609).

[†]Temple Balsall was a dependent chapelry of Hampton-in-Arden until 1863, when it became a separate parish.

St Mary. Like the chancel of an abbey church, large and spacious, and all of one date and style, i.e. Late Geometrical. Moreover it is everything it seems notwithstanding *George Gilbert Scott*'s much-maligned restoration in 1848–9. Its texture is perhaps too crisp, but in detail it is entirely faithful. For Scott this was a comparatively early work, and it shows that even then he could be a careful restorer. Outside, his embellishments were limited to the gabled tops of the buttresses with beasts and pinnacles above, the N and S parapets, the cresting on the E and W gables and the polygonal bell-turret. These replaced C17 work, including a stumpy oblong bell-turret, of the restoration in 1667–70 under the will of Lady Anne Holbourne.* It is built of smooth, even, red sandstone ashlar and has large windows of the most curious and occasionally scarcely believable tracery. The forms include cusped lights, and foiled circles, but also Y-tracery and spherical triangles, and – more surprising – a proper rose with cusped radiating panels in the top of the SW window. The SE window with the mullion ascending right to the apex is particularly unusual. Its form pre-dates Scott's work and would fit the 1670s, but allowing for the inventiveness displayed here it may be original. The E window is of five lights. Two figure corbels l. and r. of it. The windows are shafted outside and inside. Inside the feel is Victorian, lofty and spacious – collegiate. The roof and carved corbels are *Scott*'s. The SEDILIA and the PISCINA with its niche, triangular in plan, pre-date the restoration, but may have been reworked. Genuine the former vaulted S porch and the doorway inside it. So what is the date? Is this the church of the Templars of their successors, the Hospitallers? On historical evidence it has been argued that it was built for the Hospitallers, *c.* 1320 or later. Stylistically, though, it seems much more likely to belong to the late C13 and the Templars. – FONT, C17, reinstated as recently as 1984. – Carved stone PULPIT, by *Scott*, *c.* 1849. – ORGAN CASE, also *Scott*, 1873. Gothic, also designed by *Scott*. – STAINED GLASS. W window dated 1850, probably by *O'Connor* (AB). – E window, *Powell*, 1907.

The HOSPITAL (now Lady Katherine Housing and Care), E of the church. Founded in 1677 and originally built by *William Hurlbutt* of Warwick. Soon afterwards rebuilt on a grand scale, the main ranges by *Francis Smith*, one in 1709–13 and the other in 1725–7, and the MASTER'S HOUSE at the far end by *C. S. Smith*, 1836. It forms a long oblong courtyard, the wings turning outward at the front end to face the passage from the church with five-bay ranges. The two-storeyed wings, sixteen bays long and with three-bay coped stone pediments, are all brick with stone window dressings. The windows mullioned and those in the pedimented bays transomed too. The rebuilt Master's House fits awkwardly. Tudor Gothic, two storeys and

---

*The precise dates are uncertain, but there are papers regarding repairs by Lady Anne's executors in 1667 and the bell is dated 1670.

attic with square turrets separated by sharp gables and a big chimney, all against the backdrop of a high roof.

To the W of the church is the OLD HALL (parish office), converted to cottages and encased in brick in the C19. Inside them are hidden the remains of an aisled hall of the late C12, the aisles altered in the C14. There are three bays of it, and a cross-wing of the C15 with tie-beams and wind-braces. This belonged to the preceptory, and must represent the hall and parlour noted in the 1541 inventory of the Hospitallers' property.

S of the church is TEMPLE HOUSE, built as a bailiff's house for the governors of Lady Leveson's Hospital. *Francis Smith & William Smith II*, 1738–9. A five-bay brick house of two storeys with a hipped roof. Brick sedan porch with pilasters, pediment and urns, *c.* 1760.

Then, to complete the group in the village cluster, the SCHOOL, E of the hospital. Endowed in 1670, but rebuilt 1867 in a C17 style with long front relieved by tall gabled entrances and chimneys. Brick with stone mullioned-and-transomed windows, coats of arms. Cupola above. Alterations by *Willmot, Fowler & Willmot*, 1911. Much extended since 2005, but the main block still pleasantly unencumbered.

SPRINGFIELD HALL (now Springfield House School), ½ m. W. Built for Richard Morland by *Joseph Bonomi*, 1790–1. Brick, three-storey house, with front of seven bays. Later rusticated brick porch with inset Doric columns. Alterations by *Alan Brace*, 1913–14, including workshop block with clock turret. Numerous alterations since it became a local authority special school, including an extension by *W. G. Reed*, Birmingham City Architect, 1977.

BALSALL STREET, 1 m. NE. Two good houses in Longbrook Lane. MAGPIE FARM is an uncommonly pretty timber-framed house of the mid C16, on stone base with much close studding and oriel windows below the gable overhangs on the ends. Further N, BALSALL FARMHOUSE is late C17, brick, of three bays, with hipped dormers and window openings with keystones. FEN END LODGE, 1 m. S of these, is dated 1699. It is small, of cottage size, in mottled brickwork. It has symmetrically set small windows and a stringcourse with projecting brick corbels. Over the door a triangular pediment, also in projecting bricks.

CHADWICK MANOR, 1 m. S. Built in 1875 for Gilbert Wilkes (†1882), the proprietor of brass and copper mills near Birmingham. Brick, large, Jacobean, with shaped gables. Strong vertical emphasis, with thrusting embattled tower with higher corner turret and tall clustered chimneys. Galleried entrance hall with carved fireplace (minus its chimneypiece) inside. Additions towards the garden after it became a hotel in 1931. Now flats.

HERONFIELD HOUSE. *See* Packwood.

KNOWLE HALL. *See* Knowle.

BLYTHE HOUSE FARM. *See* Barston.

TEMPLE GRAFTON

99 ST ANDREW. 1875 by *Frederick Preedy*. Lias and golden ashlar. SW porch tower with pretty timber-framed bell-stage and shingled spire. Chancel, nave, N aisle and N vestry. The style is early C14. Inside, banded ashlar walls. – Chancel FURNISHINGS include carved stone arcading behind the altar by *Boulton*, 1875, and oak choir stalls, 1884. – Wooden REREDOS, 1923 – PULPIT. Also by *Boulton*. – E.E. carved stone FONT on clustered columns, 1875. – STAINED GLASS. E and W windows by *Preedy*, 1875, the latter with representations of Templars and Hospitallers. – Chancel S, *Clayton & Bell*, 1893. – Nave S, *Powell*, 1911.

BAPTIST CHAPEL, tucked away behind cottages and among farm buildings. 1864. By *Mr Stait* of Grafton and Birmingham, replacing a smaller chapel (1841) previously used by the Moravians. Round-headed windows. Inside, W gallery on iron columns and later C19 rostrum pulpit.

SCHOOL, also by *Preedy*, 1874, though much enlarged. Banded masonry, plate tracery and whalebone-timbered gables.

By the crossroads, the former VICARAGE, by *T. T. Allen*, 1867–9. Gabled with bold chimneys and one canted window bay in stone. In the village towards and beyond the church, Lias estate cottages of 1855. Others of 1868 and 1872, brick. Across the steep valley to the E, early C19 GRAFTON HOUSE in Lias, and C18 hip-roofed TOP FARM in brick. Shambling timber-framed cottages nearby.

TEMPLE GRAFTON COURT, ¼ m. S. Now flats. By *Preedy* and his assistant *J. S. Alder* for James W. Carlile, 1876–9, with later additions by *Alder*, 1888. Brick and stone with tile-hanging and half-timbering to the irregular gables. *Preedy*'s 1879 stained glass illustrating tales from Chaucer and Shakespeare has

Temple Grafton, Temple Grafton Court, perspective.
Photo lithograph, 1888

gone. Contemporary LODGES, one now isolated on the Evesham Road towards Stratford.

ARDENS GRAFTON, ½ m. W of crossroads, is an idyll. On high ground, dropping sharply towards Exhall and Oversley on the NW and overlooking the Avon valley to the S. Smart new houses, barn conversions and too-tidy cottages, yet still a rural charm. Nothing grand, not even C18 brick-fronted MANOR HOUSE, but much variety in the use of local Lias, timber, thatch and brick. One Carlile estate cottage, 1873. Fronting the road N of C17 CIDER MILL FARM, a weatherboarded barn on stone base with hipped roof, perhaps C18. Inside, a CIDER MILL with two presses and crushing stones intact. Further W, the OLD POST OFFICE, a decent two-storey house with gauged brickwork, later C18.

HILLBOROUGH MANOR, 1⅞ m. S. L-shaped, the N range partly early C16 with close studding. The W wing Lias and predominantly c. 1600, with evidence of plastered long gallery on the top floor. Attractively restored by *Michael Reardon*, 1969–71. SE of the house, a circular stone DOVECOTE, 24 ft (7.3 metres) in diameter, with conical roof. Probably C17. Nesting boxes for 900 pigeons.

To the E, HILLBOROUGH BARN, converted from an C18 barn and later wagon hovel into a house by *Michael Reardon* for himself, 1971.

Across fields, WEST HILLBOROUGH FARMHOUSE, dated 1605 and partly Lias with stone-mullioned windows and other early C17 details.

THURLASTON   4070

The village lies between the M45 motorway and Draycote Water.

ST EDMUND and attached CHURCH HOUSE, combining church, school and teacher's house.* By *Butterfield* and 'new in idea and practice' when built in 1849. The chancel was reserved for worship but the wider nave with square-headed windows and boarded floor was used in the week for school and for church on Sundays. Dual use continued until 1905 when the school closed. The W tower with domestic windows was the house, originally on four floors with external stair on the W, big N chimney and an enclosed wooden belfry on the E wall. It was shortened and received its present pyramid top in 1908. – Stone FONT with chevron mouldings. – STAINED GLASS. Bright E window by *Melanie Pope*, 1997, incorporating existing foliage sprigs at the top.

In Pudding Bag Lane, C15 PIPEWELL COTTAGE is cruck-built and thatched. The Main Street has C18 STANLEY'S FARM

---

*Butterfield sent designs for an identical school chapel to New Zealand in 1849 and built one other for Pitt (Hampshire) in 1857–8.

with extensive unrestored farm buildings. Behind, the brick
WINDMILL tower, 1794, adapted as a house in the 1970s. At
the N end of the village, STOCKS.

TIDDINGTON

A hamlet of Alveston within the Stratford borough boundary
since 1924. Despite the unbroken run of houses from Alveston
through to Stratford's Bridgetown area (*see* p. 613), Tiddington
still has a distinct identity along a section of the main road,
especially round the older housing (e.g. Nos. 32–42 of *c.* 1830)
and shops. In this area, the old SCHOOL, 1867, with a clock
turret added in 1897. Brightly diapered brickwork. Used as an
auction room since 1979. In School Lane, two distinctive 1950s
houses by *Yorke, Harper & Harvey* (*Robert Harvey*): THE
CEDARS, with spreading half-hipped roof and weatherboarding, and ELM GABLES, a long single-storey in painted white
brick. At the far end timber-framed OLD FARMHOUSE with
close studding and jettied gable.

Towards Alveston, the former BAPTIST CHAPEL by *A. E. Allen*
of Banbury, 1907. (Roman Catholic church, 1967–2002, now
a house.) At the other end of the road towards Stratford, set
back on the E side, the NFU MUTUAL offices, four-storey with
wide façade by *Robert Matthew, Johnson-Marshall & Partners*,
1982–4.

On the RIVERSIDE CARAVAN PARK, NW of the NFU, a clubhouse and restaurant on stilts by the River Avon. By *Emission
Zero*, 2014, in a Swiss chalet style with Russian timber, glass
and sheet metal finishes. Balconies, portholes and peaked
gables.

TIDMINGTON

CHURCH. Late C12 origins – see the S doorway with simple
carved tympanum. The N door Norman too, but restored and
plain. C13 W tower in three short stages with twin bell-openings,
pyramid roof and an original corbel table with carved heads.
Tower arch to the nave on primitive head corbels. C16 chancel
with straight-headed windows. The rest mostly of 1874–5 by
W. H. Knight, including the seating and fittings. – FONT. Tub-
shaped, with Romanesque carving of Christ in Majesty. – BENCH
END. One Perp, panelled, with poppyhead. – STAINED GLASS.
Three in chancel by *Lavers, Barraud & Westlake*, 1875–82.
– Modest early C19 MEMORIALS including two by *Gaffin* of
Regent Street, †1836 and †1851, and one by *Nelson* of Shipston,
†1847.

TIDMINGTON HOUSE. Mid-C18 front to a house of *c.* 1600. W front with two gables and a three-piece centre between. The centre of this also has a small gable, and rainwater heads dated 1765. Below the gable a tripartite lunette window. Below that a Venetian window. Below that a veranda of Tuscan columns, the colonnade said to be from the old house at Weston after 1825. To the l. and r. of the front, low one-bay pavilions of *c.* 1800 with pilasters, on the l. (now heightened) with a window and on the r. with a niche. The windows all sashed. On the E front the three gables with finials are in the original state of *c.* 1600, that on the l. now hidden behind a circular Regency bay. (Mainly C18 interiors, including an C18 carved turned baluster dog-leg staircase, dentilled cornice and doors with Chinese-style motifs on broken pediments and an Adam-style fireplace. NHLE.) N of the house, a good Tudor Gothic coach house and stable block, *c.* 1830.

BRIDGE on the Oxford road crossing the Stour, now much altered but with C18 elements and possibly including an arch of the bridge mentioned in 1615. 1 m. W on the Knee Brook, S of High Furze Farm, a PACKHORSE BRIDGE, on a disused track with a ford downstream. Two arches divided by a cutwater, one round and one slightly pointed. Only 6 ft (1.8 metres) wide. Possibly C17.

TILE HILL *see* p. 299

TREDINGTON

ST GREGORY. The church has a very impressive steeple, C14, with a C15 spire recessed behind an openwork parapet. Arch to the nave with three continuous chamfers. The tower hides a church of intense archaeological interest only revealed at the time of *Sir Arthur Blomfield*'s restoration, 1897–1900.* This is an Anglo-Saxon church, reputedly of 961, and above the present arcades between nave and aisles are the remains of four double-splayed windows and moreover of two doorways, about 13 ft (4 metres) above ground level. They must have been accessible by wooden outer stairs and have led on to a deep W gallery, for the windows W of the doorways are higher up than the others. Such galleries did exist in pre-Conquest churches: cf. e.g. Wing (Bucks.) and Jarrow (County Durham). External quoining in the E nave wall suggests that there may have been an aisle or lateral *porticus* N and S of the nave. The Saxon church was provided with Norman arcades about 1160. Round piers, square, many-scalloped capitals and square abaci. Single-step

---

*There is no mention of possible Anglo-Saxon work in the careful descriptions of the church by Glynne (*c.* 1840) or John Noake (1854).

arches, later converted to a pointed form. The w half-bay of the arcades is a later link with the tower. It is clearly visible that the w piers were originally responds. The s doorway of the church is of *c*. 1200. Round arch, stiff-leaf capitals on replacement shafts and chevrons with cinquefoiled ornaments.

The ironstone chancel was rebuilt in the early C14. A consecration took place in 1315. The w portion has stone benches against the walls. The side windows are primary, as are the two ogee-headed recesses either side of the E window, but Glynne tells us (*c*. 1840) the original tracery was 'entirely destroyed'. The sumptuous tracery in the present window belongs to the chancel restoration of 1853–4 by *Edward Gibbs* of Stratford. The aisle windows are much restored. Perp clerestory. Handsome Perp N porch of two storeys. Outer and inner doorway with fleuron enrichment. Chancel carpeted and re-seated with chairs, 2011. – Sanctuary floor laid with Minton TILES to a design by *Holland*, 1856, and panelling and ALTAR RAILS by *Blomfield*, 1900. – FONT, C15. Octagonal, with simple flat tracery patterns. – PULPIT. Splendid, Jacobean. Two tiers of the usual blank arches. Back panel and tester. – SCREEN. Base of a stone screen. On this a good Perp wooden screen of three-light divisions, with pretty quatrefoiled circles in the spandrels. – Complete set of C15 BENCHES, the ends with panel tracery and straight tops. – Very crude HOUSELING TABLE, i.e. a low table to kneel at for Communion. – LECTERN with chain. Wooden, rustic, and just possibly pre-Reformation. – COMMUNION RAIL, now under the tower arch. Late C17. – STAINED GLASS. The E window by *William Holland* of Warwick, 1853. Two tiers of small-figured scenes. – s chancel window also by *Holland*, 1856, and patterned glass in adjacent window probably contemporary. – One by *Kempe & Co.*, 1910. – MONUMENTS. Brass to Richard Cassey, rector, †1427, a 37-in. (94-cm.) figure; good. – Brass to Henry Sampson †1482, a kneeling 29½-in. (75-cm.) figure. Both in the N aisle. – Another in the s aisle, Alice, wife of William Barnes, †1568. Female figure with incomplete inscription. – Maria Parker †1715, with burning lamps, death's head, etc. – In chancel floor, two fine Parker ledger stones with inlaid shields and borders, †1751–95, including Sir Henry John Parker †1771. – To the same Sir Henry John, a tablet signed by *W. Tyler*. Vase in front of an obelisk. – The Rev. Thomas Hopkins †1838. Plain Grecian tablet by *H. Hopper*. – In the s aisle, a group of pedimented Gibbs family memorials with gold lettering on black marble, †1820–74.

Former RECTORY, now subdivided as YORK HOUSE and TREDINGTON HOUSE. By *D. R. Hill*, 1840–1, but incorporating some C15 windows from the preceding buildings of which some record is preserved in Hill's sketches. The preserved windows are mainly Perp, some square-headed. The old parsonage was a large and evidently important one, for Tredington was a wealthy living and, until 1857, a Peculiar Jurisdiction belonging to the incumbent.

A pleasant village lying mostly between the main road and the river, with small greens surrounded by houses of Cotswold limestone, some thatched. Attractive cluster of buildings SE of the church towards the old mill. Former SCHOOL in Church Lane, 1876, with bellcote, plate tracery and banded stone headers. Nearby, cob walls to LITTLE ORCHARD and thatched WHEELWRIGHT'S COTTAGE.

TALL TREES, just S of the village, by *Yorke, Harper & Harvey* (*Robert Harvey*), 1963, for the Misses Mavitta. Cotswold-style, with mahogany fittings made at the RSC Workshops in Stratford. The other house by *Harvey* here is BROOKFIELD, 1978, on the green, forced by the planners to be so conventional that it is a rather pathetic tailpiece to the career of an innovative and interesting local architect.

TYSOE

3040

Tysoe lies under the Edge Hill escarpment, on which there was once a RED HORSE, first mentioned in Camden's *Britannia* (1607 edition) and known to have been re-cut in 1800. Some traces remain and the outlines of several phases have been disclosed by aerial photography. The village is in three parts, with Upper Tysoe to the S and Lower Tysoe about ¾ m. N of the church at Middle Tysoe.

ASSUMPTION. The history of the church starts with the remains of two upper nave windows on the S. They belong to a late CII church and one bears traces of painted decoration. Then in the mid CI2 this church received a S aisle. The arcade is of three bays and has round piers with scalloped capitals and square abaci. The one-step pointed arches are an adjustment from the time in the CI3 when a fourth bay was built at the W, reusing a CI2 waterleaf respond. A little later than the S aisle appears the S doorway, with its two orders of columns with shaft-rings and waterleaf capitals. In the arch a chain of big lozenges, and above it a square panel with the Agnus Dei and foliage in the spandrels (cf. Studley and Whitchurch). But what did the one lonely beakhead belong to that is now alongside the Lamb? Dec N aisle with arcade of thin octagonal piers. The windows have intersecting and reticulated tracery side by side. Also an ogee-headed tomb recess. Dec also the whole clerestory (cf. Brailes). Eight windows, pierced parapet with shallow battlements and tall crocketed pinnacles. The parapet has quatrefoils on the S, a wavy line on the N side. The Sanctus-bell turret probably 1715: clearly a renewal, with a crocketed pinnacle on top. Late CI2 W tower up to the remaining corbel table. Perp top parts. General restoration in 1854 by *Scott*, who rebuilt the chancel in 1858. Organ chamber added 1868 (or 1872) with Dec details. Tower restoration and further work by *A. R. G. Fenning*,

1912, when the interior was scraped bare. – Good chancel
FURNISHINGS, some by *Scott*, but the CHOIR STALLS are
later, 1899. – FONT. Octagonal, C14, with figures of the
Virgin, Saints, etc., under crocketed gables. – BENCHES.
Some with minimum poppyheads (cf. Burton Dassett), and
a whole block Jacobean with blank arches. – ROYAL ARMS,
1726. – STAINED GLASS mostly by *Lavers, Barraud & Westlake* (later *Lavers & Westlake*), 1876–96. – Quarry glass in the
chancel, 1856. – One in S aisle by *Jones & Willis*, †1909.
– Fire station window by *Art of Glass*, c. 1998. – MONU-
MENTS. In the N aisle tomb recess a coffin-lid of a man, only
his head and shoes visible, the rest just the slab decorated
with a big cross. – Brass to Thomas Mastrupe, chaplain,
†1463. The figure, 14½ in. (37 cm.) long, is in Mass vestments holding a chalice. – Brass to Jane Gibbs †1598. Demi-
figure. – William Clarke †1618. Bad Elizabethan effigy. – In
the churchyard a C15 CROSS. The base with angle knobs, the
shaft with edge rolls. Part of the Crucifixus of the head.

METHODIST CHURCH. *Cripps & Stewart*, 1970. Reconstituted
stone and silly spike with cross.

The SCHOOL, N of the church, is by *Scott*, 1857–9 with additions
of 1872. Ironstone, C13 style with bellcote and teacher's house.
Also near the church, mid-C18 HOME FARM with Venetian
doorway and windows. BEECHEN TREE HOUSE (former vicarage) retains traces of the alterations by *Henry Goddard* of
Leicester, 1853. By the gate, one of Tysoe's late C19 WATER
FOUNTAINS with religious inscriptions on the arch. Ironstone
cottages in the lane W of the church, slightly grander buildings
lining the widened area of Main Street in the village centre.

THE ELMS, Sandpits Road, is dated 1613 and 'rebuilt 1856', but
basically C17 with mullioned windows and coped gables.

At UPPER TYSOE the MANOR HOUSE has a Dec two-light
upper window in its C14 hall range and original roof trusses
within. A C16 or C17 block links to a large extension of 1932–3
by *Armstrong & Gardner*. Very pretty.

On the hill S towards Compton Wynyates, TYSOE WINDMILL
with tapering multi-angular stone tower, conical cap and sails:
early C18, with machinery restored by *Derek Ogden* 1968–75.

FOUNTAIN FARM at LOWER TYSOE has been entirely remodelled but retains a re-set doorway dated 'I P 1671'. Remarkably
sumptuous. Shallowly modelled, with segmental pediment
over big lozenge-shaped hoodmould stops – a curious mixture.

UFTON

On a ridge running parallel with and E of the Fosse Way.

ST MICHAEL AND ALL ANGELS. On a steep bank above the
cutting at the top of Ufton Hill. Early C13 doorway with neat

nailhead decoration on the capitals. Of the C13 also the two blocked lowside lancets in the chancel. C14 ogee-headed priest's doorway. These features retained when the chancel was rebuilt and much reduced in height by *Ewan Christian* for the Ecclesiastical Commissioners *c.* 1855. The rest of the church was restored in 1860. The S arcade of three low bays is more probably C13 than C14, with octagonal columns and arches of two chamfered orders. The N arcade is later. It is of two bays but was meant to (or did) continue to the w. Perp w tower, restored by *P. B. Chatwin*, 1931–2. Scraped interior darkened by Victorian glass. – PULPIT with Jacobean panels. – READING DESK incorporating tracery fragments from the screen. – Two C15 BENCHES with carved buttresses on the back – one with a crocketed pinnacle the other with a lion's head – from the end of a block. – STAINED GLASS. A scheme of 1860–1 (originally thirteen windows) by *Hardman* (in N aisle), *Heaton & Butler* (by the font and nave N) and *Holland* (chancel, S aisle, W windows in tower and aisle and clerestory). – One in S aisle by *Clayton & Bell* (designer *George Daniels*), 1884. – E window by *Hardman Studios*, 1964.

CHURCHYARD CROSS. The head is preserved, with Crucifixion, the Virgin, St Chad and St Catherine. Restored by *G. T. Robinson*, 1862.

Immediately S of the churchyard, the former SCHOOL by *D. G. Squirhill*, 1853: Lias, small, with schoolroom and house. Further E towards Southam, the OLD RECTORY by *Christian*, 1862: stone, with fish-scale tile roofs, gables and chimneys and porch annexe. In Ufton Fields, COLBOURNE HOUSE, with C17 range and sandstone chimney facing the road, and irregular C19 brick entrance front. Further W on Harbury Lane is TOWN FARM (now OAK FARMHOUSE), a brick house with hipped slate roof. Built for Henry Horley and dated 1830.

ULLENHALL

1060

ST MARY. By *J. P. Seddon*, 1875, for the Newtons of Barrells Hall. Camden and Box stone. Cost: £5,000. An odd, idiosyncratic design in the E.E. style, not unlike Seddon's contemporary Ayot St Peter, Herts. Lancets and bar tracery. Clever detailing. The tower is near the SW corner, rather thin, with a broached octagonal bell-stage and a plain spire. Mosaic clock dial, 1886. N porch and N vestry transept both have rose windows. At the E end an apse, shafted at the angles and the shafts standing on the tips of horizontal crescent shapes, surely a motif without any historical authority. The apse is shafted inside too, the shafts being detached from the wall. The aisle windows have inner arcading as well, with detached shafts too. The body of the two-bay nave is framed by a rectangle with short triple columns of blue sandstone at each corner, suggested by the necessity for a strong support of the NE corner of the tower. Thin single columns between. Further E the transepts have plain arches, like those to the porch and baptistery at the W end, which stresses the matching of porch and transept already referred to. Excellent wagon roofs in the nave and – more prominently panelled – the chancel. Half-wagons in the aisles. – FITTINGS mainly by *Seddon*, 1875. – FONT. Octagonal with trefoiled panels in which, set back, appears a net with many fishes. – PULPIT and facing DESK, both with arcading and elaborate carving.

Light iron CHURCHYARD fence and gates.*

OLD CHURCH, ¾ m. ENE. Only the C13 chancel remains, restored by *W. Hawley Lloyd* and provided with a bellcote, 1877. The E window with three-light intersecting tracery and the two eastern side windows are *in situ*, but the group of three stepped ogee-trefoiled lancets came from the old nave. Lloyd also reused a lancet in his new W wall. Inside, a Victorian arch incorporating E.E. fragments. In the arch, mouldings with nailhead. Two carved capitals, one with a leaf-like fern, the other with grapes like corncob. – PANELLING. Fielded, C17 or C18. – COMMUNION RAIL. Of wrought iron, dated 1735. – Medieval encaustic TILES. – MONUMENT. Francis Throckmorton †1617. Large wall tablet. Inscription in a broad strapwork frame with two doll-like putti. Corinthian columns l. and r. Strapwork also at the foot. Arms at the top. All rather gaudily repainted. – Two large bronze tablets flanking the E window, referring to burials in the vault, †1752 to †1822. The remains were previously in a private mausoleum at Barrells (*see* below), demolished in 1830. Early C19, one (l.) signed *Chilcot*, 291 Strand, London, the other (r.) *Bryceson*, London. The type is a vigorous plain 'grotesque'.

Former SCHOOL, by *Lloyd*, 1876, converted to a house, 1995.

VILLAGE HALL, Henley Road. Vernacular revival. By *Harold S. Scott*, 1935, spoiled by flat-roofed extensions at the front.

Crescent of COUNCIL HOUSES in St Mark's Close, by *F. W. B. Yorke*, 1951, done with variety.

On Ullenhall Lane leading NW from the village, several smart houses along the ridge. They include FURTHER HILL GRANGE, by *Batemans*, 1934. Brick and Tudor. Three-storey butterfly-plan PAPILLON HALL (cf. Crimscote, Whitchurch) by *Marson Rathbone Taylor*, 2002. WOODNORTON, thatched, with circular stairwell by the entrance and kitchen wing at an angle to the main house, by *Owen P. Parsons*, c. 1930.

In Ullenhall Road towards Henley, GRIMSHAW HILL, also by *Batemans*, 1925. Also Tudor.

BARRELLS PARK, ½ m. SSE. Destroyed by fire in 1933 and in ruins until a new mansion was created in the shell, 2000–4. It was the home of the Knight family, the C18 writer and gardener Lady Luxborough, the Earls of Catherlough and, after 1856,

---

* *Seddon*'s VICARAGE, 1875, stood across a field N of the church. Dem. 1973.

the Newtons. Once noted for its gardens. The remains of the older part of the house to the N were demolished in 1954, leaving the large block added by *Joseph Bonomi*, 1792–4. Now restored, this has a nine-bay S front with a portico in place of Bonomi's two-storied loggia. Behind, the mid-C19 octagonal tower, originally in the angle between the house and former service wing, has also been retained.

UMBERSLADE PARK

1½ m. NE of Tanworth

1070

Built for Andrew Archer, 1693–8, but not by his younger brother Thomas Archer, the architect, who was abroad at the time. As Peter Reid observed, it therefore tends to disappoint. It was built by the *Smiths* of Warwick, *William* and his younger brother *Francis*, who may have also designed it. If so, it was their first house.

As illustrated by Colen Campbell in *Vitruvius Britannicus* (1731) the house was an unrelieved stone block nine bays long with a slightly recessed five-bay centre on front and back and two and a half storeys high. Quoins of vermiculated rustication, moulded window surrounds; top balustrade. It represents the Baroque of a particular time and no wonder Horace Walpole in 1751, with visions of his Strawberry Hill always present, called it 'an odious place'. Externally enlarged but little altered. The additions are the porte cochère on the E front and the colonnade on the W for G. F. Muntz Jun. before 1863, and the sympathetic low wings N and S by *W. H. Bidlake* with *R. Phené Spiers* for F. E. Muntz, 1899. Inside, some rooms retain Rococo plasterwork by *Robert Moore* and chimneypieces from improvements for Lord Archer in the 1750s. The entrance hall interior redone 1899. In a variety of uses after 1939, but converted to flats in 1976. The exterior remains unaltered in well-kept and wooded grounds.

Umberslade Park, elevation.
Engraving by Colen Campbell, 1731

In the grounds, but now separated by the motorway, a tall
OBELISK, erected for Lord Archer by *William Hiorne* in 1749.

E LODGES, once at the principal entrance but now cut off
on a disused loop of the old road by the motorway. *Ingall &
Son* of Birmingham, 1897; late classical with vermiculated
quoins, the lodges connected by a triumphal arch. Tudor-style
W and S LODGES with stone window surrounds and hoodmoulds and half-hipped gables, perhaps 1870s.

98 UMBERSLADE BAPTIST CHURCH, ⅞ m. NE of the house,
beyond the motorway, and quite on its own, which is highly
unusual for Nonconformist buildings. 1877 by *George Ingall*.
Built at the expense of G.F. Muntz Jun. of Umberslade Hall,
a Baptist convert, and much grander than its Anglican counterpart at Hockley Heath (*see* Nuthurst). Stone, white and beige
with slate roofs. SW tower with high, thin spire. N and S transepts
with rose windows and pinnacles. Polygonal apse. All Gothic
and lavish in detail. Inside, a big Gothic pulpit behind an open
baptistery. One-storeyed E extensions of 1893 by *Ingall & Son*.
Restored in 2007–8 for the Historic Chapels Trust. Just N, the
SUNDAY SCHOOL building of *c.* 1875; wooden-faced.

UMBERSLADE PARK FARM (previously LEASOWES FARM),
⅞ m. W, off the tree-lined avenue towards Tanworth, and under
the chunky stone railway bridge of 1908. C18 three-storey
farmhouse with thermal windows on the top floor and an
extensive range of farm buildings, mostly 1837, including well-
preserved piggeries, threshing barn (dated 1834) and stables.

4060   UPPER SHUCKBURGH

SHUCKBURGH HALL. The Shuckburghs have been here since
the C12. The hall stands in a lightly wooded deer park, the
house itself facing E across a wide valley towards Northamptonshire. Nestling in a hollow almost filled by the house, its
proud façade of Stockton cement by *H. E. Kendall Jun.*, 1844,
is no longer classical; nor can it be called Italianate. It is
entirely Victorian of the type called free or mixed Renaissance,
and it is worth watching how details go bulgy. It has also heavy
quoining, ornamental parapets and an Ionic colonnade. It
replaced a later C17 quoined brick front executed for Sir
Charles Shuckburgh, 2nd Baronet. This stands in front of an
older, timber-framed house which may be pre-Reformation.
The visible parts include a timber-framed gable, mullioned-
and-transomed stone windows and a brick chimney. Inside,
the reception rooms belong to Kendall's remodelling although
the fabric may still be partly C17. Some of the decoration came
later. *William Holland* worked on the library and dining

room in 1850–1, and *John Croft* was partially responsible for the decoration of the entrance hall with its Neo-Jacobean fireplace in 1858–9. Behind, an open-well staircase with twisted balusters. This has a domed ceiling with an inner circle of etched glass. In the side windows, stained glass on ancestral themes.

St John the Baptist (private estate church). In the grounds s of the house. A beautiful cedar tree comes close to it. Largely of 1849–55, but incorporating elements of a medieval church damaged in the Civil War and restored in 1651. The names given in 1853 for the work are *Holland,* who did the glass and other decoration, *Bonehill* (a stonemason) and *Watson* (the Napton builder). The architect is not mentioned. Hornton stone. Originally chancel, nave and w tower. Only the lower parts of the C13 tower are visibly ancient, the top probably rebuilt in 1864. Shuckburgh Chapel (s) added in 1852–3 and n chapel in 1906 when some of the family monuments were rearranged. Inside, elaborate hammerbeam roofs to nave and chancel, both finely done. – Decalogue, Creed and Lord's Prayer. In Gothic niches either side of the e window, the texts in books held by hands emerging from curtains. – Excellent wooden Furnishings, probably by the Warwick wood carvers (i.e. *Cookes & Sons* or *J. M. Willcox*). – Screen with openwork tracery and heavy brattishing, 1853. – Pulpit. Very rich Victorian carving, twisted columns, a kind of stiff-leaf, naturalistic leaves and fruit and Gothic tracery bits. – Lectern. Heavy Victorian Gothic, with angels and lions. – Stained Glass. In the sw window heraldic glass with a date, 1593. – e window by *Holland,* 1854, and others mainly by him, 1849, 1853 and undated. Some in windows now blocked. – Monuments. There are more in this church than in most Warwickshire churches. In the south chapel John Shuckburgh †1631 and wife. Stone monument with recumbent effigies. Two columns, flat back arch. Strapwork. – Sir Richard S. †1656. Bust in circular recess. Two cherubs blow trumpets and hold up curtains. Top with pediment and garlands. Several skulls, one at the foot above the signature *Peter Bennier* (Besnier). – In the north chapel lower half of the brass of a lady (Margaret Cotes, *c.* 1500?). The other part incised in the slab. – Thomas S. †1549 and wife. Brasses. – Sir Stukeley S. †1759. By *Mr Hiorne.* Of marbles of different colours. At the top, fine profile in oval medallion. – In the chancel on the s side: Anthony S. †1594 and wife. Brasses. – Catherine S. †1683, attributed to *James Hardy* (GF). Big tablet with very Baroque bust. One breast is bare. Three putto heads at the foot, l., r., and below the inscription. – John S. †1724, with pilasters and at the top two putti crying. Signed by *John Hunt* of North-ampton. – chancel north side. Sir Francis †1876, by *H. H. Armstead.* Bearded bust. – nave north side. Lady S. †1783. An angel lies by an urn in front of an obelisk. – Sir George Shuckburgh-Evelyn, the astronomer, †1804. By *John*

Flaxman Jun., 1805–6. Grecian, white, with a globe and an astrolabe. – Sir Stewkley S. †1809. *Flaxman* again, 1811. Oval relief with standing woman weeping over an urn. – NAVE SOUTH SIDE. Lady S. †1677, attributed to *Jasper Latham* (GF). – Lady Shuckburgh-Evelyn †1797. Also *Flaxman*, 1798. She lies on a Grecian couch; her family in grief around her, an angel hovering over her. – Lady S. †1846. Gothic stone surround, brass inscription held by a hand (cf. the Decalogue etc.). By *Robert Brown*. – NAVE WEST WALL. Sir George S. †1884, also by *Armstead*, 1886, and again bearded. – Caroline S. †1809, signed by *James Smith II*. – Gertrude S. †1835, signed by *E. H. Baily*.

Two LODGES to the park, both mid-C19. On Park Hill, plain rendered FRONT LODGE with hexagonal slate tiles. BACK LODGE, red brick and stone and with the same tiles, but bargeboarded with a little oriel in the gable.

HOME FARM, 350 yds SSE. Range of buildings, before 1812. Brick with tile roof and dentil cornice. L-plan. Dovecote on one end. Entrance archway on N side which has blind arcading enclosing high-level windows facing towards the hall.

UPPER STOKE *see* p. 303

UPTON HOUSE
1½ m. SW of Ratley

Upton was acquired by the National Trust in 1948 after the death of the 2nd Lord Bearsted, the chairman of Shell, and it is mainly for his fine art collections that it is visited. Indeed, it was chiefly to display Bearsted's collections that it was extensively remodelled in 1927–31 by *P. Morley Horder*. It is on the site of an earlier manor, remodelled and refronted for Sir Rushout Cullen, 1695, and further improved for William Bumstead in 1735. *Sanderson Miller* worked here in 1762 and possibly earlier too. Thereafter successive owners and tenants did little, and the house remained virtually unchanged until Bearsted bought it in 1927.

The approach is by a long drive from the N. The two main fronts face N and S, both impressively wide. The middle seven bays of the N front belong to Cullen's house, extended by adding one-bay towers with urns each side in the C19 and extended again by Horder to the present width of sixteen bays. Of 1695 the recessed three-bay centre and slightly projecting two-bay wings. Two storeys and attic, Hornton stone, raised quoins. Doorway with Tuscan columns and pediment of grey stone. Odd broken segmental stone pediment overall around a central attic window. The wings have balustraded parapets and carry rainwater heads with 'W B 1735', probably the date

of the pediment. These features long pre-date *Horder*'s alterations. What he did was to tidy it up by lowering the towers
and extending the parapets to bring some uniformity to the
centre of the extended façade. The s side has rainwater heads
with 'R C 1695'. It is simpler in outline and has also a
simpler, very thin doorway with segmental pediment. The
nine-bay centre has two-bay hip-roofed projecting wings each
side, to which single-storey canted bays were added l. and r.
c. 1760 and heightened during Horder's remodelling and
extension.

The interior of the house is nearly completely C20, but all of the
highest quality. The exception is the C17 balusters of the main
STAIRCASE, very handsome, twisted, with leaf-bulbs at the
foot. *Horder* created the LONG GALLERY along the s front.
He also designed the extraordinary Art Deco vaulted BATH-
ROOM, with its red and silver décor, doubtless influenced by
Basil Ionides, Bearsted's brother-in-law. In the galleries, the
handling of the LIBRARY with its curved balcony overlooking
the double-height PICTURE ROOM is particularly successful.
The PICTURE GALLERY with natural lighting was created in
the former squash courts by *Messrs Joseph*, the architects of
Shell Mex House in London, in 1936.

In the forecourt, a COACH HOUSE adapted for Andrew Motion,
who bought Upton in 1898, with a cupola to house a bell and
clock brought from Faulkbourne Hall, Essex. Among the trees
to the NE, the classical PAVILION RESTAURANT. By *S. T.
Walker & Duckham*, 2002, with a MURAL by *Alan Gourley*,
c. 1940, bequeathed to the Trust at his death in 1991 and
erected at Upton in 2004.

s of the house a square lawn, the ground falling away steeply s
and N. The lower grounds with terraces and pools. Cullen and
Bumstead established the gardens and *Sanderson Miller* was
probably responsible for landscaping improvements after 1757.
The C18 layout shown on an estate map of 1774 survives, but
the present appearance owes much to *Kitty Lloyd Jones* and
Lady Bearsted whose restoration and redesign was completed
in 1927–32. Among the features, BOG COTTAGE, a late C17
banqueting house, and a walled kitchen garden on the s
terrace.

UPTON VIVA, in separate grounds to the E, by *Julian Bicknell* for
the Waley-Cohen family, 1982–6: Neo-Georgian with pedimented centre, linked pavilions and low curving ranges to
entrance front. Surprisingly traditional. Cornucopia carving
over the door (alluding to the first Lord Bearsted and the Shell
Oil Company) by *Laurence Tindall*.

TEMPLE POOL, at the s end of the Upton Viva estate, ½ m.
downstream from the Mirror Pool within the grounds of the
house. *Sanderson Miller* designed the original temple, probably
after 1757. This was at the N end of the pool. The present
temple is at the other end, and its front of thin Tuscan columns
1–2–2–1 is unlike the building shown in a painting of *c.* 1803.

When it was moved and who built the present temple remain unknown but it was restored by *Shoebridge & Rising* for Andrew Motion in 1899.

WALSGRAVE-ON-SOWE *see* p. 303

see p. 303

2050

WALTON

In the pleasantly wooded Dene valley, the Walton estate has been owned by the Mordaunts and their successors since the reign of Elizabeth I. There were originally two settlements, Walton Mauduit (the present village) and Walton d'Eivile which lay s of Walton Hall. Walton d'Eivile is represented by slight undulations in Town Field now thought to be the site of the medieval village, although Roman finds have also been reported nearby.

ST JAMES. By the hall and in the graveyard of the former church. Built for Sir Charles Mordaunt as a chapel in 1750: classical, ashlar, and originally only two bays with entrance at the pedimented w end. Portico with Doric columns, triglyph frieze and pediment. Seamlessly enlarged to three bays and given a short chancel with Venetian e window and w bellcote by *Harvey Eginton* in 1842–3 when it became a parish church. Further altered in 1906 by *W.D.* Caröe who inserted the Diocletian window above the entrance. The windows have simple moulded surrounds with entablatures, the form also repeated inside in plaster. Fine plaster ceilings, 1842, coved and panelled over the nave, and an almost Neo-Palladian coffered barrel vault over the chancel. – Plain tub FONT, dug up on site in 1842. – w organ GALLERY with Grecian details by *Caröe*, extended by *Rayner & Fedeski* while Walton Hall was used as a girls' school, 1967. – STAINED GLASS. e and chancel side windows, *Clayton & Bell*, 1906–7. – One n window by *F. Holt & Co.*, 1902. – Another by *G. Maile & Son*, 1933. – The s windows have mid-C19 patterned glass.

p. 67 WALTON HALL. Now a hotel. Ostensibly all of 1858–62 by *G. G. Scott*, but said to enclose a house of *c.* 1720 with additions by *Henry Hakewill*, *c.* 1810. The clerk of works here was *Walter Scott* (cf. Wroxall). *Scott*'s remodelling cost Sir Charles Mordaunt £30,000, twice the outlay on Prichard's contemporary Ettington Park nearby. For his money Mordaunt got a thoroughly practical and well-planned large stone mansion, if not one as imaginatively composed and detailed as Ettington. The style chosen is English Middle Pointed, i.e. of *c.* 1300, but with hints of French Gothic too – a combination Scott developed for the Foreign Office competition in 1856. The entrance side is L-shaped with a five-storeyed tower in the angle and the projecting wing ending in a minor tower. Both towers have pyramid roofs. Porch with marble columns and trefoil arch within a semicircular surround. The entrance hall is represented to the outside by three Gothic windows above the porch. To the l., two specially tall windows lighting the staircase. Otherwise the main windows are straight-headed and have surrounds of leaf and flowers. To the garden a colonnade, again with trefoil arches, runs nearly all along the front. The r. end however has no columns but a canted bay and a gable instead. There is a second gable, but varied in position and size. On the w, a stone conservatory with shouldered arches on shafts, brattishing, and domed roof of French type. Iron framework.

Inside, the entrance hall has marble colonnades on two sides with richly carved foliage stone capitals and trefoil arches. The central passageway lies beyond. The principal staircase on the l. has a rather starved iron railing. More marble colonnades on the landing. The hall and stairway adorned with armorial stained glass by *William Holland*. Carved stone chimneypieces in the hallway and elsewhere, but few contemporary fittings remain. The dining room has an original ceiling, and the obligatory carved wooden buffet (cf. Alscot, Charlecote and Warwick Castle), here by *T. H. Kendall* of Warwick, 1863.

NE service range round a quadrangle with a free-standing game larder in the middle. Spired clock turret over archway leading to the C18 STABLES, much altered in the 1860s, and High Victorian estate houses for the head gardener and head groom, 1869. Beyond, three blocks of timeshare and hotel accommodation by *Sayer Chester & Associates*, 1987–8, around the old kitchen garden.

Well-landscaped grounds, with the main approach to the hall over a BRIDGE of three stone arches, doubtless by *Scott*, and probably *c.* 1876 when the lake was created. The garden terrace walls also contemporary.

On the hillside in the woods NE of the hall, the BATH HOUSE designed for Sir Charles Mordaunt by *Sanderson Miller* and erected by *William Hitchcox*, 1749. Thoughtfully restored by *Hawkes & Cave* for the Landmark Trust, 1987–91. Of cyclopean stonework standing on precipitous ground, with a cold plunge bath in the basement chamber and an octagonal plastered room above. The upper room has a stalactite ribbed vault and shellwork swags originally designed by *Mary Delany* and installed by *Robert Moore* in 1754. Suggestions that the bath itself might be Roman have been found groundless.

Walton is a charming estate village, its varied-style COTTAGES not by Scott (NHLE) but mostly by *Horace Gundry*, a one-time employee of Prichard & Seddon, 1867–75. The former SCHOOL, 1863, may, however, be the work of a junior in *Scott*'s office. Set well back from the road the big-chimneyed and bargeboarded OLD RECTORY by *William Kendall*, 1843.

3060

WAPPENBURY

St John the Baptist. Rebuilt, apart from the chancel and tower, by *A. E. Lloyd Oswell* of Shrewsbury, 1885–6. A ruthless job. Red sandstone. Good E.E. chancel, well restored in 1883. Three stepped lancets in the E wall, one hoodmould going round the three of them. Widely spaced lancets in the side walls. Trefoil-headed priest's doorway and PISCINA, the latter with the arch on two orders of short shafts. Victorian chancel arch. Perp SW tower with one bell-opening, late C13 and reused. Tall arch towards the nave, lower arch towards the aisle. A large, pained face by the door to the tower stairs. Animals' heads on the N face support the nave roof. Outside the tower has grotesque gargoyles and where the base of the stair-turret is corbelled out a man lies on his chest, his chin in his hands. The details are in the Coventry style (e.g. St John's and Holy Trinity). – PULPIT. Open Victorian stone balustrade. – STAINED GLASS. Two by *Hardman*: E window 1890, W 1898.

In the CHURCHYARD, the base of a C14 cross S of the church. On the N, a handsome Celtic cross memorial, †1898.

St Anne (R.C.). Established in the C18 and a new chapel and presbytery built after 1795. The chancel, with its panelled four-centred Gothic roof of *c.* 1830, probably belongs to the earlier chapel, but the nave is of 1849. Simple stone tracery within brick lancets. Cubical glass porch, 2014. – STAINED GLASS. *Frederick Burrow*, 1853. – MEMORIAL BRASS, Fr Richard Austin Marsh †1856, probably by *Hardman*.

Wappenbury Hall. For George Darlinson, a Coventry silk manufacturer, 1894, extended on the E by *Harry Quick*, 1897. Cotswold-style in brick, with stone ball finials on the coped gables. Extensive contemporary stables and outbuildings to the E.

Wappenbury Camp. The roughly rectangular earthwork encloses the modern village. The rampart has been almost obliterated by ploughing on the E and by river erosion on the W. Numerous gaps now exist in the fortifications, but probably only that on the SW corner, which is deeply inturned, is original. The earthworks are certainly post-Roman and may represent a stronghold of the Mercian period. The site overlies an Iron Age settlement and pottery production site.

4040

WARMINGTON

St Michael. Outside the village, on a steep bank above the Edge Hill road cutting. Hornton stone. The S aisle with the S doorway is late C13. The doorway has continuous rolls etc., also with fillets. Good S aisle E window with three circles in bar tracery. Dec N aisle, its N windows with mouchettes in the tracery and ogee hoodmoulds outside, the E window of three uneven lights, the higher ones framing a circle with a penta-gram. Dec also the chancel, but partly refenestrated. The priest's doorway has an ogee head outside, and inside the SEDILIA have crocketed ogee arches too. But these are not entirely original.* The pinnacles on the Dec NE vestry are of similar style. This is two-storey, detached from the aisle, with priest's room above. It has an ogee-headed doorway from the chancel, barred windows (one of them typically Dec), and an ogee-headed PISCINA. In the *domus inclusi* above a fireplace and NW garderobe. A little window allowed the priest to look into the chancel. Dec to Perp W tower with blunt parapet. However, the nave arcades are both Norman: both are im-pressive and were originally of three bays. Their sequence is arguable. The N arcade (directly comparable with nearby Shotteswell) has circular piers, square abaci, flat multi-scallop capitals, and unmoulded pointed arches, perhaps single-stepped originally. The S arcade is the same, but the capitals are much bigger and especially higher, and the pointed arches have a slight chamfer. So the evidence is contradictory. A further bay was added to the E when the chancel was built. The mouldings correspond and match those of the wide chancel arch; the junction is awkward. No clerestory. Chancel restoration begun by *R. C. Hussey*, 1866, and the whole church restored by 1871, apparently under the direction of members of *Scott*'s staff. – SCREEN. Part of the C15 base. – Original DOORS to the vestry stair. – ORGAN CASE. *W. Talbot Brown*, 1893. – STAINED GLASS. E window, two in chancel and another in nave by *Clayton & Bell*, †1870 to †1926, illustrating stylistic development over almost five decades. – W tower window, *F. Holt & Co.*, 1877.

In the CHURCHYARD many carved ironstone headstones and table tombs, from the 1630s onwards, with a range of scrollwork, foliage, winged heads, skulls and other decoration. An impressive array.

METHODIST CHAPEL. 1811 (closed in 2011) but with a later C19 rendered front with round-headed windows. Fittings mainly 1811, including gallery and seating. Adjoining C18 cottage used as schoolroom.

PERAMBULATION. Warmington centres on a large green with a pond surrounded by houses of Hornton stone, some thatched but a surprising number re-roofed in Welsh slate. Mainly C17–C18. Several with mullioned windows.

Above the pond, the MANOR HOUSE fronts directly on the green without any garden. Probably built for Richard Cooper. It is a fully floored hall house of *c.* 1600, symmetrical front but with the doorway and the chimney-breast in their medieval positions. Two gables for solar and service wings, two-storey

---

*Alan Brooks and Andy Foster have pointed out that the upper parts look like mid-C18 remodelling in the style of *Sanderson Miller*.

with attics. Mullioned windows. Stone slate roof. Narrow gabled bay on the w elevation with three-light staircase windows. (Screens passage preserved. Stairs with original shaped splat balusters and moulded finials.)

Just off to the s is GROVE FARM HOUSE, probably built for William Claridge. Dated to 1700 by Nat Alcock, it is the earliest four-square double-pile house yet known in the county. Five bays and two storeys with a hipped roof, the windows with wooden crosses. The doorway has lost its original hood. Inside an open-well staircase with turned balusters and a handsome, curvy handrail.

On the w side of the green the former RECTORY. Partly c15–c16, but with good early c18 front. Of two storeys and five bays with a one-bay projection. This has quoins of even length. The angles of the house have pilasters. (Good interior.)

At the N corner CAMBRAY HOUSE has an imposing central block of c. 1835 with flanking c18 wings.

SW of the green the Mollington Lane narrows towards Church Hill, with cottages on steeply rising ground opposite the VILLAGE HALL (former school) by *W.E. Mills* of Banbury, 1879. Further c17 houses in Chapel Street and School Lane. SPRINGFIELD HOUSE, School Lane, has a date-stone, 1539.

2000

WARTON

HOLY TRINITY. By *Thomas Johnson* of Lichfield, 1841. It cost £1,275. Very short chancel, N vestry, w porch and wide aisleless nave with a bellcote on the w gable. Lancet style, with triple lancet E window. Interior reordered in 1998, with some of the Gothic woodwork of 1841 reused in the chancel and w end. – DECALOGUE etc. Carved stone panels, E wall. 1841. Rather incongruous in their present setting. – PAINTED BOARD. Handsome ICBS grant board, 1841. – STAINED GLASS. E window of 1901 by *Clayton & Bell*. One s nave window by *Hardman*, 1950. Three others by *W. Pearce & Cutler*, 1930–6.

Former NETHERSOLE'S SCHOOL, Maypole Road. Teacher's residence of 1856–7 by *Robert Jennings* of Atherstone with a separate infants' school of 1905 by *R. Scrivener* behind. These overlook the well-designed school of 1975 by the *County Architect's Department*.

Just N of the church, the HATTERS ARMS of 1900. Brick with canted entrance and attractive window details. In AUSTREY ROAD, No. 14, a pleasant house dated 1775 with symmetrical front of three bays, the top storey raised in the c19. Open Doric porch and rusticated window heads.

WARWICK

INTRODUCTION

The *burh* of Warwick was founded by Ethelfleda in 914. This is her connection with Warwick. There is none, as far as we know, with the castle.

> The towne of Warwicke standithe on a rokky hille, risynge from est to west. The beauty and glory of the towne is in two streets whereof the one is caullyd Highe Strete and goith from the est gate to the west ... the other crossithe the midle of it, makynege Quadrivium, and goith from northe to southe.

Thus wrote John Leland around 1540, and thus still one's principal impression of this perfect county town. Its visual homogeneity is largely due to the great fire of 1694 and the rebuilding after it. It is also due to another factor, that Warwick was always an administrative centre rather than a town dependent on industry. The early factories were near the canal which skirted round the town to the N. Thus the factory area did not interfere with the town. Nor does the castle, its principal monument, and that also is visually an advantage. It is a case of ideal co-existence between two outstanding visual treasures.

The population grew quite sharply in the early C19, from 5,592 in 1801 to 10,952 in 1851, then remained relatively static at 12,000 in 1901, and 16,051 in 1961. In 2011 it stood at 30,114. The main area of C19 expansion was to the E towards Leamington, off the Coventry Road around the workhouse and along the Birmingham Road through Saltisford. Later C20 development has been on the N edge at Woodloes, to the SE across the Avon and to the SW towards the A46 by-pass, opened in 1967. The canals from Birmingham and Napton-on-the-Hill reached Warwick in 1799–1800 and the railway station on the Oxford to Birmingham line (GWR) opened in 1852.

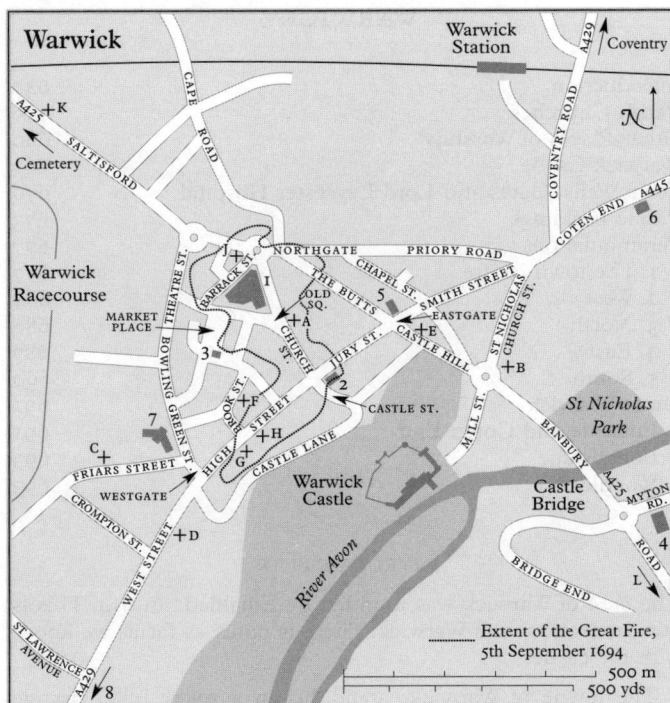

A   St Mary
B   St Nicholas
C   St Paul
D   St Mary the Immaculate (R.C.)
E   Baptist church
F   Congregational chapel (former)
G   Friends' meeting house
H   Unitarian chapel
J   Methodist church
K   Church of Jesus Christ of
    Latter Day Saints
L   Sikh Temple

1   Shire Hall complex
2   Court House
3   Market Hall
4   Warwick School
5   King's High School for
    Girls
6   Board School
7   Board School
8   Playbox Theatre

The list of Warwick architects begins in the C17 with the *Hurl-butts*, William and Roger, who, although 'of Stareton' (Stone-leigh) did much work in Warwick. After the great fire came the *Smiths*, Francis (†1738) and William (†1724), noted all over the Midlands, and then the *Hiornes*, the brothers William (†1776) and David (†1758), and William's son Francis (†1789). Other names of note are those of *Timothy Lightoler* (†1769), *Thomas Johnson*, later of Worcester (†1800), *William Eborall* (†1795) and *Job Collins* (†1800). To this list should be added the roll-call of County Surveyors, Bridgemasters and Architects. Into the C19 and beyond the main names are *Frederick Holyoake Moore* (*fl.*

1866–1920), the *Trepess* family and *Charles M.C. Armstrong* (*fl.* 1900–1940s). But Warwick was also notable for its C19 wood-carvers, *William Cookes & Sons, J.M. Willcox, T.H. Kendall,* and *Collier & Plucknett,* and for its stained glass artists, *William Holland, Tony Dury* and *Frank Holt.*

PARISH CHURCHES

St Mary, Church Street. A most impressive church, on the crown of the hill. It is visible from a distance all round and in the town most of the surrounding streets allow unobstructed views. The sight of the church from the castle towers is especially rewarding. The origins are most likely pre-Conquest. There was certainly a church here by 1123 when Roger de Newburgh made it collegiate. The outline chronology is this. First, the crypt, probably later Norman. Above it was the original chancel which was lavishly rebuilt and extended by the Beauchamps, Earls of Warwick, in the late C14. It was begun in the late 1360s and finished by 1392. The vestries and chapter house to the N are C14 too. Then comes the spectacular Beauchamp Chapel, built between 1443 and 1449 but fitted out over a longer period. It was finished in 1464 and consecrated in 1475. These parts were left largely unharmed in the great fire of 1694 but the rest of the church was destroyed, i.e. a low w tower, the medieval nave and aisles almost as long as they are now, and transepts slightly shorter than now. *Wren* and *Hawksmoor* were consulted about the rebuilding and they produced a Gothic design for a cruciform church with a low pyramid spire above the crossing and a taller w tower with spire. Instead, however, the church was rebuilt to the designs of *Sir William Wilson,* a mason-statuary who married so well that he was knighted. Rebuilding began in 1698 and was done by the *Smith* brothers, with *Samuel Dunckley* (mason), *Thomas Masters* and *John Phillips* (carpenters) and others. The tower was originally intended to stand within the w bay of the nave, but a problem with the piers when construction was under way led to a change of plan. As a result it projects into the street, occupying the position that would have been taken by a portico. For the rebuilding the town contributed £11,000, Queen Anne £1,000. The church was completed in 1704. The fabric has remained little altered since then, but there have been restorations. The eastern parts were restored internally in 1851–3, partly under the supervision of *F.J. Francis* of London. *John Gibson* produced restoration plans in 1879 but his proposals proved too expensive. When work took place in 1884–6, *William Butterfield* was in charge. He restored the nave, aisles and tower, all done faithfully to the existing style and design. Then came *J.A. Chatwin* who restored the interior, 1896–7, and his son *Philip B. Chatwin* (†1964), who served as church architect for much of the early C20. For recent work, successive architects have been *Charles Brown* and *Christopher Langstone,* working under various practice names.

Medieval

c18

Chapter House

Regimental Chapel

North Aisle

Vestry

Vestry

Tower

Nave

Chancel

Oratory

Dean's Chapel

South Aisle

Beauchamp Chapel

30 m
30 yds

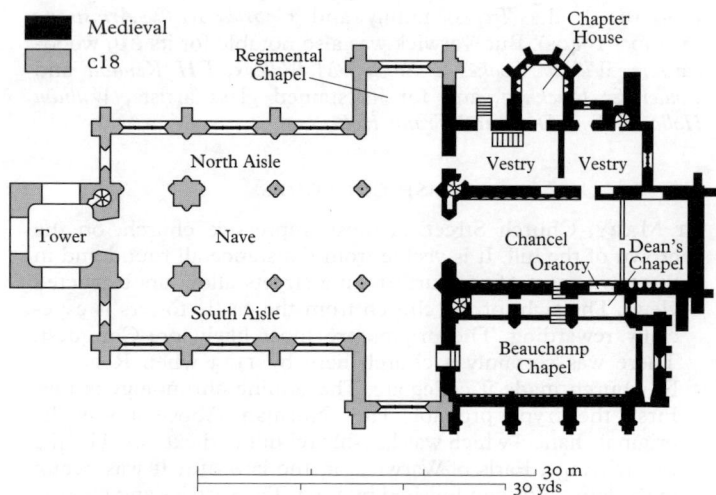

Warwick, St Mary.
Plan

Take the EXTERIOR first, beginning with the parts rebuilt after the fire, i.e the tower, nave and transepts. The style of the rebuilding, as aptly described by Terry Friedman, is an 'idiosyncratic gothic-classical mix'. The forms are Gothic, i.e. traceried windows, mainly pointed arches, but quite without Gothic authority. Some details are classical, notably the late c17 upright acanthus leaf capitals to the doorways, arches and within the window tracery. The best parallel for this stylistic mix is St Eustache, Paris, 1532–1640, though there are also mid-c17 English precedents (e.g. Brasenose College, Oxford). *Wilson* used nakedly classical forms too, including semicircular coved niches and the parapets and urns. To Glynne, *c.* 1830, this 'tasteless mixture' represented 'a style of great barbarity'. Bloxam thought it 'in miserable taste'. Yet even Glynne grudgingly allowed it to be 'in some respects handsome'. The surprise, perhaps, is that Butterfield respected and restored it all as he found it.

Rising straight up from the street, the unbuttressed WEST TOWER was built in 1700–3. It is of commanding height, visible for miles around. It has a ground stage open to the W, N and S and rises slenderly to a height of 174 ft (53 metres) including the corner pinnacles. The general *parti* is excellent, but the details are curiously tired, the forms bald. It is repetitive from tier to tier and there is a total lack of tension in the composition. In each stage, two tiers of niches, beginning above the porch piers and continuing to the top. In the lower stage blank windows with Y-tracery above the arches. Over-long shafts l. and r. Between the first and second stages a line of blind balustrading level with the parapets of the aisles. Then two stages with the same shafts and only in the centre first a giant two-light blind window, then two tiers of louvred single-light belfry windows. High parapet with arches and at the angles plinths for the pinnacles decorated with vertically placed keyed-in ovals, a typical late C17 motif. Under the tower a circular interior with a dome, decorated with pairs of ribs from the corners to a large bell-hole.*

Then the W front, with (disused) doorways l. and r. of the tower into the aisles. The doorways are pointed but have acanthus capitals. W buttresses with niches, classical again. Above, two-light traceried windows, free Gothic, too large for only two lights. So to the nave and transepts, where this mixed style continues. To the nave each side, three big three-light windows, and identical end windows to the transepts, which have no windows on the sides. In the tracery, round arches halfway up instead of a transom, round arches above supporting a big drop shape, and two squeezed-in side-pieces to fill the two-centred arch. Gothic panelling beneath the windows and on the buttresses. But the Gothic disguise slips with the top pediments with bullseye windows to the transepts, also the balustrade and urns stretching continuously to the tower. Until the later C19 restoration, there were urns on the chancel parapets too, N and S.

The S side continues with the celebrated BEAUCHAMP CHAPEL, structurally complete by c. 1449. Lavishly Perp, of course. The chapel is of three bays and a low E vestry. So the E wall is developed in two planes. The lower has an openwork quatrefoil parapet and pinnacles, the upper a seven-light window (2–3–2) and a quatrefoil parapet, and pinnacles too. There is also a quatrefoil frieze along the base. To the S are six-light windows (three plus three). There is blind panelling in the spandrels of the arches. The windows are separated by deep buttresses with decorative panelling. They carry small flying buttresses of ogee shape with a kind of two-light window to support them. Square pinnacles, also panelled.

The gap on the N side of the chapel shows that it stands apart from the church. The reason for this, and what fills part of the gap, will be seen inside. The chancel rises sheer on this side, but with stepped buttresses to all angles at the E end and a big added buttress on the S. The side windows are of four lights, with panel tracery. The ground falls away to the E, leaving the chancel high above the surrounding churchyard. The ground-level windows belong to the crypt. Higher up, the chancel has a completely blank-panelled E wall with a six-light window, also with panel tracery.

On the N, annexes of varied shape, all late C14 and contemporary with the chancel. They include the VESTRY with the

---

*Pevsner described this here, as elsewhere, as a 'large circle for the bell-ropes'. Such holes are for raising and lowering bells when necessary, and never for the ropes.

SACRISTY above, reached by the stair-turret with embattled top and integral chimney. Another massive added buttress here, and there are flying buttresses above the vestry to the chancel. In the middle of this range is the CHAPTER HOUSE, which projects N with a polygonal apse and two-light Perp windows with panel tracery. The N transept and the rest of the N side are the same as the S, already described.

So to the INTERIOR. As one enters from the W there is first the main W doorway, illustrating how Wilson tried to keep faithful to the Perp style. The mouldings are creditable and almost credible, but the capitals have the now familiar late C17 acanthus leaves again. To the NAVE and AISLES the main piers inside have the same capitals, only of course much more prominently. The abaci moreover have egg-and-dart. The piers on the other hand are pure Perp in section: four shafts and four diagonal hollows. The most remarkable thing about the interior is that it is of the hall-church type, i.e. with the aisles of the same height as the nave – a type very unusual in major English Gothic church architecture, though applied at Bristol. This was not taken over from the medieval building. But Wren used the hall-type freely, though not in Gothic terms. Another remarkable thing is that the first pair of piers from the W is considerably more massive than the others, proof that the tower was meant to go up here until its construction was abandoned in 1700. The bay of the arcade corresponding to the transepts is on the other hand not distinguished at all. The vaults are all of plaster, with their tierceron vaults and big bosses entirely Baroque in the scrolly cartouche details. With its big windows the interior is light and surprisingly successful, not least in its relationship with the old chancel beyond. It was not originally galleried and the galleries introduced in the later C18 were removed in 1896.

The rest can be taken area by area, each one described with its furnishings. One must begin with the CRYPT, reached by stairs through the vestries N of the chancel. Its building is usually connected with the fact that Roger de Newburgh made the church collegiate in 1123. But the surviving part is later in style than this, though undoubtedly Norman. Mighty piers, circular with four almost merging diagonal shafts and multi-scalloped capitals. The N row is different, far more massive, and one wonders what it was designed to support above. Perhaps a Norman tower, although this would have been an unusual place for one. The crypt is very heavily rib-vaulted, the ribs of only one slight chamfer not united in a joint keystone. At the E there are two C14 bays, connected with the building of a new chancel above. Of this period in the crypt the chief evidence is one pier, the ribs surrounding it, and some small, two-light E and S windows, with roll-moulded details.

Back upstairs to the NORTH VESTRIES and CHAPTER HOUSE, both belonging to the late C14. The vestries occupy two low vaulted rooms, divided by a medieval stone screen rediscovered and restored in 1852, the tracery being glazed by

William Holland. In the E room a Gothick fireplace, probably of *c.* 1780. The long chamber above (now the Song School) was the SACRISTY with *domus inclusi* for the lay sacristan, whose duties are known from a document of 1465. The upper room has a fireplace and also windows in the S wall overlooking the chancel. The CHAPTER HOUSE is tierceron-vaulted, and has diagonally set octagons like those in the chancel. There are arched niches all the way round the polygonal part. – STAINED GLASS. In the E window, eight small C14 figures removed from the E window in 1879 and thirteen Netherlandish roundels, *c.* 1525–40. – More roundels in the N window, but mainly C19. – Medieval fragments in light-boxes in outer vestry. – MONUMENTS. Fulke Greville, 1st Lord Brooke, †1628. By *Thomas Ashby*, 1618–19. Six-poster with two tiers of black columns. The lower carry arches, the upper stand against the blank attic storey. Top pediments and corner obelisks. Black sarcophagus, big Roman lettering, no effigy. The monument is far too big for its place in the chapter house.* In the chapter house also a large number of HELMS, GAUNTLETS, etc. – Sir Thomas Puckering †1636/7, by *Nicholas Stone*, and one of the most purely classical monuments of the date in England. Altar and reredos composition. Black-and-white marble. Two large detached columns and an open segmental pediment. No effigy, no figures, no ornament. – Francis Parker †1693. Big tablet with columns and open pediment, but entirely lacking the nobility of the former.

Now the CHANCEL. It was begun by Thomas Beauchamp, Earl of Warwick, but little was done above ground by the time he died in 1369. It was completed by his son, Thomas II, and finished by 1392. High and spacious, but rather dark as all the windows are high up with panelled walls below. It is four bays long, and most memorable for its tierceron vault with very sharp, metallic arches and ribs, the transverse arches and principal ribs being partly supported by flying ribs, a Bristol motif. The centre of each bay is an octagon set diagonally. Niches either side of E window, Easter sepulchre on the N and piscina and sedilia on the S.

REREDOS. Alabaster, by *Butterfield*, 1885, carved by *Earp*. – Complementary marble paving and alabaster ALTAR RAILS, 1894, designed by *Chatwin* and executed by *Bridgeman*. – STALLS, carved oak, by *F. J. Francis*, 1853. – STAINED GLASS. E window by *Heaton, Butler & Bayne*, 1879. – On the N, one (W) designed by *George Harris* (cf. Old Milverton) and made by *Baillie & Mayer*, 1879; one by *Heaton, Butler & Bayne*, 1902; and two by *Kempe* (1906) and *Kempe & Co.* (1911). – On the S, three more by *Kempe*, 1900, and one (W) by *Cox & Sons*, 1876. – MONUMENTS. In the middle of the chancel Thomas Beauchamp, Earl of Warwick, †1369 and his wife Catherine. Alabaster effigies, recumbent and holding hands. Against the

---

*As well as taking over the chapter house for the monument, the Grevilles also appropriated parts of the crypt below as burial vaults (not open to visitors).

tomb-chest small mourners, eleven by seven, originally identified by their arms painted on shields. Many are plaster replacements or part-replacements. The original ones are lively and extremely pretty. – Cecily Puckering †1636. A documented work of *Nicholas Stone*. Floor slab with brass inlays. – Henry Puckering †1701, by *James Hardy*. Another slab, with arms.

The chancel SOUTH DOOR with C15 blank tracery opens to a narrow passage leading down eleven steps to the Beauchamp Chapel. This is not the main entrance, of course, but one should enter this way to see what lies between. Here is the so-called DEAN'S CHAPEL, with lobbies on the W, and a small ORATORY in the wall between chapel and chancel. The chapel belongs conceptually and architecturally to the main chapel below, and must be mid-C15. However, it occupies the position of what was previously S of the chancel, an earlier two-storeyed sacristy, of which the outer mouldings of an E window remain.* The chapel and its lobbies form a series of three chambers along the N side of the Beauchamp Chapel, all originally with decorated open panels, allowing a clear view. Those in the Dean's Chapel remain, but the others are blocked by later memorials. The lobbies have panelled vaults of four-centred section. The chapel has minature fan-vaults with pendants, a tiny two-light E window, and exceptionally elaborate small canopies l. and r. with lierne-vaults inside. Below the window a frieze as finely wrought as metal. Tiny angel corbels to the vault shafts and busy traceried panelling. All delightfully delicately done. On the S side, a wooden PILLAR PISCINA. A doorway in the N wall of the chapel leads up to the late C14 ORATORY, cut into the S chancel wall as if to take a tomb-chest. It is separated from the Dean's Chapel by a solid wall and open to the chancel by a parclose of three cusped openings with grilles. Ceiling again vaulted. – STAINED GLASS. E window to Dean's Chapel by *Martin Graeme & Co.* of York, 2001. – In the lobby there are some of the original BENCHES.

Now enter the BEAUCHAMP CHAPEL through the side entrance. Directly ahead is the tomb of the founder, Richard Beauchamp, Earl of Warwick, who had died at Rouen in 1439. He had already founded a chantry and in his will he made provision for this chapel and for his tomb in it. We are uniquely well informed about the history of this building, by accounts and contracts. The cost was £2,481 4s. 7½d., of which over £1,754 had been spent by 1449/50, by when the building must have been complete. The interior is as rich and elaborate as the earl's money could make it, ostentatious in a worldly way yet built in extreme piety too. The theme of the chapel is Beauchamp's personal salvation. Represented in armour as a soldier of Christ, the effigy gazes up at a figure of the Queen of Heaven carved on the easternmost roof boss. The feet are

---

*It was once thought that the deanery stood here, hence the name. The current view is that the pre-existing structure was a sacristy. The Dean's Chapel was probably a private oratory.

to the E in anticipation of resurrection and salvation on the Day of Judgment. Behind, on the W wall, is a Judgment scene (below). Thus, as Richard Marks has observed, 'the imagery of the interior fuses the earthly and heavenly worlds'. As an example illustrating the purpose of a chantry chapel it can hardly be bettered. It is undeniably beautiful too. The chapel has panelled walls, the lowest stage with cusped ogee heads to the panels. The vault rests on thin shafts with very fine mouldings and without capitals. The vault is of a lierne type with, in the centre of each bay, curved forms, again a Bristol motif. There are plenty of bosses and much foliage. The small N doorway is reminiscent of both Bristol and Gloucester (but of course the work there is a hundred and more years older). The W wall has above the lowest panelling a frieze of square leaves and monsters. The E wall is even more ornate. Here the E window has in two orders of side and arch mouldings figure sculpture, all colourfully painted. The inner moulding is all angels (almost horizontal in the arch), the outer moulding two saints l. and two r., and the rest angels again. Angels also up the two intermediate mullions. The saints are among the best English sculpture of *c.* 1450–60 and almost up to the standard of Hans Multscher's work in Germany. In the NE and SE corners two tiers of image canopies. Doorway into the E vestry l. of the altar. A canopy above this as well, and the whole repeated r. of the altar. As Linda Monckton has shown, the architecture is distinctly provincial, specifically to the region W of Oxford and into the SW. The fittings, though, owe more to London influences, as we shall see. When leaving the chapel one passes through a projecting portal, apparently an afterthought. It has a four-centred arch, panelled inside, canopies l. and r., and a frieze of vine like a Devon screen. Up the steps on the other side, i.e. the entrance from the S transept, an equally ornate portal, a really surprising piece of Beauchamp-Chapel-Gothic pastiche, not C15 but by *Samuel Dunckley*, 1704. Even today it will deceive all but the connoisseurs. Four-centred entrance arch with fine mouldings, canopied niches l. and r. with much close decoration. Both sides of the portal partially conceal a three-light Perp window.

The chapel is exceptionally rich in FURNISHINGS. – The REREDOS with canopy is Gothick of *c.* 1765, attributed to *Timothy Lightoler* (cf. the chapel passage at Warwick Castle chapel) and the RELIEF of the Annunciation by *William Collins* is of about the same time.* It is extremely good, as English Georgian religious sculpture goes, and patently influenced by the Italian Settecento. – WALL PAINTING. On the W wall an absurd partial copy of Michelangelo's *Last Judgment*, done by *Richard Bird* of London in 1678, but some of the C15 figures which belonged to a Last Judgment too were preserved. – STAINED GLASS. The contract with *John Prudde* of

22

48

---

*This must have speedily replaced the marble altarpiece erected by *John Barnes* of Warwick in 1735 at a cost of £190 8s. 10½d.

Westminster, the king's glazier, is dated 1447. He was to use
foreign glass 'with no glass of England'. Colours were specified
and the system for working from design to finished window is
outlined. Of the original glass a fair amount survives, despite
Civil War damage etc. The E window, though much repaired,
is the original one. Richard Beauchamp (bottom middle, but
largely replaced) and his family are surrounded by saints, some
in their original positions. These are hagiographical signs of
Lancastrian allegiance. Top l., good figures of St Thomas of
Canterbury and St Alban. Top r., St Winifred of Wales and St
John of Bridlington. These are the best preserved, and of
exceptional quality. Rich in colour, with the robes and haloes
enriched with jewelled inserts, a difficult and expensive technique. In the tracery lights, the words and music of the
Gloria. – In the side windows, only the upper parts survive.
Again of the finest quality. In the first window N and S, paired
angels with musical instruments. A remarkable collection, precisely executed. Then, across two windows each side, choirs
of angels with scrolls of plainsong music, Gaudeamus on the
N and Ave Regina on the S. – STALLS. Two tiers, the lower for
the boys. Ends with simple foliage poppyheads. Animals on
the arms. The backs and the front-seat fronts with plain quatrefoils. Nothing like as elaborate and costly as the architecture.
The work was done by *Richard Bird* and *John Haynes* of
London under a contract made in 1449. The stalls were renovated by *Mr Hearn* of Leamington in 1852. – Wrought-iron
GATES to the N door, from the former chancel screen, made
by *William Marshall*, contracted for in 1699. The screen was
originally 10 ft (3 metres) high and cost £110.*

Now the MONUMENTS. – Richard Beauchamp, Earl of
Warwick, †1439. The surviving contracts tell us a number of
interesting things: first that the effigy is not a portrait, or else
the contract would not be confined to stipulating 'an image
of a man armed'; and secondly how many people were concerned with such a monument and how careful one ought to
be therefore in other cases where only one name happens to
be recorded. For the earl's tomb *John Bourde* of Corfe supplied
the Purbeck marble and *William Austen* of London cast the
effigy of latten. He appears in a contract of 1448 together with
Roger Webb, Warden of the Barber Surgeon's Company in
London, *John Massingham*, carver, and *Barthilmew Lambespring*, goldsmith and a Dutchman. What Webb was supposed
to do it is hard to decide. Massingham probably made the
model and Lambespring, as the contract explicitly states, was
to polish and gild the effigy. There is also the separate contract
with Austen, of 1449, to cast the effigy, and yet another, of
1453, for the brass plates for lid and sides and the hearse. In
this latter contract *John Essex*, marbler of London, and *Thomas*

---

* It is wrongly attributed to Nicholas Paris, c. 1716, on the nearby plaque of 1973.
Paris was, however, co-contractor with Marshall for the ironwork for the new
church.

Stevyns, coppersmith of London, appear together with Austen, and we don't know what their share was intended to be. High tomb-chest of Purbeck marble. On it, of gilded latten, the recumbent effigy of the earl, in armour, his hands in a strangely hieratic gesture of prayer – as if he were holding an invisible goblet. Long, elegant hands and a long, very English face. His head lies on a helmet; at his feet are a bear and a griffin. Over the whole lid of the tomb-chest a hooped guard of gilded latten like the framework of a covered wagon. Against the tomb-chest at the foot, enamel shields, above five by two small copper gilt figures, the traditional mourners, and between them, yet smaller and higher up, angels. There are seven male mourners and seven ladies. The style of the figurines is very Burgundian, and that of the effigy, one has reason to assume, Flemish (which was at that time of course also Burgundian). – Robert Dudley, Earl of Leicester, †1588 and his second wife, Lettice, †1634. For her an effigy, but no inscription (*see* below). Attributed to *Jasper Hollemans* of Burton upon Trent, 1599 (JB). Alabaster. Large standing wall monument. Two recumbent effigies. Coupled columns l. and r. Flat arch with much ribbonwork and the splendid motif of sixteen flags arranged radially. Top with arms and a bear. L. and r. poor statuettes and small obelisks on arched pedestals. The iron GRILLE in front is by *Nicholas Paris* of Warwick, 1716. – Robert Dudley, Lord Denbigh, 'the noble impe', †1584, aged three. Attributed to *Cornelius Cure*. Alabaster. Small standing wall monument with recumbent effigy. Strapwork and fruit above; a bear at his feet. – Ambrose Dudley, Earl of Warwick, †1590, probably from the *Cure* workshops. Alabaster and marble. Tomb-chest with pilasters and angle columns. Richly ornamented shields between. Recumbent effigy with beard and C18 coronet, on a half-rolled-up mat. Again a bear at his feet. – Lettice, Countess of Leicester, †1634. Tablet of wood made to look like brass. Signed *Gervas Clifton*. The inscription reads:

> Upon / the death of the / excellent and pious / Lady
> Lettice Countesse / of Leicester who dyed / upon
> Christmas Day / in the morning *1634.*
> Looke in this vault and search it well
> Much treasure in it lately fell
> Wee all are robd and all doe say
> Our wealth was carryed this away
> And that the theft might nere be found
> Tis buried closely under ground
> Yet if you gently stirr the mould
> There all our losse you may behould
> There may you see that face that hand
> Which once was fairest in the land
> She that in her younger yeares
> Matcht with two great English peares
> She that did supply the warrs

With thunder and the court with stars
She that in her youth had bene
Darling to the Maiden Queene
Till she was content to quitt
Her favoure for her Favoritt
Whose gould threed when she saw spunn
And the death of her brave sonn
Thought it safest to retyre
From all care and vaine desire
To a private countrie cell
Where she spent her dayes soe well
That to her the better sort
Came as to an holy court
And the poore that lived neare
Dearth nor Famine could not feare
Whilst she liv'd she lived thus
Till that God displeas'd with us
Suffred her at last to fall
Not from Him but from us all
And because she tooke delight
Christ's poore members to invite
He fully now requites her love
And sends His Angels from above
That did to Heaven her Soule convay
To solemnize His owne birth day

– Tablet commemorating the bequests of Lady Katherine Leveson (†1673/4), granddaughter of Robert Dudley, by will dated 1673. By *Joshua Marshall* to Dugdale's order. Black-and-white marble tablet, paid for in 1678. Over the door to the Dean's Chapel. Broken scroll pediment. Cherubs.

Finally, the FURNISHINGS in the REST OF THE CHURCH. Nave CHOIR STALLS, in the round. By *Christopher Langstone*, 1993. – PULPIT. By *Chatwin*, 1897. Given by the Freemasons. Carved wood on an Ashburton marble base, with canopied tester. Rather fussy. – In the S aisle, FONT, by *John Nost Sen.*, 1705. Short baluster stem with big capital; fluted bowl. – MACE RESTS, early C18, rather thickly done. By *Nicholas Paris*. – The ORGAN CASE at the W end of the nave is partly of 1719 and partly C20. The makers in 1719 were *Thomas & Henry Swarbrick*. Gibbonsesque carvings of violins and other instruments on the front. Above it, a carved wooden MITRE on a foliage bracket, probably C17 but of unknown purpose. – ROYAL ARMS of Queen Anne on one of the inner piers at the back of the nave, and a matching CLOCK on the other one, signed by *Watson*, with cherubs and scroll. Both given by Robert Abbott, Painter-Steyner of London and native of Warwick, 1714. – Wooden SCREEN with iron grilles to the Regimental Chapel (N transept), by *Chatwin*, 1937. – STAINED GLASS. Large Warwickshire Regiment memorial window in N transept, completed 1952. By *Florence & Walter Camm*, to a scheme by *P.B. Chatwin*, whose framed drawing, 1946, is displayed in the church. – In the s transept, only two lights, 1904, and a memorial panel, 1915, of a scheme by *Heaton, Butler & Bayne*, 1901. Framed design also displayed. – MONUMENTS, generally as one expects in the principal town and county church, with few highlights. Mainly in the transepts. – In the s transept, a later tablet with splendid re-set brasses to Thomas Beauchamp II †1401, and wife Margaret †1406. The figures are 6 ft 3 in. (1.9 metres) long. – To its r. William Hiorn (Hiorne), the architect-builder, †1776. Simple tablet with an urn. – Henry Beaufoy and wife, against the s wall, *c.* 1700. This replaced a monument destroyed in the fire. – By the vestry door, Thomas Oken †1573, and his wife Joan. Original brasses, re-set in a new tablet with added inscriptions after the fire. – In the n transept against the n wall, Thomas Hewitt †1737. Attributed to *Francis Smith* (Andor Gomme). Black columns and open pediment. In the pediment a still-life of books. On the pediment putti. A conservative piece. – Dr William Johnston †1733, also by *Francis Smith*. – Among the military memorials, Lt Col. Louis How Bazalgette and Major Thomas Clark †1866, by *E.J. Physick*. – Neville Frederick Mansergh †1883, by *Gaffin*, London. – In the nave, Walter Savage Landor, the poet, †1864. Signed by *J. Forsyth*.

ALL SAINTS, St Edith's Green. *See* Emscote (Outer Warwick, below).

ST NICHOLAS, Banbury Road. On the site of the medieval church. The tower dates from 1748, but was probably refaced when *Thomas Johnson* of Warwick rebuilt the church in 1779–80. The details are similar, e.g. the trefoil frieze below the parapets, the pinnacles and the coved window openings. Johnson's shallow apsed chancel was replaced in 1869 by *John Gibson* who also added the n vestry and organ chamber. In 1985 Gibson's uneventful Victorian chancel was partitioned off from the nave and sub-divided into two floors internally by *Hinton Brown Langstone*. w tower with recessed spire. The sides of the church four bays, tall narrow windows of two lights with four-centred arches. Buttresses between them. Equally typical the other motifs such as ogee-headed doorways, oddly ogee-foiled windows in the tower, round and quatrefoil windows. A pleasant, light interior. Nave and aisles of equal height. The arcade piers quatrefoil. They carry depressed plaster groin-vaults. – FURNISHINGS. Late c20 reordering involved the perhaps regrettable loss of works by Warwick craftsmen, e.g. *Collier & Plucknett* (pulpit, 1871), *Holland, Son & Holt* (reredos, 1875), and *F. Holt* (chancel décor, 1893). – FONT (s aisle). Big spiral-fluted goblet on a low foot. – WEST GALLERY, now with kitchen and toilets underneath, 1989. – STAINED GLASS. E window by *William Holland & Son*, 1871. Since the insertion of the upper floor the E window can be seen in two halves, and the upper parts of Holland's four side windows (1869–70) are wholly hidden. – One n window by *Tony Dury*, 1867, with original window design alongside. – A s window by *H.T. Bosdet*, 1924; alongside, one by *Hugh Easton*,

1935. – N again, St Nicholas, by *Norgrove Studios (Aidan McRae Thomson)*, 1999. – Many MONUMENTS, all minor, the best the brass on the E wall to Robert Willardsey, vicar, †1425, a 19½-in. (50-cm.) figure, and the tablet to Katherine Stoughton †1724, s aisle E, with cheerful putti and flaming urns.

ST PAUL, Friars Street. The abnormally long S transept was originally St Mary's cemetery chapel. It is dated 1824 and has a doorway with four-centred head and a window with Y-tracery. Perp-style side windows. This transept connects to the church through a triple archway. The rest is by *R.C. Hussey*, 1844: wide, aisleless nave and an apse as high and as wide. Lancets throughout except for the w rose window. Thin hammerbeam roof with shields. Divided internally in 1978 when the w end became the hall. E end reordered in 2001. – Carved wooden PULPIT by *T.H. Kendall*, c. 1870 – STAINED GLASS. E window by *Holland*, 1850. – Two in N side of the hall, by *Tony Dury*, 1863 and 1865. – Three w windows by *Clayton & Bell*, 1874, all faded. – One N window †1918, probably *William Pearce Ltd* (AB). – Two on N by *Jane Gray*, 1992. – The rest by *F. Holt*, 1882–8, including the Good Shepherd (now in a light-box) of 1883.

OTHER PLACES OF WORSHIP

ST MARY IMMACULATE (R.C.), West Street: 1859–60 by *E.W. Pugin*. It was here, according to Roderick O'Donnell, that Pugin devised his afterwards standard plan with narrow passage aisles allowing the whole congregation to see the altar. Brick, with lancets and plate tracery. No tower, but a spindly w bell-turret. Apse and side chapels. Windowless aisles. Porch extension with lancets by *John D. Holmes*, 1993. – Sanctuary decoration by *T.F. Norman* of Warwick, 1893. The background has been overpainted but the principal elements remain (Our Lady of Perpetual Succour, Symbols of the Evangelists and representations of the ecclesiastical history of Warwick). – REREDOS with image niches and brattishing, and ALTAR CARVING of the Last Supper. – STAINED GLASS. Series in the apse, the three in the centre by *Hardman*, 1861. The rest by *Tony Dury*, the last on N and S, 1862. – Sexfoiled side-chapel windows, also *Dury*, 1862. – Four narthex windows by *Dury*, 1865–70. – Two sexfoil side-chapel windows probably Dury too, c. 1865. – W window, *Hardman*, 1960s. – STATIONS OF THE CROSS, painted on canvas in blind openings in aisles, by *Rebecca Dering* (cf. Baddesley Clinton Hall), 1893. – MEMORIAL BRASS. Fr. Joseph Kelly †1892, doubtless by *Hardman*.

BAPTIST CHURCH, Castle Street. Design and build project by *Pettifer Construction Ltd*, 1998–9. Sandstone front rising to a corner light. Large cross mounted over incised stonework. Worship area on a diagonal plan. It replaces *George Ingall*'s 1866 chapel with a polychromatic façade.

CONGREGATIONAL CHAPEL, Brook Street (now offices). Built in 1758, enlarged in 1798 and much altered by *T.S. Whitwell*, 1825–6. Whitwell heightened the building and gave it its present front. Sides of brick with windows configured for galleries, i.e. segmental windows below, semicircular above. Stuccoed five-bay front with a pediment all across. The entrance is *in antis* with two unfluted Ionic columns. Above, five thin, arched windows with blind balustrading below. – MONUMENTS. Some preserved outside.*

FRIENDS' MEETING HOUSE, High Street. 1695, rebuilt after the 1694 fire destroyed its predecessor. It stands behind the frontage in its garden and former graveyard. Simple brick cottage with stone plinth and quoins. Wooden cross-framed windows. Some of the humble original furnishings preserved. Panelled meeting room with small gallery.

UNITARIAN CHAPEL, High Street. 1781. Gothic. Stone front with gable and windows with Y-tracery. Sides similar but brick. Added brick chancel with lancets and wheel window, 1862–3. Reordered internally in 1982–4, but the W gallery front of 1862–3 survives against a partition wall. Quarry glass windows by *Holland*, 1863. – MONUMENTS. Several, C18–C19.

METHODIST CHURCH, Northgate. Replacing earlier chapels in other parts of the town. By *Joseph Lancaster Ball*, 1893. Simple Gothic with triplet windows of plate tracery set in yellow and red banded walls. Surprisingly 'churchy', with a chancel. Reorientated with canted bay added on N as a sanctuary by *Kenneth L. Holmes*, 1992–3. – REREDOS and DECALOGUE on E wall, 1907. – STAINED GLASS. Crucifix and coloured rays in new sanctuary.

CHURCH OF JESUS CHRIST OF LATTER DAY SAINTS, Birmingham Road, Saltisford. *Fellows Burt Dalton & Associates Ltd*, 2005. Not quite the standard LDS model. Two-storey, L-plan but with the usual white fibreglass spire.

SIKH TEMPLE (Gurdwara Sahib), Tachbrook Park Drive, by the *MPC Partnership* (Kenilworth), 2008–9. Square with polygonal corners and projecting front. Three storeys, crowned with 'onion' domes.

CEMETERY, Birmingham Road. Lodge and curtain walls of blue brick with stone dressings by *Edward Holmes*, 1857. The cemetery opened in 1861 and has two similar chapels, both with simple trefoil-headed side windows. The Anglican (W) chapel has an octagonal bell-turret with later copper cap.

WARWICK CASTLE   32

Lord Torrington, who as a rule was the most unkind of travellers,[†] called Warwick Castle 'the most perfect piece of castellated

---

*Apparently lost, a memorial to Rev. James Moody, †1806, by 'his admiring friend' *J. Bacon Jun.*, who had heard Moody preach in London. Dated 1808.
[†] He thought Warwick 'one of the dullest towns I ever was in'.

antiquity in the kingdom'. Perhaps he should have placed Windsor first and Warwick second. Lower than that no one would wish to go. There is in fact much that Windsor and Warwick have in common: their scale, the mound for the keep, the mixture of periods with much stress on the C19, and the splendour of views from a distance. In some views Warwick, on its cliff above the Avon, wins over Windsor easily. The view inside the court is different from Windsor too. It is unified where Windsor is varied, and it has the great attraction of turf and ornamental trees, the work of course of the C18. But the similarity with Windsor is superficial architecturally, and Warwick relates more closely with Kenilworth, Maxstoke and the polygonal forms of castle favoured in the Midlands. The E front, with the towers and gatehouse, constitutes one of the most spectacular surviving C14 castle façades in Europe.

The castle is about 475 ft (145 metres) long and 275 ft (84 metres) wide, with the mound at the W end and the principal living quarters against one long side on the securest (S) side of the bailey. Entry is from the E through a gatehouse with the clock in its tower. The SE corner is marked by Caesar's Tower, the NE corner by Guy's Tower. In the middle of the N side is now another, low, gate feature. The towers flanking it are the Bear Tower (W) and the Clarence Tower (E). Finally, on the SW between living quarters and mound is the Watergate Tower.

Building history

In the year 1068 William the Conqueror built a motte-and-bailey castle here. It does not seem to have had any stone parts. However, in the C12 and C13 rebuilding in stone took place. In 1174 money was spent on a house in the castle. In 1191 *Ralph the Mason* was paid for repairs. Among existing parts some of the N curtain wall between the gatehouse and Guy's Tower dates from the early C13. The NE wing wall up the mound and the keep on top are later C13. According to John Rouse, writing in the later C15, the defences suffered considerable damage during the Barons' War in 1264.

The greatest building period in the Middle Ages was the C14 and it was then that Warwick underwent a transformation. Its principal features belong to an extended and largely uninterrupted campaign by the Beauchamps, Earls of Warwick, mainly from the 1330s to 1393/4. It seems possible that one family of master masons was employed for much of this period, i.e. *Thomas Montfort* (fl. 1346–7) and *John Montfort* (fl. 1376–1405) who also worked for the Beauchamps at Elmley Castle (Worcs.). Creating a setting for chivalry and entertainment, the Beauchamps were building for show as much as for defence. As John Goodall observes, the naming of the two great towers after Caesar and the legendary Guy of Warwick reflects this concern for historical heroes and chivalric romance.

Despite detailed study and analysis* the precise chronology remains uncertain. Work on the domestic range may have commenced under Guy, the 10th Earl who inherited in 1298 and died in 1315, though could be later. Due to Thomas I Beauchamp, 11th Earl (who came into his majority in 1329 and died 1369), are the gatehouse (i.e. the Clock Tower), Caesar's Tower and the wall between. The Watergate Tower is mid-C14. Thomas II, 12th Earl (†1401) completed Guy's Tower and much of the wall between it and the gatehouse. In 1423 the 13th Earl built a long-vanished stable of great size, decorated with plaster of Paris, the first recorded decorative use of the material in England. Building resumed in the later C15. After the death of Richard Neville, the 16th Earl (the 'Kingmaker'), the castle came into the possession of George, Duke of Clarence (1471–8), created Earl of Warwick in 1472. He may have built the Spy Tower. Between 1478 and 1485 his brother, later Richard III, began 'a mighty tower . . . for to shoot out gunns', represented by the half-finished Bear and Clarence towers. The castle then remained royal, until in 1547 it was granted to John Dudley, who was made Earl of Warwick. In 1590, at the death of Ambrose Dudley, the Crown had the castle back, and it was then granted in 1604 to Fulke Greville, later created Lord Brooke by James I in 1621.

Surveys in 1590 and 1601 reported the castle in poor condition. At about this time, although for whom and for what purpose is unclear, *Robert Smythson* made a plan showing the configuration of the buildings then on site. Following his acquisition in 1604, Fulke Greville refurbished the accommodation – principally the hall range – and laid out the gardens. Work was completed *c.* 1617. He spent £450 in 1610 alone, and Dugdale says that the works cost him £20,000. Of this, little visible trace remains, except perhaps in the SW range. There was damage in the Civil War, but from 1664 the 4th and 5th Lords Brooke (1658–77; 1677–1710) embarked on a substantial refurbishment programme of which much can still be seen in the state apartments, including woodwork by *Roger & William Hurlbutt* and plasterwork by *Pettifer & Pelton*. The dates were *c.* 1669–81. A phase of improvements began after the coming of age in 1740 of Francis Greville, 8th Lord Brooke (he became the 1st Earl Brooke of Warwick Castle in 1746, and 1st Earl of Warwick of the new creation in 1759). He commissioned *Capability Brown* to develop the parkland s of the river and to landscape the courtyard. Inside the castle, there were Gothick improvements mocked by Horace Walpole. The earl refurbished the chapel in 1748, and in 1763–4 engaged *Timothy Lightoler* to create a new entrance and dining room in front of the Great Hall. He also commissioned the Canaletto paintings of the castle, 1748–52. Work for the 2nd Earl (1773–1816) included the enlargement of the castle grounds with new curtain walling and lodge. *Ambrose Poynter* remodelled the

---

*Chiefly by Richard Morris in 1986 and Mark Booth and Nicholas Palmer in the 1990s.

Great Hall for the 3rd Earl in 1830–1, but this and much of the
E range were destroyed in a fire in 1871. *Anthony Salvin*, who had
previously restored parts of the castle for the 4th Earl from 1856,
undertook the restoration completed *c.* 1875. The Grevilles
retained ownership until 1978 when the castle and contents were
sold to Madame Tussauds (part of the Merlin Entertainments
Group since 2007).

Description

The MOUND of Warwick Castle, as has been said, goes back to
the time of William the Conqueror. As it now is, it is all landscaped, with walls climbing up from the NE and S sides and a
SHELL KEEP with two turrets on top. Much of this is a historicist recreation, partly of Fulke Greville's time and partly C18,
but using the surviving remains of the late C13 keep. *Job Collins*
built one of the towers in 1768, and the other is by *William*

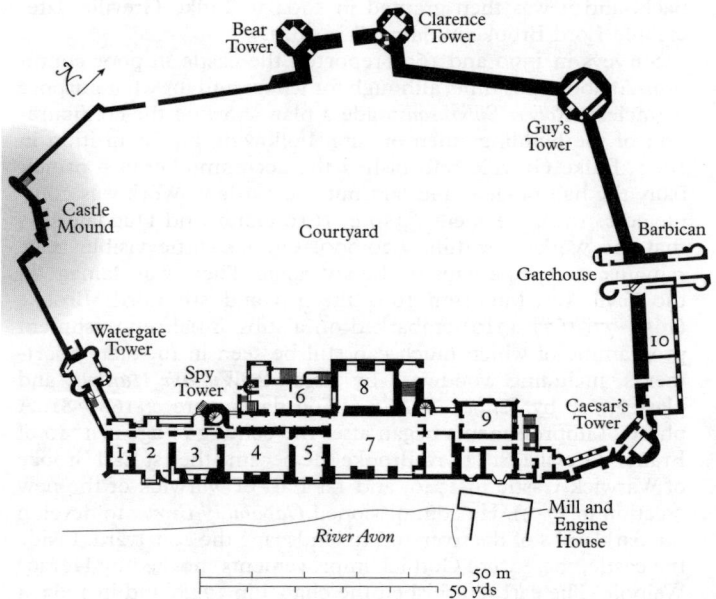

1	Blue Boudoir
2	Queen Anne Bedroom
3	Green Drawing Room
4	Cedar Drawing Room
5	Red Drawing Room
6	Chapel
7	Great Hall
8	Dining Room
9	Library
10	Brewhouse, Wash House and Laundry

Warwick, Warwick Castle.
Plan

Eborall, 1775. To the NE, a pointed archway cut into the wall in the 1760s and widened in 1775 when the gardens were developed. The CLARENCE TOWER and BEAR TOWER are both polygonal and low, and the archway between them, with the bridge over the dry moat, was made *c*. 1800. The towers themselves were originally turrets of the big gunnery tower begun by Richard III, but left unfinished. In the stretch of wall immediately E, a projecting crow's nest, probably *c*. 1430.

GUY'S TOWER, completed in 1393/4,* is 128 ft (39 metres) high. It is twelve-sided and has machicolation at the top. In two angles only, one-light windows with ogee heads and transoms. Inside, the GUARD ROOM on the fourth floor is hexagonal with radial ribs of hollow-chamfered section. Deep window reveals. Below are one room on each floor with two smaller rooms l. and r., including a garderobe. The vaults are cross-ribbed. Here we see multiple tiers of vaulted chambers (cf. Gaunt's Strong Tower at Kenilworth of *c*. 1373–80). There are two staircases, one of them (N) for express access to the top, i.e. without any openings to the intermediate floors. In the ground-floor room, a fine late C14 tiled pavement discovered in 2000 and restored in 2009.

The GATEHOUSE (or CLOCK TOWER) has an archway to the courtyard with semi-octagonal responds and a double-chamfered arch. The windows are again ogee-headed, but there is no machicolation. The angle turrets are polygonal to the inside, rounded to the outside. The gateway has two rib-vaulted bays and then to the outside a pointed tunnel-vault with oblong holes for harassing an aggressor. The upper rooms have single-chamfered ribs. A portcullis (a replica) is still in position. At the top of the newel staircases are pretty sexpartite rib-vaults (or umbrella vaults). Particularly intriguing are the bridges between the tops of the towers.

The BARBICAN consists of walls l. and r., polygonal turrets at the front, and an archway with a pointed tunnel-vault. Portcullis and murder holes again. The windows into the alley between the barbican and gatehouse are of two and three ogee-headed lights. Loopholes in the parapets, side walls and low down above the moat. It is clearly earlier than the mid-C14 gatehouse and possibly pre-dates the death of Earl Guy in 1315. When the gatehouse was built it was skilfully integrated. It seems likely, indeed, that the gatehouse and barbican constituted a single residence, as at Arundel and Alnwick.

CAESAR'S TOWER is 147 ft (45 metres) high, of irregular shape and machicolated. Its windows are like those of Guy's Tower. Inside, the apartments on two floors (the TOWER SUITES) have cross-ribbed vaults in two bays with single-chamfered ribs. These chambers have big fireplaces by *Mr Wilson*,† 1670.

---

*Payments of £395 5s. 2d. to masons and quarrymen engaged on the tower and for carriage of stone are recorded in 1393–4.

†Probably *William Wilson*, then a carver and statuary, but later the architect for rebuilding St Mary's church.

The staircase arrangement is as in Guy's Tower, with umbrella vaults like the gatehouse. In the basement, a dungeon with rib-vaults in two bays.

Outside, along the SE wall between the barbican and Caesar's Tower, is a low embattled range of 1669, originally a brew-house, washhouse and laundry, later a library and armoury. The masons were *Samuel Dunckley* and *Francis Overton*. The double windows resemble those of the contemporary altera-tions at the W end of the S range.

So to the main range of living quarters, the SOUTH RANGE. To the river it presents a dramatically high, sheer front with a variety of windows. The three main floors of the castle stand above a 35-ft (10.5-metre) buttressed stone base. The skyline punctuated by battlements, chimneys and turrets, with Cae-sar's Tower at the corner. This spectacular aspect has changed little apart from alterations to the windows, traceable through C17–C19 illustrations. In Canaletto's paintings, done in 1748–9, all the windows were sashed except for one still existing C14 twin basement window and two large ones on the first floor belonging to the Cedar Drawing Room (*see* below), which Philip Yorke described in 1748 as 'new made in the Gothic style and very pretty'. Now it is all mixed Gothic, apparently from the C13 to the C19 though largely of *Salvin*'s remodelling in 1856–75. In the SW angle, the state apartments of 1669–78 with distinctively C17 fenestration.

To understand the corresponding (i.e. N) front to the court-yard one has to appreciate that the ground level was raised by *Capability Brown* for the 1st Earl Brooke in 1753–5 (cf. the partially underground windows in the wings l. and r.). The centrepiece is an oblong three-bay projection incorporating a porch open on two sides. This is by *Timothy Lightoler*, 1763–4, but in Jacobean mode, with mullioned-and-transomed windows and battlements. It stands in front of the Great Hall and houses the State Dining Room. A painting in the style of Canaletto by John Pye, 1765, shows this front after the works were completed. Today the whole range corresponds in most respects with what Pye painted, although the details (e.g. windows) are again mostly Victorian. Taken as a whole, the range displays considerable variety. To the l. of the centre is a short stretch of two-light windows and then a block of two three-light windows and a polygonal chimney turret between. The details here are of *Salvin*'s post-1871 restoration. In the angle between this range and the present porch, a stair-turret. In Smythson's time this seems to have led off the grand entrance to the hall which was through an independent tower approached from the W by a wide outer staircase.[*] The present grand stair is Salvin's, replacing what Lightoler had provided in 1763–4.[†]

---

[*] The arrangement was confirmed by excavations under the dining room in 1992.
[†] Brown had already rebuilt the porch to the hall as recently as 1753.

To the r. is yet more of projections and recessions. This part was unharmed by the 1871 fire. First the chapel, also projecting. Another polygonal turret between two Victorian two-light windows. One low window with Y-tracery and then, standing out further into the courtyard, an early C15 two-storey square block with a stair-turret on the side. Set back to the r., the SPY TOWER, placed to one side of the SW range, largely glazed, and supporting a higher stair-turret. This is seemingly of the first half of the C16 (cf. 1530s Melbury House, Dorset), but Booth and Palmer have suggested that it was built between 1471 and 1478 during the tenure of the Duke of Clarence (†1478). The argument is that its construction was linked to Clarence's plans (as described by John Rous, writing in 1484) for a pleasance to overlook the park. The tower has a prospect or banqueting chamber on the top floor. The suggestion is supported by John Goodall who points to the details, especially the frame-like window surrounds, which are typical of buildings in the royal orbit in the time of Edward IV. The final section to the SW, embattled and generously glazed, was probably rebuilt or refronted for Fulke Greville (as suggested by Farr, Booth and Palmer) c. 1617. The elevation pleasantly complements the Spy Tower.

To see what is old, what is C17, and what is Victorian one must examine the INTERIOR. The GROUND FLOOR (now basement) has heavily rib-vaulted undercrofts extending for 200 ft (61 metres) below the state apartments from the bay E of the Great Hall right along to the Green Room. These, and by implication the original superstructures above, are of two periods. First came the great chamber block, i.e. the two-naved servants' hall with the two rooms at either end. The hall (now the restaurant) is most impressive, of four bays, with short quatrefoil piers and single-chamfered ribs. It must either pre-date Earl Guy's death in 1315 or else be soon after 1329. Later, and after 1329, are the two high-status vaulted lodging units under the hall, together with the vault under the central part of the chapel. Above ground level little survives of the Beauchamp family apartments but their arrangement is suggested by what lies below.

On the principal floor the GREAT HALL lies on the river front, lit by big three-light windows with stained glass in the tracery lights. More heraldic glass in the windows to the passage in the wall higher up. The Baronial roof of 1872–5 is *Salvin*'s. Plain ashlar walls hung with weaponry etc. Of the three E pointed arches (originally leading to the buttery and kitchens) two are substantially early C14, with two slight chamfers. Mighty chimneypiece with two lions' heads, after 1871. The elaborately carved sideboard, the Kenilworth Buffet, is a High Victorian super-piece by *Cookes & Sons*, 1851. To the N is *Lightoler*'s STATE DINING ROOM with a ceiling in Jacobean Revival style by *Robert Moore* of Warwick, 1765. Big Adamish chimneypiece. Two tremendous gilt picture frames of the same time, by *Benjamin King*.

The STATE ROOMS are on the S front W of the hall and form a suite remodelled for the 4th and 5th Lords Brooke during the last third of the C17. The alignment of the doors exemplifies an enfilade in the latest French fashion. First, the RED DRAWING ROOM, no longer C17, but largely of the 1760s. The ceiling is by *Moore*, *c*. 1765 but in an antiquarian style. After that comes the splendid CEDAR DRAWING ROOM. The cedar panelling is by *William & Roger Hurlbutt*, who were at work at the castle 1669–81 and also panelled the other state rooms. The plaster ceiling with panels and rich foliage framing is by *James Pettifer* (*Pettifer & Pelton*), early 1670s (cf. Sudbury Hall, Derbys.). Rococo sconces; large late C18 chimneypiece. In the GREEN DRAWING ROOM, the coffered ceiling of small octagons looks Early Victorian but it is by *Moore*, 1760–5, and based on a design from the ceiling of the Temple of the Sun at Palmyra illustrated by Robert Wood (1753). The colouring, by *Oram* of London, dates from *c*. 1845. The white chimneypiece is late C18. Then two rooms in the later C17 block at the SW corner. First, the QUEEN ANNE BEDROOM* again has a sumptuous late C17 ceiling, reworked in 1789 by *William Hanwell*. The pattern with small panels and a cross of broad foliated bands is unusual. Fine wall decoration too (partly concealed by tapestries). The chimneypiece is late C18, by *Richard Westmacott I*. Then, at the corner, the BLUE BOUDOIR. Small and intimate, with fine views to the park S and W. It has the most gorgeous of Pettifer's ceilings. There are also garlands etc. on the overmantel, but these are Victorian woodcarvings.

N of these, the ARMOURY PASSAGE leads back into the CHAPEL PASSAGE, leading back to the Great Hall. This has Gothick vaulting in the manner of Lightoler's Beauchamp Chapel reredos at St Mary's and must be 1750s. The CHAPEL is entered through a lobby to the l. of the passage. The walls of this are partly medieval, though altered in 1617 when the chapel was enlarged and again in the mid C18 and 1883–5. The Gothick ceiling with its shields and pendants probably dates from the 'fitting up' recorded by Philip Yorke in 1748, for which Geoffrey Tyack suggests that *Daniel Garrett*, a protégé of Lord Burlington, may have been responsible. – STAINED GLASS. Assembled bits of the C15, bits of the C16 and C17 from the Netherlands, and some in the E window of 1759.[†] – Two N windows by *Clayton & Bell*, probably 1883–5. – The Campden stone panelling at the front and the SCREEN at the back are also 1883–5, along with other FITTINGS.

The domestic wing, E of the hall, was all redone by *Salvin* after the 1871 fire. A remarkably complete set of rooms on two floors, all accessible to the public. Retiring rooms downstairs,

---

*So called after the state bed and other furnishings acquired by the 1st and 2nd Earls in the late C18. They previously belonged to Queen Anne.

[†]The E window includes some medieval glass from Tattershall (Lincs.) removed from the church in 1757, given by Lord Exeter of Burghley to the Earl of Warwick.

including the LADIES' BOUDOIR in Louis XV style. The best room is the LIBRARY, lavishly decorated by *G.E. Fox* during the post-fire reconstruction. Bookcases in the Italian Renaissance style with painted decoration on the pilasters. Much gilding. Big fireplace, rather François I than Italian. Coffered ceiling.

The WATERGATE TOWER, SE of the mound, mid-C14, has four polygonal turrets clustered round a central tower. Hexagonal entrance passage, rib-vaulted with central roundel and shield. An unusual form (cf. the gatehouses at Denbigh and Caernarvon castles and the porch of St Mary Redcliffe's church at Bristol). All restored by *Salvin*, 1859–60, including the top floor (then a BILLIARD ROOM) with its open timber roof.

STABLES COURTYARD. NE of the castle towards the town, and originally backing onto the road to the old bridge. The new stables of 1768–71 are by *Lightoler*, replacing stables built near the barbican in 1664–7. Palladian, but nothing special. Four-centred arches. U-plan, with a wide courtyard.

CONSERVATORY. 1786–7 by *Eborall*. Pointed openings with Y glazing bars. Built to display the WARWICK VASE. This C2 Roman vase decorated with silenus heads in high relief was found in fragments by Sir William Hamilton near Hadrian's Villa at Tivoli in 1770. After reconstruction, it was acquired by the 2nd Earl in 1778 and at first displayed in the courtyard. The original vase is of white marble, 5 ft 6 in. (1.7 metres) high.*

The GARDENS were laid out by *Capability Brown*. He began work in 1749, removing what remained of the C17 formal gardens. The present Rose Garden NE of the castle was recreated in 1986 to a design by *Robert Marnock*, 1868. The hexagonal Peacock or Italian Garden in front of the conservatory is also by Marnock, again restored.

At the foot of Caesar's Tower, on the river, is the MILL AND ENGINE HOUSE. There was a watermill here from the C14, rebuilt by *Lightoler*, 1767–8. Late Georgian Gothic; embattled. Restored in 2002, it contains working machinery of a type similar to what was used here from 1894 to 1940 when the building contained electrical generating plant.

CASTLE LODGE, 1796. At the entrance from the new bridge opened in 1793. Very blocky, with simple parapets and tunnel-vault. A driveway carved in the solid rock leads up to the castle. The curtain walls from here round into Castle Lane and beyond are of same period, when the grounds were enlarged by taking in parts of the town.

Lastly, the CASTLE PARK, across the river to the S. No longer part of the castle estate, but still intact as open parkland. Created between 1743 and 1789 for Francis (the 1st Earl) and his son, who acquired land between the castle and its historic

---

*It was sold by Lord Brooke in 1977 and is now in the Burrell Collection in Glasgow. The conservatory now contains a replica made for The Tussauds Group in 1991.

warren at the SW of the enlarged park. Brown was engaged in 1748 and in 1755 he was working on the Temple Park. Some of Brown's planting remains. In 1761 he dammed the Ram Brook (now the Tach Brook) to form a lake, enlarged to form the New Waters in 1787–9. The park had been enlarged to the E after the diversion of the Banbury Road in 1782–7.

A key feature of the new park was the carriage ride and circuit, made possible by the erection of a wooden bridge at Leafield in 1758. The highlight of the drive was the view from Lodge Hill across the Avon valley towards the castle (illustrated by Paul Sandby in 1776).

SPIERS LODGE, 1m. S of the castle. Set on a wooded bank at Lodge Hill on the site of a C13 hunting lodge. Gothick and said to be of 1748, although Timothy Mowl has pointed out its striking similarity to a lodge illustrated in *Lightoler*'s 1762 pattern book and suggests a later date, *c.* 1765.* Oblong and cruciform. Most windows with arched lights. Four-centred doorway. Embattled pediment. Inside one ribbed ceiling.

LEAFIELD BRIDGE (or Mylne Bridge), 350 yds W of the lodge. Designed in 1765 to replace the wooden bridge and built 1772–6. By *Robert Mylne*. Single span; rusticated. Steeply angled deck. Balustraded parapet with *Coade* stone medallions set in the piers.

TOWN WALLS, GATES AND LORD LEYCESTER HOSPITAL

The town was walled by the C14. Of the original wall there is a good section N of the West Gate facing Bowling Green Street, still visible behind the Guild Cottages (p. 684). Another short section by the East Gate towards The Butts. By the C16 much of the wall had been demolished, but the ancient E and W gates were preserved. Both have chapels on top.

EAST GATE, bestriding the junction of Jury Street and Smith Street, was built before 1426. Plain and heavy gateway with pointed tunnel-vault and machicolation over the arch, and to the N side a pedestrian arch, but above it is the delightful chapel of ST PETER (now residential). Of the medieval chapel little remains. It was probably rebuilt in the late C18† although the outline of the tower – if not the actual fabric – belongs to earlier improvements. Fulke Weale gave a turret and clock in 1729 and this is shown in the Bucks' panorama dated 1731. The tower is particularly fanciful. It has tall corner pinnacles and ends in a recessed square stage of timber with traceried sides accompanied by flying buttresses. The top renewed in 1879. On the S side, the chapel fenestration is typical of the C18 in that it is symmetrical: two lights, four lights, two lights.

---

*Tim Mowl and Brian Earnshaw, *Trumpet at a Distant Gate: The Lodge as a Prelude to the Country House* (1985) pp. 60 and 66.

†The chapel is traditionally dated to 1788 and attributed to Francis Hiorne. However, Steven Wallsgrove (*pers. com.*) has found that the Warwick Corporation records tell a different story, referring to work at the East Gate in 1774–6 and 1790, with Hiorne being mentioned only in 1776.

Battlements and corner pinnacles. To the E, windows in two tiers and a stepped gable. The mighty base was Gothicized in the later C18 too, with machicolation over the gateway, little quatrefoils in the embattled parapet and dummy cross-loops in the walls.

On the W wall below the East Gate, a DRINKING FOUNTAIN, 1859. Nearby, a cast-iron PILLAR BOX. A Greek Doric column, by *Smith & Hawkes* of the Eagle Foundry, Birmingham, 1856. Another, identical, outside the E entrance to the West Gate at the other end of the main thoroughfare.

WEST GATE, closing the W end of High Street, existed in 1123 and already had a chapel above. Both were reconstructed in the C14. The present gate is a most impressive affair. The tunnel-like archway is very long, because it consists of two different parts. Actually it represents three different periods. Inside, in the living rock are semi-octagonal wall-shafts which look C13. The vault, a pointed tunnel-vault with very closely set, slightly chamfered transverse arches, and the E entrance, two-centred, with two slight chamfers, may be early C14. The W part of the gate is an early Perp addition and has a four-centred arch and a tierceron star-vault. This part carries the tower of the CHAPEL OF ST JAMES, which now belongs to the LORD LEYCESTER HOSPITAL founded by Robert Dudley, Earl of Leicester, in 1571.

30

Leicester acquired the chapel and the adjacent buildings that had belonged to the town's medieval guilds (*see below*) and established a hospital, a Maison Dieu, with accommodation for the master and twelve brethren. Thus the buildings predate the foundation. The survival is completely fortuitous, for they escaped destruction under Henry VIII and again in the 1694 fire. Although rather altered, they form a delightful group. The fall of the street, the appearance of the hospital on a kind of terrace, and the variety of forms create a perfect ensemble.

First, the CHAPEL. It stands high above the street, raised also from the terrace. To the W, the tower presents a sheer face with the lower archway below. The tower is a Perp addition (as noted above) and projects W of the original town wall and gate. It is in three stages with angle buttresses and crenellated at the top. The chapel is reached from steps to the E; the walkway to the S entrance passes through a line of C19 flying buttresses. The ancient chapel was probably rebuilt by Thomas Beauchamp, Earl of Warwick, in the late C14, but its present appearance is largely due to restoration by *Thomas Garner* in 1865–6.* The restoration included the E window, and only the heads of the side windows are C14. The Perp arch from the tower to the chapel has sunk wave mouldings. The interior remains almost entirely as Garner designed it, complete with fittings of 1865–6; it is still used daily and lit only by candle-

---

*It was an independent commission, although Garner may have been recommended by his old master, G. G. Scott, who had inspected the chapel in 1864.

light. – *Godwin* TILES. – Alabaster REREDOS, by *R. L. Boulton*. – Excellent SCREEN and STALLS, carved by *Farmer & Brindley*. – Screen GATES and metal CANDELABRA by *Skidmore*. – STAINED GLASS, 1866. E and S windows by *Clayton & Bell*. – Annunciation window over the S door by *Morris & Co*. – Garner gave the *Hardman* ALTAR CROSS and provided the sanctuary TAPESTRY hangings, woven in France to his own design. – PAINTING. Ascension by *James Millar* of Birmingham, 1798.

The two fine timber-framed houses r. of the approach were added to the hospital estate only in the mid C20. Both are C16 with C17 additions. The one nearest the corner of Brook Street is a Wealden house, one of several in Warwick (cf. Smith Street and West Street). The other was formerly the ANCHOR INN (No. 56), with a picturesque (not wholly reliable) porch and a jettied wing (the MALT HOUSE) projecting from the back with a splendid display of Elizabethan geometrical patterning. These were restored in the 1960s to provide accommodation for the brethren.

The premises of the HOSPITAL proper begin after these with the stone ARCHWAY, Perp with a two-centred arch. In 1571 Leicester took over the premises of the combined guilds of Holy Trinity and St George. The buildings had been created in the C14, but must have been rebuilt in the late C15. The earliest known views show none of the timber framing, which was exposed during a restoration undertaken between 1830 and 1851. While much of what we see is original, some is embellished, and the splendid courtyard front of the MASTER'S HOUSE is pure C19 pastiche. Some of the C19 elaboration has since been undone. *P.B. Chatwin* restored the GUILD HALL in 1950–1, and *D.A. James* undertook a restoration of the rest of the hospital between 1958 and 1966.

The front towards the street, or rather the terrace, has the first floor oversailing on thin, concavely forward-curving brackets, and is itself provided with a moulded bressumer and closely spaced studs. One enters the courtyard through a narrow passage, timber-framed. Above this GATEWAY, two jettied storeys with bargeboarded gables and, on the inside, a little oriel in the gable. Much of this is C19. Straight ahead on the N side is the MASTER'S HOUSE, its façade of *c*. 1830 with overdone details, and especially lots of plaster bears with ragged staffs. On the W, the GREAT HALL, with stone base and simple framing above. The E range has wooden galleries on both levels, elegantly detailed with four-centred arches. The rail of the outer stair in the SE angle is Elizabethan. This also leads to the GUILD HALL on the upper floor of the street wing. It houses the Regimental Museum of the Queen's Royal Hussars. It has an open roof with collar-beams on arched braces, one of two former carved pendants, and purlins on arched braces, their spandrels with varied foliage carving. The museum extends into the Chaplain's Hall in the upper room of the E wing. This has a restored roof with some decorated spandrels. The GREAT HALL in the W range is approached from the terrace. The side walls are stone to window level. The roof has tie-beams, collar-beams and queenposts. Traceried spandrels. At the N end two blocked doorways. They belonged to the screens passage.

In the GARDEN of the hospital a re-erected late Norman ARCH with eroded chevron and nailhead decoration. This was found during the 1865–6 chapel restoration. Also a large stone URN with the date 1800, but said to be Roman and to come from Egypt. In the knot garden, a metal bear and ragged staff sculpture by *Rachel Higgins*, 1998.

PUBLIC BUILDINGS

SHIRE HALL, Market Place, etc. A complex of several buildings unified by past or present county council ownership. They include the county offices linked to the Market Place frontage, the Shire Hall on Northgate Street and the former gaol (later barracks) at the NE corner of the triangular site towards Barrack Street. Formerly associated with this group were the houses along the N side of Northgate Street, used by the education department until 2006, and the 1882–3 county offices building at their N end (*see* Perambulation 1).

Begin with the SHIRE HALL, Northgate Street. On a site used for the county courts from the C16 until 2010 when the Justice Centre opened in Leamington (p. 419). The present Shire Hall replaced an earlier one of 1676–81 by *William Hurlbutt*, sketched by Hawksmoor *c.* 1683, which survived the fire although all else around it was destroyed. Designed by *Sanderson Miller* and built by *William & David Hiorne* and *Job Collins*, 1753–8. It is a remarkable job. Hollington Stone (refaced in 1947–8), one tall storey only, nine bays, with a three-bay pediment on Corinthian half-columns. Corinthian pilasters also, doubled at the angles, and garlands in the frieze. The decoration on the pediment dates from 1948, it having been plain previously. Rusticated base and raised entrance. Inside, the whole length is one room, 93 ft by 34 ft (28.3 by 10.4 metres), stone-faced, with pilasters and Corinthian columns and another garland frieze. Coffered ceiling with plasterwork by *Robert Moore*. The two identical courtrooms are octagonal, with free-standing Corinthian columns, good stucco ceilings, octagonal lanterns and balconies with iron railings. These were open to the main hall through the columns before they were walled in, probably in 1780. At the back, an octagonal jury chamber. Below are the cells belonging to the courts, and access to the DUNGEON to the N under the former county gaol. *William Hurlbutt* built a new gaol and House of Correction in 1677–86. These were destroyed in the fire, but the dungeon survived, an octagonal vaulted room, deep in the ground. Its construction was ordered in 1680 and it was used until after John Howard's prison reforms in the late C18. Prisoners were

p. 50

shackled at night to a chain secured to eight posts in the floor. For the rebuilt gaol, *see* below.

To the s of the Shire Hall the JUDGE'S LODGING, a decent, spacious, early C19 house, ashlar-faced. Rusticated ground floor; porch with unfluted Ionic columns. The house is by *Henry Hakewill* and was built in 1814–16. Inside, a good open-well stair. Dining room fireplace of grey marble with incised Greek key decoration. Yet further s, utilitarian, ashlar-faced Neo-Georgian offices by *G.R. Barnsley* (*County Architect*) of 1955 (No. 7) and 1963 (Nos. 3–5).

At the other end, to the N, the mood changes. Here another long front, at least as impressive, but where the Shire Hall is festive, this is sombre, almost sinister. It had to be, for it was built as the COUNTY GAOL. It is by *Thomas Johnson* and dates from 1779–83. This is an astonishingly early date for a building decidedly in the Ledoux style. Elephant-grey sandstone. Eleven bays with a three-bay centre with pediment. Triple archway below. Attached, sturdy, unfluted Doric columns with the most rudely simplified details (e.g. the abaci). Full triglyph frieze. According to the model in the County Museum the columns were meant to be fluted, and they would have been among the earliest revived Greek Doric columns in England and indeed in Europe. Round the corner in Barrack Street the gaol continues, but it belongs mainly to another scheme by *Henry Couchman* (County Surveyor), 1792–3. In the middle, an entrance block of three arches (now blocked), flanked by stretches of sheer wall, originally windowless. The single bay at the N end of Johnson's Northgate Street frontage is also Couchman's, part of the 'court of safety' ordered by the justices.

Of the gaol only the outer walls to Northgate and Barrack streets remain, retained when militia barracks were erected on the gaol site in 1861–2 and later incorporated in new COUNTY COUNCIL OFFICES created within the walls by *A.C. Bunch* (County Architect), 1929–32. Two courtyard ranges, Neo-Georgian in brick with stone portals and connecting archways. Attractively and skilfully done. Carving and decorative iron-work by the *Bromsgrove Guild*, the heraldic glass in the North-gate Street entrance by *A.J. Davies*, 1932.

Then the council chamber and the offices on the s façade to Old Square, completed as the first phase of further development under *Barnsley* in 1955–8. The council chamber is polygonal to the exterior but seated inside in the round. It has armorial carving by *Walter Ritchie*, and engraved window panes by *W. Stanier*. The frontage to the Old Square offices is conventional enough. Brick with thin stone window surrounds and a corner block with stone cladding. The Market Place range adjoining, the bridge to Abbotsford (*see* Perambulation 1) and the Barrack Street façade are a Modernist continuation, by *Eric Davies* (County Architect), 1961–6. Concrete frame, Hornton stone panels and glass, with thin columns and county arms over the entrance. Facing the old courtyard behind, an abstract relief bear and staff medallion by *Davies* with *Alfred Merricks*, 1964. In front, a metal sculpture of Heron catching Perch by *Rachel Higgins*, 2000.

On the N side of Barrack Street, dominating the approach from Saltisford, is a separate county building by *Davies*, 1972–3. Three office storeys with car park below. Brutalist, concrete and glass, and quite wrong for its setting.

COURT HOUSE, Jury Street. Warwick at its best, and the grand completion of the quadrivium at the Cross envisaged by the Fire Commissioners in 1695. The old Court House (i.e. the meeting place of the Corporation) had been on this site since the late C16 but the building survived the fire. With a grander building in mind, the Corporation purchased adjoining properties from 1709 with further acquisitions in 1724–5. The present building was designed and built in 1725–6 by *Francis Smith*, with furnishing and decoration taking a little longer: final payments were made in 1731. Smith, whose portrait adorns the upper chamber, was an alderman. Other Corporation members were also involved in the building and furnishing, some of them veterans of the post-fire rebuilding. This was their showpiece and they spent too much. The cost was c. £2,254 and it left the Corporation in debt. It all ended in litigation and from 1737 to 1761 the new Court House was in sequestration. That, however, is another story. The building is of five bays and two storeys. Stone, rusticated throughout. Arched windows at ground floor, straight-headed above with moulded aprons. The upper floor has Doric pilasters and a triglyph frieze. Modillions to the eaves cornice. The parapet is balustraded and originally carried bellied obelisks. In the centre in a niche, a cast-lead figure of Justice by *Thomas Stayner* of London, 1731, with decoratively enriched coats of arms above and below. The front gates and the ironwork on the window ledges are by *Benjamin Taylor* and *Thomas Paris*, 1726. The principal upper room has fluted Ionic pilasters and a coved ceiling. Some C18 fittings remain and there is a fine later C19 fireplace and overmantel by the Warwick carver *T.H. Kendall*. The rear elevation was refaced and extended in Jacobean style in red and blueish brick with stone dressings in 1858. Adjoining Pageant House (No. 2 Jury Street, *see* p. 680) was acquired in 1908 and the combined premises back on to the PAGEANT GARDEN. In 2012–13 the Court House was refurbished with improvements to its Yeomanry Museum, ballroom and council chamber and a new visitor centre.

MARKET HALL, Market Place (Museum). By *William Hurlbutt*, 'carpenter', 1669–70. Free-standing. Sandstone ashlar. Two storeys, with hipped roof. Cupola, balustraded roof platform and dormers replaced by the county council, 1963–4. The ground floor of five by three bays is arcaded. Upper windows with moulded surrounds. Moulded eaves cornice with modillions. Inside, internal pillars and a square stone staircase block. The sides were open until 1879 when *F.H. Moore* inserted the windows. The permanent exhibits include the SHELDON

TAPESTRY, probably woven at Barcheston by *Richard Hyckes* for Ralph Sheldon, late 1580s. A topographical map of Warwickshire with miniature views of buildings, towns and landscape features.

WARWICK SCHOOL, Myton Road. 1878–9 by *John Cundall*. Symmetrical pile of brick with Bath stone dressings. Jacobean centre, but three turrets have quite un-Jacobean pyramid roofs. The HEADMASTER'S HOUSE (r.) and CHAPEL also 1878–9. The chapel was extended by adding a chancel in 1893–4, by *W.F. Unsworth*, and the w gallery and vestry in 1925. – Collegiate STALLS etc., 1894. – STAINED GLASS. E window by *Henry Holiday*, 1902–4. – w window by *Francis H. Spear*, 1925, and two s windows (moved from the vestry in 2005) also by Spear, 1926. WAY HOUSE, a little E on Myton Road, built as the junior school by *F.H. Moore*, 1888–9. Of recent additions, the best are the THORNTON BUILDING, 2008, and the HALSE SPORTS PAVILION, 2013, both by *Brown Matthews*. These face opposite sides of the playing fields. Towards the w of the site, the CHESHIRE SCIENCE BUILDING is by *Brown Matthews*, 2006–7; *Robothams* designed the MASEFIELD CENTRE, 1998–9; and the BRIDGE HOUSE THEATRE is by *Michael Reardon & Associates*, 1999–2000.

KING'S HIGH SCHOOL FOR GIRLS (KHS), Smith Street. Founded in 1879. LANDOR HOUSE in Smith Street (*see* Perambulation 4) was the original school, but the site now extends to the w along Chapel Street and The Butts. The former Chapel Street School (*F.H. Moore*, 1896) is the KHS Creative Arts Centre. New buildings include the OCTAGON BUILDING language centre, 1991, fronting Chapel Street, and the SIXTH FORM CENTRE by *Robothams*, 2006, with three-storeyed gabled elevation to The Butts and a less conformist frontage with glazed atrium to the school courtyard.

Two former BOARD SCHOOLS, both by *George H. Cox* of Birmingham, 1883–4, both with later additions by *F.H. Moore*. COTEN END is set back from the road and quite plain, but has big windows rising above the roof-line into gables. At WESTGATE, Bowling Green Street, the windows rise instead into dormers and the whole building is attractively detailed.

p. 62

Warwick, Warwick School, perspective of principal front.
Engraving, 1879

The style is Queen Anne, after Norman Shaw, with pretty pargetting in the gables and pediments. The corner block originally carried a tall and ornate cupola, removed after 1905.

PLAYBOX THEATRE, in the grounds of Aylesbury Secondary School, Stratford Road. Purpose-built performance venue for young people, by *Glenn Howells Architects*, 1998–9. Timber and metal cladding. Foyer with glass screen to covered outdoor area. Compact stage and auditorium.

WARWICK RACECOURSE, Hampton Road. There has been racing at Warwick since 1707 and part of the GRANDSTAND, although much altered and enlarged, dates from 1809. It was refurbished with a new roof canopy by *Hitchman Stone Architects*, 2010. The buildings include the PADDOCK PAVILION, by *Corstorphine & Wright*, 1989, with curved steel roof and balconies.

CASTLE BRIDGE, over the River Avon on the southern approach road diverted by Act of Parliament of 1788. Built in 1789–93 by *William Eborall*, but possibly to a design by *Robert Mylne*, who built the Leafield Bridge (p. 670) and gave advice about a new bridge in 1774.* A single-span arch of over 100 ft (30 metres) and a dignified balustrade.

PERAMBULATIONS

There are five. The historic town centre is one, and additional perambulations take in the town beyond the original walled area from the W round to the S. Warwick has no suburbs proper, except perhaps for Emscote, but the few outer districts are described at the end.

1. The town centre (the original walled town)

To explore the area of the original walled town, we begin at the West Gate (*see* p. 671) and proceed directly to the East Gate (*see* p. 670) along the main W–E thoroughfare. Warwick is built on a hill. The ground rises steeply to the High Street and then descends along Jury Street to the E. This route allows for the simplest explanation of the visual impact of the great fire of 1694 and the subsequent rebuilding.

The approach from the W is the least altered entrance to the town. As one arrives in HIGH STREET past the West Gate the road climbs sharply with raised walkways either side and two rows of timber-framed houses facing each other. On the N, the Lord Leycester Hospital (*see* p. 671). On the S Nos. 41 to the end, all C16, and the last house (No. 45), with heavy timbers and overhanging wings with gables, especially good. These escaped the great fire, but narrowly.

---

* *David and William Saunders* made a model of the new bridge in 1788 and were involved in its construction.

The fire began to the rear of No. 45, off Leycester Place, destroying the Quaker meeting house (No. 39; for its replacement *see* Churches) and quickly spreading all along the High Street on both sides (from No. 44 on the N) to the Cross and beyond. From here, all is post-1694. The rebuilding was controlled by the Fire Commissioners, whose powers allowed them to regulate the street layouts, rebuilding lines, heights of buildings, materials and – most importantly – the timetable for reconstruction, which was completed remarkably quickly. Although rebuilding continued into the early 1700s, it was well advanced when Celia Fiennes visited in 1697.

The W end of the High Street illustrates best what the Commissioners intended and what Fiennes described when she wrote that 'the streets are very handsome and the buildings regular and fine', the new buildings 'brick and coyn'd with stone and the windows the same'. The regulations limited houses to two storeys and required ground floors to be raised with steps from the street. All this can be seen here, along with illustrations of the freedom permitted in the choice of design details. The High Street and Northgate Street (below) remain fine examples of late C17 urban planning and architectural design.

The S side is less altered than the N. Especially noticeable the uniform height and fenestration of the range from the Unitarian chapel almost to the Warwick Arms Hotel beyond Back Lane. Mostly brick with stone or painted quoins, but No. 29 is ashlar. Nos. 27–27A, originally one brick house of seven bays, now divided unequally with matching pedimented doorcases. Most striking is ALDERSON HOUSE (No. 23), built as a single house for Isaac Tomkiss. Begun in 1695 and dated 1696 (rainwater head). Stone plinth. Seven bays, quoins, platband, moulded eaves cornice and dormers. Bolection-framed doorcase with semicircular fanlight. The rear is irregular, suggesting the reuse of unburnt back walls in the new house.

The N side mostly stuccoed and painted and some houses raised to three storeys. Heavy rustication to No. 46, a refronted survivor of the fire. Several later doorcases with fanlights, the best at No. 32, mid Georgian with full pediment and rosette metopes in the entablature. Then at the corner of Swan Street, the NATWEST BANK (originally National Provincial) of 1924, by *F.C.R. Palmer*, with a remarkably successful Neo-Palladian front.

Further E, the best buildings are again on the S. The WARWICK ARMS HOTEL is of *c.* 1790 (by *Eborall*), ashlar-faced, of five bays. Doorway with segmental arch and fanlight. The principal windows tripartite and under blank segmental arches – a very fine composition. Commercial Italianate at Nos. 11–13, 1860s, with Doric pillared and rusticated HSBC BANK street frontage by *T.B. Whinney*, 1919. No. 3 was built for Dorothy Weale and her son Fulke (cf. the East Gate) and largely completed by early 1696. The builders were *Thomas Masters* and *William Smith*. Described by Andor Gomme as the archetypal house of the rebuilding (cf. No. 23, above). Seven bays, stone keyblocks and platband, moulded eaves cornice and dormers. The heavy carved oak doorway is a latecomer, by *T.H. Kendall*, 1892, when the building was used as a Masonic Lodge. That explains the symbolism and the Egyptianizing columns carrying the gross semicircular pediment.

Now we reach the Cross, the true centre of the town until the closure of the old s approach via Castle Street around 1790. The fire was blown N here, leaving only the s E corner unharmed. When it came to rebuilding, the Commissioners decided exceptionally to allow three-storey buildings at each corner, all with 'cornices of wood with cantilavers answerable the one house to the other'. The three destroyed properties were replaced soon after 1695, with the old Court House at the beginning of Jury Street (*see* Public Buildings) being rebuilt on an even grander scale in 1725–8 to complete the quadrivium. So we have a grand display here, with fine buildings on all four corners.

The best (No. 1 High Street) at the s w angle is an excellent, if a little rustic, job of 1696, built for William and Mary Savage (initials and date on rainwater heads). Two and a half storeys, rendered, with hipped roof. Three by five bays. Upper Doric angle pilasters. To Castle Street the middle window has a laurel band as its surround and an open pediment. To the High Street the façade is busier and tighter. The middle window has an open and broken segmental pediment, the shanks ending in scrolls, and all the other detail is also just a little overdone. It has the required cornice, ornately done with acanthus consoles, and an iron balcony. Opposite at the NW angle, the corner house has three bays to High Street (Nos. 2–4) and three to Church Street. Unfluted Ionic giant pilasters and a richly carved eaves cornice and console brackets. Nice castiron balcony of *c.* 1825–30, as if we were at Leamington. The third, on the N E corner, has six bays to Church Street and only two on the main thoroughfare, which here becomes Jury Street. Another rich cornice, and substantial giant Corinthian angle pilasters. Taken together, the similarities (especially the treatment of the eaves) reflect compliance with the Commissioners' requirements, while the owners must have been responsible for the differences.

We should briefly explore the streets either side before continuing E. To the N, CHURCH STREET was widened after the fire and affords a perfect view of St Mary's church at the top of a gentle rise. The W side is pleasant and uneventful, two- and three-storey, mostly brick but some stuccoed or painted, with some earlier C19 rebuilding or refronting. On the E side Nos. 6–8, humble, late C18, stuccoed, with tripartite windows under blank arches. Then THE ATHENAEUM (No. 10), rebuilt in stone (cf. the unaltered rear) for Edward Heath after the fire but refronted in the mid C18. The front not large but ashlarfaced, with rusticated ground floor carrying coupled upper pilasters with Adamish details in the capitals. The centre is a tripartite window with a shallow segmental arch, above a lintel with guilloche frieze, reaching into an open pediment. Balustrading with urns. A little N, the WAR MEMORIAL, a thin Gothic tower like one of the Eleanor crosses with crocketed pinnacles, by *C. E. Bateman*, 1921. Behind is the OLD LIBRARY (No. 12), a striking office range backing onto the churchyard, almost French C18 style with segmental-headed keystoned windows, steep gables, etc. By *Robothams* for their own use, 1989.

Then S into CASTLE STREET. The view down is closed by OKEN'S HOUSE, C16, timber-framed, with overhang and gable with big diagonal strutting, all much renewed (restored 1864–5). Alongside, No. 10 has herringbone bracing on the first floor. On the r. on the way down to these, No. 8, probably by *Francis Smith c.* 1720 (Andor Gomme), ashlar-faced with rusticated plinth, of five bays, with giant angle pilasters carrying fluted capitals. Carved inscription above the door and across the platband added *c.* 1843 when it became a dispensary (established 1826). Beyond Oken's House No. 24, built as one house between 1749 and 1752 but subdivided in 1806. This is a six-bay brick house with keystoned cross-windows and dormers. Again giant angle pilasters, but here with alternating rustication. Across Castle Lane the street ends abruptly with the late C18 castle wall, the stables on the other side of it. On the l., No. 5, 'newly erected' in 1720 with quoins, and in the corner a medieval hall house (No. 9) right up against the wall.

Back to the Cross and into JURY STREET. After the Court House (*see* Public Buildings) on the S side, PAGEANT HOUSE is Late Georgian, of six (above) or seven (street level) irregular bays and three storeys with Ionic angle pilasters, a doorway with unfluted Ionic columns and no pediment. Then No. 4 of *c.* 1821, a smaller version of the same but four bays and just two-storey with panelled parapet with smaller upper angle pilasters (Ionic, unfluted). Nos. 12–14, timber-framed, with three gables and concave-sided lozenge panels. On the N, nothing notable until the long frontage of Nos. 17–19, which became LORD LEYCESTER HOTEL in the C20. It occupies two adjacent buildings, both of brick, the l. wing lower than the r. The taller section is of five bays with the carriage entrance in the fifth bay. The doorcase belongs to the time of the refronting in 1820. Here stood Jury House, a large late C17 mansion, of which some stone walls behind the hotel still remain. It was the town house of the Archers, and its forecourt halted the spread of the 1694 fire which turned N from here towards St Mary's and Northgate Street. Next door, No. 21 has a porch with Ionic columns, early C19. Then three houses of Warwick sandstone ashlar, No. 23 with platbands, keystoned windows and Tuscan pilasters.

On the S again, several good C18 houses. No. 18 with tripartite window on the first floor and Diocletian window above; No. 20 with elliptical window in the attic storey. No. 28 is stuccoed, *c.* 1770, of seven bays, with an additional half-storey and a pediment for the middle three bays. The doorcase is typical of the date, with railed steps to the street. Last, again set high up, EASTGATE HOUSE, *c.* 1730, of ashlar, three widely spaced bays and pilaster strips. Doorway and middle windows have moulded surrounds.

Lastly, on the N, No. 37 contains a C15 hall roof, a slightly earlier cross-wing and a fine kingpost roof in a bedroom. The oddly half-timbered front, however, is dated 1856, and a faintly humorous end to Warwick's main street. It has ragged staff bracing (cf. the stables at Kenilworth Castle).

With the East Gate ahead (*see* p. 670), we turn NW into THE BUTTS. On the l. a medieval wall and then a taller wall with an archway, but the town walls (*see* p. 670) stood beyond the E side of the street. On that side, Nos. 19–25, a humble block of four, rebuilt 1786/7; brick with quoins etc. Then a run of King's High School buildings, including the rear of the 2006 sixth form centre (*see* Public Buildings). On the w, the walled enclosure of the former Grammar School site and then open space until the OLD DEANERY and GLEBE HOUSE (Nos. 16–18), timber-framed and C17 (with some C15 timber inside) but much altered externally. Opposite, several decent Georgian houses in brick and stone, facing a stone-fronted terrace (Nos. 2–14) on the w. All late C18 or early C19. The best is No. 3 (E side), its ground-floor door and windows having segmental-headed reveals with keyed voussoirs. Then, opposite the Punch Bowl, two C18 stone PAVILIONS of similar design with semi-circular openings in the pediments, both with archivolts. These originally flanked the yards and rear entrances to Nos. 18–20 Northgate Street (below). Right round on the corner, facing down Cape Road, is a Shire Hall outlier, the former county offices (later the police station) by *W. Lait*, County Surveyor, 1882–3. Rather gaunt Italianate. Three storeys. Rusticated ground floor with Tuscan door surrounds. Single storey side-wing towards Northgate Street. Stark brick rear.

At the top of The Butts there is open parkland and public space on a high plateau N of the town. This is PRIORY PARK with what is left of THE PRIORY. Warwick Priory was founded by Henry de Newburgh *c.* 1114–19. After the Dissolution Thomas Hawkins (alias Fisher) built a new mansion on the site, completed *c.* 1566. In 1581 this became the home of the Puckering family who remodelled it with an early C17 w front of six great shaped gables and canted oriels. It later belonged to the Wise family. No monastic remains survive. The mansion also has gone, though not for good, for the stonework and many of the fittings were transported to America in 1927 by Alexander and Virginia Weddell.* What remains on the site is

---

*'... and good luck to them' wrote Pevsner in 1965, 'considering the losses by neglect, vandalism, and impoverishment that the major houses of England suffer every year'. The salvaged elements were used to create VIRGINIA HOUSE (now a museum) at Richmond, Virginia, designed for the Weddells by *Henry G. Morse*, 1929.

sad: a solitary wall and two subsidiary buildings, PRIORY BUNGALOW with a mullioned-and-transomed window and PRIORY HOUSE at the SW, all belonging to the low ranges that flanked the approach to the main house. Both existed by 1711. These now frame the car park of the COUNTY RECORD OFFICE, built on part of the site in 1972–3 and extended on the N in 2002–3.

Now to NORTHGATE. Across the N end of the street, facing St Mary's, is NORTHGATE HOUSE, built by Henry Puckering of The Priory in 1698 (dated rainwater head) to replace five cottages destroyed in the fire. Two houses really. Handsome front of eleven bays, brick, with a carriageway under a pediment in the centre and dormers with alternating pediment shapes. At the back still some of the original timber cross-windows. The staircases have twisted balusters, and in one of the houses is a fine upper room with pilaster panelling. The fireplaces are set diagonally, as was the fashion about 1700.

This marked the extremity of the progression of the fire, but everything to the S was lost except for part of the Shire Hall (since rebuilt) which miraculously escaped. NORTHGATE STREET was thus rebuilt between 1695 and the first decade of the C18 under the same strict regulation of the Commissioners we have seen in the High Street. Northgate has, as Alec Clifton-Taylor observed, 'the majesty of the law' on the W, i.e. the impressive group of the Shire Hall and former gaol (*see* Public Buildings). But the other side has pleasant houses throughout too. One stone, some brick but mostly stuccoed and painted. The views are closed at one end by the church, at the other by Northgate House. It is, as Clifton-Taylor observed, 'the most handsome Georgian street in the Midlands'. The best is Nos. 18–20, stuccoed, of seven bays, relatively low, with a three-bay pediment and two doorways with an arched niche between them. The proportions are *c.* 1700, the details *c.* 1775. The stone house (No. 22) belonged to *Francis Smith*, who built it in 1698. The main block of five bays, ashlar-faced, with raised ground floor and the centre bay in a shallow projection. Small one-bay projection added to the N end by Smith in 1702. Most of the properties on the E side were adapted for use as county council offices during the C20. They are now (2015) undergoing conservative restoration for return to residential use.

Turning r. by the church one comes to OLD SQUARE, still retracing the course of the fire. The square was laid out by the Fire Commissioners in 1695 'for the greater grace and ornament of the church of Saint Maries'. The church tower, of course, projects into the square in consequence of the events of 1700 noted above (*see* Churches) but the space is intimate. The houses S and W were raised to three storeys and refronted in the early C19, No. 5 with a doorcase with Tuscan columns. On the N, No. 2 is less altered. It was built by John Williams in 1696–7 for £204 and served as the vicarage until 1766. Unpainted stucco, two-storey, with Corinthian end pilasters and doorcase. To the W the street narrows. Here, a surprising and rewarding group, not Georgian or Regency but Victorian. On the r., the former POST OFFICE by *Henry Tanner* of the *Office of Works*, 1886, lightly Gothic. Alongside, the COFFEE TAVERN by *F.H. Moore*, 1880–1, with Arts and Crafts terracotta decoration. Opposite, No. 13A has later Victorian Gothic openings with good Ruskinian stone carving, inserted in the ground floor of the C18 façade. Round the corner into NEW STREET this turns seamlessly into the end bay of a Late Georgian house, No. 1, large but plain. A little S, No. 3, a very pretty miniature C18 three-bay brick house with two canted bay windows, a niche over the doorway, and a lunette window above it – all motifs one connects with grander displays.

Now W to the L-shaped MARKET PLACE. Its N end is dominated by the 1950s and 1960s extensions to the Shire Hall (*see* Public Buildings). The ground slopes gently down towards the Market Hall (Museum) (*see* Public Buildings) at the S. Imposing three-storeyed fronts on the E, Nos. 3–7 (formerly Lloyds Bank) with Grecian decoration in the semicircular first-floor window heads.* The l. section has a rainwater head dated 1826. Then No. 9, of six bays, early C19, and No. 11, two-storeyed with attic and dormers, and five infilled arches at street level. The W side is on a smaller scale and ordinary, except for the especially notable post-fire house sitting uncomfortably by the Shire Hall, to which it is linked to by a 1960s bridge. This is No. 10 (at one time known as Abbotsford), splendid and very probably by *Francis Smith*, dated 1714 (rainwater heads). Built for Job Lea, a mercer. Restored façade with some lost details reinstated. Five bays and three storeys, but on a grand scale. Stone, with giant fluted Corinthian pilasters. Doorway with broken and open segmental pediment on Corinthian columns. Segment-headed windows in moulded and lugged surrounds tied vertically in each bay by thin pilasters and panelled aprons. The middle window at first floor has sides of rich volutes. Hipped roof with dormers above a modillion cornice.

In the SW corner of the Market Place, an open space. The corner block, Nos. 40–46 (originally Woolworths), occupies the site of the Corn Exchange (*James Murray*, 1855–6; dem. *c.* 1964). It is faced with square stone panels and has on the N, at street level, abstract panels in Hornton stone by *Eric Davies*, 1964. On the steps to Theatre Street nearby, a tile mural created by Warwick children under the guidance of *Robin Wade*, 2000.

Next continue S into MARKET STREET, where the W side belongs to the first phase of a redevelopment scheme for the central area, begun in 1965. This was a borough council scheme, by the Borough Engineer (*C.E. Brown*) in association with the County Architect (*Eric Davies*) and the Civic Trust. Shops with flats over, the first group (Nos. 29–35) with first-floor

*Identical decoration can be seen in Leamington at the former Crown Hotel, No. 10 High Street.

oriels, the rest with fronts of irregular depth and height with monopitch roofing. At the corner of Bowling Green Street, an octagonal car showroom. Diagonally opposite, fronting the bus station, is WESTGATE HOUSE, a continuation of the redevelopment, completed in 1975. Pedestrian walkway with segmental arches at ground level, projecting bays and dormers above.

Now back to the Market House and the E end of Market Place which, as noted, is roughly L-shaped. N and S sides decent though ordinary. Nos. 64–66 perhaps the best. Early C19. Three-storey. Brick with rusticated and keystoned window headers. Shopfront with light cast-iron columns. At the E corner of the Market Place (Nos. 23–25), i.e. the corner of New Street, a large multi-gabled timber-framed house. A chimneypiece inside is dated 1636. Herringbone struts, panels with crosses, panels with concave-sided lozenges. At the corner three tiers of big carved heads set diagonally.

From here, a short walk down SWAN STREET brings one back to the High Street, close to where we began.

2. West

Start under the West Gate (*see* p. 671). Immediately W, the WEST-GATE ALMSHOUSES, rebuilt by *F.H. Moore*, 1889. Small-scale domestic. To the N, in Bowling Green Street, the GUILD COT-TAGES, by *Donald James Associates* for the Oken and Eyffler Charities, 1992, following the line of the TOWN WALL behind. Outside the walls here was the site of the BLACKFRIARS, established *c.* 1260. Nothing but the name Friars Street remains and so-called BLACKFRIARS HOUSE, 1815, at the corner of Bowling Green Street and West Street. Ashlar with slate roof. Three storeys. Reeded pilasters with sunk panels and stone portico with Doric pilasters and fanlight.

Opposite in WEST STREET, the MALT HOUSE with late C19 mock-Tudor half-timbering and big projecting porch with gables and oriels, replicating the Malt Shovel shown in earlier views of this site. Alongside, MALT COTTAGE (No. 23) is late C17, with stone quoins. The street here is wide, but to the W things peter out. On the W side, a decent C19 town house (No. 28), an 1880s house with strange bands of fish-scale brickwork (No. 76), and further out the only specially good building in West Street, TUDOR HOUSE INN. This is early C17 and has a jettied front with four gables, a stone plinth and some close studding on the ground floor, and concave-sided lozenge panels and herringbone struts higher up. The E side also C18 and C19 mainly, but with an interrupted run of timber-framed houses beyond the Roman Catholic church (*see* Churches) beginning at No. 49. Some are refronted rather than rebuilt (e.g. Nos. 51–53). Most have jettied fronts. TINKER'S HATCH (No. 105) has a small medieval hall (the roof now ceiled over) and a cross-wing. It is of the Wealden type. PARK COTTAGE (No. 113) has a jettied cross-wing and wattle-and-daub panels.

On the other side of the castle access road, Nos. 3–5 Stratford
Road (ST LAWRENCE PLACE) stand on the site of C12 St
Lawrence's church, used as a barn by 1669. Part stone, part
timber-framed, the house was noted as a 'new messuage' in
deeds of 1703.

At ST LAURENCE AVENUE, some early COUNCIL HOUSING by
Crouch, Butler & Savage, 1920. Nicely laid out with one side
in an arc around a green with trees. This leads through to
HAMPTON STREET and Warwick Racecourse (*see* Public
Buildings). The section of Hampton Street by the racecourse
belongs to a small 1820s development bounded by Crompton
Street on the N and West Street on the E. The area was largely
redeveloped in the 1960s, but W of Stand Street a stuccoed
row (Nos. 20–27) with gentle Regency details, e.g. incised
door pilasters. One (No. 27) has a wrought-iron balcony.
Further N, the style is Late Georgian, the material brick. The
best is No. 6, with raised entrance and railed basement.
Another good block round the corner in CROMPTON STREET,
first rated in 1825.

From here FRIARS STREET leads back towards the town, past
St Paul's church (*see* Churches) and the NEW LIFE CHURCH,
Tudor-style but now rendered, built by *F.H. Moore* as the St
Paul's Church Rooms, 1893. Behind St Paul's, accessible
either through the racecourse or from Linen Street, are the
HILL CLOSE GARDENS. In about 1846 an area of open
pasture was subdivided and laid out as detached gardens with
separate hedged plots. At first rented, the gardens were later
offered for sale as freehold plots in 1866. Development proposals in 1993 led to the rediscovery and eventual restoration of
this remarkable example of an urban amenity that achieved
great popularity in the later C19 when many town centre
houses lacked gardens. By 1877 there were thirty-seven plots,
many with their own summerhouses or pavilions. Rescue work
started in 1998, with a visitor centre by *Design Engine* of Winchester, 2007. The garden pavilions were restored under
Rodney Melville & Associates, c. 2008. The gardens are on a
sloping site, framed by the Edwardian houses of St Paul's
Street above. The pathways and hedges have been recreated
and the restored garden buildings, originally 1860s to 1880s,
are delightfully varied. Square, hexagonal and oblong. Plain
and patterned tiled roofs, some with finials. Fireplaces, seating
and stoves within. The visitor centre is triangular, faced with
terracotta panels on two sides and windowed to the gardens.
It has a sedum roof and a triangular glazed projection by the
entrance.

Leaving the gardens, follow Linen Street and Theatre Street into
COCKSPARROW STREET. Here on high ground facing W and
overlooking the racecourse is MARBLE HOUSE, a sandstone
house of impressive height, especially when looked at from a
distance. It was built for John Yardley in the early 1640s. Four
storeys plus gables by only three bays' width – plus two-bay
wings with battlements added c. 1812. The three bays are two

of canted bay windows and a porch. The bay windows are very odd in that they are set back in the wall and by their canted projection only end up flush with the wall. The house has shaped gables, two on the front and one on each end. The projecting porch has another, a little lower. THE FIRS, to the N, seems to have been built as an adjunct to Marble House, possibly in 1673, and later enlarged. The s side with recessed centre and modillion cornice is C17, stone with hipped tile roof.

In Theatre Street, one good C18 house (No. 6), brick with doorcase with open pediment and fanlight, c. 1800. Opposite, No. 33 is C17, timber-framed with square framing.

This brings us to the back of the Market Place and a good point to begin the next perambulation.

3. North

Until the 1970s the link road between the Market Place and Theatre Street had an iron bridge of 1804 over The Holloway, the main entrance to the town from the Birmingham side. The landscape was greatly changed when the area was redeveloped for the new county council offices completed in 1973 (*see* Shire Hall, p. 673). Since then, much of the approach to Warwick from the NW has been further developed with the demise of the factories that once lined Saltisford. These were served by a wharf on an arm of the Grand Union Canal near the former Eagle Works.

Down THEATRE STREET towards the roundabout, the housing on the l. belongs to two principal developments, 1979–81. The first group, by *Hinton, Brown & Langstone*, is a right-angled block, stepped up the slope and with a hipped-roof block of flats at the angle with Commaigne Close. Below, TAYLOR COURT by *Robothams* follows the line of West Rock and blends with the older buildings lower down.

In SALTISFORD, NW from the roundabout, the Eagle Engineering Works (a factory of c. 1796) has been replaced by SAINSBURY'S supermarket, and a 1980s office block, EAGLE COURT, fronts the street where Eagle House once stood. Then on the N side, the former GAS WORKS, with two octagonal gas holders of 1822 and a wall connecting them. Round-headed windows with delicate Gothic glazing bars. Converted to housing by *IDP Midlands Architects*, 2014–15. Yet further out to the NW, on the same side the C14 stone ST MICHAEL'S CHAPEL of the former Leper Hospital, with the surround of the E window visible now with reconstructed intersecting tracery. Inside, a panelled wagon roof. Behind, the timber-framed, derelict MASTER'S HOUSE with closely set studding. It has been dendro-dated to 1503–28.

Under the railway and beyond the cemetery, off Birmingham Road, a large office complex built for IBM. By *YRM*, 1979–82, and described in the contemporary architectural press as a 'slick shed'. In their familiar style (cf. Warwick University, p. 300), but with rounded corners and using vitreous steel panels rather than the familiar white tiles.

From here, walk through the IBM site to the W end of CAPE ROAD. Of *D.R. Hill*'s WARWICK PRISON (county gaol), 1853–60, only a few bits remain at the Upper Cape. The prison itself was demolished in 1934. The GOVERNOR'S HOUSE (No. 153), blue brick with stone dressings. Chunky blocks and keystones. Raised steps to the entrance. The OLD DAIRY (No. 181) is similar. Back towards town, in St Michael's Road, is ST MICHAEL'S HOSPITAL, by *Hitchman Stone Architects*, 1995–6. Opposite, the JOLLY MILLER pub (originally The Wedgenock) on Cape Road at the corner of Miller's Road. Brewer's Tudor, for Ansell's, 1935. Miller's Road leads into a large estate of COUNCIL HOUSING at Wedgnock Green, again by *Crouch, Butler & Savage*, 1920, and also well laid out with curved streets and open space (cf. St Laurence Avenue above). The estate continues towards town through Newburgh Crescent and Deerpark Drive, and then Cape Road. Past the allotments on Saltisford Common and over the railway, a group of substantial Edwardian houses on the r., and three early C20 side streets of terraced housing, VICTORIA STREET, ALBERT STREET and EDWARD STREET. After this we are back (via Cape Road) at the top of Northgate Street.

4. East

Next, E from the East Gate down SMITH STREET to St John's. In Smith Street at once, on the N side, two good houses, both now part of the King's High School for Girls (*see also* Public Buildings, schools). The first is timber-framed, with two small gables and a cross-wing with larger gable. Heavy criss-cross glazing bars. The second is LANDOR HOUSE, refronted by *Roger Hurlbutt* in 1692 and typically late C17 in style. Seven bays with recessed three-bay centre. Brick, two-storeyed, with quoins and a hipped roof. Finely carved eaves cornice and console brackets. Doorway with segmental pediment on brackets. Staircase with goodly twisted balusters. It is partly timber-framed within. Opposite Landor House is THE COTTAGE (No. 10), timber-framed, in small squares, with two gables and a dated rainwater head of 1686 shared with stone-fronted No. 12 attached. Originally one dwelling, and perhaps the date is not too late.

CHAPEL STREET on the l. lay immediately outside the town walls. In between the more recent buildings of the King's High School, it has pleasant groups of C18 and early C19 houses, especially towards the N end. To the r. of Smith Street, GERRARD STREET is similar, but there is some C17 timber-framing and the C18 and C19 houses are slightly grander, e.g. No. 17 of *c.* 1790.

Back in Smith Street, shops and variety, beginning with two tall late C19 warehouse-cum-showroom ones on the l. Mostly small-scale. Also on the N side, Nos. 27–28, a charming, small, mid-Georgian pair, of three bays only, with a pair of rusticated doorways and two Venetian windows. Lower down, No. 74 is timber-framed, with a curved brace in the centre bay suggesting that it was of the Wealden type (cf. West Street).

To the l. in PRIORY ROAD is the OLD DRILL HALL (formerly Priory House) with a long brick workshop range alongside. Built for William Holland, the noted Warwick stained glass artist and decorator, 1847. The house painted stucco, Tudorish. The workshops of seven bays with pointed windows in pairs, all with pretty patterned leading. A little W on the same side, GARDEN COTTAGE (No. 8) belonged to the gardens of The Priory. Stone with mullioned-and-transomed windows, Gothic trefoils over the doorway and a rounded stair tower with tall curved tile roof. It had a datestone, now lost. Perhaps 1860s, and possibly by *Waterhouse* who was working at The Priory for Thomas Lloyd in 1866. Extension for housing, late C20.

Now a longish detour N into COVENTRY ROAD, past the GREAT WESTERN pub at the foot of the station approach, irregular in plan and Italianate in style, mid-1850s. Beyond the railway on the r. a group of substantial Regency houses on high ground, set at an angle to the road to gain the best views of the castle, church and town. CLIFFE LODGE (No. 80) marked the entrance to the largest of these, THE CLIFFE (No. 100).* The Neoclassical lodge has Doric pilasters at angles and a portico *in antis* with fluted Greek Doric, *c.* 1830. THE CLIFFE itself is tucked away off Beech Cliffe. Stuccoed with canted bays to the front and rainwater head dated 1810. Attached and to the E, EAST CLIFFE (No. 102) is an extension by *Voysey* for M.H. Lakin (cf. Bishop's Itchington) of 1890, enlarged in 1910. The garden front is typical Voysey, low, roughcast, with unmoulded mullioned windows and an asymmetrically set, broad, shallow bow. The other Regency houses are Nos. 116 and 118 back on the main road. Fairly plain, No. 116 with projecting bay with pilasters and frieze with wreaths, No. 118 with balconied porch.

Further N, on the W side, on an island at the entrance to the GUYS CROSS PARK ESTATE, a statue of Guy and the boar by *Keith Godwin*, 1964. On the E side, approached by Nelson Lane and Cliffe Way (i.e. not directly off Coventry Road), is FIELDS COURT. This is a housing development by *Arthur Ling* and *R. Stewart Johnston*, 1966–7, in grounds landscaped by *Geoffrey Smith*. Especially successful for its grouping and for the variety in shape and style. Plum brick and white boarding. Bungalows with monopitch roofs. Houses with integral garages. Car-free open space.

*The original name was The Cliff, but the 'e' has now been added to the main house and its associated buildings. It must not be confused with Guy's Cliffe (q.v.).

Turn back now and return to the bottom of Coventry Road. To the E is Coten End with Emscote beyond (*see* Outer Warwick). Ahead is ST JOHN'S HOUSE (Museum), so called after the Hospital of St John, first mentioned in 1221. The present house, quite a mansion, was built for the Stoughton family who acquired the hospital property in 1540. A substantial house was created for Anthony Stoughton between 1615 and 1633, evidenced by a wooden panel with his initials and the date 1626 now in a doorway on the first floor of the E wing. His early C17 house was largely rebuilt and much enlarged for Nathaniel Stoughton in 1667–70, although parts of it were incorporated at the back. The front is symmetrical, with three shaped gables and two small gables between them, two canted bay windows and a central porch. Porch and bays have open-work top parapets. The windows have mullions and transoms. The arch of the porch is curious. Each voussoir block has a projecting roll along its middle, giving the impression of bulgy alternating rustication. The W and E sides have in the gable two horizontally set oval windows each. Some timber framing visible in the rear of the front block. Lower wing at the back, the E side with gables and mullioned windows of earlier C17 form. On the rear of this wing, another shaped gable. Contemporary staircase with sturdy, not at all elegant turned balusters. Good stone fireplace and some C18 oak panelling. The front garden is entered by splendid wrought-iron gates of Early Georgian date, probably by *Nicholas Paris*, between a pair of good gatepiers. Originally there was an overthrow. To the r., Nos. 2–4 ST JOHN'S, timber-framed and jettied, refronted with Georgian windows *c.* 1790.

ST NICHOLAS CHURCH STREET leads back SW towards the castle. Small scale, some timber framing and a little group of early C19 artisan dwellings (Nos. 26–30) opposite THE DOLLS HOUSE (No. 29), an ashlar Gothic building with canted W corner to St Nicholas' churchyard. Originally associated with St Nicholas church (*see* Churches) were the ST NICHOLAS PARISH ROOMS (now the Baptist Church Hall) at the SE end of GERRARD STREET. By *John Cundall*, 1885. Brick with mullioned and mullioned-and-transomed windows, stepped gable to front, low tower on the r. with statue of St Nicholas, and half-timbered and tile-hung gable with oriel at the side.

SE of the church is ST NICHOLAS PARK, with wrought-iron gates to the Banbury Road, ornamented with birds and flowers, by the *Bromsgrove Guild*, 1933. The River Avon runs along the S edge of the park and under the Castle Bridge (*see* Public Buildings). The present road from the bridge to the East Gate became the main entrance to Warwick from the S in 1793, and at that date a new wall was built along the E side of the castle estate up CASTLE HILL. The road was lowered and altered to an even gradient up the hill and the embankment on the E side also has a stone wall. Perched above, on the old street level, are OKEN'S and EYFFLER'S ALMSHOUSES, C17 and 1696, but with only some original features left.

Back now to the Castle Lodge (p. 669) to explore MILL STREET. The cobbled street runs towards (but only towards) the river and the old bridge and ends directly at the foot of the Castle. Mill Street was well out of the area of the great fire and hence has many older houses. THE MILL HOUSE (No. 4) on the r. stands on a high stone plinth with steps to the entrance. Timber-framed above, with oriel windows and jettied and gabled cross-wing. Big stone chimney on the l. side and deep projecting wing behind of brick with keystoned windows. Well restored by *Charles M.C. Armstrong*, 1902. Opposite, No. 11, late C17, painted brick with quoins, platband, cross-windows and moulded cornice. Then No. 13 and THE MALT HOUSE, both stone with mullioned windows. On the N, THEOCSBURY (No. 10) with timber-framed jettied gable. Opposite, MILL-ER'S PLACE (No. 15) is brick again, mid-C18 probably, and has a doorway with Gibbs surround. No. 18, C17, has a shell porch. Then, as the castle gets closer, a long run of timber-framed houses, especially on the l. at the end. One of this group, THE GABLES, is C19 (three equal gables); the others are *c.* 1600. ALLEN'S HOUSE (No. 39), with concave-sided lozenge panels and no gable, has a stone plaque with the date 1568 set in brickwork at the back, bearing the name of Thomas Allen. Is that too early for the panels? Then a long row of close studding, no gables, again C16. No. 43 is of one bay with overhang and No. 45 of two bays also with overhang. The Castle Mill itself lies beyond the end of the street, accessible only from the castle grounds.

Here, close to the river, the sheer force of domination of Caesar's Tower is at its most powerful – almost terrifying. This was where the old main road ran past the E front of the castle and down to the river crossing. Behind the end of Mill Street, viewable from the Mill Garden, is the OLD BRIDGE, of *c.* 1374–83. Overgrown and ruinous. One N arch, then three centre arches and two S arches. Cutwaters.

To go S of the river, one must return to the Banbury Road and cross the Castle Bridge (*see* p. 677).

5. *South*

Over the bridge, first on the r. is BRIDGE END. Here is a handsome timber-framed house with four jettied gables on its front. This is BROME'S PLACE (now subdivided as Nos. 33–35 and called Brome House and Little Brome), supposedly belonging in the mid C15 to John Brome, who also owned Baddesley Clinton. It has oriels on brackets with carved faces beneath the gables. Further W, the MILL HOUSE (No. 1), late C17, brick with stone quoins and platband. Then the road turns S and we are on the old southern approach to the town, which crossed at the Old Bridge (*see* Perambulation 4). Nothing noteworthy here, but very pleasant. At the S, between Bridge End and the Banbury Road is ARCHERY FIELDS, a well-conceived small development by *Trepess, Harley-Smith & Steel*, 1962–4. Archways at both entrances. Grouped round a landscaped courtyard with a pond. Three- and two-storeyed houses and bungalows, some with weatherboarded fronts, others tile-hung and some with light iron balconies.

The rest can be mopped up quickly. First, along Myton Road past Warwick School (*see* Public Buildings) is MYTON HAMLET. A Jacobethan LODGE by *John Gibson* dated 1883 marks the entrance to the site of Myton Grange, a large house of 1857 by *Gibson* in the same style for Thomas Heath, a Warwick solicitor. This was demolished in 1935, although part of the boilerhouse survives with big chimney and diapered brickwork. It was replaced by a children's home (now MYTON HOSPICE) by the *County Architect* (*A.C. Bunch*), 1937–8. Four similar blocks in an arc.

Back to Banbury Road and the small stone TOLLHOUSE by *William Eborall*, 1787, at the junction of Gallows Hill. Off this is WARWICK TECHNOLOGY PARK, among whose earliest buildings were WIRELESS HOUSE, built as headquarters for the BBC Transmission Group (it was Arqiva until 2014), and the ALPHA BUILDING. Both by *Alan Cooke Architects* (Norwich), 1989. In the centre of the site, which is served by a loop road, is NATIONAL GRID HOUSE.

OUTER WARWICK

EMSCOTE AND COTEN END

In the early C19 there was only a small settlement along the road towards Rugby through Coten End, E of St John's. Here a few timber-framed buildings remain, e.g. the MILLWRIGHT ARMS (No. 69 Coten End). The suburb of Emscote grew up to the E where Nelsons established their gelatine mills near the Grand Union Canal, eventually filling the triangle between Coventry Road and the River Avon which marks the boundary with Leamington on the E side of Warwick. The link with Leamington and its New Town made the Emscote Road a fashionable residential area in the mid C19.

ALL SAINTS, St Edith's Green, Emscote. *Brian Rush*, 1988–9, replacing the Victorian church demolished in 1967.* Square with a pantiled roof rising towards a glass spirelet over the sanctuary within a semi-cylindrical projection across the NE corner. – STAINED GLASS. Two in the Day Chapel, one

---

* By *James Murray*, this had been built at the expense of Miss Marianne Philips of Leamington. It was begun in 1854–6 with tower and spire added by Murray in 1861, and then remodelled and enlarged by *Bodley & Garner*, 1872. It was a lavish affair, richly furnished.

probably *Hardman*, 1989, the other *Michael Lassen*, 1990.
– From the old church, a MOSAIC by *Salviati*, 1866, and two
WAR MEMORIAL boards, one by *Comper*, 1951.

Alongside to the E are *G.T. Robinson*'s ST EDITH'S HOME,
1867–8, and No. 1 All Saints Road, built as a teacher's residence by *F.H. Moore*, 1873. The home is spiky Gothic, ornamented with carved statues and ornamental inscriptions. On
the N, the infant school (now the church centre) by *Moore*,
1887. Also in the group originally were the demolished schools
(*Murray*, 1861, and *Moore*, 1873) and a vicarage (*Murray*,
1862–3).

To the E, on the GRAND UNION CANAL towards Leamington there are aqueducts over the River Avon and over the
Great Western Railway. The river AQUEDUCT is handsome,
c. 1799–1800, with parapet renewed in concrete, 1909. The
RAILWAY AQUEDUCT is a cast-iron trough supported on
iron-rib arches concealed by the external brickwork. Built
by *Peto & Betts*, 1851. A little N the road bridge over the
Avon, PORTOBELLO BRIDGE, is by *John Nichol*, County
Surveyor, 1831, restored 1892.

The Nelson family established their canalside works, EMSCOTE
MILLS, in 1841. Parts of the factory in Wharf Street remain.
Associated with the mills were the handsome NELSON CLUB,
Charles Street, by *F.H. Moore*, 1882, and the NELSON
VILLAGE with concrete block housing in CHARLES STREET
(e.g. Nos. 46–48) erected for the workers in 1889. The concrete
blocks are laid to resemble rusticated masonry.

The Nelsons lived at THE LAWN in extensive grounds
between the Emscote Road and the mills, an Italianate
house of the 1840s enlarged to the W *c.* 1872 and on the E in
1888. The extensions and the lodge, *c.* 1869, are also built
of concrete blocks. In 1920 it became a preparatory school
which closed in 1999. The house has been converted into
apartments, with further blocks of housing built within the site
in similar style in Campriano Drive and Marne Close. The
grounds retain much good planting and a central area of open
space.

Towards Warwick there are substantial houses along EMSCOTE
ROAD, especially W of the railway bridge. Villas, mainly, and
with much variety, from *c.* 1830 onwards. Regency, Early Victorian, rock-faced and later types. A good group on the S, with
shaped gables (Nos. 14–14A), ROSE VILLA (No. 12) with
Tuscan portico, and a Regency pair (Nos. 6–8). Opposite, a
long run of blue brick villas with white stucco dressings and
wavy bargeboards (Nos. 3–17) of *c.* 1845–9, ending with No.
1 on the corner at Wharf Street facing towards Warwick. In
COTEN END, another Regency pair (Nos. 77–79) and then a
Gothic pair (Nos. 73–75) with pointed windows, hoodmoulds
and delicate glazing bars. Opposite, GREVILLE LODGE and
STOKESLEIGH (Nos. 46–48) are rock-faced. Nos. 36–38 blue
brick again, and Nos. 30–32 gabled red brick, these all with
castellated canted bays.

LONGBRIDGE MANOR. 2 m. SW, close to the motorway junction. Of C12 origin, and the home of the Stanton or Staunton family from the C15 until the 1930s. Now business premises. A puzzling house, apparently not what it seems. The timber-framed section of the N wing may belong to the 'house . . . built newly of late in Longbridge' mentioned in 1610. The S front, although rendered, resembles the front of Landor House in Warwick (1692; *see* Perambulation 4, Smith Street), with recessed centre, quoins and end bays with hipped roofs. Map evidence, however, indicates that it may be an early C19 addition. *John Standbridge* of Warwick supervised alterations here in 1784–5, and *E. F. Reynolds* made internal improvements in the 1930s.

LONGBRIDGE MONUMENT COMPLEX. In the fields S of the M40 and W and SW of Longbridge Farm. An elongated rectangular crop mark, 900 ft long (274 metres) and 100 ft (30 metres) wide, confirmed as the site of a Neolithic cursus. It lies adjacent to a large irregular enclosure also thought likely to be of Neolithic date.

WOODLOES

Of the later C20 residential area N of the town nothing need be said, but beyond the by-pass on Woodloes Lane is WOODLOES, a stone house with the date 1562 on the façade, but this façade is clearly C17, and probably not too early. It is completely symmetrical, with mullioned-and-transomed windows, a middle porch and middle gables. The chimneys also are not C16. The upper windows are curiously placed on stone brackets and project slightly.

For Guy's Cliffe *see* p. 342.

WASPERTON

2050

ST JOHN THE BAPTIST. An early work by *G. G. Scott* who created a perfect Camdenian church – 'a church as it should be' – for his Camden Society client, the Rev. Thomas Leveson Lane, vicar 1836–83. Precise dates for the main stages of the work are, in fact, uncertain, but 1843 is usually quoted. Completion was celebrated in 1852. Scott began with unpromising material, a Georgian box of 1736. How much of the old remains is unclear, although Scott had to adapt the shell of the nave to accommodate his Middle Pointed ideals. By Scott the open wooden bell-turret with spirelet, of course the windows, the S aisle, and the whole E end, including the organ recess (used as a vestry since 1959) with its spherical triangle window and the arch to the chancel, in the apex of which St Cecilia, quite large, appears hovering. Small angel corbels in the chancel. Good nave roof with crown-posts, curved braces and crenellated tie-beams. – ALTAR and SANCTUARY FLOOR with *Minton* tiles. – COMMUNION RAIL. Of wrought iron, very fine. Probably from the church of 1736. – SCREEN. By *Scott*. Simple and plain, in the style of 1300. Dated 1845. – PULPIT. With Flemish carved scenes of *c.* 1600. – STAINED GLASS. The E window by *Hardman* to a design of *Pugin*, 1852. Another by them in S aisle, 1847: St John the Baptist. – S aisle E window by *Burlison & Grylls*, 1876. – The rest by *William Holland*, pre-1852. – MEMORIALS. In the churchyard NE of the porch, to the family of Thomas Garner, Bodley's partner, who was born at Wasperton. Memorials, †1880–1 etc, by *Garner*.

CEDAR HOUSE, alongside the church, was the vicarage, enlarged by *John Nichol* in 1822 with pretty cusped bargeboards to eaves and gables and again by *William Flower* for Lane in 1837–8. Lane also built the SCHOOL (now village hall) with diaper patterning dated 1843, and a later pair of cottages alongside with brickwork resembling timber framing in the gables.

Further W is MANOR FARM: quite unpromising from outside, but inside evidence unravelled by S.R. Jones and J.T. Smith in 1958 disclosed an aisled hall of the early C14 with a speretruss and a crown-posted roof. The remaining capitals of the truss are similar to those at West Bromwich Manor House (*see Birmingham and the Black Country* volume). Wasperton belonged to Coventry Priory.

WASPERTON HOUSE at the E edge of the village is largely a classical rebuilding, *c.* 1840. Symmetrical front with shallow wings and stone colonnade across the recessed two-bay centre.

HEATHCOTE FARM, 2 m. E, is illustrated on a 1686 map, when its front with a projecting centre bay then had an oval in a central pediment and hipped dormers.

WATER ORTON

ST PETER AND ST PAUL. 1878–9 by *Bateman & Corser* in their awkward Decorated Gothic style. Rock-faced, with NW tower (its spire removed 1987) and polygonal apse. A poor job architecturally though it cost £3,885. Extensions by *Duval Brownhill Partnership*, 2001. On the S, lean-to bays with curved stone piers with panelled infill against the three W bays of the nave. N porch also 2001, along with interior reordering of the E end and restoration of the brightly stencilled apse ceiling. – STAINED GLASS. In the apse, three by *Hardman*, 1881–96. – Victorian octagonal FONT, with good carved oak cover by *Celestino Pancheri*, 1932.

METHODIST CHURCH, W of the church. 1868, polychromatic brickwork and pointed windows on entrance front. Side extension with round-headed windows, *H.H. Reynolds*, 1898. Adjoining church centre by *David Cox*, 1971–2.

In New Road E of the church, THE LINK (Water Orton community venue) by *Axon Beckett Partnership*, 2009–10. Hall with community facilities, built to an environmentally sustainable brief with borehole heating, Monodraught ventilators on the roof, and a steel-framed covered entrance.

SCHOOL, Attleborough Lane. Facing a broad green. By *Edward Holmes*, 1878. Brick with timber framing in gables and tile-hanging in window tympana. Extensive additions behind, but the attractive frontage unspoiled.

BRIDGE across the River Tame. Built about 1520 by Bishop John Vesey of Exeter (who came from nearby Sutton Coldfield). Stone. Six round arches and big, closely set cutwaters.*

RAILWAY STATION, by *A. Wheatley* for the Midland Railway, 1908. Edwardian Arts and Crafts style with corner tower.

Beyond the railway to the N, the old churchyard with the base and column of a C15 CHURCHYARD CROSS. Here was the C14 chapel of ease of Aston (Birmingham), rebuilt in the early C18 and demolished 1887.

Nearby are Regency dwellings and THE CHESTNUTS, brick with some exposed timber framing and a central brick chimney-stack. A middle hall with two wings. The hall has late-C14 crucks with an arch-braced open truss. A crosswing was added in the early C15.

WEETHLEY

ST JAMES. 1857–8 by *Edward Haycock* of Shrewsbury, replacing an earlier chapel. Paid for by Henry Miles of Downfield, Herefs., who was Haycock's father-in-law and whose son Rev. H.H. Miles was curate. Nave and apse and heavy W bellcote with shingled roof. Vestry and schoolroom on S. Lias stone; late C13 style. The chancel arch has brackets with naturalistic lilies and vine and grapes, now painted. – Small circular FONT bowl from old chapel, perhaps C14. – Bright STAINED GLASS by *Hardman* in the apse, 1858. – Panel in N window from West Bromwich, *c.* 1930, installed 1984.

A small settlement on the ridge, with a cluster of converted farm buildings N of the church. Fine views all round, especially to Bredon Hill, the Cotswolds and the Malverns.

To the S, WEETHLEY GATE on the turnpike road from Dunnington to Crabbs Cross. Octagonal with slate roof and central chimney, *c.* 1826. Sympathetic rear extension by *Cross & Harris*, 1969.

---

*An angel carving from the bridge is now displayed in Curdworth church (q.v.).

Welcombe, perspective view of principal front.
Engraving, 1882

2050

WELCOMBE

2 m. N of Stratford-upon-Avon

In a fold of the Welcombe Hills, with superb views across the
Avon valley. A hotel since 1931, Welcombe was built for Mark
Philips of Manchester. He was a cottontot, a politician and a
relation of George Philips of Weston Park (q.v.). He acquired the
estate in 1845 but chose to live at Park House, Snitterfield (q.v.),
and had the old Welcombe Hall demolished.* In 1866 Philips set
about building a new and larger house at Welcombe at a cost of
over £35,000. *Henry Clutton* prepared the designs and advertised
for tenders but the commission was taken over by *Thomas Newby*,
a young Manchester architect employed by Philips in the north-
west. Penelope Hunting† observes that the house has a number
of Clutton features as well as details chosen by Philips himself.
However, *Newby* was credited as architect in local press reports
and again when the house was illustrated in *The Builder* in 1882.
It was ready for occupation in 1870.

Jacobean-style. Brick with tall chimneys and many a shaped
    gable. The garden front is symmetrical, the entrance side out
    of symmetry by a quite excessive service wing. The S wing,
    linked by a corridor, was added by *William H. Hamlyn* in 1931.
    A modern accommodation block stands on the site of the
    Winter Garden building (conservatory) at right angles to the
    house. Inside, the wood-panelled Great Hall has a black
    marble fireplace with twisted columns. The staircase carved by
    T.H. Kendall of Warwick has a neo-C17 pierced strapwork
    balustrade leading up to a colonnade at the top landing. Exten-
    sive STABLES, converted to timeshare units and the yard

---

*An engraving of *c.* 1821 shows the house as it was then, Gothick with ogee-headed
windows, partly of *c.* 1815.
†Penelope Hunting, 'Henry Clutton's Country Houses' in *Architectural History* 16
(1983).

infilled as a spa by *Morrison Design*, Derby, 2004–5. The gardens were laid out by *W.A. Nesfield*, 1873, and restored under *Christopher Hobson*, *c.* 1994. LODGE on the Warwick Road by *Newby*, 1874.

OBELISK on Welcombe Bank, above the house. Erected in 1876 in memory of Mark Philips, †1873, but also commemorating other family members. It cost £4,000.

WELFORD-ON-AVON

ST PETER. A late Norman church with aisled nave and w tower, the chancel rebuilt in the C14 and the aisles altered in the C15. Bellcote over chancel arch. Careful restoration in 1866–7 by *G.G. Scott*. The tower is unbuttressed and Norman to the string course. Higher up are two lancets with continuous roll mouldings, i.e. an early C13 continuation, and then a Perp top restored in 1885 by *Job Stanley* of Broom after a fire. The s doorway is Norman too (with point-to-point chevron mouldings), and the N and s aisle w windows. Norman also the plain N doorway. Perp the three-light side windows in the aisles, that on the s without tracery. Small Perp E window to s aisle. Above it the coping from the E wall of the nave is oddly swept down to the original roof-line of the s aisle. Inside both arcades much more impressively Norman. Two wide bays only, with narrow aisles. Short, stubby round piers, multi-scalloped round capitals. Single-step round arches. Tower arch low, pointed, unmoulded and later than arcades. Dec chancel, restored, with C14 piscina and sedilia recess. *Scott*'s the chancel arch. One Dec window resited on E wall of N vestry and organ chamber. – FONT. Norman, supported on later balusters on C13 base. – PULPIT. Plain, C17. – SCREENS. Chancel screen in C15 style, 1926, and tower screen, 1916. Both carved in oak by *John Northcott* of Ashwater, Devon. – In the chancel, ORGAN CASE, 1931, and STALLS, 1922, by *Harold Stratton Davis*. – STAINED GLASS. Good E window by *Geoffrey Webb*, 1924. Chancel s C14 canopies re-set by *Oliver S. Mills*, 1936. Further fragments in chancel N. Chancel sw by *Mayer & Co.*, 1905.

LYCHGATE. Rebuilt 1965 in the C14 style of a previous lychgate. Two unequal bays, timber-framed on a stone base. Open sides with cusped braces below a gabled roof.

WESLEYAN CHAPEL, Chapel Street. 1913, by *Knight & Hebery* of Stratford-upon-Avon. Brick with over-large paired lancets. Extended in 2002.

Former RECTORY, w of the church. Georgian with Victorian additions.

CLEAVERS, NE of the church. Brick. 1713, of five bays and two storeys with stone quoins, with a striking porch of the 1950s by *Winston Walker*, who lived here.

In the village, many pretty timber-framed houses, many thatched and mostly C17. None especially distinguished, but together they make Welford especially picturesque. The best are to the S of the church and in nearby Boat Lane. Further groups along the High Street and other roads leading S to the village green which has a 65-foot (20-metre) MAYPOLE, said to be the tallest in England.

WELLESBOURNE

2050

Two villages, now conjoined and regarded as one. Wellesbourne Hastings with the church is on the N side of the River Dene and Wellesbourne Mountford with the hall and manor is to the S.

ST PETER. Light grey ashlar W tower, Perp, with heavy crocketed hoodmoulds. The rest mainly 1847–8 by *J.P. Harrison* for the Rev. Lord Charles Paulet. Favoured by the Tractarians, Harrison worked for the Keble brothers at Bussage (Glos.) and Hursley (Hants) in the 1840s. Here, Harrison re-shaped and largely rebuilt the old church, lengthening the nave into the chancel, enlarging the N aisle and adding the Mordaunt Chapel (the organ chamber since 1885) and vestry on the N side of the rebuilt chancel. Victorian Dec externally, excepting the W end of the S aisle and parts of the E wall. Big and worthy, though hardly distinguished. Internally the three W bays of the S arcade have shafted E.E. piers, but all the rest is rebuilt. The Victorian N arcade imitates the S. Re-set in the N wall of the chancel is the old chancel arch. This is an extremely impressive piece. The responds with big heavy single-scallop and elementary volute capitals must be late C11, but the imposts with lozenges and saltire crosses and the arches are not likely to be earlier than 1100 or 1110. The chancel arch and E end belong to the 1847–8 restoration, as do the *Minton* tiles and the elaborate wooden roof. The wide twin opening with a quatrefoil in the S side of the chancel is of 1865, when the chapel was added to house the Wellesbourne House pew. Like the chancel E window it commemorates Paulet's son (†1864). Paulet's own memorial is the splendid High Victorian REREDOS with CREDENCE and SEDILIA in the sanctuary by *T.H. Wyatt*, 1873. Pink-veined marble with coloured shafts, panels with mosaics by *Salviati* and carved central gablet. The remaining painted decoration in the church is by *William Holland* of Warwick, some 1856. – PULPIT, LECTERN, chancel STALLS and FONT all by Harrison, 1847–8. – STAINED GLASS. A rich collection based on a complete scheme of 1848. Originally all by *Holland* except one (S aisle E) by *Thomas Willement* and another (now wholly obscured by the organ) by *Ward & Nixon*. – Holland later replaced several of his own windows, the E in 1864, W in 1865, and two aisle W windows (the N exhibited at the Great

Exhibition, 1851), and inserted centre lights in four of the aisle side windows, †1853–66. – Replacements by others are the chancel s by *Kempe*, 1893. – N aisle, *Morris & Sons Ltd*, †1909. – Three in s aisle, 1871, one by *Clayton & Bell* and two by *Lavers, Barraud & Westlake*. – MONUMENT. Good brass to a knight in armour (now covered over): Sir Thomas le Straunge †1436 (although the restored inscription says †1426). The effigy is 2 ft (60 cm.) long. – In a recess, a pedestal with urn and flaming lamps, Ann †1761 and John Dewes †1786.

In the CHURCHYARD, a good table tomb to Samuel Aylworth †1670. Central section with segmental pediment. Angle pilasters with capitals.

Detached PARISH CENTRE, partly within the remodelled stables of the former rectory, with the main hall added in 1992.

CAREY MEMORIAL METHODIST CHURCH and HALL (Wesleyan), Bridge Street. *F. W. B. Yorke*, 1915. Brick with Arts and Crafts stone dressings, e.g. the chequerboard patterns in the stepped gable. Inside, the ribs of the segmental roof are decorated with pretty floral carvings. Sloping floor with bench seating.

FIRE STATION, Loxley Road, 1998. Silver and red, simple but striking.

The OLD VICARAGE, SW of the church, was built for parson Humphrey Whyle, 1698–9. Originally symmetrical with hipped roof, but spoiled by C19 canted bays added on the two main façades.

WARWICK ROAD is the main street of Wellesbourne Hastings, with a few early C19 cottages and plum brick VICTORIA HOUSE, *c.* 1840. Parallel is CHURCH STREET, with decent Walton estate cottages of 1824 in pairs with lean-to wings and carved bargeboards. Also the distinctively Victorian WORKING MEN'S CLUB, 1885, by *Frederic Kibler* of Wellesbourne. Beyond to the E in SCHOOL ROAD, No. 2 has a cruck dated to 1429–30. In the same street the former SCHOOL (now village hall), mostly 1863 with bright diapered brickwork and fishscale tiling to the wings, curly bargeboard to the centre gable. The plans are signed by local builder *James Kibler*. All around to the N, post-war development. In Kineton Road, either side of the road to Moreton Morrell, lodge-like STAPLE HILL COTTAGES by *Horace Gundry*, *c.* 1875 (cf. Walton). Half-timbered gables, big chimneys etc. On the Moreton Morrell road, STAPLE HILL HOUSE in brick with mighty chimneys, built for John Murray Mordaunt, 1863. Further out, WELLESBOURNE WATERMILL by the River Dene is dated 1834 in the brickwork and has complete working machinery inside. The MILL HOUSE, alongside, is later C18.

p. 700

The centrepiece of Wellesbourne Mountford is CHESTNUT SQUARE, delightfully surrounded by building of varied dates and styles. Timber-framed and thatched, the C17 STAG'S HEAD at the N end. More on the W near the LITTLE HOUSE, dated 1699. Brick, six bays, wooden cross-windows. Opposite, the RED HOUSE, built for T. Aylworth *c.* 1745. Of brick too,

Wellesbourne, Staple Hill Cottages, south and east elevations.
Engraving, 1875

but only three bays and compact, with the centre slightly projected under a pediment with modillions that continue along the eaves. Nicely patterned fanlight and small canted bays. Next to it, stucco-fronted PITT HOUSE is quoined with hipped roof and later porch, c. 1830. No. 6 is by *John Nichol*, civil engineer and County Surveyor, built as his own home c. 1828.

Marking the start of CHAPEL STREET, the MANOR and COOPERS alongside have diamond-pane windows, Coopers with diapering and bargeboards. Both remodelled for the Rev. John Lucy (cf. Hampton Lucy) after 1858. Another good group opposite (Nos. 2–6) including the OLD HOUSE, refronted c. 1820, the adjoining shopfront with a bow window of 1805 and the OLD SCHOOL HOUSE, refronted c. 1723. Further down, two groups of cottages with diapered and patterned brickwork by *James Kibler*, 1864 (cf. the old school). Tucked away on the N side a stud and panel GRANARY on staddlestones, the timbers dated to 1638–9.

WELLESBOURNE HALL, Stratford Road. A dignified H-plan house of c. 1700. Built for Robert Boyce (†1714). Recessed three-bay centre and somewhat projecting two-bay wings. Two storeys. Hipped roof. In the entrance hall a gallery with twisted balusters and a string with acanthus scrolls. Otherwise much of c. 1750 and later: an Adamish plaster ceiling and several fireplaces, two of them made with shellwork by *Mrs Delany*, whose sister Anne Dewes (*née* Granville) lived here. Stables with clock turret and cupola with weathervane.

WESTON

The great house at Weston is no more, but the architectural influence of south Warwickshire's grandest mansion and largest estate can still be felt. The original house, Weston Park, was built by the Sheldons, 1588, but replaced in 1827–30 by a large and rather awkward turreted three-storey mansion called Weston House, by *Edward Blore*. It was built for Sir George Philips, a Lancashire banker and mill-owner, who bought the estate in 1819. Through the following decades Philips pursued a relentless campaign of estate improvements and building, notably in Long Compton, Whichford, Little Wolford and at Weston. *Blore, James Trubshaw* and *Thomas Johnson* were his architects, *Trubshaw* and *Thomas Marklew* his clerks of works.

Blore's house was demolished in 1934. At WESTON SITE, the low wall marking three sides of the enclosure remains along with the Tudor brick STABLES, by *Trubshaw*, 1829–30. Although never formally landscaped, the park retains various significant features. From the N, a proud avenue of oaks still leads southward towards the eminence on which Weston once stood. The Cherington road was moved northwards in 1828 and the main Stratford–Oxford road to the W in the 1830s, all marked by lodges at Little Wolford (q.v.). At the S entrance to the park from Long Compton, another LODGE, 1834.

PARK HOUSE, ¾ m. SSE, is a three-bay farmhouse of *c.* 1725, enlarged as the agent's house and refronted with Gothic windows by *Marklew* in 1830–1. Matching extension in contrasting materials, 1911. Across a field to the SE, single-storey CHANTREY COTTAGE, 1838, named after Francis Chantrey, the sculptor, who – along with Thomas Harrison of Chester – was first approached by Philips about the building of the new mansion.

WESTON-IN-ARDEN

3080

OUR LADY OF THE SACRED HEART (R.C.). 1869 by *W. Gualbert Saunders* for his brother-in-law, Richard Lerins de Bary of Weston Hall. Brick, small, just outside the grounds of the hall. Chunky column and late C12-style capitals to side chapel and chancel arch. – High ALTAR and other carving by *J. L. Jaquet* of London, 1869. – STAINED GLASS. Bright E window by *Saunders & Co.*, †1869, restored 2001. – W window, *Hardman*, 1978. – N chapel window has glass of *c.* 1925 from the closed church at Wolvey.

WESTON HALL. Stone house of *c.* 1600, with a large Victorian W wing added for F.A. Newdigate in 1892–3. The original part with a recessed centre and three kneelered gables. Mullioned-and-transomed windows. On the extension, a Jacobean-style porch dated 1893 with carved decoration. Some C17 panelling inside. Weston was the home of sculptor Richard Hayward in the late C18. It became a hotel in 1970.

p. 702

Weston-in-Arden, Weston Hall, view of principal front.
Engraving, 1872

1050

WESTON-ON-AVON

ALL SAINTS. A remarkable little church, to the building of which Sir John Grevill of Milcote left £50 in 1480; the work continued under his son Thomas (†1497). Short w tower with parapet and gargoyles, nave in same style with six-light (three plus three) straight-headed windows and battlements; the details similar to other late C15 north Cotswold churches. On the s side remains of the former chapel with a squint. Its two-bay arcade has been converted into large windows with the plinth and parapet from the outer chapel walls neatly re-set, possibly in the early C18, as indicated by the big memorial (†1708) at the base of the central pier. s porch early C18 too. Chancel C15 but out of scale with the rest and different in character. Rendered and much restored in 1899 by *Glasier & Sons*, surveyors, for Lord Sackville. Perp E window. Three-light square-headed windows N and S. The lintel of the priest's doorway looks C17. Inside the mouldings of the arcade are continuous and characterized by a very wide, relatively shallow hollow. The same in the tower arch, the same in the chancel arch, the same in the doorways. Lowering of the nave roof (previously re-roofed with a steep pitch in 1688) and structural repairs by *Jethro Cossins* in 1899–1901. – C17 WAINSCOTTING in the chancel. – FURNISHINGS. Mostly of 1927 by *F. E. Howard* of Oxford, with attractive carved details. – COMMUNION RAILS. 1932. By *W. Ellery Anderson*. – TILES, by the pulpit. Medieval, with Stoneleigh patterns, heraldic emblems and floral designs. – BIER. C17. – STAINED GLASS. In middle window on N side of the nave, two lights. Late C15 glass with rebus of boats with canopies for the Cokesey family (cf. Huddington, Worcs.), whose estates were inherited by Thomas Grevill.* BRASSES. In the chancel. Two knights in armour, both wearing heraldic tabards. Sir John Grevill †1546. Effigy bearded, with broad shoes, a 3-ft 2-in. (97-cm.) figure. Excellent. – Sir Edward Grevill †1559, very similar, but 32 in. (81 cm.) and not so good. – MONUMENTS. Memorials to the Atkins family of Milcote, two of †1835–7 in Greek Revival style by *Davis* of Bidford.

Base of CHURCHYARD CROSS, now carrying a fragment of window tracery from the church.

WESTON-UNDER-WETHERLEY

3060

ST MICHAEL. Red sandstone. The church has a C13 aisle in an uncommonly complete state. Low lancets, traces of the steep former roof-line E and W, three-bay arcade with octagonal piers and arches of one chamfer and one slight chamfer. Low tomb recess. The chancel is earlier. In its E part, visible inside, are traces of Norman N and S windows. Of about 1300 the former N aisle E window with intersecting tracery (now leading into the Perp N chapel) and the chancel with just such an E window. The S windows of the nave are similar. One has Y-tracery with an encircled trefoil in the spandrel. The broad W tower has splayed lancets in the base and a cross-shaped loop higher, but the top stage is Perp. Also Perp the aisle clerestory in lighter stone and the N chapel, which is separated from the chancel by a timber ARCADE. This is Victorian but could the posts be C16? The church was restored in 1867 and the N vestry was added by *F.P. Trepess* in 1906. – FONT. Octagonal, with the main sides concave. Entirely unmoulded and undecorated, except for heads supporting the angle diagonals. They suggest a date early in the C14. – BENCH ENDS. Some C16 tracery applied in the ends of the 1867 nave seats. – STAINED GLASS. Some C15 fragments in the S window. – Three attributed to *Hardman*, the E window 1902 and S chancel 1919. – MONUMENTS. Sir Edward Saunders and wife, 1573. Of stone. Carvings mutilated. The type is German rather than English. The kneeling figures are small, and the centre of the large tablet is four inscription tablets, all with biblical passages and an oblong relief of the Resurrection in small figures and a top lunette with the relief of the Ascension of Christ. As in the Middle Ages, only the legs are visible. – Two Morgan daughters, 1584. Alabaster tablet by *Garrat Hollemans* of Burton upon Trent (JB).
Sabin Drive, ½ m. E of the church, leads to the old hospital site, redeveloped for housing. A cluster of older buildings remains around OLD COURTYARD. These mainly belong to the County

* The Cokesey connection was identified by Alan Brooks, who alerted me to its significance.

Reformatory by *D.R. Hill*, 1856. Weston became a mental hospital in 1929 and closed in 1994.

BRIDGE. *See* Hunningham.

WESTWOOD HEATH *see* p. 304

see p. 304

2040

WHATCOTE

ST PETER. Complicated by repairs in 1767 and 1820 and, surprisingly, serious wartime damage in 1940. Restoration in 1947 by *P.B. & A.B. Chatwin*, who repaired the roof and partially rebuilt the E and S walls and porch. In the nave N wall two Norman windows and a simple Norman doorway. The arch mouldings resemble the N door at Halford. In the S wall several late C13 windows. The chancel E window with intersecting tracery, *c.* 1300.* Handsomely alternating grey and brown courses to the rebuilt E wall. C13 W tower, much repaired; the four belfry windows all different, and the W face partly rebuilt in Lias. – Plain tub FONT. – PULPIT, probably 1767. – COMMUNION RAIL. C17. – BENCHES. Three Perp straight-headed ends with blank tracery. – STAINED GLASS (only the top half) and accompanying MEMORIAL to the Rev. William Sanderson Miller †1909, both by *Powell*, 1911. – BRASS. William Auldyngton †1511. The headless figure is 15 in. (38 cm.) long.

Churchyard CROSS, with C17 or early C18 sundial top and ball finial on the medieval shaft.

Big stone parsonage (now the OLD RECTORY), with gables and chimneys, largely by *William Kendall*, 1843, with side extensions 1910 and later.

2090

WHATELEY
Kingsbury

WHATELEY HALL FARM. Late C16 farmhouse with early C17 wing. L-plan. Rendered exterior. Inside, a late C17 staircase with balustrade of pierced scrolled foliage.

HOLT HALL, ½ m. S of Whateley. A C16 house, H-plan originally, with timber framing inside. Notable, the excellent open-well staircase of *c.* 1630–40 with open balustrade of S-curves and circles instead of turned balusters. Carved frieze running up the strings, with foliage, unicorn, gryphons and mythical

---

*This is shown in a drawing of *c.* 1790 (Aylesford Collection), although before the war the chancel ended in a low, square-headed C19 window.

beasts. Animal supporters on the newels. On the ceiling above the stairs, a framed panel with the arms of the Grosvenor family who owned Holt in the C17.

WHICHFORD

St Michael. The earliest feature is the Norman s doorway with one order of shafts, chevrons in the arch, and a tympanum with a rim of various small motifs. N aisle added to the Norman church in the C13: three bays, round and octagonal piers, double-chamfered arches. The e respond has stiff-leaf decoration; another capital has simple light carving. NW tower, *c.* 1300, but of more than one phase. It is connected with the aisle by an arch of three continuous chamfers. The position of the arch and the window details suggest that the aisle was widened *c.* 1300, but the details also look like a late raw attempt at copying what had been there. C13 N door with nailheads on imposts. Of *c.* 1300 also the three-bay s chapel e of the s doorway and porch. Inside this a low tomb recess. The chancel has a plain C13 priest's doorway and a contemporary piscina, but the windows were renewed *c.* 1330. Perp clerestory with three-light straight-headed windows. Big heads on the cornice above them. Restoration and re-seating by *Thomas Johnson*, 1845, and the fittings mainly of that date including the pews, some with doors. Raised row with higher fronts at the back of the church. – font. Plain, octagonal, with moulded lower half, probably early C14. – Simple arcaded altar rail, probably by *Johnson*. – stained glass. In window heads in the chancel side windows and in the s chapel early C14 pieces in black and yellow stain, some quite fine. Mohun family heraldry. Some emblems and heads. – w window, *Holland, Son & Holt*, 1874. – e and two N windows by *Heaton, Butler & Bayne*, 1900, the e window incorporating C14 Crucifixion and angels. – monuments. In the s chapel recess, coffin-lid with cross with lobed sides and a shield with the Mohun arms, *c.* 1323. – Another tomb recess in the N aisle, low, also *c.* 1300. – In the chancel a Tudor-arched N tomb recess with tomb-chest and an incised alabaster slab as a lid: John Merton, rector, †1537. – Nicholas Asheton, rector, †1582. Tomb-chest in the chancel (s) with panels of early C16 type, but a classical frieze above. Back wall with shield in medallion and two big scrolls. On the lid a brass (18½ in. (47 cm.) long). – Good assembly of C18 memorials, including Henrietta Ingram †1762, with engraved brass plate in stone surround. – War memorial triptych, by *Miss E.K. Martyn*, *c.* 1920.

Whichford House, se of the church. Former rectory. Early C18, Hornton stone, double-pile plan and with a handsome seven-bay s front with three-bay pedimented centre. The l. two matching bays were only added in 2006 by *Reg Ellis & Associates*. In the centre a doorway with moulded surround and segmental pediment. Irregular C17 work (possibly 1662, the date on a re-set lintel) on the W side. The E front again C18: five bays. Complicated inside, and much altered with imported woodwork, mid-C18.

W of the churchyard, the medieval and later OLD HOUSE has a round window with mouchette tracery and, facing the churchyard, a thatched outbuilding with a C16 four-light window with traceried head.

In the village, C17 LEASOWES FARMHOUSE with gabled dormers and attractive C19 farm buildings. Nearby, the former SCHOOL of 1850: long and low, with mullioned windows and central louvred turret.

Towards Ascott, ¼ m. E, a former mid-C19 METHODIST CHAPEL (Wesleyan) with round-headed stone windows set in red brick with blue headers. ASCOTT HOUSE and farm, built for the Weston Park estate, 1824; plans unsigned. Stone with gabled porch, mullioned windows and attached range behind with cartshed and barns. C18 WHICHFORD HILL FARMHOUSE has a fine ashlar front, three bays and three storeys.

WHICHFORD MILL, remotely situated in the upper Stour valley. Stone house dated 1711, and remains of mill pond, leat and wheel pit.

WHITCHURCH

ST MARY. Alone in a circle of trees by the River Stour. Pre-Conquest origin but the associated village was deserted by the C16. Church badly damaged in a tempest *c.* 1659, losing its roof and steeple. Restored piecemeal 1666–80, the W end in 1670–4. *Sir Arthur Blomfield & Sons* restored the chancel in 1890 and the rest in 1896. The history partially explains some of the oddities. Nave and chancel and shingled bell-turret with a pyramid roof. The nave is Norman and a puzzle. Its W part, with herringbone masonry on the N side, i.e. of the C11, is a little wider than its E part, which is C12 and ends in the C12 chancel arch. The E part has a corbel table and a N window. In the W part a C12 doorway, clearly re-set (see inside), with one order of columns. Above, a panel with a late C12 Agnus Dei, with foliage in the spandrels (cf. Tysoe and Studley). The chancel has one blocked Norman S window. The chancel arch has paired Norman demi-columns with scalloped capitals. The arch is double-chamfered and pointed and was no doubt remodelled when the chancel was rebuilt in the early C13 (see one N lancet and traces of two more inside). The large straight-sided chancel windows with panel tracery are of course late Perp, as is the big E window. This is of five lights with a two-centred arch and canopied niches within the deep hollow moulding inside. In the chancel N wall a plain Perp tomb recess. In the nave S wall a window of *c.* 1300 with intersecting tracery. Another *c.* 1670, like the W window. Big posts at the back of the church supporting the bell-turret. – PULPIT. Jacobean. – C17 HOUSELING TABLE and BENCHES (cf. Tredington and Willey). – STAINED GLASS. C15 fragments in tracery lights of Perp chancel side windows. Sacred monograms and heraldry. – E window, part *T.F. Curtis, Ward & Hughes,* 1899. – In W window and nave, glass by *Maggie Perry,* 1989 and 2002. – SCULPTURE. Anglo-Saxon interlace panel re-set in the W wall inside. Is it from a gravestone? In 1989 a further fragment – part of a cross-shaft – was found near the church. – Norman PILLAR PISCINA. – MONUMENT. In the chancel, tomb-chest with incised slab. Cross, chalice and Bible. The inscription is to William Smyth, rector, †1442.

Across the field to the W, two good houses. WHITCHURCH FARMHOUSE, *c.* 1725, with quoins, front of five bays and hipped roof. Then the OLD RECTORY by *William Kendall,* 1839, with Doric detailing to doorway. Beyond, a group of Alscot estate cottages at WIMPSTONE, 1858, but much altered.

CRIMSCOTE, ¾ m. SE, has well-preserved open field systems still farmed in the ancient manner into the early C20. At Lower Andrews, below the C17 MANOR FARM opposite, a stone DOVECOTE with coped gables and nesting recesses and stone ledges inside. The surprise is CRIMSCOTE HILL HOUSE by *Marson Rathbone Taylor,* 2008: a Cotswold-style house on a dramatic hilltop site, butterfly-plan (cf. Papillon Hall, Ullenhall) and with an embattled canted bay alongside the entrance.

WHITLEY *see* p. 305

WHOBERLEY *see* p. 306

WIBTOFT

4080

ST MARY. Medieval W wall and part of the S wall. In other parts reused medieval stones and also brick. Datestone, 1634, re-fixed in E gable. The timber-traceried Gothic windows and brickwork look early C19, probably 1811 when the church was 'put under immediate and complete repair'. The small bell-turret is probably of 1889 when Lutterworth builders *Law & King* re-roofed, re-seated and restored the building.

The site of VENONAE (partly in Leicestershire) lies ¾ m. NW on the crossing of two great Roman roads, the Fosse Way and Watling Street (A5). Nothing is now visible of the Roman settlement, but excavations have revealed a complex of post-holes, ditches, pits and gulleys indicating a widespread roadside settlement or posting station in the late C1–C4. The

colony was commemorated by the HIGH CROSS erected in
1712 at the instigation of the Earl of Denbigh and designed by
a Warwick mason, *Samuel Dunckley*. Only the square pedestal
remains, NW of the road junction. The inscription on it reads:

If, traveller, you search for the footsteps of the ancient
Romans, here you may behold them; for here their most
celebrated ways, crossing each other, extend to the utmost
boundaries of Britain. Here the Venones had their quarters
and at the distance of one mile from hence Claudius, a
certain Commander of a Cohort, seems to have had a camp
towards the Street, and towards the Fosse a tomb.

WILLENHALL *see* p. 306

WILLENHALL *see* p. 306

4080

WILLEY

ST LEONARD. A small late C14 or early C15 church, restored and
partially rebuilt by *Walter F. Lyon* (cf. nearby Bitteswell,
Leics.), 1880–5. The thin ashlar-faced Perp W tower restored
first, 1880–1, and the rest 1884–5. Most of the motifs are Victorian. Uncommonly prominent rood-loft turret on the N side.
Nave roof with timbers dated 1678. – HOUSELING TABLES (cf.
Tredington and Whitchurch) to kneel at to receive Holy Communion, C17. – STAINED GLASS. E window 1890, probably by
A. O. Hemming (AB). – MONUMENT. Early C14 effigy discovered during the restoration, when it was re-set in a new recess.
The figure partly hidden (cf. Tysoe), with three enriched elongated ogee quatrefoils cut in the surface of the slab to reveal
the head and bust, some of the drapery and the feet. The
quatrefoils connect to form part of a cross.
By the church gate, the diminutive SCHOOL (now village hall),
1866–7; diapered brickwork.

5060

WILLOUGHBY

ST NICHOLAS. A puzzling church, with more of C17 date than
at first appears. Fine W tower with large, rather harsh bell-
openings, their tracery flowing. But is it C14 Dec? The now
eroded date on the buttresses was 1636, when Deacon (1828)
says 'the steeple repaired'. But if this was the construction date
then it is a rare and fine example of Gothic survival. There was
other early C17 work here for the Clerkes, who are said to have
built the S aisle and S porch. The chancel was rebuilt in brick
(now rendered) in 1622 and shortened in 1779 when it was
given a classical E window. The present E window is Perp-style
of 1848 when the church was restored for the Rev. Richard

Tawney (vicar 1835–48). The architect may have been *J.L. Akroyd* of Coventry, who prepared an unexecuted scheme in 1843. Inside the tower arch has semicircular responds but semi-octagonal abaci. Its hoodmould with ornamental lozenge stops is very like that over the W window outside. The N and S aisle windows are Perp, and so are the N and S arcades of three bays. The thin piers are generally lozenge-shaped, but with continuous mouldings. The arches are four-centred. The chancel arch belongs to the same build, all early C16. In the S aisle – its masonry very irregular outside – all the windows (including the blocked one at the W) are in wide recesses as if re-set in blocked arcading. Of 1848 the chancel E window, roof, furnishings, reredos with texts etc., and the nave seating too. – FONT. Of cauldron shape, with the top rim partly cut away and replaced by childish E.E. carving: foliage and two demi-figures with outstretched hands (Green Men?). – PULPIT. C17, hexagonal, with carved sides, stem and stair. – STAINED GLASS. Arts and Crafts E window by *Caroline Townshend*, 1903. – E window of S aisle, probably *Burlison & Grylls*, 1920. – Large wall MONUMENT to Dr Henry Clerke, President of Magdalen College, Oxford, †1687, and wife Catherine †1669.

Down a drive across Lower Street, E of the church, the former VICARAGE and outbuildings. The house in gault brick, the stables (dated 1836) in contrasting red brick. Built for the Rev. Richard Tawney, whose father was Surveyor to the Oxford Canal Company and lived at Dunchurch. Square Regency house of three bays, two-storey with Ionic columns to porch and in the entrance hall inside. The stables have semicircular windows on the main elevation and tall blind arcading on the ends.

In the village, several farms and house built by the chief landowners, Magdalen College, Oxford, who acquired the manor and advowson in 1457, or by the well-endowed Willoughby Charity.

On the E side of Lower Street, VALE HOUSE, with brick range at right angles to the C16 timber-framed house. Charmlessly restored *c.* 2004, exposing the timber framing. Large two-storey jettied porch with Tudor arch and side screens of turned balusters, said to have come from the former manor house destroyed in 1620.

Saline springs were discovered here in the early C19 and a Spa Lodge erected in 1825. The spa was short-lived, and WILLOUGHBY HOUSE was later built on the site by Major Francis Mason. A plain house of *c.* 1860, extended in 1908.

WILMCOTE

ST ANDREW. *Harvey Eginton*, 1840–1. Built for the Rev. Edward Bowes Knottesford Fortescue of Alveston Manor, a Tractarian closely connected with the leaders of the Oxford Movement.

It was among the first churches where High Anglican teaching and practices were introduced. E.E., small. Three stepped lancets in the E wall. Vesica below W gable. The aisle roofs have the same pitch as the nave roof, but are set off just a little. Far-projecting N vestry added 1897 and enlarged 1921. Inside, round piers, rather thin, with four fillets. Heavy decorative scheme, attributed to the *Rev F. W. Doxat*, vicar 1879–86. The walls richly painted and stencilled, also the chancel ceiling. Monochrome painting on zinc panels in both aisles. – FITTINGS, mainly 1841, including stone ALTAR, FONT and PULPIT. The pulpit has later monochrome painting. – Also 1841 the CHOIR STALLS and nave SEATING. – Sanctuary tiles by *Chamberlain & Co.* of Worcester, 1841. – STAINED GLASS: E window by *Hardman*, centre light 1859, others 1865.

The church belongs in a group with the SCHOOL and former VICARAGE to the S, all erected for Fortescue. The SCHOOL is by *Butterfield*, 1845–6, but its street frontage is all but obscured by crass additions. The OLD VICARAGE is behind. Also by *Butterfield*, it was built 1846–8 and later extended S and W. These are Butterfield's first secular buildings. Both are stone, Gothic in detail yet domestic.

Former CONGREGATIONAL CHAPEL, Aston Cantlow Road. *Joseph Lattimer*, 1870. Now a house. Further N, three good rows of C19 Lias quarry workers' cottages. Opposite, an eco house (No. 89) by *Callingham Associates*, 2011.

MARY ARDEN'S FARM, Station Road.* Two C16 farmhouses and their associated farm buildings in the care of the Shakespeare Birthplace Trust and open to the public. Mary Arden was Shakespeare's mother, and the plainer brick and Lias house (GLEBE FARM) at the corner was the home of the playwright's maternal grandparents. It contains the virtually complete structure of a box-framed house, dendro-dated to 1514, with cross-wing added shortly after. To the E is PALMER'S FARM, with its impressively long front. This has close studding and a gabled wing with herringbone strutting, all delightfully irregular. The back has square large panel framing. High Lias stone plinths. The W gable-end is Lias too, but the chimneys are brick. Dendro-dating has identified three phases of construction, beginning with the gabled E wing *c.* 1569. The hall (now the central bay) was built *c.* 1580, and the kitchen bay followed *c.* 1581. In Shakespeare's time, this was the home of Adam Palmer (†1584), a yeoman farmer. Interiors furnished in C16 style, emphasizing original features.

Behind and associated with both farms, good ranges of C16–C19 agricultural buildings, including the GREAT BARN, a DOVECOTE and CIDER PRESS.

---

*The site has been reinterpreted following a detailed study by Nat Alcock and Bob Meeson in 2004 which showed that the home of the Arden family had been wrongly identified. The house referred to in the first edition of this guide (and many other guidebooks) as Mary Arden's House is now known as Palmer's Farm, while the adjacent Arden property is Glebe Farm.

The railway opened in 1860 but the present STATION buildings with awnings were erected in 1907. The lattice-girder GWR platform bridge, although dated 1883, came some years later.

WINDERTON

ST PETER AND ST PAUL. Closed in 1976 and in the care of the Feldon Trust since 1981 for community use. By *William Smith*, 1876–8. A chapel of ease in Brailes, paid for by Canon Thoyts (then vicar of Honington), and a credit to him and his architect. A serious job, and sizeable. All brown Hornton ironstone and E.E., i.e. with lancets. Nave and chancel with apse; S porch tower with gargoyles and steep shingled pyramid roof. Vaulted porch with wrought-iron gates. Inside, banded stonework in the chancel and on nave window surrounds. The chancel and apse windows and arcading have marble shafts. To the vestry a big, typical twin opening with a sexfoiled circle in the tympanum, a motif favoured by Butterfield and Street.

Winderton, St Peter and St Paul, perspective.
Engraving, 1877

The FITTINGS largely intact including pink-veined marble REREDOS. – STAINED GLASS. A complete scheme of scenes from the life of Jesus by *Lavers, Barraud & Westlake*, 1877. Among their best work and quite outstanding for its date (AB). The church lies in a fine, elevated position on a ridge high above Brailes. In the hamlet to the E a cluster of C17 stone houses with mullioned windows, some thatched.

WISHAW

Wishaw lies in pleasant countryside, now scarred by the M6 toll motorway which cuts through the village.

ST CHAD. Interesting W tower, no doubt after 1711–12 when money was raised by brief for repairs to church and steeple. Gothic in quite a serious, basic way, i.e. the pointed W window without any tracery and the paired belfry windows. But their moulded surrounds and that of the W doorway, and the big roundels on three sides, show the real date. The chancel is Dec, with ogee-headed lowside windows and an E window with reticulated tracery. S aisle C14 and plain. N aisle C15 incorporating Perp tracery in its pointed E window. Odd clerestory with pairs of round-headed windows and plain parapets. Vestry S of chancel added during restoration by *A. B. Phipson*, 1886–7, and linked to S aisle in 2007. Inside very tall and thin piers, probably heightened. The N arcade is C13 (one round, one octagonal pier), the S arcade early C14 (octagonal piers). In the E wall of the chancel inside a corbel of a man. – PULPIT. Victorian Gothic, from St Mark's, Ladywood, Birmingham, and is perhaps by *Scott*, 1841. – FONTS. A plain C18 baluster with a small bowl (disused) and an octagonal Victorian font on a polished marble column. – WALL PAINTING. Lord's Prayer, late C16, discovered behind a monument (†1673). – STAINED GLASS. All by *T. F. Curtis, Ward & Hughes*, 1908; E window and two others relocated from chancel and combined in S aisle in 2007. – Wall MONUMENTS. John Lisle †1673, with Ionic columns and scrolled pediment. – Lisle Hacket †1728, with broken pediment and obelisk. – WAR MEMORIAL. Alabaster, with carvings of St George and St Chad in niches, c. 1920.

SW of the church, ASH HOUSE (former vicarage) by *Marston & Linford*, 1930. In Church Lane to the W, the MEMORIAL HALL, by *Marcus O. Type* of Birmingham, 1923. Late Arts and Crafts style.

GROUNDS FARM, Grove Lane, 1 m. NW. Later C18 Gothic front. The best of several good farmhouses.

The old MOXHULL HALL, the seat of the Lisle and Hacket families, was demolished in 1906, leaving only the C18 stable block which became Moxhull Park House. Refronted and enlarged for E. F. Goodyear by *Sidney Davies* of Stourbridge in 1927–8, this remains as the main building of THE BELFRY hotel and golf complex developed by Jimmy Byrnes, who bought it in 1959. Later accretions of little architectural distinction.

On a hill 1¼ m. NW of the church is the successor MOXHULL HALL (now a hotel), built 1905–6 for Thomas Howard Ryland. By *Ewen Harper*, in Elizabethan style in red brick with cream terracotta and attractive leadwork. Inside, a good C17 staircase and, in the Ryland Room, a striking chimneypiece of 1877 by *Collier & Plucknett* of Warwick. Both from the old hall.

WITHYBROOK

ALL SAINTS. Short NW tower of grey stone, late C15 in appearance but with an inscribed stone inside dated 1632, when over £95 was raised 'for the Buildinge and Coveringe of the Tower . . . and for other repaires to the said church'. What, if anything, is C17 is unclear. Dec tracery remains in the E window and one S window of the S aisle. One S arcade pier has a row of fleurons in the capital. The S porch with a good ogee-panelled door with roses and fleurs-de-lys has side openings and there is evidence of an upper room or *parvise*. The rest mostly C15, with the usual addition of a Perp clerestory above the arcades of a church whose aisles were added in the C14. Perp refenestration in the chancel and in the widened N aisle, where the late C15 tracery (N and E) has transoms, but only in the middle of the three lights. Restored in 1892–3 by *Edward Turner* of Leicester, the renewed tracery of the W windows probably of that date. In the chancel a mutilated EASTER SEPULCHRE, rediscovered in 1848, with a panelled front against which sleeping soldiers were formerly carved, a recess above in which soldiers are still carved, and also a small frontal angel. Traces of colouring. – Plain circular FONT, possibly late C12. – COMMUNION RAIL. Later C17 with turned balusters. – STAINED GLASS. Many fragments in the chancel and S aisle, mostly C15. – MONUMENTS. Brass of a civilian, *c.* 1500, a 16½-in. (42-cm.) figure. – Sir Christopher Wright †1602. Tomb-chest with incised slab. Back panel with arms. On the tomb-chest an inscription by his wife reflecting on life, death and the after-life.

In Bow Lane E of the village, the former VICARAGE by *Joseph Nevill* of Coventry, 1854 for the patrons, Trinity College, Cambridge. Red brick with quoins, semicircular windows in gauged brickwork with imposts and keystones. Matching extension to the rear.

In Overstone Lane, OVERSTONE LODGE, perhaps 1840s with an extension, 1887. There are drawings by *Ernest Geldart* for unexecuted works here, *c.* 1887 and 1902. Opposite, attractive late C19 farm buildings (residential since 1993) at OVERSTONE

COURT. Possibly by the Overstone estate surveyor, *Josiah Mander* (Bruce Bailey). Red brick with banding and window surrounds in yellow and blue and keystones with corn sheaves and other agricultural symbols.

1050

WIXFORD

ST MILBURGA (a rare dedication). The s chapel restored and the rest rebuilt by *W. J. Hopkins*, 1880–1. By *Hopkins* the pretty wooden bell-turret, the porch and most of the windows at the w end. Features preserved *in situ* include two simple Norman doorways, the s one with columns. E.E. lancets in chancel, but the chancel E window simple Dec. Dec also the curious PISCINA with a plain canopy coming forward in a curve and decorated with a nodding ogee arch. In the N chancel wall a curious re-set two-light window made out of a single slab of Campden stone. It has two tiny, steep-arched lancets and, outside, a shaft in the middle carrying a head. Is this late C13? Good early C14 s chapel. Five-light Perp E window. s windows straight-headed. Two-bay arcade of standard elements. – C15 SCREENS, but only the bases remain. – STAINED GLASS. Fragments in the s chapel E window, including whole small figures, armorial shields. Further fragments in s windows – angels and music. All probably Coventry work, C15. – E window and REREDOS, *Bromsgrove Guild*, 1916. – CHEST. Dug-out, C13, with original ironwork and short posts to the legs. – BRASS, on tomb-chest in centre of s chapel. Erected by Thomas de Cruwe for his wife Juliana, †1411, and for himself (†1418). The finest brasses in the county, full-length (5-ft (1.52-metre)) figures, with complete ogee-sided canopies and inscriptions. The details, especially of her drapery, are very sensitive indeed.

In the churchyard, the square base of a CROSS; its head with the crucifix and other fragments are inside the s chapel. Also a HORSE HOUSE or parson's stable with plank walls and thatched roof; probably C18, restored 1997 by *Alan Griffiths*.

Pretty street lined with C17 crooked cottages on gently sloping ground towards the river.

78   Graceful brick and stone BRIDGE over the Arrow. By *Henry Couchman*, County Bridgemaster, 1800–1; single-span with round flood openings at each end (cf. Barford bridge).

MOOR HALL, ½ m. s of the village. A moated site of C12 origin, the home of the de Cruwes *c.* 1400. The stone ground floor of the N hall part may be early; the recessed and timber-framed upper part with close studding and diagonal bracing *c.* 1470. Extended to the s with a late C16 wing of Lias with Cotswold stone mullions, copied on the later stone front to the r. side which originally had pretty timber framing. Inside, open woodwork in the hall with cusped braces, perhaps C16.

Wixford, St Milburga.
Brass to Thomas de Cruwe †1418 and wife Juliana †1411

WOLFHAMPCOTE

5060

St Peter. In an isolated position alongside the old railway embankment. The church was abandoned in the 1950s and saved from unroofing through the intervention of the Friends of Friendless Churches. Since formal redundancy in 1972 it has been in the care of the Churches Conservation Trust, for whom it was restored by *Lyndon F. Cave*.

Low, ashlar-faced NW tower with lancets, two of them as bell-openings. The top stage was completed in 1690,* and the entire tower is probably C17 (see the squared capitals to the arch to the N aisle) rather than C13 as Pevsner suggested. The tower stands within the W end of the aisle, the last bay of the C13 N arcade being partially encased in the structure. The rest of the church mostly Dec, with good reticulated tracery in the S aisle. Perp clerestory and W window. The N windows with straight mullions clearly a later re-management (they were all square-headed in the earlier C19) of *c.* 1825. Chancel restored in 1848, but the exterior stonework and Perp tracery in the E window may be of the 1903 restoration by *J. B. Williams* of Daventry. Inside, the chancel has a fine open C14 four-bay crown-post roof with wavy struts and braces. – FONT, plain, circular, possibly C13. – SCREEN. C14, i.e. with renewed shafts with shaft-rings, not with mullions, and with intersecting shallow arches with Dec tracery. – COMMUNION RAIL. Late C17; twisted balusters. – Hexagonal PULPIT, *c.* 1790. – BENCHES. Low, one with elementary tracery on its end. – ROYAL ARMS, 1711, restored by *Eve Baker*. – Painted wooden MEMORIALS to members of the Clerke family, 1575–1801, early C19. – The HOOD MAUSOLEUM, immediately E of the church, was built for the Tibbits family (later Tibbits Hood) who acquired the living in 1794. C18 Gothick with diagonal buttresses with cinquefoiled gablets continued up as finials. Blind quatrefoil in E wall which originally had a low gable concealing a shallow slate roof below the chancel E window.

The village disappeared a long time ago. Excavations and historical research show that it stood N of the church, where earthworks are clearly visible. It was depopulated around 1500. Now only a handful of buildings remain. These include C17 WOLFHAMPCOTE HALL, H-plan with a later gabled brick front. Further W, the OLD VICARAGE of 1873, by *William Kerby* of Birmingham. Still striking are the embankments of the former Great Central and London and North Western railways which crossed here. Also the Oxford Canal with traces of the meandering route it followed before straightening in 1834.

Other settlements nearby at Flecknoe and Sawbridge (qq.v.).

WOLSTON

ST MARGARET. Cruciform. A mixture of styles and materials externally. Mainly limestone with red sandstone dressings, both transepts with banding. Re-set Norman S doorway with

---

*Deacon (1828) gives the date on the battlements as 1600.

one order of columns, much zigzag, and a hoodmould with pellets. Windows E.E. and Dec. Perp ashlar clerestory. The S transept is oddly twin-gabled. The other transept has flowing tracery on the E and an unusual mullioned N window dated 1577 with repair dates in 1624 and 1866. The low central tower is a replacement of 1760 by *Job Collins*, ashlar-faced, with bell-openings with Y-tracery. It had tall corner pinnacles originally. The E end restored 1860 with renewed Dec window. Internally the church is much more interesting. The crossing turns out to be entirely Norman. It has high W and E arches, Norman in character but known from the accounts to have been rebuilt in 1760. These are single-stepped and the capitals are decorated with small figures and (in one case) a rather wild interlace. The N and S arches are low, with small windows above, indicating that there must have been small *porticus*-like chambers of Anglo-Saxon form rather than transepts proper. The arches have normal semicircular responds and normal scalloped capitals. The S arch is round and unmoulded; the N arch must have been remodelled at the end of the C12, for it is pointed and has one step and one slight chamfer. Inside the chancel is of *c.* 1300 – see e.g. the SEDILIA and PISCINA with headstops for the hoodmoulds and cusped arches. The nave S arcade of standard elements, apparently of the early C14. The N arcade, also with standard elements, is a little later. The arches into the transepts differ, but seem both Dec. In the S transept are two big cinquecusped tomb recesses, a SEDILE, and a PISCINA. – FONT. Octagonal bowl, with very primitively carved ogee gables with crockets, probably C14 but on a C17 base. – COMMUNION RAILS. One of 1683, with enriched, strong dumb-bell balusters. The rail came from Rowington in 1931–2. – A second, with twisted balusters, in the S transept. – Chunky Victorian PULPIT and DESK, Neo-Norman, by *Jones & Willis*, 1879. – PAINTING. Virgin and Child, the child standing on the ground. By *H. Watson*, 1962, in a style inspired by Graham Sutherland. – STAINED GLASS by eight or more different artists, although some are anonymous and unidentified (suggested attributions by AB). The best are the E window, 1861, probably *Clayton & Bell*, and the S aisle †1864, probably *O'Connor*. – In the chancel, one N by *Hardman*, 1869, and S by *Herbert Bryans*, 1904. – N transept, probably *Burlison & Grylls*, 1926. – S transept, one by *Chance Brothers and Co.*, †1859, in pictorial style with bright colours, the other by *W.G. Taylor*, 1876. – Three in the N aisle by *Heaton, Butler & Bayne*, 1888, 1915 and undated. – W window, *Jones & Willis*, 1907. – MONUMENTS. In the two S transept recesses two effigies dating from *c.* 1300, one badly defaced. – In the same transept N, a monument of Purbeck marble, a familiar early C16 type with a recess, against the back wall of which were once brasses. Panelled sides and coving, canopy with quatrefoil frieze and cresting.

BAPTIST CHURCH, ¼ m. SE on Main Street. Built in 1819, enlarged in 1834 and renovated in 1867, although the dates do not readily match what one sees. It looks mid-C19. W gallery on iron columns. – MONUMENTS. One Gothic, 1830s. – Another, slate with gold lettering and topped with an urn. Stephen Mellows †1839, by *Seager* of Coventry.

In the village centre a stream flows N along MAIN STREET with little bridges to the houses on the W side. These include at the S end the so-called MANOR, an early C18 five-bay red brick house with modillion cornice, hipped roof and dormers which took the name after the real manor was demolished in 1928.

SE off SCHOOL STREET, the SURGERY, attractively designed with varied roof-lines by the *Design Team Partnership*, 1974. Further E, the former SCHOOL by *Joseph Nevill*, 1858. Much modified, although bits of the steep gables and crazy brickwork remain.

WOLSTON PRIORY. Built for Roger or William Wigston, Leicester merchants, in the late C16. The main front is of red sandstone with mullioned and mullioned-and-transomed windows. The part beyond the three-storeyed porch is altered, but the place of the kitchen fireplace survives. Inside, the screens passage is also still clearly marked. The side of the house has mullioned windows too, but is of Lias. At the back two timber-framed gables are visible either side of a chimney.

WOLVERTON

ST MARY. Nave and chancel in one. The nave C13: see the W front (with mid-buttress) and the N window of three stepped lancet lights. A chancel consecration recorded in 1316. Side windows are single lights with trefoiled heads. On the N, a C14 tomb recess adapted as an entrance to the vestry. On the S, piscina and triple sedilia. Restoration by *Thomas Garner*, 1869–70. His the present bell-turret with pierced openings, the rebuilt E end, the vestry, the wagon roofs and most of the fittings. – Marble CREED and DECALOGUE, possibly of 1738 when the chancel was wainscotted. – Victorian CHOIR STALLS, complete with carved misericords. – Light Perp wooden SCREEN, reinstated in 1884: full-height, with delicate tracery. – FONT. Octagonal, Perp, with quatrefoils. – STAINED GLASS. In one N window many fragments, C15. Bits in other windows as well, mostly re-set in grisaille glass by *Thomas Baillie & Co.*, 1869. – In a chancel S window *Morris & Co.* glass (r. panel by *W.B. Scott*, l. by *Ford Madox Brown*), 1870. – MONUMENTS. Thomas (†1664) and Elizabeth (†1707) Stanton, by *Edward Stanton*. – Opposite, two further Stanton memorials, Sarah †1701 attributed to *William Stanton* (GF) and Thomas †1715.

OLD RECTORY, at foot of path to church. A cottage purchased in 1835 and enlarged in 1846, with curly bargeboards, pinnacled gables and ridge cresting.

SCHOOL, 1876. Towards Norton Lindsey, 1 m. NE, and built for the joint School Board. Brick, with minimal stone dressings, and very plain.

WOLVERTON COURT, near the green S of the church. A surprising house, made interesting by the terrain. On the N a low C16 timber-framed range, restored by *Holtom & Yorke*, c. 1905. Above, a S-facing late C18 three-storey wing with hipped roof and to the garden two-storey canted bays. The two parts cleverly linked by *Clough Williams-Ellis* for W. Shaw, 1912. His E front is a free kind of Neo-Queen Anne, three bays, stone, three storeys, with giant pilasters with odd geometrical capitals, a hipped roof, and attenuated urns at the top. The urns and door hood made in terracotta by *Mary Seton Watts* at the Compton Pottery, Surrey. Inside, the staircase in the Williams-Ellis section incorporates old timbers from the Sheldonian Theatre in Oxford. The dining room has a big stone fireplace and a ceiling with decorated plasterwork on the coving.

WOLVEY

ST JOHN THE BAPTIST. Norman S doorway with two orders of columns and in the arch chevrons as well as fleur-de-lys-like motifs set radially. Dec aisles. Cusped intersecting Y-tracery on the S and nice parapet with blind quatrefoils. N aisle with mainly reticulated tracery. Perp W tower. C17 work in the chancel dated 1624 above the E window and the N aisle – narrowed (see its W window) after the roof collapsed in 1620 – with the date 1630 on the NW buttress. Inside, both arcades of four bays, the S a little earlier than the N. Chancel redone for Lord Overstone, 1858. Of this period the chancel arch (date and monogram on the keystone), roof and low pink-veined marble wall dividing chancel and nave. Main restoration by the *Bassett Smiths*, 1899–1900. S porch rebuilt 1909, incorporating carved C17 timbers. Nave re-pewed on Hornton stone floor, 1929. – FONT. Shallow hexagonal C17 bowl like a capital, on a pier with flatly carved arcading. – Fussy panelled TOWER SCREEN, by *H.C. Corlette*, 1937. – STAINED GLASS. E window by *C.C. Powell*, 1938; very outdated. – S aisle E, *Hemming & Co.*, 1927. – MONUMENTS. In the N aisle two effigies, he with a hood of mail and the legs parallel. Her effigy is of a type familiar in the early C14, and this is probably his date too. – Thomas Astley †1603 and wife. Two big alabaster effigies, not very good. – Elizabeth Arnold †1788. Standing, purely architectural monument, with an urn on the top.

Immediately S of the church, the octagonal MILLENNIUM ROOMS by *Michael Partridge Project Partnership Limited*, 2000.

BAPTIST CHAPEL, School Lane. Built in 1803 for a congregation established in 1789. Brick in Flemish bond with light headers and hipped slate roof. Square, originally with four bays of round-headed windows each side, those on the entrance front in two tiers. Schoolroom (enlarged 1857) and vestry added in 1818. E extension of 1863 with rose window over three unequal lights. W gallery inside, 1834.

WOLVEY HALL, Hall Lane, W of the church. Largely rebuilt by *R. & J. Goodacre* of Leicester for H. F. J. Coape-Arnold in 1889, but incorporating the staircase, fireplaces and heraldic glass from the old hall of *c.* 1676. The staircase partly of 1677 with openwork balustrade, not yet of foliage, no longer of strapwork, but of volute-like shapes interconnected. Connected at the NE, the former private chapel, also by the *Goodacres*, 1890–1. A plain brick building with lancets, used as the Roman Catholic church until 1924.* Along the short drive JACOB'S WELL, dated 1707, with a little river god, reclining.

In the village, a few C17 or C18 cottages including two with thatched roofs and eyebrow dormers. In School Lane, a blue brick gateway with bellcote above, preserved from the former SCHOOL, 1853. By the Anker just NE of the church, WOLVEY GRANGE, *c.* 1830: Flemish bond chequered brickwork and hipped roof.

WOLVEY HEATH, ¾ m. N, was once dominated by windmills. The AXE & COMPASS is a good inter-war pub on an angled site at the junction of five roads. By *Heaton & Walker* of Hinckley, 1928–9.

WOOD END, COVENTRY *see* p. 307

WOOD END
Kingsbury

A large settlement in Kingsbury parish. It grew up around the nearby brickworks and coal mine in the late C19 and its buildings are typical of those found in smaller semi-rural mining communities.

ST MICHAEL AND ALL ANGELS. A wooden mission room, 1906. – STAINED GLASS. Two in the chancel, probably by *Hardman*, *c.* 2000.

WOOTTON WAWEN

A large and ancient Forest of Arden parish, originally including Henley-in-Arden and Ullenhall. A Saxon monastery was founded

---

*St James the Less (*Fosbroke & Bedingfield* of Leicester, 1924) in Coventry Road was closed in 2011.

here early in the C8. Of this nothing survives, but the church had
been re-founded long before the Conquest when Wootton was
held by Waga or Wagen, from whom the village takes its unusual
name. By then Wootton had eleven daughter foundations. The
incoming Normans settled the church on the Benedictine abbey
of Conches, in Normandy. They established a small priory which
lay W of the church. Being an alien house its assets were confiscated after 1338 and eventually given to King's College, Cambridge, in 1443. The C15 also saw the rise of the Harewell family
as tenants of the college manors and stewards of their estates.
Wootton Hall became the seat of their Smith, Smith-Carington,
and Smythe descendants. Wootton is a linear village, strung out
along the Stratford–Birmingham road, which was turnpiked in
1725. The houses are mainly on the outside of the long curve
through the village centre.

ST PETER. Set back on a low eminence with fine open views   3
from the S and W across the field. It is a handsome, varied and
interesting building, better understood since Birmingham University's 'Wootton Project' research programme, 1983–90. The
exterior is worth describing as one would take it in as a new-
comer. Its situation invites such treatment. There is a crossing
tower oddly embedded in a church not, it seems, made for it.
The tower is Perp, one would assume, as it has twin bell-
openings each side with a transom. The nave and S aisle are
evidently Perp too, and very rich with carving in the distinctive

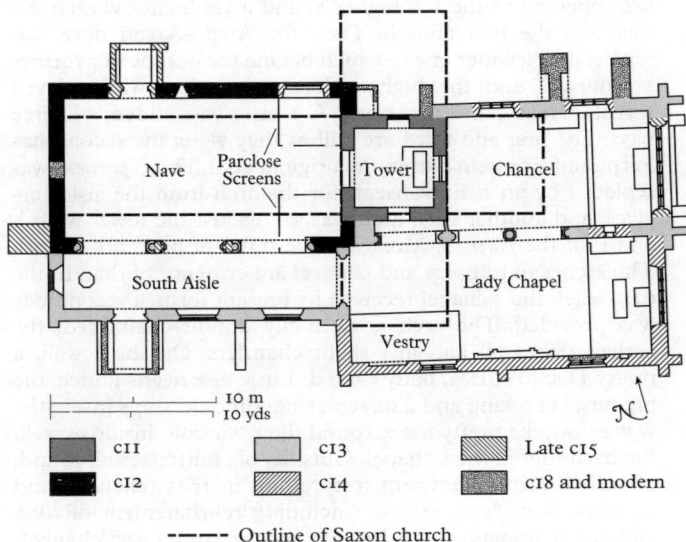

Wootton Wawen, St Peter.
Plan

style of Lapworth and Henley-in-Arden. Clerestory windows
of three lights with four-centred arches. Battlements and pinnacles. The aisle has decorated buttresses and battlements and
a Perp doorway. But the windows with their lancet lights, decorated spandrels, and straight tops must be C17.* The S chapel
is earlier than the nave and S aisle. It has a separate pitched
roof and S windows with reticulated tracery. The E window is
a group of five stepped ogee-headed lights of *c.* 1330. Then the
chancel, wider than the tower, with Dec N windows. The seven-
light Perp E window, its surround charmingly enriched by a
leaf strip, dates from the time of Robert Wodelark, provost of
King's College 1452–79. The nave W side has a tiny blocked
doorway and a large five-light Perp window. That is what
receives you, but turn the corner and on the N you have a
Norman nave wall, with some herringbone masonry, and a
small Norman window, apart from a Perp doorway and a large
late C13 window with intersecting tracery. Move further E, and
the crossing tower, here exposed, proves to be Anglo-Saxon,
now thought to be C10 or early C11. The long-and-short quoins
are unmistakable and the small doorway-like opening at
ground level clearly led into a *porticus*. Unmistakable also the
flat raised band outside the arch and concentric with it, a
barbaric substitute for mouldings. Now represented only by
stubby buttresses, the N *porticus* is shown in early illustrations
and stood to a substantial height until the mid C19.

One should enter now and verify this architectural history
by going straight into the tower space, and there it is indeed,
entirely Anglo-Saxon and entirely preserved: another such *porticus* opening to the S, a higher E, and a yet higher W arch. So
that was the first church. Then the Anglo-Saxon nave was
replaced by a wider one to which belong the outline of a former
N doorway and the higher Norman window with splayed
reveals. Next came C13 work. A S aisle was added, of three
bays. The first and third are still as they were; the second has
Perp reinforcement within the original arch. The, S *porticus* was
replaced by an E.E. transept, for the arch from the aisle survives, and another such arch was set against the tower walls l.
and r. of the *porticus*. Moreover the transept had an E chapel.
The arches to transept and chancel are evidence of that. In the
C14, when the S chapel received its present form, a second bay
was provided. The arch is normally double-chamfered; the
earlier arches all had just slight chamfers. On the S wall, a
pretty Dec PISCINA, flatly carved. Little else needs notice: the
big busts of a king and a queen as hoodmould stops inside the
W window, the pretty frieze round the E window, inside as well,
the barn roof in the S chapel. Outside, big buttresses all round,
of varied form. Significant restorations in 1635 (chancel) and
by *G. G. Scott Jun.*, 1880–1 (including reinstatement of nave
and aisle parapets), *W.H. Bidlake*, 1907–8 (tower and chancel)
and *F.W.B. Yorke*, 1948–57.

---

* It is known that some work went on in 1635, although chiefly in the chancel.

As Scott observed, the building represents 'the epitome in stone of the History of the English Nation', all periods of pre-Reformation church architecture being represented. There is architectural quality too, clearly evident from outside. Inside, the understandable compartmentalization to create usable spaces makes it harder to appreciate the whole. The narrow crossing now serves as a chancel, while the original is a separate worship area. The barn-like S chapel, filled with monuments and artefacts, is little more than a cluttered passage.

Beyond what one can readily see there are further features to note. Close examination of the Saxon masonry and roof-line analysis have confirmed that the first nave was of the same width as the tower, while the appendages N and S and the presbytery on the E were all narrower. The E side of the arch to the presbytery is exposed and largely intact. There are blocked belfry window openings in the upper stage on all four sides of the Saxon tower. Lower down there are double-splayed openings in the ringing chamber, some with pre-Conquest timber lintels and one with a contemporary wooden window frame. It is now known that the nave was rebuilt on a larger scale soon after the Conquest, perhaps *c.* 1080, and the chancel similarly in the 1130s. Their N and E walls are essentially Norman although now with later windows. A blocked window on the S side of the chancel indicates the original plan before the S chapel was enlarged in the C14.

FONT. Octagonal, early C14, with heads sticking out from the underside (cf. Aston Cantlow). – PULPIT. Perp-style, wood, with traceried panels, but probably early C17 (cf. Aston Cantlow again). The stair balustrade is C18. – SCREENS. Two complete parclose screens, and some other parts set against solid boarding on the E wall of the nave with an ogival archway around the W tower opening in the centre. The parts include brackets for images, perhaps from a reredos. – ALTAR RAILS, in the chancel, C17 with openwork splat-fret balusters. – BENCH ENDS with stunted poppyheads and coarse tracery. – CHEST of the C14 with typical legs and simple ironwork. – Against the nave W wall, two columns and coving from the former C18 W gallery, removed in the 1950s. – COMMUNION RAIL, C17, with flat, openwork balusters. – WALL PAINTINGS. In the S chapel, early C14 and still discernible although broken up by monuments. Rediscovered in 1918, the paintings include scenes from the Passion, the seven deadly sins and the lives of saints. – Hanoverian ROYAL ARMS, George I. – DECALOGUE, CREED and LORD'S PRAYER, dated 1752. – STAINED GLASS. Medieval fragments in the E window, including angels in the heads of the central lights. – More in the chancel N and nave N windows. – S aisle W and S, *Hardman*, 1897 and 1900. – W window, *Heaton, Butler & Bayne*, 1905. – Window in Saxon N *porticus* arch, by *Margaret Traherne*, 1958, in memory of F W. B. Yorke. – MONUMENTS. Recumbent effigy of a knight; alabaster, supposedly John Harewell †1428. His head on his helmet. – Tomb-chest with the brasses of John Harewell †1505, wife and children. The brasses are 3 ft (90 cm.) long. Against the tomb-chest cusped and decorated quatrefoils. – Francis Smith †1606. He lies stiffly on his side, his head on his helmet. Columns l. and r., inscription on strapwork plate, coat of arms at the top. – William Somervile †1676, attributed to *William Stanton* (GF). – Robert Knight †1744. Free-standing urn on a high pedestal (against the E window). – Henry Knight and others, 1764. Big architectural triptych, white. – John Phillips †1836, by *John Ternouth*. White tablet in a Gothic brown stone arch with rib-vault. On the tablet, a kneeling, mourning woman, presumably the widow who 'inscribes this marble'. Above an urn, a torch, and a bow with a broken string.

OUR LADY AND ST BENEDICT (R.C.), on the hill on Alcester Road, s of the station. *T.R. Donnelly*, 1904, to replace the earlier chapel at Wootton Hall (*see* below) whose altar and stained glass were transferred here in 1904.[*] Porch 1983. Inside, a lavish Gothic triptych REREDOS by *A.H. Skipworth*, 1888, brought from St Leonard's, Newark, Notts., in 1978. Crucifixion figures in alabaster. – Pictorial STAINED GLASS of the Annunciation in the gallery w window, signed by *Samuel Lowe*, 1814. – Two chancel windows of 1888 acquired in 1977 from the demolished chapel at Grove Park, Hampton-on-the-Hill, possibly by *Mayer & Co.* (AB). – In the side chapel, a panel from the Carmelite convent at Yardley (east Birmingham), in the style of *Evie Hone*, 1950s. – Other windows have panels set in cathedral glass, some from the old chapel and others brought from elsewhere in the 1970s. – MEMORIAL BRASS, Fr. James Benedict Deday †1845, by *Hardman*, 1851.

(R.C.) CEMETERY, E of the river. Created in 1852. Cemetery CROSS, designed by *A.W.N. Pugin*, with octagonal base and crucifix at the top. The CHAPEL built 1872 has STAINED GLASS by *Lavers, Barraud & Westlake* (AB).

WOOTTON HALL, in parkland E of the church, is a large, dignified mansion of 1687, now divided into flats. On the site of an older house, parts of which may be incorporated. Built for Francis Smyth, 2nd Viscount Carington, and his wife Anne. Their initials and arms are on the dated rainwater heads, and the Carington arms are boldly displayed in the pediment. Nine by nine bays, of stone with quoins. The front has a slightly projecting pedimented three-bay centre, and the ground-floor windows all have pediments, alternately triangular and segmental, the others with lugged architraves. Nicely carved modillion cornice. To the w side, which is of three storeys rather than the two of the front, a big plain Venetian window was interpolated in the C18. George Capewell Hughes acquired the hall in 1904 and is said to have redecorated the interiors in a range of then fashionable styles. He also built the Neoclassical LODGE, like an Ionic temple, re-did the approach with wrought-iron entrance gates, and provided the balustraded

*The sarcophagus-shaped 'marble' ALTAR was accidentally damaged and had to be replaced.

wall all along the Stratford road to the late C18 river BRIDGE. The cascades and pools upstream were created by Peter Holford in the 1780s and 1790s not only as improvements to the grounds but also to provide power for the mill (*see* below).

Behind the house is the former R.C. CHAPEL, built in 1813 for the Dowager Lady Smythe. Most likely by *John Tasker*, who had several Roman Catholic patrons and worked in the Greek Revival style for Sir James Smythe at Acton Burnell Hall (Shrops.) in 1814. Remarkably spacious, with plain arched windows, but inside broad giant wall pilasters, a triglyph frieze, and the altar space divided by two mighty Greek Doric columns. The ceiling is a shallow segmental vault. Fittings removed after it ceased to be a chapel in 1905.

To the N of the house and chapel is now – a comedown – a large mobile home park. Within it, a pretty DOVECOTE.

At the road junction in the village centre, a cluster of timber-framed buildings including the BULL'S HEAD. A little w the former TOLLHOUSE, erected when the Wootton to Alcester road was turnpiked in 1814. Towards Henley, MANOR FARM is timber-framed and gabled. In the centre an apsed door hood with robustly carved acanthus, flowers and much fruit. Further N and opposite, the former SCHOOL building (now a house) is by *George Clark*, the Wootton builder and architect, 1856–7.

Directly s of the church, the SEYMOUR HOMES, built in memory of the son of W.J. Fieldhouse, 1919–20. Probably by *J.P. Osborne & Son*. Pretty Arts and Crafts cottage homes, with later memorial garden and charming statue of mother and child by *Richard Goulden*, 1924, commemorating Lucy Field-house, †1921.

Beyond the river, the former MILL, converted to flats 1978. Built as a paper mill, *c.* 1766, and enlarged *c.* 1824. Brick, four storeys, and twelve bays with a three-bay pediment and segment-headed windows. Opposite, C18 PRIORY FARM, of brick, three bays and two storeys, with one-bay, one-storey wings.

Then the AQUEDUCT on the Stratford Canal, which opened in 1816. Cast-iron trough on brick piers, by *W. Whitmore*, engineer, 1813. The NAVIGATION INN of the same date.

Up the hill, AUSTY MANOR, built in 1912–13 for W.J. Fieldhouse in the style of a Cotswold manor house.

EDSTONE HALL, 1½ m. ESE, has a Grecian lodge on the main road. This belongs to the demolished mansion of *c.* 1829 for John Phillips on the site of the earlier house of the Somervilles. The present house by *F. W.B. Yorke* for Percy Pritchard, 1939, is in free Tudor style, brick with mullioned stone windows and Cotswold slate roof. Slightly angled front towards the lake. Tall mullioned-and-transomed staircase window on the entrance front. First-floor balconies on two sides. Comfortable interiors with light woodwork and soft-coloured stone fire-places. Heraldic panels by *T. W. Camm* set in clear glass in the main staircase window.

WORMLEIGHTON

An estate village, owned by the Spencers of Althorp since 1506. The village bought by John Spencer, grazier, had already been depopulated by William Cope around 1495. Spencer decided to build his new house on the present hilltop site and a new village around it. The positions of the former village and its moated manor house are clearly visible in earthworks and field systems N and W of the church.

St Peter. Of Hornton stone, mostly C13. Early the low W tower. Little heads on buttress set-offs, many heads in the corbel table. The tower has a S doorway, an unusual feature. Also early the S doorway and, inside, both aisle arcades. Three bays, round piers, octagonal abaci, pointed single-chamfered arches. Later the chancel arch. The chancel windows are Dec and Perp. Dec N aisle windows, straight-headed, and tomb recess in the aisle, Perp clerestory, small windows. Piecemeal Victorian restoration, mainly by estate craftsmen, including rebuilding S and E chancel walls, 1840, partial re-seating with enclosed pews, 1841–2, and window renewal (e.g. S aisle). – SCREEN. Perp, one of the best in the county. Said to have been brought from Southam (q.v.) in the Civil War and erected here after 1660. Tall, with ribbed coving and loft parapet. The divisions are of two lights, i.e. one arch for both but a mullion reaching up into its apex. One of the carved figures wears spectacles. – STALLS. With poppyheads: foliage, two bishops back-to-back, an angel and a dove, and also a well-endowed hound. – PANELLING by the altar. Jacobean with panels with double arches. – COMMUNION RAIL, 1664. Turned balusters and long pendant balusters between them. – BENCH BACK with fine panels of tracery from the dado of the screen. – ROYAL ARMS, 1826. – TILES. In nave and aisles, some armorial, late C13. – STAINED GLASS. E window, *Clayton & Bell*, 1880. – Chancel side windows, *Powell* quarries, 1852. – More quarries in S aisle, perhaps reused from 1851 E window. – In S aisle E by *Wailes*, 1869, and W, †1870. – MONUMENT. John Spencer †1610 at Blois. Probably by *Jasper Hollemans*, like the Spencer monuments at Brington (Bruce Bailey). Large, flat tablet. The framing of the inscription of pilasters with scrolls and shields. At the top close scrolls of big strapwork.

Manor House. The manor house of the Spencers must once have been a grand affair, perhaps as grand as Compton Wynyates. It was begun by John Spencer in 1516 and its full extent is clear from a map dated 1634. In 1645, however, it was deliberately burnt by the Royalists to prevent it falling into the hands of the Parliamentarians. What remains is one range of brick, 1516–19, with irregular battlements and large three- and four-light transomed straight-headed windows on ground floor and first floor. The lights are arched and not cusped. Round

Wormleighton, Manor House, perspective.
Engraving by W. Niven, 1878

the corner on the E, a big canted bay window with the same details. Ground floor only now, but once full height. Plain interior. The panelling from the first floor is now at Althorp, Northants.

Detached and SW of the manor is a mighty GATEHOUSE of stone, dated 1613. Built for Sir Robert, 1st Lord Spencer. The gateway is round-arched, the windows mullioned. A two-storeyed range continues to the W, a big tower of five storeys to the E. Gatehouse and tower are severely cubic in outline. Behind is early C17 CHURCH FARM, with mullioned windows.

ESTATE HOUSING. Stone, Tudor-style, gabled, and identical to others on the Althorp estates at Brington and Harlestone, Northants. Ten cottages SE of the gatehouse, all 1848, by *Blore*. Nicely grouped, with big gardens. Opposite, the VILLAGE HALL (former school), 1839, humbly extended by *George Devey*, 1882. More COTTAGES W of the school, by estate architect *Josiah Mander*, 1875–6, and N of the church, 1877 (Bruce Bailey).

WROXALL

2070

WROXALL ABBEY. Founded as a priory (it was never an abbey) for Benedictine nuns in 1141. What remains of it is part of the church and two roofless fragments of the ranges round the

cloister, uncovered and left standing when the old house was
demolished in 1866. One is a small square room with two
vaulting-shafts N and S. This is considered the chapter house,
but no more than ten could have been seated in it. It also has
a very small doorway. Perhaps it was the vestibule. The other
is the E end of what is most likely to have been the S, i.e. refectory, range of the cloister. The doorways in the N and S walls
are again tiny. These elements were incorporated into the
domestic range of the MANSION, built by the Burgoynes who
acquired the property in 1544, which joined up with the S side
of the church. This range was in stone with close-studded
timber framing to the first floor and a raised gable over the
gateway towards the church. This house later had a W front in
brick with mullioned-and-transomed stone windows and
shaped gables.

Wroxall was bought by Sir Christopher Wren in 1713, when
he was over eighty, to establish a foothold for his son and his
descendants in the Warwickshire squirearchy. What would
Wren have thought of the large and rather joyless Victorian
brick mansion that has taken the place of the venerable one he
bought? Standing to the W of the previous house, it was built
for James Dugdale of Liverpool. Dated 1866, it is in a style
between late Gothic and late Tudor with steep gables, and it
shuns all symmetry. The entrance columns of Aberdeen granite
carry – oddly and elaborately – an oriel. On the garden side
they manage to carry two oriels side by side, a feat of resourcefulness and of course without historical authority. The architect was *Walter Scott* of Liverpool and Birkenhead, previously
G.G. Scott's clerk of works at Walton (q.v.). The staircase
window, three-light mullioned-and-transomed with trefoil
heads, has stained glass by *Tony Dury*, 1867, depicting the
legend of crusader Sir Hugh de Hatton who founded the
priory. In the principal room on the garden side is a chimneypiece with granite columns. In another, a fine carved overmantel dated 1551. N of the house, gaunt Victorian STABLES
(now called Wren Court) with spiky clock tower, also by *Scott*,
1866, as is the LODGE on Birmingham Road. Wroxall was used
as a girls' school from 1936 to 1995. Since 2001 the estate has
been run by a private company and the mansion and other
buildings restored and adapted for business and hospitality
uses.

In front of the house is the CHURCH (formerly St Leonard, but
since 2009 known as Wren's Cathedral). What survives is the
N side of the nunnery church, adapted by the Burgoynes after
1544. The outline of the former S arcade can be discerned
outside and in. The E end was reopened when the organ
chamber was added, 1896–7. The E respond is original. Internally the exposed piers of two bays in the nave are clearly Dec
in form. It is assumed that the nave to which the arcade led
was the nuns' nave and the chancel and the remaining N aisle
the parishioners'. The N windows are of three steeply stepped
lights under one arch. In the spandrels are distorted cusped

pointed trefoils, and the result is slight ogees in the side arches. There are five such windows plus the W window, plus a re-set S window, but the middle one to the N has a simple doorway under, decorated with big ballflower. The E window is Perp, of five lights with panel tracery. What is the date of the rest? It is Dec obviously, and, as the church was consecrated in 1315, we may well have a key date here for stylistic comparisons (cf. Lapworth, Tanworth-in-Arden). In 1663–4 a W tower of brick was placed inside the W end. It has a round stair-turret reaching up higher than the battlements. Below the Perp-looking bell-openings on the N side is an area of dogtooth bond brickwork. Rainwater heads each side of the church signal repairs in 1663 for Sir Roger Burgoyne and in 1714 for Christopher Wren, and *Thomas Garner*'s restoration for James Dugdale, 1867–8. *Garner*, later as *Bodley & Garner*, was responsible for most of the Victorian fittings. – The carved stone REREDOS and linked Dugdale memorial in the S chapel, typically *Bodley & Garner*, 1896–7. – SCREEN and CHOIR STALLS: Dec style, probably 1868. – PULPIT also *c.* 1868 but incorporating C14 flamboyant panels, French or English. – PANELLING in the nave. Possibly C17, though installed after 1858. – STAINED GLASS. The church has one of the most complete assemblies of medieval glass in the county, well restored by *Thomas Baillie & Co.* under *Garner*, 1869. Most of it on the N side is of the original date of the windows, i.e. early C14, with unmistakable greens and yellows and big canopies. – The E window C15, with original scenes, though much restored. – Under the tower and one S window, doubtless *Burlison & Grylls*, †1876 and *c.* 1880. – MONUMENTS. Brass to a lady, *c.* 1430, a 25-in. (64-cm.) figure. – Lady Burgoyne †1693/4, attributed to *William Stanton* (GF). – Also a number of C18 tablets, some quite good. Among those commemorated are several Christopher Wrens (*see* above), †1737 to †1842. – Major H.C. Dugdale †1909 and wife, by *Clough Williams-Ellis*, 1913.

To the NE of the church in Wren's Garden is a wall almost of the crinkle-crankle type, though lobed not undulating. The GATEPIERS in the wall are of the Wren period, but the iron GATES (without their original overthrow) between them were designed by *Williams-Ellis*, *c.* 1912. He was living at Wroxall at the outbreak of the Great War and did several commissions for the estate. S of the priory ruins are remains of C18 garden walls and gatepiers, possibly surviving from landscaping undertaken by *Charles Bridgeman* for Wren after 1714. Landscaping for the Victorian house was undertaken by *Edward Milner*, 1866, as represented by stone walling for the forecourt and terraces.

Estate village, 1 m. NE of the abbey. SCHOOL dated 1863: polychromatic in coloured brick and pale stone dressings, including carved winged beasts. The blue brick N extensions are by *Williams-Ellis*, 1912. Behind, three pairs of 1860s estate cottages in similar style and the former CLUB ROOM, 1885. Further along School Lane, OLD LAUNDRY COTTAGE, 1890, flanked

by blocks of cottages. On the main road, the FORGE etc. Down
a track E of the main road N of the village is Neo-Georgian
WARREN FARM, by *Williams-Ellis*, 1912.
See also Beausale.

WYKEN *see* p. 307

GLOSSARY

Numbers and letters refer to the illustrations (by John Sambrook) on pp. 740–747.

ABACUS: flat slab forming the top of a capital (3a).

ACANTHUS: classical formalized leaf ornament (4b).

ACCUMULATOR TOWER: *see* Hydraulic power.

ACHIEVEMENT: a complete display of armorial bearings.

ACROTERION: plinth for a statue or ornament on the apex or ends of a pediment; more usually, both the plinth and what stands on it (4a).

AEDICULE (*lit.* little building): architectural surround, consisting usually of two columns or pilasters supporting a pediment.

AGGREGATE: *see* Concrete.

AISLE: subsidiary space alongside the body of a building, separated from it by columns, piers, or posts.

ALMONRY: a building from which alms are dispensed to the poor.

AMBULATORY (*lit.* walkway): aisle around the sanctuary (q.v.).

ANGLE ROLL: roll moulding in the angle between two planes (1a).

ANSE DE PANIER: *see* Arch.

ANTAE: simplified pilasters (4a), usually applied to the ends of the enclosing walls of a portico *in antis* (q.v.).

ANTEFIXAE: ornaments projecting at regular intervals above a Greek cornice, originally to conceal the ends of roof tiles (4a).

ANTHEMION: classical ornament like a honeysuckle flower (4b).

APRON: raised panel below a window or wall monument or tablet.

APSE: semicircular or polygonal end of an apartment, especially of a chancel or chapel. In classical architecture sometimes called an *exedra*.

ARABESQUE: non-figurative surface decoration consisting of flowing lines, foliage scrolls etc., based on geometrical patterns. Cf. Grotesque.

ARCADE: series of arches supported by piers or columns. *Blind arcade* or *arcading*: the same applied to the wall surface. *Wall arcade*: in medieval churches, a blind arcade forming a dado below windows. Also a covered shopping street.

ARCH: Shapes *see* 5c. *Basket arch* or *anse de panier* (basket handle): three-centred and depressed, or with a flat centre. *Nodding*: ogee arch curving forward from the wall face. *Parabolic*: shaped like a chain suspended from two level points, but inverted. Special purposes. *Chancel*: dividing chancel from nave or crossing. *Crossing*: spanning piers at a crossing (q.v.). *Relieving or discharging*: incorporated in a wall to relieve superimposed weight (5c). *Skew*: spanning responds not diametrically opposed. *Strainer*: inserted in an opening to resist inward pressure. *Transverse*: spanning a main axis (e.g. of a vaulted space). *See also* Jack arch, Triumphal arch.

ARCHITRAVE: formalized lintel, the lowest member of the classical entablature (3a). Also the moulded frame of a door or window (often borrowing the profile of a classical architrave). For *lugged* and *shouldered* architraves *see* 4b.

ARCUATED: dependent structurally on the arch principle. Cf. Trabeated.

ARK: chest or cupboard housing the

tables of Jewish law in a syn-agogue.

ARRIS: sharp edge where two surfaces meet at an angle (3a).

ASHLAR: masonry of large blocks wrought to even faces and square edges (6d).

ASTRAGAL: classical moulding of semicircular section (3f).

ASTYLAR: with no columns or similar vertical features.

ATLANTES: *see* Caryatids.

ATRIUM (plural: atria): inner court of a Roman or C20 house; in a multi-storey building, a toplit covered court rising through all storeys. Also an open court in front of a church.

ATTACHED COLUMN: *see* Engaged column.

ATTIC: small top storey within a roof. Also the storey above the main entablature of a classical façade.

AUMBRY: recess or cupboard to hold sacred vessels for the Mass.

BAILEY: *see* Motte-and-bailey.

BALANCE BEAM: *see* Canals.

BALDACCHINO: free-standing can-opy, originally fabric, over an altar. Cf. Ciborium.

BALLFLOWER: globular flower of three petals enclosing a ball (1a). Typical of the Decorated style.

BALUSTER: pillar or pedestal of bellied form. *Balusters*: vertical supports of this or any other form, for a handrail or coping, the whole being called a *balustrade* (6c). *Blind balustrade*: the same applied to the wall surface.

BARBICAN: outwork defending the entrance to a castle.

BARGEBOARDS (corruption of 'vergeboards'): boards, often carved or fretted, fixed beneath the eaves of a gable to cover and protect the rafters.

BAROQUE: style originating in Rome *c.*1600 and current in England *c.*1680–1720, characterized by dramatic massing and silhouette and the use of the giant order.

BARROW: burial mound.

BARTIZAN: corbelled turret, square or round, frequently at an angle.

BASCULE: hinged part of a lifting (or bascule) bridge.

BASE: moulded foot of a column or pilaster. For *Attic* base *see* 3b.

BASEMENT: lowest, subordinate storey; hence the lowest part of a classical elevation, below the *piano nobile* (q.v.).

BASILICA: a Roman public hall; hence an aisled building with a clerestory.

BASTION: one of a series of defens-ive semicircular or polygonal pro-jections from the main wall of a fortress or city.

BATTER: intentional inward inclina-tion of a wall face.

BATTLEMENT: defensive parapet, composed of *merlons* (solid) and *crenels* (embrasures) through which archers could shoot; some-times called *crenellation*. Also used decoratively.

BAY: division of an elevation or interior space as defined by regular vertical features such as arches, columns, windows etc.

BAY LEAF: classical ornament of overlapping bay leaves (3f).

BAY WINDOW: window of one or more storeys projecting from the face of a building. *Canted*: with a straight front and angled sides. *Bow window*: curved. *Oriel*: rests on corbels or brackets and starts above ground level; also the bay window at the dais end of a medi-eval great hall.

BEAD-AND-REEL: *see* Enrichments.

BEAKHEAD: Norman ornament with a row of beaked bird or beast heads usually biting into a roll moulding (1a).

BELFRY: chamber or stage in a tower where bells are hung.

BELL CAPITAL: *see* 1b.

BELLCOTE: small gabled or roofed housing for the bell(s).

BERM: level area separating a ditch from a bank on a hill-fort or barrow.

BILLET: Norman ornament of small half-cylindrical or rectangular blocks (1a).

BLIND: *see* Arcade, Baluster, Portico.

BLOCK CAPITAL: *see* 1a.

BLOCKED: columns, etc. inter-rupted by regular projecting

blocks (*blocking*), as on a Gibbs surround (4b).

BLOCKING COURSE: course of stones, or equivalent, on top of a cornice and crowning the wall.

BOLECTION MOULDING: covering the joint between two different planes (6b).

BOND: the pattern of long sides (*stretchers*) and short ends (*headers*) produced on the face of a wall by laying bricks in a particular way (6e).

BOSS: knob or projection, e.g. at the intersection of ribs in a vault (2c).

BOWTELL: a term in use by the C15 for a form of roll moulding, usually three-quarters of a circle in section (also called *edge roll*).

BOW WINDOW: *see* Bay window.

BOX FRAME: timber-framed construction in which vertical and horizontal wall members support the roof (7). Also concrete construction where the loads are taken on cross walls; also called *cross-wall construction*.

BRACE: subsidiary member of a structural frame, curved or straight. *Bracing* is often arranged decoratively e.g. quatrefoil, herringbone (7). *See also* Roofs.

BRATTISHING: ornamental crest, usually formed of leaves, Tudor flowers or miniature battlements.

BRESSUMER (*lit.* breast-beam): big horizontal beam supporting the wall above, especially in a jettied building (7).

BRICK: *see* Bond, Cogging, Engineering, Gauged, Tumbling.

BRIDGE: *Bowstring*: with arches rising above the roadway which is suspended from them. *Clapper*: one long stone forms the roadway. *Roving*: *see* Canal. *Suspension*: roadway suspended from cables or chains slung between towers or pylons. *Stay-suspension* or *stay-cantilever*: supported by diagonal stays from towers or pylons. *See also* Bascule.

BRISES-SOLEIL: projecting fins or canopies which deflect direct sunlight from windows.

BROACH: *see* Spire and 1c.

BUCRANIUM: ox skull used decoratively in classical friezes.

BULL-NOSED SILL: sill displaying a pronounced convex upper moulding.

BULLSEYE WINDOW: small oval window, set horizontally (cf. Oculus). Also called *œil de bœuf*.

BUTTRESS: vertical member projecting from a wall to stabilize it or to resist the lateral thrust of an arch, roof, or vault (1c, 2c). A *flying buttress* transmits the thrust to a heavy abutment by means of an arch or half-arch (1c).

CABLE OR ROPE MOULDING: originally Norman, like twisted strands of a rope.

CAMES: *see* Quarries.

CAMPANILE: free-standing bell-tower.

CANALS: *Flash lock*: removable weir or similar device through which boats pass on a flush of water. Predecessor of the *pound lock*: chamber with gates at each end allowing boats to float from one level to another. *Tidal gates*: single pair of lock gates allowing vessels to pass when the tide makes a level. *Balance beam*: beam projecting horizontally for opening and closing lock gates. *Roving bridge*: carrying a towing path from one bank to the other.

CANTILEVER: horizontal projection (e.g. step, canopy) supported by a downward force behind the fulcrum.

CAPITAL: head or crowning feature of a column or pilaster; for classical types *see* 3; for medieval types *see* 1b.

CARREL: compartment designed for individual work or study.

CARTOUCHE: classical tablet with ornate frame (4b).

CARYATIDS: female figures supporting an entablature; their male counterparts are *Atlantes* (*lit.* Atlas figures).

CASEMATE: vaulted chamber, with embrasures for defence, within a castle wall or projecting from it.

CASEMENT: side-hinged window.

CASTELLATED: with battlements (q.v.).

CAST IRON: hard and brittle, cast in a mould to the required shape.

Wrought iron is ductile, strong in tension, forged into decorative patterns or forged and rolled into e.g. bars, joists, boiler plates; *mild steel* is its modern equivalent, similar but stronger.

CATSLIDE: *See* 8a.

CAVETTO: concave classical moulding of quarter-round section (3f).

CELURE OR CEILURE: enriched area of roof above rood or altar.

CEMENT: *see* Concrete.

CENOTAPH (*lit.* empty tomb): funerary monument which is not a burying place.

CENTRING: wooden support for the building of an arch or vault, removed after completion.

CHAMFER (*lit.* corner-break): surface formed by cutting off a square edge or corner. For types of chamfers and *chamfer stops see* 6a. *See also* Double chamfer.

CHANCEL: part of the E end of a church set apart for the use of the officiating clergy.

CHANTRY CHAPEL: often attached to or within a church, endowed for the celebration of Masses principally for the soul of the founder.

CHEVET (*lit.* head): French term for chancel with ambulatory and radiating chapels.

CHEVRON: V-shape used in series or double series (later) on a Norman moulding (1a). Also (especially when on a single plane) called *zigzag*.

CHOIR: the part of a cathedral, monastic or collegiate church where services are sung.

CIBORIUM: a fixed canopy over an altar, usually vaulted and supported on four columns; cf. Baldacchino. Also a canopied shrine for the reserved sacrament.

CINQUEFOIL: *see* Foil.

CIST: stone-lined or slab-built grave.

CLADDING: external covering or skin applied to a structure, especially a framed one.

CLERESTORY: uppermost storey of the nave of a church, pierced by windows. Also high-level windows in secular buildings.

CLOSER: a brick cut to complete a bond (6e).

CLUSTER BLOCK: *see* Multi-storey.

COADE STONE: ceramic artificial stone made in Lambeth 1769–c.1840 by Eleanor Coade (†1821) and her associates.

COB: walling material of clay mixed with straw. Also called *pisé*.

COFFERING: arrangement of sunken panels (coffers), square or polygonal, decorating a ceiling, vault, or arch.

COGGING: a decorative course of bricks laid diagonally (6e). Cf. Dentilation.

COLLAR: *see* Roofs and 7.

COLLEGIATE CHURCH: endowed for the support of a college of priests.

COLONNADE: range of columns supporting an entablature. Cf. Arcade.

COLONNETTE: small medieval column or shaft.

COLOSSAL ORDER: *see* Giant order.

COLUMBARIUM: shelved, niched structure to house multiple burials.

COLUMN: a classical, upright structural member of round section with a shaft, a capital, and usually a base (3a, 4a).

COLUMN FIGURE: carved figure attached to a medieval column or shaft, usually flanking a doorway.

COMMUNION TABLE: unconsecrated table used in Protestant churches for the celebration of Holy Communion.

COMPOSITE: *see* Orders.

COMPOUND PIER: grouped shafts (q.v.), or a solid core surrounded by shafts.

CONCRETE: composition of *cement* (calcined lime and clay), *aggregate* (small stones or rock chippings), sand and water. It can be poured into *formwork* or *shuttering* (temporary frame of timber or metal) on site (*in-situ* concrete), or *pre-cast* as components before construction. *Reinforced*: incorporating steel rods to take the tensile force. *Pre-stressed*: with tensioned steel rods. Finishes include the impression of boards left by formwork (*board-marked* or *shuttered*), and texturing with steel brushes (*brushed*) or hammers (*hammer-dressed*). *See also* Shell.

CONSOLE: bracket of curved outline (4b).

COPING: protective course of masonry or brickwork capping a wall (6d).

CORBEL: projecting block supporting something above. *Corbel course*: continuous course of projecting stones or bricks fulfilling the same function. *Corbel table*: series of corbels to carry a parapet or a wall-plate or wall-post (7). *Corbelling*: brick or masonry courses built out beyond one another to support a chimney-stack, window, etc.

CORINTHIAN: *see* Orders and 3d.

CORNICE: flat-topped ledge with moulded underside, projecting along the top of a building or feature, especially as the highest member of the classical entablature (3a). Also the decorative moulding in the angle between wall and ceiling.

CORPS-DE-LOGIS: the main building(s) as distinct from the wings or pavilions.

COTTAGE ORNÉ: an artfully rustic small house associated with the Picturesque movement.

COUNTERCHANGING: of joists on a ceiling divided by beams into compartments, when placed in opposite directions in alternate squares.

COUR D'HONNEUR: formal entrance court before a house in the French manner, usually with flanking wings and a screen wall or gates.

COURSE: continuous layer of stones, etc. in a wall (6e).

COVE: a broad concave moulding, e.g. to mask the eaves of a roof. *Coved ceiling*: with a pronounced cove joining the walls to a flat central panel smaller than the whole area of the ceiling.

CRADLE ROOF: *see* Wagon roof.

CREDENCE: a shelf within or beside a piscina (q.v.), or a table for the sacramental elements and vessels.

CRENELLATION: parapet with crenels (*see* Battlement).

CRINKLE-CRANKLE WALL: garden wall undulating in a series of serpentine curves.

CROCKETS: leafy hooks. *Crocketing* decorates the edges of Gothic features, such as pinnacles, canopies, etc. *Crocket capital*: *see* 1b.

CROSSING: central space at the junction of the nave, chancel, and transepts. *Crossing tower*: above a crossing.

CROSS-WINDOW: with one mullion and one transom (qq.v.).

CROWN-POST: *see* Roofs and 7.

CROWSTEPS: squared stones set like steps, e.g. on a gable (8a).

CRUCKS (*lit.* crooked): pairs of inclined timbers (*blades*), usually curved, set at bay-lengths; they support the roof timbers and, in timber buildings, also support the walls (8b). *Base*: blades rise from ground level to a tie- or collar-beam which supports the roof timbers. *Full*: blades rise from ground level to the apex of the roof, serving as the main members of a roof truss. *Jointed*: blades formed from more than one timber; the lower member may act as a wall-post; it is usually elbowed at wall-plate level and jointed just above. *Middle*: blades rise from half-way up the walls to a tie- or collar-beam. *Raised*: blades rise from half-way up the walls to the apex. *Upper*: blades supported on a tie-beam and rising to the apex.

CRYPT: underground or half-underground area, usually below the E end of a church. *Ring crypt*: corridor crypt surrounding the apse of an early medieval church, often associated with chambers for relics. Cf. Undercroft.

CUPOLA (*lit.* dome): especially a small dome on a circular or polygonal base crowning a larger dome, roof, or turret.

CURSUS: a long avenue defined by two parallel earthen banks with ditches outside.

CURTAIN WALL: a connecting wall between the towers of a castle. Also a non-load-bearing external wall applied to a C20 framed structure.

CUSP: *see* Tracery and 2b.

CYCLOPEAN MASONRY: large irregular polygonal stones, smooth and finely jointed.

CYMA RECTA and CYMA REVERSA: classical mouldings with double curves (3f). Cf. Ogee.

DADO: the finishing (often with panelling) of the lower part of a wall in a classical interior; in origin a formalized continuous pedestal. *Dado rail*: the moulding along the top of the dado.

DAGGER: *see* Tracery and 2b.

DALLE-DE-VERRE (*lit.* glass-slab): a late C20 stained-glass technique, setting large, thick pieces of cast glass into a frame of reinforced concrete or epoxy resin.

DEC (DECORATED): English Gothic architecture *c.* 1290 to *c.* 1350. The name is derived from the type of window tracery (q.v.) used during the period.

DEMI- or HALF-COLUMNS: engaged columns (q.v.) half of whose circumference projects from the wall.

DENTIL: small square block used in series in classical cornices (3c). *Dentilation* is produced by the projection of alternating headers along cornices or stringcourses.

DIAPER: repetitive surface decoration of lozenges or squares flat or in relief. Achieved in brickwork with bricks of two colours.

DIOCLETIAN OR THERMAL WINDOW: semicircular with two mullions, as used in the Baths of Diocletian, Rome (4b).

DISTYLE: having two columns (4a).

DOGTOOTH: E.E. ornament, consisting of a series of small pyramids formed by four stylized canine teeth meeting at a point (1a).

DORIC: *see* Orders and 3a, 3b.

DORMER: window projecting from the slope of a roof (8a).

DOUBLE CHAMFER: a chamfer applied to each of two recessed arches (1a).

DOUBLE PILE: *see* Pile.

DRAGON BEAM: *see* Jetty.

DRESSINGS: the stone or brickwork worked to a finished face about an angle, opening, or other feature.

DRIPSTONE: moulded stone projecting from a wall to protect the lower parts from water. Cf. Hood-mould, Weathering.

DRUM: circular or polygonal stage supporting a dome or cupola. Also one of the stones forming the shaft of a column (3a).

DUTCH or FLEMISH GABLE: *see* 8a.

EASTER SEPULCHRE: tomb-chest used for Easter ceremonial, within or against the N wall of a chancel.

EAVES: overhanging edge of a roof; hence *eaves cornice* in this position.

ECHINUS: ovolo moulding (q.v.) below the abacus of a Greek Doric capital (3a).

EDGE RAIL: *see* Railways.

E.E. (EARLY ENGLISH): English Gothic architecture *c.* 1190–1250.

EGG-AND-DART: *see* Enrichments and 3f.

ELEVATION: any face of a building or side of a room. In a drawing, the same or any part of it, represented in two dimensions.

EMBATTLED: with battlements.

EMBRASURE: small splayed opening in a wall or battlement (q.v.).

ENCAUSTIC TILES: earthenware tiles fired with a pattern and glaze.

EN DELIT: stone cut against the bed.

ENFILADE: reception rooms in a formal series, usually with all doorways on axis.

ENGAGED or ATTACHED COLUMN: one that partly merges into a wall or pier.

ENGINEERING BRICKS: dense bricks, originally used mostly for railway viaducts etc.

ENRICHMENTS: the carved decoration of certain classical mouldings, e.g. the ovolo (qq.v.) with *egg-and-dart*, the cyma reversa with *waterleaf*, the astragal with *bead-and-reel* (3f).

ENTABLATURE: in classical architecture, collective name for the three horizontal members (architrave, frieze, and cornice) carried by a wall or a column (3a).

ENTASIS: very slight convex deviation from a straight line, used to prevent an optical illusion of concavity.

EPITAPH: inscription on a tomb.

EXEDRA: *see* Apse.

EXTRADOS: outer curved face of an arch or vault.

EYECATCHER: decorative building terminating a vista.

FASCIA: plain horizontal band, e.g. in an architrave (3c, 3d) or on a shopfront.

FENESTRATION: the arrangement of windows in a façade.

FERETORY: site of the chief shrine of a church, behind the high altar.

FESTOON: ornamental garland, suspended from both ends. Cf. Swag.

FIBREGLASS, or glass-reinforced polyester (GRP): synthetic resin reinforced with glass fibre. GRC: glass-reinforced concrete.

FIELD: *see* Panelling and 6b.

FILLET: a narrow flat band running down a medieval shaft or along a roll moulding (1a). It separates larger curved mouldings in classical cornices, fluting or bases (3c).

FLAMBOYANT: the latest phase of French Gothic architecture, with flowing tracery.

FLASH LOCK: *see* Canals.

FLÈCHE or SPIRELET (*lit.* arrow): slender spire on the centre of a roof.

FLEURON: medieval carved flower or leaf, often rectilinear (1a).

FLUSHWORK: knapped flint used with dressed stone to form patterns.

FLUTING: series of concave grooves (flutes), their common edges sharp (arris) or blunt (fillet) (3).

FOIL (*lit.* leaf): lobe formed by the cusping of a circular or other shape in tracery (2b). *Trefoil* (three), *quatrefoil* (four), *cinquefoil* (five), and *multifoil* express the number of lobes in a shape.

FOLIATE: decorated with leaves.

FORMWORK: *see* Concrete.

FRAMED BUILDING: where the structure is carried by a framework – e.g. of steel, reinforced concrete, timber – instead of by load-bearing walls.

FREESTONE: stone that is cut, or can be cut, in all directions.

FRESCO: *al fresco*: painting on wet plaster. *Fresco secco*: painting on dry plaster.

FRIEZE: the middle member of the classical entablature, sometimes ornamented (3a). *Pulvinated frieze* (*lit.* cushioned): of bold convex profile (3c). Also a horizontal band of ornament.

FRONTISPIECE: in C16 and C17 buildings the central feature of doorway and windows above linked in one composition.

GABLE: For types *see* 8a. *Gablet*: small gable. *Pedimental gable*: treated like a pediment.

GADROONING: classical ribbed ornament like inverted fluting that flows into a lobed edge.

GALILEE: chapel or vestibule usually at the W end of a church enclosing the main portal(s).

GALLERY: a long room or passage; an upper storey above the aisle of a church, looking through arches to the nave; a balcony or mezzanine overlooking the main interior space of a building; or an external walkway.

GALLETING: small stones set in a mortar course.

GAMBREL ROOF: *see* 8a.

GARDEROBE: medieval privy.

GARGOYLE: projecting water spout often carved into human or animal shape.

GAUGED or RUBBED BRICKWORK: soft brick sawn roughly, then rubbed to a precise (gauged) surface. Mostly used for door or window openings (5c).

GAZEBO (jocular Latin, 'I shall gaze'): ornamental lookout tower or raised summer house.

GEOMETRIC: English Gothic architecture *c.*1250–1310. *See also* Tracery. For another meaning, *see* Stairs.

GIANT or COLOSSAL ORDER: classical order (q.v.) whose height is that of two or more storeys of the building to which it is applied.

GIBBS SURROUND: C18 treatment of an opening (4b), seen particularly in the work of James Gibbs (1682–1754).

GIRDER: a large beam. *Box*: of hollow-box section. *Bowed*: with its top rising in a curve. *Plate*: of I-section, made from iron or steel plates. *Lattice*: with braced frame-work.

GLAZING BARS: wooden or some-times metal bars separating and supporting window panes.

GRAFFITI: *see* Sgraffito.

GRANGE: farm owned and run by a religious order.

GRC: *see* Fibreglass.

GRISAILLE: monochrome painting on walls or glass.

GROIN: sharp edge at the meeting of two cells of a cross-vault; *see* Vault and 2c.

GROTESQUE (*lit.* grotto-esque): wall decoration adopted from Roman examples in the Renaissance. Its foliage scrolls incorporate figur-ative elements. Cf. Arabesque.

GROTTO: artificial cavern.

GRP: *see* Fibreglass.

GUILLOCHE: classical ornament of interlaced bands (4b).

GUNLOOP: opening for a firearm.

GUTTAE: stylized drops (3b).

HALF-TIMBERING: archaic term for timber-framing (q.v.). Sometimes used for non-structural decorative timberwork.

HALL CHURCH: medieval church with nave and aisles of approxim-ately equal height.

HAMMERBEAM: *see* Roofs and 7.

HAMPER: in C20 architecture, a visu-ally distinct topmost storey or storeys.

HEADER: *see* Bond and 6e.

HEADSTOP: stop (q.v.) carved with a head (5b).

HELM ROOF: *see* 1C.

HENGE: ritual earthwork.

HERM (*lit.* the god Hermes): male head or bust on a pedestal.

HERRINGBONE WORK: *see* 7ii. Cf. Pitched masonry.

HEXASTYLE: *see* Portico.

HILL-FORT: Iron Age earthwork en-closed by a ditch and bank system.

HIPPED ROOF: *see* 8a.

HOODMOULD: projecting moulding above an arch or lintel to throw off water (2b, 5b). When horizontal often called a *label*. For label stop *see* Stop.

HUSK GARLAND: festoon of stylized nutshells (4b).

HYDRAULIC POWER: use of water under high pressure to work machinery. *Accumulator tower*: houses a hydraulic accumulator which accommodates fluctuations in the flow through hydraulic mains.

HYPOCAUST (*lit.* underburning): Ro-man underfloor heating system.

IMPOST: horizontal moulding at the springing of an arch (5c).

IMPOST BLOCK: block between abacus and capital (1b).

IN ANTIS: *see* Antae, Portico and 4a.

INDENT: shape chiselled out of a stone to receive a brass.

INDUSTRIALIZED or SYSTEM BUILDING: system of manufac-tured units assembled on site.

INGLENOOK (*lit.* fire-corner): recess for a hearth with provision for seating.

INTERCOLUMNATION: interval be-tween columns.

INTERLACE: decoration in relief simulating woven or entwined stems or bands.

INTRADOS: *see* Soffit.

IONIC: *see* Orders and 3c.

JACK ARCH: shallow segmental vault springing from beams, used for fireproof floors, bridge decks, etc.

JAMB (*lit.* leg): one of the vertical sides of an opening.

JETTY: in a timber-framed building, the projection of an upper storey beyond the storey below, made by the beams and joists of the lower storey oversailing the wall; on their outer ends is placed the sill of the walling for the storey above (7). Buildings can be jettied on several sides, in which case a *dragon beam* is set diagonally at the corner to carry the joists to either side.

JOGGLE: the joining of two stones to prevent them slipping by a notch in one and a projection in the other.

KEEL MOULDING: moulding used from the late C12, in section like the keel of a ship (1a).

KEEP: principal tower of a castle.

KENTISH CUSP: *see* Tracery and 2b.

KEY PATTERN: *see* 4b.

KEYSTONE: central stone in an arch or vault (4b, 5c).

KINGPOST: *see* Roofs and 7.

KNEELER: horizontal projecting stone at the base of each side of a gable to support the inclined coping stones (8a).

LABEL: *see* Hoodmould and 5b.

LABEL STOP: *see* Stop and 5b.

LACED BRICKWORK: vertical strips of brickwork, often in a contrasting colour, linking openings on different floors.

LACING COURSE: horizontal reinforcement in timber or brick to walls of flint, cobble, etc.

LADY CHAPEL: dedicated to the Virgin Mary (Our Lady).

LANCET: slender single-light, pointed-arched window (2a).

LANTERN: circular or polygonal windowed turret crowning a roof or a dome. Also the windowed stage of a crossing tower lighting the church interior.

LANTERN CROSS: churchyard cross with lantern-shaped top.

LAVATORIUM: in a religious house, a washing place adjacent to the refectory.

LEAN-TO: *see* Roofs.

LESENE (*lit.* a mean thing): pilaster without base or capital. Also called *pilaster strip*.

LIERNE: *see* Vault and 2c.

LIGHT: compartment of a window defined by the mullions.

LINENFOLD: Tudor panelling carved with simulations of folded linen. *See also* Parchemin.

LINTEL: horizontal beam or stone bridging an opening.

LOGGIA: gallery, usually arcaded or colonnaded; sometimes free-standing.

LONG-AND-SHORT WORK: quoins consisting of stones placed with the long side alternately upright and horizontal, especially in Saxon building.

LONGHOUSE: house and byre in the same range with internal access between them.

LOUVRE: roof opening, often protected by a raised timber structure, to allow the smoke from a central hearth to escape.

LOWSIDE WINDOW: set lower than the others in a chancel side wall, usually towards its W end.

LUCAM: projecting housing for hoist pulley on upper storey of warehouses, mills, etc., for raising goods to loading doors.

LUCARNE (*lit.* dormer): small gabled opening in a roof or spire.

LUGGED ARCHITRAVE: *see* 4b.

LUNETTE: semicircular window or blind panel.

LYCHGATE (*lit.* corpse-gate): roofed gateway entrance to a churchyard for the reception of a coffin.

LYNCHET: long terraced strip of soil on the downward side of prehistoric and medieval fields, accumulated because of continual ploughing along the contours.

MACHICOLATIONS (*lit.* mashing devices): series of openings between the corbels that support a projecting parapet through which missiles can be dropped. Used decoratively in post-medieval buildings.

MANOMETER or STANDPIPE TOWER: containing a column of water to regulate pressure in water mains.

MANSARD: *see* 8a.

MATHEMATICAL TILES: facing tiles with the appearance of brick, most often applied to timber-framed walls.

MAUSOLEUM: monumental building or chamber usually intended for the burial of members of one family.

MEGALITHIC TOMB: massive stone-built Neolithic burial chamber covered by an earth or stone mound.

MERLON: *see* Battlement.

METOPES: spaces between the triglyphs in a Doric frieze (3b).

MEZZANINE: low storey between two higher ones.

MILD STEEL: *see* Cast iron.

MISERICORD (*lit.* mercy): shelf on a carved bracket placed on the underside of a hinged choir stall seat to support an occupant when standing.

billet
chevron
roll moulding
beakhead
double chevron
impost block
block capital
scalloped capital
shaft
keel moulding
orders

double chamfer

shaft-ring
angle roll
fillet
nook-shaft

Nailhead
Dogtooth
Ballflower
Fleuron

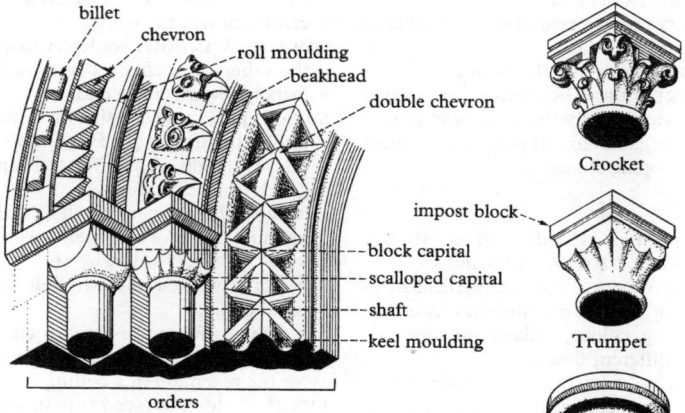

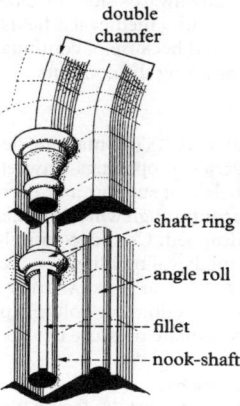

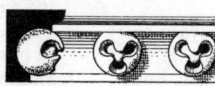

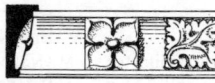

a) MOULDINGS AND ORNAMENT

Crocket
Trumpet
Bell
Stiff-leaf
Waterleaf

b) CAPITALS

Saddleback roof
Helm roof
Splay-foot spire
Broach spire

Clasping
flying
Angle
Set-back
Diagonal

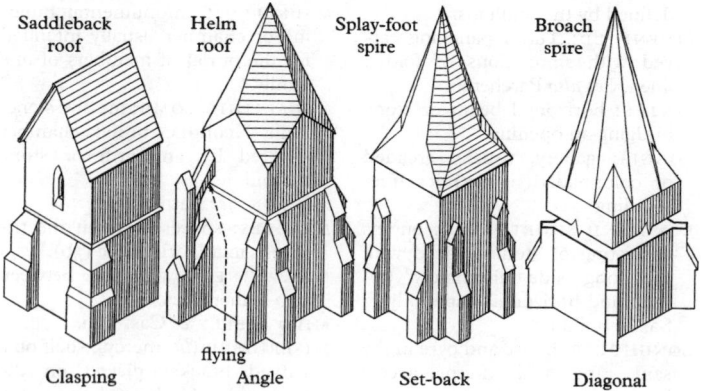

c) BUTTRESSES, ROOFS AND SPIRES

FIGURE 1: MEDIEVAL

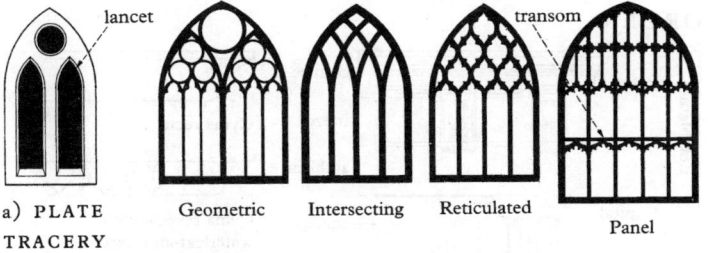

a) PLATE TRACERY

Geometric Intersecting Reticulated Panel

lancet

transom

Quatrefoil with Kentish cusps

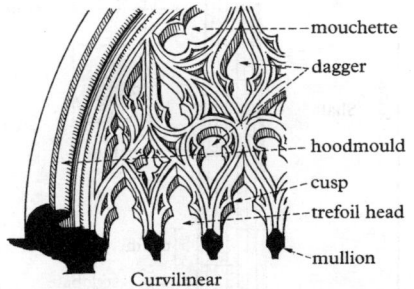

mouchette
dagger
hoodmould
cusp
trefoil head
mullion

Curvilinear

b) BAR TRACERY

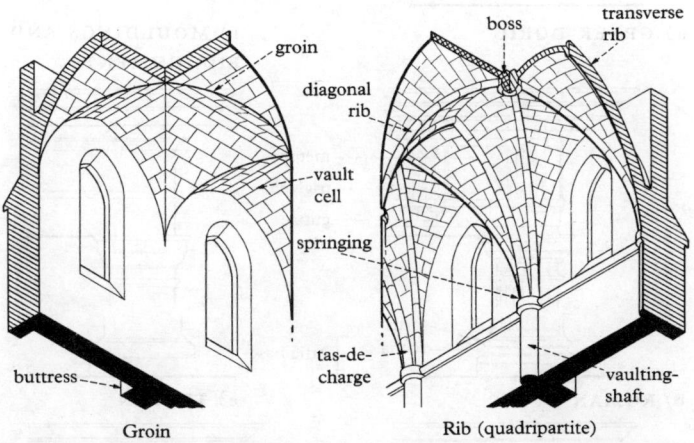

groin

diagonal rib

vault cell

springing

buttress

Groin

boss

transverse rib

tas-de-charge

vaulting-shaft

Rib (quadripartite)

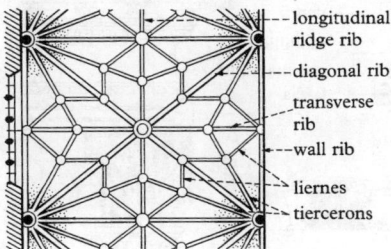

longitudinal ridge rib
diagonal rib
transverse rib
wall rib
liernes
tiercerons

Lierne

Fan

c) VAULTS

FIGURE 2: MEDIEVAL

ORDERS

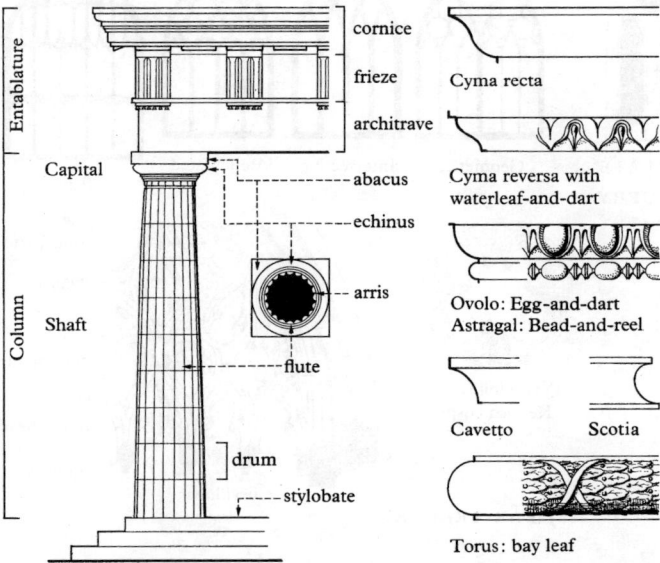

a) GREEK DORIC

f) MOULDINGS AND ENRICHMENTS

Cyma recta

Cyma reversa with waterleaf-and-dart

Ovolo: Egg-and-dart
Astragal: Bead-and-reel

Cavetto   Scotia

Torus: bay leaf

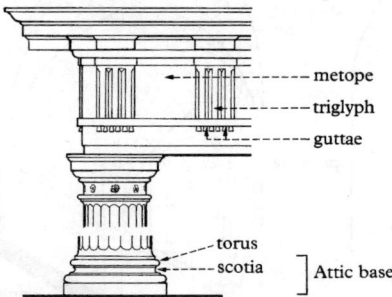

b) ROMAN DORIC

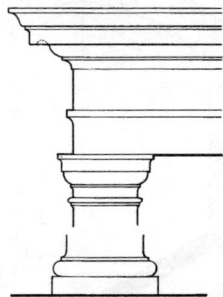

e) TUSCAN

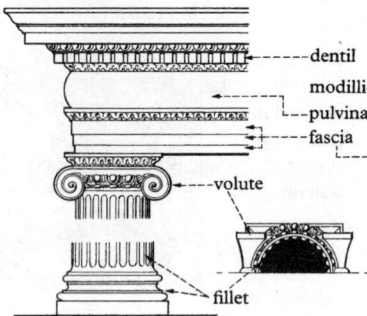

c) IONIC

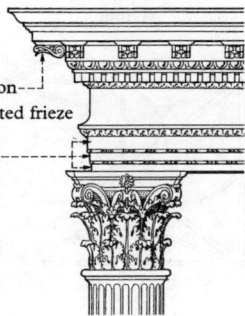

d) CORINTHIAN

FIGURE 3: CLASSICAL

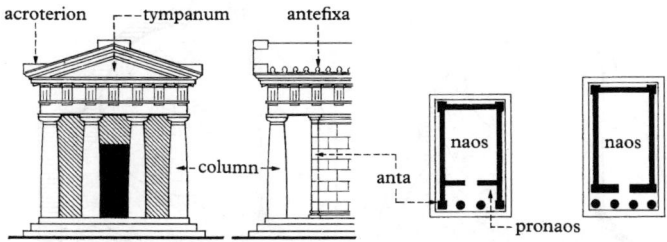

a) PORTICO

Distyle in antis   Prostyle

Anthemion & Palmette

Guilloche

Key pattern

Rinceau

Husk garland

Vitruvian scroll

Console

Diocletian window

Acanthus

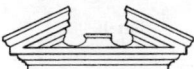

Broken pediment

Segmental pediment

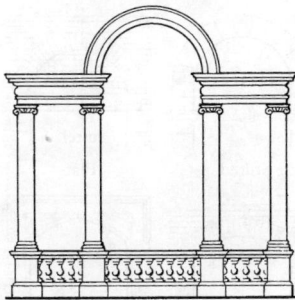

Venetian window

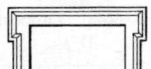

Lugged architrave

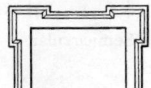

Shouldered architrave

Open pediment

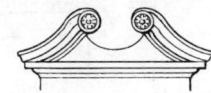

Swan-neck pediment

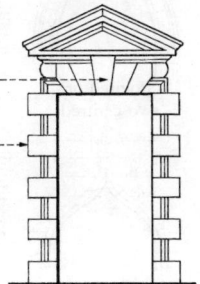

Gibbs surround

b) ORNAMENTS AND FEATURES

FIGURE 4: CLASSICAL

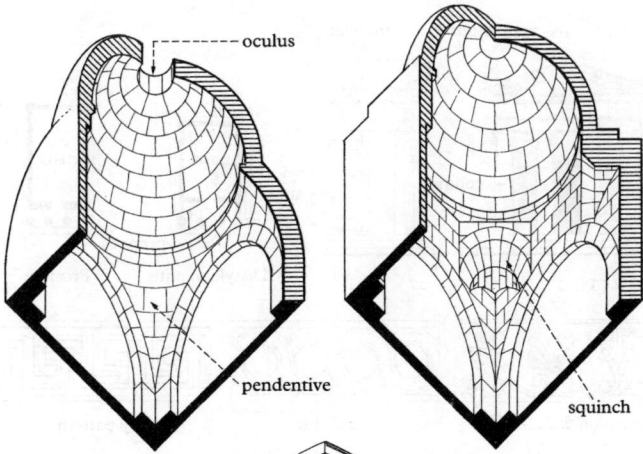

a) DOMES

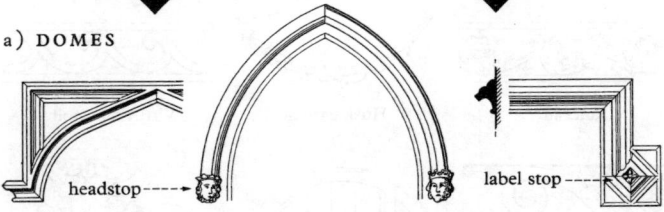

b) HOODMOULDS   Label

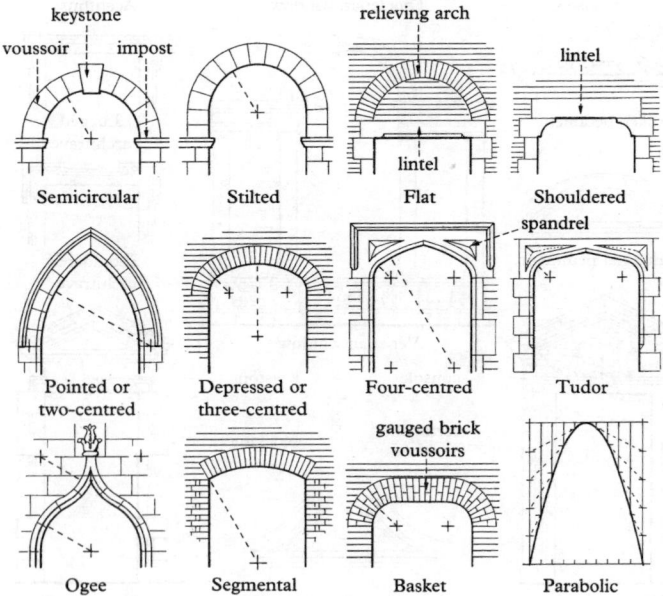

c) ARCHES

FIGURE 5: CONSTRUCTION

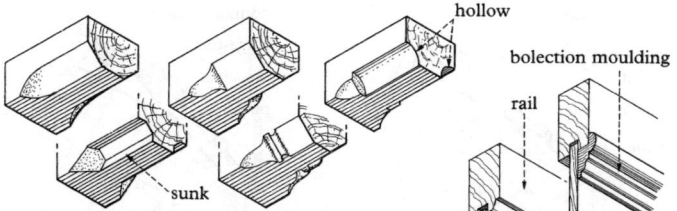

a) CHAMFERS AND CHAMFERSTOPS

hollow

sunk

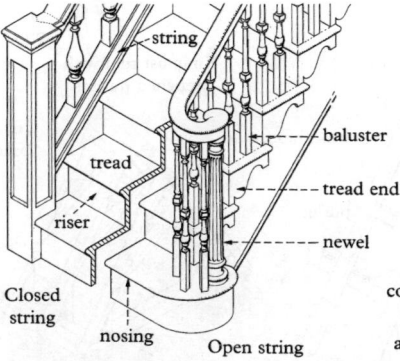

string

baluster

tread

tread end

riser

newel

Closed string

nosing

Open string

bolection moulding

rail

field

raised and fielded panel

muntin

b) PANELLING

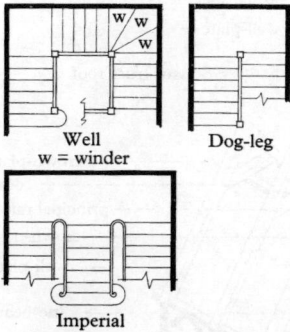

Well
w = winder

Dog-leg

Imperial

c) STAIRS

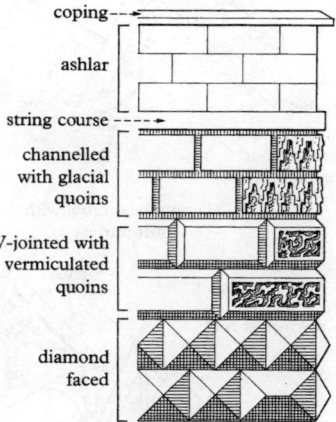

coping

ashlar

string course

channelled with glacial quoins

V-jointed with vermiculated quoins

diamond faced

d) RUSTICATION

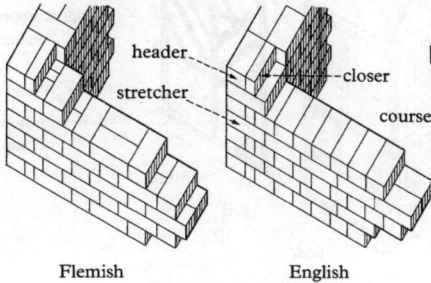

header

closer

stretcher

course

Flemish

English

e) BRICK BONDS

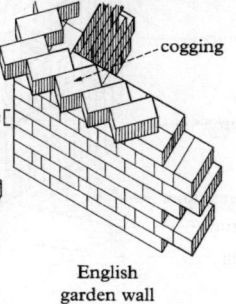

cogging

English garden wall

FIGURE 6: CONSTRUCTION

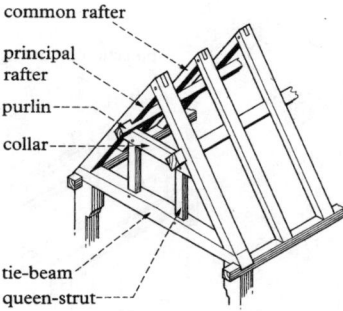

Queen-strut roof with
clasped purlins

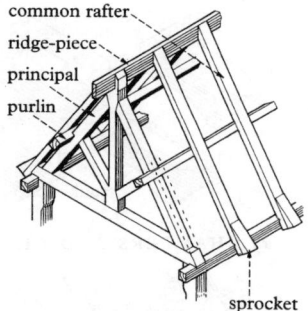

Kingpost roof with
trenched purlins

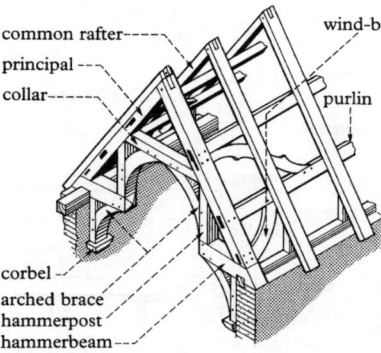

Hammerbeam roof with
butt purlins

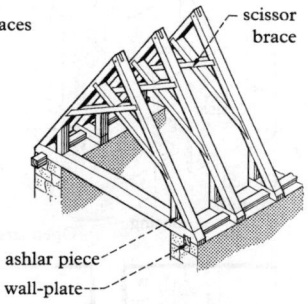

Scissor truss roof

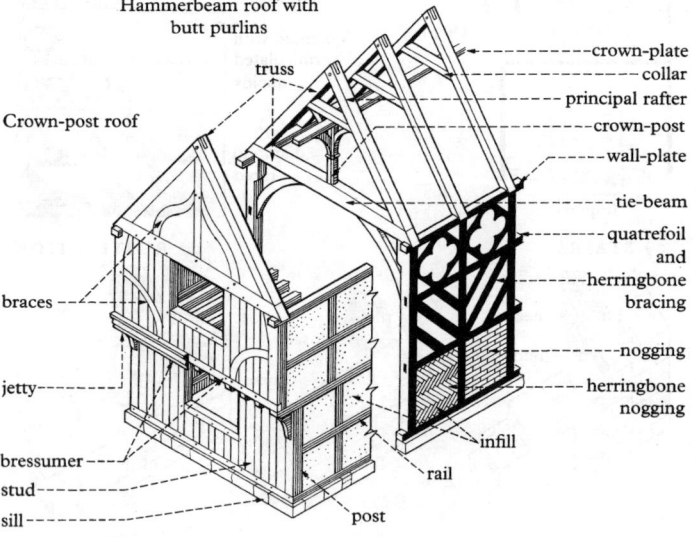

Crown-post roof

Box frame: i) Close studding   ii) Square panel

FIGURE 7: ROOFS AND TIMBER-FRAMING

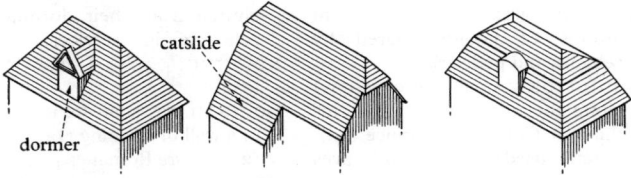

Hipped with dormer   Half-hipped with   Mansard
                         catslide

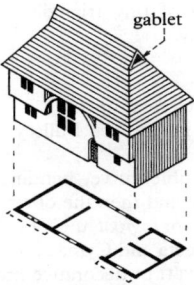

Gambrel on a
Wealden house

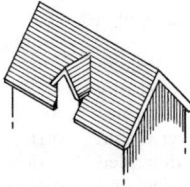

Double-pitched

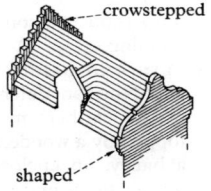

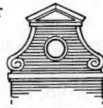

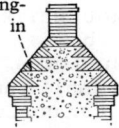

Kneelered   Flemish or Dutch   Tumbled

a) ROOF FORMS AND GABLES

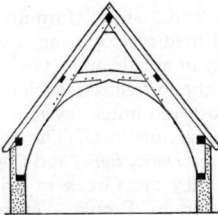

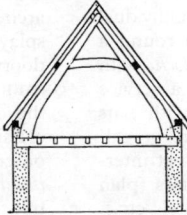

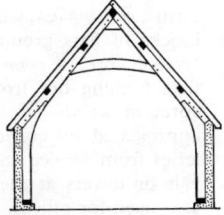

Raised   Upper   Jointed

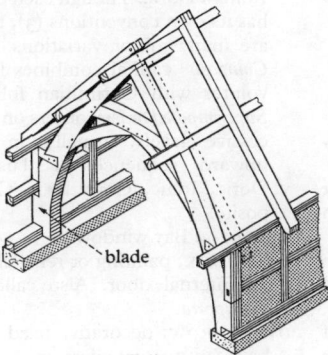

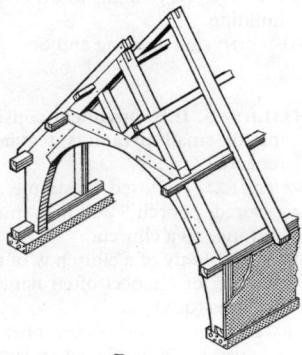

Full   Base

b) CRUCK FRAMES

FIGURE 8: ROOFS AND TIMBER-FRAMING

MIXER-COURTS: forecourts to groups of houses shared by vehicles and pedestrians.

MODILLIONS: small consoles (q.v.) along the underside of a Corinthian or Composite cornice (3d). Often used along an eaves cornice.

MODULE: a predetermined standard size for co-ordinating the dimensions of components of a building.

MOTTE-AND-BAILEY: post-Roman and Norman defence consisting of an earthen mound (motte) topped by a wooden tower within a bailey, an enclosure defended by a ditch and palisade, and also, sometimes, by an internal bank.

MOUCHETTE: see Tracery and 2b.

MOULDING: shaped ornamental strip of continuous section; see e.g. Cavetto, Cyma, Ovolo, Roll.

MULLION: vertical member between window lights (2b).

MULTI-STOREY: five or more storeys. Multi-storey flats may form a *cluster block*, with individual blocks of flats grouped round a service core; a *point block*, with flats fanning out from a service core; or a *slab block*, with flats approached by corridors or galleries from service cores at intervals or towers at the ends (plan also used for offices, hotels etc.). *Tower block* is a generic term for any very high multi-storey building.

MUNTIN: see Panelling and 6b.

NAILHEAD: E.E. ornament consisting of small pyramids regularly repeated (1a).

NARTHEX: enclosed vestibule or covered porch at the main entrance to a church.

NAVE: the body of a church w of the crossing or chancel often flanked by aisles (q.v.).

NEWEL: central or corner post of a staircase (6c). Newel stair: see Stairs.

NIGHT STAIR: stair by which religious entered the transept of their church from their dormitory to celebrate night services.

NOGGING: see Timber-framing (7).

NOOK-SHAFT: shaft set in the angle of a wall or opening (1a).

NORMAN: see Romanesque.

NOSING: projection of the tread of a step (6c).

NUTMEG: medieval ornament with a chain of tiny triangles placed obliquely.

OCULUS: circular opening.

ŒIL DE BŒUF: see Bullseye window.

OGEE: double curve, bending first one way and then the other, as in an *ogee* or *ogival arch* (5c). Cf. Cyma recta and Cyma reversa.

OPUS SECTILE: decorative mosaic-like facing.

OPUS SIGNINUM: composition flooring of Roman origin.

ORATORY: a private chapel in a church or a house. Also a church of the Oratorian Order.

ORDER: one of a series of recessed arches and jambs forming a splayed medieval opening, e.g. a doorway or arcade arch (1a).

ORDERS: the formalized versions of the post-and-lintel system in classical architecture. The main orders are *Doric*, *Ionic*, and *Corinthian*. They are Greek in origin but occur in Roman versions. Tuscan is a simple version of Roman Doric. Though each order has its own conventions (3), there are many minor variations. The *Composite* capital combines Ionic volutes with Corinthian foliage. *Superimposed orders*: orders on successive levels, usually in the upward sequence of Tuscan, Doric, Ionic, Corinthian, Composite.

ORIEL: see Bay window.

OVERDOOR: painting or relief above an internal door. Also called a *sopraporta*.

OVERTHROW: decorative fixed arch between two gatepiers or above a wrought-iron gate.

OVOLO: wide convex moulding (3f).

PALIMPSEST: of a brass: where a metal plate has been reused by turning over the engraving on the back; of a wall painting: where one overlaps and partly obscures an earlier one.

PALLADIAN: following the examples and principles of Andrea Palladio (1508–80).

PALMETTE: classical ornament like a palm shoot (4b).

PANELLING: wooden lining to interior walls, made up of vertical members (*muntins*) and horizontals (*rails*) framing panels: also called *wainscot*. *Raised and fielded*: with the central area of the panel (*field*) raised up (6b).

PANTILE: roof tile of S section.

PARAPET: wall for protection at any sudden drop, e.g. at the wall-head of a castle where it protects the *parapet walk* or wall-walk. Also used to conceal a roof.

PARCLOSE: *see* Screen.

PARGETTING (*lit.* plastering): exterior plaster decoration, either in relief or incised.

PARLOUR: in a religious house, a room where the religious could talk to visitors; in a medieval house, the semi-private living room below the solar (q.v.).

PARTERRE: level space in a garden laid out with low, formal beds.

PATERA (*lit.* plate): round or oval ornament in shallow relief.

PAVILION: ornamental building for occasional use; or projecting subdivision of a larger building, often at an angle or terminating a wing.

PEBBLEDASHING: *see* Rendering.

PEDESTAL: a tall block carrying a classical order, statue, vase, etc.

PEDIMENT: a formalized gable derived from that of a classical temple; also used over doors, windows, etc. For variations *see* 4b.

PENDENTIVE: spandrel between adjacent arches, supporting a drum, dome or vault and consequently formed as part of a hemisphere (5a).

PENTHOUSE: subsidiary structure with a lean-to roof. Also a separately roofed structure on top of a C20 multi-storey block.

PERIPTERAL: *see* Peristyle.

PERISTYLE: a colonnade all round the exterior of a classical building, as in a temple which is then said to be *peripteral*.

PERP (PERPENDICULAR): English Gothic architecture c. 1335–50 to c. 1530. The name is derived from the upright tracery panels then used (*see* Tracery and 2a).

PERRON: external stair to a doorway, usually of double-curved plan.

PEW: loosely, seating for the laity outside the chancel; strictly, an enclosed seat. *Box pew*: with equal high sides and a door.

PIANO NOBILE: principal floor of a classical building above a ground floor or basement and with a lesser storey overhead.

PIAZZA: formal urban open space surrounded by buildings.

PIER: large masonry or brick support, often for an arch. *See also* Compound pier.

PILASTER: flat representation of a classical column in shallow relief. *Pilaster strip*: *see* Lesene.

PILE: row of rooms. *Double pile*: two rows thick.

PILLAR: free-standing upright member of any section, not conforming to one of the orders (q.v.).

PILLAR PISCINA: *see* Piscina.

PILOTIS: C20 French term for pillars or stilts that support a building above an open ground floor.

PISCINA: basin for washing Mass vessels, provided with a drain; set in or against the wall to the s of an altar or free-standing (*pillar piscina*).

PISÉ: *see* Cob.

PITCHED MASONRY: laid on the diagonal, often alternately with opposing courses (*pitched and counterpitched* or *herringbone*).

PLATBAND: flat horizontal moulding between storeys. Cf. stringcourse.

PLATE RAIL: *see* Railways.

PLATEWAY: *see* Railways.

PLINTH: projecting courses at the

foot of a wall or column, generally chamfered or moulded at the top.

PODIUM: a continuous raised platform supporting a building; or a large block of two or three storeys beneath a multi-storey block of smaller area.

POINT BLOCK: *see* Multi-storey.

POINTING: exposed mortar jointing of masonry or brickwork. Types include *flush*, *recessed* and *tuck* (with a narrow channel filled with finer, whiter mortar).

POPPYHEAD: carved ornament of leaves and flowers as a finial for a bench end or stall.

PORTAL FRAME: C20 frame comprising two uprights rigidly connected to a beam or pair of rafters.

PORTCULLIS: gate constructed to rise and fall in vertical grooves at the entry to a castle.

PORTICO: a porch with the roof and frequently a pediment supported by a row of columns (4a). A portico *in antis* has columns on the same plane as the front of the building. A *prostyle* porch has columns standing free. Porticoes are described by the number of front columns, e.g. tetrastyle (four), hexastyle (six). The space within the temple is the *naos*, that within the portico the *pronaos*. *Blind portico*: the front features of a portico applied to a wall.

PORTICUS (plural: porticūs): subsidiary cell opening from the main body of a pre-Conquest church.

POST: upright support in a structure (7).

POSTERN: small gateway at the back of a building or to the side of a larger entrance door or gate.

POUND LOCK: *see* Canals.

PRESBYTERY: the part of a church lying E of the choir where the main altar is placed; or a priest's residence.

PRINCIPAL: *see* Roofs and 7.

PRONAOS: *see* Portico and 4a.

PROSTYLE: *see* Portico and 4a.

PULPIT: raised and enclosed platform for the preaching of sermons. *Three-decker*: with reading desk below and clerk's desk below that. *Two-decker*: as above, minus the clerk's desk.

PULPITUM: stone screen in a major church dividing choir from nave.

PULVINATED: *see* Frieze and 3c.

PURLIN: *see* Roofs and 7.

PUTHOLES or PUTLOG HOLES: in the wall to receive putlogs, the horizontal timbers which support scaffolding boards; sometimes not filled after construction is complete.

PUTTO (plural: putti): small naked boy.

QUARRIES: square (or diamond) panes of glass supported by lead strips (*cames*); square floor slabs or tiles.

QUATREFOIL: *see* Foil and 2b.

QUEEN-STRUT: *see* Roofs and 7.

QUIRK: sharp groove to one side of a convex medieval moulding.

QUOINS: dressed stones at the angles of a building (6d).

RADBURN SYSTEM: vehicle and pedestrian segregation in residential developments, based on that used at Radburn, New Jersey, USA, by Wright and Stein, 1928–30.

RADIATING CHAPELS: projecting radially from an ambulatory or an apse (*see* Chevet).

RAFTER: *see* Roofs and 7.

RAGGLE: groove cut in masonry, especially to receive the edge of a roof-covering.

RAGULY: ragged (in heraldry). Also applied to funerary sculpture, e.g. *cross raguly*: with a notched outline.

RAIL: *see* Panelling and 6b; also 7.

RAILWAYS: *Edge rail*: on which flanged wheels can run. *Plate rail*: L-section rail for plain unflanged wheels. *Plateway*: early railway using plate rails.

RAISED AND FIELDED: *see* Panelling and 6b.

RAKE: slope or pitch.

RAMPART: defensive outer wall of stone or earth. *Rampart walk*: path along the inner face.

REBATE: rectangular section cut out of a masonry edge to receive a shutter, door, window, etc.

REBUS: a heraldic pun, e.g. a fiery cock for Cockburn.

REEDING: series of convex mouldings, the reverse of fluting (q.v.). Cf. Gadrooning.

RENDERING: the covering of outside walls with a uniform surface or skin for protection from the weather. *Limewashing*: thin layer of lime plaster. *Pebble-dashing*: where aggregate is thrown at the wet plastered wall for a textured effect. *Roughcast*: plaster mixed with a coarse aggregate such as gravel. *Stucco*: fine lime plaster worked to a smooth surface. *Cement rendering*: a cheaper substitute for stucco, usually with a grainy texture.

REPOUSSÉ: relief designs in metalwork, formed by beating it from the back.

REREDORTER (*lit.* behind the dormitory): latrines in a medieval religious house.

REREDOS: painted and/or sculptured screen behind and above an altar. Cf. Retable.

RESPOND: half-pier or half-column bonded into a wall and carrying one end of an arch. It usually terminates an arcade.

RETABLE: painted or carved panel standing on or at the back of an altar, usually attached to it.

RETROCHOIR: in a major church, the area between the high altar and E chapel.

REVEAL: the plane of a jamb, between the wall and the frame of a door or window.

RIB-VAULT: *see* Vault and 2c.

RINCEAU: classical ornament of leafy scrolls (4b).

RISER: vertical face of a step (6c).

ROACH: a rough-textured form of Portland stone, with small cavities and fossil shells.

ROCK-FACED: masonry cleft to produce a rugged appearance.

ROCOCO: style current *c.* 1720 and *c.* 1760, characterized by a serpentine line and playful, scrolled decoration.

ROLL MOULDING: medieval moulding of part-circular section (1a).

ROMANESQUE: style current in the CII and CI2. In England often called Norman. *See also* Saxo-Norman.

ROOD: crucifix flanked by the Virgin and St John, usually over the entry into the chancel, on a beam (*rood beam*) or painted on the wall. The *rood screen* below often had a walkway (*rood loft*) along the top, reached by a *rood stair* in the side wall.

ROOFS: Shape. For the main external shapes (hipped, mansard, etc.) *see* 8a. *Helm* and *Saddleback*: *see* 1c. *Lean-to*: single sloping roof built against a vertical wall; lean-to is also applied to the part of the building beneath. Construction. *See* 7. *Single-framed* roof: with no main trusses. The rafters may be fixed to the wall-plate or ridge, or longitudinal timber may be absent altogether. *Double-framed* roof: with longitudinal members, such as purlins, and usually divided into bays by principals and principal rafters. Other types are named after their main structural components, e.g. *hammerbeam*, *crown-post* (*see* Elements below and 7).

Elements. *See* 7.

Ashlar piece: a short vertical timber connecting inner wall-plate or timber pad to a rafter.

Braces: subsidiary timbers set diagonally to strengthen the frame. *Arched braces*: curved pair forming an arch, connecting wall or post below with tie- or collar-beam above. *Passing braces*: long straight braces passing across other members of the truss. *Scissor braces*: pair crossing diagonally between pairs of rafters or principals. *Wind-braces*: short, usually curved braces connecting side purlins with principals; sometimes decorated with cusping.

Collar or *collar-beam*: horizontal transverse timber connecting a pair of rafter or cruck blades (q.v.), set between apex and the wall-plate.

Crown-post: a vertical timber set centrally on a tie-beam and supporting a collar purlin braced to it longitudinally. In an open truss lateral braces may rise to the collar-beam; in a closed truss they may descend to the tie-beam.

Hammerbeams: horizontal brackets projecting at wall-plate level like an interrupted tie-beam; the inner ends carry *hammerposts*, vertical timbers which support a purlin and are braced to a collar-beam above.

Kingpost: vertical timber set centrally on a tie- or collar-beam, rising to the apex of the roof to support a ridge-piece (cf. Strut).

Plate: longitudinal timber set square to the ground. *Wall-plate*: plate along the top of a wall which receives the ends of the rafters; cf. Purlin.

Principals: pair of inclined lateral timbers of a truss. Usually they support side purlins and mark the main bay divisions.

Purlin: horizontal longitudinal timber. *Collar purlin* or *crown plate*: central timber which carries collar-beams and is supported by crown-posts. *Side purlins*: pairs of timbers placed some way up the slope of the roof, which carry common rafters. *Butt* or *tenoned purlins* are tenoned into either side of the principals. *Through purlins* pass through or past the principal; they include *clasped purlins*, which rest on queenposts or are carried in the angle between principals and collar, and *trenched purlins* trenched into the backs of principals.

Queen-strut: paired vertical, or near-vertical, timbers placed symmetrically on a tie-beam to support side purlins.

Rafters: inclined lateral timbers supporting the roof covering. *Common rafters*: regularly spaced uniform rafters placed along the length of a roof or between principals. *Principal rafters*: rafters which also act as principals.

Ridge, ridge-piece: horizontal longitudinal timber at the apex supporting the ends of the rafters.

Sprocket: short timber placed on the back and at the foot of a rafter to form projecting eaves.

Strut: vertical or oblique timber between two members of a truss, not directly supporting longitudinal timbers.

Tie-beam: main horizontal transverse timber which carries the feet of the principals at wall level.

Truss: rigid framework of timbers at bay intervals, carrying the longitudinal roof timbers which support the common rafters.

Closed truss: with the spaces between the timbers filled, to form an internal partition.

See also Cruck, Wagon roof.

ROPE MOULDING: *see* Cable moulding.

ROSE WINDOW: circular window with tracery radiating from the centre. Cf. Wheel window.

ROTUNDA: building or room circular in plan.

ROUGHCAST: *see* Rendering.

ROVING BRIDGE: *see* Canals.

RUBBED BRICKWORK: *see* Gauged brickwork.

RUBBLE: masonry whose stones are wholly or partly in a rough state. *Coursed*: coursed stones with rough faces. *Random*: uncoursed stones in a random pattern. *Snecked*: with courses broken by smaller stones (snecks).

RUSTICATION: *see* 6d. Exaggerated treatment of masonry to give an effect of strength. The joints are usually recessed by V-section chamfering or square-section channelling (*channelled rustication*). *Banded rustication* has only the horizontal joints emphasized. The faces may be flat, but can be *diamond-faced*, like shallow pyramids, *vermiculated*, with a stylized texture like worm-casts, and *glacial* (frost-work), like icicles or stalactites.

SACRISTY: room in a church for sacred vessels and vestments.

SADDLEBACK ROOF: *see* 1c.

SALTIRE CROSS: with diagonal limbs.

SANCTUARY: area around the main altar of a church. Cf. Presbytery.

SANGHA: residence of Buddhist monks or nuns.

SARCOPHAGUS: coffin of stone or other durable material.

SAXO-NORMAN: transitional Romanesque style combining Anglo-Saxon and Norman features, current *c.* 1060–1100.

SCAGLIOLA: composition imitating marble.

SCALLOPED CAPITAL: *see* 1a.

SCOTIA: a hollow classical moulding, especially between tori (q.v.) on a column base (3b, 3f).

SCREEN: in a medieval church, usually at the entry to the chancel; *see* Rood (screen) and Pulpitum. A *parclose screen* separates a chapel from the rest of the church.

SCREENS or SCREENS PASSAGE: screened-off entrance passage between great hall and service rooms.

SECTION: two-dimensional representation of a building, moulding, etc., revealed by cutting across it.

SEDILIA (singular: sedile): seats for the priests (usually three) on the S side of the chancel.

SET-OFF: *see* Weathering.

SETTS: squared stones, usually of granite, used for paving or flooring.

SGRAFFITO: decoration scratched, often in plaster, to reveal a pattern in another colour beneath. *Graffiti*: scratched drawing or writing.

SHAFT: vertical member of round or polygonal section (1a, 3a). *Shaft-ring*: at the junction of shafts set *en delit* (q.v.) or attached to a pier or wall (1a).

SHEILA-NA-GIG: female fertility figure, usually with legs apart.

SHELL: thin, self-supporting roofing membrane of timber or concrete.

SHOULDERED ARCHITRAVE: *see* 4b.

SHUTTERING: *see* Concrete.

SILL: horizontal member at the bottom of a window or door frame; or at the base of a timber-framed wall into which posts and studs are tenoned (7).

SLAB BLOCK: *see* Multi-storey.

SLATE-HANGING: covering of overlapping slates on a wall. *Tile-hanging* is similar.

SLYPE: covered way or passage leading E from the cloisters between transept and chapter house.

SNECKED: *see* Rubble.

SOFFIT (*lit.* ceiling): underside of an arch (also called *intrados*), lintel, etc. *Soffit roll*: medieval roll moulding on a soffit.

SOLAR: private upper chamber in a medieval house, accessible from the high end of the great hall.

SOPRAPORTA: *see* Overdoor.

SOUNDING-BOARD: *see* Tester.

SPANDRELS: roughly triangular spaces between an arch and its containing rectangle, or between adjacent arches (5c). Also non-structural panels under the windows in a curtain-walled building.

SPERE: a fixed structure screening the lower end of the great hall from the screens passage. *Spere-truss*: roof truss incorporated in the spere.

SPIRE: tall pyramidal or conical feature crowning a tower or turret. *Broach*: starting from a square base, then carried into an octagonal section by means of triangular faces; and *splayed-foot*: variation of the broach form, found principally in the south-east, in which the four cardinal faces are splayed out near their base, to cover the corners, while oblique (or intermediate) faces taper away to a point (1c). *Needle spire*: thin spire rising from the centre of a tower roof, well inside the parapet: when of timber and lead often called a *spike*.

SPIRELET: *see* Flèche.

SPLAY: of an opening when it is wider on one face of a wall than the other.

SPRING or SPRINGING: level at which an arch or vault rises from its supports. *Springers*: the first stones of an arch or vaulting rib above the spring (2c).

SQUINCH: arch or series of arches thrown across an interior angle of a square or rectangular structure to support a circular or polygonal superstructure, especially a dome or spire (5a).

SQUINT: an aperture in a wall or through a pier usually to allow a view of an altar.

STAIRS: *see* 6c. *Dog-leg stair*: parallel flights rising alternately in opposite directions, without an open well. *Flying stair*: cantilevered from the walls of a stairwell, without newels; sometimes called a *Geometric* stair when the inner edge describes a curve. *Newel stair*: ascending round a central supporting newel (q.v.); called a *spiral stair* or *vice* when in a circular shaft, a *winder* when in a rectangular compartment. (Winder also applies to the steps on the turn.) *Well stair*: with flights round a square open well framed by newel posts. *See also* Perron.

STALL: fixed seat in the choir or chancel for the clergy or choir (cf. Pew). Usually with arm rests, and often framed together.

STANCHION: upright structural member, of iron, steel or reinforced concrete.

STANDPIPE TOWER: *see* Manometer.

STEAM ENGINES: *Atmospheric*: worked by the vacuum created when low-pressure steam is condensed in the cylinder, as developed by Thomas Newcomen. *Beam engine*: with a large pivoted beam moved in an oscillating fashion by the piston. It may drive a flywheel or be *non-rotative*. *Watt* and *Cornish*: single-cylinder; *compound*: two cylinders; *triple expansion*: three cylinders.

STEEPLE: tower together with a spire, lantern, or belfry.

STIFF-LEAF: type of E.E. foliage decoration. *Stiff-leaf capital see* 1b.

STOP: plain or decorated terminal to mouldings or chamfers, or at the end of hoodmoulds and labels (*label stop*), or stringcourses (5b, 6a); *see also* Headstop.

STOUP: vessel for holy water, usually near a door.

STRAINER: *see* Arch.

STRAPWORK: late C16 and C17 decoration, like interlaced leather straps.

STRETCHER: *see* Bond and 6e.

STRING: *see* 6c. Sloping member holding the ends of the treads and risers of a staircase. *Closed string*: a broad string covering the ends of the treads and risers. *Open string*: cut into the shape of the treads and risers.

STRINGCOURSE: horizontal course or moulding projecting from the surface of a wall (6d).

STUCCO: *see* Rendering.

STUDS: subsidiary vertical timbers of a timber-framed wall or partition (7).

STUPA: Buddhist shrine, circular in plan.

STYLOBATE: top of the solid platform on which a colonnade stands (3a).

SUSPENSION BRIDGE: *see* Bridge.

SWAG: like a festoon (q.v.), but representing cloth.

SYSTEM BUILDING: *see* Industrialized building.

TABERNACLE: canopied structure to contain the reserved sacrament or a relic; or architectural frame for an image or statue.

TABLE TOMB: memorial slab raised on free-standing legs.

TAS-DE-CHARGE: the lower courses of a vault or arch which are laid horizontally (2c).

TERM: pedestal or pilaster tapering downward, usually with the upper part of a human figure growing out of it.

TERRACOTTA: moulded and fired clay ornament or cladding.

TESSELLATED PAVEMENT: mosaic flooring, particularly Roman, made of *tesserae*, i.e. cubes of glass, stone, or brick.

TESTER: flat canopy over a tomb or pulpit, where it is also called a *sounding-board*.

TESTER TOMB: tomb-chest with effigies beneath a tester, either free-standing (tester with four or more columns), or attached to a wall (*half-tester*) with columns on one side only.

TETRASTYLE: *see* Portico.

THERMAL WINDOW: *see* Diocletian window.

THREE-DECKER PULPIT: *see* Pulpit.

TIDAL GATES: *see* Canals.

TIE-BEAM: *see* Roofs and 7.

TIERCERON: *see* Vault and 2c.

TILE-HANGING: *see* Slate-hanging.

TIMBER-FRAMING: *see* 7. Method of construction where the structural frame is built of interlocking timbers. The spaces are filled with non-structural material, e.g. *infill* of wattle and daub, lath and plaster, brickwork (known as *nogging*), etc. and may be covered by plaster, weatherboarding (q.v.), or tiles.

TOMB-CHEST: chest-shaped tomb, usually of stone. Cf. Table tomb, Tester tomb.

TORUS (plural: tori): large convex moulding usually used on a column base (3b, 3f).

TOUCH: soft black marble quarried near Tournai.

TOURELLE: turret corbelled out from the wall.

TOWER BLOCK: *see* Multi-storey.

TRABEATED: depends structurally on the use of the post and lintel. Cf. Arcuated.

TRACERY: openwork pattern of masonry or timber in the upper part of an opening. *Blind tracery* is tracery applied to a solid wall. *Plate tracery*, introduced *c.* 1200, is the earliest form, in which shapes are cut through solid masonry (2a).
Bar tracery was introduced into England *c.* 1250. The pattern is formed by intersecting moulded ribwork continued from the mullions. It was especially elaborate during the Decorated period (q.v.). Tracery shapes can include circles, *daggers* (elongated ogee-ended lozenges), *mouchettes* (like daggers but with curved sides) and upright rectangular *panels*. They often have *cusps*, projecting points defining lobes or *foils* (q.v.) within the main shape: *Kentish* or *split-cusps* are forked (2b).
Types of bar tracery (*see* 2b) include *geometric(al)*: *c.* 1250–1310, chiefly circles, often foiled; *Y-tracery*: *c.* 1300, with mullions branching into a Y-shape; *intersecting*: *c.* 1300, formed by interlocking mullions; *reticulated*: early C14, net-like pattern of ogee-ended lozenges; *curvilinear*: C14, with uninterrupted flowing curves; *panel*: Perp, with straight-sided panels, often cusped at the top and bottom.

TRANSEPT: transverse portion of a church.

TRANSITIONAL: generally used for the phase between Romanesque and Early English (*c.* 1175–*c.* 1200).

TRANSOM: horizontal member separating window lights (2b).

TREAD: horizontal part of a step. The *tread end* may be carved on a staircase (6c).

TREFOIL: *see* Foil.

TRIFORIUM: middle storey of a church treated as an arcaded wall passage or blind arcade, its height corresponding to that of the aisle roof.

TRIGLYPHS (*lit.* three-grooved tablets): stylized beam-ends in the Doric frieze, with metopes between (3b).

TRIUMPHAL ARCH: influential type of Imperial Roman monument.

TROPHY: sculptured or painted group of arms or armour.

TRUMEAU: central stone mullion supporting the tympanum of a wide doorway. *Trumeau figure*: carved figure attached to it (cf. Column figure).

TRUMPET CAPITAL: *see* 1b.

TRUSS: braced framework, spanning between supports. *See also* Roofs and 7.

TUMBLING or TUMBLING-IN: courses of brickwork laid at right-angles to a slope, e.g. of a gable, forming triangles by tapering into horizontal courses (8a).

TUSCAN: *see* Orders and 3e.

TWO-DECKER PULPIT: *see* Pulpit.

TYMPANUM: the surface between a lintel and the arch above it or within a pediment (4a).

UNDERCROFT: usually describes the vaulted room(s), beneath the main room(s) of a medieval house. Cf. Crypt.

VAULT: arched stone roof (sometimes imitated in timber or plaster). For types see 2c.
Tunnel or *barrel vault*: continuous semicircular or pointed arch, often of rubble masonry.

Groin-vault: tunnel vaults intersecting at right angles. *Groins* are the curved lines of the intersections.

Rib-vault: masonry framework of intersecting arches (ribs) supporting *vault cells*, used in Gothic architecture. *Wall rib* or *wall arch*: between wall and vault cell. *Transverse rib*: spans between two walls to divide a vault into bays. *Quadripartite* rib-vault: each bay has two pairs of diagonal ribs dividing the vault into four triangular cells. *Sexpartite* rib-vault: most often used over paired bays, has an extra pair of ribs springing from between the bays. More elaborate vaults may include *ridge ribs* along the crown of a vault or bisecting the bays; *tiercerons*: extra decorative ribs springing from the corners of a bay; and *liernes*: short decorative ribs in the crown of a vault, not linked to any springing point. A *stellar* or *star* vault has liernes in star formation.

Fan-vault: form of barrel vault used in the Perp period, made up of halved concave masonry cones decorated with blind tracery.

VAULTING SHAFT: shaft leading up to the spring or springing (q.v.) of a vault (2c).

VENETIAN or SERLIAN WINDOW: derived from Serlio (4b). The motif is used for other openings.

VERMICULATION: *see* Rustication and 6d.

VESICA: oval with pointed ends.

VICE: *see* Stair.

VILLA: originally a Roman country house or farm. The term was revived in England in the C18 under the influence of Palladio and used especially for smaller, compact country houses. In the later C19 it was debased to describe any suburban house.

VITRIFIED: bricks or tiles fired to a darkened glassy surface.

VITRUVIAN SCROLL: classical running ornament of curly waves (4b).

VOLUTES: spiral scrolls. They occur on Ionic capitals (3c). *Angle volute*: pair of volutes, turned outwards to meet at the corner of a capital.

VOUSSOIRS: wedge-shaped stones forming an arch (5c).

WAGON ROOF: with the appearance of the inside of a wagon tilt; often ceiled. Also called *cradle roof*.

WAINSCOT: *see* Panelling.

WALL MONUMENT: attached to the wall and often standing on the floor. *Wall tablets* are smaller with the inscription as the major element.

WALL-PLATE: *see* Roofs and 7.

WALL-WALK: *see* Parapet.

WARMING ROOM: room in a religious house where a fire burned for comfort.

WATERHOLDING BASE: early Gothic base with upper and lower mouldings separated by a deep hollow.

WATERLEAF: *see* Enrichments and 3f.

WATERLEAF CAPITAL: Late Romanesque and Transitional type of capital (1b).

WATER WHEELS: described by the way water is fed on to the wheel. *Breastshot*: mid-height, falling and passing beneath. *Overshot*: over the top. *Pitchback*: on the top but falling backwards. *Undershot*: turned by the momentum of the water passing beneath. In a *water turbine*, water is fed under pressure through a vaned wheel within a casing.

WEALDEN HOUSE: type of medieval timber-framed house with a central open hall flanked by bays of two storeys, roofed in line; the end bays are jettied to the front, but the eaves are continuous (8a).

WEATHERBOARDING: wall cladding of overlapping horizontal boards.

WEATHERING or SET-OFF: inclined, projecting surface to keep water away from the wall below.

WEEPERS: figures in niches along the sides of some medieval tombs. Also called mourners.

WHEEL WINDOW: circular, with radiating shafts like spokes. Cf. Rose window.

WROUGHT IRON: *see* Cast iron.

INDEX OF ARCHITECTS, ARTISTS, PATRONS AND RESIDENTS

Names of architects and artists working in the area covered by this volume are given in *italic*. Entries for partnerships and group practices are listed after entries for a single name.

Also indexed here are names/titles of families and individuals (not of bodies or commercial firms) recorded in this volume as having commissioned architectural work or owned, lived in, or visited properties in the area. The index includes monuments to members of such families and other individuals where they are of particular interest.

INDEX OF PLACES

Principal references are in **bold** type; demolished buildings are shown in *italic*.